# Oxford
# School
# French
# Dictionary

Editorial Manager: Valerie Grundy
New Edition: Nicholas Rollin
with the assistance of Natalie Pomier

# OXFORD
**UNIVERSITY PRESS**

# OXFORD
UNIVERSITY PRESS

Great Clarendon Street, Oxford OX2 6DP

Oxford University Press is a department of the University of Oxford.
It furthers the University's objective of excellence in research,
scholarship, and education by publishing worldwide in

Oxford New York

Auckland Bangkok Buenos Aires Cape Town Chennai
Dar es Salaam Delhi Hong Kong Istanbul Karachi Kolkata
Kuala Lumpur Madrid Melbourne Mexico City Mumbai Nairobi
São Paulo Taipei Tokyo Toronto

Oxford is a registered trade mark of Oxford University Press
in the UK and in certain other countries

© Oxford University Press 1997

First published in 1997
Revised edition 2002
This edition 2004

Database right Oxford University Press (maker)

British Library cataloguing in Publication Data available

Part of a 6-part set. Not to be sold separately.

ISBN 0-19-911201-0 (complete set)

ISBN 0-19-911265-7 *Oxford School French Dictionary* (when part
of this set)

10 9 8 7 6 5 4 3 2 1

Printed in the UK by Cox and Wyman

# INTRODUCTION

This dictionary has been specially written for students who are in their first years of learning French all the way through to preparing for exams. We have paid particular attention to making the dictionary user-friendly. With the help of bold headwords, alphabet tabs, easy-to-follow signposts and examples, the right translation can quickly be found. French verbs on both sides of the dictionary are numbered to direct the student to the appropriate verb table in the centre pages.

Throughout the writing of this dictionary we have worked in close consultation with students, teachers, inspectors, and examining boards. We gratefully acknowledge the examining boards AQA (formerly NEAB and SEG), OCR, and EDEXCEL, who have read and commented on the dictionary text.

Since the first edition of this dictionary there have been many changes in French life. Not least has been the introduction of the euro. This new edition takes full account of these changes and many new words and examples have been included in order to provide the best possible learner's dictionary of French at this level.

# HOW A BILINGUAL DICTIONARY WORKS

A bilingual dictionary contains two languages. When you look up a word in one of the languages, it gives the translation for that word in the other language. This dictionary is divided into two halves separated by a section of dark-edged pages. In the first half you look up French words, which are in alphabetical order, to find out what they mean in English and in the second half you look up English words, also in alphabetical order, to find out how to say them in French. The dark-edged pages are verb tables and you can see how to use them further on in this section.

At each entry you will find not only **translations** but other information that will help you get the right translation and use the word correctly. Here is a guide to the different things you will find in an entry:

**headword**　　a word you look up in the dictionary

translation　　translations are the only things that are in 'ordinary' type in the dictionary. They are always typed like this, and something which is typed in a different way can never be a translation

*noun*　　word class (part of speech): tells you whether the word you are looking up is a noun, a verb, an adjective, or some other part of speech. A headword can be more than one part of speech. For instance, **book** can be a noun (she was reading a book) or a verb (I've booked the seats)

| | |
|---|---|
| (*signpost*) | helpful information: to guide you to the right translation, to show you how to use the translation, or to give you extra information |
| **example** | a phrase or sentence using the word you have looked up. You should read through them carefully to see if they are close to what you want to understand or say |
| *Masc.* | gender: after a French noun, to tell you that it is masculine |
| *Fem.* | gender: after a French noun, to tell you that it is feminine. *Fem.* also shows the feminine form of some adjectives |
| ● | indicates a phrasal verb such as to carry on |
| ★ | shows an idiomatic expression such as over the moon |
| [27] | verb number – tells you which verb pattern to look at in the dark-edged centre pages of the dictionary |

# USING THE DICTIONARY

## To find out what a French word means

Suppose you want to find out what the French word **bouton** means. You need to use the first half of the dictionary to find the French words that you are looking for. To help you do this, the guide words at the top of each page show the alphabetical range of words on the pages you have open. Notice that hyphens and spaces between words in French words make no difference to the alphabetical order.

When you find the entry for **bouton** you will find the translation. But you will also see that **bouton** is a noun and because all nouns are either masculine or feminine in French, you are given the gender *Masc.* (*Masc.* = masculine, *Fem.* = feminine).

However, it often happens that a French word has more than one English translation so you will see that the translation for **bouton** is divided into sections numbered **1** and **2**.

**bouton** *noun Masc.* **1** button;
  **2** spot, pimple.

The first translation is **button** and the second is **spot** or **pimple**. You will need to look at both translations to work out which one fits the French sentence you are trying to understand. So:

**il y a quatre boutons sur ma veste** *means* there are four buttons on my jacket

BUT

**j'ai un bouton sur le nez** *means* I've got a spot on my nose

The plurals of most French nouns are formed by adding an -s, as in **boutons** in the first sentence. Exceptional plural forms can be found after the headword:

**animal** *noun* animal *Masc.* (*plural*
  **animaux**).

French like English has certain words that you would use when chatting with friends but not in more formal situations. French words like this are marked *informal* in the dictionary, like **bouquin** here:

**bouquin** *noun Masc.* (*informal*)
  book.

Note that the usual word for **book** is **livre**.

## To find an English word and how to say it in French

You can see that it is quite easy, once you know how the dictionary works, to look up a French word and find out what it means. Students usually find it harder to use the dictionary to find out how to say something in French. This dictionary is written specially to help you do this and to make it easy to find the right way of saying things in French.

Suppose you want to know how to say **garden** in French. Look up the word in the second part of the dictionary. If you follow the same method of going through the alphabetical order of the headwords as you did when you were looking up a French word, you will find **garden** on page 435.

**garden** *noun* jardin *Masc.*

Now you can see that the French word for **garden** is **jardin**. But if you want to make a sentence using a noun like **jardin** you need to know whether it is masculine or feminine. The *Masc.* after **jardin** tells you that it is masculine so *in the garden* is **dans le jardin**. It is not always as easy as this to know which French word you need. Sometimes there will be more than one French word for the English word you are looking up. When the dictionary entry gives you more than just one translation, it is very important to take the time to read through the whole entry. If you look up **plug** the entry looks like this:

**plug** *noun* **1** (*electrical*) prise *Fem.*;
  **2** (*in a bath or sink*) bonde *Fem.*; **to**
  **pull out the plug** retirer la bonde.

You can see that **1** tells you that the French word for an electrical plug is **prise** and **2** tells you that the word for a bath plug or a sink plug is **bonde**.

Remember that information which is either in brackets or italics, or both, is there to help you, but it *will never be* the translation itself. Wherever there is more than one translation, depending on what meaning of the English word you are looking for, the dictionary will always help you to choose the right one. Often it is not enough to find the translation of one word. In the case of more common words the dictionary also gives you a selection of common phrases you will often want to use. In the entry for **hair** below you can find out how to use the translation in different expressions:

**hair** *noun* **1** cheveux *Masc. plural*; **to have short hair** avoir les cheveux courts; **to brush your hair** se brosser les cheveux; **to wash your hair** se laver les cheveux; **to have your hair cut** se faire couper les cheveux; **she's had her hair cut** elle s'est fait couper les cheveux; **2 a hair** (*from the head*) un cheveu; (*from the body*) un poil.

# HOW TO USE THE VERB TABLES

On the French side of the dictionary all the headwords which are verbs look like this: **faire** *verb* [10]. On the English side of the dictionary all the verbs given as translations of English verbs look like this: **frighten** *verb* effrayer [59].

If you look at the dark-edged pages in the centre of the dictionary, you will find tables showing you how to use the different types of French verbs.

The verb **faire** above has the number 10. If you look at number 10 in the verb tables, you will see that because **faire** is a very common and very irregular verb it has a whole page to itself giving you all the tenses you will need. The verb **effrayer** has number 59 after it. When you look up verb table number 59, you will see the verb **payer**. This means that the verb endings given for **payer** will also be the endings for **effrayer**. So **payer** is there to show you the pattern that other verbs like it, such as **effrayer**, will follow.

With practice you will soon be able to find your way easily around the dictionary and identify what you are looking for in an entry. Some entries may seem long and complicated at first glance. Reading carefully through the signposts and examples will lead you to the translation you need.

# Aa

**a** *verb* SEE **avoir**.

**à** *preposition* (*note that 'à + le' becomes 'au' and 'à + les' becomes 'aux'*) **1** at; **à la maison** at home; **à l'école** at school; **au bureau** at the office; **à deux heures** at two o'clock; **2** in; **à Londres** in London; **à la campagne** in the country; **au printemps** in the spring; **3** to; **aller à Londres** to go to London; **donner quelque chose à quelqu'un** to give something to somebody; **4** by; **à la main** by hand; **à vélo** by (*or* on a) bicycle; **5** with; **une petite fille aux yeux bleus** a little girl with blue eyes; **6 à trois kilomètres d'ici** three kilometres from here; **7 ce bracelet est à Natalie** this bracelet is Natalie's.

**abandonner** *verb* [1] **1** to give up; **elle a abandonné les maths** she has given up maths; **j'abandonne** I give up; **2** to abandon; **un enfant abandonné** an abandoned child.

**abat-jour** *noun Masc.* lampshade.

**abats** *plural noun Masc.* **les abats** offal (*liver, kidneys, heart, etc*).

**abattoir** *noun Masc.* slaughterhouse.

**abattre** *verb* [21] **1** to shoot down; **deux policiers ont été abattus par des gangsters hier** two policemen were shot down by gangsters yesterday; **2** to slaughter (*an animal*); **3** to demolish (*a building*).

**abbaye** *noun Fem.* abbey; **l'abbaye de Cluny** Cluny Abbey.

**abbé** *noun Masc.* priest.

**abcès** *noun Masc.* abscess.

**abeille** *noun Fem.* bee; **une piqûre d'abeille** a bee sting.

**abîmer** *verb* [1] **1** to damage; **la pluie avait abîmé la porte** the rain had damaged the door; **tu vas t'abîmer les yeux** you'll ruin your eyesight; **des fruits abîmés** fruit which is going bad; **2 s'abîmer** to get damaged; **les pommes vont s'abîmer** the apples are going to go bad; **la viande s'abîme vite** meat goes off quickly.

**aboiement** *noun Masc.* barking; **on entendait des aboiements** we could hear dogs barking.

**abolir** *verb* [2] to abolish.

**abominable** *adjective* abominable.

**abondance** *noun Fem.* **une abondance de** plenty of, lots of; **il y a des fruits en abondance** there's plenty of fruit.

**abonné, abonnée** *noun Masc., Fem.* **1** season ticket holder; **2** subscriber (*to a magazine, journal, etc*).
**abonné** *adjective* **être abonné** to have a subscription (*to a magazine, journal, etc*); to have a season ticket (*for the bus, train, theatre, etc*).

**abonnement** *noun Masc.* **1** subscription; **2** season ticket.

**abonner** *verb* [1] **s'abonner à** to subscribe to; **je me suis abonné pour un an** I have a year's subscription.

**abord** *noun Masc.* **1 d'abord** first; **tout d'abord** first of all; **je vais**

1

**d'abord faire du thé** I'll make some tea first; **2 d'abord** at first; **j'ai d'abord cru qu'il était français** I thought at first that he was French; **3 les abords** the surroundings.

**abordable** *adjective* **1 des prix abordables** affordable prices; **2 une personne abordable** an approachable person.

**aborder** *verb* [1] **1** to tackle (*a problem, a piece of work, a subject, etc*); **2** to approach.

**aboutir** *verb* [2] **1 aboutir à** to lead to; **la rue aboutit à une petite place** the street leads to a little square; **2 aboutir à** to end up in; **nous avons abouti à Paris** we ended up in Paris; **3** to succeed, to be successful (*of discussions or negotiations*).

**aboyer** *verb* [39] to bark.

**abrégé** *noun Masc.* summary. **abrégé** *adjective* **la version abrégée** the abridged version.

**abréger** *verb* [15] to shorten.

**abréviation** *noun Fem.* abbreviation.

**abri** *noun Masc.* **1** shelter; **trouver un abri** to take shelter; **les sans-abri** the homeless; **2** shed; **3 à l'abri de** sheltered from; **à l'abri du vent** sheltered from the wind, out of the wind; **à l'abri de la lumière** in a dark place.

**abricot** *noun Masc.* apricot; **de la confiture d'abricots** apricot jam; **une tarte aux abricots** an apricot tart.

**abricotier** *noun Masc.* apricot tree.

**abriter** *verb* [1] **1** to shelter; **2 s'abriter** to take shelter.

**abrupt** *adjective* **1** steep; **une pente abrupte** a steep slope; **2** abrupt.

**abrutir** *verb* [2] **1** to deafen; **2** to stupefy.

**absence** *noun Fem.* **1** absence; **pendant mon absence** while I was out, while I was away; **2 l'absence de** the lack of.

**absent** *adjective* **1 être absent** to be out, to be away; **je serai absent pendant une heure** I'll be out for an hour; **elle a été absente tout le mois de mai** she was away for the whole of May; **2** absent; **3** absent-minded.

**absenter** *verb* [1] **s'absenter** to go out, to go away; **je m'absente quelques minutes** I'm just popping out for a few minutes.

**absolu** *adjective* absolute.

**absolument** *adverb* absolutely.

**absorbant** *adjective* **1** absorbing; **un livre absorbant** an absorbing book; **2** absorbent (*material*).

**absorber** *verb* [1] **1** to absorb; **2** to take (*food or drink*).

**abstenir** *verb* [81] **s'abstenir de** to refrain from.

**abstrait** *adjective* abstract.

**absurde** *adjective* absurd.

**absurdité** *noun Fem.* absurdity; **dire des absurdités** to talk nonsense.

**abus** *noun Masc.* abuse; **l'abus d'alcool** alcohol abuse.

**abuser** *verb* [1] **1 abuser de** to misuse; **abuser de l'alcool** to drink too much (*regularly*); **2 abuser de** to take advantage of, to exploit; **elle abuse de ta gentillesse** she's taking advantage of your kindness.

**abusif** (*Fem.* **abusive**) *adjective* **1** excessive; **2** unfair.

**acajou** *noun Masc.* mahogany; **une table en acajou** a mahogany table.

**accablant** *adjective* overwhelming.

**accabler** *verb* [1] to overwhelm.

**accéder** *verb* [24] **1 accéder à** to reach, to get to ; **pour accéder à la salle de bains, il faut passer par la chambre** to get to the bathroom you have to go through the bedroom; **2 accéder au pouvoir** to come to power.

**accélérateur** *noun Masc.* accelerator; **appuyer sur l'accélérateur** to accelerate.

**accélération** *noun Fem.* acceleration.

**accélérer** *verb* [24] **1** to speed up (*the rhythm, process, etc*); **2** to accelerate (*in a car*).

**accent** *noun Masc.* **1** accent; **un accent étranger** a foreign accent; **parler français sans accent** to speak French without an accent; **2** accent (*on a letter in written French*) **un accent aigu** an acute accent; **un accent grave** a grave accent; **un accent circonflexe** a circumflex; **3 mettre l'accent sur quelque chose** to put the emphasis on something.

**accentuer** *verb* [1] to emphasize.

**acceptation** *noun Fem.* acceptance.

**accepter** *verb* [1] **1** to accept; **accepter une invitation** to accept an invitation; **2 accepter de faire** to agree to do; **elle a accepté de m'aider** she agreed to help me.

**accès** *noun Masc.* **1** access; **accès interdit** no entry; **2 un accès de colère** a fit of anger.

**accessible** *adjective* **1** accessible; **un livre accessible** a book which is easy to read; **2 des prix accessibles** affordable prices.

**accessoire** *noun Masc.* accessory; **les accessoires** accessories (*gloves, handbags, etc*).
**accessoire** *adjective* incidental.

**accident** *noun Masc.* **1** accident; **avoir un accident** to have an accident; **un accident de la route** a road accident; **2** hitch; **il y a eu un petit accident** there's been a slight hitch.

**accidenté** *adjective* **1** injured; **2** damaged; **3 'chaussée accidentée'** 'uneven road surface'.

**acclamations** *plural noun Fem.* cheering.

**accommodant** *adjective* easy-going.

**accompagnateur**, **accompagnatrice** *noun Masc., Fem.* **1** tourist guide; **2** courier (*for a group on a package holiday*); **3** accompanying adult (*with a child*); **4** accompanist (*for example, a pianist accompanying a singer*).

3

**accompagner** *verb* [1] **1** to accompany; **je t'accompagne** I'll go with you, I'll come with you; **je t'accompagne jusqu'à chez toi** I'll see you home; **2 accompagné de** accompanied by; **elle est partie accompagnée de son frère** she left accompanied by her brother; **3** to accompany (*on the piano, for example*).

**accomplir** *verb* [2] to carry out (*a task, project, mission, etc*).

**accord** *noun Masc.* **1** agreement; **2 d'accord** all right, OK; **je suis d'accord** I agree; **je suis d'accord avec Rosie** I agree with Rosie; **Paul est d'accord pour venir avec nous** Paul's agreed to come with us; **se mettre d'accord** to come to an agreement; **ils se sont mis d'accord sur le prix** they came to an agreement over the price; **3** chord (*in music*).

**accordéon** *noun Masc.* accordeon; **jouer de l'accordéon** to play the accordeon.

**accorder** *verb* [1] **1** to grant (*a favour, permission, etc*); **2** to tune (*a musical instrument*); **3 s'accorder** to agree.

**accotement** *noun Masc.* verge (*on the edge of the road*); hard shoulder (*on the motorway*); **'accotements non stabilisés'** 'soft verges' (*as road sign*).

**accouchement** *noun Masc.* childbirth, delivery.

**accoucher** *verb* [1] to give birth.

**accoutumé** *adjective* **1** usual; **2 accoutumé à** used to, accustomed to.

**accoutumer** *verb* [1] **s'accoutumer à** to become accustomed to.

**accro** *noun Masc.* (*informal*) addict. **accro** *adjective* (*informal*) **être accro de quelque chose** to be hooked on something.

**accroc** *noun Masc.* **1** tear; **tu as un accroc à ta jupe** you've got a tear in your skirt; **2** hitch; **sans accroc(s)** without a hitch.

**accrocher** *verb* [1] **1** to hang; **accrocher un tableau au mur** to hang a picture on the wall; **accroché au mur** hanging on the wall; **2** to catch, to snag (*something on a nail or thorn, for example*).

**accroupir** *verb* [2] **s'accroupir** to crouch (down), to squat.

**accueil** *noun Masc.* **1** welcome; **un accueil chaleureux** a warm welcome; **ma famille d'accueil est très sympathique** my host family is very nice; **2** reception desk; **Madame Jones est priée de se présenter à l'accueil** would Ms Jones please go to the reception desk.

**accueillant** *adjective* **1** (*of a person*) hospitable, welcoming; **2** (*of a place*) inviting, friendly.

**accueillir** *verb* [35] **1** to welcome; **2** to receive, to greet.

**accumuler** *verb* [1] **1** to collect; **2 s'accumuler** to pile up.

**accusation** *noun Fem.* accusation.

**accusé de réception** *noun Masc.* envoyer une lettre avec accusé de réception to send a letter recorded delivery.

**accuser** *verb* [1] to accuse; **il m'a accusé d'avoir volé son stylo** he accused me of stealing his pen.

**acharner** *verb* [1] s'acharner à faire to persist in doing.

**achat** *noun Masc.* purchase; **je te montre mes achats** I'll show you what I've bought.

**acheter** *verb* [16] **1** to buy; **je vais acheter du pain** I'm going to buy some bread; **2** acheter quelque chose à quelqu'un to buy somebody something; **je t'achète un sandwich?** shall I buy you a sandwich?; **je lui ai acheté un cadeau** I bought him (*or* her) a present; **3** acheter quelque chose à quelqu'un to buy something from somebody; **j'ai vendu ma voiture – c'est Lisa qui me l'a achetée** I've sold my car – Lisa bought it from me.

**acheteur**, **acheteuse** *noun Masc., Fem.* buyer.

**achever** *verb* [50] **1** to finish (*a piece of work*); **2** to finish off (*meaning 'kill'*).

**acide** *noun Masc.* acid.
**acide** *adjective* sharp, sour.

**acier** *noun Masc.* steel.

**acné** *noun Fem.* acne.

**acoustique** *noun Fem.* acoustics.

**acquérir** *verb* [17] to acquire.

**âcre** *adjective* pungent.

**acrobate** *noun Masc. & Fem.* acrobat.

**acrobatie** *noun Fem.* acrobatics.

**acte** *noun Masc.* act.

**acte de naissance** *noun Masc.* birth certificate.

**acteur**, **actrice** *noun Masc., Fem.* actor, actress.

**actif** (*Fem.* **active**) *adjective* active; **la vie active** working life.

**action** *noun Fem.* action, act; **une bonne action** a good deed.

**activement** *adverb* actively.

**activer** *verb* [1] **1** to speed up; **2** s'activer to hurry up.

**activité** *noun Fem.* activity.

**activité professionnelle** *noun Fem.* occupation.

**actualité** *noun Fem.* **1** current affairs; **2** les actualités the news.

**actuel** (*Fem.* **actuelle**) *adjective* present, current; **la situation actuelle** the present situation.

**actuellement** *adverb* at the moment; **elle est actuellement à Rome** she's in Rome at the moment.

**adapté** *adjective* **1** suitable; **adapté à** suitable for, suited to; **2** adapted.

**adapter** *verb* [1] **1** to adapt; **2** s'adapter à to adapt to, to get used to.

**additif** *noun Masc.* additive.

**addition** *noun Fem.* **1** addition; **2** bill (*in a restaurant*) **l'addition, s'il vous plaît** can I have the bill please.

**additionner** *verb* [1] to add up.

a
b
c
d
e
f
g
h
i
j
k
l
m
n
o
p
q
r
s
t
u
v
w
x
y
z

a
b
c
d
e
f
g
h
i
j
k
l
m
n
o
p
q
r
s
t
u
v
w
x
y
z

**adhésif** (*Fem.* **adhésive**) *adjective* adhesive; **ruban adhésif** sticky tape.

**adieu** (*plural* **adieux**) *noun Masc.* goodbye, farewell (*the usual expression is 'au revoir' since 'adieu' is properly used to mean 'goodbye for ever'*).

**adjectif** *noun Masc.* adjective.

**adjoint, adjointe** *noun Masc., Fem.* **1** assistant; **2** deputy.

**admettre** *verb* [11] **1** to admit; **j'admets qu'elle a raison** I admit that she's right; **2 admettre dans** to admit to (*a restaurant, a club, etc*).

**administratif** (*Fem.* **administrative**) *adjective* administrative.

**administration** *noun Fem.* administration.

**admiratif** (*Fem.* **admirative**) *adjective* admiring; **des regards admiratifs** admiring glances.

**admiration** *noun Fem.* admiration.

**admirer** *verb* [1] to admire.

**adolescence** *noun Fem.* adolescence.

**adolescent, adolescente** *noun Masc., Fem.* teenager, adolescent.

**adolescent** *adjective* teenage, adolescent.

**adopter** *verb* [1] to adopt.

**adoptif** (*Fem.* **adoptive**) *adjective* **un enfant adoptif** an adopted child.

**adoption** *noun Fem.* adoption.

**adorable** *adjective* adorable.

**adorer** *verb* [1] to adore, to love.

**adresse** *noun Fem.* **1** address; **quelle est ton adresse?** what's your address?; **se tromper d'adresse** to get (*or* go to) the wrong address; **2** skill; **elle l'a fait avec beaucoup d'adresse** she did it very skilfully; **3** speech, address.

**adresser** *verb* [1] **1 adresser une lettre à quelqu'un** to send somebody a letter; **2 adresser la parole à quelqu'un** to speak to somebody; **3 s'adresser à** to enquire at; **adressez-vous à la réception** enquire at reception; **4 s'adresser à** to be aimed at; **le film s'adresse aux adolescents** the film is aimed at teenagers.

**adroit** *adjective* skilful.

**adulte** *noun Masc. & Fem., adjective* adult.

**adverbe** *noun Masc.* adverb.

**adversaire** *noun Masc. & Fem.* opponent.

**adverse** *adjective* opposing.

**aération** *noun Fem.* ventilation.

**aérer** *verb* [24] to air.

**aérobic** *noun Masc.* aerobics.

**aéro-club** *noun Masc.* flying club.

**aérogare** *noun Fem.* (flight) terminal (*in an airport*).

**aéronautique** *noun Fem.* aeronautics.

**aéroport** *noun Masc.* airport; **à l'aéroport** at (*or* to) the airport.

**aérosol** *noun Masc.* aerosol.

**affaire** *noun Fem.* **1** matter, business; **c'est une drôle d'affaire** it's a funny business;

**c'est une autre affaire** that's another matter; **2** affair, political crisis.

**affaires** *plural noun Fem.* **1 les affaires** business; **un homme d'affaires** a businessman; **une femme d'affaires** a businesswoman; **un voyage d'affaires** a business trip; **2** business; **occupe-toi de tes affaires!** mind your own business!; **3** belongings, things; **tu peux laisser tes affaires dans la chambre** you can leave your things in the bedroom.

**affamé** *adjective* starving.

**affamer** *verb* [1] to starve.

**affecter** *verb* [1] **1** to affect; **2 affecter de faire** to pretend to do.

**affection** *noun Fem.* affection; **j'ai beaucoup d'affection pour lui** I'm very fond of him.

**affectueusement** *adverb* affectionately.

**affectueux** (*Fem.* **affectueuse**) *adjective* affectionate.

**affiche** *noun Fem.* **1** poster; **2** notice.

**afficher** *verb* [1] to put up (*a poster or a notice*).

**affliger** *verb* [52] **1** to distress, to grieve; **2 affliger de** to afflict with.

**affluence** *noun Fem.* crowds; **aux heures d'affluence** at peak times.

**affolant** *adjective* (*informal*) frightening.

**affoler** *verb* [1] **1 affoler quelqu'un** to throw somebody into a panic;

**2 s'affoler** to panic; **ne t'affole pas** don't panic.

**affreux** (*Fem.* **affreuse**) *adjective* **1** awful, dreadful; **2** hideous.

**afin** *preposition* **1 afin de faire** in order to do; **2 afin que** in order that.

**africain** *adjective* African.

**Africain**, **Africaine** *noun Masc.*, *Fem.* African.

**Afrique** *noun Fem.* Africa; **en Afrique** in (*or* to) Africa.

**agaçant** *adjective* annoying.

**agacer** *verb* [61] to annoy.

**âge** *noun Masc.* age; **quel âge as-tu?** how old are you?; **à l'âge de cinq ans** at the age of five; **je ne sais pas son âge** I don't know how old he (*or* she) is; **il a l'âge de mon père** he's the same age as my father.

**âgé** *adjective* **1** old; **les personnes âgées** old people; **2 âgé de** aged; **une femme âgée de trente ans** a woman aged thirty.

**agence** *noun Fem.* **1** agency; **2** branch (*of a bank*).

**agence de voyages** *noun Fem.* travel agent's.

**agence immobilière** *noun Fem.* estate agent's.

**agenda** *noun Masc.* diary.

**agenouiller** *verb* [1] **s'agenouiller** to kneel down.

**agent** *noun Masc.* **1** official; **2** agent.

**agent commercial** *noun Masc.* sales representative.

**agent de police** *noun Masc.*
police officer; **une femme agent de police** a woman police officer.

**aggraver** *verb* [1] **1** to make worse; **aggraver la situation** to make things worse; **2 s'aggraver** to get worse; **la situation s'aggrave** the situation is deteriorating, things are getting worse.

**agir** *verb* [2] **1** to act; **2** to behave; **3 il s'agit de** it is about; **il s'agit de ton frère** it's about your brother; **de quoi s'agit-il?** what's it about?

**agitation** *noun Fem.* **1** hustle and bustle; **2** unrest; **3** restlessness.

**agité** *adjective* **1** restless, agitated; **2** rough (*sea*); **3** bustling (*street*); **4 mener une vie agitée** to lead a hectic life.

**agiter** *verb* [1] to shake; **agiter la main** to wave your hand.

**agneau** (*plural* **agneaux**) *noun Masc.* lamb; **un gigot d'agneau** a leg of lamb.

**agrafe** *noun Fem.* **1** staple; **2** hook (*on a garment*).

**agrafer** *verb* [1] **1** to staple; **2** to fasten.

**agrafeuse** *noun Fem.* stapler.

**agrandir** *verb* [2] to enlarge.

**agrandissement** *noun Masc.* enlargement (*of a photo*).

**agréable** *adjective* pleasant, nice.

**agréé** *adjective* **1** registered; **2** authorized.

**agréer** *verb* [32] **1** to agree to; **2 veuillez agréer l'expression de mes sentiments distingués** Yours faithfully, Yours sincerely (*this is

one of a number of fixed expressions used to end any formal or business letter*).

**agresser** *verb* [1] **1** to attack; **2** to mug.

**agresseur** *noun Masc.* attacker.

**agressif** (*Fem.* **agressive**) *adjective* aggressive.

**agression** *noun Fem.* **1** attack; **2** mugging.

**agressivité** *noun Fem.* aggressiveness.

**agricole** *adjective* agricultural.

**agriculteur**, **agricultrice** *noun Masc., Fem.* farmer.

**ahuri** *adjective* amazed, stunned.

**ai** *verb* SEE **avoir**.

**aide**[1] *noun Fem.* **1** help; **avec l'aide de Claire** with Claire's help; **venir à l'aide de quelqu'un** to help somebody; **2** aid (*financial aid given to a person or a country*).

**aide**[2] *noun Masc. & Fem.* **1** assistant; **2** helper.

**aider** *verb* [1] **1** to help; **il m'a aidé à mettre la table** he helped me set the table; **est-ce que je peux t'aider?** would you like some help?; **2** to give aid to (*financial aid to a person, group, or country*).

**aigle** *noun Masc. & Fem.* eagle.

**aiglefin** *noun Masc.* haddock.

**aigre** *adjective* **1** sour; **2** sharp.

**aigu** (*Fem.* **aiguë**) *adjective* **1** high-pitched; **2** acute.

**aiguille** *noun Fem.* **1** needle; **une aiguille à coudre** a sewing needle; **une aiguille à tricoter** a knitting needle; **2** hand (*of a clock or watch*); **dans le sens des aiguilles d'une montre** clockwise; **ça tourne dans le sens des aiguilles d'une montre** it turns clockwise.

**aiguilleur du ciel** *noun Masc.* air traffic controller.

**aiguiser** *verb* [1] to sharpen.

**ail** *noun Masc.* garlic.

**aile** *noun Fem.* wing; ★ **voler de ses propres ailes** to stand on your own two feet (*literally: to fly with your own wings*).

**ailleurs** *adverb* **1** elsewhere, somewhere else; **2 d'ailleurs** besides, moreover; **3 par ailleurs** also, in addition.

**aimable** *adjective* kind, nice; **vous êtes très aimable** that's very kind of you.

**aimant** *noun Masc.* magnet.

**aimer** *verb* [1] **1** to like; **est-ce que tu aimes les fraises?** do you like strawberries?; **aimer faire quelque chose** to like doing something; **elle aime aller au cinéma** she likes going to the cinema; **elle aimerait aller au cinéma** she'd like to go to the cinema; **2 aimer mieux** to prefer; **j'aime mieux les fraises que les framboises** I prefer strawberries to raspberries, I like strawberries better than raspberries; **j'aimerais mieux aller au cinéma** I'd prefer to go to the cinema, I'd rather go to the cinema; **3** to love; **je t'aime** I love you; **4 s'aimer** to like each other, to love each other.

**aîné, aînée** *noun Masc., Fem.* **l'aîné(e)** the eldest, the oldest (*child*).
**aîné** *adjective* elder, older (*of two*) eldest, oldest (*of more than two*); **leur fille aînée** their elder (or eldest) daughter.

**ainsi** *adverb* **1** thus; **2** in this way; **3 ainsi que** as well as, along with.

**aïoli** *noun Masc.* garlic mayonnaise.

**air** *noun Masc.* **1** air; **aller prendre l'air** to go out and get some fresh air; **2 un courant d'air** a draught; **3 avoir l'air ( ...)** to look ( ...); **avoir l'air bon** to look good; **avoir l'air fatigué** to look tired; **4 avoir l'air de** to look like; **il a l'air d'un policier** he looks like a policeman; **5 avoir l'air d'être** to look as if you are; **elle a l'air d'être perdue** she looks as if she's lost; **6 avoir l'air de faire** to look as if you are doing; **il a l'air de comprendre** he looks as if he understands; **7 sourire d'un air heureux** to smile happily; **8** tune.

**air bag™** *noun Masc.* airbag (*in a car*).

**aire de jeu** *noun Fem.* playground.

**aire de pique-nique** *noun Fem.* picnic area.

**aire de services** *noun Fem.* motorway service station.

**aise** *noun Fem.* **être à l'aise** to be comfortable, to feel at ease; **être mal à l'aise** to feel uncomfortable.

**aisselle** *noun Fem.* armpit.

**ajout** *noun Masc.* addition.

**ajouter** *verb* [1] to add; **ajoutez un œuf** add an egg.

a
b
c
d
e
f
g
h
i
j
k
l
m
n
o
p
q
r
s
t
u
v
w
x
y
z

a
b
c
d
e
f
g
h
i
j
k
l
m
n
o
p
q
r
s
t
u
v
w
x
y
z

**alarme** *noun Fem.* alarm; **sonner l'alarme** to sound the alarm.

**album** *noun Masc.* album.

**album de bandes dessinées** *noun Masc.* comic book.

**album de photos** *noun Masc.* photograph album.

**album de timbres** *noun Masc.* stamp album.

**alcool** *noun Masc.* alcohol.

**alcoolique** *noun Masc. & Fem., adjective* alcoholic.

**alcoolisé** *adjective* **une boisson alcoolisée** an alcoholic drink; **une boisson non alcoolisée** a non-alcoholic drink.

**alcootest** *noun Masc.* Breathalyzer™.

**alcôve** *noun Fem.* alcove.

**alentours** *plural noun Masc.* **1** surroundings; **2 aux alentours de** in the vicinity (*or* neighbourhood) of.

**algèbre** *noun Fem.* algebra.

**Algérie** *noun Fem.* Algeria.

**algérien** (*Fem.* **algérienne**) *adjective* Algerian.

**algues** *plural noun Fem.* seaweed.

**alibi** *noun Masc.* alibi.

**aliment** *noun Masc.* food.

**alimentaire** *adjective* **des produits alimentaires** food products; **l'industrie alimentaire** the food industry.

**alimentation** *noun Fem.* **1** groceries; **2** diet.

**allée** *noun Fem.* path, drive.

**alléger** *verb* [15] **1** to lighten; **2** to reduce.

**Allemagne** *noun Fem.* Germany.

**allemand** *noun Masc.* German (*language*).
**allemand** *adjective* German.

**Allemand, Allemande** *noun Masc., Fem.* German (*person*).

**aller**[1] *verb* [7] **1** to go; **aller à Paris** to go to Paris; **je vais à Paris** I'm going to Paris, I go to Paris; **2** (*used with another verb in much the same way as 'going to' is used in English*) **je vais écrire à ma mère ce soir** I'm going to write to my mother this evening; **3 (comment) ça va?** how are you?; **ça va bien** I'm fine; **comment va ta mère?** how's your mother?; **elle va bien** she's fine; **4** to suit; **cette robe te va bien** that dress really suits you; **est-ce que jeudi te va?** does Thursday suit you?; **5 s'en aller** to leave; **je m'en vais!** I'm off!

**aller**[2] *noun Masc.* **1 faire des allers et retours** to go to and fro; **2 un aller simple** a single ticket; **un aller-retour** a return ticket; **Avignon aller simple, s'il vous plaît** a single to Avignon please.

**allergie** *noun Fem.* allergy.

**allergique** *adjective* **être allergique à** to be allergic to; **elle est allergique aux chats** she's allergic to cats.

**alliance** *noun Fem.* **1** wedding ring; **2** alliance.

**allié, alliée** *noun Masc., Fem.* ally.

**alligator** *noun Masc.* alligator.

**allô** *exclamation* hello (*only used on the telephone*).

**allocation** *noun Fem.* benefit, allowance.

**allocation chômage** *noun Fem.* unemployment benefit.

**allocations familiales** *plural noun Fem.* family allowance.

**allonger** *verb* [52] **1** to lengthen; **2** to extend; **3 s'allonger** to lie down.

**allumer** *verb* [1] **1** to light; **allumer le feu** to light the fire; **2** to switch on; **allumer la lampe** to switch on the lamp; **3** to switch on the lights.

**allumette** *noun Fem.* match; **une boîte d'allumettes** a box of matches.

**allure** *noun Fem.* **1** speed; **à toute allure** at top speed; **2** appearance (*of a person*).

**alors** *adverb* **1** then, at that time; **elle travaillait alors à Paris** she was working in Paris then; **2** so; **alors, comment ça va?** so how are you?; **3 alors que** while; **alors qu'elle faisait ses devoirs** while she was doing her homework.

**alouette** *noun Fem.* skylark.

**Alpes** *noun Fem.* **les Alpes** the Alps.

**alphabet** *noun Masc.* alphabet.

**alphabétique** *adjective* alphabetical; **dans l'ordre alphabétique, par ordre alphabétique** in alphabetical order.

**alpin** *adjective* alpine.

**alpinisme** *noun Masc.* mountaineering.

**alsacien** (*Fem.* **alsacienne**) *adjective* from Alsace, Alsatian.

**Alsacien**, **Alsacienne** *noun Masc., Fem.* Alsatian.

**alternatif** (*Fem.* **alternative**) *adjective* alternative.

**altitude** *noun Fem.* altitude.

**alu** *noun Masc.* (*informal*) aluminium; **du papier alu** kitchen foil.

**aluminium** *noun Masc.* aluminium.

**amalgame** *noun Masc.* mixture.

**amande** *noun Fem.* **1** almond; **2** kernel (*of a fruit stone*).

**amant** *noun Masc.* lover.

**amateur** *noun Masc.* enthusiast; **un amateur de musique** a music lover. **amateur** *adjective* amateur; **un photographe amateur** an amateur photographer.

**ambassade** *noun Fem.* embassy; **l'ambassade de France** the French Embassy.

**ambassadeur** *noun Masc.* ambassador.

**ambiance** *noun Fem.* atmosphere; **une bonne ambiance** a good atmosphere.

**ambigu** (*Fem.* **ambiguë**) *adjective* ambiguous.

**ambitieux** (*Fem.* **ambitieuse**) *adjective* ambitious.

**ambition** *noun Fem.* ambition.

**ambulance** *noun Fem.* ambulance.

**ambulancier**, **ambulancière** *noun Masc., Fem.* ambulance driver.

**âme** *noun Fem.* soul.

**amélioration** *noun Fem.* improvement.

**améliorer**, **s'améliorer** *verb* [1] to improve.

**aménagé** *adjective* **1** equipped; **une cuisine aménagée** an equipped kitchen; **2** converted.

**aménager** *verb* [52] **1** to convert, to do up (*a building, a room, etc*); **2** to develop (*an area*); **3** to construct, to improve (*a road or road system*).

**amende** *noun Fem.* fine; **une amende de 500 euros** a 500-euro fine.

**amener** *verb* [50] **1** to bring; **elle a amené son cousin** she brought her cousin (with her); **2** to take; **amener un enfant à l'école** to take a child to school.

**amer** (*Fem.* **amère**) *adjective* bitter.

**américain** *adjective* American.

**Américain**, **Américaine** *noun Masc., Fem.* American.

**Amérique** *noun Fem.* America.

**ami**, **amie** *noun Masc., Fem.* friend; **un ami à moi** a friend of mine; **un ami à Lisa** a friend of Lisa's. **ami** *adjective* friendly.

**amiante** *noun Masc.* asbestos.

**amical** (*Masc. plural* **amicaux**) *adjective* friendly.

**amicale** *noun Fem.* association.

**amicalement** *adverb* **1** in a friendly way; **2** Best wishes (*at the end of a letter*).

**amitié** *noun Fem.* **1** friendship; **faire quelque chose par amitié** to do something out of friendship; **2 amitiés** love (*at the end of a letter*).

**amortisseur** *noun Masc.* shock absorber.

**amour** *noun Masc.* love.

**amoureux** (*Fem.* **amoureuse**) *adjective* in love; **être amoureux de** to be in love with.

**amour-propre** *noun Masc.* self-esteem.

**amovible** *adjective* detachable.

**amphi** *noun Masc.* (*informal*) lecture theatre (*in a university*).

**amphithéâtre** *noun Masc.* **1** amphitheatre; **2** lecture theatre.

**ample** *adjective* **1** loose-fitting (*jacket, dress, etc*); **2** ample (*quantity*).

**ampleur** *noun Fem.* size, scope.

**ampli** *noun Masc.* (*informal*) amplifier.

**amplificateur** *noun Masc.* amplifier.

**ampoule** *noun Fem.* **1** light bulb; **2** blister.

**amusant** *adjective* **1** funny; **une histoire amusante** a funny story; **2** entertaining.

**amuse-gueule** *noun Masc.* **des amuse-gueule** nibbles (*crisps, nuts, etc*).

**amuser** *verb* [1] **1** to amuse; **2** to entertain; **3 s'amuser** to play; **4 s'amuser** to enjoy oneself, to have a good time; **on s'est bien amusé** we really enjoyed ourselves, we had a really good time.

**an** *noun Masc.* year; **elle a dix ans** she's ten (years old); **le nouvel an, le jour de l'an** New Year's Day; **il va en Normandie tous les ans** he goes to Normandy every year; ★ **bon an, mal an** year in, year out (*literally: good year, bad year*).

**analgésique** *noun Masc.* analgesic, painkiller.

**analphabète** *adjective* illiterate.

**analyse** *noun Fem.* **1** analysis; **2 une analyse de sang** a blood test.

**analyser** *verb* [1] to analyse.

**ananas** *noun Masc.* pineapple.

**anatomie** *noun Fem.* anatomy.

**ancêtre** *noun Masc. & Fem.* ancestor.

**anchois** *noun Masc.* anchovy.

**ancien** (*Fem.* **ancienne**) *adjective* **1** (*coming before a noun*) former; **l'ancien président** the former president, the ex-president; **mon ancienne école** my old school; **un ancien élève** a former pupil; **2** (*coming after a noun*) old; **une maison ancienne** an old house; **une table ancienne** an antique table.

**ancien combattant** *noun Masc.* war veteran.

**ancre** *noun Fem.* anchor.

**âne** *noun Masc.* donkey.

**anémone** *noun Fem.* anemone.

**anesthésie** *noun Fem.* anaesthesia; **une anesthésie** an anaesthetic.

**anesthésiste** *noun Masc. & Fem.* anaesthetist.

**ange** *noun Masc.* angel; ★ **être aux anges** to be over the moon, to be absolutely delighted (*literally: to be at the level of the angels*).

**angine** *noun Fem.* throat infection; **avoir une angine** to have a throat infection.

**anglais** *noun Masc.* English (*language*); **parler l'anglais** to speak English.
  **anglais** *adjective* English.

**Anglais, Anglaise** *noun Masc., Fem.* Englishman, Englishwoman; **les Anglais** the English; **il y a une Anglaise dans notre classe** there's an English girl in our class.

**angle** *noun Masc.* **1** angle; **un angle droit** a right angle; **2** corner; **à l'angle de la rue** at the corner of the street; **le magasin qui fait l'angle** the shop on the corner.

**Angleterre** *noun Fem.* England; **en Angleterre** in (*or* to) England; **aller en Angleterre** to go to England.

**Anglo-Normande** *adjective* **les îles Anglo-Normandes** the Channel Islands.

**anglophone** *noun Masc. & Fem.* English speaker.
  **anglophone** *adjective* English-speaking.

**angoisse** *noun Fem.* anxiety.

**angoissé** *adjective* anxious.

**anguille** *noun Fem.* eel.

**anguleux** (*Fem.* **anguleuse**) *adjective* bony.

**animal** (*plural* **animaux**) *noun Masc.* animal.

13

a
b
c
d
e
f
g
h
i
j
k
l
m
n
o
p
q
r
s
t
u
v
w
x
y
z

**animateur, animatrice** *noun Masc., Fem.* **1** group leader; **2** organizer; **3** presenter.

**animation** *noun Fem.* **1** liveliness, life; **il y a beaucoup d'animation dans le quartier le soir** there's a lot going on in the area at night; **2** organization (*of a group, a programme, etc*).

**animé** *adjective* **1** lively (*person or discussion*); **2** busy (*place*).

**animer** *verb* [1] **1** to run (*a course*); **2** to lead (*a group* ); **3** to present (*a programme or a show*); **4** to liven up (*an occasion*); **5 s'animer** to liven up.

**anis** *noun Masc.* aniseed.

**anneau** (*plural* **anneaux**) *noun Masc.* ring.

**année** *noun Fem.* year; **l'année prochaine** next year; **l'année dernière** last year; **les années 70** the seventies; **Bonne année** Happy New Year.

**annexe** *noun Fem.* **1** appendix (*of book*); **2** annexe (*of building*).

**anniversaire** *noun Masc.* **1** birthday; **fêter son anniversaire** to celebrate one's birthday; **Bon anniversaire, Joyeux anniversaire** Happy Birthday; **2** anniversary.

**annonce** *noun Fem.* **1** advertisement; **les petites annonces** the small ads (*in a newspaper*); **2** announcement; **3** sign.

**annoncer** *verb* [61] **1** to announce; **2** to forecast; **ils annoncent de la neige pour demain** snow is forecast for tomorrow.

**annuaire** *noun Masc.* directory; **l'annuaire téléphonique** the telephone directory.

**annuel** (*Fem.* **annuelle**) *adjective* annual, yearly; **un événement annuel** a yearly event.

**annuler** *verb* [1] to cancel; **le vol a été annulé** the flight has been cancelled.

**anonyme** *adjective* anonymous.

**anorak** *noun Masc.* anorak.

**anorexie** *noun Fem.* anorexia.

**anormal** (*Masc. plural* **anormaux**) *adjective* abnormal.

**anse** *noun Fem.* handle (*of a basket, cup, jug, or teapot*).

**Antarctique** *noun Masc.* **l'Antarctique** the Antarctic.

**antenne** *noun Fem.* **1** aerial (*for a radio or television*); **2** antenna (*of an insect, a radio mast, or a spacecraft*).

**anthropologie** *noun Fem.* anthropology.

**antibiotique** *noun Masc.* antibiotic; **prendre des antibiotiques** to be on antibiotics.

**antichoc** *adjective* shockproof; **un casque antichoc** a crash helmet.

**anticiper** *verb* [1] to foresee, to anticipate.

**antidérapant** *adjective* nonslip, nonskid.

**antidote** *noun Masc.* antidote.

**antigel** *noun Masc.* antifreeze.

**antillais** *adjective* West Indian.

**Antillais, Antillaise** *noun Masc.,Fem.* West Indian.

**Antilles** *plural noun Fem.* **les Antilles** the West Indies.

**antilope** *noun Fem.* antelope.

**antipathique** *adjective* unpleasant.

**antiquaire** *noun Masc. & Fem.* antique dealer.

**antiquité** *noun Fem.* antique.

**antiseptique** *noun Masc.,* *adjective* antiseptic.

**antitabac** *adjective* antismoking.

**antiterroriste** *adjective* antiterrorist.

**antivol** *noun Masc.* anti-theft device.

**anxieux** (*Fem.* **anxieuse**) *adjective* anxious.

**août** *noun Masc.* August; **en août, au mois d'août** in August.

**apercevoir** *verb* [66] **1** to catch sight of; **2 s'apercevoir de** to notice; **s'apercevoir que** to notice that.

**aperçu** *noun Masc.* **1** insight; **2** glimpse.

**apéritif** *noun Masc.* drink (*usually alcoholic, before a meal*).

**aphte** *noun Masc.* mouth ulcer.

**aplatir** *verb* [2] **1** to flatten; **2** to smooth out.

**apostrophe** *noun Fem.* apostrophe.

**apparaître** *verb* [57] **1** to appear; **2** to seem; **il apparaît que** it seems that.

**appareil** *noun Masc.* **1** device, appliance, piece of equipment; **2** telephone; **c'est Paul à l'appareil** it's Paul speaking; **3 un appareil (dentaire)** a brace (*for teeth*).

**appareil photo** *noun Masc.* camera.

**apparemment** *adverb* apparently.

**apparence** *noun Fem.* appearance.

**apparent** *adjective* **1** visible, obvious; **2** apparent.

**apparition** *noun Fem.* appearance.

**appartement** *noun Masc.* flat; **'appartement à louer'** 'flat to let'.

**appartenir** *verb* [81] **appartenir à** to belong to; **est-ce que ce stylo t'appartient?** does this pen belong to you?, is this pen yours?; **à qui appartiennent ces chaussures?** who do these shoes belong to?

**appel** *noun Masc.* **1** call, appeal; **un appel d'aide** a call for help; **2 un appel (téléphonique)** a telephone call; **3 faire appel à** to appeal to; **4 faire l'appel** to take the register (*at school*).

**appeler** *verb* [18] **1** to call; **ils l'ont appelé Roger** they called him Roger; **2 s'appeler** to be called; **il s'appelle Frank** he's called Frank, his name is Frank; **je m'appelle Anne** my name is Anne; **comment t'appelles-tu?, tu t'appelles comment?** what's your name?; **3** to phone; **4** to call; **appeler un taxi** to call a taxi.

**appendice** *noun Masc.* appendix (*organ*).

15

a
b
c
d
e
f
g
h
i
j
k
l
m
n
o
p
q
r
s
t
u
v
w
x
y
z

**appendicite** *noun Fem.*
appendicitis.

**appétissant** *adjective* appetizing.

**appétit** *noun Masc.* appetite; **'bon
appétit'** 'enjoy your meal'.

**applaudir** *verb* [2] to applaud.

**applaudissements** *plural
noun Masc.* applause.

**application** *noun Fem.* **1** care;
**2** application.

**appliquer** *verb* [1] **1** to apply;
**2 s'appliquer** to take care;
**3 s'appliquer à** to apply to; **cela ne
s'applique pas à vous** that doesn't
apply to you.

**apporter** *verb* [1] to bring.

**apprécier** *verb* [1] to appreciate.

**appréhender** *verb* [1] **1** to arrest;
**2** to dread.

**apprenant**, **apprenante** *noun
Masc., Fem.* learner.

**apprendre** *verb* [64] **1** to learn;
**apprendre à lire** to learn to read;
**2** to hear; **j'ai appris que tu vas
partir** I hear you're leaving; **3** to
teach; **apprendre quelque chose à
quelqu'un** to teach somebody
something; **elle leur apprend le
français** she's teaching them
French; **elle leur apprend à parler
français** she's teaching them to
speak French.

**approche** *noun Fem.* approach.

**approcher** *verb* [1] **1** to move
(something) closer; **approche ta
chaise** move your chair closer;
**approche ta chaise de la table**
move your chair closer to the table;
**2 approcher quelqu'un** to go up to

somebody; **3 s'approcher de
quelque chose** to go (*or* come) near
to something.

**approprié** *adjective* appropriate.

**approuver** *verb* [1] **1** to approve of;
**2** to approve (*a document, project,
budget, etc*).

**approximatif** (*Fem.*
**approximative**) *adjective*
approximate, rough.

**approximativement** *adverb*
approximately, roughly.

**appui** *noun Masc.* support.

**appuyer** *verb* [41] **1 appuyer sur
quelque chose** to press something;
**appuie sur le bouton** press the
button; **2** to lean; **appuyer quelque
chose contre le mur** to lean
something against the wall.

**après** *adverb* afterwards, later; **une
heure après** an hour later; **peu
après** shortly afterwards;
**longtemps après** a long time
later.
**après** *preposition* **1** after; **après
dix heures** after ten o'clock; **après
l'école** after school; **2 après avoir
fait** after doing; **3 après que** after.

**après-demain** *adverb* the day
after tomorrow.

**après-midi** *noun Masc. OR Fem.*
afternoon; **cet après-midi** this
afternoon; **demain après-midi**
tomorrow afternoon; **hier après-
midi** yesterday afternoon; **tous les
après-midi** every afternoon.

**après-rasage** *noun Masc.*
aftershave.

16

**aptitude** *noun Fem.* aptitude; **son aptitude pour le dessin** his aptitude for drawing.

**aquarelle** *noun Fem.* watercolours; **une aquarelle** a watercolour (painting).

**aquarium** *noun Masc.* **1** fish tank; **2** aquarium.

**arabe** *noun Masc.* Arabic.
**arabe** *adjective* **1** Arab; **2** Arabic.

**Arabe** *noun Masc. & Fem.* Arab.

**araignée** *noun Fem.* spider; **une toile d'araignée** a spider's web.

**arbitraire** *adjective* arbitrary.

**arbitre** *noun Masc.* referee, umpire.

**arbre** *noun Masc.* tree.

**arbre généalogique** *noun Masc.* family tree.

**arc** *noun Masc.* **1** bow (*as in 'bow and arrow'*); **2** arch.

**arc-en-ciel** *noun Masc.* rainbow.

**archéologie** *noun Fem.* archeology.

**archéologue** *noun Masc. & Fem.* archeologist.

**archet** *noun Masc.* bow (*for a musical instrument such as a violin.*).

**archevêque** *noun Masc.* archbishop.

**architecte** *noun Masc. & Fem.* architect.

**architecture** *noun Fem.* architecture.

**Arctique** *noun Masc.* **l'Arctique** the Arctic.

**ardoise** *noun Fem.* slate.

**arène** *noun Fem.* **1** arena; **2** bullring.

**arête** *noun Fem.* fishbone; **ce poisson est plein d'arêtes** this fish is full of bones.

**argent** *noun Masc.* **1** money; **dépenser de l'argent** to spend money; **2** silver; **une cuillère en argent** a silver spoon.

**argent de poche** *noun Masc.* pocket money.

**argile** *noun Fem.* clay.

**argot** *noun Masc.* slang.

**aristocrate** *noun Masc. & Fem.* aristocrat.

**aristocratie** *noun Fem.* aristocracy.

**arithmétique** *noun Fem.* arithmetic.

**arme** *noun Fem.* weapon.

**armé** *adjective* **1** armed; **2** armé de armed with, equipped with.

**arme à feu** *noun Fem.* firearm.

**armée** *noun Fem.* army.

**armée de l'air** *noun Fem.* Air Force.

**armée de terre** *noun Fem.* Army.

**armoire** *noun Fem.* **1** cupboard; **2** wardrobe.

**arobase** *noun Masc.* at, @ (*in email addresses*); **jean-point-dupont-arobase-mondecom-point-com** jean-dot-dupont-at-mondecom-dot-com.

**aromates** *plural noun Masc.* herbs and spices.

a
b
c
d
e
f
g
h
i
j
k
l
m
n
o
p
q
r
s
t
u
v
w
x
y
z

**aromathérapie** *noun Fem.* aromatherapy.

**aromatisé** *adjective* flavoured.

**arôme** *noun Masc.* **1** flavouring; **2** aroma.

**arracher** *verb* [1] **1 arracher quelque chose à quelqu'un** to snatch something from somebody; **2** to rip out, to rip off (*a page or pages*); **3** to pull up (*weeds or vegetables*).

**arrangement** *noun Masc.* arrangement.

**arranger** *verb* [52] **1** to arrange; **arranger une réunion** to arrange a meeting; **2** to arrange (*flowers, books, etc*); **3** to sort out; **4** to fix; **5 s'arranger** to get better; **ça va s'arranger** it will sort itself out; **6 s'arranger avec quelqu'un** to sort it out with somebody; **tu t'arranges avec Paul** sort it out with Paul.

**arrestation** *noun Fem.* arrest.

**arrêt** *noun Masc.* **1** stop; **un arrêt de bus** a bus stop; **2 sans arrêt** non-stop.

**arrêter** *verb* [1] **1** to stop; **arrêter la voiture** to stop the car; **2** to switch off (*an engine, a machine, etc*); **3 arrêter de faire** to stop doing; **il a arrêté de fumer** he's stopped smoking; **elle n'arrête pas de travailler** she never stops working; **4 s'arrêter** to stop; **on va s'arrêter à la boulangerie** we'll stop at the baker's.

**arrhes** *plural noun Fem.* deposit; **verser des arrhes** to pay a deposit.

**arrière** *noun Masc.* back; **à l'arrière** in the back (*of a car*); **regarder en arrière** to look back.
**arrière** *adjective* back (*door, pocket, etc*).

**arrière-goût** *noun Masc.* aftertaste.

**arrière-grand-mère** *noun Fem.* great-grandmother.

**arrière-grand-père** *noun Masc.* great-grandfather.

**arrière-grands-parents** *plural noun Masc.* great-grandparents.

**arrière-petits-enfants** *plural noun Masc.* great-grandchildren.

**arrivage** *noun Masc.* **1** delivery (*of goods*); **2** batch (*of students*).

**arrivée** *noun Fem.* arrival.

**arriver** *verb* [1] **1** to arrive; **arriver à Londres** to arrive in London, to get to London; **je suis arrivé à cinq heures** I arrived at five o'clock, I got there (*or* here) at five o'clock; **j'arrive!** just coming!; **2** to happen; **un accident est arrivé** an accident has happened; **tu sais ce qui m'est arrivé?** do you know what happened to me?; **3 arriver à faire** to manage to do; **je n'arrive pas à tourner la clef** I can't manage to turn the key.

**arrogant** *adjective* arrogant.

**arrondi** *adjective* rounded.

**arrondissement** *noun Masc.* arrondissement; **elle habite à Paris dans le neuvième arrondissement** she lives in Paris in the ninth arrondissement (*large French cities are divided into numbered* administrative areas called 'arrondissements').

**arroser** verb [1] to water; **arroser les plantes** to water the plants; **on va arroser l'anniversaire de mon frère** we're going to have a few drinks to celebrate my brother's birthday.

**arrosoir** noun Masc. watering can.

**art** noun Masc. art; **une galerie d'art** an art gallery; **l'art de faire** the art of doing.

**art dramatique** noun Masc. drama.

**artère** noun Fem. **1** artery; **2** arterial road; **3** main road.

**arthrite** noun Fem. arthritis.

**artichaut** noun Masc. artichoke.

**article** noun Masc. **1** article (in a newspaper, magazine, etc); **2** item (for sale); **articles de sport** sports equipment; **articles de toilette** toiletries; **3** article (in grammar); **l'article défini** the definite article; **l'article indéfini** the indefinite article.

**articulation** noun Fem. joint; **articulation du coude/de la hanche** elbow/hip joint.

**artificiel** (Fem. **artificielle**) adjective artificial.

**artisan** noun Masc. craftsman.

**artisanal** (Masc. plural **artisanaux**) adjective **1** traditional; **2** hand-crafted.

**artisanat** noun Masc. arts and crafts.

**artiste** noun Masc. & Fem. **1** artist; **2** performer.

**as**[1] verb SEE **avoir**.

**as**[2] noun Masc. ace.

**ascenseur** noun Masc. lift; **prendre l'ascenseur** to take the lift.

**asiatique** adjective Asian.

**Asie** noun Fem. Asia.

**asile** noun Masc. **1** refuge; **2 le droit d'asile** political asylum.

**aspect** noun Masc. **1** aspect; **2** appearance; **d'un aspect bizarre** strange-looking; **3** side; **l'aspect positif** the positive side.

**asperger** verb [52] to sprinkle.

**asperges** plural noun Fem. asparagus.

**asphyxier**, **s'asphyxier** verb [1] to suffocate.

**aspirateur** noun Masc. vacuum cleaner.

**aspirine** noun Fem. aspirin.

**assaisonnement** noun Masc. **1** seasoning; **2** dressing.

**assaisonner** verb [1] **1** to season; **2** to put the dressing on (a salad).

**assassin**, **assassine** noun Masc., Fem. murderer.

**assassinat** noun Masc. murder.

**assassiner** verb [1] to murder.

**assemblée** noun Fem. meeting.

**assembler** verb [1] **1** to put together, to assemble (a kit, a machine, etc); **2** to gather together; **3 s'assembler** to gather (of a group, crowd, demonstration, etc); ★ **qui se ressemble s'assemble** birds of a feather flock together (literally: those who are similar gather together).

# asseoir

**asseoir** *verb* [20] **s'asseoir** to sit down; **s'asseoir sur une chaise** to sit down on a chair; **assieds-toi** take a seat; **asseyez-vous** do sit down SEE ALSO **assis**.

**assez** *adverb* **1 assez de** enough; **assez de pain** enough bread; **2** enough; **elle ne mange pas assez** she doesn't eat enough; **3** enough; **est-ce que l'eau est assez chaude?** is the water hot enough?; **4** quite; **leur maison est assez grande** their house is quite big; **assez souvent** quite often; **assez joli** quite pretty; **5 j'en ai assez (de)** (*informal*) I'm fed up (with).

**assiette** *noun Fem.* plate; **une assiette plate** a dinner plate; **une assiette creuse, une assiette à soupe** a soup plate; ★ **je ne suis pas dans mon assiette aujourd'hui** I'm not my usual self today.

**assis** *adjective* **être assis** to be sitting; **elle était assise dans un fauteuil** she was sitting in an armchair; **rester assis** to remain seated.

**assistance** *noun Fem.* **1** audience; **dans l'assistance** in the audience; **2** assistance.

**assistant, assistante** *noun Masc., Fem.* assistant.

**assister** *verb* [1] **1** to assist; **2** to aid (*a country, the poor, etc*); **3 assister à** to be present at, to be at; **j'ai assisté à leur mariage** I was at their wedding.

**association** *noun Fem.* association.

**associé, associée** *noun Masc., Fem.* associate, partner.

**associer** *verb* [1] **1 associer quelqu'un à quelque chose** to include somebody in something; **2 s'associer à un groupe** to join a group; **3 s'associer pour faire** to get together to do.

**assommer** *verb* [1] **1 assommer quelqu'un** to knock somebody senseless; **2 assommer quelqu'un** (*informal*) to bore somebody stiff; **3 être assommé par une nouvelle** to be stunned by a piece of news.

**assorti** *adjective* matching; **rideaux et coussins assortis** matching curtains and cushions; **une veste assortie à sa robe** a jacket to match her dress.

**assortiment** *noun Masc.* assortment, selection.

**assortir** *verb* [2] **1** to match; **2 s'assortir à** to match.

**assouplissant** *noun Masc.* fabric softener.

**assourdir** *verb* [2] **1** to deafen; **2** to muffle.

**assourdissant** *adjective* deafening.

**assumer** *verb* [1] **assumer la responsabilité de quelque chose** to take responsibility for something; **assumer une fonction** to hold a position.

**assurance** *noun Fem.* **1** confidence; **avec assurance** confidently; **2** insurance.

**assurance automobile** *noun* Fem. car insurance.

**assurance maladie** *noun* Fem. health insurance; **est-ce que vous avez une assurance maladie?** do you have health insurance?

**assurance voyage** *noun* Fem. travel insurance.

**assuré** *adjective* **1** confident; **2** insured.

**assurer** *verb* [1] **1** to assure; **je vous assure que c'est vrai** I assure you it's true; **2** to insure; **assurer sa voiture** to insure one's car; **3** to provide (*a service*); **4** to carry out (*a task or a responsibility*); **5 s'assurer** to make sure.

**astérisque** *noun* Masc. asterisk.

**asthmatique** *adjective* asthmatic.

**asthme** *noun* Masc. asthma.

**asticot** *noun* Masc. maggot.

**astiquer** *verb* [1] to polish.

**astrologie** *noun* Fem. astrology.

**astrologue** *noun* Masc. & Fem. astrologer.

**astronome** *noun* Masc. & Fem. astronomer.

**astronomie** *noun* Fem. astronomy.

**astronomique** *adjective* astronomical.

**astuce** *noun* Fem. **1** cleverness; **2 une astuce** a trick (*for managing to do something*); **il doit y avoir une astuce** there must be a trick to it.

**astucieux** (Fem. **astucieuse**) *adjective* clever; **c'était très**

astucieux de sa part de faire ça it was very crafty of her to do that.

**atelier** *noun* Masc. **1** workshop; **2** studio (*of an artist, a sculptor, etc*); **3** work group.

**athée** *noun* Masc. & Fem. atheist.

**Athènes** *noun* Athens.

**athlète** *noun* Masc. & Fem. athlete.

**athlétique** *adjective* athletic.

**athlétisme** *noun* Masc. athletics.

**Atlantique** *noun* Masc. **l'Atlantique** the Atlantic.

**atlas** *noun* Masc. atlas.

**atmosphère** *noun* Fem. atmosphere.

**atome** *noun* Masc. atom.

**atomique** *adjective* atomic.

**atomiseur** *noun* Masc. spray, atomizer.

**atout** *noun* Masc. **1** trump card; **c'est atout pique** spades are trumps; **2** asset, advantage.

**atroce** *adjective* dreadful, terrible.

**atrocité** *noun* Fem. **1** atrocity; **2** monstrosity.

**attachant** *adjective* lovable.

**attache** *noun* Fem. **1** tie, string, strap; **2 attaches familiales** family ties.

**attacher** *verb* [1] **1 attacher ses cheveux** to tie (*or* fix) your hair back; **2 s'attacher** to stick (*to the pan*).

**attaque** *noun* Fem. attack.

**attaquer** *verb* [1] **1** to attack; **2** to tackle (*a job*).

**attarder** *verb* [1] **s'attarder** to linger.

**atteindre** *verb* [60] **1** to reach; **2** to achieve.

**atteint** *adjective* **être atteint d'une maladie** to be suffering from an illness.

**attendant** *in phrase* **en attendant** meanwhile, in the meantime.

**attendre** *verb* [3] **1** to wait; **tu peux attendre deux minutes?** can you wait two minutes?; **2** to wait for; **j'attends le bus** I'm waiting for the bus; **je t'attends dehors** I'll wait for you outside; **3 s'attendre à** to expect.

**attendrissant** *adjective* touching.

**attentat** *noun Masc.* **1 un attentat (à la bombe)** a bomb attack, a bombing; **2** assassination attempt.

**attente** *noun Fem.* wait; **une attente de vingt minutes** a twenty-minute wait.

**attentif** (*Fem.* **attentive**) *adjective* **1** attentive; **2** careful.

**attention** *noun Fem.* **1** attention; **2 faire attention à** to be careful of; **faites attention aux pickpockets!** look out for pickpockets!; **3 attention!** watch out!; **attention au chien!** beware of the dog!

**atterrir** *verb* [2] to land.

**atterrissage** *noun Masc.* landing.

**attirant** *adjective* attractive.

**attirer** *verb* [1] to attract; **attirer l'attention de quelqu'un sur quelque chose** to attract (*or* draw) somebody's attention to something.

**attitude** *noun Fem.* attitude.

**attraction** *noun Fem.* attraction.

**attraper** *verb* [1] **1** to catch; **2 attraper un rhume** to catch a cold; **3** to catch hold of.

**attrayant** *adjective* attractive.

**attrister** *verb* [1] to sadden.

**au** SEE **à**.

**aubaine** *noun Fem.* godsend.

**aube** *noun Fem.* dawn; **à l'aube** at dawn.

**aubépine** *noun Fem.* hawthorn.

**auberge** *noun Fem.* inn; ★ **on n'est pas sorti de l'auberge** our problems are not over yet (*literally: we're not out of the inn*).

**auberge de jeunesse** *noun Fem.* youth hostel.

**aubergine** *noun Fem.* aubergine.

**aucun** *adjective* no; **en aucun cas** under no circumstances; **sans aucun doute** without any doubt. **aucun** *pronoun* none; **aucun des deux** neither of them; **aucun d'entre eux** none of them.

**aucunement** *adverb* in no way.

**audace** *noun Fem.* daring.

**audacieux** (*Fem.* **audacieuse**) *adjective* daring.

**au-delà de** *preposition* beyond.

**au-dessous** *adverb* **1** underneath; **2** below; **3 au-dessous de** underneath; **au-dessous de la table** underneath the table; **4 au-dessous de** below; **au-dessous de la limite** below the limit.

**au-dessus** *adverb* **1** above; **2 au-dessus de** above.

**audience** *noun Fem.* audience.

**audiovisuel** (*Fem.* **audiovisuelle**) *adjective* audiovisual.

**auditeur**, **auditrice** *noun Masc., Fem.* listener.

**audition** *noun Fem.* audition.

**augmentation** *noun Fem.* increase; **l'augmentation des prix** the increase in prices; **une augmentation de salaire** a pay rise.

**augmenter** *verb* [1] **1** to raise, to increase; **augmenter les prix** to raise prices; **2** to rise, to go up; **le prix a augmenté** the price has gone up.

**aujourd'hui** *adverb* today; **nous sommes lundi aujourd'hui** today is Monday.

**auparavant** *adverb* before, beforehand.

**auprès de** *preposition* beside, next to.

**auquel** *pronoun* **le garçon auquel je parle** the boy I'm talking to.

**aura**, **aurai**, **auras**, **aurez**, **aurons**, **auront** *verb* SEE **avoir**.

**au revoir** *exclamation* goodbye.

**aussi** *adverb* **1** also, too; **moi aussi** me too; **j'ai aussi invité ton frère** I also invited your brother, I invited your brother as well; **2 aussi ...que** as ...as; **mon panier est aussi lourd que le tien** my basket is as heavy as yours; **3 aussi bien que** as well as; **les enfants aussi bien que les**

**adultes** children as well as adults.

**aussi** *conjunction* so, therefore.

**aussitôt** *adverb* immediately.

**Australie** *noun Fem.* Australia.

**australien** (*Fem.* **australienne**) *adjective* Australian.

**Australien**, **Australienne** *noun Masc., Fem.* Australian.

**autant** *adverb* **1** as much, so much; **je n'ai jamais mangé autant** I've never eaten so much; **2 autant que** as much as, as many as; **tu en as autant que moi** you have as much (or as many) as me; **3 autant de ...que** as much ...as, as many ...as; **tu as autant de problèmes que moi** you have as many problems as I do.

**autel** *noun Masc.* altar.

**auteur** *noun Masc.* author.

**authentique** *adjective* genuine.

**auto** *noun Fem.* car.

**autobiographie** *noun Fem.* autobiography.

**autobus** *noun Masc.* bus.

**autocar** *noun Masc.* coach.

**autocollant** *noun Masc.* sticker. **autocollant** *adjective* self-adhesive.

**autodéfense** *noun Fem.* self-defence.

**auto-école** *noun Fem.* driving school.

**automate** *noun Masc.* robot.

**automatique** *adjective* automatic.

**automatiquement** *adverb* automatically.

a
b
c
d
e
f
g
h
i
j
k
l
m
n
o
p
q
r
s
t
u
v
w
x
y
z

**automne** *noun Masc.* autumn; **en automne** in autumn.

**automobile** *noun Fem.* car.
**automobile** *adjective* **l'industrie automobile** the car industry.

**automobiliste** *noun Masc. & Fem.* motorist.

**autoradio** *noun Masc.* car radio.

**autorisation** *noun Fem.*
**1** permission; **2** permit.

**autoriser** *verb* [1] **1** to allow, to authorize; **2 autoriser quelqu'un à faire** to allow somebody to do.

**autoritaire** *adjective* authoritarian, strict.

**autorité** *noun Fem.* authority.

**autoroute** *noun Fem.* motorway; **l'autoroute de l'information** the information super-highway.

**auto-stop** *noun Masc.* hitchhiking; **faire de l'auto-stop** to hitchhike.

**auto-stoppeur**, **auto-stoppeuse** *noun Masc., Fem.* hitchhiker.

**autour** *adverb* **1** around; **2 autour de** round, around; **autour de la table** round the table.

**autre** *adjective* **1** other; **l'autre couteau** the other knife; **l'autre jour** the other day; **2 un/une autre** another; **tu peux me passer un autre verre?** can you pass me another glass?; **3 quelqu'un d'autre** somebody else; **personne d'autre** nobody else.
**autre** *pronoun* **1 un/une autre** another one; **donne-moi un autre** give me another one; **2 les autres** the others; **où sont les autres?** where are the others?

**autrefois** *adverb* in the past, in the old days.

**autrement** *adverb* **1** differently; **autrement dit** in other words; **2** otherwise.

**autre part** *adverb* somewhere else.

**Autriche** *noun Fem.* Austria.

**autrichien** (*Fem.* **autrichienne**) *adjective* Austrian.

**Autrichien, Autrichienne** *noun Masc., Fem.* Austrian.

**autruche** *noun Fem.* ostrich.

**aux** SEE **à**.

**auxiliaire** *noun Masc. & Fem.*, *adjective* auxiliary.

**auxquelles** *pronoun* **les filles auxquelles je parlais** the girls I was talking to.

**auxquels** *pronoun* **les garçons auxquels je parlais** the boys I was talking to.

**avalanche** *noun Fem.* avalanche.

**avaler** *verb* [1] **1** to swallow; **2** to inhale.

**avance** *noun Fem.* **1** advance, progress; **2 je suis arrivé dix minutes en avance** I arrived ten minutes early; **avoir dix minutes d'avance** to be ten minutes early; **3 être en avance** to be early; **4 à l'avance** in advance.

**avancer** *verb* [61] **1** to move forward, to advance; **2 avancer quelque chose** to move something forward; **3 ma montre avance de cinq minutes** my watch is five minutes fast.

**avant** *adverb* **1** before; **longtemps avant** a long time before; **2** forward; **plus avant** further forward.
**avant** *preposition* **1** before; **avant Noël** before Christmas; **avant six heures** before six o'clock; **elle est arrivée avant moi** she arrived before me; **2 avant de faire** before doing; **avant de partir je vais téléphoner à ma mère** before leaving (*or* before I leave) I'll phone my mother; **3 avant que** before.
**avant** *noun Masc.* front.
**avant** *adjective* front; **la roue avant** the front wheel.

**avantage** *noun Masc.* advantage.

**avantageux** (*Fem.* **avantageuse**) *adjective* **1 des prix avantageux** attractive prices; **2 des conditions avantageuses** favourable conditions.

**avant-bras** *noun Masc.* forearm.

**avant-dernier**, **avant-dernière** *noun Masc., Fem.* **l'avant-dernier** the last but one.
**avant-dernière** *adjective* second last, last but one.

**avant-hier** *adverb* the day before yesterday.

**avare** *noun Masc. & Fem.* miser.
**avare** *adjective* mean, miserly.

**avec** *preposition* with; **avec Marie** with Marie; **avec un couteau** with a knife; **avec ça?** anything else? (*in a shop*).

**avenir** *noun Masc.* future; **l'avenir** the future; **à l'avenir** in the future.

**aventure** *noun Fem.* adventure.

**avenue** *noun Fem.* avenue.

**averse** *noun Fem.* shower.

**avertir** *verb* [2] **1** to inform; **2** to warn.

**avertissement** *noun Masc.* warning.

**aveuglant** *adjective* blinding.

**aveugle** *adjective* blind.

**aveuglément** *adverb* blindly.

**aveugler** *verb* [1] to blind.

**avez** *verb* SEE **avoir**.

**aviation** *noun Fem.* **1** aviation; **2** aircraft industry; **3** flying; **4** air force.

**avion** *noun Masc.* aeroplane, plane; **aller à Paris en avion** to go to Paris by plane, to fly to Paris; **par avion** by airmail.

**aviron** *noun Masc.* **1** rowing; **faire de l'aviron** to row; **2** oar.

**avis** *noun Masc.* **1** opinion; **à mon avis** in my opinion; **2 changer d'avis** to change one's mind; **3** notice.

**avocat**[1], **avocate** *noun Masc., Fem.* **1** solicitor; **2** barrister.

**avocat**[2] *noun Masc.* avocado (pear).

**avoine** *noun Fem.* oats; **des flocons d'avoine** porridge oats.

**avoir** *verb* [5] **1** to have (got); **elle a trois frères** she has (*or* she's got) three brothers; **tu as beaucoup de livres** you have (*or* you've got) a lot of books; **2** (*talking about age*) **avoir dix ans** to be ten; **Claudie a dix ans** Claudie's ten; **quel âge a-t-il?** how old is he?; **3 avoir chaud** to be hot; **j'ai chaud** I'm hot; **j'ai froid** I'm cold; **4** (*used with another verb, like 'have' in English, to form past tenses*) **j'ai perdu mon stylo** I have lost my

a
b
c
d
e
f
g
h
i
j
k
l
m
n
o
p
q
r
s
t
u
v
w
x
y
z

pen; **j'ai vu ta mère hier** I saw your mother yesterday; **5 j'en ai pour dix minutes** it'll take me ten minutes; **6 il y a** there is, there are; **il y a un livre sur la table** there's a book on the table; **il y a trois livres sur la table** there are three books on the table; **7 il y a** ago; **il y a trois ans** three years ago; **8 qu'est-ce qu'il y a?** what's the matter?

**avons** *verb* SEE **avoir**.

**avortement** *noun Masc.* abortion.

**avouer** *verb* [1] to confess, to admit.

**avril** *noun Masc.* April; **en avril, au mois d'avril** in April.

**azalée** *noun Fem.* azalea.

**azote** *noun Masc.* nitrogen.

# Bb

**babouin** *noun Masc.* baboon.

**baby-foot** *noun Masc.* table football; **jouer au baby-foot** to play table football; **on va faire une partie de baby-foot** we're going to have a game of table football.

**bac** *noun Masc.* **1** (*informal*) SHORT FOR **baccalauréat**; **2** tub.

**bac à glace** *noun Masc.* ice tray.

**bac à sable** *noun Masc.* sandpit.

**baccalauréat** *noun Masc.* baccalaureate (*school-leaving certificate sat at the age of 17-18 and giving access to higher education*); **passer le baccalauréat** to sit the baccalaureate; **réussir au baccalauréat** to pass the baccalaureate.

**bâche** *noun Fem.* tarpaulin.

**badaud**, **badaude** *noun Masc., Fem.* passerby, onlooker.

**baffe** *noun Fem.* (*informal*) slap.

**baffle** *noun Masc.* speaker (*on a music system*).

**bagage** *noun Masc.* **un bagage** a piece of luggage; **des bagages** luggage; **où sont tes bagages?** where is your luggage?; **j'ai fait mes bagages** I've packed.

**bagarre** *noun Fem.* fight.

**bagarrer** *verb* [1] **se bagarrer** to fight.

**bagnole** *noun Fem.* (*informal*) car.

**bague** *noun Fem.* ring.

**baguette** *noun Fem.* **1** baguette, French bread stick; **2** stick; **3** drumstick; **4** chopstick.

**baguette magique** *noun Fem.* magic wand.

**Bahamas** *noun Fem. plural* **les îles Bahamas** the Bahamas.

**baie** *noun* **1** bay (*on the sea*); **2** berry; **3 une baie vitrée** a picture window.

**baignade** *noun Fem.* swimming; **'baignade interdite'** 'no swimming'.

**baigner** *verb* [1] **se baigner** to go swimming.

**baignoire** *noun Fem.* bath.

**bail** (*plural* **baux**) *noun Masc.* lease; **un bail de trois ans** a three-year lease.

**bâiller** *verb* [1] to yawn.

**bain** *noun Masc.* bath; **prendre un bain** to have a bath.

**baiser** *noun Masc.* kiss; **bons baisers** love and kisses (*at the end of a letter*).

**baisse** *noun Fem.* drop, fall; **être en baisse** to be falling; **la température est en baisse** the temperature is falling.

**baisser** *verb* [1] **1** to lower; **baisser le store** to lower (*or* pull down) the blind; **baisser le volume** to turn down the volume; **baisser la lumière** to turn down the lights; **baisser les prix** to cut prices; **2 se baisser** to bend down.

**bal** *noun Masc.* dance; **un bal populaire** a village dance (or disco).

**balade** *noun Fem.* walk, drive; **faire une balade (à pied)** to go for a walk; **faire une balade (en voiture)** to go for a drive; **faire une balade à la campagne** to go for a walk (*or* drive) in the country.

**balader** *verb* [1] **1 se balader** to go for a walk (*or* drive); **se balader en Écosse** to tour around Scotland; **2 balader quelque chose** to carry something around.

**baladeur** *noun Masc.* Walkman™, personal stereo.

**balai** *noun Masc.* broom, (long-handled) brush; **passer le balai** to sweep the floor.

**Balance** *noun Fem.* Libra (*sign of the Zodiac*).

**balance** *noun Fem.* scales; **une balance de cuisine** kitchen scales.

**balancer** *verb* [61] **1** to sway; **2** to swing; **3** (*informal*) to throw, to chuck; **balance-moi les clés!** chuck me the keys!; **4** (*informal*) to chuck out; **je vais balancer tous ces vieux bouquins** I'm going to chuck out all these old books.

**balançoire** *noun Fem.* **1** swing; **2** seesaw.

**balayer** *verb* [59] **1** to sweep; **balayer la cuisine** to sweep the kitchen floor; **2** to sweep up; **balayer les miettes** to sweep up the crumbs.

**balayeur, balayeuse** *noun Masc., Fem.* roadsweeper.

**balbutier** *verb* [1] to mumble.

**balcon** *noun Masc.* balcony.

**baleine** *noun Fem.* whale.

**baliser** *verb* [1] **1** to signpost; **2** to mark out.

**balle** *noun Fem.* **1** ball; **2** bullet.

**ballerine** *noun Fem.* **1** ballerina; **2** ballerina shoe; **3** ballet shoe.

**ballet** *noun Masc.* ballet.

**ballon** *noun Masc.* **1** ball; **2** balloon; **3** (*informal*) Breathalyzer™; ★ **souffler dans le ballon** to be breathalyzed.

**ball-trap** *noun Masc.* clay pigeon shooting.

**balnéaire** *adjective* seaside; **une station balnéaire** a seaside resort.

**bambou** *noun Masc.* bamboo.

**banal** *adjective* ordinary; **peu banal** unusual.

**banane** *noun Fem.* **1** banana; **2** bumbag.

**banc** *noun Masc.* bench; **assis sur un banc** sitting on a bench.

**bancaire** *adjective* **1** banking; **2 une carte bancaire** a bank card.

**bancal** *adjective* **1** rickety; **2** wobbly.

**bande** *noun Fem.* **1** group; **une bande de jeunes** a group of young people; **2** gang; **une bande de criminels** a criminal gang; **3** strip (*of fabric or paper*); **4** tape (*for recording*); **5** bandage.

**bande-annonce** *noun Fem.* trailer (*for a film*).

**bandeau** (*plural* **bandeaux**) *noun Masc.* **1** headband; **2** blindfold.

**bande d'arrêt d'urgence** *noun Fem.* hard shoulder (*on motorway*).

**bande de fréquence** *noun Fem.* wavelength (*on radio*).

**bande dessinée** *noun Fem.* **1** comic strip; **2** comic book.

**bande publique** *noun Fem.* Citizen's Band, CB radio.

**bande rugueuse** *noun Fem.* rumble strip (*on motorway*).

**bande sonore** *noun Fem.* **1** soundtrack (*of film*); **2** rumble strip (*on motorway*).

**bandit** *noun Masc.* bandit.

**banditisme** *noun Masc.* crime.

**banlieue** *noun Fem.* **la banlieue** the suburbs; **une banlieue** a suburb; **une maison de banlieue** a house in the suburbs; **un train de banlieue** a commuter train.

**banque** *noun Fem.* **1** bank; **aller à la banque** to go to the bank; **2** banking; **travailler dans la banque** to work in banking.

**banquet** *noun Masc.* banquet.

**banquette** *noun Fem.* **1** wall seat (*in a café or restaurant*); **2** seat (*in a car, bus, or train*).

**banquier** *noun Masc.* banker.

**baptême** *noun Masc.* christening.

**baptiser** *verb* [1] **1** to christen; **2** to name; **3** to nickname.

**baquet** *noun Masc.* tub.

**bar** *noun Masc.* bar.

**baraque** *noun Fem.* (*informal*) house.

**Barbade** *noun Fem.* **la Barbade** Barbados.

**barbadien** (*Fem.* **barbadienne**) *adjective* Barbadian.

**Barbadien**, **Barbadienne** *noun Masc.,Fem.* Barbadian.

**barbant** *adjective* (*informal*) boring.

**barbe** *noun Fem.* beard; ★ **c'est la barbe!** what a drag!; ★ **faire quelque chose à la barbe de quelqu'un** to do something behind somebody's back (*literally: to do something in somebody's beard*).

**barbe à papa** *noun Fem.* candyfloss.

**barbecue** *noun Masc.* barbecue.

**barbelé** *noun Masc.* barbed wire.

**barbouiller** *verb* [1] **1** to smear; **tu es tout barbouillé de confiture** you've got jam all over your face;

**2** to daub; **barbouillé de slogans** daubed with slogans.

**barbu** *noun Masc.* **un barbu** a man with a beard.

**barbu** *adjective* bearded.

**barème** *noun Masc.* scale.

**barmaid** *noun Fem.* barmaid.

**barman** *noun Masc.* barman.

**baromètre** *noun Masc.* barometer.

**barque** *noun Fem.* rowing boat.

**barquette** *noun Fem.* tub, container; **une barquette de fraises** a punnet of strawberries.

**barrage** *noun Masc.* **1** dam; **2** roadblock.

**barre** *noun Fem.* bar; **une barre de fer** an iron bar; **une barre de chocolat** a chocolate bar.

**barreau** (*plural* **barreaux**) *noun Masc.* bar; **derrière les barreaux** behind bars (*in prison*).

**barrer** *verb* [1] **1** to block; **'route barrée'** 'road closed'; **2** to cross out; **barrer trois mots** to cross out three words; **3 se barrer** (*informal*) to clear off, to leave; **je me barre!** I'm off!; ★ **on est mal barré** (*informal*) we're in trouble.

**barrette** *noun Fem.* hairslide.

**barrière** *noun Fem.* **1** fence; **2** gate.

**bar-tabac** *noun Masc.* cafe (*selling cigarettes, tobacco, and stamps as well as drinks and snacks*).

**bas** *noun Masc.* **1** bottom, lower part; **en bas de la page** at the bottom of the page; **2** stocking.

**bas** *adjective* (*Fem.* **basse**) low.

**bas** *adverb* **1** low; **plus bas** further down; **parler plus bas** to lower one's voice; **2 en bas** at the bottom, down below, downstairs; **les voisins d'en bas** the neighbours in the flat below.

**bas-côté** *noun Masc.* verge (*on the roadside*).

**basculant** *adjective* **un camion à benne basculante** a dump truck.

**bascule** *noun Fem.* **1** rocker; **un fauteuil à bascule** a rocking chair; **un cheval à bascule** a rocking horse; **2** seesaw.

**basculer** *verb* [1] to topple over.

**base** *noun Fem.* **1** basis; **être à la base de quelque chose** to be at the root of something; **2** base; **à base de chocolat** chocolate-based; **3 de base** basic; **les ingrédients de base** the basic ingredients.

**base-ball** *noun Masc.* baseball.

**base de données** *noun Fem.* database.

**baser** *verb* [1] to base; **basé sur** based on.

**basilic** *noun Masc.* basil; **une sauce au basilic** a basil sauce.

**basket** *noun Masc.* **1** basketball; **2** sports shoe, trainer; ★ **lâche-moi les baskets!** (*informal*) get off my back!

**basketteur**, **basketteuse** *noun Masc., Fem.* basketball player.

**basque** *noun Masc.* Basque (*language*).

**basque** *adjective* Basque.

**Basque** *noun Masc. & Fem.* Basque (*person*).

a

**b**

c

d

e

f

g

h

i

j

k

l

m

n

o

p

q

r

s

t

u

v

w

x

y

z

**basse** *noun Fem.* bass (*in music.*).
**basse** *adjective* SEE **bas**..

**bassin** *noun Masc.* **1** pond; **2** pelvis.

**bassine** *noun Fem.* bowl.

**bassiste** *noun Masc. & Fem.* bassist.

**bataille** *noun Fem.* **1** battle; **la
bataille de Trafalgar** the Battle of
Trafalgar; **la bataille du pouvoir**
the battle for power; **une bataille de
boules de neige** a snowball fight;
**2** a card game (*similar to beggar-my-
neighbour*); ★ **avoir les sourcils en
bataille** to have bushy eyebrows;
★ **elle avait les cheveux en
bataille** her hair was all over the
place.

**bateau** (*plural* **bateaux**) *noun
Masc.* boat, ship; **faire du bateau** to
go boating (*or* sailing).

**bateau à moteur** *noun Masc.*
motorboat.

**bateau de plaisance** *noun
Masc.* pleasure boat.

**bateau-mouche** *noun Masc.*
pleasure boat (*a large river boat for
sightseeing trips*).

**bateau pneumatique** *noun
Masc.* rubber dinghy.

**bâti** *adjective* built; **bien bâti** well-
built.

**bâtiment** *noun Masc.* **1** building;
**les bâtiments de l'école** the school
buildings; **2 le bâtiment** the
building trade; **travailler dans le
bâtiment** to work in the building
trade; **3** ship.

**bâtir** *verb* [2] to build.

**bâtisse** *noun Fem.* building.

**bâton** *noun Masc.* stick.

**bâton de ski** *noun Masc.* ski stick.

**bâtonnet** *noun Masc.* stick.

**bâtonnet de poisson** *noun
Masc.* fish finger.

**bâtonnet ouaté** *noun Masc.*
cotton bud.

**batte** *noun Fem.* bat (*for cricket,
baseball, etc*).

**batterie** *noun Fem.* **1** battery;
**2** drum kit, drums.

**batterie de cuisine** *noun Fem.*
pots and pans.

**batteur** *noun Masc.* **1** drummer;
**2** whisk.

**batteur électrique** *noun Masc.*
(electric) mixer.

**battre** *verb* [21] **1** to beat (*in a game*)
**Nicole m'a battu au tennis** Nicole
beat me at tennis; **2** to beat, to
batter; **battre un chien** to beat a
dog; **3** to beat (*a mixture*); **battre les
œufs** to whisk the eggs; **battre la
crème** to whip the cream; **4 se
battre** to fight; **5 battre des mains**
to clap your hands; **6 le cœur bat**
the heart beats; **7 la porte bat** the
door bangs.

**bavard** *adjective* talkative.

**bavarder** *verb* [1] to chat, to
chatter.

**baver** *verb* [1] to dribble.

**bavure** *noun Fem.* **1** smudge;
**2** blunder.

**bazar** *noun Masc.* **1** general store;
**2** (*informal*) mess.

**BCBG** SHORT FOR **bon chic bon genre**
chic and stylish (*in appearance*).

**B.D.** *noun Fem.* comic strip SHORT FOR bande dessinée.

**beau, bel** (*before a vowel or silent 'h'*) (*Fem.* **belle**) (*Masc. plural* **beaux**) *adjective* **1** beautiful, lovely; **une belle maison** a beautiful house; **un bel homme** a handsome man; **fais de beaux rêves!** sweet dreams!; **2 il fait beau** it's a nice day; ★ **faire le beau** to sit up and beg (*of a dog*).

**beaucoup** *adverb* **1** a lot; **tu m'en as donné beaucoup** you've given me a lot; **tu ne m'en as pas donné beaucoup** you haven't given me much; **cinquante euros c'est beaucoup** fifty euros is a lot; **2** a lot; **il lit beaucoup** he reads a lot; **il ne lit pas beaucoup** he doesn't read much; **3** very much; **j'aime beaucoup ta robe** I like your dress very much, I really like your dress; **j'aime beaucoup aller au cinéma** I really like going to the cinema; **4 beaucoup de** a lot of; **beaucoup d'argent** a lot of money; **elle a beaucoup d'argent** she has a lot of money; **elle n'a pas beaucoup d'argent** she doesn't have much money; **il a beaucoup d'amis** he has a lot of friends; **il n'a pas beaucoup d'amis** he doesn't have many friends; **5 beaucoup plus** much more; **beaucoup moins** much less; **beaucoup trop** far too much; **beaucoup trop court** far too short.

**beau-fils** (*plural* **beaux-fils**) *noun Masc.* **1** son-in-law; **2** stepson.

**beau-frère** (*plural* **beaux-frères**) *noun Masc.* brother-in-law.

**beau-père** (*plural* **beau-pères**) *noun Masc.* **1** father-in-law; **2** stepfather.

**beauté** *noun Fem.* beauty.

**beaux-arts** *plural noun Masc.* fine arts; **école des beaux-arts** art school.

**beaux-parents** *plural noun Masc.* parents-in-law, in-laws.

**bébé** *noun Masc.* baby.

**bec** *noun Masc.* beak.

**bêche** *noun Fem.* spade.

**bégayer** *verb* [59] to stammer.

**beige** *adjective* beige.

**beignet** *noun Masc.* **1** fritter; **2** doughnut.

**bel** *adjective* SEE **beau**.

**belette** *noun Fem.* weasel.

**belge** *adjective* Belgian.

**Belge** *noun Masc. & Fem.* Belgian.

**Belgique** *noun Fem.* Belgium.

**bélier** *noun Masc.* ram.

**Bélier** *noun Masc.* Aries (*sign of the Zodiac*).

**belle** *noun Fem.* **1 ma belle** darling; **2 la Belle au bois dormant** Sleeping Beauty.
**belle** *adjective* SEE **beau**.

**belle-famille** *noun Fem.* in-laws.

**belle-fille** (*plural* **belles-filles**) *noun Fem.* **1** daughter-in-law; **2** stepdaughter.

**belle-mère** (*plural* **belles-mères**) *noun Fem.* **1** mother-in-law; **2** stepmother.

**belle-sœur** (*plural* **belles-sœurs**) *noun Fem.* sister-in-law.

a
**b**
c
d
e
f
g
h
i
j
k
l
m
n
o
p
q
r
s
t
u
v
w
x
y
z

**bénédiction** *noun Fem.* blessing.

**bénéfice** *noun Masc.* profit; **faire un bénéfice de dix mille euros** to make a profit of ten thousand euros.

**bénéfique** *adjective* beneficial.

**bénévole** *noun Masc. & Fem.* voluntary worker.
**bénévole** *adjective* voluntary, unpaid.

**bénir** *verb* [2] to bless.

**benne** *noun Fem.* skip (*for rubbish*).

**béquille** *noun Fem.* crutch.

**berceau** (*plural* **berceaux**) *noun Masc.* cradle.

**bercer** *verb* [61] to rock (*a baby*).

**berceuse** *noun Fem.* **1** lullaby; **2** rocking chair.

**béret** *noun Masc.* beret.

**berge** *noun Fem.* bank (*of a river or canal*).

**berger**, **bergère** *noun Masc.*, *Fem.* shepherd, shepherdess.

**berger allemand** *noun Masc.* Alsatian (dog).

**besoin** *noun Masc.* need; **avoir besoin de quelque chose** to need something; **j'ai besoin d'un marteau** I need a hammer; **avoir besoin de faire** to need to do; **j'ai vraiment besoin de me reposer** I really need to take a rest.

**bestiole** *noun Fem.* (*informal*) creepy-crawly.

**bétail** *noun Masc.* **1** livestock; **2** cattle.

**bête** *noun Fem.* animal.
**bête** *adjective* stupid.

**bêtise** *noun Fem.* stupidity; **faire une bêtise** to do something stupid.

**béton** *noun Masc.* concrete.

**bétonnière** *noun Fem.* cement mixer.

**betterave (rouge)** *noun Fem.* beetroot.

**beurre** *noun Masc.* butter; ★ **un œil au beurre noir** a black eye (*literally: an eye with black butter*).

**beurrer** *verb* [1] to butter.

**bibelot** *noun Masc.* ornament.

**biberon** *noun Masc.* (feeding) bottle.

**bible** *noun Fem.* bible; **la Bible** the Bible.

**bibliothécaire** *noun Masc. & Fem.* librarian.

**bibliothèque** *noun Fem.* **1** library; **2** bookcase.

**bic™** *noun Masc.* **un stylo bic™** a Biro™ .

**biche** *noun Fem.* doe.

**bicyclette** *noun Fem.* bicycle; **faire de la bicyclette** to cycle.

**bidet** *noun Masc.* bidet.

**bidon** *noun Masc.* can.
**bidon** *adjective* (*informal*) phoney.

**bidonville** *noun Masc.* shanty town.

**bidule** *noun Masc.* (*informal*) whatsit, thingamajig.

**bien** *noun Masc.* **1** good; **le bien et le mal** good and evil; **ça te fera du bien** that'll do you good; **2** possession; **tous leurs biens** all their possessions.
**bien** *adjective* **1** good, nice; **des gens bien** nice people; **ce sera bien de le revoir** it will be nice to see him

again; **2** well; **je ne me sens pas
bien** I don't feel well; **3** happy,
comfortable; **on est bien ici** it's nice
here; **on est très bien dans ce
fauteuil** this chair's really
comfortable.

**bien** *adverb* **1** well; **elle chante
bien** she sings well; **bien joué!** well
done!; **tu vas bien?** are you well?;
**2** well; **bien habillé** well dressed;
**cette couleur te va bien** that
colour suits you; **3** very, really; **bien
triste** really sad; **bien chaud** really
hot; **4** very much; **j'aime bien ta
robe** I like your dress very much, I
really like your dress; **j'aimerais
bien savoir** I'd really like to know;
**j'aimerais bien aller au cinéma** I'd
really like to go to the cinema;
**'veux-tu du thé?' – 'oui, je veux
bien'** 'would you like some tea?' –
'yes, I'd love some'; **'tu aimes le
poisson?' – 'oui, je l'aime bien'** 'do
you like fish?' – 'yes, I do'; **je veux
bien le faire** I'm quite happy to do it;
**5** much; **bien mieux** much better;
**bien plus chaud** much hotter;
**6 bien de** many, a number of; **bien
des gens** many people; ★ **c'est bien
fait pour elle!** serves her right!

**bien entendu** *adverb* of course.

**bien-être** *noun Masc.* well-being.

**bien que** *conjunction* although.

**bien sûr** *adverb* of course.

**bientôt** *adverb* soon; **à bientôt** see
you soon.

**bienvenu, bienvenue**[1] *noun
Masc., Fem., adjective* welcome; **soyez
le bienvenu** (*or* **la bienvenue**)**!**
welcome!

**bienvenue**[2] *noun Fem.* welcome;
**bienvenue!** welcome!; **bienvenue
en France!** welcome to France!;
**souhaiter la bienvenue à
quelqu'un** to welcome somebody.

**bière** *noun Fem.* beer; **boire de la
bière** to drink beer; **trois bières, s'il
vous plaît** three beers, please.

**bière blonde** *noun Fem.* lager.

**bière brune** *noun Fem.* brown ale.

**bifteck** *noun Masc.* steak.

**bifurcation** *noun Fem.* fork (*in the
road*).

**bigoudi** *noun Masc.* hair curler.

**bijou** (*plural* **bijoux**) *noun Masc.*
jewel, piece of jewellery.

**bijouterie** *noun Fem.* jeweller's
(shop).

**bijoutier, bijoutière** *noun Masc.,
Fem.* jeweller.

**bilan** *noun Masc.* balance sheet;
★ **faire le bilan de quelque chose**
to assess something.

**bilingue** *adjective* bilingual.

**billard** *noun Masc.* **1** billiards; **jouer
au billard** to play billiards;
**2** billiard table.

**billard américain** *noun Masc.*
pool.

**billard anglais** *noun Masc.*
snooker.

**billard électrique** *noun Masc.*
pinball machine.

**bille** *noun Fem.* **1** marble; **jouer aux
billes** to play marbles; **2** billiard
ball.

**billet** *noun Masc.* **1** note, banknote;
**un billet de cent euros** a

hundred-euro note; **2** ticket; **un billet de train** a train ticket.

**billion** *noun Masc.* billion.

**biochimie** *noun Fem.* biochemistry.

**biographie** *noun Fem.* biography.

**biologie** *noun Fem.* biology.

**biologique** *adjective* **1** biological; **2** organically grown.

**biologiste** *noun Masc. & Fem.* biologist.

**bip** *noun Masc.* beep; **'après le bip sonore'** 'after the tone' (*on an answering machine*).

**biscotte** *noun Fem.* continental toast.

**biscuit** *noun Masc.* biscuit.

**bise** *noun Fem.* (*informal*) kiss; **faire la bise à quelqu'un** to kiss somebody on the cheek; **grosses bises** lots of love.

**bissextile** *adjective* **une année bissextile** a leap year.

**bistro**, **bistrot** *noun Masc.* bistro, cafe.

**bizarre** *adjective* odd, strange.

**blague** *noun Fem.* (*informal*) **1** joke; **sans blague!** no kidding!; **2** trick; **faire une blague à quelqu'un** to play a trick on somebody.

**blaguer** *verb* [1] (*informal*) to joke.

**blaireau** (*plural* **blaireaux**) *noun Masc.* **1** badger; **2** shaving brush.

**blâmer** *verb* [1] **1** to criticize; **2** to blame.

**blanc** *noun Masc.* **1** white; **peint en blanc** painted white; **2** white meat, breast; **3** white wine; **4** blank;

**laisser un blanc** to leave a blank.

**blanc** *adjective* (*Fem.* **blanche**) **1** white; **2** blank; **une feuille blanche** a blank sheet of paper.

**Blanc**, **Blanche** *noun Masc., Fem.* white man, white woman.

**blanche** *adjective* SEE **blanc**.

**blanchir** *verb* [2] to whiten.

**blanchisserie** *noun Fem.* laundry.

**blé** *noun Masc.* wheat.

**blessé**, **blessée** *noun Masc., Fem.* injured person, casualty.
**blessé** *adjective* injured.

**blesser** *verb* [1] **1** to hurt, to injure; **2 se blesser** to hurt oneself; **tu t'es blessé?** did you hurt yourself?

**blessure** *noun Fem.* **1** injury; **2** wound.

**bleu**[1] *noun Masc.*, *adjective* blue; **peint en bleu** painted blue; **bleu marine** navy blue.

**bleu**[2] *noun Masc.* bruise.

**bleuet** *noun Masc.* cornflower.

**bloc** *noun Masc.* **1** block; **un bloc de ciment** a block of cement; **2 un bloc de papier à lettres** a writing pad.

**bloc-notes** *noun Masc.* notepad.

**blond** *adjective* blonde, fair-haired.

**bloqué** *adjective* **1** blocked; **2** jammed; **3** stuck.

**bloquer** *verb* [1] **1** to block; **2** to jam.

**blouse** *noun Fem.* overall.

**blouson** *noun Masc.* jacket.

a
**b**
c
d
e
f
g
h
i
j
k
l
m
n
o
p
q
r
s
t
u
v
w
x
y
z

**blue-jean** *noun Masc.* jeans; **j'ai acheté un blue-jean** I bought a pair of jeans.

**bobine** *noun Fem.* reel.

**bocal** (*plural* **bocaux**) *noun Masc.* jar.

**bœuf** *noun Masc.* **1** bullock; **2** beef; **est-ce que tu aimes le bœuf?** do you like beef?

**bof** *exclamation* (*informal*) 'c'était bien hier soir?' – 'bof!' 'did you have a good time last night?' – 'nothing special'.

**bohémien, bohémienne** *noun Masc., Fem.* gipsy.

**boire** *verb* [22] to drink; **qu'est-ce que tu veux boire?** what would you like to drink?; **il n'y a rien à boire** there's nothing to drink.

**bois** *noun Masc.* wood; **une table en bois** a wooden table; ★ **avoir la gueule de bois** (*informal*) to have a hangover (*literally: to have a mouth made of wood*).

**boisson** *noun Fem.* drink; **une boisson fraîche** a cold drink.

**boîte** *noun Fem.* **1** tin; **une boîte de sardines** a tin of sardines; **2** box; **une boîte d'allumettes** a box of matches; **3** (*informal*) **une boîte de nuit** a nightclub; **aller dans une boîte** to go to a club; **4** (*informal*) firm, company.

**boîte aux lettres** *noun Fem.* post box.

**boiter** *verb* [1] to limp.

**bol** *noun Masc.* **1** bowl; **un bol de riz** a bowl of rice; **2** (*informal*) luck; **un coup de bol** a stroke of luck; ★ **en avoir ras le bol** (*informal*) to be fed

up (*literally: to have a bowlful*); **j'en ai ras le bol d'attendre** I'm fed up with waiting.

**bombarder** *verb* [1] **1** to bombard; **2** to bomb, to shell.

**bombe** *noun Fem.* **1** bomb; **2** spray can (*containing hairspray, fly spray, etc*).

**bôme** *noun Fem.* boom (*of a sail*).

**bon** (*Fem.* **bonne**) *adjective* **1** good; **un bon repas** a good meal; **bon en français** good at French; **2 un bon kilomètre** a good kilometre, at least a kilometre; **3** right; **le bon numéro** the right number; **la bonne adresse** the right address; **c'est bon** it's OK, it's fine.

**bon** *noun* **1** voucher; **2 cela a du bon** that has its good points; **pour de bon** for good.

**bon** *adverb* **sentir bon** to smell good (*or nice*); **il fait bon aujourd'hui** it's a nice day today; **il fait bon dans mon appartement** it's lovely and warm in my flat.

**bon anniversaire** *greeting* happy birthday.

**bon appétit** *exclamation* enjoy your meal.

**bonbon** *noun Masc.* sweet.

**bonbonne** *noun Fem.* **1 une bonbonne à gaz** a gas cylinder; **2** demijohn.

**bond** *noun Masc.* leap; **se lever d'un bond** to leap to your feet.

**bondé** *adjective* crowded, packed; **bondé d'étudiants** packed with students.

**bondir** *verb* [2] to leap; **bondir de joie** to jump for joy.

a
b
c
d
e
f
g
h
i
j
k
l
m
n
o
p
q
r
s
t
u
v
w
x
y
z

**bonheur** *noun Masc.* **1** happiness; **2** pleasure; **avoir le bonheur de faire** to have the pleasure of doing.

**bonhomme** (*plural* **bonshommes**) *noun Masc.* fellow, man.

**bonhomme de neige** *noun Masc.* snowman.

**bonjour** *greeting* hello, good morning, good afternoon; ★ **être simple comme bonjour** to be really easy, to be as easy as pie (*literally: to be as simple as hello*).

**bon marché** *adjective* cheap.

**bonne** *noun Fem.* maid.
**bonne** *adjective* SEE **bon**.

**bonne année** *greeting* happy New Year.

**bonne chance** *exclamation* good luck.

**bonne heure** *in phrase* **de bonne heure** early.

**bonne nuit** *greeting* goodnight.

**bonnet** *noun Masc.* hat, bonnet.

**bon retour** *exclamation* safe journey back.

**bon sens** *noun Masc.* common sense.

**bonsoir** *greeting* good evening.

**bonté** *noun Fem.* kindness.

**bon voyage** *exclamation* have a good trip.

**boom** *noun Masc.* boom (*time of prosperity*).

**bord** *noun Masc.* **1** edge (*of a table, cliff, etc*); **2** rim (*of a glass, cup, vase, etc*); **3** side, edge (*of a road, path, etc*); **au bord de la route** on the edge of the road; **4** bank (*of a stream or lake*); **5** **au bord de la mer** at the seaside.

**bordeaux** *adjective* maroon.

**border** *verb* [1] **1** to line; **bordé d'arbres** tree-lined; **2** to edge, to trim.

**bordure** *noun Fem.* **1** border; **2** edge; **3** **en bordure de** on the edge of.

**borne** *noun Fem.* **1** kilometre marker (*the equivalent of a milestone*); **2** bollard.

**Bosnie** *noun Fem.* Bosnia.

**bosse** *noun Fem.* bump.

**bosser** *verb* [1] (*informal*) to work.

**botanique** *noun Fem.* botany.
**botanique** *adjective* **les jardins botaniques** the botanic gardens.

**botte** *noun Fem.* **1** boot; **des bottes de cuir** leather boots; **des bottes de caoutchouc** wellington boots; **2** **une botte de foin** a bale of hay.

**bottine** *noun Fem.* ankle boot.

**bouc** *noun Masc.* billy goat.

**boucan** *noun Masc.* (*informal*) din, racket.

**bouc émissaire** *noun Masc.* scapegoat.

**bouche** *noun Fem.* mouth.

**bouche-à-bouche** *noun Masc.* mouth-to-mouth resuscitation.

**bouche d'égout** *noun Fem.* manhole.

**bouchée** *noun Fem.* mouthful.

**boucher**[1] *verb* [1] **1** to cork (*a bottle*); **2** to block up, to fill (*a hole, gap, or crack*); **3** **se boucher** to get blocked up; **4 se boucher le nez** to hold one's nose.

**boucher**[2] *noun Masc., Fem.* butcher.

**boucherie** *noun Fem.* butcher's (shop).

**bouchon** *noun Masc.* **1** cork; **2** screw-cap; **3** traffic jam.

**boucle** *noun Fem.* **1** buckle; **2** curl.

**bouclé** *adjective* curly.

**boucle d'oreille** *noun Fem.* earring.

**Bouddha** *noun Masc.* Buddha.

**bouddhisme** *noun Masc.* Buddhism.

**bouder** *verb* [1] **1** to sulk; **2 bouder quelque chose** to stay away from something.

**boudin** *noun Masc.* black pudding.

**boudin blanc** *noun Masc.* white pudding.

**boue** *noun Fem.* mud.

**bouée** *noun Fem.* **1** rubber ring; **2** buoy.

**bouée de sauvetage** *noun Fem.* lifebelt.

**boueux** (*Fem.* **boueuse**) *adjective* muddy.

**bouffe** *noun Fem.* (*informal*) food.

**bouffée** *noun Fem.* **une bouffée d'air frais** a breath of fresh air.

**bouffer** *verb* [1] (*informal*) to eat.

**bougeoir** *noun Masc.* candlestick.

**bouger** *verb* [52] to move.

**bougie** *noun Fem.* **1** candle; **2** spark plug.

**bouillabaisse** *noun Fem.* Mediterranean fish soup (*made with several varieties of fish and vegetables*).

**bouillant** *adjective* boiling; **faire cuire à l'eau bouillante** cook in boiling water.

**bouillir** *verb* [23] to boil; **faire bouillir le lait** to boil the milk; **le lait bout** the milk is boiling.

**bouilloire** *noun Fem.* kettle.

**bouillon** *noun Masc.* stock (*made with meat, fish, or vegetables*).

**bouillon-cube** *noun Masc.* stock cube.

**bouillotte** *noun Fem.* hot-water bottle.

**boulanger, boulangère** *noun Masc., Fem.* baker.

**boulangerie** *noun Fem.* bakery, baker's.

**boule** *noun Fem.* **1** bowl; **jouer aux boules** to play bowls; **2** scoop (*of ice-cream*); **vous voulez combien de boules?** how many scoops would you like?

**bouleau** (*plural* **bouleaux**) *noun Masc.* birch tree.

**boule de neige** *noun Fem.* snowball.

**boulette** *noun Fem.* pellet.

**boulette de viande** *noun Fem.* meatball.

**boulevard** *noun Masc.* boulevard.

**boulevard périphérique** *noun Masc.* ring road.

**bouleverser** *verb* [1] **1** to overwhelm, to shatter; **être bouleversé** to be overwhelmed (*or* shattered); **2** to disrupt (*a schedule, plans, etc*); **3** to turn upside down.

a
**b**
c
d
e
f
g
h
i
j
k
l
m
n
o
p
q
r
s
t
u
v
w
x
y
z

# boulot

**boulot** *noun Masc. (informal)*
**1** work; **j'ai trop de boulot** I've got too much work to do; **c'est un boulot immense** it's a huge amount of work; **2** job; **elle cherche du boulot** she's looking for a job.

**boum** *noun Fem. (informal)* party.

**bouquet** *noun Masc.* bunch, bouquet (*of flowers or herbs*).

**bouquin** *noun Masc. (informal)* book.

**bouquiner** *verb* [1] (*informal*) to read.

**bouquiniste** *noun Masc. & Fem.* secondhand bookseller.

**bourdon** *noun Masc.* bumblebee.

**bourg** *noun Masc.* market town.

**bourgeois, bourgeoise** *noun Masc., Fem.* middle-class person.
**bourgeois** *adjective* middle-class.

**bourgeon** *noun Masc.* bud.

**Bourgogne** *noun Fem.* Burgundy.

**bourratif** (*Fem.* **bourrative**) *adjective* very filling.

**bourré** *adjective* **1** **bourré de** crammed with, stuffed with; **2** drunk.

**bourrer** *verb* [1] to cram.

**bourse** *noun Fem.* grant.

**Bourse** *noun Fem.* stock exchange.

**bousculer** *verb* [1] to push, to jostle.

**boussole** *noun Fem.* compass.

**bout** *noun Masc.* **1** end; **au bout de** at the end of; **2** tip (*of nose or finger*); **3** **un bout de papier** a scrap of paper; **un petit bout de fromage** a little bit of cheese; **4** **au bout de** after; **au bout d'une demi-heure** after half an hour.

**bouteille** *noun Fem.* bottle.

**boutique** *noun Fem.* shop.

**bouton** *noun Masc.* **1** button; **2** spot, pimple.

**bouton d'or** *noun Masc.* buttercup.

**boxe** *noun Fem.* boxing.

**boxeur** *noun Masc.* boxer.

**bracelet** *noun Masc.* **1** bracelet; **2** bangle.

**bracelet-montre** *noun Masc.* wristwatch.

**braise** *noun Fem.* embers (*of a fire*).

**brancard** *noun Masc.* stretcher.

**branche** *noun Fem.* branch.

**branché** *adjective (informal)* trendy.

**brancher** *verb* [1] **1** to plug in (*an iron, a television, etc*); **2** to connect (*electricity, gas, water, telephone*).

**bras** *noun Masc.* sleeve; **en bras de chemise** in one's shirtsleeves.

**bras de fer** *noun Masc.* arm wrestling.

**brasse** *noun Fem.* breaststroke.

**brasserie** *noun Fem.* **1** brasserie, cafe-restaurant; **2** brewery.

**brave** *adjective* nice (*person*).

**break** *noun Masc.* estate car.

**brebis** *noun Fem.* ewe.

**bref** (*Fem.* **brève**) *adjective* short, brief.

**Brésil** *noun Masc.* Brazil.

**brésilien** *noun Masc.* Brazilian Portuguese (*language*).

**brésilien**, **brésilienne** *adjective* Brazilian.

**Brésilien**, **Brésilienne** *noun* Masc., Fem. Brazilian.

**Bretagne** *noun Fem.* Brittany.

**bretelle** *noun Fem.* **1** strap; **2** slip road; **3** des bretelles braces.

**breton** *noun Masc.* Breton (*language*).

**Breton**, **Bretonne** *noun Masc., Fem.* Breton.
   **breton** (*Fem.* **bretonne**) *adjective* Breton.

**brevet** *noun Masc.* certificate.

**bribes** *plural noun Fem.* bits, fragments.

**bricolage** *noun Masc.* DIY, do-it-yourself.

**bricoler** *verb* [1] to do DIY.

**bricoleur**, **bricoleuse** *noun Masc., Fem.* DIY enthusiast.

**brièvement** *adverb* briefly.

**brillamment** *adverb* brilliantly.

**brillant** *adjective* **1** shiny; **2** brilliant.

**briller** *verb* [1] to shine.

**brin** *noun Masc.* sprig (*of herb or plant*); un brin d'herbe a blade of grass.

**brindille** *noun Fem.* twig.

**brioche** *noun Fem.* brioche, bun.

**brique** *noun Fem.* **1** brick; **2** carton (*of fruit-juice, milk, etc*).

**briquet** *noun Masc.* lighter.

**brise** *noun Fem.* breeze.

**briser** *verb* [1] to break.

**britannique** *adjective* British.

**Britannique** *noun Masc. & Fem.* British person; les Britanniques the British.

**brocante** *noun Fem.* **1** junk shop; **2** second-hand goods.

**broche** *noun Fem.* **1** brooch; **2** spit (*for roasting*).

**brochet** *noun Masc.* pike.

**brochette** *noun Fem.* **1** skewer; **2** kebab; une brochette de viande a meat kebab.

**brochure** *noun Fem.* **1** booklet; **2** brochure.

**brocolis** *plural noun Masc.* broccoli.

**broder** *verb* [1] to embroider.

**broderie** *noun Fem.* embroidery; des broderies embroidery.

**bronchite** *noun Fem.* bronchitis; avoir une bronchite to have bronchitis.

**bronzage** *noun Masc.* suntan.

**bronzer** *verb* [1] to tan.

**brosse** *noun Fem.* brush.

**brosse à cheveux** *noun Fem.* hairbrush.

**brosse à dents** *noun Fem.* toothbrush.

**brosser** *verb* [1] **1** to brush; **2** se brosser les dents to brush your teeth.

**brouette** *noun Fem.* wheelbarrow.

**brouillard** *noun Masc.* fog.

**brouillon** *noun Masc.* rough draft.

**bru** *noun Fem.* daughter-in-law.

**brugnon** *noun Masc.* nectarine.

**bruit** *noun Masc.* **1** noise; entendre un bruit to hear a noise; entendre le

**brûlant**

FRENCH-ENGLISH

**bruit d'une voiture** to hear the sound of a car; **2** rumour.

**brûlant** *adjective* **1** boiling hot; **2** burning hot.

**brûlé** *noun Masc.* **un goût de brûlé** a burnt taste; **ça sent le brûlé** there's a smell of burning.

**brûler** *verb* [1] **1** to burn; **2 se brûler** to burn yourself.

**brûlure** *noun Fem.* burn.

**brume** *noun Fem.* mist.

**brun** *adjective* **1** brown; **2** dark-haired.

**brushing** *noun Masc.* blow-dry; **se faire faire un brushing** to have a blow-dry.

**brut** *adjective* **1** raw (*material*); **2** crude (*oil*); **3** gross (*income*); **4** dry (*champagne*).

**brutal** (*Masc. plural* **brutaux**) *adjective* **1** violent, brutal; **2** sudden.

**brutalement** *adverb* **1** suddenly; **2** violently.

**Bruxelles** *noun* Brussels.

**bruyant** *adjective* noisy, loud.

**bruyère** *noun Fem.* heather.

**bu** *verb* SEE **boire**.

**bûche** *noun Fem.* log.

**budget** *noun Masc.* budget.

**buffet** *noun Masc.* **1** sideboard; **2** buffet.

**buisson** *noun Masc.* bush.

**buissonnière** *adjective* **faire l'école buissonnière** to play truant.

**Bulgarie** *noun Fem.* Bulgaria.

**bulle** *noun Fem.* bubble.

**bulletin** *noun Masc.* report, bulletin.

**bulletin de salaire** *noun Masc.* payslip.

**bulletin scolaire** *noun Masc.* school report.

**bureau** (*plural* **bureaux**) *noun Masc.* **1** desk; **elle est à son bureau** she is at her desk; **2** office; **au bureau** at (*or* to) the office.

**bureaucratie** *noun Fem.* bureaucracy.

**bureau de poste** *noun Masc.* post office.

**bureau de tabac** *noun Masc.* tobacconist's.

**bureau de tourisme** *noun Masc.* tourist information office.

**burin** *noun Masc.* chisel.

**bus** *noun Masc.* bus.

**buse** *noun Fem.* buzzard.

**buste** *noun Masc.* bust.

**but** *noun Masc.* **1** goal, aim, purpose; **2** goal (*in football, hockey*); **marquer un but** to score a goal; **3** target.

**buté** *adjective* stubborn.

**buvable** *adjective* drinkable.

**buvard** *noun Masc.* blotter; **du papier buvard** blotting paper.

**buvette** *noun Fem.* bar (*at a dance, village fair, etc*).

**buvez, buvons** *verb* SEE **boire**.

# Cc

**ça** *pronoun* **1** that, this; **donne-moi ça** give me that; **ça c'est un**

moineau that's a sparrow;
**2 comment ça va?,ça va?** how are
you?; **ça va bien merci** I'm fine
thanks; **3 c'est ça** that's right; **ça
ne fait rien** it doesn't matter.

**çà** *adverb* **çà et là** here and there.

**cabane** *noun Fem.* hut, shed.

**cabas** *noun Masc.* shopping bag.

**cabillaud** *noun Masc.* cod.

**cabine** *noun Fem.* **1** cubicle; **cabine
de douche** shower cubicle; **cabine
d'essayage** fitting room (*in a
clothes shop*); **2** cabin (*on a ship*);
**3** cab (*on a lorry*).

**cabinet** *noun Masc.* **1** office (*of a
solicitor*); **2** surgery (*of a doctor or
dentist*); **3 cabinet de médecins**
medical practice.

**cabine téléphonique** *noun
Fem.* phone box.

**cabinets** *plural noun Masc.* toilet.

**câble** *noun Masc.* **1** cable; **2** rope.

**câblé** *adjective* **être câblé** to have
cable television.

**cabosser** *verb* [1] to dent.

**cacahuète** *noun Fem.* peanut; **des
cacahuètes grillées** roasted
peanuts.

**cacao** *noun Masc.* cocoa.

**cache** *noun Fem.* hiding place.

**caché** *adjective* hidden.

**cache-cache** *noun Masc.* **jouer à
cache-cache** to play hide and seek.

**cachemire** *noun Masc.*
**1** cashmere; **2 motif cachemire**
paisley pattern.

**cache-nez** *noun Masc.* (thick)
scarf.

**cache-pot** *noun Masc.* flowerpot
holder.

**cacher** *verb* [1] **1** to hide; **cacher
quelque chose** to hide something;
**elle a caché son portefeuille dans
un tiroir** she's hidden her wallet in a
drawer; **2 se cacher** to hide; **il s'est
caché derrrière la porte** he hid
behind the door.

**cachet** *noun Masc.* **1** tablet; **un
cachet d'aspirine** an aspirin;
**2** official stamp (*made with a rubber
stamp*); **3 le cachet de la poste** the
postmark.

**cachette** *noun Fem.* **1** hiding
place; **2 en cachette** secretly, on
the sly.

**cachot** *noun Masc.* dungeon.

**cactus** *noun Masc.* cactus.

**cadavre** *noun Masc.* corpse, body.

**caddie** *noun Masc.* trolley (*in the
supermarket*).

**cadeau** (*plural* **cadeaux**) *noun
Masc.* present; **faire un cadeau à
quelqu'un** to give somebody a
present; **du papier cadeau**
wrapping-paper; **je vous fais un
paquet-cadeau?** shall I gift-wrap it
for you?

**cadenas** *noun Masc.* padlock.

**cadence** *noun Fem.* rhythm.

**cadet**, **cadette** *noun Masc., Fem.*
younger child, youngest child.
**cadet** (*Fem.* **cadette**) *adjective*
younger, youngest.

**cadran** *noun Masc.* **1** face (*of a
watch or clock*); **2** dial (*on an*

a
b
c
d
e
f
g
h
i
j
k
l
m
n
o
p
q
r
s
t
u
v
w
x
y
z

*instrument such as the speedometer in a car).*

**cadran solaire** *noun Masc.* sundial.

**cadre** *noun Masc.* **1** frame (*of a picture, mirror, or window*); **2** surroundings, setting; **3** executive (*a person with a management job in a company*); **4** frame (*of a bicycle*).

**cafard** *noun Masc.* **1** cockroach; **2** depression; **avoir le cafard** to be down in the dumps.

**café** *noun Masc.* **1** coffee; **café instantané, café soluble** instant coffee; **café moulu** ground coffee; **café en grains** coffee beans; **café au lait** coffee with milk; **prendre un café** to have a coffee; **2** cafe.

**café-crème** *noun Masc.* white coffee.

**caféine** *noun Fem.* caffeine.

**cafétéria** *noun Fem.* cafeteria.

**cafetière** *noun Fem.* **1** coffee pot; **2** coffee maker.

**cage** *noun Fem.* cage.

**cageot** *noun Masc.* crate.

**cagibi** *noun Masc.* store cupboard.

**cagnotte** *noun Fem.* **1** kitty (*of money*); **2** jackpot.

**cagoule** *noun Fem.* hood.

**cahier** *noun Masc.* **1** exercise book; **2** notebook.

**caille** *noun Fem.* quail.

**cailler** *verb* [1] to curdle.

**caillou** (*plural* **cailloux**) *noun Masc.* pebble, stone.

**caisse** *noun Fem.* **1** till, cash register; **2** cash desk; **3** checkout (*in a supermarket*); **4** box, crate.

**caisse à outils** *noun Fem.* toolbox.

**caisse d'épargne** *noun Fem.* savings bank.

**caissier, caissière** *noun Masc., Fem.* **1** checkout assistant; **2** cashier.

**cajou** *noun* **une noix de cajou** a cashew nut.

**cake** *noun Masc.* fruit cake.

**calamité** *noun Fem.* disaster, calamity.

**calcaire** *noun Masc.* **1** limestone; **2** furring (*the sediment which clogs up kettles, steam irons, etc*). **calcaire** *adjective* **eau calcaire** hard water; **l'eau ici est très calcaire** the water here is very hard.

**calcium** *noun Masc.* calcium.

**calcul** *noun Masc.* **1** calculation; **2** arithmetic.

**calculatrice** *noun Fem.* pocket calculator.

**calculer** *verb* [1] to calculate, to work out.

**calculette** *noun Fem.* pocket calculator.

**caleçon** *noun Masc.* **1** boxer shorts; **2** leggings.

**calembour** *noun Masc.* pun, play on words.

**calendrier** *noun Masc.* **1** calendar; **2** schedule.

**calepin** *noun Masc.* notebook.

**caler** *verb* [1] **1** to wedge; **2** to prop up; **3 ma voiture a calé** my car stalled.

**calibre** *noun Masc.* **1** size, grade (*of eggs, fruit, or vegetables*); **2** calibre, bore (*of a gun*).

**câlin** *noun Masc.* cuddle; **fais-moi un câlin** give me a cuddle (*usually said to a child*); **fais un calin à ta grand-mère** give your gran a cuddle. **câlin** *adjective* affectionate.

**câliner** *verb* [1] to cuddle.

**calmant** *noun Masc.* sedative. **calmant** *adjective* soothing.

**calmar** *noun Masc.* squid.

**calme** *noun Masc.* peace and quiet. **calme** *adjective* **1** calm; **2** quiet.

**calmement** *adverb* calmly.

**calmer** *verb* [1] **1 calmer quelqu'un** to calm somebody down; **2 se calmer** to calm down; **calme-toi** calm down; **3** to soothe; **l'aspirine a calmé la douleur** the aspirin soothed the pain.

**calorie** *noun Fem.* calorie.

**calque** *noun Masc.* **un calque** a tracing; **papier-calque** tracing paper.

**calvados** *noun Masc.* calvados (*apple brandy made in Normandy*).

**camarade** *noun Masc. & Fem.* friend; **camarade de classe** classmate.

**cambriolage** *noun Masc.* burglary.

**cambrioler** *verb* [1] **cambrioler une maison** to burgle a house; **ils ont été cambriolés** they were burgled.

**cambrioleur**, **cambrioleuse** *noun Masc., Fem.* burglar.

**caméra** *noun Fem.* cine-camera.

**caméscope** *noun Masc.* camcorder.

**camion** *noun Masc.* truck, lorry.

**camion-citerne** *noun Masc.* tanker lorry.

**camionnette** *noun Fem.* van.

**camionneur** *noun Masc.* lorry driver, truck driver.

**camp** *noun Masc.* camp.

**campagnard**, **campagnarde** *noun Masc., Fem.* country person. **campagnard** *adjective* country; **la vie campagnarde** country life.

**campagne** *noun Fem.* **1** country, countryside; **à la campagne** in the country, in the countryside; **aller se promener à la campagne** to go for a country walk; **2** campaign.

**camper** *verb* [1] to camp.

**campeur**, **campeuse** *noun Masc., Fem.* camper.

**camping** *noun Masc.* **1** camping; **faire du camping** to go camping; **2 un camping, un terrain de camping** a campsite.

**camping-car** *noun Masc.* camper van.

**camping-gaz**™ *noun Masc.* camping stove.

**Canada** *noun Masc.* Canada; **au Canada** in (*or* to) Canada.

**canadien** (*Fem.* **canadienne**) *adjective* Canadian.

**Canadien**, **Canadienne** *noun Masc., Fem.* Canadian.

**canal** (*plural* **canaux**) *noun Masc.* canal.

**canapé** *noun Masc.* sofa.

**canapé-lit** *noun Masc.* sofa bed.

**canard** *noun Masc.* duck.

**canari** *noun Masc.* canary.

**cancer** *noun Masc.* cancer; **avoir un cancer** to have cancer.

**Cancer** *noun Masc.* Cancer (*sign of the Zodiac*).

**candidat**, **candidate** *noun Masc., Fem.* **1** candidate; **2** applicant.

**candidature** *noun Fem.* **poser sa candidature à un poste** to apply for a job.

**cane** *noun Fem.* female duck.

**caneton** *noun Masc.* duckling.

**canette** *noun Fem.* **une canette de bière** a small bottle of beer.

**canevas** *noun Masc.* canvas.

**caniche** *noun Masc.* poodle.

**canicule** *noun Fem.* **1** scorching heat; **2** heat wave.

**canif** *noun Masc.* penknife.

**caniveau** (*plural* **caniveaux**) *noun Masc.* gutter.

**canne** *noun Fem.* walking stick.

**canne à pêche** *noun Fem.* fishing rod.

**canne à sucre** *noun Fem.* sugar cane.

**cannelle** *noun Fem.* cinnamon.

**canoë** *noun Masc.* **1** canoe; **2** **faire du canoë** to go canoeing.

**canon** *noun Masc.* **1** gun; **2** barrel (*of a gun*); **3** cannon.

**canot** *noun Masc.* small boat, dinghy; **un canot pneumatique** a rubber (*or* inflatable) dinghy.

**canot de sauvetage** *noun Masc.* lifeboat.

**cantatrice** *noun Fem.* opera singer.

**cantine** *noun Fem.* canteen; **manger à la cantine** to have school lunch.

**caoutchouc** *noun Masc.* **1** rubber; **des bottes en caoutchouc** wellington boots; **2** rubber band.

**cap** *noun Masc.* **1** cape, headland; **2** course (*of a ship*).

**capable** *adjective* capable; **être capable de faire** to be capable of doing.

**capacité** *noun Fem.* **1** ability; **2** capacity.

**cape** *noun Fem.* cape, cloak.

**capitaine** *noun Masc.* captain; **le capitaine des pompiers** the chief fire officer.

**capital** (*plural* **capitaux**) *noun Masc.* capital (*financial*).
**capital** *adjective* **1** **d'une importance capitale** of major importance; **2** **une question capitale** a key question; **3** **la peine capitale** capital punishment.

**capitale** *noun Fem.* capital city; **la capitale française** the French capital.

**capot** *noun Masc.* bonnet (*of a car*).

**câpre** *noun Fem.* caper.

**caprice** *noun Masc.* **1** whim; **2** tantrum; **faire un caprice** to throw a tantrum.

**Capricorne** *noun Masc.* Capricorn (*sign of the Zodiac*).

**capsule** *noun Fem.* **1** cap, top (*of a bottle*); **2** capsule.

**capter** *verb* [1] **1 capter une chaîne (de télévision)** to get a (television) channel; **2 capter l'attention de quelqu'un** to catch somebody's attention.

**captif**, **captive** *noun Masc., Fem.* captive.

**captivant** *adjective* **1** fascinating; **2** gripping, riveting.

**captivité** *noun Fem.* captivity; **être gardé en captivité** to be kept in captivity.

**capturer** *verb* [1] to capture.

**capuche** *noun Fem.* hood.

**capuchon** *noun Masc.* **1** hood; **2** top, cap (*of a pen*).

**capucine** *noun Fem.* nasturtium.

**car**[1] *conjunction* because.

**car**[2] *noun Masc.* coach, bus; **voyager en car** to travel by coach; **un voyage en car** a coach journey.

**carabine** *noun Fem.* rifle.

**caractère** *noun Masc.* **1** character, nature; **avoir mauvais caractère** to be bad-tempered; **2** character; **leur maison a beaucoup de caractère** their house has a lot of character; **3** character, letter; **en gros caractères** in large print.

**caractéristique** *noun Fem.*, *adjective* characteristic.

**carafe** *noun Fem.* carafe, jug (*for wine or water*).

**Caraïbes** *noun plural Fem.* **les îles Caraïbes** the Caribbean Islands; **aller aux Caraïbes** to go to the Caribbean.

**caramel** *noun Masc.* **1** caramel; **2** toffee.

**caravane** *noun Fem.* caravan.

**carbone** *noun Masc.* **1** carbon; **2** carbon paper.

**carbonisé** *adjective* burnt to a cinder.

**carburant** *noun Masc.* fuel.

**carburateur** *noun Masc.* carburettor.

**carcasse** *noun Fem.* carcass.

**cardiaque** *adjective* **une crise cardiaque** a heart attack.

**cardinal** (*plural* **cardinaux**) *noun Masc.* **1** cardinal; **2** cardinal number.

**carême** *noun Masc.* Lent.

**caresser** *verb* [1] to stroke, to caress.

**cargaison** *noun Fem.* cargo.

**caricature** *noun Fem.* caricature.

**caricaturiste** *noun Masc. & Fem.* caricaturist, cartoonist.

**carie** *noun Fem.* **la carie dentaire** tooth decay; **avoir une carie** to have a hole in your tooth.

**carillon** *noun Masc.* **1** church bells; **2** wind chimes.

**caritatif** (*Fem.* **caritative**) *adjective* charitable; **une association caritative** a charity.

**carnaval** *noun Masc.* carnival.

a
b
c
d
e
f
g
h
i
j
k
l
m
n
o
p
q
r
s
t
u
v
w
x
y
z

**carnet** *noun Masc.* **1** notebook; **2** book (*of tickets or stamps*).

**carnet de chèques** *noun Masc.* chequebook.

**carotte** *noun Fem.* carrot.

**carpe** *noun Fem.* carp.

**carpette** *noun Fem.* rug.

**carré** *noun Masc., adjective* square; **un mètre carré** a square metre.

**carreau** (*plural* **carreaux**) *noun Masc.* **1** floor tile; **2** wall tile; **3** windowpane; **4 du tissu à carreaux** checked fabric; **5 du papier à carreaux** squared paper; **6** diamonds (*suit of playing cards*); **le roi de carreau** the king of diamonds.

**carrefour** *noun Masc.* crossroads, junction.

**carrelage** *noun Masc.* **1** tiled floor; **2** tiling, tiles.

**carrelet** *noun Masc.* plaice.

**carrément** *adverb* downright, completely; **c'est carrément malhonnête** it's downright dishonest.

**carrière** *noun Fem.* **1** career; **2** quarry.

**carrosserie** *noun Fem.* **1** bodywork (*of car, etc*); **2** bodywork repairs.

**cartable** *noun Masc.* **1** satchel, schoolbag; **2** briefcase.

**carte** *noun Fem.* **1** card; **2** playing card; **jouer aux cartes** to play cards; **un jeu de cartes** a pack of cards, a card game; **3** map; **4** menu.

**carte à jouer** *noun Fem.* playing card.

**carte à mémoire** *noun Fem.* smart card.

**carte à microprocesseur** *noun Fem.* smart card.

**carte à puce** *noun Fem.* smart card.

**carte bancaire** *noun Fem.* bank card.

**carte d'abonnement** *noun Fem.* season ticket.

**carte d'anniversaire** *noun Fem.* birthday card.

**carte de crédit** *noun Fem.* credit card.

**carte d'embarquement** *noun Fem.* boarding card.

**carte de fidelité** *noun Fem.* loyalty card.

**carte d'identité** *noun Fem.* identity card.

**carte de séjour** *noun Fem.* resident's permit.

**carte des vins** *noun Fem.* wine list.

**carte de téléphone** *noun Fem.* telephone card.

**carte de visite** *noun Fem.* business card.

**carte de vœux** *noun Fem.* greetings card.

**carte postale** *noun Fem.* postcard.

**carte routière** *noun Fem.* road map.

**carte SIM** *noun Fem.* SIM card.

**carte téléphonique** *noun Fem.* phonecard.

**carton** *noun Masc.* **1** cardboard; **une chemise en carton** a cardboard folder; **carton ondulé** corrugated cardboard; **2** cardboard box.

**cartouche** *noun Fem.* cartridge.

**cas** *noun Masc.* **1** case; **au cas où tu oublierais** in case you forget; **en aucun cas** on no account; **en tout cas** in any case, at any rate; **2** case; **trois cas de rougeole** three cases of measles.

**cascade** *noun Fem.* **1** waterfall; **2** stunt.

**cascadeur, cascadeuse** *noun Masc., Fem.* stuntman, stuntwoman.

**case** *noun Fem.* **1** square (*on a board game*); **2** box (*on a form*); **3** hut.

**casher** *adjective* kosher.

**casier** *noun Masc.* **1** pigeonhole; **2** locker; **3** rack.

**casino** *noun Masc.* casino.

**casque** *noun Masc.* **1** crash helmet; **2** safety helmet, hard hat; **3** headphones, headset.

**casquette** *noun Fem.* cap; **une casquette de base-ball** a baseball cap.

**casse-croûte** *noun Masc.* snack.

**casse-noisettes** *noun Masc.* nutcrackers.

**casse-pieds** *adjective* (*informal*) **elle est casse-pieds!** she's a pain in the neck!

**casser** *verb* [1] **1** to break; **casser un verre** to break a glass; **2 se casser** to break; **le verre s'est cassé** the glass broke; **3 se casser la jambe** to break your leg; ★ **se**

**casser la tête** to go to a lot of trouble (*literally: to break your head*); **ne te casse pas la tête!** don't go to a lot of trouble!.

**casserole** *noun Fem.* saucepan.

**casse-tête** *noun Masc.* **1** puzzle; **2** problem.

**cassette** *noun Fem.* cassette, tape.

**cassis** *noun Masc.* blackcurrant; **sirop de cassis** blackcurrant cordial.

**cassoulet** *noun Masc.* oven-baked beans (*with meat and sausage*).

**castor** *noun Masc.* beaver.

**catalogue** *noun Masc.* catalogue.

**catastrophe** *noun Fem.* disaster, catastrophe.

**catch** *noun Masc.* wrestling.

**catcheur, catcheuse** *noun Masc., Fem.* wrestler.

**catégorie** *noun Fem.* category.

**cathédrale** *noun Fem.* cathedral.

**catholicisme** *noun Masc.* (Roman) Catholicism.

**catholique** *noun Masc. & Fem., adjective* (Roman) Catholic.

**cauchemar** *noun Masc.* nightmare; **faire un cauchemar** to have a nightmare.

**cause** *noun Fem.* **1** cause; **la cause du problème** the cause of the problem; **2 à cause de** because of; **3 la cause de quelque chose** the reason for something; **fermé pour cause de maladie** closed for reasons of illness; **4** cause; **une bonne cause** a good cause.

a
b
**c**
d
e
f
g
h
i
j
k
l
m
n
o
p
q
r
s
t
u
v
w
x
y
z

**causer** *verb* [1] **1** to cause; **2** to talk, to chat; **causer de quelque chose** to talk (*or* chat) about something; **causer avec quelqu'un** to talk (*or* chat) to somebody.

**caution** *noun Fem.* **1** deposit (*when renting a flat or house*); **2** bail.

**cavalier**, **cavalière** *noun Masc., Fem.* rider.

**cave** *noun Fem.* cellar.

**caveau** (*plural* **caveaux**) *noun Masc.* vault.

**caverne** *noun Fem.* cave.

**ce**[1], **cet** (*before a vowel or mute 'h'*) (*Fem.* **cette**) *adjective* **1** this, that; **ce stylo ne marche pas** this pen doesn't work; **cette semaine** this week; **ce couteau-ci** this knife; **2** that; **passe-moi cette assiette** pass me that plate; **cette chaise-là** that chair; **3** **cette nuit** last night, tonight.

**ce**[2], **c'** (*before an 'e'*) *pronoun* **1** this, that, it; **qui est-ce?** who is it?; **c'est moi** it's me; **qu'est-ce que c'est?** what is it?; **c'est la première maison à gauche** it's the first house on the left; **2** he, she, they; **c'est un médecin** he's a doctor; **ce sont les enfants de Paul** they're Paul's children; **3** **ce qui** what; **mange ce qui reste** eat what's left; **4** **ce que** what; **prends ce que tu veux** take what you want; **5** **c'est tout ce qui reste** that's all that's left; **prends tout ce que tu veux** take everything you want.

**ceci** *pronoun* this; **ceci n'est pas à moi** this is not mine.

**cécité** *noun Fem.* blindness.

**céder** *verb* [24] **1** to give in; **2** 'cédez le passage' 'give way' (*at a road junction*); **3** **céder sa place** to give up your seat; **4** **céder à quelque chose** to give in to something.

**cédille** *noun Fem.* cedilla.

**cèdre** *noun Masc.* cedar.

**ceinture** *noun Fem.* **1** belt; **2** waistband; **3** waist.

**ceinture de sauvetage** *noun Fem.* lifebelt.

**ceinture de sécurité** *noun Fem.* seatbelt.

**cela** *pronoun* this, that, it (*'cela' is used in the same way as 'ça' but is more formal*); **cela ne me concerne pas** that does not concern me; **cela ne fait rien** that doesn't matter.

**célébration** *noun Fem.* celebration.

**célèbre** *adjective* famous.

**célébrer** *verb* [24] to celebrate.

**céleri** *noun Masc.* celery.

**célibataire** *noun Masc. & Fem.* **1** bachelor; **2** single woman. **célibataire** *adjective* single; **elle est célibataire** she's single.

**celle** *pronoun* SEE **celui**.

**celle-ci** *pronoun* SEE **celui-ci**.

**celle-là** *pronoun* SEE **celui-là**.

**celles** *pronoun* SEE **ceux**.

**celles-ci** *pronoun* SEE **ceux-ci**.

**celles-là** *pronoun* SEE **ceux-là**.

**cellule** *noun Fem.* **1** (prison) cell; **2** cell (*in biology and medicine*); **3** unit.

**celui**, **celle** *pronoun* the one; **'quel livre?' – 'celui qui est sur la table'** 'which book?' – 'the one on the table'; **'quelle casserole?' – 'celle qui est sur la cuisinière'** 'which saucepan?' – 'the one on the cooker'.

**celui-ci**, **celle-ci** *pronoun* this one.

**celui-là**, **celle-là** *pronoun* that one.

**cendre** *noun Fem.* ash; **les cendres** the ashes.

**cendrier** *noun Masc.* ashtray.

**Cendrillon** *noun* Cinderella.

**censé** *adjective* supposed; **être censé faire/être** to be supposed to do/be; **je suis censé être là à dix heures** I'm supposed to be there at ten o'clock.

**cent**[1] *number* a hundred, one hundred; **trois cents personnes** three hundred people; **deux cent cinquante personnes** two hundred and fifty people (*note that there is no 's' on 'cent' when it is followed by another number*).

**cent**[2] *noun Masc.* cent (*one hundredth of a euro or dollar*).

**centaine** *noun Fem.* **une centaine de personnes** a hundred people, a hundred or so people; **plusieurs centaines de personnes** several hundred people; **des centaines de lettres** hundreds of letters.

**centenaire** *noun Masc.* centenary.

**centième** *number* hundredth.

**centime** *noun Masc.* **1** cent (*one hundredth of a euro*); **2** centime (*one hundredth of former French currency: the franc*).

**centimètre** *noun Masc.* **1** centimetre; **un centimètre carré** a square centimetre; **un centimètre cube** a cubic centimetre; **2** tape measure.

**central** *noun Masc.* **un central téléphonique** a telephone exchange.
**central** *adjective* (*Masc. plural* **centraux**) **1** central; **2** main.

**centrale** *noun Fem.* power station; **une centrale nucléaire** a nuclear power station.

**centraliser** *verb* [1] to centralize.

**centre** *noun Masc.* centre; **au centre de** in the centre of.

**centre commercial** *noun Masc.* shopping centre, mall.

**centre de loisirs** *noun Masc.* leisure centre.

**centre sportif** *noun Masc.* sports centre.

**centre-ville** *noun Masc.* town centre, city centre.

**cependant** *adverb* however.

**cercle** *noun Masc.* circle; **en cercle** in a circle.

**cercueil** *noun Masc.* coffin.

**céréale** *noun Fem.* cereal, grain.

**cérémonie** *noun Fem.* ceremony.

**cerf** *noun Masc.* stag.

**cerf-volant** *noun Masc.* kite.

**cerise** *noun Fem.* cherry.

**cerisier** *noun Masc.* cherry tree.

**certain** *adjective* **1** certain, sure; **être certain de** to be certain (*or* sure) of; **2** certain; **un certain nombre de** a certain number of; **3** some; **certaines personnes** some people.

**certains** *pronoun* some; **certains de mes amis** some of my friends.

**certainement** *adverb* **1** most probably; **2** certainly; **3** of course.

**certes** *adverb* admittedly.

**certificat** *noun Masc.* certificate.

**certifier** *verb* [1] to certify.

**cerveau** (*plural* **cerveaux**) *noun Masc.* **1** brain; **2** mind.

**ces** *adjective* **1** these; **c'est Sara qui m'a acheté ces fleurs** it was Sara who bought me these flowers; **2** those; **ces livres que je t'ai prêtés** those books I lent you; **ces arbres-là** those trees.

**CES** *noun Masc.* (*Collège d'enseignement secondaire*) secondary school (*from 11 to 15, when students can go on to a 'lycée' for a further 3 years*).

**cesse** *noun Fem.* **sans cesse** constantly.

**cesser** *verb* [1] to stop; **cesser de faire** to stop doing.

**cessez-le-feu** *noun Masc.* ceasefire.

**c'est-à-dire** *phrase* that is, that's to say.

**cet**, **cette** *adjective* SEE **ce**.

**ceux**, **celles** *pronoun* the ones; **'quels livres?'** – **'ceux qui sont sur la table'** 'which books?' – 'the ones on the table'; **'quelles chaussettes?'** – **'celles que tu m'as prêtées hier'** 'which socks?' – 'the ones you lent me yesterday' SEE **celui**.

**ceux-ci**, **celles-ci** *pronoun* these ones.

**ceux-là**, **celles-là** *pronoun* those ones.

**chacal** *noun Masc.* jackal.

**chacun**, **chacune** *pronoun* **1** each; **ils ont chacun un billet** they each have a ticket; **2** everyone; **comme chacun sait** as everyone knows.

**chagrin** *noun Masc.* grief.

**chaîne** *noun Fem.* **1** chain; **2** channel (*on TV*).

**chaîne hi-fi** *noun Fem.* hi-fi system.

**chaîne laser** *noun Fem.* CD player.

**chaîne stéréo** *noun Fem.* stereo system.

**chair** *noun Fem.* **1** flesh; **2** meat; **la chair à saucisse** sausage meat; ★ **avoir la chair de poule** to have goose pimples (*literally: to have hen's flesh*).

**chaise** *noun Fem.* chair.

**châle** *noun Masc.* shawl.

**chalet** *noun Masc.* chalet.

**chaleur** *noun Fem.* heat, warmth.

**chaleureux** (*Fem.* **chaleureuse**) *adjective* warm.

**chambre** *noun Fem.* **1** bedroom; **dans ma chambre** in my bedroom; **2** (hotel) room; **une chambre pour une personne** a single room; **une**

**chambre pour deux personnes** a double room; **3 la musique de chambre** chamber music.

**chambre d'amis** *noun Fem.* spare bedroom.

**chambre de commerce** *noun Fem.* chamber of commerce.

**chambres d'hôte** *plural noun Fem.* bed and breakfast.

**chameau** (*plural* **chameaux**) *noun Masc.* camel.

**champ** *noun Masc.* field.

**champagne** *noun Masc.* champagne.

**champ de bataille** *noun Masc.* battlefield.

**champ de courses** *noun Masc.* racetrack.

**champignon** *noun Masc.* **1** mushroom; **des champignons de Paris** button mushrooms; **2** fungus.

**champion, championne** *noun Masc., Fem.* champion.

**championnat** *noun Masc.* championship.

**chance** *noun Fem.* **1** luck; **un coup de chance** a stroke of luck; **Bonne chance!** Good luck!; **j'ai eu la chance de pouvoir passer un an en France** I was lucky enough to be able to spend a year in France; **avoir de la chance** to be lucky; **tu as de la chance d'avoir une sœur pareille!** you're lucky to have a sister like that!; **2** chance.

**chancelier** *noun Masc.* chancellor.

**chandail** *noun Masc.* jumper.

**chandelier** *noun Masc.* **1** candlestick; **2** candelabra.

**change** *noun Masc.* exchange rate; **bureau de change** bureau de change (*for changing money*).

**changeant** *adjective* changeable.

**changement** *noun Masc.* change.

**changer** *verb* [52] **1** to change; **tu n'as pas changé** you haven't changed; **2 changer quelque chose** to change something; **changer les draps** to change the sheets; **changer une prise** to change a plug; **3 changer quelque chose** to exchange something (*in a shop*); **4 changer de** to change; **changer de train** to change trains; **changer d'avis** to change your mind; **j'ai changé d'avis** I've changed my mind; **5 se changer** to get changed, to change your clothes.

**chanson** *noun Fem.* song.

**chant** *noun Masc.* **1** singing; **2** song.

**chantage** *noun Masc.* blackmail.

**chanter** *verb* [1] to sing.

**chanteur, chanteuse** *noun Masc., Fem.* singer.

**chantier** *noun Masc.* **1** building site; **2** roadworks.

**chantonner** *verb* [1] to hum.

**chaos** *noun Masc.* chaos.

**chaotique** *adjective* chaotic.

**chapeau** (*plural* **chapeaux**) *noun Masc.* **1** hat; **2 chapeau!** well done!

**chapeau melon** *noun Masc.* bowler hat.

**chapelle** *noun Fem.* chapel.

**chapelure** *noun Fem.*
breadcrumbs.

**chapiteau** (*plural* **chapiteaux**)
*noun Masc.* **1** marquee; **2** big top
(*circus tent*).

**chapitre** *noun Masc.* chapter.

**chaque** *adjective* each, every.

**char** *noun Masc.* **1** (military) tank;
**2** carnival float.

**charabia** *noun Masc.* (*informal*)
gobbledygook, rubbish.

**charade** *noun Fem.* riddle.

**charbon** *noun Masc.* coal.

**charbon de bois** *noun Masc.*
charcoal.

**charcuterie** *noun Fem.* **1** pork
butcher's (*selling salads and ready-
prepared dishes as well as pork,
bacon, ham, sausages, etc*); **2** pork
products (*ham, salami, pâté, etc*).

**charcutier**, **charcutière** *noun
Masc.*, *Fem.* pork butcher.

**chardon** *noun Masc.* thistle.

**charge** *noun Fem.* **1** load;
**2** responsibility; **avoir la charge de**
to be responsible for; **3 charges**
costs, charges.

**charger** *verb* [52] **1** to load; **2** to
charge (*a battery*).

**chariot** *noun Masc.* **1** trolley (*in a
supermarket*); **1** waggon.

**charité** *noun Fem.* charity.

**charmant** *adjective* charming.

**charme** *noun Masc.* **1** charm;
**2** spell.

**charmer** *verb* [1] to charm.

**charnière** *noun Fem.* hinge.

**charpentier** *noun Masc.*
carpenter.

**charrette** *noun Fem.* cart.

**charrue** *noun Fem.* plough.

**charte** *noun Fem.* charter.

**charter** *adjective* **un vol charter** a
charter flight.

**chasse** *noun Fem.* hunting,
shooting.

**chasse d'eau** *noun Fem.* (toilet)
flush; **tirer la chasse d'eau** to flush
the toilet.

**chasse-neige** *noun Masc.*
snowplough.

**chasser** *verb* [1] to chase off.

**chasseur** *noun Masc.* hunter.

**chat** *noun Masc.* cat.

**châtaigne** *noun Fem.* sweet
chestnut.

**châtaignier** *noun Masc.* sweet
chestnut tree.

**châtain** *adjective* **les cheveux
châtains** brown hair.

**château** (*plural* **châteaux**) *noun
Masc.* **1** castle; **2** large country
house.

**château d'eau** *noun Masc.* water
tower.

**chatouiller** *verb* [1] to tickle.

**chatroom** *noun Masc.* chatroom.

**chatte** *noun Fem.* (female) cat.

**chaud** *adjective* hot, warm; **du lait
chaud** hot milk; **un pull chaud** a
warm jumper; **j'ai chaud** I'm hot; **il
fait chaud ici** it's hot here.

**chaudière** *noun Fem.* boiler; **une
chaudière à gaz** a gas boiler.

**chauffage** *noun Masc.* heating.

**chauffage central** *noun Masc.* central heating.

**chauffe-eau** *noun Masc.* water heater.

**chauffer** *verb* [1] **1** to heat, to heat up; **2** to warm.

**chauffeur** *noun Masc.* **1** driver; **un chauffeur de taxi** a taxi driver; **2** chauffeur.

**chaumière** *noun Fem.* thatched cottage.

**chaussée** *noun Fem.* roadway.

**chaussette** *noun Fem.* sock.

**chausson** *noun Masc.* **1** slipper; **2** ballet shoe.

**chaussure** *noun Fem.* shoe.

**chauve** *adjective* bald.

**chauve-souris** *noun Fem.* bat.

**chavirer** *verb* [1] to capsize.

**chef** *noun Masc.* **1** leader; **2** head; **3** boss; **4 chef de cuisine** chef.

**chef-d'œuvre** *noun Masc.* masterpiece.

**chemin** *noun Masc.* **1** country road; **2** track, path; **3** way; **perdre son chemin** to lose your way; **en chemin** on the way.

**chemin de fer** *noun Masc.* railway.

**cheminée** *noun Fem.* **1** chimney; **2** fireplace; **3** mantlepiece.

**cheminot** *noun Masc.* railway worker.

**chemise** *noun Fem.* shirt.

**chemise de nuit** *noun Fem.* nightdress.

**chemisier** *noun Masc.* blouse.

**chêne** *noun Masc.* **1** oak tree; **2** oak; **une table en chêne** an oak table.

**chenil** *noun Masc.* **1** dog kennel; **2** kennels.

**chenille** *noun Fem.* caterpillar.

**chèque** *noun Masc.* cheque; **un carnet de chèques** a cheque book.

**chèque de voyage** *noun Masc.* traveller's cheque.

**chéquier** *noun Masc.* cheque book.

**cher** (*Fem.* **chère**) *adjective* **1** dear; **Chère Anne** Dear Anne; **2** expensive, dear; **pas trop cher** reasonably priced.
**cher** *adverb* **coûter cher** to be expensive.

**chercher** *verb* [1] **1** to look for; **qu'est-ce que tu cherches?** what are you looking for?; **je cherche mes lunettes** I'm looking for my glasses; **je cherche un emploi** I'm looking for a job; **2 chercher quelque chose** to look something up (*in a dictionary, for example*); **3 aller chercher** to go and get (*or* fetch) (*somebody or something*); **je vais chercher des verres** I'll go and get some glasses; **4** to pick up; **je viendrai te chercher à l'école** I'll come and pick you up from school; **5 chercher à faire** to try to do.

**chercheur**, **chercheuse** *noun Masc., Fem.* scientist.

**chéri**, **chérie** *noun Masc., Fem.* darling.

**chérir** *verb* [2] to cherish.

**cheval** (*plural* **chevaux**) *noun Masc.* **1** horse; **à cheval** on horseback; **monter à cheval** to ride a horse; **2 faire du cheval** to go horseriding.

**cheval à bascule** *noun Masc.* rocking horse.

**chevalet** *noun Masc.* easel.

**chevet** *noun Masc.* **1** bedhead; **au chevet de quelqu'un** at somebody's bedside; **un livre de chevet** a bedside book; **une lampe de chevet** a bedside lamp; **2** bedside table.

**cheveu** (*plural* **cheveux**) *noun Masc.* **1 un cheveu** a hair; **2 les cheveux** hair; **il a les cheveux blonds** he has blond hair; ★ **avoir un cheveu sur la langue** to have a lisp (*literally: to have a hair on one's tongue*); ★ **couper les cheveux en quatre** to split hairs (*literally: to cut hairs in four*).

**cheville** *noun Fem.* ankle.

**chèvre**[1] *noun Fem.* goat, nanny-goat.

**chèvre**[2] *noun Masc.* goat's cheese.

**chèvrefeuille** *noun Masc.* honeysuckle.

**chevreuil** *noun Masc.* **1** roe deer; **2** venison.

**chez** *preposition* **1 chez quelqu'un** at (*or* to) somebody's house; **je vais chez Paul ce soir** I'm going to Paul's this evening; **elle est chez les Brown** she's at the Browns'; **viens chez moi** come round to my place; **il est chez lui** he's at home; **je rentre chez moi maintenant** I'm going home now; **fais comme chez toi** make yourself at home; **2 chez le boucher** at (*or* to) the butcher's; **je l'ai rencontrée chez le coiffeur**

**hier** I met her at the hairdresser's yesterday; **je vais chez le coiffeur demain** I'm going to the hairdresser's tomorrow.

**chic** *adjective* **1** chic, well-dressed; **2** nice; **c'était vachement chic de ta part** it was really nice of you; **3 Chic!** (*informal*) Cool!.

**chicorée** *noun Fem.* **1** endive; **2** chicory powder (*for adding to coffee*).

**chien** *noun Masc.* dog; **'chien méchant'** 'beware of the dog'.

**chien d'aveugle** *noun Masc.* guide dog.

**chien de berger** *noun Masc.* sheepdog.

**chien de garde** *noun Masc.* guard dog.

**chienne** *noun Fem.* (female) dog, bitch.

**chiffon** *noun Masc.* **1** rag; **2** duster.

**chiffre** *noun Masc.* figure; **un numéro à cinq chiffres** a five-figure number.

**chignon** *noun Masc.* bun, chignon.

**chimie** *noun Fem.* chemistry.

**chimique** *adjective* chemical.

**chimpanzé** *noun Masc.* chimpanzee.

**Chine** *noun Fem.* China.

**chinois** *noun Masc.* Chinese (*language*).
**chinois** *adjective* Chinese.

**Chinois**, **Chinoise** *noun Masc.*, *Fem.* Chinese man, Chinese woman; **les Chinois** the Chinese.

**chiot** *noun Masc.* puppy.

**chips** *noun Fem.* crisp; **un paquet de chips** a packet of crisps.

**chirurgical** (*Masc. plural* **chirurgicaux**) *adjective* surgical; **une intervention chirurgicale** an operation.

**chirurgie** *noun Fem.* surgery.

**chirurgie au laser** *noun Fem.* laser surgery.

**chirurgien** *noun Masc.* surgeon.

**chirurgien-dentiste** *noun Masc.* dental surgeon.

**choc** *noun Masc.* **1** shock; **ça m'a fait un choc** it gave me a shock; **2** crash.

**chocolat** *noun Masc.* chocolate; **chocolat au lait** milk chocolate; **chocolat blanc** white chocolate; **chocolat en poudre** drinking chocolate; **un gâteau au chocolat** a chocolate cake; **un chocolat chaud** a hot chocolate.

**chœur** *noun Masc.* **1** choir (*professional*); **2** chorus.

**choisir** *verb* [2] to choose.

**choix** *noun Masc.* **1** choice; **un bon choix** a good choice; **2 un grand choix** a wide choice (*or* variety).

**chômage** *noun Masc.* unemployment; **être au chômage** to be unemployed.

**chômeur**, **chômeuse** *noun Masc., Fem.* unemployed person.

**chope** *noun Fem.* beer mug.

**choquer** *verb* [1] to shock.

**chorale** *noun Fem.* choir (*amateur*).

**choriste** *noun Masc. & Fem.* **1** member of a choir; **2** member of a chorus; **3** backing singer.

**chose** *noun Fem.* thing; **les choses qui m'intéressent** the things that interest me; **j'ai plusieurs choses à te dire** I have several things to tell you; **je prends la même chose** I'll have the same.

**chou** (*plural* **choux**) *noun Masc.* cabbage.

**chouchou**[1], **chouchoute** *noun Masc., Fem.* teacher's pet.

**chouchou**[2] *noun Masc.* scrunchy (*for holding back your hair*).

**choucroute** *noun Fem.* sauerkraut (*pickled cabbage with different types of sausage, ham, and bacon*).

**chou de Bruxelles** *noun Masc.* Brussels sprout.

**chouette** *noun Fem.* owl. **chouette** *adjective* (*informal*) great; **c'est chouette!** that's great!; **leur maison est très chouette** their house is really lovely.

**chou-fleur** (*plural* **choux-fleurs**) *noun Masc.* cauliflower.

**chrétien**, **chrétienne** *noun Masc., Fem., adjective* Christian.

**christianisme** *noun Masc.* Christianity.

**chrome** *noun Masc.* chromium.

**chronique** *noun Fem.* **1** column, page (*devoted to a particular journalist in a newspaper*); **2** (radio) programme. **chronique** *adjective* chronic.

a
b
c
d
e
f
g
h
i
j
k
l
m
n
o
p
q
r
s
t
u
v
w
x
y
z

**chronomètre** *noun Masc.* stopwatch.

**chrysanthème** *noun Masc.* chrysanthemum.

**chuchoter** *verb* [1] to whisper.

**chut** *exclamation* shh!

**chute** *noun Fem.* **1** fall; **faire une chute de 5 mètres** to fall 5 metres; **2 chutes de neige** snowfall; **chutes de pluie** rainfall; **3** fall, drop (*in price, value, temperature*).

**chuter** *verb* [1] to fall, to drop.

**Chypre** *noun Fem.* Cyprus.

**ci** *adverb* **ce mois-ci** this month; **ces timbres-ci** these stamps; **ces jours-ci** these last few days.

**cible** *noun Fem.* target.

**ciboulette** *noun Fem.* **de la ciboulette** chives.

**cicatrice** *noun Fem.* scar.

**ci-contre** *adverb* opposite.

**ci-dessous** *adverb* below.

**ci-dessus** *adverb* above.

**cidre** *noun Masc.* cider.

**ciel** (*plural* **cieux**) *noun Masc.* **1** sky; **au ciel** in the sky; **2** heaven.

**cigale** *noun Fem.* cicada.

**cigare** *noun Masc.* cigar.

**cigarette** *noun Fem.* cigarette.

**cigogne** *noun Fem.* stork.

**ci-inclus** *adjective* enclosed; **la copie ci-incluse** the enclosed copy. **ci-inclus** *adverb* enclosed.

**ci-joint** *adverb* **veuillez trouver ci-joint** please find enclosed (*in a letter*).

**cil** *noun Masc.* eyelash.

**ciment** *noun Masc.* cement.

**cimetière** *noun Masc.* **1** cemetery; **2** graveyard.

**cinéaste** *noun Masc. & Fem.* film director.

**ciné-club** *noun Masc.* film club.

**cinéma** *noun Masc.* **1** cinema; **aller au cinéma** to go to the cinema; **2** (*informal*) play-acting; **arrête ton cinéma!** stop that nonsense!.

**cinéphile** *noun Masc. & Fem.* keen cinema-goer.

**cinglé** *adjective* (*informal*) crazy.

**cinq** *number* five; **Lucie a cinq ans** Lucie's five; **à cinq heures** at five o'clock; **le cinq avril** the fifth of April.

**cinquantaine** *noun Fem.* **une cinquantaine (de)** about fifty; **une cinquantaine de personnes** about fifty people; **avoir la cinquantaine** to be about fifty.

**cinquante** *number* fifty.

**cinquantième** *number* fiftieth.

**cinquième** *noun Fem.* (*in a French school*) the equivalent of Year 8. **cinquième** *noun Masc.* **au cinquième** on the fifth floor. **cinquième** *adjective* fifth.

**cintre** *noun Masc.* clothes hanger.

**cirage** *noun Masc.* shoe polish.

**circonférence** *noun Fem.* circumference.

**circonflexe** *noun Masc.* **un accent circonflexe** a circumflex.

**circonstance** *noun Fem.* circumstance.

**circuit** *noun Masc.* **1** circuit (*in an athletics stadium*); **2** tour; **3** (electrical) circuit.

**circulaire** *noun Fem.*, *adjective* circular.

**circulation** *noun Fem.* **1** traffic; **il y a beaucoup de circulation ce soir** there's a lot of traffic this evening; **2** circulation.

**circuler** *verb* [1] **1** to run (*of a bus or train*); **ce train ne circule pas le dimanche** that train doesn't run on Sundays; **2** to circulate.

**cire** *noun Fem.* wax.

**cirer** *verb* [1] to polish.

**cirque** *noun Masc.* circus; **au cirque** at (*or* to) the circus.

**ciseaux** *plural noun Masc.* scissors; **une paire de ciseaux** a pair of scissors.

**citadin**, **citadine** *noun Masc.*, *Fem.* city dweller.

**citation** *noun Fem.* quotation.

**cité** *noun Fem.* **1** city, town; **2** housing estate; **3 une cité universitaire** university halls of residence.

**citer** *verb* [1] to quote.

**citerne** *noun Fem.* tank.

**citoyen**, **citoyenne** *noun Masc.*, *Fem.* citizen.

**citron** *noun Masc.* lemon; **une tarte au citron** a lemon tart.

**citronnade** *noun Fem.* still lemonade.

**citronnier** *noun Masc.* lemon tree.

**citron vert** *noun Masc.* lime.

**citrouille** *noun Fem.* pumpkin.

**civet** *noun Masc.* stew.

**civil** *noun Masc.* **1** civilian; **2 un policier en civil** a plain-clothes policeman.
**civil** *adjective* **1** civilian; **2 un mariage civil** a civil wedding (*as opposed to a church wedding*).

**civilisation** *noun Fem.* civilization.

**civique** *adjective* civic.

**clair** *adjective* **1** light; **bleu clair** light blue; **2 la chambre est très claire** the bedroom is very light; **3** clear.
**clair** *adverb* clearly; **voir clair** to see clearly.

**clair de lune** *noun Masc.* moonlight.

**clairement** *adverb* clearly.

**clapier** *noun Masc.* rabbit hutch.

**claque** *noun Fem.* slap.

**claqué** *adjective* (*informal*) exhausted, wiped out.

**claquer** *verb* [1] **claquer la porte** to slam the door.

**clarifier** *verb* [1] to clarify.

**clarinette** *noun Fem.* clarinet; **jouer de la clarinette** to play the clarinet.

**clarté** *noun Fem.* **1** light; **2** clarity.

**classe** *noun Fem.* **1** class; **elle est dans ma classe à l'école** she's in my class (or year) at school; **en classe** in class; **2** classroom; **3 première/deuxième classe** first/second class; **4** (social) class.

**classement** *noun Masc.* **1** classification; **2** placing; **3** grading; **4** filing.

a
b
c
d
e
f
g
h
i
j
k
l
m
n
o
p
q
r
s
t
u
v
w
x
y
z

# classer

**classer** *verb* [1] **1** to classify; **2** to grade; **3** to file.

**classeur** *noun Masc.* **1** ring binder, file; **2** filing cabinet.

**classique** *adjective* **1** classical; **2** classic; **3** usual; **c'est classique!** that's typical!

**clavier** *noun Masc.* keyboard.

**clé** *noun Fem.* **1** key; **fermer quelque chose à clé** to lock something; **2** spanner.

**clef** = CLÉ.

**clémentine** *noun Fem.* clementine.

**clic** *noun Masc.* click (*with mouse*); **un clic sur le bouton droit de la souris** a right-click; **un clic sur le bouton gauche de la souris** a left-click.

**client, cliente** *noun Masc., Fem.* **1** customer; **2** client.

**clientèle** *noun Fem.* customers.

**cligner** *verb* [1] **cligner des yeux** to blink.

**clignotant** *noun Masc.* indicator (*on a motor vehicle*).

**clignoter** *verb* [1] to flash.

**climat** *noun Masc.* climate.

**climatisation** *noun Fem.* air-conditioning.

**climatisé** *adjective* air-conditioned.

**clin d'œil** *noun Masc.* wink; **faire un clin d'œil à quelqu'un** to wink at somebody; ★ **en un clin d'œil** in a flash.

**clinique** *noun Fem.* clinic, private hospital.

**clip** *noun Masc.* **1** video clip; **2** clip brooch; **3** clip-on earring.

**cliquer** *verb* [1] **cliquer sur quelque chose** to click on something (*using a computer mouse*); **cliquer en appuyant sur le bouton gauche de la souris** to left-click; **cliquer deux fois sur l'icône** to double-click the icon.

**cliqueter** *verb* [48] **1** to jingle; **2** to rattle.

**clochard, clocharde** *noun Masc., Fem.* tramp, down-and-out.

**cloche** *noun Fem.* bell.

**clocher** *noun Masc.* **1** steeple; **2** bell tower.

**cloison** *noun Fem.* **1** partition; **2** partition wall; **3** screen.

**cloître** *noun Masc.* cloister.

**clos** *adjective* closed.

**clôture** *noun Fem.* **1** fence; **2** close; **3** closing.

**clou** *noun Masc.* **1** nail; **2** stud.

**clou de girofle** *noun Masc.* clove.

**clouer** *verb* [1] **clouer quelque chose** to nail something down.

**clown** *noun Masc.* clown.

**club** *noun Masc.* club; **un club de foot** a football club.

**cobaye** *noun Masc.* guinea pig.

**Coca™** *noun Masc.* Coke™.

**cocaïne** *noun Fem.* cocaine.

**coccinelle** *noun Fem.* ladybird.

**cocher** *verb* [1] to tick.

**cochon** *noun Masc.* pig.
**cochon** *adjective* (*Fem.* **cochonne**) (*informal*) dirty (*joke, story*).

**cochon d'Inde** *noun Masc.* guinea pig.

**cocktail** *noun Masc.* **1** cocktail; **2** cocktail party.

**coco** *noun Masc.* **une noix de coco** a coconut.

**cocorico** *noun Masc.* cock-a-doodle-do.

**cocotte** *noun Fem.* **1** casserole; **2** hen (*in baby talk*); **3** chocolate hen (*traditionally sold at Easter*).

**cocotte-minute™** *noun Fem.* pressure cooker.

**code** *noun Masc.* **1** code; **le code de la route** the highway code; **2 codes** dipped headlights.

**code postal** *noun Masc.* postcode.

**cœur** *noun Masc.* **1** heart; **2** hearts (*suit of playing cards*); **le roi de cœur** the king of hearts; **3 par cœur** by heart; **apprendre quelque chose par cœur** to learn something by heart; ★ **avoir mal au cœur** to feel sick.

**coffre** *noun Masc.* **1** chest; **2** safe; **3** boot (*of a car*).

**coffre-fort** *noun Masc.* safe.

**cogner** *verb* [1] to bump, to bang; **se cogner la tête** to bang your head.

**coiffer** *verb* [1] **se coiffer** to brush (*or* comb) your hair.

**coiffeur**, **coiffeuse**[1] *noun Masc.*, *Fem.* hairdresser.

**coiffeuse**[2] *noun Fem.* dressing table.

**coiffure** *noun* **1** hairdressing; **2** hairstyle; **tu as changé de coiffure** you've changed your hairstyle.

**coin** *noun Masc.* **1** corner; **au coin** in the corner; **au coin de** in the corner of; **2 le café du coin** the local cafe; **les gens du coin** the local people; ★ **au coin du feu** by the fireside (*literally: in the corner of the fire*).

**coincé** *adjective* stuck, jammed.

**coincer** *verb* [61] to jam.

**coïncidence** *noun Fem.* coincidence.

**col** *noun Masc.* **1** collar; **2** neck; **3** (mountain) pass.

**colère** *noun Fem.* anger; **être en colère** to be angry.

**colin** *noun Masc.* hake.

**colique** *noun Fem.* diarrhoea.

**colis** *noun Masc.* parcel.

**collant** *noun Masc.* **un collant** (a pair of) tights.
**collant** *adjective* sticky.

**colle** *noun Fem.* **1** glue; **2** detention; **une heure de colle** an hour's detention.

**collecte** *noun Fem.* collection (*of money*).

**collection** *noun Fem.* collection.

**collectionner** *verb* [1] to collect.

**collectionneur**, **collectionneuse** *noun Masc.*, *Fem.* collector.

**collège** *noun Masc.* secondary school (*from 11 to 15, when students can either leave school altogether or go on to a 'lycée' for a further 3 years*).

a
b
c
d
e
f
g
h
i
j
k
l
m
n
o
p
q
r
s
t
u
v
w
x
y
z

**collégien**, **collégienne** *noun*
Masc., Fem. schoolboy, schoolgirl.

**collègue** *noun Masc. & Fem.*
colleague.

**coller** *verb* [1] **1** to stick; **2** to stick
down; **3** to glue; **4** to press.

**collier** *noun Masc.* **1** necklace;
**2** collar (*for a dog, cat, etc*).

**colline** *noun Fem.* hill.

**collision** *noun Fem.* collision.

**colombe** *noun Fem.* dove.

**colonel** *noun Masc.* colonel.

**colonie** *noun Fem.* colony.

**colonie de vacances** *noun*
Fem. holiday camp (*for children*).

**colonne** *noun Fem.* column.

**colonne vertébrale** *noun Fem.*
spine.

**colorant** *noun Masc.* colouring.

**coloré** *adjective* **1** coloured;
**2** colourful.

**colorer** *verb* [1] to colour.

**colorier** *verb* [1] to colour in.

**coloris** *noun Masc.* colour; **existe
en plusieurs coloris** several
colours available.

**combat** *noun Masc.* **1** fighting; **2** **un
combat de boxe** a boxing match.

**combattant** *noun Masc.* **un
ancien combattant** a war veteran.

**combattre** *verb* [21] to fight.

**combien** *adverb* **1** how much; **tu
en veux combien?** how much do
you want?; **c'est combien?** how
much is it?; **ça coûte combien?**
how much does it cost?; **je vous dois
combien?** how much do I owe you?,
how much is that?; **2** how many; **tu**
en veux combien? how many do
you want?; **3 combien de** how
much; **combien d'argent?** how
much money?; **4 combien de** how
many; **combien de tasses?** how
many cups?; ★ **nous sommes le
combien aujourd'hui?** what's the
date today? (*literally: we are the how
many today?*).

**combinaison** *noun Fem.*
**1** combination; **2** jumpsuit;
**3** overalls; **4** slip, petticoat.

**combiné** *noun Masc.* receiver (*of a
telephone*).

**comble** *noun Masc.* **1 le comble
de** the height of; **le comble du
luxe** the height of luxury; **2 ça
c'est le comble!** that's the last
straw!

**comédie** *noun Fem.* comedy.

**comédien**, **comédienne** *noun*
Masc., Fem. actor, actress.

**comestible** *adjective* edible.

**comique** *noun Masc.* comic,
comedian.
**comique** *adjective* funny.

**comité** *noun Masc.* committee.

**commandant** *noun Masc.*
**1** major; **2** squadron leader;
**3 commandant-en-chef**
commander in chief.

**commande** *noun Fem.* order; **sur
commande** to order.

**commander** *verb* [1] **1** to order;
**avez-vous commandé?** have you
ordered?; **2** to be in charge.

**comme** *preposition* **1** like; **une
montre comme la tienne** a watch
like yours; **2** like; **comme ça** like
this; **3** as a; **travailler comme**

**serveur dans un café** to work as a waiter in a cafe; **4 qu'est-ce que tu veux comme glace?** what kind of ice cream would you like?

**comme** *conjunction* **1** as; **comme tu veux** as you like; **2** as, since; **comme je suis malade** as (*or* since) I'm ill; **3** as; **comme je fermais la porte** as I was closing the door; **4 comme si** as if.

**comme** *adverb* **comme il est gentil!** he's so nice!; **comme c'est bon!** it's so good!; **comme il fait chaud!** it's so hot!; ★ **blanc comme la neige** as white as snow; ★ **fort comme un bœuf** as strong as an ox.

**commencement** *noun Masc.* beginning, start.

**commencer** *verb* [61] **1** to begin, to start; **le film a commencé** the film has started; **2 commencer à faire, commencer de faire** to start (*or* begin) to do; **elle a commencé à faire ses devoirs** she's started to do her homework; **je commence à comprendre** I'm beginning to understand; **il commence à pleuvoir** it's starting to rain.

**comment** *adverb* **1** how; **comment as-tu fait ce gâteau?** how did you make this cake?; **je ne sais pas comment le faire** I don't know how to do it; **2 comment vas-tu?** how are you?; **comment ça va?** how are you?; **comment va ta mère?** how's your mother?; **3 comment t'appelles-tu?** what's your name?; **il s'appelle comment, ton frère?** what's your brother's name?; **4** pardon?; **5 comment est leur maison?, elle est comment,**

**leur maison?** what's their house like?

**commentaire** *noun Masc.* **1** comment; **2** commentary.

**commenter** *verb* [1] **commenter quelque chose** to comment on something.

**commerçant, commerçante** *noun Masc., Fem.* shopkeeper.

**commerce** *noun Masc.* **1** shop; **2 le commerce** business; **je fais des études de commerce** I'm doing business studies; **3 le commerce** trade.

**commercial** (*Masc. plural* **commerciaux**) *adjective* **1** commercial; **2 un centre commercial** a shopping centre.

**commettre** *verb* [11] **1 commettre une erreur** to make a mistake; **2 commettre un crime** to commit a crime.

**commissariat** *noun Masc.* police station.

**commission** *noun Fem.* **1** committee; **2** commission; **3** message; **4** errand; **5 faire les commissions** to do the shopping.

**commode** *noun Fem.* chest of drawers.

**commode** *adjective* **1** convenient, handy; **2** easy.

**commun** *adjective* **1** common; **2** shared; **3** joint; **4 en commun** in common; **ils n'ont rien en commun** they have nothing in common; **5 en commun** jointly, together; **6 les transports en commun** public transport.

a
b
c
d
e
f
g
h
i
j
k
l
m
n
o
p
q
r
s
t
u
v
w
x
y
z

**communauté** *noun Fem.*
community.

**communication** *noun Fem.*
**1 une communication
téléphonique** a telephone call;
**2** communication; **se mettre en
communication avec quelqu'un** to
get in touch with someone.

**communion** *noun Fem.*
communion.

**communiquer** *verb* [1] **1** to
communicate; **2 communiquer
quelque chose** to pass something
on.

**communisme** *noun Masc.*
communism.

**communiste** *noun Masc. & Fem.*,
*adjective* communist.

**compact** *adjective* **1** dense;
**2** compact; **3 un disque compact** a
compact disc, a CD.

**compagnie** *noun Fem.* **1** company,
firm; **2** company; **elle m'a tenu
compagnie** she kept me company.

**compagnie aérienne** *noun
Fem.* airline.

**compagnon** *noun Masc.*
companion.

**comparable** *adjective*
comparable.

**comparaison** *noun Fem.*
comparison; **en comparaison de** in
comparison with.

**comparatif** (*Fem.* **comparative**)
*adjective* comparative.

**comparé** *adjective* **comparé à**
compared to (*or* with).

**comparer** *verb* [1] to compare.

**compartiment** *noun Masc.*
compartment.

**compas** *noun Masc.* compass.

**compatir** *verb* [2] to sympathize.

**compensation** *noun Fem.*
compensation.

**compenser** *verb* [1] **compenser
quelque chose** to compensate for
something.

**compétence** *noun Fem.* **1** ability;
**2** skill; **3** competence.

**compétent** *adjective* competent.

**compétitif** (*Fem.* **compétitive**)
*adjective* competitive.

**compétition** *noun Fem.*
competition.

**complémentaire** *adjective*
further, supplementary.

**complet** *noun Masc.* suit.
**complet** *adjective* (*Fem.* **complète**)
**1** complete; **2** total; **3** full (*speaking
of a hotel or a train*); **4 le pain
complet** wholemeal bread.

**complètement** *adverb*
completely.

**compléter** *verb* [24] **1** to complete;
**2** to fill in (*a form*).

**complexe** *noun Masc.*, *adjective*
complex.

**complication** *noun Fem.*
complication.

**complice** *noun Masc. & Fem.*
accomplice.

**compliment** *noun Masc.*
compliment; **faire des
compliments à quelqu'un** to
compliment somebody.

**compliqué** *adjective* complicated.

**compliquer** *verb* [1] to complicate.

**complot** *noun Masc.* plot.

**comportement** *noun Masc.* behaviour.

**comporter** *verb* [1] **1** to include; **2** to consist of; **3 se comporter** to behave.

**composé** *adjective* **1 composé de** made up of; **2 une salade composée** a mixed salad.

**composer** *verb* [1] **1** to make up; **2** to put together; **3** to compose (*music*); **4 composer un numéro (de téléphone)** to dial a (telephone) number; **composez le 00 44 pour le Royaume Uni** dial 00 44 for the United Kingdom.

**compositeur**, **compositrice** *noun Masc., Fem.* composer.

**composition** *noun Fem.* composition.

**composter** *verb* [1] to punch (*a ticket*); **'n'oubliez pas de composter votre billet'** remember to punch your ticket (*in France it is an offence not to punch your ticket on trains and buses at the start of your journey in one of the machines provided for this*).

**compote** *noun Fem.* stewed fruit; **la compote de pommes** apple puree.

**compréhensible** *adjective* understandable.

**compréhensif** (*Fem.* **compréhensive**) *adjective* understanding.

**compréhension** *noun Fem.* comprehension; **un test de compréhension** a comprehension test.

**comprendre** *verb* [64] **1** to understand; **je comprends** I understand; **j'ai compris** I understood; **j'ai mal compris** I misunderstood; **2** to include; **3 se comprendre** to understand each other; **4 ça se comprend** that's understandable.

**comprimé** *noun Masc.* tablet.

**compris** *adjective* **1** included; **service compris** service included; **non compris** not included; **2 y compris** including; **tout le monde y compris les enfants** everybody including the children.

**compromis** *noun Masc.* compromise.

**comptabilité** *noun Fem.* accounting, accountancy.

**comptable** *noun Masc. & Fem.* accountant.

**compte** *noun Masc.* **1** account; **un compte bancaire** a bank account; **un compte d'épargne** a savings account; **j'ai cent livres sur mon compte** I have a hundred pounds in my account; **2 le compte est bon** the amount is correct; **3 se rendre compte de quelque chose** to realize something; **se rendre compte que** to realize that; **je me suis rendu compte que j'avais oublié mes clés** I realized I had forgotten my keys; **4 tenir compte de quelque chose** to take something into account; **5 en fin de compte** all things considered.

**compter** *verb* [1] **1** to count; **compter les visiteurs** to count the visitors; **2 compter sur quelqu'un** to count on somebody; **3** to count (*to be valid*); **ça ne compte pas** that doesn't count.

**compte rendu** *noun Masc.* report.

**compteur** *noun Masc.* meter.

**compteur de vitesse** *noun Masc.* speedometer.

**comptine** *noun Fem.* nursery rhyme.

**comptoir** *noun Masc.* **1** counter; **2** bar.

**concentré** *adjective* concentrated.

**concentré de tomate** *noun Masc.* tomato puree.

**concentrer** *verb* [1] **se concentrer (sur)** to concentrate (on).

**conception** *noun Fem.* design.

**concernant** *preposition* concerning.

**concerner** *verb* [1] to concern; **en ce qui me concerne** as far as I'm concerned.

**concert** *noun Masc.* concert; **un concert de rock** a rock concert.

**concessionnaire** *noun Masc. & Fem.* dealer, agent.

**concierge** *noun Masc. & Fem.* caretaker.

**conclure** *verb* [25] to conclude.

**conclusion** *noun Fem.* conclusion.

**concombre** *noun Masc.* cucumber.

**concours** *noun Masc.* competition.

**concret** (*Fem.* **concrète**) *adjective* **1** concrete; **2** practical.

**concurrence** *noun Fem.* competition; **il y a beaucoup de concurrence** there's a lot of competition.

**concurrent, concurrente** *noun Masc., Fem.* competitor.

**condamner** *verb* [1] to sentence (*a criminal*).

**condition** *noun Fem.* **1** condition; **en bonne condition** in good condition; **2 à condition de/que** provided that; **tu peux emprunter mon vélo à condition de me le rendre ce soir** you can borrow my bike provided you let me have it back this evening; **3 dans ces conditions** in that case.

**conditionnel** *noun Masc.* conditional tense.

**conditionner** *verb* [1] to package.

**conducteur, conductrice** *noun Masc., Fem.* driver.

**conduire** *verb* [26] **1** to drive; **apprendre à conduire** to learn to drive; **un permis de conduire** a driving licence; **je te conduis à la gare** I'll drive you to the station; **2** to take; **je vous conduis à votre chambre** I'll take you to your room; **3 se conduire** to behave.

**conduite** *noun Fem.* behaviour; **mauvaise conduite** bad behaviour.

**conférence** *noun Fem.* **1** lecture; **2** conference.

**confesser** *verb* [1] **se confesser** to go to confession.

**confiance** *noun Fem.* **1** trust; **avoir confiance en quelqu'un, faire confiance à quelqu'un** to trust somebody; **je te fais confiance** I'll leave it to you; **2** confidence.

**confiant** *adjective* confident.

**confidence** *noun Fem.* secret.

**confier** *verb* [1] **1 confier quelque chose à quelqu'un** to entrust something to somebody; **2 se confier à quelqu'un** to confide in somebody.

**confirmation** *noun Fem.* confirmation.

**confirmer** *verb* [1] to confirm.

**confiserie** *noun Fem.* **1** sweet shop; **1** confectionery.

**confisquer** *verb* [1] to confiscate.

**confit** *adjective* **les fruits confits** crystallized fruits.

**confiture** *noun Fem.* jam; **la confiture d'abricots** apricot jam.

**conflit** *noun Masc.* conflict.

**confondre** *verb* [69] to confuse, to mix up.

**confort** *noun Masc.* comfort; **tout confort** with all mod cons.

**confortable** *adjective* comfortable.

**confrontation** *noun Fem.* **1** confrontation; **2** clash.

**confus** *adjective* **1** confused; **2** embarrassed.

**confusion** *noun Fem.* **1** confusion; **2** embarrassment.

**congé** *noun Masc.* **1** holiday (*from work*); **Robert est en congé aujourd'hui** Robert's on holiday today; **quel est ton jour de congé?** when's your day off?; **je pars en congé le dix** I'm on holiday from the tenth; **prendre une semaine de congé** to take a week's holiday; **2** leave; **Sylvie est en congé de maladie** Sylvie is on sick leave.

**congélateur** *noun Masc.* freezer.

**congeler** *verb* [45] to freeze.

**congère** *noun Fem.* snowdrift.

**congestion** *noun Fem.* congestion.

**congrès** *noun Masc.* conference.

**conifère** *noun Masc.* conifer.

**conjoint, conjointe** *noun Masc., Fem.* spouse (*husband or wife*).

**conjonctivite** *noun Fem.* conjunctivitis.

**conjugaison** *noun Fem.* conjugation.

**connaissance** *noun Fem.* **1** knowledge; **tes connaissances en français** your knowledge of French; **2** acquaintance; **3** consciousness; **perdre connaissance** to lose consciousness.

**connaître** *verb* [27] **1** to know; **est-ce que tu connais Gaby?** do you know Gaby?; **je ne connais pas Londres** I don't know London; **je la connais depuis trois ans** I've known her for three years; **2 se connaître** to know each other; **on se connaît** we know each other; **3 s'y**

**connaître en quelque chose** to know about something; **je ne m'y connais pas du tout en informatique** I know absolutely nothing about computers.

**connecter** verb [1] to connect.

**connexion** noun Fem. connection.

**connu** adjective well-known; **elle est très connue en France** she's very well-known in France.

**consacrer** verb [1] to devote.

**consciemment** adverb consciously.

**conscience** noun Fem. conscience; **avoir mauvaise conscience** to have a guilty conscience.

**consciencieux** (Fem. **consciencieuse**) adjective conscientious.

**conscient** adjective 1 aware; **être conscient de quelque chose** to be aware of something; 2 conscious.

**conseil** noun Masc. 1 advice; **un conseil** a piece of advice; **donner un conseil à quelqu'un** to give someone a piece of advice; **des conseils** advice; **suivre les conseils de quelqu'un** to follow someone's advice; 2 council.

**conseiller**[1], **conseillère** noun Masc., Fem. adviser.

**conseiller**[2] verb [1] 1 to advise; **conseiller à quelqu'un de faire** to advise somebody to do; **je te conseille de voir un médecin** I advise you to see a doctor; 2 to recommend; **pouvez-vous me conseiller un dentiste?** Can you recommend me a dentist?

**consentement** noun Masc. consent.

**consentir** verb [58] **consentir à quelque chose** to agree to something.

**conséquence** noun Fem. 1 consequence; 2 **en conséquence** consequently.

**conséquent** adjective **par conséquent** consequently.

**conservateur**, **conservatrice** noun Masc., Fem. 1 conservative; 2 (museum) curator.

**conservation** noun Fem. 1 conservation; 2 **lait longue conservation** long-life milk.

**conserve** noun Fem. 1 **les conserves** canned food; 2 **en conserve** canned; **des légumes en conserve** canned vegetables.

**conserver** verb [1] 1 to keep; **je t'ai conservé une place** I've kept you a seat; **'à conserver au frais'** 'keep in a cool place'; 2 **se conserver** to keep; **ce fromage se conserve bien** this cheese keeps well.

**considérable** adjective considerable; **un pourcentage considérable des étudiants** a considerable percentage of the students.

**considérablement** adverb considerably.

**considération** noun Fem. consideration.

**considérer** verb [24] to consider.

**consigne** noun Fem. 1 left luggage office; 2 deposit (on a returnable *bottle*); **3** instructions; **consignes à suivre en cas d'incendie** fire regulations.

**consistant** *adjective* substantial; **un repas consistant** a substantial meal.

**consister** *verb* [1] **consister en** to consist of, to consist in.

**consommateur**, **consommatrice** *noun Masc., Fem.* **1** consumer; **2** customer (*in a café*).

**consommation** *noun Fem.* **1** consumption (*of fuel, electricity, gas*); **2** drink.

**consommer** *verb* [1] **1** to use (*fuel*); **2** to have a drink (*in a café*).

**consonne** *noun Fem.* consonant.

**conspiration** *noun Fem.* conspiracy.

**conspirer** *verb* [1] to conspire, to plot.

**constamment** *adverb* constantly.

**constant** *adjective* constant.

**constater** *verb* [1] to notice.

**constipé** *adjective* constipated.

**construction** *noun Fem.* construction, building.

**construire** *verb* [26] to build; **construire une maison** to build a house; **faire construire une maison** to have a house built.

**consul** *noun Masc.* consul.

**consulat** *noun Masc.* consulate.

**consultation** *noun Fem.* **1** consultation; **2** (doctor's) surgery hours.

**consulter** *verb* [1] **1** to consult; **2** to hold surgery.

**contact** *noun Masc.* contact; **prendre contact avec quelqu'un** to contact somebody.

**contacter** *verb* [1] to contact.

**contagieux** (*Fem.* **contagieuse**) *adjective* infectious.

**contamination** *noun Fem.* contamination.

**contaminer** *verb* [1] to contaminate.

**conte** *noun Masc.* tale, story; **un conte de fées** a fairy tale.

**contempler** *verb* [1] to look at, to contemplate.

**contemporain**, **contemporaine** *noun Masc., Fem., adjective* contemporary.

**contenant** *noun Masc.* container.

**conteneur** *noun Masc.* container.

**contenir** *verb* [77] to contain; **'ne contient pas de sucre'** 'does not contain sugar'.

**content** *adjective* pleased, glad, happy; **être content de quelque chose** to be pleased with something; **elle est très contente de son nouveau travail** she's very pleased with her new job; **je suis content de te voir** I'm pleased to see you.

**contenter** *verb* [1] **1** to satisfy; **2 se contenter de faire** to content oneself with doing.

**contenu** *noun Masc.* contents.

**contesté** *adjective* controversial.

**contester** *verb* [1] to dispute, to challenge, to question.

a
b
c
d
e
f
g
h
i
j
k
l
m
n
o
p
q
r
s
t
u
v
w
x
y
z

a
b
c
d
e
f
g
h
i
j
k
l
m
n
o
p
q
r
s
t
u
v
w
x
y
z

**contexte** *noun Masc.* context.

**continent** *noun Masc.* continent.

**continu** *adjective* continuous.

**continuation** *noun Fem.* continuation.

**continuer** *verb* [1] to continue, to go on (with); **continue!** go on!; **elle a continué son histoire** she went on with her story; **continuer à faire, continuer de faire** to go on doing; **elle a continué à parler** she went on talking.

**contour** *noun Masc.* outline, contour.

**contourner** *verb* [1] to go round.

**contraceptif** *noun Masc.* contraceptive.

**contraception** *noun Fem.* contraception.

**contractuel, contractuelle** *noun Masc., Fem.* traffic warden.

**contradiction** *noun Fem.* contradiction.

**contradictoire** *adjective* contradictory.

**contraindre** *verb* [31] to force.

**contraire** *noun Masc.* **1 le contraire** the opposite; **c'est le contraire de ce que je pensais** it's the opposite of what I thought; **2 au contraire** on the contrary. **contraire** *adjective* opposite.

**contrairement** *adverb* **contrairement à** contrary to, unlike; **contrairement à ce qu'il nous a dit** contrary to what he told us.

**contrariant** *adjective* annoying.

**contrarier** *verb* [1] **1** to upset; **2** to annoy.

**contraste** *noun Masc.* contrast.

**contraster** *verb* [1] to contrast.

**contrat** *noun Masc.* contract.

**contravention** *noun Fem.* **1** parking ticket; **2** speeding ticket.

**contre** *preposition* **1** against; **contre le mur** against the wall; **2 être contre quelque chose** to be against something; **je suis plutôt contre** on the whole, I'm against it; **3 jouer contre quelqu'un** to play against somebody; **4** versus; **5 échanger quelque chose contre** to exchange something for (*something else*); **6 par contre** on the other hand; ★ **le pour et le contre** the pros and cons.

**contrebande** *noun Fem.* **1** smuggling; **2** smuggled goods.

**contrebasse** *noun Fem.* double bass.

**contredire** *verb* [47] to contradict.

**contrefaçon** *noun Fem.* **1** forgery; **méfiez-vous des contrefaçons** beware of forgeries; **2** forged signature; **3** counterfeit banknote.

**contremaître** *noun Masc.* foreman.

**contremaîtresse** *noun Fem.* supervisor.

**contreplaqué** *noun Masc.* plywood.

**contribuable** *noun Masc. & Fem.* taxpayer.

**contribuer** *verb* [1] **contribuer à** to contribute to.

**contribution** *noun Fem.* contribution.

**contrôle** *noun Masc.* **1** control; **2** class test (*at school*); **j'ai un contrôle de français cet après-midi** I've got a French test this afternoon; **3 contrôle de police** police check; **4 contrôle des passeports** passport control; **contrôle des billets** ticket inspection.

**contrôle continu** *noun Masc.* continuous assessment.

**contrôle des naissances** *noun Masc.* birth control.

**contrôler** *verb* [1] **1** to check; **2** to control.

**contrôleur, contrôleuse** *noun Masc., Fem.* ticket inspector.

**contrôleur aérien, contrôleuse aérienne** *noun Masc., Fem.* air traffic controller.

**controversé** *adjective* controversial; **une décision controversée** a controversial decision.

**convaincant** *adjective* convincing.

**convaincre** *verb* [79] **1** to convince; **je ne suis pas convaincu** I'm not convinced; **2** to persuade; **je l'ai convaincu d'acheter un ordinateur** I persuaded him to buy a computer.

**convenable** *adjective* **1** suitable; **2** decent.

**convenir** *verb* [81] **1 convenir à** to suit, to be suitable for; **est-ce que dix heures te convient?** does ten o'clock suit you?; **2 convenir de faire** to agree to do.

**convention** *noun Fem.* **1** agreement; **2** convention.

**conversation** *noun Fem.* conversation.

**convertir** *verb* [2] to convert.

**conviction** *noun Fem.* conviction.

**convive** *noun Masc. & Fem.* guest.

**convivial** (*Masc. plural* conviviaux) *adjective* **1** friendly; **une atmosphère conviviale** a friendly atmosphere; **2** user-friendly.

**convoi** *noun Masc.* **1** convoy; **2** 'convoi exceptionnel' 'dangerous load'.

**convoquer** *verb* [1] **1** to invite (*to a meeting*); **2** to summon.

**coopératif** (*Fem.* coopérative) *adjective* cooperative.

**coopération** *noun Fem.* cooperation.

**coopérative** *noun Fem.* cooperative.

**coopérer** *verb* [24] to cooperate.

**coordonnées** *plural noun Fem.* address and telephone number.

**coordonner** *verb* [1] to coordinate.

**copain** *noun Masc.* **1** friend, mate (*male*); **je sors avec les copains** I'm going out with my mates; **2** boyfriend; **elle est partie en vacances avec son copain** she's gone on holiday with her boyfriend.

**copie** *noun Fem.* **1** copy; **2** paper (*on which an exam or class exercise has been written*); **j'ai un tas de copies**

a b c d e f g h i j k l m n o p q r s t u v w x y z

**à corriger ce soir** I've got a pile of marking to do this evening.

**copier** *verb* [1] to copy.

**copier-coller** *verb* [1] to cut and, paste; **copiez-collez le tableau** cut and paste the table.

**copieux** (*Fem.* **copieuse**) *adjective* hearty; **un petit déjeuner copieux** a hearty breakfast.

**copine** *noun Fem.* **1** friend, mate (*female*); **je sors avec les copines** I'm going out with my mates; **2** girlfriend; **il est parti en vacances avec sa copine** he's gone on holiday with his girlfriend.

**coq** *noun Masc.* cockerel.

**coque** *noun Fem.* **1** hull (*of a boat*); **2** shell (*of a nut*); **3 un œuf à la coque** a soft-boiled egg.

**coquelicot** *noun Masc.* poppy.

**coqueluche** *noun Fem.* whooping-cough.

**coquet** (*Fem.* **coquette**) *adjective* **1** flirtatious; **2** pretty.

**coquetier** *noun Masc.* eggcup.

**coquillage** *noun Masc.* **1** shellfish; **2** seashell.

**coquille** *noun Fem.* **1** shell; **2** misprint.

**coquille Saint-Jacques** *noun Fem.* scallop.

**coquin** *adjective* cheeky, naughty.

**cor** *noun Masc.* horn (*musical instrument*).

**corail** (*plural* **coraux**) *noun Masc.* coral.

**Coran** *noun Masc.* **le Coran** the Koran.

**corbeau** *noun Masc.* crow.

**corbeille** *noun Fem.* basket; **une corbeille à papier** a wastepaper basket; **une corbeille à linge** a linen basket.

**corbillard** *noun Masc.* hearse.

**corde** *noun Fem.* **1** rope; **2** string (*of a racket, a bow, or an instrument such as a guitar or violin*); ★ **pleuvoir des cordes** to be pouring down (*literally: to be raining ropes*).

**corde à linge** *noun Fem.* clothes line.

**corde à sauter** *noun Fem.* skipping rope.

**corde d'attache** *noun Fem.* guy rope.

**cordial** (*Masc. plural* **cordiaux**) *adjective* warm, cordial.

**cordialement** *adverb* **1** warmly; **2 cordialement à vous** Yours sincerely.

**cordonnerie** *noun Fem.* shoe repairer's.

**cordonnier** *noun Masc.* shoe repairer.

**corne** *noun Fem.* horn.

**cornemuse** *noun Fem.* bagpipes; **jouer de la cornemuse** to play the bagpipes.

**cornet** *noun Masc.* **1 un cornet de glace** an ice cream cone; **2 un cornet de frites** a bag of chips (*in fact sold in a cardboard cornet*).

**corniche** *noun Fem.* **1** ledge; **2** cornice; **3 (route de) corniche** coastal road.

**cornichon** *noun Masc.* gherkin.

**Cornouailles** *noun Fem.*
Cornwall.

**corps** *noun Masc.* body.

**correct** *adjective* **1** correct;
**2** reasonable, fine; **à un prix
correct** at a reasonable price; **le
repas était tout à fait correct** the
meal was absolutely fine.

**correctement** *adverb*
**1** correctly; **est-ce que vous avez
rempli le formulaire
correctement?** have you filled in
the form correctly?; **2** properly;
**3** reasonably well.

**correcteur
orthographique** *noun Masc.*
spell checker.

**correction** *noun Fem.* correction.

**correspondance** *noun Fem.*
**1** letters, correspondence;
**2 acheter quelque chose par
correspondance** to buy something
by mail order; **3** connection (*a train
or flight*); **j'ai raté ma
correspondance** I missed my
connection; **un vol en
correspondance** a connecting
flight.

**correspondant,
correspondante** *noun Masc.,
Fem.* pen friend.

**correspondre** *verb* [3] to
correspond.

**corrida** *noun Fem.* bullfight.

**corriger** *verb* [52] **1** to correct; **2** to
mark; **elle est en train de corriger
ses copies** she's doing her
marking.

**corsage** *noun Masc.* **1** blouse;
**2** bodice.

**corse** *adjective* Corsican.

**Corse**[1] *noun Fem.* Corsica.

**Corse**[2] *noun Masc. & Fem.* Corsican
(*person*).

**corsé** *adjective* full-bodied, strong.

**corvée** *noun Fem.* chore.

**cosmétiques** *plural noun Masc.*
cosmetics.

**costaud** *adjective* strong, sturdy.

**costume** *noun Masc.* **1** suit;
**2** costume.

**côte** *noun Fem.* **1** coast; **2** hill; **3** rib;
**4** chop; **une côte d'agneau** a lamb
chop.

**côté** *noun Masc.* **1** side; **de l'autre
côté (de)** on the other side (of); **de
l'autre côté de la rue** on the other
side of the street; **2 d'un autre côté**
on the other hand; **3 à côté** nearby;
**mon frère habite à côté** my
brother lives nearby; **4 à côté de**
next to, beside; **elle était assise à
côté de moi** she was sitting next to
me.

**Côte d'Azur** *noun Fem.* French
Riviera.

**côtelette** *noun Fem.* chop; **une
côtelette de porc** a pork chop.

**cotisation** *noun Fem.*
**1** subscription; **2** contribution.

**coton** *noun Masc.* **1** cotton; **un pull
en coton** a cotton jumper; **2** sewing
cotton; **3** cotton wool.

**cou** *noun Masc.* neck.

**couchage** *noun Masc.* **un sac de
couchage** a sleeping bag.

**couchant** *adjective* **le soleil
couchant** the setting sun; **au soleil
couchant** at sunset.

a
b
c
d
e
f
g
h
i
j
k
l
m
n
o
p
q
r
s
t
u
v
w
x
y
z

71

**couche** *noun Fem.* **1** layer; **2** coat (*of paint*); **3** nappy.

**couche d'ozone** *noun Fem.* ozone layer.

**coucher** *verb* [1] **1** to sleep; **tu peux coucher chez Sophie** you can sleep at Sophie's house; **2 se coucher** to go to bed; **elle se couche à dix heures** she goes to bed at ten o'clock; **se coucher avec quelqu'un** to sleep with someone; **3 coucher un enfant** to put a child to bed.

**coucher de soleil** *noun Masc.* sunset; **un coucher de soleil magnifique** a magnificent sunset.

**coucou** *noun Masc.* **1** cuckoo; **2** cowslip.

**coude** *noun Masc.* elbow.

**coudre** *verb* [28] to sew; **coudre un bouton** to sew on a button.

**couette** *noun Fem.* duvet, continental quilt.

**couler** *verb* [1] **1** to flow; **2 avoir le nez qui coule** to have a runny nose; **3 faire couler un bain** to run a bath; **4** to sink.

**couleur** *noun Fem.* colour; **de quelle couleur est ta voiture?** what colour is your car?

**couleuvre** *noun Fem.* grass snake.

**coulisses** *plural noun Fem.* wings (*in a theatre*).

**couloir** *noun Masc.* corridor.

**couloir d'autobus** *noun Masc.* bus lane.

**coup** *noun Masc.* blow; **il a reçu un coup à l'estomac** he was hit in the stomach; ★ **boire un coup** (*informal*) to have a drink; ★ **donner un coup de balai** to sweep the floor; ★ **un coup de peinture** a lick of paint; ★ **sur le coup** at first; ★ **tenir le coup** to last out; ★ **tout d'un coup** all of a sudden.

**coupable** *noun Masc. & Fem.* culprit. **coupable** *adjective* guilty.

**coup d'œil** *noun Masc.* glance; **jeter un coup d'œil à quelque chose** to have a quick look at something.

**coup de chance** *noun Masc.* stroke of luck.

**coup de feu** *noun Masc.* (gun)shot.

**coup de main** *noun Masc.* **donner un coup de main à quelqu'un** to give somebody a hand.

**coup de pied** *noun Masc.* kick.

**coup de poing** *noun Masc.* punch.

**coup de soleil** *noun Masc.* **attraper un coup de soleil** to get sunburnt.

**coup de téléphone** *noun Masc.* phone call.

**coup de tonnerre** *noun Masc.* clap of thunder:

**coup de vent** *noun Masc.* gust of wind.

**coupe** *noun Fem.* **1** cup (*for sports*); **la Coupe du Monde** the World Cup; **2** haircut; **3** fruit dish.

**couper** *verb* [1] **1** to cut; **se faire couper les cheveux** to have your hair cut; **2 se couper** to cut yourself; **se couper le doigt** to cut your finger; **3** to cut off, to turn off (*gas, electricity*); **4 excuse-moi, je**

**t'ai coupé la parole** sorry, I interrupted you.

**coup franc** *noun Masc.* free kick.

**couple** *noun Masc.* couple.

**couplet** *noun Masc.* **1** verse (*of song*); **2** couplet.

**coupon** *noun Masc.* **1** remnant (*of fabric*); **2** coupon.

**coupure** *noun Fem.* cut; **une coupure de courant** a power cut.

**cour** *noun Fem.* **1** school playground; **2** inner courtyard (*in an apartment block or hotel*); **3** court (*of a king or queen*); **4** law court.

**courage** *noun Masc.* **1** courage, bravery; **2** energy; **avoir le courage de faire** to have the energy to do; **3 bon courage!** good luck!.

**courageux** (*Fem.* **courageuse**) *adjective* brave.

**couramment** *adverb* fluently.

**courant** *noun Masc.* **1 être au courant de quelque chose** to know about something; **est-ce que ta sœur est au courant?** does your sister know?; **je te tiens au courant** I'll let you know what happens; **2** current; **3** electricity; **couper le courant** to cut off (*or* turn off) the electricity; **une panne de courant** a power cut.
**courant** *adjective* **1** common; **2** usual; **3** current.

**courant d'air** *noun Masc.* draught.

**courbe** *noun Fem.* curve.

**courber** *verb* [1] to bend.

**coureur**, **coureuse** *noun Masc., Fem.* runner.

**courge** *noun Fem.* (vegetable) marrow.

**courgette** *noun Fem.* courgette.

**courir** *verb* [29] **1** to run; **traverser la rue en courant** to run across the street; **2 courir un risque** to run a risk.

**couronne** *noun Fem.* crown.

**courrier** *noun Masc.* mail, post.

**courrier électronique** *noun Masc.* electronic mail, email.

**cours** *noun Masc.* **1** class, lesson; **le cours de français** the French lesson; **suivre des cours d'espagnol** to go to Spanish classes; **2** course (*of events*); **au cours de** in the course of.

**course** *noun Fem.* **1** race; **2** running; **3 les courses** shopping; **faire des courses** to do some shopping; **je fais mes courses à midi** I do my shopping at lunchtime.

**courses hippiques** *plural noun Fem.* horse racing.

**court** *adjective* short.

**court-circuit** *noun Masc.* short-circuit.

**court de tennis** *noun Masc.* tennis court.

**couru** *verb* SEE **courir**.

**cousin**, **cousine** *noun Masc., Fem.* cousin; **mon cousin germain** my first cousin.

**coussin** *noun Masc.* cushion.

**coût** *noun Masc.* cost; **le coût de la vie** the cost of living.

a
b
c
d
e
f
g
h
i
j
k
l
m
n
o
p
q
r
s
t
u
v
w
x
y
z

**couteau** (*plural* **couteaux**) *noun Masc.* knife; **un couteau à pain** a bread knife.

**coûter** *verb* [1] to cost; **ça coûte combien?** how much is it?; **ça coûte dix euros** it's ten euros; **coûter cher** to be expensive; **est-ce que ça t'a coûté cher?** was it expensive?

**coutume** *noun Fem.* custom.

**couture** *noun Fem.* **1** sewing, dressmaking; **faire de la couture** to sew; **2** seam.

**couturier** *noun Masc.* fashion designer.

**couturière** *noun Fem.* dressmaker.

**couvent** *noun Masc.* convent.

**couvercle** *noun Masc.* **1** lid; **2** screwtop.

**couvert** *noun Masc.* place setting; **les couverts** the cutlery; **mettre les couverts** to set the table.
**couvert** *adjective* **1** covered; **un marché couvert** a covered market; **2** **couvert de** covered with; **3** overcast, cloudy.

**couverture** *noun Fem.* **1** blanket; **2** cover (*of a book*).

**couvre-lit** *noun Masc.* bedspread.

**couvrir** *verb* [30] **1** to cover; **2 se couvrir** to cloud over; **ça s'est couvert dans l'après-midi** it clouded over in the afternoon.

**crabe** *noun Masc.* crab.

**cracher** *verb* [1] to spit.

**crachin** *noun Masc.* drizzle.

**craie** *noun Fem.* chalk.

**craindre** *verb* [31] to be afraid of.

**crainte** *noun Fem.* fear.

**crampe** *noun Fem.* cramp.

**crâne** *noun Masc.* skull; **avoir mal au crâne** (*informal*) to have a headache.

**crâner** *verb* [1] (*informal*) to show off.

**crapaud** *noun Masc.* toad.

**craquement** *noun Masc.* creak.

**craquer** *verb* [1] **1** to split; **2** to creak; **3** (*informal*) to crack up; ★ **j'ai craqué** I couldn't resist it!

**crasse** *noun Fem.* filth.

**cravate** *noun Fem.* tie.

**crawl** *noun Masc.* crawl (*in swimming*); **nager le crawl** to swim crawl.

**crayon** *noun Masc.* pencil.

**créatif** (*Fem.* **créative**) *adjective* creative.

**création** *noun Fem.* creation.

**créativité** *noun Fem.* creativity.

**crèche** *noun Fem.* **1** crèche, day nursery; **2** nativity scene (*as a Christmas decoration*).

**crédit** *noun Masc.* **1** credit; **2** funding.

**crédit immobilier** *noun Masc.* mortgage.

**créer** *verb* [32] to create.

**crémaillère** *noun Fem.* chimney hook (*used in olden times to hang a pot for cooking over the fire*); ★ **pendre la crémaillère** to have a house-warming party (*literally: to hang the chimney hook*).

**crème** *noun Fem.*, *adjective* cream.

**crème anglaise** *noun Fem.* custard.

**créme Chantilly** *noun Fem.* whipped cream.

**crémerie** *noun Fem.* cheese shop.

**crémeux** (*Fem.* **crémeuse**) *adjective* creamy.

**crêpe** *noun Fem.* pancake.

**crépon** *noun Masc.* crepe paper.

**crépuscule** *noun Masc.* twilight.

**cresson** *noun Masc.* watercress.

**creuser** *verb* [1] **1** to dig; **2** to hollow out; ★ **se creuser la cervelle** (*informal*) to rack your brains.

**creux** *noun Masc.* hollow. **creux** *adjective* (*Fem.* **creuse**) **1** hollow; **2 une assiette creuse** a soup plate.

**crevaison** *noun Fem.* puncture.

**crevé** *adjective* **1** burst; **2** (*informal*) knackered.

**crever** *verb* [50] **1** to burst; **un pneu crevé** a burst tyre, a puncture; **2** (*informal*) to die; **je crève de faim!** I'm starving!

**crevette** *noun Fem.* prawn.

**cri** *noun Masc.* cry, shout.

**criard** *adjective* garish.

**cric** *noun Masc.* (car) jack.

**cricket** *noun Masc.* cricket; **jouer au cricket** to play cricket.

**crier** *verb* [1] **1** to shout; **2** to scream.

**crime** *noun Masc.* crime.

**criminel, criminelle** *noun Masc., Fem., adjective* criminal.

**crinière** *noun Fem.* mane.

**criquet** *noun Masc.* grasshopper.

**crise** *noun Fem.* **1** crisis; **2** attack (*of an illness*).

**crise cardiaque** *noun Fem.* heart attack.

**cristal** (*plural* **cristaux**) *noun Masc.* crystal.

**critère** *noun Masc.* criterion.

**critique**[1] *noun Masc.* critic.

**critique**[2] *noun Fem.* **1** criticism; **les critiques** criticism; **2** review (*of a film, book, etc*).

**critique**[3] *adjective* critical.

**critiquer** *verb* [1] to criticize.

**Croatie** *noun Fem.* Croatia.

**croche-pied** *noun Masc.* **faire un croche-pied à quelqu'un** (*informal*) to trip somebody up.

**crochet** *noun Masc.* **1** hook; **2** detour; **3** crochet.

**crocodile** *noun Masc.* crocodile.

**croire** *verb* [33] **1 croire que** to think that; **je crois qu'il est parti** I think he's left; **tu crois que c'est trop tard?** do you think it's too late?; **je ne crois pas** I don't think so; **2** to believe; **je n'arrive pas à le croire** I can't believe it; **3 croire à** to believe in; **4 je n'en croyais pas mes yeux!** I couldn't believe my eyes!

**croiser** *verb* [1] **1** to cross; **croiser les jambes** to cross your legs; **croiser les bras** to fold your arms; **2 croiser quelqu'un** to bump into somebody (*meet by chance*); **j'ai croisé Odile devant la banque** I bumped into Odile outside the bank.

**croisière** *noun Fem.* cruise.

**croissance** *noun Fem.* growth.

**croissant** *noun Masc.* croissant.

a
b
c
d
e
f
g
h
i
j
k
l
m
n
o
p
q
r
s
t
u
v
w
x
y
z

a

b

c

d

e

f

g

h

i

j

k

l

m

n

o

p

q

r

s

t

u

v

w

x

y

z

**croître** *verb* [34] to grow.

**croix** *noun Fem.* cross.

**Croix-Rouge** *noun Fem.* Red Cross.

**croquant** *adjective* crunchy.

**croque-monsieur** *noun Masc.* toasted ham sandwich with cheese sauce on top.

**croque-mort** *noun* (*informal*) *Masc.* undertaker.

**croquer** *verb* [1] to munch.

**croquis** *noun Masc.* sketch.

**crottes** *plural noun Fem.* droppings; **des crottes de chien** dog dirt.

**croustillant** *adjective* crispy.

**croûte** *noun Fem.* **1** crust; **2** rind (*of cheese*); **3** scab.

**croûton** *noun Masc.* crouton.

**croyance** *noun Fem.* belief.

**cru**[1] *verb* SEE **croire**.

**cru**[2] *adjective* raw, uncooked.

**cruauté** *noun Fem.* cruelty; **ils ont été traités avec beaucoup de cruauté** they were treated with great cruelty.

**cruche** *noun Fem.* (large) jug.

**crudités** *plural noun Fem.* raw vegetables (*served with dips as a starter*).

**cruel** (*Fem.* **cruelle**) *adjective* cruel.

**crustacé** *noun Masc.* shellfish.

**crypte** *noun Fem.* crypt.

**Cuba** *noun Fem.* Cuba.

**cubain** *adjective Fem.* Cuban.

**Cubain**, **Cubaine** *noun Masc.*, *Fem.* Cuban.

**cube** *noun Masc.* cube.
**cube** *adjective* cubic; **un mètre cube** a cubic metre.

**cueillir** *verb* [35] to pick (*fruit or flowers*).

**cuiller** *noun Fem.* **1** spoon; **2** spoonful.

**cuillère** *noun Fem.* = **cuiller**.

**cuillerée** *noun Fem.* spoonful.

**cuir** *noun Masc.* leather; **des chaussures en cuir** leather shoes.

**cuir chevelu** *noun Masc.* scalp.

**cuire** *verb* [36] to cook.

**cuisine** *noun Fem.* **1** kitchen; **2** cooking; **faire la cuisine** to cook, to do the cooking.

**cuisiner** *verb* [1] to cook.

**cuisinier**, **cuisinière**[1] *noun Masc.*, *Fem.* cook.

**cuisinière**[2] *noun Fem.* cooker; **une cuisinière à gaz** a gas cooker; **une cuisinière à électrique** an electric cooker.

**cuisse** *noun Fem.* thigh.

**cuisse de poulet** *noun Fem.* chicken leg, chicken thigh.

**cuit** *adjective* cooked; **bien cuit** well done (*meat*).

**cuivre** *noun Masc.* copper.

**cuivre jaune** *noun Masc.* brass; **un chandelier en cuivre jaune** a brass candlestick.

**culot** *noun Masc.* (*informal*) cheek; **quel culot!** what a cheek!, what a nerve!; **elle a du culot!** she's got a nerve!

**culotte** *noun Fem.* **une (petite) culotte** knickers, panties.

**culpabilité** *noun Fem.* guilt.

**cultivateur**, **cultivatrice** *noun Masc., Fem.* farmer.

**cultiver** *verb* [1] **1** to grow; **2** to cultivate.

**culture** *noun Fem.* **1** farming; **2** growing; **de culture biologique** organically produced; **3** crop; **4** culture.

**culturel** (*Fem.* **culturelle**) *adjective* cultural.

**culturisme** *noun Masc.* body-building.

**cure** *noun Fem.* course of treatment.

**curé** *noun Masc.* parish priest.

**cure-dents** *noun Masc.* toothpick.

**curer** *verb* [1] **se curer les ongles** to clean your nails; **se curer les dents** to pick your teeth.

**curieux** (*Fem.* **curieuse**) *adjective* **1** strange, odd; **2** curious, inquisitive.

**curiosité** *noun Fem.* curiosity.

**curseur** *noun Masc.* cursor (*on a computer screen*).

**cuve** *noun Fem.* vat, tank.

**cuvette** *noun Fem.* bowl; **la cuvette des wc** the lavatory bowl.

**cybercafé** *noun Masc.* Internet cafe; **où est-ce qu'il y a un cybercafé?** where is there an Internet cafe?

**cybernaute** *noun Masc. & Fem.* web surfer, cybernaut.

**cyclable** *adjective* **une piste cyclable** a cycle track.

**cycle** *noun Masc.* cycle.

**cyclisme** *noun Masc.* cycling.

**cycliste** *noun Masc. & Fem.* cyclist.

**cyclone** *noun Masc.* hurricane.

**cygne** *noun Masc.* swan.

**cylindre** *noun Masc.* **1** cylinder; **2** roller.

**cynique** *adjective* cynical.

**cyprès** *noun Masc.* cypress (tree).

# Dd

**d'** *preposition* SEE **de**.

**dactylo** *noun Masc. & Fem.* typist.

**dactylographie** *noun Fem.* typing.

**daigner** *verb* [1] to deign.

**daim** *noun Masc.* **1** suede; **des chaussures en daim** suede shoes; **2** fallow deer.

**dalle** *noun Fem.* paving slab.

**daltonien** (*Fem.* **daltonienne**) *adjective* colour-blind.

**dame** *noun Fem.* **1** lady; **2** queen (*in cards or chess*).

**dames** *plural noun Fem.* draughts; **jouer aux dames** to play draughts.

**dancing** *noun Masc.* dance hall.

**Danemark** *noun Masc.* Denmark; **au Danemark** to (*or* in) Denmark.

**danger** *noun Masc.* danger.

**dangereux** (*Fem.* **dangereuse**) *adjective* dangerous.

**danois** *noun Masc.* Danish (*language*).
**danois** *adjective* Danish.

**Danois**, , **Danoise** *noun Masc., Fem.* Danish.

a
b
c
d
e
f
g
h
i
j
k
l
m
n
o
p
q
r
s
t
u
v
w
x
y
z

a
b
c
**d**
e
f
g
h
i
j
k
l
m
n
o
p
q
r
s
t
u
v
w
x
y
z

**dans** *preposition* **1** in; **elle est dans la cuisine** she's in the kitchen; **2** into; **va dans la cuisine** go into the kitchen; **3 dans trois mois** in three months' time; **4 boire dans un verre** to drink out of a glass.

**danse** *noun Fem.* **1** dance; **2** dancing; **faire de la danse** to go to dancing classes.

**danse classique** *noun Fem.* ballet.

**danser** *verb* [1] to dance.

**danseur**, **danseuse** *noun Masc.*, *Fem.* dancer.

**d'après** *preposition* **1** according to; **d'après le ministre** according to the minister; **2** based on; **un film d'après le roman de** a film based on the novel by; **3** in the style of; **un tableau d'après Degas** a painting in the style of Degas.

**date** *noun Fem.* date.

**date de naissance** *noun Fem.* date of birth.

**date limite** *noun Fem.* closing date.

**date limite de vente** *noun Fem.* sell-by date.

**datte** *noun Fem.* date (*fruit*).

**dauphin** *noun Masc.* dolphin.

**davantage** *adverb* **1** more; **2** longer.

**de**, **d'** (*before a vowel or a silent 'h'*) (*note that 'de + le' becomes 'du' and 'de + les' becomes 'des'*).

**de** *preposition* **1** of; **une boîte d'allumettes** a box of matches; **le pied de la table** the leg of the table, the table leg; **2 le père de Marie** Marie's father; **la maison de tes parents** your parents' house; **3** from; **elle vient de Paris** she comes from Paris; **elle rentre du bureau à six heures** she comes home from the office at six o'clock; **4** made from; **une table de bois** a wooden table; **5** by; **le prix a augmenté de vingt euros** the price has gone up (by) twenty euros.

**de** *determiner* **du café** (some) coffee; **veux-tu du café?** would you like (some) coffee?; **je n'ai pas de café** I don't have any coffee; **nous avons des pommes et des oranges** we have apples and oranges; **veux-tu de l'eau?** would you like some water?

**dé** *noun Masc.* **1** dice; **2 un dé à coudre** a thimble.

**dealer** *noun Masc.* drug pusher.

**déballer** *verb* [1] to unpack.

**débardeur** *noun Masc.* camisole top, vest-style top.

**débarquer** *verb* [1] **1** to disembark; **2** to land; **3** (*informal*) to turn up; **elle a débarqué chez moi** she turned up at my place.

**débarras** *noun Masc.* junk room; ★ **bon débarras!** good riddance!

**débarrasser** *verb* [1] **1** to clear out (*a room*); **débarrasser la table** to clear the table; **2 se débarrasser de quelque chose** to get rid of something; **je me suis débarrassé de tous ces vieux bouquins** I got rid of all those old books.

**débat** *noun Masc.* debate.

**débattre** *verb* [21] to discuss, to negotiate; **'prix à débattre'** 'price negotiable'.

**débile** *adjective* (*informal*) stupid, crazy; **tu es débile ou quoi?** are you stupid or something?; **c'est complètement débile!** that's completely crazy!

**déblayer** *verb* [59] to clear.

**débordé** *adjective* **être débordé** to be up to your eyes in work.

**débordement** *noun Masc.* **1** overflowing; **2** flood.

**déborder** *verb* [1] to overflow.

**débouché** *noun Masc.* job prospect; **il y a peu de/beaucoup de débouchés pour les jeunes diplômés** there are few/many openings for recent graduates.

**déboucher** *verb* [1] **1** to uncork (*a bottle*); **2** to unblock (*a drain or pipe*); **3 déboucher sur** to lead into.

**déboussoler** *verb* [1] (*informal*) to confuse.

**debout** *adverb* **1** standing; **rester debout** to remain standing; **je suis resté debout toute la journée** I've been on my feet all day; **se mettre debout** to stand up; **tout le monde s'est mis debout** everybody stood up; **2** upright; **mettre quelque chose debout** to stand something upright; **3** up (*out of bed*); **je suis debout à six heures tous les jours** I'm up at six every day; ★ **ça ne tient pas debout** it doesn't make any sense (*literally: it doesn't stand upright*).

**déboutonner** *verb* [1] to unbutton.

**débrancher** *verb* [1] **1** to unplug (*an iron, a television set, etc*); **2** to disconnect (*the electricity, gas, water, telephone*).

**débris** *noun Masc.* **1** fragment; **2** piece of wreckage.

**débrouiller** *verb* [1] **se débrouiller** to manage; **je peux me débrouiller tout seul** I can manage by myself; **débrouille-toi!** get on with it!

**début** *noun Masc.* beginning, start; **le début de** the beginning of; **au début** at the beginning, to start with; **on commencera début mars** we'll start at the beginning of March; **en début d'après-midi** in the early afternoon.

**débutant**, **débutante** *noun Masc., Fem.* beginner.

**débuter** *verb* [1] to begin, to start.

**décaféiné** *adjective* decaffeinated.

**décalage** *noun Masc.* **1** gap; **2** discrepancy.

**décalage horaire** *noun Masc.* time difference (*between time zones*); **il y a une heure de décalage horaire entre la France et la Grande-Bretagne** there's an hour's time difference between France and Britain.

**décaler** *verb* [1] to move (*forward or back*).

**décapiter** *verb* [1] to behead.

**décapotable** *adjective* **une voiture décapotable** a convertible (car).

a
b
c
**d**
e
f
g
h
i
j
k
l
m
n
o
p
q
r
s
t
u
v
w
x
y
z

**a**
**décapsuleur** *noun Masc.* (bottle) opener.

**b**
**décéder** *verb* [24] to die; **elle est décédée au mois de novembre** she died in November.

**c**

**d**
**décembre** *noun Masc.* December; **en décembre, au mois de décembre** in December.

**e**

**décemment** *adverb* decently.

**f**
**décennie** *noun Fem.* decade.

**g**

**décent** *adjective* decent.

**h**
**déception** *noun Fem.* disappointment.

**i**
**décès** *noun Masc.* death.

**j**
**décevant** *adjective* disappointing.

**k**
**décevoir** *verb* [66] to disappoint.

**l**
**décharge** *noun Fem.* (public) rubbish tip.

**m**
**décharger** *verb* [52] to unload.

**n**
**déchets** *plural noun Masc.* **1** waste; **les déchets nucléaires** nuclear waste; **2** rubbish.

**o**

**p**
**déchiffrer** *verb* [1] to decipher.

**q**
**déchirant** *adjective* heart-rending.

**r**
**déchirer** *verb* [1] **1** to tear; **j'ai déchiré mon pantalon** I've torn my trousers; **2** to tear up; **déchirer une enveloppe** to tear up an envelope; **3** to tear off; **déchirer une feuille** to tear off a sheet of paper; **4** to tear out; **déchirer une page** to tear out a page; **5 se déchirer** to tear, to rip.

**s**

**t**

**u**

**v**

**w**
**décidé** *adjective* determined.

**x**
**décidément** *adverb* really.

**y**
**décider** *verb* [1] **1** to decide; **décider de faire** to decide to do; **j'ai décidé de vendre mon vélo** I've

**z**

decided to sell my bike; **2 se décider** to make up your mind; **il faut qu'on se décide une fois pour toutes** we must make up our minds once and for all; **3 se décider à faire** to decide to do.

**décimal** (*Masc. plural* **décimaux**) *adjective* decimal.

**décimale** *noun Fem.* decimal.

**décision** *noun Fem.* decision.

**déclaration** *noun Fem.* **1** statement; **2** declaration.

**déclarer** *verb* [1] to declare.

**déclencher** *verb* [1] **1** to cause; **2** to set off; **déclencher l'alarme** to set off the alarm.

**déclic** *noun Masc.* click.

**décliner** *verb* [1] to decline.

**décollage** *noun Masc.* takeoff (*of a plane*).

**décollé** *adjective* ★ **avoir les oreilles décollées** to have sticking-out ears (*literally: to have ears which have come unstuck*).

**décoller** *verb* [1] **1** to take off (*of a plane*); **2 décoller quelque chose** to peel something off; **3 se décoller** to come unstuck, to peel off; **le papier peint est en train de se décoller** the wallpaper's peeling off.

**décolleté** *adjective* low-cut.

**décolorer** *verb* [1] **se décolorer** to fade; **se faire décolorer les cheveux** to have your hair lightened.

**décombres** *plural noun Masc.* rubble.

**décongeler** *verb* [45] to defrost.

**déconseillé** *adjective* not recommended; **'déconseillé pour les enfants'** 'not recommended for children'.

**déconseiller** *verb* [1] déconseiller à quelqu'un de faire to advise somebody not to do; **nous lui avons déconseillé de voyager toute seule** we advised her not to travel alone.

**décontracté** *adjective* relaxed, laid-back; **mon patron est très décontracté** my boss is very laid-back.

**décontracter** *verb* [1] **se décontracter** to relax.

**décor** *noun Masc.* **1** decor; **2** setting.

**décorateur, décoratrice** *noun Masc., Fem.* interior designer.

**décoratif** (*Fem.* **décorative**) *adjective* **1** ornamental; **2** decorative.

**décoration** *noun Fem.* **1** decorating; **2** interior design.

**décorer** *verb* [1] to decorate.

**découper** *verb* [1] **1** to cut out; **découper un article dans un journal** to cut an article out of a newspaper; **2** to carve (*meat*); **c'est Marie-Laure qui va découper le poulet** Marie-Laure's going to carve the chicken.

**décourageant** *adjective* discouraging.

**décourager** *verb* [52] to discourage.

**découvert** *noun Masc.* overdraft.

**découverte** *noun Fem.* discovery.

**découvrir** *verb* [30] to discover.

**décrire** *verb* [38] to describe.

**décrocher** *verb* [1] **1** to lift the receiver (*of a telephone*); **'décrochez'** 'lift the receiver'; **il faut décrocher avant de composer le numéro** you have to lift the receiver before dialling; **2** to take down (*a picture, curtains, etc*).

**déçu** *adjective* disappointed; **nous sommes tous très déçus** we're all very disappointed.

**dedans** *adverb* inside **1** elle a ouvert la boîte mais il n'y avait rien dedans she opened the box but there was nothing in it; **2 là-dedans** in there.

**dédommager** *verb* [52] to compensate.

**déduction** *noun Fem.* deduction.

**déduire** *verb* [26] **1** to deduce; **2** to deduct.

**déesse** *noun Fem.* goddess.

**défaire** *verb* [10] **1** to undo, to untie; **2 se défaire** to come undone; **3 se défaire de** to get rid of.

**défaite** *noun Fem.* defeat.

**défaut** *noun Masc.* **1** flaw, defect; **2 à défaut de** for want of.

**défavorisé** *adjective* underprivileged; **les défavorisés** the underprivileged.

**défectueux** (*Fem.* **défectueuse**) *adjective* faulty; **une prise défectueuse** a faulty plug.

**défendre** *verb* [3] **1** to forbid; **2** to defend.

**défendu** *adjective* forbidden.

**défense** *noun* **1 défense de fumer** no smoking; **2** defence;

81

**défi**

FRENCH-ENGLISH

3 protection; **la défense de l'environnement** the protection of the environment; 4 tusk (*of an elephant*).

**défi** *noun Masc.* challenge.

**déficit** *noun Masc.* deficit.

**défigurer** *verb* [1] to disfigure.

**défilé** *noun Masc.* 1 parade; 2 procession; 3 march.

**défiler** *verb* [1] 1 to parade; 2 to march; 3 to come and go.

**définir** *verb* [2] to define.

**définitif** (*Fem.* **définitive**) *adjective* final, definitive.

**définition** *noun Fem.* definition.

**définitivement** *adverb* 1 for good; 2 definitely.

**défoncer** *verb* [61] to smash in (*a door*).

**déformer** *verb* [1] 1 to bend out of shape; 2 to distort; 3 to stretch (*a garment or shoes*).

**défouler** *verb* [1] 1 **se défouler** to let off steam; 2 to unwind.

**défunt** *noun Masc.* **le défunt** the deceased.

**dégagé** *adjective* 1 clear; 2 casual.

**dégager** *verb* [52] 1 to clear; 2 to free (*a trapped person*).

**dégâts** *plural noun Masc.* damage.

**dégel** *noun Masc.* thaw.

**dégeler** *verb* [45] to thaw.

**dégénérer** *verb* [24] 1 to degenerate; 2 to go from bad to worse.

**dégivrer** *verb* [1] 1 to defrost; 2 to de-ice.

**dégonfler** *verb* [1] to let down (*a tyre, an airbed, etc*).

**dégouliner** *verb* [1] to trickle.

**dégourdi** *adjective* smart, bright; **un gamin dégourdi** a bright kid.

**dégoût** *noun Masc.* disgust.

**dégoûtant** *adjective* 1 filthy; **tes mains sont dégoûtantes** your hands are filthy; 2 disgusting.

**dégoûté** *adjective* disgusted.

**dégoûter** *verb* [1] 1 to disgust; 2 **dégoûter quelqu'un de quelque chose** to put somebody off something; **ça m'a dégoûté du poisson** that put me off fish.

**dégrader** *verb* [1] 1 to damage; 2 **se dégrader** to deteriorate.

**dégraisser** *verb* [1] to dryclean.

**degré** *noun Masc.* degree.

**dégringoler** *verb* [1] (*informal*) to tumble down.

**déguisé** *adjective* 1 in fancy dress, in disguise; 2 **une soirée déguisée** a fancy-dress party; 3 disguised.

**déguiser** *verb* [1] 1 to disguise; 2 **se déguiser** to dress up in fancy dress.

**dégustation** *noun Fem.* tasting; **'dégustation de glaces'** 'a fine selection of ice creams'.

**déguster** *verb* [1] 1 to savour, to enjoy; 2 to taste (*wine, cheese, etc*).

**dehors** *adverb* 1 outside; **je t'attends dehors** I'll wait for you outside; **j'ai passé toute la journée dehors** I've been outside all day; 2 **en dehors de** apart from; **en dehors de la salade, tout est prêt**

everything's ready apart from the salad.

**déjà** *adverb* **1** already; **tu pars déjà?** are you leaving already?; **je t'ai déjà dit de ne pas faire ça!** I told you not to do that!; **2** before; **tu es déjà venu ici?** have you been here before?

**déjeuner** *noun Masc.* lunch; **petit déjeuner** breakfast.
**déjeuner** *verb* [1] **1** to have lunch; **nous déjeunons à une heure** we have lunch at one o'clock; **2** to have breakfast.

**délabré** *adjective* dilapidated.

**délacer** *verb* [61] to unlace.

**délai** *noun Masc.* period of time, waiting period.

**délavé** *adjective* **1** faded; **2** washed-out.

**délecter** *verb* [1] **se délecter à faire** to delight in doing.

**délégué**, **déléguée** *noun Masc., Fem.* **1** delegate; **2** representative.

**délibéré** *adjective* deliberate.

**délibérer** *verb* [24] to discuss.

**délicat** *adjective* **1** delicate; **2** tactful.

**délice** *noun Masc.* delight; **c'est un vrai délice!** it's absolutely delicious!

**délicieux** (*Fem.* **délicieuse**) *adjective* delicious.

**délinquance** *noun Fem.* **1** crime; **2** delinquency.

**délinquant**, **délinquante** *noun Masc., Fem.* offender.

**délirant** *adjective* (*informal*) crazy; **c'est complètement délirant!** it's completely crazy!

**délire** *noun Masc.* **1** (*informal*) madness; **2** frenzy.

**délirer** *verb* [1] (*informal*) to be crazy; **il délire!** he's crazy!

**délit** *noun Masc.* criminal offence.

**délivrer** *verb* [1] to free, to liberate.

**déloyal** (*Masc. plural* **déloyaux**) *adjective* disloyal.

**deltaplane** *noun Masc.* **1** hang-glider; **2 faire du deltaplane** to go hang-gliding.

**déluge** *noun Masc.* **1** downpour; **2 le Déluge** the Flood (*in the Bible*).

**demain** *adverb* tomorrow; **à demain!** see you tomorrow!; **après-demain** the day after tomorrow.

**demande** *noun Fem.* **1** request; **2** demand; **3** application; **faire une demande d'emploi** to apply for a job; **'demandes d'emplois'** 'situations wanted'; **4** claim; **faire une demande de remboursement auprès d'une compagnie d'assurance** to make a claim on insurance.

**demandé** *adjective* **très demandé** very much in demand, very popular.

**demander** *verb* [1] **1 demander quelque chose** to ask for something; **2 demander quelque chose à quelqu'un** to ask somebody (for) something; **demande à ton père!** ask your father!; **il m'a demandé ton adresse** he asked me for your address; **3 demander à quelqu'un de faire** to ask somebody to do; **elle m'a demandé de**

a
b
c
d
e
f
g
h
i
j
k
l
m
n
o
p
q
r
s
t
u
v
w
x
y
z

**téléphoner** she asked me to phone; **4 se demander** to wonder; **je me demande ce qu'elle est en train de faire** I wonder what she's doing.

**demandeur d'emploi** *noun Masc.* job-seeker.

**démangeaison** *noun Fem.* itch.

**démanger** *verb* [52] **ça me démange** it itches.

**démanteler** *verb* [45] to dismantle.

**démaquillant** *noun Masc.* make-up remover.

**démaquiller** *verb* [1] **se démaquiller** to remove your make-up.

**démarche** *noun Fem.* **1** walk; **2** step.

**démarrer** *verb* [1] **1** to start (*of engine or car*); **la voiture ne veut pas démarrer** the car won't start; **2** to drive off; **3** to start up, to start off; **le projet va démarrer en juin** the project will start up in June.

**démarreur** *noun Masc.* starter (*in a car*).

**démêler** *verb* [1] to untangle.

**déménagement** *noun Masc.* (house) move, removal.

**déménager** *verb* [52] **1** to move (house); **2** to move out; **nous déménageons la semaine prochaine** we're moving out next week; **3 déménager quelque chose** to move something.

**déménageur** *noun Masc.* removal man.

**dément** *adjective* crazy.

**démentir** *verb* [53] **1** to deny; **2** to refute.

**démesuré** *adjective* excessive.

**demeure** *noun Fem.* residence, mansion.

**demeurer** *verb* [1] to reside, to live.

**demi**[1] *adjective* **1** half; **trois et demi** three and a half; **elle a trois ans et demi** she's three and a half; **une heure et demie** an hour and a half; **2 une demi-pomme** half an apple; **une demi-bouteille** half a bottle; **3 à deux heures et demie** at half past two; **à trois heures et demie** at half past three.

**demi**[2] *noun Masc.* half (*of beer*).

**demi-cercle** *noun Masc.* semicircle.

**demi-douzaine** *noun Fem.* half a dozen.

**demie** *noun Fem.* half-hour; **à la demie** on the half-hour.

**demi-écrémé** *adjective* semi-skimmed.

**demi-finale** *noun Fem.* semifinal.

**demi-frère** *noun Masc.* half brother.

**demi-heure** *noun Fem.* **une demi-heure** half an hour; **toutes les demi-heures** every half hour.

**demi-journée** *noun Fem.* half a day.

**demi-litre** *noun Masc.* half a litre.

**demi-pension** *noun Fem.* half board.

**demi-sel** *adjective* slightly salted.

**demi-sœur** *noun Fem.* half sister.

**démission** *noun Fem.* resignation; **donner sa démission** to resign.

**démissionner** *verb* [1] to resign.

**demi-tarif** *adjective* half-price.

**demi-tour** *noun Masc.* **faire demi-tour** to turn back.

**démocrate** *noun Masc. & Fem.* democrat.
**démocrate** *adjective* democratic.

**démocratie** *noun Fem.* democracy.

**démocratique** *adjective* democratic.

**démodé** *adjective* old-fashioned.

**demoiselle** *noun Fem.* young lady.

**demoiselle d'honneur** *noun Fem.* bridesmaid.

**démolir** *verb* [2] to demolish, to wreck.

**démolition** *noun Fem.* demolition.

**démon** *noun Masc.* demon.

**démonstrateur**, **démonstratrice** *noun Masc., Fem.* demonstrator (*for products*).

**démonstratif** (*Fem.* **démonstrative**) *adjective* demonstrative.

**démonstration** *noun Fem.* **1** demonstration (*of a product, appliance, etc*); **2** display.

**démonter** *verb* [1] to dismantle, to take apart.

**démontrer** *verb* [1] to demonstrate, to prove.

**démoraliser** *verb* [1] to demoralize.

**démouler** *verb* [1] to turn out (*a cake, mousse, etc, from a tin or mould*).

**démuni** *adjective* **1** poverty stricken; **2** penniless.

**dénoncer** *verb* [61] to denounce.

**dénouer** *verb* [1] to undo.

**denrée** *noun Fem.* foodstuff.

**dense** *adjective* dense.

**densité** *noun Fem.* density.

**dent** *noun Fem.* tooth; **avoir mal aux dents** to have toothache.

**dentaire** *adjective* dental.

**dent de sagesse** *noun Fem.* wisdom tooth.

**dentelé** *adjective* **1** jagged; **2** serrated; **3** perforated.

**dentelle** *noun Fem.* lace.

**dentier** *noun Masc.* denture, false teeth.

**dentifrice** *noun Masc.* toothpaste.

**dentiste** *noun Masc. & Fem.* dentist.

**déodorant** *noun Masc.* deodorant.

**dépannage** *noun Masc.* repair; 'dépannages' 'emergency repairs'; **le service de dépannage** the breakdown service; **un véhicule de dépannage** a breakdown vehicle.

**dépanner** *verb* [1] **1** to fix, to repair; **2 dépanner quelqu'un** (*informal*) to help somebody out.

**dépanneuse** *noun Fem.* breakdown truck.

**départ** *noun Masc.* **1** departure; **je t'appellerai avant mon départ** I'll phone you before I leave; **elle m'a appelé avant son départ** she

a
b
c
d
e
f
g
h
i
j
k
l
m
n
o
p
q
r
s
t
u
v
w
x
y
z

a b **c** d e f g h i j k l m n o p q r s t u v w x y z

phoned me before she left; **2 au départ** at first, to start with.

**département** *noun Masc.* department (*As well as other sorts of department, this is a French numbered administrative area, rather like a county in Britain. The two numbers on the end of vehicle registrations in France show the number of the department where the car is registered*).

**dépassé** *adjective* outdated, old-fashioned.

**dépasser** *verb* [1] **1** to overtake; **2** to exceed; **3 ça me dépasse!** it's beyond me!

**dépêcher** *verb* [50] **se dépêcher** to hurry up; **dépêche-toi!** hurry up!

**dépendance** *noun Fem.* outbuilding.

**dépendre** *verb* [3] **1 dépendre de** to depend on; **ça dépend de l'heure** it depends on the time; **ça dépend** it depends; **2** to be dependent on.

**dépenser** *verb* [1] to spend.

**dépenses** *plural noun Fem.* **1** expenses; **2** spending.

**dépensier** (*Fem.* **dépensière**) *adjective* extravagant.

**dépilatoire** *adjective* **une crème dépilatoire** a hair-removing cream.

**dépistage** *noun Masc.* screening.

**dépit** *noun Masc.* **en dépit de** in spite of.

**déplacé** *adjective* out of place.

**déplacement** *noun Masc.* trip; **les frais de déplacement** travel expenses.

**déplacer** *verb* [61] **1** to move; **2 se déplacer** to travel.

**déplaire** *verb* [62] **déplaire à quelqu'un** to be displeasing to somebody; **cela me déplaît** I don't like that.

**déplaisant** *adjective* unpleasant.

**dépliant** *noun Masc.* leaflet.

**déplier** *verb* [1] to unfold.

**déporter** *verb* [1] to deport.

**déposer** *verb* [1] **1** to put down; **2** to drop off; **il m'a déposé à la gare** he dropped me off at the station; **3 déposer un chèque** to pay in a cheque.

**dépôt** *noun Masc.* **1** warehouse; **2** depot; **3** deposit.

**dépôt d'ordures** *noun Masc.* rubbish tip.

**dépoussiérer** *verb* [24] to dust.

**dépressif** (*Fem.* **dépressive**) *adjective* depressive.

**dépression** *noun Fem.* depression; **une dépression nerveuse** a nervous breakdown.

**déprimant** *adjective* depressing.

**déprimer** *verb* [1] **1** to depress; **2** to get depressed; **elle déprime en ce moment** she's depressed at the moment.

**depuis** *preposition* **1** since; **depuis vendredi** since Friday; **je suis à Paris depuis mardi** I've been in Paris since Tuesday; **j'habite à Londres depuis avril** I've been living in London since April; **2** for;

**elle habite à Londres depuis cinq ans** she's lived in London for five years; **je le connais depuis longtemps** I've known him for a long time; **3 tu es là depuis combien de temps?** how long have you been here?; **tu le sais depuis combien de temps?** how long have you known?; **depuis quand es-tu à Paris?** how long have you been in Paris?; **4 depuis que** since; **depuis que ton frère est à Londres** since your brother's been in London.
**depuis** *adverb* since; **je ne l'ai pas revu depuis** I haven't seen him since.

**député** *noun Masc.* deputy (*the French equivalent of a member of Parliament*).

**déraciner** *verb* [1] to uproot.

**déranger** *verb* [52] to disturb; **'ne pas déranger'** 'do not disturb'; **excusez-moi de vous déranger** sorry to bother you ; **est-ce que cela vous dérange si j'ouvre la fenêtre?** do you mind if I open the window?; **cela ne me dérange pas du tout** I don't mind at all; **ça vous dérange de venir me chercher?** do you mind coming to pick me up?

**déraper** *verb* [1] **1** to skid; **2** to get out of control.

**dérisoire** *adjective* pathetic, trivial; **je l'ai acheté pour une somme dérisoire** I bought it for next to nothing.

**dériveur** *noun Masc.* sailing dinghy.

**dermatologue** *noun Masc. & Fem.* dermatologist.

**dernier** (*Fem.* **dernière**) *adjective* **1** last; **le dernier train part à minuit** the last train leaves at midnight; **jeudi dernier** last Thursday; **la semaine dernière** last week; **l'année dernière** last year; **2** latest; **leur dernier album** their latest album; **3 en dernier** last; **il est arrivé en dernier** he arrived last.

**dernier cri** *noun Masc.* latest fashion; **le dernier cri en matière d'équipement hifi** the latest in audio equipment.

**dernièrement** *adverb* recently.

**dérouler** *verb* [1] **1** to unroll, to unwind; **2 se dérouler** to take place; **ça s'est très bien déroulé** it went very well.

**déroutant** *adjective* puzzling.

**derrière** *noun Masc.* **1** back (*of an object or a house*); **2** bottom, backside.
**derrière** *preposition* behind; **derrière la porte** behind the door.
**derrière** *adverb* behind; **être derrière** to be in the back (*of the car*).

**des** *article* some, any SEE **de, un**.

**dès** *preposition* **1** from; **dès l'âge de cinq ans** from the age of five; **2 dès que** as soon as.

**désagréable** *adjective* unpleasant.

**désarroi** *noun Masc.* confusion.

**désastre** *noun Masc.* disaster.

**désavantage** *noun Masc.* disadvantage.

**désavouer** *verb* [1] **1** to deny; **2** to disown.

a
b
c
d
e
f
g
h
i
j
k
l
m
n
o
p
q
r
s
t
u
v
w
x
y
z

a
b
c
**d**
e
f
g
h
i
j
k
l
m
n
o
p
q
r
s
t
u
v
w
x
y
z

**descendre** *verb* [3] **1** to go down; **descendre les escaliers** to go down the stairs; **2** to come down; **je descends dans trois secondes!** I'll be down in a second!; **3** to get off (*a train or bus*); **je descends à Dijon** I'm getting off at Dijon; **4** to get down; **pouvez-vous descendre ma valise, s'il vous plaît?** could you get my case down for me, please?; **5** to take (*or* bring) downstairs; **je vais descendre mes bagages** I'm going to take my luggage downstairs; **est-ce que tu peux descendre une chaise de là-haut?** could you bring a chair down from upstairs?

**descente** *noun Fem.* descent.

**descriptif** (*Fem.* **descriptive**) *adjective* descriptive.

**description** *noun Fem.* description.

**déséquilibrer** *verb* [1] **déséquilibrer quelqu'un** to throw somebody off balance.

**désert** *noun Masc.* desert.
**désert** *adjective* deserted.

**déserter** *verb* [1] to desert.

**désespéré** *adjective* **1** desperate; **2** in despair; **3** une situation **désespérée** a hopeless situation.

**désespérer** *verb* [24] to despair, to give up hope.

**désespoir** *noun Masc.* despair.

**déshabiller** *verb* [1] **1 se déshabiller** to undress, to get undressed; **2 déshabiller quelqu'un** to undress somebody.

**désherbant** *noun Masc.* weedkiller.

**désherber** *verb* [1] to weed.

**déshérité** *noun Masc.* **les déshérités** the underprivileged.

**déshériter** *verb* [1] to disinherit.

**déshydraté** *adjective* dehydrated.

**désigner** *verb* [1] **1** to point out; **2** to denote.

**désinfectant** *noun Masc.* disinfectant.

**désinfecter** *verb* [1] to disinfect.

**désir** *noun Masc.* **1** wish; **2** desire.

**désirer** *verb* [1] to want; **que désirez-vous?** what would you like?

**désobéir** *verb* [2] **1** to be disobedient; **2 désobéir à quelqu'un** to disobey somebody.

**désobéissant** *adjective* disobedient.

**désobligeant** *adjective* unpleasant.

**désodorisant** *noun Masc.* air freshener.

**désolé** *adjective* **être désolé** to be sorry; **je suis désolé** I'm sorry; **désolé de te déranger** sorry to disturb you.

**désopilant** *adjective* hilarious.

**désordonné** *adjective* untidy.

**désordre** *noun Masc.* **1** untidiness, mess; **être en désordre** to be in a mess; **2** disorder.

**désorganisé** *adjective* disorganized.

**désorienté** *adjective* disorientated, confused.

**désormais** *adverb* **1** from now on; **2** from then on.

**détendu**

**desquels, desquelles**
*pronoun* (= *de lesquels, de lesquelles*)
of which, of whom.

**dessécher** *verb* [24] **1** to dry out;
**2 se dessécher** to dry out.

**desserrer** *verb* [1] to loosen.

**dessert** *noun Masc.* dessert,
pudding.

**desservir** *verb* [58] **le train
dessert Vienne et Valence** the
train calls at Vienne and Valence.

**dessin** *noun Masc.* **1** drawing; **un
cours de dessin** a drawing class;
**2 un dessin** a drawing; **3** design.

**dessin animé** *noun Masc.*
(animated) cartoon.

**dessiner** *verb* [1] to draw.

**dessin humoristique** *noun
Masc.* cartoon.

**dessous** *noun Masc.* **1** underside;
**le dessous du pied** the sole of the
foot; **2 les voisins du dessous** the
neighbours below; **3 les dessous**
underwear; **4 en dessous**
underneath; **5 en dessous de**
below.
**dessous** *adverb* underneath.

**dessous-de-plat** *noun Masc.*
table mat (*for dish*).

**dessus** *noun Masc.* **1** top; **le dessus
du carton** the top of the box; **un
pantalon gris et un dessus rose**
grey trousers and a pink top; **2 les
voisins du dessus** the neighbours
above; **3 en dessus** above; **4 au
dessus de** above.
**dessus** *adverb* on top; **quelqu'un a
écrit dessus** somebody's written on
it.

**dessus-de-lit** *noun Masc.*
bedspread.

**destin** *noun Masc.* **1** fate; **2** destiny.

**destinataire** *noun Masc. & Fem.*
addressee.

**destination** *noun Fem.*
destination; **le train à destination
de Nice** the train for Nice; **les
passagers à destination de Rome**
passengers travelling to Rome.

**destiner** *verb* [1] **1 destiner
quelque chose à** to design
something for; **2 être destiné à** to
be intended for; **3 être destiné à
faire** to be intended to do.

**détachable** *adjective* detachable.

**détachant** *noun Masc.* stain
remover.

**détacher** *verb* [1] **1** to untie; **2** to
undo; **3** to tear off; **4** to remove; **5** to
remove the stains from; **6 se
détacher** to come off, to come
undone.

**détail** *noun Masc.* **1** detail; **en détail**
in detail; **2 regarder quelque
chose dans le détail** to look closely
at something; **3** retail.

**détailler** *verb* [1] to detail, to
itemize; **une facture détaillée** an
itemized bill.

**détecter** *verb* [1] to detect.

**détective** *noun Masc.* detective.

**déteindre** *verb* [60] **1** to fade; **2** to
run (*in the wash*).

**détendre** *verb* [3] **1** to be relaxing;
**2** to relax; **3 se détendre** to relax.

**détendu** *adjective* relaxed.

a
b
c
**d**
e
f
g
h
i
j
k
l
m
n
o
p
q
r
s
t
u
v
w
x
y
z

**détenir**

**détenir** *verb* [81] **1** to detain; **2** to keep.

**détente** *noun Fem.* relaxation.

**détenu**, **détenue** *noun Masc., Fem.* prisoner, detainee.

**détergent** *noun Masc.* detergent.

**détériorer** *verb* [1] **se détériorer** to deteriorate.

**détermination** *noun Fem.* determination.

**déterminer** *verb* [1] to fix.

**détestable** *adjective* appalling, revolting.

**détester** *verb* [1] to hate.

**détour** *noun Masc.* detour; ★ **ça vaut le détour** it's well worth seeing (*literally: it's worth the detour*).

**détournement** *noun Masc.* **un détournement d'avion** a highjacking.

**détourner** *verb* [1] **1** to divert; **2 détourner un avion** to highjack a plane; **3 détourner les yeux** to look away.

**détritus** *plural noun Masc.* rubbish, refuse.

**détruire** *verb* [26] to destroy.

**dette** *noun Fem.* debt.

**deuil** *noun Masc.* **1** bereavement; **2** mourning.

**deux** *number* **1** two; **deux enfants** two children; **elle a deux ans** she's two; **il est deux heures** it's two o'clock; **2 deux fois** twice; **3** second (*in dates*); **le deux juin** the second of June; **4** both; **les deux frères** both brothers; **tous les deux, toutes les deux** both; **ils sont malades tous les deux, tous les deux sont**

malades they're both ill, both of them are ill.

**deuxième** *noun* **au deuxième** on the second floor.
**deuxième** *adjective* **pour la deuxième fois** for the second time.

**deuxièmement** *adverb* secondly.

**deux-points** *noun Masc.* colon.

**dévaliser** *verb* [1] to rob.

**dévaluer** *verb* [1] to devalue.

**devant** *noun Masc.* front.
**devant** *preposition* **1** in front of; **elle était devant moi dans la queue** she was in front of me in the queue; **il l'a dit devant ses parents** he said it in front of his parents; **2** outside; **devant la boulangerie** outside the baker's.

**développement** *noun Masc.* development; **les pays en voie de développement** developing countries.

**développer** *verb* [1] **1** to develop; **2** to expand; **3 se développer** to expand; **la ville se développe** the town is expanding.

**devenir** *verb* [81] to become; **elle est devenue médecin/infirmière** she went into medicine/nursing.

**déverser** *verb* [1] **1** to pour out; **2** to tip out.

**déviation** *noun Fem.* diversion.

**deviner** *verb* [1] **1** to guess; **2** to foresee.

**devinette** *noun Fem.* riddle.

**devis** *noun Masc.* quote, estimate.

**devises** *plural noun Fem.* (foreign) currency.

**dévisser** *verb* [1] to unscrew.

**devoir** *noun Masc.* **1** exercise, test; **2 devoirs** homework; **faire ses devoirs** to do your homework; **3** duty.

**devoir** *verb* [8] **1** to owe; **elle me doit vingt euros** she owes me twenty euros; **je vous dois combien?** how much do I owe you?; **2** to have to; **je dois partir à dix heures** I have to (*or* I must) leave at ten o'clock; **3 tu dois être fatigué** you must be tired; **elle doit avoir quarante ans** she must be forty; **il a dû oublier** he must have forgotten; **4 tu devrais partir** you ought to leave, you should leave; **tu aurais dû partir** you should have left; **5 elle doit arriver à cinq heures** she's supposed to arrive at five o'clock.

**dévorer** *verb* [1] to devour.

**dévoué** *adjective* devoted.

**dévouement** *noun Masc.* devotion.

**dévouer** *verb* [1] **se dévouer à** to devote oneself to.

**diabète** *noun Masc.* diabetes.

**diabétique** *noun Masc. & Fem.*, *adjective* diabetic.

**diable** *noun Masc.* devil.

**diabolo** *noun Masc.* fruit cordial and lemonade; **un diabolo menthe** a mint cordial and lemonade.

**diagnostic** *noun Masc.* diagnosis.

**diagnostique** *adjective* diagnostic.

**diagnostiquer** *verb* [1] to diagnose.

**diagonal** (*Masc. plural* **diagonaux**) *adjective* diagonal.

**diagonale** *noun Fem.* diagonal; **en diagonale** diagonally.

**diagramme** *noun Masc.* graph.

**dialecte** *noun Masc.* dialect.

**dialogue** *noun Masc.* dialogue.

**dialyse** *noun Fem.* dialysis.

**diamant** *noun Masc.* diamond.

**diamètre** *noun Masc.* diameter.

**diapo** *noun Fem.* (*informal*) slide SHORT FOR **diapositive**.

**diapositive** *noun Fem.* slide.

**diarrhée** *noun Fem.* diarrhoea.

**dico** *noun Masc.* (*informal*) dictionary SHORT FOR **dictionnaire**.

**dictateur** *noun Masc.* dictator.

**dictature** *noun Fem.* dictatorship.

**dictée** *noun Fem.* dictation.

**dicter** *verb* [1] to dictate.

**dictionnaire** *noun Masc.* dictionary.

**dicton** *noun Masc.* saying.

**diesel** *noun Masc.* diesel.

**diététique** *noun Fem.* **un magasin de diététique** a health-food shop. **diététique** *adjective* dietary.

**dieu** (*plural* **dieux**) *noun Masc.* god.

**Dieu** *noun Masc.* God; **mon Dieu!** good heavens!

**différemment** *adverb* differently.

**différence** *noun Fem.* **1** difference; **quelle est la différence (entre)?**

what's the difference (between)?; **2 à la différence de** unlike.

**différend** *noun Masc.* disagreement.

**différent** *adjective* **1** different; **différent de** different from; **2** various, different; **différentes personnes** various people, different people.

**difficile** *adjective* **1** difficult, hard; **difficile à faire** difficult to do; **leur maison est difficile à trouver** their house is difficult to find; **c'est difficile à imaginer** it's hard to imagine; **2** hard to please, fussy.

**difficilement** *adverb* with difficulty.

**difficulté** *noun Fem.* difficulty; **avoir de la difficulté à faire** to have difficulty in doing; **j'ai eu de la difficulté à vous joindre** I had difficulty getting in touch with you.

**difforme** *adjective* deformed, misshapen.

**difformité** *noun Fem.* deformity.

**diffuser** *verb* [1] **1** to broadcast; **2** to distribute; **3** to spread.

**digérer** *verb* [24] to digest.

**digestif** *noun Masc.* (after-dinner) liqueur.

**digestion** *noun Fem.* digestion.

**digital** (*Masc. plural* **digitaux**) *adjective* digital.

**digne** *adjective* **1** worthy; **digne de** worthy of; **digne de foi** trustworthy; **2** dignified.

**dignité** *noun Fem.* dignity.

**digue** *noun Fem.* **1** sea wall; **2** dyke.

**dilemme** *noun Masc.* dilemma.

**diligent** *adjective* diligent.

**diluant** *noun Masc.* thinner.

**diluer** *verb* [1] **1** to dilute; **2** to thin (*paint*).

**dimanche** *noun Masc.* **1** Sunday; **nous sommes dimanche aujourd'hui** it's Sunday today; **dimanche dernier** last Sunday; **dimanche prochain** next Sunday; **2** on Sunday; **je t'appellerai dimanche soir** I'll ring you on Sunday evening; **3 le dimanche** on Sundays; **fermé le dimanche** closed on Sundays; **4 tous les dimanches** every Sunday.

**dimension** *noun Fem.* size.

**diminuer** *verb* [1] **1** to reduce; **2** to come (*or* go) down; **3** to decrease; **4** to die down.

**dinde** *noun Fem.* turkey (*as meat*).

**dindon** *noun Masc.* turkey (*when alive*).

**dîner** *noun Masc.* dinner, supper; **inviter quelqu'un à dîner** to invite somebody to dinner.
**dîner** *verb* [1] to have dinner; **viens dîner chez nous ce soir** come to dinner with us this evening.

**dingue** *adjective* (*informal*) crazy.

**dinosaure** *noun Masc.* dinosaur.

**diplomate** *noun Masc. & Fem.* diplomat.
**diplomate** *adjective* diplomatic.

**diplomatie** *noun Fem.* diplomacy.

**diplomatique** *adjective* diplomatic.

**diplôme** *noun Masc.* **1** diploma, certificate; **2** (university) degree.

**diplômé** *adjective* qualified.

**dire** *verb* [9] **1** to say; **elle dit qu'elle est malade** she says she's ill; **2** to tell; **dire quelque chose à quelqu'un** to tell somebody something; **j'ai dit à Anne que tu l'appellerais** I told Anne you'd ring her; **dire à quelqu'un de faire** to tell somebody to do; **je leur ai dit de venir à cinq heures** I told them to come at five o'clock; **on dirait qu'il va pleuvoir** it looks like rain; **dire la vérité** to tell the truth; **dire l'heure** to tell the time; **dire des mensonges** to tell lies.

**direct** *adjective* **1** direct; **un vol direct** a direct flight; **2** (*in broadcasting*) **en direct de** live from.

**directement** *adverb* **1** directly; **2 aller directement à** to go straight to.

**directeur**, **directrice** *noun Masc., Fem.* **1** director; **2** manager; **3** head (*of a school*).

**directeur général**, **directrice générale** *noun Masc.,Fem.* managing director.

**direction** *noun Fem.* **1** direction; **en direction de** towards, in the direction of; **2** management; **3** steering (*of a vehicle*).

**dirigeant**, **dirigeante** *noun Masc., Fem.* leader.

**diriger** *verb* [52] **1** to direct; **2** to manage; **3** to conduct (*an orchestra*); **4 se diriger vers** to make for; **elle s'est dirigée vers la porte** she made for the door.

**discerner** *verb* [1] **1** to make out; **2** to detect.

**discipline** *noun Fem.* **1** discipline; **2** subject (*of study*).

**discipliner** *verb* [1] **1** to discipline; **2** to control.

**disco** *noun Masc.* **1** disco; **2** disco music.

**discothèque** *noun Fem.* **1** disco, discotheque; **2** music library.

**discours** *noun Masc.* speech.

**discret** (*Fem.* **discrète**) *adjective* **1** discreet; **2** quiet; **3** subtle.

**discrétion** *noun Fem.* discretion.

**discrimination** *noun Fem.* discrimination.

**discussion** *noun Fem.* discussion.

**discutable** *adjective* questionable; **une décision discutable** a questionable decision.

**discuter** *verb* [1] **1** to talk; **on peut discuter tranquillement chez moi** we can talk in peace at my house; **2** to argue; **ça se discute** it's arguable; **3 discuter de quelque chose** to discuss something; **on va en discuter demain** we'll discuss it tomorrow.

**disparaître** *verb* [27] **1** to disappear; **2 faire disparaître quelque chose** to get rid of something; **3** to die; **4** to die out (*traditions, customs*).

**disparition** *noun Fem.* **1** disappearance; **2 une espèce en voie de disparition** an endangered species; **3** death.

**disparu**, **disparue** *noun Masc., Fem.* **1** missing person; **2 les disparus** the dead.

a
b
c
d
e
f
g
h
i
j
k
l
m
n
o
p
q
r
s
t
u
v
w
x
y
z

**dispenser**

b
c
d
e
f
g
h
i
j
k
l
m
n
o
p
q
r
s
t
u
v
w
x
y
z

**FRENCH-ENGLISH**

**disparu** *adjective* **1** missing; **2** lost; **3** dead; **4** extinct.

**dispenser** *verb* [1] **1** to hand out; **2** to give; **3 dispenser quelqu'un de** to exempt somebody from.

**disperser** *verb* [1] **1** to break up (*a crowd or demonstration*); **2 se disperser** to break up; **la foule s'est dispersée** the crowd broke up.

**disponibilité** *noun Fem.* availability.

**disponible** *adjective* available.

**disposé** *adjective* **1** arranged, laid out; **2 être disposé à faire** to be willing to do.

**disposer** *verb* [1] **1** to arrange, to lay out; **2 disposer de quelque chose** to have something (at your disposal).

**dispositif** *noun Masc.* **1** device; **2** system.

**disposition** *noun Fem.* **1** arrangement, layout; **2 à ta disposition** at your disposal; **3** measure.

**dispute** *noun Fem.* argument.

**disputé** *adjective* **1** contested; **2** controversial.

**disputer** *verb* [1] **1 se disputer** to argue; **ils se sont disputés** they had an argument; **2 se disputer quelque chose** to fight over something; **3 se faire disputer** (*informal*) to get told off; **je me suis fait disputer par mon patron** I got told off by my boss.

**disqualifier** *verb* [1] to disqualify.

**disque** *noun Masc.* **1** record; **passer un disque** to play a record (or CD); **2** disc; **3** (computer) disk.

**disque compact** *noun Masc.* compact disc, CD.

**disque dur** *noun Masc.* hard disk (*of a computer*).

**disquette** *noun Fem.* (computer) diskette.

**disséquer** *verb* [24] to dissect.

**dissertation** *noun Fem.* essay.

**dissident**, **dissidente** *noun Masc., Fem.* dissident.

**dissimuler** *verb* [1] to conceal.

**dissocier** *verb* [1] to separate.

**dissolvant** *noun Masc.* **1** nail polish remover; **2** solvent.

**dissoudre** *verb* [67] **1 dissoudre quelque chose** to dissolve something; **2 se dissoudre** to dissolve.

**dissuader** *verb* [1] **1 dissuader quelqu'un de faire** to persuade somebody not to do, to put somebody off doing; **il m'a dissuadé d'y aller** he persuaded me not to go; **2** to deter; **pour dissuader les voleurs** in order to deter thieves.

**distance** *noun Fem.* **1** distance; **une distance de cinq kilomètres** a distance of five kilometres; **c'est à quelle distance d'ici?** how far is it from here?; **à distance** from a distance; **l'enseignement à distance** distance learning; **2** gap.

**distant** *adjective* distant; **distant de** far away from; **un village distant**

94

**de trois kilomètres** a village three kilometres away.

**distiller** *verb* [1] to distil.

**distillerie** *noun Fem.* distillery.

**distinct** *adjective* distinct.

**distinctif** (*Fem.* **distinctive**) *adjective* distinctive.

**distinction** *noun Fem.* distinction.

**distingué** *adjective* distinguished.

**distinguer** *verb* [1] **1** to make out; **j'ai distingué un bateau à l'horizon** I made out a boat on the horizon; **2 distinguer entre** to distinguish between.

**distraction** *noun Fem.*
**1** entertainment; **on a besoin d'un peu de distraction** we need a bit of entertainment; **2** leisure; **3** leisure activity, form of entertainment; **4** absent-mindedness.

**distraire** *verb* [78] **1** to amuse, to entertain; **ça m'a distrait un peu** that cheered me up a bit; **2** to distract; **3 se distraire** to amuse yourself, to enjoy yourself.

**distrait** *adjective* absent-minded.

**distribuer** *verb* [1] **1** to hand out, to distribute; **2 distribuer les cartes** to deal (*in a card game*); **3 distribuer le courrier** to deliver the mail.

**distributeur** *noun Masc.*
**1** distributor; **2 un distributeur automatique** a vending machine; **3 un distributeur de tickets** a ticket machine; **4 un distributeur de billets** a cash dispenser.

**distribution** *noun Fem.*
**1** distribution; **2** handing out;

**3** delivery (*of mail*); **4** cast (*of a play*).

**diverger** *verb* [52] to diverge.

**divers** *adjective* various; **dans divers pays** in various countries.

**divertir** *verb* [2] **1** to amuse, to entertain; **2 se divertir** to amuse oneself.

**divertissant** *adjective* amusing, entertaining.

**divin** *adjective* divine.

**diviser** *verb* [1] to divide.

**division** *noun Fem.* division.

**divorce** *noun Masc.* divorce.

**divorcé** *adjective* divorced; **mes parents sont divorcés** my parents are divorced.

**divorcer** *verb* [61] to get divorced; **ils ont divorcé après dix ans de mariage** they got divorced after being married for ten years.

**dix** *number* ten; **elle a dix ans** she's ten; **il est dix heures** it's ten o'clock; **le dix juillet** the tenth of July.

**dix-huit** *number* eighteen; **il a dix-huit ans** he's eighteen; **à dix-huit heures** at six p.m.

**dixième** *noun Masc.* **au dixième** on the tenth floor.
**dixième** *adjective* tenth.

**dix-neuf** *number* nineteen; **elle a dix-neuf ans** she's nineteen; **à dix-neuf heures** at seven p.m.

**dix-sept** *number* seventeen; **elle a dix-sept ans** she's seventeen; **à dix-sept heures** at five p.m.

a
b
c
d
e
f
g
h
i
j
k
l
m
n
o
p
q
r
s
t
u
v
w
x
y
z

a b c **d** e f g h i j k l m n o p q r s t u v w x y z

**dizaine** *noun Fem.* **1** ten; **2 une dizaine de personnes** about ten people.

**docteur** *noun Masc.* doctor.

**document** *noun Masc.* document.

**documentaire** *noun Masc.*, *adjective* documentary.

**documentaliste** *noun Masc. & Fem.* librarian.

**documentation** *noun Fem.* **1** documentation; **2** material; **3** research.

**documenter** *verb* [1] **se documenter sur quelque chose** to gather information on something.

**dodo** *noun Masc.* **faire dodo** (*baby talk*) to sleep; **on va faire dodo** time to tuck up in bed.

**dogmatique** *adjective* dogmatic.

**doigt** *noun Masc.* finger; **se couper le doigt** to cut your finger; **avoir mal au doigt** to have a sore finger; ★ **être à deux doigts de** to be within an inch of (*literally: to be two fingers away from*).

**doigt de pied** *noun Masc.* toe.

**domaine** *noun Masc.* **1** estate; **2** field, domain.

**dôme** *noun Masc.* dome.

**domestique** *noun Masc. & Fem.* servant.

**domestique** *adjective* domestic.

**domicile** *noun Masc.* **1** place of residence; **2 à domicile** at home; **travailler à domicile** to work at home.

**dominant** *adjective* **1** dominant; **2** main.

**dominer** *verb* [1] **1** to dominate; **2** to control.

**Dominicain, Dominicaine** *noun Masc.,Fem.* Dominican.

**dominicain** *adjective* Dominican; **la République dominicaine** the Dominican Republic.

**domino** *noun Masc.* domino; **jouer aux dominos** to play dominoes.

**dommage** *noun Masc.* **1 c'est dommage** it's a pity; **c'est dommage qu'elle n'y soit pas allée** it's a pity she didn't go; **2 les dommages** damage.

**dompter** *verb* [1] to tame.

**DOM-TOM** SHORT FOR **départements et territoires d'outre-mer** (*French overseas departments and territories*).

**don** *noun Masc.* **1** gift; **faire don de** to give; **2** donation; **dons en argent** cash donations; **3** gift, talent; **elle a un don pour les langues** she has a gift for languages; **avoir le don de faire quelque chose** to have the gift of doing something.

**donc** *conjunction* so, therefore.

**donne** *noun Fem.* deal (*in card games*).

**donné** *adjective* given; **étant donné que** given that.

**donnée** *noun Fem.* **1** fact; **2 données** data.

**donner** *verb* [1] **1** to give; **donner quelque chose à quelqu'un** to give somebody something; **elle m'a donné dix euros** she gave me ten euros; **donne-moi ton adresse** give me your address; **2** to give away; **il a donné tous ses livres** he gave away all his books; **3 ma fenêtre donne sur la rue** my window looks onto the street; **4 se donner à quelque chose** to devote yourself to something.

**dont** *relative pronoun* whose, of which; **une personne dont j'ai oublié le nom** a person whose name I've forgotten; **la maison dont je parle** the house I'm talking about; **six verres dont l'un est cassé** six glasses, one of which is broken.

**doré** *adjective* **1** gold; **2** gilt; **3** golden.

**dorénavant** *adverb* from now on; **dorénavant je serai là tous les jours** from now on I'll be here every day.

**dorer** *verb* [1] **1** to gild; **2** **faire dorer** to brown (*meat or vegetables*).

**dormir** *verb* [37] to sleep; **tu as bien dormi?** did you sleep well?; **elle va dormir chez moi** she's going to spend the night at my house; **il dort** he's asleep.

**dortoir** *noun Masc.* dormitory.

**dos** *noun Masc.* back; **avoir mal au dos** to have backache; **faire quelque chose dans le dos de quelqu'un** to do something behind somebody's back; **elle me tournait le dos** she had her back to me; **il m'a tourné le dos** he turned his back on me.

**dosage** *noun Masc.* **1** amount; **2** mixture.

**dose** *noun Fem.* **1** dose; **2** measure.

**dossier** *noun Masc.* **1** file; **2** application form; **remplir un dossier** to fill in an application form; **3 dossier médical** medical records; **4 le dossier d'une chaise** the back of a chair.

**douane** *noun Fem.* **la douane** customs; **passer la douane** to go through customs.

**douanier** *noun Masc.* customs officer.

**double** *noun Masc.* **1 le double (de)** twice as much, twice as many; **2** copy, duplicate; **3** double. **double** *adjective* double.

**doublé** *adjective* **1** lined; **2** dubbed (*film*).

**doublement** *adverb* doubly.

**doubler** *verb* [1] **1** to double; **2** to overtake; **il m'a doublé dans un virage** he overtook me on a bend; **3** to line (*a garment*); **4** to dub (*a film*).

**doublure** *noun Fem.* lining.

**douce** *adjective* SEE **doux**.

**doucement** *adverb* **1** gently; **2** slowly; **3** softly.

**douceur** *noun Fem.* **1** softness; **2** gentleness; **3** mildness (*of weather*).

**douche** *noun Fem.* shower; **prendre une douche** to take a shower.

**doucher** *verb* [1] **se doucher** to have a shower.

**doué** *adjective* gifted; **être doué pour quelque chose** to have a gift for something.

**douillet** (*Fem.* **douillette**) *adjective* cosy.

**douleur** *noun Fem.* **1** pain; **2** grief.

**douloureux** (*Fem.* **douloureuse**) *adjective* painful.

**doute** *noun Masc.* **1** doubt; **2 sans doute** probably.

**douter** *verb* [1] **1** to doubt; **douter de** to have doubts about; **2 se douter de** to suspect; **je m'en doutais** I thought as much.

**douteux** (*Fem.* **douteuse**) *adjective* **1** doubtful; **2** dubious.

**Douvres** *noun* Dover.

**doux** (*Fem.* **douce**) *adjective* **1** soft; **2** gentle; **3** mild; **4** sweet.

**douzaine** *noun Fem.* **1** dozen; **2 une douzaine (de)** a dozen or so.

**douze** *number* twelve; **elle a douze ans** she's twelve; **le douze juillet** the twelfth of July.

**douzième** *noun Masc.* **au douzième** on the twelfth floor. **douzième** *adjective* twelfth.

**dragée** *noun Fem.* sugared almond.

**draguer** *verb* [1] (*informal*) **draguer quelqu'un** to chat somebody up; **il est toujours en train de draguer les nanas** he's always chatting up the girls; **se faire draguer** to get chatted up; **Carole s'est fait draguer par ton copain** Carole got chatted up by your mate.

**dramatique** *adjective* **1** tragic; **2** dramatic; **l'art dramatique** drama.

**drame** *noun Masc.* **1** tragedy; **2** drama; **il en a fait tout un drame** he made a big scene about it.

**drap** *noun Masc.* sheet.

**drapeau** (*plural* **drapeaux**) *noun Masc.* flag.

**drap-housse** *noun Masc.* fitted sheet.

**dresser** *verb* [1] **1** to train (*an animal*); **2** to put up (*a tent*); **3** to draw up (*a list*); **4 se dresser** to stand up.

**drogue** *noun Fem.* drug; **la drogue** drugs; **les drogues douces** soft drugs; **les drogues dures** hard drugs.

**droguer** *verb* [1] **1** to drug, to give drugs to; **2 se droguer** to take drugs.

**droguerie** *noun Fem.* hardware shop.

**droit** *noun Masc.* **1** right; **les droits de l'homme** human rights; **2 avoir le droit de faire** to be allowed to do; **je n'ai pas le droit de sortir ce soir** I'm not allowed to go out tonight; **3 avoir le droit de faire** to have the right to do; **tu n'as pas le droit de me critiquer** you have no right to criticize me; **4 le droit** law; **un étudiant en droit** a law student; **5** fee; **les droits d'inscription** enrolment fees.
**droit** *adjective* **1** straight; **une ligne droite** a straight line; **cette ligne n'est pas droite** this line is crooked; **2** right; **ma main droite** my right hand; **3 un angle droit** a right angle.

**droit** *adverb* straight; **continuez tout droit** go straight ahead.

**droite** *noun Fem.* **1** right; **à droite** on the right; **tourner à droite** to turn right; **à ta droite** on your right; **2 la droite** the right (*in politics*).

**droitier** (*Fem.* **droitière**) *adjective* right-handed.

**drôle** *adjective* **1** funny; **une histoire drôle** a funny story; **un film très drôle** a really funny film; **2** odd; **un drôle de film** an odd film.

**drôlement** *adverb* **1** (*informal*) really; **c'était drôlement bon!** it was really good!; **2** oddly, peculiarly.

**dû**, **due**, **dus** *verb* SEE **devoir**.

**du** *article* some, any SEE **de**.

**duc** *noun Masc.* duke.

**duchesse** *noun Fem.* duchess.

**dune** *noun Fem.* dune.

**duo** *noun Masc.* duet.

**duplex** *noun Masc.* maisonette.

**duquel** *pronoun* (= *de lequel*).

**dur** *adjective* **1** hard; **2** tough (*meat*); **3** difficult, hard.
**dur** *adverb* **travailler dur** to work hard.

**durant** *preposition* **1** for; **des années durant** for years; **2** during.

**durcir** *verb* [2] **1** to harden; **2 se durcir** to harden.

**durée** *noun Fem.* length.

**durement** *adverb* harshly.

**durer** *verb* [1] **1** to last; **2 durer pendant trois mois** to go on for three months.

**dureté** *noun Fem.* **1** hardness; **2** toughness; **3** difficulty.

**duvet** *noun Masc.* sleeping bag.

**DVD** *noun Masc.* DVD.

**dynamique** *adjective* dynamic, lively.

**dyslexique** *noun Masc. & Fem.* dyslexic.

# Ee

**eau** *noun Fem.* water; **est-ce que tu veux de l'eau?** would you like some water?; **un verre d'eau** a glass of water; **eau gazeuse** sparkling mineral water; **eau plate** still mineral water; **'eau potable'** 'drinking water'; **'eau non potable'** 'not drinking water'; ★ **tomber à l'eau** to fall through (*literally: to fall into the water*); **nos projets sont tombés à l'eau** our plans have fallen through; ★ **mettre l'eau à la bouche de quelqu'un** to make somebody's mouth water; **ta sauce sent tellement bon que ça me met l'eau à la bouche** your sauce smells so good it's making my mouth water.

**eau de Javel** *noun Fem.* bleach.

**eau de toilette** *noun Fem.* toilet water.

**eau minérale** *noun Fem.* mineral water.

a
b
c
d
e
f
g
h
i
j
k
l
m
n
o
p
q
r
s
t
u
v
w
x
y
z

a
b
c
d
e
f
g
h
i
j
k
l
m
n
o
p
q
r
s
t
u
v
w
x
y
z

**ébaucher** *verb* [1] **1** to sketch; **2** to outline.

**ébéniste** *noun Masc. & Fem.* cabinet maker.

**éblouir** *verb* [2] to dazzle.

**éblouissant** *adjective* dazzling.

**éboueur** *noun Masc.* refuse collector.

**ébouillanter** *verb* [1] to scald.

**ébranler** *verb* [1] to shake.

**ébullition** *noun Fem.* boiling point; **porter à ébullition** to bring to the boil.

**écaille** *noun Fem.* **1** scale (*of a fish or reptile*); **2** tortoiseshell.

**écailler** *verb* [1] **s'écailler** to flake; **la peinture s'écaille** the paint's flaking.

**écart** *noun Masc.* **1** gap, distance; **faire un écart** to swerve; **la voiture a fait un écart pour éviter le chien** the car swerved to avoid the dog; **2** difference; **3 à l'écart de** away from.

**écarté** *adjective* **1 un village écarté** a remote village; **2 les jambes écartées** with legs apart; **3 les bras écartés** with arms outstretched.

**écarter** *verb* [1] **1** to move apart; **écarter les rideaux** to open the curtains; **2** to move back.

**échafaudage** *noun Masc.* scaffolding.

**échalote** *noun Fem.* shallot.

**échange** *noun Masc.* exchange; **en échange (de)** in exchange (for), in return (for).

**échanger** *verb* [52] to exchange, to swap; **nous avons échangé nos adresses** we exchanged addresses.

**échangeur** *noun Masc.* (motorway) interchange.

**échantillon** *noun Masc.* sample.

**échapper** *verb* [1] **1 échapper à** to escape, to escape from, to get away from; **le week-end nous échappons à la ville** at weekends we get away from the town; **2 s'échapper** to escape.

**écharde** *noun Fem.* splinter.

**écharpe** *noun Fem.* scarf.

**échasse** *noun Fem.* stilt.

**échec** *noun Masc.* failure.

**échecs** *plural noun Masc.* chess; **jouer aux échecs** to play chess.

**échelle** *noun Fem.* **1** ladder; **2** scale.

**échelon** *noun Masc.* **1** rung; **2** grade.

**échiquier** *noun Masc.* chessboard.

**écho** *noun Masc.* **1** echo; **2 des échos** rumours.

**échographie** *noun Fem.* (medical) scan; **passer une échographie** to have a scan.

**échouer** *verb* [1] to fail; **échouer à un examen** to fail an exam.

**éclabousser** *verb* [1] to splash.

**éclair** *noun Masc.* **1** flash of lightning; **2 un éclair au chocolat** a chocolate eclair.

**éclairage** *noun Masc.* lighting.

**éclairagiste** *noun Masc. & Fem.* lighting engineer.

**éclaircie** *noun Fem.* sunny interval.

**éclairer** *verb* [1] to light (up).

**éclat** *noun Masc.* **1** splinter, fragment; **2** brightness; **3** splendour; **4 un éclat de rire** a roar of laughter.

**éclatant** *adjective* brilliant; **des murs d'une blancheur éclatante** brilliant white walls.

**éclater** *verb* [1] **1** to burst; **un pneu a éclaté** a tyre has burst; **2** to shatter; **l'ampoule a éclaté** the bulb shattered; **3** to break out (*war or fighting*); **4 éclater de rire** to burst out laughing; **éclater en sanglots** to burst into tears.

**éclipse** *noun Fem.* eclipse.

**écluse** *noun Fem.* lock (*on a canal or river*).

**écœurant** *adjective* sickly.

**écœurer** *verb* [1] to make (somebody) feel sick.

**école** *noun Fem.* school; **aller à l'école** to go to school.

**école de conduite** *noun Fem.* driving school.

**école de langue** *noun Fem.* language, school.

**école maternelle** *noun Fem.* (state) nursery school (*age 2 – 6*).

**école primaire** *noun Fem.* primary school (*age 6 –11*).

**écolier, écolière** *noun Masc., Fem.* schoolchild.

**écologie** *noun Fem.* ecology.

**écologique** *adjective* **1** ecological; **2** environmentally friendly.

**écologiste** *noun Masc. & Fem.* ecologist.

**économe** *noun Masc.* potato peeler.
**économe** *adjective* economical.

**économie** *noun Fem.* **1** economy; **2** economics; **3 les économies** savings; **faire des économies** to save up.

**économique** *adjective* **1** economical; **2** economic.

**économiser** *verb* [1] to save.

**économiste** *noun Masc. & Fem.* economist.

**écorce** *noun Fem.* **1** bark (*of a tree*); **2** peel (*of an orange or a lemon*).

**écorcher** *verb* [1] **s'écorcher le genou** to graze your knee.

**écorchure** *noun Fem.* graze.

**écossais** *noun Masc.* tartan (cloth). **écossais** *adjective* **1** Scottish; **2** tartan; **une jupe écossaise** a tartan skirt.

**Écossais, Écossaise** *noun Masc., Fem.* Scotsman, Scotswoman, Scot; **les Écossais** the Scots.

**Écosse** *noun Fem.* Scotland; **elle habite en Écosse** she lives in Scotland.

**écourter** *verb* [1] to shorten.

**écouter** *verb* [1] to listen to; **j'écoute beaucoup la radio** I listen to the radio a lot; **écoute-moi** listen to me.

**écouteur** *noun Masc.* **1** receiver (*on a telephone*); **2** headphones.

**écran** *noun Masc.* **1** screen; **à l'écran** on the screen; **le petit écran** television; **2 la crème écran total** sun block.

a
b
c
d
**e**
f
g
h
i
j
k
l
m
n
o
p
q
r
s
t
u
v
w
x
y
z

**écrasant** *adjective* crushing, overwhelming; **une victoire/ défaite écrasante** a crushing victory/defeat.

**écraser** *verb* [1] **1** to crush; **écrasez les noix** crush the walnuts; **2** to squash; **tu vas écraser les pêches!** you'll squash the peaches!; **3 écraser une cigarette** to stub out a cigarette; **4 se faire écraser** to get run over; **Attention! Tu vas te faire écraser!** Watch out! You'll get run over!; **5 s'écraser** to crash; **leur voiture s'est écrasée contre un mur** their car crashed into a wall.

**écrémé** *adjective* **le lait écrémé** skimmed milk; **le lait demi-écrémé** semi-skimmed milk.

**écrevisse** *noun Fem.* crayfish.

**écrire** *verb* [38] **1** to write; **elle m'a écrit une lettre** she wrote me a letter; **2 s'écrire** to write to each other; **ils s'écrivent tous les jours** they write to each other every day; **3 s'écrire** to be spelled; **comment ça s'écrit?** how do you spell it?

**écrit** *noun Masc.* **1** (piece of) writing; **2** written paper (*of an exam*); **il a réussi à l'oral mais il a raté l'écrit** he passed the oral but failed the written paper; **3 à l'écrit** in writing. **écrit** *adjective* written.

**écriture** *noun Fem.* handwriting.

**écrivain** *noun Masc.* writer.

**écrou** *noun Masc.* nut (*screwed onto a bolt*).

**écrouler** *verb* [1] **s'écrouler** to collapse.

**écume** *noun Fem.* **1** foam, froth; **2** scum.

**écureuil** *noun Masc.* squirrel.

**écurie** *noun Fem.* stable.

**eczéma** *noun Masc.* eczema.

**EDF** SHORT FOR **Électricité de France** French electricity company.

**Édimbourg** *noun* Edinburgh.

**éditer** *verb* [1] to publish.

**éditeur** *noun Masc.* publisher.

**édition** *noun Fem.* **1** publishing; **elle travaille dans l'édition** she works in publishing; **2** edition; **une édition de poche** a paperback edition.

**édredon** *noun Masc.* eiderdown.

**éducateur**, **éducatrice** *noun Masc., Fem.* special needs teacher.

**éducatif** (*Fem.* **éducative**) *adjective* educational.

**éducation** *noun Fem.* education; **elle a reçu une bonne éducation** she had a good education.

**éducation physique** *noun Fem.* physical education, PE.

**éduquer** *verb* [1] to educate.

**effacer** *verb* [61] to rub out.

**effaceur** *noun Masc.* correction pen.

**effarant** *adjective* amazing.

**effarer** *verb* [1] to alarm.

**effectivement** *adverb* indeed (*used to show agreement with what someone has just said*); **il est effectivement extrêmement gentil** he is indeed extremely nice; **oui, elle m'a effectivement téléphoné hier** yes, that's right, she did phone me yesterday; **'Tu as oublié tes clés'** – **'Ah oui, effectivement!'** 'You've left your keys behind' – 'Oh yes, so I have!'; **'Il est maintenant trop tard pour y aller'** – **'Oui, effectivement'** 'It's too late to go now' – 'Yes, so it is.'

**effectuer** *verb* [1] to make, to carry out.

**effet** *noun Masc.* **1** effect; **2 en effet** indeed (*used to show agreement with what someone has just said*); **elle avait en effet raison** she was indeed right; **'il fait très froid'** – **'Oui, en effet'** 'It's very cold' – 'Yes, it is, isn't it?'; **'Tu as laissé la porte ouverte'** – **'Oui, en effet'** 'You've left the door open' – 'Yes, so I have'.

**efficace** *adjective* **1** efficient; **elle est très efficace** she's very efficient; **2** effective; **c'est un remède très efficace** it's a very effective remedy.

**efficacité** *noun Fem.* **1** efficiency; **il est connu pour son efficacité** he's known for his efficiency; **2** effectiveness.

**effondrer** *verb* [1] **s'effondrer** to collapse.

**efforcer** *verb* [61] **s'efforcer de faire** to try hard to do; **elle s'efforce de rester calme** she tries hard to remain calm.

**effort** *noun Masc.* effort; **faire un effort** to make an effort; **il n'a même pas fait l'effort de m'appeler** he couldn't even be bothered to phone me.

**effrayant** *adjective* frightening.

**effrayer** *verb* [59] to frighten.

**effroi** *noun Masc.* terror.

**effronté** *adjective* cheeky.

**effroyable** *adjective* dreadful.

**égal**, **égale** (*Masc. plural* **égaux**) *noun Masc., Fem.* equal.
**égal** *adjective* **1** equal; **une distance égale** an equal distance; **des quantités égales** equal quantities; **être égal à** to be equal to; **2 ça m'est égal** I don't mind; **'Tu veux aller au cinéma ou rester à la maison?'** – **'Ça m'est égal'** 'Do you want to go to the cinema or stay at home?' – 'I don't mind'.

**également** *adverb* also; **elle est également prof d'allemand** she's also a German teacher.

**égaler** *verb* [1] to equal; **trois plus cinq égale huit** three plus five equals eight.

**égaliser** *verb* [1] to equalize; **ils ont égalisé dans la dernière minute** they equalized in the last minute.

**égalité** *noun Fem.* **1** equality; **2 les deux joueurs sont à égalité** the two players are level.

**égard** *noun Masc.* **1 à l'égard de** towards; **à mon égard** towards me; **2 à cet égard** in this respect.

**égaré** *adjective* stray; **un chien égaré** a stray dog.

**égarer** *verb* [1] **1** to mislay; **j'ai égaré mes lunettes** I've mislaid my glasses; **2 s'égarer** to get lost; **nous nous sommes égarés dans les petites rues** we got lost in the back streets.

**égayer** *verb* [59] **1** to brighten up; **j'ai acheté quelques fleurs pour égayer la pièce** I've bought some flowers to brighten up the room; **2** to cheer up; **un peu de musique va nous égayer un peu** a bit of music will cheer us up a bit.

**églantine** *noun Fem.* wild rose.

**églefin** *noun Masc.* haddock.

**église** *noun Fem.* church; **aller à l'église** to go to church.

**égoïsme** *noun Masc.* selfishness.

**égoïste** *adjective* selfish.

**égout** *noun Masc.* sewer.

**égoutter** *verb* [1] **1** to drain (*vegetables*); **2** to strain (*pasta*); **3** to drip.

**égratignure** *noun Fem.* scratch.

**Égypte** *noun Fem.* Egypt.

**eh bien** *exclamation* well; **eh bien, ça me fait plaisir de te revoir** well, it's nice to see you again.

**élancer** *verb* [61] **s'élancer** to dash.

**élargir** *verb* [2] to widen.

**élastique** *noun Masc.* **1** rubber band; **2** elastic.
**élastique** *adjective* **1** elastic; **2** elasticated.

**électeur**, **électrice** *noun Masc., Fem.* voter.

**élection** *noun Fem.* election; **une élection présidentielle** a presidential election; **se présenter aux élections** to be a candidate in the elections.

**électricien**, **électricienne** *noun Masc., Fem.* electrician.

**électricité** *noun Fem.* electricity.

**électrique** *adjective* **1** electric; **2** electrical.

**électronique** *noun Fem.* electronics.
**électronique** *adjective* electronic.

**élégant** *adjective* elegant.

**élément** *noun Masc.* **1** element; **2** part.

**élémentaire** *adjective* basic, elementary.

**éléphant** *noun Masc.* elephant.

**élevage** *noun Masc.* **1** farming (*of livestock*); **2** farm; **un élevage de porcs** a pig farm.

**élevé** *adjective* high; **une note élevée** a high mark.

**élève** *noun Masc. & Fem.* student, pupil.

**élever** *verb* [50] **1** **élever un enfant** to bring up a child; **elle a été élevée en Écosse** she was brought up in Scotand; **2** to breed (*animals*); **3** **élever la voix** to raise one's voice; **4** **s'élever** to rise; **5** **s'élever à** to amount to; **la facture s'élève à cinq cents euros** the bill amounts to five hundred euros.

**éleveur**, **éleveuse** *noun Masc., Fem.* breeder.

**éliminer** *verb* [1] **1** to eliminate; **2** to rule out; **nous ne pouvons pas éliminer cette possibilité** we cannot rule out that possibility.

**élire** *verb* [51] to elect.

**elle** *pronoun* **1** she; **où est Sylvie? — elle est dans la cuisine** where's Sylvie? — she's in the kitchen; **2** her; **Paul est avec elle** Paul's with her; **3** it (*when referring to an object which is feminine in French*); **où est ma tasse? — elle est sur la table** where's my cup? — it's on the table.

**elle-même** *pronoun* **1** herself; **elle me l'a dit elle-même** she told me herself; **2** itself (*referring to an object which is feminine in French*); **la pièce elle-même est jolie mais les meubles sont hideux** the room itself is pretty but the furniture is hideous.

**elles** *pronoun* they, them **1** they (*referring to female people or feminine objects*); **elles sont arrivées** they've arrived; **2** them; **avec elles** with them.

**éloigné** *adjective* distant; **la colline la plus éloignée** the most distant hill.

**éloigner** *verb* [1] **s'éloigner (de)** to move away (from).

**Élysée** *noun Masc.* the Élysée Palace (*the official residence of the French President*).

**émail** *noun Masc.* enamel.

**emballage** *noun Masc.* wrapping.

**emballer** *verb* [1] **1** to wrap, to pack; **2** (*informal*) to get enthusiastic; **elle s'est vraiment emballée pour son nouveau boulot** she's got really enthusiastic about her new job; **ça ne m'emballe pas vraiment** I'm not that keen.

**embarquement** *noun Masc.* boarding; **une carte d'embarquement** a boarding card.

**embarquer** *verb* [1] **1** (*informal*) to go off with; **elle a embarqué toutes mes chaises** she's gone off with all my chairs; **2** **s'embarquer** to board.

**embarras** *noun Masc.* **1** embarrassment; **2** dilemma.

**embarrassé** *adjective* **1** embarrassed; **2** cluttered.

**embarrasser** *verb* [1] **1** to embarrass; **2** to clutter up.

**embaucher** *verb* [1] to take on (*an employee*); **ils embauchent en ce moment** they're taking people on at the moment.

**embêtant** *adjective* annoying; **c'est vraiment embêtant!** it's really annoying!

**embêter** *verb* [1] **1** to annoy; **arrête de m'embêter!** stop annoying me!; **2** **s'embêter** to be bored; **on ne s'embête pas ici** there's plenty going on here; **on ne s'embête pas!** we're having a great time!

**embouteillage** *noun Masc.* traffic jam.

**embrasser** *verb* [1] to kiss; **je t'embrasse** lots of love (*at the end of a letter or said on the phone to a friend*).

**embrayage** *noun Masc.* clutch (*in a vehicle*).

**émeraude** *noun Fem.* emerald.

a
b
c
d
e
f
g
h
i
j
k
l
m
n
o
p
q
r
s
t
u
v
w
x
y
z

**émerger** *verb* [52] to emerge.

**émeute** *noun Fem.* riot.

**émission** *noun Fem.* programme (*on television or radio*).

**emménager** *verb* [52] to move in (*to a flat or house*); **nous avons emménagé la semaine dernière** we moved in last week.

**emmener** *verb* [50] to take; **c'est sa sœur qui l'emmène à l'école** it's his sister who takes him to school; **tu veux que je t'emmène?** would you like a lift?

**émotif** (*Fem.* **émotive**) *adjective* emotional.

**émotion** *noun Fem.* emotion.

**émouvant** *adjective* moving.

**emparer** *verb* [1] **s'emparer de** to seize.

**empêcher** *verb* [1] **1** to prevent, to stop; **rien ne t'empêche d'essayer** there's nothing to stop you trying; **2 elle n'a pas pu s'empêcher de rire** she couldn't help laughing.

**empereur** *noun Masc.* emperor.

**empiler** *verb* [1] to pile up.

**empirer** *verb* [1] to get worse.

**emplacement** *noun Masc.* site.

**emploi** *noun Masc.* **1** job; **2** use; **le mode d'emploi** instructions for use.

**emploi du temps** *noun Masc.* timetable (*at school*).

**employé**, **employée** *noun Masc., Fem.* employee.

**employer** *verb* [39] **1** to employ; **2** to use.

**employeur**, **employeuse** *noun Masc., Fem.* employer.

**empoisonné** *adjective* poisoned.

**empoisonner** *verb* [1] to poison.

**emporter** *verb* [1] to take (away); **'plats à emporter'** 'takeaway meals'.

**empreinte** *noun Fem.* footprint.

**empreinte digitale** *noun Fem.* fingerprint.

**emprisonner** *verb* [1] to imprison.

**emprunt** *noun Masc.* loan.

**emprunter** *verb* [1] to borrow.

**emprunt-logement** *noun Masc.* mortgage.

**EMT** *noun* (= *éducation manuelle et technique*) technology (*at school*).

**ému** *adjective* moved.

**en** *preposition* **1** in; **elle habite en Écosse** she lives in Scotland; **en été** in summer; **en avril** in April; **un livre en anglais** a book in English; **habillé en noir** dressed in black; **j'étais en pyjama** I was in my pyjamas; **2** into; **aller en ville** to go into town; **traduire en anglais** to translate into English; **3** to; **aller en Italie** to go to Italy; **4** by; **en avion** by plane; **5** made of; **une table en bois** a table made of wood, a wooden table; **6 en vacances** on holiday; **7 en ami** as a friend; **8 en rentrant à la maison j'ai rencontré Tom** as I was coming home I met Tom; **je me suis brûlé en repassant ma chemise** I burned myself (while) ironing my shirt.

**en** *pronoun* **1 j'en ai** I've got some; **je n'en veux pas** I don't want any;

**tu en as combien?** how many (of them) do you have?, how much (of it) do you have?; **elle en a quatre** she's got four; **'qui a un stylo?' — 'j'en ai un'** 'who's got a pen?' — 'I've got one' (*notice that in this sort of expression 'en' is often not translated at all*); **2 elle m'en a parlé** she told me about it; **3 j'ai emprunté ton fer à repasser — est-ce que tu en as besoin?** I borrowed your iron — do you need it?

**encadrement** *noun Masc.* **1** frame; **2** framing; **3** door frame.

**encadrer** *verb* [1] to frame.

**enceinte** *noun Fem.* **1** surrounding wall; **2** enclosed space; **3** loudspeaker.
**enceinte** *adjective* pregnant.

**encens** *noun Masc.* incense.

**encercler** *verb* [1] to surround, to circle.

**enchanté** *adjective* **1** delighted; **2** (*when meeting someone*) **enchanté/enchantée** pleased to meet you.

**enchère** *noun Fem.* bid; **une vente aux enchères** an auction sale.

**encombrant** *adjective* bulky.

**encombrer** *verb* [1] **1** to clutter; **2** to obstruct.

**encore** *adverb* **1** still; **elle est encore au bureau** she's still at the office; **il reste encore de la viande** there's still some meat left; **2 pas encore** not yet; **il n'est pas encore rentré** he hasn't come home yet, he's not home yet; **3** again; **je l'ai encore oublié** I've forgotten it again; **4** more; **encore un peu** a little more; **encore une fois** one more time; **attendre encore une semaine** to wait for another week; **5** even; **encore mieux** even better.

**encourageant** *adjective* encouraging.

**encouragement** *noun Masc.* encouragement.

**encourager** *verb* [52] **1** to encourage; **elle m'a encouragé à suivre des cours de dessin** she encouraged me to go to drawing classes; **2** to cheer on (*a team*).

**encre** *noun Fem.* ink.

**encyclopédie** *noun Fem.* encyclopedia.

**endive** *noun Fem.* chicory.

**endommager** *verb* [52] to damage.

**endormi** *adjective* asleep.

**endormir** *verb* [37] **1 endormir quelqu'un** to send somebody to sleep; **2 s'endormir** to fall asleep, to go to sleep.

**endroit** *noun Masc.* **1** place; **un bon endroit pour** a good place for; **2** the right side (*of a garment*); **3 à l'endroit** the right way up.

**énergie** *noun Fem.* energy.

**énergique** *adjective* energetic.

**énervé** *adjective* irritated, annoyed.

**énerver** *verb* [1] **1** to irritate, to annoy; **ça m'énerve!** this is getting on my nerves!; **2 s'énerver** to get annoyed.

**enfance** *noun Fem.* childhood.

a
b
c
d
e
f
g
h
i
j
k
l
m
n
o
p
q
r
s
t
u
v
w
x
y
z

**enfant** *noun Masc. & Fem.* child; **un enfant unique** an only child.

**enfantin** *adjective* **1** easy; **2** childish.

**enfer** *noun Masc.* hell.

**enfermer** *verb* [1] **1** to shut up; **2 s'enfermer** to shut yourself up; **elle s'est enfermée dans sa chambre** she shut herself up in her room.

**enfiler** *verb* [1] **1** to put on; **je vais juste enfiler mon pull** I'll just put my jumper on; **2 enfiler une aiguille** to thread a needle.

**enfin** *adverb* **1** at last; **je l'ai enfin fini** I've finished it at last; **2** finally; **elle a enfin réussi** she finally succeeded.

**enflé** *adjective* swollen; **il a le genou enflé** his knee is swollen.

**enflure** *noun Fem.* swelling.

**enfoncer** *verb* [61] **1** to push in; **2 s'enfoncer dans** to sink into.

**enfreindre** *verb* [2] to disobey; **elle a enfreint les règles** she disobeyed the rules.

**engagement** *noun Masc.* commitment.

**engager** *verb* [52] **1** to take on (*an employee*); **2** to commit; **3 s'engager à faire** to promise to do; **je me suis engagé à organiser le repas** I promised to organize the meal.

**engelure** *noun Fem.* chilblain.

**engin** *noun Masc.* device.

**engourdi** *adjective* numb; **j'ai les doigts engourdis par le froid** my fingers are numb with cold.

**engourdir** *verb* [2] **s'engourdir** to go numb.

**engrais** *noun Masc.* fertilizer.

**engueuler** *verb* [1] (*informal*) to tell off; **elle m'a engueulé** she gave me a telling off; **se faire engueuler** to get a telling off.

**énième** *adjective* umpteenth; **pour la énième fois** for the umpteenth time.

**énigme** *noun Fem.* riddle.

**enivrer** *verb* [1] **1 enivrer quelqu'un** to make somebody drunk; **2 s'enivrer** to get drunk.

**enjeu** (*plural* **enjeux**) *noun Masc.* **1** stake (*in a gambling game*); **2** what is at stake.

**enlèvement** *noun Masc.* kidnapping.

**enlever** *verb* [50] **1** to take off (*garment*); **il a enlevé sa veste** he took off his jacket; **2** to remove; **enlever une tache** to remove a stain; **tu peux enlever les assiettes** you can clear the plates; **3** to kidnap.

**enneigé** *adjective* **1** snowy; **2** snow-covered.

**ennemi, ennemie** *noun Masc., Fem.* enemy.

**ennui** *noun Masc.* **1** boredom; **2** problem; **avoir des ennuis** to have problems.

**ennuyé** *adjective* **1** bored; **2** embarrassed.

**ennuyer** *verb* [41] **1** to bore; **son discours m'a ennuyé** I found his speech boring; **2** to bother; **je t'ennuie?** am I bothering you?;

**3 s'ennuyer** to be (*or* get) bored; **j'ai fini par m'ennuyer** I got bored in the end; **on s'ennuie ici** it's boring here.

**ennuyeux** (*Fem.* **ennuyeuse**) *adjective* **1** boring; **2** annoying; **ça c'est vraiment ennuyeux** that's really annoying.

**énorme** *adjective* huge.

**énormément** *adverb* **1** tremendously; **2 énormément de** masses of; **j'ai énormément de choses à faire avant de partir** I've got masses of things to do before I leave.

**enquête** *noun Fem.* **1** investigation; **2** inquiry; **3** survey.

**enregistrement** *noun Masc.* **1** recording; **2** check-in (*at airport*).

**enregistrer** *verb* [1] **1** to record; **2** to register; **3** to check in (*at airport*).

**enrhumer** *verb* [1] **s'enrhumer** to catch a cold; **être enrhumé** to have a cold.

**enrichir** *verb* [2] **1** to make rich; **2** to enrich.

**enrichissant** *adjective* rewarding.

**enrouler** *verb* [1] to wind.

**enseignant**, **enseignante** *noun Masc., Fem.* teacher.

**enseigne** *noun Fem.* sign; **enseigne lumineuse** neon sign.

**enseignement** *noun Masc.* **1** teaching; **2** education.

**enseigner** *verb* [1] to teach.

**ensemble** *noun Masc.* **1** outfit; **j'ai acheté un joli ensemble pour le**

mariage I've bought a lovely outfit for the wedding; **2 l'ensemble de** the whole of; **3 dans l'ensemble** on the whole.

**ensemble** *adverb* together; **on va y aller ensemble** we'll go together; **ils sont ensemble depuis trois ans** they've been together for three years.

**ensoleillé** *adjective* sunny.

**ensommeillé** *adjective* sleepy.

**ensuite** *adverb* then; **on va aller à la banque et ensuite chez Marianne** we'll go to the bank and then to Marianne's.

**entamer** *verb* [1] to start; **ce paquet n'a pas encore été entamé** this packet hasn't been started yet.

**entasser** *verb* [1] to pile up.

**entendre** *verb* [3] **1** to hear; **est-ce que tu l'entends?** can you hear it?; **se faire entendre** to make yourself heard; **2 j'ai entendu dire que …** I've heard that …; **3** to mean; **qu'est-ce que tu entends par là?** what do you mean by that?; **4 s'entendre bien** to get on well.

**entendu** *exclamation* **1** okay, fine; **2 bien entendu** of course.

**entente** *noun Fem.* **1** understanding; **2** agreement.

**enterrement** *noun Masc.* funeral, burial.

**enterrer** *verb* [1] to bury.

**entêté** *adjective* stubborn.

**entêter** *verb* [1] **s'entêter à faire** to persist in doing.

## enthousiasme

**enthousiasme** *noun Masc.* enthusiasm.

**enthousiasmer** *verb* [1] **s'enthousiasmer** to get enthusiastic.

**enthousiaste** *adjective* enthusiastic.

**entier** (*Fem.* **entière**) *adjective* **1** whole; **une pomme entière** a whole apple; **le monde entier** the whole world; **2 je n'ai pas lu sa lettre en entier** I haven't read his letter right through; **3 le lait entier** full-fat milk.

**entièrement** *adverb* completely, entirely.

**entorse** *noun Fem.* sprain; **se faire une entorse à la cheville** to sprain your ankle.

**entouré** *adjective* **entouré de** surrounded by; **elle est entourée d'amis** she's surrounded by friends.

**entourer** *verb* [1] to surround; **entourer de** to surround with.

**entracte** *noun Masc.* interval (*at the theatre*).

**entraînement** *noun Masc.* **1** training; **2** practice.

**entraîner** *verb* [1] **1** to lead to; **entraîner des problèmes** to lead to problems; **2** to take; **il m'a entraîné chez sa copine** he took me off to his girlfriend's; **3 entraîner une équipe** to train a team; **4** to drag; **5 s'entraîner** to train; **elle s'entraîne tous les matins** she trains every morning.

**entre** *preposition* **1** between; **entre la porte et la fenêtre** between the door and the window; **on va le**

**partager entre nous** we'll share it between us; **2** among; **entre eux** among themselves; **3 l'un d'entre eux** one of them.

**entrée** *noun Fem.* **1** entrance; **à l'entrée de** at the entrance to; **billets à l'entrée** tickets at the door; **2** hall(way); **3** admission; **4** starter, first course.

**entremets** *noun Masc.* dessert.

**entrepôt** *noun Masc.* warehouse.

**entreprendre** *verb* [64] **1** to undertake; **2** to start.

**entreprise** *noun Fem.* firm, business.

**entrer** *verb* [1] **1** to go in; **entrer dans un magasin** to go into a shop; **entrer à l'hôpital** to go into hospital; **2** to come in; **entrer dans** to come into; **Entrez!** Come in!

**entre-temps** *adverb* meanwhile.

**entretenir** *verb* [81] **1** to maintain (*a building, a road, etc*); **2** to support.

**entretien** *noun Masc.* **1** interview; **elle a été convoquée à un entretien** she's been invited for interview; **2** discussion; **j'ai eu un entretien avec mon patron** I had a discussion with my boss; **3** upkeep; **l'entretien de la maison** the upkeep of the house.

**entrevue** *noun Fem.* interview.

**entrouvert** *adjective* ajar, half-open.

**envahir** *verb* [2] to invade.

**enveloppe** *noun Fem.* envelope; **une enveloppe matelassée** a padded envelope.

**envelopper** *verb* [1] to wrap up.

**envers** *noun Masc.* **1** wrong side; **2 à l'envers** upside down, inside out, back to front.

**envers** *preposition* towards, to.

**envie** *noun Fem.* **1** urge; **avoir envie de faire** to want to do, to feel like doing; **j'ai envie de te voir** I want to see you; **j'ai envie d'aller au cinéma** I feel like going to the cinema; **2 avoir envie de quelque chose** to feel like something; **j'ai envie d'une glace** I feel like an ice cream; **3 ces frites me font envie** I fancy some of those chips.

**envier** *verb* [1] to envy.

**envieux** (*Fem.* **envieuse**) *adjective* envious.

**environ** *adverb* about; **environ trente personnes** about thirty people.

**environnement** *noun Masc.* environment.

**environs** *plural noun Masc.* surroundings; **aux environs de** near.

**envisager** *verb* [52] **envisager de faire** to plan to do; **qu'est-ce que vous envisagez de faire?** what are you planning to do?

**envoi** *noun Masc.* **1** dispatch; **faire un envoi de** to send; **2** consignment.

**envoler** *verb* [1] **s'envoler** to fly away.

**envoyer** *verb* [40] to send; **envoyer quelque chose à quelqu'un** to send somebody something; **elle m'a envoyé une carte** she sent me a card; **elle m'a envoyé chercher les verres** she sent me to get the glasses.

**épais** (*Fem.* **épaisse**) *adjective* thick; **une tranche épaisse** a thick slice.

**épaisseur** *noun Fem.* thickness.

**épargne** *noun Fem.* savings; **une banque d'épargne** a savings bank; **un compte d'épargne** a savings account.

**épatant** *adjective* (*informal*) fantastic, great.

**épaule** *noun Fem.* shoulder.

**épaulette** *noun Fem.* **1** shoulder strap; **2** shoulder pad.

**épave** *noun Fem.* wreck.

**épée** *noun Fem.* sword.

**épeler** *verb* [18] to spell.

**éphémère** *adjective* fleeting.

**épi** *noun Masc.* ear (*of corn*); **un épi de maïs** a corn cob.

**épice** *noun Fem.* spice.

**épicé** *adjective* spicy, hot; **je n'aime pas les choses épicées** I don't like spicy food.

**épicerie** *noun Fem.* grocer's (shop); **à l'épicerie** at the grocer's.

**épicier**, **épicière** *noun Masc.*, *Fem.* grocer.

**épidémie** *noun Fem.* epidemic.

**épilepsie** *noun Fem.* epilepsy.

**épiler** *verb* [1] **s'épiler les sourcils** to pluck your eyebrows; **une pince à épiler** eyebrow tweezers; **s'épiler les jambes** to shave your legs (*or use wax or cream to remove hair*).

a
b
c
d
e
f
g
h
i
j
k
l
m
n
o
p
q
r
s
t
u
v
w
x
y
z

**épinards** *plural noun Masc.* spinach; **est-ce que tu aimes les épinards?** do you like spinach?

**épine** *noun Fem.* thorn.

**épineux** (*Fem.* **épineuse**) *adjective* prickly.

**épingle** *noun Fem.* pin; **une épingle de sûreté** a safety pin.

**épingler** *verb* [1] to pin.

**éplucher** *verb* [1] to peel.

**épluchures** *plural noun Fem.* peelings.

**éponge** *noun Fem.* **1** sponge; **2** towelling.

**éponger** *verb* [52] **1** to mop up; **2** to sponge.

**époque** *noun Fem.* time; **à cette époque-là** at that time.

**épouse** *noun Fem.* wife.

**épouser** *verb* [1] to marry.

**épouvantable** *adjective* dreadful.

**épouvantail** *noun Masc.* scarecrow.

**épouvante** *noun Fem.* terror; **un film d'épouvante** a horror film.

**épouvanter** *verb* [1] to terrify.

**époux** *noun Masc.* husband.

**épreuve** *noun Fem.* **1** test; **2** exam; **l'épreuve de français** the French exam; **3** event (*sports*); **4** ordeal.

**éprouver** *verb* [1] to feel, to experience.

**éprouvette** *noun Fem.* test tube.

**EPS** *noun* (*éducation physique et sportive*) PE.

**épuisant** *adjective* exhausting; **c'est un travail épuisant** it's exhausting work.

**épuisé** *adjective* **1** exhausted, worn out; **je suis épuisé** I'm worn out; **2** out of stock; **3** out of print.

**épuiser** *verb* [1] to wear out; **cette discussion m'a épuisé** that discussion's worn me out.

**équateur** *noun Masc.* equator.

**équestre** *adjective* **un centre équestre** a riding school.

**équilibré** *adjective* balanced.

**équilibre** *noun Masc.* balance.

**équipage** *noun Masc.* crew.

**équipe** *noun Fem.* team.

**équipé** *adjective* **1** equipped; **2** **une cuisine équipée** a fitted kitchen.

**équipement** *noun Masc.* equipment.

**équipements** *plural noun Masc.* **les équipements sportifs** sports facilities.

**équitation** *noun Fem.* riding.

**équivalent** *adjective* equivalent.

**érable** *noun Masc.* maple tree; **le sirop d'érable** maple syrup.

**errer** *verb* [1] to wander.

**erreur** *noun Fem.* mistake; **par erreur** by mistake.

**es** *verb* SEE **être**[2].

**escabeau** *noun Masc.* stepladder.

**escalade** *noun Fem.* rock-climbing.

**escalier** *noun Masc.* **1** stairs; **dans l'escalier** on the stairs; **2** staircase; **3** **un escalier mécanique, un escalier roulant** an escalator.

**escargot** *noun Masc.* snail.

**escarpin** *noun Masc.* court shoe.

**esclavage** *noun Masc.* slavery.

**esclave** *noun Masc. & Fem.* slave.

**escompte** *noun Masc.* discount; **un escompte de 10%** a 10% discount.

**escorter** *verb* [1] to escort.

**escrime** *noun Fem.* fencing (*the sport*).

**escroc** *noun Masc.* crook, swindler.

**escroquer** *verb* [1] to swindle.

**escroquerie** *noun Fem.* swindle; **quelle escroquerie!** what a swindle!

**espace** *noun Masc.* space.

**espacer** *verb* [61] to space out.

**espadon** *noun Masc.* swordfish.

**espadrille** *noun Fem.* espadrille.

**Espagne** *noun Fem.* Spain.

**espagnol** *noun Masc.* Spanish (*language*).
**espagnol** *adjective* Spanish.

**Espagnol**, **Espagnole** *noun Masc., Fem.* Spaniard; **les Espagnols** the Spanish.

**espèce** *noun Fem.* **1** sort; **une espèce de** a sort of; **on a mangé du poisson avec une espèce de sauce épicée** we had fish with a sort of spicy sauce; **2** species; **3 espèce d'idiot!** you idiot!; **4 en espèces** in cash.

**espérer** *verb* [24] to hope; **ils espèrent pouvoir venir** they're hoping to be able to come; **j'espère qu'elle n'a pas oublié** I hope she hasn't forgotten; **j'espère bien!** I certainly hope so.

**espiègle** *adjective* mischievous.

**espion**, **espionne** *noun Masc., Fem.* spy.

**espionnage** *noun Masc.* spying, espionage.

**espionner** *verb* [1] to spy on.

**espoir** *noun Masc.* hope.

**esprit** *noun Masc.* **1** mind; **ça ne m'est pas venu à l'esprit** it didn't cross my mind; **2** wit; **avoir de l'esprit** to be witty.

**esquimau™** (*plural* **esquimaux**) *noun Masc.* ice lolly.

**esquisse** *noun Fem.* sketch.

**esquisser** *verb* [1] to sketch.

**essai** *noun Masc.* **1** trial; **2** test; **3** attempt, try.

**essaim** *noun Masc.* swarm.

**essayer** *verb* [59] **1** to try; **essayer de faire** to try to do; **j'ai essayé de t'appeler** I tried to phone you; **2** to try on; **essayer une robe** to try on a dress; **voulez-vous l'essayer?** would you like to try it on?; **3** to test.

**essence** *noun Fem.* **1** petrol; **essence sans plomb** unleaded petrol; **2** essential oil.

**essentiel** (*Fem.* **essentielle**) *adjective* essential; **c'est l'essentiel** that's the main thing.

**essentiellement** *adverb* **1** mainly; **2** essentially.

**essorage** *noun Masc.* spin-dry.

**essorer** *verb* [1] to spin-dry.

**essoufflé** *adjective* out of breath.

**essuie-glace** *noun Masc.* windscreen wiper.

a
b
c
d
e
f
g
h
i
j
k
l
m
n
o
p
q
r
s
t
u
v
w
x
y
z

**essuie-tout**

a
b
c
d
**e**
f
g
h
i
j
k
l
m
n
o
p
q
r
s
t
u
v
w
x
y
z

**essuie-tout** noun Masc. (paper) kitchen towel.

**essuyer** verb [41] to wipe; **essuyer la vaisselle** to do the drying-up; **s'essuyer les mains** to dry your hands.

**est**[1] verb SEE **être**[2].

**est**[2] noun Masc. east; **l'est de Paris** the east of Paris; **dans l'est de la France** in the east of France; **l'Europe de l'Est** Eastern Europe. **est** adjective **1** east; **2** eastern.

**est-ce que** (used for asking questions) **est-ce qu'il pleut?** is it raining?; **est-ce que Julie est partie?** has Julie left?; **où est-ce qu'il habite?** where does he live?

**esthéticienne** noun Fem. beautician.

**estime** noun Fem. respect.

**estimer** verb [1] **1** to esteem; **2** to value; **3 j'estime que ...** I think that ....

**estival** (Masc. plural **estivaux**) adjective summer.

**estivant**, **estivante** noun Masc., Fem. summer visitor.

**estomac** noun Masc. stomach; **avoir mal à l'estomac** to have stomachache.

**Estonie** noun Fem. Estonia.

**estrade** noun Fem. platform.

**estragon** noun Masc. tarragon; **une sauce à l'estragon** a tarragon sauce.

**et** conjunction and.

**établir** verb [2] **1** to establish; **2 établir une liste** to draw up a list;

**3 s'établir à son compte** to set up in business.

**établissement** noun Masc. **1** institution; **établissement scolaire** school; **2** organization.

**étage** noun Masc. floor; **au premier étage** on the first floor; **au dernier étage** on the top floor; **à l'étage** upstairs.

**étagère** noun Fem. **1** shelf; **2** set of shelves.

**étain** noun Masc. **1** tin; **2** pewter.

**étalage** noun Masc. window display.

**étaler** verb [1] **1** to spread; **2** to spread out; **3** to roll out (pastry).

**étanche** adjective **1** watertight; **2** waterproof.

**étang** noun Masc. pond.

**étape** noun Fem. **1** stage; **2** stopping place.

**état** noun Masc. state, condition; **en mauvais état** in a bad state; **en bon état** in good condition; **en état de marche** in working order; **être dans tous ses états** to be in a state.

**État** noun Masc. state, State.

**États-Unis** plural noun Masc. **les États-Unis** the United States; **aux États-Unis** in (or to) the United States.

**été**[1] verb SEE **être**[2].

**été**[2] noun Masc. summer; **en été** in summer; **l'été dernier** last summer; **des vêtements d'été** summer clothes.

**éteindre** verb [60] **1** to turn off, to switch off; **éteindre la lumière** to turn out the lights; **2** to put out (*a fire or cigarette*); **3 s'éteindre** to go out.

**éteint** *adjective* extinct (*volcano*).

**étendre** *verb* [3] **1** to spread out; **2** to stretch out (*your arms or legs*); **3 étendre le linge** to hang out the washing; **4 s'étendre** to stretch; **5 s'étendre** to spread.

**éternel** (*Fem.* **éternelle**) *adjective* eternal.

**éternité** *noun Fem.* eternity.

**éternuement** *noun Masc.* sneeze.

**éternuer** *verb* [1] to sneeze.

**êtes** *verb* SEE **être**[2].

**ethnie** *noun Fem.* ethnic group.

**ethnique** *adjective* ethnic.

**étinceler** *verb* [18] to sparkle, to twinkle.

**étincelle** *noun Fem.* spark.

**étiquette** *noun Fem.* **1** label; **2** etiquette.

**étirer** *verb* [1] to stretch.

**étoffe** *noun Fem.* fabric.

**étoile** *noun Fem.* star; **une étoile filante** a shooting star.

**étonnant** *adjective* **1** surprising; **2** astonishing.

**étonnement** *noun Masc.* **1** surprise; **2** astonishment.

**étonner** *verb* [1] **1** to surprise; **ça m'a beaucoup étonné** that really surprised me; **ça ne m'étonne pas du tout** that doesn't surprise me at all; **2 s'étonner** to be surprised; **s'étonner de quelque chose** to be surprised at something.

**étouffant** *adjective* stifling.

**étouffer** *verb* [1] **1** to stifle; **2** to suffocate; **3 s'étouffer** to choke.

**étourderie** *noun Fem.* **1** absent-mindedness; **2 une étourderie** a careless mistake.

**étourdi**, **étourdie** *noun Masc., Fem.* scatterbrain. **étourdi** *adjective* scatterbrained.

**étourdir** *verb* [2] to daze, to stun.

**étourneau** *noun Masc.* starling.

**étrange** *adjective* strange.

**étranger**[1], **étrangère** *noun Masc., Fem.* **1** foreigner; **2** stranger. **étranger**, **étrangère** *adjective* foreign; **un pays étranger** a foreign country.

**étranger**[2] *noun Masc.* **à l'étranger** abroad.

**étrangler** *verb* [1] **1** to strangle; **2** to choke.

**être**[1] *noun Masc.* being; **un être humain** a human being.

**être**[2] *verb* [6] **1** to be; **nous sommes dans la cuisine** we're in the kitchen; **elle est malade** she's ill; **c'est moi** it's me; **2 elle est infirmière** she's a nurse; **3 être à quelqu'un** to belong to somebody, to be somebody's; **ce livre est à Paul** this book is Paul's; **ce livre est à moi** this book is mine; **4 il est 6 heures** it's 6 o'clock; **5 nous sommes le 7 mars** it's the 7th of March (today); **6** (*used with certain verbs to form past tenses: for a list of these, see the centre pages*) **je suis allé à Paris** I went to Paris; **nous sommes rentrés à 7 heures** we got home at 7 o'clock; **7** (*used to form the passive of verbs*) **ses robes sont**

## étroit

**faites par sa mère** her dresses are made by her mother.

**étroit** *adjective* **1** narrow; **2** close.

**étroitement** *adverb* closely.

**étude** *noun Fem.* **1** study; **2 études** studies; **faire des études de médecine** to study medicine.

**étudiant**, **étudiante** *noun Masc.*, *Fem.* student.

**étudier** *verb* [1] to study.

**étui** *noun Masc.* case.

**eu** *verb* SEE **avoir**.

**euro** *noun Masc.* euro; **l'euro est divisé en cents/centimes** the euro is divided into cents.

**Europe** *noun Fem.* Europe; **en Europe** in (*or* to) Europe.

**européen** (*Fem.* **européenne**) *adjective* European.

**euthanasie** *noun Fem.* euthanasia.

**eux** *pronoun* **1** them; **avec eux** with them; **des amis à eux** friends of theirs; **2** they.

**eux-mêmes** *pronoun* themselves.

**évacuer** *verb* [1] to evacuate; **la police a fait évacuer l'immeuble** the police evacuated the building.

**évader** *verb* [1] **s'évader** to escape.

**évaluer** *verb* [1] to assess.

**évanouir** *verb* [2] **s'évanouir** to faint.

**évaporer** *verb* [1] **s'évaporer** to evaporate.

**évasion** *noun Fem.* escape.

**éveillé** *adjective* awake.

**éveiller** *verb* [1] **1** to arouse; **2** to awaken.

**événement** *noun Masc.* event.

**éventail** *noun Masc.* fan.

**éventualité** *noun Fem.* possibility.

**éventuel** (*Fem.* **éventuelle**) *adjective* possible.

**éventuellement** *adverb* **1** possibly; **2** if necessary.

**évêque** *noun Masc.* bishop.

**évidemment** *adverb* of course.

**évidence** *noun Fem.* **être en évidence** to be clearly visible; **de toute évidence** clearly; **de toute évidence il a oublié de venir** he's clearly forgotten to come; **mettre quelque chose en évidence** to reveal something.

**évident** *adjective* obvious.

**évier** *noun Masc.* sink.

**éviter** *verb* [1] to avoid; **éviter de faire** to avoid doing; **ça t'évitera de sortir** that'll save you having to go out.

**évolué** *adjective* advanced.

**évoluer** *verb* [1] **1** to develop; **nous ne savons pas comment la situation va évoluer** we do not know how the situation will develop; **2** to progress; **l'informatique a beaucoup évolué ces dernières années** computer science has progressed a great deal in recent years; **3** to change; **les choses ont évolué depuis** things have changed since.

**évolution** *noun Fem.* **1** development; **2** progress; **3** evolution.

**exact** *adjective* **1** correct; **c'est exact** that's absolutely right; **2** exact, precise.

**exactement** *adverb* exactly.

**exagéré** *adjective* **1** exaggerated; **2** excessive.

**exagérer** *verb* [24] **1** to exaggerate; **2** to go too far.

**examen** *noun Masc.* **1** exam; **passer un examen** to sit an exam; **réussir à un examen** to pass an exam; **un examen blanc** a mock exam; **2 un examen médical** a medical examination.

**examinateur, examinatrice** *noun Masc., Fem.* examiner.

**examiner** *verb* [1] to examine.

**exaspérant** *adjective* exasperating.

**exaspérer** *verb* [24] to exasperate.

**excellence** *noun Fem.* excellence.

**excellent** *adjective* excellent.

**excentrique** *noun Masc. & Fem.*, *adjective* eccentric.

**excepté** *preposition* except.

**exception** *noun Fem.* exception; **à l'exception de** with the exception of.

**exceptionnel** (*Fem.* **exceptionnelle**) *adjective* **1** exceptional; **2** special.

**exceptionnellement** *adverb* exceptionally.

**excès** *noun Masc.* excess.

**excès de vitesse** *noun Masc.* speeding.

**excessif** (*Fem.* **excessive**) *adjective* excessive.

**excessivement** *adverb* excessively; **il est excessivement timide** he's incredibly shy.

**excitant** *noun Masc.* stimulant. **excitant** *adjective* exciting.

**excitation** *noun Fem.* excitement.

**excité** *adjective* **1** frenzied; **2** over-excited; **3** thrilled.

**exciter** *verb* [1] **s'exciter** to get excited.

**exclamation** *noun Fem.* exclamation.

**exclamer** *verb* [1] **s'exclamer** to exclaim.

**exclu** *adjective* **il n'est pas exclu que** ... it's not impossible that ....

**exclusif** (*Fem.* **exclusive**) *adjective* exclusive.

**excursion** *noun Fem.* excursion, trip.

**excuse** *noun* **1** apology; **présenter ses excuses** to apologize; **2** excuse.

**excuser** *verb* [1] **1** to forgive; **excusez-moi!** sorry!; **excusez-moi de vous déranger** sorry to disturb you; **2 s'excuser** to apologize; **je m'excuse** I'm sorry; **je m'excuse d'être en retard** sorry I'm late.

**exécuter** *verb* [1] **1** to execute; **2** to carry out.

**exemplaire** *noun Masc.* copy; **six exemplaires du dictionnaire** six copies of the dictionary.

**exemple** *noun Masc.* example; **par exemple** for example; **donner l'exemple** to set an example.

a b c d e f g h i j k l m n o p q r s t u v w x y z

a
b
c
d
**e**
f
g
h
i
j
k
l
m
n
o
p
q
r
s
t
u
v
w
x
y
z

**exercer** *verb* [61] **1** to exercise (*a right*); **2** to practise (*an art or a profession*); **3** to exert (*authority*); **4** s'exercer to practise.

**exercice** *noun Masc.* exercise; **exercices de mise en forme** fitness exercises.

**exhiber** *verb* [1] **1** to show off; **2** to display.

**exhibitionniste** *noun Masc.* flasher.

**exigeant** *adjective* hard to please.

**exiger** *verb* [52] **1** to demand; **2** to require.

**exil** *noun Masc.* exile.

**exilé**, **exilée** *noun Masc., Fem.* exile.

**existence** *noun Fem.* existence.

**exister** *verb* [1] to exist.

**exotique** *adjective* exotic.

**expansion** *noun Fem.* **1** expansion; **2** growth.

**expédier** *verb* [1] to send (off); **expédier un paquet** to send off a package.

**expéditeur**, **expéditrice** *noun Masc., Fem.* sender.

**expédition** *noun Fem.* expedition.

**expérience** *noun Fem.* **1** experience; **avoir de l'expérience** to be experienced; **2** experiment; **faire une expérience** to carry out an experiment.

**expérimenté** *adjective* experienced.

**expert** *noun Masc.* expert.

**explication** *noun Fem.* explanation.

**explicite** *adjective* explicit.

**expliquer** *verb* [1] to explain.

**exploit** *noun Masc.* **1** achievement; **2** feat.

**exploiter** *verb* [1] **1** to exploit; **2** to use, to make use of.

**explorer** *verb* [1] to explore.

**exploser** *verb* [1] to explode, to blow up.

**explosif** (*Fem.* **explosive**) *adjective* explosive.

**explosion** *noun Fem.* **1** explosion; **2** boom.

**export** *noun Masc.* export.

**exportateur**, **exportatrice** *noun Masc., Fem.* exporter.

**exportation** *noun Fem.* export.

**exporter** *verb* [1] to export; **la Russie exporte beaucoup de pétrole** Russia exports a lot of oil.

**exposé** *noun Masc.* talk; **Gaby a fait un exposé sur le Japon** Gaby gave a talk about Japan.
**exposé** *adjective* **1** exposed; **2** on display.

**exposer** *verb* [1] **1** to exhibit; **2** to expose; **3** to explain.

**exposition** *noun Fem.* **1** exhibition; **une exposition d'art africain** an exhibition of African art; **2** exposure.

**exprès** *adjective* express.
**exprès** *adverb* **1** deliberately; **tu l'as fait exprès** you did it deliberately, you did it on purpose; **il a fait exprès de le casser** he broke it on purpose; **c'est fait exprès** it's

meant to be like that; **2** specially; **je suis venu exprès pour te voir** I've come specially to see you.

**express** *noun Masc.* **1** fast train; **2** espresso coffee.

**expression** *noun Fem.* expression.

**exprimer** *verb* [1] **1** to express; **2 s'exprimer** to express yourself; **je m'exprime mal** I'm expressing myself badly.

**expulser** *verb* [1] **1** to evict; **2** to expel.

**exquis** *adjective* exquisite, delightful.

**extase** *noun Fem.* ecstasy.

**extensif** (*Fem.* **extensive**) *adjective* extensive.

**extension** *noun Fem.* extension.

**extérieur** *noun Masc.* **1** outside; **à l'extérieur** outside; **2** exterior. **extérieur** *adjective* **1** outside; **2** outer.

**externat** *noun Masc.* day school.

**externe** *noun Masc. & Fem.* day pupil.

**extincteur** *noun Masc.* fire extinguisher.

**extinction** *noun Fem.* extinction; **une espèce en voie d'extinction** an endangered species.

**extra** *adjective* (*informal*) great, fantastic; **ta sauce est vraiment extra!** your sauce is really fantastic!

**extraction** *noun Fem.* **1** extraction; **2** mining.

**extraire** *verb* [78] **1** to extract; **2** to mine.

**extrait** *noun Masc.* extract.

**extraordinaire** *adjective* extraordinary, amazing.

**extra-terrestre** *noun Masc. & Fem.* extra-terrestrial, alien (*from outer space*).

**extravagant** *adjective* **1** eccentric; **des vêtements extravagants** eccentric clothes; **2** extravagant.

**extrême** *noun Masc.*, *adjective* extreme.

**extrêmement** *adverb* extremely.

**Extrême-Orient** *noun Masc.* the Far East.

**extrémité** *noun Fem.* **1** end; **2** tip; **3** edge; **4** extreme.

# Ff

**F** SHORT FOR **francs**; **30 F** 30 francs.

**fabricant** *noun Masc.* manufacturer.

**fabrication** *noun Fem.* manufacture.

**fabriquer** *verb* [1] to make; **fabriqué en France** made in France; **qu'est-ce que tu fabriques?** (*informal*) what are you up to?

**fabuleux** (*Fem.* **fabuleuse**) *adjective* fabulous.

**fac** *noun Fem.* (*informal*) university; **être en fac d'anglais** to be doing a degree in English.

**face** *noun Fem.* **1** face; **face à face** face to face; **2 en face** opposite; **en face de l'école** opposite the school;

a
b
c
d
e
f
g
h
i
j
k
l
m
n
o
p
q
r
s
t
u
v
w
x
y
z

la maison d'en face the house opposite; le magasin en face de chez nous the shop opposite our house; 3 faire face à quelque chose to face up to something; 4 façe à facing; face au mur facing the wall; 5 pile ou face? heads or tails?

**fâché** *adjective* 1 angry; elle est fâchée contre moi she's angry with me; 2 il est fâché avec son frère he's fallen out with his brother.

**fâcher** *verb* [1] 1 se fâcher to get angry; se fâcher contre quelqu'un to get angry with somebody; elle s'est fâchée contre moi she got angry with me; 2 se fâcher avec quelqu'un to fall out with somebody.

**facile** *adjective* easy; c'est facile it's easy; c'est facile à comprendre it's easy to understand.

**facilement** *adverb* easily.

**facilité** *noun Fem.* easiness.

**faciliter** *verb* [1] to make (something) easier; ça devrait nous faciliter les choses that should make things easier for us.

**façon** *noun Fem.* 1 way; il y a plusieurs façons de le faire there are several ways of doing it; d'une façon extraordinaire in an extraordinary way; de quelle façon? in what way?; 2 de toute façon anyway.

**façonner** *verb* [1] 1 to make; 2 to shape.

**facteur**[1] *noun Masc.* factor.

**facteur**[2] *noun Masc.* postman; est-ce que le facteur est passé? has the postman been?

**factrice** *noun Fem.* postwoman.

**facture** *noun Fem.* bill; la facture d'électricité the electricity bill.

**facultatif** (*Fem.* facultative) *adjective* optional.

**faculté** *noun Fem.* faculty.

**fade** *adjective* tasteless; la sauce est un peu fade the sauce is a bit tasteless.

**faible** *noun Masc.* avoir un faible pour to have a soft spot for.
**faible** *adjective* 1 weak; elle est encore très faible she's still very weak; 2 elle est faible en chimie she's not very good at chemistry; 3 un faible bruit a faint noise.

**faiblesse** *noun Fem.* weakness.

**faiblir** *verb* [2] 1 to weaken; 2 le vent a faibli the wind's died down a bit.

**faïence** *noun Fem.* earthenware; des assiettes en faïence earthenware plates.

**faillir** *verb* [42] faillir faire to nearly do; j'ai failli tomber I nearly fell; j'ai failli rater le train I nearly missed the train.

**faillite** *noun Fem.* bankruptcy; faire faillite to go bankrupt.

**faim** *noun Fem.* hunger; avoir faim to be hungry; j'ai très faim I'm really hungry; je meurs de faim! I'm starving!; je n'ai plus faim I've had enough to eat; ces gâteaux me donnent faim those cakes make me feel hungry.

**fainéant** *adjective* lazy.

**faire** *verb* [10] **1** to make; **faire un gâteau** to make a cake; **je vais me faire un café** I'm going to make myself a coffee; **faire du bruit** to make a noise; **2** to do; **qu'est-ce que tu fais?** what are you doing?; **il est en train de faire ses devoirs** he's doing his homework; **faire du français** to do French; **fais comme tu veux** do as you like; **3** **qu'as-tu fait du couteau?** what have you done with the knife?; **4** **il fait froid** it's cold; **il fait chaud** it's hot; **5** **quel temps fait-il?** what's the weather like?; **il fait beau** it's a nice day; **il fait beau en été ici** the weather's nice here in summer; **6** **ça ne fait rien** it doesn't matter; **7** **faire faire quelque chose** to have (*or* get) something done; **elle a fait réparer son vélo** she got her bike repaired; **il s'est fait couper les cheveux** he's had his hair cut; **8** **faire chauffer de l'eau** to heat some water; **faire cuire quelque chose** to cook something; **9** **ne t'en fais pas** don't worry.

**faire-part** *noun Masc.* announcement (*of birth, marriage, or death*).

**fais** *verb* SEE **faire**.

**faisan** *noun Masc.* pheasant.

**faisons** *verb* SEE **faire**.

**fait**[1] *verb* SEE **faire**.

**fait**[2] *noun Masc.* **1** fact; **en fait** actually; **en fait je l'ai vu hier** in fact I saw him yesterday; **2** **au fait** by the way; **au fait, est-ce que tu as fermé la porte?** by the way, did you shut the door?

**fait d'actualité** *noun Masc.* news item.

**faites** *verb* SEE **faire**.

**falaise** *noun Fem.* cliff.

**fallait** *verb* SEE **falloir**.

**falloir** *impersonal verb* [43] **1** **il faut le faire** it has to be done, you must do it; **il ne faut pas faire ça** you mustn't do that; **il ne fallait pas faire ça** you shouldn't have done that; **il faudra partir à six heures** we'll have to leave at six o'clock; **2** **il me faut un stylo** I need a pen; **il leur faut une voiture** they need a car; **qu'est-ce qu'il te faut?** what do you need?; **3** **il faut que tu le fasses** (*subjunctive*) you must do it; **il faut que tu prennes tes clés** you must take your keys; **4** **comme il faut** properly; **tu ne l'as pas fait comme il faut** you haven't done it properly; **marche comme il faut!** walk properly.

**famé** *adjective* **un quartier mal famé** a rough area.

**fameux** (*Fem.* **fameuse**) *adjective* first-rate; **le repas n'était pas fameux** the meal wasn't great.

**familial** (*Masc. plural* **familiaux**) *adjective* family; **la vie familiale** family life; **les allocations familiales** child benefit.

**familiariser** *verb* [1] **se familiariser avec** to become familiar with.

**familiarité** *noun Fem.* familiarity.

a
b
c
d
e
f
g
h
i
j
k
l
m
n
o
p
q
r
s
t
u
v
w
x
y
z

**familier** (*Fem.* **familière**) *adjective* familiar; **un endroit familier** a familiar place.

**famille** *noun Fem.* **1** family; **un déjeuner en famille** a family lunch; **une famille nombreuse** a big family; **2** relatives; **j'ai de la famille à Londres** I have relatives in London.

**famille monoparentale** *noun Fem.* single-parent family.

**fanatique** *noun Masc. & Fem.* fanatic.

**faneé** *adjective* withered; **les fleurs sont fanées** the flowers are withered.

**fanfare** *noun Fem.* brass band.

**fantaisie** *noun Fem.* **1** imagination; **2 des bijoux de fantaisie** costume jewellery.

**fantaisiste** *adjective* **1** unreliable; **il est un peu fantaisiste** he's rather unreliable; **2 une idée fantaisiste** a wild idea.

**fantastique** *adjective* fantastic.

**fantôme** *noun Masc.* ghost.

**farce** *noun Fem.* **1** practical joke; **un magasin de farces et attrapes** a joke shop; **2** stuffing (*for a chicken, for example*).

**farci** *adjective* stuffed; **des tomates farcies** stuffed tomatoes.

**farcir** *verb* [2] to stuff (*a chicken, for example*).

**fard à paupières** *noun Masc.* eye shadow.

**fardeau** (*plural* **fardeaux**) *noun Masc.* burden.

**farfelu** *adjective* bizarre; **c'est un type farfelu** he's a bizarre bloke; **elle a toujours des idées farfelues** she always has crazy ideas.

**farine** *noun Fem.* **1** flour; **2** baby cereal.

**fascinant** *adjective* fascinating; **son histoire était absolument fascinante** his story was absolutely fascinating.

**fascination** *noun Fem.* fascination.

**fasciner** *verb* [1] to fascinate; **ça me fascine** I find that fascinating.

**fascisme** *noun Masc.* fascism.

**fast-food** *noun Fem.* fast food.

**fastidieux** (*Fem.* **fastidieuse**) *adjective* tedious; **c'est un travail fastidieux** it's tedious work.

**fatal** *adjective* **1** inevitable; **c'était fatal** it was bound to happen; **2** fatal.

**fatalité** *noun Fem.* fate.

**fatidique** *adjective* fateful.

**fatigant** *adjective* tiring.

**fatigue** *noun Fem.* tiredness.

**fatigué** *adjective* tired; **je suis fatigué** I'm tired; **tu as l'air fatigué** you look tired.

**fatiguer** *verb* [1] **1** to tire (somebody) out; **la promenade m'a fatigué** the walk tired me out; **2 se fatiguer** to get tired.

**faubourg** *noun Masc.* suburb.

**fauché** *adjective* (*informal*) broke; **je suis fauché cette semaine** I'm broke this week.

**faucher** *verb* [1] **1** to mow, to scythe; **2** (*informal*) to nick; **quelqu'un m'a fauché mon vélo** somebody's nicked my bike.

**faucon** *noun Masc.* falcon, hawk.

**faudra**, **faudrait** *verb* SEE **falloir**.

**faufiler** *verb* [1] **se faufiler à travers la foule** to thread your way through the crowd.

**faune** *noun Fem.* wildlife.

**fausse** *adjective* SEE **faux** [1].

**faussement** *adverb* wrongly.

**fausser** *verb* [1] **1** to distort; **2** to bend.

**faut** *verb* SEE **falloir**.

**faute** *noun Fem.* **1** mistake, error; **faire une faute** to make a mistake; **une faute d'orthographe** a spelling mistake; **2** fault; **c'est (de) ma faute** it's my fault; **c'est la faute de Sophie** it's Sophie's fault; **3 faute de** for lack of; **faute de temps** for lack of time; **faute de mieux** for want of anything better; **4 sans faute** without fail.

**fauteuil** *noun Masc.* armchair.

**fauteuil roulant** *noun Masc.* wheelchair.

**fautif** (*Fem.* **fautive**) *adjective* faulty.

**fauve** *noun Masc.* wild animal. **fauve** *adjective* tawny.

**faux** [1] (*Fem.* **fausse**) *adjective* **1** wrong; **c'est faux** it's wrong; **2** untrue; **c'est totalement faux** it's totally untrue; **3** false; **une fausse barbe** a false beard; **4** imitation; **une table en faux marbre** an imitation marble table; **5 chanter faux** to sing out of tune.

**faux** [2] *noun Masc.* fake, forgery; **cette pièce est un faux** this coin's a forgery.

**faux** [3] *noun Fem.* scythe.

**faux ami** *noun Masc.* false friend (*a word in a foreign language which looks very like a word in your own language but does not mean the same thing at all*).

**faux-filet** *noun Masc.* sirloin.

**faveur** *noun Fem.* favour; **en faveur de** in favour of.

**favorable** *adjective* favourable.

**favorablement** *adverb* favourably.

**favori** (*Fem.* **favorite**) *adjective* favourite.

**favoriser** *verb* [1] to favour.

**fax** *noun Masc.* **1** fax; **envoyer un fax** to send a fax; **2** fax machine.

**fédéral** (**fédéraux**) **fédéral** *adjective* federal.

**fédération** *noun Fem.* federation.

**fée** *noun Fem.* fairy; ★ **avoir des doigts de fée** to have nimble fingers (*literally: to have the fingers of a fairy*).

**féerique** *adjective* magical.

**feignant** *adjective* (*informal*) lazy.

**fêler** *verb* [1] **se fêler** to crack.

**félicitations** *plural noun Fem.* congratulations.

**féliciter** *verb* [1] to congratulate.

**fêlure** *noun Fem.* crack.

**femelle** *noun Fem.*, *adjective* female (*animal*).

a
b
c
d
e
f
g
h
i
j
k
l
m
n
o
p
q
r
s
t
u
v
w
x
y
z

a b c d e f g h i j k l m n o p q r s t u v w x y z

féminin *noun* Masc. **le féminin** the feminine (*in French and other grammars*); **au féminin** in the feminine.
féminin *adjective* **1** female; **le sexe féminin** the female sex; **2** feminine; **elle est très féminine** she's very feminine; **3** women's; **les vêtements féminins** women's clothing; **la presse féminine** women's magazines; **les questions féminines** women's issues.

féministe *noun* Masc. & Fem. feminist.

femme *noun* Fem. **1** woman; **c'est une femme très intéressante** she's a very interesting woman; **2** wife; **la femme de David** David's wife.

femme au foyer *noun* Fem. housewife.

femme d'affaires *noun* Fem. businesswoman.

femme de ménage *noun* Fem. cleaning lady.

fendre *verb* [3] **1** to split; **2** to crack.

fenêtre *noun* Fem. window; **regarder par la fenêtre** to look out the window; ★ **jeter l'argent par les fenêtres** to throw your money away (*literally: to throw money out of the windows*).

fenouil *noun* Masc. fennel.

fente *noun* Fem. **1** slit; **2** slot; **3** crack.

fer *noun* Masc. iron.

fer à cheval *noun* Masc. horseshoe.

fer à repasser *noun* Masc. iron (*for ironing things with*).

fer forgé *noun* Masc. wrought iron.

férié *adjective* **un jour férié** a public holiday.

ferme[1] *noun* Fem. **1** farm; **2** farmhouse.

ferme[2] *adjective* firm.

fermé *adjective* closed; **'fermé le dimanche'** closed on Sundays.

ferme d'éoliennes *noun* Fem. wind farm.

fermenter *verb* [1] to ferment.

fermer *verb* [1] **1** to close, to shut; **peux-tu fermer la porte, s'il te plaît** shut the door please; **il a fermé les yeux** he closed his eyes; **2** to turn off (*the lights, the tap, the water, etc*); **n'oublie pas de fermer les robinets** don't forget to turn off the taps; **3 se fermer** to close, to shut.

fermeture *noun* Fem. **1** closing; **heures de fermeture** closing times; **2** fastening (*on a garment*).

fermeture annuelle *noun* Fem. annual closure.

fermeture éclair *noun* Fem. zip.

fermier, **fermière** *noun* Masc., Fem. **1** farmer; **2 la fermière** the farmer's wife.
fermière *adjective* farm; **produits fermiers** farm produce; **un poulet fermier** a free-range chicken.

fermoir *noun* Masc. clasp.

féroce *adjective* **1** fierce; **2** ferocious.

ferraille *noun* Fem. scrap metal.

**ferroviaire** *adjective* rail; **le réseau ferroviaire** the rail network.

**fertile** *adjective* fertile.

**fertilité** *noun Fem.* fertility.

**fesse** *noun Fem.* buttock; **fesses** bottom.

**festin** *noun Masc.* feast.

**festival** *noun Masc.* festival.

**fête** *noun Fem.* **1** public holiday; **2** party; **faire la fête** to celebrate; **3 les fêtes de fin d'année** the festive season; **4** fête, fair; **5** saint's name day (*in France each day of the year is associated with the name of a saint and many people still celebrate the day of the saint they are named after*).

**fête des Mères** *noun Fem.* Mother's Day (*in France on the last Sunday in May*).

**fête des Pères** *noun Fem.* Father's Day.

**fête foraine** *noun Fem.* funfair.

**Fête Nationale** *noun Fem.* Bastille Day.

**fêter** *verb* [1] to celebrate.

**feu** *noun Masc.* **1** fire; **faire du feu** to light a fire; **prendre feu** to catch fire; **2** light; **as-tu du feu?** have you got a light?; **3 les feux de signalisation** the traffic lights; **un feu rouge** a red light; **4 faire cuire à feu doux** cook on a gentle heat; ★ **il n'y a pas le feu** there's no hurry (*literally: there isn't a fire*).

**feu d'artifice** *noun Masc.* **1** firework; **2** firework display.

**feuillage** *noun Masc.* leaves.

**feuille** *noun Fem.* **1** leaf; **2** une **feuille de papier** a sheet of paper.

**feuilleté** *noun Masc.* savoury pasty. **feuilleté** *adjective* **de la pâte feuilletée** puff pastry.

**feuilleter** *verb* [48] **feuilleter un livre** to leaf through a book.

**feuilleton** *noun Masc.* serial, soap (*on television*).

**feutre** *noun Masc.* **1** felt; **2 un feutre** a felt-tip pen.

**fève** *noun Fem.* broad bean.

**février** *noun Masc.* February; **en février, au mois de février** in February.

**fiable** *adjective* reliable.

**fiançailles** *plural noun Fem.* engagement (*to be married*).

**fiancé**, **fiancée** *noun Masc., Fem.* fiancé, fiancée. **fiancé** *adjective* **être fiancé à quelqu'un** to be engaged to somebody.

**fiancer** *verb* [61] **se fiancer** to get engaged.

**fibre** *noun Fem.* fibre.

**ficeler** *verb* [18] to tie up.

**ficelle** *noun Fem.* **1** string; **2** thin baguette (*of French bread*).

**fiche** *noun Fem.* **1** form; **remplir une fiche** to fill in a form; **2** index card; **3** plug.

**fiche d'inscription** *noun Fem.* registration form.

**ficher** *verb* (*informal*) [1] **1** to do; **qu'est-ce que tu fiches?** what do you think you're doing?; **2 je m'en fiche!** I don't care!; **3 fiche-moi la paix!** leave me alone!

**fichier** *noun* Masc. file.

**fichu** *adjective* (*informal*) done for; **ma voiture est fichue** my car's had it.

**fiction** *noun* Fem. fiction.

**fidèle** *adjective* 1 faithful; 2 loyal.

**fier**[1] (Fem. **fière**) *adjective* proud.

**fier**[2] *verb* [1] **se fier à** to trust.

**fierté** *noun* Fem. pride.

**fièvre** *noun* Fem. fever; **avoir de la fièvre** to have a temperature.

**figer** *verb* [52] 1 **se figer** to congeal; 2 to freeze to the spot.

**figue** *noun* Fem. fig.

**figuier** *noun* Masc. fig tree.

**figure** *noun* Fem. 1 face; 2 figure.

**figurer** *verb* [1] 1 to appear; 2 **se figurer** to imagine.

**fil** *noun* Masc. 1 thread; **du fil à coudre** sewing thread; 2 wire, flex (*of a telephone or electrical appliance*); 3 **un coup de fil** (*informal*) a phone call; **passer un coup de fil** to make a phone call; **passe-moi un coup de fil** give me a ring.

**fil de fer** *noun* Masc. wire; **fil de fer barbelé** barbed wire.

**file** *noun* Fem. 1 **une file d'attente** a queue; 2 lane (*on a road*).

**filer** *verb* [1] 1 to speed along; 2 (*informal*) to give; **elle m'a filé deux CD** she gave me two CDs (*which she didn't want any more*).

**filet** *noun* Masc. 1 net; 2 fillet; **un filet de poisson** a fish fillet.

**fille** *noun* Fem. 1 girl; **une petite fille** a little girl; **une jeune fille** a young woman; 2 daughter.

**fillette** *noun* Fem. little girl.

**filleul, filleule** *noun* Masc., Fem. godson, goddaughter.

**film** *noun* Masc. film.

**film comique** *noun* Masc. comedy (*film*).

**film d'épouvante** *noun* Masc. horror film.

**filmer** *verb* [1] to film.

**film policier** *noun* Masc. thriller.

**fils** *noun* Masc. son.

**filtre** *noun* Masc. filter.

**filtrer** *verb* [1] to filter.

**fin**[1] *noun* Fem. end; **à la fin** in the end; **à la fin du film** at the end of the film; **sans fin** endless.

**fin**[2] *adjective* 1 fine; 2 slender.

**final** (Masc. *plural* **finaux**) *adjective* final.

**finale** *noun* Fem. final, cup final.

**finalement** *adverb* 1 in the end, finally; 2 after all.

**finance** *noun* Fem. finance.

**financer** *verb* [61] to finance.

**fines herbes** *plural noun* Fem. mixed herbs.

**finir** *verb* [2] 1 to finish, to end; **le film finit à dix heures** the film finishes at ten o'clock; 2 **finir de faire** to finish doing; **j'ai fini de faire la vaisselle** I've finished doing the washing-up; 3 **finir quelque chose** to finish something; **as-tu**

**fluide**

**fini tes devoirs?** have you finished your homework?; **j'ai fini le sucre** I've finished the sugar, I've used up all the sugar; **4 finir par faire** to end up doing; **il a fini par accepter** he accepted in the end.

**finlandais** *noun Masc.* Finnish (*language*).

**finlandais** *adjective* Finnish.

**Finlande** *noun Fem.* Finland.

**firme** *noun Fem.* firm.

**fisc** *noun Masc.* tax office.

**fissure** *noun Fem.* crack.

**fixe** *adjective* **1** fixed; **2 un emploi fixe** a steady job; **3 aux heures fixes** at set times.

**fixer** *verb* [1] **1** to fix (*to attach*); **2** to set (*a date, a price*); **fixer les élections legislatives** to set the date for the general elections.

**flacon** *noun Masc.* (small) bottle.

**flamand** *noun Masc.* Flemish (*language*).

**flamand** *adjective* Flemish.

**Flamand, Flamande** *noun Masc., Fem.* Fleming (*Dutch-speaking Belgian*).

**flamant** *noun Masc.* flamingo.

**flamber** *verb* [1] to blaze.

**flamme** *noun Fem.* flame.

**flan** *noun Masc.* custard tart.

**flanc** *noun Masc.* side.

**flâner** *verb* [1] to stroll.

**flaque** *noun Fem.* **une flaque d'eau** a puddle.

**flash** *noun Masc.* **1** flash (*on a camera*); **2** newsflash.

**flatter** *verb* [1] to flatter.

**flatteur** (*Fem.* **flatteuse**) *adjective* flattering.

**flèche** *noun Fem.* **1** arrow; **2** spire.

**fléchette** *noun Fem.* dart; **jouer aux fléchettes** to play darts.

**fléchir** *verb* [2] **1** to bend; **2** to weaken.

**fleur** *noun Fem.* flower; **un tissu à fleurs** a flower-patterned fabric; **être en fleurs** to be in flower.

**fleuri** *adjective* **1** flowery; **du tissu fleuri** flowery material; **2 ton jardin est très fleuri** you've got lots of flowers in your garden.

**fleurir** *verb* [2] **1** to flower, to blossom; **2** to flourish.

**fleuriste** *noun Masc. & Fem.* florist.

**fleuve** *noun Masc.* river.

**flexible** *adjective* flexible.

**flic** *noun Masc.* (*informal*) policeman, cop.

**flipper** *noun Masc.* pinball machine.

**flirter** *verb* [1] to flirt.

**flocon** *noun Masc.* flake; **un flocon de neige** a snowflake.

**flocons d'avoine** *plural noun Masc.* porridge oats.

**floral** (*Masc. plural* **floraux**) *adjective* floral.

**flotte** *noun Fem.* fleet (*of ships*).

**flotter** *verb* [1] to float.

**flou** *adjective* **1** blurred; **une image floue** a blurred image; **2** vague; **ses projets sont un peu flous** her plans are a bit vague.

**fluide** *noun Masc., adjective* fluid.

a
b
c
d
e
**f**
g
h
i
j
k
l
m
n
o
p
q
r
s
t
u
v
w
x
y
z

**fluo** *adjective* (*informal*) fluorescent; **vert fluo** fluorescent green.

**fluor** *noun Masc.* fluorine.

**fluorescent** *adjective* fluorescent.

**flûte** *noun Fem.* flute; **jouer de la flûte** to play the flute.

**flûte à bec** *noun Fem.* recorder.

**focaliser** *verb* [1] to focus.

**foi** *noun Fem.* faith.

**foie** *noun Masc.* liver; **une crise de foie** an upset stomach.

**foin** *noun Masc.* hay.

**foire** *noun Fem.* fair.

**fois** *noun Fem.* **1** time; **une fois** once; **deux fois** twice; **trois fois** three times; **trois fois dix** three times ten; **plusieurs fois** several times; **la première fois** the first time; **trois fois plus grand** three times as big; **2 à la fois** at the same time; **trois à la fois** three at a time; **3 une fois que** once; **une fois que j'aurai pris une douche** once I've had a shower; **4 j'ai vu une fois** ... I once saw ...; **il était une fois** ... once upon a time ...; **5 à chaque fois** whenever, each time; **à chaque fois que nous sortons, nous verrouillons la porte** whenever we go out, we lock the door.

**folie** *noun Fem.* madness; **c'est de la folie!** it's crazy!

**folk** *noun Masc.* folk music.

**folle** *noun Fem.*, *adjective* SEE **fou**.

**foncer** *verb* [61] (*informal*) to rush; **tout le monde a foncé vers la porte** everybody rushed for the door.

**fonction** *noun Fem.* **1** job; **une voiture de fonction** a company car; **2** function.

**fonctionnaire** *noun Masc. & Fem.* civil servant.

**fonctionnel** (*Fem.* **fonctionnelle**) *adjective* functional.

**fonctionnement** *noun Masc.* working; **comprendre le fonctionnement de quelque chose** to understand how something works.

**fonctionner** *verb* [1] to work.

**fonction publique** *noun Fem.* civil service.

**fond** *noun Masc.* **1** bottom; **au fond du lac** at the bottom of the lake; **au fond de la bouteille** in the bottom of the bottle; **2** back; **au fond du tiroir** at the back of the drawer; **au fond de la salle** at the back of the room; **3** end; **au fond du couloir** at the end of the corridor; **4** background; **5 au fond** basically.

**fondamental** (*Masc. plural* **fondamentaux**) *adjective* basic, fundamental.

**fondateur**, **fondatrice** *noun Masc.*, *Fem.* founder.

**fondation** *noun Fem.* foundation.

**fond de teint** *noun Masc.* make-up, foundation.

**fonder** *verb* [1] **1** to found; **2** to base.

**fondre** *verb* [3] to melt.

**fondu** *adjective* melted.

**font** *verb* SEE **faire**.

**fontaine** *noun Fem.* **1** fountain; **2** drinking fountain.

**fonte** noun Fem. **1** cast iron; **une poêle en fonte** a cast iron frying pan; **2** melting (of metal); **3** thawing (of ice).

**foot** noun (informal) **un match de foot** a football match; **jouer au foot** to play football.

**football** noun Masc. football.

**footballeur** noun Masc. footballer.

**footing** noun Masc. jogging; **faire du footing** to go jogging.

**forain** noun Masc. fairground worker.
**forain** adjective **une fête foraine** a funfair.

**force** noun Fem. **1** strength; **2** force; **de force** by force; **3** force; **force de vente** sales force; **4** à **force de** by; **à force de travailler toute la nuit, elle a fini sa dissertation** she finished her essay by working all night.

**forcément** adverb **1** inevitably; **il y a forcément une solution** there has to be a solution; **2 pas forcément** not necessarily.

**forcer** verb [61] **1** to force; **2 se forcer** to force yourself.

**forêt** noun Fem. forest.

**forfait** noun Masc. fixed price.

**forgeron** noun Masc. blacksmith.

**formalité** noun Fem. formality.

**format** noun Masc. format, size.

**formation** noun Fem. training; **elle a une formation d'infirmière** she's a trained nurse.

**formation continue** noun Fem. continuing education.

**forme** noun Fem. **1** shape, form; **2 être en forme** to be on form; **se mettre en forme** to get fit; **tu as l'air en forme** you're looking well.

**formel** (Fem. **formelle**) adjective **1** positive, categorical; **2** formal.

**formellement** adverb strictly; **formellement interdit** strictly forbidden.

**former** verb [1] **1** to form; **2** to train, to educate.

**formidable** adjective (informal) great, fantastic; **le film était formidable** the film was fantastic.

**formulaire** noun Masc. form; **remplir un formulaire** to fill in a form.

**formule** noun Fem. **1** formula; **Formule Un** Formula One (car racing); **2** form; **3** format.

**fort** adjective **1** strong; **il est très fort** he's very strong; **le café est très fort** the coffee's very strong; **2 être fort en quelque chose** to be good at something; **elle est très forte en maths** she's very good at maths; **3** stout.
**fort** adverb **1** extremely; **c'était fort bon** it was extremely good; **2** hard; **frapper fort** to knock (or hit) hard; **3** loudly; **chanter fort** to sing loudly; **parle plus fort** speak louder.

**forteresse** noun Fem. fortress.

**fortifiant** noun Masc. tonic.

**fortifier** verb [1] **1** to strengthen; **2** to fortify.

**fortuit** adjective accidental.

**fortune** noun Fem. **1** fortune; **faire fortune** to make a fortune; **2 de**

**fortune** makeshift; **un lit de fortune** a makeshift bed.

**fossé** *noun Masc.* ditch.

**fossette** *noun Fem.* dimple.

**fou, folle** *noun Masc., Fem.* madman, madwoman; **un fou m'a doublé dans un virage** a madman overtook me on a bend.
**fou** (*Fem.* **folle**) *adjective* **1** mad; **devenir fou** to go mad; **2** crazy, amazing; **on a passé une soirée folle** we had an amazing evening; **il y avait un monde fou** there were masses of people; **3 être fou de** to be mad about; ★ **attraper un fou rire** to get the giggles.

**foudre** *noun Fem.* lightning; **être frappé par la foudre** to be struck by lightning.

**fouet** *noun Masc.* **1** whip; **2** whisk (*for eggs, cream, etc*).

**fouetter** *verb* [1] **1** to whip; **2** to whisk (*eggs, cream, etc*); ★ **avoir d'autres chats à fouetter** to have other fish to fry (*literally: to have other cats to whip*).

**fougère** *noun Fem.* **1** fern; **2** bracken.

**fouille** *noun Fem.* search.

**fouiller** *verb* [1] **1** to search; **fouiller quelqu'un** to search somebody; **la police a fouillé la chambre/la maison** the police searched the room/house; **2 fouiller dans quelque chose** to rummage through something.

**fouillis** *noun Masc.* mess.

**foulard** *noun Masc.* scarf.

**foule** *noun Fem.* **1** crowd; **2 une foule de** masses of.

**four** *noun Masc.* oven; **cuit au four** roasted, baked.

**four à micro-ondes** *noun Masc.* microwave oven.

**fourche** *noun Fem.* garden fork, pitchfork.

**fourchette** *noun Fem.* fork.

**fourgon** *noun Masc.* van.

**fourgonnette** *noun Fem.* (small) van.

**fourmi** *noun Fem.* ant; ★ **avoir des fourmis dans les jambes** to have pins and needles in your legs (*literally: to have ants in your legs*).

**fourmiller** *verb* [1] **fourmiller de** to be swarming with.

**fourneau** (*plural* **fourneaux**) *noun Masc.* stove.

**fournée** *noun Fem.* batch (*of cakes, bread*).

**fournir** *verb* [2] to supply.

**fournisseur** *noun Masc.* supplier.

**fournitures** *plural noun Fem.* stationery; **les fournitures de bureau** office stationery; **les fournitures scolaires** school equipment (*stationery, school bags etc*).

**fourré** *adjective* **1** filled; **fourré au chocolat** with a chocolate filling; **2** fur-lined.

**fourrure** *noun Fem.* **1** fur; **2** fur coat.

**foyer** *noun Masc.* **1** home; **rester au foyer** to stay at home (*rather than going out to work*); **une femme au foyer** a housewife; **2** hearth; **3** household; **4** hostel.

**fracas** *noun Masc.* crash.

**fracasser** *verb* [1] to smash.

**fraction** *noun Fem.* fraction.

**fracture** *noun Fem.* fracture.

**fracturer** *verb* [1] **1** to break open; **2** to fracture.

**fragile** *adjective* **1** fragile; **2** frail.

**fragment** *noun Masc.* fragment.

**fraîche** *adjective* SEE **frais**².

**fraîcheur** *noun Fem.* **1** coolness; **2** freshness.

**frais**¹ *plural noun Masc.* **1** expenses; **les frais de déplacement** travel expenses; **2** costs.

**frais**² (*Fem.* **fraîche**) *adjective* **1** cool, cold; **il fait frais ce matin** it's a chilly morning; **2** cool; **'boissons fraîches'** 'cool drinks'; **servir frais** serve chilled; **conserver au frais** keep in a cool place; **3** fresh; **des légumes frais** fresh vegetables; **'peinture fraîche'** 'wet paint'.

**fraise** *noun Fem.* strawberry; **une glace à la fraise** a strawberry ice cream.

**framboise** *noun Fem.* raspberry; **un yaourt à la framboise** a raspberry yoghurt.

**franc**¹ *noun Masc.* franc (*the currency of Switzerland; name of the currencies used in France, Belgium and Luxembourg until replaced by the euro; 100 French francs = 15.24 euros*).

**franc**² (*Fem.* **franche**) *adjective* frank.

**français** *noun Masc.* French; **j'apprends le français** I'm learning French; **Laura parle français** Laura speaks French.

**français** *adjective* French; **un film français** a French film.

**Français, Française** *noun Masc., Fem.* Frenchman, Frenchwoman; **les Français** the French.

**France** *noun Fem.* France; **aller en France** to go to France; **habiter en France** to live in France.

**franche** *adjective* SEE **franc**².

**franchement** *adverb* **1** frankly; **franchement, je ne le crois pas** frankly, I don't believe him; **2** really; **le film était franchement nul** the film was really awful.

**franchir** *verb* [2] to cross.

**franchise** *noun Fem.* **1** frankness, honesty; **2** franchise.

**francophone** *adjective* French-speaking.

**frange** *noun Fem.* fringe.

**frangin** *noun Masc.* (*informal*) brother.

**frangine** *noun Fem.* (*informal*) sister.

**frangipane** *noun Fem.* almond cream.

**franglais** *noun Masc.* Franglais (*a mixture of French and English*).

**frapper** *verb* [1] **1** to hit; **2 frapper à la porte** to knock on the door; **3** to strike; **être frappé par** to be struck by; **ça m'a beaucoup frappé** that made a big impression on me; **4 frappé par le chômage** hit by unemployment.

**fraude** *noun Fem.* **1** fraud; **2** cheating.

a
b
c
d
e
f
g
h
i
j
k
l
m
n
o
p
q
r
s
t
u
v
w
x
y
z

**fredonner** *verb* [1] to hum.

**freezer** *noun Masc.* freezer compartment (*in a fridge*).

**frein** *noun Masc.* brake; **les freins** the brakes; **le frein à main** the handbrake.

**freiner** *verb* [1] **1** to brake; **2** to slow down.

**frêle** *adjective* frail.

**frelon** *noun Masc.* hornet.

**frémir** *verb* [2] **1** to shudder; **2** to tremble.

**frêne** *noun Masc.* ash tree.

**fréquemment** *adverb* frequently.

**fréquence** *noun Fem.* frequency.

**fréquenté** *adjective* **1** busy; **un restaurant très fréquenté** a very busy restaurant; **2 un quartier mal fréquenté** a rough area.

**fréquenter** *verb* [1] **1** to go around with (*people*); **2** to go often to (*a place*).

**frère** *noun Masc.* brother.

**fric** *noun Masc.* (*informal*) money.

**frictionner** *verb* [1] to rub.

**frigidaire™** *noun Masc.* fridge.

**frigo** *noun Masc.* (*informal*) fridge; **au frigo** in the fridge.

**frileux** (*Fem.* **frileuse**) *adjective* **être frileux** to feel the cold; **je ne suis pas frileuse** I don't feel the cold.

**frime** *noun Fem.* (*informal*) **c'est de la frime!** it's all show!

**fringues** *plural noun Fem.* (*informal*) clothes.

**fripé** *adjective* crumpled.

**frire** *verb* [74] **faire frire quelque chose** to fry something.

**frisé** *adjective* **1** curly; **2** curly-haired.

**frisée** *noun Fem.* curly endive, frisée (*a sort of lettuce*).

**friser** *verb* [1] to curl.

**frisson** *noun Masc.* shiver.

**frissonner** *verb* [1] **1** to shiver; **2** to shudder.

**frit** *adjective* fried.

**frite** *noun Fem.* chip, French fry; **steak frites** steak and chips.

**friture** *noun Fem.* **friture de poissons** fried fish.

**froid** *noun Masc.* **1 le froid** the cold; **2 avoir froid** to be cold; **j'ai froid** I'm cold; **3 il fait froid aujourd'hui** it's cold today; **4 prendre froid** to catch a chill.
**froid** *adjective* cold; **tes mains sont froides** your hands are cold.

**froidement** *adverb* coldly.

**froideur** *noun Fem.* coldness.

**froisser** *verb* [1] **1** to crease; **2 se froisser** to crease; **la soie se froisse facilement** silk crushes easily; **3 se froisser** to take offence; **4 se froisser** to strain (*a muscle*).

**frôler** *verb* [1] to brush against.

**fromage** *noun Masc.* cheese.

**fromagerie** *noun Fem.* cheese shop.

**froment** *noun Masc.* wheat.

**froncer** *verb* [61] **froncer les sourcils** to frown.

**front** *noun Masc.* **1** forehead; **2** **faire front à** to face up to.

**frontière** *noun Fem.* border; **nous avons passé la frontière à Bâle** we crossed the border at Basle.

**frotter** *verb* [1] to rub; **se frotter les yeux** to rub your eyes.

**fruit** *noun Masc.* **les fruits** fruit; **acheter des fruits** to buy some fruit; **un fruit** a piece of fruit; **veux-tu un fruit?** would you like some fruit?

**fruité** *adjective* fruity.

**fruits de mer** *plural noun Masc.* seafood; **une omelette aux fruits de mer** a seafood omelette.

**frustrant** *adjective* frustrating.

**frustrer** *verb* [1] **1** to thwart; **2** to frustrate.

**fugue** *noun Fem.* **1** **faire une fugue** to run away; **2** fugue.

**fuir** *verb* [44] **1** to run away, to flee; **2** **fuir quelque chose** to run away from something; **3** to leak; **la bouilloire fuit** the kettle's leaking.

**fuite** *noun Fem.* **1** flight; **2** **prendre la fuite** to flee; **3** leak.

**fulgurant** *adjective* dazzling.

**fumé** *adjective* smoked; **du saumon fumé** smoked salmon.

**fumée** *noun Fem.* smoke; ★ **il n'y a pas de fumée sans feu** there's no smoke without fire.

**fumer** *verb* [1] **1** to smoke; **2** **fumer une cigarette** to smoke a cigarette; **il fume la pipe** he smokes a pipe; ★ **fumer comme un pompier** to smoke like a chimney (*literally: to smoke like a fireman*).

**fumeur, fumeuse** *noun Masc., Fem.* smoker; **zone non-fumeur** no-smoking area.

**fumier** *noun Masc.* manure.

**funambule** *noun Masc. & Fem.* tightrope walker.

**funèbre** *adjective* **1** funeral; **pompes funèbres** undertaker's; **2** gloomy.

**funérailles** *plural noun Fem.* funeral.

**funiculaire** *noun Masc.* funicular.

**fur** *noun Masc.* **1** **au fur et à mesure** as you go along; **je corrige les erreurs au fur et à mesure** I correct the mistakes as I go along; **2** **au fur et à mesure que** as.

**furet** *noun Masc.* ferret.

**fureur** *noun Fem.* **1** rage, fury; **2** frenzy; ★ **faire fureur** to be all the rage; **ces boucles d'oreilles font fureur en ce moment** these earrings are all the rage at the moment.

**furibond** *adjective* furious.

**furieusement** *adverb* furiously.

**furieux** (*Fem.* **furieuse**) *adjective* furious; **elle est furieuse contre son copain** she's furious with her boyfriend.

**furoncle** *noun Masc.* boil.

**fusain** *noun Masc.* charcoal (*for drawing*).

**fuseau** *noun Masc.* ski pants.

**fusée** *noun Fem.* rocket.

**fusible** *noun Masc.* fuse.

**fusil** *noun Masc.* gun.

**fusiller** *verb* [1] to shoot.

a
b
c
d
e

g
h
i
j
k
l
m
n
o
p
q
r
s
t
u
v
w
x
y
z

a

**fusionner** *verb* [1] to merge.

**fût** *noun Masc.* cask, barrel.

b

**futé** *adjective* **1** crafty; **2** bright, clever.

c

d

**futur** *noun Masc.* future (*tense*).
**futur** *adjective* future; **son futur mari** her husband-to-be.

e

# Gg

g

h

**gâcher** *verb* [1] **1** to waste; **gâcher la nourriture** to waste food; **2** to spoil; **ça m'a gâché la journée!** that's spoiled my day!

i

j

k

**gâchis** *noun Masc.* waste.

l

**gadget** *noun Masc.* gadget.

**gaffe** *noun Fem.* (*informal*) blunder; **j'ai fait une gaffe** I've done something stupid; ★ **fais gaffe!** watch out!.

m

n

o

**gage** *noun Masc.* forfeit (*in a game*).

**gagnant**, **gagnante** *noun Masc., Fem.* winner.

p

**gagnant** *adjective* winning.

q

**gagner** *verb* [1] **1** to win; **il a gagné** he's won; **gagner le match** to win the match; **2** to earn (*money*); **elle gagne bien sa vie** she makes a good living; **3 gagner du temps** to save time.

r

s

t

u

**gai** *adjective* cheerful.

v

**gaieté** *noun Fem.* cheerfulness.

**gain** *noun Masc.* **1** earnings; **2 c'est un gain de temps** it saves time.

w

x

**galaxie** *noun Fem.* galaxy.

**galerie** *noun Fem.* gallery.

y

**galerie marchande** *noun Fem.* shopping arcade.

z

**galet** *noun Masc.* pebble.

**galette** *noun Fem.* **1** biscuit; **2** round flat cake or loaf.

**galette des Rois** *noun Fem.* Twelfth Night cake (*a cake eaten on Twelfth Night; it contains a 'fève', literally a bean, but usually a small ceramic figure; the person who gets this is the king or queen and is given a cardboard crown to wear*).

**galipette** *noun Fem.* somersault (*child's*).

**Galles** *noun* **le pays de Galles** Wales.

**Gallois, Galloise** *noun Masc., Fem.* Welshman, Welshwoman; **les Gallois** the Welsh.

**gallois** *noun Masc.* Welsh (*language*).
**gallois** *adjective* Welsh.

**galoper** *verb* [1] to galop.

**gamba** *noun Fem.* king prawn.

**gamin, gamine** *noun Masc., Fem.* (*informal*) kid; **elle a trois gamins** she has three kids.

**gamme** *noun Fem.* **1** range; **la nouvelle gamme de produits de beauté** the new range of beauty products; **2** scale (*in music*).

**gammé** *adjective* **la croix gammée** the swastika.

**gangster** *noun Masc.* gangster.

**gant** *noun Masc.* glove.

**gant de boxe** *noun Masc.* boxing glove.

**gant de ménage** *noun Masc.* rubber glove.

**gant de toilette** *noun Masc.* facecloth.

**garage** *noun Masc.* garage.

**garagiste** *noun Masc. & Fem.*
1 garage owner; 2 motor mechanic.

**garantie** *noun Fem.* guarantee.

**garantir** *verb* [2] to guarantee.

**garçon** *noun Masc.* 1 boy; 2 young
man; **un brave garçon** a nice chap;
3 waiter; 4 **un vieux garçon** a
bachelor.

**garçon de café** *noun Masc.*
waiter (*in a cafe*).

**garde** *noun Masc. & Fem.* 1 guard;
2 nurse; 3 **être de garde** to be on
duty; **la pharmacie de garde** the
duty chemist's; **mettre quelqu'un
en garde** to warn somebody;
★ **prends garde!** watch out, be
careful!

**garder** *verb* [1] 1 to keep; **est-ce
que tu peux garder mon sac?** can
you keep my bag for me?; **je t'ai
gardé du gâteau** I've kept you some
cake; **je t'ai gardé une place** I've
kept you a seat; 2 to keep on; **elle a
gardé son manteau** she kept her
coat on; 3 to look after; **je garde
mon petit-fils ce soir** I'm looking
after my grandson this evening;
4 **garder la maison** to guard the
house.

**garderie** *noun Fem.* day nursery.

**garde-robe** *noun Fem.* wardrobe.

**gardien, gardienne** *noun Masc.,
Fem.* 1 security guard; 2 caretaker;
3 attendant (*in a car park or
museum*).

**gardien de but** *noun Masc.*
goalkeeper.

**gardien de la paix** *noun Masc.*
policeman.

**gare** *noun Fem.* (railway) station.

**garer** *verb* [1] 1 **garer une voiture**
to park a car; 2 **se garer** to park.

**gare routière** *noun Fem.* coach
station.

**garni** *adjective* **bien garni** full, well-
stocked.

**garnir** *verb* [2] 1 to decorate; 2 to
stock (*shelves, fridge*).

**garniture** *noun Fem.* 1 side-dish;
2 filling (*for sandwich*); 3 topping
(*for pizza*); 4 trimming, decoration.

**gars** *noun Masc.* (*informal*) guy.

**Gascogne** *noun Fem.* Gascony.

**gasoil** *noun Masc.* diesel (oil).

**gaspiller** *verb* [1] to waste.

**gastronome** *noun Masc. & Fem.*
gourmet.

**gastronomie** *noun Fem.*
gastronomy.

**gâteau** (*plural* **gâteaux**) *noun
Masc.* cake; **un gâteau au chocolat** a
chocolate cake.

**gâter** *verb* [1] 1 to spoil; 2 **se gâter**
to go bad; **la viande se gâte** the
meat is going bad; **le temps se gâte**
the weather's breaking.

**gauche** *noun Fem.* 1 left; **à gauche**
on the left; **les Anglais conduisent
à gauche** the English drive on the
left; **tournez à gauche** turn left; **à
ma gauche** on my left; 2 **la gauche**
the Left (*in politics*); **des idées de
gauche** left-wing ideas.
**gauche** *adjective* left, left-hand; **sa
main gauche** his left hand.

**gaucher** (*Fem.* **gauchère**) *adjective*
left-handed.

**gaufre**

FRENCH-ENGLISH

a

**gaufre** *noun Fem.* waffle.

**gaufrette** *noun Fem.* wafer.

b

**gaz** *noun Masc.* gas; **le chauffage à gaz** gas central heating; **nous nous chauffons au gaz** we have gas heating.

c

d

e

**gazeux** (*Fem.* **gazeuse**) *adjective* fizzy; **eau gazeuse** fizzy mineral water.

f

**gazole** *noun Masc.* diesel (oil).

g

**gazon** *noun Masc.* grass, lawn.

**géant, géante** *noun Masc., Fem.* giant.

h

**géant** *adjective* huge.

i

**gel** *noun Masc.* **1** frost; **2 le gel des prix** the price freeze; **3** gel.

j

k

**gelé** *adjective* frozen.

l

**gelée** *noun Fem.* **1** jelly; **œuf en gelée** egg in aspic; **2** frost.

m

**geler** *verb* [45] to freeze; **il gèle dehors** it's freezing outside.

n

**gélule** *noun Fem.* capsule.

o

**Gémeaux** *plural noun Masc.* Gemini (*sign of the Zodiac*).

p

q

**gémir** *verb* [2] to moan.

r

**gênant** *adjective* **1** annoying; **ce bruit est très gênant** that noise is very annoying; **2** awkward; **c'est une situation gênante** it's an awkward situation.

s

t

**gencive** *noun Fem.* gum (*part of your mouth*).

u

v

**gendarme** *noun Masc.* policeman.

w

**gendarmerie** *noun Fem.* police station.

x

**gendarmerie nationale** *noun Fem.* (French) national police force.

y

z

**gendre** *noun Masc.* son-in-law.

**gêne** *noun Fem.* **1** embarrassment; **2** inconvenience; **3** discomfort.

**gêné** *adjective* embarrassed.

**gêner** *verb* [1] **1** to bother; **est-ce que mon sac vous gêne?** is my bag in your way?; **2** to embarrass; **3** to block (*traffic*); **ta voiture gêne** your car's in the way.

**général** (*plural* **généraux**) *noun Masc.* general; **le général Dubois** General Dubois.
**général** (*Masc. plural* **gènèraux**) *adjective* general; **en général** in general, generally; **de façon générale** generally.

**généralement** *adverb* generally.

**génération** *noun Fem.* generation.

**généreux** (*Fem.* **généreuse**) *adjective* generous.

**générique** *noun Masc.* (film) credits.

**générosité** *noun Fem.* generosity.

**genêt** *noun Masc.* broom (*the bush*).

**génétique** *noun Fem.* genetics.

**Genève** *noun* Geneva.

**génial** (*Masc. plural* **géniaux**) *adjective* **1** brilliant; **une idée géniale** a brilliant idea; **2** (*informal*) great; **c'était génial!** it was great!.

**génie** *noun Masc.* **1** genius; **2** engineering.

**genou** (*plural* **genoux**) *noun Masc.* knee; **avoir mal au genou** to have a sore knee; **être à genoux** to be kneeling; **se mettre à genoux** to kneel down; **sur mes genoux** on my lap.

136

**genre** *noun Masc.* kind; **un genre de sauce épicée** a kind of spicy sauce; **un peu dans le genre de ton pull** a bit like your sweater.

**gens** *plural noun Masc.* people; **beaucoup de gens** lots of people; **les gens disent que** ... people say that ....

**gentil** (*Fem.* **gentille**) *adjective* **1** kind, nice; **elle est très gentille** she's really nice; **2** kind; **c'est très gentil de ta part** it's very kind of you; **3** good; **sois gentil et mange ta viande** be a good boy and eat up your meat.

**gentillesse** *noun Fem.* kindness.

**gentiment** *adverb* **1** nicely; **demande gentiment** ask nicely; **2** kindly.

**géographie** *noun Fem.* geography.

**géologie** *noun Fem.* geology.

**géométrie** *noun Fem.* geometry.

**gérant**, **gérante** *noun Masc., Fem.* manager, manageress.

**gérer** *verb* [24] to manage, to run.

**germain** *adjective* **un cousin germain** a first cousin.

**gésier** *noun Masc.* gizzard.

**geste** *noun Masc.* gesture.

**gestion** *noun Fem.* management; **gestion de fichiers** file management (*on a computer*).

**gibier** *noun Masc.* game (*for example, venison, pheasant*).

**gifle** *noun Fem.* slap (*in the face*).

**gifler** *verb* [1] to slap (*in the face*).

**gigantesque** *adjective* huge, gigantic; **un repas gigantesque** a huge meal.

**gigaoctet** *noun Masc.* gigabyte; **un disque dur de 20 gigaoctets** a twenty gigabyte hard disk.

**gigot** *noun Masc.* leg of lamb.

**gilet** *noun Masc.* **1** cardigan; **2** waistcoat.

**gilet de sauvetage** *noun Masc.* life-jacket.

**gingembre** *noun Masc.* ginger.

**girafe** *noun Fem.* giraffe.

**gitan**, **gitane** *noun Masc., Fem.* gipsy.

**gîte (rural)** *noun Masc.* holiday house.

**glaçage** *noun Masc.* **1** glazing; **2** icing.

**glace** *noun Fem.* **1** ice cream; **une glace au chocolat** a chocolate ice cream; **2** ice; **3** mirror; **se regarder dans la glace** to look at yourself in the mirror; **4** window (*in a car*).

**glacé** *adjective* **1** icy cold; **j'ai les mains glacées** my hands are freezing; **2** **un thé glacé** an iced tea.

**glacier** *noun Masc.* glacier.

**glacière** *noun Fem.* cool-box.

**glaçon** *noun Masc.* ice cube.

**glissant** *adjective* slippery.

**glisser** *verb* [1] to slip, to slide; **attention, ça glisse!** be careful, it's slippery!

**global** (*Masc. plural* **globaux**) *adjective* total.

**globalisation** *noun Fem.* globalization.

**gloire** *noun Fem.* fame, glory.

**glorieux** (*Fem.* **glorieuse**) *adjective* glorious.

**glossaire** *noun Masc.* glossary.

**gobelet** *noun Masc.* cup, tumbler; **un gobelet en carton** a paper cup.

**godasse** *noun Fem.* (*informal*) shoe.

**gogo** (*informal*) **à gogo** as much as you like; **pizza à gogo** as much pizza as you can eat.

**golden** *noun Fem.* Golden Delicious (apple).

**golf** *noun Masc.* **1** golf; **jouer au golf** to play golf; **2** golf course.

**golfe** *noun Masc.* gulf.

**golfeur**, **golfeuse** *noun Masc., Fem.* golfer.

**gomme** *noun Fem.* rubber.

**gommer** *verb* [1] to rub out.

**gonfler** *verb* [1] **1** to pump up (*tyres*); **2** to blow up (*a balloon*).

**gorge** *noun Fem.* **1** throat; **j'ai mal à la gorge** I've got a sore throat; **j'avais la gorge serrée** I had a lump in my throat; **il chantait à pleine gorge** he was singing at the top of his voice; **2** gorge.

**gorgée** *noun Fem.* sip; **une gorgée de thé** a sip of tea.

**gorille** *noun Masc.* gorilla.

**gosse** *noun Masc. & Fem.* kid.

**goudron** *noun Masc.* tar.

**gourde** *noun Fem.* water bottle.

**gourmand** *adjective* greedy.

**gourmandise** *noun Fem.* **1** greed; **2 elle aime les gourmandises** she likes sweet things.

**gousse** *noun Fem.* **une gousse d'ail** a clove of garlic.

**goût** *noun Masc.* taste; **ça a un goût bizarre** it has a strange taste; **de bon goût** in good taste; ★ **chacun ses goûts** it takes all sorts to make a world.

**goûter** *noun Masc.* **1** teatime snack; **2** children's party.
**goûter** *verb* [1] **1** to taste, to try; **est-ce que tu as goûté le gâteau?** have you tried the cake?; **2** to have a teatime snack.

**goutte** *noun Fem.* drop; **une goutte de** a drop of; **goutte à goutte** drop by drop.

**gouvernement** *noun Masc.* government.

**gouverner** *verb* [1] to govern, to rule.

**grâce** *noun Fem.* **grâce à** thanks to; **la soirée a été un grand succès grâce à toi** the evening was a great success thanks to you.

**gracieux** (*Fem.* **gracieuse**) *adjective* graceful.

**grade** *noun Masc.* rank; **monter en grade** to be promoted.

**gradins** *plural noun Masc.* terraces (*in a stadium*).

**graduel** (*Fem.* **graduelle**) *adjective* gradual.

**graffiti** *plural noun Masc.* graffiti.

**grain** *noun Masc.* **1** grain; **un grain de sable** a grain of sand; **2 du poivre en grains** peppercorns; **3 du**

**café en grains** coffee beans; **4 un grain de beauté** a beauty spot; **5 un grain de raisin** a grape.

**graine** *noun Fem.* seed.

**graisse** *noun Fem.* fat, grease.

**grammaire** *noun Fem.* grammar.

**gramme** *noun Masc.* gramme.

**grand** *adjective* **1** big; **une grande maison** a big house; **c'est ma grande sœur** she's my big sister; **2** tall; **un grand arbre** a tall tree; **ton frère est très grand** your brother's very tall; **elle est plus grande que moi** she's taller than me; **3** great; **un grand artiste** a great artist; **un grand ami** a great friend; **4** main; **les grandes lignes** main (railway) lines.

**grand** *adverb* wide; **la porte était grande ouverte** the door was wide open.

**grand bassin** *noun Masc.* main pool (*for experienced swimmers*).

**grand-chose** *pronoun* much; **pas grand-chose** not much; **il ne reste pas grand-chose** there's not much left.

**Grande-Bretagne** *noun Fem.* Great Britain.

**grande personne** *noun Fem.* grown-up.

**grande surface** *noun Fem.* hypermarket.

**grandes vacances** *plural noun Fem.* summer holidays.

**grandeur** *noun Fem.* size; **grandeur nature** life-size.

**grandir** *verb* [2] to grow, to grow up.

**grand magasin** *noun Masc.* department store.

**grand-mère** (*plural* **grands-mères**) *noun Fem.* grandmother.

**grand-père** (*plural* **grands-pères**) *noun Masc.* grandfather.

**grands espaces** *plural noun Masc.* open spaces.

**grands-parents** *plural noun Masc.* grandparents.

**grange** *noun Fem.* barn.

**graphiste** *noun Masc. & Fem.* graphic designer.

**grappe** *noun Fem.* **une grappe de raisin** a bunch of grapes.

**gras** (*Fem.* **grasse**) *adjective* **1** fatty, greasy; **40% matière grasse** 40% fat (*on cheese or yoghurt label*); **2 une peau grasse** oily skin; ★ **faire la grasse matinée** to have a lie-in.

**gratitude** *noun Fem.* gratitude.

**gratte-ciel** *noun Masc.* skyscraper.

**gratter** *verb* [1] **1 gratter quelque chose** to scratch something; **2 se gratter** to scratch (yourself); **3** to itch; **ça gratte** it itches.

**gratuit** *adjective* free; **le concert est gratuit** the concert's free; **'entrée gratuite'** 'admission free'.

**grave** *adjective* **1** serious; **un grave accident** a serious accident; **2 ce n'est pas grave** it doesn't matter; **3** serious; **une expression grave** a serious expression; **4** deep; **une voix grave** a deep voice.

**gravement** *adverb* seriously; **elle est gravement malade** she's seriously ill.

**gravure** *noun Fem.* engraving, print.

a
b
c
d
e
f
g
h
i
j
k
l
m
n
o
p
q
r
s
t
u
v
w
x
y
z

**a**

**gré** *noun Masc.* **contre son gré** against his will.

**b**

**grec** *noun Masc.* Greek (*language*).
**grec** (*Fem.* **grecque**) *adjective* Greek.

**c**

**d**

**Grec**, **Grecque** *noun Masc., Fem.* Greek (person).

**e**

**Grèce** *noun Fem.* Greece.

**f**

**grêle** *noun Fem.* hail.

**g**

**grelotter** *verb* [1] to shiver.

**h**

**grenade** *noun Fem.* **1** grenade; **2** pomegranate.

**i**

**grenadine** *noun Fem.* grenadine (*pomegranate cordial*).

**j**

**k**

**grenier** *noun Masc.* attic, loft; **au grenier** in the attic.

**l**

**grenouille** *noun Fem.* frog; **les cuisses de grenouille** frogs' legs.

**m**

**n**

**grève** *noun Fem.* strike; **une grève des trains** a train strike; **le métro est en grève** the underground's on strike; **faire grève** to go (*or* be) on strike.

**o**

**p**

**gréviste** *noun Masc. & Fem.* striker.

**q**

**grièvement** *adverb* seriously; **grièvement blessé** seriously injured.

**r**

**s**

**griffe** *noun Fem.* claw.

**t**

**griffonner** *verb* [1] to scribble.

**grillade** *noun Fem.* grilled meat, meat for grilling; **une grillade de porc** a pork steak.

**u**

**v**

**grillage** *noun Masc.* wire netting.

**w**

**grille** *noun Fem.* **1** metal gate; **2** railings; **3** wire fence.

**x**

**y**

**grillé** *adjective* **1** grilled; **2** toasted; **du pain grillé** toast.

**z**

**grille-pain** *noun Masc.* toaster.

**griller** *verb* [1] **1** to grill; **2** to toast.

**grillon** *noun Masc.* cricket (*the creature not the game*).

**grimace** *noun Fem.* **faire des grimaces** to make faces.

**grimper** *verb* [1] to climb; **grimper dans un arbre** to climb a tree.

**grincer** *verb* [61] to creak, to squeak.

**grincheux** (*Fem.* **grincheuse**) *adjective* grumpy.

**grippe** *noun Fem.* flu; **avoir la grippe** to have flu; **une grippe intestinale** gastric flu.

**gris** *adjective* grey.

**grisaille** *noun Fem.* dull overcast weather.

**grogner** *verb* [1] **1** to growl; **2** to grumble.

**gronder** *verb* [1] **1** **gronder quelqu'un** to tell somebody off; **se faire gronder** to get a telling-off; **2** to rumble (*thunder, for example*).

**gros** (*Fem.* **grosse**) *adjective* **1** big; **un gros morceau** a big piece; **un gros problème** a big problem; **2** fat; **un gros monsieur** a fat man; **3** **un gros rhume** a bad cold; **4** **un gros fumeur** a heavy smoker; **5** **un gros mot** a swear word; **6** **en gros** roughly.

**groseille** *noun Fem.* redcurrant.

**groseille à maquereau** *noun Fem.* gooseberry.

**grosse** *adjective* SEE **gros**.

**grossesse** *noun Fem.* pregnancy.

**grosseur** *noun Fem.* **1** lump; **2** size.

**grossier** (*Fem.* **grossière**) *adjective* **1** rude; **2** crude; **une idée grossière de** a rough idea of; **une erreur grossière** a bad mistake.

**grossir** *verb* [2] to put on weight; **il a beaucoup grossi** he's put on a lot of weight.

**grosso modo** *adverb* roughly.

**grotesque** *adjective* ridiculous.

**grotte** *noun Fem.* cave.

**groupe** *noun Masc.* group; **travailler/voyager en groupe** to work/travel in a group.

**grouper** *verb* [1] **1** to group; **2 se grouper** to gather, to form a group.

**groupe sanguin** *noun Masc.* blood group.

**grue** *noun Fem.* crane.

**guépard** *noun Masc.* cheetah.

**guêpe** *noun Fem.* wasp.

**guère** *adverb* **ne ...guère** hardly; **je ne l'ai guère vu depuis Noël** I've hardly seen him since Christmas.

**guérir** *verb* [2] **1** to cure; **le médecin l'a guéri** the doctor cured him; **2** to get better; **j'ai été malade mais je suis maintenant guéri** I've been ill but I'm better now.

**guérison** *noun Fem.* recovery (*from an illness or injury*).

**guerre** *noun Fem.* war; **le pays est actuellement en guerre** the country is at war at the moment; **la Seconde Guerre mondiale** World War II.

**guetter** *verb* [1] to watch out for.

**gueule** *noun Fem.* mouth (*of an animal; considered rude if used of a person*); **(ferme) ta gueule!** (*rude*) shut up!

**gueule de bois** *noun Fem.* (*informal*) **avoir la gueule de bois** to have a hangover.

**gueuler** *verb* [1] (*informal*) to yell.

**gui** *noun Masc.* mistletoe.

**guichet** *noun Masc.* **1** ticket office (*in a station or museum*); **2** box office (*in a theatre or cinema*); **3** counter, window (*in a bank or post office*).

**guichet automatique** *noun Masc.* cashpoint.

**guide** *noun Masc.* guide.

**guider** *verb* [1] to guide.

**guidon** *noun Masc.* handlebars.

**guillemets** *plural noun Masc.* inverted commas; **entre guillemets** in inverted commas.

**guirlande** *noun Fem.* **des guirlandes** tinsel; **des guirlandes en papier** paper chains.

**guirlande électrique** *noun Fem.* fairy lights, Christmas-tree lights.

**guitare** *noun Fem.* guitar; **jouer de la guitare** to play the guitar.

**guitariste** *noun Masc. & Fem.* guitarist.

**gym** *noun Fem.* (*informal*) PE, gymnastics.

**gymnase** *noun Masc.* gym; **je te verrai au gymnase** I'll see you in the gym.

**gymnastique** *noun Fem.* gymnastics, exercises.

a
b
c
d
e
f
g
h
i
j
k
l
m
n
o
p
q
r
s
t
u
v
w
x
y
z

# Hh

**habile** *adjective* clever; **elle est habile de ses mains** she's clever with her hands; **de manière habile** cleverly.

**habillé** *adjective* **1** dressed; **je ne suis pas encore habillé** I'm not dressed yet; **2** smart (*for example, a dress or suit*).

**habiller** *verb* [1] **1 habiller quelqu'un** to dress somebody; **2 s'habiller** to get dressed; **habille-toi vite!** get dressed quick!; **3 s'habiller** to dress up; **s'habiller en clown** to dress up as a clown.

**habitant**, **habitante** *noun Masc., Fem.* inhabitant.

**habitation** *noun Fem.* house.

**habiter** *verb* [1] to live; **ils habitent à Paris** they live in Paris.

**habitude** *noun Fem.* **1** habit; **c'est une mauvaise habitude** it's a bad habit; **2 d'habitude** usually; **d'habitude il arrive à midi** he usually arrives at twelve; **3 comme d'habitude** as usual; **j'ai pris le bus comme d'habitude** I took the bus as usual; **4 avoir l'habitude de faire** to be used to doing; **j'ai l'habitude de travailler le soir** I'm used to working in the evening.

**habitué**, **habituée** *noun Masc., Fem.* regular (*in a café, shop, etc*).

**habitué** *adjective* **être habitué à quelque chose** to be accustomed to something.

**habituel** (*Fem.* **habituelle**) *adjective* usual.

**habituer** *verb* [1] **s'habituer à quelque chose** to get used to something; **je m'y suis habituée** I've got used to it.

**hache** *noun Fem.* axe.

**haché** *adjective* chopped; **du bœuf haché** mince.

**hacher** *verb* [1] **1** to chop (*vegetables*); **2** to mince (*meat*).

**hachis Parmentier** *noun Masc.* shepherd's pie.

**haddock** *noun Masc.* smoked haddock.

**haie** *noun Fem.* **1** hedge; **2 les haies** hurdles (*sport*).

**haine** *noun Fem.* hatred.

**haïr** *verb* [46] to hate.

**Haïti** *noun Masc.* Haiti.

**haïtien** *Fem.* **haïtienne** *adjective* Haitian.

**Haïtien**, **Haïtienne** *noun Masc., Fem.* Haitian.

**haleine** *noun Fem.* breath; **être hors d'haleine** to be out of breath.

**hall** *noun Masc.* **1** (entrance) hall; **2** concourse (*in a station*).

**halles** *plural noun Fem.* covered market.

**halogène** *adjective* halogen; **une lampe halogène** a halogen lamp.

**halte** *noun Fem.* stop; **halte!** stop!; **faire une halte** to stop somewhere.

**halte-garderie** *noun Fem.* playgroup.

**haltérophilie** *noun Fem.* weightlifting.

**hamac** *noun Masc.* hammock.

**hameau** (*plural* **hameaux**) *noun*
Masc. group of houses.

**hameçon** *noun Masc.* fish hook.

**hamster** *noun Masc.* hamster.

**hanche** *noun Fem.* hip.

**handball** *noun Masc.* handball;
**jouer au handball** to play handball.

**handicap** *noun Masc.* handicap.

**handicapé, handicapée** *noun*
Masc., Fem. handicapped person.
**handicapé** *adjective* handicapped,
disabled.

**hanté** *adjective* haunted.

**harceler** *verb* [45] **1** to pester; **2** to
harass.

**hareng** *noun Masc.* herring.

**haricot** *noun Masc.* bean; **haricot
vert** French bean; **haricot blanc**
haricot bean.

**harmonica** *noun Masc.* mouth
organ; **jouer de l'harmonica** to play
the mouth organ.

**harmonie** *noun Fem.* harmony.

**harmoniser** *verb* [1] to
coordinate, to harmonize.

**harnais** *noun Masc.* harness.

**harpe** *noun Fem.* harp.

**hasard** *noun Masc.* **1** chance; **par
hasard** by chance; **je l'ai rencontré
par hasard** I met him by chance;
**2 au hasard** at random; **elle a
choisi un livre au hasard** she chose
a book at random; **3 à tout hasard**
just in case; **prends un manteau à
tout hasard** take a coat just in case;
**4 à tout hasard** on the off chance.

**hasardeux** (*Fem.* **hasardeuse**)
*adjective* risky.

**hâte** *noun Fem.* **à la hâte** hurriedly;
**elle est partie à la hâte** she left in
a rush.

**hausse** *noun Fem.* increase, rise;
**une hausse des prix** a rise in
prices; **les prix sont en hausse**
prices are rising.

**hausser** *verb* [1] **1** to raise;
**2 hausser les épaules** to shrug
your shoulders.

**haut** *noun Masc.* **1** top; **le haut de
l'échelle** the top of the ladder;
**regarder quelqu'un de haut en
bas** to look somebody up and down;
**2 l'arbre fait 10 mètres de haut**
the tree is 10 metres high; **3 en haut**
upstairs; **elle est en haut** she's
upstairs; **4 en haut de** at the top of;
**en haut de l'escalier** at the top of
the stairs.
**haut** *adjective* **1** high; **la branche
la plus haute** the highest branch;
**2 à haute voix** aloud; **lire à haute
voix** to read aloud.
**haut** *adverb* high; **plus haut dans
l'arbre** higher up the tree; **'voir plus
haut'** 'see above' (*in a book*); **haut
les mains!** hands up!

**hautbois** *noun Masc.* oboe.

**hauteur** *noun Fem.* height; **la
hauteur de la pièce** the height of
the room; **dans le sens de la
hauteur** upright; **l'avion prend de
la hauteur** the plane's gaining
height; **il n'est pas à la hauteur de
son travail** he's not up to his job.

**haut-parleur** *noun Masc.* loudspeaker.

**Haye** *noun* **La Haye** The Hague.

**hebdomadaire** *noun Masc.* weekly magazine.

**héberger** *verb* [52] to put up; **Jess va nous héberger** Jess'll put us up.

**hein** *exclamation* (*informal*) what?, eh?

**hélas** *exclamation* unfortunately; **elle est déjà partie, hélas** she's already left, unfortunately; **hélas non** I'm afraid not.

**hélicoptère** *noun Masc.* helicopter.

**hémorragie** *noun Fem.* haemorrhage.

**hennir** *verb* [2] to neigh.

**herbe** *noun Fem.* 1 **l'herbe** grass; 2 herb; **les fines herbes** mixed herbs; **les herbes de Provence** mixed herbs; 3 **une mauvaise herbe** a weed.

**hérisson** *noun Masc.* hedgehog.

**héritage** *noun Masc.* inheritance.

**hériter** *verb* [1] to inherit.

**hermétique** *adjective* airtight.

**héroïne** *noun Fem.* 1 heroine; 2 heroin.

**héros** *noun Masc.* hero.

**hésitation** *noun Fem.* hesitation.

**hésiter** *verb* [1] to hesitate; **à ta place, je n'hésiterais pas!** if I were you, I wouldn't hesitate!; **j'ai beaucoup hésité avant d'accepter** I thought about it for a long time before I agreed; **j'hésite entre le poulet et le poisson** I can't decide whether to have the chicken or the fish.

**hêtre** *noun Masc.* 1 beech tree; 2 beech wood.

**heure** *noun Fem.* 1 hour; **une heure plus tard** an hour later; **deux heures de train** two hours in the train; **une demi-heure** half an hour; **une heure et demie** an hour and a half; **Londres est à une heure d'avion de Paris** London is an hour from Paris by air; **toutes les quatre heures** every four hours; **toutes les heures: il y a des trains toutes les heures** there are trains every hour; **payé à l'heure** paid by the hour; **cent kilomètres à l'heure** a hundred kilometres an hour; 2 time; **quelle heure est-il?** what time is it?; **il est sept heures** it's seven o'clock; **à huit heures du matin** at eight o'clock in the morning; **tu te lèves à quelle heure demain?** what time are you getting up tomorrow?; **à neuf heures** at nine o'clock; **à six heures et demie** at half past six; 3 **être à l'heure** to be on time; 4 **à l'heure du déjeuner** at lunchtime; ★ **de bonne heure** early; **je me lève de bonne heure demain** I'm getting up early tomorrow.

**heures d'affluence** *plural noun Fem.* peak time, rush hour.

**heureusement** *adverb* fortunately.

**heureux** (*Fem.* **heureuse**) *adjective* 1 happy; **elle est heureuse d'être ici** she's happy to be here; 2 lucky, fortunate.

**heurter** *verb* [1] to hit, to bump into; **la voiture a heurté un camion** the car collided with a lorry.

**heurtoir** *noun Masc.* (door) knocker.

**hexagone** *noun Masc.* **1** hexagon; **2 l'Hexagone** France (*French journalists often refer to France as l'Hexagone as it has a six-sided shape on the map*).

**hibou** (*plural* **hiboux**) *noun Masc.* owl.

**hideux** (*Fem.* **hideuse**) *adjective* hideous.

**hier** *adverb* yesterday; **je l'ai vue hier** I saw her yesterday; **hier matin** yesterday morning; **avant-hier** the day before yesterday.

**hi-fi** *noun Fem.* hi-fi; **une chaîne hi-fi** a stereo system.

**hippique** *adjective* equestrian; **un concours hippique** a horse show; **un club hippique** a riding school.

**hippodrome** *noun Masc.* racecourse.

**hippopotame** *noun Masc.* hippopotamus.

**hirondelle** *noun Fem.* swallow.

**histoire** *noun Fem.* **1** history; **l'histoire française** French history; **2** story; **l'histoire de ma vie** the story of my life; **3** matter; **c'est une histoire d'argent** it's a matter of money; ★ **faire des histoires** to kick up a fuss.

**historique** *adjective* **1** historic; **un monument historique** a historic monument; **2** historical.

**hit-parade** *noun Masc.* **le hit-parade** the charts (*pop music*).

**hiver** *noun Masc.* winter; **en hiver** in winter.

**HLM** *noun Masc. OR Fem.* (= *habitation à loyer modéré*) council flat; **nous habitons dans un HLM à Valence** we live in a council flat in Valence; **les HLM** council housing.

**hocher** *verb* [1] **hocher la tête** to shake your head, to nod.

**hockey** *noun Masc.* hockey; **jouer au hockey** to play hockey; **le hockey sur glace** ice hockey.

**hollandais** *noun Masc.* Dutch (*language*).
**hollandais** *adjective* Dutch.

**Hollandais**, **Hollandaise** *noun Masc., Fem.* Dutchman, Dutchwoman; **les Hollandais** the Dutch.

**Hollande** *noun Fem.* Holland; **en Hollande** in (*or* to) Holland.

**homard** *noun Masc.* lobster.

**homéopathique** *adjective* homeopathic.

**hommage** *noun Masc.* tribute, homage; **rendre hommage à quelqu'un/quelque chose** to pay tribute to someone/something.

**homme** *noun Masc.* man; **l'homme de la rue** the man in the street; **l'homme moderne est plus grand que ses ancêtres** modern man is taller than his ancestors.

**homme d'affaires** *noun Masc.* businessman.

**homme d'État** *noun Masc.* statesman.

**homogénéisé** *adjective* homogenized.

a
b
c
d
e
f
g
h
i
j
k
l
m
n
o
p
q
r
s
t
u
v
w
x
y
z

145

**homosexuel, homosexuelle** *noun, Masc., Fem.*
**homosexuelle** *adjective* homosexual.

**Hongrie** *noun Fem.* Hungary.

**hongrois** *noun Masc.* Hungarian (*language*).
**hongrois** *adjective* Hungarian.

**honnête** *adjective* honest, respectable.

**honnêtement** *adverb* honestly, frankly; **honnêtement je ne sais pas ce que tu veux dire** I honestly don't know what you mean.

**honnêteté** *noun Fem.* honesty; **en toute honnêteté** in all honesty.

**honneur** *noun Masc.* honour.

**honorer** *verb* [1] to honour.

**honte** *noun Fem.* shame; **avoir honte de quelque chose** to be ashamed of something; **j'ai vraiment honte** I'm really ashamed of myself; **tu n'as pas honte!** what a thing to say (*or* do)!

**honteux** (*Fem.* **honteuse**) *adjective* disgraceful.

**hôpital** *noun Masc.* hospital; **être à l'hôpital** to be in hospital.

**hoquet** *noun Masc.* hiccup; **avoir le hoquet** to have hiccups.

**horaire** *noun Masc.* timetable, schedule; **les horaires de train** the train timetable.

**horizon** *noun Masc.* horizon; **à l'horizon** on the horizon.

**horizontal** (*Masc. plural* **horizontaux**) *adjective* horizontal.

**horloge** *noun Fem.* clock.

**horodateur** *noun Masc.* parking ticket machine.

**horoscope** *noun Masc.* horoscope.

**horreur** *noun Fem.* **1** horror; **quelle horreur!** how awful!; **2 avoir horreur de quelque chose** to hate something; **j'ai horreur d'être en retard** I hate being late. **j'ai horreur des escargots!** I can't stand snails!

**horrible** *adjective* horrible.

**horrifier** *verb* [1] to horrify.

**hors** *preposition* **1 hors de** outside; **hors de France** outside France; **2 être hors jeu** to be offside; **3 les boutiques hors taxe** the duty-free shops; ★ **être hors de soi** to be beside yourself; **j'étais hors de moi** I was beside myself.

**hors-d'œuvre** *noun Masc.* starter (*to a meal*).

**hortensia** *noun Masc.* hydrangea.

**hospitalier** *adjective* **un centre hospitalier** a hospital.

**hospitaliser** *verb* [1] **elle a été hospitalisée** she's been taken into hospital.

**hospitalité** *noun Fem.* hospitality.

**hostilité** *noun Fem.* hostility.

**hôte**[1] *noun Masc.* host.

**hôte**[2] *noun Masc., Fem.* **1** guest; **hôte payant** paying guest; **2** host.

**hôtel** *noun Masc.* hotel; **un hôtel de luxe** a luxury hotel; **passer deux nuits à l'hôtel** to spend two nights in a hotel.

**hôtel de ville** *noun Masc.* town hall.

**hôtesse** *noun Fem.* **1** hostess; **2** receptionist.

**hôtesse d'accueil** *noun Fem.* receptionist.

**hôtesse de l'air** *noun Fem.* flight attendant.

**housse** *noun Fem.* cover (*for a chair or a machine*); **une housse de couette** a duvet cover.

**houx** *noun Masc.* holly.

**hublot** *noun Masc.* **1** window (*in a plane*); **2** porthole (*in a boat*).

**huer** *verb* [1] to boo; **la foule a huè l'arbitre** the crowd booed the referee.

**huile** *noun Fem.* oil; **huile de tournesol** sunflower oil; **huile d'olive** olive oil; **huile solaire** suntan oil.

**huit** *number* **1** eight; **Paul a huit ans** Paul's eight; **le huit juillet** the eighth of July; **2 huit jours** a week; **il y a huit jours** a week ago.

**huitième** *noun Masc.* **au huitième** on the eighth floor.
**huitième** *adjective* eighth.

**huître** *noun Fem.* oyster.

**humain** *adjective* human.

**humanitaire** *adjective* humanitarian.

**humeur** *noun Fem.* mood; **il est de bonne humeur** he's in a good mood; **elle est de mauvaise humeur** she's in a bad mood; **je ne suis pas d'humeur à faire ça** I'm not in the mood to do that.

**humide** *adjective* damp.

**humidité** *noun Fem.* damp.

**humoristique** *adjective* humorous; **un dessin humoristique** a cartoon.

**humour** *noun Masc.* humour; **avoir de l'humour** to have a sense of humour.

**hurler** *verb* [1] to yell, to howl.

**hutte** *noun Fem.* hut.

**hydratant** *adjective* moisturizing.

**hygiène** *noun Fem.* hygiene.

**hygiénique** *adjective* **1** hygienic; **2 une serviette hygiénique** a sanitary towel; **3 du papier hygiénique** toilet paper.

**hymne** *noun Masc.* hymn; **l'hymne national** the national anthem.

**hypermarché** *noun Masc.* hypermarket.

**hypermétrope** *adjective* long-sighted.

**hypertension** *noun Fem.* high blood pressure.

**hypnotiser** *verb* [1] to hypnotize.

**hypocondriaque** *noun Masc. & Fem., adjective* hypochondriac.

**hypocrite** *noun Masc. & Fem.* hypocrite.

**hypothèse** *noun Fem.* hypothesis.

**hystérie** *noun Fem.* hysteria.

# Ii

**iceberg** *noun Masc.* iceberg.

**ici** *adverb* **1** here; **il y a trop de monde ici** there are too many people here; **les gens d'ici** the local

a
b
c
d
e
f
g
h
i
j
k
l
m
n
o
p
q
r
s
t
u
v
w
x
y
z

people; **2 jusqu'ici** this far; **les bus ne viennent pas jusqu'ici** the buses don't come this far; **3 jusqu'ici** so far; **jusqu'ici il a fait beau** so far the weather's been good.

**icône** *noun Fem.* icon.

**idéal** (*plural* **idéaux**) *noun Masc.*, *adjective* ideal; **l'idéal serait de louer une voiture** the ideal thing would be to hire a car.

**idée** *noun Fem.* idea; **quelle bonne idée!** what a good idea!; **je n'ai aucune idée** I've no idea; **se faire des idées** to imagine things.

**identifier** *verb* [1] to identify.

**identique** *adjective* identical.

**identité** *noun Fem.* identity; **une carte d'identité** an identity card.

**idiot**, **idiote** *noun Masc., Fem.* idiot; **ne fais pas l'idiot!** don't fool around!
**idiot** *adjective* stupid; **c'est vraiment idiot!** it's really stupid!

**ignorance** *noun Fem.* ignorance.

**ignorant** *adjective* ignorant.

**ignorer** *verb* [1] **1** not to know; **j'ignore leur adresse** I don't know their address; **j'ignore les détails** I don't know the details; **2** to ignore; **ils l'ont ignoré** they ignored him.

**il** *pronoun* **1** he; **il parle français** he speaks French; **2** it; **'où est mon sac?' – 'il est sur la chaise'** 'where's my bag?' – 'it's on the chair; **il pleut** it's raining.

**île** *noun Fem.* island.

**illégal** (*Masc. plural* **illégaux**) *adjective* illegal.

**illimité** *adjective* unlimited.

**illisible** *adjective* illegible.

**illumination** *noun Fem.* floodlighting; **les illuminations de Noël** the Christmas lights.

**illuminer** *verb* [1] to floodlight.

**illusion** *noun Fem.* illusion; **elle se fait des illusions** she's fooling herself.

**illustration** *noun Fem.* illustration.

**illustré** *noun Masc.* comic.
**illustré** *adjective* illustrated.

**illustrer** *verb* [1] to illustrate.

**ils** *pronoun* they; **ils sont en vacances** they're on holiday.

**il y a** SEE **avoir**.

**image** *noun Fem.* picture; **il y a de belles images dans ton livre** there are some lovely pictures in your book.

**imaginaire** *adjective* imaginary.

**imagination** *noun Fem.* imagination.

**imaginer** *verb* [1] to imagine; **je n'arrive pas à l'imaginer** I can't imagine it; **elle va appeler, j'imagine** I suppose she'll phone.

**imbattable** *adjective* unbeatable.

**imbécile** *noun Masc. & Fem.* fool; **faire l'imbécile** to fool around.
**imbécile** *adjective* idiotic.

**imitation** *noun Fem.* imitation.

**imiter** *verb* [1] to imitate.

**immangeable** *adjective* inedible.

**immanquablement** *adverb* inevitably.

**immatriculation** *noun Fem.* registration (*of a car*); **une plaque d'immatriculation** a numberplate.

**immédiat** *adjective* immediate; **dans l'immédiat** for the time being; **je n'ai pas de projets dans l'immédiat** I don't have any plans for the time being.

**immédiatement** *adverb* immediately.

**immense** *adjective* huge.

**immeuble** *noun Masc.* **1** block of flats; **2** building; **un immeuble de six étages** a six-storey building; **3 un immeuble de bureaux** an office block.

**immigration** *noun Fem.* immigration.

**immigré, immigrée** *noun Masc., Fem.* immigrant.

**immobile** *adjective* motionless.

**immobilier** (*Fem.* **immobilière**) **une agence immobilière** an estate agent's.

**immobiliser** *verb* [1] to immobilize.

**immodéré** *adjective* excessive.

**immoral** (*Masc. plural* **immoraux**) *adjective* immoral.

**immuniser** *verb* [1] to immunize.

**impact** *noun Masc.* impact.

**impair** *adjective* odd; **un nombre impair** an odd number.

**impardonnable** *adjective* unforgivable.

**imparfait** *noun Masc.* imperfect (tense); **à l'imparfait** in the imperfect.
**imparfait** *adjective* imperfect.

**impasse** *noun Fem.* dead end.

**impatience** *noun Fem.* impatience.

**impatient** *adjective* impatient.

**impeccable** *adjective* **1** perfect; **un accent français impeccable** a perfect French accent; **2** spotless; **l'appartement est impeccable** the flat's spotless; **3** (*informal*) great; **'je viendrai te chercher chez toi à midi'** – **'impeccable!'** 'I'll come and pick you up at your place at twelve' – 'great!'

**impensable** *adjective* unthinkable.

**imper** *noun Masc.* (*informal*) SHORT FOR **imperméable** raincoat.

**impératif** *noun Masc.* imperative; **à l'impératif** in the imperative.

**impératrice** *noun Fem.* empress.

**imperfection** *noun Fem.* imperfection.

**imperméable** *noun Masc.* raincoat.

**impertinent** *adjective* cheeky.

**impitoyable** *adjective* merciless.

**impliquer** *verb* [1] **1** to mean; **cela implique que nous n'aurons pas assez d'argent** this means that we won't have enough money; **2 être impliqué dans quelque chose** to be involved in something.

**impoli** *adjective* rude.

**importance** *noun Fem.* importance; **ça n'a pas d'importance** it doesn't matter.

**important** *adjective* **1** important; **il est important de savoir que ...** it's important to know that ...;

a
b
c
d
e
f
g
h
i
j
k
l
m
n
o
p
q
r
s
t
u
v
w
x
y
z

**2** considerable; **une réduction importante** a considerable reduction; **il y aura des retards importants** there will be considerable delays.

**importations** *plural noun Fem.* imports.

**importer** *verb* [1] **1** to import (*goods*); **2** to matter; **'lequel veux-tu?' – 'n'importe!'** 'which one do you want?' – 'it doesn't matter!'; **n'importe où** anywhere; **viens n'importe quand** come any time; **n'importe qui sait faire ça** anyone can do that; **il dit n'importe quoi** he's talking nonsense; **elle le fait n'importe comment** she does it any old how.

**imposant** *adjective* imposing.

**imposer** *verb* [1] **1** to impose; **imposer à quelqu'un de faire quelque chose** to make somebody do something; **la maman de Katy lui a imposé de rester à la maison** Katy's mum made her stay at home; **2 s'imposer** to establish oneself.

**impossibilité** *noun Fem.* impossibility.

**impossible** *adjective* impossible. **impossible** *noun* **faire l'impossible** to do your utmost; **nous ferons l'impossible pour les contacter** we'll do our utmost to contact them.

**impôt** *noun Masc.* tax.

**imprécis** *adjective* vague.

**impression** *noun Fem.* impression; **sa première impression** his first impression; **elle a fait très bonne impression** she made a very good impression; **j'ai l'impression qu'il n'est pas heureux** I have a feeling he's not happy.

**impressionnant** *adjective* impressive.

**impressionner** *verb* [1] to impress.

**imprévisible** *adjective* unpredictable.

**imprévu** *adjective* unexpected.

**imprimante** *noun Fem.* printer (*for a computer*).

**imprimante laser** *noun Fem.* laser printer.

**imprimé** *noun Masc.* form (*to fill in*). **imprimé** *adjective* printed.

**imprimer** *verb* [1] to print.

**improviser** *verb* [1] to improvise.

**improviste** *noun* **à l'improviste** unexpectedly; **mon oncle est arrivé à l'improviste** my uncle arrived unexpectedly.

**imprudent** *adjective* **1** careless; **2** rash.

**impuissant** *adjective* helpless.

**impulsif** (Fem. **impulsive**) *adjective* impulsive.

**inabordable** *adjective* **1** inaccessible; **2 des prix inabordables** prohibitive prices.

**inacceptable** *adjective* unacceptable.

**inaccessible** *adjective* inaccessible.

**inachevé** *adjective* unfinished.

**inadapté** *adjective* unsuitable.

**inadmissible** *adjective* intolerable.

**inaperçu** *adjective* **passer inaperçu** to go unnoticed; **son départ est passé inaperçu** her departure went unnoticed.

**inattendu** *adjective* unexpected; **une visite inattendue** an unexpected visit.

**inattention** *noun Fem.* lack of attention; **une faute d'inattention** a careless mistake.

**inaudible** *adjective* inaudible.

**inauguration** *noun Fem.* inauguration, opening.

**inaugurer** *verb* [1] **1** to open (*an exhibition, a new building*); **2** to unveil (*a monument*).

**incapable** *adjective* **1** incapable; **je suis incapable de bouger!** I'm incapable of moving!; **2** incompetent; **il est complètement incapable** he's completely incompetent.

**incassable** *adjective* unbreakable.

**incendiaire** *noun Masc. & Fem.* arsonist.
**incendiaire** *adjective* **une bombe incendiaire** an incendiary bomb.

**incendie** *noun Masc.* fire; **l'incendie a détruit l'église** the fire destroyed the church.

**incertain** *adjective* **1** uncertain; **le résultat est toujours incertain** the result is still uncertain; **2** unsettled (*weather*).

**incertitude** *noun Fem.* uncertainty.

**incident** *noun Masc.* incident; **en cas d'incident** if anything should happen.

**inciter** *verb* [1] to encourage; **le père d'André l'a incité à apprendre la guitare** André's father encouraged him to learn to play the guitar.

**inclure** *verb* [25] **1** to include; **2** to enclose.

**inclus** *adjective* including; **il y aura trente invités, enfants inclus** there will be thirty guests, including children; **jusqu'à samedi inclus** up to and including Saturday.

**incollable** *adjective* **le riz incollable** easy-cook rice.

**incolore** *adjective* colourless.

**incommode** *adjective* **1** awkward; **2** uncomfortable.

**incomparable** *adjective* incomparable.

**incompétent** *adjective* incompetent.

**incompréhensible** *adjective* incomprehensible.

**inconditionnel, inconditionnelle** *noun Masc., Fem.* devotee; **c'est un inconditionnel du jazz** he's a real jazz fan.
**inconditionnel** (*Fem.* **inconditionnelle**) *adjective* unconditional.

**inconfortable** *adjective* uncomfortable.

**inconnu, inconnue** *noun Masc., Fem.* stranger.
**inconnu** *adjective* unknown; **elle m'est inconnue** I don't know her.

a
b
c
d
e
f
g
h
i
j
k
l
m
n
o
p
q
r
s
t
u
v
w
x
y
z

a
b
c
d
e
f
g
h
**i**
j
k
l
m
n
o
p
q
r
s
t
u
v
w
x
y
z

**inconsciemment** *adverb* unconsciously.

**inconscient** *adjective* **1** unthinking; **2** unconscious (*in a faint*).

**incontestable** *adjective* unquestionable.

**incontournable** *adjective* unavoidable; **c'est un fait incontournable** it's an undeniable fact.

**inconvénient** *noun Masc.* **1** drawback; **il y a plusieurs inconvénients** there are several drawbacks; **2 l'inconvénient, c'est que** ... the difficulty is that ...; **3 si vous n'y voyez pas d'inconvénient** if you have no objection.

**incorporer** *verb* [1] to blend in (*ingredients in cooking*); **incorporez l'huile une goutte à la fois** blend in the oil drop by drop.

**incorrect** *adjective* **1** incorrect; **2** rude.

**incrédule** *adjective* incredulous.

**incroyable** *adjective* incredible; **elle a des connaissances incroyables** her knowledge is incredible.

**inculper** *verb* [1] **inculper quelqu'un de** to charge somebody with (*a crime*); **elle a été inculpée de vol** she was charged with theft.

**Inde** *noun Fem.* India; **en Inde** in (*or* to) India.

**indécis** *adjective* **1** undecided; **elle est toujours indécise** she hasn't decided yet; **2** indecisive.

**indemne** *adjective* unharmed.

**indemnisation** *noun Fem.* compensation; **une demande d'indemnisation** a claim for compensation.

**indemniser** *verb* [1] to compensate; **demander à être indemnisé** to demand compensation.

**indéniable** *adjective* undeniable.

**indépendamment** *adverb* independently.

**indépendance** *noun Fem.* independence.

**indépendant** *adjective* **1** independent; **2 cuisine indépendante** separate kitchen; **3 une maison indépendante** a detached house.

**index** *noun Masc.* **1** index; **2** forefinger.

**indicateur** *noun Masc.* **1** timetable (*in a rail or coach station*); **l'indicateur des départs** the departures board; **2** street directory; **3** gauge (*for example, for oil levels*); **4 un panneau indicateur** a road sign.

**indicateur de pression** *noun Masc.* pressure gauge.

**indicatif** *noun Masc.* **1** dialling code; **l'indicatif pour l'Espagne est 34** the dialling code for Spain is 34; **2** theme tune; **3** indicative (*of a verb*).

**indications** *plural noun Fem.* directions.

**indice** *noun Masc.* clue.

**indien** (*Fem.* **indienne**) *adjective* Indian.

**indifférent** *adjective* indifferent.

**indigène** *adjective* native; **les indigènes** the locals.

**indigeste** *adjective* indigestible.

**indigestion** *noun Fem.* indigestion; **avoir une indigestion** to have indigestion.

**indignation** *noun Fem.* indignation.

**indigne** *adjective* 1 unworthy; 2 disgraceful.

**indigner** *verb* [1] **s'indigner** to get indignant.

**indiqué** *adjective* recommended; **ce n'est pas très indiqué** it's not a very good idea.

**indiquer** *verb* [1] to point out, to show; **pouvez-vous m'indiquer la gare?** can you show me the way to the station?; **le nom est indiqué sur un grand panneau** the name is on a big sign; **cela indique que** ... this shows that ....

**indirect** *adjective* indirect.

**indiscipliné** *adjective* unruly.

**indiscret** (*Fem.* **indiscrète**) *adjective* 1 indiscreet; **ne le lui dis pas, elle est très indiscrète** don't tell her, she can't keep a secret; 2 **si ce n'est pas indiscret** if it's not being nosy.

**indiscutable** *adjective* unquestionable.

**indispensable** *adjective* essential; **les vêtements indispensables** essential clothing; **il est indispensable** it's essential.

**indisposé** *adjective* unwell.

**individu** *noun Masc.* individual; **c'est un drôle d'individu** he's a funny bloke.

**individuel** (*Fem.* **individuelle**) *adjective* 1 individual; 2 separate; **une chambre individuelle** a single room; **une maison individuelle** a detached house.

**indolore** *adjective* painless.

**indulgent** *adjective* indulgent; **notre prof de maths est trop indulgent avec nous** our maths teacher isn't strict enough with us.

**industrialisé** *adjective* **les pays industrialisés** the industrialized countries.

**industrie** *noun Fem.* industry.

**industriel** (*Fem.* **industrielle**) *adjective* industrial; **une ville industrielle** an industrial city.

**inédit** *adjective* 1 unpublished; 2 new.

**inefficace** *adjective* 1 inefficient; **en tant que patron il est très inefficace** as a boss he's very inefficient; 2 ineffective; **un remède inefficace** an ineffective remedy.

**inégal** (*Masc. plural* **inégaux**) *adjective* 1 uneven; 2 unequal.

**inespéré** *adjective* unhoped-for; **un succès inespéré** an unhoped-for success.

**inévitable** *adjective* 1 inevitable; **c'était inévitable** it was bound to happen; 2 unavoidable; **des problèmes inévitables** unavoidable problems.

**inexact** *adjective* 1 incorrect; 2 inaccurate.

a
b
c
d
e
f
g
h
i
j
k
l
m
n
o
p
q
r
s
t
u
v
w
x
y
z

**inexpérimenté** *adjective* inexperienced.

**infarctus** *noun Masc.* heart attack.

**infect** *adjective* foul; **le repas était infect!** the meal was foul!

**infecter** *verb* [1] **1** to infect; **2 s'infecter** to go septic.

**infection** *noun Fem.* infection.

**inférieur** *adjective* **1** lower; **sur une marche inférieure** on a lower step; **des prix inférieurs à la moyenne** lower than average prices; **2** smaller; **la taille inférieure** the smaller size; **3** inferior, worse; **de qualité inférieure** of a lower quality.

**infernal** (*Masc. plural* **infernaux**) *adjective* frightful, dreadful.

**infini** *adjective* infinite.

**infinitif** *noun Masc.* infinitive (*in grammar*); **à l'infinitif** in the infinitive.

**infirme** *noun* **les infirmes** the disabled.
**infirme** *adjective* disabled; **est-il infirme?** does he have a disability?

**infirmerie** *noun Fem.* medical room.

**infirmier, infirmière** *noun Masc., Fem.* nurse.

**infirmité** *noun Fem.* disability.

**inflammable** *adjective* flammable.

**inflation** *noun Fem.* inflation.

**influence** *noun Fem.* influence; **il a une bonne influence sur son frère** he's a good influence on his brother.

**influencer** *verb* [61] to influence.

**informaticien, informaticienne** *noun Masc., Fem.* computer scientist.

**information** *noun Fem.* **1** information; **une information très utile** a very useful piece of information; **2 les informations** the news (*on TV or radio*); **les informations sont à vingt heures** the news is at eight o'clock.

**informatique** *noun Fem.* computer science, IT.
**informatique** *adjective* computer; **un système informatique** a computer system.

**informatiser** *verb* [1] to computerize.

**informer** *verb* [1] **1** to inform; **2 s'informer** to find out; **je peux m'informer si tu veux** I can find out if you like.

**infrarouge** *adjective* infra-red.

**infusion** *noun Fem.* herbal tea.

**ingénierie** *noun Fem.* engineering.

**ingénieur** *noun Masc.* engineer; **faire des études d'ingénieur** to study engineering.

**ingénieux** (*Fem.* **ingénieuse**) *adjective* ingenious; **c'était très ingénieux de sa part** that was very ingenious of her.

**ingrat** *adjective* **1** ungrateful; **2 un travail ingrat** unrewarding work.

**ingrédient** *noun Masc.* ingredient.

**inhabité** *adjective* uninhabited.

**inhabituel** (*Fem.* **inhabituelle**) *adjective* unusual.

**inhalateur** *noun Masc.* inhaler.

**inhumain** *adjective* inhuman.

**inimaginable** *adjective* unimaginable, unthinkable.

**ininterrompu** *adjective* **1** uninterrupted; **2** continuous.

**initial** (*Masc. plural* **initiaux**) *adjective* initial.

**initiale** *noun Fem.* initial; **mes initiales sont là-dessus** my initials are on it.

**initiation** *noun Fem.* introduction (*to a new place or skill*); **une journée d'initiation** an introductory day (*to a course, for example*); **une initiation à l'anglais** an introduction to English.

**initiative** *noun Fem.* initiative.

**initier** *verb* [1] **1 initier quelqu'un à** to introduce somebody to (*a skill*); **2** to initiate (*an idea or plan*); **3 s'initier à quelque chose** to learn about something; **elle s'initie à la photo** she's starting to learn photography.

**injecter** *verb* [1] to inject.

**injection** *noun Fem.* injection.

**injure** *noun Fem.* insult.

**injurier** *verb* [1] to insult; **il m'a injurié** he swore at me.

**injuste** *adjective* unfair.

**innocent** *adjective* innocent.

**innombrable** *adjective* countless.

**innovation** *noun Fem.* innovation.

**innover** *verb* [1] to break new ground.

**inoccupé** *adjective* empty.

**inondation** *noun Fem.* flood; **des inondations** flooding.

**inonder** *verb* [1] to flood.

**inoubliable** *adjective* unforgettable.

**inouï** *adjective* incredible.

**inox** *noun Masc.* stainless steel; **une casserole en inox** a stainless steel pan.

**inoxydable** *adjective* **un évier en acier inoxydable** a stainless steel sink.

**inquiet** (*Fem.* **inquiète**) *adjective* anxious, worried.

**inquiétant** *adjective* worrying.

**inquiéter** *verb* [24] **1** to worry; **je ne veux pas t'inquiéter** I don't want to worry you; **ça m'inquiète un peu** I find that a bit worrying; **ce qui m'inquiète, c'est qu'elle n'a pas téléphoné** what I find worrying is the fact that she hasn't phoned; **2 s'inquiéter** to worry, to be worried; **elle va s'inquiéter si nous sommes en retard** she'll worry if we're late; **ne t'inquiète pas!** don't worry!

**inquiétude** *noun Fem.* anxiety.

**insatisfait** *adjective* dissatisfied.

**inscription** *noun Fem.* **1** enrolment (*for a course or in a school*); **2** registration.

**inscrire** *verb* [38] **1** to enrol, to register (*someone for a course or school*); **elle m'a inscrit pour l'examen** she's entered me for the exam; **2 s'inscrire** to enrol; **s'inscrire au club de foot** to join the football club.

**insecte** *noun Masc.* insect.

**insérer** *verb* [24] to, insert.

a
b
c
d
e
f
g
h
i
j
k
l
m
n
o
p
q
r
s
t
u
v
w
x
y
z

a b c d e f g h i j k l m n o p q r s t u v w x y z

**insertion** *noun Fem.* **1** insertion (*of an advertisement in a paper, for example*); **2** integration (*when somebody joins a new community*); **l'insertion des jeunes dans la société** the integration of young people into society.

**insignifiant** *adjective* insignificant.

**insister** *verb* [1] to insist; **il faut insister** keep on trying; **la clé est un peu tordue, il faut insister un peu** the key's a bit bent, you have to push it really hard.

**insolation** *noun Fem.* sunstroke; **attraper une insolation** to get sunstroke.

**insolent** *adjective* insolent.

**insoutenable** *adjective* unbearable.

**inspecter** *verb* [1] to inspect.

**inspecteur, inspectrice** *noun Masc., Fem.* inspector.

**inspection** *noun Fem.* **1** inspection; **2** inspectorate (*an official department*).

**inspiration** *noun Fem.* inspiration.

**inspirer** *verb* [1] **1** to inspire; **ça ne m'inspire pas** that doesn't appeal to me; **2** to breathe in; **inspire fort!** breathe in deep!; **3 s'inspirer** to be inspired by; **il s'est inspiré de Picasso** he was inspired by Picasso.

**instable** *adjective* unstable; **il fait un temps instable** the weather's unsettled.

**installation** *noun Fem.* **1** installation, putting in; **2** move (*to a house or town*); **avant son installation à Paris** before he

moved to Paris; **3 des installations sportives** sports facilities.

**installer** *verb* [1] **1** to install, to put in (*central heating or a dishwasher, for example*); **2** to connect (*gas, electricity, a phone*); **3 s'installer** to settle, to settle in; **installez-vous** do sit down; **je me suis installée à mon bureau** I settled down at my desk.

**instant** *noun Masc.* moment; **pour l'instant** for the moment; **à tout instant** all the time.

**instantané** *adjective* instant; **du café instantané** instant coffee.

**instinct** *noun Masc.* instinct.

**institut** *noun Masc.* institute; **un institut de beauté** a beautician's.

**instituteur, institutrice** *noun Masc., Fem.* primary school teacher.

**institution** *noun Fem.* **1** institution; **2** private school.

**institutrice** *noun Fem.* SEE **instituteur**.

**instructeur, instructrice** *noun Masc., Fem.* instructor.

**instruction** *noun Fem.* **1** education; **instruction civique** civics; **2 instructions** instructions; **instructions de lavage** washing instructions.

**instruire** *verb* [26] **1** to teach, to train; **2 s'instruire** to learn.

**instruit** *adjective* educated.

**instrument** *noun Masc.* **1** instrument; **un instrument de mesure** a measuring instrument; **les instruments de bord** the controls; **2 un instrument de**

**musique** a musical instrument; **un instrument à cordes** a string instrument.

**insu** *noun* **à mon insu** without my knowing.

**insuffisance** *noun Fem.* shortage.

**insuffisant** *adjective*
**1** insufficient; **2** inadequate; **c'est insuffisant** it's not good enough.

**insultant** *adjective* insulting.

**insulte** *noun Fem.* insult.

**insulter** *verb* [1] to insult.

**insupportable** *adjective* unbearable; **je la trouve insupportable** I can't stand her.

**intact** *adjective* intact.

**intégral** (*Masc. plural* **intégraux**) *adjective* complete.

**intégrale** *noun Fem.* complete works (*usually music*); **l'intégrale des Beatles** the complete Beatles collection.

**intellectuel**, **intellectuelle** *noun Masc., Fem., adjective* intellectual.

**intelligence** *noun Fem.* intelligence.

**intelligent** *adjective* clever, intelligent.

**intendance** *noun Fem.* administration (*in a school*).

**intense** *adjective* intense.

**intensif** (*Fem.* **intensive**) *adjective* intensive.

**intention** *noun Fem.* intention; **avoir l'intention de faire** to mean to do; **j'avais l'intention d'y aller**

mais je n'ai pas pu I meant to go but I wasn't able to.

**interdiction** *noun Fem.* ban; 'interdiction de fumer' 'no smoking'.

**interdire** *verb* [47] to forbid; **je t'interdis de le faire** I forbid you to do it.

**interdit** *adjective* forbidden; 'entrée interdite' 'no entry'; **il est interdit de fumer dans la salle** smoking is forbidden in the theatre.

**intéressant** *adjective*
**1** interesting; **c'est un film très intéressant** it's a very interesting film; **2 à un prix intéressant** at a good price.

**intéressé**[1] *adjective* interested; **être intéressé par quelque chose** to be interested in something.

**intéressé**[2], **intéressée** *noun Masc., Fem.* person concerned.

**intéresser** *verb* [1] **1** to interest; **ça ne m'intéresse pas** that doesn't interest me; **2 s'intéresser à** to be interested in; **elle s'intéresse beaucoup à l'informatique** she's very interested in computing.

**intérêt** *noun Masc.* **1** interest; **ce livre est sans intérêt** this book is really boring; **2 tu as intérêt à faire** you'd better do; **tu as intérêt à le finir avant ce soir!** you'd better get it finished by this evening!

**intérieur** *noun Masc.* inside, interior; **l'intérieur du placard** the inside of the cupboard; **où est-elle? – à l'intérieur** where is she? – inside (*in the house*).

a
b
c
d
e
f
g
h
i
j
k
l
m
n
o
p
q
r
s
t
u
v
w
x
y
z

a
b
c
d
e
f
g
h
i
j
k
l
m
n
o
p
q
r
s
t
u
v
w
x
y
z

**intérieur** *adjective* inside, internal; **le côté intérieur** the inside.

**intermédiaire** *noun Masc. & Fem.* go-between.
**intermédiaire** *adjective* intermediate; **avez-vous la taille intermédiaire?** do you have the size in between?

**internat** *noun Masc.* boarding school.

**international** (*Masc. plural* **internationaux**) *adjective* international.

**interne** *noun Masc. & Fem.* boarder (*in a school.*).
**interne** *adjective* internal.

**Internet** *noun Masc.* Internet; **sur Internet** on the Internet.

**interpeller** *verb* [1] **1** to call out to; **2 la police l'a interpellé** the police have taken him in for questioning.

**interphone™** *noun Masc.* entry phone.

**interprète** *noun Masc. & Fem.* **1** (*in the theatre*) actor; (*in music*) performer, soloist; **2** interpreter.

**interpréter** *verb* [24] **1** to perform, to play (*a role in the theatre or a piece of music*), to sing (*a song*); **2** to interpret (*a language or a remark*).

**interrogatif** *noun Masc.* interrogative.

**interrogation** *noun Fem.* **1** test (*at school*); **2** questioning.

**interroger** *verb* [52] **1** to question, to ask; **il m'a interrogé sur mon séjour en France** he asked me about my stay in France; **2** to test (*at school*).

**interrompre** *verb* [69] to interrupt; **interrompre quelqu'un** to interrupt somebody; **il a interrompu son travail** he broke off his work.

**interrupteur** *noun Masc.* switch.

**interruption** *noun Fem.* **1** interruption; **2 sans interruption** without stopping.

**intervalle** *noun Masc.* **1** interval; **2 dans l'intervalle** in the meantime.

**intervenir** *verb* [81] to intervene.

**intervention** *noun Fem.* intervention.

**interview** *noun Fem.* interview (*on TV, radio, for a magazine*).

**intestin** *noun Masc.* intestine.

**intime** *adjective* intimate; **un journal intime** a diary (*kept by somebody*).

**intimider** *verb* [1] to intimidate.

**intimité** *noun Fem.* intimacy; **dans l'intimité** in private.

**intolérable** *adjective* intolerable.

**intolérant** *adjective* intolerant.

**intoxication** *noun Fem.* poisoning.

**intoxiquer** *verb* [1] to poison.

**intrigue** *noun Fem.* plot (*of a novel, play, etc*).

**introduction** *noun Fem.* introduction.

**introduire** *verb* [26] **1** to introduce (*an idea, a measure, a new product*); **2 s'introduire** to get into; **un cambrioleur s'est introduit dans**

**l'appartement** a burglar got into the flat.

**intrus**, **intruse** noun Masc., Fem. intruder.

**intuitif** (Fem. **intuitive**) adjective intuitive.

**intuition** noun Fem. intuition.

**inusable** adjective hard-wearing.

**inutile** adjective pointless; **il est inutile de l'appeler** there's no point telephoning him; **inutile de dire que** ... needless to say ....

**inutilement** adverb pointlessly; **je l'ai cherché inutilement** I looked for it in vain.

**inutilisable** adjective unusable.

**invalide** noun Masc. & Fem. disabled person.

**invasion** noun Fem. invasion.

**inventer** verb [1] to invent.

**invention** noun Fem. invention.

**inverse** noun Masc. **l'inverse** the opposite; **l'inverse est vrai** the opposite is true.
**inverse** adjective opposite; **en sens inverse** in the opposite direction; **dans l'ordre inverse** in reverse order.

**investigation** noun Fem. investigation.

**investissement** noun Masc. investment.

**invisible** adjective invisible.

**invitation** noun Fem. invitation.

**invité**, **invitée** noun Masc., Fem. guest; **nous avons des invités ce soir** we have people coming round this evening.

**inviter** verb [1] to invite; **ils m'ont invité à dîner** they invited me to dinner.

**involontaire** adjective unintentional.

**invraisemblable** adjective
1 unlikely; **une explication invraisemblable** an unlikely explanation; 2 (informal) amazing.

**ira**, **irai**, **iraient**, **irais**, **irait**, **iras** verb SEE **aller**.

**iris** noun Masc. iris.

**irlandais** noun Masc.,
**irlandais** adjective Irish.

**Irlandais**, **Irlandaise** noun Masc., Fem. Irishman, Irishwoman; **les Irlandais** the Irish.

**Irlande** noun Fem. Ireland; **la République d'Irlande** the Republic of Ireland.

**Irlande du Nord** noun Fem. Northern Ireland.

**ironie** noun Fem. irony.

**ironique** adjective ironic.

**irons**, **iront** verb SEE **aller**[1].

**irradier** verb [1] to irradiate.

**irréel**, **irréelle** adjective unreal.

**irréfléchi** adjective thoughtless.

**irrégularité** noun Fem. irregularity.

**irrégulier** (Fem. **irrégulière**) adjective irregular.

**irrésistible** adjective irresistible.

**irresponsable** adjective irresponsible.

**irritable** adjective irritable.

**irritation** noun Fem. irritation.

a

**irriter** *verb* [1] **1** to irritate; **cela m'irrite** that makes me cross; **2 s'irriter** to get irritated.

b

**islamique** *adjective* Islamic.

c

**isolation** *noun Fem.* insulation; **isolation acoustique** soundproofing.

d

e

**isolé** *adjective* **1** remote; **2** lonely.

f

**isoler** *verb* [1] **1** to insulate (*a room or building*); **2** to isolate (*a sick person or a prisoner*).

g

h

**Israël** *noun Masc.* Israel.

i

**israélien** (*Fem.* **israélienne**) *adjective* Israeli.

j

**issue** *noun Fem.* exit; **issue de secours** emergency exit; **une rue sans issue** a dead end.

k

**Italie** *noun Fem.* Italy; **en Italie** in (*or* to) Italy.

l

m

**italien** *noun Masc.* Italian (*language*).
**italien** *adjective* Italian.

n

**Italien, Italienne** *noun Masc., Fem.* Italian (*person*).

o

p

**itinéraire** *noun Masc.* route.

q

**itinérant** *adjective* travelling.

r

**ivoire** *noun Masc., adjective* ivory.

s

**ivre** *adjective* drunk.

**ivresse** *noun Fem.* drunkenness.

t

**ivrogne** *noun Masc. & Fem.* drunkard.

u

v

# Jj

w

x

**j'** *pronoun* SEE **je**.

y

**J.-C.** *noun Masc.* short for Jésus-Christ; **200 avant J.-C.** 200 BC; **400 après J.-C.** 400 AD.

z

**jacinthe** *noun Fem.* hyacinth.

**jalousie** *noun Fem.* **1** jealousy; **2** slatted blind.

**jaloux** (*Fem.* **jalouse**) *adjective* jealous; **elle est jalouse de mes résultats d'examen** she's jealous of my exam results.

**jamaïquain** *adjective* Jamaican.

**Jamaïquain, Jamaïquaine** *noun Masc., Fem.* Jamaican.

**Jamaïque** *noun Fem.* Jamaica.

**jamais** *adverb* **1** never; **elle ne fume jamais** she never smokes; **on ne sait jamais** you never know; **jamais plus!** never again!; **2** ever; **plus grand que jamais** bigger than ever; **si jamais il pleut** if by any chance it rains; **à jamais** forever.

**jambe** *noun Fem.* leg; **se casser la jambe** to break your leg.

**jambon** *noun Masc.* ham; **jambon blanc** cooked ham; **jambon de pays** cured raw ham.

**janvier** *noun Masc.* January; **en janvier, au mois de janvier** in January.

**Japon** *noun Masc.* Japan; **au Japon** in (*or* to) Japan.

**japonais** *noun Masc.* Japanese (*language*).
**japonais** *adjective* Japanese.

**Japonais, Japonaise** *noun Masc., Fem.* Japanese (*person*).

**jardin** *noun Masc.* garden; **Patrick est au jardin** Patrick's in the garden; **une chaise de jardin** a garden chair.

**jardinage** *noun Masc.* gardening.

**jardinier, jardinière**¹ *noun Masc., Fem.* gardener.

**jardinière**² *noun Fem.* (large) plant pot.

**jardin public** *noun Masc.* park (*in a town*).

**jaune** *noun Masc.* **1** yellow; **2 un jaune d'œuf** an egg-yolk.
**jaune** *adjective* yellow; **une robe jaune** a yellow dress.

**jaunisse** *noun Fem.* jaundice.

**Javel** *noun* **eau de Javel** bleach.

**jazz** *noun Masc.* jazz; **j'aime le jazz** I like jazz.

**je, j'** (*before a vowel or silent 'h'*) *pronoun* I; **je sais où il habite** I know where he lives; **j'habite à Lyon** I live in Lyons.

**jean** *noun Masc.* **1** (pair of) jeans; **j'ai acheté un jean** I've bought some jeans; **2** denim; **une jupe en jean** a denim skirt.

**jet** *noun Masc.* **1** jet (*of water or steam*); **les jets d'eau de Versailles** the fountains at Versailles; **2** jet (plane).

**jetée** *noun Fem.* jetty.

**jeter** *verb* [48] **1** to throw; **jette-moi le ballon** throw me the ball; **2** to throw away; **j'ai jeté ces vieilles chaussures** I've thrown away those old shoes; **3 jeter un coup d'œil** to have a look; **est-ce que tu peux jeter un coup d'œil aux pommes de terre?** can you have a look at the potatoes?

**jeton** *noun Masc.* **1** counter (*for a board game*); **2** token (*for a machine*).

**jeu** (*plural* **jeux**) *noun Masc.* **1** game; **faire un jeu** to play a game; **gagner par trois jeux à deux** to win by three games to two; **2** gambling; **3** acting; ★ **ce n'est pas du jeu!** (*informal*) that's not fair!

**jeu-concours** *noun Masc.* competition.

**jeu de cartes** *noun Masc.* **1** pack of cards; **2** game of cards.

**jeu de hasard** *noun Masc.* game of chance.

**jeu de mots** *noun Masc.* pun.

**jeu de société** *noun Masc.* board game.

**jeudi** *noun Masc.* **1** Thursday; **nous sommes jeudi aujourd'hui** it's Thursday today; **jeudi prochain** next Thursday; **jeudi dernier** last Thursday; **2** on Thursday; **je l'ai vu jeudi soir** I saw him on Thursday evening; **3 le jeudi** on Thursdays; **fermé le jeudi** closed on Thursdays; **4 tous les jeudis** every Thursday.

**jeune** *noun Masc. & Fem.* young person; **une émission destinée aux jeunes** a programme aimed at young people.
**jeune** *adjective* young; **un jeune homme** a young man; **une jeune femme** a young woman; **une jeune fille** a girl.

**jeunesse** *noun Fem.* **1** young people; **la jeunesse d'aujourd'hui** young people today; **2** youth; **dans ma jeunesse** in my youth.

**jeu-vidéo** *noun Masc.* video game.

a
b
c
d
e
f
g
h
i
**j**
k
l
m
n
o
p
q
r
s
t
u
v
w
x
y
z

**a**

**jogging** *noun Masc.* **1** faire du jogging to go jogging; **2** un jogging a track-suit.

**b**

**joie** *noun Fem.* joy.

**c**

**joindre** *verb* [49] **1** to get hold of (*often by telephone*); je n'ai pas pu la joindre I wasn't able to get hold of her; **2** to enclose (*in a letter or parcel*); **3** to put together; les pieds joints feet together; ★ joindre les deux bouts to make ends meet (*financially*).

**d**

**e**

**f**

**g**

**h**

**joli** *adjective* pretty.

**i**

**jongler** *verb* [1] to juggle.

**j**

**jongleur, jongleuse** *noun Masc., Fem.* juggler.

**k**

**jonquille** *noun Fem.* daffodil.

**l**

**joue** *noun Fem.* cheek.

**m**

**jouer** *verb* [1] **1** to play; elle joue avec le chien she's playing with the dog; à toi de jouer! your go!; bien joué! well done!; **2** jouer à to play (*a sport*); on va jouer au foot we're going to play football; **3** jouer de to play (*an instrument*); Robert joue de la guitare Robert plays the guitar; **4** to act; il joue bien dans ce film he's really good in this film.

**n**

**o**

**p**

**q**

**r**

**jouet** *noun Masc.* toy.

**s**

**joueur, joueuse** *noun Masc., Fem.* player.

**t**

**jour** *noun Masc.* **1** day; les jours de la semaine the days of the week; trois jours plus tard three days later; le jour où the day when; un de ces jours one of these days; **2** de nos jours nowadays; de nos jours, ils sont assez fréquents nowadays they are quite common; **3** mettre quelque chose à jour to bring

**u**

**v**

**w**

**x**

**y**

**z**

something up to date; **4** daylight, light; il fait jour it's daylight; en plein jour in broad daylight; jour et nuit night and day.

**jour de l'an** *noun Masc.* New Year's Day.

**jour férié** *noun Masc.* public holiday.

**journal** (*plural* journaux) *noun Masc.* **1** newspaper, magazine; le journal du soir the evening paper; du papier journal newspaper (*for wrapping*); **2** news (*on TV or radio*); le journal de vingt-deux heures the ten o'clock news; **3** un journal intime a diary.

**journalisme** *noun Masc.* journalism.

**journaliste** *noun Masc. & Fem.* journalist.

**journée** *noun Fem.* day; toute la journée all day, the whole day; il est payé à la journée he's paid by the day.

**jour ouvrable** *noun Masc.* working day.

**joyeux** (*Fem.* joyeuse) *adjective* happy; Joyeux Anniversaire Happy Birthday; Joyeux Noël Merry Christmas.

**judaïsme** *noun Masc.* Judaism.

**judicieux** (*Fem.* judicieuse) *adjective* sensible; un choix judicieux a wise choice.

**judo** *noun Masc.* judo.

**juge** *noun Masc.* judge.

**juge d'instruction** noun Masc. examining magistrate.

**juge de ligne** noun Masc. line judge (in tennis).

**juge de touche** noun Masc. linesman (in football, rugby).

**jugement** noun Masc. judgement.

**juger** verb [52] to judge.

**juif, juive** noun Masc., Fem. Jew. **juif, juive** adjective Jewish.

**juillet** noun Masc. July; **en juillet, au mois de juillet** in July; **le quatorze juillet** Bastille Day (July 14, a national holiday to celebrate the taking of the Bastille prison in Paris by the people at the beginning of the French Revolution in 1789).

**juin** noun Masc. June; **en juin, au mois de juin** in June.

**juive** noun Fem., adjective SEE **juif**.

**jumeau** (plural **jumeaux**) **jumelle** noun Masc., Fem. twin; **des vrais jumeaux** identical twins.

**jumeler** verb [18] to twin (towns); **Oxford est jumelé avec Grenoble** Oxford is twinned with Grenoble.

**jumelles** plural noun Fem. 1 binoculars; 2 SEE **jumeau**.

**jument** noun Fem. mare.

**jungle** noun Fem. jungle.

**jupe** noun Fem. skirt.

**jupon** noun Masc. petticoat.

**jurer** verb [1] to swear.

**juridique** adjective legal; **le système juridique** the legal system.

**jury** noun Masc. 1 jury; 2 board of examiners.

**jus** noun Masc. 1 juice; **un jus d'orange** an orange juice; 2 gravy.

**jus de fruits** noun Masc. fruit juice.

**jusqu'à** preposition 1 as far as (a place); **ce train va jusqu'à Paris** this train goes as far as Paris; **nous avons marché jusqu'à la mer** we walked as far as the sea; **il m'a accompagné jusqu'à chez moi** he took me all the way home; 2 until; **elle reste jusqu'à mardi** she's staying until Tuesday; **jusqu'à quand reste-t-il?** how long is he staying for?; **jusqu'à présent, jusqu'à maintenant** up to now; 3 **jusqu'à ce que** until.

**juste** adjective 1 right, correct; **le mot juste** the right word; **ce que tu dis est juste** what you say is right; 2 fair; **ce n'est pas juste!** it's not fair!; 3 in tune; **elle chante juste** she sings in tune; 4 **c'est un peu juste** it's a bit tight; **une heure est un peu juste** an hour's a bit tight. **juste** adverb just; **juste à temps** just in time; **il vient tout juste d'arriver** he's only just arrived.

**justement** adverb 1 precisely; 2 just; **je parlais justement de toi** I was just talking about you; 3 correctly; **comme elle a dit très justement** as she so rightly said.

**justesse** noun Fem. 1 correctness; 2 **de justesse** only just; **il a eu son avion, mais de justesse** he caught his plane, but only just.

**justice** noun Fem. justice.

a b c d e f g h i j k l m n o p q r s t u v w x y z

**a b c d e f g h i j k l m n o p q r s t u v w x y z**

**justifier** *verb* [1] to justify.

**juteux** (*Fem.* **juteuse**) *adjective* juicy.

**juvénile** *adjective* youthful.

# Kk

**K.O.** *adjective* **1** **mettre quelqu'un K.O.** to knock somebody out (*in boxing*); **2 je suis complètement K.O.** (*informal*) I'm completely knackered.

**kaki** *noun Masc.* persimmon.
**kaki** *adjective* khaki.

**kangourou** *noun Masc.* kangaroo.

**karaté** *noun Masc.* karate.

**karting** *noun Masc.* go-karting.

**kascher** *adjective* kosher.

**kermesse** *noun Fem.* (school) fête.

**ketchup** *noun Masc.* ketchup.

**kidnapper** *verb* [1] to kidnap.

**kidnappeur**, **kidnappeuse** *noun Masc., Fem.* kidnapper.

**kilo** *noun Masc.* kilo; **deux kilos de pommes** two kilos of apples; **j'ai pris trois kilos** I've put on three kilos.

**kilogramme** *noun Masc.* kilogramme.

**kilométrage** *noun Masc.* mileage.

**kilomètre** *noun Masc.* kilometre; **à dix kilomètres d'ici** ten kilometres from here; **Paris est à combien de kilomètres de Dijon?** how many kilometres is it from Paris to Dijon?; **elle a combien de kilomètres**

**votre voiture?** what's the mileage on your car?

**kinésithérapeute** *noun Masc. & Fem.* physiotherapist.

**kinésithérapie** *noun Fem.* physiotherapy.

**kiosque** *noun Masc.* kiosk.

**kiwi** *noun Masc.* kiwi (*the bird and the fruit*).

**klaxon™** *noun Masc.* horn (*on a car*).

**klaxonner** *verb* [1] to sound the horn (*in a car*).

**km** SHORT FOR **kilomètre**; **km/h** kph (*kilometres per hour*).

**koala** *noun Masc.* koala bear.

**kraft** *noun Masc.* **le papier kraft** brown paper.

**K-way™** *noun Masc.* cagoule.

# Ll

**la, l'** (*before a vowel or silent 'h'*) *definite article, pronoun* SEE **le**.

**là** *adverb* **1** there; **est-ce que Paul est là?** is Paul there?; **c'est là qu'habite mon frère** that's where my brother lives; **2** here; **viens là** come here; **Danielle n'est pas là en ce moment** Danielle's not here at the moment; **3** then; **c'est là que j'ai pensé à toi** that's when I thought of you.

**-là** *adverb* **cette maison-là** that house; **ces gens-là** those people; **à ce moment-là** at that moment.

**là-bas** *adverb* **1** there; **qu'est-ce que vous avez fait là-bas?** what did you do there?; **2** over there; **notre maison est là-bas** our house is over there.

**labo** *noun Masc.* (*informal*) lab.

**laboratoire** *noun Masc.* laboratory.

**laboratoire de langues** *noun Masc.* language laboratory.

**labourer** *verb* [1] to plough.

**labyrinthe** *noun Masc.* maze, labyrinth.

**lac** *noun Masc.* lake; **le lac d'Annecy** Lake Annecy.

**lacer** *verb* [61] **lacer ses chaussures** to tie your shoelaces.

**lacet** *noun Masc.* lace (*for shoes*); **des chaussures à lacets** lace-up shoes.

**lâche** *adjective* **1** cowardly; **2** loose (*a belt or rope, for example*).

**lâcher** *verb* [1] **1** to drop (*an object*), to let go of (*a rope or branch*); **lâche-moi!** let go of me!; **ne lâche pas la corde!** don't let go of the rope!; **2** to drop; **elle a lâché son sac** she dropped her bag; **3** to give way; **la corde a lâché** the rope gave way.

**lâcheté** *noun Fem.* cowardice.

**lacrymogène** *adjective* **le gaz lacrymogène** teargas.

**là-dedans** *adverb* in there; **il y a un oiseau là-dedans** there's a bird in there; **il n'y a rien là-dedans** there's nothing inside.

**là-dessous** *adverb* under there; **les verres sont là-dessous** the glasses are under there.

**là-dessus** *adverb* **1** on there; **tu peux mettre les assiettes là-dessus** you can put the plates on there; **2** about it; **ils sont d'accord là-dessus** they agree about it; **a-t-il dit quelque chose là-dessus?** did he say anything about it?; **3** with that; **là-dessus il est sorti** with that, he went out.

**là-haut** *adverb* **1** up here, up there; **il est là-haut dans l'arbre** he's up there in the tree; **2** upstairs; **maman est là-haut** Mum's upstairs.

**laid** *adjective* ugly.

**laideur** *noun Fem.* ugliness.

**laine** *noun Fem.* wool; **un pull en laine** a woollen jumper.

**laine vierge** *noun Fem.* pure new wool.

**laïque** *adjective* **une école laïque** a state school.

**laisse** *noun Fem.* lead (*for a dog*).

**laisser** *verb* [1] **1** to leave; **j'ai laissé mes clés chez toi** I've left my keys at your house; **bon, je vous laisse** right, I must be off now; **2 laisser quelqu'un faire** to let somebody do; **laisse-le parler!** let him speak!; **laissez-la faire, elle reviendra** leave her alone, she'll come back; **3 il se laisse insulter** he puts up with being insulted; **elle s'est laissée aller** she's let herself go.

**laisser-aller** *noun Masc.* carelessness.

**lait** *noun Masc.* milk; **un thé au lait** a cup of tea with milk; **un café au lait** a white coffee.

**lait demi-écrémé** *noun Masc.* semi-skimmed milk.

**lait écrémé** *noun Masc.* skimmed milk.

**laitier** (*Fem.* **laitière**) *adjective* **les produits laitiers** milk products (*such as yoghurt*).

**laiton** *noun Masc.* brass.

**laitue** *noun Fem.* lettuce.

**lame** *noun Fem.* blade.

**lamelle** *noun Fem.* thin strip.

**lamentable** *adjective* awful.

**lampadaire** *noun Masc.* **1** standard lamp; **2** street lamp.

**lampe** *noun Fem.* lamp, light; **allumer la lampe** to turn on the lamp.

**lampe de poche** *noun Fem.* torch.

**lampe électrique** *noun Fem.* torch.

**lance** *noun Fem.* spear.

**lancement** *noun Masc.* launch.

**lancer** *verb* [61] **1** to throw; **il m'a lancé le ballon** he threw the ball to me; **2** to launch (*a product, a spacecraft*); **ils vont lancer leur nouveau produit en juin** they're going to launch their new product in June; **3 se lancer dans quelque chose** to embark on something.

**landau** *noun Masc.* pram.

**lande** *noun Fem.* moor.

**langage** *noun Masc.* language, type of language; **le langage administratif** official jargon.

**langouste** *noun Fem.* crayfish.

**langue** *noun Fem.* **1** tongue; **tirer la langue** to stick your tongue out; **2** language; **une langue étrangère** a foreign language; **ma langue maternelle** my mother tongue; ★ **je l'ai sur le bout de la langue** it's on the tip of my tongue.

**lanière** *noun Fem.* strap.

**lapin** *noun Masc.* rabbit; ★ **il m'a posé un lapin** (*informal*) he stood me up.

**laque** *noun Fem.* **1** hairspray; **2** lacquer, gloss paint.

**laquelle** *pronoun* SEE **lequel**.

**lard** *noun Masc.* streaky bacon.

**lardons** *plural noun Masc.* diced bacon; **salade aux lardons fumés** green salad with diced smoked bacon.

**large** *noun Masc.* open sea; **au large** offshore.
**large** *adjective* wide; **un large sourire** a broad smile; **être large de deux mètres** to be two metres wide.

**largement** *adverb* **c'est largement suffisant** that's more than enough; **j'ai largement le temps** I've got plenty of time.

**largeur** *noun Fem.* width.

**larme** *noun Fem.* tear; **en larmes** in tears; **rire aux larmes** to laugh till you cry.

**laryngite** *noun Fem.* laryngitis.

**lasagnes** *plural noun Fém.* lasagna; **manger des lasagnes** to eat lasagna.

**laser** *noun Masc.* laser; **une platine laser** a compact disc player.

**lasser** *verb* [1] **se lasser** to get tired.

**lassitude** *noun Fem.* weariness.

**latin** *noun Masc.*, *adjective* Latin.

**lauréat**, **lauréate** *noun Masc.*, *Fem.* winner; **un lauréat du prix Nobel** a Nobel Prize winner.

**laurier** *noun Masc.* laurel; **un laurier commun** a bay tree; **une feuille de laurier** a bay leaf.

**laurier-rose** *noun Masc.* oleander.

**lavable** *adjective* washable; **lavable en machine** machine-washable.

**lavabo** *noun Masc.* washbasin.

**lavage** *noun Masc.* **1** washing; **2** wash (*on a washing-machine programme*); **3** car wash.

**lavande** *noun Fem.* lavender.

**lave-linge** *noun Masc.* washing machine.

**laver** *verb* [1] **1** to wash; **2 se laver** to wash; **se laver les mains** to wash your hands; **se laver les dents** to brush your teeth.

**laverie** *noun Fem.* launderette.

**lave-vaisselle** *noun Masc.* dish washer.

**le**, **la**, **l'**, **les** *definite article* **1** the; **le chat** the cat; **la maison** the house; **les enfants** the children; **'quelle chemise?'** – **'la verte'** 'which shirt?' – 'the green one'; **2** (*'les' is often not translated*) **je n'aime pas les chiens** I don't like dogs; **elle se lave les cheveux** she's washing her hair; **3 le père de mon ami** my friend's father; **4** a, an; **cinq euros le kilo** five euros a kilo.

**le**, **la**, **l'**, **les** *pronoun* him, her, it, them; **je la vois tous les soirs** I see her every evening; **je le vois tous les soirs** I see him every evening; **où est-ce que tu les as mis?** where did you put them?; **il l'a acheté chez Meyer** he bought it at Meyer's.

**lécher** *verb* [24] to lick.

**lèche-vitrines** *noun Masc.* **faire du lèche-vitrines** to go window-shopping.

**leçon** *noun Fem.* lesson; **une leçon de géographie** a geography lesson.

**lecteur**, **lectrice** *noun Masc.*, *Fem.* **1** reader (*of a book*); **2** foreign language assistant (*in a university*).

**lecteur de cassettes** *noun Masc.* cassette player.

**lecteur de disquettes** *noun Masc.* floppy disk drive.

**lecteur laser** *noun Masc.* CD player.

**lecture** *noun Fem.* reading; **j'aime la lecture** I like reading; **le soir il fait de la lecture** he reads in the evenings.

**légal** (*Masc. plural* **légaux**) *adjective* legal.

**légende** *noun Fem.* **1** caption (*to a picture*); **2** key (*to a map*); **3** legend.

**léger** (*Fem.* **légère**) *adjective* **1** light; **une veste légère** a light jacket; **un repas léger** a light meal; **2** slight; **un léger retard** a slight delay; **3** weak; **un café léger** a weak coffee; ★ **faire quelque chose à la légère** to do something without thinking.

a
b
c
d
e
f
g
h
i
j
k
l
m
n
o
p
q
r
s
t
u
v
w
x
y
z

**légèrement** *adverb* **1** lightly; **légèrement parfumé** lightly perfumed; **2** slightly; **il est légèrement blessé** he's slightly hurt; **elle est légèrement plus grande que moi** she's slightly taller than me.

**légèreté** *noun Fem.* lightness.

**législatif** (*Fem.* **législative**) *adjective* legislative; **les élections législatives** the general election.

**légume** *noun Masc.* vegetable; **des légumes verts** green vegetables.

**lendemain** *noun Masc.* **le lendemain** the next day; **Marc est arrivé le lendemain** Marc arrived the next day; **le lendemain matin** the next morning; **le lendemain de l'accident** the day after the accident.

**lent** *adjective* slow.

**lentement** *adverb* slowly.

**lenteur** *noun Fem.* slowness; **avec lenteur** slowly.

**lentille** *noun Fem.* **1** lentil; **soupe aux lentilles** lentil soup; **2** lens; **lentilles de contact** contact lenses; **elle met ses lentilles** she's putting in her contact lenses.

**léopard** *noun Masc.* leopard.

**lequel, laquelle, lesquels, lesquelles** *pronoun* **1** which one?, which?; **'passe-moi les verres' – 'lesquels?'** 'pass me the glasses' – 'which ones?'; **2** which, who; **la voiture dans laquelle ils roulaient** the car they were driving in, the car in which they were driving; **le monsieur avec lequel je discutais** the man to whom I was talking (*often not translated*), the man I was talking to.

**les** *definite article,, pronoun* SEE **le**.

**lesquelles, lesquelles** SEE **lequel**.

**lessive** *noun Fem.* **1** washing; **faire la lessive** to do the washing; **2** washing powder, washing liquid.

**lettre** *noun Fem.* **1** letter; **écrire une lettre** to write a letter; **2** letter (*of the alphabet*); **une lettre minuscule** a small letter; **une lettre majuscule** a capital letter; ★ **il prend tout ce qu'on lui dit à la lettre** he takes everything you say literally.

**lettres** *plural noun Fem.* arts (*at university*).

**leur** *pronoun* them (*meaning 'to them'*); **je leur donne de l'argent** I give them money.
**leur** *adjective* (*plural* **leurs**) their; **leur voiture** their car; **leurs enfants** their children.
**leur** *pronoun* **le leur, la leur, les leurs** theirs; **ça, c'est notre maison, et ça, c'est la leur** that's our house and that's theirs; **nous avons appelé nos parents et ils ont appelé les leurs** we phoned our parents and they phoned theirs.

**levant** *adjective* **le soleil levant** the rising sun.

**lever**[1] *verb* [50] **1** to lift, to raise; **levons nos verres!** let's raise our glasses!; **levez la main!** put your hand up!; **il a levé les yeux** he looked up; **2 se lever** to get up (*out of bed or from a chair*); **je me lève à sept heures** I get up at seven o'clock; **nous nous sommes levés**

**tôt** we got up early; **quand le soleil se lève** when the sun rises.

**lever**[2] *noun Masc.* **au lever du soleil** at sunrise.

**lève-tard** *noun Masc.* late riser.

**lève-tôt** *noun Masc.* early riser.

**levier** *noun Masc.* lever.

**lèvre** *noun Fem.* lip.

**lévrier** *noun Masc.* greyhound.

**levure** *noun Fem.* yeast.

**lexique** *noun Masc.* word list.

**lézard** *noun Masc.* lizard.

**liaison** *noun Fem.* **1** link, connection; **une liaison routière** a road link; **une liaison radio** radio contact; **une liaison satellite** a satellite link; **2** (love) affair.

**liasse** *noun Fem.* wad, bundle (*of papers or banknotes*).

**libellule** *noun Fem.* dragonfly.

**libération** *noun Fem.* release, liberation; **la libération des femmes** women's liberation; **la Libération (de 1944)** the Liberation (of 1944) (*the end of the German occupation of France*).

**libérer** *verb* [24] **1** to free, to release (*a prisoner or hostage*); **2** to vacate (*a hotel room or flat*).

**liberté** *noun Fem.* freedom.

**libraire** *noun Masc. & Fem.* bookseller.

**librairie** *noun Fem.* bookshop.

**librairie-papeterie** *noun Fem.* bookseller's and stationer's.

**libre** *adjective* **1** free; **vous êtes libre de partir** you are free to go; **2** free (*of a seat or telephone*); **est-ce que cette place est libre?** is this seat free?

**librement** *adverb* freely.

**libre-service** *noun Masc.* self service, self-service shop or restaurant; **un libre-service bancaire** a cash dispenser.

**licence** *noun Fem.* degree (*at university*); **elle a une licence de chimie** she has a chemistry degree.

**licencier** *verb* [1] **licencier quelqu'un** to make somebody redundant.

**lien** *noun Masc.* link; **mes liens avec la famille** my links with my family; **un lien d'amitié** a bond of friendship.

**lierre** *noun Masc.* ivy.

**lieu** (*plural* **lieux**) *noun Masc.* **1** place; **un lieu public** a public place; **date et lieu de naissance** date and place of birth; **lieu de travail** place of work; **2 en premier lieu** in the first place; **3 avoir lieu** to take place; **le mariage aura lieu en juin** the marriage will take place in June; **4 au lieu de** instead of; **au lieu de prendre le bus, il est parti à pied** instead of taking the bus, he went off on foot; **5 les lieux** the premises; **peut-on visiter les lieux?** can one visit the premises?; **la police est arrivée sur les lieux** the police are now at the scene.

**lieutenant** *noun Masc.* lieutenant.

**lièvre** *noun Masc.* hare.

**lifting** *noun Masc.* face-lift.

a
b
c
d
e
f
g
h
i
j
k
l
m
n
o
p
q
r
s
t
u
v
w
x
y
z

**ligne** *noun Fem.* **1** line; **une ligne droite** a straight line; **une ligne blanche** a white line (*on the road*); **à la ligne!** new paragraph! (*in a dictation*); **2** line (*of a bus or train*); **la ligne Paris-Dijon** the Paris-Dijon line; **une ligne de chemin de fer** a railway line; **les grandes lignes** the main lines (*sign at a railway station*); **3** cable; **ligne électrique** electric cable; **4** (telephone) line; **la ligne est mauvaise** it's a bad line; **restez en ligne, monsieur** hold the line, sir; **5** figure; **pour garder la ligne** to keep your figure, to stay slim; **6** fishing line.

**ligne d'arrivée** *noun Fem.* finishing line.

**ligne de touche** *noun Fem.* touch line.

**lilas** *noun Masc.* lilac.

**limace** *noun Fem.* slug.

**lime** *noun Fem.* file; **une lime à ongles** a nail file.

**limite** *noun Fem.* **1** limit; **une limite d'âge** an age limit; **2 la date limite** the closing date; **3 sans limites** endless; **une patience sans limites** endless patience; **4 à la limite** if it comes to it, at a pinch; **à la limite, je peux te prêter l'argent** if it comes to it, I can lend you the money; **5 dans la limite de** within the limits of; **dans la limite des places disponibles** subject to available seating space; **dans la limite du possible** as far as possible; **6** boundary; **les limites du village** the village boundaries; **7** maximum, last; **vitesse limite** maximum speed; **âge limite** maximum age; **date limite de vente** sell-by date.

**limiter** *verb* [1] **1** to limit; **2 se limiter** to limit oneself; **je me limite à deux cafés par jour** I limit myself to two coffees a day.

**limonade** *noun Fem.* lemonade.

**lin** *noun Masc.* linen; **une jupe en lin** a linen skirt.

**linge** *noun Masc.* **1** linen (*sheets, towels, etc*); **linge de maison** household linen; **du linge sale** dirty linen; **2** washing; **as-tu du linge pour la machine?** have you any washing for the machine?; **une corde à linge** a washing line; ★ **elle était blanche comme un linge** she was white as a sheet.

**lingerie** *noun Fem.* lingerie.

**Lion** *noun Masc.* Leo (*sign of the Zodiac*).

**lion** *noun Masc.* lion.

**liqueur** *noun Fem.* liqueur.

**liquidation** *noun Fem.* clearance sale, closing-down sale; **'liquidation totale!'** 'everything must go!'

**liquide** *noun Masc.* **1** liquid; **2** cash; **payer quelque chose en liquide** to pay cash for something.
**liquide** *adjective* liquid.

**lire** *verb* [51] to read; **lire un roman** to read a novel; **elle sait lire maintenant** she can read now; **elle m'a lu une histoire** she read me a story; **un auteur qui est très lu** a popular author; **lire à haute voix** to read aloud; ★ **lire entre les lignes** to read between the lines.

**lis** *verb* SEE **lire**.

**lisible** *adjective* legible.

**lisse** *adjective* smooth.

**liste** *noun Fem.* list; **faire une liste** to make a list; **faire la liste de** to make a list of.

**liste d'attente** *noun Fem.* waiting list.

**lit**[1] *verb* SEE **lire**.

**lit**[2] *noun Masc.* bed; **aller au lit** to go to bed; **faire son lit** to make one's bed; **un lit à une place** a single bed; **un lit à deux places** a double bed; **une chambre à deux lits** a twin-bedded room; **au lit!** bedtime!

**literie** *noun Fem.* bedding.

**litière** *noun Fem.* litter (*for an animal's bed*); **la litière pour chat** cat litter.

**litre** *noun Masc.* litre; **un litre d'eau** a litre of water.

**littéralement** *adverb* literally.

**littérature** *noun Fem.* literature; **la littérature française** French literature.

**livraison** *noun Fem.* delivery; **'livraisons à toute heure'** 'we deliver any time'; **'livraisons à domicile'** 'we deliver'.

**livre**[1] *noun Masc.* book; **un livre pour enfants** a children's book; **un livre de poche** a paperback.

**livre**[2] *noun Fem.* **1** pound (*in money*); **une livre sterling** a pound sterling; **2** pound (*in France = 500 grammes*); **une livre de tomates** a pound of tomatoes.

**livrer** *verb* [1] **1** to deliver; **2** to hand over; **3 se livrer** to surrender.

**livret** *noun Masc.* booklet.

**livret de famille** *Masc.*, **livret de famille** *noun* family record book (*with details of births, marriages, and deaths*).

**livret scolaire** *noun Masc.* school report book.

**local** (*plural* **locaux**) *noun Masc.* place (*usually a building*); **locaux commerciaux** business premises; **dans les locaux du lycée** on school premises.
**local** (*Masc. plural* **locaux**) *adjective* local; **un journal local** a local paper; **dix heures heure locale** ten a.m. local time.

**localement** *adverb* locally.

**locataire** *noun Masc. & Fem.* tenant.

**location** *noun Fem.* **1** renting; **un appartement de location** a rented flat; **'locations'** 'to rent'; **2** hire, rental; **location de voitures** car hire; **location de vidéos** video rental; **3** reservation, booking (*of theatre seats*).

**locomotive** *noun Fem.* engine, locomotive.

**loge** *noun Fem.* **1** lodge (*for the caretaker in a block of flats*); **2** (*in a theatre*) dressing-room (*for an actor*), box (*for a spectator*).

**logement** *noun Masc.*
**1** accommodation; **il a trouvé un logement tout près** he's found somewhere to live just nearby;
**2** housing; **la crise du logement** the housing crisis.

**loger** *verb* [52] **1** to put up; **peux-tu me loger ce soir?** can you put me up tonight?; **2** to stay; **pour l'instant**

a
b
c
d
e
f
g
h
i
j
k
l
m
n
o
p
q
r
s
t
u
v
w
x
y
z

elle loge chez mes parents for the moment she's staying with my parents.

**logiciel** *noun Masc.* **1** software; **2** program (*for a computer*); un logiciel de jeux a games program; un logiciel antivirus antivirus software.

**logique** *noun Fem.* logic.
**logique** *adjective* logical.

**loi** *noun Fem.* law.

**loin** *adverb* **1** (*in distance*) a long way, far off; c'est loin it's a long way; c'est trop loin it's too far; c'est loin d'ici it's a long way from here; le cinéma est plus loin the cinema is further on; nous ne sommes pas allés plus loin that's the farthest we went; **2** (*in time*) far off; les vacances sont loin the holidays are a long way off; il n'est pas loin de midi it's almost twelve; **3** de loin from a long way off; on voit leur maison de loin you can see their house from a long way off; **4** de loin by far; c'est de loin le plus cher it's by far the most expensive; **5** au loin in the distance.

**lointain** *adjective* distant.

**loisirs** *plural noun Masc.* **1** spare time; je dessine pendant mes loisirs I draw in my spare time; **2** spare-time activities.

**Londonien, Londonienne** *noun Masc., Fem.* Londoner.

**Londres** *noun* London; à Londres in (*or* to) London; les rues de Londres the streets of London.

**long** *noun Masc.* **1** une corde de cinq mètres de long a rope five metres long; **2** le long de all along; le long de la route all along the road; **3** tout le long du film all the way through the film.
**long** (*Fem.* longue) *adjective* long; une longue vie a long life; un long silence a long silence; un long voyage a long journey; la rue la plus longue de Paris the longest street in Paris; une chemise à manches longues a long-sleeved shirt; la pièce est longue de quatre mètres, la pièce fait quatre mètres de long the room is four metres long; ★ marcher de long en large to walk up and down; ★ à la longue in the long run.

**longtemps** *adverb* (for) a long time; elle est restée longtemps she stayed for a long time; longtemps après a long time after; elle est là depuis longtemps she's been here for a long time; j'y suis allé, mais il y a longtemps I've been there, but a long time ago; ça fait longtemps qu'on ne s'est pas vu! it's ages since we've seen each other!; je n'en ai pas pour longtemps I won't be long.

**longuement** *adverb* for a long time.

**longueur** *noun Fem.* **1** length; de quelle longueur est le couloir? how long is the corridor?; **2** avoir des longueurs to drag; le film est intéressant mais il a des longueurs it's an interesting film but it drags in places.

**longueur d'onde** *noun Fem.* wavelength.

**lorsque, lorsqu'** (*before a vowel or silent 'h'*) *conjunction* when; **lorsque j'étais petite** when I was a little girl.

**lot** *noun Masc.* **1** batch; **un lot de trois boîtes** a pack of three cans; **2** prize (*in a lottery*); **elle a gagné le gros lot** she won the jackpot.

**lot** *noun Masc.* batch (*in computing*).

**loterie** *noun Fem.* **1** lottery; **2** raffle.

**lotion** *noun Fem.* lotion.

**lotissement** *noun Masc.* housing estate.

**loto** *noun Masc.* lottery.

**lotte** *noun Fem.* monkfish.

**louche**¹ *noun Fem.* ladle.

**louche**² *adjective* fishy; **il y a un type louche à la porte** there's a fishy-looking guy at the door.

**louer** *verb* [1] **1** to let (*a house or flat*); **pendant mon absence j'ai loué mon appartement** while I was away I let my flat; **'à louer'** 'to let'; **2** to rent; **nous avons loué un appartement à Lille** we've rented a flat in Lille; **3** to hire; **nous avons loué une voiture** we hired a car; **4** to praise.

**loup** *noun Masc.* wolf; ★ **j'ai une faim de loup** I'm absolutely starving (*literally: I'm as hungry as a wolf*); ★ **quand on parle du loup (on en voit la queue)** speak of the devil (*literally: when you speak of the wolf (you see its tail)*).

**loupe** *noun Fem.* magnifying glass.

**louper** *verb* [1] (*informal*) **1** to miss (*a train*); **on a loupé le train de dix heures** we missed the ten o'clock train; **2** to fail; **elle a loupé son permis** she failed her driving test.

**loup-garou** *noun Masc.* werewolf.

**lourd** *adjective* **1** heavy; **ta valise est très lourde** your case is very heavy; **le repas était un peu lourd** the meal was a bit heavy; **2 une lourde erreur** a serious mistake.

**loutre** *noun Fem.* otter.

**loyal** (*Masc. plural* **loyaux**) *adjective* faithful.

**loyauté** *noun Fem.* loyalty.

**loyer** *noun Masc.* rent; **payer le loyer** to pay the rent.

**lu** *verb* SEE **lire**.

**lucarne** *noun Fem.* skylight.

**luge** *noun Fem.* sledge.

**lugubre** *adjective* gloomy.

**lui** *pronoun* **1** him; **c'est lui** it's him; **Hélène travaille avec lui** Hélène works with him; **est-ce qu'il a aimé le bouquin que je lui ai prêté?** did he like the book I lent him?; **2** to him; **Pierre est en colère – qu'est-ce que tu lui as dit?** Pierre's angry – what did you say to him?; **3** to her; **Nadine est en colère – qu'est-ce que tu lui as dit?** Nadine's angry – what did you say to her?; **4** (*for emphasis*) **lui, il n'est jamais content!** he's never pleased!

**lui-même** *pronoun* **1** himself; **il l'a fait lui-même** he did it himself; **2** (*on telephone*) **'Monsieur**

a b c d e f g h i j k l m n o p q r s t u v w x y z

Dubois?' – 'lui-même' 'Monsieur Dubois?' – 'speaking'.

**lumière** *noun Fem.* light.

**lumineux** (*Fem.* **lumineuse**) *adjective* luminous; **un panneau lumineux** an electronic display board; **une enseigne lumineuse** a neon sign.

**lunch** *noun Masc.* buffet (*lunch or supper*).

**lundi** *noun Masc.* **1** Monday; **nous sommes lundi aujourd'hui** it's Monday today; **lundi prochain** next Monday; **lundi dernier** last Monday; **2** on Monday; **je l'ai vu lundi soir** I saw him on Monday evening; **3 le lundi** on Mondays; **fermé le lundi** closed on Mondays; **4 tous les lundis** every Monday.

**lune** *noun Fem.* moon; ★ **il est dans la lune** he's got his head in the clouds; ★ **il m'a promis la lune** he promised me the earth.

**lune de miel** *noun Fem.* honeymoon.

**lunettes** *plural noun Fem.* glasses; **une paire de lunettes** a pair of glasses; **mets tes lunettes!** put on your glasses!; **je porte des lunettes pour lire** I wear glasses for reading.

**lunettes de natation** *plural noun Fem.* swimming goggles.

**lunettes de soleil** *plural noun Fem.* sun-glasses.

**lutte** *noun Fem.* fight, struggle; **la lutte contre la drogue** the fight against drugs.

**lutter** *verb* [1] to fight, to struggle; **ils luttaient pour la liberté et contre l'oppression** they were fighting for freedom and against oppression.

**luxe** *noun Masc.* luxury; **une voiture de luxe** a luxury car.

**luxueux** (*Fem.* **luxueuse**) *adjective* luxurious.

**lycée** *noun Masc.* secondary school (*for ages 15-18*).

**lycéen**, **lycéenne** *noun Masc., Fem.* secondary school student.

# Mm

**M.** SHORT FOR **Monsieur**; **M. Dupont** Mr Dupont.

**ma** *adjective* my; SEE **mon**.

**macaronis** *plural noun Masc.* macaroni; **manger des macaronis** to have macaroni.

**mâche** *noun Fem.* lamb's lettuce.

**mâcher** *verb* [1] to chew.

**machin** *noun Masc.* (*informal*) whatsit, thingumajig; **tu n'as pas un machin pour ouvrir les enveloppes?** don't you have a whatsit for opening envelopes with?

**machine** *noun Fem.* **1** machine; **2 taper à la machine** to type.

**machine à coudre** *noun Fem.* sewing machine.

**machine à écrire** *noun Fem.* typewriter.

**machine à laver** *noun Fem.* washing machine.

**machine à sous** *noun Fem.* fruit machine.

**mâchoire** *noun Fem.* jaw.

**mâchonner** *verb* [1] to chew.

**maçon** *noun Masc.* **1** builder;
**2** bricklayer.

**Madame** (*plural* **Mesdames**)
*noun Fem.* **1 Madame Jones** Ms
Jones, Mrs Jones; **2 Madame, ...**
Dear Madam, ...; **3 bonsoir**
**madame** good evening (*when*
*greeting a person you do not know*
*well in French, it is polite to add*
*'Madame', 'Monsieur', or*
*'Mademoiselle' to the greeting*).

**Mademoiselle** (*plural*
**Mesdemoiselles**) *noun Fem.* **1** Miss,
Ms; **2 bonsoir mademoiselle** good
evening. SEE ALSO **Madame**.

**magasin** *noun Masc.* shop; **un**
**grand magasin** a department store;
**un magasin de vêtements** a
clothes shop; **un magasin de sport**
a sports shop; **faire les magasins** to
go round the shops.

**magazine** *noun Masc.* magazine.

**maghrébin** *adjective* North
African.

**Maghrébin**, **Maghrébine**
*noun Masc., Fem.* North African.

**magicien**, **magicienne** *noun*
*Masc., Fem.* magician.

**magie** *noun Fem.* magic.

**magique** *adjective* **1** magic;
**2** magical.

**magistral** (*Masc. plural*
**magistraux**) *adjective* **un cours**
**magistral** a lecture (*at university*).

**magnétique** *adjective* magnetic.

**magnétiser** *verb* [1] **1** to
magnetize; **2** to hypnotize.

**magnétophone** *noun Masc.* tape
recorder.

**magnétoscope** *noun Masc.* video
recorder.

**magnifique** *adjective* splendid.

**magouille** *noun Fem.* (*informal*)
fiddling.

**magret de canard** *noun Masc.*
duck breast.

**mai** *noun Masc.* May; **en mai, au**
**mois de mai** in May; **le premier**
**mai** May Day.

**maigre** *adjective* thin, skinny;
★ **maigre comme un clou** as thin
as a rake (*literally: as thin as a nail*).

**maigrir** *verb* [2] to lose weight; **il a**
**beaucoup maigri** he's lost a lot of
weight.

**maille** *noun Fem.* stitch (*in knitting*).

**maillot** *noun Masc.* **1** shirt, jersey
(*in sports such as football*); **2 maillot**
**(de corps)** vest.

**maillot de bain** *noun Masc.*
**1** swimsuit; **2** swimming trunks.

**main** *noun Fem.* hand; **avoir**
**quelque chose à la main** to have
something in your hand; **serrer la**
**main à quelqu'un** to shake hands
with somebody; **se serrer la main** to
shake hands; **nous nous sommes**
**serré la main** we shook hands; **se**
**donner la main** to hold hands; **haut**
**les mains!** hands up!; **donner un**
**coup de main à quelqu'un** to give
somebody a hand; **tu veux un coup**
**de main?** do you want a hand?; **fait**
**à la main** handmade.

a
b
c
d
e
f
g
h
i
j
k
l
m
n
o
p
q
r
s
t
u
v
w
x
y
z

175

a
b
c
d
e
f
g
h
i
j
k
l
**m**
n
o
p
q
r
s
t
u
v
w
x
y
z

**main-d'œuvre** *noun Fem.* labour.

**maintenant** *adverb* **1** now; **il est maintenant trop tard pour sortir** it's too late to go out now; **2** nowadays; **maintenant presque tout le monde a le téléphone** nowadays nearly everybody has a phone..

**maintenir** *verb* [81] **1** to maintain; **2** to support.

**maire** *noun Masc.* mayor.

**mairesse** *noun Fem.* mayoress.

**mairie** *noun Fem.* **1** town hall; **2** town council.

**mais** *conjunction* **1** but; **j'ai essayé de t'appeler mais tu n'étais pas là** I tried to phone you but you weren't there; **2 mais oui** yes of course; **mais non** of course not.

**maïs** *noun Masc.* **1** maize; **2** sweetcorn; **3 des épis de maïs** corn on the cob.

**maison** *noun Fem.* **1** house; **leur maison est petite mais très confortable** their house is small but very comfortable; **2** home; **rester à la maison** to stay at home; **rentrer à la maison** to go home.

**maison de la culture** *noun Fem.* cultural centre, arts centre.

**maison de retraite** *noun Fem.* old people's home.

**maître, maîtresse** *noun Masc., Fem.* **1** master, mistress; **2** teacher.

**maître-nageur** *noun Masc.* swimming instructor.

**maîtresse** *noun Fem.* **1** SEE **maître**; **2** lover.

**maîtrise** *noun Fem.* **1** mastery; **2** command; **la maîtrise de soi** self-control; **3** master's degree.

**maîtriser** *verb* [1] **1** to control; **2** to master.

**majestueux** (*Fem.* **majestueuse**) *adjective* majestic.

**majeur** *adjective* **1** major; **2 être majeur** to be over 18.
**majeur** *noun* middle finger.

**majorité** *noun Fem.* majority.

**majuscule** *noun Fem.* capital (letter); **en majuscules** in block capitals; **un R majuscule** a capital R.

**mal** (*plural* **maux**) *noun Masc.* **1** pain, ache; **faire mal** to hurt; **se faire mal** to hurt yourself; **avoir mal à la gorge** to have a sore throat; **j'ai mal au dos** my back hurts; **ça fait mal** it hurts; **2 faire mal à quelqu'un** to hurt somebody; **aïe! tu me fais mal!** ouch! you're hurting me!; **3 avoir du mal à faire** to have difficulty in doing; **j'ai du mal à comprendre ce qu'il dit** I have difficulty in understanding what he says; **se donner du mal à faire** to go to a lot of trouble to do; **elle s'est donné beaucoup de mal pour contacter tout le monde** she went to a lot of trouble to contact everybody; **4** evil.
**mal** *adjective* **1 pas mal** not bad; **2 être mal** to be uncomfortable.
**mal** *adverb* **1** badly; **écrire mal** to write badly; **2 je t'entends mal** I can't hear you very well; **3 j'ai mal compris** I misunderstood; **4 être mal à l'aise** to feel uncomfortable.

**malade** *noun Masc. & Fem.* patient.
**malade** *adjective* ill, sick; **tomber malade** to fall ill.

**maladie** *noun Fem.* **1** illness; **2** disease.

**maladresse** *noun Fem.*
**1** clumsiness; **2** blunder.

**maladroit** *adjective* clumsy.

**malaise** *noun Masc.* **1 avoir un malaise** to feel faint, to pass out; **2 créer un malaise** to make people feel uncomfortable; **ça a créé un malaise** it made everybody feel uncomfortable.

**malaxer** *verb* [1] **1** to knead; **2** to cream.

**malchance** *noun Fem.* bad luck.

**mal de mer** *noun Masc.* **avoir le mal de mer** to be seasick.

**mal du pays** *noun Masc.* **avoir le mal du pays** to be homesick.

**mâle** *noun Masc., adjective* male.

**malédiction** *noun Fem.* curse.

**malencontreux** (*Fem.* **malencontreuse**) *adjective* unfortunate.

**malentendu** *noun Masc.* misunderstanding.

**malfaiteur** *noun Masc.* criminal.

**mal famé** *adjective* **un quartier mal famé** a rough area.

**malgré** *preposition* **1** in spite of; **malgré le froid** in spite of the cold; **2 malgré tout** all the same; **mais malgré tout nous avons décidé d'y aller** but we decided to go all the same.

**malheur** *noun Masc.* misfortune; **porter malheur** to bring bad luck.

**malheureusement** *adverb* unfortunately; **Vincent était déjà parti, malheureusement** unfortunately, Vincent had already left.

**malheureux, malheureuse** *noun Masc., Fem.* poor thing; **la malheureuse!** poor woman! **malheureux** (*Fem.* **malheureuse**) *adjective* **1** unhappy; **avoir l'air malheureux** to look unhappy; **rendre quelqu'un malheureux** to make somebody unhappy; **2** unfortunate; **un choix malheureux** an unfortunate choice.

**malhonnête** *adjective* dishonest.

**malice** *noun Fem.* mischief.

**malicieux** (*Fem.* **malicieuse**) *adjective* mischievous.

**malin** (*Fem.* **maligne**) *adjective* **1** clever; **ce n'était pas très malin ça** that wasn't very clever; **elle se croit maligne** she thinks she's clever; **2** malignant (*tumour*).

**malle** *noun Fem.* trunk.

**malodorant** *adjective* smelly.

**malpoli** *adjective* rude.

**malpropre** *adjective* dirty.

**malsain** *adjective* unhealthy.

**maltraiter** *verb* [1] to ill-treat; **les enfants maltraités** battered children.

**malveillance** *noun Fem.* malice.

**malveillant** *adjective* malicious.

**maman** *noun Fem.* mum, mummy.

**mamie** *noun Fem.* granny, gran, nan.

**mammifère** *noun Masc.* mammal.

177

**manager** *verb* [52] to manage.

**manageur** *noun Masc.* manager.

**manche**[1] *noun Masc.* handle (*of a tool*).

**manche**[2] *noun Fem.* **1** sleeve; **une chemise à manches courtes** a short-sleeved shirt; **sans manches** sleeveless; **2** leg (*of a match*).

**Manche** *noun Fem.* **la Manche** the Channel; **le tunnel sous la Manche** the Channel Tunnel.

**mandarine** *noun Fem.* mandarin orange.

**mandat** *noun Masc.* money order.

**manège** *noun Masc.* **1** merry-go-round; **2** riding school.

**manette** *noun Fem.* lever.

**mangeable** *adjective* edible.

**manger** *noun Masc.* food.
**manger** *verb* [52] to eat; **qu'est-ce qu'on va manger?** what shall we have to eat?; **manger au restaurant** to go out for a meal; **j'ai déjà mangé** I've already eaten; **j'ai assez mangé** I'm full, I've had enough; **donner à manger à** to feed; **ils mangent trois fois par jour** they have three meals a day; ★ **manger ses mots** to mumble (*literally: to eat your words*).

**mangue** *noun Fem.* mango.

**maniaque** *noun Masc. & Fem.* fusspot.
**maniaque** *adjective* extremely fussy.

**manie** *noun Fem.* **1** odd habit; **2** mania.

**manier** *verb* [1] to handle.

**manière** *noun Fem.* **1** way; **une manière plus facile** an easier way; **on ne peut pas le faire d'une manière plus facile?** isn't there an easier way of doing it?; **de cette manière** like this, like that; **d'une autre manière** in another way; **d'une manière ou d'une autre** one way or another; **d'une certaine manière** in a way; **2 de toute manière** in any case; **3 de manière à faire** so as to do; **de manière à éviter de dépenser de l'argent** so as to avoid spending money; **4 manières** manners; **ne fais pas de manières!** don't make a fuss!

**manifestant, manifestante** *noun Masc., Fem.* demonstrator.

**manifestation** *noun Fem.* demonstration; **une manifestation contre le racisme** a demonstration against racism.

**manifester** *verb* [1] **1** to demonstrate, to take part in a demonstration; **2 manifester quelque chose** to express something.

**manipuler** *verb* [1] **1** to handle; **2** to manipulate.

**manivelle** *noun Fem.* handle.

**mannequin** *noun Masc.* **1** fashion model; **2** dummy (*either in a shop window or as used by a dressmaker*).

**manoir** *noun Masc.* manor house.

**manque** *noun Masc.* **manque de** lack of, shortage of; **leur manque d'imagination** their lack of imagination; **être en manque d'affection** to be in need of affection.

**manqué** *adjective* **1** failed; **un acteur manqué** a failed actor; **2** missed; **une occasion manquée** a missed opportunity.

**manquer** *verb* [1] **1 manquer quelque chose** to miss something; **il a manqué son train** he missed his train; **2 manquer un examen** to fail an exam; **3 manquer à quelqu'un** to be missed by somebody; **tu me manques** I miss you; **Londres leur manque** they miss London; **4 il manque quelque chose** something's missing; **il manque trois fourchettes** there are three forks missing, we're three forks short; **5 manquer de** to lack; **nous ne manquons pas de verres** there's no shortage of glasses; **6 manquer de faire** to fail to do; **il a manqué de fermer la porte à clé** he failed to lock the door.

**mansarde** *noun Fem.* attic room.

**manteau** (*plural* **manteaux**) *noun Masc.* coat.

**manuel** *noun Masc.* **1** manual; **2** textbook; **un manuel scolaire** a school book.
**manuel** *adjective* (*Fem.* **manuelle**) manual.

**manufacture** *noun Fem.* **1** factory; **2** manufacture.

**manuscrit** *noun Masc.* manuscript.
**manuscrit** *adjective* handwritten; **un petit mot manuscrit** a handwritten note.

**maquereau** (*plural* **maquereaux**) *noun Masc.* mackerel.

**maquette** *noun Fem.* scale model.

**maquillage** *noun Masc.* make-up.

**maquiller** *verb* [1] **se maquiller** to put on your make-up.

**marais** *noun Masc.* marsh.

**marathon** *noun Masc.* marathon.

**marbre** *noun Masc.* marble; **une cheminée en marbre** a marble fireplace.

**marc de café** *noun Masc.* coffee grounds.

**marchand**, **marchande** *noun Masc., Fem.* **1** shopkeeper; **la marchande de fromage** the woman in the cheese shop; **2** stallholder (*on a market*).

**marchand de journaux** *noun Masc.* newsagent.

**marchander** *verb* [1] to haggle (over).

**marchandise** *noun Fem.* goods.

**marche** *noun Fem.* **1** walking; **faire de la marche** to go walking; **2** march; **3** step; **les marches d'escalier** the stairs; **attention à la marche** mind the step; **4 mettre en marche** to start up (*a machine*); **être en état de marche** to be in working order.

**marché** *noun Masc.* **1** market; **aller au marché** to go to market; **le marché aux fleurs** the flower market; **un marché aux puces** a flea market; **le marché de l'emploi** the job market; **2** deal.

a
b
c
d
e
f
g
h
i
j
k
l
m
n
o
p
q
r
s
t
u
v
w
x
y
z

a
b
c
d
e
f
g
h
i
j
k
l
**m**
n
o
p
q
r
s
t
u
v
w
x
y
z

**marche arrière** *noun Fem.* reverse; **faire marche arrière** to reverse.

**marchepied** *noun Masc.* step (*on a train*).

**marcher** *verb* [1] **1** to walk; **on va marcher jusqu'à la gare** we'll walk as far as the station; **2 marcher dans quelque chose** to tread in something; **marcher sur quelque chose** to tread on something; **3** to march; **4** to work; **ça a marché** it worked; **la machine à laver ne marche pas** the washing machine doesn't work; **les trains ne marchent pas aujourd'hui** the trains are not running today; **5 et ton boulot, ça marche?** (*informal*) and is your job going all right?; ★ **faire marcher quelqu'un** to pull somebody's leg.

**marcheur, marcheuse** *noun Masc., Fem.* walker.

**mardi** *noun Masc.* **1** Tuesday; **nous sommes mardi aujourd'hui** it's Tuesday today; **mardi prochain** next Tuesday; **mardi dernier** last Tuesday; **2** on Tuesday; **je t'appellerai mardi soir** I'll ring you on Tuesday evening; **3 le mardi** on Tuesdays; **c'est fermé le mardi** it's closed on Tuesdays; **4 tous les mardis** every Tuesday.

**Mardi gras** *noun Masc.* Shrove Tuesday.

**mare** *noun Fem.* pond.

**marécage** *noun Masc.* swamp.

**marée** *noun Fem.* tide; **la marée monte** the tide's coming in; **la marée descend** the tide's going out.

**marée noire** *noun Fem.* oil slick.

**margarine** *noun Fem.* margarine.

**marge** *noun Fem.* **1** margin; **2 en marge de** on the fringe of.

**marguerite** *noun Fem.* **1** marguerite; **2** oxeye daisy.

**mari** *noun Masc.* husband; **le mari de Claire** Claire's husband.

**mariage** *noun Masc.* **1** marriage; **2** wedding; **être invité à un mariage** to be invited to a wedding.

**Marianne** *noun Fem.* Marianne (*a female figure representing the French Republic in statues and paintings*).

**marié, mariée** *noun Masc., Fem.* bridegroom, bride; **les jeunes mariés** the newlyweds.
**marié** *adjective* married.

**marier** *verb* [1] **1 se marier** to get married; **ils se sont mariés à Londres** they got married in London; **elle s'est mariée avec Frank** she married Frank; **2 le prêtre qui les a mariés** the priest who married them.

**marin** *noun Masc.* sailor.
**marin** *adjective* sea.

**marine** *adjective* **bleu marine** navy blue.

**mariner** *verb* [1] to marinate.

**marionnette** *noun Fem.* puppet.

**marjolaine** *noun Fem.* marjoram.

**marketing** *noun Masc.* marketing.

**marmelade** *noun Fem.* **marmelade d'oranges amères** orange marmalade.

**marmite** *noun Fem.* cooking pot.

**marmonner** *verb* [1] to mutter, to mumble.

**Maroc** *noun Masc.* Morocco.

**marocain** *adjective* Moroccan.

**Marocain**, **Marocaine** *noun Masc., Fem.* Moroccan (*person*).

**maroquinerie** *noun Fem.*
**1** leather shop; **2** leather goods.

**marquant** *adjective* outstanding.

**marque** *noun Fem.* **1** brand; **une marque de nourriture pour chats** a brand of cat food; **2** make; **c'est une marque de jean bien connue** it's a well-known make of jeans; **3** mark; **4** point.

**marque déposée** *noun Fem.* registered trademark.

**marquer** *verb* [1] **1** to mark; **2** to write down; **j'ai marqué ton nom** I've written down your name; **3 marquer un but** to score a goal.

**marqueur** *noun Masc.* marker pen.

**marraine** *noun Fem.* godmother.

**marrant** *adjective* (*informal*) funny.

**marre** *adverb* (*informal*) **j'en ai marre** I'm fed up; **j'en ai marrre d'écrire** I'm fed up with writing.

**marrer** *verb* [1] **1 se marrer** to have a great time; **2 se marrer** to have a good laugh.

**marron** *noun Masc.* **1** (sweet) chestnut; **2** (horse) chestnut.
**marron** *adjective* brown; **des chaussures marron** brown shoes; **marron clair** light brown; **marron foncé** dark brown.

**marronnier** *noun Masc.* chestnut tree.

**mars** *noun Masc.* March; **en mars, au mois de mars** in March.

**Marseillaise** *noun Fem.* **la Marseillaise** the Marseillaise (*the French national anthem*).

**Marseille** *noun* Marseilles.

**marteau** (*plural* **marteaux**) *noun Masc.* **1** hammer; **2** doorknocker.

**marteau piqueur** *noun Masc.* pneumatic drill.

**marteler** *verb* [45] to hammer.

**martinet** *noun Masc.* swift.

**martin-pêcheur** *noun Masc.* kingfisher.

**martyrisé** *adjective* **un enfant martyrisé** a battered child.

**mascotte** *noun Fem.* mascot.

**masculin** *noun Masc.* masculine (*in French and other grammars*); **au masculin** in the masculine.
**masculin** *adjective* **1** male; **le sexe masculin** the male sex; **2** men's; **les vêtements masculins** men's clothing; **3** masculine.

**masque** *noun Masc.* mask.

**masquer** *verb* [1] to hide.

**massacre** *noun Masc.* massacre.

**massacrer** *verb* [1] to massacre.

**massage** *noun Masc.* massage; **faire un massage à quelqu'un** to give somebody a massage.

**masse** *noun Fem.* **1** mass; **2 une masse de** (*informal*) masses of; **j'ai une masse de boulot à faire avant lundi** I've got masses of work to do for Monday.

a
b
c
d
e
f
g
h
i
j
k
l
m
n
o
p
q
r
s
t
u
v
w
x
y
z

a

**masser** *verb* [1] **1** to massage; **2 se masser** to assemble.

b

**massif** (*Fem.* **massive**) *adjective*
**1** solid; **une table en pin massif** a solid pine table; **2** massive.

c

d

**mass media** *plural noun Masc.* **les mass media** the mass media.

e

f

**mastic** *noun Masc.* **1** putty; **2** filler.

g

**mastiquer** *verb* [1] **1** to chew; **2** to putty (*a window*); **3** to fill (*a crack*).

h

**mat** *adjective* matt.

i

**mât** *noun Masc.* **1** mast; **2** pole.

j

**match** *noun Masc.* match; **un match de foot** a football match; **faire match nul** to draw.

k

l

**matelas** *noun Masc.* mattress.

m

**matelassé** *adjective* quilted.

n

**matelot** *noun Masc.* sailor.

o

**matériaux** *plural noun Masc.* materials; **les matériaux de construction** building materials.

p

q

**matériel** *noun Masc.* equipment; **matériel de sport** sports equipment.

r

s

**maternel** (*Fem.* **maternelle**) *adjective* **1** motherly; **2** maternal; **ma tante maternelle** my aunt on my mother's side of the family.

t

u

**maternelle** *noun Fem.* (state) nursery school (*for ages 2 - 6*); **aller en maternelle** to go to nursery school.

v

w

x

**maternité** *noun Fem.*
**1** motherhood; **2** pregnancy; **être en congé de maternité** to be on maternity leave; **3** maternity unit.

y

z

**mathématiques** *plural noun Fem.* mathematics.

**matheux, matheuse** *noun Masc., Fem.* maths genius.

**maths** *plural noun Fem.* maths.

**matière** *noun Fem.* subject; **la matière que j'aime le mieux c'est l'histoire** the subject I like best is history; **en matière de: la politique du gouvernement en matière de l'éducation** the government's education policy.

**matières grasses** *plural noun Fem.* fat (*in food*).

**matin** *noun Masc.* morning; **à quelle heure est-ce que tu te lèves le matin?** what time do you get up in the morning?; **à six heures du matin** at six o'clock in the morning; **du matin au soir** from morning till night; **de bon matin** early in the morning.

**matinal** (*Masc. plural* **matinaux**) **matinal** *adjective* **1** morning; **2 être matinal** to be an early riser.

**matinée** *noun Fem.* **1** morning; **au cours de la matinée** during the morning; **2** matinée.

**matou** *noun Masc.* tomcat.

**matraque** *noun Fem.* truncheon, club.

**matrimonial** (*Masc. plural* **matrimoniaux**) *adjective* **une agence matrimoniale** a marriage bureau.

**maturité** *noun Fem.* maturity.

**maudire** *verb* to curse.

**maussade** *adjective* **1** sullen; **2** dull, dreary (*weather*).

**mauvais** *adjective* **1** bad; **une mauvaise expérience** a bad experience; **ça sent mauvais ici** there's a nasty smell here; **ça a mauvais goût** it tastes horrible; **c'est du mauvais goût** it's bad taste; **2** wrong; **le mauvais numéro** the wrong number; **la mauvaise adresse** the wrong address; **3 il fait mauvais** the weather's bad; **4 elle a mauvaise mine** she doesn't look well.

**mauvaise herbe** *noun Fem.* weed.

**maux** *plural noun Masc.* SEE **mal**.

**maximum** *noun Masc., adjective* maximum; **au maximum** as much as possible; **au maximum** at the most; **faire le maximum** to do your utmost.

**mayonnaise** *noun Fem.* mayonnaise.

**mazout** *noun Masc.* fuel oil.

**me, m'** *(before a vowel or silent 'h')* *pronoun* me **1 elle me déteste** she hates me; **il m'a vu** he saw me; **2** to me; **elle ne me parle jamais** she never speaks to me; **elle m'a donné son adresse** she gave me her address; **il me l'a donné** he gave it to me; **3** myself; **je me fais une salade** I'm making myself a salad; **je me suis blessé** I hurt myself; **je me lève à sept heures** I get up at seven o'clock; **je me brosse les dents** I brush my teeth (*literally: I brush to myself the teeth*).

**mec** *noun Masc.* (*informal*) guy.

**mécanicien, mécanicienne** *noun Masc., Fem.* **1** mechanic; **2** train driver.

**mécanique** *noun Fem.* **1** mechanics; **2** mechanism. **mécanique** *adjective* **1** mechanical; **2** clockwork.

**mécanisme** *noun Masc.* mechanism.

**méchamment** *adverb* spitefully, nastily.

**méchanceté** *noun Fem.* **1** nastiness; **2** spite.

**méchant** *adjective* **1** nasty; **elle a été vraiment méchante avec moi** she was really nasty to me; **2** spiteful; **3** vicious; **'chien méchant'** 'beware of the dog'.

**mèche** *noun Fem.* **1** lock (*of hair*); **2** wick.

**méconnaissable** *adjective* unrecognizable.

**mécontent** *adjective* dissatisfied.

**mécontentement** *noun Masc.* **1** annoyance; **2** displeasure.

**médaille** *noun Fem.* medal.

**médecin** *noun Masc.* doctor; **aller chez le médecin** to go to the doctor's.

**médecine** *noun Fem.* medicine; **faire des études de médecine** to go to medical school.

**médias** *plural noun Masc.* **les médias** the media.

**médiathèque** *noun Fem.* multimedia library.

**médical** (*Masc. plural* **médicaux**) *adjective* medical.

**médicament** *noun Masc.* drug.

a
b
c
d
e
f
g
h
i
j
k
l
m
n
o
p
q
r
s
t
u
v
w
x
y
z

**médiéval** (*Masc. plural* médiévaux) *adjective* medieval.

**médiocre** *adjective* second-rate, poor; **un travail médiocre** a second-rate piece of work.

**méditation** *noun Fem.* meditation.

**méditer** *verb* [1] **1** to meditate; **2 méditer quelque chose** to mull something over.

**Méditerranée** *noun Fem.* **la Méditerranée** the Mediterranean.

**méditerranéen** (*Fem.* méditerranéenne) *adjective* Mediterranean; **la cuisine méditerranéenne** Mediterranean cooking.

**méduse** *noun Fem.* jellyfish.

**méfait** *noun Masc.* **1** crime; **2 les méfaits de la pollution** the detrimental effects of pollution.

**méfiance** *noun Fem.* suspicion.

**méfiant** *adjective* suspicious.

**méfier** *verb* [1] **se méfier de quelqu'un** not to trust somebody; **méfie-toi!** watch out!

**mégère** *noun Fem.* shrew.

**mégot** *noun Masc.* cigarette end.

**meilleur** *noun Masc.* best; **c'est le meilleur** it's the best one; **le meilleur des deux** the better of the two.

**meilleur** *adjective* **1** better; **le climat est bien meilleur au sud** the climate's much better in the south; **meilleur que** better than; **ton écriture est meilleure que la mienne** your writing's better than mine; **c'est meilleur que l'autre** it's better than the other one; **2** best; **le**

**meilleur** the best moment; **c'est ma meilleure amie** she's my best friend; **meilleurs voeux** best wishes.

**mélange** *noun Masc.* mixture.

**mélanger** *verb* [52] **1** to mix; **2** to mix up; **j'ai mélangé les dates** I got the dates mixed up.

**mélasse** *noun Fem.* black treacle.

**mêlée** *noun Fem.* scrum.

**mêler** *verb* [1] **1 se mêler à** to mingle with; **2 se mêler de** to meddle in; ★ **mêle-toi de ce qui te regarde!** mind your own business!.

**mélodie** *noun Fem.* melody, tune.

**mélomane** *noun Masc. & Fem.* music lover.

**melon** *noun Masc.* **1** melon; **2 un chapeau melon** a bowler hat.

**membre** *noun Masc.* **1** member; **2** limb.

**même** *adjective* **1** same; **j'ai le même anniversaire que toi** I have the same birthday as you; **ils avaient des chapeaux de la même couleur** they had the same colour hats; **2 en même temps** at the same time; **3 tout de même** all the same. **même** *adverb* even; **il n'a même pas demandé** he didn't even ask.

**mémé** *noun* (*informal*) *Fem.* **1** granny; **2 une vieille mémé** an old lady.

**mémoire** *noun Fem.* memory.

**mémoriser** *verb* [1] to memorize.

**menace** *noun Fem.* threat.

**menacer** *verb* [61] to threaten.

**ménage** *noun Masc.* **1** housework; **faire le ménage** to do the cleaning; **une femme de ménage** a cleaning lady; **2** household.

**ménager**[1] *verb* [52] **ménager quelqu'un** to handle somebody tactfully.

**ménager**[2] (*Fem.* **ménagère**) *adjective* household; **les appareils ménagers** household appliances; **les travaux ménagers** housework.

**mendiant**, **mendiante** *noun Masc.*, *Fem.* beggar.

**mendier** *verb* [1] to beg.

**mener** *verb* [50] **1** to lead; **mener à** to lead to; **le chemin qui mène à la ferme** the track which leads to the farm; **2 mener une société** to run a company; **3 mener une campagne** to conduct a campaign.

**méningite** *noun Fem.* meningitis.

**menottes** *plural noun Fem.* handcuffs.

**mensonge** *noun Masc.* lie; **dire des mensonges** to tell lies.

**mensualité** *noun Fem.* monthly payment.

**mensuel** (*Fem.* **mensuelle**) *adjective* monthly.

**mental** (*Masc. plural* **mentaux**) *adjective* mental.

**mentalité** *noun Fem.* mentality.

**menteur**, **menteuse** *noun Masc.*, *Fem.* liar.
**menteur** (*Fem.* **menteuse**) *adjective* untruthful.

**menthe** *noun Fem.* mint; **le sirop de menthe** mint cordial.

**mention** *noun Fem.* **1** mention; **2** grade (*in an exam or a degree*); **elle a eu son bac avec mention bien** she got a grade B plus pass in her baccalaureate.

**mentionner** *verb* [1] to mention.

**mentir** *verb* [53] to lie, to tell lies.

**menton** *noun Masc.* chin.

**menu**[1] *noun Masc.* menu; **qu'est-ce qu'il y a au menu?** what's on the menu?; **le menu du jour** today's menu; **est-ce qu'il y un menu à prix fixe?** is there a set menu?

**menu**[2] *adjective* very small.

**menuiserie** *noun Fem.* woodwork.

**menuisier** *noun Masc.* joiner.

**mépris** *noun Masc.* contempt.

**mépriser** *verb* [1] to despise.

**mer** *noun Fem.* sea; **aller à la mer** to go to the seaside; **au bord de la mer** at the seaside; **la mer du Nord** the North Sea; **la mer des Antilles** the Caribbean (Sea).

**mercerie** *noun Fem.* haberdashery.

**merci**[1] *exclamation* thank you, thanks; **merci beaucoup, merci bien** thank you very much; **merci de m'avoir rappelé** thank you for calling me back.

**merci**[2] *noun Fem.* mercy.

**mercredi** *noun Masc.* **1** Wednesday; **nous sommes mercredi aujourd'hui** it's Wednesday today; **mercredi prochain** next Wednesday; **mercredi dernier** last Wednesday; **2** on Wednesday; **je t'appellerai mercredi soir** I'll ring you on

a
b
c
d
e
f
g
h
i
j
k
l
m
n
o
p
q
r
s
t
u
v
w
x
y
z

**mercure**

Wednesday evening; **3 le mercredi** on Wednesdays; **c'est fermé le mercredi** it's closed on Wednesdays; **tous les mercredis** every Wednesday.

**mercure** *noun Masc.* mercury.

**mère** *noun Fem.* mother; **la mère de Sophie** Sophie's mother.

**merguez** *noun Fem.* spicy lamb sausage.

**méridional** (*Masc. plural* **méridionaux**) *adjective* southern.

**meringue** *noun Fem.* meringue.

**mérite** *noun Fem.* merit.

**mériter** *verb* [1] to deserve.

**merlan** *noun Masc.* whiting.

**merle** *noun Masc.* blackbird.

**merveille** *noun Fem.* **1** wonder; **ton gâteau est une vraie merveille** your cake's absolutely wonderful; **2 à merveille** wonderfully.

**merveilleux** (*Fem.* **merveilleuse**) *adjective* marvellous.

**mes** *adjective* SEE **mon**.

**Mesdames** *noun* SEE **Madame**.

**Mesdemoiselles** *noun* SEE **Mademoiselle**.

**mesquin** *adjective* petty, mean.

**message** *noun Masc.* message.

**messager**, **messagère** *noun Masc., Fem.* messenger.

**messe** *noun Fem.* mass; **aller à la messe** to go to mass.

**Messieurs** *noun* SEE **Monsieur**.

**mesure** *noun Fem.* **1** measurement; **prendre les mesures de la pièce** to take the measurements of the room; **2 sur mesure** tailor-made; **3** measure; **prendre des mesures pour faire** to take measures to do; **le conseil municipal va prendre des mesures pour contrôler la pollution** the town council is going to take measures to control pollution; **4 être en mesure de faire** to be in a position to do; **nous ne sommes pas en mesure de vous aider** we are not in a position to help you.

**mesurer** *verb* [1] to measure.

**met** *verb* SEE **mettre**.

**métal** (*plural* **métaux**) *noun Masc.* metal.

**métallique** *adjective* metallic.

**métallisé** *adjective* metallic; **bleu métallisé** metallic blue.

**météo** *noun Fem.* weather forecast.

**méthode** *noun Fem.* **1** method; **une méthode de faire** a method of doing; **2** manual, tutor.

**métier** *noun Masc.* **1** job; **2 un métier à tisser** a weaving loom.

**mètre** *noun Masc.* **1** metre; **2** metre rule.

**métrique** *adjective* metric.

**métro** *noun Masc.* underground; **une station de métro** an underground station.

**mets** *verb* SEE **mettre**.

**metteur en scène** *noun Masc.* **1** director (*of a film*); **2** producer (*of a play*).

**mettre** *verb* [11] **1** to put; **où as-tu mis le sel?** where have you put the salt?; **2** to put on; **je vais mettre mon manteau** I'm going to put my coat on; **3** to wear; **mets ta jupe rose** wear your pink skirt; **4** to turn on (*radio, television, heating*); **mettre le réveil** to set the alarm clock; **5 mettre quelqu'un en colère** to make somebody angry; **6 j'ai mis trois heures pour le faire** it took me three hours to do it; **7 se mettre quelque part** to stand (or sit) somewhere; **8 se mettre debout** to stand up; **9 se mettre à faire** to start to do; **elle s'est mise à chanter** she started to sing.

**meublé** *adjective* furnished.

**meuble** *noun Masc.* **1 des meubles** furniture; **2 un meuble** a piece of furniture.

**meule** *noun Fem.* **1** millstone; **2 une meule de foin** a haystack.

**meurtre** *noun Masc.* murder.

**meurtrier**, **meurtrière** *noun Masc., Fem.* murderer.
**meurtrier** (*Fem.* **meurtrière**) *adjective* **1** deadly; **2** fatal.

**mexicain** *adjective* Mexican.

**Mexicain**, **Mexicaine** *noun Masc. & Fem.* Mexican.

**Mexico** *noun* Mexico City.

**Mexique** *noun Masc.* Mexico; **aller au Mexique** to go to Mexico.

**mi-** *prefix* **1** half-; **mi-clos** half-shut; **2** mid-; **à la mi-février** in mid-February.

**mi-bas** *noun Masc.* knee sock.

**mi-chemin** *noun* **à mi-chemin** halfway.

**micro** *noun Masc.* microphone.

**microbe** *noun Masc.* germ.

**micro-ondes** *noun Masc.* microwave; **faire cuire quelque chose au micro-ondes** to cook something in the microwave.

**micro-ordinateur** *noun Masc.* microcomputer.

**microscope** *noun Masc.* microscope.

**midi** *noun Masc.* **1** midday, noon; **il est midi vingt** it's twenty past twelve; **je viendrai vers midi** I'll come around twelve; **2** lunchtime; **je fais mes courses à midi** I do my shopping in my lunch hour.

**Midi** *noun Masc.* **le Midi** the South of France.

**miel** *noun Masc.* honey.

**mien**, **mienne**, **miens**, **miennes** *pronoun* le mien, la mienne, les miens, les miennes mine; **'à qui sont ces chaussures?'** – **'ce sont les miennes'** 'whose shoes are these?' – 'they're mine'; **puis-je t'emprunter ton vélo? le mien est chez moi** can I borrow your bike? mine's at home.

**miette** *noun Fem.* crumb.

**mieux** *adjective, adverb* **1** better; **tu la connais mieux que moi** you know her better than I do; **je me sens mieux** I feel better; **mon père va mieux maintenant** my father's better now; **c'est mieux comme ça** it's better like that; **2 il vaut mieux que tu restes chez toi** it would be better if you stayed at home; **3** best; **c'est le rouge que j'aime le mieux** I like the red one

187

a
b
c
d
e
f
g
h
i
j
k
l
**m**
n
o
p
q
r
s
t
u
v
w
x
y
z

best, I prefer the red one.

**mieux** *noun Masc.* **le mieux est de revenir** the best thing is to come back; **au mieux** at best, at least; **pour le mieux** for the best.

**mignon** (*Fem.* **mignonne**) *adjective* sweet.

**migraine** *noun Fem.* headache, migraine.

**mijoter** *verb* [1] to simmer.

**milieu** *noun Masc.* **1** middle; **au milieu de** in the middle of; **2** background; **il vient d'un milieu pauvre** he comes from a poor background; **3** environment.

**militaire** *noun Masc.* serviceman. **militaire** *adjective* military; **le service militaire** military service.

**mille** *number* a thousand; **mille personnes** a thousand people; **deux mille personnes** two thousand people.

**millefeuille** *noun Masc.* vanilla slice.

**millénaire** *noun Masc.* millennium.

**mille-pattes** *noun Masc.* centipede.

**milliard** *noun Masc.* thousand million.

**milliardaire** *noun Masc. & Fem.* multimillionaire.

**millier** *noun Masc.* thousand; **des milliers de euros** thousands of euros.

**milligramme** *noun Masc.* milligramme.

**millimètre** *noun Masc.* millimetre.

**million** *noun Masc.* million; **deux millions de euros** two million euros.

**millionnaire** *noun Masc. & Fem.* millionaire.

**mime** *noun Masc. & Fem.* mime artist.

**mimer** *verb* [1] **1** to mime; **2** to mimic.

**minable** *adjective* (*informal*) **1** pathetic; **ses plaisanteries sont minables** her jokes are pathetic; **2** crummy; **un film minable** a crummy film.

**mince** *adjective* **1** thin; **une mince tranche de viande** a thin slice of meat; **2** slim; **3 mince alors!** (*informal*) oh bother!.

**minceur** *noun Fem.* **1** thinness; **2** slimness.

**mine** *noun Fem.* **1 avoir bonne mine** to look well; **tu as mauvaise mine** you don't look well; **2** expression; **3** mine; **une mine de charbon** a coalmine; **4** pencil lead.

**minéral** (*plural* **minéraux**) *noun Masc.* mineral. **minéral** *adjective* mineral; **eau minérale** mineral water.

**minet**, **minette** *noun Masc., Fem.* pussycat.

**mineur**[1] *noun Masc.* miner.

**mineur**[2], **mineure** *noun Masc., Fem.* minor, person under 18. **mineure** *adjective* **1** minor; **2** under 18.

**minijupe** *noun Fem.* mini-skirt.

**minimal** (*Masc. plural* **minimaux**) *adjective* minimal.

**minimiser** *verb* [1] **1** to minimize; **2** to play down.

**minimum** *noun Masc., adjective* minimum; **au minimum** at the very least.

**ministère** *noun Masc.* ministry.

**ministre** *noun Masc.* minister.

**Minitel™** *noun Masc. (Minitel is France Telecom's online data service; subscribers have a small computer linked to the telephone and can use it to access a large number of services including the telephone directories).*

**minorité** *noun Fem.* minority.

**minou** *noun Masc.* pussycat.

**minuit** *noun Masc.* midnight; **à minuit** at midnight.

**minuscule** *noun Fem.* small letter *(as opposed to a capital letter).* **minuscule** *adjective* tiny.

**minute** *noun Fem.* minute; **dans dix minutes** in ten minutes; **dix minutes plus tard** ten minutes later; **d'une minute à l'autre** any minute now.

**minuterie** *noun Fem.* time-switch.

**minutieux** (*Fem.* **minutieuse**) *adjective* thorough.

**mirabelle** *noun Fem.* small yellow plum.

**miracle** *noun Masc.* miracle; **par miracle** miraculously. **miracle** *adjective* wonder.

**miraculeux** (*Fem.* **miraculeuse**) *adjective* miraculous.

**miroir** *noun Masc.* mirror; **au miroir** in the mirror.

**mis** *verb* SEE **mettre**.

**miser** *verb* [1] to bet.

**misérable** *adjective* poor.

**misère** *noun Fem.* destitution, extreme poverty.

**missile** *noun Masc.* missile.

**missionnaire** *noun Masc. & Fem.* missionary.

**mistral** *noun Masc.* mistral (*a strong cold north wind which blows down the Rhône valley to the Mediterranean*).

**mite** *noun Fem.* clothes moth.

**mi-temps**[1] *noun Masc.* part-time job; **travailler à mi-temps** to work part-time.

**mi-temps**[2] *noun Fem.* half-time (*in a match*).

**miteux** (*Fem.* **miteuse**) *adjective* seedy, shabby.

**mitraillette** *noun Fem.* submachine gun.

**mixage** *noun Masc.* sound mixing.

**mixer** *verb* [1] to mix.

**mixte** *adjective* **1** mixed; **2** coeducational.

**Mlle** SHORT FOR **Mademoiselle**.

**Mme** SHORT FOR **Madame**.

**mobile** *noun Masc.* **1** motive; **2** mobile. **mobile** *adjective* **1** mobile; **2** **feuilles mobiles** loose sheets (*as opposed to a pad of paper*).

**mobilier** *noun Masc.* furniture.

**mobylette** *noun Fem.* moped.

**mocassin** *noun Masc.* **1** loafer; **2** moccasin.

**moche** *adjective* (*informal*) **1** awful; **2** ugly.

a

**mode**[1] *noun Fem.* fashion; **être à la mode** to be fashionable.

b

**mode**[2] *noun Masc.* way, mode.

c

**mode d'emploi** *noun Masc.* instructions for use.

d

**mode de vie** *noun Masc.* way of life.

e

**modèle** *noun Masc.* **1** model; **2** style; **ce modèle existe en plusieurs coloris** this style is available in several colours.

f

g

**modéré** *adjective* moderate.

h

**moderne** *adjective* modern.

i

**moderniser** *verb* [1] to modernize.

j

**modernité** *noun Fem.* modernity.

k

**modeste** *adjective* **1** modest; **2** humble.

l

**modestie** *noun Fem.* modesty.

m

**modifier** *verb* [1] to change.

**modiste** *noun Fem.* milliner.

n

**module** *noun Masc.* **1** module; **2** kitchen unit.

o

**moelle** *noun Fem.* marrow (*of bone*).

p

**moelleux** (*Fem.* **moelleuse**) *adjective* **1** soft; **2** mellow.

q

r

**mœurs** *plural noun Fem.* **1** customs; **2** morals.

s

**moi** *pronoun* **1** me; **c'est pour moi** it's for me; **pas moi** not me; **2 moi, je pense que ...** I think that ...; **3 à moi** mine; **ce n'est pas à moi** it's not mine; **un ami à moi** a friend of mine.

t

u

v

w

**moi-même** *pronoun* myself; **je l'ai fait moi-même** I did it myself.

x

**moindre** *adjective* slightest; **le moindre problème** the slightest problem; **je n'ai pas la moindre idée** I haven't the slightest idea.

y

z

**moine** *noun Masc.* monk.

**moineau** (*plural* **moineaux**) *noun Masc.* sparrow.

**moins** *preposition* **1** minus; **sept moins deux égale cinq** seven minus two equals five; **2 il est dix heures moins cinq** it's five to ten. **moins** *adverb* **1** less; **tu en as moins que moi** you've got less than me; **de moins en moins** less and less; **il est moins grand que son frère** he's not as tall as his brother; **c'est moins loin** it's not as far; **j'aime moins le bleu** I don't like the blue one as much; **2 le moins** the least; **le moins difficile** the least difficult; **le moins gros** the smallest; **3 moins de** less, fewer; **moins de beurre** less butter; **moins de voitures** fewer cars; **4 au moins** at least; **5 du moins** at least; **6 à moins que** (+ *subjunctive*) unless; **à moins qu'elle soit malade** unless she's ill.

**mois** *noun Masc.* month; **au mois de mai** in May; **le mois dernier** last month; **le mois prochain** next month.

**moisi** *noun Masc.* mould.
**moisi** *adjective* mouldy.

**moisir** *verb* [2] to go mouldy.

**moisson** *noun Fem.* harvest.

**moite** *adjective* **1** damp; **2** muggy.

**moitié** *noun Fem.* **1** half; **la moitié d'une pomme** half an apple; **donne-moi la moitié** give me half; **la moitié du temps** half the time; **2 à moitié** half; **à moitié vide** half empty.

**moitié-moitié** *adverb* half-and-half; **partager moitié-moitié** to go halves.

**molaire** *noun Fem.* molar, back tooth.

**molle** *adjective* SEE **mou**.

**mollet** *noun Masc.* calf (*of the leg*). **mollet** *adjective* **un œuf mollet** a soft-boiled egg.

**molleton** *noun Masc.* flannel, flannelette.

**môme** *noun Masc. & Fem.* (*informal*) kid.

**moment** *noun Masc.* moment; **un moment, s'il vous plaît** just a moment please; **en ce moment** at the moment; **par moments** at times; **pour le moment** for the moment; **au moment où** just when; **à ce moment-là** just at that moment, just then; **j'ai attendu un bon moment** I waited for a good while.

**mon**, **ma**, **mes** *adjective* my; **mon fils** my son; **ma fille** my daughter; **mes enfants** my children.

**monarchie** *noun Fem.* monarchy.

**monastère** *noun Masc.* monastery.

**monde** *noun Masc.* **1** world; **2** people; **il y a beaucoup de monde** there are a lot of people; **peu de monde** not many people; **tout le monde** everybody.

**mondial** (*Masc. plural* **mondiaux**) *adjective* **1** world; **la Seconde Guerre mondiale** the Second World War; **2** worldwide.

**monétique** *noun Fem.* electronic banking.

**moniteur**[1] *noun Masc.* monitor.

**moniteur**[2], **monitrice** *noun Masc., Fem.* **1** instructor (*sports or driving*); **un moniteur de ski** a ski instructor; **2** camp leader.

**monnaie** *noun Fem.* **1** currency; **2 une pièce de monnaie** a coin; **3** change; **je n'ai pas de monnaie** I don't have any change.

**monopoliser** *verb* [1] to monopolize.

**monotone** *adjective* monotonous.

**Monsieur** (*plural* **Messieurs**) *noun Masc.* **1 Monsieur Lejay** Mr Lejay; **bonsoir monsieur** good evening (*when greeting somebody you do not know well in French it is polite to add 'Monsieur', 'Madame', or 'Mademoiselle' to the greeting*); **2** man; **un grand monsieur** a tall man; **les deux messieurs assis à la table** the two men sitting at the table.

**monstre** *noun Masc.* monster. **monstre** *adjective* huge; **un travail monstre** a huge amount of work.

**monstrueux** (*Fem.* **monstrueuse**) *adjective* monstrous.

**mont** *noun Masc.* mountain; **le mont Blanc** Mont Blanc.

**montagne** *noun Fem.* **1** mountain; **la montagne** the mountains; **2 une montagne de** a mountain of.

**montagneux** (*Fem.* **montagneuse**) *adjective* mountainous.

a
b
c
d
e
f
g
h
i
j
k
l
**m**
n
o
p
q
r
s
t
u
v
w
x
y
z

**montant** *noun Masc.* sum.
**montant** *adjective* rising.

**montée** *noun Fem.* **1** ascent, way up; **2** rise, increase; **3** slope; **en montée** uphill.

**monter** *verb* [1] **1** to go up, to come up; **monter l'escalier** to go (*or* come) up the stairs; **monter la colline** to go up the hill; **monter se coucher** to go up to bed; **2 monter dans** to get on (*a bus, train, etc*); **3 monter quelque chose** to bring (*or* take) something up; **je vais monter tes valises** I'll take your cases up; **4** to assemble (*a kit*); **5** to rise; **les prix ont monté** prices have risen; **6** to increase; **7 monter à cheval** to ride a horse.

**montgolfière** *noun Fem.* hot-air balloon.

**montre** *noun Fem.* watch.

**montrer** *verb* [1] **1** to show; **montrer quelque chose à quelqu'un** to show somebody something; **montre-moi ton cadeau** show me your present; **2** to point out; **montrer quelque chose du doigt** to point to something.

**monture** *noun Fem.* frames (*of glasses*).

**monument** *noun Masc.* **1** monument; **un monument aux morts** a war memorial; **2** historic building.

**moquer** *verb* [1] **1 se moquer de** to make fun of; **tout le monde s'est moqué de moi** everybody made fun of me; **2 se moquer de** not to care

about; **je m'en moque** I couldn't care less.

**moquette** *noun Fem.* fitted carpet.

**moqueur** (*Fem.* **moqueuse**) *adjective* mocking.

**moral** (*plural* **moraux**) *noun Masc.* morale; **je n'ai pas le moral** I'm feeling really down.
**moral** (*Masc. plural* **moraux**) *adjective* **1** moral; **2** mental.

**morale** *noun Fem.* **1** moral; **2** morality.

**morceau** (*plural* **morceaux**) *noun Masc.* piece, bit; **un morceau de pain** a piece of bread; **un morceau de sucre** a sugar lump.

**mordre** *verb* [3] to bite.

**mordu** *adjective* **être mordu de quelque chose** (*informal*) to be mad about something.

**morne** *adjective* **1** gloomy; **2** dismal, dreary.

**morsure** *noun Fem.* bite.

**mort**[1] *noun Fem.* death; **trois mois avant sa mort** three months before he died.

**mort**[2], **morte** *noun Masc., Fem.* dead man, dead woman.
**mort** *adjective* dead.

**mort-aux-rats** *noun Fem.* rat poison.

**mortel** (*Fem.* **mortelle**) *adjective* **1** deadly; **2** fatal.

**morue** *noun Fem.* **1** cod; **2** salt cod.

**mosaïque** *noun Fem.* mosaic.

**Moscou** *noun* Moscow.

**mosquée** *noun Fem.* mosque.

**mot** *noun Masc.* **1** word; **mot à mot** word for word; **2 un petit mot** a note.

**motard**, **motarde** *noun Masc., Fem.* (*informal*) motorcyclist.

**mot de passe** *noun Masc.* password.

**moteur** *noun Masc.* engine.

**motif** *noun Masc.* **1** motive; **2** pattern.

**motiver** *verb* [1] to motivate.

**moto** *noun Fem.* motorbike; **je suis venu en moto** I came by motorbike.

**motocycliste** *noun Masc. & Fem.* motorcyclist.

**mots croisés** *plural noun Masc.* crossword.

**motte** *noun Fem.* **1** lump; **2** slab.

**mou, mol** (*before a vowel*) (*Fem.* **molle**) *adjective* **1** soft; **2** flabby.

**mouche** *noun Fem.* fly.

**moucher** *verb* [1] **se moucher** to blow your nose.

**moucheron** *noun Masc.* midge.

**mouchoir** *noun Masc.* **1** handkerchief; **2** tissue.

**moue** *noun Fem.* pout; **faire la moue** to pout.

**mouette** *noun Fem.* seagull.

**mouiller** *verb* [1] **1** to wet; **2 se mouiller** to get wet.

**moulant** *adjective* tight-fitting.

**moule**[1] *noun Masc.* mould.

**moule**[2] *noun Fem.* mussel.

**mouler** *verb* [1] to mould.

**moulin** *noun Masc.* mill.

**moulin à vent** *noun Masc.* windmill.

**moulu** *adjective* ground; **le café moulu** ground coffee.

**moulure** *noun Fem.* moulding.

**mourir** *verb* [54] to die; **elle est morte en février** she died in February; **je meurs de faim!** I'm starving!; **je meurs d'envie d'y aller** I'm dying to go there.

**mousquetaire** *noun Masc.* musketeer.

**moussant** *adjective* foaming.

**mousse** *noun Fem.* **1** foam; **mousse à raser** shaving foam; **2** lather; **3** froth; **4 mousse au chocolat** chocolate mousse; **5** moss.

**mousser** *verb* [1] to foam.

**mousseux** (*Fem.* **mousseuse**) *adjective* **du vin mousseux** sparkling wine.

**moustache** *noun Fem.* moustache.

**moustique** *noun Masc.* mosquito.

**moutarde** *noun Fem.* mustard.

**mouton** *noun Masc.* **1** sheep; **2** mutton.

**mouvement** *noun Masc.* **1** movement; **2** activity, bustle.

**mouvementé** *adjective* hectic, eventful; **j'ai eu une semaine mouvementée** I've had a hectic week.

**Moyen-Âge** *noun Masc.* Middle Ages.

**moyen** *noun Masc.* **1** means; **un moyen de transport** a means of transport; **un moyen de faire** a means of doing; **je n'ai aucun moyen de le contacter** I have no

a b c d e f g h i j k l m n o p q r s t u v w x y z

means of contacting him; **2 les moyens** the means, the wherewithal; **je n'ai pas les moyens de m'acheter un ordinateur** I can't afford to buy a computer; **3** way.

**moyen** (*Fem.* **moyenne**) *adjective* **1** medium; **2** medium-sized; **3** average.**un équipe de niveau très moyen** a very average team.

**moyenne** *noun Fem.* **1** average; **en moyenne** on average; **2 avoir la moyenne** to pass (*an exam*).

**Moyen-Orient** *noun Masc.* Middle East.

**muet** (*Fem.* **muette**) *adjective* **1** speechless, dumb; **2** silent.

**muguet** *noun Masc.* lily of the valley.

**mulet** *noun Masc.* mule.

**multifonction** *adjective* multipurpose.

**multiple** *adjective* **1** multiple; **2** various.

**multiplication** *noun Fem.* **1** multiplication; **2 multiplication de** increase in the number of.

**multiplier** *verb* [1] **1** to multiply; **2** to increase.

**municipal** (*Masc. plural* **municipaux**) *adjective* **1** local, town; **2** municipal.

**municipalité** *noun Fem.* **1** town (*or* local) council; **2** municipality.

**munition** *noun Fem.* ammunition.

**mûr** *adjective* **1** ripe; **2** mature.

**mur** *noun Masc.* wall.

**muraille** *noun Fem.* (defensive) wall; **la Grande Muraille de Chine** the Great Wall of China.

**mûre** *noun Fem.* blackberry.

**mûrir** *verb* [2] **1** to ripen; **2** to mature; **3** to develop.

**murmure** *noun Masc.* murmur.

**murmurer** *verb* [1] to murmur.

**musc** *noun Masc.* musk.

**muscade** *noun Fem.* nutmeg; **une noix de muscade** a nutmeg.

**muscle** *noun Masc.* muscle.

**musclé** *adjective* muscular.

**musculation** *noun Fem.* bodybuilding.

**museau** (*plural* **museaux**) *noun Masc.* muzzle, snout.

**musée** *noun Masc.* museum.

**musical** (*Masc. plural* **musicaux**) *adjective* musical.

**musicien, musicienne** *noun Masc., Fem.* musician.

**musique** *noun Fem.* music; **mettre de la musique** to put on some music.

**musulman, musulmane** *noun Masc., Fem., adjective* Muslim.

**mutuel** (*Fem.* **mutuelle**) *adjective* mutual.

**myope** *adjective* short-sighted; ★ **être myope comme une taupe** to be as blind as a bat (*literally: to be as short-sighted as a mole*).

**myopie** *noun Fem.* short-sightedness.

**myosotis** *noun Masc.* forget-me-not.

**myrtille** *noun Fem.* bilberry.

**mystère** *noun Masc.* mystery.

**mystérieux** (*Fem.* **mystérieuse**) *adjective* mysterious.

**mystifier** *verb* [1] to fool.

**mystique** *adjective* mystical.

**mythe** *noun Masc.* myth.

**mythologie** *noun Fem.* mythology.

# Nn

**n'** *adverb* SEE **ne.**

**nacre** *noun Fem.* mother-of-pearl.

**nage** *noun Fem.* swimming.

**nager** *verb* [52] to swim.

**nageur, nageuse** *noun Masc., Fem.* swimmer.

**naïf** (*Fem.* **naïve**) *adjective* naïve.

**nain, naine** *noun Masc., Fem., adjective* dwarf.

**naissance** *noun Fem.* birth; **date de naissance** date of birth.

**naître** *verb* [55] to be born; **elle est née en 1975** she was born in 1975.

**nana** *noun Fem.* (*informal*) girl.

**naphtaline** *noun Fem.* mothballs.

**nappe** *noun Fem.* tablecloth.

**narcisse** *noun Masc.* narcissus.

**narine** *noun Fem.* nostril.

**natal** *adjective* native; **mon pays natal** my native country.

**natalité** *noun Fem.* **le taux de natalité** the birthrate.

**natation** *noun Fem.* swimming; **faire de la natation** to go swimming.

**natif** (*Fem.* **native**) *adjective* native.

**nation** *noun Fem.* nation.

**national** (*Masc. plural* **nationaux**) *adjective* national.

**nationaliser** *verb* [1] to nationalize.

**nationalité** *noun Fem.* nationality.

**nativité** *noun Fem.* Nativity.

**natte** *noun Fem.* **1** plait; **2** mat.

**nature** *noun Fem.* nature.
**nature** *adjective* **yaourt nature** plain yoghurt; **un thé nature** a cup of tea without milk or sugar.

**naturel** *noun Masc.* **1** nature; **2 au naturel** plain.
**naturel** (*Fem.* **naturelle**) *adjective* natural.

**naturellement** *adverb* of course.

**nausée** *noun Fem.* nausea; **avoir la nausée** to feel sick.

**nautique** *adjective* water; **faire du ski nautique** to go water-skiing.

**navet** *noun Masc.* turnip.

**navette** *noun Fem.* shuttle; **j'ai pris la navette de l'aéroport** I took the shuttle from the airport; **faire la navette** to travel back and forth.

**naviguer** *verb* [1] to sail.

**navire** *noun Masc.* ship.

**navire-citerne** *noun Masc.* oil tanker.

**navire-école** *noun Masc.* training ship.

**navré** *adjective* sorry; **je suis vraiment navré** I'm terribly sorry.

**né, née** *verb* SEE **naître.**

**ne, n'** (*before a vowel or silent 'h'*) *adverb* **1** ne + pas not; **je n'aime**

a
b
c
d
e
f
g
h
i
j
k
l
m
n
o
p
q
r
s
t
u
v
w
x
y
z

**pas le lait** I don't like milk; **2 ne + jamais** never; **je ne vais jamais à Londres** I never go to London; **3 ne + que** only; **je n'ai que dix euros** I only have ten euros; **4 ne + plus** no longer; **elle n'habite plus à Londres** she no longer lives in London; **5 ne + rien** nothing; **il ne mange rien** he eats nothing; **rien ne t'empêche d'y aller** there's nothing to stop you going; **6 ne + personne** nobody; **il n'y a personne** there's nobody; **personne n'a compris** nobody understood.

**néanmoins** *adverb* nevertheless.

**nécessaire** *noun Masc.* **faire le nécessaire** to do the necessary.
**nécessaire** *adjective* necessary; **il est nécessaire de faire** it is necessary to do; **est-ce qu'il est nécessaire de réserver?** is it necessary to book?

**nécessairement** *adverb* necessarily.

**nécessité** *noun Fem.* necessity.

**nécessiter** *verb* [1] to require.

**nectarine** *noun Fem.* nectarine.

**néerlandais** *noun Masc.* Dutch (*language*).
**néerlandais** *adjective* Dutch.

**nef** *noun Fem.* nave (*of a church*).

**négatif** *noun Masc.* negative.
**négatif** (*Fem.* **négative**) *adjective* negative.

**négligé** *adjective* scruffy.

**négligent** *adjective* careless.

**négliger** *verb* [52] **1** to neglect; **2 il a négligé de le faire** he didn't bother to do it.

**négociant** *noun Masc.* merchant.

**négocier** *verb* [1] to negotiate.

**neige** *noun Fem.* snow; **un bonhomme de neige** a snowman.

**neiger** *verb* [52] to snow; **il neige** it's snowing.

**neigeux** (*Fem.* **neigeuse**) *adjective* snowy.

**nénuphar** *noun Masc.* waterlily.

**néon** *noun Masc.* neon.

**néo-zélandais** *adjective* New Zealand.

**Néo-Zélandais**, **Néo-Zélandaise** *noun Masc., Fem.* New Zealander.

**nerf** *noun Masc.* nerve.

**nerveux** (*Fem.* **nerveuse**) *adjective* nervous.

**n'est-ce pas?** *adverb* **il fait froid ce soir, n'est-ce pas?** it's cold this evening, isn't it?; **il habite à Paris, n'est ce pas?** he lives in Paris, doesn't he?; **tu as déjà mangé, n'est-ce pas?** you've already eaten, haven't you?

**net** (*Fem.* **nette**) *adjective* **1** clear; **c'est très net** it's quite clear; **2** distinct; **une nette différence** a distinct difference; **une nette amélioration** a distinct improvement.
**net** *adverb* **1 s'arrêter net** to stop dead; **2 refuser net** to refuse flatly.

**nettement** *adverb* far; **nettement meilleur** much better.

**nettoyage** *noun Masc.* cleaning; **le nettoyage à sec** dry cleaning.

**nettoyer** *verb* [39] to clean.

**neuf**[1] *number* nine; **il est neuf heures du matin** it's nine o'clock in the morning; **Julie a neuf ans** Julie's nine; **le neuf juillet** the ninth of July.

**neuf**[2] (*Fem.* **neuve**) *adjective* new; **une voiture toute neuve** a brand new car.

**neutre** *adjective* neutral.

**neuvième** *noun Masc.* **au neuvième** on the ninth floor. **neuvième** *adjective* ninth.

**neveu** (*plural* **neveux**) *noun Masc.* nephew.

**nez** *noun Masc.* nose.

**ni** *conjunction* **ni ...ni** neither ...nor; **ni lui ni son frère** neither he nor his brother; **il n'y a ni pain ni lait** there's neither bread nor milk; **ni Frank ni Paul ne le sait** neither Frank nor Paul knows; **ni moi non plus** me neither.

**niche** *noun Fem.* **1** kennel; **2** niche.

**nid** *noun Masc.* nest.

**nièce** *noun Fem.* niece.

**nier** *verb* [1] to deny.

**n'importe** *adverb* **1** either, it doesn't matter; **'tu veux une aile ou une cuisse?' – 'n'importe'** 'do you want a wing or a leg?' – 'either, it doesn't matter'; **2 n'importe qui** anybody; **n'importe qui peut le faire** anybody can do it; **3 n'importe quoi** anything; **je ferai n'importe quoi pour t'aider** I'll do absolutely anything to help you; **elle a fait n'importe quoi** she's made a real mess of it; **tu dis n'importe quoi** you're talking complete rubbish; **4 n'importe quand** any time; **tu**

peux m'appeler n'importe quand you can ring me any time; **5 n'importe comment** any old how; **tu peux jeter tous ces papiers dans un tiroir n'importe comment** you can throw all these papers into a drawer any old how; **6 n'importe où** anywhere; **pose tes valises n'importe où** put your cases down anywhere you like; **je ne peux pas habiter n'importe où** I can't live just anywhere.

**niveau** (*plural* **niveaux**) **niveau** *noun Masc.* level; **au même niveau** at the same level.

**niveau de vie** *noun Masc.* standard of living.

**noble** *adjective* noble.

**noces** *plural noun Fem.* wedding.

**nocif** (*Fem.* **nocive**) *adjective* harmful.

**nocturne** *noun Fem.* late-night opening. **nocturne** *adjective* nocturnal.

**Noël** *noun Masc.* Christmas; **Joyeux Noël** Merry Christmas; **un cadeau de Noël** a Christmas present; **le sapin de Noël** the Christmas tree.

**nœud** *noun Masc.* knot; **faire un nœud** to tie a knot.

**noir** *noun Masc.* **1** black; **2 le noir** the dark. **noir** *adjective* **1** black; **2** dark; **il fait noir** it's dark.

**Noir**, **Noire** *noun Masc., Fem.* black man, black woman; **les Noirs** black people.

**noirceur** *noun Fem.* blackness.

**noircir** *verb* [2] to blacken.

a
b
c
d
e
f
g
h
i
j
k
l
m
n
o
p
q
r
s
t
u
v
w
x
y
z

**noisette** *noun Fem.* hazelnut.

**noix** *noun Fem.* **1** walnut; **2 une noix de beurre** a knob of butter.

**noix de cajou** *noun Fem.* cashew nut.

**noix de coco** *noun Fem.* coconut.

**nom** *noun Masc.* **1** name; **nom de famille** surname; **nom de jeune fille** maiden name; **2 au nom de: au nom de la famille Dupont** on behalf of the Dupont family; **3** noun.

**nombre** *noun Masc.* number; **bon nombre de** a good many; **le nombre de victimes s'élève à 25** the number of dead is 25.

**nombreux** (*Fem.* **nombreuse**) *adjective* many; **de nombreuses personnes** many people; **ils étaient nombreux** there were a lot of them; **ils étaient peu nombreux** there weren't many of them; **une famille nombreuse** a big family.

**nombril** *noun Masc.* navel.

**nommer** *verb* [1] **1** to appoint; **2** to name.

**non** *adverb* **1** no; **elle a dit non** she said no; **2 non seulement** not only; **non loin de** not far from; **moi non plus** me neither.

**non-** *combining form* **un non-fumeur** a nonsmoker.

**nord** *noun Masc.* north; **le nord de l'Espagne** northern Spain; **le vent du nord** the north wind.
**nord** *adjective* north, northern; **le côté nord** the north side.

**nord-américain** *adjective* North American.

**Nord-Américain**, **Nord-Américaine** *noun Masc., Fem.* North American.

**nord-est** *noun Masc.* north-east.

**nord-ouest** *noun Masc.* north-west.

**normal** (*Masc. plural* **normaux**) *adjective* **1** normal; **2 c'est normal** it's natural; **3 ce n'est pas normal** it's not right.

**normalement** *adverb* **1** normally; **2** according to plan; **normalement, elle doit être à Rome actuellement** if things have gone according to plan, she should be in Rome at the moment.

**normand** *adjective* Norman; **la côte normande** the Normandy coast.

**Normand**, **Normande** *noun Masc., Fem.* Norman.

**Normandie** *noun Fem.* Normandy.

**norme** *noun Fem.* **1** norm; **2** standard; **selon les normes européennes** according to European standards.

**Norvège** *noun Fem.* Norway.

**norvégien** (*Fem.* **norvégienne**) *adjective* Norwegian.

**nos** *adjective* SEE **notre**.

**notaire** *noun Masc.* notary public.

**notamment** *adverb* in particular.

**note** *noun Fem.* **1** bill; **la note, s'il vous plaît** can I have the bill please; **2** mark; **j'ai eu une bonne note en allemand** I got a good mark in German; **3 prendre des notes** to take notes.

**noter** *verb* [1] **1** to write down; **2** to notice.

**notice** *noun Fem.* instructions.

**notion** *noun Fem.* **1** idea; **2 des notions** basic knowledge; **j'ai des notions d'espagnol** I have a basic knowledge of Spanish.

**notre** (*plural* **nos**) *adjective* our; **notre fille** our daughter; **nos enfants** our children.

**nôtre** *pronoun* **le nôtre, la nôtre, les nôtres** ours.

**nouer** *verb* [1] to tie, to knot.

**nougat** *noun Masc.* nougat.

**nouilles** *plural noun Fem.* noodles, pasta.

**nounours** *noun Masc.* (*baby talk*) teddy bear.

**nourrice** *noun Fem.* childminder.

**nourrir** *verb* [2] to feed.

**nourrissant** *adjective* nourishing.

**nourrisson** *noun Masc.* infant.

**nourriture** *noun Fem.* food.

**nous** *pronoun* **1** we; **nous apprenons le français** we are learning French; **2** us; **viens avec nous** come with us; **elle nous aide** she helps us; **elle nous a aidés** she helped us; **3** to us; **elle ne nous a pas parlé** she didn't speak to us; **elle nous a donné son adresse** she gave us her address; **4** ourselves; **nous nous ferons une salade** we'll make ourselves a salad; **5** (*reflexive*) **nous nous levons à sept heures** we get up at seven o'clock.

**nous-mêmes** *pronoun* ourselves.

**nouveau, nouvel** (*before a vowel or silent 'h'*) (*Fem.* **nouvelle**) (*Masc.*

*plural* **nouveaux**) *adjective* **1** new; **viens voir mon nouvel appartement** come and see my new flat; **2 à nouveau, de nouveau** again.

**nouveauté** *noun Fem.* **1** novelty; **2** new release.

**Nouvel An** *noun Masc.* New Year.

**nouvelle** *adjective* SEE **nouveau**
**nouvelle** *noun Fem.* **1 une nouvelle** news; **j'ai une bonne nouvelle!** I've got good news!; **2** short story; **nous étudions une nouvelle de Camus** we're doing a Camus short story; **3 des nouvelles** news; **nous n'avons pas de nouvelles pour l'instant** we have no news for the moment; **as-tu des nouvelles de lui?** have you heard from him?

**Nouvelle-Zélande** *noun Fem.* New Zealand.

**novembre** *noun Masc.* November; **en novembre, au mois de novembre** in November.

**noyau** (*plural* **noyaux**) *noun Masc.* **1** stone (*in fruit*); **2** nucleus.

**noyer**[1] *verb* [39] **1** to drown; **2 se noyer** to drown, to drown oneself.

**noyer**[2] *noun Masc.* **1** walnut tree; **2** walnut; **une table en noyer** a walnut table.

**nu** *adjective* **1** naked; **2** bare.

**nuage** *noun Masc.* cloud.

**nuageux** (*Fem.* **nuageuse**) *adjective* cloudy.

**nuance** *noun Fem.* **1** shade (*of a colour*); **2** nuance.

a
b
c
d
e
f
g
h
i
j
k
l
m
n
o
p
q
r
s
t
u
v
w
x
y
z

# nucléaire

**nucléaire** *adjective* nuclear; **l'énergie nucléaire** nuclear power.

**nœud ferroviaire** *noun Masc.* (railway) junction.

**nuisible** *adjective* harmful.

**nuit** *noun Fem.* **1** night; **cette nuit** last night, tonight; **dans la nuit** in the night; **toute la nuit** all night; **travailler la nuit** to work at night; **2 il fait nuit** it's dark; **avant la nuit** before dark; **la nuit tombe à sept heures** it gets dark at seven o'clock.

**nul** (*Fem.* **nulle**) *adjective* **1** (*informal*) hopeless, awful; **le film était nul** the film was awful; **je suis nul en histoire** I'm hopeless at history; **2 un match nul** a draw.

**nulle part** *adverb* nowhere; **je ne trouve nulle part mon dictionnaire** I can't find my dictionary anywhere.

**numéro** *noun Masc.* number; **ils habitent au numéro vingt-cinq** they live at number twenty-five.

**numéro de téléphone** *noun Masc.* telephone number.

**nu-pied** *noun Masc.* open sandal.

**nurse** *noun Fem.* nanny.

**nutritif** (*Fem.* **nutritive**) *adjective* nourishing, nutritious; **valeur nutritive** nutritional value.

**nutrition** *noun Fem.* nutrition.

**nylon** *noun Masc.* nylon.

# Oo

**oasis** *noun Fem.* oasis.

**obéir** *verb* [2] **obéir à** to obey.

**obéissance** *noun Fem.* obedience.

**obéissant** *adjective* obedient.

**objectif** *noun Masc.* objective. **objectif** (*Fem.* **objective**) *adjective* objective.

**objection** *noun Fem.* objection.

**objet** *noun Masc.* object.

**objets trouvés** *plural noun Masc.* lost property; **aller aux objets trouvés** to go to the lost property office.

**obligatoire** *adjective* compulsory.

**obligé** *adjective* **être obligé de faire** to have to do; **je suis obligé de partir** I have to go.

**obliger** *verb* [52] **obliger quelqu'un à faire** to force somebody to do.

**obscène** *adjective* obscene.

**obscur** *adjective* **1** dark; **2** obscure.

**obscurité** *noun Fem.* **1** darkness; **dans l'obscurité** in the dark; **2** obscurity.

**obséder** *verb* [24] to obsess; **être obsédé par quelque chose** to be obsessed by something.

**obsèques** *plural noun Fem.* funeral.

**observateur, observatrice** *noun Masc., Fem.* observer. **observateur** (*Fem.* **observatrice**) *adjective* observant.

**observation** *noun Fem.* **1** comment; **2** remark.

**office**

**observatoire** *noun Masc.* observatory.

**observer** *verb* [1] **1** to watch; **elle nous observait de loin** she was watching us from a distance; **2** to observe (*rules*).

**obsession** *noun Fem.* obsession.

**obstacle** *noun Masc.* obstacle.

**obstination** *noun Fem.* obstinacy.

**obstiné** *adjective* stubborn.

**obtenir** *verb* [77] to get.

**occasion** *noun Fem.*
**1** opportunity; **avoir l'occasion de faire** to have the opportunity to do; **2 acheter quelque chose d'occasion** to buy something second hand; **une voiture d'occasion** a second-hand car; **3** bargain; **une bonne occasion** a good bargain; **4** occasion; **à l'occasion de** on the occasion of; **5 à l'occasion** some time.

**occasionner** *verb* [1] to cause.

**Occident** *noun Masc.* **l'Occident** the West.

**occidental** (*Masc. plural* **occidentaux**) *adjective* western.

**occupation** *noun Fem.* occupation; **trouver une occupation** to find something to do.

**occupé** *adjective* **1** busy; **je suis occupé en ce moment** I'm busy at the moment; **2** engaged (*of a telephone line or toilet*); **3 cette place est occupée** this seat is taken.

**occuper** *verb* [1] **1** to occupy; **2 s'occuper** to keep yourself busy; **3 s'occuper de** to deal with, to see to; **je vais m'occuper du dîner** I'll go and see to dinner; **je m'en occupe** I'll see to it; **4 s'occuper de quelqu'un** to attend to somebody; **est-ce qu'on s'occupe de vous?** are you being attended to?

**occurrence** *noun Fem.* **1** case; **plusieurs occurrences de typhoïde** several cases of typhoid; **2** occurrence.

**océan** *noun Masc.* ocean.

**octet** *noun Masc.* byte (*in computing*).

**octobre** *noun Masc.* October; **en octobre, au mois d'octobre** in October.

**odeur** *noun Fem.* smell; **des odeurs de cuisine** cooking smells.

**odorat** *noun Masc.* sense of smell.

**œil** (*plural* **yeux**) *noun Masc.* eye; ★ **cela saute aux yeux** it's obvious (*literally: it jumps into your eyes*).

**œillet** *noun Masc.* carnation.

**œuf** *noun Masc.* egg; **un œuf à la coque** a boiled egg; **un œuf dur** a hard-boiled egg; **un œuf mollet** a soft-boiled egg; **un œuf sur le plat** a fried egg; **des œufs brouillés** scrambled eggs.

**œuvre** *noun Fem.* work (*of art or literature*); **une œuvre d'art** a work of art.

**offenser** *verb* [1] to offend.

**office** *noun Masc.* **1** office; **2 office religieux** religious service.

a
b
c
d
e
f
g
h
i
j
k
l
m
n
o
p
q
r
s
t
u
v
w
x
y
z

a b c d e f g h i j k l m **n** **o** p q r s t u v w x y z

**officiel** *noun Masc.* official.
**officiel** (*Fem.* **officielle**) *adjective*
official.

**officier** *noun Masc.* officer.

**offre** *noun Fem.* **1** offer; **2** '**offres**
**d'emploi**' 'situations vacant'.

**offrir** *verb* [56] **1** offrir quelque
chose à quelqu'un to give
something to somebody; **elle m'a**
**offert une montre pour mon**
**anniversaire** she gave me a watch
for my birthday; **2** s'offrir quelque
chose to treat yourself to
something; **je vais m'offrir un**
**nouveau dictionnaire** I'm going to
treat myself to a new dictionary;
**3** to offer.

**oie** *noun Fem.* goose.

**oignon** *noun Masc.* onion.

**oiseau** (*plural* **oiseaux**) *noun Masc.*
bird.

**olive** *noun Fem.* olive; **l'huile d'olive**
olive oil.

**olivier** *noun Masc.* olive tree.

**ombragé** *adjective* shaded (*from
the sun*).

**ombre** *noun Fem.* **1** shade; **à**
**l'ombre** in the shade; **2** shadow.

**ombre à paupières** *noun Fem.*
eyeshadow.

**ombrelle** *noun Fem.* sun umbrella.

**omelette** *noun Fem.* omelette; **une**
**omelette aux champignons** a
mushroom omelette.

**omettre** *verb* [11] to omit, to leave
out; **omettre de faire quelque**
**chose** to fail to do something.

**omoplate** *noun Fem.* shoulder
blade.

**on** *pronoun* **1** we; **on va au cinéma**
we're going to the cinema; **on a**
**oublié de fermer la porte** we forgot
to shut the door; **2** you; **de la**
**terrasse on voit la mer** from the
terrace you can see the sea; **on ne**
**devrait pas mentir** you shouldn't
tell lies; **3** on leur a dit que ... they
were told that ...; **on a volé leur**
**voiture** their car's been stolen.

**oncle** *noun Masc.* uncle.

**onde** *noun Fem.* wave (*on radio*).

**ondée** *noun Fem.* shower (*of rain*).

**onéreux** (*Fem.* **onéreuse**) *adjective*
costly.

**ongle** *noun Masc.* nail; **se faire les**
**ongles** to do your nails; **je me suis**
**coupé les ongles** I've cut my
nails.

**ongle de pied** *noun Masc.* toenail.

**ONU** *noun Fem.* SHORT FOR
**Organisation des Nations unies**
UN, United Nations.

**onze** *number* eleven; **onze**
**personnes** eleven people; **Marie-**
**Ange a onze ans** Marie-Ange is
eleven; **le onze juillet** the eleventh
of July.

**onzième** *noun Masc.* **au onzième**
on the eleventh floor.
**onzième** *adjective* eleventh.

**opéra** *noun Masc.* **1** opera; **2** opera
house.

**opérateur, opératrice** *noun*
*Masc., Fem.* operator.

**opération** *noun Fem.* **1** operation;
**2** calculation.

**opérer** *verb* [24] to operate; **opérer**
**quelqu'un** to operate on somebody;

**est-ce qu'il va falloir opérer?** will they have to operate; **se faire opérer** to have an operation.

**opinion** *noun Fem.* opinion.

**opposant, opposante** *noun Masc., Fem.* opponent.

**opposé** *noun* **l'opposé** the opposite.
**opposé** *adjective* **1** opposite; **2 être opposé à quelque chose** to be opposed to something.

**opposer** *verb* [1] **1 le match de samedi prochain oppose les Anglais et les Français** the English are playing the French in next Saturday's match; **2 s'opposer à quelque chose** to oppose something; **ils s'opposent à un changement des règles** they are opposed to a change in the rules.

**opposition** *noun Fem.* opposition.

**opter** *verb* [1] to opt.

**opticien, opticienne** *noun Masc., Fem.* optician.

**optimisme** *noun Masc.* optimism.

**optimiste** *noun Masc. & Fem.* optimist.
**optimiste** *adjective* optimistic.

**option** *noun Fem.* option.

**optionnel** (*Fem.* **optionnelle**) *adjective* optional.

**or**[1] *noun Masc.* **1** gold; **une montre en or** a gold watch; **2 une occasion en or** a golden opportunity.

**or**[2] *conjunction* now.

**orage** *noun Masc.* storm.

**orageux** (*Fem.* **orageuse**) *adjective* **1** stormy; **2** thundery.

**oral** (*plural* **oraux**) *noun Masc.* oral (exam); **l'oral de français** the French oral.
**oral** (*Masc. plural* **oraux**) *adjective* oral; **une épreuve orale** an oral exam.

**orange** *noun Fem., adjective* orange.

**oranger** *noun Masc.* orange tree.

**orbite** *noun Fem.* orbit.

**orchestral** (*Masc. plural* **orchestraux**) *adjective* orchestral.

**orchestre** *noun Masc.* **1** orchestra; **2** band.

**orchidée** *noun Fem.* orchid.

**ordinaire** *noun Masc.* **1** 2-star petrol; **2 sortir de l'ordinaire** to be out of the ordinary; **ça sort un peu de l'ordinaire** it's a bit out of the ordinary; **3 à l'ordinaire, d'ordinaire** usually.
**ordinaire** *adjective* ordinary; **une journée ordinaire** an ordinary day.

**ordinateur** *noun Masc.* computer; **un ordinateur portable** a portable computer.

**ordonnance** *noun Fem.* prescription.

**ordonné** *adjective* tidy.

**ordonner** *verb* [1] to order.

**ordre** *noun Masc.* **1** order; **donner des ordres** to give orders; **2** order; **par ordre alphabétique** in alphabetical order; **mettre de l'ordre** to tidy up; **mettre en ordre** to tidy.

**ordures** *plural noun Fem.* rubbish.

a
b
c
d
e
f
g
h
i
j
k
l
m
n
o
p
q
r
s
t
u
v
w
x
y
z

**oreille** *noun Fem.* ear.

**oreiller** *noun Masc.* pillow.

**oreillons** *plural noun Masc.* mumps.

**organe** *noun Masc.* organ (*of the body*).

**organique** *adjective* organic.

**organisateur**, **organisatrice** *noun Masc., Fem.* organizer.

**organisation** *noun Fem.* organization.

**organiser** *verb* [1] **1** to organize; **2** s'organiser to get organized.

**organisme** *noun Masc.* **1** organization; **2** body; **3** organism.

**organiste** *noun Masc. & Fem.* organist.

**orge** *noun Fem.* barley; **le sucre d'orge** barley sugar.

**orgeat** *noun Masc.* **le sirop d'orgeat** barley water.

**orgue** *noun Fem.* organ; **jouer de l'orgue** to play the organ.

**orgueil** *noun Masc.* pride.

**orgueilleux** (*Fem.* **orgueilleuse**) *adjective* proud.

**Orient** *noun Masc.* **l'Orient** the East.

**oriental** (*Masc. plural* **orientaux**) *adjective* **1** eastern; **2** oriental.

**orientation** *noun Fem.* **1** orientation; **2** l'orientation professionnelle careers advice; **3** avoir le sens de l'orientation to have a good sense of direction.

**orienter** *verb* [1] **1** to position; **2** to direct; **3** s'orienter to get one's bearings; **4** s'orienter vers to move towards; **Bernard s'oriente vers** les langues Bernard's going in for languages.

**originaire** *adjective* **être originaire de** to be a native of; **Giselle est originaire de Dijon** Giselle comes from Dijon.

**original** (*plural* **originaux**) *noun Masc.* original.
**original** (*Masc. plural* **originaux**) *adjective* **1** original; **le film est en version originale** the film isn't dubbed; **2** eccentric; **c'est une vieille dame assez originale** she's rather an eccentric old lady.

**originalité** *noun Fem.* **1** originality; **2** eccentricity.

**origine** *noun Fem.* **1** origin; **2** elle est d'origine écossaise she's Scottish; **3** à l'origine originally; à l'origine la maison appartenait à mon oncle the house originally belonged to my uncle.

**orme** *noun Masc.* elm tree.

**orné** *adjective* **orné de** decorated with.

**ornemental** (*Masc. plural* **ornementaux**) *adjective* ornamental.

**orphelin**, **orpheline** *noun Masc., Fem.* orphan.

**orphelinat** *noun Masc.* orphanage.

**orteil** *noun Masc.* toe; **gros orteil** big toe.

**orthographe** *noun Fem.* spelling.

**ortie** *noun Fem.* nettle.

**os** *noun Masc.* bone.

**osé** *adjective* daring; **c'était un peu osé de dire ça** it was a bit daring to say that.

**oseille** *noun Fem.* sorrel.

**oser** *verb* [1] to dare.

**osier** *noun Masc.* wicker; **un panier en osier** a wicker basket.

**osseux** (*Fem.* **osseuse**) *adjective* bony (*knees, arms*).

**otage** *noun Masc.* hostage; **être pris en otage** to be taken hostage.

**OTAN** *noun Fem.* SHORT FOR **Organisation du traité de l'Atlantique Nord** NATO.

**ôter** *verb* [1] **1** to take off; **je vais ôter ma veste** I'll take off my jacket; **2** to take away; **3** to remove.

**otite** *noun Fem.* earache; **avoir une otite** to have earache.

**ou** *conjunction* **1** or; **est-ce que vous voulez le fromage ou le dessert?** would you like cheese or dessert?; **2 ou ...ou** either ...or; **c'est ou dans ma chambre ou dans le salon** it's either in my bedroom or in the sitting-room; **3 ou bien** or else; **on peut se retrouver au cinéma ou bien chez moi, si tu veux** we can meet at the cinema or else at my place, if you like.

**où** *adverb* where; **où es-tu?** where are you?; **ton frère habite où?** where does your brother live?; **tu l'as trouvé où ton sac?** where did you find your bag?; **je sais où elle habite** I know where she lives. **où** *pronoun* **1** where; **le village où elle habite** the village where she lives; **la ville d'où il vient** the town he comes from; **2** when, that; **le jour où je suis arrivé** the day I arrived.

**ouate** *noun Fem.* cotton wool.

**oubli** *noun Masc.* **1** forgetfulness; **2 l'oubli de quelque chose** forgetting something; **3** oversight; **c'était un oubli** I (*or* you, etc.) forgot about it.

**oublier** *verb* [1] **1** to forget; **j'ai oublié leur adresse** I've forgotten their address; **2** to leave; **j'ai oublié mes clefs chez Jérôme** I've left my keys at Jérôme's.

**ouest** *noun Masc.* west; **à l'ouest de Paris** west of Paris; **dans l'ouest de la France** in the west of France; **l'Ouest** the West; **l'Europe de l'Ouest** Western Europe. **ouest** *adjective* **1** west; **le côté ouest** the west coast; **2** western.

**ouf** *exclamation* phew!

**oui** *adverb* yes; **elle a dit oui** she said yes; **dire oui de la tête** to nod.

**ouragan** *noun Masc.* hurricane.

**ourlet** *noun Masc.* hem.

**ours** *noun Masc.* bear.

**oursin** *noun Masc.* sea urchin.

**outil** *noun Masc.* tool.

**outré** *adjective* outraged.

**outre** *preposition* in addition to.

**outremer** *noun Masc.*, *adjective* ultramarine.

**outre-mer** *adverb* overseas.

**ouvert** *adjective* **1** open; **laisse la porte ouverte** leave the door open; **'ouvert le dimanche'** 'open on Sundays'; **2 laisser le robinet ouvert** to leave the tap on.

**ouvertement** *adverb* openly.

**ouverture** *noun Fem.* **1** opening; **les heures d'ouverture** opening

a
b
c
d
e
f
g
h
i
j
k
l
m
n
**o**
p
q
r
s
t
u
v
w
x
y
z

hours; **2** openness; **ouverture d'esprit** open-mindedness.

**ouvre-boîte** *noun Masc.* tin-opener.

**ouvre-bouteille** *noun Masc.* bottle-opener.

**ouvrier**, **ouvrière** *noun Masc., Fem.* worker.
**ouvrier** (*Fem.* **ouvrière**) *adjective* **la classe ouvrière** the working class.

**ouvrir** *verb* [30] **1** to open; **ouvrir la fenêtre** to open the window; **2 ouvrir le robinet** to turn on the tap; **3 elle n'a pas ouvert la bouche** she didn't say a word; **4 s'ouvrir** to open; **ça s'ouvre comment?** how do you open it?

**ovale** *adjective* oval.

**overdose** *noun Fem.* overdose; **une overdose d'héroïne** an overdose of heroine.

**ovni** *noun Masc.* SHORT FOR **objet volant non identifié** UFO.

**oxygène** *noun Masc.* oxygen.

**ozone** *noun Fem.* ozone.

# Pp

**Pacifique** *noun Masc.* **l'océan Pacifique** the Pacific Ocean.

**pagaille** *noun Fem.* (*informal*) mess; **quelle pagaille!** what a mess!

**page** *noun Fem.* page; **à la première/dernière page** on the first/last page; **les Pages Jaunes** the Yellow Pages.

**paie** *noun Fem.* pay; **un bulletin de paie, une fiche de paie** a payslip.

**paiement** *noun Masc.* payment.

**paillasson** *noun Masc.* doormat.

**paille** *noun Fem.* straw.

**pain** *noun Masc.* **1** bread; **une tranche de pain** a slice of bread; **2 un pain** a loaf of bread; **trois pains** three loaves of bread; **un petit pain** a roll; ★ **ils se vendent comme des petits pains** they're selling like hot cakes (*literally: like rolls*).

**pain au chocolat** *noun Masc.* chocolate pastry.

**pain complet** *noun Masc.* wholemeal bread.

**pain d'épices** *noun Masc.* gingerbread.

**pain de mie** *noun Masc.* sandwich loaf.

**pain de seigle** *noun Masc.* rye bread.

**pain grillé** *noun Masc.* toast.

**pair** *adjective* **1** even (*number*); **2 au pair** au pair; **une jeune fille au pair** an au pair; **travailler au pair** to work as an au pair.

**paire** *noun Fem.* pair; **une paire de chaussures** a pair of shoes.

**paix** *noun Fem.* peace.

**pakistanais** *adjective* Pakistani.

**Pakistanais**, **Pakistanaise** *noun Masc., Fem.* Pakistani.

**palais** *noun Masc.* **1** palace; **2** palate.

**palais de justice** *noun Masc.* law courts.

**pâle** *adjective* pale; **bleu pâle** pale blue.

**Palestine** *noun Fem.* Palestine.

**palier** *noun Masc.* landing (*on a staircase*).

**pâlir** *verb* [2] **1** to turn pale; **2** to fade.

**palme** *noun Fem.* flipper (*for swimming*).

**palmier** *noun Masc.* palm tree.

**palpitant** *adjective* thrilling.

**pamplemousse** *noun Masc.* grapefruit.

**panaché** *noun Masc.* shandy. **panaché** *adjective* **une salade panachée** a mixed salad.

**pancarte** *noun Fem.* notice, sign.

**pané** *adjective* coated in breadcrumbs.

**panier** *noun Masc.* basket.

**panier à salade** *noun Masc.* salad shaker.

**panique** *noun Fem.* panic.

**paniquer** *verb* [1] to panic.

**panne** *noun Fem.* breakdown (*of a car or machine*); **la voiture est en panne** the car's broken down; **la photocopieuse est en panne** the photocopier's not working; **tomber en panne** to break down; **nous sommes en panne d'essence** we've run out of petrol; **une panne de courant** a power cut.

**panneau** (*plural* **panneaux**) *noun Masc.* sign, notice board.

**panneau indicateur** *noun Masc.* signpost.

**panneau publicitaire** *noun Masc.* advertisement hoarding.

**panorama** *noun Masc.* **1** panorama; **2** viewpoint.

**pansement** *noun Masc.* **1** sticking plaster; **2** dressing.

**panser** *verb* [1] to put a dressing on (*a wound*).

**pantalon** *noun Masc.* trousers; **mon pantalon gris** my grey trousers; **un pantalon neuf** a new pair of trousers; **deux pantalons** two pairs of trousers.

**panthère** *noun Fem.* panther.

**pantoufle** *noun Fem.* slipper.

**paon** *noun Masc.* peacock.

**papa** *noun Masc.* Dad, Daddy, father.

**pape** *noun Masc.* pope.

**paperasse** *noun Fem.* (*informal*) paperwork, bumph.

**papeterie** *noun Fem.* **1** stationer's shop; **2** stationery.

**papi** *noun Masc.* (*informal*) granddad.

**papier** *noun Masc.* paper; **du papier blanc** white paper; **vos papiers, s'il vous plaît monsieur** your (identity) papers please, sir.

**papier à lettres** *noun Masc.* writing paper.

**papier aluminium** *noun Masc.* kitchen foil.

**papier cadeau** *noun Masc.* gift wrap.

**papier-calque** *noun Masc.* tracing paper.

**papier hygiénique** *noun Masc.* toilet paper.

a
b
c
d
e
f
g
h
i
j
k
l
m
n
o
**p**
q
r
s
t
u
v
w
x
y
z

a
b
c
d
e
f
g
h
i
j
k
l
m
n
o
**p**
q
r
s
t
u
v
w
x
y
z

**papier peint** *noun Masc.* wallpaper.

**papiers d'identité** *plural noun Masc.* identity papers.

**papillon** *noun Masc.* butterfly.

**paquebot** *noun Masc.* liner.

**pâquerette** *noun Fem.* daisy.

**Pâques** *noun Masc.* Easter; **à Pâques** at Easter; **un œuf de Pâques** an Easter egg; **les vacances de Pâques** the Easter holidays; **le lundi de Pâques** Easter Monday.

**paquet** *noun Masc.* **1** packet; **un paquet de sucre** a packet of sugar; **2** parcel; **il y a un paquet pour vous** there's a parcel for you; **3** bundle (*of clothes or papers*).

**paquet-cadeau** *noun Masc.* gift-wrapped parcel; **est-ce que je vous fais un paquet-cadeau?** shall I gift-wrap it for you?

**par** *preposition* **1** by; **par moi** by me; **par la poste** by post; **payer par chèque** to pay by cheque; **par accident** by accident; **par hasard** by chance; **deux par deux** two by two; **jeter quelque chose par la fenêtre** to throw something out of the window; **aller par Paris** to go via (*or* by) Paris; **par ennui** out of boredom; **2** in; **par endroits** in places; **par cette chaleur** in this heat; **3** per; **50 euros par personne** 50 euros per person; **deux repas par jour** two meals a day; **deux fois par semaine** twice a week.

**parachute** *noun Masc.* parachute.

**parachutiste** *noun Masc. & Fem.* parachutist.

**paradis** *noun Masc.* heaven.

**paragraphe** *noun Masc.* paragraph.

**paraître** *verb* [57] **1** to seem; **ça me paraît étrange** that seems strange to me; **il paraît qu'il est mort** it seems he's dead; **2 paraît-il** apparently; **elle est à Nice, paraît-il** she's in Nice, apparently; **3** to appear; **paraître en public** to appear in public; **4** (*of a book*) to come out, to be published; **le roman va paraître en juin** the novel will come out in June.

**parallèle** *adjective* parallel.

**paralysé** *adjective* paralysed.

**parapente** *noun Masc.* **1** paraglider; **2** paragliding.

**parapluie** *noun Masc.* umbrella.

**parasite** *noun Masc.* **1** parasite; **2 des parasites** interference (*on TV or radio*).

**parasol** *noun Masc.* parasol.

**parc** *noun Masc.* **1** park; **aller au parc** to go to the park; **2** grounds (*of a large house*); **3** fleet (*of vehicles*).

**parc d'attractions** *noun Masc.* amusement park.

**parce que** *conjunction* because; **parce qu'elle est malade** because she's ill; **c'est parce que je t'aime** it's because I love you.

**par-ci** *adverb* **par-ci par-là** here and there.

**parcmètre** *noun Masc.* parking meter.

**parc naturel** *noun Masc.* nature park.

**parcourir** *verb* [29] to go all over, to travel all over; **j'ai parcouru l'Europe** I travelled all over Europe.

**parcours** *noun Masc.* **1** route (*for a bus or a traveller*); **2** course (*for a race*).

**par-derrière** *adverb* from the back, behind; **elle est passée par-derrière** she went round the back.

**par-dessous** *adverb* underneath.

**par-dessus** *adverb* **1** on top; **2** over it; **il a sauté par-dessus** he jumped over it.

**par-dessus** *preposition* over; **elle a sauté par-dessus le ruisseau** she jumped over the stream; **j'aime ça par-dessus tout!** I like that best of all!

**pardessus** *noun Masc.* overcoat.

**par-devant** *adverb* by the front.

**pardon** *noun Masc.* **1** pardon, forgiveness; **je te demande pardon** I'm sorry; **2** excuse me, sorry.

**pardonner** *verb* [1] to forgive; **je ne lui pardonnerai jamais** I'll never forgive him.

**pare-balles** *adjective* bullet-proof; **un gilet pare-balles** a bullet-proof vest.

**pare-brise** *noun Masc.* windscreen.

**pare-chocs** *noun Masc.* bumper (*on a car*).

**pareil** (*Fem.* **pareille**) *adjective* **1** the same; **les deux voitures sont presque pareilles** the two cars are almost the same; **c'est toujours pareil** it's always the same; **mais ce n'est pas du tout pareil!** but it's not the same at all!; **2** such; **je n'ai jamais dit une chose pareille** I never said any such thing; **tu ne**

**peux pas sortir par un temps pareil** you can't go out in weather like this.

**parent** *noun Masc.* **1** parent; **mes parents** my parents; **2** relation; **parents et amis** friends and relations.

**parenthèse** *noun Fem.* bracket; **entre parenthèses** in brackets.

**paresse** *noun Fem.* laziness.

**paresseux** (*Fem.* **paresseuse**) *adjective* lazy.

**parfait** *adjective* perfect.

**parfaitement** *adverb* **1** perfectly; **tu le sais parfaitement!** you know perfectly well!; **parfaitement faux** totally wrong; **2 parfaitement!** absolutely!

**parfois** *adverb* sometimes.

**parfum** *noun Masc.* **1** perfume; **2** flavour; **tu veux quel parfum de yaourt?** what flavour yoghurt would you like?

**parfumé** *adjective* **1** perfumed, fragrant; **parfumé à la lavande** lavender-scented; **2** flavoured; **une glace parfumée au chocolat** a chocolate ice cream.

**parfumerie** *noun Fem.* perfume shop.

**pari** *noun Masc.* bet; **faire un pari** to make a bet.

**parier** *verb* [1] to bet.

**Paris** *noun* Paris; **à Paris** in (*or* to) Paris.

**parisien** (*Fem.* **parisienne**) *adjective* **1** Parisian; **2** Paris; **un restaurant parisien** a Paris restaurant.

a
b
c
d
e
f
g
h
i
j
k
l
m
n
o
p
q
r
s
t
u
v
w
x
y
z

a
b
c
d
e
f
g
h
i
j
k
l
m
n
o
**p**
q
r
s
t
u
v
w
x
y
z

**Parisien, Parisienne** *noun*
*Masc., Fem.* Parisian.

**parking** *noun Masc.* car park; **dans
le parking** in the car park.

**Parlement** *noun Masc.* parliament.

**parler** *verb* [1] **1** to speak; **parler
(le) français** to speak French;
**parler en italien** to speak in Italian;
**parler fort/doucement** to speak
loudly/softly; **parler à quelqu'un** to
speak to someone; **2** to talk; **il parle
très vite** he talks very fast; **parler
cinéma** to talk (about) films;
**3 parler de** to talk about, to
mention; **tout le monde en parle**
everyone's talking about it; **non, il
n'en a pas parlé** no, he didn't
mention it; **n'en parlons plus!** let's
say no more about it!; **4 se parler** to
talk to each other; ★ **tu parles!**
(*informal*) you must be joking!.

**parmi** *preposition* among; **parmi les
invités** among the guests.

**parole** *noun Fem.* **1 les paroles** the
lyrics; **les paroles de la chanson**
the lyrics of the song; **2 elle m'a
donné sa parole** she gave me her
word; **3** speech; **perdre la parole** to
lose the power of speech.

**parquet** *noun Masc.* **1** wooden floor;
**2** parquet.

**parrain** *noun Masc.* godfather.

**parrainer** *verb* [1] to sponsor.

**parsemer** *verb* [50] to sprinkle.

**part** *noun Fem.* **1** portion, helping;
**une part de pizza** a portion of pizza;
**2** share; **il a payé sa part** he paid
his share; **elle a fait sa part du
travail** she did her share of the work;
**3** side; **de toutes parts** from all

sides; **4 pour ma part, je pense
que ...** for my part, I think that ...;
**5 à part** separate, separately; **une
chambre à part** a separate
bedroom; **j'ai mis l'argent à part** I
put the money aside; **à part ça,
qu'est-ce qu'il t'a dit?** apart from
that, what did he tell you?; **6 de la
part de quelqu'un** on behalf of
somebody, for somebody; **c'est de
la part de qui?** who's calling?; **dis-
lui bonjour de ma part** say hello to
him from me.

**partager** *verb* [52] **1** to share
(*possessions or food*); **2** to divide; **je
partage mon temps entre mon
travail et les enfants** I divide my
time between my job and the children.

**partenaire** *noun Masc. & Fem.*
partner.

**parterre** *noun Masc.* **1** flower bed;
**2** stalls (*in a theatre*).

**parti** *noun Masc.* **1** party, group; **le
parti communiste** the communist
party; **2** side.

**participation** *noun Fem.*
participation.

**participe** *noun Masc.* participle;
**participe passé** past participle.

**participer** *verb* [1] **participer à
quelque chose** to take part in
something.

**particulier** *noun Masc.* private
individual.
**particulier** (*Fem.* **particulière**)
*adjective* **1** special; **rien de
particulier** nothing special;
**2** private; **une voiture particulière**
a private car; **3 en particulier** in
particular; **rien en particulier**

nothing in particular; **4 en particulier** in private.

**particulièrement** *adverb* particularly.

**partie** *noun Fem.* **1** part; **une partie de ma vie** part of of my life; **la première partie** the first part; **2 en partie** partly; **3 faire partie de quelque chose** to be part of something; **ce bâtiment fait partie du musée** this building is part of the museum; **elle fait partie de la famille** she's one of the family; **4** game; **faire une partie de tennis** to have a game of tennis; **gagner la partie** to win the game.

**partir** *verb* [58] **1** to leave, to go; **partir à pied** to go on foot; **tu pars déjà?** are you leaving already?; **elle est partie en Italie** she's gone to Italy; **il est parti à Londres** he's gone to London; **elle est partie au travail** she's left for work; **partir en vacances** to go away on holiday; **elle est partie pour huit jours** she's gone away for a week; **ils sont partis en courant** they ran off; **2 à partir de** from; **à partir de lundi** from Monday (onwards).

**partition** *noun Fem.* score (*in music*).

**partout** *adverb* **1** everywhere; **j'ai cherché partout** I've looked everywhere; **2 un peu partout: ça se trouve un peu partout** you can find it/them almost anywhere; **3 trois buts partout** three goals all.

**parvenir** *verb* [81] **1 parvenir à** to reach; **2 parvenir à faire** to manage to do; **il est parvenu à ouvrir la porte** he managed to open the door.

**pas**[1] *adverb* **1** (*used with 'ne' to put verbs into the negative*) **je ne suis pas** I am not; **je n'ai pas de stylo** I don't have a pen; **je ne pense pas** I don't think so; **ils n'ont pas le téléphone** they're not on the phone; **2** not; **c'est lui qui paie, pas moi** he's paying, not me; **pas du tout** not at all; **pas vraiment** not really; **une radio pas chère** a cheap radio; **pas de chance!** bad luck!; **pas possible!** I don't believe it!

**pas**[2] *noun Masc.* **1** step; **faire un grand/petit pas** to take a big/small step; **j'habite à deux pas d'ici** I live very near here; **2** pace; **ralentir le pas** to slow down; **'roulez au pas!'** 'dead slow' (*road sign*).

**passage** *noun Masc.* **1** traffic; **une rue où il y a beaucoup de passage** a street where there's a lot of traffic; **passage interdit** no through traffic; **2** visit; **je peux te prendre au passage** I can pick you up on my way.

**passage à niveau** *noun Masc.* level crossing.

**passage pour piétons** *noun Masc.* pedestrian crossing.

**passager, passagère** *noun Masc., Fem.* passenger.
**passager** (*Fem.* **passagère**) *adjective* passing, temporary.

**passage souterrain** *noun Masc.* subway (*under a road*).

**passant, passante** *noun Masc., Fem.* passer-by.

**passé** *noun Masc.* **1** past; **c'est dans le passé** it's in the past now; **2** past tense; **le passé composé** the present perfect.

**passé** *adjective* **1** l'année passée last year; **2** past; il est dix heures passées it's past ten o'clock.

**passeport** *noun Masc.* passport.

**passer** *verb* [1] **1** to pass; le temps passe vite time passes quickly; **2** to spend (*time*); j'ai passé deux jours à Paris I spent two days in Paris; **3** en passant in passing; **4** passer quelque chose à quelqu'un to pass somebody something; passe-moi le sel pass me the salt; **5** to cross; passer le pont to cross the bridge; **6** to drop in; Pierre est passé ce matin Pierre dropped in this morning; est-ce que le facteur est passé? has the postman been?; je passerai te prendre à huit heures I'll pick you up at eight; **7** to get through; laissez passer l'ambulance! let the ambulance through!; **8** to be on, to be showing (*films*); le film est passé à la télé lundi the film was on telly on Monday; **9** to go; passer à la caisse to go to the checkout; passons au salon let's go through to the sitting room; **10** to give; il m'a passé son vélo he gave me his bike; **11** to put through, to hand over to (*on the telephone*); je vous passe le responsable I'll put you through to the manager; **12** to put (on) (*a garment*); **13** passer l'aspirateur to vacuum; **14** to take, to sit (*a test or an exam*); **15** passer par to go through; nous sommes passés par Paris we went through (or via) Paris; **16** se passer to happen; qu'est-ce qui se passe? what's happening?; ça s'est passé en Chine it happened in China; **17** se

passer de to do without; se passer d'un manteau to do without a coat.

**passerelle** *noun Fem.* **1** footbridge; **2** gangway.

**passe-temps** *noun Masc.* hobby.

**passif** *noun Masc.* passive (*in grammar*).
**passif** (*Fem.* **passive**) *adjective* passive.

**passion** *noun Fem.* passion.

**passionnant** *adjective* exciting.

**passionné**, **passionnée** *noun Masc., Fem.* enthusiast; c'est un passionné de tennis he's a tennis enthusiast.
**passionné** *adjective* keen; c'est une musicienne passionnée she's a keen musician.

**passionner** *verb* [1] l'histoire me passionne history fascinates me.

**passoire** *noun Fem.* strainer.

**patate** *noun Fem.* (*informal*) potato.

**pâte** *noun Fem.* **1** pastry; pâte feuilletée puff pastry; **2** dough; **3** batter; pâte à crêpes pancake batter; **4** paste; **5** les pâtes pasta; on va manger des pâtes ce soir we're having pasta tonight.

**pâte à modeler** *noun Fem.* Plasticine™.

**patience** *noun Fem.* patience.

**patient**, **patiente** *noun Masc., Fem., adjective* patient.

**patienter** *verb* [1] to wait; patientez, s'il vous plaît please hold the line?

**patin** *noun Masc.* skate.

**patinage** *noun Masc.* skating; patinage artistique figure skating.

**patin à glace** *noun Masc.* **1** ice skate; **2** ice skating.

**patin à roulettes** *noun Masc.* roller skate.

**patiner** *verb* [1] to skate.

**patineur, patineuse** *noun Masc., Fem.* skater.

**patinoire** *noun Fem.* ice rink.

**pâtisserie** *noun Fem.* **1** cake shop; **2** cake.

**patois** *noun Masc.* dialect.

**patrie** *noun Fem.* homeland, country.

**patron**[1] *noun Masc.* pattern (*for dressmaking*).

**patron**[2]**, patronne** *noun Masc., Fem.* boss.

**patronner** *verb* [1] to sponsor.

**patrouille** *noun Fem.* patrol.

**patte** *noun Fem.* **1** paw; **2** leg (*of an animal*); ★ **à quatre pattes** on all fours.

**paume** *noun Fem.* palm (*of the hand*).

**paumer** *verb* [1] (*informal*) **1** to lose; **2 se paumer** to get lost.

**paupière** *noun Fem.* eyelid; **le fard à paupières** eyeshadow.

**pause** *noun Fem.* **1** break; **faire une pause** to take a break; **la pause café** the coffee break; **2** pause.

**pauvre** *noun Masc. & Fem.* poor man, poor woman; **les pauvres** the poor; **le pauvre!** poor thing! **pauvre** *adjective* poor.

**pauvreté** *noun Fem.* poverty.

**pavé** *noun Masc.* cobblestone.

**pavillon** *noun Masc.* **1** detached house; **un pavillon de banlieue** a house in the suburbs; **2** wing (*in a hospital*).

**payant** *adjective* **1** (*of a show or event*) not free; **c'est payant?** do you have to pay to get in?; **un parking payant** a pay-and-display car park; **2 un hôte payant** a paying guest.

**paye** *noun Fem.* wages.

**payer** *verb* [59] **1** to pay (*a bill or a person*); **c'est moi qui paie** I'm paying; **être mal payé** to be badly paid; **être payé à l'heure** to be paid by the hour; **2** to pay for; **il a payé le repas** he paid for the meal; **3** (*informal*) **je te paie à boire** I'll buy you a drink; **4 je me suis payé une semaine à Paris** I treated myself to a week in Paris.

**pays** *noun Masc.* **1** country; **la France est un beau pays** France is a beautiful country; **2** region; **des fruits du pays** locally grown fruit.

**paysage** *noun Masc.* landscape.

**paysan, paysanne** *noun Masc., Fem.* farmer.

**Pays-Bas** *plural noun Masc.* **les Pays-Bas** the Netherlands.

**pays de Galles** *noun Masc.* Wales; **au pays de Galles** in (*or* to) Wales.

**PC** *noun Masc.* PC, personal computer.

**péage** *noun Masc.* **1** toll; **autoroute à péage** toll motorway (*motorists have to pay to travel on motorways in France*); **2** tollbooth.

**peau** (*plural* **peaux**) *noun Fem.* **1** skin; **avoir la peau sèche** to have

a
b
c
d
e
f
g
h
i
j
k
l
m
n
o
p
q
r
s
t
u
v
w
x
y
z

213

dry skin; **2** peel (*of fruit*); **peau d'orange** orange peel.

**pêche** *noun Fem.* **1** peach; **2** fishing; **aller à la pêche** to go fishing.

**péché** *noun Masc.* sin.

**pêcher**[1] *verb* [1] **1** to fish for (*trout, salmon, etc*); **2** to catch; **Denise a pêché trois truites** Denise caught three trout.

**pêcher**[2] *noun Masc.* peach tree.

**pêcheur** *noun Masc.* fisherman.

**pédagogique** *adjective* educational; **méthode pédagogique** teaching method.

**pédale** *noun Fem.* pedal; ★ **perdre les pédales** (*informal*) to lose your grip.

**pédaler** *verb* [1] to pedal.

**pédalo**™ *noun Masc.* pedalo, pedal boat.

**pédestre** *adjective* **faire une randonnée pédestre** to go walking (*on a long-distance public footpath*).

**peigne** *noun Masc.* comb.

**peigner** *verb* [1] **1** to comb; **2 se peigner** to comb your hair.

**peindre** *verb* [60] to paint.

**peine** *noun Fem.* **1** effort, trouble; **se donner de la peine** to go to a lot of trouble; **il n'a même pas pris la peine d'appeler** he didn't even take the trouble to ring; **2 ce n'est pas la peine** it's not worth it; **3** difficulty; **elle a eu beaucoup de peine à trouver un logement** she had a lot of difficulty finding somewhere to live; **4 faire de la peine à quelqu'un** to upset somebody; **5** penalty (*in law*); **sous peine**

**d'amende** offenders will be fined; **6 à peine** hardly, scarcely; **je le connais à peine** I hardly know him; **il était à peine cinq heures** it was barely five o'clock.

**peine de mort** *noun Fem.* death penalty.

**peintre** *noun Masc.* painter.

**peintre-décorateur** *noun Masc.* decorator.

**peinture** *noun Fem.* **1** paint; **'peinture fraîche'** 'wet paint'; **2** painting; **faire de la peinture** to paint; **3 une peinture** a painting.

**pèlerin** *noun Masc.* pilgrim.

**pèlerinage** *noun Masc.* pilgrimage; **faire un pèlerinage** to go on a pilgrimage.

**pelle** *noun Fem.* **1** spade; **2** shovel.

**pelle à poussière** *noun Fem.* dustpan.

**pelle mécanique** *noun Fem.* mechanical digger.

**pellicule** *noun Fem.* **1** film (*for a camera*); **une pellicule couleur** a colour film; **2 les pellicules** dandruff.

**pelouse** *noun Fem.* lawn; **'pelouse interdite'** 'keep off the grass'.

**peluche** *noun Fem.* soft toy.

**pencher** *verb* [1] **1** to tilt; **2** to lean; **3 se pencher** to bend down; **4 se pencher par la fenêtre** to lean out of the window.

**pendant** *preposition* **1** for; **je t'ai attendu pendant deux heures** I waited for you for two hours; **2** during; **pendant l'hiver** during the winter; **3 pendant que** while;

214

**pendant que les enfants sont à l'école** while the children are at school; **4 pendant ce temps là** meanwhile; **pendant ce temps là elle attendait à la gare** meanwhile she was waiting at the station.

**pendentif** *noun Masc.* pendant.

**penderie** *noun Fem.* wardrobe, hanging cupboard.

**pendre** *verb* [3] **1** to hang; **2 pendre quelque chose** to hang something up; **3** to hang down.

**pendule** *noun Fem.* clock.

**pénétrer** *verb* [24] **1 pénétrer dans** to enter; **un voleur a pénétré dans le bureau** a thief got into the office; **2** to penetrate.

**pénible** *adjective* **1** difficult, hard; **2 il est pénible** he's a pain.

**péniche** *noun Fem.* barge.

**pénis** *noun Masc.* penis.

**pensée** *noun Fem.* **1** thought; **2** pansy.

**penser** *verb* [1] **1** to think; **je pense que tu as raison** I think you're right; **oui, je pense** yes, I think so; **je ne pense pas** I don't think so; **2** to intend; **il pense arriver mardi** he's intending to arrive on Tuesday; **3 penser de** to think of; **qu'est-ce que tu penses de mon idée?** what do you think of my idea?; **4 penser à** to think about; **à quoi penses-tu?** what are you thinking about?; **5 cette chanson me fait penser à ta mère** this song reminds me of your mother; **6** to remember; **pendant que j'y pense** while I remember; **fais-moi penser à**

**acheter des citrons** remind me to buy lemons.

**pension** *noun Fem.* **1** boarding school; **2** boarding house; **3** pension; **4 pension complète** full board; **demi-pension** half board, dinner, bed and breakfast.

**pension de famille** *noun Fem.* family hotel.

**pensionnaire** *noun Masc. & Fem.* boarder.

**pensionnat** *noun Masc.* boarding school.

**pente** *noun Fem.* slope; **en pente** sloping.

**Pentecôte** *noun Fem.* Whitsun; **à la Pentecôte** at Whitsun.

**pépin** *noun Masc.* **1** (grape) pip; **2** (*informal*) slight problem.

**perçant** *adjective* **1** piercing; **2** sharp.

**perce-neige** *noun Masc. OR Fem.* snowdrop.

**percer** *verb* [61] to pierce; **avoir les oreilles percées** to have pierced ears; **se faire percer les oreilles** to have your ears pierced; **percer un trou** to make a hole.

**perceuse** *noun Fem.* drill.

**perdant, perdante** *noun Masc., Fem.* loser.

**perdre** *verb* [3] **1** to lose; **notre équipe a perdu** our team lost; **2 perdre quelque chose** to lose something; **j'ai perdu mes clefs** I've lost my keys; **j'ai perdu mon chemin** I've lost my way; **3 être perdu** to be lost; **4 se perdre** to get lost; **je me suis perdu dans les**

a
b
c
d
e
f
g
h
i
j
k
l
m
n
o
p
q
r
s
t
u
v
w
x
y
z

petites **rues** I got lost in the back streets; **5 perdre du temps** to waste time.

**perdrix** *noun Fem.* (*invariable*) partridge.

**perdu** *adjective* **1** lost; **un enfant perdu** a lost child; **je suis perdu** I'm lost; **vous êtes perdu?** are you lost?; **2** stray; **un chien perdu** a stray dog; **3 c'est du temps perdu** it's a waste of time.

**père** *noun Masc.* father; **le père Noël** Father Christmas.

**perfectionner** *verb* [1] to perfect.

**performant** *adjective* **1** efficient; **2** high-performance.

**périmé** *adjective* out-of-date.

**période** *noun Fem.* period.

**périphérique** *noun Masc.* ring road.

**perle** *noun Fem.* **1** pearl; **2** bead.

**permanence** *noun Fem.* **1** service; **'permanence de 8h à 19h'** 'open from 8 a.m. to 7 p.m.'; **2 en permanence** permanently, all the time.

**permanent** *adjective* **1** permanent; **2** continuous.

**permettre** *verb* [11] **permettre à quelqu'un de faire** to allow someone to do; **elle leur a permis de partir** she allowed them to leave; **permettez-moi de vous aider** let me help you.

**permis** *noun Masc.* permit, licence.

**permis de conduire** *noun Masc.* driving licence; **passer son permis** to sit your driving test.

**permission** *noun Fem.* **1** permission; **2** leave (*from the army*).

**perroquet** *noun Masc.* parrot.

**perruche** *noun Fem.* budgie.

**perruque** *noun Fem.* wig.

**persécution** *noun Fem.* persecution.

**persévérer** *verb* [24] to persevere.

**persil** *noun Masc.* parsley.

**persister** *verb* [1] to persist.

**personnage** *noun Masc.* **1** character (*in a book, film, or play*); **2** figure, person; **un personnage célèbre** a famous person.

**personnalité** *noun Fem.* personality.

**personne**[1] *pronoun* **1** nobody; **personne ne sait** nobody knows; **2** anybody; **je ne vois personne** I can't see anybody; **je n'ai parlé à personne** I didn't speak to anybody.

**personne**[2] *noun Fem.* person; **vingt personnes** twenty people; **les personnes âgées** the elderly; **en personne** in person.

**personnel** *noun Masc.* **1** staff; **2 le service du personnel** the personnel department.
**personnel** (*Fem.* **personnelle**) *adjective* personal.

**personnellement** *adverb* personally.

**perspective** *noun Fem.* **1** perspective; **2** view; **3** prospect.

**persuader** *verb* [1] **1** to persuade; **persuader quelqu'un de faire** to persuade somebody to do; **2 être persuadé** to be sure.

**perte** *noun Fem.* **1** loss; **2** waste; **une perte de temps** a waste of time.

**perturber** *verb* [1] to disrupt.

**pesanteur** *noun Fem.* gravity.

**pèse-personne** *noun Masc.* bathroom scales.

**peser** *verb* [50] **1** **peser quelque chose** to weigh something; **2** to weigh; **je pèse 60 kilos** I weigh 60 kilos.

**pessimiste** *noun Masc. & Fem.* pessimist.
**pessimiste** *adjective* pessimistic.

**pétale** *noun Masc.* petal.

**pétanque** *noun Fem.* bowls (*the French version, played outdoors with metal bowls; also called 'boules'*).

**pétard** *noun Masc.* firecracker, banger.

**pétillant** *adjective* sparkling (*wine or mineral water*).

**petit**[1] *adjective* **1** little, small; **une petite fille** a little girl; **une toute petite maison** a tiny house; **2** short; **une petite distance** a short distance; ★ **petit à petit** little by little.

**petit**[2] *noun Masc.* little boy; **les petits** the children.

**petite** *noun Fem.* little girl; **les petites** the little girls.

**petit ami** *noun Masc.* boyfriend.

**petit bassin** *noun Masc.* shallow pool (*for non-swimmers*).

**petit déjeuner** *noun Masc.* breakfast.

**petite amie** *noun Fem.* girlfriend.

**petite annonce** *noun Fem.* small ad.

**petite-fille** *noun Fem.* granddaughter.

**petit-fils** *noun Masc.* grandson.

**petit mot** *noun Masc.* note.

**petit pois** *noun Masc.* garden pea.

**petits-enfants** *plural noun Masc.* grandchildren.

**pétrole** *noun Masc.* **1** oil, petroleum; **2** paraffin.

**pétrolier** *noun Masc.* **1** oil tanker, ship; **2** petroleum engineer.

**peu** *adverb* **1** not much; **il dort peu** he doesn't sleep much; **elle gagne très peu** she earns very little; **2** not very; **peu intéressant** not very interesting; **peu réaliste** unrealistic; **3** **peu de** not much, not many; **il reste peu de temps** there's not much time left; **peu de voitures** not many cars; **4** **un peu de** a little, a bit; **il reste un peu de café** there's a bit of coffee left; **un tout petit peu de sel** a tiny amount of salt; **5** **parle un peu plus fort** speak a little louder; **juste un petit peu** just a little; **6** **à peu près** about; **il y avait à peu près vingt personnes** there were about twenty people.

**peuple** *noun Masc.* people, nation.

**peuplier** *noun Masc.* poplar.

**peur** *noun Fem.* fear; **avoir peur de** to be afraid of; **Nadine a peur des souris** Nadine's afraid of mice; **n'ayez pas peur!** don't be afraid!; **faire peur à quelqu'un** to frighten somebody; **tu m'as fait peur!** you gave me a fright!

**peut** *verb* SEE **pouvoir**[1].

a
b
c
d
e
f
g
h
i
j
k
l
m
n
o
**p**
q
r
s
t
u
v
w
x
y
z

a **peut-être** *adverb* perhaps.

b **peuvent**, **peux** *verb* SEE **pouvoir**[1].

c **phare** *noun Masc.* **1** headlight; **allumer les phares** to turn the headlights on; **2** lighthouse.

d **pharmacie** *noun Fem.* chemist's.

e **pharmacien**, **pharmacienne** *noun Masc., Fem.* chemist, pharmacist.

f **phénomène** *noun Masc.* phenomenon.

g **philo** *noun Fem.* (*informal*) SHORT FOR **philosophie**.

h **philosophie** *noun Fem.* philosophy.

j **phoque** *noun Masc.* seal.

k **photo** *noun Fem.* **1** photo, photograph; **une photo d'identité** a passport photo; **2** photography.

l **photocopie** *noun Fem.* photocopy.

m **photocopier** *verb* [1] to photocopy.

n **photocopieuse** *noun Fem.* photocopier.

o **photographe** *noun Masc. & Fem.* photographer; **Sean est photographe** Sean's a photographer.

p **photographie** *noun Fem.* **1** photography; **2** photograph.

q **photographier** *verb* [1] to photograph.

r **photomaton**™ *noun Masc.* photo booth.

s **phrase** *noun Fem.* sentence.

t **physique**[1] *noun Fem.* physics.

u **physique**[2] *adjective* physical.

v **pianiste** *noun Masc. & Fem.* pianist.

**piano** *noun Masc.* piano; **jouer du piano** to play the piano.

**piano à queue** *noun Masc.* grand piano.

**pichet** *noun Masc.* jug.

**pièce** *noun Fem.* **1** room; **notre maison a quatre pièces** our house has four rooms; **2** coin; **une pièce de deux euros** a two-euro coin; **3** play; **une pièce de Molière** a play by Molière; **4** bit, piece; **les pièces d'un puzzle** the pieces of a jigsaw; **5** item; **dix euros (la) pièce** ten euros each; **6** patch (*for repairs*).

**pièce détachée** *noun Fem.* spare part.

**pièce de théâtre** *noun Fem.* play.

**pièce d'identité** *noun Fem.* identification (*such as a passport or identity card*).

**pièce jointe** *noun Fem.* attachment.

**pied** *noun Masc.* **1** foot; **être pieds nus** to be barefoot; **aller à pied** to go on foot; **un coup de pied** a kick; **donner un coup de pied à quelqu'un** to kick someone; **2** bottom, foot; **au pied du lit** at the foot of the bed; **3** **le pied de la table** the table leg; **4** (*in swimming*) **j'ai pied** I can touch the bottom; **je n'ai plus pied** I'm out of my depth.

**piège** *noun Masc.* trap.

**piéger** *verb* [15] to trap; **une voiture piégée** a car bomb.

**pierre** *noun Fem.* stone.

**pierre précieuse** *noun Fem.* precious stone.

**piéton, piétonne** *noun Masc., Fem.* pedestrian; **un passage pour piétons** a pedestrian crossing.

**piétonnier** (*Fem.* **piétonnière**) *adjective* pedestrian; **une rue piétonnière** a pedestrian street.

**pieuvre** *noun Fem.* octopus.

**pigeon** *noun Masc.* pigeon.

**pile**[1] *noun Fem.* **1** battery; **2** pile; **une pile de vêtements** a pile of clothes; **3** tails (*when tossing a coin*); **pile ou face?** heads or tails?

**pile**[2] *adverb* (*informal*) **1** exactly; **à dix heures pile** at ten o'clock on the dot; **2 s'arrêter pile** to stop dead.

**pilône** *noun Masc.* pylon.

**pilote** *noun Masc.* **1** pilot; **2 un pilote de course** a racing driver.

**piloter** *verb* [1] to fly (*a plane*).

**pilule** *noun Fem.* pill.

**piment** *noun Masc.* chilli.

**pin** *noun Masc.* pine tree; **une pomme de pin** a pine cone.

**pince** *noun Fem.* **1 une pince** a pair of pliers; **2** dart (*in a garment*); **3** pincer (*of a crab*).

**pince à épiler** *noun Fem.* tweezers.

**pince à linge** *noun Fem.* clothes peg.

**pinceau** (*plural* **pinceaux**) *noun Masc.* paintbrush.

**pincée** *noun Fem.* pinch (*of salt, for example*).

**pincer** *verb* [61] to pinch.

**pingouin** *noun Masc.* penguin.

**ping-pong** *noun Masc.* ping-pong.

**pintade** *noun Fem.* guinea fowl.

**pion**[1] *noun Masc.* **1** counter (*in a board game*); **2** pawn (*in chess*); **3** piece (*in draughts*).

**pion**[2] *noun Masc. & Fem.* student supervisor of school pupils (*colloquial*) SEE **surveillant**.

**pipe** *noun Fem.* pipe; **fumer la pipe** to smoke a pipe.

**pipi** *noun Masc.* (*informal*) wee; **faire pipi** to have a wee.

**piquant** *adjective* **1** prickly; **2** spicy.

**pique** *noun Masc.* spades (*in a pack of cards*); **le trois de pique** the three of spades.

**pique-nique** *noun Masc.* picnic.

**pique-niquer** *verb* [1] to have a picnic.

**piquer** *verb* [1] **1** to sting; **j'ai été piqué par une guêpe** I've been stung by a wasp; **2** to bite; **piqué par des moustiques** bitten by mosquitoes; **3 se piquer** to prick yourself; **je me suis piqué le doigt** I've pricked my finger; **4** (*informal*) to pinch; **quelqu'un a piqué mon stylo** somebody's pinched my pen; ★ **piquer une crise (de nerfs)** (*informal*) to throw a fit.

**piquet** *noun Masc.* **1** post; **2** peg.

**piqûre** *noun Fem.* **1** injection; **faire une piqûre à quelqu'un** to give somebody an injection; **2** bite, sting (*of an insect*).

**pirate** *noun Masc.* pirate.

**pirate de l'air** *noun Masc.* hijacker (*of plane*).

**pirate de la route** *noun Masc.* hijacker (*of lorry*).

a
b
c
d
e
f
g
h
i
j
k
l
m
n
o
p
q
r
s
t
u
v
w
x
y
z

**pirate informatique** *noun* *Masc.* computer hacker.

**pire** *adjective* **1** worse; **pire que** worse than; **c'est pire que ça!** it's worse than that!; **c'est encore pire** it's even worse; **2** worst; **le pire** the worst; **au pire** if the worst comes to the worst.

**pis** *in phrase* **tant pis** too bad; **tant pis pour lui!** that's his bad luck!

**piscine** *noun* *Fem.* swimming-pool; **est-ce que la piscine est surveillée?** is there a lifeguard at the swimming pool?

**pissenlit** *noun* *Masc.* dandelion.

**pistache** *noun* *Fem.* pistachio.

**piste** *noun* *Fem.* **1** trail (*left by an animal or fugitive*); **la police est sur sa piste** the police are on his trail; **2** track (*for racing or sport*); **faire un tour de piste** to do a lap; **3** piste, trail (*in skiing*); **4** runway (*at an airport*).

**piste cyclable** *noun* *Fem.* cycle lane.

**pistolet** *noun* *Masc.* pistol.

**pitié** *noun* *Fem.* pity; **avoir pitié de quelqu'un** to feel sorry for someone.

**pittoresque** *adjective* picturesque.

**pizza** *noun* *Fem.* pizza; **vous voulez une pizza à quoi?** what kind of pizza would you like?

**placard** *noun* *Masc.* cupboard.

**place** *noun* *Fem.* **1** space, room; **il y a assez de place pour deux** there's enough room for two; **2** seat (*in a theatre, cinema, train, or bus*); **trois places pour ce soir** two seats for this evening's performance; **3** place; **remettez tous les livres à leur place!** put all the books back in their places!; **si j'étais à ta place** if I were you; **4** place; **en troisième place** in third place; **5** square; **la place Rouge** the Red Square; **la place du village** the village square; **6 à la place de** instead of; **il y est allé à ma place** he went instead of me; **7 être sur place** to be on the spot.

**placer** *verb* [61] **1** to place; **2** to seat (*a person*); **elle m'a placé à côté de Louis** she put me next to Louis.

**plafond** *noun* *Masc.* ceiling.

**plage** *noun* *Fem.* beach; **on va à la plage** we're going to the beach.

**plaie** *noun* *Fem.* wound.

**plaindre** *verb* [31] **1** to feel sorry for; **je te plains** I feel sorry for you; **2 se plaindre** to complain; **je ne me plains pas** I'm not complaining; **elle s'est plainte de la qualité du service auprès du responsable** she complained to the manager about the standard of service.

**plaine** *noun* *Fem.* plain.

**plainte** *noun* *Fem.* complaint; **porter plainte** to complain.

**plaire** *verb* [62] **1 s'il te plaît, s'il vous plaît** please; **deux billets, s'il vous plaît** two tickets, please; **2 le tissu me plaît** I like the material; **la chambre vous plaît?** do you like your room?; **le film a beaucoup plu à mon père** my father liked the film very much.

**plaisanter** *verb* [1] to joke.

**plaisanterie** *noun* *Fem.* joke.

**plaisir** *noun Masc.* pleasure; **le plaisir de lire** the pleasure of reading; **'vous venez avec nous?' — 'oui, avec plaisir'** 'will you come too?' — 'yes, with pleasure'; **faire plaisir à quelqu'un** to please someone; **j'y suis allé pour faire plaisir à ma mère** I went to please my mother.

**plan** *noun Masc.* **1** map (*of a town or underground system*); **le plan du métro** the underground map; **2** plan; **le plan du bâtiment** the plan of the building; **3 au premier plan** in the foreground, in the forefront.

**planche** *noun Fem.* plank.

**planche à repasser** *noun Fem.* ironing board.

**planche à roulettes** *noun Fem.* skateboard.

**planche à voile** *noun Fem.* **1** windsurfing board; **2** windsurfing; **faire de la planche à voile** to go windsurfing.

**plancher** *noun Masc.* floor.

**plan d'eau** *noun Masc.* artificial lake (*often for swimming and other water sports*).

**planer** *verb* [1] **1** to glide; **2** (*informal*) to have your head in the clouds.

**planète** *noun Fem.* planet.

**plante** *noun Fem.* plant; **une plante verte** a house-plant.

**planter** *verb* [1] **1** to plant (*a tree, shrub, or plant*); **2** to hammer in (*a nail*); **3 se planter** (*informal*) to make a blunder.

**plaquage** *noun Masc.* **1** tackle; **2** tackling.

**plaqué** *adjective* **plaqué or** gold-plated; **plaqué argent** silver-plated.

**plaque** *noun Fem.* **1** patch (*of damp or ice*); **2** plate, sheet (*of metal or glass*).

**plaque d'immatriculation** *noun Fem.* number plate (*on a car*).

**plastique** *noun Masc.* plastic; **un sac en plastique** a plastic bag.

**plat** *noun Masc.* **1** dish; **un plat chaud/froid** a hot/cold dish; **le plat du jour** the dish of the day; **2** course (*of a meal*); **le plat principal** the main course; ★ **faire tout un plat de quelque chose** (*informal*) to make a big deal of something.
**plat** *adjective* **1** flat; **à plat ventre** flat on your stomach; **2 l'eau plate** still water.

**platane** *noun Masc.* plane tree.

**plateau** (*plural* **plateaux**) *noun Masc.* **1** tray; **2** plateau.

**plate-bande** *noun Fem.* flower bed.

**plâtre** *noun Masc.* plaster; **il a une jambe dans le plâtre** he has a leg in plaster.

**plein** *adjective* **1** full; **le panier est plein** the basket's full; **elle est pleine d'idées** she's full of ideas; **2 en pleine nuit** in the middle of the night; **en plein été** at the height of summer; **en plein centre-ville** right in the middle of town; **en pleine mer** on the open sea.
**plein** *noun Masc.* **faire le plein** to fill up (*a car with petrol*); **le plein, s'il vous plaît** a full tank, please.
**plein** *adverb* **plein de** (*informal*)

loads of; **elle a plein d'amis** she's got loads of friends.

**pleurer** *verb* [1] to cry.

**pleut** *verb* SEE **pleuvoir**.

**pleuvoir** *verb* [63] to rain; **il pleut** it's raining; **il va pleuvoir** it's going to rain; **il a plu cette nuit** it rained last night.

**pli** *noun Masc.* **1** fold; **2** pleat; **3** crease (*in trousers*).

**plier** *verb* [1] **1** to fold; **2** to bend (*your arm or leg, or a stem*); ★ **être plié en deux/en quatre** (*informal*) to be doubled up (*with laughter or pain*).

**plomb** *noun Masc.* **1** lead; **de l'essence sans plomb** unleaded petrol; **2** fuse; **faire sauter les plombs** to blow the fuses.

**plombage** *noun Masc.* filling (*in a tooth*).

**plombier** *noun Masc.* plumber.

**plongée** *noun Fem.* diving; **faire de la plongée** to go diving.

**plongeoir** *noun Masc.* diving board.

**plonger** *verb* [52] **1** to dive; **2** to plunge.

**plongeur**, **plongeuse** *noun Masc., Fem.* **1** diver; **2** washer-up.

**plu** *verb* SEE **plaire**; **pleuvoir**.

**pluie** *noun Fem.* rain; **un jour de pluie** a rainy day; **sous la pluie** in the rain.

**plume** *noun Fem.* **1** feather; **2** ink pen.

**plupart** *noun Fem.* **la plupart de** most; **la plupart des gens** most people; **la plupart du temps** most of the time.

**pluriel** *noun Masc.* plural; **au pluriel** in the plural.

**plus** *adverb* **1 plus de** more; **voulez-vous un peu plus de fromage?** would you like a little more cheese?; **2 plus de** more than; **il y avait plus de cent personnes** there were more than a hundred people; **3 plus que** more than; **il mange plus que moi** he eats more than I do; **le film est plus intéressant que le livre** the film's more interesting than the book; **leur maison est plus grande que la nôtre** their house is bigger than ours; **4 le plus rapide** the fastest; **le plus joli** the prettiest; **5 plus ...plus** the more ...the more; **plus je gagne, plus je dépense** the more I earn the more I spend; **6 en plus** more; **il nous faut trois côtelettes en plus** we need three more chops; **7 de plus** more; **trois chaises de plus** three more chairs; **une fois de plus** one more time; **8 de plus en plus** more and more; **elle fume de plus en plus** she smokes more and more; **je deviens de plus en plus fatigué** I'm getting more and more tired; **il fait de plus en plus chaud** it's getting hotter and hotter; **9 plus ou moins** more or less; **la cuisine est plus ou moins propre** the kitchen's more or less clean; **10 le plus** the most; **c'est lui qui gagne le plus** he earns the most; **au plus** at the most; **11 ne ... plus** no longer; **elle n'habite plus ici** she no longer lives here; **12 je ne veux plus y aller** I don't want to go there any more; **14 il n'y a plus de lait** there's no milk left; **15** plus;

**deux plus trois égalent cinq** two plus three is five.

**plusieurs** *adjective* several; **plusieurs personnes** several people; **plusieurs fois** several times.

**plutôt** *adverb* 1 rather; **prends le jaune plutôt que le vert** take the yellow one rather than the green one; 2 instead; **demande plutôt à Anne** ask Anne instead; 3 pretty; **le repas était plutôt bon** the meal was pretty good; **plutôt bien** pretty good; 4 rather; **elle est plutôt maigre** she's rather thin.

**pluvieux** (*Fem.* **pluvieuse**) *adjective* rainy.

**pneu** *noun Masc.* tyre.

**pneumopathie atypique** *noun Fem.* SARS (*the disease*).

**poche** *noun Fem.* pocket; **un livre de poche** a paperback; **l'argent de poche** pocket money; ★ **c'est dans la poche** (*informal*) it's in the bag; ★ **je connais Paris comme ma poche** (*informal*) I know Paris like the back of my hand.

**poêle**[1] *noun Masc.* stove (*for heating*); **un poêle à bois** a wood-burning stove.

**poêle**[2] *noun Fem.* frying pan.

**poème** *noun Masc.* poem.

**poésie** *noun Fem.* poetry.

**poète** *noun Masc.* poet.

**poids** *noun Masc.* weight; **prendre du poids** to put on weight; **perdre du poids** to lose weight.

**poids lourd** *noun Masc.* lorry.

**poignée** *noun Fem.* 1 handful; **une poignée de cailloux** a handful of pebbles; 2 handle; 3 **une poignée de main** a handshake.

**poignet** *noun Masc.* wrist.

**poil** *noun Masc.* hair; **un poil** a hair; **le chat perd ses poils** the cat's moulting; ★ **être de bon/mauvais poil** to be in a good/bad mood.

**poilu** *adjective* hairy.

**poing** *noun Masc.* fist; **un coup de poing** a punch.

**point** *noun Masc.* 1 point; **et mon dernier point** and my last point; **un point de détail** a minor point; **un point faible** a weak point; 2 **un point de rencontre** a meeting-place; 3 **être sur le point de faire** to be just about to do; **j'étais sur le point de t'appeler** I was on the point of phoning you; 4 dot; **un petit point sur la carte** a tiny dot on the map; 5 full stop; 6 point (*when scoring*); **six points contre sept** six points to seven; **marquer/perdre des points** to win/lose points; 7 mark (*in a test*); 8 **à point** just in time; **tu es arrivé à point** you arrived just in time; **un steak cuit à point** a medium-rare steak.

**point chaud** *noun Masc.* trouble spot.

**point de départ** *noun Masc.* starting point.

**point d'exclamation** *noun Masc.* exclamation mark.

**point de vue** *noun Masc.* point of view; **d'un point de vue politique** from a political point of view.

**point d'interrogation** *noun Masc.* question mark.

**pointe** *noun Fem.* **1** point; **la pointe d'un couteau** the point of a knife; **sur la pointe des pieds** on tip-toe; **être en pointe** to be pointed; **2 les heures de pointe** the rush hour, peak time; **3 une pointe de** a touch of; **une pointe d'ail** a touch of garlic; ★ **être à la pointe du progrès** to be in the forefront of progress.

**pointillé** *noun Masc.* dotted line.

**point mort** *noun Masc.* neutral (*gear*); **tu es au point mort** you're in neutral.

**pointu** *adjective* pointed.

**pointure** *noun Fem.* size (*of shoes*); **quelle est votre pointure?** what size do you take?

**point-virgule** *noun Masc.* semi-colon.

**poire** *noun Fem.* pear.

**poireau** (*plural* **poireaux**) *noun Masc.* leek.

**poirier** *noun Masc.* pear tree; **faire le poirier** to stand on your head.

**pois** *noun Masc.* **1** pea; **des petits pois** (garden) peas; **2 à pois** spotted; **un tissu à pois** a spotted fabric.

**pois chiche** *noun Masc.* chick pea.

**pois de senteur** *noun Masc.* sweet pea.

**poison** *noun Masc.* poison.

**poisson** *noun Masc.* fish; **j'aime le poisson** I like fish.

**poisson d'avril** *noun Masc.* April fool; **il m'a fait un poisson d'avril** he played an April fool trick on me.

**poissonnerie** *noun Fem.* fishmonger's.

**poissonnier**, **poissonnière** *noun Masc., Fem.* fishmonger.

**poisson rouge** *noun Masc.* goldfish.

**Poissons** *plural noun Masc.* Pisces (*sign of the Zodiac*).

**poitrine** *noun Fem.* **1** chest; **2** bust; **quel est votre tour de poitrine?** what is your bust size?

**poivre** *noun Masc.* pepper; **poivre noir en grains** whole black peppercorns.

**poivrier** *noun Masc.* pepper pot.

**poivron** *noun Masc.* pepper (*red, green, or yellow*).

**poker** *noun Masc.* poker.

**polar** *noun Masc.* (*informal*) detective story.

**pôle** *noun Masc.* pole; **le pôle Nord/Sud** the North/South Pole.

**poli** *adjective* polite; **être poli avec quelqu'un** to be polite to somebody.

**police** *noun Fem.* **1** police; **appeler la police** to call the police; **2** (insurance) policy.

**policier** *noun Masc.* police officer; **une femme policier** a woman police officer.
**policier** *adjective* **un roman policier** a detective story.

**poliment** *adverb* politely.

**politesse** *noun Fem.* politeness; **par politesse** out of politeness.

**politicien**, **politicienne** *noun Masc., Fem.* politician.

**politique** *noun Fem.* **1** politics; **2** policy; **la politique sociale/étrangère** social/foreign policy.

**politique** *adjective* **1** political; **2 un homme politique** a politician.

**polluer** *verb* [1] to pollute.

**pollution** *noun Fem.* pollution.

**polo** *noun Masc.* polo shirt.

**Pologne** *noun Fem.* Poland; **en Pologne** in (*or* to) Poland.

**polonais** *noun, Masc.* Polish (*language*).
**polonais** *adjective* Polish.

**Polonais, Polonaise** *noun Masc., Fem.* Pole.

**pommade** *noun Fem.* ointment.

**pomme** *noun Fem.* **1** apple; **une tarte aux pommes** an apple tart; **2** potato; **pommes frites** chips; ★ **tomber dans les pommes** (*informal*) to faint (*literally: to fall into the apples*).

**pomme de terre** *noun Fem.* potato.

**pommier** *noun Masc.* apple tree.

**pompe** *noun Fem.* pump.

**pompe à essence** *noun Fem.* petrol pump.

**pompes funèbres** *plural noun Fem.* undertaker's.

**pompier** *noun Masc.* fire fighter; **appeler les pompiers** to call the fire brigade.

**pompiste** *noun Masc. & Fem.* petrol pump attendant.

**poncer** *verb* [61] to sand (*wood*).

**ponctuation** *noun Fem.* punctuation.

**poney** *noun Masc.* pony.

**pont** *noun Masc.* **1** bridge; **2** deck (*of a ship*); ★ **faire le pont** to take a long weekend (*usually when the Thursday before or the Tuesday after is a public holiday*).

**populaire** *adjective* **1** working-class (*family, housing, or area*); **2** popular (*art or writing*); **3** folk; **la culture populaire** folk culture; **4** popular.

**population** *noun Fem.* population.

**porc** *noun Masc.* **1** pig; **un élevage de porcs** a pig farm; **2** pork; **manger un rôti de porc** to have roast pork.

**porcelaine** *noun Fem.* china, porcelain.

**porcherie** *noun Fem.* pigsty; **ta chambre est une vraie porcherie** your room is a real pigsty.

**port** *noun Masc.* **1** port; **2** harbour.

**portable** *adjective* portable; **un ordinateur portable** a laptop computer.

**portail** *noun Masc.* gate.

**portatif** (*Fem.* **portative**) *adjective* portable.

**porte** *noun Fem.* **1** door; **la porte d'entrée** the front door; **2** gate (*in an airport*); **la porte numéro douze** gate number twelve; **3 l'entreprise a fermé ses portes** the business has closed down; **mettre quelqu'un à la porte** to sack somebody.

**porte-bagages** *noun Masc.* luggage rack.

**porte-clés** *noun Masc.* key-ring.

**portée** *noun Fem.* **à portée de main** within reach.

**porte-fenêtre** *noun Fem.* French window.

a
b
c
d
e
f
g
h
i
j
k
l
m
n
o
p
q
r
s
t
u
v
w
x
y
z

**portefeuille** *noun Masc.* wallet; **une jupe en portefeuille** a wrapover skirt.

**porte-jarretelles** *noun Masc.* suspender belt.

**portemanteau** (*plural* **portemanteaux**) *noun Masc.* coat rack.

**portemine** *noun Masc.* propelling pencil.

**porte-monnaie** *noun Masc.* purse.

**porte-parole** *noun Masc.* spokesperson.

**porter** *verb* [1] **1** to carry; **porter une valise** to carry a suitcase; **2** to take; **porter un paquet à la poste** to take a parcel to the post office; **3** to wear; **elle portait une robe bleue** she was wearing a blue dress; **4 se porter bien** to be well; **se porter mal** to be in a bad way; ★ **porter bonheur/malheur** to bring good/bad luck.

**portière** *noun Fem.* door (*of a car*).

**portion** *noun Fem.* portion, helping.

**porto** *noun Masc.* port (*wine*).

**portoricain** *adjective* Puerto Rican.

**Portoricain, Portoricaine** *noun Masc., Fem.* Puerto Rican (*person*).

**Porto Rico** *noun Fem.* Puerto Rico.

**portrait** *noun Masc.* portrait.

**portugais** *noun Masc.* Portuguese (*language*).
  **portugais** *adjective* Portuguese.

**Portugais, Portugaise** *noun Masc., Fem.* Portuguese (*person*).

**Portugal** *noun Masc.* Portugal; **au Portugal** in (*or* to) Portugal.

**poser** *verb* [1] **1** to put down; **il a posé sa tasse sur la table** he put his cup down on the table; **pose ta valise** put your case down; **2 cela nous pose un problème** that's a problem for us; **3 poser une question** to ask a question.

**positif** (*Fem.* **positive**) *adjective* positive.

**position** *noun Fem.* position.

**posséder** *verb* [24] to own.

**possessif** (*Fem.* **possessive**) *adjective* possessive.

**possibilité** *noun Fem.* **1** possibility; **c'est une possibilité** it's a possibility; **2** opportunity; **la possibilité de voyager** the opportunity to travel.

**possible** *adjective* possible; **aussi grand que possible** as big as possible; **le moins possible** as little as possible; **dès que possible** as soon as possible; **ce n'est pas possible!** I don't believe it!; ★ **faire tout son possible** to do your best.

**poste**[1] *noun Masc.* **1** job, post; **un poste de secrétaire** a job as a secretary; **2 un poste de radio/ télévision** a radio/television set; **3** extension (*on a telephone system*); **le poste 578, s'il vous plaît** extension 578, please.

**poste**[2] *noun Fem.* post office; **il travaille pour la poste** he works for the post office; **mettre quelque chose à la poste** to post something.

**poste de police** *noun Masc.* police station.

**pot** *noun Masc.* **1** jar; **un pot de confiture** a jar of jam; **2** carton; **un**

**pot de crème** a carton of cream; **3 un pot de peinture** a tin of paint; ★ **prendre un pot** to have a drink.

**potable** *adjective* **eau (non) potable** (not) drinking water.

**potage** *noun Masc.* soup; **potage aux légumes** vegetable soup.

**potager** *noun Masc.* vegetable garden.

**pot-au-feu** *noun Masc.* boiled beef with vegetables.

**pot d'échappement** *noun Masc.* exhaust, silencer (*for a car*).

**poteau** (*plural* **poteaux**) *noun Masc.* post.

**poteau télégraphique** *noun Masc.* telegraph pole.

**potelé** *adjective* chubby.

**poterie** *noun Fem.* **1** pottery; **2** piece of pottery.

**pou** (*plural* **poux**) *noun Masc.* louse; ★ **chercher des poux** (*informal*) to nitpick.

**poubelle** *noun Fem.* dustbin; **mettre quelque chose à la poubelle** to throw something in the dustbin.

**pouce** *noun Masc.* **1** thumb; **2** inch; ★ **se tourner les pouces** (*informal*) to twiddle your thumbs.

**poudre** *noun Fem.* powder.

**pouffer** *verb* [1] **pouffer de rire** to burst out laughing.

**poulain** *noun Masc.* foal.

**poule** *noun Fem.* hen; ★ **quand les poules auront des dents** (*informal*) when pigs can fly (*literally: when hens have teeth*).

**poulet** *noun Masc.* chicken; **une cuisse de poulet** a chicken leg ; **du poulet rôti** roast chicken.

**poulet fermier** *noun Masc.* free-range chicken.

**pouls** *noun Masc.* pulse; **le médecin a pris mon pouls** the doctor took my pulse.

**poumon** *noun Masc.* lung; **crier à pleins poumons** to shout at the top of your voice.

**poupée** *noun Fem.* doll.

**pour** *preposition* **1** for; **un cadeau pour Marie-Laure** a present for Marie-Laure; **un billet pour Calais** a ticket for Calais; **le train pour Londres** the train for London; **ce sera prêt pour samedi?** will it be ready for Saturday?; **être pour** to be in favour; **je n'y suis pour rien** I had nothing to do with it; **je n'en ai pas pour longtemps** it won't take long; **2 pour faire cela** in order to do that; **je suis allé au marché pour acheter des légumes** I went to the market to buy some vegetables; **je suis là pour t'aider** I'm here to help you; **c'était juste pour rire!** it was only meant as a joke!; **pour ainsi dire** so to speak; ★ **le pour et le contre** the pros and cons;

**pourboire** *noun Masc.* tip.

**pour cent** *noun Masc.* per cent; **dix pour cent** ten per cent.

**pourcentage** *noun Masc.* percentage.

**pourquoi** *adverb* why; **pourquoi ont-ils refusé?** why did they refuse?; **je veux savoir pourquoi**

I want to know why; **pourquoi pas?** why not?

**pourri** *adjective* rotten.

**pourrir** *verb* [2] to go bad.

**poursuivre** *verb* [75] **1** to chase; **2** to continue.

**pourtant** *adverb* **1** though; **et pourtant c'est vrai** it's true though; **2** yet; **et pourtant ça aurait pu être bien** and yet it could have been good.

**pourvu que** *conjunction* (*followed by subjunctive*) **1** providing, as long as; **pourvu que tu reviennes samedi** providing you come back on Saturday; **2** let's hope that; **pourvu que ça dure!** let's hope it lasts!

**pousser** *verb* [1] **1** to push; **elle a poussé la porte** she pushed the door shut (*or* open); **2 pousser un cri** to let out a cry, to cry out; **3** to grow (*of a child, hair, or a plant*); **mes tomates poussent bien** my tomatoes are growing well; **4 se pousser** to move over; **pousse-toi!** move over!

**poussette** *noun* Fem. pushchair.

**poussière** *noun* Fem. dust; ★ **dix euros et des poussières** ten euros something, just over 10 euros.

**poutre** *noun* Fem. beam.

**pouvez** *verb* SEE **pouvoir**[1].

**pouvoir**[1] *verb* [12] can; **je peux être là à dix heures** I can be there at ten; **peux-tu m'aider?** can you help me?; **je ne peux pas l'ouvrir** I can't open it; **ils ne pouvaient pas téléphoner avant** they couldn't phone before; **je n'ai pas pu réserver** I wasn't able to book; **elle aurait pu nous le dire** she could have told us; **puis-je**

parler à Cécile, s'il vous plaît may I speak to Cécile, please; **tu peux toujours essayer** there's no harm in trying.

**pouvoir**[2] *noun* Masc. power; **après dix ans au pouvoir** after ten years in power.

**pouvons** *verb* SEE **pouvoir**[1].

**prairie** *noun* Fem. meadow.

**pratique** *noun* Fem. practice; **mettre quelque chose en pratique** to put something into practice; **il manque de pratique** he lacks practical experience.
**pratique** *adjective* practical, convenient; **cet ouvre-boîte n'est pas très pratique** this can opener isn't very practical; **le nouvel appartement est très pratique pour les magasins** the new flat's very handy for the shops.

**pratiquement** *adverb* practically; **c'est pratiquement fini** it's practically finished.

**pratiquer** *verb* [1] **1** to play, to do (*a sport or hobby*); **je pratique le yoga** I do yoga; **2** to practise; **pendant mon séjour à Lille j'aurai la possibilité de pratiquer mon français** during my stay in Lille I'll be able to practise my French.

**pré** *noun* Masc. meadow.

**préalable** *adjective* prior; **une condition préalable** a prior condition.

**précaution** *noun* Fem. precaution; **par précaution** as a precaution; **prendre ses précautions** to take precautions.

**prendre**

**précédent** *adjective* previous; **l'année précédente** the previous year, the year before.

**précieux** (*Fem.* **précieuse**) *adjective* precious, valuable; **une pierre précieuse** a precious stone; **des renseignements précieux** extremely useful information.

**précipice** *noun Masc.* precipice.

**précipitation** *noun Fem.* **1** haste; **2 précipitations** rainfall.

**précipiter** *verb* [1] **se précipiter** to rush; **ils se sont précipités vers la porte** they rushed for the door.

**précis** *adjective* **1** precise; **2** accurate; **3** specific.

**précisément** *adverb* precisely.

**préciser** *verb* [1] **1** to specify (*details or one's intentions*); **2** to explain; **pouvez-vous préciser comment?** could you explain exactly how?

**précision** *noun Fem.* **1** precision; **2** detail; **voici quelques précisions sur le voyage** here are some details about the journey.

**précuit** *adjective* precooked.

**préfecture** *noun Fem.* prefecture (*France is divided into 96 'départements', which are roughly equivalent to British counties. The administration of each of these is done at the local level from the prefecture*).

**préfecture de police** *noun Fem.* (local) police headquarters.

**préférable** *adjective* preferable.

**préféré** *adjective* favourite; **mon plat préféré** my favourite dish.

**préférence** *noun Fem.* **1** preference; **2 de préférence** preferably; **de préférence avant le dix mai** preferably before the tenth of May.

**préférer** *verb* [24] to prefer; **elle préfère le poisson à la viande** she prefers fish to meat.

**préfet** *noun Masc.* prefect (*official with overall responsibility for running a French territorial department*); **le préfet de police** the chief of police; SEE ALSO **préfecture**.

**préjugé** *noun Masc.* prejudice.

**prélavage** *noun Masc.* prewash.

**prématuré** *adjective* premature.

**premier** (*Fem.* **première**) *adjective* **1** first; **la première fois** the first time; **c'est la première fois que je le fais** it's the first time I've done it; **Michel, tu passes le premier** Michel, you go first; **le premier juin** the first of June; **2** top; **de première qualité** top quality; **3 au premier étage** on the first floor; **4 en premier** first; **arriver en premier** to arrive first.

**première** *noun Fem.* **1** première (*of a film or play*); **2 une première mondiale** a world first (*an important event or achievement*); **3 voyager en première** to travel first-class; **4** (*in a French school*) the equivalent of Year 12.

**premièrement** *adverb* firstly.

**premier ministre** *noun Masc.* prime minister.

**prendre** *verb* [64] **1** to take; **prends celui-ci!** take this one!; **prendre un taxi** to take a taxi; **2 prendre**

a
b
c
d
e
f
g
h
i
j
k
l
m
n
o
p
q
r
s
t
u
v
w
x
y
z

# prénom

quelque chose à quelqu'un to take something from somebody; **qui m'a pris mon vélo?** who's taken my bike?; **3** to have (*something to eat or drink*); **je prends une bière** I'll have a beer; **qu'est-ce que tu prends?** what would you like?; **4** to bring; **est-ce que tu as pris ton parapluie?** did you bring your umbrella?; **5 passer prendre quelqu'un** to pick somebody up; **je passerai te prendre à dix heures** I'll pick you up at ten; ★ **c'est à prendre ou à laisser** take it or leave it.

**prénom** *noun Masc.* first name.

**préparatifs** *plural noun Masc.* preparations; **les préparatifs du voyage** the preparations for the journey.

**préparation** *noun Fem.* preparation, training.

**préparer** *verb* [1] **1** to prepare; **je vais préparer les légumes** I'll go and prepare the vegetables; **Françoise est en train de préparer le dîner** Françoise is busy making dinner; **as-tu préparé tes affaires pour le matin?** have you got your things ready for the morning?; **on a préparé une petite surprise pour elle** we've got a little surprise ready for her; **des plats préparés** ready-to-eat meals; **2 se préparer** to get ready; **je vais me préparer pour partir** I'll go and get ready to leave.

**préposition** *noun Fem.* preposition.

**près** *adverb* **1** nearby; **il y a un village tout près** there's a village nearby; **2 près de** near; **près de la gare** near the station; **près de toi** near you; **près de chez nous** near our house, near where we live; **3 près de** nearly, almost; **près de mille euros** nearly a thousand euros; **4 de près** closely; **regarder quelque chose de près** to look closely at something; **5 à peu près** more or less; **à peu près deux heures** two hours, more or less; **j'ai à peu près fini** I've more or less finished.

**prescrire** *verb* [38] **1** to prescribe; **2** to stipulate.

**présence** *noun Fem.* presence.

**présent** *noun Masc.* **1** present (tense); **au présent** in the present; **2 à présent** now; **à présent je n'ai pas le temps** I haven't got time just now.
**présent** *adjective* present (*at an event*); **toute la famille était présente** the whole family was there.

**présentateur, présentatrice** *noun Masc., Fem.* **1** presenter (*of a broadcast or programme*); **2** newsreader.

**présentation** *noun Fem.* **1** presentation; **2** introduction (*to someone you haven't met before*).

**présenter** *verb* [1] **1** to introduce; **je vous présente mon père** may I introduce my father?; **Alain, je te présente Raphaël** Alain, this is Raphaël; **2** to present (*a ticket, pass, or document*); **il faut présenter votre passeport** you must show your passport; **3 présenter ses excuses** to apologize; **4 se présenter** to go, to come; **en arrivant, présentez-vous à la réception** when you get there (*or* here), go (*or* come) to reception; **5 se**

**présenter à quelqu'un** to introduce yourself to somebody.

**préservatif** *noun Masc.* condom.

**préservation** *noun Fem.*
1 preservation; 2 conservation.

**préserver** *verb* [1] to protect, to preserve.

**président** *noun Masc.* 1 president; 2 chairman.

**présidente** *noun Fem.* 1 president; 2 chairwoman.

**présidentielles** *plural noun Fem.* **les présidentielles** the presidential elections.

**presque** *adverb* 1 nearly; **j'ai presque fini** I've nearly finished; 2 **presque rien** hardly anything; **il ne reste presque rien** there's hardly anything left; 3 **presque pas de** hardly any; **il ne reste presque pas de lait** there's hardly any milk left.

**presqu'île** *noun Fem.* peninsula.

**pressant** *adjective* urgent.

**presse** *noun Fem.* **la presse** the press, the newspapers; **que dit la presse?** what do the papers say?

**pressé** *adjective* 1 **être pressé** to be in a hurry; 2 urgent; **ce n'est pas pressé** it's not urgent; 3 **un citron pressé** a fresh lemon juice (*served with water and sugar*).

**presser** *verb* [1] 1 to urge (*someone to do something*); 2 to squeeze; **presser une orange** to squeeze an orange; 3 **ça ne presse pas** there's no hurry; **presser le pas** to hurry (on); 4 **se presser** to hurry.

**pressing** *noun Masc.* dry cleaner's.

**pression** *noun Fem.* 1 pressure; **sous pression** pressurized; 2 press stud; 3 (*informal*) draught beer; **un demi pression** a half of draught beer.

**prestidigitateur**, **prestidigitatrice** *noun Masc., Fem.* conjurer.

**prestige** *noun Masc.* prestige.

**prestigieux** (*Fem.* **prestigieuse**) *adjective* prestigious.

**présumer** *verb* [1] to assume, to presume.

**prêt** *noun Masc.* loan. **prêt** *adjective* ready; **le dîner est prêt!** dinner's ready!; **être prêt à partir** to be ready to leave.

**prêt-à-porter** *noun Masc.* ready-to-wear (clothes).

**prétendre** *verb* [3] to claim; **elle prétend que ce n'est pas sa faute** she claims it's not her fault.

**prêter** *verb* [1] 1 to lend; **prêter quelque chose à quelqu'un** to lend somebody something; **je te prêterai mon vélo** I'll lend you my bike; 2 **prêter attention** to pay attention; 3 **prêter l'oreille** to listen.

**prétexte** *noun Masc.* excuse.

**prêtre** *noun Masc.* priest.

**preuve** *noun Fem.* 1 proof; **la preuve, c'est que ...** the proof is that ...; 2 **faire preuve de** to show; **ils ont fait preuve de beaucoup d'intelligence** they showed considerable intelligence.

**prévenir** *verb* [81] 1 to tell (*in advance*); **préviens-moi de ta visite** tell me when you're coming; **ils arrivent toujours sans nous**

a b c d e f g h i j k l m n o p q r s t u v w x y z

**prévenir** they always arrive without letting us know; **2** to call (*the police or a doctor*); **3** to warn; **je te préviens** I warn you.

**prévention** *noun Fem.* prevention.

**prévision** *noun Fem.* forecast, forecasting; **les prévisions météorologiques** the weather forecast.

**prévoir** *verb* [65] **1** to predict (*an event or change*); **2** to plan (*a journey or an arrangement*); **3** tout a été prévu everything's been taken care of; **4 le départ est prévu pour huit heures** departure is scheduled for eight o'clock; **5** to allow (*time or money*); **prévoyez 10 euros pour le taxi** allow 10 euros for the taxi.

**prier** *verb* [1] **1** prier quelqu'un de faire to ask someone to do; **il m'a prié d'excuser son retard** he asked me to forgive him for being late; **les clients sont priés de ne pas fumer** customers are kindly requested not to smoke; **2 je vous en prie** you're welcome, it's nothing; **'merci beaucoup' – 'je vous en prie'** 'thank you very much' – 'you're welcome'; **3** to pray.

**prière** *noun Fem.* **1** prayer; **2** request; **'prière de fermer la porte'** 'please close the door'.

**primaire** *adjective* primary; **l'école primaire** primary school.

**prime** *noun Fem.* **1** bonus; **2** free gift.

**primevère** *noun Fem.* primrose.

**prince** *noun Masc.* prince; **le prince Charles** Prince Charles.

**princesse** *noun Fem.* princess.

**principal** (*Masc. plural* **principaux**) *adjective* principal, chief.

**principe** *noun Masc.* **1** principle; **2 en principe** as a rule; **en principe je rentre à six heures** as a rule I get back at six; **3 en principe** in theory; **en principe tout le monde a été informé** in theory, everybody's been informed.

**printanier** (*Fem.* **printanière**) *adjective* spring-like (*weather*).

**printemps** *noun Masc.* spring; **au printemps** in (the) spring.

**priorité** *noun Fem.* **1** priority; **2** right of way; **'vous n'avez pas la priorité'** 'you do not have right of way' (*sign at a roundabout*).

**pris** *verb* SEE **prendre**
**pris** *adjective* **1** busy; **je suis très prise ce matin** I'm very busy this morning; **2** taken; **toutes les places sont prises** all the seats are taken; **3** overcome (*with an emotion or a feeling*); **être pris de panique** to be panic-stricken.

**prise** *noun Fem.* **1** socket, plug (*for an electric appliance*); **2** capture; **la prise de la Bastille** the storming of the Bastille.

**prise de courant** *noun Fem.* power point.

**prise de sang** *noun Fem.* blood test.

**prise multiple** *noun Fem.* adaptor plug.

**prison** *noun Fem.* prison.

**prisonnier**, **prisonnière** *noun Masc., Fem.* prisoner.

**privé** *noun Masc.* **1** private sector (*of business or the school system*); **2 en privé** in private, off the record. **privé** *adjective* **1** private; **'propriété privée'** 'private property'; **2** without; **nous sommes privés d'électricité** we are without electricity; **privé de sens** senseless.

**priver** *verb* [1] **1 priver quelqu'un de quelque chose** to deprive someone of something; **2 se priver de quelque chose** to do without something.

**privilège** *noun Masc.* privilege.

**privilégié** *adjective* privileged, special, fortunate.

**privilégier** *verb* [1] **1** to favour; **2** to give priority to.

**prix** *noun Masc.* **1** price; **quel est le prix des places?** what price are the seats?; **le prix a augmenté** the price has gone up; **2 à tout prix** at all costs; **3** prize; **le premier prix** first prize.

**probable** *adjective* likely; **c'est peu probable** it's unlikely.

**probablement** *adverb* probably.

**problème** *noun Masc.* problem; **sans problème!** no problem!

**procédé** *noun Masc.* process.

**procès** *noun Masc.* **1** trial; **2** lawsuit.

**procession** *noun Fem.* procession.

**prochain** *adjective* next; **la prochaine fois** the next time; **le mois prochain** next month; **jeudi prochain** next Thursday; **à la prochaine!** see you soon!

**prochainement** *adverb* soon.

**proche** *adjective* **1** near; **la ville la plus proche est Valence** the nearest town is Valence; **2** close; **c'est une amie très proche de Julie** she' a very close friend of Julie's; **3 proche de** near; **ils ont acheté une maison proche de Nice** they've bought a house near Nice.

**Proche-Orient** *noun Masc.* **le Proche-Orient** the Middle East.

**proches** *plural noun Masc.* close family and friends.

**procurer** *verb* [1] **se procurer quelque chose** to get something.

**producteur, productrice** *noun Masc., Fem.* producer.

**production** *noun Fem.* production.

**produire** *verb* [26] **1** to produce; **2 se produire** to happen; **ça s'est produit au mois de mai** that happened in May.

**produit** *noun Masc.* product; **les produits de beauté** beauty products; **les produits d'entretien** household products; **les produits laitiers** dairy produce; **les produits congelés** frozen foods; **les produits d'exportation** export products.

**prof** *noun Masc.* (*informal*) SHORT FOR **professeur** teacher; **notre prof de français** our French teacher.

**professeur** *noun Masc.* **1** teacher; **ma sœur est professeur de physique** my sister's a physics teacher; **2** university lecturer; **3** university professor.

**profession** *noun Fem.* profession, occupation.

a
b
c
d
e
f
g
h
i
j
k
l
m
n
o
p
q
r
s
t
u
v
w
x
y
z

**professionnel** (*Fem.* **professionnelle**) *adjective* professional.

**profil** *noun Masc.* profile.

**profit** *noun Masc.* **1** profit; **les profits de la société** the company's profits; **2 au profit de** in aid of; **au profit des sans-abri** in aid of the homeless.

**profiter** *verb* [1] **1 profiter de** to take advantage of (*an opportunity*); **j'ai profité des soldes pour m'acheter un manteau** I took advantage of the sales to buy myself a coat; **2** to make the most of; **profite bien de tes vacances!** make the most of your holiday!; **3 profiter à** to benefit.

**profond** *adjective* deep; **un trou profond de 3 mètres** a hole three metres deep; **la France profonde** provincial France.

**profondément** *adverb* deeply, profoundly.

**profondeur** *noun Fem.* depth; **la piscine a une profondeur de 3 mètres** the swimming pool is 3 metres deep; **étudier quelque chose en profondeur** to study something in depth.

**programmateur**[1] *noun Masc.* **1** timer; **2** programme selector (*on appliance*).

**programmateur**[2], **programmatrice** *noun Masc., Fem.* programmer (*on radio, tv*).

**programme** *noun Masc.* **1** programme; **ce n'est pas au programme** it's not on the programme; **2** program (*for a computer*); **3** syllabus; **le programme de maths** the maths syllabus.

**programmer** *verb* [1] **1** to schedule; **2** to program (*on a computer*).

**programmeur**, **programmeuse** *noun Masc., Fem.* (computer) programmer.

**progrès** *noun Masc.* progress; **les progrès de l'informatique** advances in computer science; **faire des progrès** to make progress.

**progresser** *verb* [1] **1** to progress; **2** to make progress.

**projecteur** *noun Masc.* **1** floodlight; **2** spotlight; **3** projector.

**projet** *noun Masc.* **1** plan; **mes projets pour l'été** my plans for the summer; **2** project; **3** rough draft.

**projeter** *verb* [48] **1** to throw, to hurl; **le choc l'a projeté de sa voiture** the impact hurled him out of his car; **2** to show (*a film*); **3** to cast (*a shadow*); **4 projeter de faire** to plan to do.

**prolongation** *noun Fem.* **1** continuation; **2** extension; **3** extra time; **jouer les prolongations** to go into extra time.

**prolongé** *adjective* lengthy; **une discussion prolongée** a lengthy discussion.

**prolonger** *verb* [52] **1** to extend; **elle a prolongé son congé de maladie** she's extended her sick leave; **2 se prolonger** to go on; **les discussions se sont prolongées**

jusqu'à 23 h discussions went on till 11 p.m.

**promenade** *noun Fem.* **1** walk; **faire une promenade** to go for a walk; **une promenade en voiture** a drive; **une promenade à vélo** a bike ride; **une promenade en bateau** a boat trip; **2** promenade (*by the sea*).

**promener** *verb* [50] **1 promener un enfant** to take a child for a walk; **promener le chien** to walk the dog; **2 promener quelque chose** to carry something around; **3 se promener** to go for a walk; **se promener en voiture** to go for a drive; **se promener à vélo** to go for a bike ride.

**promesse** *noun Fem.* promise; **il m'a fait une promesse** he made me a promise; **tenir sa promesse** to keep your promise.

**prometteur** (*Fem.* **prometteuse**) *adjective* promising.

**promettre** *verb* [11] to promise; **promettre de faire** to promise to do; **il a promis de téléphoner ce soir** he promised to ring this evening; **j'ai promis à ma mère de lui écrire une fois par semaine** I promised my mother I would write to her once a week.

**promotion** *noun Fem.* **1** special offer; **les fraises sont en promotion cette semaine** strawberries are on special offer this week; **2** promotion (*to a higher job*); **avoir une promotion** to be promoted.

**pronom** *noun Masc.* pronoun.

**prononcer** *verb* [61] **1** to pronounce (*a word*); **2** to mention (*a name*), to say (*a word or phrase*); **3** to make (*a speech*); **4 se prononcer pour/contre quelque chose** to declare oneself for/against something.

**prononciation** *noun Fem.* pronunciation.

**propagande** *noun Fem.* propaganda.

**proportion** *noun Fem.* proportion; **en proportion de** in proportion to.

**propos** *noun Masc.* **1 à propos** by the way; **à propos, as-tu appelé maman?** by the way, did you ring Mum?; **2 à propos de** about; **il n'a rien dit à propos de son père** he said nothing about his father; **3 des propos** remarks.

**proposer** *verb* [1] **1 proposer quelque chose à quelqu'un** to suggest something to somebody; **je leur ai proposé une petite promenade** I suggested we went for a little walk; **2 proposer quelque chose à quelqu'un** to offer somebody something; **on lui a proposé un poste de technicien** she (*or* he) has been offered a job as a technician.

**proposition** *noun Fem.* offer.

**propre** *adjective* **1** (*when it comes after the noun*) clean; **une chemise propre** a clean shirt; **2** (*when it comes before the noun*) own; **ma propre voiture** my own car; **leurs propres enfants** their own children.

**proprement**

**proprement** *adverb* **1** properly; **mange proprement!** eat properly!; **2 à proprement parler** strictly speaking.

**propreté** *noun Fem.* cleanliness.

**propriétaire** *noun Masc. & Fem.* **1** owner (*usually of a building or a business*); **2** landlord, landlady.

**propriété** *noun Fem.* **1** property; **propriété privée** private property; **2** ownership.

**prospectus** *noun Masc.* leaflet.

**prospère** *adjective* prosperous.

**prostituée** *noun Fem.* prostitute.

**protecteur, protectrice** *noun Masc., Fem.* protector.
**protecteur** (*Fem.* **protectrice**) *adjective* protective; **une crème protectrice** protective cream.

**protection** *noun Fem.* protection; **des lunettes de protection** protective goggles.

**protéger** *verb* [15] to protect; **pour protéger l'environnement** to protect the environment; **se protéger du soleil** to protect yourself from the sun.

**protestant, protestante** *noun Masc., Fem., adjective* Protestant.

**protestation** *noun Fem.* protest.

**protester** *verb* [1] to protest; **protester contre quelque chose** to protest against something.

**prouver** *verb* [1] to prove.

**provenance** *noun Fem.* origin; **du fromage en provenance de France** cheese from France; **un passager en provenance de Madrid** a passenger arriving from Madrid.

**provençal** (*plural* **provençaux**) *adjective* from Provence, Provençal.

**proverbe** *noun Masc.* proverb.

**province** *noun Fem.* province; **en province** in the provinces; **une ville de province** a provincial town.

**provision** *noun Fem.* **1** supply; **nous avons fait provision de bois** we've laid in a supply of wood; **2 des provisions** food; **maman est partie prendre des provisions** Mum's gone off shopping for food.

**provisoire** *adjective* temporary.

**provocateur, provocatrice** *noun Masc., Fem.* agitator.
**provocateur** (*Fem.* **provocatrice**) *adjective* provocative.

**provoquer** *verb* [1] **1** to cause; **provoquer un accident** to cause an accident; **provoquer une discussion** to spark off a discussion; **2 provoquer quelqu'un** to provoke somebody.

**proximité** *noun Fem.* nearness; **à proximité de** near.

**prudemment** *adjective* carefully.

**prudence** *noun Fem.* caution; **conduisez avec prudence!** drive carefully!

**prudent** *adjective* **1** careful; **soyez prudents par mauvais temps!** be careful in bad weather!; **2** wise; **il est plus prudent de réserver** it's wiser to book.

**prune** *noun Fem.* plum.

**pruneau** (*plural* **pruneaux**) *noun Masc.* prune.

236

**prunier** *noun Masc.* plum tree.

**psychanalyste** *noun Masc. & Fem.* psychoanalyst.

**psychiatre** *noun Masc. & Fem.* psychiatrist.

**psychologie** *noun Fem.* psychology.

**psychologique** *adjective* psychological.

**psychologue** *noun Masc. & Fem.* psychologist.

**pu** *verb* SEE **pouvoir**[1].

**pub** *noun Fem.* (*informal*) SHORT FOR **publicité** advert.

**public** *noun Masc.* **1** public; **en public** in public; **ouvert au public** open to the public; **'interdit au public'** 'no admission'; **2** audience, spectators; **pour un public jeune** for a young audience; **3** fans (*of a performer*).

**public** (*Fem.* **publique**) *adjective* public; **dans un lieu public** in a public place; **une école publique** a state school.

**publicitaire** *adjective* **1** advertising; **une campagne publicitaire** an advertising campaign; **2** promotional (*material*).

**publicité** *noun Fem.* **1** advertising; **elle travaille dans la publicité** she works in advertising; **faire de la publicité** to advertise; **2** advertisement, ad (*in a magazine, a newspaper, on television, or at the cinema*).

**publier** *verb* [1] to publish.

**puce** *noun Fem.* **1 une puce électronique** a microchip; **une carte à puce** a smart card; **2** flea; **un marché aux puces** a fleamarket.

**puer** *verb* [1] to stink.

**puis** *adverb* then; **nous allons à Cannes, puis à Nice** we're going to Cannes, then Nice.

**puisque**, **puisqu'** (*before a vowel or silent 'h'*) *conjunction* since; **puisqu'il pleut je prendrai le bus** since it's raining I'll take the bus.

**puissance** *noun Fem.* power; **un moteur d'une forte puissance** a high-power engine; **une puissance étrangère** a foreign power.

**puissant** *adjective* powerful, strong.

**puits** *noun Masc.* well.

**pull**, **pull-over** *noun Masc.* jumper.

**pulvérisateur** *noun Masc.* spray.

**punaise** *noun Fem.* **1** drawing-pin; **2** bug.

**punir** *verb* [2] to punish.

**punition** *noun Fem.* punishment.

**pur** *adjective* **1** pure; **un shampooing très doux, très pur** an ultra-mild, ultra-pure shampoo; **un croissant pur beurre** an all-butter croissant; **2** sheer, total; **c'est de la folie pure** it's sheer madness.

**purée** *noun Fem.* mashed potatoes.

**puzzle** *noun Masc.* jigsaw puzzle.

**PV** *noun Masc.* SHORT FOR **procès verbal** parking ticket.

**pyjama** *noun Masc.* (pair of) pyjamas; **où est mon pyjama?** where are my pyjamas?; **un pyjama propre** a clean pair of pyjamas.

**pyramide** *noun Fem.* pyramid.

**Pyrénées** *plural noun Fem.* Pyrenees.

a
b
c
d
e
f
g
h
i
j
k
l
m
n
o
**p**
q
r
s
t
u
v
w
x
y
z

# Qq

**qu'est-ce que** SEE **que**.

**qu'est-ce qui** SEE **qui**.

**quai** *noun Masc.* **1** platform; **le train à destination de Paris va arriver au quai numéro trois** the train for Paris is about to arrive at platform number three; **2** quay.

**qualifié** *adjective* **1** qualified; **2** skilled.

**qualifier** *verb* [1] to qualify.

**qualité** *noun Fem.* quality; **des fruits de première qualité** top quality fruit.

**quand** *conjunction, adverb* when; **quand est-ce que ton frère arrive?** when is your brother arriving?; **quand tu auras dix-sept ans, tu pourras apprendre à conduire** when you're seventeen you'll be able to learn to drive.

**quand même** *adverb* all the same; **il pleut mais je vais sortir quand même** it's raining but I'm going to go out all the same; **quand même!** honestly!

**quant à** *preposition* as for; **quant à moi, je reste** as for me, I'm staying here.

**quantité** *noun Fem.* amount.

**quarantaine** *noun Fem.* **1** about forty; **une quarantaine de personnes** about forty people; **j'approche la quarantaine** I'll soon be forty; **2** quarantine.

**quarante** *number* forty.

**quart** *noun Masc.* **1** (*in time expressions*) quarter; **un quart d'heure** a quarter of an hour; **dix heures et quart** quarter past ten; **2** quarter; **le quart du gâteau** a quarter of the cake; **un quart d'eau minérale** a quarter-litre bottle of mineral water; **trois quarts** three quarters; **les trois quarts du temps** most of the time.

**quart de finale** *noun Masc.* quarter-final.

**quartier** *noun Masc.* area (*of a town*); **un quartier résidentiel** a residential area; **les gens du quartier** the local people.

**quartier général** *Masc.* headquarters.

**quartz** *noun Masc.* quartz.

**quasi** *adverb* almost; **quasi parfait** almost perfect.

**quasiment** *adverb* **1** practically; **c'est quasiment neuf** it's practically new; **2 quasiment jamais** hardly ever; **il n'est quasiment jamais chez lui** he's hardly ever at home.

**quatorze** *number* fourteen; **Céline a quatorze ans** Céline's fourteen; **le quatorze juin** the fourteenth of June.

**quatre** *number* four; **Louis a quatre ans** Louis is four; **le quatre mars** the fourth of March.

**quatre-vingt-dix** *number* ninety; **quatre-vingt-dix-neuf** ninety-nine.

**quatre-vingts** *number* eighty; **quatre-vingts personnes** eighty people; **quatre-vingt-trois** eighty-three (*note that the 's' is dropped when another number is added*); **quatre-vingt-seize** ninety-six.

**quatrième** *noun Fem.* (*in a French school*) the equivalent of Year 9.
**quatrième** *noun Masc.* **au quatrième** on the fourth floor.
**quatrième** *adjective* fourth.

**que** *conjunction, pronoun, adverb*
**1** that (*often left out in English*); **elle dit que c'est vrai** she says (that) it's true; **je sais qu'il y habite** I know he lives there; **je veux que tu sois heureux** I want you to be happy; **2** whether; **qu'ils arrivent demain ou mardi, n'importe** whether they come tomorrow or on Tuesday, it doesn't matter; **3 que tout le monde se lève!** everybody stand up!; **4 plus ...que** more ...than; **elle est plus grande que Marie** she's taller than Marie; **5 aussi ...que** as ...as; **elle est aussi grande que moi** she's as tall as me; **6 ne ...que** only; **je n'ai que dix euros** I've only got ten euros; **7** that, which, whom (*often left out in English*); **le livre que je lis** the book (that) I'm reading; **la chemise qu'il a achetée** the shirt (which) he's bought; **8** what; **que veut-il?** what does he want?; **je ne sais pas ce qu'il veut** I don't know what he wants; **9 qu'est-ce que ...?** what ...?; **qu'est-ce que tu as trouvé?** what have you found?; **qu'est-ce que c'est?** what's that?; **qu'est-ce qu'il y a?** what's the matter?; **qu'est-ce qu'elle a?** what's the matter with her?; **10** how (*in an*

exclamation); **que tu as grandi!** how you've grown!

**Québec** *noun Masc.* **le Québec** Quebec.

**québécois** *noun Masc.* Canadian French (*language*).
**québécois** *adjective* from Quebec, Quebecker.

**Québécois**, **Québécoise** *noun Masc., Fem.* French Canadian, Quebecker; **les Québécois** the French Canadians, the Quebeckers.

**quel**, **quelle** *adjective* **1** (*in a question*) what, which; **quel livre?** which book?; **quelle voiture?** which car?; **quelle heure est-il?** what time is it?; **quel âge as-tu?** how old are you?; **dans quels pays?** in which countries?; **pour quelles raisons?** for what reasons?; **2** (*in an exclamation*) what; **quel beau temps!** what lovely weather!; **quelle coïncidence!** what a coincidence!; **quelle horreur!** how dreadful!

**quelconque** *adjective* any; **si tu as un problème quelconque** if you have any sort of a problem; **si pour une raison quelconque** if for any reason.

**quelle** *adjective* SEE **quel**.

**quelque chose** *pronoun*
**1** something; **il faut manger quelque chose, Claire** you must eat something, Claire; **il y a quelque chose de bizarre** there's something strange; **voulez-vous boire quelque chose?** would you like something to drink?; **2** anything; **est-ce que tu as vu quelque chose?** did you see anything?

a b c d e f g h i j k l m n o p q r s t u v w x y z

239

a

b

c

d

e

f

g

h

i

j

k

l

m

n

o

p

**q**

r

s

t

u

v

w

x

y

z

**quelquefois** *adverb* sometimes.

**quelque part** *adverb*
1 somewhere; **quelque part dans le jardin** somewhere in the garden; 2 anywhere; **est-ce que tu as vu mes lunettes quelque part?** have you seen my glasses anywhere?

**quelques** *plural adjective* 1 some; **je vais te donner quelques cerises** I'll give you some cherries; 2 a few; **il reste quelques fraises** there are a few strawberries left; **elle est partie pour quelques jours** she's gone away for a few days.

**quelqu'un** *pronoun* 1 somebody; **quelqu'un a appelé pour toi** somebody rang for you; **quelqu'un d'autre** somebody else; 2 anybody; **il y a quelqu'un?** is there anybody there?

**quelques-uns, quelques-unes** *plural pronoun* some; **quelques-uns des enfants** some of the children.

**quels, quelles** *adjective* SEE **quel**.

**querelle** *noun Fem.* quarrel.

**question** *noun Fem.* 1 question; **poser une question à quelqu'un** to ask somebody a question; **elle n'a pas répondu à mes questions** she didn't answer my questions; 2 matter, question; **c'est une question de goût** it's a matter of taste; **c'est hors de question** it's out of the question; **pas question!** no way!.

**questionnaire** *noun Masc.* questionnaire.

**questionner** *verb* [1] to question.

**queue** *noun Fem.* 1 tail; **la queue du chat** the cat's tail; 2 queue; **faire la queue** to queue; 3 **la queue du train** the rear of the train; 4 stalk (*of a flower or a fruit*).

**queue de cheval** *noun Fem.* ponytail.

**qui** *pronoun* 1 who; **qui a fermé la porte?** who closed the door?; **qui voulez-vous voir?** who do you want to see?; **la personne qui vous a écrit n'est pas là aujourd'hui** the person who wrote to you is not here today; 2 that; **prends la casserole qui est sur l'évier** take the pan that's on the sink; 3 **à qui?** whose?; **à qui est ce pull?** whose is this jumper?; 4 **à qui parles-tu?** who are you talking to?; 5 **qu'est-ce qui ...?** what ...?; **qu'est-ce qui t'amène?** what brings you here?

**quincaillerie** *noun Fem.* hardware shop.

**quinzaine** *noun Fem.* 1 about fifteen; **une quinzaine d'enfants** about fifteen children; 2 **une quinzaine de jours** a fortnight; **dans une quinzaine** two weeks from now.

**quinze** *number* 1 fifteen; **Marise a quinze ans** Marise is fifteen; **le quinze juillet** the fifteenth of July; 2 **quinze jours** two weeks; **tous les quinze jours** every two weeks.

**quitter** *verb* [1] 1 to leave; **je quitte le bureau à cinq heures** I leave the office at five; **j'ai quitté l'école à seize ans** I left school at sixteen; 2 **se quitter** to part; 3 **ne quittez pas** hold the line please (*on the telephone*).

**quoi** *pronoun* **1** what; **quoi encore?** what now?; **tu es sourd ou quoi?** are you deaf or what?; **à quoi penses-tu?** what are you thinking about?; **pour quoi faire?** what for?; **à quoi bon continuer?** what's the point in going on?; **il n'y a pas de quoi se fâcher** there's no reason to get angry; **il n'y a pas de quoi** don't mention it; **2** which; **après quoi, il est parti** after which, he left.

**quoique** *conjunction* although, though; **quoique petit, il est fort** although he's small he's strong.

**quotidien** (*Fem.* **quotidienne**) *adjective* daily; **la vie quotidienne** daily life; **sa visite quotidienne** her daily visit.
**quotidien** *noun Masc.* daily newspaper.

**quotidiennement** *adverb* daily; **les livraisons s'effectuent quotidiennement** deliveries are made daily.

# Rr

**rabais** *noun Masc.* discount; **au rabais** at a discount.

**raccompagner** *verb* [1] **raccompagner quelqu'un** to see somebody home.

**raccourci** *noun Masc.* short cut.

**raccourcir** *verb* [2] to shorten.

**raccrocher** *verb* [1] to hang up (*telephone*).

**race** *noun Fem.* **1** race; **la race humaine** the human race; **2** breed; **un chien de race** a pedigree dog.

**racheter** *verb* [16] **1** to buy more; **il faut racheter du pain** we'll have to buy more bread; **2** **il m'a racheté ma voiture** he bought my car off me.

**racine** *noun Fem.* root.

**raciste** *noun Masc. & Fem., adjective* racist; **des propos racistes** racist remarks.

**racler** *verb* [1] to scrape.

**raconter** *verb* [1] to tell (*a story*); **raconte-nous ce qui s'est passé** tell us what happened.

**radar** *noun Masc.* radar.

**radeau** (*plural* **radeaux**) *noun Masc.* raft.

**radiateur** *noun Masc.* radiator.

**radio** *noun Fem.* **1** radio; **je l'ai entendu à la radio** I heard it on the radio; **2** X-ray; **passer une radio** to have an X-ray.

**radiocassette** *noun Masc. OR Fem.* radio cassette player.

**radio-réveil** *noun Masc.* clock radio.

**radis** *noun Masc.* radish.

**rafale** *noun Fem.* gust (*of wind or rain*), flurry (*of snow*).

**raffoler** *verb* [1] **raffoler de** to be mad about; **je ne raffole pas des huîtres** I'm not mad about oysters.

**rafraîchir** *verb* [2] **1** **le temps se rafraîchit** the weather's getting cooler; **2** to cool (somebody) down.

**rafraîchissement** *noun Masc.* **1** refreshment; **2** drop in temperature.

a b c d e f g h i j k l m n o p **q r** s t u v w x y z

**rage** *noun Fem.* **1** rabies; **2 une rage de dents** raging toothache.

**ragoût** *noun Masc.* stew.

**raide** *adjective* **1** stiff (*body, arm, leg*); **2** straight (*hair*); **3 une pente raide** a steep slope.

**raie** *noun Fem.* **1** parting (*in your hair*); **2** skate (*the fish*).

**rail** *noun Masc.* rail (*for trains*); ★ **remettre quelque chose sur les rails** to put something back on the right track.

**raisin** *noun Masc.* grapes; **j'ai acheté du raisin noir** I bought some black grapes; **une grappe de raisin** a bunch of grapes; **un grain de raisin** a grape; **le jus de raisin** grape juice.

**raisin de Corinthe** *noun Masc.* currant.

**raisin sec** *noun Masc.* raisin.

**raison** *noun Fem.* **1** reason; **pour cette raison** for this reason; **pour raisons de santé** for health reasons; **2 avoir raison** to be right; **oui, tu as raison** yes, you're right.

**raisonnable** *adjective* sensible.

**raisonnement** *noun Masc.* reasoning.

**rajouter** *verb* [1] to add; **on peut rajouter de l'eau si on veut** you can add water if you want.

**ralentir** *verb* [2] to slow down.

**ralentissement** *noun Masc.* slowing down.

**ralentisseur** *noun Masc.* speed bump.

**râler** *verb* [1] (*informal*) to moan; **arrête de râler!** stop moaning!

**rallonge** *noun Fem.* **1** extension cord; **2** extra leaf (*for a table*).

**ramasser** *verb* [1] **1** to pick up; **est-ce que tu peux ramasser tous ces papiers, s'il te plaît** can you pick up all these papers please; **2** to pick (*fruit*); **ils ont déjà ramassé les framboises** they've already picked the raspberries; **3** to collect; **on va ramasser des châtaignes dans les bois** we're going to go and collect chestnuts in the woods; **4** collect in (*books, homework*); **Anne, veux-tu ramasser tous les cahiers?** Anne, would you collect in all the exercise books?

**rame** *noun Fem.* **1** oar; **2 une rame de métro** an underground train.

**rameau** (*plural* **rameaux**) *noun Masc.* branch; **le dimanche des Rameaux** Palm Sunday.

**ramener** *verb* [50] **1 ramener quelqu'un (en voiture)** to give somebody a lift home; **tu veux que je te ramène?** do you want a lift home?; **elle m'a ramené en voiture** she gave me a lift back; **2** to take back; **je dois ramener les livres à la bibliothèque** I must take these books back to the library.

**ramer** *verb* [1] to row.

**rampe** *noun Fem.* **1** banister; **2** ramp.

**rançon** *noun Fem.* ransom.

**rancune** *noun Fem.* resentment, grudge.

**randonnée** *noun Fem.* hike, walk; **faire une randonnée pédestre** to go on a hike (*on public footpaths*); **on a fait une randonnée de vingt**

**kilomètres** we did a twenty-kilometre walk; **faire une randonnée à cheval** to go pony-trekking; **une randonnée à vélo** a long-distance bike ride.

**randonneur**, **randonneuse** *noun Masc., Fem.* **1** hiker, walker, rambler; **2** touring cyclist.

**rang** *noun Masc.* row; **au cinquième rang** in the fifth row.

**rangée** *noun Fem.* row; **une rangée de maisons** a row of houses.

**ranger** *verb* [52] **1** to put away; **ranger la vaisselle** to put away the dishes; **2** to tidy; **je vais ranger ma chambre** I'm going to tidy my room; **3** to arrange; **il range ses livres par ordre alphabétique** he arranges his books alphabetically.

**râper** *verb* [1] to grate; **le fromage râpé** grated cheese.

**rapide** *noun Masc.* express train. **rapide** *adjective* quick; **prends le métro, c'est plus rapide** take the underground, it's quicker.

**rapidement** *adverb* quickly, rapidly.

**rappel** *noun Masc.* **1** reminder (*for a bill*); **'dernier rappel'** 'final demand'; **2** booster (*vaccination*).

**rappeler** *verb* [18] **1** to remind; **rappelle-moi de passer par la banque** remind me to go to the bank; **le paysage me rappelle la France** the countryside reminds me of France; **2** to ring back (*on the telephone*); **il va te rappeler dans une heure** he'll ring you back in a hour; **3 se rappeler** to remember; **je ne me rappelle plus** I can't

remember; **je me rappelle qu'elle avait les cheveux longs** I remember she had long hair.

**rapport** *noun Masc.* **1** report; **un rapport officiel** an official report; **2** connection; **je ne vois pas le rapport** I don't see the connection; **3 être en rapport avec quelqu'un** to be in touch with someone; **4 avoir de bons/mauvais rapports avec quelqu'un** to be on good/bad relations with someone; **5 par rapport à** compared with; **il a fait très beau par rapport à l'année dernière** the weather's been very good compared with last year.

**rapporter** *verb* [1] **1** to bring back; **est-ce que tu peux le rapporter demain?** can you bring it back tomorrow?; **2** to bring in; **son travail ne rapporte pas beaucoup** her job doesn't bring in much money.

**rapprocher** *verb* [1] **1** to move (something) closer; **peux-tu rapprocher la lampe de ma chaise?** can you move the lamp closer to my chair?; **2** to bring together (*different people*); **des efforts pour rapprocher les deux pays** efforts to bring the two countries together; **3 se rapprocher** to come (*or* go) closer; **elle s'est rapprochée de la table** she moved closer to the table.

**raquette** *noun Fem.* **1** racket (*for tennis*); **2** bat (*for ping-pong*).

**rare** *adjective* rare; **une fleur rare** a rare flower; **il est rare qu'elle arrive à l'heure** she hardly ever arrives on time.

a
b
c
d
e
f
g
h
i
j
k
l
m
n
o
p
q
r
s
t
u
v
w
x
y
z

# rarement

b
c
d
e
f
g
h
i
j
k
l
m
n
o
p
q
r
s
t
u
v
w
x
y
z

**rarement** *adverb* rarely.

**ras** *adjective* **1** short (*hair or fur*); **il a les cheveux coupés ras** his hair is cut short; **2 en rase campagne** in open country; **3 au ras de l'eau/du sol** at water/ground level; ★ **j'en ai ras le bol!** (*informal*) I'm fed up!

**raser** *verb* [1] **1** to shave, to shave off; **il a rasé sa barbe** he's shaved off his beard; **la mousse à raser** shaving foam; **2 se raser** to shave; **se raser les jambes** to shave your legs.

**ras-le-cou** *noun Masc.* crew-neck sweater.

**rasoir** *noun Masc.* razor.

**rassemblement** *noun Masc.* meeting, rally.

**rassembler** *verb* [1] to gather (together); **j'ai rassemblé les enfants près de l'entrée** I gathered all the children together by the main entrance; **tout le village s'est rassemblé pour l'écouter** the whole village gathered to listen to him.

**rassis** *adjective* **du pain rassis** stale bread.

**rassurer** *verb* [1] **1** to reassure; **ah, cela me rassure!** oh, that sets my mind at rest!; **2 rassure-toi** don't worry.

**rat** *noun Masc.* rat.

**râteau** (*plural* **râteaux**) *noun Masc.* rake.

**rater** *verb* [1] **1** to fail; **Sophie a raté son permis** Sophie failed her driving test; **2** to miss; **j'ai raté mon train** I've missed my train.

**rationner** *verb* [1] to ration.

**RATP** *noun Fem.* SHORT FOR **Régie autonome des transports parisiens** (*Paris city-transport system*).

**rattacher** *verb* [1] **1** to (re)fasten; **rattache ta ceinture** (re)fasten your seat-belt; **2** to attach; **plus rien ne me rattache ici** I no longer have any ties here.

**rattraper** *verb* [1] **1** to catch up with (*a person*); **ne t'inquiète pas, ils nous rattraperont** don't worry, they'll catch up with us; **2** to make up for (*lost time*); **3 se rattraper** to make up for it; **j'ai très peu joué cet été mais je vais me rattraper** I've played very little this summer but I'll make up for it.

**rature** *noun Fem.* crossing-out.

**ravi** *adjective* delighted; **je suis ravi de vous voir** I'm delighted to see you.

**ravisseur**, **ravisseuse** *noun Masc., Fem.* kidnapper.

**rayé** *adjective* striped (*fabric*).

**rayer** *verb* [59] **1** to cross out (*a mistake*); **j'ai rayé ton nom de la liste** I crossed your name off the list; **2** to scratch (*a surface*).

**rayon** *noun Masc.* **1** shelf; **un rayon pour mes livres** a shelf for my books; **2** department (*in a department store*); section (*in a supermarket*); **au rayon fraîcheur** in the chilled foods section; **3** ray; **un rayon de soleil** a ray of sunshine; **un rayon laser** a laser beam; **les rayons X** X-rays; **4** radius.

**rayure** *noun Fem.* **1** stripe; **2** scratch.

**RC** *noun Masc.* SHORT FOR **rez-de-chaussée** ground floor.

**réacteur** *noun Masc.* **1** **un réacteur nucléaire** a nuclear reactor; **2** jet engine.

**réaction** *noun Fem.* reaction..

**réagir** *verb* [2] to react; **elle n'a pas réagi** she didn't react.

**réalisateur**, **réalisatrice** *noun Masc., Fem.* director (*of a film or TV programme*).

**réalisation** *noun Fem.* **1** carrying out (*of a plan or project*); **2** production (*of a film or a radio/TV programme*).

**réaliser** *verb* [1] **1** to carry out (*a project*); **2** to fulfil; **réaliser un rêve** to fulfil a dream; **3** to make (*a film*); **4** to realize.

**réaliste** *adjective* realistic.

**réalité** *noun Fem.* reality; **en réalité** in reality.

**réanimation** *noun Fem.* resuscitation; **(service de) réanimation** intensive care (unit).

**rebelle** *noun Masc. & Fem.* rebel.

**rébellion** *noun Fem.* rebellion.

**rebondir** *verb* [2] to bounce.

**rebord** *noun Masc.* **1** **le rebord de la fenêtre** the window ledge; **2** edge; **le rebord de la baignoire** the edge of the bath.

**récemment** *adverb* recently.

**récent** *adjective* recent.

**réception** *noun Fem.* **1** reception desk; **demandez la clé à la réception** ask for the key at the reception desk; **2** reception (*party*).

**réceptionniste** *noun Masc. & Fem.* receptionist.

**recette** *noun Fem.* recipe; **la recette du gâteau** the recipe for the cake.

**recevoir** *verb* [66] **1** to receive, to get; **j'ai reçu ta lettre** I got your letter; **2** to welcome (*a visitor or guest*); **3** to see (*a patient or client*); **le dentiste reçoit entre 9h et 17h** the dentist sees patients between 9 a.m. and 5 p.m.; **4** **être reçu à un examen** to pass an exam; **elle a été reçue première à l'examen** she came top in the exam.

**rechange** *noun Masc.* **de rechange** spare; **une pièce de rechange** a spare part.

**recharge** *noun Fem.* refill.

**réchaud** *noun Masc.* stove.

**réchauffer** *verb* [1] **1** to warm up (*food*); **peux-tu mettre la soupe à réchauffer?** can you put the soup on to warm?; **2** to warm (*hands or feet*); **3** **se réchauffer** to get warm; **va te réchauffer près du feu** go and get warm by the fire.

**recherche** *noun Fem.* **1** research; **2** **être à la recherche de quelque chose** to be looking for something; **je suis à la recherche d'un logement** I'm looking for somewhere to live.

**rechercher** *verb* [1] to look for; **la police le recherche** the police are looking for him; **elle recherche un travail plus flexible** she's looking for a more flexible job.

**récipient** *noun Masc.* container.

**réciproque** *adjective* mutual.

a b c d e f g h i j k l m n o p q r s t u v w x y z

**récit** *noun Masc.* story; **il nous a fait le récit de son voyage** he told us all about his journey.

**réciter** *verb* [1] to recite.

**réclamation** *noun Fem.* claim (*for compensation*).

**réclame** *noun Fem.*
1 advertisement; **une réclame pour le nouveau modèle** an advertisement for the new model; **2 en réclame** on (special) offer; **le jambon est en réclame cette semaine** the ham is on special offer this week.

**réclamer** *verb* [1] to demand; **ils réclament trois jours de plus de vacances** they're demanding three more days' holiday.

**récolte** *noun Fem.* **1** harvest; **2** crop; **faire la récolte** to get the harvest in.

**récolter** *verb* [1] **1** to harvest; **récolter le blé** to harvest the wheat; **2** to collect (*money*); **3** (*informal*) to get; **récolter une amende** to get a fine.

**recommandation** *noun Fem.* recommendation.

**recommandé** *adjective* registered; **une lettre recommandée** a registered letter; **je voudrais l'envoyer en recommandé** I'd like to send it by registered post.

**recommander** *verb* [1] **1** to advise; **je te recommande de ne rien dire** I advise you to say nothing; **2** to recommend.

**recommencer** *verb* [61] **1** to start again; **j'ai recommencé ma lettre** I started my letter again; **il a recommencé à neiger** it's started snowing again; **2** to do it again; **si tu ne fais pas attention, elle va recommencer** if you don't watch out, she'll do it again; **ça recommence!** here we go again!

**récompense** *noun Fem.* reward.

**récompenser** *verb* [1] to reward.

**réconcilier** *verb* [1] **se réconcilier avec quelqu'un** to make it up with somebody.

**réconfortant** *adjective* comforting.

**reconnaissable** *adjective* recognizable.

**reconnaissance** *noun Fem.*
1 gratitude; **en reconnaissance de** in appreciation of; **2** recognition.

**reconnaissant** *adjective* grateful.

**reconnaître** *verb* [27] **1** to recognize; **je ne l'ai pas reconnue** I didn't recognize her; **je l'ai reconnu à sa voix** I recognized him by his voice; **2** to admit; **il faut reconnaître que c'est difficile** it must be admitted that it's difficult; **elle reconnaît qu'elle a menti** she admits she lied.

**reconstruire** *verb* [26] to rebuild.

**recopier** *verb* [1] to copy out.

**record** *noun Masc.* record; **un record mondial** a world record; **battre un record** to break a record.

**recouvrir** *verb* [30] to cover.

**récréation** *noun Fem.* break; **la cour de récréation** the playground.

**rectangle** *noun Masc.* rectangle.

**rectangulaire** *adjective* rectangular.

**rectifier** *verb* [1] to correct.

**reçu** *noun* Masc. receipt.
**reçu** *verb* SEE **recevoir**.

**recueil** *noun* Masc. collection (*of poems or essays*).

**reculer** *verb* [1] **1** to move back; **elle a reculé de quelques pas** she moved back a few steps; **2** to reverse (*in a car*); **3 reculer la date d'une réunion** to postpone a meeting.

**reculons** *in phrase* **à reculons** backwards.

**récupérer** *verb* [24] **1** to get back; **je vais chez Brigitte pour récupérer le bouquin que je lui ai prêté** I'm going round to Brigitte's to get back the book I lent her; **2** to recover (*from an illness*).

**recycler** *verb* [1] to recycle.

**rédaction** *noun* Fem. essay.

**redemander** *verb* [1] **1** to ask again; **tu devrais redemander** you should ask again; **2** to ask for more; **il faut qu'on redemande des cahiers** we'll have to ask for more exercise books.

**redescendre** *verb* [3] **1** to go (or come) back down; **elle est redescendue à la cave** she went back down to the cellar; **je monte à Glasgow demain et je redescends lundi** I'm going up to Glasgow tomorrow and I'm coming back down on Monday; **2** to bring or take back down; **est-ce que tu peux redescendre ma valise?** can you bring my suitcase back down?

**rédiger** *verb* [52] to write (*an article*), to write up (*notes*).

**redonner** *verb* [1] to give again; **je leur ai redonné mon adresse** I gave them my address again; **est-ce que je te redonne un peu de salade?** can I give you a bit more salad?

**redoubler** *verb* [1] to repeat a year (*at school*).

**redresser** *verb* [1] **1** to straighten up; **2** to put right; **3 se redresser** to recover.

**réduction** *noun* Fem. **1** reduction; **une réduction du nombre d'étudiants** a reduction in the number of students; **2** (price) reduction; **une réduction de 20%** a 20% reduction.

**réduire** *verb* [68] to cut (*prices*); **réduire les impôts** to cut taxes; **des vêtements à prix réduits** cut-price clothing.

**rééducation** *noun* Fem. physiotherapy.

**réel** (*Fem.* **réelle**) *adjective* real.

**réellement** *adverb* really.

**refaire** *verb* [10] **1** to redo; **je dois refaire mon devoir de maths** I have to redo my maths homework; **c'est tout à refaire** it has to be completely redone; **il ne faut pas refaire la même erreur** we mustn't make the same mistake again; **2** to make more; **elle est en train de refaire du café** she's making some more coffee.

**référence** *noun* Fem. reference; **faire référence à quelque chose** to refer to something.

a
b
c
d
e
f
g
h
i
j
k
l
m
n
o
p
q
r
s
t
u
v
w
x
y
z

# réfléchi

b
c
d
e
f
g
h
i
j
k
l
m
n
o
p
q
**r**
s
t
u
v
w
x
y
z

**réfléchi** *adjective* **1** reflexive (*verb*); **2** considered (*decision*).

**réfléchir** *verb* [2] to think; **il faut bien réfléchir avant d'accepter** you should think carefully before accepting; **j'ai réfléchi au problème** I've thought about the problem.

**reflet** *noun Masc.* **1** reflection; **2 des cheveux aux reflets blonds** hair with blond highlights.

**refléter** *verb* [24] to reflect.

**réflexe** *noun Masc., adjective* reflex.

**réflexion** *noun Fem.* **1** thought; **2** comment; **il m'a fait des réflexions désagréables** he made some nasty comments to me.

**refrain** *noun Masc.* chorus.

**réfrigérateur** *noun Masc.* refrigerator.

**refroidir** *verb* [2] to cool down.

**refroidissement** *noun Masc.* drop in temperature.

**refuge** *noun Masc.* **1** mountain hut (*for climbers*); **2** animal sanctuary; **3** traffic island; **4** refuge.

**réfugié, réfugiée** *noun Masc., Fem.* refugee.

**réfugier** *verb* [1] **se réfugier** to take shelter, to take refuge.

**refus** *noun Masc.* refusal; ★ **ce n'est pas de refus** I wouldn't say no; **'veux-tu boire quelque chose?'** – **'ce n'est pas de refus'** 'would you like a drink?' – 'I wouldn't say no'.

**refuser** *verb* [1] **1** to refuse; **refuser de faire** to refuse to do; **elle a refusé de répondre** she refused to answer; **2** to turn down; **ils ont**

refusé sa **candidature** they turned him down for the job.

**regagner** *verb* [1] **nous avons regagné nos places** we went back to our seats.

**régal** *noun Masc.* feast; **ça a été un véritable régal** it was a real feast.

**régaler** *verb* [1] **on s'est vraiment régalé!** the food was absolutely wonderful!

**regard** *noun Masc.* look.

**regarder** *verb* [1] **1** to look at; **je vais regarder la carte** I'll look at the map; **2** to watch; **regarder la télé** to watch telly; **veux-tu regarder le film?** do you want to watch the film?; **3** to look; **regarder par la fenêtre** to look out of the window; **regarde!** look!; **4** to concern; **cela ne nous regarde pas** that doesn't concern us; **cela ne le regarde pas** that's none of his business.

**régate** *noun Fem.* regatta.

**régime** *noun Masc.* **1** diet; **un régime sans sel** a salt-free diet; **je fais un régime** I'm on a diet; **2 un régime de bananes** a bunch of bananas; **3** régime.

**région** *noun Fem.* region; **les vins de la région** the local wines.

**régional** (*Masc. plural* **régionaux**) *adjective* regional.

**registre** *noun Masc.* register.

**réglable** *adjective* adjustable.

**règle** *noun Fem.* **1** ruler; **2** rule; **selon les règles** according to the rules; **les règles de sécurité** the safety regulations; **en règle générale** as a general rule; **3 en**

**règle** in order (*valid*); **4 les règles** period (*menstruation*); **j'ai mes règles** I've got my period.

**règlement** *noun Masc.* regulations.

**régler** *verb* [24] **1** to pay (*a debt or a bill*); **vous réglez comment, monsieur?** how would you like to pay, sir?; **2** to sort out (*details or a problem*); **3** to adjust; **on peut régler la hauteur** you can adjust the height.

**réglisse** *noun Fem.* liquorice.

**règne** *noun Masc.* reign.

**régner** *verb* [24] to reign.

**regret** *noun Masc.* regret; **avec/ sans regret** with/without regret; **mille regrets** I'm terribly sorry.

**regretter** *verb* [1] **1** to be sorry; **je regrette** I'm sorry; **nous regrettons beaucoup de partir** we're very sorry to be leaving; **2** to regret; **elles regrettent avoir quitté Paris** they regret having left Paris; **je ne regrette rien** I have no regrets; **3** to miss; **je regrette la vie à Paris** I miss the Parisian way of life.

**regrouper** *verb* [1] **1** to group together; **les débutants sont regroupés ensemble** beginners are grouped together; **2 se regrouper** to regroup; **les enfants se sont regroupés autour d'elle** the children gathered around her.

**régularité** *noun Fem.* regularity.

**régulier** (*Fem.* **régulière**) *adjective* **1** regular; **à intervalles réguliers** at regular intervals; **2 vols réguliers à New York** scheduled flights to New York.

**régulièrement** *adverb* regularly.

**rein** *noun Masc.* **1** kidney; **2 les reins** the back; **j'ai mal aux reins** I've got back-ache.

**reine** *noun Fem.* queen; **la reine Elisabeth** Queen Elizabeth.

**reine-claude** *noun Fem.* greengage.

**rejeter** *verb* [48] to reject.

**rejoindre** *verb* [49] **1** to meet up with; **je vous rejoins au bar** I'll meet you in the bar; **2** to join (*other people, a group, or a movement*); **3 se rejoindre** to meet up; **alors on se rejoint à onze heures?** so shall we meet up at eleven?; **4 se rejoindre** to merge (*motorways, lanes*).

**rejouer** *verb* [1] to replay.

**relâcher** *verb* [1] **1** to loosen (*a grip or hold*); **2** to set free (*a prisoner, hostage, or animal*); **3** to relax (*your attention or discipline*).

**relais** *noun Masc.* **1** restaurant, hotel; **2 prendre le relais (de quelqu'un)** to take over (from someone); **il a pris le relais au volant** he took over the driving; **3** relay race.

**relatif** (*Fem.* **relative**) *adjective* relative.

**relation** *noun Fem.* **1** connection; **en relation avec** in connection with; **2** acquaintance; **une relation de mon frère** an acquaintance of my brother's; **3** relationship; **il a de bonnes relations avec son patron** he has a good relationship with his boss; **4 les relations publiques** public relations.

a
b
c
d
e
f
g
h
i
j
k
l
m
n
o
p
q
**r**
s
t
u
v
w
x
y
z

**relativement** *adverb* relatively;
**relativement à** in relation to.

**relax** *adjective* (*informal*) casual,
laid back.

**relaxer** *verb* [1] to relax.

**relent** *noun* Masc. lingering smell.

**relevé** *noun* Masc. **1 faire le relevé
de quelque chose** to make a list of
something; **2 un relevé de compte**
a bank statement.

**relever** *verb* [50] **1** to raise;
**2 relever la tête** to look up; **3** to
notice (*details, mistakes, or
interesting facts*); **4 relever le
compteur** to read the meter; **5 se
relever** to pick yourself up (*after a
fall*).

**relier** *verb* [1] **1** to link; **2** to match
up.

**religieux, religieuse** *noun*
Masc., Fem. monk, nun.
**religieux** (*Fem.* **religieuse**)
*adjective* religious.

**religion** *noun* Fem. religion.

**relire** *verb* [51] to re-read, to read
over.

**remarié** *adjective* remarried.

**remarquable** *adjective*
remarkable, striking.

**remarque** *noun* Fem. remark,
comment.

**remarquer** *verb* [1] **1** to notice; **je
n'ai rien remarqué** I didn't notice
anything; **j'ai remarqué qu'elle est
arrivée en retard** I noticed she
arrived late; **2 se faire remarquer**
to draw attention to yourself; **il
n'aime pas se faire remarquer** he
doesn't like drawing attention to

himself; **3 faire remarquer
quelque chose à quelqu'un** to
point something out to somebody;
**elle lui a fait remarquer que
c'était déjà trop tard** she pointed
out to him that it was already too
late.

**rembobiner** *verb* [1] to rewind (*a
tape or video*).

**remboursement** *noun* Masc.
repayment, refund.

**rembourser** *verb* [1] **1** to pay
back; **je te rembourserai demain**
I'll pay you back tomorrow; **2** to
refund the price of; **ils m'ont
remboursé les billets** they
refunded me the price of the tickets;
**3** to reimburse; **nous vous
rembourserons le voyage** we'll pay
your travelling expenses.

**remède** *noun* Masc. remedy.

**remerciement** *noun* Masc.
thanks; **tous mes remerciements**
many thanks; **une lettre de
remerciement** a thank-you letter.

**remercier** *verb* [1] **1** to thank; **je
l'ai remerciée pour les fleurs** I
thanked her for the flowers;
**2 remercier quelqu'un d'avoir fait
quelque chose** to thank somebody
for doing something; **il nous a
remerciés de l'avoir aidé** he
thanked us for helping him.

**remettre** *verb* [11] **1** to put back;
**remets la bouteille au frigo** put the
bottle back in the fridge; **il a remis
la photo sur la table** he put the
photo back on the table; **as-tu remis
tous les livres à leur place?** have
you put all the books back in their
place?; **2** to put back on; **je vais**

**remettre ma veste** I'm going to put my jacket back on; **3** to hand over; **pouvez-vous me remettre les clés demain?** can you hand over the keys to me tomorrow?; **4** to put off; **ils ont remis la réunion à jeudi** they've put the meeting off until Thursday; **5 se remettre** to start again; **elle s'est remise au piano** she's started playing the piano again; **il s'est remis à pleuvoir** it's started raining again; **6 se remettre de** to recover; **ils ne se sont toujours pas remis du choc** they still haven't recovered from the shock.

**remise** *noun Fem.* **1** handing out; **la remise des prix** the prizegiving; **2** discount; **nous faisons une remise de 20% sur tous les CD** we're giving a 20% discount on all CDs; **3** garden shed.

**remonte-pente** *noun Masc.* ski lift.

**remonter** *verb* [1] **1** to go (*or* come) back up; **Nathalie est remontée dans sa chambre** Nathalie's gone back up to her room; **je descends à Londres ce soir et je remonte lundi** I'm going down to London tonight and coming back up on Monday; **2** to take (*or* bring) back up; **veux-tu remonter les chaises?** would you take the chairs back upstairs?; **3** to put back up; **il m'a remonté ma valise au filet** he put my case up in the luggage rack for me; **4 remonter la pente** to go back up the hill; **5** to get or climb back in; **ils sont remontés dans le car** they got back into the coach; **6 remonter quelqu'un, remonter le moral à quelqu'un** to cheer someone up.

**remords** *noun Masc.* remorse.

**remorque** *noun Fem.* **1** trailer (*for a car*); **2** tow-rope.

**remplaçant, remplaçante** *noun Masc., Fem.* **1** replacement (*for another person*); **2** supply teacher.

**remplacer** *verb* [61] **1** to stand in for (*a person*); **2** to replace; **il faut remplacer les piles** you need to replace the batteries.

**remplir** *verb* [2] **1** to fill; **il a rempli son verre de vin** he filled his glass with wine; **la salle était remplie de jeunes** the hall was full of young people; **2 remplir un formulaire** to fill in a form; **3** to carry out (*a duty or a role*).

**remue-ménage** *noun Masc.* commotion.

**remuer** *verb* [1] **1** to move (*your head or hand, for example*); **le vent remuait les branches** the wind was shaking the branches; **2** to stir; **peux-tu remuer la sauce, s'il te plaît?** can you stir the sauce, please?

**rémunérer** *verb* [24] to pay (*a person*), to pay for (*work*).

**renard** *noun Masc.* fox.

**rencontre** *noun Fem.* **1** meeting; **elle est venue à ma rencontre** she came to meet me; **2** (*in sport*) match; **la rencontre entre la France et l'Allemagne** the match between France and Germany.

**rencontrer** *verb* [1] **1** to meet (*a person*); **je l'ai rencontrée en 1993** I met her in 1993; **2** to play (*an opponent or a team*); **3 se rencontrer** to meet; **nous nous**

a
b
c
d
e
f
g
h
i
j
k
l
m
n
o
p
q
r
s
t
u
v
w
x
y
z

sommes rencontrés à Londres we met in London.

**rendez-vous** *noun Masc.*
**1** appointment; **prendre rendez-vous** to make an appointment; **j'ai rendez-vous chez le dentiste** I've got a dentist's appointment; **le médecin voit les malades sur rendez-vous** the doctor sees patients by appointment; **2** date; **Marc a rendez-vous avec sa copine à trois heures** Marc's got a date with his girlfriend at three; **3 donner rendez-vous à quelqu'un** to arrange to meet somebody; **il m'a donné rendez-vous au café** he arranged to meet me at the cafe.

**rendormir** *verb* [37] **se rendormir** to go back to sleep; **elle s'est rendormie** she went back to sleep.

**rendre** *verb* [3] **1** to give back; **je te rendrai les clés demain** I'll give you back the keys tomorrow; **2 rendre quelqu'un heureux** to make somebody happy; **3** to hand in (*homework*); **4 se rendre** to give oneself up, to surrender; **les voleurs se sont rendus à la police** the thieves gave themselves up to the police; **5 se rendre compte de quelque chose** to realize something; **je me suis rendu compte du fait que j'avais oublié mes clés** I realized I had forgotten my keys.

**renifler** *verb* [1] to sniff.

**renne** *noun Masc.* reindeer.

**renommé** *adjective* famous.

**renoncer** *verb* [61] **1** to give up; **c'est trop difficile, je renonce!** it's too difficult, I give up!; **2 renoncer à** quelque chose to give something up.

**renouveler** *verb* [18] to renew (*a passport or a subscription, for example*).

**rénover** *verb* [1] **1** to renovate (*a house*); **2** to restore (*furniture*).

**renseignement** *noun Masc.* **1** un renseignement a piece of information; **un renseignement utile** a useful piece of information; **2 les renseignements** information; **je cherche des renseignements** I'm looking for information; **adressez-vous aux renseignements** ask at the information desk; **3 renseignements** directory enquiries.

**renseigner** *verb* [1] **1 renseigner quelqu'un** to give someone information; **la brochure vous renseigne sur les horaires** the brochure gives you timetable information; **il était très bien renseigné sur le projet** he was very well-informed about the project; **2 se renseigner** to find out; **je vais me renseigner au bureau de tourisme** I'm going to find out at the tourist office.

**rentable** *adjective* profitable.

**rentrée** *noun Fem.* la rentrée (des classes) the start of the new school year.

**rentrer** *verb* [1] **1** to get home; **Maman rentre à dix-huit heures** Mum will be home at six; **je vais rentrer chez moi** I'm going home; **2** to get back; **ils rentrent de Paris jeudi** they'll be back from Paris on

Thursday; **3** to come (*or* go) in; **rentrez!** do come in!; **elles sont rentrées dans un magasin** they've gone into a shop; **4 rentrer dans quelque chose** to go in something; **tout ça ne rentrera jamais dans ton sac!** all that will never go in your bag!; **5 rentrer dans quelque chose** to crash into something; **la voiture est rentrée dans un mur** the car crashed into a wall; **6 rentrer quelque chose** to bring something in (*from outside*); **rentre les chaises, il pleut!** bring the chairs in, it's raining!

**renverser** *verb* [1] **1** to knock over; **il a renversé sa chaise** he knocked his chair over; **2 être renversé par une voiture** to be knocked down by a car; **3** to spill; **j'ai renversé mon thé** I've spilled my tea. '

**renvoyer** *verb* [40] **1** to send back; **as-tu renvoyé le formulaire?** have you sent back the form?; **on m'a renvoyé à l'hôpital** they sent me back to hospital; **2** to throw back (*a ball*); **3** to dismiss; **la secrétaire a été renvoyée** the secretary has been dismissed.

**réouverture** *noun Fem.* reopening.

**répandu** *adjective* widespread.

**réparation** *noun Fem.* repair.

**réparer** *verb* [1] to repair.

**repartir** *verb* [58] **1** to go off again; **ils ont déposé les enfants et ils sont repartis** they dropped the children and went off again; **2** to go again; **je suis reparti chez moi** I went home again; **3 repartir à zéro** to start from scratch.

**repas** *noun Masc.* meal; **le repas de midi** lunch; **le repas du soir** the evening meal.

**repassage** *noun Masc.* ironing.

**repasser** *verb* [1] **1** to drop in again; **il a dit qu'il repasserait demain** he said he'd drop in again tomorrow; **2** to iron; **Frank est en train de repasser sa chemise** Frank's busy ironing his shirt; **une planche à repasser** an ironing board; **3** to resit (*an exam or test*); **4** to replay (*a video*).

**repeindre** *verb* [60] to repaint.

**repère** *noun Masc.* **un point de repère** a landmark, a reference point.

**repérer** *verb* [24] **1** (*informal*) to spot; **j'ai repéré trois erreurs dans son article** I spotted three mistakes in his article; **2** to locate (*a place*).

**répertoire** *noun Masc.* notebook (*with a thumb index*); **un répertoire d'adresses** an address book.

**répéter** *verb* [24] **1** to repeat; **elle l'a répété trois fois** she repeated it three times; **faire des essais répétés** to make repeated attempts; **2** to rehearse (*a play*); **3** to practise (*a piece of music*); **4 se répéter** to repeat oneself; **5 se répéter** to happen again; **espérons que cela ne se répètera pas** let's hope it doesn't happen again.

**répétition** *noun Fem.* **1** rehearsal; **la répétition générale** the dress rehearsal; **2** repetition.

**replier** *verb* [1] **1** to fold up; **elle a replié la carte** she folded up the map (*a sheet*); **2 elle a replié ses**

a
b
c
d
e
f
g
h
i
j
k
l
m
n
o
p
q
r
s
t
u
v
w
x
y
z

a
b
c
d
e
f
g
h
i
j
k
l
m
n
o
p
q
r
s
t
u
v
w
x
y
z

**jambes** she tucked her legs up (under her).

**répondeur** *noun Masc.* answering machine; **j'ai laissé un message sur le répondeur** I left a message on the answering machine.

**répondre** *verb* [3] **1** to answer; **il n'a pas répondu** he didn't answer; **je ne lui ai pas répondu** I didn't answer him; **2 répondre à une question** to answer a question; **3 répondre à une lettre** to reply to a letter.

**réponse** *noun Fem.* answer; **donner la bonne/mauvaise réponse** to give the right/wrong answer.

**reportage** *noun Masc.* **1** report; **un reportage sur la drogue** a report on drugs; **2** (news) story.

**reporter**[1] *verb* [1] to postpone; **on a reporté le match à jeudi** the match has been postponed until Thursday.

**reporter**[2] *noun Masc.* reporter.

**repos** *noun Masc.* rest; **dix jours de repos** ten days' rest.

**reposant** *adjective* restful.

**reposer** *verb* [1] **1 reposer quelque chose** to put something back down; **elle a reposé le livre sur la table** she put the book back down on the table; **2 se reposer** to have a rest; **j'ai besoin de me reposer** I need a rest; **repose-toi bien!** have a good rest!

**repousser** *verb* [1] **1** to grow again; **tes cheveux ont vite repoussé** your hair's grown quickly; **2** to push back; **3** to postpone; **le match a été repoussé** the match has been postponed.

**reprendre** *verb* [64] **1** to have some more (*food or drink*); **reprends du poulet** have some more chicken; **2** to take back; **est-ce que je peux reprendre les verres que je t'avais prêtés?** can I take back the glasses I lent you?; **3** to start again; **l'école reprend en septembre** school starts again in September; **4 reprendre le travail** to go back to work; **j'ai repris le travail lundi** I went back to work on Monday; **5 reprendre la route** to set off again.

**représentant, représentante** *noun Masc., Fem.* sales rep.

**représentation** *noun Fem.* performance (*of a play*); **prochaine représentation à 20h** next performance 8 p.m.

**représenter** *verb* [1] **1** to depict; **2** to represent.

**réprimander** *verb* [1] to tell off, to reprimand.

**réprimer** *verb* [1] to suppress.

**reprise** *noun Fem.* **1** resumption (*of work or discussions*); **2** rerun (*of a play or film*), repeat (*of a broadcast*); **3 à plusieurs reprises** on several occasions.

**reproche** *noun Masc.* criticism; **il m'a fait des reproches** he criticized me.

**reprocher** *verb* [1] **1** to criticize; **il a reproché à son fils de ne pas travailler** he criticized his son for not working; **2 se reprocher** to blame oneself.

**reproduction** *noun Fem.* reproduction.

**reproduire** *verb* [26] **1** to reproduce; **2 se reproduire** to happen again.

**républicain** *adjective* republican.

**république** *noun Fem.* republic; **la République française** the French Republic.

**répugnant** *adjective* revolting.

**réputation** *noun Fem.* reputation; **il a la réputation d'être très sévère** he has a reputation for being very strict.

**requin** *noun Masc.* shark.

**RER** *noun Masc.* SHORT FOR **réseau express régional** (*the fast suburban network on the Paris underground*).

**rescousse** *noun Fem.* **aller à la rescousse de quelqu'un** to go to someone's rescue.

**réseau** (*plural* **réseaux**) *noun Masc.* network.

**réservation** *noun Fem.* reservation.

**réservé** *adjective* reserved.

**réserve** *noun Fem.* **1** stock; **des réserves de charbon** stocks of coal; **j'ai deux bouteilles en réserve** I have put aside two bottles; **2** reserve (*for birds or animals*); **une réserve ornithologique** a bird sanctuary.

**réserver** *verb* [1] **1** to reserve, to book; **j'ai réservé deux places pour ce soir** I've booked two seats for this evening; **2** to keep; **Philippe t'a réservé du poulet** Philippe's kept some chicken for you.

**réservoir** *noun Masc.* **1** tank; **réservoir à essence** petrol tank; **2** reservoir.

**résidence** *noun Fem.* **1** home, residence; **une résidence secondaire** a holiday home; **2** block of flats.

**résidence universitaire** *noun Fem.* hall of residence.

**résident, résidente** *noun Masc., Fem.* resident.

**résidentiel** (*Fem.* **résidentielle**) *adjective* residential.

**résistant, résistante** *noun Masc., Fem.* Resistance fighter (*in France during World War II*). **résistant** *adjective* tough.

**résister** *verb* [1] **résister à** to resist.

**résolu** *adjective* **1** determined; **elle est résolue à démissionner** she is determined to resign; **2** resolved; **le problème est résolu** the problem is resolved.

**résoudre** *verb* [67] **1** to solve (*a problem*); **2 se résoudre à faire** to make up one's mind to do; **elle s'est résolue à partir** she made up her mind to leave.

**respect** *noun Masc.* respect.

**respecter** *verb* [1] to respect.

**respectueux** (*Fem.* **respectueuse**) *adjective* respectful.

**respiration** *noun Fem.* breathing.

**respirer** *verb* [1] to breathe.

**responsabilité** *noun Fem.* **1** responsibility; **2 avoir la responsabilité de quelque chose** to be responsible for something; **il a la responsabilité des livraisons** he's responsible for deliveries.

a b c d e f g h i j k l m n o p q r s t u v w x y z

**responsable** *noun Masc. & Fem.*
**1** person in charge; **le responsable du projet** the person in charge of the project; **2** person responsible; **les responsables de la catastrophe** those responsible for the disaster.

**responsable** *adjective*
responsible; **il est responsable de l'accident** he's responsible for the accident.

**ressemblance** *noun Fem.*
similarity.

**ressembler** *verb* [1]
**1 ressembler à** to look like; **elle ressemble beaucoup à sa mère** she looks very like her mother; **cela ressemble à du bois mais c'est du plastique** it looks like wood but it's plastic; **2 se ressembler** to be alike; **les deux sœurs ne se ressemblent pas du tout** the two sisters are not at all alike.

**ressentiment** *noun Masc.*
resentment.

**resserrer** *verb* [1] **1** to tighten (*a knot or screw, for example*); **2 se resserrer** to move closer together; **resserrez-vous un peu!** squeeze up a bit!

**resservir** *verb* [58] **1** to give another helping; **je vous ressers un peu?** shall I give you a little more?; **2 se resservir** to help yourself to more; **ressers-toi de la salade** help yourself to some more salad; **je me suis déjà resservi, merci** I've already helped myself to more, thank you.

**ressort** *noun Masc.* spring (*in a bed or a chair*).

**ressortir** *verb* [58] to go out again; **il est revenu pour les clés et il est ressorti** he came back for the keys and went out again.

**ressource** *noun Fem.* **1** resource; **des ressources énergétiques** energy resources; **2 il est sans ressources** he has no means of support.

**restaurant** *noun Masc.* restaurant; **on mange au restaurant ce soir** we're going out for a meal tonight.

**restauration** *noun Fem.*
**1** catering; **la restauration rapide** the fast-food industry; **2** restoration.

**restaurer** *verb* [1] to restore.

**reste** *noun Masc.* **1 le reste** the rest; **le reste du temps** the rest of the time; **et tout le reste, tu le sais déjà** and you know all the rest already; **2 les restes** the leftovers; **j'ai fait un curry avec les restes du poulet** I made a curry with the leftover chicken.

**rester** *verb* [1] **1** to stay; **reste là, je reviens tout de suite!** stay there, I'll be right back!; **Camille est restée à la maison** Camille stayed at home; **je ne peux pas rester longtemps** I can't stay long; **hier je suis resté sans manger** I didn't have anything to eat yesterday; **2 rester debout** to remain standing; **je préfère rester debout** I prefer to stand; **3 rester assis** to remain seated; **je suis resté assis toute la journée** I've been sitting down all day; **4** to be left; **il reste du fromage** there's some cheese left; **il nous reste combien d'argent?** how much money have we got left?; **il**

ne reste pas beaucoup à faire there's not much left to do.

**restriction** *noun Fem.* restriction.

**résultat** *noun Masc.* result; **les résultats des examens** the exam results.

**résulter** *verb* [1] **résulter de** to result from.

**résumé** *noun Masc.* summary, résumé.

**résumer** *verb* [1] to summarize, to sum up.

**rétablir** *verb* [2] **1** to restore; **2 se rétablir** to recover (*after an illness*).

**retaper** *verb* [1] to do up (*a house*).

**retard** *noun Masc.* **1** delay; **ils annoncent un retard d'une heure sur notre vol** they say there's an hour's delay on our flight; **sans retard** without delay; **2 avoir du retard** to be late; **excusez mon retard** I'm sorry I'm late; **ils sont arrivés avec trois heures de retard** they arrived three hours late; **3 être en retard** to be late; **nous sommes en retard** we're late.

**retarder** *verb* [1] **1** to hold up, to delay; **la grève nous a retardés** the strike held us up; **l'avion était retardé** the plane was delayed; **2** to put off, to postpone; **il a retardé son départ** he put off his departure.

**retenir** *verb* [77] **1** to hold up; **j'ai été retenu au bureau** I was held up at the office; **je ne vous retiendrai pas longtemps** I won't keep you long; **2 retenir son souffle** to hold your breath; **elle ne pouvait pas retenir ses larmes** she couldn't hold back her tears; **3** to book; **j'ai**

**retenu des places** I've booked seats; **4** to remember; **je ne retiens jamais leur adresse** I can never remember their address.

**réticence** *noun Fem.* **1** reluctance; **2** reticence.

**retirer** *verb* [1] **1** to take off; **je vais d'abord retirer ma veste** I'll take my jacket off first; **2** to take away; **ils ont retiré son permis** they took away his licence; **3 retirer de l'argent** to take out some money (*from your bank account*).

**retouche** *noun Fem.* alteration (*to a garment*).

**retour** *noun Masc.* **1** return; **un billet aller-retour** a return ticket; **dès mon retour** as soon as I get back; **2 être de retour** to be back; **elle sera de retour vers onze heures** she'll be back about eleven.

**retourner** *verb* [1] **1** to go back; **elle est retournée à l'école** she went back to school; **je n'y suis jamais retourné** I've never been back there; **2** to turn over; **est-ce que je retourne les steaks?** shall I turn the steaks over?; **3** to overturn.

**retraite** *noun Fem.* retirement; **prendre sa retraite** to retire; **une maison de retraite** an old people's home.

**retraité, retraitée** *noun Masc., Fem.* pensioner.

**rétrécir** *verb* [2] to shrink.

**retrousser** *verb* [1] **1** to hitch up; **2** to roll up; **il a retroussé ses manches** he rolled up his sleeves.

**retrouver** *verb* [1] **1** to find; **as-tu retrouvé tes clés?** did you find

a
b
c
d
e
f
g
h
i
j
k
l
m
n
o
p
q
r
s
t
u
v
w
x
y
z

your keys?; **2** to meet; **je te retrouve
à la sortie** I'll meet you at the exit;
**3 se retrouver** to meet; **on se
retrouve devant le cinéma?** shall
we meet outside the cinema?; **on se
retrouvera à Noël** we'll see each
other again at Christmas; **4 se
retrouver** to end up; **on s'est
retrouvé chez Amanda** we ended
up at Amanda's place; **5 se
retrouver** to find one's way around;
**je n'arrive jamais à me retrouver à
Londres** I can never find my way
around London.

**rétroviseur**, **rétro** *noun Masc.*
rearview mirror.

**réunion** *noun Fem.* **1** meeting;
**2** reunion; **3** gathering;
**4** reunification.

**réunir** *verb* [2] **se réunir** to meet; **on
s'est réuni pour discuter du
problème** we met to discuss the
problem.

**réussi** *adjective* successful.

**réussir** *verb* [2] **1** to succeed;
**j'espère qu'elle va réussir** I hope
she'll succeed; **2 réussir un
examen** to pass an exam; **3** to be
successful; **ça a très bien réussi**
that was very successful; **4 réussir
à faire** to manage to do; **je n'ai pas
réussi à les persuader** I didn't
manage to persuade them.

**réussite** *noun Fem.* success.

**réutilisable** *adjective* reusable.

**revanche** *noun Fem.* **1** return
match; **2 prendre sa revanche** to
get your own back; **3 en revanche**
on the other hand.

**rêve** *noun Masc.* dream; **faire un
rêve** to have a dream; **votre maison
de rêve** your dream house.

**réveil** *noun Masc.* alarm clock.

**réveille-matin** *noun Masc.* alarm
clock.

**réveiller** *verb* [1] **1** réveiller
quelqu'un to wake somebody up;
**elle m'a réveillé à sept heures** she
woke me at seven; **2 se réveiller** to
wake up; **d'habitude je me réveille
à sept heures** I usually wake up at
seven.

**réveillon** *noun Masc.* **le réveillon
du Nouvel An** the New Year's Eve
celebrations.

**réveillonner** *verb* [1] **1** to
celebrate Christmas Eve; **2** to see
the New Year in.

**révéler** *verb* [24] to reveal.

**revenant**, **revenante** *noun
Masc., Fem.* ghost.

**revendre** *verb* [3] to sell, to resell.

**revenir** *verb* [81] **1** to come back;
**elles sont revenues très tard** they
came back very late; **tu reviendras
nous voir?** will you come back and
see us?; **2** to come to; **ça revient à
quinze euros** that comes to fifteen
euros; **ça revient au même** it comes
to the same thing; **3 je n'en reviens
pas!** I can't get over it!

**revenu** *noun Masc.* income.

**rêver** *verb* [1] to dream.

**réverbère** *noun Masc.* street lamp.

**revers** *noun Masc.* **1** lapel (*on a
jacket*); turn-up (*of trousers,*); cuff
(*on a sleeve*); **2** backhand (*in tennis*);

**3** setback; **4 le revers de la médaille** the other side of the coin.

**réviser** *verb* [1] **1** to revise; **2** to service (*a car or machine*).

**révision** *noun Fem.* **1** revision; **2** service (*for a car*).

**revoici** *preposition* (*informal*) **me revoici!** here I am again!

**revoir**[1] *verb* [13] **1** to see again; **et nous ne l'avons jamais revue** and we never saw her again; **2** to revise; **je dois revoir ma chimie** I have to revise my chemistry.

**revoir**[2] *noun Masc.* **au revoir** goodbye.

**révoltant** *adjective* appalling.

**révolte** *noun Fem.* revolt, rebellion.

**révolter** *verb* [1] to appal.

**révolution** *noun Fem.* revolution.

**révolutionner** *verb* [1] to revolutionize.

**revolver** *noun Masc.* revolver, handgun.

**revouloir** *verb* [14] to have a second helping of; **est-ce que tu reveux des frites?** would you like a second helping of chips?

**revue** *noun Fem.* magazine; **une revue d'art** an art magazine; **une revue scientifique** a scientific journal.

**rez-de-chaussée** *noun Masc.* ground floor (*literally: level with the road*); **la réception est au rez-de-chaussée** reception is on the ground floor.

**RF** SHORT FOR **République française** French Republic.

**Rhin** *noun Masc.* **le Rhin** the Rhine.

**rhinocéros** *noun Masc.* rhinoceros.

**rhubarbe** *noun Fem.* rhubarb.

**rhum** *noun Masc.* rum.

**rhume** *noun Masc.* cold; **attraper un rhume** to catch a cold; **un rhume de cerveau** a head cold.

**rhume des foins** *noun Masc.* hay fever.

**ri** *verb* SEE **rire**.

**ricaner** *verb* [1] to snigger, to giggle.

**riche** *adjective* **1** well-off; **nous ne sommes pas très riches** we're not terribly well-off; **2** rich; **riche en vitamines** rich in vitamins.

**richesse** *noun Fem.* **1** wealth; **2 les richesses naturelles** natural resources.

**ride** *noun Fem.* wrinkle (*on skin*), ripple (*on water*).

**rideau** (*plural* **rideaux**) *noun Masc.* curtain.

**ridicule** *adjective* ridiculous; **mais c'est totalement ridicule!** but that's completely ridiculous!

**rien**[1] *pronoun* **1** nothing; **'qu'est-ce qu'elle a dit?' – 'rien'** 'what did she say?' – 'nothing'; **il n'a rien** he has nothing; **je n'ai rien vu** I didn't see anything; **ce n'est rien** it's nothing; **il ne reste plus rien** there's nothing left; **rien du tout** nothing at all; **'merci' – 'de rien'** 'thank you' – 'it's nothing'; **rien d'autre** nothing else; **rien de bon** nothing good; **2 rien que** just; **rien que les livres pèsent 20 kilos** the books by themselves weigh 20 kilos; **'que reste-t-il à faire?' – 'rien que la vaisselle'** 'what's left to do?' – 'just the washing-up'; ★ **rien à faire!** it's no good!

a
b
c
d
e
f
g
h
i
j
k
l
m
n
o
p
q
r
s
t
u
v
w
x
y
z

**rien**[2] *noun Masc.* little thing; **elle se met à hurler pour un rien** the slightest thing starts her shouting.

**rigide** *adjective* rigid, stiff.

**rigoler** *verb* [1] (*informal*) **1** to laugh; **elle en a beaucoup rigolé** she had a good laugh about it; **2** to have a good time; **nous avons bien rigolé** we had a great time; **3** to be joking; **je rigolais!** I was only joking!

**rigolo** (*Fem.* **rigolote**) *adjective* (*informal*) funny.

**rigoureux** (*Fem.* **rigoureuse**) *adjective* **1** rigorous; **2** strict; **3** harsh.

**rillettes** *plural noun Fem.* **les rillettes de porc** potted pork.

**rime** *noun Fem.* rhyme.

**rimer** *verb* [1] to rhyme.

**rincer** *verb* [61] to rinse; **se rincer les cheveux** to rinse one's hair.

**rire** *noun Masc.* laughter; **un rire** a laugh.
**rire** *verb* [68] **1** to laugh; **il nous fait rire** he makes us laugh; **2** to have fun; **on va rire ce soir** we'll have some fun this evening; **c'était pour rire** it was meant as a joke.

**ris** *noun Masc.* **les ris de veau** calf's sweetbreads.

**risque** *noun Masc.* risk; **risque d'incendie** fire risk; **c'est sans risque** it's safe.

**risqué** *adjective* risky.

**risquer** *verb* [1] **1** to risk; **vas-y, tu ne risques rien** go on, it's quite safe; **2 il risque de pleuvoir** it might well rain; **tu risques de te brûler** you might burn yourself.

**rivage** *noun Masc.* shore.

**rival, rivale** *noun Masc., Fem.* (*Masc. plural* **rivaux**) rival.

**rive** *noun Fem.* **1** bank (*of a river*); **la Rive gauche** the Left Bank (*when talking about the Seine in Paris and other rivers which flow through cities, the left bank is the left side of the river when you are facing downstream*); **2** shore (*by the sea*).

**rivière** *noun Fem.* river.

**riz** *noun Masc.* rice; **riz cantonais** fried rice; **gâteau de riz** rice pudding.

**RN** *noun Fem.* SHORT FOR **route nationale** A road.

**robe** *noun Fem.* dress; **une robe d'été** a summer dress; **une robe de mariée** a wedding dress.

**robe de chambre** *noun Fem.* dressing gown.

**robinet** *noun Masc.* tap; **l'eau du robinet** tap water.

**robot** *noun Masc.* robot; **robot ménager** food processor.

**robuste** *adjective* robust, sturdy.

**roche** *noun Fem.* rock.

**rocher** *noun Masc.* rock.

**rock** *noun Masc.* rock (music).

**rôder** *verb* [1] to prowl.

**rognons** *plural noun Masc.* kidneys (*for cooking*).

**roi** *noun Masc.* king; **le roi Charles** King Charles; **les Rois mages** the Three Wise Men; **la fête des Rois** Twelfth Night.

**rôle** *noun Masc.* role.

**roller** *noun Masc.* **1** roller-skating; **2** roller-skate.

**romain** *adjective* Roman.

**roman** *noun Masc.* novel; **un roman policier** a detective story.

**romancier**, **romancière** *noun Masc., Fem.* novelist.

**romantique** *adjective* romantic.

**romarin** *noun Masc.* rosemary.

**rompre** *verb* [69] to split up; **Claire et David ont rompu** Claire and David have split up; **Anne a rompu avec son copain** Anne's broken up with her boyfriend; **rompre ses fiançailles** to break off your engagement.

**ronce** *noun Fem.* bramble.

**rond** *noun Masc.* circle; **tourner en rond** to go round in circles.
**rond** *adjective* round.

**rondelle** *noun Fem.* **1** slice; **une rondelle de tomate** a slice of tomato; **2** washer (*for a tap or screw*).

**rond-point** *noun Masc.* roundabout.

**ronfler** *verb* [1] to snore.

**ronger** *verb* [52] **1** to gnaw; **2 se ronger les ongles** to bite one's nails.

**ronronner** *verb* [1] to purr.

**rosbif** *noun Masc.* roast beef.

**rose** *noun Fem.* rose.
**rose** *adjective* pink; **rose pâle** pale pink.

**rosé** *noun Masc.* rosé (wine); **un verre de rosé** a glass of rosé.

**rosée** *noun Fem.* dew.

**rosier** *noun Masc.* rosebush.

**rossignol** *noun Masc.* nightingale.

**rôti** *noun Masc.* roast; **du rôti de bœuf** roast beef; **un rôti de bœuf** a joint of beef.

**rôtir** *verb* [2] to roast.

**roucouler** *verb* [1] to coo.

**roue** *noun Fem.* wheel; **la roue de secours** the spare wheel; ★ **faire la roue** to turn a cartwheel.

**rouge** *noun Masc.* **1** (the colour) red; **le rouge ne me va pas** red doesn't suit me; **2** red traffic light; **il est passé au rouge** he jumped the lights; **le feu est passé au rouge** the light changed to red; **3** red wine; **un verre de rouge** a glass of red wine.
**rouge** *adjective* red; **tes chaussettes rouges** your red socks.

**rouge à lèvres** *noun Masc.* lipstick.

**rouge-gorge** *noun Masc.* robin.

**rougeur** *noun Fem.* redness.

**rougir** *verb* [2] **1** to blush; **2** to turn red.

**rouille** *noun Fem.* rust.

**rouillé** *adjective* rusty.

**rouiller**, **se rouiller** *verb* [1] to go rusty.

**roulade** *noun Fem.* **1** stuffed rolled meat; **2** somersault, roll.

**roulant** *adjective* **un fauteuil roulant** a wheelchair.

a
b
c
d
e
f
g
h
i
j
k
l
m
n
o
p
q
**r**
s
t
u
v
w
x
y
z

a
b
c
d
e
f
g
h
i
j
k
l
m
n
o
p
q
**r**
s
t
u
v
w
x
y
z

**rouleau** (*plural* **rouleaux**) *noun* Masc. roll; **un rouleau d'essuie-tout** a roll of kitchen towel.

**rouleau à pâtisserie** *noun* Masc. rolling pin.

**rouler** *verb* [1] **1** to go; **nous roulons très vite** we're going very fast; **2** to drive; **il faut rouler à droite en France** in France you must drive on the right; **nous avons roulé toute la nuit** we drove all night; **3** to roll; **4** to roll up; **il faut rouler le tapis** we must roll up the carpet; **5** (*informal*) to cheat; **on m'a roulé!** I've been done!

**Roumanie** *noun* Fem. Romania.

**rousse** *adjective* SEE **roux**.

**route** *noun* Fem. **1** road; **une grande route** a main road; **un accident de la route** a road accident; **Rouen est à trois heures de route d'ici** Rouen is three hours' drive from here; **2** route; **il a changé de route à cause de la neige** he changed his route because of the snow; **3 en route** on the way; **être en route** to be on the way; **nous sommes en route pour Nice** we're on our way to Nice; **4 se mettre en route** to set off; **5 bonne route!** safe journey!

**route à quatre voies** *noun* Fem. dual carriageway.

**route départementale** *noun* Fem. secondary road, B road.

**route nationale** *noun* Fem. A road.

**routier**, **routière** *noun* Masc. Fem. lorry driver.

**routier** (Fem. **routière**) *adjective* road; **le transport routier** road

transport; **la gare routière** the bus station.

**routine** *noun* Fem. routine.

**roux** (Fem. **rousse**) *adjective* red-haired, ginger.

**royal** (*plural* **royaux**) *adjective* royal.

**royaume** *noun* Masc. kingdom.

**Royaume-Uni** *noun* Masc. United Kingdom.

**ruban** *noun* Masc. ribbon.

**ruban adhésif** *noun* Masc. sticky tape.

**rubéole** *noun* Fem. German measles.

**ruche** *noun* Fem. beehive.

**rudement** *adverb* (*informal*) really; **il est rudement bon ton gâteau** your cake's really good.

**rue** *noun* Fem. street; **une rue piétonne** a pedestrian street; ★ **mettre quelqu'un à la rue** to put someone out on the street.

**rugby** *noun* Masc. rugby; **jouer au rugby** to play rugby.

**rugbyman** (*plural* **rugbymen**) *noun* Masc. rugby player.

**ruine** *noun* Fem. ruin; **une maison en ruine(s)** a ruined house.

**ruiner** *verb* [1] to ruin.

**ruisseau** (*plural* **ruisseaux**) *noun* Masc. stream.

**rumeur** *noun* Fem. **1** rumour; **2** murmur.

**rumsteck** *noun* Masc. rump steak.

**rupture** *noun* Fem. break-up.

**rural** (Masc. *plural* **ruraux**) *adjective* country; **la vie rurale** country life.

**ruse** *noun Fem.* **1** trick; **les ruses du métier** the tricks of the trade; **2** cunning.

**rusé** *adjective* cunning, crafty.

**russe** *noun Masc.* Russian (*language*).
**russe** *adjective* Russian.

**Russe** *noun Masc., Fem.* Russian (*person*).

**Russie** *noun Fem.* Russia.

**rythme** *noun Masc.* rhythm; **marquer le rythme** to beat time.

# Ss

**s'** *pronoun* SEE **se**.

**sa** *adjective* SEE **son**.

**sable** *noun Masc.* sand.

**sablé** *noun Masc.* shortbread biscuit.
**sablé** *adjective* **la pâte sablée** shortcrust pastry.

**sac** *noun Masc.* **1** bag; **un sac de sucre** a bag of sugar; **un sac de sport** a sports bag; **2** sack; **un sac de charbon** a sack of coal; ★ **vider son sac** (*informal*) to get something off one's chest (*literally: to empty one's bag*).

**sac à dos** *noun Masc.* rucksack.

**sac à main** *noun Masc.* handbag.

**sac de congélation** *noun Masc.* freezer bag.

**sac de couchage** *noun Masc.* sleeping bag.

**sachet** *noun Masc.* sachet; **un sachet de thé** a teabag.

**sacoche** *noun Fem.* **1** bag; **la sacoche du facteur** the postman's bag; **2** pannier (*for a bike*).

**sacré** *adjective* **1** (*informal*) **c'est un sacré problème** it's a hell of a problem; **elle a eu une sacrée chance** she's been damn lucky; **2** sacred.

**sacrifice** *noun Masc.* sacrifice.

**sacrifier** *verb* [1] to sacrifice.

**sage** *adjective* **1** good, well-behaved; **Tom, sois sage** be a good boy, Tom; **2** wise, sensible; **il serait sage de se renseigner sur le prix** it would be wise to enquire about the price.

**sage-femme** *noun Fem.* midwife.

**sagesse** *noun Fem.* wisdom; **une dent de sagesse** a wisdom tooth.

**Sagittaire** *noun Masc.* Sagittarius (*sign of the Zodiac*).

**saignant** *adjective* rare (*beef*).

**saigner** *verb* [1] to bleed.

**sain** *adjective* healthy; ★ **sain et sauf** safe and sound.

**saint**, **sainte** *noun Masc., Fem.* saint.
**saint** *adjective* holy; **le Saint-Esprit** the Holy Spirit; **le vendredi saint** Good Friday; **la Sainte Vierge** the Virgin Mary.

**Saint-Jacques** *noun* **une coquille Saint-Jacques** a scallop.

**Saint-Jean** *noun Fem.* Midsummer's Day (*June 24th*).

**Saint-Sylvestre** *noun Fem.* New Year's Eve.

**Saint-Valentin** *noun Fem.* St Valentine's Day.

**sais** *verb* SEE **savoir**[1].

**saisir** *verb* [2] **1** to grab; **il m'a saisi par le bras** he grabbed my arm; **2 saisir l'occasion** to seize the opportunity; **3** to understand; **je n'ai pas tout à fait saisi** ... I didn't entirely understand ...; **4** to catch, (*to hear*); **je n'ai pas saisi votre nom** I didn't catch your name.

**saison** *noun Fem.* season; **il fait froid pour la saison** it's cold for the time of year.

**sait** *verb* SEE **savoir**[1].

**salade** *noun Fem.* **1** lettuce; **une salade** a lettuce ; **2** salad; **une salade de fruits** a fruit salad.

**saladier** *noun Masc.* salad bowl.

**salaire** *noun Masc.* salary, wages.

**salarié**, **salariée** *noun Masc., Fem.* salaried employee.

**sale** *adjective* **1** (*after the noun*) dirty; **les mains sales** dirty hands; **2** (*before the noun*) (*informal*) horrible; **quel sale temps!** what horrible weather!; **il a une sale tête** he looks awful.

**salé** *adjective* **1** salty; **la sauce est un peu trop salée** the sauce is a bit salty; **2** savoury; **des petits gâteaux salés** savoury biscuits; **3 du beurre salé** salt butter.

**saler** *verb* [1] to salt.

**saleté** *noun Fem.* dirt.

**salir** *verb* [2] to dirty, to get (something) dirty; **tu vas salir ta robe** you'll get your dress dirty.

**salive** *noun Fem.* saliva.

**salle** *noun Fem.* **1** room ('*salle*' by itself is no longer used to mean a room in a house); **2** dining-room (*in a restaurant*); **3** hall; **4** auditorium (*in a theatre or cinema*).

**salle à manger** *noun Fem.* **1** dining room; **2** dining-room suite.

**salle d'attente** *noun Fem.* waiting room.

**salle d'eau** *noun Fem.* shower room.

**salle de bains** *noun Fem.* bathroom.

**salle de classe** *noun Fem.* classroom.

**salle de jeux** *noun Fem.* games room.

**salle d'embarquement** *noun Fem.* departure lounge.

**salle de séjour** *noun Fem.* living room.

**salle des fêtes** *noun Fem.* community centre.

**salon** *noun Masc.* **1** sitting room; **2** living-room suite; **3** trade fair; **4** salon; **salon de coiffure** hair salon.

**salon de thé** *noun Masc.* tea-room.

**salopette** *noun Fem.* **1** dungarees; **2** overalls.

**saluer** *verb* [1] **1** to say hello to; **je l'ai salué, mais il ne m'a pas entendu** I said hello to him but he didn't hear; **elle l'a salué de la main** she waved at him; **2** to say goodbye to.

**salut** *greeting Masc.* Hi!

**samedi** *noun Masc.* **1** Saturday; **samedi prochain** next Saturday; **samedi dernier** last Saturday; **2** on Saturday; **samedi soir** on Saturday evening; **3 le samedi** on Saturdays;

**fermé le samedi** closed on Saturdays; **4 tous les samedis** every Saturday.

**SAMU** *noun Masc.* SHORT FOR **Service d'assistance médicale d'urgence** ambulance service.

**sandale** *noun Fem.* sandal.

**sandwich** *noun Masc.* sandwich; **un sandwich au jambon** a ham sandwich.

**sandwicherie** *noun Fem.* snack bar.

**sang** *noun Masc.* blood; **être en sang** to be covered in blood.

**sang-froid** *noun Masc.* calm.

**sanglier** *noun Masc.* wild boar.

**sanglot** *noun Masc.* sob; **éclater en sanglots** to burst into tears.

**sanisette™** *noun Fem.* automatic public lavatory.

**sanitaire** *adjective* **les conditions sanitaires** sanitary conditions; **les règlements sanitaires** health regulations.
**sanitaire** *noun Masc.* **les sanitaires** the toilet block (*in a campsite*).

**sans** *preposition* without; **une maison sans téléphone** a house without a telephone; **un café sans sucre** a coffee with no sugar; **sans hésiter** without hesitating.

**sans-abri** *noun Masc. & Fem.* homeless person; **les sans-abri** the homeless.

**sans-emploi** *noun Masc. & Fem.* unemployed person; **les sans-emploi** the unemployed.

**santé** *noun Fem.* **1** health; **être en bonne santé** to be in good health; **2 à votre santé!** cheers!

**sapeur-pompier** *noun Masc.* fireman; **appeler les sapeurs-pompiers** to call the fire brigade.

**sapin** *noun Masc.* fir tree; **un sapin de Noël** a Christmas tree.

**sarcasme** *noun Masc.* sarcasm.

**sardine** *noun Fem.* sardine.

**satellite** *noun Masc.* satellite.

**satin** *noun Masc.* satin.

**satisfaction** *noun Fem.* satisfaction.

**satisfaire** *verb* [10] to satisfy.

**satisfaisant** *adjective* satisfactory.

**satisfait** *adjective* satisfied; **êtes-vous satisfaits de votre séjour?** are you satisfied with your stay?

**sauce** *noun Fem.* **1** sauce; **2** gravy.

**saucisse** *noun Fem.* sausage.

**saucisson** *noun Masc.* salami.

**sauf**[1] *preposition* **1** except; **tous les jours sauf le lundi** every day except Monday; **sauf quand il pleut** except when it rains; **2 sauf si** unless; **c'est tout, sauf s'il y a des questions?** that's all, unless there are any questions?; **3 sauf que** except that; **tout va bien, sauf que ta sur n'est pas encore arrivée** everything's fine, except that your sister hasn't arrived yet.

**sauf**[2] *adjective* SEE **sain**.

**saule** *noun Masc.* willow; **un saule pleureur** a weeping willow.

**saumon** *noun Masc.* salmon.

a
b
c
d
e
f
g
h
i
j
k
l
m
n
o
p
q
r
s
t
u
v
w
x
y
z

a

**saupoudrer** *verb* [1] to sprinkle.

b

**saut** *noun* Masc. jump.

c

**saut à la perche** *noun* Masc. pole vault.

d

**saut à l'élastique** *noun* Masc. bungee jumping.

e

f

**saut en hauteur** *noun* Masc. high jump.

g

**saut en longueur** *noun* Masc. long jump.

h

**sauter** *verb* [1] **1** to jump, to jump over; **elle a sauté la barrière** she jumped over the gate; **elle a sauté dans un taxi** she jumped into a taxi; **2 sauter à la corde** to skip (*with a rope*); **3** to skip; **nous avons sauté trois pages** we've skipped three pages; **4** to blow up; **les terroristes ont fait sauter l'avion** the terrorists blew up the plane; **faire sauter les plombs** to blow the fuses; ★ **ça saute aux yeux!** it's blindingly obvious!

i

j

k

l

m

n

o

p

**sauterelle** *noun* Fem. grasshopper.

q

**sauvage** *noun* Masc., Fem. savage. **sauvage** *adjective* **1** wild; **2** savage.

r

s

**sauvegarder** *verb* [1] **1** to safeguard; **2** to save, to back up (*on a computer*).

t

u

**sauver** *verb* [1] **1** to save; **vous m'avez sauvé la vie** you saved my life; **2 se sauver** to run away; **ils se sont sauvés** they ran away; **3 je me sauve!** (*informal*) I'm off!

v

w

x

**sauvetage** *noun* Masc. rescue, life-saving.

y

z

**savent, savez** *verb* SEE **savoir**[1].

**savoir**[1] *verb* [70] **1** to know; **je sais qu'il habite à Londres** I know he lives in London; **je ne savais pas qu'elle était médecin** I didn't know she was a doctor; **tu sais très bien que ...** you know very well that ...; **je n'en sais rien** I know nothing about it; **comment l'avez-vous su?** how did you find out about it?; **allez savoir!** who knows!; **2 savoir faire** to know how to do; **je ne sais pas le faire** I don't know how to do it; **savoir lire et écrire** to be able to read and write; **tu sais jouer du piano?** can you play the piano?.

**savoir**[2] *noun* Masc. knowledge.

**savoir-faire** *noun* Masc. know-how.

**savon** *noun* Masc. soap.

**savonnette** *noun* Fem. cake of soap.

**savons** *verb* SEE **savoir**[1].

**savoureux** (Fem. **savoureuse**) *adjective* tasty.

**scandale** *noun* Masc. scandal; **le discours du ministre a fait scandale** the minister's speech caused a scandal.

**scandinave** *adjective* Scandinavian.

**Scandinavie** *noun* Fem. Scandinavia.

**scanner** *noun* Masc. scanner (*in medicine and for documents*); **passer un scanneur** to have a scan.

**scarabée** *noun* Masc. beetle.

**scénariste** *noun* Masc. & Fem. scriptwriter.

**scène** *noun Fem.* **1** stage (*in a theatre*); **être sur scène** to be on stage; **mettre en scène** to stage (*a play*), to direct (*a film*); **2** scene; **sur la scène politique** on the political scene; **des scènes de panique** scenes of panic; **faire (toute) une scène** to throw a fit.

**sceptique** *adjective* sceptical.

**schéma** *noun Masc.* diagram.

**scie** *noun Fem.* saw.

**science** *noun Fem.* science.

**sciences naturelles** *plural noun Fem.* biology.

**scientifique** *noun Masc. & Fem.* scientist.
**scientifique** *adjective* scientific.

**scier** *verb* [1] to saw.

**scolaire** *adjective* school; **les vacances scolaires** the school holidays; **le livret scolaire** the school report.

**scolarité** *noun Fem.* schooling, education.

**Scorpion** *noun Masc.* Scorpio (*sign of the Zodiac*).

**Scotch™** *noun Masc.* Sellotape™.

**scout, scoute** *noun Masc., Fem.* boy scout, girl guide.

**scrutin** *noun Masc.* **1** ballot; **2** polls; **le jour du scrutin** polling day.

**sculpteur** *noun Masc.* sculptor.

**sculpteuse** *noun Fem.* sculptress.

**sculpture** *noun Fem.* sculpture.

**SDF** *noun Masc. & Fem.* SHORT FOR **sans domicile fixe** of no fixed abode; **les SDF** the homeless.

**se, s'** (*before a vowel or silent 'h'*) *reflexive pronoun* **1** himself; **il se regarde** he's looking at himself; **2** herself; **elle se regarde** she's looking at herself; **3** itself; **le chien s'est fait mal** the dog has hurt itself; **4** themselves; **ils se sont fait mal** they've hurt themselves; **5** each other; **ils se regardaient** they were looking at each other; **6** yourself, oneself; **se faire mal** to hurt yourself (or oneself); **7** (*sometimes not translated*) **Claudie se lave les cheveux** Claudie's washing her hair; **Jules se brosse les dents** Jules is brushing his teeth.

**séance** *noun Fem.* **1** session; **2** showing (*of a film*); **la séance de vingt heures** the eight o'clock showing.

**seau** (*plural* **seaux**) *noun Masc.* bucket.

**sec** (*Fem.* **sèche**) *adjective* **1** dry; **mes cheveux ne sont pas secs** my hair's not dry; **un vin blanc sec** a dry white wine; **2** dried; **des abricots secs** dried apricots.

**sèche-cheveux** *noun Masc.* hair dryer.

**sèche-linge** *noun Masc.* tumble dryer.

**sèche-mains** *noun Masc.* hand dryer.

**sécher** *verb* [1] to dry; **des fleurs séchées** dried flowers.

**sécheresse** *noun Fem.* drought.

**second** *noun Masc.* **au second** on the second floor; **il est arrivé en second** he arrived second.

a
b
c
d
e
f
g
h
i
j
k
l
m
n
o
p
q
r
**s**
t
u
v
w
x
y
z

**second** *adjective* second; **la seconde fois** the second time.

**secondaire** *adjective* secondary; **une école secondaire** a secondary school; **des effets secondaires** side effects.

**seconde** *noun Fem.* **1** second; **je reviens dans une seconde** I'll be back in a moment; **2** second class; **voyager en seconde** to travel second class; **un billet de seconde** a second class ticket; **3** (*in a French school*) the equivalent of Year 11.

**secouer** *verb* [1] to shake; **secouer la tête** to shake your head.

**secourir** *verb* [29] to rescue.

**secourisme** *noun Masc.* first aid.

**secouriste** *noun Masc. & Fem.* first aider.

**secours** *noun Masc.* **1** help; **au secours!** help!; **elle a crié au secours** she shouted for help; **2** ; **les premiers secours** first aid; **3 une sortie de secours** an emergency exit; **4 la roue de secours** the spare wheel.

**secret** *noun Masc.* secret; **garder un secret** to keep a secret; **en secret** in secret.
**secret** (*Fem.* **secrète**) *adjective* secret.

**secrétaire**[1] *noun Masc., Fem.* secretary.

**secrétaire**[2] *noun Masc.* writing desk.

**secrétariat** *noun Masc.* secretary's office.

**secteur** *noun Masc.* sector; **dans le secteur privé** in the private sector;

dans le secteur public in the public sector.

**sécu** *noun Fem.* (*informal*) SHORT FOR **Sécurité sociale** Social Security.

**sécurité** *noun Fem.* **1** safety; **pour votre sécurité** for your own safety; **les règles de sécurité** safety regulations; **la sécurité routière** road safety; **une ceinture de sécurité** a seatbelt; **2 être en sécurité** to be safe; **3** security; **un système de sécurité** a security system; **la sécurité de l'emploi** job security.

**Sécurité sociale** *noun Fem.* Social Security.

**séduisant** *adjective* attractive, appealing.

**seigle** *noun Masc.* rye; **le pain de seigle** rye bread.

**seigneur** *noun Masc.* lord; **le Seigneur** the Lord.

**sein** *noun Masc.* **1** breast; **avoir un cancer du sein** to have breast cancer; **2** within; **au sein du gouvernement** within the government.

**seize** *number* sixteen; **Corinne a seize ans** Corinne's sixteen; **le seize juillet** the sixteenth of July.

**seizième** *number* sixteenth.

**séjour** *noun Masc.* **1** stay; **pendant votre séjour en France** during your stay in France; **2 la salle de séjour** the living room.

**sel** *noun Masc.* salt; **une pincée de sel** a pinch of salt.

**sélection** *noun Fem.* **1** selection; **2** choice; **3** team; **la sélection française** the French team.

**sélectionner** *verb* [1] to select.

**self** *noun Masc.* (*informal*) self-service restaurant.

**self-service** *noun Masc.* (*informal*) self-service restaurant.

**selle** *noun Fem.* saddle.

**selon** *preposition* according to; **selon la météo, il va pleuvoir** according to the forecast, it's going to rain.

**semaine** *noun Fem.* week; **cette semaine** this week; **la semaine prochaine/dernière** next/last week; **une/deux fois par semaine** once/twice a week; **elle est payée à la semaine** she's paid by the week.

**semblable** *adjective* similar.

**semblant** *noun Masc.* **faire semblant de faire** to pretend to do; **elle fait semblant de ne pas entendre** she's pretending not to hear.

**sembler** *verb* [1] to seem; **la maison semble vide** the house seems empty; **il semble bon d'attendre leur retour** it seems a good idea to wait till they get back.

**semelle** *noun Fem.* sole (*of a shoe*).

**semer** *verb* [1] **1** to sow (*seeds*); **2 semer la panique** to spread panic.

**semestre** *noun Masc.* semester.

**semi-remorque** *noun Masc.* articulated truck.

**semoule** *noun Fem.* semolina; **le sucre semoule** caster sugar.

**sens** *noun Masc.* **1** direction; **dans les deux sens** in both directions; **dans le sens Calais-Paris** in the Calais-Paris direction; **dans tous les sens** in all directions; **sens dessus dessous** upside down; **mets-le dans le bon sens!** put it the right way up!; **2** meaning; **le sens d'un mot** the meaning of a word; **cela n'a pas de sens** it doesn't make sense, it's absurd.

**sensation** *noun Fem.* **1** feeling; **2** sensation; **le film a fait sensation à Cannes** the film was a sensation at Cannes.

**sensationnel** (*Fem.* **sensationnelle**) *adjective* sensational, fantastic.

**sens commun** *noun Masc.* common sense.

**sens de l'humour** *noun Masc.* sense of humour; **avoir le sens de l'humour** to have a sense of humour.

**sensé** *adjective* sensible.

**sensibiliser** *verb* [1] **sensibiliser les gens à un problème** to increase people's awareness of a problem.

**sensibilité** *noun Fem.* **1** sensitivity; **2** sensibility.

**sensible** *adjective* **1** sensitive; **c'est une fille très sensible** she's a very sensitive girl; **je suis sensible au froid** I feel the cold; **2** noticeable; **une différence sensible** a noticeable difference.

**sensiblement** *adverb* noticeably.

**sens interdit** *noun Masc.* no entry sign, one-way street.

**sens unique** *noun Masc.* one-way street.

**sentier** *noun Masc.* path.

**sentier de randonnée** *noun*
Masc. long-distance footpath (*a
marked route for ramblers*).

**sentiment** *noun* Masc. feeling;
**sentiments affectueux** best
wishes; **veuillez croire à mes
sentiments les meilleurs** yours
sincerely, yours faithfully (*one of a
number of fixed formulae for ending
a formal letter*).

**sentimental** (*Masc. plural*
**sentimentaux**) *adjective*
sentimental.

**sentir** *verb* [58] **1** to smell; **ça sent
bon!** that smells good!; **2** to smell of;
**ça sent les roses** it smells of roses;
**tu sens la cigarette** you smell of
cigarettes; **3** to feel; **je ne sens rien**
I can't feel anything; **on sent que
l'hiver s'approche** you can feel it
will soon be winter; **je sens qu'elle
est sincère** I feel she's sincere; **4 se
sentir** to feel; **je ne me sens pas
bien** I don't feel well; ★ **je ne peux
pas le sentir!** I can't stand him!

**séparé** *adjective* **1** separated; **mes
parents sont séparés** my parents
are separated; **2** separate; **dans une
chambre séparée** in a separate
bedroom.

**séparément** *adverb* separately.

**séparer** *verb* [1] **1** to separate;
**séparez les œufs** separate the eggs;
**séparer les filles des garçons** to
separate the girls from the boys;
**2 se séparer** to separate, to split up;
**mes parents se sont séparés** my
parents have separated.

**sept** *number* seven; **Yasmin a sept
ans** Yasmin's seven; **il est sept
heures** it's seven o'clock; **le sept
mars** the seventh of March.

**septante** *number* seventy (*used in
Belgium and Switzerland, instead of
soixante-dix*); **septante-sept**
seventy-seven.

**septembre** *noun* Masc. September;
**en septembre, au mois de
septembre** in September.

**septième** *noun* Masc. **au septième**
on the seventh floor.
**septième** *adjective* seventh.

**sera**, **serai**, **seras**, **serez** *verb*
SEE **être**[1].

**série** *noun* Fem. series.

**sérieusement** *adverb* seriously.

**sérieux** *noun* **prendre quelque
chose au sérieux** to take
something seriously.
**sérieux** (*Fem.* **sérieuse**) *adjective*
**1** serious; **vraiment? tu es
sérieux?** really? are you serious?;
**2** responsible; **Camilla est une
jeune fille sérieuse** Camilla is a
responsible young woman;
**3** reliable; **il n'est pas sérieux** he's
unreliable; **4 un travail sérieux** a
careful piece of work; ★ **garder son
sérieux** to keep a straight face.

**serin** *noun* Masc. canary.

**seringue** *noun* Fem. syringe.

**séronégatif** (*Fem.* **séronégative**)
*adjective* HIV-negative.

**serons**, **seront** *verb* SEE **être**[1].

**séropositif** (*Fem.* **séropositive**)
*adjective* HIV-positive.

**serpent** *noun* Masc. snake.

**serpillière** *noun* Fem. floorcloth.

270

**serre** *noun Fem.* greenhouse; **l'effet de serre** the greenhouse effect.

**serré** *adjective* **1** tight; **ma jupe est trop serrée** my skirt's too tight; **un budget serré** a tight budget; **2** close (*match or competition*).

**serrer** *verb* [1] **1** to grip; **elle serrait le volant** she gripped the steering wheel; **il m'a serrée dans ses bras** he hugged me; **2 serrer la main à quelqu'un** to shake somebody's hand; **nous nous sommes serré la main** we shook hands; **3 serrer quelqu'un dans ses bras** to hug somebody; **4 serrer les poings** to clench your fists; **5** to tighten (*a screw or belt*); **6** to be too tight; **mes chaussures me serrent** my shoes are too tight; **7** to push closer together; **serrez les tables** move the tables closer together; **8 se serrer** to squeeze up; **serrez-vous un peu!** squeeze up a bit!

**serrure** *noun Fem.* lock.

**serveur, serveuse** *noun Masc., Fem.* waiter, waitress.

**service** *noun Masc.* **1** favour; **peux-tu me rendre un petit service?** could you do me a small favour?; **2** service (*bus, train*); **service de dimanche** Sunday service; **3 être en service** to be working; **il n'y a qu'un ascenseur en service** there's only one lift working; **être hors service** to be out of order; **l'ascenseur est hors service** the lift is out of order; **4** duty, service; **la pharmacie de service** the duty chemist; **je suis de service ce soir** I am on duty this evening; **le service militaire** national service;

**5** service (*charge*); **le service est compris** service is included; **6** department (*in a town hall or hospital, for example*); **le service des urgences** the casualty department.

**service après-vente** *noun Masc.* after-sales service.

**service clientèle** *noun Masc.* customer services.

**serviette** *noun Fem.* **1** towel; **une serviette de bain** a bath towel; **2** napkin; **3** briefcase.

**serviette hygiénique** *noun Fem.* sanitary towel.

**servir** *verb* [71] **1** to serve (*in a shop, for example*); **merci, on me sert** thank you, I'm being served; **2** to serve (*with food or drink*); **est-ce que je peux vous servir du poulet?** can I give you some chicken?; **'servir frais'** 'serve chilled'; **3 se servir** to help yourself; **sers-toi de riz** help yourself to rice; **4 se servir de** to use; **est-ce que tu sais te servir d'une machine à coudre?** do you know how to use a sewing machine?; **5** to serve (*in tennis or in the army*); **à toi de servir!** your service!; **6 servir à** to be used for; **à quoi ça sert?** what's it for?; **ça ne sert à rien!** it's no use!; **ça ne sert à rien de pleurer** there's no point in crying; **7 se servir** to be served (*food or drink*); **ce vin se sert frais** this wine should be served chilled.

**ses** *adjective* SEE **son**.

**set de table** *noun Masc.* place mat.

a
b
c
d
e
f
g
h
i
j
k
l
m
n
o
p
q
r
s
t
u
v
w
x
y
z

**seul** *adjective* **1** only; **la seule personne** the only person; **c'est le seul Anglais que je connaisse** he's the only English person I know; **j'étais le seul à aimer le film** I was the only one who liked the film; **2** alone; **il ne faut pas y aller seul** you mustn't go there alone; **j'étais tout seul à la maison** I was all alone in the house; **3 se sentir seul** to feel lonely; **4 tout seul** all by yourself; **il l'a fait tout seul** he did it all by himself; **Sophie sait s'habiller toute seule maintenant** Sophie can get dressed all by herself now.

**seulement** *adverb* **1** only; **trois fois seulement** only three times; **2 non seulement ...mais** not only ...but; **non seulement elle n'est pas venue, mais elle n'a même pas appelé** not only did she not come, but she didn't even phone; **3 si seulement je l'avais su** if only I'd known.

**sévère** *adjective* strict.

**sexe** *noun Masc.* **1** sex; **2** genitals.

**sexuel** (*Fem.* **sexuelle**) *adjective* **1** sexual; **2 l'éducation sexuelle** sex education.

**shampooing** *noun Masc.* shampoo.

**short** *noun Masc.* (pair of) shorts; **où est mon short?** where are my shorts?; **trois shorts** three pairs of shorts.

**si**, **s'** (*before 'il' or 'ils'*) *conjunction* if; **si tu veux** if you like; **s'il pleut** if it rains.
**si** *adverb* **1** so; **je suis si fatigué!** I'm so tired!; **tu chantes si bien!**

you sing so well!; **2** yes (*when you are contradicting somebody*); **'tu ne viens pas avec nous?' –'si!'** 'you're not coming with us?' – 'yes I am!'; **'il ne reste pas manger' – 'mais si!'** 'he's not staying for a meal' – 'of course he is!'; **elle ne les aime pas du tout, moi si** she doesn't like them at all, but I do.

**Sicile** *noun Fem.* Sicily.

**sida** *noun Masc.* SHORT FOR **syndrome immuno-déficitaire acquis** AIDS; **avoir le sida** to have AIDS.

**siècle** *noun Masc.* century; **au vingtième siècle** in the twentieth century.

**siège** *noun Masc.* **1** seat; **le siège d'avant** the front seat; **2** head office (*of a company*); **3** siege (*in war*).

**sien**, **sienne**, **siens**, **siennes** *pronoun* le sien, la sienne, les siens, les siennes **1** his; **j'ai prêté mon vélo à Paul, le sien est chez lui** I've lent Paul my bike, his is at home; **'est-ce que ces chaussures sont à Bernard?' – 'oui, ce sont les siennes'** 'are these shoes Bernard's?' – 'yes, they're his'; **2** hers; **j'ai prêté mon vélo à Annie, le sien est chez elle** I've lent Annie my bike, hers is at home; **'est-ce que ces chaussures sont à Nathalie?' – 'oui, ce sont les siennes'** 'are these shoes Nathalie's?' – 'yes, they're hers'.

**sieste** *noun Fem.* nap; **faire la sieste** to have a nap.

**siffler** *verb* [1] to whistle.

**sifflet** *noun Masc.* whistle.

**signal** (*plural* **signaux**) *noun Masc.* signal.

**signaler** *verb* [1] **1** to point out; **je vous signale que je serai absent ce jour-là** I'd like to point out that I shall be away that day; **2** to report; **3** to indicate (*roadworks or danger, for example*).

**signalisation** *noun Fem.* signalling, signals.

**signalisation routière** *noun Fem.* road signs and markings.

**signature** *noun Fem.* signature; **je vous demande une petite signature** just sign here, would you?

**signe** *noun Masc.* sign; **c'est bon/ mauvais signe** it's a good/bad sign; **faire signe à quelqu'un** to wave to someone; **il m'a fait signe de m'approcher** he beckoned me over to him; **d'un signe de main elle a montré la sortie** she pointed to the exit; **de quel signe êtes-vous?** what star sign are you?

**signe astrologique** *noun Masc.* star sign.

**signer** *verb* [1] **1** to sign; **2 se signer** to cross oneself.

**signification** *noun Fem.* meaning.

**signifier** *verb* [1] to mean.

**silence** *noun Masc.* silence; **en silence** in silence.

**silencieux** (*Fem.* **silencieuse**) *adjective* silent.

**silhouette** *noun Fem.* **1** silhouette, outline; **2** figure.

**similarité** *noun Fem.* similarity.

**simple** *noun Masc.* **le simple messieurs/dames** the men's/ women's singles (*in tennis*).
**simple** *adjective* simple; **un repas simple** a simple meal; **un simple coup de téléphone** just one telephone call.

**simplement** *adverb* simply.

**simplicité** *noun Fem.* simplicity.

**simplifier** *verb* [1] to simplify.

**simuler** *verb* [1] to simulate.

**simultané** *adjective* simultaneous.

**sincère** *adjective* sincere.

**sincérité** *noun Fem.* sincerity.

**singe** *noun Masc.* monkey; **un grand singe** an ape.

**singulier** *noun Masc.* singular; **au singulier** in the singular.

**sinistre** *noun Masc.* accident, disaster (*for example, a fire or flood*).
**sinistre** *adjective* **1** sinister; **2** gloomy.

**sinistré**, **sinistrée** *noun Masc., Fem.* disaster victim.
**sinistrée** *adjective* stricken; **de l'aide pour les familles sinistrées** help for the families stricken by the disaster.

**sinon** *conjunction* otherwise; **il faut partir, sinon on sera en retard** we must leave, otherwise we'll be late.

**sirène** *noun Fem.* **1** siren; **une sirène d'alarme** a fire alarm; **2** mermaid.

**sirop** *noun Masc.* **1** syrup; **sirop pectoral** cough mixture; **2 sirop de menthe** mint cordial.

**site** *noun Masc.* site, area; **site touristique** place of interest (*to visit*); **site classé** conservation area.

a
b
c
d
e
f
g
h
i
j
k
l
m
n
o
p
q
r
s
t
u
v
w
x
y
z

273

**site internet** *noun Masc.* web site.

**sitôt** *adverb* as soon as; **sitôt rentrée, elle s'est couchée** as soon as she got home, she went to bed; **sitôt après** immediately afterwards; ★ **sitôt dit, sitôt fait** no sooner said than done.

**situation** *noun Fem.* **1** situation; **2** job; **il a perdu sa situation** he's lost his job.

**situer** *verb* [1] **1 être situé** to be situated; **l'hôtel est situé au bord de la mer** the hotel is situated by the sea; **bien situé** well situated; **2 se situer** to be situated; **la maison se situe dans un quartier résidentiel** the house is in a residential area; **3 se situer** to be set; **le roman se situe à Moscou** the novel is set in Moscow.

**six** *number* six; **Rosie a six ans** Rosie's six; **il est six heures** it's six o'clock; **le six juillet** the sixth of July.

**sixième** *noun Fem.* (*in a French school*) the equivalent of Year 7. **sixième** *noun Masc.* **au sixième** on the sixth floor. **sixième** *adjective* sixth.

**skate** *noun Masc.* **1** skate-boarding; **2** skate-board.

**ski** *noun Masc.* **1** ski; **où sont mes skis?** where are my skis?; **2** skiing; **il adore le ski** he loves skiing; **on va faire du ski ce week-end** we're going skiing this weekend.

**ski de fond** *noun Masc.* cross-country skiing.

**ski de piste** *noun Masc.* downhill skiing.

**skier** *verb* [1] to ski; **il skie plutôt bien** he skis pretty well; **skier hors piste** to ski off-piste.

**skieur, skieuse** *noun Masc., Fem.* skier.

**ski nautique** *noun Masc.* water-skiing.

**slip** *noun Masc.* **1** underpants; **2** knickers.

**Slovaquie** *noun Fem.* Slovakia.

**Slovénie** *noun Fem.* Slovenia.

**SMIC** *noun Masc.* SHORT FOR **Salaire minimum interprofessionnel de croissance** guaranteed minimum wage; **elle touche le SMIC** she's on the legal minimum wage.

**smoking** *noun Masc.* dinner jacket.

**snack** *noun Masc.* snack bar.

**SNCF** *noun Fem.* SHORT FOR **Société nationale des chemins de fer français** (*French national railways*).

**snob** *noun Masc. & Fem.* snob. **snob** *adjective* snobbish (*of a person*), posh (*of a restaurant*).

**sobre** *adjective* sober.

**sociable** *adjective* friendly, sociable.

**social** (*Masc. plural* **sociaux**) *adjective* social.

**socialiste** *noun Masc., Fem.*, *adjective* socialist.

**société** *noun Fem.* **1** society; **dans notre société** in our society; **2** company; **il travaille pour une grande société** he works for a big company.

**société anonyme** *noun Fem.* public company.

**sociologie** *noun Fem.* sociology.

**socquette** *noun Fem.* ankle sock.

**sœur** *noun Fem.* sister; **ma grande sœur** my big sister, my older sister.

**soi** *pronoun* 1 one, oneself; **des amis autour de soi** friends around one; 2 **avoir confiance en soi** to have confidence in oneself; 3 itself; **pas très intéressant en soi** not very interesting in itself; **cela va de soi** that goes without saying.

**soi-disant** *adjective* 1 so-called; **c'est le soi-disant champion** he's the so-called champion; 2 supposedly; **elle est soi-disant malade** she's supposedly ill.

**soie** *noun Fem.* silk; **un foulard en soie** a silk scarf; **le papier de soie** tissue paper.

**soif** *noun Masc.* thirst; **avoir soif** to be thirsty.

**soigner** *verb* [1] to look after.

**soigneusement** *adverb* carefully.

**soi-même** *pronoun* yourself, oneself; **il faut le faire soi-même** you have to do it yourself.

**soin** *noun Masc.* 1 care; 2 **prendre soin de quelque chose** to take care of something; 3 **les soins** treatment; 4 **les premiers soins** first aid.

**soir** *noun Masc.* evening, night; **ce soir** tonight; **hier soir** last night; **demain soir** tomorrow night; **je sors tous les samedis soirs** I go out every Saturday night; **par un beau soir d'été** one fine summer's evening; **à six heures du soir** at six

in the evening; **à ce soir!** see you tonight!

**soirée** *noun Fem.* 1 evening; **pendant la soirée** during the evening; 2 party; **elle donne une petite soirée** she's having a little party; 3 **en tenue de soirée** in evening dress.

**soirée dansante** *noun Fem.* dance.

**sois** *verb* SEE **être**[1]; **sois gentil** be good.

**soit** *conjunction* **soit ...soit** either ...or; **soit demain, soit jeudi** either tomorrow or Thursday.

**soixantaine** *noun Fem.* 1 about sixty; **une soixantaine de personnes** about sixty people; 2 **avoir la soixantaine** to be in your sixties.

**soixante** *number* sixty.

**soixante-dix** *number* seventy; **soixante-dix-huit** seventy-eight.

**soja** *noun Masc.* soya bean; **la sauce de soja** soy sauce.

**sol** *noun Masc.* 1 floor; 2 soil.

**solaire** *adjective* 1 solar; 2 **la crème solaire** sun cream.

**soldat** *noun Masc.* soldier.

**solde** *noun Masc.* 1 **les soldes** the sales; **faire les soldes** to go round the sales; 2 **être en solde** to be reduced; **les pulls sont en solde** the jumpers are reduced; 3 balance (*in a bank account*).

**soldé** *adjective* reduced.

**sole** *noun Fem.* sole (*fish*).

**soleil** *noun Masc.* sun; **au soleil** in the sun; **il fait soleil** it's sunny; **en**

a
b
c
d
e
f
g
h
i
j
k
l
m
n
o
p
q
r
s
t
u
v
w
x
y
z

plein soleil in full sun; **attraper un coup de soleil** to get sunburnt.

**solfège** *noun Masc.* musical theory.

**solide** *adjective* **1** strong; **2** solid.

**soliste** *noun Masc. & Fem.* soloist.

**solitaire** *adjective* **1** lonely, isolated; **2 un navigateur solitaire** a solo yachtsman.

**solitude** *noun Fem.* **1** loneliness; **2** solitude.

**solution** *noun Fem.* solution.

**sombre** *adjective* dark, gloomy.

**somme**[1] *noun Fem.* sum; **une somme d'argent** a sum of money.

**somme**[2] *noun Masc.* nap; **faire un somme** to have a nap.

**sommeil** *noun Masc.* sleep; **avoir sommeil** to feel sleepy; **je n'ai plus sommeil** I'm not sleepy any more.

**sommes** *verb* SEE **être**[1].

**sommet** *noun Masc.* summit.

**somnambule** *noun Masc. & Fem.* sleepwalker; **être somnambule** to walk in your sleep.

**son**[1], **sa**, **ses** *adjective* **1** his; **son fils** his son; **sa fille** his daughter; **ses enfants** his children; **2** her; **son fils** her son; **sa fille** her daughter; **ses enfants** her children; **3** its; **le chat a perdu son collier** the cat's lost its collar.

**son**[2] *noun Masc.* **1** sound; **le son d'un piano** the sound of a piano; **2** volume (*on a radio or hi-fi*); **baisser le son** to turn the volume down; **3** bran.

**sondage** *noun Masc.* survey; **un sondage d'opinion** an opinion poll.

**sonner** *verb* [1] to ring; **le téléphone sonne** the phone's ringing; **on sonne à la porte** somebody's ringing the doorbell.

**sonnerie** *noun Fem.* bell; **la sonnerie d'alarme** the alarm bell; **la sonnerie du téléphone** the ring of the telephone.

**sonnette** *noun Fem.* bell, doorbell.

**sono** *noun Fem.* (*informal*) sound system.

**Sonotone**™ *noun Masc.* hearing aid.

**sophistiqué** *adjective* sophisticated.

**sorbet** *noun Masc.* sorbet; **un sorbet au cassis** a blackcurrant sorbet.

**sorcière** *noun Fem.* witch.

**sort** *noun Masc.* fate; ★ **tirer au sort** to draw lots.

**sorte** *noun Fem.* sort; **c'est une sorte de poudre** it's a sort of powder; **toutes sortes d'activités** all sorts of activities.

**sortie** *noun Fem.* **1** exit; **il nous attend à la sortie** he's waiting for us at the exit; **sortie de secours** emergency exit; **2** outing; **3** launch (*of a new product*), release (*of a film*), publication (*of a book*).

**sortir** *verb* [72] **1** to go out; **tout le monde est sorti dans la rue** everybody went out into the street; **ils sont sortis déjeuner** they've gone out for lunch; **elle est sortie en courant** she ran out; **2** to come out; **c'est l'heure où les gens sortent du cinéma** it's the time when people are coming out of the cinema; **son nouveau film sortira**

en mai her new film is coming out
in May; **3** to go out (*for pleasure*);
**mes parents sortent peu** my
parents don't go out much; **4 sortir
avec** to be going out with; **il sort
avec ma sœur** he's going out with
my sister; **5** to take out; **elle a sorti
une bouteille du frigo** she took a
bottle out of the fridge; **j'ai oublié
de sortir le chien** I forgot to take
the dog out; **6 s'en sortir** to manage;
**je m'en sortirai d'une manière ou
d'une autre** I'll manage one way or
another.

**sottise** *noun Fem.* **1** silliness; **2 dire
des sottises** to talk nonsense; **ne
fais pas de sottises** don't do
anything silly.

**sou** *noun Masc.* **j'ai dépensé tous
mes sous** I've spent all my money;
**je n'ai pas un sou** I'm broke; **une
machine à sous** a fruit machine;
★ **être près de ses sous** to be tight-
fisted.

**souci** *noun Masc.* **1** worry,; **se faire
du souci** to worry; **mon fils me
donne bien des soucis** my son's a
great worry to me; **j'ai d'autres
soucis à présent** I've got other
problems just now; **2** marigold.

**soucieux** (*Fem.* **soucieuse**)
*adjective* worried.

**soucoupe** *noun Fem.* saucer.

**soudain** *adjective* sudden.
**soudain** *adverb* suddenly.

**souffle** *noun Masc.* breath; **être à
bout de souffle** to be out of breath;
**couper le souffle à quelqu'un** to
take someone's breath away.

**soufflé** *noun Masc.* soufflé; **un
soufflé au fromage** a cheese
soufflé.

**souffler** *verb* [1] **1** to blow; **le vent
soufflait fort** there was a strong
wind; **2** to blow out (*a candle*); **3** to
whisper; **elle me soufflait quelque
chose à l'oreille** she was
whispering something in my ear;
★ **souffler dans le ballon**
(*informal*) to be breathalysed.

**souffrance** *noun Fem.* **1** suffering;
**2** misery.

**souffrir** *verb* [73] **1** to suffer; **a-t-
elle beaucoup souffert?** did she
suffer much?; **il souffre souvent du
dos** he often has back pain; **2 je ne
peux pas le souffrir!** (*informal*) I
can't stand him!

**souhait** *noun Masc.* wish; ★ **à tes
souhaits!** bless you! (*when
somebody sneezes*).

**souhaiter** *verb* [1] to wish; **je te
souhaite bonne chance** I wish you
luck; **il nous a souhaité la
bienvenue** he welcomed us; **il
souhaite se marier** he'd like to get
married.

**soûl** *adjective* drunk.

**soulagé** *adjective* relieved.

**soulagement** *noun Masc.* relief.

**soulager** *verb* [52] to relieve.

**soulever** *verb* [50] **1** to lift; **je
n'arrive pas à soulever ta valise** I
can't lift your case; **2** to raise
(*problems, objections, or difficulties*);
**personne n'a soulevé la question**
nobody raised the question.

**soulier** *noun Masc.* shoe.

a **souligner** *verb* [1] **1** to underline; **2** to emphasize.

b **soupçon** *noun Masc.* **1** suspicion; **2** spot, drop (*of food or drink*); **juste un soupçon de lait** just a drop of milk.

c
d

e **soupçonner** *verb* [1] to suspect.

f **soupe** *noun Fem.* soup; **la soupe aux oignons** onion soup.

g **souper** *verb* [1] to have supper.

h **soupir** *noun Masc.* sigh.

i **soupirer** *verb* [1] to sigh.

**souple** *adjective* **1** supple (*person*); **2** flexible (*system*); **3** soft (*hair or clean washing*).

j
k

l **source** *noun Fem.* spring; **l'eau de source** spring water.

m **sourcil** *noun Masc.* eyebrow.

n **sourd** *adjective* **1** deaf; **2** dull, muffled (*noise*); ★ **faire la sourde oreille** to turn a deaf ear.

o

**souriant** *adjective* cheerful.

p **sourire** *noun Masc.* smile; **il faut garder le sourire** you must keep smiling.
q **sourire** *verb* [68] to smile; **sourire à quelqu'un** to smile at somebody.

r
s **souris** *noun Fem.* mouse (*also for a computer*).

t

u **sous** *preposition* under, underneath; **sous la chaise** under the chair; **sortir sous la pluie** to go out in the rain; **sous terre** underground; ★ **sous peu** before long.

v
w

x **sous-entendu** *noun Masc.* innuendo.

y
z **sous-entendu** *adjective* implied.

**sous-estimer** *verb* [1] to underestimate.

**sous-marin** *noun Masc.* submarine.
**sous-marin** *adjective* under-water, deep-sea.

**sous-sol** *noun Masc.* basement; **au sous-sol** in the basement.

**sous-tasse** *noun Fem.* saucer.

**sous-titre** *noun Masc.* subtitle.

**soustraction** *noun Fem.* subtraction.

**sous-vêtements** *plural noun Masc.* underwear.

**soutenir** *verb* [77] **1** to support; **elle m'a soutenu à la réunion** she supported me at the meeting; **2 soutenir que** to maintain that; **3 soutenir une conversation** to keep up a conversation; **4** to withstand (*a shock or attack*).

**souterrain** *adjective* underground.

**soutien** *noun Masc.* support.

**soutien-gorge** *noun Masc.* bra.

**soutif** *noun Masc.* (*informal*) bra.

**souvenir** *noun Masc.* **1** memory; **mes souvenirs de Londres** my memories of London; **garder un bon souvenir de quelque chose** to have happy memories of something; **je n'ai aucun souvenir de l'avoir rencontrée** I have no memory of meeting her; **2** souvenir.

**souvenir** *verb* [81] **se souvenir de** to remember; **je me souviens d'elle** I remember her; **je me souviens de l'avoir rencontrée** I remember meeting her; **t'en souviens-tu?** do you remember that?

**souvent** *adverb* often; **je ne la vois pas très souvent** I don't see her very often; **le plus souvent** more often than not.

**spacieux** (*Fem.* **spacieuse**) *adjective* spacious.

**spaghettis** *plural noun Masc.* spaghetti; **manger des spaghettis** to have spaghetti.

**sparadrap** *noun Masc.* sticking plaster.

**speaker**, **speakerine** *noun Masc., Fem.* announcer.

**spécial** (*Masc. plural* **spéciaux**) *adjective* **1** special; **rien de spécial** nothing special; **les effets spéciaux** special effects; **2** odd; **il est vraiment très spécial** he's really very odd.

**spécialement** *adverb* specially.

**spécialiser** *verb* [1] **se spécialiser** to specialize; **elle se spécialise dans la génétique** she's specializing in genetics.

**spécialiste** *noun Masc. & Fem.* specialist.

**spécialité** *noun Fem.* speciality.

**spécifier** *verb* [1] to specify.

**spectacle** *noun Masc.* show.

**spectaculaire** *adjective* spectacular.

**spectateur**, **spectatrice** *noun Masc., Fem.* **1** member of the audience; **2** spectator.

**spéléologie** *noun Fem.* potholing.

**spirituel**, **spirituelle** *adjective* **1** witty; **2** spiritual.

**splendeur** *noun Fem.* splendour.

**splendide** *adjective* magnificent.

**sponsoriser** *verb* [1] to sponsor.

**spontané** *adjective* spontaneous.

**sport** *noun Masc.* sport, sports; **aimez-vous le sport?** do you like sport?; **il fait beaucoup de sport** he does a lot of sport; **mon maillot de sport** my sports shirt; **les sports d'hiver** winter sports; **être bon en sport** to be good at sports.

**sportif**, **sportive** *noun Masc., Fem.* sportsman, sportswoman. **sportif** (*Fem.* **sportive**) *adjective* **1** sports; **un club sportif** a sports club; **une rencontre sportive** a sports meeting; **2** sporty, athletic.

**spot** *noun Masc.* **1** spotlight; **2 un spot publicitaire** a commercial.

**square** *noun Masc.* public garden.

**squelette** *noun Masc.* skeleton.

**stable** *adjective* **1** stable; **2 un emploi stable** a steady job.

**stade** *noun Masc.* stadium.

**stage** *noun Masc.* **1** course; **un stage intensif d'anglais** an intensive English course; **faire un stage de formation** to go on a training course; **2 un stage professionnel** work experience; **j'aimerais faire un stage professionnel dans une société française** I'd like to do work experience in a French company.

**stagiaire** *noun Masc. & Fem.* **1** trainee; **2** person on a work experience placement.

**stand** *noun Masc.* **1** stand (*in a market or an exhibition*); **2** stall (*in a fairground*).

a b c d e f g h i j k l m n o p q r s t u v w x y z

**standard** *noun Masc.* switchboard;
**il faut passer par le standard** you
have to go through the switchboard.

**standardiste** *noun Masc. & Fem.*
switchboard operator.

**standing** *noun Masc.* **un**
**appartement de standing** a luxury
flat.

**star** *noun Fem.* star (*in a film or*
*show*).

**starter** *noun Masc.* choke (*in a car*).

**station** *noun Fem.* **1 une station de**
**métro** an underground station;
**2 une station de taxis** a taxi rank;
**3** resort; **une station de ski** a ski
resort; **4 une station de radio** a
radio station.

**station de travail** *noun Fem.*
(computer) work station.

**stationnaire** *adjective*
**1** stationary; **2** stable.

**stationnement** *noun Masc.*
parking; **'stationnement interdit'**
'no parking'.

**stationner** *verb* [1] to park.

**station-service** *noun Fem.*
service station.

**statistique** *noun Fem.* statistic(s).

**statue** *noun Fem.* statue.

**statut** *noun Masc.* **1** statute;
**2** status.

**steak** *noun Masc.* steak; **un steak**
**frites** steak and chips; **un steak**
**haché** a burger steak.

**sténodactylo** *noun Masc. & Fem.*
shorthand typist.

**stéréo** *noun Fem., adjective* stereo.

**stérile** *adjective* sterile.

**stériliser** *verb* [1] to sterilize.

**steward** *noun Masc.* flight
attendant (*male*).

**stimulant** *adjective* stimulating.

**stock** *noun Masc.* stock; **en stock** in
stock.

**stop** *noun Masc.* **1** stop sign; **2 faire**
**du stop** to hitch-hike.

**stopper** *verb* [1] to stop.

**store** *noun Masc.* **1** blind; **2** awning.

**strapontin** *noun Masc.* fold-down
seat.

**stratégie** *noun Fem.* strategy.

**stratégique** *adjective* strategic.

**stress** *noun Masc.* stress.

**stressant** *adjective* stressful.

**stressé** *adjective* stressed; **elle**
**avait l'air stressé** she looked
stressed; **je suis très stressé en ce**
**moment** I'm stressed out at the
moment.

**strict** *adjective* **1** strict; **2** severe.

**studieux** (*Fem.* **studieuse**)
*adjective* studious.

**studio** *noun Masc.* **1** studio flat;
**2** studio.

**stupéfait** *adjective* astounded.

**stupéfiants** *plural noun Masc.*
narcotics.

**stupeur** *noun Fem.* astonishment.

**stupide** *adjective* stupid.

**stupidité** *noun Fem.* stupidity.

**style** *noun Masc.* style; **c'est bien**
**son style!** that's just like him!

**styliste** *noun Masc. & Fem.* designer.

**stylo** *noun Masc.* fountain pen.

**stylo-bille** *noun Masc.* ball-point pen.

**stylo-feutre** *noun Masc.* felt pen.

**stylo-plume** *noun Masc.* fountain pen.

**su** *verb* SEE **savoir**[1].

**subir** *verb* [2] **1** to be subjected to (*change, violence, or pressure*); **2** to suffer (*defeat or damage*); **3 subir une opération** to have an operation.

**subitement** *adverb* suddenly.

**subjonctif** *noun Masc.* subjunctive; **au subjonctif** in the subjunctive.

**subordonné, subordonnée** *noun Masc., Fem.* subordinate.

**substituer** *verb* [1] to substitute.

**subtil** *adjective* subtle.

**subvention** *noun Fem.* subsidy.

**succès** *noun Masc.* success; **c'est un grand succès!** it's a great success!

**succursale** *noun Fem.* branch (*of a company*).

**sucer** *verb* [61] to suck.

**sucette** *noun Fem.* lollipop.

**sucre** *noun Masc.* **1** sugar; **du jus d'orange sans sucre** unsweetened orange juice; **2 un sucre** a lump of sugar.

**sucré** *adjective* sweet; **c'est trop sucré pour moi** it's too sweet for me.

**sucre cristallisé** *noun Masc.* granulated sugar.

**sucre d'orge** *noun Masc.* barley sugar.

**sucre en morceaux** *noun Masc.* sugar lumps.

**sucre en poudre** *noun Masc.* caster sugar.

**sucre glace** *noun Masc.* icing sugar.

**sucrerie** *noun Fem.* **des sucreries** sweet things.

**sucre roux** *noun Masc.* brown sugar.

**sucrier** *noun Masc.* sugar bowl.

**sud** *noun Masc.* south; **au sud de l'Écosse** in the south of Scotland; **au sud de Calais** south of Calais; **un vent du sud** a south wind. **sud** *adjective* **1** south; **la côte sud** the south coast; **2** southern; **la partie sud** the southern part.

**sud-africain** *adjective* South African.

**Sud-Africain, Sud-Africaine** *noun Masc., Fem.* South African.

**sud-américain** *adjective* South American.

**Sud-Américain, Sud-Américaine** *noun Masc., Fem.* South American.

**sud-est** *noun Masc., adjective* south-east.

**sud-ouest** *noun Masc., adjective* south-west.

**Suède** *noun Fem.* Sweden.

**suédois** *noun Masc.* Swedish (*language*). **suédois** *adjective* Swedish.

**Suédois, Suédoise** *noun Masc., Fem.* Swede.

**suer** *verb* [1] to sweat.

**sueur** *noun Fem.* sweat; **je suis en sueur** I'm sweating.

**suffire** *verb* [74] **1** to be enough; **un kilo suffit** one kilo's enough; **ça suffit!** that's enough!; **2 il suffit de faire** all you have to do is; **il suffit de nous téléphoner** all you have to do is give us a call.

**suffisamment** *adverb* enough; **ce n'est pas suffisamment cuit** it's not cooked enough; **il n'y a pas suffisamment de verres** there aren't enough glasses.

**suffisant** *adjective* **1** sufficient; **c'est bien suffisant!** that's quite enough!; **2** smug; **je la trouve un peu suffisante** I find her a bit smug.

**suffoquer** *verb* [1] to suffocate, to choke.

**suggérer** *verb* [24] to suggest.

**suggestion** *noun Fem.* suggestion.

**suicider** *verb* [1] **se suicider** to commit suicide.

**suis** *verb* SEE **être**[1]; SEE **suivre**.

**suisse** *adjective* Swiss.

**Suisse** *noun Fem.* Switzerland; **en Suisse** in (or to) Switzerland; **la Suisse romande** French-speaking Switzerland; **la Suisse allemande** German-speaking Switzerland.

**suite** *noun Fem.* **1** rest; **je te raconterai la suite plus tard** I'll tell you the rest later; **et on connaît la suite** and we all know what happened next; **2** continuation; **'suite page 67'** 'continued on page 67'; **regardez la suite jeudi** watch the next instalment on Thursday; **3** suite (*in a hotel*); **4** in succession; **trois fois de suite** three times in succession; **5 tout de suite** straightaway; **j'arrive tout de suite!** I'll be right there!; **6 par la suite** later; **on s'est rendu compte par la suite que c'était une erreur** we realized later that it was a mistake.

**suivant, suivante** *noun Masc., Fem.* next one; **pas ce lundi mais le suivant** not this Monday but the next.

**suivant** *adjective* following; **le jour suivant** the following day.

**suivre** *verb* [75] **1** to follow; **suivez-moi** follow me; **2 suivre l'actualité** to keep up with the news; **3 'à suivre'** 'to be continued'; **4 faire suivre son courrier** to have your mail forwarded; **5 suivre un cours** to do a course; **6 suivre un régime** to be on a diet.

**sujet** *noun Masc.* **1** subject; **au sujet de** about; **c'est au sujet de votre fils** it's about your son; **c'est à quel sujet?** what's it about?; **un sujet de conversation** a topic of conversation; **2 un sujet d'examen** an exam question.

**sujet** *adjective* (*Fem.* **sujette**) **être sujet à** to suffer from; **elle est sujette à des crises d'asthme** she suffers from asthma attacks.

**super** *noun Masc.* four-star petrol.
**super** *adjective* (*informal*) fantastic; **mais c'est super!** but that's fantastic!

**superficie** *noun Fem.* area.

**superficiel** (*Fem.* **superficielle**) *adjective* superficial.

**supérieur, supérieure** *noun Masc., Fem.* superior.
**supérieur** *adjective* **1** upper; **l'étage supérieur** the upper floor; **la lèvre supérieure** the upper lip;

**2** greater; **la taille supérieure** the bigger size; **à une vitesse supérieure** at a faster speed; **à une température supérieure** at a higher temperature; **un prix supérieur** a higher price; **3** better, superior (*work, quality*); **c'est de loin supérieur à l'autre!** it's much better than the other one!; **4 supérieur à** greater than; **un nombre supérieur à trois** a number higher than three.

**superlatif** *noun Masc.* superlative.

**supermarché** *noun Masc.* supermarket.

**superposer** *verb* [1] **1** to stack up; **des lits superposés** bunk beds; **2** to superimpose (*an image*).

**superstitieux** (Fem. **superstitieuse**) *adjective* superstitious.

**superstition** *noun Fem.* superstition.

**supplément** *noun Masc.* extra charge; **le vin est en supplément** wine is extra.

**supplémentaire** *adjective* **1** additional; **2 faire des heures supplémentaires** to do overtime.

**supplice** *noun Masc.* torture.

**supplier** *verb* [1] to beg.

**support** *noun Masc.* **1** support; **2** back-up (material); **un support audiovisuel** audiovisual aids.

**supportable** *adjective* bearable.

**supporter** *verb* [1] **1** to stand; **il ne supporte pas qu'on le critique** he can't stand being criticized; **je ne peux plus la supporter!** I can't

stand any more of her!; **2** to support (*a weight*).

**supposer** *verb* [1] to suppose.

**supprimer** *verb* [1] **1** to get rid of; **2 supprimer des emplois** to cut jobs; **supprimer un train** to cancel a train.

**sur** *preposition* **1** on; **c'est sur ton lit** it's on your bed; **un débat sur le racisme** a discussion on racism; **le cinéma est sur la droite** the cinema's on the right; **2** over; **un pont sur la Loire** a bridge over the Loire; **3** by (*in measurements*); **c'est deux mètres sur trois** it's two metres by three; **4** out of; **trois femmes sur cinq** three women out of five; **5** out of; **j'ai eu douze sur vingt en géographie** I got twelve out of twenty in geography.

**sûr** *adjective* **1** sure; **tu es sûr?** are you sure?; **oui, bien sûr!** yes, of course!; **sûr et certain** certain; **j'en étais sûr!** I knew it!; **2 sûr de soi, de lui, d'elle** (*etc*) self-confident; **elle est très sûre d'elle** she's very self-confident; **3** safe; **en lieu sûr** in a safe place; **le plus sûr est de tout fermer à clé** the safest thing is to lock everything.

**surcharger** *verb* [52] to overload.

**surdité** *noun Fem.* deafness.

**surdose** *noun Fem.* overdose (*of medicine*).

**sûrement** *adverb* **1** certainly; **sûrement pas!** certainly not!; **2 il doit sûrement arriver à tout instant** he's bound to arrive at any moment; **elle est sûrement partie** she's bound to have left.

**sûreté** *noun Fem.* safety, security.

**surf** *noun Masc.* surfing; **faire du surf** to go surfing.

**surface** *noun Fem.* **1** surface; **2** area; **3 une grande surface** a hypermarket.

**surface de réparation** *noun Fem.* penalty area.

**surf des neiges** *noun Masc.* snowboarding; **faire du surf des neiges** to go snowboarding.

**surfer** *verb* [1] **surfer Internet/le web** to surf the Net/Web.

**surfeur, surfeuse** *noun Masc., Fem.* surfer (*on the sea*).

**surgelé** *noun Masc.* **les surgelés** frozen food.
   **surgelé** *adjective* frozen; **les légumes surgelés** frozen vegetables.

**sur-le-champ** *adverb* right away.

**surlendemain** *noun Masc.* **elle est arrivée le surlendemain** she arrived two days later.

**surmonter** *verb* [1] to overcome.

**surnaturel** (*Fem.* **surnaturelle**) *adjective* supernatural.

**surnom** *noun Masc.* nickname.

**surnommer** *verb* [1] to nickname.

**surpeuplé** *adjective* overpopulated.

**surprenant** *adjective* surprising.

**surprendre** *verb* [64] **1** to surprise; **ça m'a beaucoup surpris** I found that really surprising; **2 surprendre quelqu'un en train de faire quelque chose** to catch somebody doing something; **je l'ai surprise en train de lire mon courrier** I caught her reading my mail.

**surpris** *adjective* surprised; **je suis surpris de te voir** I'm surprised to see you.

**surprise** *noun Fem.* surprise; **quelle surprise!** what a surprise!; **à ma grande surprise elle a accepté** to my great surprise she agreed; **faire une surprise à quelqu'un** to give somebody a surprise.

**surréaliste** *noun Masc. & Fem.* surrealist.
   **surréaliste** *adjective* surreal.

**surtout** *adverb* **1** especially; **il y a beaucoup de touristes, surtout en été** there are lots of tourists, especially in the summer; **2** above all; **il faut surtout rester calme** above all, we must stay calm.

**surveillant, surveillante** *noun Masc., Fem.* supervisor (*in a school, responsible for maintaining school discipline outside the classroom*).

**surveiller** *verb* [1] **1** to watch, to keep an eye on; **est-ce que tu peux surveiller mon sac deux secondes?** can you keep an eye on my bag for a couple of minutes?; **2 surveiller une maison** to keep a house under surveillance; **3** to supervise; **surveiller le travail des élèves** to supervise the students' work (*work or progress*); **4 surveiller un examen** to invigilate an exam; **5 je surveille ma ligne** I'm watching my figure.

**survêtement** *noun Masc.* tracksuit.

**survie** *noun Fem.* survival.

**survivant**, **survivante** *noun Masc.*, *Fem.* survivor.

**survivre** *verb* [82] to survive; **survivre à un accident** to survive an accident.

**survoler** *verb* [1] to fly over.

**suspect**, **suspecte** *noun Masc.*, *Fem.* suspect.
**suspect** *adjective* suspicious.

**suspense** *noun Masc.* suspense (*as in a thriller*).

**suture** *noun Fem.* **un point de suture** a stitch (*in a wound*).

**svelte** *adjective* slender.

**SVP** SHORT FOR **s'il vous plaît** please.

**sweat** *noun Masc.* SEE **sweatshirt**.

**sweatshirt** *noun Masc.* sweatshirt.

**syllabe** *noun Fem.* syllable.

**symbole** *noun Masc.* symbol.

**symbolique** *adjective* symbolic; **un geste symbolique** a token gesture.

**sympa** *adjective* (*informal*) nice; **je le trouve très sympa, ton copain** he's really nice, your boyfriend.

**sympathie** *noun Fem.* **j'ai beaucoup de sympathie pour elle** I like her a lot.

**sympathique** *adjective* nice; **c'est un type sympathique** he's a nice guy.

**sympathiser** *verb* [1] **sympathiser avec quelqu'un** to get on well with someone.

**symptôme** *noun Masc.* symptom.

**synagogue** *noun Fem.* synagogue.

**syndicat** *noun Masc.* trade union.

**syndicat d'initiative** *noun Masc.* tourist information office.

**synthétique** *adjective* synthetic.

**synthétiseur** *noun Masc.* synthesizer.

**système** *noun Masc.* system; **un système d'éclairage** a lighting system.

# Tt

**ta** *adjective* SEE **ton**[1].

**tabac** *noun Masc.* **1** tobacco; **2 un bureau de tabac** a tobacconist's.

**tabagisme** *noun Masc.* addiction to tobacco.

**table** *noun Fem.* table; **à table!** dinner's ready!; **se mettre à table** to sit down to eat; **mettre la table** to lay the table.

**tableau** *noun Masc.* **1** painting; **un tableau de Renoir** a painting by Renoir; **2 le tableau noir** the blackboard; **3 le tableau d'affichage** the notice board.

**tableau de bord** *noun Masc.* dashboard.

**table de chevet**, **table de nuit** *noun Fem.* bedside table.

**table des matières** *noun Fem.* (list of) contents (*in a book*).

**tablette** *noun Fem.* **une tablette de chocolat** a bar of chocolate.

**tablier** *noun Masc.* apron.

**tabouret** *noun Masc.* stool.

**tache** *noun Fem.* **1** stain; **2** spot.

a
b
c
d
e
f
g
h
i
j
k
l
m
n
o
p
q
r
s
t
u
v
w
x
y
z

**tâche** *noun Fem.* task.

**tache de rousseur** *noun Fem.* freckle.

**tacher** *verb* [1] to stain.

**tacle** *noun Masc.* tackle (*in rugby*).

**tact** *noun Masc.* tact; **il l'a fait avec beaucoup de tact** he did it very tactfully.

**tactique** *noun Fem.* tactics. **tactique** *adjective* tactical.

**tagueur** *noun Masc.* graffiti artist.

**taie** *noun Fem.* **une taie d'oreiller** a pillowcase.

**taille** *noun Fem.* **1** size; **qu'est-ce que vous avez à ma taille?** what have you got in my size?; **quelle taille faites-vous?** what size are you?; **'taille unique'** 'one size'; **la taille au-dessus/au-dessous** the next size up/down; **2** height; **un homme de grande taille** a tall man; **3** waist; **avoir la taille fine** to have a slim waist.

**taille-crayon** *noun Masc.* pencil sharpener.

**tailler** *verb* [1] **1** to cut; **2** to carve; **3** to prune; **4** to sharpen (*a pencil*).

**tailleur** *noun Masc.* **1** suit (*for a woman*); **2** tailor; ★ **s'asseoir en tailleur** to sit cross-legged (*literally: like a tailor*).

**taire** *verb* [76] **se taire** to stop talking; **taisez-vous!** be quiet!

**talent** *noun Masc.* talent; **c'est un jeune musicien de talent** he's a talented young musician.

**talon** *noun Masc.* **1** heel (*of your foot or a shoe*); **2** stub (*of a ticket or cheque book*).

**talon aiguille** *noun Masc.* stiletto heel.

**tambour** *noun Masc.* drum.

**tambourin** *noun Masc.* tambourine.

**Tamise** *noun Fem.* **la Tamise** the Thames.

**tampon** *noun Masc.* **1** pad (*for sponging*); **un tampon à récurer** a scouring pad; **2** **un tampon (hygiénique)** a tampon.

**tamponneuse** *adjective* **les autos tamponneuses** the dodgems.

**tandis que** *conjunction* while.

**tant** *adverb* **1** so much; **j'ai tant mangé que ...** I've eaten so much that ...; **ce qu'elle avait tant espéré** what she had so much hoped for; **je ne les aime pas tant que ça** I don't like them as much as that; **2** **tant de** so much, so many; **tant d'argent** so much money; **tant d'amis** so many friends; **tant de monde** so many people; **3** **tant pis** never mind; **4** **tant mieux** so much the better; **5** **tant que** while; **tant que tu y es, passe-moi un stylo** while you're there, pass me a pen; **6** **tant que** as long as; **tant que Jacques ne sera pas rentré, je ne peux pas sortir** I can't go out until Jacques gets back.

**tante** *noun Fem.* aunt.

**tantôt** *adverb* sometimes; **tantôt chez elle, tantôt chez moi** sometimes at her place and sometimes at mine.

**taper** *verb* [1] **1** **taper quelqu'un** to hit somebody; **ça tape aujourd'hui** the sun's really beating down today; **2** **taper à la machine** to type; **taper**

une lettre to type a letter; **3 taper des mains** to clap your hands; **taper du pied** to tap your foot; **4 taper à la porte** to knock on the door; **5** (*informal*) **se taper dessus** to knock each other about.

**tapis** *noun Masc.* carpet.

**tapis de bain** *noun Masc.* bathmat.

**tapis roulant** *noun Masc.* **1** walkway; **2** carousel (*for airport luggage*); **3** conveyor belt.

**tapisser** *verb* [1] **1** to wallpaper; **2** to upholster.

**tapisserie** *noun Fem.* **1** tapestry; **2** wallpaper.

**taquiner** *verb* [1] to tease.

**tard** *adverb* late; **couche-toi, il est tard** go to bed, it's late; **plus tard** later; **trop tard** too late; **pas plus tard que mardi** no later than Tuesday; **ce sera pour plus tard** there'll be other times.

**tarder** *verb* [1] to be a long time; **ta mère ne va pas tarder** your mother won't be long.

**tardif** (*Fem.* **tardive**) *adjective* late.

**tarif** *noun Masc.* **1** rate; **tarif de nuit** night rate (*for the phone*); **2** fare; **plein tarif** full fare; **tarif réduit** reduced fare; **3** price list.

**tarte** *noun Fem.* tart; **une tarte aux abricots** an apricot tart.

**tartine** *noun Fem.* slice of bread and butter (*and/or jam*).

**tartiner** *verb* [1] to spread (*on bread*).

**tas** *noun Masc.* **1** pile; **un tas de bois** a pile of wood; **2** batch; **un tas de**

lettres a batch of letters; **3** (*informal*) **un tas de** stacks of; **j'ai un tas de choses à faire ce soir** I've got stacks of things to do tonight.

**tasse** *noun Fem.* cup; **une tasse de thé** a cup of tea.

**tatie** *noun Fem.* (*informal*) auntie.

**taupe** *noun Fem.* mole (*animal*).

**taupinière** *noun Fem.* mole hill.

**taureau** (*plural* **taureaux**) *noun Masc.* bull.

**Taureau** *noun Masc.* Taurus (*sign of the Zodiac*).

**taux** *noun Masc.* rate; **le taux mensuel** the monthly rate; **le taux de change** the exchange rate.

**taxe** *noun Fem.* tax; **la boutique hors taxes** the duty-free shop.

**taxi** *noun Masc.* taxi; **appeler un taxi** to call a taxi.

**tchèque** *adjective* Czech; **la République tchèque** the Czech Republic.

**te, t'** (*before a vowel or silent 'h'*) *pronoun* you **1 Gaby te cherche** Gaby's looking for you; **il t'a vu** he saw you; **il te l'a donné** he gave it to you; **2** to you; **3** yourself; **tu peux te faire une salade** you can make yourself a salad; **tu t'es blessé?** have you hurt yourself?; **tu te lèves quand?** what time do you get up?

**technicien, technicienne** *noun Masc., Fem.* technician.

**technique** *noun Fem.* technique. **technique** *adjective* technical.

**technologie** *noun Fem.* technology.

a
b
c
d
e
f
g
h
i
j
k
l
m
n
o
p
q
r
s
**t**
u
v
w
x
y
z

**teckel** *noun Masc.* dachshund.

**tee-shirt** *noun Masc.* T-shirt.

**teint** *noun Masc.* complexion; **avoir le teint clair** to have a fair complexion.

**teinturier**, **teinturière** *noun Masc., Fem.* dry-cleaner's.

**tel**, **telle** *adjective* **1** such; **avec un tel intérêt** with such interest; **une telle aventure** such an adventure; **de tels mensonges** such lies; **2 tel que** such as; **les grandes villes telles que Paris et Lyon** large towns such as Paris and Lyons; **3 rien de tel que** nothing like; **il n'y a rien de tel qu'un bon repas** there's nothing like a good meal; **4 servir le saumon tel quel** serve the salmon just as it is; **je l'ai acheté tel quel** I bought it just as it was.

**télé** *noun Fem.* (*informal*) telly; **je l'ai vu à la télé** I saw it on telly.

**télécabine** *noun Masc.* cable car.

**télécarte™** *noun Fem.* phonecard.

**télécommande** *noun Fem.* remote control.

**télécopie** *noun Fem.* fax.

**télécopieur** *noun Masc.* fax machine, fax.

**téléphérique** *noun Masc.* cable car.

**téléphone** *noun Masc.* telephone; **un numéro de téléphone** a phone number; **Bruno est au téléphone** Bruno's on the phone.

**téléphone portable** *noun Masc.* mobile phone.

**téléphoner** *verb* [1] to phone; **je vais téléphoner à Robert** I'll phone Robert.

**téléphone sans fil** *noun Masc.* cordless phone.

**téléphonique** *adjective* **une cabine téléphonique** a phone box; **un appel téléphonique** a phone call.

**télésiège** *noun Masc.* chairlift.

**téléski** *noun Masc.* ski-tow.

**téléspectateur**, **téléspectatrice** *noun Masc., Fem.* viewer (*of TV*).

**téléviser** *verb* [1] to televize.

**téléviseur** *noun Masc.* television (set); **un téléviseur couleur** a colour television.

**télévision** *noun Fem.* television; **à la télévision** on television.

**telle** *adjective* SEE **tel**.

**tellement** *adverb* **1** so; **c'est tellement compliqué!** it's so complicated!; **2** so much; **c'est tellement mieux payé** it's so much better paid; **'tu aimes lire?'** – **'pas tellement'** 'do you like reading?' – 'not much'; **3 tellement de** so much, so many; **j'ai tellement de travail!** I've got so much work!; **il y a tellement de choses à voir!** there are so many things to see!; **il y avait tellement de monde** there were so many people there.

**tels**, **telles** *adjective* SEE **tel**.

**témoignage** *noun Masc.* **1** story, account; **selon les témoignages de l'accident** according to accounts of the accident; **2** evidence (*in court*);

**3 un témoignage d'amitié** a token of friendship.

**témoigner** *verb* [1] to give evidence.

**témoin** *noun Masc.* witness.

**température** *noun Fem.* temperature.

**tempête** *noun Fem.* storm.

**temple** *noun Masc.* **1** temple; **2** (Protestant) church.

**temporaire** *adjective* temporary.

**temps** *noun Masc.* **1** weather; **quel temps fait-il?** what's the weather like?; **par temps de pluie** in rainy weather; **2** time; **je n'ai pas le temps** I haven't got time; **il est temps de partir** it's time to go; **arriver à temps** to arrive in (*or* on) time; **de temps en temps** from time to time; **en même temps** at the same time; **ça a pris beaucoup de temps** it took a long time; **il nous reste combien de temps?** how much time do we have left?; **c'est du temps perdu** it's a waste of time; **il était temps!** about time too!; **ces derniers temps** recently; **un travail à plein temps** a full-time job; **un travail à temps partiel** a part-time job; **3** tense (*of a verb*).

**tendance** *noun Fem.* **1** tendency; **avoir tendance à faire** to tend to do; **2** trend.

**tendre**[1] *verb* [3] **1** to stretch (*something elastic*); **2** to hold out; **elle m'a tendu un crayon** she held out a pencil to me; **tendre la main à quelqu'un** to hold out one's hand to someone; **3 tendre le bras** to reach out.

**tendre**[2] *adjective* tender.

**tendresse** *noun Fem.* tenderness.

**tendu** *adjective* tense.

**tenir** *verb* [77] **1** to hold; **peux-tu tenir la corde?** can you hold the rope?; **elle tenait l'enfant par la main** she was holding the child by the hand; **2** to run (*a shop, a business*); **le stand est tenu par des bénévoles** the stand is run by volunteers; **3** to keep; **elle tenait les yeux baissés** she kept her eyes down; **'tenir hors de la portée des enfants'** 'keep out of reach of children'; **4** to take up; **cela tient la place de deux personnes** it takes up the space of two people; **5 tenir à** to be attached to; **elle tient beaucoup à ses petits-enfants** she's very attached to her grandchildren; **6 tenir à faire quelque chose** to be determined to do something; **je tiens à le finir aujourd'hui** I'm determined to finish it today; **7 tiens!** oh!; **tiens, il est déjà midi!** oh, it's twelve already!; **tiens! est-ce que je t'ai raconté ...?** listen! have I told you ...?; **tiens, tiens, c'est toi!** well, well, it's you!; **tiens, prends le mien** here, take mine; **8 tenir de quelqu'un** to take after someone; **elle tient de sa mère** she takes after her mother; **9 se tenir** to hold; **ils se tenaient par la main** they were holding each other by the hand; **10 se tenir** to stand; **elle se tenait devant l'entrée** she was standing by the entrance; **tiens-toi tranquille!** be quiet!; **tiens-toi droit!** stand up straight!; **11 se tenir pour**

a b c d e f g h i j k l m n o p q r s t u v w x y z

289

to think yourself; **il se tient pour un génie** he thinks he's a genius.

**tennis** *noun Masc.* **1** tennis; **jouer au tennis** to play tennis; **un terrain de tennis, un tennis** a tennis court; **tennis de table** table tennis; **2** tennis shoe.

**tension** *noun Fem.* **1** tension; **2** blood pressure.

**tentant** *adjective* tempting.

**tentation** *noun Fem.* temptation.

**tentative** *noun Fem.* attempt.

**tente** *noun Fem.* tent.

**tenter** *verb* [1] **1** to attempt; **il a tenté de s'échapper** he tried to escape; **tenter sa chance, tenter le coup** (*informal*) to give it a try; **2** to tempt.

**tenu** *adjective* **1** **bien/mal tenu** well/badly cared for; **2** **être tenu de faire** to be required to do.

**tenue** *noun Fem.* clothes; **être en tenue de sport** to be in sports kit; **en tenue de soirée** in evening dress.

**terme** *noun Masc.* **1** word, term; **un terme technique** a technical term; **les termes du contrat** the terms of the contract; **2** end; **à court terme** short-term; **à long terme** long-term.

**terminaison** *noun Fem.* ending.

**terminale** *noun Fem.* (*in a French school*) the equivalent of Year 13.

**terminer** *verb* [1] **1** to finish; **2** to end; **la réunion s'est terminée à dix-huit heures** the meeting ended at six p.m.; **ça va mal se terminer!** it'll end in tears!

**terminus** *noun Masc.* terminus.

**terrain** *noun Masc.* **1** ground, land; **il a acheté du terrain** he's bought some land; **2** pitch, ground (*for sports*); **un terrain de football** a football pitch; **un terrain de golf** a golf course; **3** piece of ground; **un terrain à bâtir** a building plot.

**terrain de camping** *noun Masc.* campsite.

**terrain de jeu(x)** *noun Masc.* playground.

**terrain de sport(s)** *noun Masc.* sports ground.

**terrain vague** *noun Masc.* waste ground.

**terrasse** *noun Fem.* terrace.

**terre** *noun Fem.* **1** ground; **s'asseoir par terre** to sit on the floor; **tomber par terre** to fall down; **2** **la Terre** the Earth; **3** soil; **4** land (*not sea*); **aller à terre** to go ashore.

**terre cuite** *noun Fem.* terracotta.

**terrible** *adjective* **1** terrible; **des événements terribles** terrible events; **2** (*informal*) terrific; **'c'était bien, le film?' – 'pas terrible'** 'was the film any good?' – 'not great'.

**terrifiant** *adjective* terrifying.

**terrifier** *verb* [1] terrify.

**terrine** *noun Fem.* pâté.

**territoire** *noun Masc.* **1** territory; **2** country; **il fera beau sur l'ensemble du territoire** the weather will be fine throughout the country.

**terrorisme** *noun Masc.* terrorism.

**terroriste** *noun Masc. & Fem.* terrorist.

**tes** *adjective* your; SEE **ton**[1].

**test** *noun Masc.* test.

**testament** *noun Masc.* will.

**tester** *verb* [1] to test.

**tétanos** *noun Masc.* tetanus.

**têtard** *noun Masc.* tadpole.

**tête** *noun Fem.* **1** head; **se laver la tête** to wash your hair; **j'ai la tête qui tourne** my head's spinning; **2** face; **je n'aime pas sa tête** I don't like his face; **3** top; **tu es en tête de la liste** you're first on the list; **4** mind; **j'ai quelque chose en tête** I have something in mind; **où avais-tu la tête?** what were you thinking of?; **5** front (*of a train*); **les deux wagons de tête sont à destination de Bourges** the two front coaches are for Bourges; ★ **faire la tête** to sulk; ★ **un dîner en tête à tête** a private dinner for two; ★ **j'en ai par-dessus la tête!** I'm fed up to the back teeth!

**têtu** *adjective* stubborn.

**texte** *noun Masc.* text.

**texto™** *noun Masc.* text message; **envoyer un texto à quelqu'un** to text someone.

**TGV** *noun Masc.* SHORT FOR **train à grande vitesse** high-speed train.

**thalassothérapie** *noun Fem.* sea-water treatment (*at a health spa*).

**thé** *noun Masc.* tea; **un thé au lait** tea with milk.

**théâtre** *noun Masc.* **1** theatre; **des costumes de théâtre** stage costumes; **un coup de théâtre** a dramatic turn of events; **2** plays; **le théâtre de Molière** Molière's plays;

**3 faire du théâtre** to belong to a drama group.

**théière** *noun Fem.* teapot.

**thème** *noun Masc.* **1** subject; **2** prose (*a text to translate into the foreign language*).

**théorie** *noun Fem.* theory.

**thérapie** *noun Fem.* **1** (medical) treatment; **2** therapy.

**thermal** (*Masc. plural* **thermaux**) *adjective* thermal; **une station thermale** a spa.

**thermomètre** *noun Masc.* thermometer.

**thermos™** *noun Masc.* vacuum flask, thermos™.

**thon** *noun Masc.* tuna.

**thym** *noun Masc.* thyme.

**tibia** *noun Masc.* **1** shin; **2** shinbone.

**tic** *noun Masc.* nervous twitch.

**ticket** *noun Masc.* **1** ticket; **un ticket de métro** an underground ticket; **2 un ticket de caisse** a till receipt.

**tiède** *adjective* **1** warm; **2** lukewarm.

**tien, tienne, tiens, tiennes** *pronoun* **le tien, la tienne, les tiens, les tiennes** yours; **est-ce que ce stylo est le tien?** is this pen yours?; **ma voiture et la tienne** my car and yours; **mes lettres et les tiennes** my letters and yours.

**tiens** *verb* SEE **tenir**
**tiens** *pronoun* SEE **tien**.

**tiers** *noun Masc.* third; **les deux tiers de la population** two-thirds of the population.
**tiers** (*Fem.* **tierce**) *adjective* third.

# tiers-monde

**tiers-monde** *noun Masc.* Third World.

**tige** *noun Fem.* stem.

**tigre** *noun Masc.* tiger.

**tilleul** *noun Masc.* 1 lime tree; 2 lime flower tea.

**timbre** *noun Masc.* stamp.

**timide** *adjective* 1 shy; 2 self-conscious.

**timidité** *noun Fem.* shyness.

**tiquer** *verb* [1] **sans tiquer** without batting an eyelid.

**tir** *noun Masc.* 1 shooting; 2 shot (*in football*).

**tirage** *noun Masc.* **le tirage au sort** the draw (*in a lottery, for example*); **par tirage au sort** by drawing lots.

**tir à l'arc** *noun Masc.* archery.

**tire-bouchon** *noun Masc.* corkscrew.

**tirelire** *noun Fem.* money box.

**tirer** *verb* [1] 1 to pull; **il m'a tiré par le bras** he pulled my arm; **elle m'a tiré les cheveux** she pulled my hair; 2 to draw; **tirer les rideaux** to draw the curtains; **il a tiré la lettre de sa poche** he drew the letter from his pocket; **tirer un trait** to draw a line; **tirer des conclusions** to draw conclusions; **tirer au sort** to draw lots; 3 to fire; **ils ont tiré sur les policiers** they fired on the police; **tirer plusieurs coups de feu** to fire several shots.

**tiret** *noun Masc.* dash.

**tiroir** *noun Masc.* drawer.

**tisane** *noun Fem.* herbal tea.

**tisonnier** *noun Masc.* poker (*for fire*).

**tissu** *noun Masc.* material, fabric.

**titre** *noun Masc.* 1 title; 2 headline; **les titres de l'actualité** the news headlines; 3 **à juste titre** quite rightly; **à titre d'exemple** as an example.

**titre de transport** *noun Masc.* travel ticket.

**tituber** *verb* [1] to stagger.

**toast** *noun Masc.* 1 piece of toast; **servir avec des toasts** serve with toast; 2 toast (*to someone's health*).

**toboggan** *noun Masc.* slide.

**toi** *pronoun* you; **c'est toi!** it's you!; **avec toi** with you; **plus grand que toi** bigger than you; **c'est à toi de jouer** it's your turn; **assieds-toi** sit down; **est-ce que ces chaussettes sont à toi?** are these socks yours?

**toile** *noun Fem.* 1 cloth; **toile de lin** linen; **une toile cirée** an oilcloth; 2 painting, canvas; **une toile de Picasso** a painting by Picasso.

**Toile** *noun Fem.* **la Toile** the Web.

**toile d'araignée** *noun Fem.* spider's web, cobweb.

**toilette** *noun Fem.* 1 **faire sa toilette** to have a wash; 2 outfit; **je me suis acheté une toilette pour le mariage de ma sœur** I've bought an outfit for my sister's wedding.

**toilettes** *plural noun Fem.* toilet; **aller aux toilettes** to go to the toilet.

**toi-même** *pronoun* yourself; **l'as-tu fait toi-même?** did you make it yourself?

**toit** *noun Masc.* roof.

**tolérant** *adjective* tolerant.

**tolérer** *verb* [24] to tolerate.

**tomate** *noun Fem.* tomato; **une salade de tomates** a tomato salad.

**tombe** *noun Fem.* grave.

**tombeau** (*plural* **tombeaux**) *noun Masc.* tomb.

**tomber** *verb* [1] **1** to fall; **attention, tu vas tomber!** careful, you'll fall!; **la chaise est tombée** the chair fell over; **Noël tombe un lundi** Christmas falls on a Monday; **2 laisser tomber** to drop; **j'ai laissé tomber mon porte-monnaie** I've dropped my purse; **3 laisser tomber** to give up (*an activity*); **elle a laissé tomber l'espagnol** she's given up Spanish; **4 tomber malade** to fall ill; **tomber amoureux** to fall in love; **5 tomber sur** to bump into; **je suis tombé sur Georges devant la poste** I bumped into Georges outside the post office; **6 ça tombe bien** that's lucky; ★ **je tombe de sommeil** I can't keep my eyes open (*literally: I'm dropping with sleep*).

**tombola** *noun Fem.* tombola, lottery.

**ton**[1], **ta**, **tes** *adjective* your; **ton chat** your cat; **ta sœur** your sister; **tes pieds** your feet.

**ton**[2] *noun Masc.* **1** tone of voice; **2** colour.

**tondeuse** *noun Fem.* lawnmower.

**tondre** *verb* [3] to mow.

**tonique** *adjective* bracing.

**tonne** *noun Fem.* tonne, metric ton (*1,000 kg*); ★ **j'ai des tonnes de choses à faire** (*informal*) I've loads of things to do.

**tonneau** (*plural* **tonneaux**) *noun Masc.* barrel.

**tonnerre** *noun Masc.* thunder.

**tonton** *noun Masc.* (*informal*) uncle.

**tonus** *noun Masc.* **1** energy (*for a person*); **2** tone (*for your muscles*).

**toque** *noun Fem.* chef's hat.

**torchon** *noun Masc.* cloth, tea towel.

**tordre** *verb* [3] to twist; **se tordre la cheville** to twist your ankle.

**tordu** *adjective* **1** bent; **2** crooked; **3** weird; **une histoire tordue** a weird story.

**tornade** *noun Fem.* tornado.

**torrent** *noun Masc.* waterfall, mountain stream.

**torse** *noun Masc.* chest, upper body; **il s'est mis torse nu** he stripped to the waist.

**tort** *noun Masc.* **1 avoir tort** to be wrong; **je crois que tu as tort** I think you're wrong; **il a tort de dire ça** he's wrong to say that; **2 à tort** wrongly; **à tort ou à raison** rightly or wrongly.

**torticolis** *noun Masc.* stiff neck; **avoir le torticolis** to have a stiff neck.

**tortiller** *verb* [1] **se tortiller** to wriggle.

**tortue** *noun Fem.* tortoise, turtle.

**torture** *noun Fem.* torture.

**torturer** *verb* [1] to torture.

**tôt** *adverb* **1** early; **on va partir tôt** we're leaving early; **tôt le matin** early in the morning; **2** soon; **le plus tôt possible** as soon as possible; **tôt ou tard** sooner or later.

a

**total** (*plural* **totaux**) *noun Masc.*
total; **au total** in total.
**total** (*Masc. plural* **totaux**) *adjective*
total.

b

c

**totalement** *adverb* totally.

d

**totalité** *noun Fem.* **la totalité des
élèves** all the pupils; **la totalité du
groupe** the whole group.

e

f

**touchant** *adjective* touching.

g

**touche** *noun Fem.* **1** key (*on a piano
or keyboard*); **2** button (*on a
machine*); **la touche
d'enregistrement** the record
button; **appuyez sur la touche**
press the button; **3** (**ligne de**)
**touche** touchline.

h

i

j

k

**toucher** *verb* [1] **1** to touch; **ne
touche pas à ma peinture** don't
touch my painting; **2** to touch; **cette
histoire m'a beaucoup touché** that
story really touched me; **3** to affect,
to concern; **ce problème nous
touche tous** this problem affects us
all; **4** to get (*money or wages*); **il
touche 350 euros par semaine**
he's getting 350 euros a week.

l

m

n

o

p

**touffu** *adjective* bushy, thick.

q

r

**toujours** *adverb* **1** always; **il est
toujours en retard** he's always late;
**comme toujours** as always; **2** still;
**nous habitons toujours au même
endroit** we're still living in the same
place; **ton paquet n'est toujours
pas arrivé** your parcel still hasn't
come; **3 pour toujours** for ever.

s

t

u

v

**tour**[1] *noun Masc.* **1 faire le tour de** to
go round; **faire le tour des
magasins** to go round all the shops;
**faire le tour du monde** to go round
the world; **2 faire un tour** to go for a

w

x

y

z

walk; **on va faire un petit tour** we'll
go for a little walk; **3 faire un tour à
vélo** to go for a bike ride; **4 faire un
tour en voiture** to go for a drive;
**5** turn; **c'est ton tour de jouer** it's
your turn to play; **à qui le tour?**
whose turn is it?

**tour**[2] *noun Fem.* **1** tower; **la tour
Eiffel** the Eiffel Tower; **2** tower
block; **3** castle, rook (*in chess*).

**tourbillon** *noun Masc.* whirlwind,
whirlpool.

**tourisme** *noun Masc.* tourism.

**touriste** *noun Masc. & Fem.* tourist.

**touristique** *adjective* **un guide
touristique** a tourist guide(book);
**une ville touristique** a town which
attracts tourists.

**tourmenter** *verb* [1] to tease.

**tournant** *noun Masc.* **1** bend (*in a
road*); **2** turning-point.

**tourne-disque** *noun Masc.* record
player.

**tournée** *noun Fem.* **1** round (*of a
postman or baker, for example*);
**2** round (*of drinks*); **c'est ma
tournée** it's my round; **3** tour (*of a
performer*); **être en tournée** to be on
tour.

**tourner** *verb* [1] **1** to turn; **tournez
à gauche à l'église** turn left at the
church; **2** to toss (*a salad*); **3 mal
tourner** to go wrong; **4 se tourner** to
turn; **elle s'est tournée vers moi**
she turned to face me; **5 tourner le
dos à quelqu'un** to have your back
to somebody.

**tournesol** *noun Masc.* sunflower.

**tournevis** *noun Masc.* screwdriver.

**tournis** *noun Masc.* **avoir le tournis** to feel dizzy; **j'ai le tournis** I'm feeling dizzy.

**tournoi** *noun Masc.* tournament.

**tourterelle** *noun Fem.* turtle dove.

**tous** *adjective, pronoun* SEE **tout**.

**Toussaint** *noun Fem.* All Saints' Day (*November 1st*).

**tousser** *verb* [1] to cough.

**tout**, **toute**, **tous**, **toutes** *adjective* 1 all; **tout le pain** all the bread; **toute la classe** all the class, the whole class; **tous les garçons** all the boys; **toutes les filles** all the girls; **tout le monde** everybody; **toute la journée** all day; **tous les deux** both; **je les achète tous les trois** I'll buy all three of them; **pendant toute une année** for a whole year; 2 any; **à tout âge** at any age; **à tout instant** at any moment; **'service à toute heure'** 'service at any time'; 3 every; **tous les jours** every day; **prenez un comprimé toutes les quatre heures** take one pill every four hours.

**tout**, **toutes**, **tous**, **toutes** *pronoun* 1 everything; **ils ont tout pris** they took everything; **tout va bien** everything's fine; 2 all; **tous ensemble** all together; **elles étaient toutes là** they were all there; **54 en tout** 54 in all; **et tout ça** and all that; **tout ce que je sais, c'est que ...** all I know is that ...; **3 pas du tout** not at all.

**tout** *adverb* **c'est tout prêt** it's all ready; **il est tout seul** he's all alone; **tout doucement** very slowly; **tout droit** straight ahead.

**tout à coup** *adverb* suddenly.

**tout à fait** *adverb* completely, absolutely; **ce n'est pas tout à fait sec** it's not absolutely dry.

**tout à l'heure** *adverb* 1 just now; **je l'ai vu tout à l'heure** I saw him just now; 2 in a little while; **à tout à l'heure!** see you later!.

**tout de même** *adverb* all the same; **c'est tout de même bizarre** all the same, it is odd.

**tout de suite** *adverb* at once; **fais-le tout de suite!** do it at once!

**tout d'un coup** *adverb* suddenly.

**toutefois** *adverb* however.

**toutes** *adjective, pronoun* SEE **tout**.

**toux** *noun Fem.* cough.

**toxicomane** *noun Masc. & Fem.* drug addict.

**toxique** *adjective* poisonous, toxic.

**trac** *noun Masc.* (*informal*) **avoir le trac** to feel nervous.

**trace** *noun Fem.* 1 tracks; **des traces de skis** ski-tracks; **des traces de pas** footprints; 2 mark; **des traces de doigts** finger marks.

**tracer** *verb* [61] to draw.

**tracteur** *noun Masc.* tractor.

**tradition** *noun Fem.* tradition.

**traditionnel** (*Fem.* **traditionnelle**) *adjective* traditional.

**traducteur**, **traductrice** *noun Masc., Fem.* translator.

**traduction** *noun Fem.* translation.

**traduire** *verb* [26] to translate; **traduire en français** to translate into French.

**trafic** *noun Masc.* 1 **le trafic de drogue** drug dealing; 2 traffic.

a
b
c
d
e
f
g
h
i
j
k
l
m
n
o
p
q
r
s
t
u
v
w
x
y
z

a
b
c
d
e
f
g
h
i
j
k
l
m
n
o
p
q
r
s
t
u
v
w
x
y
z

**trafiquant, trafiquante** *noun Masc., Fem.* dealer (*in drugs or arms*).

**tragédie** *noun Fem.* tragedy.

**tragique** *adjective* tragic.

**trahir** *verb* [2] to betray.

**trahison** *noun Fem.* betrayal.

**train** *noun Masc.* 1 train; **monter dans le train** to get on the train; **descendre du train** to get off the train; **le train de dix heures** the ten o'clock train; 2 **être en train de faire** to be (busy) doing; **Henri est en train de faire la vaisselle** Henri's doing the washing-up.

**traîner** *verb* [1] 1 to wander round; 2 to lie around; **il laisse ses affaires traîner partout** he leaves his things lying around everywhere; 3 to dawdle; **ne traînez pas, le train arrive** don't be long, the train's coming; 4 to drag on; **j'ai des projets qui traînent** I've got some projects that are dragging on; 5 to drag; **elle traînait sa valise derrière elle** she was dragging her suitcase behind her; 6 **traîner les pieds** to drag your feet.

**traire** *verb* [78] to milk.

**trait** *noun Masc.* 1 line; 2 **les traits** features (*of a face*); **avoir les traits fins** to have delicate features; 3 **d'un seul trait** at one go; **il l'a bu d'un seul trait** he drank it all at one go.

**trait d'union** *noun Masc.* hyphen.

**traité** *noun Masc.* treaty.

**traitement** *noun Masc.* 1 treatment; 2 processing; **le traitement de texte** word processing; 3 salary.

**traiter** *verb* [1] 1 to treat; **il la traite très mal** he treats her very badly; **le médecin qui me traite** the doctor who's treating me; 2 to deal with (*a question or problem*); 3 **traiter de** to call; **il m'a traité de menteur** he called me a liar.

**traiteur** *noun Masc.* caterer.

**trajet** *noun Masc.* 1 journey; **c'est un trajet de deux heures** it's a two-hour journey; 2 route.

**trampoline** *noun Masc.* trampoline; **faire du trampoline** to trampoline.

**tramway** *noun Masc.* tram, tramway.

**tranchant** *adjective* sharp.

**tranche** *noun Fem.* 1 slice; **deux tranches de jambon** two slices of ham; 2 phase, period (*of time*).

**trancher** *verb* [1] 1 to slice; 2 to decide.

**tranquille** *adjective* 1 quiet; **une rue tranquille** a quiet street; **tiens-toi tranquille!** be quiet!; 2 **laisse-moi tranquille!** leave me alone!; 3 **maman n'est pas tranquille si je n'appelle pas** Mum worries if I don't ring.

**tranquillité** *noun Fem.* peace.

**transat** *noun Masc.* (*informal*) deck chair.

**transférer** *verb* [24] to transfer.

**transfert** *noun Masc.* transfer.

**transformer** *verb* [1] 1 to change; **ils ont transformé leur jardin** they've completely changed their garden; **nous avons transformé cette chambre en bureau** we've

turned this bedroom into a study;
**2 se transformer en** to change into;
**le têtard se transforme en
grenouille** the tadpole changes into
a frog.

**transfusion** *noun Fem.* **une
transfusion sanguine** a blood
transfusion.

**transistor** *noun Masc.* transistor.

**transmettre** *verb* [11]
**1 transmettre quelque chose à
quelqu'un** to pass something on to
somebody; **2** to transmit.

**transpiration** *noun Fem.*
perspiration, sweat.

**transpirer** *verb* [1] to sweat.

**transplantation** *noun Fem.*
**1** transplant (*medical*);
**2** transplantation (*of plants*).

**transport** *noun Masc.* **1** transport;
**les frais de transport** transport
costs; **2 les transports en commun**
public transport.

**transporter** *verb* [1] **1** to
transport; **2** to carry.

**trappe** *noun Fem.* trap door.

**travail** (*plural* **travaux**) *noun Masc.*
**1** work; **j'ai beaucoup de travail à
faire** I've got a lot of work to do;
**2** job; **je cherche un travail** I'm
looking for a job.

**travailler** *verb* [1] to work;
**travailler dans la banque** to work
in banking.

**travailleur, travailleuse**
*noun Masc., Fem.* worker.
**travailleur** (*Fem.* **travailleuse**)
*adjective* hard-working.

**travailliste** *adjective* Labour; **le
parti travailliste** the Labour party
(*in Britain*).

**travaux** *plural noun Masc.* **1** work;
**des travaux de construction**
building work; **ils font faire des
travaux chez eux** they're having
some work done on the house;
**2** roadworks; **3 les travaux
ménagers** housework; **4 les
travaux dirigés** classwork; **les
travaux manuels** handicrafts.

**travée** *noun Fem.* bay (*for coaches*).

**travers** *noun* **1 à travers** through;
**j'ai regardé à travers les rideaux** I
looked through the curtains;
**voyager à travers le monde** to
travel all over the world; **2 de
travers** crooked; **le tableau est de
travers** the picture's crooked; **3 de
travers** wrongly; **c'est boutonné
de travers** it's buttoned up wrongly.

**traversée** *noun Fem.* crossing; **une
traversée de l'Atlantique** an
Atlantic crossing.

**traverser** *verb* [1] **1** to cross;
**regarde avant de traverser la rue**
look before you cross the road; **2** to
go through; **traverser la France
pour aller en Italie** to go through
France on the way to Italy; **la pluie a
traversé ma veste** the rain's gone
right through my jacket; **ils ont
traversé une crise** they went
through a crisis.

**traversin** *noun Masc.* bolster.

**trébucher** *verb* [1] to stumble.

**trèfle** *noun Masc.* **1** clover; **2** clubs
(*in cards*); **la dame de trèfle** the
queen of clubs.

**treize** *number* thirteen; **Aurélie a treize ans** Aurélie's thirteen; **à treize heures** at one p.m.; **le treize juillet** the thirteenth of July.

**treizième** *number* thirteenth.

**tremblement de terre** *noun Masc.* earthquake.

**trembler** *verb* [1] to shake, to tremble.

**trempé** *adjective* soaked.

**tremper** *verb* [1] to soak.

**tremplin** *noun Masc.* springboard.

**trentaine** *noun Fem.* **1** about thirty; **une trentaine de personnes** about thirty people; **2 elle a la trentaine** she's in her thirties.

**trente** *number* thirty; **elle a trente ans** she's thirty; **le trente juillet** the thirtieth of July.

**très** *adverb* very; **très heureux** very happy; **j'ai très faim** I'm very hungry; **très bien fait** very well done.

**trésor** *noun Masc.* treasure.

**tresse** *noun Fem.* plait.

**tréteau** (*plural* **tréteaux**) *noun Masc.* trestle.

**triangulaire** *adjective* triangular.

**tribu** *noun Fem.* tribe.

**tribunal** (*plural* **tribunaux**) *noun Masc.* court; **paraître devant le tribunal** to appear in court (*on a charge*).

**tricher** *verb* [1] to cheat.

**tricolore** *adjective* three-coloured; **le drapeau tricolore** the French flag (*which is three-coloured, blue, white, and red, in vertical stripes*).

**tricoter** *verb* [1] to knit.

**trier** *verb* [1] to sort (out); **hier soir nous avons trié toutes les photos** last night we sorted out all the photographs.

**trimestre** *noun Masc.* term.

**trinidadien** (*Fem.* **trinidadienne**) *adjective* Trinidadian.

**Trinidadien, Trinidadienne** *noun Masc., Fem.* Trinidadian.

**Trinité** *noun Fem.* **(l'île de) la Trinité** Trinidad.

**triomphe** *noun Masc.* triumph.

**triompher** *verb* [1] to triumph.

**tripes** *plural noun Fem.* tripe.

**triple** *noun Masc.* **le triple** three times as much.

**tripler** *verb* [1] to treble; **le prix a triplé** the price has tripled.

**triplés** *plural noun Masc.* triplets.

**triste** *adjective* sad.

**tristesse** *noun Fem.* sadness.

**trognon** *noun Masc.* **un trognon de pomme** an apple core.

**trois** *number* three; **Tom a trois ans** Tom's three; **à trois heures** at three o'clock; **le trois mars** the third of March; ★ **être haut comme trois pommes** to be knee-high to a grasshopper (*literally: as tall as three apples*).

**troisième** *noun Fem.* (*in a French school*) the equivalent of Year 10. **troisième** *noun Masc.* **au troisième** on the third floor. **troisième** *adjective* third.

**trombone** *noun Masc.* **1** trombone; **2** paperclip (*because of its shape*).

**trompe** *noun Fem.* trunk (*elephant's*).

**tromper** *verb* [1] **1** to deceive; **2 se tromper** to make a mistake; **il s'est trompé** he made a mistake; **je me suis trompé de train** I got the wrong train; **vous vous êtes trompé de numéro** you've got the wrong number.

**trompette** *noun Fem.* trumpet; **jouer de la trompette** to play the trumpet.

**tronc** *noun Masc.* trunk (*of a tree*).

**tronçonneuse** *noun Fem.* chain saw.

**trop** *adverb* **1** too; **c'est trop loin** it's too far; **c'est beaucoup trop cher** it's much too expensive; **2** too much; **j'ai trop mangé** I've eaten too much; **tu m'en as donné trop** you've given me too much; **3 trop de** too much, too many; **trop de pain** too much bread; **trop de tomates** too many tomatoes; **trop de monde** too many people; **4 de trop** too many, too much; **il y a une chaise de trop** there's one chair too many; **il y a dix euros de trop** that's ten euros too much.

**tropique** *noun Masc.* tropic.

**trottoir** *noun Masc.* pavement.

**trou** *noun Masc.* hole; **le trou dans la couche d'ozone** the hole in the ozone layer.

**troublant** *adjective* disturbing.

**trou d'incendie** *noun Masc.* fire hydrant.

**trou de serrure** *noun Masc.* keyhole.

**trouer** *verb* [1] to make a hole in; **des chaussettes trouées** socks with holes in them.

**trouille** *noun Fem.* **avoir la trouille** (*informal*) to be scared.

**troupe** *noun Fem.* **1 une troupe de théâtre** a theatre company; **2** flock (*of birds*); **3** troop (*of tourists or children*).

**troupeau** (*plural* **troupeaux**) *noun Masc.* herd (*of cattle*), flock (*of sheep*).

**trousse** *noun Fem.* pencil case.

**trousseau** (*plural* **trousseaux**) *noun Masc.* **un trousseau de clés** a bunch of keys.

**trousse de maquillage** *noun Fem.* make-up bag.

**trousse de secours** *noun Fem.* first-aid kit.

**trousse de toilette** *noun Fem.* toilet bag.

**trouver** *verb* [1] **1** to find; **as-tu trouvé ton passeport?** did you find your passport?; **2** to think; **j'ai trouvé le film passionnant** I thought the film was wonderful; **3 se trouver** to be (*in a place*); **les gens qui se trouvaient autour de moi** the people who were around me; **savez-vous où se trouve la gare routière?** do you know where the bus station is?

**truc** *noun Masc.* (*informal*) **1** thing; **un petit truc en bois** a little thing made of wood; **il y a un truc qui ne va pas** something's wrong; **le jazz, ce n'est pas mon truc** jazz just isn't my thing; **2** trick; **il doit y avoir un truc** there must be a trick to it.

a
b
c
d
e
f
g
h
i
j
k
l
m
n
o
p
q
r
s
t
u
v
w
x
y
z

a
b
c
d
e
f
g
h
i
j
k
l
m
n
o
p
q
r
s
**t**
**u**
v
w
x
y
z

**truite** *noun Fem.* trout.

**tsigane** *noun Masc. & Fem.* gipsy.

**TSVP** SHORT FOR **tournez s'il vous plaît** PTO (*please turn over*).

**TTC** SHORT FOR **toutes taxes comprises** inclusive of tax.

**tu** *pronoun* you (*'tu' is used when talking to family members, people you know well, and people of your own age; otherwise 'vous' is used for 'you'*).

**tube** *noun Masc.* **1** tube; **2** (*informal*) hit (*a pop song*).

**tuer** *verb* [1] **1** to kill; **2 se tuer** to be killed; **elle s'est tuée dans un accident de voiture** she was killed in a car accident; **3 se tuer** to kill yourself.

**tue-tête** *in phrase* **crier à tue-tête** to shout at the top of your voice.

**tuile** *noun Fem.* **1** tile; **2** thin almond biscuit.

**tulipe** *noun Fem.* tulip.

**Tunisie** *noun Fem.* Tunisia.

**tunisien** (*Fem.* **tunisienne**) *adjective* Tunisian.

**tunnel** *noun Masc.* tunnel; **le tunnel sous la Manche** the Channel Tunnel.

**turban** *noun Masc.* turban.

**turc** *noun Masc.* Turkish (*language*). **turc** (*Fem.* **turque**) *adjective* Turkish.

**Turc**, **Turque** *noun Masc., Fem.* Turk.

**Turquie** *noun Fem.* Turkey.

**tuteur**, **tutrice** *noun Masc., Fem.* **1** guardian; **2** tutor.

**tutoyer** *verb* [39] to address somebody as 'tu' (*rather than 'vous'*); **il ne faut pas tutoyer ton professeur** you mustn't address your teacher as 'tu'; **et si on se tutoyait?** shall we say 'tu' to each other?

**tuyau** (*plural* **tuyaux**) *noun Masc.* **1** pipe; **2** (*informal*) tip (*a helpful hint*).

**tuyau d'arrosage** *noun Masc.* hosepipe.

**TVA** *noun Fem.* SHORT FOR **taxe à la valeur ajoutée** VAT.

**type** *noun Masc.* **1** kind; **quel type de papier?** what type of paper?; **2** (*informal*) guy; **le type qui a ouvert la porte** the guy who opened the door.

**typique** *adjective* typical.

**tyranniser** *verb* [1] to bully.

**tzigane** *noun Masc. & Fem., adjective* gypsy.

# Uu

**ulcère** *noun Masc.* ulcer.

**un**, **une** (*plural* **des**) *article, pronoun, number* **1** a, an; **un lion** a lion; **une fraise** a strawberry; **des cerises** (some) cherries; **2** one; **un pour moi** one for me; **un par un** one by one; **trente et une personnes** thirty-one people; **les uns pensent que ...** some think that ...; **un jour sur deux** every other day; **3 l'un(e) et l'autre** the one and the other; **l'un est français et l'autre est**

**allemand** one's French and the other's German; **4 l'un(e) ou l'autre** either of them; **tu peux prendre l'un ou l'autre, ça n'a pas d'importance** you can take either of them, it doesn't matter.

**uni** *adjective* **1** close-knit (*family or group*); **2** plain (*not patterned*); **un tissu uni** a plain fabric.

**uniforme** *noun Masc.* uniform.

**union** *noun Fem.* union; **l'ex-Union soviétique** the former Soviet Union.

**Union européenne** *noun Fem.* European Union.

**unique** *adjective* **1** only; **elle est fille unique** she's an only child; **il est fils unique** he's an only child; **l'unique raison** the only reason; **2** single; **'prix unique'** 'all one price'; **3** unique.

**uniquement** *adverb* only.

**unité** *noun Fem.* **1** unity; **2** unit (*of currency, measurement, etc*).

**unité de disques** *noun Fem.* disk drive.

**univers** *noun Masc.* universe.

**universitaire** *adjective* university (*degree, town*), academic (*work*).

**université** *noun Fem.* university.

**urbanisme** *noun Masc.* town planning.

**urgence** *noun Fem.* **1** urgency; **il y a urgence!** it's urgent!; **2 d'urgence** immediately, at once; **il faut téléphoner d'urgence** you must phone at once; **3** emergency; **les urgences, le service des**

**urgences** accident and emergency, the casualty department.

**urgent** *adjective* urgent.

**USA** *plural noun Masc.* USA; **aux USA** in (*or* to) the USA.

**usage** *noun Masc.* **1** use; **à l'usage** with use; **en usage** in use; **à usage externe** for external use only; **2 'hors d'usage'** 'not in service'.

**usagé** *adjective* **1** worn; **2** used.

**usager** *noun Masc.* user.

**usé** *adjective* worn.

**user** *verb* [1] to wear out (*shoes, clothing*).

**usine** *noun Fem.* factory.

**ustensile** *noun Masc.* utensil.

**utile** *adjective* useful.

**utilisable** *adjective* usable.

**utilisateur, utilisatrice** *noun Masc., Fem.* user.

**utiliser** *verb* [1] to use.

**utilité** *noun Fem.* usefulness; **un livre d'une grande utilité** a very useful book.

**va** *verb* SEE **aller**.

**vacances** *plural noun Fem.* holidays; **les vacances scolaires** the school holidays; **les grandes vacances** the summer holidays; **être en vacances** to be on holiday; **bonnes vacances!** have a good holiday!

**vacancier**, **vacancière** noun Masc., Fem. holiday-maker.

**vacarme** noun Masc. din; **ils faisaient un vacarme pas possible!** they were making an amazing din!

**vaccination** noun Fem. vaccination.

**vacciner** verb [1] to vaccinate; **se faire vacciner** to be vaccinated.

**vache** noun Fem. cow.
**vache** adjective mean.

**vachement** adverb (informal) really; **c'était vachement bien!** it was really good!

**va-et-vient** noun Masc. coming and going.

**vagabond** noun Masc. tramp.

**vagin** noun Masc. vagina.

**vague**¹ noun Fem. wave (in the sea).

**vague**² adjective vague.

**vaguement** adverb vaguely.

**vain** adjective **1** useless; **2 en vain** in vain.

**vaincre** verb [79] **1** to defeat; **2** to overcome.

**vainqueur** noun Masc. winner.

**vais** verb SEE **aller**.

**vaisseau** (plural **vaisseaux**) noun Masc. vessel.

**vaisselle** noun Fem. dishes; **faire la vaisselle** to do the washing-up.

**valable** adjective valid.

**valet** noun Masc. jack; **le valet de pique** the jack of spades.

**valeur** noun Fem. value; **des objets de valeur** valuables; **c'est sans valeur** it's of no value.

**valider** verb [1] to stamp (a ticket).

**valise** noun Fem. suitcase; **faire ses valises** to pack.

**vallée** noun Fem. valley.

**valoir** verb [80] **1** to be worth; **ça vaut combien?** how much is it worth?; **ce tableau vaut cher** that painting's worth a lot; **2 valoir la peine** to be worth it; **ça ne vaut pas la peine d'y aller s'il pleut** it's not worth going if it's raining; **ça vaudrait la peine d'essayer** it would be worth a try; **3 il vaut mieux faire** it would be better to do; **il vaut mieux téléphoner avant** it would be better to phone first.

**valse** noun Fem. waltz.

**vampire** noun Masc. vampire.

**vandalisme** noun Masc. vandalism.

**vanille** noun Fem. vanilla; **une glace à la vanille** a vanilla ice cream.

**vanter** verb [1] **se vanter** to boast.

**vapeur** noun Fem. steam; **faire cuire des légumes à la vapeur** to steam vegetables.

**vaporisateur** noun Masc. (perfume) spray.

**variable** adjective variable, changeable.

**varicelle** noun Fem. chickenpox; **avoir la varicelle** to have chickenpox.

**varié** adjective varied, various; **'sandwichs variés'** 'a selection of sandwiches'.

**varier** verb [1] to vary.

**variété** *noun Fem.* **1** variety; **2 un spectacle de variétés** a variety show.

**vas** *verb* SEE **aller**.

**vase**[1] *noun Masc.* vase.

**vase**[2] *noun Fem.* mud.

**vaste** *adjective* large, enormous.

**va-vite** *adverb Fem.* **à la va-vite** in a rush.

**veau** (*plural* **veaux**) *noun Masc.* **1** calf; **2** veal.

**vécu** *verb* SEE **vivre**.

**vedette** *noun Fem.* star; **une vedette de cinéma** a film star.

**végétal** *adjective* vegetable; **l'huile végétale** vegetable oil.

**végétarien**, **végétarienne** *noun Masc., Fem.*
**végétarien** (*Fem.* **végétarienne**) *adjective* vegetarian.

**véhicule** *noun Masc.* vehicle.

**veille** *noun Fem.* **la veille** the day before; **je l'avais rencontrée la veille de mon départ** I met her the day before my departure; **la veille de Noël** Christmas Eve; **la veille du jour de l'an** New Year's Eve.

**veilleuse** *noun Fem.* **1** night-light; **2** pilot light.

**veinard** *noun Masc.* (*informal*) **petit veinard!** you lucky little devil!

**veine** *noun Fem.* **1 avoir de la veine** (*informal*) to be lucky; **2** vein.

**vélo** *noun Masc.* bike; **je suis venu à vélo** I came by bike; **faire du vélo** to go cycling.

**vélodrome** *noun Masc.* cycle-racing track, velodrome.

**vélomoteur** *noun Masc.* moped.

**vélo tout-terrain** *noun Masc.* mountain bike.

**velours** *noun Masc.* **1** velvet; **2** corduroy.

**velouté** *noun Masc.* cream soup; **velouté de champignons** cream of mushroom soup.

**vendanges** *plural noun Fem.* grape harvest.

**vendeur**, **vendeuse** *noun Masc., Fem.* **1** shop assistant; **2** salesperson; **3** seller.

**vendre** *verb* [3] to sell; **vendre quelque chose à quelqu'un** to sell somebody something; **j'ai vendu mon ordinateur à Colette** I've sold my computer to Colette; **'à vendre'** 'for sale'; **'vendu'** 'sold'.

**vendredi** *noun Masc.* **1** Friday; **nous sommes vendredi aujourd'hui** it's Friday today; **vendredi dernier** last Friday; **vendredi prochain** next Friday; **2** on Friday; **je l'ai vu vendredi soir** I saw him on Friday evening; **3** on Fridays; **fermé le vendredi** closed on Fridays; **4 tous les vendredis** every Friday; **le vendredi saint** Good Friday.

**vénéneux** (*Fem.* **vénéneuse**) *adjective* poisonous (*plant*).

**vengeance** *noun Fem.* revenge.

**venger** *verb* [52] **se venger** to have your revenge.

**venimeux** (*Fem.* **venimeuse**) *adjective* poisonous (*snake, spider*).

**venir** *verb* [81] **1** to come; **il vient de Provence** he comes from Provence; **elles sont venues mardi** they came

a
b
c
d
e
f
g
h
i
j
k
l
m
n
o
p
q
r
s
t
u
v
w
x
y
z

on Tuesday; **viens voir!** come and see!; **2 faire venir** to send for; **il faut faire venir le médecin** we must send for the doctor; **3 venir de faire** to have just done; **ils viennent d'arriver** they have just arrived; **elle venait de partir** she had just left.

**vent** *noun Masc.* wind; **un vent du sud** a south wind.

**vente** *noun Fem.* sale; **être en vente** to be on sale.

**vente aux enchères** *noun Fem.* auction sale.

**ventilateur** *noun Masc.* fan.

**ventre** *noun Masc.* stomach; **avoir mal au ventre** to have stomachache.

**venu** *verb* SEE **venir**.

**ver** *noun Masc.* worm.

**verbe** *noun Masc.* verb.

**verdict** *noun Masc.* verdict.

**verger** *noun Masc.* orchard.

**verglas** *noun Masc.* black ice.

**vérifier** *verb* [1] to check.

**véritable** *adjective* real.

**vérité** *noun Fem.* truth.

**vernir** *verb* [2] to varnish.

**vernis à ongles** *noun Masc.* nail varnish.

**verre** *noun Masc.* **1** glass; **un verre de vin** a glass of wine; **2** glass; **un vase en verre** a glass vase; **3** lens (*of spectacles*).

**verrou** *noun Masc.* bolt (*on a door*).

**verrouiller** *verb* [1] to bolt (*a door*).

**verrue** *noun Fem.* wart.

**vers**[1] *preposition* **1** towards; **il montait vers l'église** he was going up towards the church; **2** about (*a time*); **vers midi** about twelve; **vers la fin du mois** around the end of the month.

**vers**[2] *noun Masc.* line of poetry; **des vers** poetry.

**Verseau** *noun Masc.* Aquarius (*sign of the Zodiac*).

**versement** *noun Masc.* payment.

**verser** *verb* [1] **1** to pour; **Sylvie m'a versé une tasse de thé** Sylvie poured me a cup of tea; **2** to pay in; **j'ai versé 300 euros sur mon compte** I paid 300 euros into my account.

**version** *noun Fem.* **1** version; **2** translation (*into your own language*).

**verso** *noun Masc.* back (*of a piece of paper*); **voir au verso** see overleaf.

**vert** *adjective* green; ★ **avoir la main verte** to have green fingers.

**vertical** (*Masc. plural* **verticaux**) *adjective* vertical, upright.

**vertige** *noun Masc.* vertigo.

**verveine** *noun Fem.* verbena tea.

**veste** *noun Fem.* jacket.

**vestiaire** *noun Masc.* **1** cloakroom (*in a theatre, restaurant, etc*); **2** changing room (*in a gym, sports ground*).

**vêtement** *noun Masc.* garment; **les vêtements** clothes; **'vêtements pour enfants'** 'children's wear'.

**vétérinaire** *noun Masc. & Fem.* vet.

**veuf**, **veuve** *noun Masc., Fem.* widower, widow.

**vexer** *verb* [1] to annoy, to offend.

**viande** *noun Fem.* meat.

**vibrer** *verb* [1] to vibrate.

**victime** *noun Fem.* victim.

**victoire** *noun Fem.* victory.

**vide** *adjective* empty.
**vide** *noun Masc.* **1** space; **dans le vide** in(to) space; **2** vacuum; **emballé sous vide** vacuum-packed.

**vidéo** *noun Fem.* video; **une cassette vidéo** a video cassette; **une caméra vidéo** a video camera; **un jeu vidéo** a video game.

**vidéoclip** *noun Masc.* music video.

**vidéoclub** *noun Masc.* video shop.

**vidéothèque** *noun Fem.* video library.

**vider** *verb* [1] to empty.

**vie** *noun Fem.* life; **toute ma vie** all my life; **il est encore en vie** he's still alive; **ton mode de vie** your lifestyle; ★ **c'est la vie** that's life, that's the way it goes.

**vieil** *adjective* SEE **vieux**.

**vieillard**, **vieillarde** *noun Masc.*, *Fem.* old man, old woman.

**vieille** *adjective* SEE **vieux**.

**vieillesse** *noun Fem.* old age.

**vieillir** *verb* [2] to age; **il a beaucoup vieilli récemment** he's aged a lot recently.

**vierge** *noun Fem.* virgin; **la Sainte Vierge** the Virgin Mary.
**vierge** *adjective* **1** blank; **une cassette vierge** a blank cassette; **2 laine vierge** pure new wool; **l'huile d'olive vierge** virgin olive oil.

**Vierge** *noun Fem.* Virgo (*sign of the Zodiac*).

**vieux**, **vieil** (*before a vowel or silent 'h'*) (*Fem.* **vieille**) (*Masc. plural* **vieux**) *adjective* old; **une vieille ville** an old town; **un vieil arbre** an old tree.
**vieux**, **vieille** *noun Masc., Fem.* **un vieux** an old man; **une vieille** an old woman.

**vieux garçon** *noun Masc.* bachelor.

**vif** (*Fem.* **vive**) *adjective* **1** bright; **rose vif** bright pink; **2** lively; **une vive discussion** a lively discussion; **3 avoir l'esprit vif** to be quick-witted.

**vigne** *noun Fem.* vine, vineyard.

**vigneron**, **vigneronne** *noun Masc., Fem.* wine-grower.

**vignette** *noun Fem.* **1** label; **2** tax disc.

**vignoble** *noun Masc.* vineyard.

**vilain** *adjective* **1** ugly; **2** naughty; **c'est vilain, ça!** that's naughty!

**villa** *noun Fem.* detached house, villa.

**village** *noun Masc.* village.

**ville** *noun Fem.* town, city; **une grande ville** a city; **en ville** in (*or* into) town.

**vin** *noun Masc.* wine.

**vinaigre** *noun Masc.* vinegar.

**vinaigrette** *noun Fem.* French dressing.

**vingt** *number* twenty; **Marion a vingt ans** Marion's twenty; **le vingt juillet** the twentieth of July; **à vingt heures** at 8 p.m.; **vingt et un** twenty-one.

**vingtaine** *noun Fem.* about twenty; **une vingtaine de personnes** about twenty people.

a
b
c
d
e
f
g
h
i
j
k
l
m
n
o
p
q
r
s
t
u
v
w
x
y
z

**vingtième** *adjective* twentieth.

**viol** *noun Masc.* rape.

**violemment** *adjective* violently.

**violence** *noun Fem.* violence.

**violent** *adjective* violent.

**violer** *verb* [1] to rape.

**violet** (*Fem.* **violette**¹) *adjective* purple.

**violette**² *noun Fem.* violet (*the flower*).

**violon** *noun Masc.* violin; **jouer du violon** to play the violin.

**violoncelle** *noun Masc.* cello; **jouer du violoncelle** to play the cello.

**vipère** *noun Fem.* adder, viper.

**virage** *noun Masc.* bend (*in the road*).

**virement** *noun Masc.* transfer (*of money*).

**virer** *verb* [1] **1** to transfer (*money*); **2** to turn; **3** to turn (right) around.

**virgule** *noun Fem.* **1** comma; **2** decimal point; **sept virgule trois** seven point three.

**virus** *noun Masc.* virus.

**vis**¹ *verb* SEE **vivre**.

**vis**² *noun Fem.* screw.

**visa** *noun Masc.* visa.

**visage** *noun Masc.* face.

**viser** *verb* [1] **1** to aim; **2** to aim at (*a target*).

**visibilité** *noun Fem.* visibility.

**visible** *adjective* visible, obvious.

**visite** *noun Fem.* visite; **une visite chez nos cousins** a visit to our cousins; **rendre visite à quelqu'un** to visit somebody; **elle a de la visite** she's got visitors.

**visiter** *verb* [1] to visit (*a place*); **on peut visiter l'appartement?** can we see round the flat?

**visiteur**, **visiteuse** *noun Masc., Fem.* visitor.

**visualisation graphique** *noun Fem.* graphics.

**vit** *verb* SEE **vivre**.

**vitamine** *noun Fem.* vitamin.

**vite** *adverb* **1** fast; **tu conduis trop vite** you drive too fast; **parle moins vite** speak more slowly; **2** quick; **vite! le bus arrive!** quick! here's the bus!; **ce sera vite fait** it won't take long; **3** soon; **on sera vite arrivé** we'll soon be there; **elle a vite compris** she understood immediately.

**vitesse** *noun Fem.* **1** speed; **elle est partie à toute vitesse** she rushed off; **2** gear; **en deuxième vitesse** in second gear.

**vitrail** (*plural* **vitraux**) *noun Masc.* stained glass window.

**vitre** *noun Fem.* window.

**vitrine** *noun Fem.* shop window.

**vivant** *adjective* **1** living; **2** lively.

**vive**¹ *adjective* SEE **vif**.

**vive**² *exclamation* **Vive le roi!** Long live the king!

**vivement** *adverb* **1** **réagir vivement** to react strongly; **2** **vivement les vacances!** roll on the holidays!

**vivre** *verb* [82] to live; **ils vivent ensemble** they live together; **ils ont vécu dans plusieurs pays**

**différents** they've lived in several different countries.

**vocabulaire** *noun Masc.* vocabulary.

**vœu** *noun* (*plural* **vœux**) *Masc.* **1** wish; **faire un vœu** to make a wish; **meilleurs vœux!** best wishes! (*especially at the New Year*); **2** vow.

**vogue** *noun Fem.* fashion; **en vogue** in fashion.

**voici** *preposition* **1** here is, here are; **voici l'addition** here's the bill; **voici les clés** here are the keys; **me voici!** here I am!; **2** this is; **voici ma sœur** this is my sister.

**voie** *noun Fem.* **1** way; **être sur la bonne voie** to be on the right track; **2** track (*for trains*); **la voie ferrée** the railway track; **le train de Bourges entre en gare voie dix** the train from Bourges is now arriving at platform ten; **3** lane (*on a main road*); **une route à trois voies** a three-lane road.

**voilà** *preposition* **1** there is, there are; **voilà tes lunettes, là-bas sur la table** there are your glasses, over there on the table; **la voilà devant la boulangerie** there she is outside the baker's; **2** here is, here are; **voilà Anna qui arrive** here's Anna coming now; **voilà ton café** here's your coffee; **voilà, c'est tout** right, that's all; **3** that is; **voilà ma fille** that's my daughter; **et voilà pourquoi** and that's why.

**voile**[1] *noun Masc.* veil.

**voile**[2] *noun Fem.* sail; **des cours de voile** sailing lessons.

**voilier** *noun Masc.* sailing boat.

**voir** *verb* [13] **1** to see; **je ne vois rien** I can't see anything; **je viendrai te voir un de ces jours** I'll come and see you one of these days; **oui, je vois, tu veux dire que ...** yes, I see, you mean that ...; **un film à voir** a film worth seeing; **peut-être, on verra** perhaps, we'll see; **2** **se voir** to be noticeable; **ça ne se verra pas** nobody will notice; **3** **se voir** to see each other; **ils se voient à Noël** they see each other at Christmas; **4** **faire voir quelque chose à quelqu'un** to show somebody something; **je te ferai voir mes photos de vacances** I'll show you my holiday photos; **fais voir!** let's have a look!; **5** **ça n'a rien à voir avec mon problème** that's got nothing to do with my problem; ★ **il ne voit pas plus loin que le bout de son nez** he can't see any further than the end of his nose; ★ **elle ne peut pas le voir (en peinture)** she can't stand him (*literally: she can't bear to see him (in a painting)*); ★ **j'en ai vu d'autres** I've seen worse.

**voisin, voisine** *noun Masc., Fem.* neighbour; **Claire est chez les voisins** Claire's round at the neighbours'; **ma voisine de table** the girl sitting next to me at table.

**voisinage** *noun Masc.* neighbourhood.

**voiture** *noun Fem.* **1** car; **en voiture** by car; **2** carriage (*on a train*).

**voix** *noun Fem.* **1** voice; **à haute voix** aloud; **à voix basse** softly; **2** vote; **elle a eu 20 voix** she got 20 votes.

**vol** *noun Masc.* **1** flight; **le vol pour Milan** the Milan flight; **2** theft; ★ **à vol d'oiseau** as the crow flies (*literally: by bird flight*).

**volaille** *noun Fem.* poultry; **les foies de volaille** chicken livers.

**volant** *noun Masc.* **1** steering wheel; **qui était au volant?** who was driving?; **2** shuttlecock.
**volant** *adjective* flying.

**volcan** *noun Masc.* volcano.

**volée** *noun Fem.* volley.

**voler** *verb* [1] **1** to fly; **2** to steal; **voler quelque chose à quelqu'un** to steal something from someone; **on leur a volé leur voiture** their car's been stolen; **3 voler quelqu'un** to rob somebody.

**volet** *noun Masc.* shutter.

**voleur**, **voleuse** *noun Masc., Fem.* thief.

**volley** *noun Masc.* volleyball; **jouer au volley** to play volleyball.

**volontaire** *noun Masc. & Fem.* volunteer.

**volonté** *noun Fem.* **1** will; **la bonne volonté** goodwill; **2 à volonté** unlimited; **'pizza à volonté'** 'as much pizza as you want'.

**volontiers** *adverb* gladly; **'tu viens avec nous?'** – **'volontiers'** 'will you come too?' – 'I'd love to'; **'tu me le prêtes?'** – **'volontiers'** 'will you lend it to me?' – 'of course'.

**volume** *noun Masc.* volume.

**vomir** *verb* [2] to be sick, to vomit.

**vos** *adjective* SEE **votre**.

**voter** *verb* [1] to vote; **elle vote toujours pour les Verts** she always votes for the Greens.

**votre** (*plural* **vos**) *adjective* your; **nous connaissons votre fils** we know your son; **vos billets, monsieur** your tickets, sir.

**vôtre** *pronoun* **le vôtre, la vôtre, les vôtres** yours; **une maison comme la vôtre** a house like yours; **mes parents et les vôtres** my parents and yours; ★ **à la vôtre!** cheers!.

**vouloir** *verb* [14] **1** to want; **elle ne veut rien** she doesn't want anything; **veux-tu venir avec nous?** do you want to come with us?; **je n'ai pas voulu arriver trop tôt** I didn't want to arrive too early; **il veut qu'elle l'appelle** he wants her to phone him; **il m'a vexé sans le vouloir** he annoyed me without meaning to; **2** to like; **si tu veux** if you like; **je voudrais visiter Versailles** I'd like to go to Versailles; **'encore du café?'** – **'oui, je veux bien'** 'more coffee?' – 'yes, I'd love some'; **3 voulez-vous m'excuser?** would you excuse me?; **veux-tu fermer la porte?** would you shut the door?; **veux-tu te taire!** will you be quiet!; **4 vouloir dire** to mean; **qu'est-ce que tu veux dire?** what do you mean?; **si tu vois ce que je veux dire** if you see what I mean; **qu'est-ce que ce mot veut dire?** what does this word mean?; **5 en vouloir à quelqu'un** to bear a grudge against someone; **elle leur en veut** she's never forgiven them; ★ **vouloir c'est pouvoir** where there's a will there's a way (*literally: to want is to be able*).

**voulu** *verb* SEE **vouloir**.

**vous** *pronoun* **1** you; **avec vous** with you; **est-ce que ce sac est à vous?** is this your bag?; **à vous de jouer!** your turn to play!; **2** to you; **je vous écrirai** I'll write to you; **3** yourself; **ne vous coupez pas!** don't cut yourself!

**vous-même(s)** *pronoun* yourself, yourselves; **vous me l'avez dit vous-même** you told me yourself; **est-ce que vous l'avez fait vous-mêmes?** did you make it yourselves?

**voûte** *noun Fem.* vault, arch.

**vouvoyer** *verb* [39] to use 'vous' to mean 'you' (*rather than 'tu' which you use when talking to friends, family, and people of your own age*); **ils se connaissent depuis des années mais ils continuent à se vouvoyer** they've known each other for years but they still address each other as 'vous'.

**voyage** *noun Masc.* journey; **bon voyage!** have a good trip!

**voyage organisé** *noun Masc.* package tour.

**voyager** *verb* [52] to travel.

**voyageur, voyageuse** *noun Masc., Fem.* passenger.

**voyelle** *noun Fem.* vowel.

**voyou** *noun Masc.* hooligan.

**vrac** *adverb* **acheter des olives en vrac** to buy olives loose (*as opposed to pre-packaged*).

**vrai** *adjective* **1** true; **c'est une histoire vraie** it's a true story;

**2** real; **c'est un vrai problème** it's a real problem; **c'est vrai?** really?; **pour de vrai** for real; **3 à vrai dire** to tell the truth.

**vraiment** *adverb* really.

**vraisemblable** *adjective* likely; **peu vraisemblable** unlikely.

**vraisemblablement** *adverb* probably.

**VTT** *noun Masc.* SHORT FOR **vélo tout-terrain** mountain bike.

**vu** *verb* SEE **voir**

**vu** *adjective* **1 vu que** seeing that; **vu qu'il pleut, ce n'est pas la peine d'y aller** seeing it's raining, there's no point in going; **2 être mal vu** to be disapproved of; **il est plutôt mal vu** people don't think much of him; **c'est mal vu de faire beaucoup de bruit** they don't like people making a lot of noise; **cette critique a été mal vue** this criticism didn't go down well; **3 être bien vu** to be well thought of; **elle est très bien vue dans la société** people in the company think highly of her.

**vue** *noun Fem.* **1** eyesight; **perdre la vue** to lose your eyesight; **2** sight; **je le connais de vue** I know him by sight; **nous l'avons perdue de vue** we've lost touch with her; **rien qu'à la vue de la viande** at the very sight of meat; **3** view; **une chambre avec vue sur le lac** a room with a view of the lake.

**vulgaire** *adjective* **1** vulgar; **2** common.

a
b
c
d
e
f
g
h
i
j
k
l
m
n
o
p
q
r
s
t
u
v
w
x
y
z

# Ww

**wagon** *noun Masc.* **1** railway carriage; **2** waggon.

**wagon-lit** *noun Masc.* sleeper (*on a train*).

**wagon-restaurant** *noun Masc.* restaurant car.

**wallon** *noun Masc.* Wallon (*language*).
**wallon** (*Fem.* **wallonne**) *adjective* Walloon (*of French-speaking Belgium*).

**Wallon, Wallone** *noun Masc., Fem.* Walloon (*French-speaking Belgian*).

**WC** (*pronounced 'vaysay'*) *plural noun Masc.* toilet; **aller aux WC** to go to the toilet; **il est aux WC** he's in the loo.

**web** *noun Masc.* **le web** the Web.

# Xx

**xylophone** *noun Masc.* xylophone; **jouer du xylophone** to play the xylophone.

# Yy

**y** *pronoun,, adverb* **1** there; **j'y vais demain** I'm going there tomorrow; **2 il y a** there is, there are; **il y a un café à côté** there's a cafe next door; **il y a des tomates dans le frigo** there are some tomatoes in the fridge; **3 j'y pensais** I was thinking of it; **tu n'y peux rien** you can't do anything about it.

**yaourt** *noun Masc.* yoghurt.

**yeux** *plural noun Masc.* SEE **œil**.

**yoga** *noun Masc.* yoga.

**yougoslave** *adjective* Yugoslavian.

**Yougoslavie** *noun Fem.* Yugoslavia; **l'ex-Yougoslavie** the former Yugoslavia.

# Zz

**zapper** *verb* [1] to channel hop.

**zèbre** *noun Masc.* zebra.

**zéro** *noun Masc.* zero, nil, love (*in tennis*); **trois à zéro** three-nil; **zéro heure** midnight; **elle a le moral à zéro** she's really depressed; ★ **il faut tout reprendre à zéro** we'll have to start again from scratch.

**zézayer** *verb* [59] to lisp.

**zigzag** *noun Masc.* zigzag; **une route en zigzag** a winding road; **faire des zigzags** to zigzag.

**zodiaque** *noun Masc.* zodiac.

**zone** *noun Fem.* **1** zone, area; **2 la zone** the slums; **un enfant de la zone** a child who grew up in the slums.

**zone euro** *noun Fem.* eurozone.

**zone industrielle** *noun Fem.* industrial estate.

**zoo** *noun Masc.* zoo.

**zoologique** *adjective* zoological.

**zut** *exclamation* (*informal*) damn!

# VERB TABLES AND FORMS

## aimer
to like *or* to love

### Imperative
aime
aimons
aimez

### Past participle
aimé

### Present
j' aime
tu aimes
il aime
nous aimons
vous aimez
ils aiment

### Present subjunctive
j' aime
tu aimes
il aime
nous aimions
vous aimiez
ils aiment

### Perfect
j' ai aimé
tu as aimé
il a aimé
nous avons aimé
vous avez aimé
ils ont aimé

### Imperfect
j' aimais
tu aimais
il aimait
nous aimions
vous aimiez
ils aimaient

### Future
j' aimerai
tu aimeras
il aimera
nous aimerons
vous aimerez
ils aimeront

### Conditional
j' aimerais
tu aimerais
il aimerait
nous aimerions
vous aimeriez
ils aimeraient

2

| **Imperative** | **Past participle** | **finir** |
|---|---|---|
| finis | fini | to finish |
| finissons | | |
| finissez | | |

## Present

| je | finis |
|---|---|
| tu | finis |
| il | finit |
| nous | finissons |
| vous | finissez |
| ils | finissent |

## Present subjunctive

| je | finisse |
|---|---|
| tu | finisses |
| il | finisse |
| nous | finissions |
| vous | finissiez |
| ils | finissent |

## Perfect

| j' | ai fini |
|---|---|
| tu | as fini |
| il | a fini |
| nous | avons fini |
| vous | avez fini |
| ils | ont fini |

## Imperfect

| je | finissais |
|---|---|
| tu | finissais |
| il | finissait |
| nous | finissions |
| vous | finissiez |
| ils | finissaient |

## Future

| je | finirai |
|---|---|
| tu | finiras |
| il | finira |
| nous | finirons |
| vous | finirez |
| ils | finiront |

## Conditional

| je | finirais |
|---|---|
| tu | finirais |
| il | finirait |
| nous | finirions |
| vous | finiriez |
| ils | finiraient |

## attendre
to wait

**Imperative**

attends
attendons
attendez

**Past participle**

attendu

### Present

j' attends
tu attends
il attend
nous attendons
vous attendez
ils attendent

### Perfect

j' ai attendu
tu as attendu
il a attendu
nous avons attendu
vous avez attendu
ils ont attendu

### Future

j' attendrai
tu attendras
il attendra
nous attendrons
vous attendrez
ils attendront

### Present subjunctive

j' attende
tu attendes
il attende
nous attendions
vous attendiez
ils attendent

### Imperfect

j' attendais
tu attendais
il attendait
nous attendions
vous attendiez
ils attendaient

### Conditional

j' attendrais
tu attendrais
il attendrait
nous attendrions
vous attendriez
ils attendraient

4

## Imperative
lave-toi
lavons-nous
lavez-vous

## Past participle
lavé

## se laver
to wash (oneself)

## Present
| | |
|---|---|
| je | me lave |
| tu | te laves |
| il | se lave |
| nous | nous lavons |
| vous | vous lavez |
| ils | se lavent |

## Present subjunctive
| | |
|---|---|
| je | me lave |
| tu | te laves |
| il | se lave |
| nous | nous lavions |
| vous | vous laviez |
| ils | se lavent |

## Perfect
| | |
|---|---|
| je | me suis lavé |
| tu | t'es lavé |
| il | s'est lavé |
| elles | s'est lavée |
| nous | nous sommes lavés |
| vous | vous êtes lavé(s) |
| ils | se sont lavés |
| elles | se sont lavées |

## Imperfect
| | |
|---|---|
| je | me lavais |
| tu | te lavais |
| il | se lavait |
| nous | nous lavions |
| vous | vous laviez |
| ils | se lavaient |

## Future
| | |
|---|---|
| je | me laverai |
| tu | te laveras |
| il | se lavera |
| nous | nous laverons |
| vous | vous laverez |
| ils | se laveront |

## Conditional
| | |
|---|---|
| je | me laverais |
| tu | te laverais |
| il | se laverait |
| nous | nous laverions |
| vous | vous laveriez |
| ils | se laveraient |

**avoir**
to have

**Imperative**
aie
ayons
ayez

**Past participle**
eu

## Present
j' ai
tu as
il a
nous avons
vous avez
ils ont

## Present subjunctive
j' aie
tu aies
il ait
nous ayons
vous ayez
ils aient

## Perfect
j' ai eu
tu as eu
il a eu
nous avons eu
vous avez eu
ils ont eu

## Imperfect
j' avais
tu avais
il avait
nous avions
vous aviez
ils avaient

## Future
j' aurai
tu auras
il aura
nous aurons
vous aurez
ils auront

## Conditional
j' aurais
tu aurais
il aurait
nous aurions
vous auriez
ils auraient

6

| Imperative | Past participle | être |
|---|---|---|
| sois | été | to be |
| soyons | | |
| soyez | | |

## Present

je **suis**
tu **es**
il **est**
nous **sommes**
vous **êtes**
ils **sont**

## Perfect

j' ai **été**
tu as **été**
il a **été**
nous avons **été**
vous avez **été**
ils ont **été**

## Future

je **serai**
tu **seras**
il **sera**
nous **serons**
vous **serez**
ils **seront**

## Present subjunctive

je **sois**
tu **sois**
il **soit**
nous **soyons**
vous **soyez**
ils **soient**

## Imperfect

j' **étais**
tu **étais**
il **était**
nous **étions**
vous **étiez**
ils **étaient**

## Conditional

je **serais**
tu **serais**
il **serait**
nous **serions**
vous **seriez**
ils **seraient**

# aller
## to go

**Imperative**
va
allons
allez

**Past participle**
allé

## Present

| | |
|---|---|
| je | **vais** |
| tu | **vas** |
| il | **va** |
| nous | **allons** |
| vous | **allez** |
| ils | **vont** |

## Present subjunctive

| | |
|---|---|
| j' | **aille** |
| tu | **ailles** |
| il | **aille** |
| nous | **allions** |
| vous | **alliez** |
| ils | **aillent** |

## Perfect

| | |
|---|---|
| je | suis **allé** |
| tu | es **allé** |
| il | est **allé** |
| nous | sommes **allés** |
| vous | êtes **allé(s)** |
| ils | sont **allés** |

## Imperfect

| | |
|---|---|
| j' | **allais** |
| tu | **allais** |
| il | **allait** |
| nous | **allions** |
| vous | **alliez** |
| ils | **allaient** |

## Future

| | |
|---|---|
| j' | **irai** |
| tu | **iras** |
| il | **ira** |
| nous | **irons** |
| vous | **irez** |
| ils | **iront** |

## Conditional

| | |
|---|---|
| j' | **irais** |
| tu | **irais** |
| il | **irait** |
| nous | **irions** |
| vous | **iriez** |
| ils | **iraient** |

8

| Imperative | Past participle |
|---|---|
| dois | du |
| devons | |
| devez | |

**devoir**
to have to

## Present

| | |
|---|---|
| je | **dois** |
| tu | **dois** |
| il | **doit** |
| nous | de**vons** |
| vous | de**vez** |
| ils | **doivent** |

## Present subjunctive

| | |
|---|---|
| je | **doive** |
| tu | **doives** |
| il | **doive** |
| nous | de**vions** |
| vous | de**viez** |
| ils | **doivent** |

## Perfect

| | | |
|---|---|---|
| j' | ai | **dû** |
| tu | as | **dû** |
| il | a | **dû** |
| nous | avons | **dû** |
| vous | avez | **dû** |
| ils | ont | **dû** |

## Imperfect

| | |
|---|---|
| je | de**vais** |
| tu | de**vais** |
| il | de**vait** |
| nous | de**vions** |
| vous | de**viez** |
| ils | de**vaient** |

## Future

| | |
|---|---|
| je | dev**rai** |
| tu | dev**ras** |
| il | dev**ra** |
| nous | dev**rons** |
| vous | dev**rez** |
| ils | dev**ront** |

## Conditional

| | |
|---|---|
| je | dev**rais** |
| tu | dev**rais** |
| il | dev**rait** |
| nous | dev**rions** |
| vous | dev**riez** |
| ils | dev**raient** |

## dire
to say

**Imperative**
dis
disons
dites

**Past participle**
dit

**Present**

| | |
|---|---|
| je | dis |
| tu | dis |
| il | dit |
| nous | disons |
| vous | dites |
| ils | disent |

**Present subjunctive**

| | |
|---|---|
| je | dise |
| tu | dises |
| il | dise |
| nous | disions |
| vous | disiez |
| ils | disent |

**Perfect**

| | | |
|---|---|---|
| j' | ai | dit |
| tu | as | dit |
| il | a | dit |
| nous | avons | dit |
| vous | avez | dit |
| ils | ont | dit |

**Imperfect**

| | |
|---|---|
| je | disais |
| tu | disais |
| il | disait |
| nous | disions |
| vous | disiez |
| ils | disaient |

**Future**

| | |
|---|---|
| je | dirai |
| tu | diras |
| il | dira |
| nous | dirons |
| vous | direz |
| ils | diront |

**Conditional**

| | |
|---|---|
| je | dirais |
| tu | dirais |
| il | dirait |
| nous | dirions |
| vous | diriez |
| ils | diraient |

| Imperative | Past participle | **faire** |
|---|---|---|
| fais | fait | to do *or* to make |
| faisons | | |
| faites | | |

## Present

| je | fais |
|---|---|
| tu | fais |
| il | fait |
| nous | faisons |
| vous | faites |
| ils | font |

## Perfect

| j' | ai fait |
|---|---|
| tu | as fait |
| il | a fait |
| nous | avons fait |
| vous | avez fait |
| ils | ont fait |

## Future

| je | ferai |
|---|---|
| tu | feras |
| il | fera |
| nous | ferons |
| vous | ferez |
| ils | feront |

## Present subjunctive

| je | fasse |
|---|---|
| tu | fasses |
| il | fasse |
| nous | fassions |
| vous | fassiez |
| ils | fassent |

## Imperfect

| je | faisais |
|---|---|
| tu | faisais |
| il | faisait |
| nous | faisions |
| vous | faisiez |
| ils | faisaient |

## Conditional

| je | ferais |
|---|---|
| tu | ferais |
| il | ferait |
| nous | ferions |
| vous | feriez |
| ils | feraient |

## mettre
### to put

| Imperative | Past participle |
|---|---|
| mets | mis |
| mettons | |
| mettez | |

### Present
| | |
|---|---|
| je | mets |
| tu | mets |
| il | met |
| nous | mettons |
| vous | mettez |
| ils | mettent |

### Present subjunctive
| | |
|---|---|
| je | mette |
| tu | mettes |
| il | mette |
| nous | mettions |
| vous | mettiez |
| ils | mettent |

### Perfect
| | | |
|---|---|---|
| j' | ai | mis |
| tu | as | mis |
| il | a | mis |
| nous | avons | mis |
| vous | avez | mis |
| ils | ont | mis |

### Imperfect
| | |
|---|---|
| je | mettais |
| tu | mettais |
| il | mettait |
| nous | mettions |
| vous | mettiez |
| ils | mettaient |

### Future
| | |
|---|---|
| je | mettrai |
| tu | mettras |
| il | mettra |
| nous | mettrons |
| vous | mettrez |
| ils | mettront |

### Conditional
| | |
|---|---|
| je | mettrais |
| tu | mettrais |
| il | mettrait |
| nous | mettrions |
| vous | mettriez |
| ils | mettraient |

## 12

## Imperative

the imperative of **pouvoir** is not used

## Past participle

pu

## pouvoir
to be able

## Present

| | |
|---|---|
| je | **peux** |
| tu | **peux** |
| il | **peut** |
| nous | pouv**ons** |
| vous | pouv**ez** |
| ils | **peuvent** |

## Perfect

| | | |
|---|---|---|
| j' | ai | **pu** |
| tu | as | **pu** |
| il | a | **pu** |
| nous | avons | **pu** |
| vous | avez | **pu** |
| ils | ont | **pu** |

## Future

| | |
|---|---|
| je | **pourrai** |
| tu | **pourras** |
| il | **pourra** |
| nous | **pourrons** |
| vous | **pourrez** |
| ils | **pourront** |

## Present subjunctive

| | |
|---|---|
| je | **puisse** |
| tu | **puisses** |
| il | **puisse** |
| nous | **puissions** |
| vous | **puissiez** |
| ils | **puissent** |

## Imperfect

| | |
|---|---|
| je | pouv**ais** |
| tu | pouv**ais** |
| il | pouv**ait** |
| nous | pouv**ions** |
| vous | pouv**iez** |
| ils | pouv**aient** |

## Conditional

| | |
|---|---|
| je | **pourrais** |
| tu | **pourrais** |
| il | **pourrait** |
| nous | **pourrions** |
| vous | **pourriez** |
| ils | **pourraient** |

## voir
to see

| **Imperative** | **Past participle** |
|---|---|
| vois | vu |
| voyons | |
| voyez | |

### Present

je vois
tu vois
il voit
nous **voyons**
vous **voyez**
ils voient

### Perfect

j' ai **vu**
tu as **vu**
il a **vu**
nous avons **vu**
vous avez **vu**
ils ont **vu**

### Future

je **verrai**
tu **verras**
il **verra**
nous **verrons**
vous **verrez**
ils **verront**

### Present subjunctive

je **voie**
tu **voies**
il **voie**
nous **voyions**
vous **voyiez**
ils **voient**

### Imperfect

je **voyais**
tu **voyais**
il **voyait**
nous **voyions**
vous **voyiez**
ils **voyaient**

### Conditional

je **verrais**
tu **verrais**
il **verrait**
nous **verrions**
vous **verriez**
ils **verraient**

# 14

## Imperative
veuille
veuillons
veuillez

## Past participle
voulu

## vouloir
to want

## Present
je veux
tu veux
il veut
nous voulons
vous voulez
ils veulent

## Present subjunctive
je veuille
tu veuilles
il veuille
nous voulions
vous vouliez
ils veuillent

## Perfect
j' ai voulu
tu as voulu
il a voulu
nous avons voulu
vous avez voulu
ils ont voulu

## Imperfect
je voulais
tu voulais
il voulait
nous voulions
vous vouliez
ils voulaient

## Future
je voudrai
tu voudras
il voudra
nous voudrons
vous voudrez
ils voudront

## Conditional
je voudrais
tu voudrais
il voudrait
nous voudrions
vous voudriez
ils voudraient

## French irregular verb forms

The list shows the main forms of other irregular verbs. The number before the infinitive is the number given after verbs in the dictionary which follow this pattern.

**(1)** = Present      **(3)** = Imperfect

**(2)** = Past participle      **(4)** = Future

15 **abréger** (1) j'abrège, nous abrégeons, ils abrègent (2) abrégé (3) j'abrégeais (4) j'abrégerai

16 **acheter** (1) j'achète, nous achetons, ils achètent (2) acheté (3) j'achetais (4) j'achèterai

17 **acquérir** (1) j'acquiers, il acquiert, nous acquérons, vous acquérez ils acquièrent (2) acquis (3) j'acquérais (4) j'acquerrai

18 **appeler** (1) j'appelle, nous appelons (2) appelé (3) j'appelais (4) j'appellerai

19 **apprendre** (1) j'apprends, nous apprenons, vous apprenez, ils apprennent (2) appris (3) j'apprenais (4) j'apprendrai

20 **s'asseoir** (1) je m'assieds, nous nous asseyons, vous vous asseyez, ils s'asseyent (2) assis (3) je m'asseyais (4) je m'assiérai

21 **battre** (1) je bats, il bat, nous battons (2) battu (3) je battais (4) je battrai

22 **boire** (1) je bois, nous buvons, ils boivent (2) bu (3) je buvais (4) je boirai

23 **bouillir** (1) je bous, nous bouillons (2) bouilli (3) je bouillais (4) je bouillirai

24 **céder** (1) je cède, nous cédons, ils cèdent (2) cédé (3) je cédais (4) je céderai

25 **conclure** (1) je conclus, nous concluons (2) conclu (3) je concluais (4) je conclurai

26 **conduire** (1) je conduis, nous conduisons (2) conduit (3) je conduisais (4) je conduirai

27 **connaître** (1) je connais, nous connaissons (2) connu (3) je connaissais (4) je connaîtrai

28 **coudre** (1) je couds, nous cousons, vous cousez, ils cousent (2) cousu (3) je cousais (4) je coudrai

29 **courir** (1) je cours, nous courons (2) couru (3) je courais (4) je courrai

30 **couvrir** (1) je couvre, nous couvrons (2) couvert (3) je couvrais (4) je couvrirai

31 **craindre** (1) je crains, nous craignons (2) craint (3) je craignais (4) je craindrai

32 **créer** (1) je crée, nous créons (2) créé (3) je créais (4) je créerai

33 **croire** (1) je crois, nous croyons, ils croient (2) cru (3) je croyais (4) je croirai

34 **croître** (1) je croîs, nous croissons (2) crû, crue (3) je croissais (4) je croîtrai

35 **cueillir** (1) je cueille, nous cueillons (2) cueilli (3) je cueillais (4) je cueillerai

36 **cuire** (1) je cuis, nous cuisons, ils cuisent (2) cuit (3) je cuisais (4) je cuirai

37 **dormir** (1) je dors, nous dormons (2) dormi (3) je dormais (4) je dormirai

38 **écrire** (1) j'écris, nous écrivons (2) écrit (3) j'écrivais (4) j'écrirai

39 **employer** (1) j'emploie, nous employons, vous employez, ils emploient (2) employé (3) j'employais (4) j'emploierai

40 **envoyer** (1) j'envoie, nous envoyons, vous envoyez, ils envoient (2) envoyé (3) j'envoyais (4) j'enverrai

41 **essuyer** (1) j'essuie, nous essuyons, vous essuyez, ils essuient (2) essuyé (3) j'essuyais (4) j'essuierai

42 **faillir** (1) je faille (2) failli

43 **falloir** (1) je il faut (2) fallu (3) il fallait (4) il faudra

44 **fuir** (1) je fuis, nous fuyons, ils, fuient (2) fui (3) je fuyais (4) je fuirai

45 **geler** (1) je gèle, nous gelons, vous gelez, ils gèlent (2) gelé (3) je gelais (4) je gèlerai

46 **haïr** (1) je hais, nous haïssons, ils haïssent (2) haï (3) je haïssais (4) je haïrai

47 **interdire** (1) j'interdis, nous interdisons, vous interdisez (2) interdit (3) j'interdisais (4) j'interdirai

48 **jeter** (1) je jette, nous jetons, ils jettent (2) jeté (3) je jetais (4) je jetterai

49 **joindre** (1) je joins, nous joignons (2) joint (3) je joignais (4) je joindrai

50 **lever** (1) je lève, nous levons, ils lèvent (2) levé (3) je levais (4) je lèverai

51 **lire** (1) je lis, nous lisons (2) lu (3) je lisais (4) je lirai

52 **manger** (1) je mange, nous mangeons (2) mangé (3) je mangeais (4) je mangerai

53 **mentir** (1) je mens, nous mentons (2) menti (3) je mentais (4) je mentirai

54 **mourir** (1) je meurs, nous mourons, ils meurent (2) mort (3) je mourais (4) je mourrai

55 **naître** (1) je nais, il naît, nous naissons (2) né (3) je naissais (4) je naîtrai

56 **offrir** (1) j'offre, nous offrons (2) offert (3) j'offrais (4) j'offrirai

57 **paraître** (1) je parais, il paraît, nous paraissons (2) paru (3) je paraissais (4) je paraîtrai

**58 partir** (1) je pars, nous partons (2) parti (3) je partais (4) je partirai

**59 payer** (1) je paie/je paye, nous payons, vous payez, ils paient/ils payent (2) payé (3) je payais (4) je paierai/je payerai

**60 peindre** (1) je peins, nous peignons (2) peint (3) je peignais (4) je peindrai

**61 placer** (1) je place, nous plaçons (2) placé (3) je plaçais (4) je placerai

**62 plaire** (1) je plais, il plaît, nous plaisons (2) plu (3) je plaisais (4) je plairai

**63 pleuvoir** (1) je il pleut (2) plu (3) il pleuvait (4) il pleuvra

**64 prendre** (1) je prends, nous prenons, ils prennent (2) pris (3) je prenais (4) je prendrai

**65 prévoir** (1) je prévois, nous prévoyons, vous prévoyez, ils prévoient (2) prévu (3) je prévoyais (4) je prévoirai

**66 recevoir** (1) je reçois, il reçoit, ils reçoivent (2) reçu (3) je recevais (4) je recevrai

**67 résoudre** (1) je résous, nous résolvons, vous résolvez, ils résolvent (2) résolu (3) je résolvais (4) je résoudrai

**68 rire** (1) je ris, nous rions (2) ri (3) je riais (4) je rirai

**69 rompre** (1) je romps, il rompt, nous rompons (2) rompu (3) je rompais (4) je romprai

**70 savoir** (1) je sais, nous savons, ils savent (2) su (3) je savais (4) je saurai (5) pres subj je sache

**71 servir** (1) je sers, nous servons (2) servi (3) je servais (4) je servirai

**72 sortir** (1) je sors, nous sortons (2) sorti (3) je sortais (4) je sortirai

**73 souffrir** (1) je souffre, nous souffrons (2) souffert (3) je souffrais (4) je souffrirai

**74 suffire** (1) je suffis, nous suffisons (2) suffi (3) je suffisais (4) je suffirai

**75 suivre** (1) je suis, nous suivons (2) suivi (3) je suivais (4) je suivrai

**76 taire** (1) je me tais, nous nous taisons (2) tu (3) je me taisais (4) je me tairai

**77 tenir** (1) je tiens, nous tenons, ils tiennent (2) tenu (3) je tenais (4) je tiendrai

**78 traire** (1) je trais, nous trayons, ils traient (2) trait (3) je trayais (4) je trairai

**79 vaincre** (1) je vaincs, il vainc, nous vainquons (2) vaincu (3) je vainquais (4) je vaincrai

**80 valoir** (1) je vaux, il vaut, nous valons (2) valu (3) je valais (4) je vaudrai

**81 venir** (1) je viens, nous venons, ils viennent (2) venu (3) je venais (4) je viendrai

**82 vivre** (1) je vis, nous vivons (2) vécu (3) je vivais (4) je vivrai

# Aa

**a** *indefinite article* **1** (*before a noun which is masculine in French*) un; **a tree** un arbre; **2** (*before a noun which is feminine in French*) une; **a table** une table; **3 five euros a kilo** cinq euros le kilo; **4 fifty kilometres an hour** cinquante kilomètres l'heure; **5 three times a day** trois fois par jour.

**abandon** *verb* abandonner [1].

**abbey** *noun* abbaye *Fem.*; **Westminster Abbey** l'Abbaye de Westminster.

**abbreviation** *noun* abréviation *Fem.*

**abide** *verb* **I can't abide ...** je ne supporte pas ....

**ability** *noun* capacité *Fem.*; **the ability to do** la capacité de faire.

**able** *adjective* **to be able to do** pouvoir [12] faire; **she wasn't able to come** elle n'a pas pu venir.

**abnormal** *adjective* anormal (*Masc. plural* anormaux).

**abolish** *verb* abolir [2].

**abortion** *noun* avortement *Masc.*

**about** *preposition* **1** (*on the subject of*) sur; **a film about Picasso** un film sur Picasso; **2 what's it about?** de quoi s'agit-il?; **3** (*concerning or in relation to*) au sujet de; **he wants to talk to you about your exam** il veut te parler au sujet de ton examen; **4 to talk about something** parler de quelque chose; **what is she talking about?** de quoi parle-t-elle?; **5 to think about something/**

**somebody** penser à quelque chose/quelqu'un; **I'm thinking about you** je pense à toi.

**about** *adverb* **1** (*approximately*) environ, à peu près; **there are about sixty people** il y a environ soixante personnes, il y a à peu près soixante personnes; **2** (*when talking about the time*) vers; **about three o'clock** vers trois heures; ★ **to be about to do** être sur le point de faire; **I'm (just) about to leave** je suis sur le point de partir.

**above** *preposition* **1** au dessus de; **above the table** au dessus de la table; **2 above all** surtout.

**abroad** *adverb* à l'étranger; **to go abroad** aller à l'étranger; **to live abroad** vivre à l'étranger.

**abscess** *noun* abcès *Masc.*

**abseiling** *noun* descente *Fem.* en rappel.

**absent** *adjective* absent; **to be absent from** être absent de.

**absent-minded** *adjective* distrait.

**absolute** *adjective* complet (*Fem.* complète); **an absolute disaster** un désastre complet.

**absolutely** *adverb* **1** absolument; **it's absolutely dreadful** c'est absolument affreux; **2** tout à fait; **you're absolutely right** tu as tout à fait raison.

**absorb** *verb* absorber [1].

**abuse** *noun* **1 alcohol abuse** abus *Masc.* d'alcool; **drug abuse** usage *Masc.* des stupéfiants; **2** (*violent treatment of a person*) mauvais traitement *Masc.*; **3** (*insulting words*)

a
b
c
d
e
f
g
h
i
j
k
l
m
n
o
p
q
r
s
t
u
v
w
x
y
z

injures *Fem. plural*.

**abuse** *verb* **to abuse somebody** maltraiter [1] quelqu'un.

**academic** *adjective* **the academic year** l'année universitaire.

**accelerate** *verb* accélérer [24].

**accelerator** *noun* accélérateur *Masc.*

**accent** *noun* accent *Masc.*; **she has a French accent** elle a l'accent français.

**accept** *verb* accepter [1].

**acceptable** *adjective* acceptable.

**acceptance** *noun* acceptation *Fem.*

**access** *noun* accès *Masc.*
**access** *verb* **to access something** accéder [24] à quelque chose.

**accessory** *noun* accessoire *Masc.*

**accident & emergency** *noun* les urgences *Fem. plural*.

**accident** *noun* **1** accident *Masc.*; **to have an accident** avoir un accident; **a road accident** un accident de la route; **a car accident** un accident de voiture; **2** (*chance*) hasard *Masc.*; **by accident** par hasard; **I found it by accident** je l'ai trouvé par hasard.

**accidental** *adjective* fortuit; **an accidental discovery** une découverte fortuite.

**accidentally** *adverb* **1** (*without meaning to*) accidentellement; **I accidentally knocked over his glass** j'ai accidentellement renversé son verre; **2** (*by chance*) par hasard;

**I accidentally discovered that ...** j'ai découvert par hasard que ....

**accommodate** *verb* recevoir [66]; **the centre can accommodate sixty people** le centre peut recevoir soixante personnes.

**accommodation** *noun* logement *Masc.*; **I'm looking for accommodation** je cherche un logement.

**accompany** *verb* **to accompany somebody** accompagner [1] quelqu'un.

**according** *in phrase* **according to** selon; **according to Sophie** selon Sophie.

**accordion** *noun* accordéon *Masc.*

**account** *noun* **1** (*in a bank, shop, or post office*) compte *Masc.*; **a bank account** un compte bancaire; **to open an account** ouvrir un compte; **I have fifty pounds in my account** j'ai cinquante livres sur mon compte; **2** (*a description of an experience or event*) compte rendu *Masc.*; **3 on account of** à cause de; **the station is closed on account of the strike** la gare est fermée à cause de la grève; **4 to take something into account** tenir compte de quelque chose; **we will take his illness into account** nous tiendrons compte de sa maladie.

**accountant** *noun* comptable *Masc. & Fem.*; **she is an accountant** elle est comptable.

**accuracy** *noun* précision *Fem.*

**accurate** *adjective* précis.

**accurately** *adverb* avec précision.

**accuse** *verb* accuser [1]; **to accuse somebody of something** accuser quelqu'un de quelque chose; **to accuse someone of doing something** accuser quelqu'un d'avoir fait quelque chose; **she accused me of stealing her pen** elle m'a accusé d'avoir volé son stylo.

**accustomed to** *adjective* ; **to be accustomed to something** être [6] habitué à; **she's accustomed to having lots of homework** elle a l'habitude d'avoir beaucoup de devoirs.

**ace** *noun* as *Masc.*; **the ace of hearts** l'as de cœur.
**ace** *adjective* super (*informal*); **he's an ace drummer** c'est un super batteur.

**ache** *verb* **my arm aches** j'ai mal au bras; **my head aches** j'ai mal à la tête.

**achieve** *verb* **1** accomplir [2]; **she's achieved a great deal** elle a beaucoup accompli; **2 to achieve an ambition** réaliser [1] une ambition; **3 to achieve an aim** atteindre [60] un objectif; **4 to achieve success** réussir [2].

**achievement** *noun* **1** réussite *Fem.*; **it's a great achievement** c'est une grande réussite; **2 a sense of achievement** un sentiment de satisfaction.

**acid** *noun* acide *Masc.*

**acid rain** *noun* pluies *Fem. plural* acides.

**acne** *noun* acné *Fem.*

**acorn** *noun* gland *Masc.*

**acrobat** *noun* acrobate *Masc. & Fem.*

**across** *preposition* **1** (*over to the other side of*) **to walk across something** traverser [1] quelque chose; **we walked across the park** nous avons traversé le parc; **to run across the road** traverser la route en courant; **2** (*on the other side of*) de l'autre côté de; **the house across the street** la maison de l'autre côté de la rue; **3 across from** en face de; **she was sitting across from me** elle était assise en face de moi.

**acrylic** *noun* acrylique *Masc.*

**act** *noun* acte *Masc.*
**act** *verb* **1** (*in a play or film*) jouer [1]; **to act the part of** jouer le rôle de; **2** (*to take action*) agir [2].

**acting** *noun* jeu *Masc.*; **she wants to go into acting** elle veut devenir actrice; **the acting was terrible/sensational** les acteurs jouaient très mal/bien.

**action** *noun* action *Fem.*

**action replay** *noun* répétition *Fem.* d'une séquence.

**active** *adjective* actif (*Fem.* active).

**activity** *noun* activité *Fem.*

**activity holiday** *noun* vacances *Fem. plural* sportives.

**actor** *noun* acteur *Masc.*; **who's your favourite actor?** qui est votre acteur préféré?

**actress** *noun* actrice *Fem.*; **she's my favourite actress** c'est mon actrice préférée.

**actual** *adjective* **his actual words** ses paroles précises; ★ **in actual fact** en fait.

a
b
c
d
e
f
g
h
i
j
k
l
m
n
o
p
q
r
s
t
u
v
w
x
y
z

**a**
**b**
**c**
**d**
**e**
**f**
**g**
**h**
**i**
**j**
**k**
**l**
**m**
**n**
**o**
**p**
**q**
**r**
**s**
**t**
**u**
**v**
**w**
**x**
**y**
**z**

**actually** *adverb* **1** (*in fact, as it happens*)) en fait; **actually, I've changed my mind** en fait, j'ai changé d'avis; **he's not actually here at the moment** en fait il n'est pas là en ce moment; **2** (*really and truly*) vraiment; **did she actually say that?** est-ce qu'elle a vraiment dit ça?

**acupuncture** *noun* acupuncture *Fem.*

**acute** *adjective* **1** (*pain*) vif (*Fem.* vive); **2 an acute accent** un accent aigu.

**ad** *noun* **1** pub *Fem.* (*informal*); **2** (*in a newspaper*) annonce *Fem.*; **to put an ad in the paper** mettre une annonce dans le journal; **the small ads** les petites annonces.

**AD** *abbreviation* après Jésus-Christ, apr. J-C; **in 400 AD** en quatre cents après Jésus-Christ.

**adapt** *verb* **1 to adapt something** adapter [1] quelque chose (*a book or film*); **2 to adapt to something** s'adapter [1] à quelque chose; **she's adapted to the new system** elle s'est adaptée au nouveau système.

**adaptor** *noun* adaptateur *Masc.*

**add** *verb* ajouter [1]; **add three eggs** ajoutez trois œufs.

● **to add something up** additionner [1] quelque chose.

**addict** *noun* **1** (*drug addict*) drogué, droguée *Masc., Fem.*; **2** accro *Masc. & Fem.* (*informal*); **she's a telly addict** c'est une accro de la télé; **he's a football addict** c'est un accro du foot.

**addicted** *adjective* **1 to become addicted to heroin** former une dépendance à l'héroïne; **2 I'm addicted to tomatoes** je raffole des tomates.

**addition** *noun* **1** (*adding up*) addition *Fem.*; **2 in addition** en plus; **3 in addition to** en plus de.

**additional** *adjective* supplémentaire; **additional costs** les frais supplémentaires.

**additive** *noun* additif *Masc.*

**address** *noun* adresse *Fem.*; **what's your address?** quelle est ton adresse?; **to change address** changer d'adresse.

**address book** *noun* carnet *Masc.* d'adresses.

**adequate** *adjective* suffisant.

**adhesive** *noun* colle *Fem.*
**adhesive** *adjective* collant; **adhesive tape** du papier collant.

**adjective** *noun* adjectif *Masc.*

**adjust** *verb* **1 to adjust something** régler [24] quelque chose; **to adjust the height** régler la hauteur; **2 to adjust to something** s'adapter [1] à quelque chose.

**adjustable** *adjective* réglable.

**administration** *noun* administration *Fem.*

**admiral** *noun* amiral *Masc.*

**admiration** *noun* admiration *Fem.*

**admire** *verb* admirer [1].

**admission** *noun* entrée *Fem.*; **'no admission'** 'entrée interdite'; **'admission free'** 'entrée gratuite'.

**admit** *verb* **1** (*confess*) reconnaître [27]; **she admits she lied** elle

reconnaît qu'elle a menti;
2 (*concede*) admettre [11]; **I must admit that** ... j'admets que ...;
3 (*allow to enter*) laisser [1] entrer; **to admit somebody to a restaurant** laisser entrer quelqu'un dans un restaurant; **4 to be admitted to hospital** être [6] hospitalisé.

**adolescence** *noun* adolescence *Fem.*

**adolescent** *noun* adolescent *Masc.*, adolescente *Fem.*

**adopt** *verb* adopter [1].

**adopted** *adjective* adoptif (*Fem.* adoptive).

**adoption** *noun* adoption *Fem.*

**adore** *verb* adorer [1].

**Adriatic Sea** *noun* **the Adriatic Sea** la mer Adriatique.

**adult** *noun* adulte *Masc. & Fem.*
**adult** *adjective* adulte; **the adult population** la population adulte.

**Adult Education** *noun* enseignement *Masc.* pour adultes.

**advance** *noun* progrès *Masc.*; **advances in technology** des progrès dans le domaine de la technologie.
**advance** *verb* **1** (*make progress*) progresser [1]; **2** (*move forward*) avancer [61].

**advanced** *adjective* avancé.

**advantage** *noun* **1** avantage *Masc.*; **there are several advantages** il y a plusieurs avantages; **2 to take advantage of something** profiter de quelque chose; **I took advantage of the sales to buy myself some shoes** j'ai profité des soldes pour

m'acheter des chaussures; **3 to take advantage of somebody** (*unfairly*) exploiter quelqu'un.

**Advent** *noun* Avent *Masc.*

**adventure** *noun* aventure *Fem.*

**adventurous** *adjective* aventureux (*Fem.* aventureuse).

**adverb** *noun* adverbe *Masc.*

**advert, advertisement** *noun* **1** (*at the cinema or on television*) publicité *Fem.*; **2** (*commercial advertisement in a newspaper*) annonce *Fem.*; **3** (*small ad in a newspaper advertising a job, an article for sale, etc*) petite annonce *Fem.*

**advertise** *verb* **1 to advertise something in the newspaper** (*in the small ads*) mettre [11] une annonce pour quelque chose dans le journal; **I saw a bike advertised in the paper** j'ai vu une annonce pour un vélo dans le journal; **2 to advertise a product** faire [10] de la publicité pour un produit.

**advertising** *noun* publicité *Fem.*

**advice** *noun* conseils *Masc. plural*; **to ask for advice about something** demander des conseils à propos de quelque chose; **a piece of advice** un conseil.

**advise** *verb* conseiller [1]; **to advise somebody to do** conseiller à quelqu'un de faire; **I advised him to stop** je lui ai conseillé d'arrêter; **I advised her not to wait** je lui ai conseillé de ne pas attendre.

**adviser** *noun* conseiller *Masc.*, conseillère *Fem.*

**aerial** *noun* antenne *Fem.*

a
b
c
d
e
f
g
h
i
j
k
l
m
n
o
p
q
r
s
t
u
v
w
x
y
z

**aerobics** *noun* aérobic *Masc.*; **to do aerobics** faire de l'aérobic.

**aeroplane** *noun* avion *Masc.*

**aerosol** *noun* **an aerosol can** une bombe.

**affair** *noun* **1** (*event*) affaire *Fem.*; **international affairs** les affaires internationales; **2 a love affair** une aventure amoureuse.

**affect** *verb* affecter [1].

**affectionate** *adjective* affectueux (*Fem.* affectueuse).

**afford** *verb* **to be able to afford to do** avoir [5] les moyens de faire; **we can't afford to go out much** nous n'avons pas les moyens de sortir beaucoup; **I can't afford a new bike** je n'ai pas les moyens de m'acheter un nouveau vélo.

**afraid** *adjective* **1 to be afraid of something** avoir peur de quelque chose; **she's afraid of dogs** elle a peur des chiens; **2 I'm afraid there's no milk left** je suis désolé mais il ne reste plus de lait; **I'm afraid so** hélas oui; **I'm afraid not** hélas non.

**Africa** *noun* Afrique *Fem.*; **in Africa** en Afrique; **to Africa** en Afrique.

**African** *noun* Africain *Masc.*, Africaine *Fem.*.

**African** *adjective* africain (*Fem.* africaine).

**after** *preposition, adverb, conjunction* après; **after 10 o'clock** après dix heures; **after lunch** après le déjeuner; **after school** après l'école; **the day after tomorrow** après-demain; **soon after** peu après; **after I've finished my homework** après que j'aurai fini mes devoirs; **to run after somebody** courir après quelqu'un.

**after all** *adverb* après tout; **after all, she's only six** elle n'a que six ans après tout.

**afternoon** *noun* après-midi *Masc.* or *Fem.*; **this afternoon** cet après-midi; **tomorrow afternoon** demain après-midi; **yesterday afternoon** hier après-midi; **on Saturday afternoon** samedi après-midi; **on Saturday afternoons** le samedi après-midi; **at four o'clock in the afternoon** à quatre heures de l'après-midi; **every afternoon** tous les après-midi.

**afters** *noun* dessert *Masc.*

**after-shave** *noun* après-rasage *Masc.*

**afterwards** *adverb* après; **shortly afterwards** peu de temps après.

**again** *adverb* **1** (*one more time*) encore une fois; **try again** essaie encore une fois; **I've forgotten it again** je l'ai oublié encore une fois; **2** (*once more*) de nouveau; **she's ill again** elle est de nouveau malade; **3 I saw her again yesterday** je l'ai revue hier; **you should ask again** tu devrais redemander; **4 I don't want to see her again** je ne veux plus la revoir; **never again!** jamais plus!

**against** *preposition* contre; **against the wall** contre le mur; **to lean against the wall** s'appuyer contre le mur; **I'm against the idea** je suis contre l'idée; **the fight against racism** la lutte contre le racisme.

334

**age** *noun* âge *Masc.* **1 at the age of fifteen** à l'âge de quinze ans; **she's the same age as me** elle a le même âge que moi; **to be under age** être mineur; **2 I haven't seen Johnny for ages** ça fait une éternité que je n'ai pas vu Johnny; **I haven't been to London for ages** ça fait une éternité que je ne suis pas allé à Londres.

**aged** *adjective* âgé de; **a woman aged thirty** une femme âgée de trente ans.

**agenda** *noun* ordre *Masc.* du jour.

**agent** *noun* agent *Masc.*; **an estate agent** un agent immobilier; **a travel agent's** une agence de voyage.

**aggressive** *adjective* agressif (*Fem.* agressive).

**ago** *adverb* **an hour ago** il y a une heure; **three days ago** il y a trois jours; **five years ago** il y a cinq ans; **a long time ago** il y a longtemps; **not long ago** il n'y a pas longtemps; **how long ago was it?** c'était il y a combien de temps?

**agree** *verb* **1 to agree with somebody** être [6] d'accord avec quelqu'un; **I agree with Laura** je suis d'accord avec Laura; **I don't agree** je ne suis pas d'accord; **2 I agree that ...** je suis d'accord sur le fait que ...; **I agree that it's too late now** je suis d'accord sur le fait qu'il est maintenant trop tard; **3 to agree to do** accepter [1] de faire; **Steve's agreed to help me** Steve a accepté de m'aider; **4 coffee doesn't agree with me** je ne supporte pas le café.

**agreement** *noun* accord *Masc.*

**agricultural** *adjective* agricole.

**agriculture** *noun* agriculture *Fem.*

**ahead** *adverb* **1 go ahead!** allez-y!; **2 straight ahead** tout droit; **go straight ahead until you get to the crossroads** allez tout droit jusqu'au carrefour; **3 our team was ten points ahead** notre équipe avait dix points d'avance; **4 to be ahead of time** être en avance.

**aid** *noun* **1** aide *Fem.*; **aid to developing countries** l'aide aux pays en voie de développement; **2 in aid of** au profit de; **in aid of the homeless** au profit des sans-abri.

**AIDS** *noun* sida *Masc.* (*short for: syndrome immunodéficitaire acquis*); **to have AIDS** avoir le sida.

**aim** *noun* objectif *Masc.*; **their aim is to control pollution** leur objectif est de contrôler la pollution.
**aim** *verb* **1 to aim to do** avoir [5] l'intention de faire; **we're aiming to finish it today** nous avons l'intention de le finir aujourd'hui; **2 a campaign aimed at young people** une campagne qui vise les jeunes; **3 to aim a gun at somebody** braquer [1] un révolver sur quelqu'un.

**air** *noun* **1** air *Masc.*; **in the open air** en plein air; **to go out for a breath of air** sortir prendre l'air; **2 to travel by air** voyager en avion.

**airbag** *noun* (*in a car*) airbag *Masc.*

**air-conditioned** *adjective* climatisé.

**air conditioning** *noun* climatisation *Fem.*

---

**Air Force** noun Armée Fem. de l'air.

**air hostess** noun hôtesse Fem. de l'air; **she's an air hostess** elle est hôtesse de l'air.

**airline** noun compagnie Fem. aérienne.

**airmail** noun **by airmail** par avion.

**airport** noun aéroport Masc.

**aisle** noun allée Fem. centrale.

**alarm** noun alarme Fem.; **a fire alarm** une alarme incendie; **a burglar alarm** une alarme contre le vol.

**alarm clock** noun réveil Masc.

**album** noun album Masc.

**alcohol** noun alcool Masc.

**alcoholic** noun alcoolique Masc. & Fem.

**alcoholic** adjective alcoolisé; **alcoholic drinks** les boissons alcoolisées.

**alert** adjective vif (Fem. vive) noun **on the alert: you must be on the alert for pickpockets** faites attention aux pickpockets.

**A levels** noun plural baccalauréat Masc., bac Masc. (informal) (Students take 'le bac' at the same age as A levels are taken in Britain. You can explain A levels briefly as follows: Les A levels sont répartis en deux niveaux, AS et A2. On passe les examens AS au bout d'une année de préparation, généralement dans quatre ou cinq matières. On passe les examens A2 un an plus tard, dans un plus petit nombre de matières, en choisissant parmi celles qui ont déjà fait l'objet d'un examen AS. La meilleure note que l'on peut obtenir est A et la note la plus basse est N. Les A levels permettent de s'inscrire à l'université); SEE **baccalauréat**.

**Algeria** noun Algérie Fem.; **to Algeria** en Algérie; **in Algeria** en Algérie.

**alibi** noun alibi Masc.

**alien** noun **1** (foreigner) étranger Masc., étrangère Fem.; **2** (from outer space) extra-terrestre Masc. & Fem.

**alike** adjective pareil (Fem. pareille) **1 they're all alike** ils sont tous pareils; **2 to look alike** se ressembler; **the two brothers look alike** les deux frères se ressemblent.

**alive** adjective vivant.

**all along** adverb depuis le début; **I knew it all along** je le savais depuis le début.

**allergic** adjective allergique; **to be allergic to something** être allergique à quelque chose.

**allergy** noun allergie Fem.; **she has an allergy to cats** elle est allergique aux chats.

**alligator** noun alligator Masc.

**allow** verb **1 to allow somebody to do** permettre [11] à quelqu'un de faire; **the teacher allowed them to go out** le prof leur a permis de sortir; **2 to be allowed to do** avoir [5] le droit de faire; **I'm not allowed to go out during the week** je n'ai pas le droit de sortir en semaine.

**all right** adverb **1** (yes) d'accord; **'come round to my house around six'–'all right'** 'passe chez moi vers six heures'–'d'accord'; **2** (fine) bien; **is everything all right?** est-ce que tout va bien?; **she's all right now** elle va bien maintenant; **it's all right by me** ça ne me dérange pas; **3** (*not bad*) pas mal; **the meal was all right** le repas n'était pas mal; **4 are you all right?** ça va?; **5 is it all right to ...?** est-ce qu'on peut ...?; **is it all right to leave the door open?** est-ce qu'on peut laisser la porte ouverte?

**ally** *noun* allié *Masc.*, alliée *Fem.*

**almond** *noun* amande *Fem.*

**almost** *adverb* presque; **almost every day** presque tous les jours; **almost everybody** presque tout le monde; **she's almost five** elle a presque cinq ans.

**alone** *adjective* **1** seul; **he lives alone** il habite seul; **2 leave me alone!** laisse-moi tranquille!; **3 leave these papers alone!** ne touche pas à ces papiers!

**along** *preposition* **1** le long de; **there are trees all along the road** il y a des arbres tout le long de la route; **2** (*there is often no direct translation for 'along' so the sentence has to be expressed differently*) **she lives along the road from me** elle habite dans la même rue que moi; **to go for a walk along the beach** aller se promener sur la plage.

**aloud** *adverb* à haute voix; **to read something aloud** lire quelque chose à haute voix.

**alphabet** *noun* alphabet *Masc.*

**alphabetical** *adjective* alphabétique; **in alphabetical order** par ordre alphabétique.

**Alps** *plural noun* **the Alps** les Alpes.

**already** *adverb* déjà; **they've already left** ils sont déjà partis; **it's six o'clock already!** il est déjà six heures!

**Alsatian** *noun* (*dog*) berger *Masc.* allemand.

**also** *adverb* aussi; **I've also invited Karen** j'ai aussi invité Karen.

**alter** *verb* changer [52].

**alternate** *adjective* **on alternate days** un jour sur deux.

**alternative** *noun* **1** possibilité *Fem.*; **there are several alternatives** il y a plusieurs possibilités; **2 we have no alternative** nous n'avons pas le choix.
**alternative** *adjective* autre; **to find an alternative solution** trouver une autre solution.

**alternatively** *adverb* sinon; **alternatively, we could go together on Saturday** sinon, on pourrait y aller ensemble samedi.

**alternative medicine** *noun* médecine *Fem.* douce.

**although** *conjunction* bien que (*followed by subjunctive*); **although she's ill, she's willing to help us** bien qu'elle soit malade, elle est prête à nous aider.

**altitude** *noun* altitude *Fem.*

**altogether** *adverb* **1** en tout; **I've spent thirty pounds altogether** j'ai dépensé trente livres en tout; **2** (*completely*) complètement; **I'm not altogether convinced** je ne suis pas complètement convaincu.

**aluminium** *noun* aluminium *Masc.*

a b c d e f g h i j k l m n o p q r s t u v w x y z

**always** *adverb* toujours; **I always leave at five** je pars toujours à cinq heures.

**am** *verb* SEE **be**.

**a.m.** *abbreviation* du matin; **at 8 a.m.** à huit heures du matin.

**amateur** *noun* amateur *Masc.*; **amateur dramatics** théâtre *Masc.* amateur.

**amaze** *verb* surprendre [64]; **what amazes me is** ... ce qui me surprend c'est ....

**amazed** *adjective* stupéfait; **I was amazed to see her** j'étais stupéfait de la voir.

**amazement** *noun* stupéfaction *Fem.*; **to my amazement: to my amazement she agreed** à ma grande surprise elle s'est mise d'accord.

**amazing** *adjective* **1** (*terrific*) fantastique; **your dress is amazing!** ta robe est fantastique!; **they've got an amazing house** ils ont une maison fantastique; **2** (*extraordinary*) extraordinaire; **she has an amazing number of friends** elle a un nombre extraordinaire d'amis; **he told me an amazing story** il m'a raconté une histoire extraordinaire.

**ambassador** *noun* ambassadeur *Masc.*, ambassadrice *Fem.*.

**ambition** *noun* ambition *Fem.*

**ambitious** *adjective* ambitieux (*Fem.* ambitieuse).

**ambulance** *noun* ambulance *Fem.*

**ambulance driver** *noun* ambulancier *Masc.*, ambulancière *Fem.*

**amenities** *plural noun* équipements *Masc. plural.*

**America** *noun* Amérique *Fem.*; **in America** en Amérique; **to America** en Amérique.

**American** *noun* Américain *Masc.*, Américaine *Fem.*.
**American** *adjective* américain (*Fem.* américaine).

**ammunition** *noun* munition *Fem.*

**among, amongst** *preposition* **1** parmi; **I found it amongst my books** je l'ai trouveé parmi mes livres; **2** (*between*) entre; **you can decide amongst yourselves** vous pouvez décider entre vous.

**amount** *noun* **1** quantité *Fem.*; **an enormous amount of bread** une énorme quantité de pain; **a huge amount of work** un travail énorme; **2** (*of money*) somme *Fem.*; **a large amount of money** une grosse somme d'argent.
**amount** *verb* **to amount to** s'élever [50] à; **the bill amounts to five hundred euros** la facture s'élève à cinq cents euros.

**amp** *noun* **1** (*electricity*) ampère *Masc.*; **2** (*amplifier*) ampli *Masc.* (*informal*).

**amplifier** *noun* amplificateur *Masc.*

**amuse** *verb* amuser [1].

**amusement arcade** *noun* salle *Fem.* de jeux électroniques.

**amusing** *adjective* amusant.

**an** *article* SEE **a**.

**anaesthetic** *noun* anesthésie *Fem.*

**analyse** *verb* analyser [1].

**analysis** *noun* analyse *Fem.*

**ancestor** *noun* ancêtre *Masc. & Fem.*

**anchor** *noun* ancre *Fem.*

**anchovy** *noun* anchois *Masc.*

**ancient** *adjective* **1** (*historic*) ancien (*Fem.* ancienne); **an ancient abbey** une abbaye ancienne; **2** (*very old*) très vieux (*Fem.* très vieille); **an ancient pair of jeans** un très vieux jean; **3 ancient Greece** la Grèce antique.

**and** *conjunction* **1** et; **Sean and Anna** Sean et Anna; **Rosie and I** Rosie et moi; **your shoes and socks** tes chaussures et tes chaussettes; **2 louder and louder** de plus en plus fort.

**angel** *noun* ange *Masc.*

**anger** *noun* colère *Fem.*

**angle** *noun* angle *Masc.*

**angrily** *adverb* avec colère.

**angry** *adjective* **to be angry** être en colère; **she was angry with me** elle était en colère contre moi; **to get angry** se fâcher [1].

**animal** *noun* animal *Masc.* (*plural* animaux).

**ankle** *noun* cheville *Fem.*; **to break your ankle** se casser la cheville.

**anniversary** *noun* anniversaire *Masc.*; **a wedding anniversary** un anniversaire de mariage.

**announce** *verb* annoncer [61].

**announcement** *noun* annonce *Fem.*

**annoy** *verb* agacer [61]; **to be annoyed** être [6] agacé; **to get annoyed** se fâcher [1]; **she got annoyed** elle s'est fâchée.

**annoying** *adjective* agaçant.

**annual** *adjective* annuel (*Fem.* annuelle).

**anorak** *noun* anorak *Masc.*

**anorexia** *noun* anorexie *Fem.*

**another** *adjective* **1** un autre (*Fem.* une autre); **would you like another cup of tea?** voulez-vous une autre tasse de thé?; **2** encore; **another two years** encore deux ans; **we need another three chairs** il nous faut encore trois chaises.

**answer** *noun* **1** réponse *Fem.*; **the right answer** la bonne réponse; **the wrong answer** la mauvaise réponse; **2 the answer to a problem** la solution à un problème.
**answer** *verb* **1** répondre [3] à; **he hasn't answered our letter** il n'a pas répondu à notre lettre; **2 to answer the door** aller [5] ouvrir la porte.

**answering machine** *noun* répondeur *Masc.*; **to leave a message on the answering machine** laisser un message au répondeur.

**ant** *noun* fourmi *Fem.*

**Antarctic** *noun* Antarctique *Masc.*

**anthem** *noun* **the national anthem** l'hymne national.

**antibiotic** *noun* antibiotique *Fem.*

**antique** *noun* **antiques** les antiquités *Fem.*
**antique** *adjective* ancien (*Fem.* ancienne); **an antique table** une table ancienne.

**antique shop** *noun* magasin *Masc* d'antiquités.

a
b
c
d
e
f
g
h
i
j
k
l
m
n
o
p
q
r
s
t
u
v
w
x
y
z

**antiseptic** *noun* antiseptique *Masc.*

**anxious** *adjective* inquiet (*Fem.* inquiète).

**anxiously** *adverb* avec inquiétude.

**any** *adjective, adverb, pronoun* **1** du, de l', de la, des; **is there any butter?** y a-t-il du beurre?; **is there any oil?** y a-t-il de l'huile?; **is there any flour?** y a-t-il de la farine?; **are there any eggs?** y a-t-il des œufs?; **2** de (*used in negative sentences*); **there isn't any flour** il n'y a pas de farine; **there aren't any eggs** il n'y a pas d'œufs; **3** en (*when 'any' is used on its own without a noun*); **I don't want any** je n'en veux pas; **4** **not** ...**any more** ne ...plus; **there isn't any more butter** il n'y a plus de beurre; **I don't go there any more** je n'y vais plus.

**anybody, anyone** *pronoun* **1** (*in questions and after 'if'*) quelqu'un; **is anybody in?** est-ce qu'il y a quelqu'un?; **if anybody wants some beer, it's in the fridge** si quelqu'un veut de la bière, elle est au frigo; **does anybody want some tea?** qui veut du thé?; **2** **not** ...**anybody** ne ...personne; **there isn't anybody in her office** il n'y a personne dans son bureau; **3** (*absolutely anybody*) n'importe qui; **anybody can go** n'importe qui peut y aller.

**anyhow** *adverb* SEE **anyway**.

**anyone** *pronoun* SEE **anybody**.

**anything** *pronoun* **1** (*in questions*) quelque chose; **is there anything I can do to help?** est-ce que je peux faire quelque chose pour t'aider?; **2** **not** ...**anything** ne ...rien; **there isn't anything on the table** il n'y a rien sur la table; **3** (*anything at all*) n'importe quoi; **anything could happen** il pourrait arriver n'importe quoi.

**anyway, anyhow** *adverb* de toute façon; **anyway, I'll ring you before I leave** de toute façon, je t'appellerai avant de partir.

**anywhere** *adverb* **1** (*in questions*) quelque part; **have you seen my keys anywhere?** est-ce que tu as vu mes clés quelque part?; **are you going anywhere tomorrow?** est-ce que tu vas quelque part demain?; **2** **not** ...**anywhere** ne ...nulle part; **I can't find my keys anywhere** je ne trouve nulle part mes clés; **3** (*absolutely anywhere*) n'importe où; **put your cases down anywhere** pose tes valises n'importe où.

**apart** *adjective, adverb* **1** (*separate*) séparé; **we don't like being apart** nous n'aimons pas être séparés; **2** **to be two metres apart** être à deux mètres l'un de l'autre; **3 apart from** à part; **apart from Judy everybody was there** à part Judy tout le monde y était.

**apartheid** *noun* apartheid *Masc.*

**apartment** *noun* appartement *Masc.*

**ape** *noun* (grand) singe *Masc.*

**apologize** *verb* s'excuser [1]; **he apologizes for his behaviour** il s'excuse de son comportement; **he apologized to Tanya** il s'est excusé auprès de Tanya.

**apology** noun excuses Fem. plural.

**apostrophe** noun apostrophe Fem.

**apparatus** noun 1 (in a gym) agrès Masc. plural; 2 (in a lab) matériel Masc.

**apparent** adjective apparent.

**apparently** adverb apparemment.

**appeal** noun appel Masc.
**appeal** verb 1 to appeal for lancer [61] un appel pour; 2 to appeal to somebody tenter [1] quelqu'un; horror films don't appeal to me les films d'épouvante ne me tentent pas.

**appear** verb 1 apparaître [57]; Mick appeared at the door Mick est apparu à la porte; 2 to appear on television passer [1] à la télévision; 3 (seem) paraître [57]; it appears that somebody has stolen the key il paraît que quelqu'un a volé la clé.

**appendicitis** noun appendicite Fem.

**appendix** noun 1 (of book) annexe Fem.; 2 (organ) appendice Masc.

**appetite** noun appétit Masc.; it'll spoil your appetite ça te coupera l'appétit.

**applaud** verb applaudir [2].

**applause** noun applaudissements Masc. plural.

**apple** noun pomme Fem.

**apple core** noun trognon Masc. de pomme.

**apple tree** noun pommier Masc.

**applicant** noun candidat Masc., candidate Fem.

**application** noun a job application une candidature.

**application form** noun (for a job) dossier Masc. de candidature.

**apply** verb 1 to apply for a job poser [1] sa candidature à un poste; 2 to apply for a course faire [10] une demande d'inscription à un cours; 3 to apply to s'appliquer [1] à; that doesn't apply to students cela ne s'applique pas aux étudiants.

**appointment** noun rendez-vous Masc.; to make a dental appointment prendre rendez-vous chez le dentiste; I've got a hair appointment at four j'ai rendez-vous chez le coiffeur à seize heures.

**appreciate** verb I appreciate your advice je vous suis reconnaissant de vos conseils; I'd appreciate it if you could tidy up afterwards je te serais reconnaissant de ranger après.

**apprentice** noun apprenti Masc., apprentie Fem..

**apprenticeship** noun apprentissage Masc.

**approach** verb (come near to) 1 s'approcher de [1]; we were approaching Paris nous nous approchions de Paris; 2 (tackle) aborder [1] (a task or problem).

**appropriate** adjective approprié.

**approval** noun approbation Fem.

**approve** verb to approve of apprécier [1]; they don't approve of her friends ils n'apprécient pas ses amis.

**approximate** adjective approximatif (Fem. approximative).

**a**

**approximately** *adverb* environ; **approximately fifty people** environ cinquante personnes.

**apricot** *noun* abricot *Masc.*

**apricot tree** *noun* abricotier *Masc.*

**April** *noun* avril *Masc.*; **in April** en avril.

**April Fool** *noun* poisson *Masc.* d'avril.

**April Fool's Day** *noun* le premier avril.

**apron** *noun* tablier *Masc.*

**aquarium** *noun* aquarium *Masc.*

**Aquarius** *noun* Verseau *Masc.*; **Sharon's Aquarius** Sharon est Verseau.

**Arab** *noun* Arabe *Masc. & Fem.* **Arab** *adjective* arabe; **the Arab countries** les pays arabes.

**arch** *noun* arche *Fem.*

**archaeologist** *noun* archéologue *Masc. & Fem.*; **she's an archaeologist** elle est archéologue.

**archaeology** *noun* archéologie *Fem.*

**archbishop** *noun* archevêque *Masc.*

**architect** *noun* architecte *Masc. & Fem.*; **he's an architect** il est architecte.

**architecture** *noun* architecture *Fem.*

**Arctic** *noun* Arctique *Masc.*

**are** *verb* SEE be.

**area** *noun* **1** (*part of a town*) quartier; **a nice area** un quartier bien; **a rough area** un quartier mal

fréquenté; **2** (*region*) région *Fem.*; **in the Leeds area** dans la région de Leeds.

**argue** *verb* se disputer [1] **1** there's no point in arguing ce n'est pas la peine de se disputer; **2 to argue about something** discuter [1] de quelque chose; **they're arguing about the result** ils sont en train de discuter du résultat.

**argument** *noun* dispute *Fem.*; **to have an argument** se disputer.

**Aries** *noun* Bélier *Masc.*; **Pauline's Aries** Pauline est Bélier.

**arithmetic** *noun* arithmétique *Fem.*

**arm** *noun* bras *Masc.*; **to fold your arms** croiser les bras; **arm in arm** bras dessus bras dessous; **to break your arm** se casser le bras.

**armchair** *noun* fauteuil *Masc.*

**armed** *adjective* armé.

**armpit** *noun* aisselle *Fem.*

**army** *noun* armée *Fem.*; **to join the army** s'engager dans l'armée.

**around** *preposition, adverb* **1** (*with time*) vers; **we'll be there around ten** on va arriver vers dix heures; **2** (*with ages or amounts*) environ; **she's around fifteen** elle a environ quinze ans; **we need around six kilos** il nous faut environ six kilos; **3** (*surrounding*) autour de; **the countryside around Edinburgh** le paysage autour d'Édimbourg; **4** (*near*) **is there a post office around here?** est-ce qu'il y a un bureau de poste près d'ici?; **is Phil around?** est-ce que Phil est là?; **5** (*wrapped around*) autour de; **she**

**had a scarf around her neck** elle avait une écharpe autour du cou.

**arrange** *verb* **to arrange to do** prévoir [65] de faire; **we've arranged to see a film on Saturday** nous avons prévu de voir un film samedi.

**arrangement** *noun* **1** (*of things*) disposition *Fem.*; **2** (*agreement*) accord *Masc.*

**arrest** *noun* **to be under arrest** être en état d'arrestation.
**arrest** *verb* arrêter [1].

**arrival** *noun* arrivée *Fem.*

**arrive** *verb* arriver [1]; **they arrived at 3 p.m.** ils sont arrivés à quinze heures.

**arrow** *noun* flèche *Fem.*

**art** *noun* **1** art *Masc.*; **modern art** l'art moderne; **2** (*school subject*) dessin *Masc.*; **the art class** le cours de dessin.

**artery** *noun* artère *Fem.*

**art gallery** *noun* (*public*) musée *Masc.* des beaux arts.

**artichoke** *noun* artichaut *Masc.*

**article** *noun* article *Masc.*

**artificial** *adjective* artificiel (*Fem.* artificielle).

**artist** *noun* artiste *Masc. & Fem.*; **he's an artist** c'est un artiste.

**artistic** *adjective* artistique.

**art school** *noun* école *Fem.* de beaux arts.

**as** *conjunction, adverb, preposition* **1** comme; **as you know** comme vous le savez; **as usual** comme d'habitude; **as I told you** comme je t'avais dit; **2** (*because*) puisque; **as**

there were no trains, we took the bus puisqu'il n'y avait pas de trains, nous avons pris le bus; **3 as ...as** aussi ...que; **he's as tall as his brother** il est aussi grand que son frère; **you must be as tired as I am** tu dois être aussi fatigué que moi; **4 as much ...as** autant de ...que; **you have as much time as I do** tu as autant de temps que moi; **5 as many ...as** autant de ...que; **we have as many problems as he does** nous avons autant de problèmes que lui; **6 as long as** pourvu que (*with subjunctive*); **we'll go tomorrow, as long as it's a nice day** on va y aller demain, pourvu qu'il fasse beau; **7 for as long as** aussi longtemps que; **you can stay for as long as you like** tu peux rester aussi longtemps que tu veux; **8 as soon as possible** dès que possible; **9 to work as** travailler comme; **he works as a taxi driver in the evenings** il travaille comme chauffeur de taxi le soir.

**asbestos** *noun* amiante *Fem.*

**ash** *noun* cendre *Fem.*

**ashamed** *adjective* **to be ashamed** avoir honte; **you should be ashamed of yourself!** tu devrais avoir honte!

**ashtray** *noun* cendrier *Masc.*

**Asia** *noun* Asie *Fem.*; **in Asia** en Asie.

**Asian** *noun* **1** (*from the Far East*) Asiatique *Masc. & Fem.*; **2** (*from India*) Indien *Masc.*, Indienne *Fem.*; **3** (*from Pakstan*) Pakistanais *Masc.*, Pakistanaise *Fem.*
**Asian** *adjective* **1** asiatique (*from Asia*); **2** (*from India*) indien (*Fem.*

# ask

indienne); **3** (*from Pakistan*)
pakistanais (*Fem.* pakistanaise).

**ask** *verb* **1** demander [1]; **you can ask at reception** tu peux demander à l'accueil; **to ask somebody something** demander quelque chose à quelqu'un; **I asked him where he lives** je lui ai demandé où il habite; **to ask for something** demander quelque chose; **I asked for three coffees** j'ai demandé trois cafés; **to ask somebody for something** demander quelque chose à quelqu'un; **to ask somebody to do** demander à quelqu'un de faire; **ask Danny to give you a hand** demande à Danny de te donner un coup de main; **2 to ask somebody a question** poser [1] une question à quelqu'un; **I asked you a question!** je t'ai posé une question!; **3** inviter [1]; **they've asked us to a party at their house** ils nous ont invité à une soirée chez eux; **4 Paul's asked Janie out on Friday** Paul a invité Janie à sortir avec lui vendredi.

**asleep** *adjective* **to be asleep** dormir [37]; **the baby's asleep** le bébé dort; **to fall asleep** s'endormir [37].

**asparagus** *noun* asperges *Fem.* plural.

**aspirin** *noun* aspirine *Fem.*

**assembly** *noun* (*at school*) rassemblement *Masc.*

**assess** *verb* évaluer [1].

**assignment** *noun* (*at school*) devoir *Masc.*

**assist** *verb* aider [1].

**assistance** *noun* aide *Fem.*

**assistant** *noun* **1** assistant *Masc.*, assistante *Fem.*; **2 a shop assistant** un vendeur, une vendeuse.

**association** *noun* association *Fem.*

**assorted** *adjective* variés (*Fem.* variées).

**assortment** *noun* mélange *Masc.*

**assume** *verb* supposer [1].

**assure** *verb* assurer [1].

**asterisk** *noun* astérisque *Masc.*

**asthma** *noun* asthme *Masc.*; **she has asthma** elle souffre de l'asthme.

**astonishing** *adjective* étonnant; **her knowledge is astonishing** elle a des connaissances incroyables.

**astrologer** *noun* astrologue *Masc.* & *Fem.*

**astrology** *noun* astrologie *Fem.*

**astronaut** *noun* astronaute *Masc.* & *Fem.*

**astronomer** *noun* astronome *Masc.* & *Fem.*.

**astronomy** *noun* astronomie *Fem.*

**at** *preposition* **1** à (*note that 'à + le' always becomes 'au' and 'à + les' always becomes 'aux'*); **at home** à la maison; **at school** à l'école; **at my office** à mon bureau; **at the market** au marché; **at meetings** aux réunions; **2** (*talking about the time*) à; **at eight o'clock** à huit heures; **3 at night** la nuit; **at the weekend** le weekend; **4 at Emma's house** chez Emma; **she's at her brother's this evening** elle est chez son frère ce soir; **at the hairdresser's** chez le coiffeur; **5 at last** enfin; **he's found**

**a job at last** il a enfin trouvé un emploi; **1** (@ *in e-mail addresses*) arobase *Masc.*; **john-dot-smith@easycom-dot-com** john-point-smith-arobase-easycom-point-com.

**athlete** *noun* athlète *Masc. & Fem.*

**athletic** *adjective* athlétique.

**athletics** *noun* athlétisme *Masc.*

**Atlantic** *noun* Atlantique *Masc.*

**atlas** *noun* atlas *Masc.*

**atmosphere** *noun* atmosphère *Fem.*

**atom** *noun* atome *Masc.*

**atomic** *adjective* atomique.

**attach** *verb* attacher [1].

**attached** *adjective* **to be attached to** être [6] attaché à.

**attachment** *noun* pièce *Fem.* jointe.

**attack** *noun* attaque *Fem.*
**attack** *verb* attaquer [1].

**attacker** *noun* agresseur *Masc.*

**attempt** *noun* tentative *Fem.*; **at the first attempt** à la première tentative.
**attempt** *verb* **to attempt to do** essayer [59] de faire.

**attend** *verb* assister [1] à; **to attend a class** assister à un cours.

**attention** *noun* attention *Fem.*; **to pay attention to** faire attention à; **I wasn't paying atttention** je ne faisais pas attention.

**attic** *noun* grenier *Masc.*; **in the attic** au grenier.

**attitude** *noun* attitude *Fem.*

**attract** *verb* attirer [1].

**attraction** *noun* attraction *Fem.*

**attractive** *adjective* séduisant.

**aubergine** *noun* aubergine *Fem.*

**auction** *noun* vente *Fem.* aux enchères.

**audience** *noun* public *Masc.*

**August** *noun* août *Masc.*; **in August** en août.

**aunt**, **auntie** *noun* tante *Fem.*

**au pair** *noun* jeune fille *Fem.* au pair; **I'm looking for a job as an au pair** je cherche un emploi de jeune fille au pair.

**Australia** *noun* Australie *Fem.*; **in Australia** en Australie; **to Australia** en Australie.

**Australian** *noun* Australien *Masc.*, Australienne *Fem.*
**Australian** *adjective* australien (*Fem.* australienne).

**Austria** *noun* Autriche *Fem.*; **in Austria** en Autriche; **to Austria** en Autriche.

**Austrian** *noun* Autrichien *Masc.*, Autrichienne *Fem.*
**Austrian** *adjective* autrichien (*Fem.* autrichienne).

**author** *noun* auteur *Masc.*

**autobiography** *noun* autobiographie *Fem.*

**autograph** *noun* autographe *Masc.*

**automatic** *adjective* automatique.

**automatically** *adverb* automatiquement.

**autumn** *noun* automne *Masc.*; **in autumn** en automne.

**availability** *noun* disponibilité *Fem.*

a
b
c
d
e
f
g
h
i
j
k
l
m
n
o
p
q
r
s
t
u
v
w
x
y
z

**available** *adjective* disponible.

**avalanche** *noun* avalanche *Fem.*

**avenue** *noun* avenue *Fem.*

**average** *noun* moyenne *Fem.*; **on average** en moyenne; **above average** au-dessus de la moyenne. **average** *adjective* moyen (*Fem.* moyenne); **the average height** la hauteur moyenne.

**avocado** *noun* avocat *Masc.*

**avoid** *verb* éviter [1]; **she avoided me** elle m'a évité; **to avoid doing** éviter de faire; **I avoid speaking to him** j'évite de lui parler.

**awake** *adjective* **to be awake** être réveillé; **is Lola awake?** est-ce que Lola est réveillée?; **are you still awake?** tu ne dors pas?

**award** *noun* prix *Masc.*; **to win an award** remporter un prix.

**aware** *adjective* **to be aware of a noise** être conscient d'un bruit; **to be aware of a problem** être au courant d'un problème; **as far as I'm aware** à ma connaissance.

**away** *adverb* **1 to be away** être absent; **I'll be away next week** je serai absent la semaine prochaine; **2 to go away** partir; **Laura's gone away for a week** Laura est partie pour une semaine; **go away!** va-t-en!; **3 to run away** partir en courant; **the thieves ran away** les voleurs sont partis en courant; **4 the school is two kilometres away** l'école est à deux kilomètres d'ici; **how far away is it?** c'est à quelle distance d'ici?; **not far away** pas loin d'ici; **5 to put something away** ranger quelque chose; **I'll just**

**put my books away** je vais juste ranger mes livres; **6 to give something away** donner quelque chose; **she's given away all her tapes** elle a donné toutes ses cassettes.

**away match** *noun* match *Masc.* à l'extérieur.

**awful** *adjective* **1** affreux (*Fem.* affreuse); **the film was awful!** le film était affreux!; **2 I feel awful** (*ill*) je ne me sens pas bien du tout; **3 I feel awful about it** ça m'ennuie vraiment; **4 an awful lot of** énormément de.

**awkward** *adjective* **1** difficile; **it's an awkward situation** c'est une situation difficile; **it's a bit awkward** c'est un peu difficile; **an awkward child** un enfant difficile; **2 an awkward question** une question gênante.

**axe** *noun* hache *Fem.*

# Bb

**baby** *noun* bébé *Masc.*

**babysit** *verb* faire [10] du babysitting.

**babysitter** *noun* babysitter *Masc. & Fem.*

**babysitting** *noun* babysitting *Masc.*

**bachelor** *noun* célibataire *Masc.*

**back** *noun* **1** (*of a person or animal*) dos *Masc.*; **to do something behind someone's back** faire quelque chose dans le dos de quelqu'un; **2** (*of* *a piece of paper, your hand, or a garment*) dos *Masc.*; **on the back** au dos; **3** (*of a car, a plane, or a building*) arrière *Masc.*; **we have seats at the back** nous avons des places à l'arrière; **a garden at the back of the house** un jardin à l'arrière de la maison; **4 the children at the back of the room** les enfants au fond de la salle; **5** (*of a chair or sofa*) dossier *Masc.*; **6** (*in football or hockey*) arrière *Masc.*; **left back** arrière gauche.

**back** *adjective* **1** arrière (*a wheel or seat*); **the back seat of the car** le siège arrière de la voiture; **2 the back gate** la porte de derrière; **the back garden** le jardin de derrière.

**back** *adverb* **1 to go back** rentrer; **to go back to school** rentrer à l'école; **Lisa's gone back to London** Lisa est rentrée à Londres; **2 to come back** rentrer; **they've come back from Italy** ils sont rentrés d'Italie; **she's back at work** elle a repris le travail; **Sue's not back yet** Sue n'est pas encore rentrée; **we went by bus and walked back** nous avons pris le bus pour y aller et nous sommes rentrés à pied; **3 to phone back** rappeler; **I'll ring back later** je rappellerai plus tard; **4 to give something back to somebody** rendre quelque chose à quelqu'un; **I gave him back his cassettes** je lui ai rendu ses cassettes; **give it back!** rends-le-moi!

**back** *verb* **1** (*to support*) soutenir [81] (*a candidate, for example*); **2** (*to bet on*) parier [1] sur (*a horse*).

● **to back up** (*computing*) **to back up**

**a file** sauvegarder [1] un fichier sur disquette.

● **to back somebody up** soutenir [77] quelqu'un.

**backache** *noun* mal *Masc.* de dos.

**backbone** *noun* colonne *Fem.* vertébrale.

**back door** *noun* **1** (*of a building*) porte *Fem.* de derrière; **2** (*of a car*) porte *Fem.* arrière.

**backfire** *verb* (*turn out badly*) échouer [1].

**background** *noun* **1** (*of a person*) (*social*) milieu *Masc.*; **2** (*of events or a situation*) contexte *Masc.*; **3** (*in a picture or view*) arrière-plan *Masc.*; **the trees in the background** les arbres à l'arrière-plan; **4 background music** la musique d'ambiance; **5 background noise** les bruits *Masc. plural* de fond.

**backhand** *noun* revers *Masc.*

**backing** *noun* **1** (*on sticky-back plastic, for example*) revêtement *Masc.* intérieur; **2** (*moral support*) soutien *Masc.*; **3** (*in music*) **a backing group** un groupe d'accompagnement.

**backpack** *noun* sac *Masc.* à dos. **backpack** *verb* **to go backpacking** partir [58] en voyage avec son sac à dos.

**back seat** *noun* siège *Masc.* arrière.

**backside** *noun* derrière *Masc.*

**backstage** *adverb* **to go backstage** aller dans les coulisses.

**backstroke** *noun* dos *Masc.* crawlé.

347

**back to front** *adverb* à l'envers; **your jumper's back to front** ton pull est à l'envers.

**backup** *noun* **1** (*support*) soutien *Masc.*; **2** (*in computing*) **a backup disk** un disque de sauvegarde.

**backwards** *adverb* (*to lean or fall*) en arrière.

**bacon** *noun* **1** (*French streaky bacon*) lard *Masc.*; **2** (*thin-sliced British-type*) bacon *Masc.*; **bacon and eggs** œufs au bacon.

**bad** *adjective* **1** (*not good*) mauvais (*goes before the noun*) **bad work** du mauvais travail; **a bad meal** un mauvais repas; **his new film's not bad** son nouveau film n'est pas mauvais; **it's bad for your health** c'est mauvais pour la santé; **I'm bad at physics** je suis mauvais en physique; **2** (*serious*) grave; **a bad accident** un accident grave; **a bad cold** un gros rhume; **3** (*rotten*) pourri; **a bad apple** une pomme pourrie; **to go bad** se gâter; **4** (*rude*) **bad language** du langage grossier; **5** (*naughty*) vilain; **bad dog!** vilain!; **bad girl!** vilaine! ★ **too bad!** (*I'm sorry for you*) pas de chance!; (*I don't care*) tant pis!

**badge** *noun* badge *Masc.*

**badly** *adverb* **1** mal; **he writes badly** il écrit mal; **I slept badly** j'ai mal dormi; **the exam went badly** l'examen s'est mal passé; **2** (*seriously*) (*to hurt or damage*) gravement; **the car was badly damaged** la voiture a été gravement endommagée; **badly hurt** grièvement blessé.

**bad-mannered** *adjective* mal élevé.

**badminton** *noun* badminton *Masc.*; **to play badminton** jouer au badminton.

**bad-tempered** *adjective* **1** (*for a little while*) irrité; **2** (*always*) **she's very bad-tempered** elle a très mauvais caractère.

**bag** *noun* sac *Masc.*

**baggage** *noun* bagages *Masc. plural.*

**baggage allowance** *noun* franchise *Fem.* de bagages.

**baggage reclaim** *noun* réception *Fem.* des bagages.

**bagpipes** *plural noun* cornemuse *Fem.*; **to play the bagpipes** jouer de la cornemuse.

**bags** *plural noun* bagages *Masc. plural*; **to pack your bags** faire ses bagages; ★ **to have bags under your eyes** avoir des valises sous les yeux (*informal*) .

**Bahaman** *adjective* des Bahamas.

**Bahamas** *noun* (*plural*) **the Bahamas** les Bahamas; **the Bahamas Islands** les îles Bahamas.

**bake** *verb* **to bake a cake** faire [10] un gâteau; **to bake vegetables** faire [10] cuire des légumes au four.

**baked** *adjective* **1** (*fish or fruit*) au four; **baked apples** les pommes au four; **2 a baked potato** une pomme de terre au four.

**baked beans** *plural noun* les haricots blancs à la sauce tomate.

**baker** *noun* boulanger *Masc.*, boulangère *Fem.*; **to go to the baker's** aller à la boulangerie.

**bakery** *noun* boulangerie *Fem.*

**balance** *noun* **1** équilibre *Masc.*; **to lose your balance** perdre l'équilibre; **2** (*money in your bank account*) solde *Masc.*

**balanced** *adjective* équilibré.

**balcony** *noun* balcon *Masc.*

**bald** *adjective* chauve.

**ball** *noun* **1** (*for tennis or golf*) balle *Fem.*; **2** (*for football or volleyball*) ballon *Masc.*; **3** (*of string or wool*) pelote *Fem.*

**ballet** *noun* ballet *Masc.*

**ballet dancer** *noun* danseur *Masc.* de ballet, danseuse *Fem.* de ballet.

**ballet shoe** *noun* chausson *Masc.* de danse.

**balloon** *noun* **1** ballon *Masc.*; **2** (*hot air*) montgolfière *Fem.*

**ballot** *noun* scrutin *Masc.*

**ballpoint (pen)** *noun* stylo *Masc.* à bille.

**ban** *noun* interdiction *Fem.*; **a ban on smoking** une interdiction de fumer.
**ban** *verb* interdire [47].

**banana** *noun* banane *Fem.*; **a banana yoghurt** un yaourt à la banane.

**band** *noun* **1** (*playing music*) groupe *Masc.*; **a rock band** un groupe de rock; **2 a jazz band** un orchestre de jazz; **3 a brass band** une fanfare; **4 a rubber band** un élastique.

**bandage** *noun* bandage *Masc.*
**bandage** *verb* mettre [11] un bandage à.

**bang** *noun* **1** (*noise*) boum *Masc.*; **2** (*of a door, shutter, or window, etc*) claquement *Masc.*

**bang** *verb* **1** (*to hit*) taper [1] sur (*a drum, for example*); **he banged his fist on the table** il a tapé du poing sur la table; **2** (*to knock*) cogner [1]; **to bang on the door** cogner à la porte; **I banged my head on the door** je me suis cogné la tête contre la porte; **I banged into the table** j'ai heurté la table; **3 to bang the door** claquer [1] la porte.

**bang** *exclamation* (*like a gun*) pan!

**bangle** *noun* bracelet *Masc.*

**banister(s)**, **bannister(s)** (*plural*) *noun* rampe *Fem.* (d'escalier).

**bank** *noun* **1** (*for money*) banque *Fem.*; **I'm going to the bank** je vais à la banque; **2** (*of a river or lake*) bord *Masc.*

**bank account** *noun* compte *Masc.* bancaire.

**bank balance** *noun* solde *Masc.* bancaire.

**bank card** *noun* carte *Fem.* bancaire.

**bank holiday** *noun* jour *Masc.* férié.

**banking** *noun* banque *Fem*; milieu *Masc.* bancaire.

**banknote** *noun* billet *Masc.* de banque.

**bank statement** *noun* relevé *Masc.* de compte.

**baptize** *verb* baptiser [1].

**bar** *noun* **1** (*selling drinks*) bar *Masc.*; **Janet works in a bar** Janet travaille dans un bar; **2** (*the counter*) comptoir *Masc.*; **on the bar** sur le bar; **3 a bar of chocolate** une tablette de chocolat; **4 a bar of soap**

a
**b**
c
d
e
f
g
h
i
j
k
l
m
n
o
p
q
r
s
t
u
v
w
x
y
z

une savonnette; **5** (*made of wood or metal*) barre *Fem.*; **a metal bar** une barre en métal; **6** (*in music*) mesure *Fem.*

**bar** *verb* **1** (*to block physically*) barrer [1]; **to bar someone's way** barrer le passage à quelqu'un; **2** (*to ban from an activity*) exclure [25].

**Barbadian** *noun* Barbadien *Masc.*, Barbadienne *Fem.*

**Barbadian** *adjective* de la Barbade.

**Barbados** *noun* la Barbade.

**barbecue** *noun* barbecue *Masc.*; **there's a barbecue tonight** il y a un barbecue ce soir.

**barbecue** *verb* **to barbecue a chicken** faire [10] griller un poulet au barbecue; **barbecued chicken** du poulet grillé au barbecue.

**barbed wire** *noun* barbelé *Masc.*

**bare** *adjective* nu.

**barefoot** *adjective* **to be barefoot** être nu-pieds; **to walk barefoot** marcher pieds nus.

**bargain** *noun* (*a good buy*) affaire *Fem.*; **I got a bargain** j'ai fait une affaire; **it's a bargain!** c'est une bonne affaire!

**barge** *noun* péniche *Fem.*

**bark** *noun* **1** (*of a tree*) écorce *Fem.*; **2** (*of a dog*) aboiement *Masc.*

**bark** *verb* aboyer [39].

**barley** *noun* orge *Masc.*

**barmaid** *noun* barmaid *Fem.*

**barman** *noun* barman *Masc.*

**barn** *noun* grange *Fem.*

**barometer** *noun* baromètre *Masc.*

**barrel** *noun* tonneau *Masc.* (*plural* tonneaux).

**barrier** *noun* barrière *Fem.*

**base** *noun* base *Fem.*

**baseball** *noun* base-ball *Masc.*; **a baseball cap** une casquette de base-ball.

**based** *adjective* **1 to be based on** être fondé sur; **the film is based on a true story** le film est fondé sur une histoire vraie; **2 to be based in** être basé à; **he's based in Bristol** il est basé à Bristol.

**basement** *noun* sous-sol *Masc.*; **in the basement** au sous-sol.

**bash** *noun* **1** bosse *Fem.*; **it's got a bash on the wing** il y a une bosse à l'aile; **2 I'll have a bash** je vais essayer un coup.

**bash** *verb* cogner [1]; **I bashed my head** je me suis cogné la tête.

**basic** *adjective* **1** de base; **basic knowledge** des connaissances de base; **her basic salary** son salaire de base; **2 the basic facts** les faits essentiels; **3** (*not luxurious*) rudimentaire; **the flat's a bit basic** l'appartement est un peu rudimentaire.

**basically** *adverb* **1** au fond; **it's basically all right** au fond ça va; **2** à vrai dire; **basically, I don't want to go** à vrai dire, je ne veux pas y aller.

**basics** *noun* rudiments *Masc. plural.*

**basin** *noun* (*washbasin*) lavabo *Masc.*

**basis** *noun* **1** base *Fem.*; **2 on the basis of** sur la base de; **on a regular basis** régulièrement.

**basket** noun 1 (for shopping) panier Masc.; 2 (other) corbeille Fem.; **a waste-paper basket** une corbeille à papier; **a linen basket** une corbeille à linge.

**basketball** noun basketball Masc.; **to play basketball** jouer au basketball.

**bass** noun 1 basse Fem.; **to play bass** jouer de la basse; **2 a double bass** une contrebasse.

**bass drum** noun grosse caisse Fem.

**bass guitar** noun guitare Fem. basse.

**bassoon** noun basson Masc.; **to play the bassoon** jouer du basson.

**bat** noun 1 (for cricket or baseball) batte Fem.; 2 (for table tennis) raquette Fem.; 3 (animal) chauve-souris Fem.

**batch** noun 1 (of cakes) fournée Fem.; 2 (of letters) tas Masc.; **a batch of letters** un tas de lettres; 3 (in computing) lot Masc.

**bath** noun 1 bain Masc.; **to have a bath** prendre un bain; **I was in the bath** j'étais dans mon bain; 2 (bathtub) baignoire Fem.; **the bath's pink** la baignoire est rose.

**bathe** verb 1 laver [1] (a wound); 2 (go swimming) se baigner [1].

**bathroom** noun salle Fem. de bains (plural salles de bains).

**baths** plural noun piscine Fem.

**bath towel** noun serviette Fem. de bain.

**batter** noun (for frying) pâte Fem. à frire; **fish in batter** des beignets de poisson; **pancake batter** la pâte à crêpes.

**battery** noun 1 (for a torch or radio, for example) pile Fem.; 2 (for a car) batterie Fem.

**battle** noun bataille Fem.

**bay** noun 1 (on the coast) baie Fem.; 2 (for coaches) travée Fem.

**B.C.** (short for: before Christ) av. J.-C.

**be** verb 1 être [6]; **Melanie is in the kitchen** Melanie est dans la cuisine; **where is the butter?** où est le beurre?; **I'm tired** je suis fatigué; **when we were in France** quand nous étions en France; 2 (with jobs and professions) être; **she's a teacher** elle est professeur (note that 'a' is not translated); **he's a taxi driver** il est chauffeur de taxi; 3 (in clock times) être; **it's three o'clock** il est trois heures; **it's half past five** il est cinq heures et demie; 4 (days of the week and dates) **what day is it today?** nous sommes quel jour aujourd'hui?; **it's Tuesday today** nous sommes mardi aujourd'hui; **it's the twentieth of May** nous sommes le vingt mai; 5 (talking about age) avoir [5]; **how old are you?** quel âge as-tu?; **I'm fifteen** j'ai quinze ans; **Harry's twenty** Harry a vingt ans; 6 (cold, hot, hungry) avoir [5]; **I'm hot** j'ai chaud; **I'm cold** j'ai froid; **I'm hungry** j'ai faim; 7 (weather) faire [10]; **it's cold today** il fait froid aujourd'hui; **it's a nice day** il fait beau; 8 **I've never been to Paris** je ne suis jamais allé à Paris; **have you been to Britain before?** est-ce que tu es déjà venu en Grande Bretagne?; 9 **to be loved**

351

être aimé; **he has been killed** il a été tué.

**beach** *noun* plage *Fem.*; **to go to the beach** aller à la plage; **on the beach** sur la plage.

**bead** *noun* perle *Fem.*

**beak** *noun* bec *Masc.*

**beam** *noun* **1** (*of light*) rayon *Masc.*; **2** (*for a roof*) poutre *Fem.*

**bean** *noun* haricot *Masc.*; **baked beans** les haricots à la sauce tomate; **green beans** les haricots verts.

**bear** *noun* ours *Masc.*
**bear** *verb* **1** supporter [1]; **I can't bear him** je ne peux pas le supporter; **I can't bear the idea** je ne supporte pas l'idée; **2 to bear something in mind** tenir [77] compte de quelque chose; **I'll bear it in mind** je ne l'oublierai pas.

● **to bear up** tenir [77] le coup.

**beard** *noun* barbe *Fem.*

**bearded** *adjective* barbu.

**bearings** *plural noun* **to get one's bearings** se repérer [24].

**beast** *noun* **1** (*animal*) bête *Fem.*; **2 you beast!** chameau!

**beat** *noun* rythme *Masc.*
**beat** *verb* **1** (*defeat*) battre [21]; **we beat them!** on les a battus!; **2 to beat the eggs** battre les œufs; **3 you can't beat a good meal** rien ne vaut un bon repas.

● **to beat somebody up** tabasser [1] quelqu'un (*informal*).

**beautician** *noun* esthéticien *Masc.*, esthéticienne *Fem.*

**beautiful** *adjective* beau (*Fem.* belle) (*Masc. plural* beaux) (*goes before the noun*); **a beautiful day** un beau jour; **a beautiful girl** une belle fille; **beautiful pictures** de beaux tableaux; **a beautiful place** un bel endroit (*'bel' for masculine nouns beginning with a vowel or silent 'h'*).

**beautifully** *adverb* admirablement.

**beauty** *noun* beauté *Fem.*

**beauty spot** *noun* (*for tourists*) beau site *Masc.*

**because** *conjunction* **1** parce que; **because it's you** parce que c'est toi; **because it's cold** parce qu'il fait froid; **2 because of** à cause de; **because of the accident** à cause de l'accident.

**become** *verb* devenir [81].

**bed** *noun* **1** lit *Masc.*; **a double bed** un grand lit; **in bed** au lit; **to go to bed** aller se coucher; **2** (*flower bed*) parterre *Masc.*

**bedclothes** *plural noun* couvertures *Fem. plural*.

**bedding** *noun* literie *Fem.*

**bedroom** *noun* chambre *Fem.*; **bedroom furniture** les meubles de chambre; **my bedroom window** la fenêtre de ma chambre.

**bedside** *noun* **a bedside table** une table de chevet.

**bedsit**, **bedsitter** *noun* chambre *Fem.* meublée.

**bedspread** *noun* dessus-de-lit *Masc.*

**bedtime** *noun* **it's bedtime** c'est l'heure d'aller se coucher.

**bee** *noun* abeille *Fem.*

**beech** *noun* hêtre *Masc.*

**beef** *noun* bœuf *Masc.*; **we had roast beef** on a mangé du rôti de bœuf.

**beefburger** *noun* hamburger *Masc.*

**beer** *noun* bière *Fem.*; **two beers please** deux bières s'il vous plaît; **a beer can** une canette de bière.

**beetle** *noun* scarabée *Masc.*

**beetroot** *noun* betterave *Fem.*

**before** *preposition, adverb* **1** avant; **before Monday** avant lundi; **he left before me** il est parti avant moi; **2 the day before** la veille; **the day before the wedding** la veille du mariage; **the day before yesterday** avant-hier; **the week before** la semaine d'avant; **3** (*already*) déjà; **I've seen him before somewhere** je l'ai déjà vu quelque part; **I had seen the film before** j'avais déjà vu le film.

**before** *conjunction* **1** avant de; **before doing** avant de faire; **I closed the windows before leaving** (or **before I left**) j'ai fermé les fenêtres avant de partir; **2** avant que; **phone me before they leave** appelle-moi avant qu'ils s'en aillent; **oh, before I forget** ... avant que j'oublie ....

**beforehand** *adverb* (*ahead of time*) à l'avance; **phone beforehand** appelle à l'avance.

**beg** *verb* **1** (*ask for money*) mendier [1]; **2** (*ask*) supplier [1]; **she begged me not to leave** elle m'a supplié de ne pas partir; **I beg your pardon** je vous demande pardon.

**begin** *verb* **1** commencer [61]; **the meeting begins at ten** la réunion commence à dix heures; **the words beginning with P** les mots qui commencent par un P; **2 to begin to do** commencer à faire; **I'm beginning to understand** je commence à comprendre.

**beginner** *noun* débutant *Masc.*, débutante *Fem.*

**beginning** *noun* début *Masc.*; **at the beginning** au début; **at the beginning of the holidays** au début des vacances.

**behalf** *noun* **on behalf of** pour.

**behave** *verb* **1** se comporter [1]; **he behaved badly** il s'est mal comporté; **2 to behave yourself** être sage; **behave yourselves!** soyez sages!

**behaviour** *noun* comportement *Masc.*

**behind** *adverb, preposition* **1** derrière; **behind the sofa** derrière le canapé; **behind them** derrière eux; **the car behind** la voiture de derrière; **2** (*not making progress*) **he's behind in class** il a du retard en classe; **3 to leave something behind** oublier quelque chose; **I've left my keys behind** j'ai oublié mes clés.

**behind** *noun* derrière *Masc.*

**beige** *adjective* beige.

**Belgian** *noun* Belge *Masc. & Fem.* **Belgian** *adjective* belge.

**Belgium** *noun* Belgique *Fem.*; **to Belgium** en Belgique; **in Belgium** en Belgique.

a
**b**
c
d
e
f
g
h
i
j
k
l
m
n
o
p
q
r
s
t
u
v
w
x
y
z

a
**b**
c
d
e
f
g
h
i
j
k
l
m
n
o
p
q
r
s
t
u
v
w
x
y
z

**belief** *noun* conviction *Fem.*; **his political beliefs** ses convictions politiques.

**believe** *verb* **1** croire [33]; **I believe you** je te crois; **they believed what I said** ils ont cru ce que j'ai dit; **I don't believe you!** ce n'est pas vrai!; **2 to believe in** croire à; **to believe in ghosts** croire aux fantômes; **to believe in God** croire en Dieu.

**bell** *noun* **1** (*in a church*) cloche *Fem.*; **2** (*on a door*) sonnette *Fem.*; **ring the bell!** appuyez sur la sonnette!; **3** (*for a cat or toy*) grelot *Masc*; ★ **that name rings a bell** ce nom me dit quelque chose (*literally: says something to me*).

**belong** *verb* **1 to belong to** appartenir [81] à; **that belongs to Richard** cela appartient à Richard; **2 to belong to a club** faire [10] partie d'un club; **3** (*go*) aller [5]; **that chair belongs in the study** cette chaise va dans le bureau; **where does this vase belong?** ce vase va où?

**belongings** *plural noun* affaires *Fem. plural*; **all my belongings are in London** toutes mes affaires sont à Londres.

**below** *preposition* au-dessous de; **below the window** au-dessous de la fenêtre; **the flat below yours** l'appartement au-dessous du tien.
**below** *adverb* **1** (*further down*) en bas; **shouts came from below** des cris venaient d'en bas; **2 the flat below** l'appartement de dessous.

**belt** *noun* ceinture *Fem.*

**bench** *noun* banc *Masc.*

**bend** *noun* **1** (*in a road*) virage *Masc.*; **2** (*in a river*) courbe *Fem.*
**bend** *verb* **1** (*to make a bend in*) plier [1] (*your arm or leg, or a wire*); **2** (*to curve*) (*a road or path*) tourner [1]; **3 to bend down** or **forwards** se pencher [1]; **she bent down to look** elle s'est penchée pour regarder.

**beneath** *preposition* sous.

**benefit** *noun* **1** avantage *Masc.*; **2 unemployment benefit** les allocations *Fem. plural* de chômage.

**bent** *adjective* tordu.

**beret** *noun* béret *Masc.*

**berry** *noun* baie *Fem.*

**berth** *noun* couchette *Fem.*

**beside** *preposition* (*next to*) à côté de; **she was sitting beside me** elle était assise à côté de moi; ★ **that's beside the point** ça n'a rien à voir.

**besides** *adverb* **1** (*anyway*) d'ailleurs; **besides, it's too late** d'ailleurs, il est trop tard; **2** (*as well*) en plus; **four dogs, and six cats besides** quatre chiens et six chats en plus.

**best** *adjective* **1** meilleur; **it's the best** c'est le meilleur; **that's the best car** cette voiture-là est la meilleure; **she's my best friend** c'est ma meilleure amie; **2 she's the best at tennis** c'est elle la meilleure en tennis; **the best thing to do is to phone them** la meilleure chose à faire, c'est de les appeler.
**best** *adverb* le mieux; **he plays best** il joue le mieux; **I like Paris best** c'est Paris que j'aime le mieux; **best of all** mieux que tout; ★ **all the best!** (*good luck*) bonne chance!

(*cheers*) à ta santé!; ★ **it's the best I can do** je ne peux pas faire mieux; ★ **to do your best to do** faire de son mieux pour faire;; **I did my best to help her** j'ai fait de mon mieux pour l'aider.

**best man** *noun* garçon *Masc.* d'honneur.

**bet** *noun* pari *Masc.*
**bet** *verb* parier [1]; **to bet on a horse** parier sur un cheval; **I bet you he'll forget!** je te parie qu'il va oublier!

**better** *adjective, adverb* **1** meilleur; **she's found a better flat** elle a trouvé un meilleur appartement; **this road's better than the other one** cette route est meilleure que l'autre; **2** mieux; **this pen writes better** ce stylo écrit mieux; **it works better than the other one** ça fonctionne mieux que l'autre; **3 even better** encore mieux; **it's even better than before** c'est encore mieux qu'avant; **4** (*less ill*) **to be better** aller mieux; **he's a bit better today** il va un peu mieux aujourd'hui; **to feel better** se sentir mieux; **I feel better** je me sens mieux; **5 to get better** s'améliorer; **my French is getting better** mon français s'améliore; **6 so much the better** tant mieux; **the sooner the better** le plus vite possible.
**better** *adverb* **you had better phone at once** tu ferais mieux d'appeler tout de suite; **he'd better not go** il ferait mieux de ne pas y aller; **I'd better go now** je dois partir maintenant.

**better off** *adjective* **1** (*richer*) plus riche; **they're better off than us** ils sont plus riches que nous; **2** (*more comfortable*) mieux; **you'd be better off in bed** tu serais mieux au lit.

**between** *preposition* entre; **between London and Dover** entre Londres et Douvres; **between Monday and Friday** entre lundi et vendredi; **between the two** entre les deux.

**beware** *verb* **beware of the dog!** attention au chien!

**beyond** *preposition* **1** (*in space and time*) au-delà de; **beyond the border** au-delà de la frontière; **2 it's beyond me!** ça me dépasse!

**Bible** *noun* **the Bible** la Bible.

**bicycle** *noun* vélo *Masc.*; **by bicycle** à vélo.

**bicycle lane** *noun* piste *Fem.* cyclable.

**big** *adjective* **1** grand (*goes before the noun*); **a big house** une grande maison; **a big city** une grande ville; **my big sister** ma grande sœur; **it's too big for me** c'est trop grand pour moi; **2** gros (*Fem.* grosse) (*before the noun*); **a big dog** un gros chien; **a big car** une grosse voiture; **a big mistake** une grosse erreur.

**bigheaded** *adjective* **to be bigheaded** avoir la grosse tête.

**big screen** *noun* grand écran *Masc.*

**big toe** *noun* gros orteil *Masc.*

**bike** *noun* **1** (*with pedals*) vélo *Masc.*; **by bike** à vélo; **2** (*with motor*) moto *Fem.*

**bikini** *noun* bikini *Masc.*

a b c d e f g h i j k l m n o p q r s t u v w x y z

**bilingual** *adjective* bilingue.

**bill** *noun* 1 (*in a restaurant*) addition *Fem.*; **can we have the bill, please** l'addition, s'il vous plaît; 2 (*for gas, electricity, etc.*) facture *Fem.*

**billiards** *noun* billard *Masc.*; **to play billiards** jouer au billard.

**billion** *noun* milliard *Masc.*

**bin** *noun* poubelle *Fem.*

**binoculars** *noun* jumelles *Fem.* plural.

**biochemistry** *noun* biochimie *Fem.*

**biography** *noun* biographie *Fem.*

**biologist** *noun* biologiste *Masc. & Fem.*

**biology** *noun* biologie *Fem.*

**bird** *noun* oiseau *Masc.* (*plural* oiseaux).

**bird sanctuary** *noun* réserve *Fem.* ornithologique.

**birdwatching** *noun* **to go birdwatching** observer les oiseaux.

**Biro™** *noun* bic™ *Masc.*

**birth** *noun* naissance *Fem.*

**birth certificate** *noun* acte *Masc.* de naissance.

**birth control** *noun* contraception *Fem.*

**birthday** *noun* 1 anniversaire *Masc.*; **happy birthday!** joyeux anniversaire!; 2 **a birthday present** un cadeau d'anniversaire.

**birthday party** *noun* 1 (*for a child*) goûter *Masc.* d'anniversaire; 2 (*for an adult*) soirée *Fem.* d'anniversaire.

**biscuit** *noun* biscuit *Masc.*

**bishop** *noun* évêque *Masc.*

**bit** *noun* 1 (*of bread, cheese, wood*) morceau *Masc.*; **a bit of chocolate** un morceau de chocolat; 2 (*of string, paper, garden*) bout *Masc.*; **a bit of string** un bout de ficelle; **with a little bit of garden** avec un petit bout de jardin; 3 (*a small amount*) **a bit of** un peu de; **a bit of sugar** un peu de sucre; **with a bit of luck** avec un peu de chance; **a bit of news** une nouvelle; **to have a bit of trouble with** avoir un petit problème avec; 4 (*in a book or film, for example*) passage *Masc.*; **this bit is brilliant!** ce passage est génial!; 5 **to fall to bits** tomber en morceaux; 6 **a bit** un peu; **a bit hot** un peu chaud; **a bit early** un peu trop tôt; **wait a bit!** attends un peu!; 7 (*for a horse*) mors *Masc*; ★ **bit by bit** petit à petit.

**bite** *noun* 1 (*snack*) morceau *Masc.*; **I'll just have a bite before I go** je vais juste manger un morceau avant de partir; 2 (*from an insect*) piqûre *Fem.*; **a mosquito bite** une piqûre de moustique; 3 (*from a dog*) morsure *Fem.*

**bite** *verb* 1 (*a person or a dog*) mordre [3]; 2 (*an insect*) piquer [1]; ★ **to bite one's nails** se ronger [52] les ongles.

**bitter** *adjective* (*taste*) amer (*Fem.* amère).

**black** *adjective* 1 noir; **my black jacket** ma veste noire; **to turn black** noircir [2]; 2 **a Black man** un Noir; **a Black woman** une Noire; 3 **a black coffee** un café noir.

**blackberry** *noun* mûre *Fem.*

**blackbird** *noun* merle *Masc.*

**blow**

**blackboard** *noun* tableau *Masc.* noir.

**blackcurrant** *noun* cassis *Masc.*

**black eye** *noun* œil *Masc.* au beurre noir.

**black pudding** *noun* boudin *Masc.* noir.

**blade** *noun* lame *Fem.*

**blame** *noun* responsabilité *Fem.*; **to take the blame for something** prendre la responsabilité de quelque chose.
 **blame** *verb* **to blame someone for something** tenir [77] quelqu'un responsable de quelque chose; **they blamed him for the accident** ils l'ont tenu responsable de l'accident; **she is to blame for it** elle en est responsable; **I blame the parents!** à mon avis c'est la faute des parents!; **I don't blame you!** je te comprends!

**blank** *noun* blanc *Masc.*
 **blank** *adjective* **1** (*a page or piece of paper, or a cheque*) blanc (*Fem.* blanche); (*a tape or disk*) vierge (*a screen*) vide; **2 my mind went blank** j'ai eu un trou de mémoire.

**blanket** *noun* couverture *Fem.*

**blast** *noun* **1** (*an explosion*) explosion *Fem.*; **2** (*of air*) souffle *Masc.*; **3 to play music at full blast** jouer de la musique à plein volume.

**blaze** *noun* incendie *Masc.*
 **blaze** *verb* brûler [1].

**blazer** *noun* blazer *Masc.*

**bleach** *noun* eau *Fem.* de javel.

**bleed** *verb* saigner [1]; **my nose is bleeding** je saigne du nez.

**blend** *noun* mélange *Masc.*

**blender** *noun* mixer *Masc.*

**bless** *verb* bénir [2]; **bless you!** (*after a sneeze*) à tes souhaits!

**blind** *noun* (*in a window*) store *Masc.*
 **blind** *adjective* aveugle; **to go blind** perdre la vue.

**blindness** *noun* cécité *Fem.*

**blink** *verb* (*your eyes*) cligner [1] des yeux.

**blister** *noun* ampoule *Fem.*

**blizzard** *noun* tempête *Fem.* de neige.

**blob** *noun* goutte *Fem.*

**block** *noun* **1 a block of flats** un immeuble; **an office block** un immeuble de bureaux; **2** (*a square group of buildings*) **to run** (or **drive**) **round the block** faire le tour du pâté de maisons.
 **block** *verb* **1** bloquer [1] (*an exit or a road*); **2** boucher [1] (*a drain or a hole*); **the sink's blocked** l'évier est bouché.

**blonde** *adjective* blond.

**blood** *noun* sang *Masc.*

**blood test** *noun* prise *Fem.* de sang.

**blossom** *noun* fleurs *Fem.* plural; **to be in blossom** être en fleurs.

**blot** *noun* tache *Fem.*

**blotchy** *adjective* (*skin*) marbré.

**blouse** *noun* chemisier *Masc.*

**blow** *noun* coup *Masc.*
 **blow** *verb* **1** (*the wind or a person*) souffler [1]; **2** (*in an explosion*) **the bomb blew a hole in the wall** la bombe a fait un trou dans le mur; **3 to blow your nose** se moucher [1].

a
b
c
d
e
f
g
h
i
j
k
l
m
n
o
p
q
r
s
t
u
v
w
x
y
z

- **to blow something out** souffler [1] (*a candle*), éteindre [60] (*flames*).

- **to blow up** (*explode*) exploser [1].

- **to blow something up** gonfler [1] (*a balloon or tyre*), faire [10] sauter (*a building*); **they blew up the president's residence** ils ont fait sauter la résidence du président.

**blow-dry** *noun* brushing *Masc.*; **a cut and blow dry** une coupe brushing.

**blue** *adjective* bleu; **blue eyes** les yeux bleus.

**bluebell** *noun* jacinthe *Fem.* des bois.

**blues** *plural noun* le blues *Masc.* singular.

**blunder** *noun* gaffe *Fem.*

**blunt** *adjective* **1** (*a knife or scissors*) émoussé; **2** (*a pencil*) mal taillé; **3** (*person*) brusque.

**blurred** *adjective* **1** indistinct; **2** (*photo*) flou.

**blush** *verb* rougir [2].

**board** *noun* **1** (*plank*) planche *Fem.*; **2** (*blackboard*) tableau *Masc.* noir; **3** (*notice board*) panneau *Masc.* d'affichage; **4** (*for a board game*) jeu *Masc.*; **5** a chess board un échiquier; **6** (*accommodation in a hotel*) **full board** pension *Fem.* complète; **half board** demi-pension *Fem.*; **7** on board à bord; **they were on board the ferry** ils étaient à bord du ferry.

**boarder** *noun* (*in a school*) interne *Masc. & Fem.*

**board game** *noun* jeu *Masc.* de société (*plural* jeux de société).

**boarding** *noun* embarquement *Masc.*

**boarding card** *noun* carte *Fem.* d'embarquement.

**boarding school** *noun* école *Fem.* privée avec internat.

**boast** *verb* se vanter [1]; **he was boasting about his new bike** il se vantait de son nouveau vélo.

**boat** *noun* **1** (*in general*) bateau *Masc.*; **2** (*sailing boat*) voilier *Masc.*; **3** (*rowing boat*) barque *Fem.*

**body** *noun* **1** corps *Masc.*; **2** (*corpse*) cadavre *Masc.*

**bodybuilding** *noun* culturisme *Masc.*

**bodyguard** *noun* garde *Masc.* du corps.

**boil** *noun* **1 bring the water to the boil** portez l'eau à ébullition; **2** (*swelling*) furoncle *Masc.* **boil** *verb* **1** bouillir [23]; **the water's boiling** l'eau bout; **2** faire [10] bouillir; **I'm going to boil some water** je vais faire bouillir de l'eau; **to boil vegetables** faire [10] cuire des légumes à l'eau bouillante; **to boil an egg** faire cuire un œuf.

- **to boil over** déborder [1].

**boiled egg** *noun* œuf *Masc.* à la coque.

**boiler** *noun* (*for central heating*) chaudière *Fem.*

**boiling** *adjective* **1** (*water*) bouillant; **2 it's boiling hot today!** il fait une chaleur infernale aujourd'hui!

**bolt** *noun* (*on a door*) verrou *Masc.* **bolt** *verb* (*to lock*) verrouiller [1] (*a door*).

**bomb** *noun* bombe *Fem.*
**bomb** *verb* bombarder [1].

**bombing** *noun* 1 (*in a war*) bombardement *Masc.*; 2 (*a terrorist attack*) attentat *Masc.* à la bombe.

**bone** *noun* 1 os *Masc.*; 2 (*of a fish*) arête *Fem.*

**bonfire** *noun* 1 (*for rubbish*) feu *Masc.* de jardin; 2 (*for a celebration*) feu *Masc.* de joie.

**bonnet** *noun* capot *Masc.* (*of a car*).

**bony** *adjective* 1 (*fish*) plein d'arêtes; 2 (*body*) anguleux (*Fem.* anguleuse); 3 (*knee*) osseux (*Fem.* osseuse).

**boo** *verb* huer [1]; **the crowd booed the referee** la foule a hué l'arbitre.

**book** *noun* 1 (*that you read*) livre *Masc.*; **a book about dinosaurs** un livre sur les dinosaures; **a biology book** un livre de biologie; **2 an exercise book** un cahier; **3** (*of cheques, stamps, tickets, etc*) carnet *Masc.*; **a cheque book** un carnet de chèques.
**book** *verb* réserver [1]; **I booked a table for 8 p.m.** j'ai réservé une table pour vingt heures.

**bookcase** *noun* bibliothèque *Fem.*

**booking** *noun* (*for a theatre or a holiday, for example*) réservation *Fem.*

**booking office** *noun* bureau *Masc.* de location.

**booklet** *noun* brochure *Fem.*

**bookshelf** *noun* étagère *Fem.*

**bookshop** *noun* librairie *Fem.*

**boom** *noun* 1 (*of a sail*) bôme *Fem.*; 2 (*time of prosperity*) boom *Masc.*

**boot** *noun* 1 (*for football, walking, climbing, or skiing*) chaussure *Fem.*; **walking boots** des chaussures de randonnée; 2 (*short fashion boot*) bottine *Fem.*; 3 (*knee-high boots or wellingtons*) botte *Fem.*; 4 (*of a car*) coffre *Masc.*

**border** *noun* (*between countries*) frontière *Fem.*; **we crossed the border at Basel** nous avons passé la frontière à Bâle.

**bore** *noun* 1 (*a boring person*) raseur *Masc.*, raseuse *Fem.* (*informal*); 2 (*a nuisance*) **what a bore!** quelle barbe!

**bored** *adjective* **to be bored** s'ennuyer; **je m'ennuie** I'm bored; **to get bored** s'ennuyer.

**boring** *adjective* ennuyeux (*Fem.* ennuyeuse).

**born** *adjective* né; **to be born** naître [55]; **she was born in June** elle est née en juin.

**borrow** *verb* emprunter [1]; **can I borrow your bike?** puis-je t'emprunter ton vélo?; **to borrow something from someone** emprunter quelque chose à quelqu'un; **I'll borrow some money from Dad** je vais emprunter de l'argent à Papa.

**Bosnia** *noun* Bosnie *Fem.*

**boss** *noun* patron *Masc.*, patronne *Fem.*

**bossy** *adjective* autoritaire.

**both** *pronoun* 1 (*of people*) tous les deux (*Fem.* toutes les deux); **they both came** ils sont venus tous les deux; **both my sisters were there** mes sœurs y étaient toutes les deux;

a
b
c
d
e
f
g
h
i
j
k
l
m
n
o
p
q
r
s
t
u
v
w
x
y
z

**2** (*of things*) les deux; **they are both sold** les deux sont vendus; **both my feet** mes deux pieds; **3 both at home and at school** à la maison comme à l'école; **both in summer and in winter** en été comme en hiver.

**bother** *noun* ennui *Masc.*; **I've had a lot of bother with the car** j'ai eu beaucoup d'ennuis avec la voiture; **it's too much bother** c'est trop de tracas; **it's no bother** ce n'est pas un problème; **without any bother** sans aucune difficulté.

**bother** *verb* **1** (*to disturb*) déranger [52]; **I'm sorry to bother you** je suis désolé de vous déranger; **2** (*to worry*) inquiéter [24]; **that doesn't bother me at all** ça ne m'inquiète pas du tout; **don't bother about dinner** ne t'inquiète pas pour le dîner; **3 she didn't even bother to come** elle n'a même pas pris la peine de venir; **don't bother!** ce n'est pas la peine!

**bottle** *noun* bouteille *Fem.*

**bottle bank** *noun* conteneur *Masc.* à verre.

**bottle opener** *noun* ouvre-bouteille *Masc.*

**bottom** *noun* **1** (*of a hill, a wall, or steps*) pied *Masc.*; **at the bottom of the ladder** au pied de l'échelle; **2** (*of a bag or a bottle, a hole, a stretch of water, or a garden*) fond *Masc.*; **at the bottom of the lake** au fond du lac; **3 at the bottom of the page** en bas de la page; **4** (*buttocks*) derrière *Masc.*

**bottom** *adjective* **1** inférieur; **the bottom shelf** le rayon inférieur;

**2** (*a division, team, or place*) dernier (*Fem.* dernière); **3 the bottom sheet** le drap de dessous; **the bottom flat** l'appartement du rez-de-chaussée.

**bounce** *verb* rebondir [2].

**bouncer** *noun* videur *Masc.*

**bound** *adjective* (*certain*) **he's bound to be late** il va sûrement être en retard; **that was bound to happen** cela devait arriver.

**boundary** *noun* limite *Fem.* (*for sports*) limites *Fem. plural* du terrain.

**bow** *noun* **1** (*in a shoelace or ribbon*) nœud *Masc.*; **2** (*for a violin*) archet *Masc.*; **3 a bow and arrow** un arc et une flèche.

**bowels** *plural noun* intestins *Masc. plural.*

**bowl** *noun* **1** (*for cereal, for example*) bol *Masc.*; **2** (*larger, for salad or mixing*) saladier *Masc.*; **3** (*for washing up*) cuvette *Fem.*
**bowl** *verb* lancer [61] (*a ball*).

**bowler** *noun* (*in cricket*) lanceur *Masc.*

**bowling** *noun* (*tenpin*) bowling *Masc.*; **to go bowling** jouer au bowling.

**bow tie** *noun* nœud *Masc.* papillon.

**box** *noun* **1** boîte *Fem.*; **a box of chocolates** une boîte de chocolats; **2 a cardboard box** un carton; **3** (*on an application form*) case *Fem.*

**boxer** *noun* **1** (*fighter*) boxeur *Masc.*; **2** (*dog*) boxer *Masc.*

**boxer shorts** *plural noun* caleçon *Masc. singular.*

**boxing** *noun* **1** boxe *Fem.*; **2 a boxing match** un match de boxe.

**Boxing Day** *noun* le lendemain de Noël.

**box office** *noun* guichet *Masc.*

**boy** *noun* garçon *Masc.*; **a little boy** un petit garçon.

**boyfriend** *noun* copain *Masc.*

**bra** *noun* soutien-gorge *Masc.*

**brace** *noun* (*for teeth*) appareil *Masc.*

**bracelet** *noun* bracelet *Masc.*

**bracket** *noun* **in brackets** entre parenthèses.

**brain** *noun* cerveau *Masc.* (*plural* cerveaux).

**brainwave** *noun* idée *Fem.* géniale.

**brake** *noun* frein *Masc.*
**brake** *verb* freiner [1].

**bramble** *noun* ronce *Fem.*

**branch** *noun* **1** (*of a tree*) branche *Fem.*; **2** (*of a shop*) succursale *Fem.*; **our Oxford branch** notre succursale à Oxford; **3** (*of a bank*) agence *Fem.*

**brand** *noun* marque *Fem.*

**brand new** *adjective* tout neuf (*Fem.* toute neuve).

**brandy** *noun* cognac *Masc.*

**brass** *noun* laiton *Masc.*, cuivre *Masc.* jaune; **a brass candlestick** un chandelier en cuivre jaune.

**brass band** *noun* fanfare *Fem.*

**brave** *adjective* courageux (*Fem.* courageuse).

**bravery** *noun* courage *Masc.*

**Brazilian** *noun* Brésilien *Masc.*, Brésilienne *Fem.*
**Brazilian** *adjective* brésilien (*Fem.* brésilienne).

**bread** *noun* pain *Masc.*; **a slice of bread** une tranche de pain.

**break** *noun* **1** (*a short rest*) pause *Fem.*; **fifteen minutes' break** une pause de quinze minutes; **to take a break** faire une pause; **2** (*in school*) récréation *Fem.*; **3 the Christmas break** les vacances de Noël.

**break** *verb* **1** casser [1]; **he broke a glass** il a cassé un verre; **I broke a tooth/my arm** je me suis cassé une dent/le bras; **2** se casser [1]; **the eggs broke** les œufs se sont cassés; **3 to break your arm** se casser le bras; **4 to break your promise** manquer [1] à sa promesse; **he broke the rules** il n'a pas respecté les règlements; **you mustn't break the rules** il faut respecter les règlements; **5 to break a record** battre [21] un record; **6 to break the news** annoncer [61] la nouvelle.

● **to break down** tomber [1] en panne; **the car broke down** la voiture est tombée en panne.

● **to break in** (*a thief*) entrer [1] par effraction.

● **to break out 1** (*a fire*) se déclarer [1]; **2** (*a fight or a storm*) éclater [1]; **3** (*a prisoner*) s'évader [1].

● **to break up 1** (*a family or couple*) se séparer [1]; **2** (*a crowd or clouds*) se disperser [1]; **3** (*for the holidays*) **we break up on Thursday** les cours finissent jeudi.

**breakdown** *noun* **1** (*of a vehicle*) panne *Fem.*; **we had a breakdown on the motorway** nous sommes tombés en panne sur l'autoroute; **2** (*in talks or negotiations*) rupture *Fem.*; **3** (*a nervous collapse*) dépression *Fem.*; **to have a**

a
**b**
c
d
e
f
g
h
i
j
k
l
m
n
o
p
q
r
s
t
u
v
w
x
y
z

**(nervous) breakdown** faire une dépression.

**breakdown truck** *noun* camion *Masc.* de dépannage.

**breakfast** *noun* petit déjeuner *Masc.*; **we have breakfast at eight** nous prenons le petit déjeuner à huit heures.

**break-in** *noun* cambriolage *Masc.*

**breast** *noun* **1** (*a woman's*) sein *Masc.*; **2** (*of a chicken or other fowl*) blanc *Masc.*

**breaststroke** *noun* brasse *Fem.*

**breath** *noun* **1** (*when you breathe in*) souffle *Masc.*; **out of breath** à bout de souffle; **to get one's breath** reprendre son souffle; **to take a deep breath** respirer profondément; **2** (*when you breathe out*) haleine *Fem.*; **to have bad breath** avoir mauvaise haleine.

**breathe** *verb* respirer [1].

**breathing** *noun* respiration *Fem.*

**breed** *noun* (*of dog, for example*) race *Fem.*
**breed** *verb* **1** élever [50] (*animals*); **2** (*to have babies*) se reproduire [26]; **rabbits breed fast** les lapins se reproduisent vite.

**breeze** *noun* brise *Fem.*

**brew** *verb* **1** préparer [1] (*tea*); **2** brasser [1] (*beer*).

**brewery** *noun* brasserie *Fem.*

**brick** *noun* brique *Fem.*; **a brick wall** un mur de briques.

**bride** *noun* mariée *Fem.*; **the bride and groom** les mariés *Masc. plural.*

**bridegroom** *noun* marié *Masc.*

**bridesmaid** *noun* demoiselle *Fem.* d'honneur.

**bridge** *noun* **1** (*over a river*) pont *Masc.*; **a bridge over the Thames** un pont sur la Tamise; **2** (*card game*) bridge *Masc.*; **to play bridge** jouer au bridge.

**bridle** *noun* bride *Fem.*

**brief** *adjective* bref (*Fem.* brève).

**briefcase** *noun* serviette *Fem.*

**briefly** *adjective* brièvement.

**briefs** *plural noun* slip *Masc.*

**bright** *adjective* **1** (*colour, light*) vif (*Fem.* vive); **bright green socks** des chaussettes vert vif; **2 bright sunshine** un soleil éclatant; **3** (*clever*) intelligent; **she's not very bright** elle n'est pas très intelligente; ★ **to look on the bright side** voir le bon côté des choses.

**brighten up** *verb* **the weather's brightening up** le temps s'éclaircit.

**brilliant** *adjective* **1** (*very clever*) brillant; **a brilliant surgeon** un chirurgien brillant; **he's brilliant at maths** il est très doué en maths; **2** (*wonderful*) génial (*Masc. plural* géniaux) (*informal*); **the party was brilliant!** la boum était géniale!

**bring** *verb* **1** apporter [1] (*something you carry*); **they brought a present** ils ont apporté un cadeau; **bring your camera!** apporte ton appareil-photo!; **it brings good luck** ça porte bonheur; **2** amener [50] (*a person or an animal*); **she's bringing all the children** elle va amener tous les enfants; **3 to bring something back** rapporter [1] quelque chose;

**4 to bring up** élever [50] (*children*); he was brought up by his aunt il a été élevé par sa tante.

**bristle** *noun* poil *Masc.*

**Britain, Great Britain** *noun* Grande-Bretagne *Fem.*; **in Britain** en Grande-Bretagne; **to Britain** en Grande-Bretagne; **Britain is sending aid** la Grande-Bretagne envoie de l'aide.

**British** *plural noun* **the British** les Britanniques; **the British love animals** les Britanniques adorent les animaux.
**British** *adjective* britannique; **the British army** l'armée britannique; **the British Isles** les îles Britanniques.

**Brittany** *noun* Bretagne *Fem.*; **in Brittany** en Bretagne; **to Brittany** en Bretagne.

**broad** *adjective* (*wide*) large.

**broad bean** *noun* fève *Fem.*

**broadcast** *noun* émission *Fem.*
**broadcast** *verb* diffuser [1] (*a programme*).

**broccoli** *noun* brocolis *Masc. plural*; **to eat broccoli** manger des brocolis.

**brochure** *noun* brochure *Fem.*

**broke** *adjective* **to be broke** (*no money*) être fauché (*informal*).

**broken** *adjective* cassé; **the window's broken** la vitre est cassée; **to have a broken leg** avoir la jambe cassée.

**bronchitis** *noun* bronchite *Fem.*; **to have bronchitis** avoir une bronchite.

**brooch** *noun* broche *Fem.*

**broom** *noun* **1** (*for sweeping*) balai *Masc.*; **2** (*bush*) genêt *Masc.*

**brother** *noun* frère *Masc.*; **my little brother** mon petit frère; **my mother's brother** le frère de ma mère.

**brother-in-law** *noun* beau-frère *Masc.* (*plural* beaux-frères).

**brown** *adjective* **1** marron (*does not change in the feminine or plural*); **my brown jacket** ma veste marron; **your brown shoes** tes chaussures marron; **light brown** marron clair; **dark brown** marron foncé; **2** châtain (*hair*); **3** (*tanned in the sun*) bronzé; **to go brown** bronzer.

**brown bread** *noun* pain *Masc.* complet.

**brown sugar** *noun* sucre *Masc.* brun.

**bruise** *noun* **1** (*on a person*) bleu *Masc.*; **2** (*on fruit*) tache *Fem.*

**brush** *noun* **1** (*for your hair, clothes, nails, or shoes*) brosse *Fem.*; **my hair brush** ma brosse à cheveux; **2** (*for sweeping*) balai *Masc.*; **3** (*paintbrush*) pinceau *Masc.*
**brush** *verb* brosser [1] (*the floor or your clothes*); **to brush your hair** se brosser les cheveux; **she brushed her hair** elle s'est brossé les cheveux; **to brush your teeth** se brosser les dents.

**Brussels** *noun* Bruxelles.

**Brussels sprout** *noun* chou *Masc.* de Bruxelles.

**bubble** *noun* bulle *Fem.*

**bubble bath** *noun* bain *Masc.* moussant.

a
b
c
d
e
f
g
h
i
j
k
l
m
n
o
p
q
r
s
t
u
v
w
x
y
z

**a**

**b**

**c**

**d**

**e**

**f**

**g**

**h**

**i**

**j**

**k**

**l**

**m**

**n**

**o**

**p**

**q**

**r**

**s**

**t**

**u**

**v**

**w**

**x**

**y**

**z**

**bucket** *noun* seau *Masc.* (*plural* seaux).

**buckle** *noun* boucle *Fem.*

**Buddhism** *noun* bouddhisme *Masc.*

**Buddhist** *noun* bouddhiste *Masc.* & *Fem.*

**budget** *noun* budget *Masc.*

**budgie** *noun* perruche *Fem.*

**buffet** *noun* buffet *Masc.*

**buffet car** *noun* voiture *Fem.* bar.

**bug** *noun* 1 (*insect*) bestiole *Fem.* (*informal,*); 2 (*germ*) microbe *Fem.*; a **stomach bug** une gastroentérite; 3 (*in a computer*) bug *Masc.*

**build** *verb* construire [26]; **they are building three houses over there** ils construisent trois maisons là-bas.

**builder** *noun* maçon *Masc.*

**building** *noun* bâtiment *Masc.*; (*with offices or flats*) immeuble *Masc.*

**building site** *noun* chantier *Masc.*

**building society** *noun* société *Fem.* d'investissement et de crédit immobilier.

**built-up** *adjective* urbanisé; a **built-up area** une agglomération.

**bulb** *noun* 1 (*for a light*) ampoule *Fem.*; 2 (*that you plant*) bulbe *Masc.*

**bull** *noun* taureau *Masc.* (*plural* taureaux).

**bulldozer** *noun* bulldozer *Masc.*

**bullet** *noun* balle *Fem.*

**bulletin** *noun* bulletin *Masc.*; a **news bulletin** un bulletin d'informations.

**bullfight** *noun* corrida *Fem.*

**bully** *noun* brute *Fem.*; **he's a bully** c'est une brute.

**bully** *verb* tyranniser [1].

**bum** *noun* (*bottom*) derrière *Masc.*

**bump** *noun* 1 (*that sticks up*) bosse *Fem.*; a **bump on the head** une bosse à la tête; a **bump in the road** une bosse sur la route; 2 (*jolt*) secousse *Fem.*; 3 (*noise*) bruit *Masc.* sourd.

**bump** *verb* 1 (*to bang*) cogner [1]; I **bumped my head** je me suis cogné la tête; 2 to **bump into something** rentrer [1] dans quelque chose; 3 to **bump into somebody** (*meet by chance*) croiser [1] quelqu'un.

**bumper** *noun* pare-chocs *Masc.*

**bumpy** *adjective* 1 accidenté (*road*); 2 agité (*plane landing*).

**bun** *noun* 1 (*for a burger*) petit pain *Masc.*; 2 (*sugary*) petit cake *Masc.*

**bunch** *noun* 1 (*of flowers*) bouquet *Masc.*; 2 (*of carrots or radishes*) botte *Fem.*; 3 (*of keys*) trousseau *Masc.*; 4 a **bunch of grapes** une grappe de raisin.

**bundle** *noun* tas *Masc.*

**bungalow** *noun* pavillon *Masc.*

**bunk** *noun* 1 (*on a train or boat*) couchette *Fem.*; 2 **bunk beds** des lits superposés.

**bureau** *noun* agence *Fem.*

**burger** *noun* hamburger *Masc.*

**burglar** *noun* cambrioleur *Masc.*

**burglar alarm** *noun* sonnerie *Fem.* d'alarme.

**burglary** *noun* cambriolage *Masc.*

**burn** *noun* brûlure *Fem.*

**burn** *verb* 1 brûler [1]; I've **burned the rubbish** j'ai brûlé les ordures;

the fire's burning well le feu brûle bien; **she burnt herself on the grill** elle s'est brûlée au grill; **you'll burn your finger!** tu vas te brûler le doigt!; **2** laisser [1] brûler (*something you're cooking*); **Mum's burnt her cake** maman a laissé brûler son gâteau; **3** (*through sunburn*) **I burn easily** j'attrape facilement des coups de soleil.

**burnt** *adjective* brûlé.

**burst** *verb* **1** crever [50] (*a balloon or tyre, for example*); **a burst tyre** un pneu crevé; **2 to burst out laughing** éclater [1] de rire; **3 to burst into tears** fondre [3] en larmes; **4 to burst into flames** prendre [64] feu.

**bury** *verb* enterrer [1].

**bus** *noun* **1** (*public transport*) autobus *Masc.*, bus *Masc.*; **we'll take the bus** on va prendre le bus; **on the bus** dans le bus; **a bus ticket** un ticket de bus; **2** (*coach*) car *Masc.*; **to go to London by bus** aller à Londres en car.

**bus conductor** *noun* receveur *Masc.* d'autobus.

**bus driver** *noun* conducteur de bus *Masc.*, conductrice de bus *Fem.*

**bush** *noun* buisson *Masc.*

**business** *noun* **1** (*commercial dealings*) affaires *Fem. plural*; **to be in business** être dans les affaires; **he's in Leeds on business** il est à Leeds en voyage d'affaires; **he's in the insurance business** il travaille dans l'assurance; **a business letter** une lettre d'affaires; **2** (*firm or company*) entreprise *Fem.*; **small businesses** les petites entreprises;

**3 mind your own business!** occupe-toi de tes affaires!; **that's my business!** ça me regarde!

**business class** *noun* classe *Fem.* affaires.

**businessman** *noun* homme *Masc.* d'affaires.

**business trip** *noun* voyage *Masc.* d'affaires.

**businesswoman** *noun* femme *Fem.* d'affaires.

**bus lane** *noun* couloir *Masc.* d'autobus.

**bus pass** *noun* carte *Fem.* de bus.

**bus route** *noun* ligne *Fem.* d'autobus.

**bus shelter** *noun* abribus™ *Masc.*

**bus station** *noun* gare *Fem.* routière.

**bus stop** *noun* arrêt *Masc.* de bus.

**bust** *noun* **bust size** tour *Masc.* de poitrine.

**busy** *adjective* **1** occupé (*a person*), chargé (*a day or week*); **2 don't disturb him, he's busy** ne le dérange pas, il est occupé; **a busy day** une journée chargée; **3** (*full of cars or people*) très fréquenté (*a road*); **the shops were busy** il y avait beaucoup de monde dans les magasins; **4** (*phone*) **the line's busy** la ligne est occupée.

**but** *conjunction* mais; **small but strong** petit mais fort; **not Thursday but Friday** pas jeudi mais vendredi; **I'll try, but it's difficult** j'essaierai, mais c'est difficile.

**but** *preposition* sauf; **anything but that** tout, sauf ça; **everyone but**

a
**b**
c
d
e
f
g
h
i
j
k
l
m
n
o
p
q
r
s
t
u
v
w
x
y
z

**Roger** tout le monde sauf Roger; **the last but one** l'avant-dernier.

**butcher** *noun* boucher *Masc.*; **he's a butcher** il est boucher; **the butcher's** la boucherie.

**butter** *noun* beurre *Masc.*
**butter** *verb* beurrer [1].

**buttercup** *noun* bouton *Masc.* d'or.

**butterfly** *noun* papillon *Masc.*

**button** *noun* bouton *Masc.*; **the record button** la touche d'enregistrement.

**buttonhole** *noun* boutonnière *Fem.*

**buy** *noun* **a good buy** une bonne affaire; **a bad buy** une mauvaise affaire.
**buy** *verb* acheter [16]; **I bought the tickets** j'ai acheté les billets; **to buy something for somebody** acheter quelque chose à quelqu'un; **Sarah bought him a sweater** Sarah lui a acheté un pull; **to buy something from someone** acheter quelque chose à quelqu'un; **I bought my bike from Tim** j'ai acheté mon vélo à Tim.

**buyer** *noun* acheteur *Masc.*, acheteuse *Fem.*

**buzz** *verb* (*a fly or bee*) bourdonner [1].

**buzzer** *noun* sonnerie *Fem.*

**by** *preposition* **1** par; **by telephone** par téléphone; **to take somebody by the hand** prendre quelqu'un par la main; **eaten by a dog** mangé par un chien; **by mistake** par erreur; **2** (*travel*) en; **to come by bus** venir en bus; **to leave by train** partir en train; **by bike** en vélo; **3** (*near*) à

côté de; **by the fire** à côté du feu; **by the sea** au bord de la mer; **close by** tout près; **4** (*before*) avant; **ready by Monday** prêt avant lundi; **Kevin was back by four** Kevin est rentré avant quatre heures; **5 by yourself** tout seul; **I was by myself in the house** j'étais tout seul chez moi; **she did it by herself** elle l'a fait toute seule; **6 by the way** au fait; **7 to go by** passer.

**bye** *exclamation* au revoir; **bye for now!** à bientôt!

**bypass** *noun* rocade *Fem.*

# Cc

**cab** *noun* **1** taxi *Masc.*; **to call a cab** appeler un taxi; **2** (*on a lorry*) cabine *Fem.*

**cabbage** *noun* chou *Masc.* (*plural* choux).

**cabin** *noun* cabine *Fem.*

**cable** *noun* câble *Masc.*

**cable car** *noun* téléphérique *Masc.*

**cable television** *noun* télévision *Fem.* par câble.

**cactus** *noun* cactus *Masc.*

**cafe** *noun* café *Masc.*

**cage** *noun* cage *Fem.*

**cagoule** *noun* K-way™ *Masc.*

**cake** *noun* gâteau *Masc.* (*plural* gâteaux); **would you like a piece of cake?** veux-tu un morceau de gâteau?

**calculate** *verb* calculer [1].

**calculation** *noun* calcul *Masc.*

**calculator** *noun* calculatrice *Fem*.

**calendar** *noun* calendrier *Masc*.

**calf** *noun* **1** (*animal*) veau *Masc*.; **2** (*of your leg*) mollet.

**call** *noun* (*telephone*) appel *Masc*.; **I had several calls this morning** j'ai eu plusieurs appels ce matin; **thank you for your call** merci de votre appel; **a phone call** un coup de téléphone.
**call** *verb* **1** appeler [18]; **to call a taxi** appeler un taxi; **to call the doctor** appeler le médecin; **they called the police** ils ont appelé la police; **call this number** appelez ce numéro; **thank you for calling** merci de votre appel; **I'll call you back later** je te rappellerai plus tard; **2** appeler [18]; **they've called the baby Julie** ils ont appelé le bébé Julie; **3 to be called** s'appeler [18]; **she has a brother called Dan** elle a un frère qui s'appelle Dan; **what's he called?** il s'appelle comment?

• **to call in** passer [1]; **I'll call in on the way back from school** je passerai en rentrant de l'école.

**call box** *noun* cabine *Fem*. téléphonique.

**calm** *adjective* calme.
**calm** *verb* calmer [1].

• **to calm down** se calmer; **he's calmed down a bit** il s'est calmé un peu.

• **to calm somebody down** calmer quelqu'un; **I tried to calm her down** j'ai essayé de la calmer.

**calmly** *adverb* calmement.

**calorie** *noun* calorie *Fem*.

**camcorder** *noun* caméscope *Masc*.

**camel** *noun* chameau *Masc*. (*plural* chameaux).

**camera** *noun* **1** appareil *Masc*. photo (*plural* appareils photo); **2** (*film or TV camera*) caméra.

**cameraman** *noun* caméraman *Masc*.

**camp** *noun* camp *Masc*.
**camp** *verb* camper [1].

**campaign** *noun* campagne *Fem*.

**camper van** *noun* camping-car *Masc*.

**camping** *noun* camping *Masc*.; **to go camping** faire du camping; **we're going camping in Brittany this summer** nous allons faire du camping en Bretagne cet été.

**campsite** *noun* terrain *Masc*. de camping.

**can**[1] *noun* **1** boîte *Fem*.; **a can of tomatoes** une boîte de tomates; **2** (*for petrol or oil*) bidon *Masc*.

**can**[2] *verb* **1** pouvoir [12]; **I can't/cannot be there before ten** je ne peux pas y être avant dix heures; **you can leave your bag here** tu peux laisser ton sac ici; **can you open the door, please?** peux-tu ouvrir la porte, s'il te plaît?; **can I help you?** est-ce que je peux vous aider?; **they couldn't come** ils n'ont pas pu venir; **you could ring back tomorrow** tu pourrais rappeler demain; **you could have told me** tu aurais pu me le dire; **2** (*not translated*) **can you hear me?** est-ce que tu m'entends?; **I can't see him** je ne le vois pas; **I can't remember** je ne me souviens pas; **I can't find my keys** je ne trouve pas mes clés;

a
b
c
d
e
f
g
h
i
j
k
l
m
n
o
p
q
r
s
t
u
v
w
x
y
z

**3** (*know how to*) savoir [70]; **she can't drive** elle ne sait pas conduire; **can you play the piano?** est-ce que tu sais jouer du piano?

**Canada** *noun* Canada *Masc.*; **to Canada** au Canada; **in Canada** au Canada.

**Canadian** *noun* Canadien *Masc.*, Canadienne *Fem.*. **Canadian** *adjective* canadien (*Fem.* canadienne).

**canal** *noun* canal *Masc.* (*plural* canaux).

**canary** *noun* canari *Masc.*

**cancel** *verb* annuler [1]; **the concert's been cancelled** le concert a été annulé.

**cancer** *noun* cancer *Masc.*; **to have lung cancer** avoir un cancer du poumon.

**Cancer** *noun* Cancer *Masc.*; **I'm Cancer** je suis Cancer.

**candidate** *noun* candidat *Masc.*, candidate *Fem.*

**candle** *noun* bougie *Fem.*

**candlestick** *noun* bougeoir *Masc.*

**candyfloss** *noun* barbe *Fem.* à papa.

**canned** *adjective* en conserve; **canned tomatoes** les tomates en conserve.

**cannon** *noun* canon *Masc.*

**cannot** *verb* can[2].

**canoe** *noun* canoë *Masc.*

**canoeing** *noun* **to go canoeing** faire du canoë; **I like canoeing** j'aime faire du canoë.

**can-opener** *noun* ouvre-boîte *Masc.*

**canteen** *noun* cantine *Fem.*

**canvas** *noun* toile *Fem.*

**cap** *noun* **1** (*hat*) casquette *Fem.*; **a baseball cap** une casquette de baseball; **2** (*on a bottle or tube*) bouchon *Masc.*

**capable** *adjective* capable.

**capacity** *noun* capacité *Fem.*

**capital** *noun* **1** (*city*) capitale *Fem.*; **Paris is the capital of France** Paris est la capitale de la France; **2** (*letter*) majuscule *Fem.*; **in capitals** en majuscules.

**capitalism** *noun* capitalisme *Masc.*

**Capricorn** *noun* Capricorne *Masc.*; **Linda's Capricorn** Linda est Capricorne.

**capsize** *verb* chavirer [1].

**captain** *noun* capitaine *Masc.*

**captivity** *noun* captivité *Fem.*; **to be kept in captivity** être gardé en captivité.

**capture** *verb* capturer [1].

**car** *noun* voiture *Fem.*; **in the car** dans la voiture; **to park the car** garer la voiture; **we're going by car** nous y allons en voiture; **a car crash** un accident de voiture.

**caramel** *noun* caramel *Masc.*

**caravan** *noun* caravane *Fem.*

**card** *noun* carte *Fem.*; **un jeu de cartes** a card game, a pack of cards; **faire une partie de cartes** to have a game of cards.

**cardboard** *noun* carton *Masc.*

**cardigan** *noun* cardigan *Masc.*

**cardphone** *noun* téléphone *Masc.* à carte.

**care** *noun* **1** soin *Masc.*; **to take care to do** prendre soin de faire; **2 to take care of somebody** s'occuper de quelqu'un; **3 take care!** (*be careful*) fais attention!, (*when saying goodbye*) à bientôt!
**care** *verb* **1 to care about** se soucier de [1]; **to care about pollution** se soucier de la pollution; **2 she doesn't care** ça lui est égal; **I couldn't care less!** ça m'est complètement égal!

**career** *noun* carrière *Fem.*

**careful** *adjective* prudent **1 a careful driver** un conducteur prudent; **2 be careful!** fais attention!

**carefully** *adverb* **1 read the instructions carefully** lisez attentivement les instructions; **listen carefully** écoutez bien; **2** (*handle*) avec précaution; **she put the vase down carefully** elle a posé le vase avec précaution; **3 to copy something carefully** recopier soigneusement quelque chose; **4 drive carefully!** sois prudent!

**careless** *adjective* **1 he's very careless** il ne fait pas du tout attention à ce qu'il fait; **2 this is careless work** c'est du travail peu soigné; **a careless mistake** une faute d'inattention; **3 careless driving** la conduite imprudente.

**caretaker** *noun* gardien *Masc.*, gardienne *Fem.*

**car ferry** *noun* ferry *Masc.*

**cargo** *noun* cargaison *Fem.*

**car hire** *noun* location *Fem.* de voitures.

**Caribbean** *noun* **1 the Caribbean (islands)** les Caraïbes; **2 the Caribbean** (*sea*) la mer des Caraïbes.

**carnation** *noun* œillet *Masc.*

**carnival** *noun* carnaval *Masc.*

**car park** *noun* parking *Masc.*

**carpenter** *noun* menuisier *Masc.*

**carpentry** *noun* menuiserie *Fem.*

**carpet** *noun* **1** (*fitted*) moquette *Fem.*; **2** (*loose*) tapis *Masc.*

**car phone** *noun* téléphone *Masc.* de voiture.

**car radio** *noun* autoradio *Masc.*

**carriage** *noun* (*of a train*) voiture *Fem.*

**carrier bag** *noun* sac *Masc.* en plastique.

**carrot** *noun* carotte *Fem.*

**carry** *verb* **1** porter [1]; **she was carrying a parcel** elle portait un paquet; **2** (*vehicle, plane*) transporter [1]; **the coach was carrying schoolchildren** le car transportait des écoliers.

● **to carry on** continuer [1]; **they carried on talking** ils ont continué à parler.

**carrycot** *noun* porte-bébé *Masc.*

**carsick** *adjective* **to be carsick** avoir le mal de la route.

**cart** *noun* charrette *Fem.*

**carton** *noun* **1** (*of cream or yoghurt*) pot *Masc.*; **2** (*of milk or orange*) brique *Fem.*

a b c d e f g h i j k l m n o p q r s t u v w x y z

**cartoon** *noun* **1** (*a film*) dessin *Masc.* animé; **2** (*a comic strip*) bande *Fem.* dessinée; **3** (*an amusing drawing*) dessin *Masc.* humoristique.

**cartridge** *noun* (*for a pen or a video*) cartouche *Fem.*

**carve** *verb* découper [1] (*meat*).

**case**[1] *noun* **1** (*suitcase*) valise *Fem.*; **to pack a case** faire une valise; **2** (*a large wooden box, for wine for example*) caisse *Fem.*; **3** (*for spectacles or small things*) étui *Masc.*

**case**[2] *noun* **1** cas *Masc.*; **in that case** en ce cas; **that's not the case** ce n'est pas le cas; **a case of flu** un cas de grippe; **2 in case** au cas où; **in case he's late** au cas où il serait en retard; **check first, just in case** vérifie d'abord, au cas où; **3 in any case** de toute façon; **in any case, it's too late** de toute façon, c'est trop tard.

**cash** *noun* **1** (*money in general*) argent *Masc.*; **I haven't any cash on me** je n'ai pas d'argent; **2** (*money rather than a cheque*) espèces *Fem. plural*; **to pay in cash** payer en espèces; **£50 in cash** cinquante livres en espèces.

**cash card** *noun* carte *Fem.* de retrait.

**cash desk** *noun* caisse *Fem.*; **pay at the cash desk** payez à la caisse.

**cash dispenser** *noun* guichet *Masc.* automatique.

**cashew** *noun* cajou *Masc.*

**cashier** *noun* caissier *Masc.*, caissière *Fem.*

**cash point** *noun* = cash dispenser.

**cassette** *noun* cassette *Fem.*

**cassette recorder** *noun* magnétophone *Masc.* à cassettes.

**cast** *noun* les acteurs *Masc. plural*; **the cast were on stage** les acteurs étaient sur scène.

**castle** *noun* **1** château *Masc.* (*plural* châteaux); **2** (*in chess*) tour *Fem.*

**casual** *adjective* décontracté.

**casualty** *noun* **1** (*in an accident*) victime *Fem.*; **there are 47 casualties** il y a 47 victimes; **2** (*hospital department*) urgences *Fem. plural*; **he's in casualty** il est aux urgences.

**cat** *noun* chat *Masc.*; (*female*) chatte *Fem.*; **a big black cat** un gros chat noir; ★ **it's raining cats and dogs** il pleut des cordes (*literally: it's raining in ropes*).

**catalogue** *noun* catalogue *Masc.*

**catastrophe** *noun* catastrophe *Fem.*

**catch** *noun* **1** (*on a door*) fermeture *Fem.*; **2** (*a drawback*) piège *Masc.*; **what's the catch?** où est le piège? **catch** *verb* **1** attraper [1]; **Tom caught the ball** Tom a attrapé le ballon; **you can't catch me!** vous ne m'attraperez pas!; **can you catch hold of the branch?** peux-tu attraper la branche?; **2 to catch somebody doing** attraper quelqu'un en train de faire; **he was caught stealing money** il a été attrapé en train de voler de l'argent; **3** prendre [64] (*a bus or plane*); **did Tim catch his plane?** est-ce que Tim a pris son avion?; **4** attraper [1] (*an illness*); **he's caught chickenpox** il a attrapé la varicelle;

**I've caught a cold** j'ai attrapé un rhume; **5** saisir [2] (*what somebody says*); **I didn't catch your name** je n'ai pas saisi votre nom.

● **to catch up with somebody** rattraper [1] quelqu'un.

**category** *noun* catégorie *Fem.*

**catering** *noun* restauration *Fem.*

**caterpillar** *noun* chenille *Fem.*

**cathedral** *noun* cathédrale *Fem.*; **Winchester cathedral** la cathédrale de Winchester.

**Catholic** *noun, adjective* catholique *Masc. & Fem.*

**cattle** *plural noun* bétail *Masc. singular.*

**cauliflower** *noun* chou-fleur *Masc.* (*plural* choux-fleurs); **cauliflower cheese** un gratin de chou-fleur.

**cause** *noun* cause *Fem.*; **the cause of the accident** la cause de l'accident; **for a good cause** pour une bonne cause.
**cause** *verb* **1** causer [1] (*damage or problems*); **to cause problems** causer des problèmes; **2** provoquer [1] (*chaos or disease*); **the strike caused delays** la grève a provoqué des retards.

**caution** *noun* prudence *Fem.*

**cautious** *adjective* prudent.

**cave** *noun* grotte *Fem.*

**caving** *noun* spéléologie *Fem.*; **to go caving** faire de la spéléologie.

**CD** *noun* CD *Masc.*

**CD player** *noun* platine *Fem.* laser.

**CD-ROM** *noun* CD-ROM *Masc.*

**ceiling** *noun* plafond *Masc.*; **on the ceiling** au plafond.

**celebrate** *verb* fêter [1]; **I'm celebrating my birthday** je fête mon anniversaire.

**celebrity** *noun* célébrité *Fem.*

**celery** *noun* céleri *Masc.*

**cell** *noun* cellule *Fem.*

**cellar** *noun* cave *Fem.*

**cello** *noun* violoncelle *Masc.*; **to play the cello** jouer du violoncelle.

**cement** *noun* ciment *Masc.*

**cemetery** *noun* cimetière *Masc.*

**cent** *noun* **1** (*in euro system*) centime *Masc.* (d'euro) (*unofficial term*); cent *Masc.* (*official term*); **2** (*in dollar system*) cent *Masc.*

**centenary** *noun* centenaire *Masc.*

**centigrade** *adjective* centigrade; **ten degrees centigrade** dix degrés centigrade.

**centimetre** *noun* centimètre *Masc.*

**central** *adjective* central (*Masc. plural* centraux); **central London** le centre de Londres; **the office is very central** le bureau est en plein centre-ville.

**central heating** *noun* chauffage *Masc.* central.

**centre** *noun* centre *Masc.*; **in the centre of** au centre de; **in the town centre** en centre-ville; **a shopping centre** un centre commercial.

**century** *noun* siècle *Masc.*; **in the twentieth century** au vingtième siècle; **the twenty-first century** le vingt-et-unième siècle.

**cereal** *noun* **breakfast cereal** céréales *Fem. plural* pour le petit déjeuner; **to have cereal for**

a
b
c
d
e
f
g
h
i
j
k
l
m
n
o
p
q
r
s
t
u
v
w
x
y
z

breakfast prendre des céréales au petit déjeuner.

**ceremony** *noun* cérémonie *Fem.*

**certain** *adjective* certain; **a certain number of** un certain nombre de; **are you certain of the address?** es-tu certain de l'adresse?; **I'm certain of it** j'en suis certain; **to be certain that** être sûr que; **Nicola's certain you're wrong** Nicola est sûre que tu as tort; **nobody knows for certain** personne ne sait au juste.

**certainly** *adverb* certainement; **certainly not** certainement pas.

**certificate** *noun* 1 certificat *Masc.*; 2 **a birth certificate** un acte de naissance.

**chain** *noun* chaîne *Fem.*

**chair** *noun* 1 (*upright*) chaise *Fem.*; **a kitchen chair** une chaise de cuisine; 2 (*with arms*) fauteuil *Masc.*

**chair lift** *noun* télésiège *Masc.*

**chalet** *noun* 1 (*in the mountains*) chalet *Masc.*; 2 (*in a holiday camp*) bungalow *Masc.*

**chalk** *noun* craie *Fem.*

**challenge** *noun* 1 (*that excites you*) challenge *Masc.*; **the challenge of new ideas** le challenge des nouvelles idées; 2 (*that is difficult*) épreuve *Fem.*; **the exam was a real challenge** l'examen était une vraie épreuve.

**champion** *noun* champion *Masc.*, championne *Fem.*; **world champion** champion du monde.

**chance** *noun* 1 (*an opportunity*) occasion *Fem.*; **to have the chance to do** avoir l'occasion de faire; **if you have the chance to go to New York** si tu as l'occasion d'aller à New York; **I haven't had the chance to write to him** je n'ai pas eu l'occasion de lui écrire; 2 (*likelihood*) chance *Fem.*; **there's little chance of winning** il y a peu de chance de gagner; 3 (*luck*) **by chance** par hasard; **do you have her address, by any chance?** aurais-tu par hasard son adresse?

**change** *noun* 1 changement *Masc.*; **a change of plan** un changement de programme; **they've made some changes to the house** ils ont fait des changements dans la maison; **for a change, let's eat out** mangeons au restaurant pour changer; **it makes a change from hamburgers** cela change un peu des hamburgers; 2 **a change of clothes** des vêtements de rechange; 3 (*cash*) monnaie *Fem.*; **I haven't any change** je n'ai pas de monnaie.

**change** *verb* 1 (*transform completely*) changer [52]; **it changed my life** cela m'a changé la vie; **Liz never changes** Liz ne change jamais; 2 (*to switch from one thing to another*) changer [52] de; **we changed trains at Crewe** nous avons changé de train à Crewe; **I must change my shirt** je dois changer de chemise; **they changed places** ils ont changé de place; **to change your mind** changer d'avis; 3 (*to exchange in a shop*) échanger [52]; **can I change it for the larger size?** puis-je l'échanger contre la taille au-dessus?; 4 (*to change your clothes*) se changer [52]; **Mike's gone up to change** Mike est monté se changer.

**changing room** *noun* (*for sport or swimming*) **1** vestiaire *Masc.*; **2** (*in a shop*) salon *Masc.* d'essayage.

**channel** *noun* **1** (*on TV*) chaîne *Fem.*; **to change channels** changer de chaîne; **2 the Channel** la Manche.

**Channel Islands** *plural noun* îles *Fem.* *plural* Anglo-Normandes.

**Channel Tunnel** *noun* tunnel *Masc.* sous la Manche.

**chaos** *noun* pagaille *Fem.* (*informal*); **it was chaos!** c'était la pagaille!

**chapel** *noun* chapelle *Fem.*

**chapter** *noun* chapitre *Masc.*; **in chapter two** au chapitre deux.

**character** *noun* **1** (*personality*) caractère *Masc.*; **a house with a lot of character** une maison qui a du caractère; **2** (*somebody in a book, play, or film*) personnage *Masc.*; **the main character** le personnage principal.

**characteristic** *adjective* caractéristique.

**charcoal** *noun* **1** (*for burning*) charbon *Masc.* de bois; **2** (*for drawing*) fusain *Masc.*

**charge** *noun* **1** (*what you pay*) frais *Masc. plural*; **a booking charge** des frais de réservation; **an extra or additional charge** un supplément; **there's no charge** c'est gratuit; **2 to be in charge** être responsable; **who's in charge of these children?** qui est responsable de ces enfants?; **3 to be on a charge of theft** être inculpé de vol.

**charge** *verb* **1** (*to ask a specific sum*) prendre [64]; **they charge fifteen pounds an hour** ils prennent quinze livres de l'heure; **how much do you charge for one day?** combien prenez-vous pour une journée?; **2** (*to ask people to pay*) faire [10] payer; **we don't charge, it's free** nous ne faisons pas payer les gens, c'est gratuit; **3 to charge somebody with** inculper [1] quelqu'un de (*a crime*).

**charity** *noun* organisation *Fem.* caritative.

**charm** *noun* charme *Masc.*

**charming** *adjective* charmant.

**chart** *noun* **1** (*table*) tableau *Masc.*; **2 the weather chart** la carte du temps; **3 the charts** le hit-parade; **number one in the charts** numéro un au hit-parade.

**charter flight** *noun* vol *Masc.* charter.

**chase** *noun* poursuite *Fem.*; **a car chase** une poursuite en voiture.

**chase** *verb* pourchasser [1] (*a person or animal*).

**chat** *noun* conversation *Fem.*; **to have a chat with somebody** bavarder avec quelqu'un.

**chatroom** *noun* chatroom *Masc.*

**chat show** *noun* talk-show *Masc.*

**chatter** *verb* **1** (*gossip*) bavarder [1]; **2 my teeth are chattering** je claque des dents.

**cheap** *adjective* pas cher (*Fem.* pas chère); **cheap shoes** des chaussures pas chères; **that's very cheap!** ce n'est vraiment pas cher!

**cheaper** *adjective* moins cher (*Fem.* moins chère).

a
b
c
d
e
f
g
h
i
j
k
l
m
n
o
p
q
r
s
t
u
v
w
x
y
z

**cheaply** *adverb* pas cher; **to eat cheaply** manger pas cher.

**cheap rate** *adjective* à tarif réduit; **a cheap rate phone call** un appel à tarif réduit.

**cheat** *noun* tricheur *Masc.*, tricheuse *Fem.*
**cheat** *verb* tricher [1].

**check** *noun* 1 (*in a factory or at border controls*) contrôle *Masc.*; **passport check** contrôle des passeports; 2 (*by a doctor*) examen *Masc.*; 3 (*in chess*) **check!** échec au roi!
**check** *verb* (*to make sure*) vérifier [1]; **he checked the time** il a vérifié l'heure; **check they're all back** vérifiez qu'ils sont tous rentrés; **check with your father** demande à ton père.

- **to check in** 1 (*at the airport*) enregistrer [1]; 2 (*at a hotel*) arriver [1] à l'hôtel; **he checked in at five o'clock** il est arrivé à l'hôtel à cinq heures.

- **to check out** quitter [1] l'hôtel; **he checked out at 8.30** il a quitté l'hôtel à 8h30.

**check-in** *noun* enregistrement *Masc.*

**checkout** *noun* caisse *Fem.*; **at the checkout** à la caisse.

**check-up** *noun* examen *Masc.* médical.

**cheek** *noun* 1 (*part of face*) joue *Fem.*; 2 (*nerve*) **what a cheek!** quel culot! (*informal*).

**cheeky** *adjective* 1 coquin; 2 (*rude*) impoli.

**cheer** *noun* 1 **three cheers for Tom!** faisons un ban à Tom!; 2 (*when you have a drink*) **cheers!** à la vôtre!
**cheer** *verb* (*to shout hurray*) applaudir [2].
- **to cheer on** encourager.
- **to cheer up: cheer up!** courage!
- **to cheer somebody up** remonter [1] le moral à quelqu'un; **your visit's cheered me up** ta visite m'a remonté le moral.

**cheerful** *adjective* gai.

**cheese** *noun* fromage *Masc.*; **blue cheese** le fromage bleu; **a cheese sandwich** un sandwich au fromage.

**cheesecake** *noun* cheesecake *Masc.*

**chef** *noun* chef *Masc.* cuisinier.

**chemical** *noun* produit *Masc.* chimique.
**chemical** *adjective* chimique.

**chemist** *noun* 1 pharmacien *Masc.*, pharmacienne *Fem.*; 2 **chemist's** pharmacie *Fem.*; **at the chemist's** à la pharmacie; 3 (*scientist*) chimiste *Masc. & Fem.*

**chemistry** *noun* chimie *Fem.*

**cheque** *noun* chèque *Masc.*; **to pay by cheque** payer par chèque; **to write a cheque** faire un chèque.

**chequebook** *noun* carnet *Masc.* de chèques.

**cherry** *noun* cerise *Fem.*

**chess** *noun* échecs *Masc. plural*; **to play chess** jouer aux échecs.

**chessboard** *noun* échiquier *Masc.*

**chest** *noun* 1 (*part of the body*) poitrine *Fem.*; 2 (*box*) coffre *Masc.*;

**3 a chest of drawers** une commode.

**chestnut** *noun* marron *Masc.*

**chestnut tree** *noun* **1** (*horse-chestnut*) marronnier *Masc.*; **2** (*sweet chestnut*) châtaignier *Masc.*

**chew** *verb* mâcher [1] (*food*).

**chewing gum** *noun* chewing-gum *Masc.*

**chick** *noun* (*of a hen*) poussin *Masc.*

**chicken** *noun* poulet *Masc.*; **roast chicken** du poulet rôti; **chicken thighs** des cuisses de poulet; **a chicken sandwich** un sandwich au poulet.

**chickenpox** *noun* varicelle *Fem.*

**chicory** *noun* endive *Fem.*

**chief** *noun* chef *Masc.*; **the chief of police** le préfet de police.

**child** *noun* enfant *Masc. & Fem.*; **Jenny's children** les enfants de Jenny.

**childish** *adjective* puéril.

**child-minder** *noun* nourrice *Fem.*

**chill** *noun* fraîcheur *Fem.*

**chilled** *adjective* (*wine*) bien frais.

**chilli** *noun* piment *Masc.*

**chilly** *adjective* frisquet (*Fem.* frisquette); **it's chilly today** il fait frisquet aujourd'hui.

**chimney** *noun* cheminée *Fem.*

**chimpanzee** *noun* chimpanzé *Masc.*

**chin** *noun* menton *Masc.*

**China** *noun* Chine *Fem.*; **in China** en Chine.

**china** *noun* porcelaine *Fem.*; **a china plate** une assiette en porcelaine.

**Chinese** *noun* **1 the Chinese** (*people*) les Chinois; **2** (*language*) chinois *Masc.*

**Chinese** *adjective* chinois; **a Chinese man** un Chinois; **a Chinese woman** une Chinoise; **a Chinese meal** un repas chinois.

**chip** *noun* **1** (*fried potato*) frite *Fem.*; **I'd like some chips** j'aimerais des frites; **2** (*microchip*) puce *Fem.*; **3** (*in glass or china*) ébréchure *Fem.*

**chipped** *adjective* ébréché.

**chives** *noun* ciboulette *Fem. singular.*

**chocolate** *noun* chocolat *Masc.*; **a chocolate ice cream** une glace au chocolat; **hot chocolate** chocolat *Masc.* chaud; **a box of chocolates** une boîte de chocolats.

**choice** *noun* choix *Masc.*; **you have a choice of two flights** vous avez le choix entre deux vols.

**choir** *noun* **1** (*in a school*) chorale *Fem.*; **I sing in the choir** je fais partie de la chorale; **2** (*professional*) chœur *Masc.*

**choke** *noun* (*on a car*) starter *Masc.*
**choke** *verb* **1** (*by yourself*) s'étouffer [1]; **she was choking on a bone** elle s'éttouffait avec une arête; **2** (*smoke or fumes*) étouffer [1].

**choose** *verb* choisir [2]; **you chose well** tu as bien choisi; **Cathy chose the red one** Cathy a choisi le rouge; **it's hard to choose from all these colours** il est difficile de choisir parmi toutes ces couleurs.

**chop** *noun* côtelette *Fem.*; **a lamb chop** une côtelette d'agneau.
**chop** *verb* hacher [1].

**chopstick** *noun* baguette *Fem.*

a
b
c
d
e
f
g
h
i
j
k
l
m
n
o
p
q
r
s
t
u
v
w
x
y
z

**a**
**b**
**c**
**d**
**e**
**f**
**g**
**h**
**i**
**j**
**k**
**l**
**m**
**n**
**o**
**p**
**q**
**r**
**s**
**t**
**u**
**v**
**w**
**x**
**y**
**z**

**chord** *noun* accord *Masc.*

**chorus** *noun* 1 (*when you all join in the song*) refrain *Masc.*; 2 (*a group of singers*) chœur *Masc.*

**Christ** *noun* le Christ.

**christening** *noun* baptême *Masc.*

**Christian** *noun, adjective* chrétien *Masc.*, chrétienne *Fem.*

**Christian name** *noun* prénom *Masc.*

**Christmas** *noun* Noël *Masc.*; **at Christmas** à Noël; **Happy Christmas!** Joyeux Noël!

**Christmas card** *noun* carte *Fem.* de Noël.

**Christmas carol** *noun* chant *Masc.* de Noël.

**Christmas cracker** *noun* diablotin *Masc.*

**Christmas Day** *noun* jour *Masc.* de Noël.

**Christmas dinner** *noun* repas *Masc.* de Noël.

**Christmas Eve** *noun* veille *Fem.* de Noël; **on Christmas Eve** la veille de Noël.

**Christmas present** *noun* cadeau *Masc.* de Noël.

**Christmas tree** *noun* sapin *Masc.* de Noël.

**chunk** *noun* morceau *Masc.*

**church** *noun* église *Fem.*; **to go to church** aller à l'église.

**churchyard** *noun* cimetière *Masc.*

**chute** *noun* (*in a swimming pool or playground*) toboggan *Masc.*

**cider** *noun* cidre *Masc.*

**cigar** *noun* cigare *Masc.*

**cigarette** *noun* cigarette *Fem.*; **to light a cigarette** allumer une cigarette.

**cinema** *noun* cinéma *Masc.*; **to go to the cinema** aller au cinéma.

**circle** *noun* cercle *Masc.*; **to sit in a circle** s'asseoir en cercle; **to go round in circles** tourner en rond.

**circuit** *noun* 1 (*for athletes*) piste *Fem.*; 2 (*for cars*) circuit *Masc.*

**circumference** *noun* circonférence *Fem.*

**circumflex** *noun* accent *Masc.* circonflexe.

**circumstances** *plural noun* **under the circumstances** dans ces circonstances.

**circus** *noun* cirque *Masc.*

**citizen** *noun* citoyen *Masc.*, citoyenne *Fem.*

**city** *noun* (grande) ville *Fem.*; **the city of Paris** la ville de Paris.

**city centre** *noun* centre-ville *Masc.*; **in the city centre** au centre-ville.

**civilian** *noun* civil *Masc.*, civile *Fem.*

**civilization** *noun* civilisation *Fem.*

**civil servant** *noun* fonctionnaire *Masc. & Fem.*; **he's a civil servant** il est fonctionnaire.

**civil service** *noun* fonction *Fem.* publique.

**civil war** *noun* guerre *Fem* civile.

**claim** *noun* 1 (*statement*) déclaration *Fem.*; 2 (*for compensation*) réclamation *Fem.*; **to make a claim on insurance** faire une demande de remboursement auprès d'une compagnie

**claim** *verb* prétendre [3]; **he claimed to know** il prétendait savoir.

**clap** *verb* **1** applaudir [2]; **everyone clapped** tout le monde a applaudi; **2 to clap your hands** battre [21] des mains.

**clapping** *noun* applaudissements *Masc. plural.*

**clarinet** *noun* clarinette *Fem.*; **to play the clarinet** jouer de la clarinette.

**clash** *noun* (*for example, between police and demonstrators*) affrontement *Masc.*
**clash** *verb* **1** (*rival groups*) s'affronter [1]; **2** (*colours*) jurer [1]; **the curtains clash with the wallpaper** les rideaux jurent avec le papier peint.

**clasp** *noun* (*of a necklace*) fermoir *Masc.*

**class** *noun* **1** (*a group of students or pupils*) classe *Fem.*; **she's in the same class as me** elle est dans la même classe que moi; **2** (*a lesson*) cours *Masc.*; **an art class** un cours de dessin; **in class** en cours; **3** (*division*) classe *Fem.*; **a social class** une classe sociale.

**classic** *adjective* classique.

**classical** *adjective* classique; **classical music** la musique classique.

**classmate** *noun* camarade *Masc. & Fem.* de classe.

**classroom** *noun* classe *Fem.*

**claw** *noun* **1** (*of a cat or dog*) griffe *Fem.*; **2** (*of a crab*) pince *Fem.*

**clay** *noun* **1** (*for modelling*) argile *Fem.*; **2 a clay court** (*in tennis*) un terrain en terre battue.

**clean** *adjective* **1** propre; **a clean shirt** une chemise propre; **my hands are clean** j'ai les mains propres; **2** (*germ-free*) pur (*air or water*).
**clean** *verb* nettoyer [39] **1 I cleaned the whole house** j'ai nettoyé toute la maison; **2 to clean your teeth** se laver [1] les dents; **I'm going to clean my teeth** je vais me laver les dents.

**cleaner** *noun* **1** (*in a public place*) agent *Masc.* de nettoyage; **2** (*cleaning lady*) femme *Fem.* de ménage; **3 a dry cleaner's** un pressing.

**cleaning** *noun* **to do the cleaning** faire le ménage.

**cleanser** *noun* **1** (*for the house*) produit *Masc.* d'entretien; **2** (*for your face*) démaquillant *Masc.*

**clear** *adjective* **1** (*that you can see through*) transparent; **clear glass** du verre transparent; **2** (*cloudless*) clair; **3** (*easy to understand*) clair; **clear instructions** des instructions claires; **is that clear?** est-ce que c'est clair?; **it's clear that** ... il est clair que ....
**clear** *verb* **1** enlever [50] (*papers, rubbish, or clothes*); **have you cleared your stuff out of your room?** as-tu enlevé tes affaires de ta chambre?; **2** débarrasser [1] (*a table or a room*); **can I clear the table?** puis-je débarrasser la table?; **3** dégager [52] (*a road or path*); **4** (*fog or snow*) se dissiper [1]; **and then the fog cleared** et puis le

a

b

c

d

brouillard s'est dissipé; **5 to clear your throat** se racler [1] la gorge.

• **to clear something up** ranger [52] quelque chose; **I'll just clear up my books** je vais juste ranger mes livres.

e

f

g

**clearly** *adjective* **1** (*to think, speak, or hear*) clairement; **2** (*obviously*) manifestement; **she was clearly worried** manifestement, elle était inquiète.

h

**clementine** *noun* clémentine *Fem.*

i

j

k

l

**clever** *adjective* **1** intelligent; **their children are all very clever** leurs enfants sont tous très intelligents; **2** (*ingenious*) astucieux (*Fem.* astucieuse); **a clever idea** une idée astucieuse.

m

n

o

p

**click** *noun* **1** (*noise*) petit bruit *Masc.*, déclic *Masc.*; **2** (*with mouse*) clic *Masc.*; **a double-click** un double-clic. **click** *verb* **to click on something**: cliquer [1] sur quelque chose; **click on the icon twice** cliquer deux fois sur l'icône.

q

**client** *noun* client *Masc.*, cliente *Fem.*

r

**cliff** *noun* falaise *Fem.*

**climate** *noun* climat *Masc.*

s

t

u

**climb** *verb* **1** monter [1] (*a hill, stairs*); **2** faire [10] l'escalade de (*a mountain*); **we climbed Mont Blanc** nous avons fait l'escalade du Mont Blanc.

v

**climber** *noun* alpiniste *Masc. & Fem.*

w

x

**climbing** *noun* escalade *Fem.*; **they go climbing in Italy** ils font de l'escalade en Italie.

y

z

**clinic** *noun* centre *Masc.* médical (*plural* centres médicaux).

**clip** *noun* **1** (*from a film*) extrait *Masc.*; **2** (*for your hair*) barrette *Fem.* **clip** *verb* **1** (*to cut*) couper [1]; **2** (*to fasten*) attacher [1].

**cloakroom** *noun* (*for coats*) vestiaire *Masc.*

**clock** *noun* (*large*) horloge *Fem.*; (*smaller*) pendule *Fem.*; **an alarm clock** un réveil; **to put the clocks forward an hour** avancer les pendules d'une heure; **to put the clocks back** reculer les pendules.

**clock radio** *noun* radio-réveil *Masc.*

**clockwise** *adverb* dans le sens des aiguilles d'une montre; **it turns clockwise** ça tourne dans le sens des aiguilles d'une montre.

**close**[1] *adjective, adverb* **1** (*result*) serré; **2** (*friend or relation*) proche; **3** (*near*) près; **the station's very close** la gare est tout près; **she lives close by** elle habite tout près; **close to the cinema** près du cinéma; **not very close** pas très près.

**close**[2] *noun* fin *Fem.*; **at the close** à la fin.
**close** *verb* fermer [1]; **close your eyes!** ferme les yeux!; **she closed the door** elle a fermé la porte; **the post office closes at six** la poste ferme à six heures.

**closed** *adjective* fermé; **'closed on Mondays'** 'fermé le lundi'.

**closely** *adverb* de près; **to examine something closely** regarder quelque chose de près.

**closing date** *noun* date *Fem.* limite; **the closing date for entries** la date limite pour les inscriptions.

**closing-down sale** *noun* liquidation *Fem.*

**closing time** *noun* heure *Fem.* de fermeture.

**cloth** *noun* **1** (*for the floor*) serpillière *Fem.*; **2** (*for polishing*) chiffon *Masc.*; **3** (*for drying up*) torchon *Masc.*; **4** (*fabric by the metre*) tissu *Masc.*

**clothes** *plural noun* vêtements *Masc. plural*; **to put your clothes on** s'habiller; **to take your clothes off** se déshabiller; **to change your clothes** se changer.

**clothes hanger** *noun* cintre *Masc.*

**clothes line** *noun* corde *Fem.* à linge.

**clothes peg** *noun* pince *Fem.* à linge.

**clothing** *noun* vêtements *Masc.* plural.

**cloud** *noun* nuage *Masc.*

● **to cloud over** se couvrir [30]; **it clouded over in the afternoon** ça s'est couvert dans l'après-midi.

**cloudy** *adjective* nuageux (*Fem.* nuageuse).

**clove** *noun* **1** clou *Masc.* de girofle; **2 a clove of garlic** une gousse d'ail.

**clown** *noun* clown *Masc.*

**club** *noun* **1** (*association*) club *Masc.*; **he's in the football club** il fait partie du club de foot; **2** (*in cards*) trèfle *Masc.*; **the four of clubs** le quatre de trèfle; **3** (*golfing iron*) crosse *Fem.*

**clue** *noun* **1** indice *Masc.*; **they have a few clues** ils ont quelques indices;

**2** (*in a crossword*) définition *Fem.*; ★ **I haven't a clue** je n'ai aucune idée.

**clumsy** *adjective* maladroit.

**clutch** *noun* (*in a car*) embrayage *Masc.*

**clutch** *verb* **to clutch something** tenir [77] quelque chose fermement.

**coach** *noun* **1** (*bus*) car *Masc.*; **by coach** en car; **on the coach** dans le car; **to travel by coach** voyager en car; **2** (*sports trainer*) entraîneur *Masc.*, entraîneuse *Fem.*; **3** (*railway carriage*) wagon *Masc.*

**coach station** *noun* gare *Fem.* routière.

**coach trip** *noun* excursion *Fem.* en car; **to go on a coach trip** faire une excursion en car.

**coal** *noun* charbon *Masc.*

**coal mine** *noun* mine *Fem.* de charbon.

**coal miner** *noun* mineur *Masc.*

**coarse** *adjective* grossier (*Fem.* grossière).

**coast** *noun* côte *Fem.*; **on the east coast** sur la côte est.

**coat** *noun* **1** manteau *Masc.* (*plural* manteaux); **2 a coat of paint** une couche de peinture.

**coat hanger** *noun* cintre *Masc.*

**cobweb** *noun* toile *Fem.* d'araignée.

**cockerel** *noun* coq *Masc.*

**cocoa** *noun* (*drink*) chocolat *Masc.* (chaud); (*powder*) cacao *Masc.*

**coconut** *noun* noix *Fem.* de coco.

**cod** *noun* cabillaud *Masc.*

**code** *noun* **1** code *Masc.*; **the highway code** le code de la route;

a
b
**c**
d
e
f
g
h
i
j
k
l
m
n
o
p
q
r
s
t
u
v
w
x
y
z

2 the dialling code for Cambridge l'indicatif pour Cambridge.

**coffee** *noun* café *Masc.*; **a cup of coffee** un café; **a black coffee, please** un café, s'il vous plaît; **a white coffee** un café au lait.

**coffee break** *noun* pause-café *Fem.*

**coffee cup** *noun* tasse *Fem.* à café.

**coffee machine** *noun* cafetière *Fem.*; (*electric*) cafetière *Fem.* électrique.

**coffee table** *noun* table *Fem.* basse.

**coffin** *noun* cercueil *Masc.*

**coin** *noun* pièce *Fem.* de monnaie; **a pound coin** une pièce d'une livre.

**coincidence** *noun* coïncidence *Fem.*

**Coke™** *noun* coca *Masc.*; **two Cokes™ please** deux cocas s'il vous plaît.

**colander** *noun* passoire *Fem.*

**cold** *noun* 1 (*cold weather*) froid *Masc.*; **to be out in the cold** être dehors dans le froid; 2 (*illness*) rhume *Masc.*; **to have a cold** être enrhumé; **Carol's got a cold** Carol est enrhumée; **a bad cold** un gros rhume.

**cold** *adjective* 1 froid; **your hands are cold** tu as les mains froides; **cold milk** du lait froid; 2 (*weather, temperature*) **it's cold today** il fait froid aujourd'hui; **it's cold in the kitchen** il fait froid dans la cuisine; 3 (*feeling*) **I'm cold** j'ai froid.

**cold sore** *noun* bouton *Masc.* de fièvre.

**collapse** *verb* 1 (*a roof or a wall*) s'écrouler [1]; 2 (*a person*) **he collapsed in his office** il a eu un malaise dans son bureau.

**collar** *noun* 1 (*on a garment*) col *Masc.*; 2 (*for a dog*) collier *Masc.*

**collarbone** *noun* clavicule *Fem.*

**colleague** *noun* collègue *Masc.* & *Fem.*

**collect** *verb* 1 (*as a hobby*) collectionner [1]; **I collect stamps** je collectionne les timbres; 2 aller [7] chercher (*a person*); **she collects the children from school** elle va chercher les enfants à la sortie de l'école; 3 passer [64] prendre (*thing*); **I have to collect a book at the library** je dois passer prendre un livre à la bibliothèque; 4 encaisser [1] (*fares or money*); 5 **to collect in the exercise books** ramasser [1] les cahiers.

**collection** *noun* 1 (*of stamps, CDs, etc*) collection *Fem.*; 2 (*of money*) collecte *Fem.*

**collector** *noun* collectionneur *Masc.*, collectionneuse *Fem.*

**college** *noun* 1 (*for higher education*) établissement *Masc.* d'études supérieures; **to go to college** faire des études supérieures; 2 (*a school*) collège *Masc.*

**collie** *noun* colley *Masc.*

**collision** *noun* collision *Fem.*

**colonel** *noun* colonel *Masc.*

**colour** *noun* couleur *Fem.*; **what colour is your car?** de quelle couleur est ta voiture?; **what colour is it?** c'est de quelle couleur?; **do**

**you have it in a different colour?** est-ce que vous l'avez dans une autre couleur?.

**colour** *verb* (*with paints or crayons*) colorier [1]; **to colour something red** colorier quelque chose en rouge.

**colour blind** *adjective* daltonien (*Fem.* daltonienne).

**colour film** *noun* pellicule *Fem.* couleur (*plural* pellicules couleur).

**colourful** *adjective* en couleurs vives.

**colouring book** *noun* album *Masc.* à colorier.

**colour scheme** *noun* couleurs *Fem. plural.*

**colour supplement** *noun* supplément *Masc.* illustré.

**column** *noun* colonne *Fem.*

**comb** *noun* peigne *Masc.*
**comb** *verb* **to comb your hair** se peigner [1]; **I'll just comb my hair** je vais juste me peigner.

**combination** *noun* combinaison *Fem.*

**combine** *verb* combiner [1] (*two separate things*); **they don't combine well** ils ne se combinent pas bien.

**come** *verb* **1** venir [81]; **come quick!** viens vite!; **come and see!** venez voir!; **Nick came by bike** Nick est venu à vélo; **did Jess come to school yesterday?** est-ce que Jess est venue à l'école hier?; **Alan comes from Scotland** Alan vient de l'Ecosse; **can you come over for a coffee?** peux-tu venir prendre un café?; **2** arriver [1]; **coming!** j'arrive!; **the bus is**

**coming** le bus arrive; **3 to come down** descendre [3] (*the stairs or the street*); **4 to come up** monter [1]; **can you come up a moment?** peux-tu monter un instant?; **5 to come in** entrer [1]; **come in!** entrez!; **she came into the kitchen** elle est entrée dans la cuisine; **6 to come for** passer [1] prendre (*a person*); **my father's coming for me** mon père passe me prendre; **7 come along!** dépêche-toi!

● **to come apart** (*to break*) se casser [1]; **the door handle came apart in my hands** la poignée m'est restée dans la main; (*a book*) se déchirer [1].

● **to come back** revenir [81]; **he's coming back to collect us** il revient nous chercher.

● **to come off** (*a button or handle, for example*) se détacher [1], (*a lid*) s'enlever [50].

● **to come out 1** sortir [72]; **they came out when I called** ils sont sortis quand j'ai appelé; **the CD's coming out soon** le CD sort bientôt; **2** (*the sun or moon*) se montrer [1].

● **to come up to somebody** aborder [1] quelqu'un.

**comedian** *noun* comique *Masc.*

**comedy** *noun* comédie *Fem.*

**comfortable** *adjective*
**1** confortable; **this chair's really comfortable** ce fauteuil est très confortable; **2 to feel comfortable** (*a person*) se sentir à l'aise; **are you comfortable there?** êtes-vous bien là?

**comfortably** *adverb* confortablement.

**comic** *noun* (*magazine*) illustré *Masc.*

**comic strip** *noun* bande *Fem.* dessinée.

**comma** *noun* virgule *Fem.*

**command** *noun* ordre *Masc.*

**comment** *noun* (*in a conversation*) remarque *Fem.*; **he made some rude comments about my friends** il a fait des remarques impolies sur mes amis.

**commentary** *noun* reportage *Masc.* en direct; **the commentary of the match** le reportage du match.

**commentator** *noun* commentateur *Masc.*, commentatrice *Fem.*; **a sports commentator** un commentateur sportif.

**commercial** *noun* spot *Masc.* publicitaire.
**commercial** *adjective* commercial (*Masc. plural* commerciaux).

**commit** *verb* **1** commettre [11] (*a crime*); **2 to commit yourself** s'engager [52].

**committee** *noun* comité *Masc.*

**common** *adjective* **1** courant; **it's a common problem** c'est un problème courant; **2 in common** en commun; **they have nothing in common** ils n'ont rien en commun.

**common sense** *noun* bon sens *Masc.*

**communicate** *verb* communiquer [1].

**communication** *noun* **1** (*message*) communication *Fem.*; **2 communications**

communications *Fem* (*plural*); **the communications are good** les communications sont bonnes.

**communion** *noun* communion *Fem.*

**communism** *noun* communisme *Masc.*

**communist** *noun, adjective* communiste *Masc. & Fem.*

**community** *noun* communauté *Fem.*; **the European Community** la Communauté Européenne.

**commute** *verb* **to commute between Oxford and London** faire [10] le trajet entre Oxford et Londres tous les jours.

**commuter** *noun* navetteur *Masc.*, navetteuse *Fem.*

**compact disc** *noun* disque *Masc.* compact.

**compact disc player** *noun* platine *Fem.* laser.

**company** *noun* **1** (*business*) société *Fem.*; **an insurance company** une société d'assurances; **she's set up a company** elle a monté une société; **2** compagnie *Fem.*; **an airline company** une compagnie aérienne; **a theatre company** une compagnie théâtrale; **3 to keep somebody company** tenir compagnie à quelqu'un; **the dog keeps me company** le chien me tient compagnie.

**comparatively** *adverb* relativement.

**compare** *verb* comparer [1]; **if you compare the French with the English** si on compare les Français aux Anglais; **our house is small**

**compared with yours** notre maison est petite par rapport à la vôtre.

**comparison** *noun* comparaison *Fem.*; **in comparison with** par rapport à.

**compartment** *noun* compartiment *Masc.*

**compass** *noun* boussole *Fem.*

**compatible** *adjective* (*computing*) compatible.

**compensation** *noun* indemnisation *Fem.*

**compete** *verb* **1 to compete in something** participer [1] à quelque chose (*race, event*); **2 to compete for something** se disputer [1] quelque chose (*jobs, places*); **thirty people competing for one job** trente personnes qui se disputent un seul emploi.

**competent** *adjective* compétent.

**competition** *noun* concours *Masc.*; **a fishing competition** un concours de pêche.

**competitor** *noun* concurrent *Masc.*, concurrente *Fem.*

**complain** *verb* se plaindre [31]; **we complained about the hotel and the meals** nous nous sommes plaints de l'hôtel et des repas.

**complaint** *noun* plainte *Fem.*; **to make a complaint** se plaindre [31]; **she made a complaint to the manager about the poor service** elle s'est plainte de la qualité du service auprès du responsable.

**complete** *adjective* complet (*Fem.* complète); **the complete collection** la collection complète.

**complete** *verb* (*to finish*) compléter [24].

**completely** *adverb* complètement.

**complexion** *noun* teint *Masc.*

**complicated** *adjective* compliqué.

**compliment** *noun* compliment *Masc.*; **to pay somebody a compliment** faire un compliment à quelqu'un.

**compose** *verb* composer [1]; **composed of** composé de.

**composer** *noun* compositeur *Masc.*, compositrice *Fem.*

**comprehension** *noun* compréhension *Fem.*; **a comprehension test** un test de compréhension.

**compromise** *noun* compromis *Masc.*

**compulsory** *adjective* obligatoire.

**computer** *noun* ordinateur *Masc.*; **to work on a computer** travailler sur ordinateur; **to have something on computer** avoir quelque chose sur ordinateur.

**computer engineer** *noun* technicien *Masc.* en informatique, technicienne *Fem.* en informatique.

**computer game** *noun* jeu *Masc.* électronique (*plural* jeux électroniques).

**computer program** *noun* programme *Masc.* informatique, logiciel *Masc.*

**computer programmer** *noun* programmeur *Masc.*, programmeuse *Fem.*

a
b
c
d
e
f
g
h
i
j
k
l
m
n
o
p
q
r
s
t
u
v
w
x
y
z

**computer science** *noun* informatique *Fem.*

**computing** *noun* informatique *Fem.*

**conceited** *adjective* vaniteux (*Fem.* vaniteuse).

**concentrate** *verb* se concentrer [1]; **I can't concentrate** je n'arrive pas à me concentrer; **I was concentrating on the film** je me concentrais sur le film.

**concentration** *noun* concentration *Fem.*

**concern** *noun* (*worry*) inquiétude *Fem.*; **there is no cause for concern** il n'y a pas lieu de s'inquiéter. **concern** *verb* 1 (*to affect*) concerner [1]; **this doesn't concern you** ceci ne te concerne pas; **2 as far as I'm concerned** en ce qui me concerne.

**concert** *noun* 1 concert *Masc.*; **to go to a concert** aller à un concert; **2 a concert ticket** un billet de concert.

**conclusion** *noun* conclusion *Fem.*

**concrete** *noun* béton *Masc.*; **a concrete floor** un sol en béton.

**condemn** *verb* condamner [1].

**condition** *noun* 1 condition *Fem.*; **in good condition** en bonne condition; **weather conditions** les conditions météorologiques; **2** (*something you agree to*) condition *Fem.*; **the conditions of sale** les conditions de vente; **on condition that you let me pay** à condition que tu me laisses payer.

**conditional** *noun* conditionnel *Masc.*

**conditioner** *noun* (*for your hair*) après-shampooing *Masc.*

**condom** *noun* préservatif *Masc.*

**conduct** *noun* conduite *Fem.* **conduct** *verb* diriger [52] (*an orchestra or a piece of music*).

**conductor** *noun* (*of an orchestra*) chef *Masc.* d'orchestre.

**cone** *noun* 1 (*for ice cream*) cornet *Masc.*; **2** (*for traffic*) balise *Fem.*

**confectionery** *noun* confiserie *Fem.*

**conference** *noun* conférence *Fem.*

**confess** *verb* avouer [1].

**confession** *noun* confession *Fem.*

**confidence** *noun* 1 (*self-confidence*) assurance *Fem.*; **to be lacking in confidence** manquer d'assurance; **2** (*faith in somebody else*) confiance *Fem.*; **to have confidence in somebody** avoir confiance en quelqu'un.

**confident** *adjective* 1 (*sure of yourself*) assuré; **2** (*sure that something will happen*) sûr.

**confirm** *verb* confirmer [1]; **we'll confirm the date** nous confirmerons la date.

**confuse** *verb* 1 troubler [1] (*a person*); **2** confondre [69]; **I confuse him with his brother** je le confonds avec son frère.

**confused** *adjective* 1 confus; **he gave us a confused story** il nous a raconté une histoire confuse; **2 I'm confused about the holiday dates** je ne comprends pas bien les dates des vacances; **now I'm completely**

confused! là je ne comprends plus rien!

**confusing** *adjective* pas clair; **the instructions are confusing** les instructions ne sont pas claires.

**confusion** *noun* confusion *Fem.*

**congratulate** *verb* féliciter [1]; **I congratulated Tim on his success** j'ai félicité Tim de son succès; **we congratulate you on winning** nous vous félicitons d'avoir gagné.

**congratulations** *plural noun* félicitations *Fem. plural*; **congratulations on the baby!** félicitations pour le bébé!

**conjurer** *noun* prestidigitateur *Masc.*

**connect** *verb* (*to plug in to the mains*) brancher [1] (*a dishwasher or TV, for example*).

**connection** *noun* 1 (*between two ideas or events*) rapport *Masc.*; **there's no connection between his letter and my decision** il n'y a aucun rapport entre sa lettre et ma décision; 2 (*between trains or planes*) correspondance *Fem.*; **Sally missed her connection** Sally a raté sa correspondance; 3 (*electrical*) contact; **a faulty connection** un mauvais contact.

**conscience** *noun* conscience *Fem.*; **to have a guilty conscience** avoir mauvaise conscience.

**conscious** *adjective* conscient.

**consequence** *noun* conséquence *Fem.*

**consequently** *adverb* par conséquent.

**conservation** *noun* (*of nature*) protection *Fem.*

**conservative** *noun, adjective* conservateur *Masc.*, conservatrice *Fem.*

**conservatory** *noun* jardin *Masc.* d'hiver.

**consider** *verb* 1 (*to give thought to*) considérer [24] (*a suggestion or idea*); 2 (*to think you might do*) envisager [52]; **we are considering buying a flat** nous envisageons d'acheter un appartement; 3 **all things considered** tout compte fait.

**considerable** *adjective* considérable; **a considerable number of the students** un pourcentage considérable des étudiants.

**considerate** *adjective* attentionné (*person*).

**consideration** *noun* considération *Fem.*; **no consideration was given to their safety** on ne s'est pas soucié de leur sécurité.

**considering** *preposition* étant donné; **considering her age** étant donné son âge; **considering he did it all himself** étant donné qu'il a tout fait lui-même.

**consist** *verb* **to consist of** être [6] composé de.

**consistent** *adjective* régulier, constant.

**consonant** *noun* consonne *Fem.*

**constant** *adjective* permanent.

**constipated** *adjective* constipé.

**construct** *verb* construire [26].

a
b
c
d
e
f
g
h
i
j
k
l
m
n
o
p
q
r
s
t
u
v
w
x
y
z

**construction** *noun* construction *Fem.*

**consul** *noun* consul *Masc.*

**consulate** *noun* consulat *Masc.*

**consult** *verb* consulter [1].

**consumer** *noun* consommateur *Masc.*, consommatrice *Fem.*

**consumption** *noun* consommation *Fem.*

**contact** *noun* 1 (*touch*) contact *Masc.*; **to be in contact with somebody** être en contact avec quelqu'un; **we've lost contact** nous avons perdu contact; 2 (*a person you know*) connaissance *Fem.*; **Rob has contacts in the music business** Rob a des connaissances dans le monde de la musique.
**contact** *verb* contacter [1]; **I'll contact you tomorrow** je te contacterai demain.

**contact lens** *noun* lentille *Fem.* de contact (*plural* lentilles de contact).

**contain** *verb* contenir [77].

**container** *noun* récipient *Masc.*

**contaminate** *verb* contaminer [1].

**contemporary** *adjective* 1 (*around today*) contemporain; 2 (*modern*) moderne.

**contents** *plural noun* contenu *Masc.*; **the contents of my suitcase** le contenu de ma valise.

**contest** *noun* concours *Masc.*

**contestant** *noun* concurrent *Masc.*, concurrente *Fem.*

**context** *noun* contexte *Masc.*

**continent** *noun* continent *Masc.*; **on the Continent** en Europe continentale.

**continental** *adjective* **a continental holiday** des vacances en Europe continentale.

**continue** *verb* continuer [1]; **we continued (with) our journey** nous avons continué notre voyage; **Jill continued chatting** Jill a continué de bavarder; **'to be continued'** 'à suivre'.

**continuous** *adjective* continu; **continuous assessment** le contrôle continu.

**contraception** *noun* contraception *Fem.*

**contraceptive** *noun* contraceptif *Masc.*

**contract** *noun* contrat *Masc.*

**contradict** *verb* contredire [47].

**contradiction** *noun* contradiction *Fem.*

**contrary** *noun* contraire *Masc.*; **on the contrary** au contraire.

**contrast** *noun* contraste *Masc.*

**contribute** *verb* donner [1] (*money*).

**contribution** *noun* (*to charity or an appeal*) don *Masc.*

**control** *noun* (*of a crowd or animals*) contrôle *Masc.*; **the police have lost control** la police a perdu le contrôle; **keep your dogs under control** maîtrisez vos chiens; **everything's under control** tout va bien; **the fire was out of control** on ne maîtrisait plus l'incendie.
**control** *verb* 1 maîtriser [1] (*a*

crowd, animals, or a fire, for example); **2 to control oneself** se contrôler [1].

**controversial** *adjective* discutable; **a controversial decision** une décision discutable.

**convenient** *adjective* **1** commode; **frozen vegetables are very convenient** les légumes congelés sont très commodes; **2 to be convenient for somebody** convenir à quelqu'un; **if that's convenient for you** si cela vous convient; **3 the house is convenient for shops and schools** la maison est bien située par rapport aux magasins et aux écoles.

**convent** *noun* couvent *Masc.*

**conventional** *adjective* **1** conventionnel (*Fem.* conventionnelle); **2** (*person*) conformiste.

**conversation** *noun* conversation *Fem.*

**convert** *verb* transformer [1]; **we're going to convert the garage into a workshop** nous allons transformer le garage en atelier.

**convince** *verb* convaincre [79]; **I'm convinced you're wrong** je suis convaincu que tu as tort.

**convincing** *adjective* convaincant.

**cook** *noun* cuisinier *Masc.*, cuisinière *Fem.*
**cook** *verb* **1** faire [10] la cuisine; **who's cooking tonight?** qui fait la cuisine ce soir?; **I like cooking** j'aime faire la cuisine; **2** faire [10] cuire (*vegetables, pasta, etc*); **cook

the carrots for five minutes** faites cuire les carottes pendant cinq minutes; **3** préparer [1] (*a meal*); **Fran's busy cooking supper** Fran est en train de préparer le dîner; **4** (*food*) cuire [36]; **the sausages are cooking** les saucisses sont en train de cuire; **is the chicken cooked?** est-ce que le poulet est cuit?

**cooker** *noun* cuisinière *Fem.*; **an electric cooker** une cuisinière électrique; **a gas cooker** une cuisinière à gaz.

**cookery** *noun* cuisine *Fem.*

**cookery book** *noun* livre *Masc.* de cuisine.

**cooking** *noun* cuisine *Fem.*; **to do the cooking** faire la cuisine; **Italian cooking** la cuisine italienne.

**cool** *noun* **1** (*coldness*) fraîcheur *Fem.*; **stay in the cool** reste à la fraîcheur; **2** (*calm*) **to lose one's cool** perdre son sang-froid; **he kept his cool** il a gardé son sang-froid.
**cool** *adjective* **1** (*cold*) frais (*Fem.* fraîche); **a cool drink** une boisson fraîche; **it's cool inside** il fait frais dans la maison; **2** (*laid-back*) décontracté; **3** (*sophisticated*) branché (*informal*).
**cool** *verb* refroidir [2]; **while the engine was cooling (down)** pendant que le moteur refroidissait.

**cooperate** *verb* coopérer [24].

**cop** *noun* flic *Masc.* (*informal*).

**cope** *verb* **1** (*to manage*) se débrouiller [1]; **she copes well** elle se débrouille bien; **2 to cope with** s'occuper [1] de (*children or work*);

**I'll cope with the dishes** je m'occuperai de la vaisselle; **3** faire [10] face à (*problems*); **she's had a lot to cope with** elle a été obligée de faire face à beaucoup de choses; **he can't cope any more** il n'arrive plus à faire face.

**copper** *noun* cuivre *Masc.*

**copy** *noun* **1** copie *Fem.*; **make ten copies of this letter** faites dix copies de cette lettre; **2** (*of a book*) exemplaire *Masc.*
**copy** *verb* copier [1]; **I copied (down) the address** j'ai copié l'adresse.

**cord** *noun* (*for a blind, for example*) cordon *Masc.*

**cordless telephone** *noun* téléphone *Masc.* sans fil.

**core** *noun* (*of an apple or a pear*) trognon *Masc.*

**cork** *noun* **1** (*in a bottle*) bouchon *Masc.*; **2** (*material*) liège *Masc.*

**corkscrew** *noun* tire-bouchon *Masc.*

**corn** *noun* **1** (*wheat*) blé *Masc.*; **2** (*sweetcorn*) maïs *Masc.*

**corner** *noun* coin *Masc.*; **in a corner of the kitchen** dans un coin de la cuisine; **at the corner of the street** au coin de la rue; **out of the corner of your eye** du coin de l'œil; **it's just round the corner** c'est tout près.

**cornflakes** *noun* corn-flakes *Masc. plural.*

**Cornwall** *noun* Cornouailles *Fem.*; **in Cornwall** en Cornouailles.

**corpse** *noun* cadavre *Masc.*

**correct** *adjective* **1** exact; **yes, that's correct** oui, c'est exact; **2** bon (*Fem.* bonne); **the correct sum** la bonne somme; **the correct answer** la bonne réponse; **the correct choice** le bon choix.
**correct** *verb* corriger [52].

**correction** *noun* correction *Fem.*

**correctly** *adverb* correctement; **have you filled in the form correctly?** est-ce que vous avez rempli le formulaire correctement?; **she answered correctly** elle a donné la bonne réponse.

**correspond** *verb* correspondre [3].

**corridor** *noun* couloir *Masc.*

**Corsica** *noun* Corse *Fem.*; **to Corsica** en Corse.

**cosmetics** *plural noun* produits *Masc. plural* de beauté.

**cost** *noun* prix *Masc.*; **the cost of a new computer** le prix d'un nouvel ordinateur; **the cost of living** le coût de la vie.
**cost** *verb* coûter [1]; **how much does it cost?** combien est-ce que ça coûte?; **the tickets cost £10** les billets coûtent dix livres; **it costs too much** cela coûte trop cher.

**costume** *noun* costume *Masc.*

**cosy** *adjective* (*a bed or room*) douillet (*Fem.* douillette); **it's cosy by the fire** on est bien à côté du feu.

**cot** *noun* lit *Masc.* d'enfant.

**cottage** *noun* petite maison *Fem.*

**cotton** *noun* **1** (*fabric*) coton *Masc.*; **a cotton shirt** une chemise en coton; **2** (*thread*) fil *Masc.* de coton.

**cotton wool** *noun* ouate *Fem.* de coton.

**couch** *noun* canapé *Masc.*

**cough** *noun* toux *Fem.*; **a nasty cough** une mauvaise toux; **to have a cough** tousser.
**cough** *verb* tousser [1].

**could** *verb* **1 if he could pay** s'il pouvait payer; **I couldn't open it** je ne pouvais pas l'ouvrir; **they couldn't smoke there** ils ne pouvaient pas fumer là; **she did all she could** elle a fait tout ce qu'elle pouvait; **2** (*knew how to*) **he couldn't drive** il ne savait pas conduire; **I couldn't swim** je ne savais pas nager; **3** (*with seeing; hearing, or smelling*) **I could hear the police car** j'entendais la voiture de police; **she couldn't see anything** elle ne voyait rien; **4** (*might*) **could I speak to David?** pourrais-je parler à David?; **you could try telephoning** tu pourrais téléphoner.

**council** *noun* conseil *Masc.*; **the town council** le conseil municipal.

**councillor** *noun* **1** (*of town council*) membre *Masc.*, du conseil municipal; **2** (*local council*) membre *Masc.*, du conseil régional.

**count** *verb* **1** (*reckon up*) compter [1]; **I counted my money** j'ai compté mon argent; **thirty-five not counting the children** trente-cinq sans compter les enfants; **2 to count as** être [6] considéré comme; **children over twelve count as adults** les enfants au-dessus de douze ans sont considérés comme adultes; **3** (*to be allowed*) compter [1]; **that doesn't count** ça ne compte pas.

**counter** *noun* **1** (*in a shop or café*) comptoir *Masc.*; **2** (*in a post office or bank*) guichet *Masc.*; **3** (*in a big store*) rayon *Masc.*; **on the cheese counter** au rayon fromagerie; **4** (*for board games*) jeton *Masc.*

**country** *noun* **1** (*France, England, etc*) pays *Masc.*; **a foreign country** un pays étranger; **from another country** d'un autre pays; **2** (*not town*) campagne *Fem.*; **to live in the country** vivre à la campagne; **a country walk** une promenade à la campagne; **a country road** une route de campagne.

**country dancing** *noun* danse *Fem.* folklorique.

**countryside** *noun* campagne *Fem.*

**county** *noun* comté *Masc.*

**couple** *noun* **1** (*a pair*) couple *Masc.*; **2 a couple of** deux ou trois; **a couple of times** deux ou trois fois; **I've got a couple of things to do** j'ai deux ou trois choses à faire.

**courage** *noun* courage *Masc.*

**courgette** *noun* courgette *Fem.*

**courier** *noun* **1** (*on a package holiday*) accompagnateur *Masc.*, accompagnatrice *Fem.*; **2** (*delivery service*) coursier *Masc.*; **by courier** par coursier.

**course** *noun* **1** (*lessons*) cours *Masc.*; **a beginners' course** un cours pour débutants; **a computer course** un cours d'informatique; **to go on a course** suivre un cours; **2** (*part of a meal*) plat *Masc.*; **the main course** le plat principal; **a golf course** un golf;

a b c d e f g h i j k l m n o p q r s t u v w x y z

**a**

**3 of course** bien sûr; **yes, of course!** oui, bien sûr!; **he's forgotten, of course** il a oublié, bien sûr.

**b**

**c**

**court** noun **1** (for tennis or squash) court Masc.; **2** (for basketball) terrain Masc.

**d**

**e**

**courtyard** noun cour Fem.

**f**

**cousin** noun cousin Masc., cousine Fem.; **my cousin Sonia** ma cousine Sonia.

**g**

**h**

**cover** noun **1** (for a book) couverture Fem.; **2** (for a duvet or cushion) housse Fem.; **a duvet cover** une housse de couette.

**i**

**j**

**cover** verb **1** (to protect or cover up) couvrir [30]; **cover the wound** couvrez la blessure; **he was covered in spots** il était couvert de boutons; **2** (with leaves, snow, or fabric) recouvrir [30]; **the ground was covered with snow** le sol était recouvert de neige.

**k**

**l**

**m**

**n**

**o**

**cow** noun vache Fem.; **mad cow disease** maladie Fem. de la vache folle.

**p**

**q**

**coward** noun lâche Masc. & Fem.

**r**

**cowboy** noun cowboy Masc.

**s**

**crab** noun crabe Masc.

**t**

**crack** noun **1** (in a wall or cup) fêlure Fem.; **2** (a cracking noise) craquement Masc.

**u**

**v**

**crack** verb **1** (to make a crack in) fêler [1] (a cup, a chair, or a bone); **2** (to break) casser [1] (a nut or an egg); **3** (to split by itself: ice, for example) se fêler [1]; **4** (to make a noise) (a twig) craquer [1].

**w**

**x**

**y**

**z**

**cracker** noun **1** (biscuit) cracker Masc.; **2** (Christmas cracker) diablotin Masc.

**crackle** verb crépiter [1].

**craft** noun (at school) travaux Masc. plural manuels.

**crafty** adjective ingénieux (Fem. ingénieuse); **that was very crafty of her** c'était très ingénieux de sa part.

**cramp** noun crampe Fem.; **to have cramp in your leg** avoir une crampe à la jambe.

**crane** noun grue Fem.

**crash** noun **1** (an accident) accident Masc.; **a car crash** un accident de voiture; **2** (smashing noise) fracas Masc.; **a crash of broken glass** un fracas de verre brisé.

**crash** verb **1** (a car or plane) s'écraser [1]; **the plane crashed** l'avion s'est écrasé; **2 to crash into something** rentrer [1] dans quelque chose; **the car crashed into a tree** la voiture est rentrée dans un arbre.

**crash course** noun cours Masc. intensif.

**crash helmet** noun casque Masc.

**crate** noun **1** (for bottles or china) caisse Fem.; **2** (for fruit) cageot Masc.

**crawl** noun (in swimming) crawl Masc.

**crawl** verb **1** (a person, a baby) marcher [1] à quatre pattes; **2** (cars in a jam) rouler [1] au pas; **we were crawling along** nous roulions au pas.

**crayon** noun **1** (wax) crayon Masc. gras; **2** (coloured pencil) crayon Masc. de couleur.

**craze** noun vogue Fem.; **the craze for rollerblades** la vogue des rollers.

**crazy** adjective fou (Fem. folle).

**creak** verb (a hinge) grincer [61] (a floorboard) craquer [1].

**cream** noun crème Fem.; **strawberries and cream** des fraises à la crème.

**cream cheese** noun fromage Masc. à tartiner.

**crease** noun pli Masc.

**creased** adjective froissé.

**create** verb créer [32].

**creative** adjective créatif (Fem. créative) (a person).

**creature** noun créature Fem.

**crèche** noun crèche Fem.

**credit** noun crédit Masc.; **to buy something on credit** acheter quelque chose à crédit.

**credit card** noun carte Fem. de crédit.

**cress** noun cresson Masc.

**crew** noun 1 (on a ship or plane) équipage Masc.; 2 (rowing or filming) équipe Fem.

**crew cut** noun cheveux Masc. plural en brosse.

**cricket** noun 1 (game) cricket Masc.; **to play cricket** jouer au cricket; 2 (insect) grillon Masc.

**cricket bat** noun batte Fem. de cricket.

**crime** noun 1 crime Masc.; **murder is a crime** le meurtre est un crime; 2 (within society) criminalité Fem.;

**the fight against crime** la lutte contre la criminalité.

**criminal** noun, adjective criminel Masc., criminelle Fem.

**crimson** adjective pourpre.

**crisis** noun crise Fem.

**crisp** noun chip Fem.; **a packet of (potato) crisps** un sachet de chips. **crisp** adjective 1 (biscuit) croustillant; 2 (apple) croquant.

**critical** adjective 1 critique (a remark or somebody's condition); 2 décisif (Fem. décisive) (a moment).

**criticism** noun critique Fem.

**criticize** verb critiquer [1].

**Croatia** noun Croatie Fem.

**crockery** noun vaisselle Fem.

**crocodile** noun crocodile Masc.

**crook** noun (criminal) escroc Masc.

**crooked** adjective de travers; **the picture is crooked** le tableau est de travers; **a crooked line** une ligne pas droite.

**crop** noun récolte Fem.

**cross** noun croix Fem.
**cross** adjective fâché; **she's very cross** elle est très fâchée; **I'm cross with you** je suis fâché contre toi.
**cross** verb 1 (to cross over) traverser [1]; **to cross the road** traverser la rue; 2 **to cross your legs** croiser [1] les jambes; 3 **to cross into Italy** passer [1] en Italie; 4 (to cross each other) se croiser [1]; **the two roads cross here** les deux routes se croisent ici.

● **to cross out** rayer [59] (a mistake, for example).

a b c d e f g h i j k l m n o p q r s t u v w x y z

a

b

c

d

e

f

g

h

i

j

k

l

m

n

o

p

q

r

s

t

u

v

w

x

y

z

**cross-Channel** *adjective* trans-Manche; **a cross-Channel ferry** un ferry trans-Manche.

**cross-country** *noun* **1** cross *Masc.*; **2 cross-country skiing** le ski de fond.

**crossing** *noun* **1** (*from one place to another*) traversée *Fem.*; **a Channel crossing** une traversée trans-Manche; **2 a pedestrian crossing** un passage piétons; **a level crossing** un passage à niveau.

**cross-legged** *adjective* **to sit cross-legged** être assis en tailleur.

**crossroads** *noun* carrefour *Masc.*; **at the crossroads** au carrefour.

**crossword** *noun* mots *Masc. plural* croisés; **to do the crossword** faire les mots croisés.

**crouch** *verb* s'accroupir [2].

**crow** *noun* corbeau *Masc.*; ★ **ten kilometres as the crow flies** dix kilomètres à vol d'oiseau.
**crow** *verb* (*a cock*) chanter [1].

**crowd** *noun* foule *Fem.*; **in the crowd** dans la foule; **a crowd of 5,000** une foule de cinq mille.
**crowd** *verb* **to crowd into** or **onto** s'entasser [1] dans (*a room or bus, for example*); **we all crowded into the train** nous nous sommes tous entassés dans le train.

**crowded** *adjective* bondé.

**crown** *noun* couronne *Fem.*

**crude** *adjective* **1** (*rough and ready*) rudimentaire; **2** (*vulgar*) grossier (*Fem.* grossière).

**cruel** *adjective* cruel (*Fem.* cruelle).

**cruelty** *noun* cruauté *Fem.*; **they were treated with great cruelty** ils ont été traités avec beaucoup de cruauté.

**cruise** *noun* croisière *Fem.*; **to go on a cruise** faire une croisière.

**crumb** *noun* miette *Fem.*

**crumple** *verb* froisser [1].

**crunch** *verb* croquer [1] (*an apple*).

**crunchy** *adjective* croquant.

**crush** *verb* écraser [1].

**crust** *noun* croûte *Fem.*

**crusty** *adjective* croustillant (*bread*).

**crutch** *noun* béquille *Fem.*; **to be on crutches** marcher avec des béquilles.

**cry** *noun* cri *Masc.*
**cry** *verb* **1** (*weep*) pleurer [1]; **2** (*call out*) crier [1].

**crystal** *noun* cristal *Masc.*

**cub** *noun* **1** (*animal*) petit *Masc.*; **2** (*scout*) louveteau *Masc.*

**Cuba** *noun* Cuba *Fem.*

**Cuban** *noun* Cubain *Masc.*, Cubaine *Fem.*
**Cuban** *adjective* cubain.

**cube** *noun* cube *Masc.*; **an ice cube** un glaçon.

**cubic** *adjective* (*for measurements*) cube; **three cubic metres** trois mètres cube.

**cubicle** *noun* **1** (*in a changing room*) cabine *Fem.*; **2** (*in a public lavatory*) cabinet *Masc.*

**cuckoo** *noun* coucou *Masc.*

**cucumber** *noun* concombre *Masc.*

**cuddle** *noun* to give somebody a **cuddle** faire un câlin à quelqu'un. **cuddle** *verb* câliner [1].

**cue** *noun* (*billiards, pool, snooker*) queue *Fem.* de billard.

**cuff** *noun* (*on a shirt*) manchette *Fem.*

**cul-de-sac** *noun* impasse *Fem.*

**culture** *noun* culture *Fem.*

**cunning** *adjective* rusé.

**cup** *noun* 1 (*for drinking*) tasse *Fem.*; a cup of tea une tasse de thé; 2 (*a trophy*) coupe *Fem.*

**cupboard** *noun* placard *Masc.*; in the kitchen cupboard dans le placard de la cuisine.

**cup tie** *noun* match *Masc.* de coupe.

**cure** *noun* remède *Masc.* **cure** *verb* guérir [2].

**curiosity** *noun* curiosité *Fem.*

**curious** *adjective* curieux (*Fem.* curieuse).

**curl** *noun* boucle *Fem.* **curl** *verb* friser [1] (*hair*).

**currant** *noun* raisin *Masc.* de Corinthe.

**currency** *noun* foreign currency les devises étrangères.

**current** *noun* (*of electricity or water*) courant *Masc.* **current** *adjective* actuel (*Fem.* actuelle) (*a situation, for example*).

**current affairs** *noun* actualité *Fem.*

**curriculum** *noun* programme *Masc.*

**curry** *noun* curry *Masc.*; chicken curry le curry de poulet.

**cursor** *noun* curseur *Masc.*

**curtain** *noun* rideau *Masc.* (*plural* rideaux*).

**cushion** *noun* coussin *Masc.*

**custard** *noun* 1 (*runny*) crème *Fem.* anglaise; 2 (*baked*) flan *Masc.*

**custom** *noun* coutume *Fem.*

**customer** *noun* client *Masc.*, cliente *Fem.*; customer services le service clientèle.

**customs** *plural noun* douane *Fem. singular*; to go through customs passer à la douane.

**customs hall** *noun* douane *Fem.*

**customs officer** *noun* douanier *Masc.*, douanière *Fem.*

**cut** *noun* 1 (*injury*) coupure *Fem.*; 2 (*haircut*) coupe *Fem.* **cut** *verb* 1 couper [1]; I've cut the bread j'ai coupé le pain; you'll cut yourself! tu vas te couper!; Kevin's cut his finger Kevin s'est coupé le doigt; 2 to cut the grass tondre [3] le gazon; 3 to get your hair cut se faire [10] couper les cheveux; Anne's had her hair cut Anne s'est fait couper les cheveux; 4 to cut prices baisser les prix.

● to cut down something abattre [21] (*a tree*).

● to cut out something 1 découper [1] (*a shape, a newspaper article*); 2 supprimer (*sugar, fatty food, etc.*).

● to cut up something couper [1] (*food*).

**cutlery** *noun* couverts *Masc. plural*.

**CV** *noun* CV *Masc.*

**cycle** *noun* (*bike*) vélo *Masc.* **cycle** *verb* faire [10] du vélo; do you like cycling? est-ce que tu aimes

a
b
c
d
e
f
g
h
i
j
k
l
m
n
o
p
q
r
s
t
u
v
w
x
y
z

faire du vélo?; **we cycle to school** nous allons à l'école à vélo.

**cycle lane** *noun* piste *Fem.* cyclable.

**cycle race** *noun* course *Fem.* cycliste.

**cycling** *noun* cyclisme *Masc.*

**cycling holiday** *noun* vacances *Fem. plural* à vélo.

**cyclist** *noun* cycliste *Masc. & Fem.*

**cylinder** *noun* cylindre *Masc.*

# Dd

**dad** *noun* **1** père *Masc.*; **Anna's dad** le père d'Anna; **my dad works in a bank** mon père travaille dans une banque; **2** (*within the family*) papa *Masc.*; **Dad's not home yet** Papa n'est pas encore rentré.

**daffodil** *noun* jonquille *Fem.*

**daily** *adjective* quotidien (*Fem.* quotidienne); **his daily visit** sa visite quotidienne.

**daily** *adverb* quotidiennement; **she visits him daily** elle lui rend visite tous les jours.

**dairy products** *plural noun* les produits *Masc. plural* laitiers.

**daisy** *noun* paquerette *Fem.*

**dam** *noun* barrage *Masc.*

**damage** *verb* abîmer [1].

**damage** *noun* dégâts *Masc. plural*; **there's no damage** il n'y a pas de dégâts.

**damage** *verb* endommager [52].

**damn** *noun* **he doesn't give a damn** il s'en fiche complètement (*informal*).

**damn** *exclamation* **damn!** zut! (*informal*).

**damp** *adjective* humide.

**damp** *noun* humidité *Fem.*; **because of the damp** à cause de l'humidité.

**dance** *noun* **1** (*art form*) danse *Fem.*; **a folk dance** une danse traditionnelle; **2** (*occasion*) soirée *Fem.* dansante.

**dance** *verb* danser [1].

**dancer** *noun* danseur *Masc.*, danseuse *Fem.*

**dancing** *noun* danse *Fem.*; **I like dancing** j'aime danser.

**dancing class** *noun* cours *Masc.* de danse; **to go to dancing classes** suivre des cours de danse.

**dandruff** *noun* pellicules *Fem. plural.*

**danger** *noun* danger *Masc.*; **to be in danger** être en danger.

**dangerous** *adjective* dangereux (*Fem.* dangereuse); **it's dangerous to drive too fast** il est dangereux de conduire trop vite.

**Danish** *noun* danois *Masc.*

**Danish** *adjective* danois.

**dare** *verb* **1** oser [1]; **to dare to do** oser faire; **I didn't dare suggest it** je n'ai pas osé le suggérer; **2 don't you dare tell her I'm here!** je t'interdis de lui dire que je suis là!; **3 I dare you!** chiche que tu y vas! (*informal*); **I dare you to tell him!** chiche que tu le lui dises! (*informal*).

**daring** *adjective* osé; **that was a bit daring!** c'était un peu osé!

**dark** *noun* in the dark dans l'obscurité; **after dark** après la tombée de la nuit; **to be afraid of the dark** avoir peur du noir.
**dark** *adjective* **1** (*colour*) foncé; **a dark blue skirt** une jupe bleu foncé; **2 she has dark brown hair** elle est brune; **3 it's dark already** il fait nuit déjà; **it gets dark around five** la nuit commence à tomber vers cinq heures; **4** (*room*) sombre; **the kitchen's a bit dark** la cuisine est plutôt sombre; **it's dark in here** il fait sombre ici.

**darkness** *noun* obscurité *Fem.*; **in darkness** dans l'obscurité.

**darling** *noun* chéri *Masc.*, chérie *Fem.*; **see you later, darling!** à tout à l'heure, chéri!

**dart** *noun* fléchette *Fem.*; **to play darts** jouer aux fléchettes.

**data** *plural noun* données *Fem. plural.*

**database** *noun* base *Fem.* de données.

**date** *noun* **1** date *Fem.*; **the date of the meeting** la date de la réunion; **to fix a date for** fixer une date pour; **2 what's the date today?** nous sommes le combien aujourd'hui?; **3 out of date** (*passport, driving licence, etc*) périmé; (*technology, method, information, etc*) dépassé; **my passport's out of date** mon passeport est périmé; **4** (*appointment*) **Laura's got a date with Frank tonight** Laura sort avec Frank ce soir; **5** (*fruit*) datte *Fem.*

**date of birth** *noun* date *Fem.* de naissance.

**daughter** *noun* fille *Fem.*; **Tina's daughter** la fille de Tina.

**daughter-in-law** *noun* belle-fille *Fem.* (*plural* belles-filles).

**dawn** *noun* aube *Fem.*

**day** *noun* **1** jour *Masc.*; **three days later** trois jours plus tard; **the day I went to London** le jour où je suis allé à Londres; **2** (*just from morning until evening*) journée *Fem.*; **we spent the day in London** nous avons passé la journée à Londres; **it rained all day** il a plu pendant toute la journée; **3 it's going to be a nice day tomorrow** il va faire beau demain; **4 the day after** le lendemain; **the day after the wedding** le lendemain du mariage; **the day after tomorrow** après-demain; **my sister's arriving the day after tomorrow** ma sœur arrive après-demain; **5 the day before** la veille; **the day before the wedding** la veille du mariage; **the day before yesterday** avant-hier; **my sister arrived the day before yesterday** ma sœur est arrivée avant-hier.

**day off** *noun* jour *Masc.* de congé; **when's your day off?** quel est ton jour de congé?

**dead** *adjective* mort; **her father's dead** son père est mort.
**dead** *adverb* (*really*) vachement (*informal*); **he's dead nice** il est vachement gentil; **it was dead good** c'était vachement bien; **it's dead easy** c'est vachement facile; **you're dead right** tu as absolument raison; **she arrived dead on time** elle est arrivée à l'heure pile.

a
b
c
d
e
f
g
h
i
j
k
l
m
n
o
p
q
r
s
t
u
v
w
x
y
z

**dead end** *noun* impasse *Fem.*

**deadline** *noun* date *Fem.* limite.

**deaf** *adjective* sourd.

**deafening** *adjective* assourdissant.

**deal** *noun* **1** (*involving money*) affaire; **it's a good deal** c'est une bonne affaire; **2** marché *Masc.*; **I'll make a deal with you** je ferai un marché avec toi; **it's a deal!** marché conclu!; **3 a great deal of** beaucoup de; **I don't have a great deal of time** je n'ai pas beaucoup de temps. **deal** *verb* (*in cards*) donner [1]; **it's you to deal** c'est à toi de donner.

● **to deal with something** s'occuper [1] de quelque chose; **Linda deals with the accounts** Linda s'occupe de la comptabilité; **I'll deal with it as soon as possible** je m'en occuperai dès que possible.

**dear** *adjective* **1** cher (*Fem.* chère); **Dear Sylvie** Chère Sylvie; **2** (*expensive*) cher (*Fem.* chère).

**death** *noun* mort *Fem.*; **after his father's death** après la mort de son père; ★ **you'll frighten him to death** tu lui feras une peur bleue; ★ **I'm bored to death** je m'ennuie à mourir; ★ **I'm sick to death of it** j'en ai marre (*informal*) .

**death penalty** *noun* peine *Fem.* de mort.

**debate** *noun* débat *Masc.* **debate** *verb* débattre [21].

**debt** *noun* dette *Fem.*; **to get into debt** s'endetter.

**decade** *noun* décennie *Fem.*

**decaffeinated** *adjective* décaféiné.

**deceive** *verb* tromper [1].

**December** *noun* décembre *Masc.*; **in December** en décembre.

**decent** *adjective* **1** convenable; **a decent salary** un salaire convenable; **2 a decent meal** un bon repas; **3 he seems a decent enough guy** il semble être un type plutôt bien (*informal*).

**decide** *verb* décider [1]; **to decide to do** décider de faire; **she's decided to buy a car** elle a décidé d'acheter une voiture; **she's decided not to buy a car** elle a décidé de ne pas acheter une voiture.

**decimal** *adjective* décimal (*Masc. plural* décimaux).

**decimal point** *noun* virgule *Fem.*

**decision** *noun* décision *Fem.*; **the right decision** la bonne décision; **the wrong decision** la mauvaise décision; **to make a decision** prendre une décision.

**deck** *noun* (*on a ship*) pont *Masc.*

**deckchair** *noun* transat *Masc.*

**declare** *verb* déclarer [1].

**decorate** *verb* **1** décorer [1]; **to decorate the Christmas tree** décorer le sapin de Noël; **2** peindre; **we're decorating the kitchen this weekend** on va peindre la cuisine ce weekend.

**decoration** *noun* décoration *Fem.*

**decorator** *noun* peintre-décorateur *Masc.*

**decrease** *noun* diminution *Fem.*; **a decrease in the number of** une

diminution du nombre de.
**decrease** *verb* diminuer [1].

**deduct** *verb* déduire [26].

**deep** *adjective* profond; **a deep feeling of gratitude** un profond sentiment de reconnaissance; **the river is very deep here** la rivière est très profonde ici; **how deep is the swimming pool?** quelle est la profondeur de la piscine?; **a hole two metres deep** un trou de deux mètres de profondeur.

**deep end** *noun* **the deep end** (*of a swimming pool*) le grand bassin.

**deep freeze** *noun* congélateur *Masc.*

**deeply** *adverb* profondément.

**deer** *noun* **1** (*red deer*) cerf *Masc.*; **2** (*roe deer*) chevreuil *Masc.*; **3** (*fallow deer*) daim *Masc.*

**defeat** *noun* défaite *Fem.*
**defeat** *verb* battre [21].

**defect** *noun* défaut *Masc.*

**defence** *noun* défense *Fem.*

**defend** *verb* défendre [3].

**defender** *noun* défenseur. *Masc.*

**define** *verb* définir [2].

**definite** *adjective* **1** net (*Fem.* nette) (*before the noun*); **a definite change** un net changement; **a definite improvement** une nette amélioration; **2** (*certain*) sûr; **it's not definite yet** ce n'est pas encore sûr; **3** (*exact*) précis; **a definite answer** une réponse précise; **I don't have a definite idea of what I want** je n'ai pas une idée précise de ce que je veux.

**definite article** *noun* article *Masc.* défini.

**definitely** *adverb* **1** (*when giving your opinion about something*) sans aucun doute; **the blue one is definitely the biggest** le bleu est sans aucun doute le plus grand; **your French is definitely better than mine** ton français est sans aucun doute meilleur que le mien; **'are you sure you like this one better?' – 'definitely!'** 'tu es sûr que tu préfères celui-ci?' – 'sans aucun doute!'; **2** **she's definitely going to be there** elle va y être, c'est sûr; **I'm definitely not going** c'est décidé, je n'y vais pas.

**definition** *noun* définition *Fem.*

**degree** *noun* **1** degré *Masc.*; **thirty degrees** trente degrés; **2** **a university degree** un diplôme universitaire.

**delay** *noun* retard *Masc.*; **a two-hour delay** un retard de deux heures.
**delay** *verb* **1** (*make late*) retarder [1]; **the flight was delayed by bad weather** le vol a été retardé par le mauvais temps; **2** (*postpone*) différer [24]; **the decision has been delayed until Thursday** la décision a été différée juqu'à jeudi.

**delete** *verb* effacer [61].

**deliberate** *adjective* délibéré.

**deliberately** *adverb* exprès; **you did it deliberately** tu l'as fait exprès; **he left it there deliberately** il a fait exprès de le laisser là.

**delicate** *adjective* délicat.

**delicatessen** *noun* épicerie *Fem.* fine.

a
b
c
d
e
f
g
h
i
j
k
l
m
n
o
p
q
r
s
t
u
v
w
x
y
z

**delicious** *adjective* délicieux (*Fem.* délicieuse).

**delighted** *adjective* ravi; **they're delighted with their new flat** ils sont ravis de leur nouvel appartement; **I'm delighted to hear you can come** je suis ravi d'apprendre que vous pouvez venir.

**deliver** *verb* **1** livrer [1]; **they're delivering the washing machine tomorrow** ils vont livrer la machine à laver demain; **2** distribuer [1] (*mail*).

**delivery** *noun* livraison *Fem.*

**demand** *noun* demande *Fem.* **demand** *verb* exiger [52].

**demo** *noun* (*protest*) manif *Fem.* (*informal*).

**democracy** *noun* démocratie *Fem.*

**democratic** *adjective* démocratique.

**demolish** *verb* démolir [2].

**demonstrate** *verb* **1** faire [10] la démonstration de (*a machine, product, or technique*); **2** (*protest*) manifester [1]; **to demonstrate against something** manifester contre quelque chose.

**demonstration** *noun* **1** (*of machine, product, technique*) démonstration *Fem.*; **2** (*protest*) manifestation.

**demonstrator** *noun* (*in protest*) manifestant *Masc.*, manifestante *Fem.*

**denim** *noun* jean *Masc.*; **a denim jacket** un blouson en jean.

**Denmark** *noun* Danemark *Masc.*; **in Denmark** au Danemark; **to Denmark** au Danemark.

**dense** *adjective* dense.

**dent** *noun* bosse *Fem.* **dent** *verb* cabosser [1].

**dental** *adjective* **1** dentaire; **dental floss** du fil dentaire; **dental hygiene** l'hygiène dentaire; **2 a dental appointment** un rendez-vous chez le dentiste.

**dental surgeon** *noun* chirurgien-dentiste *Masc.*

**dentist** *noun* dentiste *Masc. & Fem.*; **my mum's a dentist** ma mère est dentiste.

**deny** *verb* nier [1].

**deodorant** *noun* déodorant *Masc.*

**depart** *verb* partir [58].

**department** *noun* **1** (*in school, university*) département *Masc.*; **the language department** le département de langues; **2** (*in a shop*) rayon *Masc.*; **the men's department** le rayon hommes.

**department store** *noun* grand magasin *Masc.*

**departure** *noun* départ *Masc.*

**departure lounge** *noun* salle *Fem.* d'embarquement.

**depend** *verb* **to depend on** dépendre [3] de; **it depends on the price** ça dépend du prix; **it depends on what you want** ça dépend de ce que tu veux; **it depends** ça dépend.

**deposit** *noun* **1** (*when renting or hiring*) caution *Fem.*; **2** (*when booking a holiday or hotel room*) arrhes *Fem. plural*; **to pay a deposit** verser des arrhes; **3** (*on a bottle*) consigne *Fem.*

**depressed** *adjective* déprimé.

**depressing** *adjective* déprimant.

**depth** *noun* profondeur *Fem.*

**deputy** *noun* adjoint *Masc.*, adjointe *Fem.*.

**deputy head** *noun* directeur *Masc.* adjoint, directrice *Fem.* adjointe.

**descend** *verb* descendre [3].

**describe** *verb* décrire [38].

**description** *noun* description *Fem.*

**desert** *noun* désert *Masc.*; **in the desert** dans le désert.

**desert island** *noun* île *Fem.* déserte.

**deserve** *verb* mériter [1].

**design** *noun* **1** conception *Fem.*; **the design of the plane** la conception de l'avion; **2** (*artistic design*) design *Masc.*; **fashion design** le stylisme; **3** (*pattern*) motif *Masc.*; **a floral design** un motif floral.
**design** *verb* **1** concevoir [66] (*a machine, plane, system*); **2** créer [32] (*costumes, clothes, fabric, scenery*).

**designer** *noun* **1** (*fashion designer*) styliste *Masc. & Fem.*; **2** (*graphic designer*) graphiste *Masc. & Fem.*

**desire** *noun* désir *Masc.*
**desire** *verb* désirer [1].

**desk** *noun* **1** (*in office or at home*) bureau *Masc.*; **2** (*pupil's*) table *Fem.*; **3 the reception desk** la réception; **the information desk** le bureau des renseignements.

**despair** *noun* désespoir *Masc.*
**despair** *verb* **to despair of doing** désespérer [24] de faire.

**desperate** *adjective* **1** désespéré; **a desperate attempt** une tentative désespérée; **2 to be desperate to do** avoir très envie de faire; **I'm desperate to see you** j'ai très envie de te voir.

**despise** *verb* mépriser [1].

**dessert** *noun* dessert *Masc.*; **what's for dessert?** qu'est-ce qu'il y a comme dessert?

**destination** *noun* destination *Fem.*

**destroy** *verb* détruire [26].

**destruction** *noun* destruction *Fem.*

**detached house** *noun* maison *Fem.* individuelle.

**detail** *noun* détail *Masc.*

**detailed** *adjective* détaillé.

**detective** *noun* **1** (*police*) inspecteur *Masc.* de police; **2 a private detective** un détective.

**detective story** *noun* roman *Masc.* policier.

**detention** *noun* retenue *Fem.*

**detergent** *noun* détergent *Masc.*

**determined** *adjective* résolu; **he's determined to leave** il est résolu de partir.

**detour** *noun* détour *Masc.*

**develop** *verb* **1** développer [1]; **to get a film developed** faire développer une pellicule; **2** se développer; **how children develop** comment les enfants se développent.

**developing country** *noun* pays *Masc.* en voie de développement.

**development** *noun* développement *Masc.*

**devil** *noun* diable *Masc.*

**devoted** *adjective* dévoué.

**dew** *noun* rosée *Fem.*

**diabetes** *noun* diabète *Masc.*

**diabetic** *noun*, *adjective* diabète *Masc. & Fem.*; **to be (a) diabetic** être diabète.

**diaeresis** *noun* tréma *Masc.*

**diagnosis** *noun* diagnostic *Masc.*

**diagonal** *adjective* diagonal (*Masc. plural* diagonaux).

**diagram** *noun* schéma *Masc.*

**dial** *verb* composer [1] le numéro; **lift the receiver and dial 142** décrochez et composez le 142; **dial 00 33 for France** faîtes le 00 33 pour la France.

**dialling tone** *noun* tonalité *Fem.*

**dialogue** *noun* dialogue *Masc.*

**diameter** *noun* diamètre *Masc.*

**diamond** *noun* **1** diamant *Masc.*; **2** (*in cards*) carreau; **the jack of diamonds** le valet de carreau; **3** (*shape*) losange *Masc.*

**diarrhoea** *noun* diarrhée *Fem.*; **to have diarrhoea** avoir la diarrhoée.

**diary** *noun* **1** agenda *Masc.*; **j'ai marqué la date de la réunion dans mon agenda** I've noted the date of the meeting in my diary; **2** journal intime; **to keep a diary** tenir un journal (intime).

**dice** *noun* dé *Masc.*; **to throw the dice** jeter le dé.

**dictation** *noun* dictée *Fem.*

**dictionary** *noun* dictionnaire *Masc.*; **to look up a word in the dictionary** chercher un mot dans le dictionnaire.

**did** *verb* SEE **do**.

**die** *verb* **1** mourir [54]; **my grannie died in January** ma grand-mère est morte en janvier; **2 to be dying to do** mourir d'envie de faire; **I'm dying to see them!** je meurs d'envie de les voir!

● **to die out** disparaître [27].

**diesel** *noun* **1** gazole *Masc.*; **2 a diesel engine** un moteur diesel; **a diesel car** une voiture diesel.

**diet** *noun* **1** alimentation *Fem.*; **to have a healthy diet** avoir une alimentation saine; **2** (*slimming or special*) régime *Masc.*; **to be on a diet** être au régime; **a salt-free diet** un régime sans sel.

**difference** *noun* **1** différence *Fem.*; **I can't see any difference between the two** je ne vois pas la différence entre les deux; **what's the difference between ...?** quelle est la différence entre ...?; **2 it makes a difference** ça change quelque chose; **it makes no difference** ça ne change rien; **it makes no difference what I say** je peux dire ce que je veux, ça ne change rien.

**different** *adjective* différent; **the two sisters are very different** les deux sœurs sont très différentes; **she's very different from her sister** elle est très différente de sa sœur.

**difficult** *adjective* difficile; **it's really difficult** c'est vraiment difficile; **it's difficult to decide** il est difficile de décider.

**difficulty** *noun* **1** difficulté *Fem.*; **2 to have difficulty doing** avoir du mal à faire; **I had difficulty finding your house** j'ai eu du mal à trouver ta maison.

**dig** *verb* **to dig a hole** creuser [1] un trou.

**digestion** *noun* digestion *Fem.*

**digital** *adjective* numérique; **a digital recording** un enregistrement numérique; **a digital watch** une montre à affichage numérique.

**dim** *adjective* **1 a dim light** une lumière faible; **2 she's a bit dim** elle est un peu bouchée (*informal*).

**dimension** *noun* dimension *Fem.*

**din** *noun* vacarme *Masc.*; **they were making a dreadful din** ils faisaient un vacarme pas possible; **stop making such a din!** arrêtez de faire ce vacarme!

**dinghy** *noun* **1 a sailing dinghy** un dériveur; **2 a rubber dinghy** un canot pneumatique.

**dining room** *noun* salle *Fem.* à manger ; **in the dining room** dans la salle à manger.

**dinner** *noun* **1** (*evening*) dîner *Masc.*; **to invite somebody to dinner** inviter quelqu'un à dîner; **2** (*midday*) déjeuner *Masc.*; **to have school dinner** manger à la cantine.

**dinner party** *noun* dîner *Masc.*

**dinner time** *noun* **1** (*evening*) l'heure du dîner; **2** (*midday*) l'heure du déjeuner.

**dinosaur** *noun* dinosaure *Masc.*

**diploma** *noun* diplôme *Masc.*

**direct** *adjective* direct; **a direct flight** un vol direct.

**direct** *adverb* directement; **the bus goes direct to the airport** le bus est direct pour l'aéroport.
**direct** *verb* **1** réaliser [1] (*programme, film*); **2** mettre en scène (*play*); **3** régler (*traffic*).

**direction** *noun* **1** direction *Fem.*; **in the other direction** dans l'autre direction; **2 to ask somebody for directions** demander son chemin à quelqu'un; **3 directions for use** mode *Masc.* d'emploi.

**directly** *adverb* **1** directement; **2 directly afterwards** immédiatement après.

**director** *noun* **1** (*of a company*) directeur *Masc.*, directrice *Fem.*; **2** (*of a programme or film*) réalisateur *Masc.*, réalisatrice *Fem.*; **3** (*of a play*) metteur *Masc.* en scène.

**directory** *noun* annuaire *Masc.*; **to be ex-directory** être sur la liste rouge.

**dirt** *noun* saleté *Fem.*

**dirty** *adjective* sale; **my hands are dirty** j'ai les mains sales; **to get something dirty** salir quelque chose; **you'll get your dress dirty** tu vas salir ta robe; **to get dirty** se salir; **the curtains get dirty quickly** les rideaux se salissent vite.

**disability** *noun* infirmité *Fem.*, handicap *Masc.*; **does he have a disability?** est-il infirme?

**disabled** *adjective* handicapé; **disabled people** les handicapés.

**disadvantage** *noun* **1** désavantage *Masc.*; **2 to be at a disadvantage** être désavantagé.

a
b
c
d
e
f
g
h
i
j
k
l
m
n
o
p
q
r
s
t
u
v
w
x
y
z

a
b
c
**d**
e
f
g
h
i
j
k
l
m
n
o
p
q
r
s
t
u
v
w
x
y
z

**disagree** *verb* **I disagree** je ne suis pas d'accord; **I disagree with James** je ne suis pas d'accord avec James.

**disappear** *verb* disparaître [27].

**disappearance** *noun* disparition *Fem.*

**disappointed** *adjective* déçu; **I was disappointed with my marks** j'ai été déçu par mes notes.

**disappointment** *noun* déception *Fem.*

**disaster** *noun* désastre *Masc.*; **it was a complete disaster** ça a été un désastre complet.

**disastrous** *adjective* désastreux (*Fem.* désastreuse).

**disc** *noun* **1 a compact disc** un disque compact; **2 a slipped disc** une hernie discale; **3 a tax disc** (*for a vehicle*) une vignette.

**discipline** *noun* discipline *Fem.*

**disc-jockey** *noun* disc-jockey *Masc.*

**disco** *noun* **1** soirée *Fem.* disco; **they're having a disco** ils font une soirée disco; **2** (*club*) discothèque.

**disconnect** *verb* **1** (*the telephone, electricity*) couper [1]; **have you disconnected the electricity?** est-ce que vous avez coupé l'électricité?; **2** (*appliance*) débrancher [1].

**discount** *noun* réduction *Fem.*

**discourage** *verb* décourager [52].

**discover** *verb* découvrir [30].

**discovery** *noun* découverte *Fem.*

**discreet** *adjective* discret (*Fem.* discrète).

**discrimination** *noun* discrimination *Fem.*; **racial discrimination** la discrimination raciale.

**discuss** *verb* **to discuss something** discuter [1] de quelque chose; **we'll discuss the problem tomorrow** nous discuterons du problème demain; **I'm going to discuss it with Phil** je vais en discuter avec Phil.

**discussion** *noun* discussion *Fem.*

**disease** *noun* maladie *Fem.*

**disgraceful** *adjective* scandaleux (*Fem.* scandaleuse).

**disguise** *noun* déguisement *Masc.*; **to be in disguise** être déguisé. **disguise** *verb* déguiser [1]; **disguised as a woman** déguisé en femme.

**disgust** *noun* dégoût *Masc.*

**disgusted** *adjective* dégoûté.

**disgusting** *adjective* dégoûtant.

**dish** *noun* **1** plat *Masc.*; **a large white dish** un grand plat blanc; **he cooked my favourite dish** il a préparé mon plat favori; **2 to do the dishes** faire la vaisselle.

**dishcloth** *noun* (*for drying up*) torchon *Masc.*

**dishonest** *adjective* malhonnête.

**dishonesty** *noun* malhonnêteté *Fem.*

**dish towel** *noun* torchon *Masc.*

**dishwasher** *noun* lave-vaisselle *Masc.*

**disinfect** *verb* désinfecter [1].

**disinfectant** *noun* désinfectant *Masc.*

**disk** *noun* disque *Masc.*; **a floppy disk** une disquette; **the hard disk** le disque dur.

**disk drive** *noun* unité *Fem.* de disque; **the floppy disk drive** le lecteur de disquettes.

**diskette** *noun* disquette *Fem.*

**dislike** *verb* ne pas aimer [1]; **I dislike sport** je n'aime pas le sport.

**dismay** *noun* consternation *Fem.*

**dismiss** *verb* licencier [1] (*an employee*).

**disobedient** *adjective* désobéissant.

**disobey** *verb* désobéir à [2] (*a person*); enfreindre [60] (*a rule*); **she disobeyed the rules** elle a enfreint les régles.

**display** *noun* 1 exposition *Fem.*; **a handicrafts display** une exposition d'artisanat; **to be on display** être exposé; **2 a window display** une vitrine; **3 a firework display** un feu d'artifice.
**display** *verb* exposer [1].

**disposable** *adjective* jetable.

**dispute** *noun* dispute *Fem.*

**disqualify** *verb* disqualifier [1].

**disrupt** *verb* perturber [1].

**dissolve** *verb* dissoudre [67].

**distance** *noun* distance *Fem.*; **from a distance** de loin; **in the distance** au loin; **it's within walking distance** on peut y aller à pied.

**distant** *adjective* lointain.

**distinct** *adjective* net (*Fem.* nette).

**distinctly** *adverb* 1 distinctement; 2 **it's distinctly odd** c'est vraiment bizarre.

**distract** *verb* distraire [78].

**distribute** *verb* distribuer [1].

**district** *noun* 1 (*in town*) quartier *Masc.*; **a poor district of Paris** un quartier pauvre de Paris; 2 (*in the country*) région *Fem.*

**disturb** *verb* déranger [52]; **sorry to disturb you** je suis désolé de vous déranger; **do not disturb** ne pas déranger.

**ditch** *noun* fossé *Masc.*
**ditch** *verb* **to ditch somebody** plaquer [1] quelqu'un (*informal*).

**dive** *noun* plongeon *Masc.*
**dive** *verb* plonger [52].

**diver** *noun* plongeur *Masc.*, plongeuse *Fem.*.

**diversion** *noun* (*traffic*) déviation *Fem.*

**divide** *verb* diviser [1].

**diving** *noun* plongée *Fem.*

**diving board** *noun* plongeoir *Masc.*

**division** *noun* division *Fem.*

**divorce** *noun* divorce *Masc.*
**divorce** *verb* divorcer [61]; **they divorced in Mexico** ils ont divorcé au Mexique.

**divorced** *adjective* divorcé; **my parents are divorced** mes parents sont divorcés.

**DIY** *noun* bricolage *Masc.*; **to do DIY** faire du bricolage; **a DIY shop** un magasin de bricolage.

**dizzy** *adjective* **I feel dizzy** j'ai la tête qui tourne.

**DJ** *noun* disc jockey *Masc.*

**do** *verb* **1** faire [10]; **what are you doing?** qu'est-ce que tu fais?; **I'm doing my homework** je fais mes devoirs; **what have you done with the hammer?** qu'est-ce que tu as fait du marteau?; **2** (*questions in French are formed either with 'est-ce que' or by putting the pronoun subject after the verb and a hyphen between them*) **do you want some strawberries?** est-ce que tu veux des fraises?, veux-tu des fraises?; **when does it start?** quand est-ce que ça commence?; **how did you open the door?** comment as-tu ouvert la porte?; **3** (*in negative sentences*) **don't, doesn't, didn't** ne ...pas; **I don't like mushrooms** je n'aime pas les champignons; **Rosie doesn't like spinach** Rosie n'aime pas les épinards; **you didn't shut the door** tu n'as pas fermé la porte; **it doesn't matter** ça ne fait rien; **4** (*when it refers back to another verb, 'do' is not translated*) **'do you live here?'** – **'yes, I do'** est-ce que tu habites ici?' – 'oui'; **she has more money than I do** elle a plus d'argent que moi; **'I live in Oxford'** – **'so do I'** 'j'habite à Oxford' – 'moi aussi'; **'I didn't phone Gemma'** – **'neither did I'** 'je n'ai pas appelé Gemma' – 'moi non plus'; **5 don't you?, doesn't he?** etc. n'est-ce pas?; **you know Helen, don't you?** tu connais Helen, n'est-ce pas?; **she left on Thursday, didn't she?** elle est partie jeudi, n'est-ce pas?; **6 that'll do** ça ira; **it'll do like that** ça ira comme ça.

● **to do something up 1** lacer [61]

(*shoes*); **2** boutonner [1] (*cardigan, jacket*); **3** retaper [1] (*house*).

● **to do with 1** regarder [1]; **it has nothing to do with him/you** ça ne le/te regarde pas; **2 to do with something: I could do with a rest** j'aurai bien besoin de me reposer.

● **to do without** se passer [1] de; **we can do without knives** on peut se passer de couteaux.

**doctor** *noun* médecin *Masc.*; **her mother's a doctor** sa mère est médecin.

**document** *noun* document *Masc.*

**documentary** *noun* documentaire *Masc.*

**dodgems** *plural noun* **the dodgems** les autos *Fem. plural* tamponneuses.

**dog** *noun* chien *Masc.*; (*female*) chienne *Fem.*

**do-it-yourself** *noun* bricolage *Masc.*

**dole** *noun* allocations *Fem. plural* chômage; **to be on the dole** être au chômage.

**doll** *noun* poupée *Fem.*

**dollar** *noun* dollar *Masc.*

**dolphin** *noun* dauphin *Masc.*

**Dominican** *noun* Dominicain *Masc.*, Dominicaine *Fem.*
**Dominican** *adjective* dominicain.

**Dominican Republic** *noun* République *Fem.* dominicaine.

**domino** *noun* domino *Masc.*; **to play dominoes** jouer aux dominos.

**don't** SEE **do**.

**donation** *noun* don *Masc.*

**donkey** *noun* âne *Masc.*

**door** *noun* 1 porte *Fem.*; **to open the door** ouvrir la porte; **to shut the door** fermer la porte; 2 (*of a vehicle or train*) portière *Fem.*

**doorbell** *noun* sonnerie *Fem.*; **to ring the doorbell** sonner à la porte; **there's the doorbell!** on sonne!

**doorstep** *noun* pas *Masc.* de la porte.

**dormitory** *noun* dortoir *Masc.*

**dot** *noun* 1 (*written*) point *Masc.*; 2 (*on fabric*) pois *Masc.*; 3 **at ten on the dot** à dix heures pile.

**double** *adjective, adverb* 1 double; **a double helping** une double portion; **a double whisky** un double whisky; 2 le double; **double the time** le double du temps; **double the price** le double du prix; 3 **a double room** une chambre pour deux personnes; 4 **a double bed** un grand lit.

**double bass** *noun* contrebasse *Fem.*; **to play the double bass** jouer de la contrebasse.

**double-breasted** *adjective* **a double-breasted jacket** une veste croisée.

**double-decker bus** *noun* autobus *Masc.* à impériale.

**double glazing** *noun* double vitrage *Masc.*

**doubles** *noun* (*in tennis*) double *Masc.*; **to play a game of doubles** faire un double.

**doubt** *noun* doute *Masc.*; **there's no doubt about it** il n'y a aucun doute là-dessus; **I have my doubts** j'ai des doutes.

**doubt** *verb* **to doubt something** douter [1] de quelque chose; **I doubt it** j'en doute; **I doubt that** douter que (+ *subjunctive*); **I doubt they'll do it** je doute qu'ils le fassent.

**doubtful** *adjective* 1 pas sûr; **it's doubtful** ce n'est pas sûr; 2 **to be doubtful about doing** hésiter à faire; **I'm doubtful about inviting them together** j'hésite à les inviter ensemble.

**dough** *noun* pâte *Fem.*

**doughnut** *noun* beignet *Masc.*

**Dover** *noun* Douvres; **to Dover** à Douvres.

**down** *adverb, preposition* 1 en bas; **he's down in the cellar** il est en bas dans la cave; 2 **down the road** (*nearby*) à côté; **there's a chemist's just down the road** il y a une pharmacie juste à côté; 3 **to go down** descendre; **I went down to the kitchen** je suis descendu dans la cuisine; **to walk down the street** descendre la rue; **to run down the stairs** descendre les escaliers en courant; 4 **to come down** descendre; **she came down from her bedroom** elle est descendue de sa chambre; 5 **to sit down** s'asseoir; **she sat down on the sofa** elle s'est assise sur le canapé.

**downstairs** *adverb* 1 en bas; **she's downstairs in the sitting-room** elle est en bas dans le salon; **the dog sleeps downstairs** le chien dort en bas; 2 du dessous; **the flat downstairs** l'appartement du dessous; **the people downstairs** les voisins du dessous.

**doze** *verb* sommeiller [1].

405

a
b
c
d
e
f
g
h
i
j
k
l
m
n
o
p
q
r
s
t
u
v
w
x
y
z

**a**  **dozen** *noun* douzaine *Fem.*; **a dozen eggs** une douzaine d'œufs.

**b**  **drag** *noun* **what a drag!** quelle barbe! (*informal*); **she's a bit of a drag** elle n'est pas marrante (*informal*).
  **drag** *verb* traîner [1].

**c**

**d**  **dragon** *noun* dragon *Masc.*

**e**  **drain** *noun* égout *Masc.*
  **drain** *verb* égoutter [1] (*vegetables*).

**f**  **drama** *noun* **1** (*subject*) art *Masc.* dramatique; **2 he made a big drama about it** il en a fait tout un cinéma (*informal*).

**g**

**h**  **dramatic** *adjective* spectaculaire.

**i**  **draught** *noun* courant *Masc.* d'air.

**j**  **draughts** *noun* dames *Fem. plural*; **to play draughts** jouer aux dames.

**k**

**l**  **draw** *noun* **1** (*in a match*) match nul *Masc.*; **it was a draw** ils ont fait match nul; **2** (*lottery*) tirage *Masc.* au sort.
  **draw** *verb* **1** dessiner [1]; **I can't draw horses** je ne sais pas dessiner les chevaux; **she can draw really well** elle dessine vraiment bien; **2 to draw a picture** faire [10] un dessin; **3 to draw the curtains** tirer [1] les rideaux; **4 to draw a crowd** attirer [1] une foule de spectateurs; **5** (*in a match*) faire [10] match nul; **we drew three all** nous avons fait match nul trois à trois; **6 to draw lots** tirer [1] au sort.

**m**

**n**

**o**

**p**

**q**

**r**

**s**

**t**

**u**

**v**

**w**  **drawback** *noun* inconvénient *Masc.*

**x**  **drawer** *noun* tiroir *Masc.*

**y**  **drawing** *noun* dessin *Masc.*

**z**  **drawing pin** *noun* punaise *Fem.*

**dreadful** *adjective* affreux (*Fem.* affreuse).

**dreadfully** *adverb* terriblement; **I'm dreadfully late** je suis terriblement en retard; **I'm dreadfully sorry** je suis vraiment navré.

**dream** *noun* rêve *Masc.*; **to have a dream** faire un rêve; **I had a horrible dream last night** j'ai fait un rêve horrible cette nuit.
  **dream** *verb* rêver [1]; **to dream about something** rêver de quelque chose.

**drenched** *adjective* trempé; **to get drenched** se faire tremper; **we got drenched on the way home** on s'est fait tremper en rentrant.

**dress** *noun* robe *Fem.*
  **dress** *verb* **to dress a child** habiller [1] un enfant.
  ● **to dress up** se déguiser [1]; **to dress up as a vampire** se déguiser en vampire.

**dressed** *adjective* **1** habillé; **is Tom dressed yet?** est-ce que Tom est habillé?; **she was dressed in black trousers and a yellow shirt** elle était habillée d'un pantalon noir et d'une chemise jaune; **2 to get dressed** s'habiller; **I got dressed quickly** je me suis vite habillé.

**dresser** *noun* (*for dishes*) vaisselier *Masc.*

**dressing gown** *noun* robe *Fem.* de chambre.

**dressing table** *noun* coiffeuse *Fem.*

**drier** *noun* **a hair drier** un sèche-cheveux; **a tumble drier** un sèche-linge.

**drift** *noun* **a snow drift** une congère.

**drill** *noun* perceuse *Fem.*

**drink** *noun* **1** boisson *Fem.*; **a hot drink** une boisson chaude; **a cold drink** une boisson fraîche; **2 would you like a drink?** tu veux boire quelque chose?; **3 to go out for a drink** aller prendre un pot (*informal*).
**drink** *verb* boire [22]; **he drank a glass of water** il a bu un verre d'eau.

**drive** *noun* **1 to go for a drive** faire un tour en voiture; **2** (*up to a house*) allée *Fem.*
**drive** *verb* **1** conduire [26]; **she drives very fast** elle conduit très vite; **to drive a car** conduire une voiture; **I'd like to learn to drive** j'aimerais apprendre à conduire; **can you drive?** tu sais conduire?; **2** aller en voiture; **we drove to Paris** nous somes allés à Paris en voiture; **3 to drive somebody (to a place)** emmener [50] quelqu'un en voiture; **Mum drove me to the station** Maman m'a emmené en voiture à la gare; **to drive somebody home** raccompagner [1] quelqu'un; ★ **she drives me mad!** elle me rend folle!

**driver** *noun* **1** conducteur *Masc.*, conductrice *Fem.*; **2** (*of a taxi or bus*) chauffeur *Masc.*

**driving instructor** *noun* moniteur *Masc.* d'auto-école.

**driving lesson** *noun* leçon *Fem.* de conduite.

**driving licence** *noun* permis *Masc.* de conduire.

**driving school** *noun* école *Fem.* de conduite.

**driving test** *noun* permis *Masc.* de conduire; **to take your driving test** passer son permis; **Jenny's passed her driving test** Jenny a eu son permis.

**drop** *noun* goutte *Fem.*
**drop** *verb* **1 to drop something** laisser [1] tomber quelque chose; **I dropped my glasses** j'ai laissé tomber mes lunettes; **I'm going to drop history next year** je vais laisser tomber l'histoire l'année prochaine; **drop it!** laisse tomber!; **2** déposer [1] (*a person*); **could you drop me at the station?** est-ce que tu peux me déposer à la gare?

**drought** *noun* sécheresse *Fem.*

**drown** *verb* se noyer [39]; **she drowned in the lake** elle s'est noyée dans le lac.

**drug** *noun* **1** (*medicine*) médicament *Masc.*; **2** (*illegal*) **drugs** la drogue.

**drug abuse** *noun* usage *Masc.* des stupéfiants.

**drug addict** *noun* toxicomane *Masc. & Fem.*

**drug addiction** *noun* toxicomanie *Fem.*

**drum** *noun* **1** tambour *Masc.*; **2 drums** la batterie; **to play drums** jouer de la batterie.

**drum kit** *noun* batterie *Fem.*

**drummer** *noun* batteur *Masc.*, batteuse *Fem.*

a

**drunk** *noun* ivrogne *Masc. & Fem.*
**drunk** *adjective* ivre.

b

**dry** *adjective* sec (*Fem.* sèche).
**dry** *verb* 1 sécher [24]; **to let**
**something dry** laisser [1] sécher
quelque chose; 2 **to dry your hair** se
sécher les cheveux; 3 **to dry your**
**hands** s'essuyer [41] les mains; **to**
**dry the dishes** s'essuyer [41] la
vaisselle; 4 **to dry the washing**
faire [10] sécher le linge.

c

d

e

f

g

**dry cleaner's** *noun* teinturerie
*Fem.*

h

**dryer** *noun* SEE **drier.**

i

**dual carriageway** *noun* route
*Fem.* à quatre voies.

j

k

**dubbed** *adjective* **a dubbed film** un
film doublé.

l

**duck** *noun* canard *Masc.*

m

**due** *adjective, adverb* 1 **to be due to**
**do** devoir faire; **we're due to leave**
**on Thursday** nous devons partir
jeudi; **Paul's due back soon** Paul
doit bientôt revenir; 2 **due to** en
raison de; **the match has been**
**cancelled due to bad weather** le
match a été annulé en raison du
mauvais temps.

n

o

p

q

r

**duke** *noun* duc *Masc.*

s

**dull** *adjective* 1 **dull weather** un
temps maussade; **it's a dull day**
**today** il fait un temps maussade
aujourd'hui; 2 (*boring*) ennuyeux
(*Fem.* ennuyeuse).

t

u

v

**dumb** *adjective* 1 muet (*Fem.*
muette); **to be deaf and dumb** être
sourd-muet; 2 (*stupid*) bête; **he**
**asked some dumb questions** il a
posé des questions bêtes.

w

x

y

z

**dummy** *noun* (*for a baby*) tétine
*Fem.*

**dump** *verb* 1 jeter [48] (*rubbish*);
2 plaquer [1] (*a person*) (*informal*);
**she's dumped her boyfriend** elle a
plaqué son copain.

**dune** *noun* dune *Fem.*

**dungarees** *plural noun* salopette
*Fem. singular.*

**dungeon** *noun* cachot *Masc.*

**Dunkirk** *noun* Dunkerque.

**during** *preposition* pendant; **during**
**the night** pendant la nuit; **I saw her**
**during the holidays** je l'ai vue
pendant les vacances.

**dusk** *noun* **at dusk** à la nuit
tombante.

**dust** *noun* poussière *Fem.*
**dust** *verb* épousseter [48].

**dustbin** *noun* poubelle *Fem.*; **to put**
**something in the dustbin** jeter
quelque chose à la poubelle.

**dustman** *noun* éboueur *Masc.*

**dusty** *adjective* poussiéreux (*Fem.*
poussiéreuse).

**Dutch** *noun* 1 (*language*)
hollandais *Masc.*; 2 **the Dutch**
(*people*) les Hollandais *Masc. plural.*
**Dutch** *adjective* hollandais.

**duty** *noun* 1 devoir *Masc.*; **to have a**
**duty to do** avoir le devoir de faire;
**you have a duty to inform us** vous
avez le devoir de nous informer; 2 **to**
**be on duty** être de service; **to be on**
**night duty** être de service de nuit;
**I'm off duty tonight** je ne suis pas
de service ce soir.

**duty-free** *adjective* hors taxes; **the**
**duty-free shops** les boutiques hors

taxes; **duty-free purchases** les achats hors taxes.

**duvet** *noun* couette *Fem.*

**duvet cover** *noun* housse *Fem.* de couette.

**DVD** *noun* DVD *Masc.*

**dwarf** *noun* nain *Masc.*, naine *Fem.*

**dye** *noun* teinture *Fem.*

**dye** *verb* teindre [60]; **to dye your hair** se teindre les cheveux; **I'm going to dye my hair pink** je vais me teindre les cheveux en rose.

**dynamic** *adjective* dynamique.

**dyslexia** *noun* dyslexie *Fem.*

**dyslexic** *adjective* dyslexique.

# Ee

**each** *adjective* chaque; **each time** chaque fois; **curtains for each window** des rideaux pour chaque fenêtre.

**each** *pronoun* chacun (*Fem.* chacune); **my sisters each have a computer** mes sœurs ont chacune un ordinateur; **she gave us an apple each** elle nous a donné une pomme à chacun; **each of you** chacun de vous, chacune de vous; **we each got a present** chacun de nous a reçu un cadeau; **the tickets cost ten pounds each** les billets coûtent dix livres chacun.

**each other** *pronoun* ('*each other*' *is usually translated using a reflexive pronoun*) **they love each other** ils s'aiment; **we know each other** nous nous connaissons; **do you often see each other?** est-ce que vous vous voyez souvent?

**eagle** *noun* aigle *Masc.*

**ear** *noun* oreille *Fem.*

**earache** *noun* **to have earache** avoir une otite.

**earlier** *adverb* **1** (*a while ago*) tout à l'heure; **your brother phoned earlier** ton frère a appelé tout à l'heure; **2** (*not as late*) plus tôt; **we should have started earlier** nous aurions dû commencer plus tôt; **earlier in the morning** plus tôt le matin.

**early** *adverb* **1** (*in the morning*) tôt; **to get up early** se lever tôt; **it's too early** il est trop tôt; **2** (*for an appointment*) en avance; **we're early, the train doesn't leave until ten** nous sommes en avance, le train ne part qu'à dix heures; **Grandma likes to be early** Grand-mère aime être en avance.

**early** *adjective* **1** (*one of the first*) premier (*Fem.* première); **in the early months** pendant les premiers mois; **I'm getting the early train** je prends le premier train; **2 to have an early lunch** déjeuner tôt; **Jan's having an early night** Jan va se coucher tôt; **we're making an early start** nous partons tôt; **3 in the early afternoon** en début d'après-midi; **in the early hours** au petit matin.

**earn** *verb* gagner [1] (*money*); **Richard earns four pounds an hour** Richard gagne quatre livres de l'heure.

**earnings** *plural noun* salaire *Masc.*

a b c d e f g h i j k l m n o p q r s t u v w x y z

a
b
c
d
**e**
f
g
h
i
j
k
l
m
n
o
p
q
r
s
t
u
v
w
x
y
z

**earphones** *noun* casque *Masc.*

**earring** *noun* boucle *Fem.* d'oreille.

**earth** *noun* terre *Fem.*; **life on earth** la vie sur terre; ★ **what on earth are you doing?** mais qu'est-ce que tu fais là?

**earthquake** *noun* tremblement *Masc.* de terre.

**easily** *adverb* **1** (*without difficulty*) facilement; **2** (*by far*) de loin; **he's easily the best** il est de loin le meilleur.

**east** *noun* est *Masc.*; **in the east** à l'est.

**east** *adjective, adverb* est; **the east side** le côté est; **an east wind** un vent d'est; **east of Paris** à l'est de Paris.

**Easter** *noun* Pâques *Masc.*; **they're coming at Easter** ils viennent à Pâques; **Happy Easter** Joyeuses Pâques.

**Easter Day** *noun* dimanche *Masc.* de Pâques.

**Easter egg** *noun* œuf *Masc.* de Pâques.

**Eastern Europe** *noun* Europe *Fem.* de l'Est.

**easy** *adjective* facile; **it's easy!** c'est facile!; **it was easy to make** c'était facile à faire.

**eat** *verb* **1** manger [52]; **he was eating a banana** il mangeait une banane; **we're going to have something to eat** nous allons manger quelque chose; **2** prendre [64] (*a meal*); **we were eating breakfast** nous prenions le petit déjeuner; **3 to eat out** manger au restaurant.

**EC** *noun* (*short for European Community*) CE *Fem.*, Communauté *Fem.* européenne.

**echo** *noun* écho *Masc.*
**echo** *verb* retentir [2].

**eclipse** *noun* éclipse *Fem.*

**ecological** *adjective* écologique.

**ecologist** *noun* écologiste *Masc. & Fem.*

**ecology** *noun* écologie *Fem.*

**economic** *adjective* **1** (*to do with the economy*) économique; **2** (*profitable*) rentable.

**economical** *adjective* **1** économe (*a person*); **2** économique (*way of doing something*); **it's more economical to buy a big one** c'est plus économique d'acheter un grand.

**economics** *noun* économie *Fem.*

**economy** *noun* économie *Fem.*

**eczema** *noun* eczéma *Masc.*

**edge** *noun* **1** bord *Masc.*; **the edge of the table** le bord de la table; **at the edge of the lake** au bord du lac; **2 to be on edge** être énervé.

**edible** *adjective* comestible.

**Edinburgh** *noun* Édimbourg.

**edit** *verb* éditer [1].

**editor** *noun* (*of a newspaper*) rédacteur *Masc.* en chef, rédactrice *Fem.* en chef.

**educate** *verb* (*a teacher*) instruire [26].

**education** *noun* éducation *Fem.*

**educational** *adjective* éducatif (*Fem.* éducative).

**effect** *noun* effet *Masc.*; **the effect of the accident** l'effet de l'accident; **to have an effect on** avoir un effet sur; **it had a good effect on the whole family** ça a eu un bon effet sur toute la famille; **special effects** les effets spéciaux.

**effective** *adjective* efficace.

**efficient** *adjective* efficace.

**effort** *noun* effort *Masc.*; **to make an effort** faire un effort; **David made an effort to help us** David a fait un effort pour nous aider; **he didn't even make the effort to apologize** il n'a même pas fait l'effort pour s'excuser.

**e.g.** par ex.

**egg** *noun* œuf *Masc.*; **a dozen eggs** une douzaine d'œufs; **a fried egg** un œuf au plat; **two boiled eggs** deux œufs à la coque; **a hard-boiled egg** un œuf dur; **scrambled eggs** les œufs brouillés.

**egg-cup** *noun* coquetier *Masc.*

**eggshell** *noun* coquille *Fem.* d'œuf.

**egg-white** *noun* blanc *Masc.* d'œuf.

**egg-yolk** *noun* jaune *Masc.* d'œuf.

**eight** *number* huit *Masc.*; **Maya's eight** Maya a huit ans; **at eight o'clock** à huit heures.

**eighteen** *number* dix-huit *Masc.*; **Jason's eighteen** Jason a dix-huit ans.

**eighth** *number* **1** huitième; **2 the eighth of July** le huit juillet; **on the eighth floor** au huitième étage.

**eighty** *number* quatre-vingts; **eighty-five** quatre-vingt-cinq (*note* that the 's' disappears when another number follows).

**Eire** *noun* la République d'Irlande; **in Eire** en République d'Irlande.

**either** *pronoun* **1** (*one or the other*) l'un ou l'autre; **choose either (of them)** choisis l'un ou l'autre; **I don't like either (of them)** je n'aime ni l'un ni l'autre; **2** (*both*) les deux; **either is possible** tous les deux sont possibles.

**either** *conjunction* **1 either … or** ou … ou; **either Thursday or Friday** ou jeudi ou vendredi; **either Susie or Judy** ou Susie ou Judy; **he either wrote or phoned** il a ou écrit ou appelé; **2** (*with a negative*) non plus; **he doesn't want to either** il ne veut pas non plus; **I don't know them either** je ne les connais pas non plus.

**elastic** *noun, adjective* élastique *Masc.*

**elastic band** *noun* élastique *Masc.*

**elbow** *noun* coude *Masc.*

**elder** *adjective* aîné; **her elder brother** son frère aîné.

**elderly** *adjective* âgé; **the elderly** les personnes *Fem. plural* âgées.

**eldest** *adjective* aîné; **her eldest brother** son frère aîné.

**elect** *verb* élire [51]; **she has been elected** elle a été élue.

**election** *noun* élection *Fem.*; **in the election** aux élections; **to call a general election** fixer les élections législatives.

**electric** *adjective* électrique.

**electrical** *adjective* électrique.

a
b
c
d
e
f
g
h
i
j
k
l
m
n
o
p
q
r
s
t
u
v
w
x
y
z

a
b
c
d
e
f
g
h
i
j
k
l
m
n
o
p
q
r
s
t
u
v
w
x
y
z

**electrician** *noun* électricien *Masc.*, électricienne *Fem.*

**electricity** *noun* électricité *Fem.*; **to turn off the electricity** couper le courant.

**electronic** *adjective* électronique.

**electronic mail** *noun* courrier *Masc.* électronique.

**electronics** *noun* électronique *Fem.*

**elegant** *adjective* élégant.

**element** *noun* élément *Masc.*

**elephant** *noun* éléphant *Masc.*

**eleven** *number* onze *Masc.*; **Josh is eleven** Josh a onze ans; **at eleven o'clock** à onze heures; **a football eleven** une équipe de football.

**eleventh** *number* onzième; **the eleventh of May** le onze mai; **on the eleventh floor** à l'onzième étage.

**eliminate** *verb* éliminer [1].

**else** *adverb* **1** d'autre; **somebody else** quelqu'un d'autre; **did you see anyone else?** as-tu vu quelqu'un d'autre?; **nothing else** rien d'autre; **I don't want anything else** je ne veux rien d'autre; **2 something else** autre chose; **would you like something else?** désirez-vous autre chose?; **3 somewhere else** ailleurs; **4 or else** sinon; **hurry up, or else we'll be late** dépêche-toi, sinon nous serons en retard.

**e-mail** *noun* courrier *Masc.* électronique.

**embankment** *noun* **1** (*by a river*) quai *Masc.*; **2** (*by a railway*) remblai *Masc.*

**embarrassed** *adjective* gêné; **I was terribly embarrassed** j'étais très gêné.

**embarrassing** *adjective* gênant.

**embarrassment** *noun* embarras *Masc.*, gêne *Fem.*

**embassy** *noun* ambassade *Fem.*; **the French Embassy** l'ambassade de France.

**embroider** *verb* broder [1].

**embroidery** *noun* broderie *Fem.*

**emergency** *noun* cas *Masc.* d'urgence; **in an emergency, break the glass** en cas d'urgence, cassez la vitre; **it's an emergency!** c'est urgent!

**emergency exit** *noun* sortie *Fem.* de secours.

**emergency landing** *noun* atterrissage *Masc.* d'urgence.

**emotion** *noun* émotion *Fem.*

**emotional** *adjective* **1** ému (*a person*); **she was quite emotional** elle était tout émue; **2** (*a speech or an occasion*) chargé d'émotion.

**emperor** *noun* empereur *Masc.*

**emphasis** *noun* accent *Masc.*

**emphasize** *verb* **he emphasized that it wasn't compulsory** il a insisté sur le fait que ce n'était pas obligatoire.

**empire** *noun* empire *Masc.*; **the Roman Empire** l'Empire Romain.

**employ** *verb* employer [39].

**employee** *noun* salarié *Masc.*, salariée *Fem.*

**employer** *noun* employeur *Masc.*, employeuse *Fem.*

**employment** *noun* travail *Masc.*

**empress** *noun* impératrice *Fem.*

**empty** *adjective* vide; **an empty bottle** une bouteille vide; **the room was empty** la pièce était vide. **empty** *verb* vider [1]; **I emptied the teapot into the sink** j'ai vidé la théière dans l'évier.

**enchanting** *adjective* ravissant.

**enclose** *verb* (*in a letter*) joindre [49]; **please find enclosed a cheque** veuillez trouver ci-joint un chèque.

**encore** *noun* bis *Masc.*; **to give an encore** jouer un bis.

**encourage** *verb* encourager [52]; **to encourage somebody to do something** encourager quelqu'un à faire quelque chose; **Mum encouraged me to try again** Maman m'a encouragé à recommencer.

**encouragement** *noun* encouragement *Masc.*

**encouraging** *adjective* encourageant.

**encyclopedia** *noun* encyclopédie *Fem.*

**end** *noun* 1 (*last part*) fin *Fem.*; **'The End'** 'Fin'; **at the end of the film** à la fin du film; **by the end of the day** à la fin de la journée; **in the end I went home** finalement je suis rentré chez moi; **Sally's coming at the end of June** Sally viendra fin juin; 2 (*of a table, garden, stick, or road, for example*) bout *Masc.*; **hold the other end** tiens l'autre bout; **at the end of the street** au bout de la rue; 3 (*in tennis or football*) côté *Masc.*; **to change ends** changer de côté.

**end** *verb* 1 (*to put an end to*) mettre [11] fin à (*an arrangement*); **they've ended the strike** ils ont mis fin à la grève; 2 (*to come to an end*) se terminer [1]; **the day ended with a dinner** la journée s'est terminée par un dîner.

● **to end up** 1 **to end up doing** finir [2] par faire; **we ended up taking a taxi** nous avons fini par prendre un taxi; 2 **to end up somewhere** se retrouver [1] quelque part; **Rob ended up in San Francisco** Rob s'est retrouvé à San Francisco.

**endangered** *adjective* menacé; **an endangered species** une espèce en voie d'extinction.

**ending** *noun* fin *Fem.*

**endless** *adjective* interminable (*a day or a journey, for example*).

**enemy** *noun* ennemi *Masc.*, ennemie *Fem.*; **to make enemies** se faire des ennemis.

**energetic** *adjective* énergique.

**energy** *noun* énergie *Fem.*

**engaged** *adjective* 1 (*to be married*) fiancé; **they're engaged** ils sont fiancés; **to get engaged** se fiancer [61]; 2 (*a phone or toilet*) occupé; **it's engaged, I'll ring later** c'est occupé, j'appellerai plus tard.

**engagement** *noun* (*to marry*) fiançailles *Fem. plural.*

**engagement ring** *noun* bague *Fem.* de fiançailles.

**engine** *noun* 1 (*in a car*) moteur *Masc.*; 2 (*pulling a train*) locomotive *Fem.*

a
b
c
d
e
f
g
h
i
j
k
l
m
n
o
p
q
r
s
t
u
v
w
x
y
z

**engineer** *noun* **1** (*who comes for repairs*) technicien *Masc.*; **2** (*who builds roads and bridges*) ingénieur *Masc.*

**engineering** *noun* ingénierie *Fem.*; **to study engineering** faire des études d'ingénieur.

**England** *noun* Angleterre *Fem.*; **in England** en Angleterre; **to England** en Angleterre; **I am from England** je suis anglais.

**English** *noun* **1** (*the language*) anglais *Masc.*; **do you speak English?** parlez-vous anglais?; **he answered in English** il a répondu en anglais; **2** (*English people*) **the English** les Anglais *Masc. plural*. **English** *adjective* **1** (*of or from England*) anglais; **the English team** l'équipe anglaise; **2 an English lesson** un cours d'anglais; **our English teacher** notre professeur d'anglais.

**English Channel** *noun* **the English Channel** la Manche.

**Englishman** *noun* Anglais *Masc.*

**Englishwoman** *noun* Anglaise *Fem.*

**enjoy** *verb* **1** aimer [1]; **did you enjoy the party?** as-tu aimé la soirée?; **we really enjoyed the concert** nous avons beaucoup aimé le concert; **2 to enjoy doing** aimer faire; **I enjoy swimming** j'aime nager; **do you enjoy living in York?** aimez-vous vivre à York?; **3 to enjoy oneself** s'amuser [1]; **we really enjoyed ourselves** nous nous sommes très bien amusés; **enjoy yourselves!** amusez-vous bien!; **did**

**you enjoy yourself?** tu t'es bien amusé?

**enjoyable** *adjective* agréable.

**enlarge** *verb* agrandir [2] (*a photo, for example*).

**enlargement** *noun* (*of a photo*) agrandissement *Masc.*

**enormous** *adjective* énorme.

**enough** *adverb, pronoun* **1** assez; **there's enough for everyone** il y en a assez pour tout le monde; **2** (*followed by a noun*) assez de; **is there enough bread?** est-ce qu'il y a assez de pain?; **3** (*followed by an adjective or adverb*) suffisamment; **big enough** suffisamment grand; **slowly enough** suffisamment lentement; **4 that's enough** ça suffit.

**enquire** *verb* se renseigner [1]; **I'm going to enquire about the trains** je vais me renseigner sur les trains.

**enquiry** *noun* demande *Fem.* de renseignements; **to make enquiries about something** demander des renseignements sur quelque chose.

**enrol** *verb* s'inscrire [38]; **I want to enrol on the course** je veux m'inscrire au cours.

**enter** *verb* **1** (*to go inside*) entrer [1] dans (*a room or building*); **we all entered the church** nous sommes tous entrés dans l'église; **2 to enter for** s'inscrire [38] à (*an exam or competition*); s'inscrire pour (*a race*).

**entertain** *verb* **1** (*to keep amused*) divertir [2]; **something to entertain the children** quelque chose pour divertir les enfants; **2** (*to have people* *round*) recevoir [66]; **they don't entertain much** ils reçoivent peu.

**entertaining** *noun* **they do a lot of entertaining** ils reçoivent beaucoup.

**entertaining** *adjective* amusant.

**entertainment** *noun* (*fun*) distractions *Fem. plural*; **there wasn't much entertainment in the evenings** il n'y avait pas beaucoup de distractions le soir.

**enthusiasm** *noun* enthousiasme *Masc.*

**enthusiast** *noun* passionné *Masc.*, passionnée *Fem.*; **he's a rugby enthusiast** c'est un passionné de rugby.

**enthusiastic** *adjective* enthousiaste.

**entire** *adjective* entier (*Fem.* entière); **the entire class** la classe entière.

**entirely** *adverb* complètement.

**entrance** *noun* entrée *Fem.*

**entry** *noun* (*the way in*) entrée *Fem.*; **'no entry'** 'défense d'entrer'.

**entry phone** *noun* interphone *Masc.*

**envelope** *noun* enveloppe *Fem.*

**envious** *adjective* envieux (*Fem.* envieuse); **he's envious of my exam results** il est jaloux de mes résultats d'examen.

**environment** *noun* environnement *Masc.*

**environmental** *adjective* écologique.

**environment-friendly** *adjective* écologique.

**envy** *noun* envie *Fem.*

**epidemic** *noun* épidémie *Fem.*

**epileptic** *noun* épileptique *Masc. & Fem.*

**episode** *noun* épisode *Masc.*

**equal** *adjective* égal (*Masc. plural* égaux); **in equal quantities** en quantités égales.

**equal** *verb* égaler [1].

**equality** *noun* égalité *Fem.*

**equalize** *verb* égaliser [1]; **they equalized in the last minute** ils ont égalisé dans la dernière minute.

**equally** *adverb* (*to share*) en parts égales; **we divided it equally** nous l'avons divisé en parts égales.

**equator** *noun* équateur *Masc.*

**equip** *verb* équiper [1]; **well equipped for the hike** bien équipé pour la randonnée; **equipped with rucksacks** équipés de sacs à dos.

**equipment** *noun* **1** (*for sport*) équipement *Masc.*; **2** matériel *Masc.*; **laboratory equipment** le matériel de laboratoire; **3** (*for sports*) équipement *Masc.*

**equivalent** *adjective* **to be equivalent to** être équivalent à.

**error** *noun* **1** (*in spelling or typing*) faute *Fem.*; **a spelling error** une faute d'orthographe; **2** (*in maths or on a computer*) erreur *Fem.*

**error message** *noun* message *Masc.* d'erreur.

**escalator** *noun* escalier *Masc.* mécanique.

**escape** *noun* (*from prison*) évasion *Fem.*

a
b
c
d
e
f
g
h
i
j
k
l
m
n
o
p
q
r
s
t
u
v
w
x
y
z

**escape** *verb* **1** (*a person*) s'évader [1]; **2** (*an animal*) s'échapper [1].

**escort** *noun* escorte *Fem.*; **a police escort** une escorte de police.

**especially** *adjective* **1** (*above all*) surtout; **there are lots of tourists, especially in August** il y a beaucoup de touristes, surtout en août; **2** (*unusually*) particulièrement; **'is he rich?' – 'not especially'** 'est-il riche?' – 'pas particulièrement'.

**essay** *noun* rédaction *Fem.*; **an essay on pollution** une rédaction sur la pollution.

**essential** *adjective* essentiel (*Fem.* essentielle); **it's essential to reply quickly** il est essentiel de répondre vite.

**establishment** *noun* (*an organization*) établissement *Masc.*

**estate** *noun* **1** (*a housing estate*) cité *Fem.*; **2** (*a big house and grounds*) domaine *Masc.*

**estate agent's** *noun* agence *Fem.* immobilière.

**estate car** *noun* break *Masc.*

**estimate** *noun* **1** (*a quote for work*) devis *Masc.*; **2** (*a rough guess*) estimation *Fem.*
**estimate** *verb* évaluer [1].

**etc** etc.

**ethnic** *adjective* ethnique; **an ethnic minority** une minorité ethnique.

**EU** *noun* (SHORT FOR **European Union**) Union *Fem.* européenne.

**euro** *noun* euro *Masc.*; **the euro is divided into cents** l'euro est divisé en centimes.

**Europe** *noun* Europe *Fem.*; **in Europe** en Europe; **to Europe** en Europe.

**European** *noun* Européen *Masc.*, Européenne *Fem.*
**European** *adjective* européen (*Fem.* européenne).

**European Union** *noun* Union *Fem.* européenne.

**eurozone** *noun* zone *Fem.* euro.

**evacuate** *verb* faire [10] évacuer; **the police evacuated the building** la police a fait évacuer l'immeuble.

**evaporate** *verb* s'évaporer [1].

**eve** *noun* **Christmas Eve** la veille de Noël; **New Year's Eve** la Saint-Sylvestre.

**even**[1] *adverb* **1** même; **even Lisa didn't like it** même Lisa ne l'a pas aimé; **without even asking** sans même demander; **2 even if** même si; **even if they arrive** même s'ils arrivent; **3 not even** même pas; **I don't like animals, not even dogs** je n'aime pas les animaux, même pas les chiens; **4 even bigger** encore plus grand; **even more embarrassing** encore plus gênant; **even faster** encore plus vite; **5 even more than** encore plus que; **I liked the song even more than their last one** j'ai aimé la chanson encore plus que leur dernière; **6 even so** quand même; **even so, we had a good time** nous nous sommes bien amusés quand même.

**even**[2] *adjective* 1 (*a surface or layer*) régulier (*Fem.* régulière); 2 (*a number*) pair; **six is an even number** six est un numéro pair; 3 (*with the same score*) à égalité (*competitors*); **Lee and Blair are even** Lee et Blair sont à égalité.

**evening** *noun* 1 soir *Masc.*; **this evening** ce soir; **at six o'clock in the evening** à six heures du soir; **tomorrow evening** demain soir; **on Thursday evening** jeudi soir; **the evening before** la veille au soir; **every evening** tous les soirs; **I work in the evening(s)** je travaille le soir; **the evening meal** le repas du soir; 2 (*from beginning to end*) soirée *Fem.*; **during the evening** pendant la soirée; **an evening with Pavarotti** une soirée avec Pavarotti.

**evening class** *noun* cours *Masc.* du soir.

**event** *noun* 1 (*a happening*) évènement *Masc.*; 2 (*in athletics*) épreuve *Fem.*; **track events** les épreuves de vitesse; 3 **in any event, at all events** de toute façon.

**eventful** *adjective* mouvementé (*a day or an outing*).

**eventually** *adverb* finalement.

**ever** *adverb* 1 (*at any time*) jamais; **hardly ever** presque jamais; **have you ever noticed that?** as-tu jamais remarqué ça?; **no-one ever came** personne n'est jamais venu; **hotter than ever** plus chaud que jamais; **more slowly than ever** plus lentement que jamais; 2 (*always*) toujours; **as cheerful as ever** toujours aussi gai; **the same as ever** toujours le même; 3 **ever since** depuis; **and it's been raining ever since** et depuis il pleut tout le temps.

**every** *adjective* 1 tous (*Fem.* toutes); **every house has a garden** toutes les maisons ont un jardin; **every day** tous les jours; **every Monday** tous les lundis; **every ten kilometres** tous les dix kilomètres; **I've seen every one of his films** j'ai vu tous ses films; 2 (*each*) chaque; **every time** chaque fois; 3 **every now and then** de temps en temps.

**everybody**, **everyone** *pronoun* tout le monde; **everybody knows that** ... tout le monde sait que ...; **everyone else** tous les autres.

**everything** *pronoun* tout; **everything is ready** tout est prêt; **everything's fine** tout va bien; **everything else** tout le reste; **everything you said** tout ce que tu as dit.

**everywhere** *adverb* partout; **there was mud everywhere** il y avait de la boue partout; **everywhere she went** partout où elle allait; **everywhere else** partout ailleurs.

**evidently** *adverb* manifestement.

**evil** *noun* mal *Masc.*
**evil** *adjective* mauvais.

**exact** *adjective* exact; **the exact amount** la somme exacte; **it's the exact opposite** c'est exactement le contraire.

**exactly** *adverb* exactement; **they're exactly the same age** ils ont exactement le même âge; **yes, exactly** oui, exactement.

417

**exaggerate** *verb* exagérer [24].

**exaggeration** *noun* exagération *Fem.*

**exam** *noun* examen *Masc.*; **a history exam** un examen d'histoire; **to sit an exam** passer un examen; **to pass an exam** réussir un examen; **to fail an exam** échouer à un examen.

**examination** *noun* examen *Masc.*

**examine** *verb* examiner [1].

**examiner** *noun* examinateur *Masc.*, examinatrice *Fem.*

**example** *noun* exemple *Masc.*; **for example** par exemple; **to set a good example** donner l'exemple.

**excellent** *adjective* excellent.

**except** *preposition* **1** sauf; **except in March** sauf au mois de mars; **every day except Tuesday** tous les jours sauf le mardi; **except when it rains** sauf quand il pleut; **2 except for** sauf; **except for the children** sauf les enfants.

**exception** *noun* exception *Fem.*; **without exception** sans exception; **with the exception of** à l'exception de.

**exchange** *noun* échange *Masc.*; **in exchange for his help** en échange de son aide; **an exchange visit** un voyage d'échange.

**exchange** *verb* échanger [52]; **can I exchange this shirt for a smaller one?** puis-je échanger cette chemise contre une plus petite?

**exchange rate** *noun* taux *Masc.* d'échange.

**excite** *verb* exciter [1].

**excited** *adjective* **1** excité (*a person or animal*); **the children are excited** les enfants sont excités; **2 to get excited** s'exciter; **the dogs get excited when they hear the car** les chiens s'excitent quand ils entendent la voiture.

**excitement** *noun* excitation *Fem.*

**exciting** *adjective* passionnant; **a really exciting film** un film vraiment passionnant.

**exclamation mark** *noun* point *Masc.* d'exclamation.

**excursion** *noun* excursion *Fem.*

**excuse** *noun* excuse *Fem.*; **Gary has a good excuse** Gary a une bonne excuse; **that's no excuse** ce n'est pas une excuse.

**excuse** *verb* (*apologizing*) **excuse me!** excusez-moi!

**execute** *verb* exécuter [1].

**exercise** *noun* exercice *Masc.*; **a maths exercise** un exercice de maths; **physical exercise** l'exercice physique.

**exercise bicycle** *noun* vélo *Masc.* d'appartement.

**exercise book** *noun* cahier *Masc.*; **my French exercise book** mon cahier de français.

**exhaust (pipe)** *noun* pot *Masc.* d'échappement.

**exhausted** *adjective* épuisé.

**exhaust fumes** *noun* gaz *Masc. plural* d'échappement.

**exhibition** *noun* exposition *Fem.*; **the Cézanne exhibition** l'exposition Cézanne.

**exist** *verb* exister [1].

**exit** *noun* sortie *Fem.*

**expand** *verb* s'agrandir [2]; **the town is expanding** la ville se développe.

**expect** *verb* **1** attendre [3] (*guests or a baby*); **we're expecting thirty people** nous attendons trente personnes; **2** s'attendre [3] à (*something to happen*); **I didn't expect that** je ne m'attendais pas à ça; **I didn't expect it at all** je ne m'y attendais pas du tout; **3** (*as a supposition*) imaginer [1]; **I expect you're tired** j'imagine que tu es fatigué; **I expect she'll bring her boyfriend** j'imagine qu'elle amènera son copain; **yes, I expect so** oui, j'imagine.

**expedition** *noun* expédition *Fem.*

**expel** *verb* **to be expelled** (*from school*) se faire [10] renvoyer.

**expenses** *noun* frais *Masc. plural.*

**expensive** *adjective* cher (*Fem.* chère); **those shoes are too expensive for me** ces chaussures sont trop chères pour moi; **the most expensive CDs** les CDs les plus chers.

**experience** *noun* expérience *Fem.*

**experienced** *adjective* expérimenté.

**experiment** *noun* expérience *Fem.*; **to do an experiment** faire une expérience.

**expert** *noun* spécialiste *Masc. & Fem.*; **he's a computer expert** c'est un spécialiste en informatique.

**expire** *verb* expirer [1].

**expiry date** *noun* date *Fem.* d'expiration.

**explain** *verb* expliquer [1].

**explanation** *noun* explication *Fem.*

**explode** *verb* exploser [1].

**explore** *verb* explorer [1].

**explosion** *noun* explosion *Fem.*

**export** *noun* exportation *Fem.*; **our chief export is wool** la laine est notre premier produit d'exportation.

**export** *verb* exporter [1]; **Russia exports a lot of oil and timber** la Russie exporte beaucoup de pétrole et de bois.

**exposure** *noun* (*of a film*) pose *Fem.*; **a 24-exposure film** une pellicule de vingt-quatre poses.

**express** *noun* (*a train*) rapide *Masc.* **express** *verb* **1** exprimer [1]; **2 to express yourself** s'exprimer.

**expression** *noun* expression *Fem.*

**extend** *verb* agrandir [2] (*a building*).

**extension** *noun* **1** (*to a house*) addition *Fem.*; **2** (*telephone*) poste *Masc.*; **can I have extension 2347 please?** est-ce que je peux avoir le poste vingt-trois quarante-sept, s'il vous plaît? (*note that in spoken French telephone numbers are usually broken down into groups of two figures; this applies to longer numbers as well*); **3** (*electrical*) rallonge *Fem.*

**extension lead** *noun* rallonge *Fem.*

**extension number** *noun* numéro *Masc.* de poste.

**exterior** *adjective* extérieur.

a
b
c
d
e
f
g
h
i
j
k
l
m
n
o
p
q
r
s
t
u
v
w
x
y
z

a
b
c
d
e
f
g
h
i
j
k
l
m
n
o
p
q
r
s
t
u
v
w
x
y
z

**extinct** *adjective* **1** (*species*) disparu; **2** (*volcano*) éteint.

**extinguish** *verb* éteindre [60].

**extinguisher** *noun* (*fire extinguisher*) extincteur *Masc.*

**extra** *adjective* supplémentaire; **extra homework** des devoirs supplémentaires; **wine is extra** le vin est en supplément; **you have to pay extra** il faut payer un supplément; **at no extra charge** sans supplément.
**extra** *adverb* **extra hot** extra-chaud; **extra large** extra-grand.

**extraordinary** *adjective* extraordinaire.

**extra-special** *adjective* exceptionnel (*Fem.* exceptionnelle).

**extra time** *noun* (*in football*) prolongation *Fem.*; **to go into extra time** jouer les prolongations.

**extravagant** *adjective* dépensier (*Fem.* dépensière) (*a person*).

**extreme** *noun* extrême *Masc.*; **to go to extremes** pousser les choses à l'extrême.
**extreme** *adjective* extrême.

**extremely** *adverb* extrêmement; **extremely fast** extrêmement vite.

**eye** *noun* œil *Masc.* (*plural* yeux); **my left eye** mon œil gauche; **a girl with blue eyes** une fille aux yeux bleus; **shut your eyes!** ferme les yeux!; ★ **to keep an eye on something** surveiller quelque chose; ★ **to make eyes at somebody** faire les yeux doux à quelqu'un.

**eyebrow** *noun* sourcil *Masc.*

**eyelash** *noun* cil *Masc.*

**eyelid** *noun* paupière *Fem.*

**eyeliner** *noun* eye-liner *Masc.*

**eye make-up** *noun* maquillage *Masc.* pour les yeux.

**eye shadow** *noun* fard *Masc.* à paupières.

**eyesight** *noun* vue *Fem.*

# Ff

**fabric** *noun* (*cloth*) tissu *Masc.*

**fabulous** *adjective* sensationnel (*Fem.* sensationnelle).

**face** *noun* **1** (*of a person*) visage *Masc.*; **you've got chocolate on your face** tu as du chocolat sur le visage; **2 to pull a face** faire une grimace; **3** (*of a clock or watch*) cadran *Masc.*
**face** *verb* **1** (*a person*) faire [10] face à; **she faced her attacker** elle a fait face à son agresseur; **2 the house faces the park** la maison donne sur le jardin public; **3** (*to stand the idea of*) avoir [5] le courage de; **I can't face going back** je n'ai pas le courage de rentrer; **4 to face up to something** faire face à quelque chose.

**face cloth** *noun* gant *Masc.* de toilette.

**facilities** *plural noun* **1 the school has good sports facilities** l'école dispose d'un bon ensemble sportif; **2 the flat has cooking facilities** l'appartement a une cuisine équipée.

**false**

**fact** *noun* fait *Masc.*; **the fact is that** ... le fait est que ...; **in fact** en fait; **is that a fact?** vraiment?

**factory** *noun* usine *Fem.*

**fade** *verb* **1** (*fabric*) se décolorer [1]; **faded jeans** un jean délavé; **2 the colours have faded** les couleurs ont passé.

**fail** *verb* **1** rater [1] (*a test or exam*); **I failed my driving test** j'ai raté mon permis; **2** échouer [1]; **three students failed** trois étudiants ont échoué; **3** (*not to do*) **to fail to do** manquer [1] de faire; **he failed to contact us** il a manqué de nous contacter; ★ **without fail** sans faute; **ring me without fail** appelle-moi sans faute.

**failure** *noun* **1** échec *Masc.*; **it was a terrible failure** c'était un échec terrible; **2** (*a breakdown in a machine*) panne *Fem.*; **a power failure** une panne de courant.

**faint** *adjective* **1 to feel faint** se sentir [58] mal; **2** (*slight*) léger (*Fem.* légère); **a faint smell of gas** une légère odeur de gaz; **I haven't the faintest idea** je n'en ai pas la moindre idée; **3** (*a voice or sound*) faible.

**faint** *verb* s'évanouir [2]; **Lisa fainted** Lisa s'est évanouie.

**fair** *noun* foire *Fem.*

**fair** *adjective* **1** (*not unfair*) juste; **it's not fair!** ce n'est pas juste!; **2** (*hair*) blond; **he's fair-haired** il a les cheveux blonds; **3** (*skin*) clair; **people with fair skin** les gens qui ont la peau claire; **4** (*fairly good*) assez bon (*Fem.* assez bonne) (*a chance, condition, or performance*)

her **history is fair** son histoire est assez bonne; **5** (*weather*) **if it's fair tomorrow** s'il ne pleut pas demain.

**fairground** *noun* champ *Masc.* de foire.

**fairly** *adverb* (*quite*) assez; **she's fairly happy** elle est assez contente.

**fairy** *noun* fée *Fem.*

**fairy tale** *noun* conte *Masc.* de fées.

**faith** *noun* **1** (*trust*) confiance *Fem.*; **to have faith in somebody** avoir confiance en quelqu'un; **2** (*religious belief*) foi *Fem.*

**faithful** *adjective* fidèle.

**faithfully** *adverb* **yours faithfully** veuillez agréer, Monsieur (*or* Madame) mes salutations distinguées.

**fake** *noun* faux *Masc.*; **the diamonds were fakes** les diamants étaient des faux.

**fake** *adjective* faux (*Fem.* fausse) (*goes before the noun*); **a fake passport** un faux passeport.

**fall** *noun* chute *Fem.*; **to have a fall** tomber.

**fall** *verb* **1** tomber [1]; **mind, you'll fall** attention, tu vas tomber; **Tony fell off his bike** Tony est tombé de son vélo; **she fell downstairs** elle est tombée dans l'escalier; **my jacket fell on the floor** ma veste est tombée par terre; **2** (*the temperature*) descendre [3]; **it fell to minus eleven last night** il est descendu à moins onze cette nuit; **3** (*prices*) baisser [1].

**false** *adjective* faux (*Fem.* fausse) (*goes before the noun*); **a false alarm** une fausse alerte.

a
b
c
d
e
f
g
h
i
j
k
l
m
n
o
p
q
r
s
t
u
v
w
x
y
z

a
b
c
d
e
**f**
g
h
i
j
k
l
m
n
o
p
q
r
s
t
u
v
w
x
y
z

**false teeth** *plural noun* dentier *Masc.*

**fame** *noun* renommée *Fem.*

**familiar** *adjective* familier (*Fem.* familière); **your face is familiar** votre visage m'est familier.

**family** *noun* famille *Fem.*; **a family of six** une famille de six personnes; **Ben's one of the family** Ben fait partie de la famille; **the Barnes family** la famille Barnes.

**family name** *noun* nom *Masc.* de famille.

**famous** *adjective* célèbre.

**fan** *noun* **1** fan *Masc. & Fem.* (*informal,*); **Diana's an Oasis fan** Diana est une fan de Oasis; **2** (*of a team*) supporter *Masc.*; **Brian's a Chelsea fan** Brian est un supporter de Chelsea; **3** (*electric, for cooling*) ventilateur *Masc.*; **4** (*that you hold in your hand*) éventail *Masc.*

**fanatic** *noun* fanatique *Masc. & Fem.*

**fancy** *noun* **to take someone's fancy** faire envie à quelqu'un; **the picture took his fancy** le tableau lui a fait envie.

**fancy** *adjective* (*equipment*) sophistiqué.

**fancy** *verb* **1** (*to want*) **(do you) fancy a coffee?** tu veux un café?; **do you fancy going to the new film?** ça te dirait d'aller voir le nouveau film?; **2 I really fancy him** il me plaît beaucoup; **3 (just) fancy that!** pas possible!; **fancy you being here!** tiens donc, toi ici!

**fancy dress** *noun* **in fancy dress** déguisé; **a fancy-dress party** une soirée déguisée.

**fantastic** *adjective* génial (*Masc. plural* géniaux) (*informal*); **really? that's fantastic!** vraiment? c'est génial!; **a fantastic holiday** des vacances géniales.

**far** *adverb, adjective* **1** loin; **it's not far** ce n'est pas loin; **is it far to Carlisle?** est-ce que Carlisle est loin d'ici?; **how far is it to Bristol?** Bristol est à quelle distance d'ici?; **he took us as far as Newport** il nous a accompagnés jusqu'à Newport; **2 by far** de loin; **the prettiest by far** de loin le plus joli; **3** (*much*) beaucoup; **far better** beaucoup mieux; **far faster** beaucoup plus vite; **far too many people** beaucoup trop de monde; **4 so far** jusqu'ici; **so far everything's going well** jusqu'ici tout va bien; ★ **as far as I know** pour autant que je sache.

**fare** *noun* **1** (*on a bus or the underground*) prix *Masc.* du ticket; **2** (*on a train or plane*) prix *Masc.* du billet; **half fare** demi-tarif *Masc.*; **full fare** plein tarif *Masc.*; **the return fare to Cardiff** le prix d'un aller-retour à Cardiff.

**Far East** *noun* Extrême-Orient *Masc.*

**farm** *noun* ferme *Fem.*

**farmer** *noun* agriculteur *Masc.*, agricultrice *Fem.*

**farmhouse** *noun* ferme *Fem.*

**farming** *noun* agriculture *Fem.*

**farthest** *adjective* le plus éloigné; **the farthest hill** la colline la plus éloignée.

**farthest** *adverb* le plus loin; **that's**

the farthest we went that day
nous ne sommes pas allés plus loin
ce jour-là.

**fascinating** *adjective* fascinant.

**fashion** *noun* mode *Fem.*; **in fashion**
à la mode; **out of fashion** démodé.

**fashionable** *adjective* à la mode.

**fashion model** *noun* mannequin
*Masc.*

**fashion show** *noun* présentation
*Fem.* de collection.

**fast** *adjective* 1 rapide; **a fast car**
une voiture rapide; **2 my watch is
fast** ma montre avance; **you're ten
minutes fast** ta montre avance de
dix minutes.

**fast** *adverb* 1 vite; **he swims fast** il
nage vite; **2 to be fast asleep** être
profondément endormi.

**fast food** *noun* fast-food *Masc.*

**fast forward** *noun* avance *Fem.*
rapide.

**fat** *noun* 1 (*butter, cream, etc*)
matières *Fem. plural* grasses; 2 (*on
meat*) gras *Masc.*; 3 (*on your body*)
graisse *Fem.*

**fat** *adjective* gros (*Fem.* grosse) (*goes
before the noun*); **a fat man** un gros
monsieur; **to get fat** grossir.

**fatal** *adjective* (*accident*) mortel
(*Fem.* mortelle).

**Father's Day** *noun* fête *Fem.* des
Pères.

**father** *noun* père *Masc.*; **my father's
office** le bureau de mon père.

**Father Christmas** *noun* le père
Noël.

**father-in-law** *noun* beau-père
*Masc.*

**fault** *noun* 1 (*when you are
responsible*) faute *Fem.*; **it's
Stephen's fault** c'est la faute de
Stephen; **it's not my fault** ce n'est
pas ma faute; 2 (*a defect*) défaut
*Masc.*; **there's a fault in this
sweater** il y a un défaut dans ce pull;
3 (*in tennis*) faute *Fem.*

**favour** *noun* 1 (*a kindness*) service
*Masc.*; **to do somebody a favour**
rendre service à quelqu'un; **can you
do me a favour?** peux-tu me rendre
service?; **to ask a favour of
somebody** demander un service à
quelqu'un; 2 **to be in favour of
something** être pour quelque chose.

**favourite** *adjective* préféré; **my
favourite band** mon groupe préféré.

**fax** *noun* fax *Masc.*

**fear** *noun* peur *Fem.*
**fear** *verb* craindre [31]; **to fear the
worst** craindre le pire.

**feather** *noun* plume *Fem.*

**feature** *noun* 1 (*of your face*) trait
*Masc.*; **to have delicate features**
avoir les traits délicats; 2 (*of a car or
a machine*) caractéristique *Fem.*

**February** *noun* février *Masc.*; **in
February** en février.

**fed up** *adjective* **I'm fed up** j'en ai
marre (*informal*); **I'm fed up with
working every day** j'en ai marre de
travailler tous les jours.

**feed** *verb* donner [1] à manger à;
**have you fed the dog?** est-ce que tu
as donné à manger au chien?

**feel** *verb* 1 se sentir [58]; **I feel tired**
je me sens fatigué; **I don't feel well**
je ne me sens pas bien; 2 sentir [58];
**I didn't feel a thing** je n'ai rien

a b c d e **f** g h i j k l m n o p q r s t u v w x y z

senti; **3 to feel afraid** avoir [5] peur; **to feel cold** avoir froid; **to feel thirsty** avoir soif; **4 to feel like doing** avoir envie de faire; **I feel like going to the cinema** j'ai envie d'aller au cinéma; **5** (*touch*) toucher [1].

**feeling** *noun* **1** (*in your mind*) sentiment *Masc.*; **a feeling of embarrassment** un sentiment de gêne; **to show your feelings** montrer ses sentiments; **to hurt somebody's feelings** blesser quelqu'un; **2** (*in your body*) sensation *Fem.*; **a dizzy feeling** une sensation de vertige; **3** (*an impression or intuition*) impression *Fem.*; **I have the feeling James doesn't like me** j'ai l'impression que James ne m'aime pas.

**felt-tip (pen)** *noun* feutre *Masc.*

**female** *noun* (*animal*) femelle *Fem.* **female** *adjective* **1** féminin (*person, population*); **2** femelle (*animal, insect*).

**feminine** *adjective* féminin.

**feminist** *noun, adjective* féministe *Masc. & Fem.*

**fence** *noun* (*round a field*) clôture *Fem.*

**fern** *noun* fougère *Fem.*

**ferry** *noun* ferry *Masc.*

**fertilizer** *noun* engrais *Masc.*

**festival** *noun* (*for films, art, or music*) festival *Masc.*

**fetch** *verb* aller [7] chercher; **Tom's fetching the children** Tom est allé chercher les enfants; **fetch me the other knife!** va me chercher l'autre couteau!

**fever** *adjective* fièvre *Fem.*

**few** *adjective, pronoun* **1** peu de; **few people think that** ... peu de gens pensent que ...; **very few houses have a swimming-pool** très peu de maisons ont une piscine; **2 a few** (*followed by a noun*) quelques; **a few weeks earlier** quelques semaines plus tôt; **in a few minutes** dans quelques minutes; **3 a few** (*by itself*) quelques-uns (*Fem.* quelques-unes); **have you any tomatoes? we want a few for the salad** avez-vous des tomates? nous en voulons quelques-unes pour la salade; **4 quite a few** pas mal de; **there were quite a few questions** il y avait pas mal de questions.

**fewer** *adjective* moins de; **there are fewer tourists this year** il y a moins de touristes cette année.

**fiancé** *noun* fiancé *Masc.*

**fiancée** *noun* fiancée *Fem.*

**fiction** *noun* **I read a lot of fiction** je lis beacoup de romans.

**field** *noun* **1** (*with grass or crops*) champ *Masc.*; **a field of wheat** un champ de blé; **2** (*for sport*) terrain *Masc.*; **3** (*the kind of work you do*) domaine *Masc.*

**fierce** *adjective* **1** féroce (*an animal or person*); **2** violent (*a storm or a battle*).

**fifteen** *number* quinze; **Lara's fifteen** Lara a quinze ans.

**fifth** *number* cinquième; **the fifth of January** le cinq janvier; **on the fifth floor** au cinquième étage.

**fifty** *number* cinquante *Masc.*; **my uncle's fifty** mon oncle a cinquante ans.

**fig** *noun* figue *Fem.*

**fight** *noun* **1** (*a scuffle*) bagarre *Fem.*; **2** (*in boxing*) combat *Masc.*; **3** (*against illness*) lutte *Fem.*

**fight** *verb* **1** (*to have a fight*) se battre [21]; **they were fighting** ils se battaient; **2** (*to quarrel*) se disputer [1]; **they're always fighting** ils sont toujours en train de se disputer; **3** (*struggle against*) lutter [1] contre (*poverty or a disease*).

**fighting** *noun* **1** (*in the streets or a pub, for example*) bagarre *Fem.*; **2** (*in war*) combat *Masc.*

**figure** *noun* **1** (*number*) chiffre *Masc.*; **a four-figure number** un nombre de quatre chiffres; **2** (*body shape*) ligne *Fem.*; **good for your figure** bon pour la ligne; **3** (*a person*) personnage *Masc.*; **a familiar figure** un personnage familier; **4** (*diagram*) figure *Fem.*

**file** *noun* **1** (*for records of a person or case*) dossier *Masc.*; **2** (*ring binder*) classeur *Masc.*; **3** (*cardboard folder*) chemise *Fem.*; **4** (*on a computer*) fichier *Masc.*; **5 a nail file** une lime.
**file** *verb* **1** classer [1] (*documents*); **2 to file your nails** se limer [1] les ongles.

**fill** *verb* remplir [2] (*a container*); **she filled my glass** elle a rempli mon verre; **a smoke-filled room** une pièce remplie de fumée.

● **to fill in** remplir [2] (*a form*).

● **to fill in for someone** remplacer [61] quelqu'un.

**filling** *noun* **1** (*for a sandwich*) garniture *Fem.*; (*of meat, vegetables*) farce *Fem.*; **with an apricot filling** fourré à l'abricot; **2** (*in tooth*) plombage *Masc.*

**film** *noun* **1** (*in a cinema*) film *Masc.*; **shall we go and see a film?** si on allait voir un film?; **the new film about Picasso** le nouveau film au sujet de Picasso; **2** (*for a camera*) pellicule *Fem.*; **a 24-exposure colour film** une pellicule couleur de 24 poses.

**film star** *noun* vedette *Fem.* de cinéma.

**filter** *noun* filtre *Masc.*

**filthy** *adjective* dégoûtant.

**fin** *noun* nageoire *Fem.*

**final** *noun* (*in sport*) finale *Fem.*
**final** *adjective* dernier (*Fem.* dernière); **the final instalment** le dernier épisode; **the final result** le résultat final.

**finally** *adverb* finalement.

**find** *verb* trouver [1]; **did you find your passport?** as-tu trouvé ton passeport?; **I can't find my keys** je ne trouve pas mes clefs.

● **to find out 1** (*to enquire*) se renseigner [1]; **I don't know, I'll find out** je ne sais pas, je me renseignerai; **2 to find something out** découvrir [30] (*the facts or an answer*); **when Lucy found out the truth** quand Lucy a découvert la vérité.

**fine** *noun* amende *Fem.* (*for parking or speeding*) contravention *Fem.*
**fine** *adjective* **1** (*in good health*) bien; **'how are you?' – 'fine,**

## finely

thanks' 'comment ça va?' – 'très bien merci'; **2** (*very good*) excellent; **she's a fine athlete** c'est une excellente athlète; **3** (*convenient*) très bien; **ten o'clock? yes, that's fine** dix heures? oui, très bien; **Friday will be fine** vendredi sera très bien; **4** (*sunny*) beau (*Fem.* belle) (*weather or a day*); **if it's fine** s'il fait beau; **5** (*not coarse or thick*) fin; **in fine wool** en laine fine.

**finely** *adjective* (*chopped or grated*) finement.

**finger** *noun* doigt *Masc.*; ★ **I'll keep my fingers crossed for you** je croise les doigts pour toi.

**fingernail** *noun* ongle *Masc.*

**finish** *noun* **1** (*end*) fin *Fem.*; **2** (*in a race*) arrivée *Fem.*

**finish** *verb* **1** finir [2]; **wait, I haven't finished** attends, je n'ai pas fini; **when does school finish?** à quelle heure finit l'école?; **2** (*to finish off*) terminer [1] (*work or a project*); **have you finished the book?** est-ce que tu as terminé le livre?; **3 to finish doing** finir de faire; **have you finished telephoning?** as-tu fini de téléphoner?

• **to finish with** finir avec; **have you finished with the computer?** as-tu fini avec l'ordinateur?.

**finishing line** *noun* ligne *Fem.* d'arrivée.

**Finland** *noun* Finlande *Fem.*; **in Finland** en Finlande; **to Finland** en Finlande.

**Finnish** *noun* finnois *Masc.* (*the language*).

**Finnish** *adjective* finlandais.

**fire** *noun* **1** (*in a grate*) feu *Masc.*; **to light a fire** allumer un feu; **sitting by the fire** assis près du feu; **2 to catch fire** prendre feu; **3** (*accidental*) incendie *Masc.*; **a fire in a factory** un incendie dans une usine.

**fire** *verb* **1** (*to shoot*) tirer [1]; **the soldiers were firing** les soldats tiraient; **to fire at somebody** tirer sur quelqu'un; **2** décharger (*a gun*).

**fire alarm** *noun* alarme *Fem.* incendie.

**fire brigade** *noun* pompiers *Masc. plural.*

**fire engine** *noun* voiture *Fem.* des pompiers.

**fire escape** *noun* escalier *Masc.* de secours.

**fire extinguisher** *noun* extincteur *Masc.*

**fire fighter** *noun* pompier *Masc.*

**fireplace** *noun* cheminée *Fem.*

**fire station** *noun* caserne *Fem.* de pompiers.

**firework** *noun* feu *Masc.* d'artifice (*plural* feux d'artifice); **there will be a firework display** il y aura un feu d'artifice.

**firm** *noun* (*business*) entreprise *Fem.*
**firm** *adjective* ferme.

**first** *adjective, adverb* **1** premier (*Fem.* première); **Susan's the first** Susan est la première; **the first of May** le premier mai; **for the first time** pour la première fois; **I came first in the 200 metres** je suis arrivé premier aux 200 mètres; **2** (*to begin with*) d'abord; **first, I'm going to make some tea** d'abord je vais faire du thé; **3 at first** au début; **at first he was shy** au début il était timide.

**first aid** *noun* premiers secours *Masc. plural.*

**first-aid kit** *noun* trousse *Fem.* de secours.

**first class** *adjective* **1** de première classe (*a ticket, carriage, or hotel*); **a first-class compartment** un compartiment de première classe; **he always travels first class** il voyage toujours en première; **2** au tarif rapide (*a letter or stamp*); **six first-class stamps** six timbres au tarif rapide.

**first floor** *noun* premier étage *Masc.*; **on the first floor** au premier étage.

**firstly** *adverb* premièrement.

**first name** *noun* prénom *Masc.*

**fir tree** *noun* sapin *Masc.*

**fish** *noun* poisson *Masc.*; **do you like fish?** aimez-vous le poisson? **fish** *verb* pêcher [1]; **Dad was fishing for trout** Papa pêchait la truite.

**fish and chips** *noun* poisson *Masc.* frit avec des frites.

**fisherman** *noun* pêcheur *Masc.*

**fishing** *noun* pêche *Fem.*; **I love fishing** j'adore la pêche; **to go fishing** aller à la pêche.

**fishing rod** *noun* canne *Fem.* à pêche.

**fishing tackle** *noun* matériel *Masc.* de pêche.

**fist** *noun* poing *Masc.*

**fit** *noun* **1** (*of rage*) **to have a fit** piquer une crise; **your dad'll have a fit when he sees your hair!** ton père va piquer une crise quand il va voir tes cheveux!; **2 an epileptic fit** une crise d'épilepsie.

**fit** *adjective* (*healthy*) en forme; **I feel really fit** je me sens vraiment en forme; **to keep fit** se maintenir en forme.

**fit** *verb* **1** (*to be the right size for*) (*a garment*) être [6] de la taille de (*a person*); (*shoes*) être à la pointure de; **this skirt doesn't fit me** cette jupe n'est pas à ma taille; **2** (*be able to be put into*) aller [7] dans; **will my cases all fit in the car?** est-ce que mes valises iront dans la voiture?; **the key doesn't fit in the lock** la clé ne va pas dans la serrure; **3** (*install*) installer [1]; **they've fitted an alarm** ils ont installé une alarme.

**fitness** *noun* forme *Fem.*; **fitness training** exercices *Masc. plural* de mise en forme.

**fitted carpet** *noun* moquette *Fem.*

**fitted kitchen** *noun* cuisine *Fem.* intégrée.

**fitting room** *noun* cabine *Fem.* d'essayage.

**five** *number* cinq *Masc.*; **Belinda's five** Belinda a cinq ans; **it's five o'clock** il est cinq heures.

**fix** *verb* **1** (*repair*) réparer [1]; **Mum's fixed the computer** Maman a réparé l'ordinateur; **2** (*to decide on*) fixer [1]; **to fix a date** fixer une date; **at a fixed price** à prix fixe; **3** préparer [1] (*a meal*); **I'll fix supper** c'est moi qui vais préparer le repas du soir.

a
b
c
d
e
f
g
h
i
j
k
l
m
n
o
p
q
r
s
t
u
v
w
x
y
z

**fizzy** *adjective* gazeux (*Fem.* gazeuse); **fizzy water** eau *Fem.* gazeuse.

**flag** *noun* drapeau *Masc.* (*plural* drapeaux).

**flame** *noun* flamme *Fem.*

**flamingo** *noun* flamant *Masc.* rose.

**flan** *noun* tarte *Fem.*; **an onion flan** une tarte à l'oignon.

**flap** *verb* battre [21]; **the bird flapped its wings** l'oiseau battait des ailes.

**flash** *noun* **1 a flash of lightning** un éclair; **2 to do something in a flash** faire quelque chose en un clin d'œil; **3** (*on a camera*) flash *Masc.*
**flash** *verb* **1** (*a light*) clignoter [1]; **2 to flash by or past** passer [1] comme un éclair; **3 to flash your headlights** faire [10] un appel de phares.

**flashback** *noun* flash-back *Masc.*

**flask** *noun* **1** (*insulated bottle*) thermos™ *Masc. or Fem.*; **2** (*container*) flacon *Masc.*

**flat** *noun* appartement *Masc.*; **a third-floor flat** un appartement au troisième étage.
**flat** *adjective* **1** plat; **flat shoes** des chaussures plates; **a flat landscape** un paysage plat; **2 a flat tyre** un pneu crevé.

**flatmate** *noun* colocataire *Masc.* & *Fem.*

**flatter** *verb* flatter [1].

**flattering** *adjective* flatteur (*Fem.* flatteuse).

**flavour** *noun* **1** (*taste*) goût *Masc.*; **the sauce had no flavour** la sauce n'avait aucun goût; **2** (*of drink, ice cream, etc.*) parfum *Masc.*; **what flavour of ice cream would you like?** tu veux quel parfum de glace? **flavour** *verb* parfumer [1]; **vanilla-flavoured** parfumé à la vanille.

**flea** *noun* puce *Fem.*

**flea market** *noun* marché *Masc.* aux puces.

**fleet** *noun* **1** (*of ships*) flotte *Fem.*; **2** (*of vehicles*) parc *Masc.*

**flesh** *noun* chair *Fem.*

**flex** *noun* fil *Masc.*

**flexible** *adjective* flexible (*an arrangement*).

**flight** *noun* **1** vol *Masc.*; **a charter flight** un vol charter; **the flight from Moscow is delayed** le vol de Moscou est retardé; **2 a flight of stairs** un escalier; **four flights of stairs** quatre étages.

**flight attendant** *noun* **1** (*male*) steward *Masc.*; **2** (*female*) hôtesse *Fem.* de l'air.

**fling** *verb* lancer [61].

**flipper** *noun* (*for a swimmer*) palme *Fem.*

**flirt** *verb* flirter [1].

**float** *verb* flotter [1].

**flood** *noun* **1** (*of water*) inondation *Fem.*; **the floods in the south** les inondations au sud; **to be in floods of tears** verser des torrents de larmes; **2** (*of letters or complaints*) déluge *Masc.*
**flood** *verb* inonder [1].

**floodlight** *noun* projecteur *Masc.*

**floor** *noun* **1** (*wooden*) plancher *Masc.* (*concrete*) sol *Masc.*; **to sweep**

the floor balayer; **to sweep the kitchen floor** balayer la cuisine; **your glasses are on the floor** tes lunettes sont par terre; **2** (*a storey*) étage *Masc.*; **on the second floor** au deuxième étage.

**floppy disk** *noun* disquette *Fem.*

**florist** *noun* fleuriste *Masc. & Fem.*

**flour** *noun* farine *Fem.*

**flow** *verb* couler [1].

**flower** *noun* fleur *Fem.*; **a bunch of flowers** un bouquet.
**flower** *verb* fleurir [2].

**flu** *noun* grippe *Fem.*; **to have flu** avoir la grippe.

**fluent** *adjective* **she speaks fluent Italian** elle parle couramment l'italien.

**fluently** *adverb* couramment.

**fluid** *noun* liquide *Masc.*

**flush** *verb* **1** (*to go red*) rougir [2]; **2 to flush the lavatory** tirer [1] la chasse.

**flute** *noun* flûte *Fem.*; **to play the flute** jouer de la flûte.

**fly** *noun* mouche *Fem.*
**fly** *verb* **1** (*a bird, a bee, or a plane*) voler [1]; **2** (*in a plane*) prendre [64] l'avion; **we flew to Edinburgh** nous sommes allés à Édimbourg en avion; **we flew from Gatwick** nous sommes partis de Gatwick; **3** faire [10] voler (*a kite*); **4** (*to pass quickly*) (*time*) passer [1] très vite.

**fly spray** *noun* bombe *Fem.* insecticide.

**foam** *noun* **1** (*foam rubber*) mousse *Fem.*; **a foam mattress** un matelas mousse; **2** (*on a drink*) mousse *Fem.*

**focus** *noun* **to be in focus** être au point; **to be out of focus** être flou.
**focus** *verb* mettre [11] au point (*a camera*).

**fog** *noun* brouillard *Masc.*

**foggy** *adjective* brumeux (*Fem.* brumeuse) (*weather*); **it was foggy** il y avait du brouillard.

**foil** *noun* (*kitchen foil*) papier *Masc.* aluminium.

**fold** *noun* pli *Masc.*
**fold** *verb* **1** plier [1]; **to fold something up** plier quelque chose; **2 to fold your arms** croiser [1] les bras.

**folder** *noun* chemise *Fem.*

**folding** *adjective* pliant; **a folding table** une table pliante.

**follow** *verb* suivre [75]; **follow me!** suivez-moi!; **followed by a dinner** suivi d'un dîner; **do you follow me?** vous me suivez?

**following** *adjective* suivant; **the following year** l'année suivante.

**fond** *adjective* **to be fond of somebody** aimer beaucoup quelqu'un; **I'm very fond of him** je l'aime beaucoup.

**food** *noun* **1** nourriture *Fem.*; **to buy food** acheter à manger; **I like French food** j'aime la cuisine française; **2** (*stocks*) provisions *Fem. plural*; **we bought food for the holiday** nous avons acheté des provisions pour les vacances.

**food poisoning** *noun* intoxication *Fem.* alimentaire.

**fool** *noun* idiot *Masc.*, idiote *Fem.*

a b c d e **f** g h i j k l m n o p q r s t u v w x y z

a
b
c
d
e
**f**
g
h
i
j
k
l
m
n
o
p
q
r
s
t
u
v
w
x
y
z

**foot** *noun* **1** pied *Masc.*; **Lucy came on foot** Lucy est venue à pied; **2** (*the bottom*) **at the foot of the stairs** en bas de l'escalier.

**football** *noun* **1** (*the game*) football *Masc.*; **to play football** jouer au football; **2** (*ball*) ballon *Masc.* de football.

**footballer** *noun* joueur *Masc.* de football, joueuse *Fem.* de football.

**footpath** *noun* sentier *Masc.*

**footprint** *noun* empreinte *Fem.*

**footstep** *noun* pas *Masc.*

**for** *preposition* **1** pour; **a present for my mother** un cadeau pour ma mère; **petrol for the car** de l'essence pour la voiture; **sausages for lunch** des saucisses pour le déjeuner; **it's for cleaning** c'est pour nettoyer; **what's it for?** c'est pour quoi faire?; **2** (*time expressions in the past or future*) pendant; **I studied French for six years** (*but I no longer do*) j'ai étudié le français pendant six ans; **I'll be away for four days** je serai absent pendant quatre jours; **3** (*time expressions in the past but continuing in the present*) depuis; **I've been waiting here for an hour** (*and I'm still waiting*) j'attends ici depuis une heure; **my brother's been living in Paris for three years** (*and he still lives there*) mon frère habite à Paris depuis trois ans; **4 I sold my bike for fifty pounds** j'ai vendu mon vélo cinquante livres; **5 what's the French for 'bee'?** comment dit-on 'bee' en français?

**forbid** *verb* défendre [3]; **to forbid somebody to do something** défendre à quelqu'un de faire

quelque chose; **I forbid you to go out** je te défends de sortir.

**forbidden** *adjective* défendu.

**force** *noun* force *Fem.*
**force** *verb* forcer [61]; **to force somebody to do** forcer quelqu'un à faire.

**forecast** *noun* (*weather forecast*) météo *Fem.*

**forefinger** *noun* index *Masc.*

**foreground** *noun* premier plan *Masc.*; **in the foreground** au premier plan.

**forehead** *noun* front *Masc.*

**foreign** *adjective* étranger (*Fem.* étrangère); **in a foreign country** dans un pays étranger.

**foreigner** *noun* étranger *Masc.*, étrangère *Fem.*

**foresee** *verb* prévoir [65].

**forest** *noun* forêt *Fem.*

**forever** *adverb* **1** pour toujours; **I'd like to stay here forever** j'aimerais rester là pour toujours; **2** (*non-stop*) sans arrêt; **he's forever asking questions** il pose sans arrêt des questions.

**forgery** *noun* **1** (*picture*) faux *Masc.*; **2** (*signature, banknote*) contrefaçon *Fem.*

**forget** *verb* oublier [1]; **I forget his name** j'oublie son nom; **we've forgotten the bread!** nous avons oublié le pain!; **to forget to do** oublier de faire; **I forgot to phone** j'ai oublié d'appeler; **to forget about something** oublier quelque chose.

**forgive** *verb* pardonner [1] à; **to forgive somebody** pardonner à quelqu'un; **I forgave him** je lui ai pardonné; **to forgive somebody for doing** pardonner à quelqu'un d'avoir fait; **I forgave her for losing my ring** je lui ai pardonné d'avoir perdu ma bague.

**fork** *noun* fourchette *Fem.*

**form** *noun* **1** formulaire *Masc.*; **to fill in a form** remplir un formulaire; **2** (*shape or kind*) forme *Fem.*; **in the form of** sous form de; **3 to be on form** être en forme; **4** (*in school*) classe *Fem.*
**form** *verb* former [1].

**formal** *adjective* officiel (*Fem.* officielle) (*invitation, event, complaint, etc.*).

**format** *noun* format *Masc.*

**former** *adjective* ancien (*Fem.* ancienne) (*goes before the noun*); **a former pupil** un ancien élève.

**formula** *noun* formule *Fem.*

**fortnight** *noun* quinze jours *Masc. plural*; **we're going to Spain for a fortnight** nous allons passer quinze jours en Espagne.

**fortress** *noun* forteresse *Fem.*

**fortunate** *adjective* **to be fortunate** avoir [5] de la chance.

**fortunately** *adverb* heureusement.

**fortune** *noun* fortune *Fem.*; **to make a fortune** gagner [1] beaucoup d'argent.

**forty** *number* quarante; **my aunt's forty** ma tante a quarante ans.

**forward** *noun* (*in sport*) avant *Masc.*
**forward** *adverb* **to move forward** avancer; **a seat further forward** une place plus en avant.

**foster child** *noun* enfant *Masc.* adoptif, enfant *Fem.* adoptive.

**foul** *noun* (*in sport*) faute *Fem.*
**foul** *adjective* infect; **the weather's foul** il fait un temps infect.

**fountain** *noun* fontaine *Fem.*

**fountain pen** *noun* stylo *Masc.* à encre.

**four** *number* quatre *Masc.*; **Simon's four** Simon a quatre ans; **it's four o'clock** il est quatre heures; ★ **on all fours** à quatre pattes.

**fourteen** *number* quatorze *Masc.*; **Susie's fourteen** Susie a quatorze ans.

**fourth** *number* quatrième; **the fourth of July** le quatre juillet; **on the fourth floor** au quatrième étage.

**fox** *noun* renard *Masc.*

**fracture** *noun* fracture *Fem.*

**fragile** *adjective* fragile.

**frame** *noun* **1** (*of picture*) cadre *Masc.*; **2** (*of door*) encadrement *Masc.*

**franc** *noun* franc *Masc.*; (*the currency of Switzerland; name of the currencies used in France, Belgium and Luxembourg until replaced by the euro; 100 French francs = 15.24 euros*).

**France** *noun* France *Fem.*; **in France** en France; **to France** en France; **I like France** j'aime la France; **Nadine's from France** Nadine est française.

431

a
b
c
d
e
f
g
h
i
j
k
l
m
n
o
p
q
r
s
t
u
v
w
x
y
z

a b c d e f g h i j k l m n o p q r s t u v w x y z

**frantic** *adjective* **1** (*very upset*) fou (*Fem.* folle); **Mum was frantic with worry** Maman était folle d'inquiétude; **2** (*desperate*) désespéré (*efforts or a search*).

**freckle** *noun* tache *Fem.* de rousseur.

**free** *adjective* **1** (*when you don't pay*) gratuit; **the bus is free** le bus est gratuit; **a free ticket** un billet gratuit; **2** (*not occupied*) libre; **are you free on Thursday?** es-tu libre jeudi?; **3** sugar-free sans sucre; **lead-free** sans plomb.
**free** *verb* libérer [24].

**freedom** *noun* liberté *Fem.*

**free gift** *noun* cadeau *Masc.* (*plural* cadeaux).

**free kick** *noun* coup *Masc.* franc.

**freeze** *verb* **1** (*in a freezer*) congeler [45]; **frozen peas** des petits pois congelés; **2** (*in cold weather*) geler [45]; **it's freezing outside** il gèle dehors.

**freezer** *noun* congélateur *Masc.*

**freezing** *noun* zéro *Masc.*; **three degrees below freezing** trois degrés en-dessous de zéro.
**freezing** *adjective* **I'm freezing** je suis gelé (*informal*); **it's freezing outside** il fait très froid dehors.

**French** *noun* **1** (*the language*) français *Masc.*; **to speak French** parler français; **say it in French** dis-le en français; **to learn French** apprendre le français; **2** (*the people*) **the French** les Français *Masc. plural*; **most of the French** la plupart des Français.

**French** *adjective* **1** français; **Jean-**

Marc is French Jean-Marc est français; **2** de français (*a teacher or a lesson*); **the French class** le cours de français.

**French bean** *noun* haricot *Masc.* vert.

**French dressing** *noun* vinaigrette *Fem.*

**French fries** *plural noun* frites *Fem. plural.*

**Frenchman** *noun* Français *Masc.*

**French stick** *noun* baguette *Fem.*

**French window** *noun* porte-fenêtre *Fem.* (*plural* portes-fenêtres).

**Frenchwoman** *noun* Française *Fem.*

**frequent** *adjective* fréquent.

**frequently** *adverb* souvent.

**fresh** *adjective* frais (*Fem.* fraîche); **fresh eggs** des œufs frais; **I'm going out for some fresh air** je vais prendre de l'air.

**Friday** *noun* vendredi *Masc.*; **next Friday** vendredi prochain; **last Friday** vendredi dernier; **on Friday** vendredi; **I'll phone you on Friday evening** je t'appellerai vendredi soir; **on Fridays** le vendredi; **closed on Fridays** fermé le vendredi; **every Friday** tous les vendredis; **Good Friday** le Vendredi saint.

**fridge** *noun* frigo *Masc.* (*informal*); **put it in the fridge** mets-le au frigo.

**friend** *noun* ami *Masc.*, amie *Fem.*; **a friend of mine** un ami (*or* une amie) à moi; **to make friends** (*in a general way*) se faire des amis; **he made friends with Danny** il est devenu ami avec Danny.

**friendly** *adjective* sympathique.

**friendship** *noun* amitié *Fem*.

**fries** *plural noun* frites *Fem. plural*.

**fright** *noun* peur *Fem.*; **to have** or **get a fright** avoir peur; **you gave me a fright!** tu m'as fait peur!

**frighten** *verb* effrayer [59].

**frightened** *adjective* **to be frightened** avoir peur; **Martin's frightened of snakes** Martin a peur des serpents.

**frightening** *adjective* effrayant.

**fringe** *noun* frange *Fem*.

**frog** *noun* grenouille *Fem*.

**from** *preposition* de; **a letter from Tom** une lettre de Tom; **100 metres from the cinema** à cent mètres du cinéma; **from Monday to Friday** du lundi jusqu'au vendredi; **he comes from Dublin** il vient de Dublin; **two years from now** d'ici deux ans; **from seven o'clock onwards** à partir de sept heures.

**front** *noun* **1** (*of a building, a garment, or a cupboard*) devant *Masc.*; **2** (*of a car*) avant *Masc.*; **sitting in the front** assis à l'avant; **3** (*of a train or a queue*) tête *Fem.*; **there are seats at the front of the train** il y a des places en tête du train; **4** (*of a card or envelope*) recto *Masc.*; **the address is on the front** l'adresse est au recto; **5** (*in a theatre, cinema, or class*) premier rang *Masc.*; **seats at the front** des places au premier rang; **6 in front of** devant; **in front of the TV** devant la télé; **in front of me** devant moi.

**front** *adjective* **1** de devant; **his front paw** sa patte de devant; **in the front row** au premier rang; **2** avant; **the front seat** (*of a car*) le siège avant; **the front wheel** la roue avant.

**front door** *noun* porte *Fem.* d'entrée.

**frontier** *noun* frontière *Fem*.

**frost** *noun* gel *Masc*.

**frosty** *adjective* **1 it's frosty this morning** il gèle ce matin; **2** couvert de givre (*windscreen, grass, etc.*).

**frown** *verb* froncer [61] les sourcils; **he frowned at us** il nous a regardés en fronçant les sourcils.

**frozen** *adjective* (*in a freezer*) surgelé; **a frozen pizza** une pizza surgelée.

**fruit** *noun* fruits *Masc. plural* (*note that in French 'un fruit' is a piece of fruit, whereas 'fruit' in English meaning several pieces of fruit always has to be 'fruits' in the plural in French*) **we bought cheese and fruit** nous avons acheté du fromage et des fruits; **fruit juice** le jus de fruits.

**fruit machine** *noun* machine *Fem.* à sous.

**fruit salad** *noun* salade *Fem.* de fruits.

**frustrated** *adjective* frustré.

**frustrating** *adjective* frustrant.

**fry** *verb* faire [10] frire; **we fried the fish** nous avons fait frire les poissons; **a fried egg** un œuf au plat.

**frying pan** *noun* poêle *Fem*.

**fuel** *noun* (*for a vehicle or plane*) carburant *Masc*.

**full** *adjective* **1** plein; **this glass is full** ce verre est plein; **the train was**

a b c d e **f** g h i j k l m n o p q r s t u v w x y z

**full of tourists** le train était plein de touristes; **2** complet (*Fem.* complète) (*a hotel or flight*); **3** (*top*) **at full speed** à toute vitesse; **at full volume** à plein volume; **4 I'm full** j'ai assez mangé; **5 to write something out in full** écrire quelque chose en toutes lettres.

**full stop** *noun* point *Masc.*

**full-time** *adjective* **a full-time job** un travail à plein temps.

**full time** *noun* (*in sport*) fin *Fem.* du match.

**fully** *adjective* entièrement.

**fun** *noun* plaisir *Masc.*; **to have fun** s'amuser; **have fun!** amusez-vous bien!; **we had fun catching the ponies** nous nous sommes beaucoup amusés en attrapant les poneys; **skiing is fun** c'est amusant de faire du ski; **I do it for fun** je le fais pour m'amuser; ★ **to make fun of somebody** se moquer de quelqu'un.

**funds** *plural noun* fonds *Masc. plural.*

**funeral** *noun* enterrement *Masc.*

**funfair** *noun* fête *Fem.* foraine.

**funny** *adjective* **1** (*when you laugh*) drôle; **how funny you are!** que tu es drôle!; **a funny story** une histoire drôle; **2** (*strange*) bizarre; **that's funny, I'm sure I paid** c'est bizarre, je suis certain que j'ai payé; **a funny noise** un bruit bizarre.

**fur** *noun* **1** (*on an animal*) poils *Masc. plural*; **2** (*for a coat*) fourrure *Fem.*; **a fur coat** un manteau de fourrure.

**furious** *adjective* furieux (*Fem.* furieuse); **she was furious with**

**Steve** elle était furieuse contre Steve.

**furniture** *noun* meubles *Masc. plural*; **to buy some furniture** acheter des meubles; **a piece of furniture** un meuble.

**further** *adverb* plus loin; **further than the station** plus loin que la gare; **ten kilometres further on** dix kilomètres plus loin; **further forward** plus en avant; **further back** plus en arrière.

**fuse** *noun* fusible *Masc.*

**fuss** *noun* histoires *Fem. plural*; **to make a fuss** faire des histoires; **to make a fuss about the bill** faire toute une histoire à propos de l'addition.

**fussy** *adjective* **to be fussy about something** être difficile sur quelque chose (*food, for example*).

**future** *noun* **1** avenir *Masc.*; **in future** à l'avenir; **in the future** dans l'avenir; **2** (*in grammar*) futur *Masc.*; **a verb in the future** un verbe au futur.

# Gg

**gadget** *noun* gadget *Masc.*

**gain** *verb* **1** gagner [1]; **in order to gain time** pour gagner du temps; **we have nothing to gain** nous n'avons rien à gagner; **2 to gain speed** prendre de la vitesse; **to gain weight** prendre du poids.

**galaxy** *noun* galaxie *Fem.*

**gale** *noun* vent *Masc.* violent.

**gallery** *noun* **an art gallery** (*public*) un musée; (*private*) une galerie.

**gamble** *verb* jouer [1].

**gambling** *noun* jeu *Masc.*

**game** *noun* **1** jeu *Masc.*; **children's games** les jeux d'enfant; **a game of chance** un jeu de hasard; **a board game** un jeu de société; **2 a game of** une partie de; **to have a game of cards** faire une partie de cartes; **3** match *Masc.*; **a game of football** un match de foot; **to be good at games: Jack's very good at games** Jack est très bon en sport.

**gang** *noun* bande *Fem.*; **all the gang were there** toute la bande y était.

**gangster** *noun* gangster *Masc.*

**gap** *noun* **1** (*hole*) trou *Masc.*; **2** (*in time*) intervalle *Masc.*; **a two-year gap** un intervalle de deux ans; **3 an age gap** une différence d'âge.

**gap year** *noun* année *Fem.* sabbatique avant d'entrer à l'université.

**garage** *noun* garage *Masc.*

**garden** *noun* jardin *Masc.*

**gardener** *noun* jardinier *Masc.*; **he wants to be a gardener** il veut être jardinier.

**gardening** *noun* jardinage *Masc.*

**garlic** *noun* ail *Masc.*

**garlic mayonnaise** *noun* aïoli *Masc.*

**garment** *noun* vêtement *Masc.*

**gas** *noun* gaz *Masc.*

**gas cooker** *noun* cuisinière *Fem.* à gaz.

**gas fire** *noun* radiateur *Masc.* à gaz.

**gas meter** *noun* compteur *Masc.* à gaz.

**gate** *noun* **1** (*garden*) portail *Masc.*; **2** (*field*) barrière *Fem.*; **3** (*at the airport*) porte *Fem.*

**gather** *verb* **1** (*people*) se rassembler [1]; **a crowd gathered** une foule s'est rassemblée; **2** cueillir [35] (*fruit, vegetables, flowers*); **3 as far as I can gather** autant que je sache.

**gay** *adjective* homosexuel (*Fem.* homosexuelle).

**gaze** *verb* **to gaze at something** regarder [1] quelque chose.

**GCSEs** *noun plural* You can explain GCSEs briefly as follows: Ce sont des examens que l'on passe à environ 16 ans dans un certain nombre de matières (12 au maximum). La meilleure note que l'on peut obtenir est A-star et la note la plus basse est N. Une fois qu'ils ont obtenu leurs GCSEs, de nombreux étudiants se préparent pour les A levels; SEE **A levels**.

**gear** *noun* **1** (*in a car*) vitesse *Fem.*; **to change gear** changer de vitesse; **2** (*equipment*) matériel *Masc.*; **camping gear** du matériel de camping; **3** (*things*) affaires; **I've left all my gear at Gary's** j'ai laissé toutes mes affaires chez Gary.

**gear lever** *noun* levier *Masc.* de vitesses.

**gel** *noun* **hair gel** le gel pour les cheveux.

**Gemini** *noun* Gémeaux *Masc. plural*; **Steph's Gemini** Steph est Gémeaux.

a
b
c
d
e
f
g
h
i
j
k
l
m
n
o
p
q
r
s
t
u
v
w
x
y
z

a
b
c
d
e
f
**g**
h
i
j
k
l
m
n
o
p
q
r
s
t
u
v
w
x
y
z

**gender** *noun* (*of a word*) genre
Masc.; **what is the gender of
'maison'?** quel est le genre de
'maison'?

**general** *noun* général Masc. (*plural*
généraux); **General Jackson** le
général Jackson.
**general** *adjective* général (*Masc.
plural* généraux); **in general** en
général.

**general election** *noun*
élections Fem. plural législatives.

**general knowledge** *noun*
connaissances Fem. plural générales.

**generally** *adverb* généralement.

**generation** *noun* génération Fem.

**generator** *noun* générateur Masc.

**generous** *adjective* généreux (*Fem.*
généreuse).

**genetics** *noun* génétique Fem.

**Geneva** *noun* Genève; **to Geneva** à
Genève; **in Geneva** à Genève; **Lake
Geneva** le lac Léman.

**genius** *noun* génie Masc.; **Lisa,
you're a genius!** Lisa, tu es un
génie!

**gentle** *adjective* doux (*Fem.* douce).

**gentleman** *noun* monsieur Masc.
(*plural* messieurs); **ladies and
gentlemen** mesdames et messieurs.

**gently** *adverb* doucement.

**gents** *noun* toilettes Fem. plural,
(*marked on the door*) 'Messieurs';
**where's the gents?** où sont les
toilettes?

**genuine** *adjective* 1 (*real*)
véritable; **a genuine diamond** un
véritable diamant; 2 (*authentic*)
authentique; **a genuine signature**

une signature authentique;
3 sincère (*person*); **she's very
genuine** elle est très sincère.

**geography** *noun* géographie Fem.

**geology** *noun* géologie Fem.

**geometry** *noun* géométrie Fem.

**germ** *noun* microbe Masc.

**German** *noun* 1 Allemand Masc.,
Allemande Fem.; 2 (*language*)
allemand.
**German** *adjective* allemand.

**Germany** *noun* Allemagne Fem.; **to
Germany** en Allemagne; **in
Germany** en Allemagne.

**get** *verb* 1 (*have, receive*) avoir [5];
**he's got lots of money** il a
beaucoup d'argent; **she's got long
hair** elle a les cheveux longs; **I got a
bike for my birthday** j'ai eu un vélo
pour mon anniversaire; **I got your
letter yesterday** j'ai eu ta lettre
hier; **I got fifteen for my French
homework** j'ai eu quinze pour mon
devoir français; 2 (*fetch*) chercher
[1]; **I'll go and get some bread**
j'irai chercher du pain; **I'll get your
bag for you** je te chercherai ton sac;
3 (*obtain*) trouver [1]; **Fred's got a
job** Fred a trouvé un emploi; **where
did you get that jacket?** où est-ce
que tu as trouvé cette veste?; 4 **to
have got to do** devoir [8] faire; **I've
got to phone before midday** je
dois appeler avant midi; 5 **to get to
somewhere** arriver [1] quelque
part; **when we got to London**
quand nous sommes arrivés à
Londres; **to get here** (or there)
arriver; **we got here this morning**
nous sommes arrivés ce matin;
**what time did they get there?** ile

sont arrivés à quelle heure?;
**6** (*become*) commencer [61] à être;
**I'm getting tired** je commence à
être fatigué; **it's getting late** il
commence à être tard; **it's getting
dark** il commence à faire nuit; **I'm
getting hungry** je commence à
avoir faim; **7 to get something
done** faire [10] faire quelque chose;
**I'm getting my hair cut this
afternoon** je vais me faire couper
les cheveux cet après-midi.

● **to get back** rentrer [1]; **Mum gets
back at six** Maman rentre à six
heures.

● **to get something back** récupérer
[24] quelque chose; **did you get your
books back?** est-ce que tu as
récupéré tes livres?

● **to get into something** monter [1]
dans quelque chose (*a vehicle*); **he
got into the car** il est monté dans la
voiture.

● **to get off something** descendre [3]
de quelque chose; **I got off the train
at Banbury** je suis descendu du
train à Banbury.

● **to get on** aller [7]; **how's Amanda
getting on?** comment va Amanda?

● **to get on something** monter [1]
dans quelque chose (*vehicle*); **she
got on the train at Reading** elle est
montée dans le train à Reading.

● **to get on with somebody**
s'entendre [3] avec quelqu'un; **she
doesn't get on with her brother**
elle ne s'entend pas avec son frère.

● **to get out of something** descendre
[3] de quelque chose (*vehicle*); **Laura
got out of the car** Laura est
descendue de la voiture.

● **to get something out** sortir [72]

quelque chose; **Robert got his
guitar out** Robert a sorti sa guitare.

● **to get together** se voir; [13]; **we
must get together soon** il faut
qu'on se voie bientôt.

● **to get up** se lever; [50]; **I get up at
seven** je me lève à sept heures.

**ghost** *noun* fantôme *Masc.*

**giant** *noun* géant *Masc.*, géante *Fem.*
**giant** *adjective* énorme; **a giant
lorry** un énorme camion.

**giddy** *adjective* **to feel giddy** avoir
[5] le tournis; **I'm feeling giddy** j'ai
le tournis.

**gift** *noun* **1** cadeau *Masc.* (*plural*
cadeaux); **a Christmas gift** un
cadeau de Noël; **2 to have a gift for
something** être doué pour quelque
chose; **Jo has a real gift for
languages** Jo est vraiment douée
pour les langues.

**gifted** *adjective* doué.

**gig** *noun* concert *Masc.* de rock.

**gigabyte** *noun* gigaoctet *Masc.*; **a
twenty gigabyte hard disk** un
disque dur de 20 gigaoctets.

**gigantic** *adjective* gigantesque.

**gin** *noun* gin *Masc.*

**ginger** *noun* gingembre *Masc.*

**gipsy** *noun* **1** (*in general*) bohémien
*Masc.*, bohémienne *Fem.*; **2** (*from
Spain*) gitan *Masc.*, gitane *Fem.*;
**3** (*from Eastern Europe*) tsigane
*Masc. & Fem.*

**giraffe** *noun* giraffe *Fem.*

**girl** *noun* **1** fille *Fem.*; **three boys and
four girls** trois garçons et quatre
filles; **a little girl** une petite fille;
**when I was a little girl** quand

a
b
c
d
e
f
**g**
h
i
j
k
l
m
n
o
p
q
r
s
t
u
v
w
x
y
z

j'étais petite; **2** (*a teenager or young woman*) jeune fille *Fem.*; **an eighteen-year-old girl** une jeune fille de dix-huit ans.

**girlfriend** *noun* copine *Fem.*; **Darren's gone out with his girlfriend** Darren est sorti avec sa copine; **Lizzie and her girlfriends have gone to the cinema** Lizzie et ses copines sont allées au cinéma.

**give** *verb* donner [1]; **to give something to somebody** donner quelque chose à quelqu'un; **I'll give you my address** je te donnerai mon adresse; **give me the key** donne-moi la clé; **Yasmin's dad gave her the money** le père de Yasmin lui a donné l'argent.

● **to give something away** donner quelque chose; **she's given away all her books** elle a donné tous ses livres.

● **to give something back to somebody** rendre [3] quelque chose à quelqu'un; **I gave her back the keys** je lui ai rendu les clés.

● **to give in** céder [24]; **my mum said no but she gave in in the end** maman a dit non, mais elle a fini par céder.

● **to give up** abandonner [1]; **I give up!** j'abandonne!

● **to give up doing** arrêter [1] de faire; **she's given up smoking** elle a arrêté de fumer.

**glacier** *noun* glacier *Masc.*

**glad** *adjective* content; **I'm glad to hear he's better** je suis content d'apprendre qu'il va mieux; **I'm glad to be back** je suis content d'être de retour.

**glamorous** *adjective* **1** (*life*) luxueux (*Fem.* luxueuse); **2** (*job*) prestigieux (*Fem.* prestigieuse); **3** (*woman*) élégant.

**glance** *noun* coup d'œil *Masc.* **glance** *verb* **to glance at something** jeter [48] un coup d'œil à quelque chose; **Sara glanced at the envelope** Sara a jeté un coup d'œil à l'enveloppe.

**glass** *noun* verre *Masc.*; **a glass of water** un verre d'eau; **a glass table** une table en verre.

**glasses** *plural noun* lunettes *Fem. plural*; **to wear glasses** porter des lunettes.

**glider** *noun* planeur *Masc.*

**global** *adjective* mondial (*Masc. plural* mondiaux).

**global warming** *noun* le réchauffement de la planète.

**globe** *noun* globe *Masc.*

**gloomy** *adjective* **1** (*expression*) lugubre; **2** (*weather*) déprimant.

**glory** *noun* gloire *Fem.*

**glove** *noun* gant *Masc.*; **a pair of gloves** une paire de gants.

**glove compartment** *noun* boîte *Fem.* à gants.

**glue** *noun* colle *Fem.*

**go** *noun* **1** (*in a game*) **whose go is it?** c'est à qui de jouer?; **it's my go** c'est à moi de jouer; **2 to have a go at doing** essayer de faire; **I'll have a go at mending it for you** j'essaierai de le réparer pour toi.
**go** *verb* **1** aller [7]; **we're going to London tomorrow** nous allons à Londres demain; **Mark's gone to**

the dentist's Mark est allé chez le dentiste; **to go for a walk** aller se promener; **2** (*with another verb*) aller; **I'm going to make some tea** je vais faire du thé; **he was going to phone me** il allait m'appeler; **3** (*leave*) partir [58]; **Pauline's already gone** Pauline est déjà partie; **we're going on holiday tomorrow** nous partons en vacances demain; **4** (*an event*) se passer [1]; **did the party go well?** est-ce que la soirée s'est bien passée?

- **to go away** s'en aller [7]; **go away!** va-t-en!

- **to go back 1** retourner [1]; **I'm going back to France in March** je retourne en France en mars; **I'm not going back there again!** je n'y retourne plus!; **2** (*to home, school, office*) rentrer [1]; **I went back home** je suis rentré chez moi

- **to go down 1** descendre [3]; **she's gone down to the kitchen** elle est descendue dans la cuisine; **to go down the stairs** descendre l'escalier; **2** (*price, temperature*) baisser [1]; **prices have gone down** les prix ont baissé; **3** (*tyre, balloon, airbed*) se dégonfler [1].

- **to go in** entrer [1]; **he went in and shut the door** il est entré et il a fermé la porte.

- **to go into 1** (*person*) entrer dans; **Fran went into the kitchen** Fran est entrée dans la cuisine; **2** (*object*) rentrer [1] dans; **this file won't go into my bag** ce classeur ne rentre pas dans mon sac

- **to go off 1** (*bomb*) exploser [1]; **2** (*alarm clock*) sonner [1]; **my alarm clock went off at six** mon réveil a sonné à six heures; **3** (*fire or burglar alarm*) se déclencher [1]; **the fire alarm went off** l'alarme d'incendie s'est déclenchée

- **to go on 1** se passer [1]; **what's going on?** qu'est-ce qui se passe?; **2 to go on doing** continuer [1] à faire; **she went on talking** elle a continué à parler; **3 to go on about something** ne pas arrêter [1] de parler de quelque chose; **he's always going on about his dog** il n'arrête pas de parler de son chien

- **to go out 1** sortir [72]; **I'm going out tonight** je sors ce soir; **she went out of the kitchen** elle est sortie de la cuisine; **2 to be going out with somebody** sortir avec quelqu'un; **she's going out with my brother** elle sort avec mon frère; **3** (*light, fire*) s'éteindre [60]; **the light went out** la lumière s'est éteinte

- **to go past something** passer [1] devant quelque chose; **we went past your house** nous sommes passés devant chez toi.

- **to go round: to go round to somebody's house** aller [7] chez quelqu'un; **I went round to Fred's last night** je suis allé chez Fred hier soir.

- **to go round something 1** faire [10] le tour de (*building, park, garden*); **2** visiter [1] (*museum, monument*).

- **to go through** passer [1] par; **the train went through Dijon** le train est passé par Dijon; **you can go through my office** tu peux passer par mon bureau.

- **to go up 1** (*person*) monter [1]; **she's gone up to her room** elle est

439

montée dans sa chambre; **to go up the stairs** monter l'escalier; **2** (*prices*) augmenter [1]; **the price of petrol has gone up** le prix de l'essence a augmenté

**goal** *noun* but *Masc.*; **to score a goal** marquer un but; **to win by three goals to two** gagner trois buts à deux.

**goalkeeper** *noun* gardien *Masc.* de but.

**goat** *noun* chèvre *Fem.*; **goat's cheese** le fromage de chèvre.

**God** *noun* Dieu *Masc.*; **to believe in God** croire en Dieu.

**god** *noun* dieu *Masc.* (*plural* dieux).

**godchild** *noun* filleul *Masc.*, filleule *Fem.*

**goddaughter** *noun* filleule *Fem.*

**goddess** *noun* déesse *Fem.*

**godfather** *noun* parrain *Masc.*

**godmother** *noun* marraine *Fem.*

**godson** *noun* filleul *Masc.*

**goggles** *plural noun* lunettes *Fem. plural*; **swimming goggles** les lunettes de plongée; **skiing goggles** les lunettes de ski.

**go-karting** *noun* karting *Masc.*; **to go go-karting** faire du karting.

**gold** *noun* or *Masc.*; **a gold bracelet** un bracelet en or.

**goldfish** *noun* poisson *Masc.* rouge.

**golf** *noun* golf *Masc.*; **to play golf** jouer au golf.

**golf club** *noun* **1** (*place*) club *Masc.* de golf; **2** (*iron*) crosse *Fem.* de golf.

**golf course** *noun* terrain *Masc.* de golf.

**golfer** *noun* golfeur *Masc.*, golfeuse *Fem.*

**good** *adjective* **1** bon (*Fem.* bonne); **she's a good teacher** c'est un bon professeur; **the cherries are very good** les cerises sont très bonnes; **2 to be good for you** être bon pour la santé; **tomatoes are good for you** les tomates sont bonnes pour la santé; **3 to be good at** être bon en; **she's good at art** elle est bonne en dessin; **4** (*well-behaved*) sage; **be good!** sois sage!; **5** (*kind*) gentil (*Fem.* gentille); **she's been very good to me** elle a été très gentille avec moi; **6 for good** pour de bon; **I've stopped smoking for good** j'ai arrêté de fumer pour de bon.

**good afternoon** *exclamation* bonjour.

**goodbye** *exclamation* au revoir.

**good evening** *exclamation* bonsoir.

**Good Friday** *noun* le Vendredi saint.

**good-looking** *adjective* beau (*Fem.* belle) (*Masc. plural* beaux); **Maya's boyfriend's really good-looking** le copain de Maya est très beau.

**good morning** *exclamation* bonjour.

**goodness** *exclamation* mon Dieu!; **for goodness sake!** au nom du ciel!

**goodnight** *exclamation* bonne nuit.

**goods** *plural noun* marchandises *Fem. plural*.

**goods train** *noun* train *Masc.* de marchandises.

**goose** *noun* oie *Fem.*

**goose pimples** *noun* chair *Fem.* de poule.

**gorgeous** *adjective* superbe; **a gorgeous dress** une robe superbe; **it's a gorgeous day** il fait un temps superbe.

**gorilla** *noun* gorille *Masc.*

**gorse** *noun* ajoncs *Masc. plural.*

**gosh** *exclamation* ça alors!

**gossip** *noun* **1** (*person*) bavard *Masc.*, bavarde *Fem.*; **2** (*news*) nouvelles *Fem. plural*; **what's the latest gossip?** quoi de neuf? **gossip** *verb* bavarder [1].

**government** *noun* gouvernement *Masc.*

**grab** *verb* **1** saisir [2]; **she grabbed my arm** elle m'a saisi par le bras; **2 to grab something from somebody** arracher [1] quelque chose à quelqu'un; **he grabbed the book from me** il m'a arraché le livre.

**graceful** *adjective* élégant.

**grade** *noun* (*mark*) note *Fem.*; **to get good grades** avoir de bonnes notes.

**gradual** *adjective* progressif (*Fem.* progressive).

**gradually** *adverb* petit à petit; **the weather got gradually better** le temps s'est amélioré petit à petit.

**graffiti** *plural noun* graffiti *Masc. plural.*

**grain** *noun* grain *Masc.*

**grammar** *noun* grammaire *Fem.*

**grammar school** *noun* (*from age 11 to 15*) collège *Masc.*; (*from age 15 to 18*) lycée *Masc.*

**grammatical** *adjective* **a grammatical error** une faute de grammaire.

**gramme** *noun* gramme *Masc.*

**gran** *noun* mamie *Fem.* (*informal*).

**grandchildren** *plural noun* petits-enfants *Masc. plural.*

**granddad** *noun* papy *Masc.* (*informal*).

**granddaughter** *noun* petite-fille *Fem.*

**grandfather** *noun* grand-père *Masc.*

**grandma** *noun* mamie *Fem.* (*informal*).

**grandmother** *noun* grand-mère *Fem.*

**grandpa** *noun* papi *Masc.* (*informal*).

**grandparents** *plural noun* grandparents *Masc. plural.*

**grandson** *noun* petit-fils *Masc.*

**granny** *noun* mamie *Fem.* (*informal*).

**grape** *noun* **a grape** un grain de raisin; **to buy some grapes** acheter du raisin; **do you like grapes?** est-ce que tu aimes le raisin?; **a bunch of grapes** une grappe de raisin.

**grapefruit** *noun* pamplemousse *Masc.*

**graph** *noun* graphique *Masc.*

**graphic designer** *noun* graphiste *Masc. & Fem.*

**graphics** *noun* visualisation *Fem.* graphique.

**grasp** *verb* saisir [2].

a
b
c
d
e
f
**g**
h
i
j
k
l
m
n
o
p
q
r
s
t
u
v
w
x
y
z

a **grass** *noun* 1 herbe *Fem.*; **sitting on the grass** assis sur l'herbe; 2 (*lawn*)
b pelouse *Fem.*; **to cut the grass** tondre la pelouse.
c **grasshopper** *noun* sauterelle
d *Fem.*

e **grate** *verb* râper [1]; **grated cheese** du fromage râpé.

f **grateful** *adjective* reconnaissant.

g **grater** *noun* râpe *Fem.*

h **grave**[1] *noun* tombe *Fem.*

i **grave**[2] *noun* accent *Masc.* grave.

**gravel** *noun* gravillons *Masc. plural.*

j **graveyard** *noun* cimetière *Masc.*

k **gravity** *noun* pesanteur *Fem.*

l **gravy** *noun* sauce *Fem.* au jus de rôti.

**grease** *noun* graisse *Fem.*

m **greasy** *adjective* gras (*Fem.* grasse);
n **to have greasy skin** avoir la peau grasse; **I hate greasy food** je déteste
o la nourriture grasse.

p **great** *adjective* 1 grand; **a great poet** un grand poète; 2 (*terrific*)
q génial (*Masc. plural* géniaux); **it was a great party!** ça a été une soirée
r géniale!; **great!** génial!; 3 **a great deal of** beaucoup de; **a great many**
s beaucoup de; **there are a great many things still to be done** il
t reste beaucoup de choses à faire.

u **Great Britain** *noun* Grande-Bretagne *Fem.*; **in Great Britain** en
v Grande-Bretagne; **to Great Britain** en Grande-Bretagne; **to be from**
w **Great Britain** être britannique.

x **Greece** *noun* Grèce *Fem.*; **to Greece** en Grèce; **in Greece** en
y Grèce.

z

**greedy** *adjective* (*with food*) gourmand.

**Greek** *noun* 1 (*person*) Grec *Masc.*, Grecque *Fem.*; 2 (*language*) grec *Masc.*
**Greek** *adjective* grec (*Fem.* grecque).

**green** *noun* 1 (*colour*) vert *Masc.*; **a pale green** un vert pâle; 2 **greens** (*vegetables*) les légumes verts; 3 **the Greens** (*ecologists*) les Verts *Masc. plural.*
**green** *adjective* 1 vert; **a green door** une porte verte; 2 écologiste; **the Green Party** le parti écologiste.

**greengrocer** *noun* marchand *Masc.* de fruits et légumes.

**greenhouse** *noun* serre *Fem.*

**greenhouse effect** *noun* effet *Masc.* de serre.

**greetings** *plural noun* **Season's Greetings** meilleurs vœux *Masc. plural.*

**greetings card** *noun* carte *Fem.* de vœux.

**grey** *adjective* gris; **a grey skirt** une jupe grise; **to have grey hair** avoir les cheveux gris.

**greyhound** *noun* lévrier *Masc.*

**grid** *noun* 1 (*grating*) grille *Fem.*; 2 (*network*) réseau *Masc.* (*plural* réseaux).

**grief** *noun* chagrin *Masc.*

**grill** *noun* (*of a cooker*) gril *Masc.*
**grill** *verb* **to grill something** faire [10] griller quelque chose; **I grilled the sausages** j'ai fait griller les saucisses.

**grim** *adjective* sinistre.

**grin** noun sourire Masc.
**grin** verb sourire [68].

**grip** noun prise Fem.
**grip** verb serrer [1].

**grit** noun (for roads) gravillons Masc. plural.

**groan** noun 1 (of pain) gémissement Masc.; 2 (of disgust, boredom) grognement Masc.
**groan** verb 1 (in pain) gémir [2]; 2 (in disgust, boredom) grogner [1].

**grocer's** noun épicerie Fem.; **I met Jake in the grocer's** j'ai rencontré Jake à l'épicerie.

**grocer** noun épicier Masc.; **my dad's a grocer** mon père est épicier.

**groceries** plural noun provisions Fem. plural; **to buy some groceries** acheter des provisions.

**groom** noun (bridegroom) marié Masc.; **the bride and groom** les jeunes mariés.

**gross** adjective **1 a gross injustice** une injustice flagrante; **2 a gross error** une erreur grossière; **3** (disgusting) dégoûtant; **the food was gross!** la nourriture était dégoûtante!

**ground** noun **1** terre Fem.; **to sit on the ground** s'asseoir par terre; **to throw something on the ground** jeter quelque chose par terre; **2** (for sport) terrain Masc.; **a football ground** un terrain de foot.
**ground** adjective moulu; **ground coffee** du café moulu.

**ground floor** noun rez-de-chaussée Masc.; **they live on the ground floor** ils habitent au rez-de-chaussée.

**group** noun groupe Masc.

**grow** verb **1** (plant, hair) pousser [1]; **you hair's grown!** tes cheveux ont poussé!; **2** (person) grandir [2]; **my little sister's grown a lot this year** ma petite sœur a beaucoup grandi cette année; **3** (number) augmenter [1]; **the number of students has grown** le nombre d'étudiants a augmenté; **4** faire [10] pousser (fruit, vegetables); **our neighbours grow strawberries** nos voisins font pousser des fraises; **5 to grow a beard** se laisser [1] pousser la barbe; **6 to grow old** vieillir [2].

● **to grow up** grandir [2]; **the children are growing up** les enfants grandissent; **she grew up in Scotland** elle a grandi en Écosse.

**growl** verb grogner [1].

**grown-up** noun adulte Masc. & Fem.

**growth** noun croissance Fem.

**grudge** noun **to bear a grudge against somebody** en vouloir à quelqu'un; **she bears me a grudge** elle m'en veut.

**gruesome** adjective horrible.

**grumble** verb se plaindre [31]; **she's always grumbling** elle est toujours en train de se plaindre; **to grumble about something** se plaindre de quelque chose.

**guarantee** noun garantie Fem.; **a year's guarantee** une garantie d'un an.
**guarantee** verb garantir [2].

a
b
c
d
e
f
g
h
i
j
k
l
m
n
o
p
q
r
s
t
u
v
w
x
y
z

a
b
c
d
e
f
**g**
**h**
i
j
k
l
m
n
o
p
q
r
s
t
u
v
w
x
y
z

**guard** *noun* **1 a prison guard** un gardien de prison; **2** (*on a train*) chef *Masc.* de train; **3 a security guard** un vigile.
**guard** *verb* surveiller [1].

**guard dog** *noun* chien *Masc.* de garde.

**guardian** *noun* (*of child*) tuteur *Masc.*, tutrice *Fem.*

**guess** *noun* **have a guess!** devine!; **it's a good guess** tu as deviné.
**guess** *verb* deviner [1]; **guess who I saw last night!** devine qui j'ai vu hier soir!; **you'll never guess!** tu ne devineras jamais!

**guest** *noun* **1** invité *Masc.*, invitée *Fem.*; **we've got guests coming tonight** nous avons des invités ce soir; **2** (*in a hotel*) client *Masc.*, cliente *Fem.*; **3 a paying guest** un hôte payant.

**guesthouse** *noun* pension *Fem.* de famille.

**guide** *noun* **1** (*person or book*) guide *Masc.*; **2** (*girl guide*) guide *Fem.*, (*belonging to a church company of girl guides*) éclaireuse *Fem.*

**guidebook** *noun* guide *Masc.*

**guide dog** *noun* chien *Masc.* d'aveugle.

**guideline** *noun* indication *Fem.*

**guilty** *adjective* coupable; **to feel guilty** se sentir coupable.

**guinea pig** *noun* (*pet*) cochon *Masc.* d'Inde; (*in an experiment*) cobaye *Masc.*; **they want me to be a guinea pig** ils veulent que je serve de cobaye.

**guitar** *noun* guitare *Fem.*; **to play the guitar** jouer de la guitare; **on the guitar** à la guitare.

**guitarist** *noun* guitariste *Masc. & Fem.*

**gum** *noun* **1** (*in mouth*) gencive *Fem.*; **2** (*chewing gum*) chewing-gum *Masc.*

**gun** *noun* **1** revolver *Masc.*; **2** (*rifle*) fusil *Masc.*

**gust** *noun* **a gust of wind** une rafale de vent.

**gutter** *noun* (*in the street*) caniveau (*plural* caniveaux).

**guy** *noun* type *Masc.* (*informal*); **he's a nice guy** c'est un type sympa; **a guy from Newcastle** un type qui vient de Newcastle.

**guy rope** *noun* corde *Fem.* d'attache.

**gym** *noun* gym *Fem.*; **to go to the gym** aller à la gym.

**gymnasium** *noun* gymnase *Masc.*

**gymnast** *noun* gymnaste *Masc. & Fem.*

**gymnastics** *noun* gymnastique *Fem.*

**gym shoe** *noun* tennis *Masc.*

# Hh

**habit** *noun* habitude *Fem.*; **to be in the habit of doing** avoir l'habitude de faire; **it's a bad habit** c'est une mauvaise habitude.

**haddock** *noun* églefin *Masc.*; **smoked haddock** haddock *Masc.*

**hail** *noun* grêle *Fem.*

**hailstone** *noun* grêlon *Masc.*

**hailstorm** *noun* averse *Fem.* de grêle.

**hair** *noun* **1** cheveux *Masc. plural*; **to have short hair** avoir les cheveux courts; **to brush your hair** se brosser les cheveux; **to wash your hair** se laver les cheveux; **to have your hair cut** se faire couper les cheveux; **she's had her hair cut** elle s'est fait couper les cheveux; **2 a hair** (*from the head*) un cheveu; (*from the body*) un poil.

**hairbrush** *noun* brosse *Fem.* à cheveux.

**haircut** *noun* **1** coupe *Fem.*; **I like your new haircut** j'aime bien ta nouvelle coupe; **2 to have a haircut** se faire couper les cheveux.

**hairdresser** *noun* coiffeur *Masc.*, coiffeuse *Fem.*; **she's a hairdresser** elle est coiffeuse; **at the hairdresser's** chez le coiffeur.

**hair drier** *noun* sèche-cheveux *Masc.*

**hair gel** *noun* gel *Masc.* pour les cheveux.

**hairgrip** *noun* pince *Fem.* à cheveux.

**hair remover** *noun* crème *Fem.* dépilatoire.

**hairslide** *noun* barrette *Fem.*

**hairspray** *noun* laque *Fem.*

**hairstyle** *noun* coiffure *Fem.*

**hairy** *adjective* poilu.

**Haiti** *noun* Haïti *Masc.*

**Haitian** *noun* Haïtien *Masc.*, Haïtienne *Fem.*
**Haitian** *adjective* haïtien (*Fem.* haïtienne).

**half** *noun* **1** moitié *Fem.*; **half of** la moitié de; **I gave him half of the money** je lui ai donné la moitié de l'argent; **half an apple** la moitié d'une pomme; **you've only eaten half of it** tu n'en as mangé que la moitié; **half the people** la moitié des gens; **2 to cut something in half** couper quelque chose en deux; **3** (*as a fraction*) demi; **three and a half** trois et demi; **she's five and a half** elle a cinq ans et demi; **4** (*in time*) demi, demie; **half an hour** une demi-heure; **an hour and a half** une heure et demie; **it's half past three** il est trois heures et demie; **5** (*in weights and measures*) demi, demie; **half a litre** un demi-litre; **half a cup** une demi-tasse.

**half hour** *noun* demi-heure *Fem.*; **every half hour** toutes les demi-heures.

**half price** *adjective, adverb* à moitié prix; **half-price CDs** des CD à moitié prix; **I bought it half price** je l'ai acheté à moitié prix.

**half-time** *noun* mi-temps *Fem.*; **at half-time** à la mi-temps.

**halfway** *adverb* **1** à mi-chemin; **halfway between Paris and Dijon** à mi-chemin entre Paris et Dijon; **2 to be halfway through doing** avoir à moitié fini de faire; **I'm halfway through my homework** j'ai à moitié fini mes devoirs.

**hall** *noun* **1** (*in a house*) entrée *Fem.*; **2** (*public*) salle *Fem.*; **the village hall** la salle des fêtes; **a concert hall** une salle de concert.

a
b
c
d
e
f
g
h
i
j
k
l
m
n
o
p
q
r
s
t
u
v
w
x
y
z

a
b
c
d
e
f
g
**h**
i
j
k
l
m
n
o
p
q
r
s
t
u
v
w
x
y
z

**Hallowe'en** *noun* la veille de la Toussaint (*the French do not have any particular customs for this date*).

**ham** *noun* jambon *Masc.*; **a slice of ham** une tranche de jambon; **a ham sandwich** un sandwich au jambon.

**hamburger** *noun* hamburger *Masc.*

**hammer** *noun* marteau *Masc.* (*plural* marteaux).

**hammock** *noun* hamac *Masc.*

**hamster** *noun* hamster *Masc.*

**hand** *noun* 1 main *Fem.*; **to have something in your hand** avoir quelque chose à la main; **to hold somebody's hand** tenir quelqu'un par la main; 2 **to give somebody a hand** donner un coup de main à quelqu'un; **can you give me a hand to move the table?** est-ce que tu peux me donner un coup de main pour déplacer la table?; **do you need a hand?** est-ce que tu as besoin d'un coup de main?; 3 **on the other hand** ... par contre ...; 4 (*of a watch or clock*) aiguille *Fem.*; **the hour hand** l'aiguille des heures. **hand** *verb* **to hand something to somebody** passer [1] quelque chose à quelqu'un; **I handed him the keys** je lui ai passé les clés.

● **to hand something in** rendre [3] quelque chose; **I've handed in my homework** j'ai rendu mon devoir.

● **to hand something out** distribuer [1] quelque chose; **Claire handed out the exercise books** Claire a distribué les cahiers.

**handbag** *noun* sac *Masc.* à main (*plural* sacs à main).

**handcuffs** *plural noun* menottes *Fem. plural*.

**handful** *noun* **a handful of** une poignée de.

**handicapped** *adjective* handicapé.

**handkerchief** *noun* mouchoir *Masc.*

**handle** *noun* 1 (*of a door or drawer*) poignée *Fem.*; 2 (*on a cup or basket*) anse *Fem.*; 3 (*of a knife, tool, or saucepan*) manche *Masc.*; 4 (*of a frying pan*) queue *Fem.*
**handle** *verb* 1 s'occuper [1] de; **Gina handles the accounts** Gina s'occupe de la comptabilité; 2 **she's good at handling people** elle a un bon contact avec les gens; 3 **I can't handle any more problems!** j'ai assez de problèmes comme ça!

**handlebars** *plural noun* guidon *Masc.*

**hand luggage** *noun* bagages *Masc. plural* à main.

**handmade** *adjective* fait à la main.

**handsome** *adjective* beau (*Fem.* belle); **he's a handsome guy** c'est un beau type.

**handwriting** *noun* écriture *Fem.*

**handy** *adjective* 1 pratique; **this little knife's very handy** ce petit couteau est très pratique; 2 sous la main; **I always keep a notebook handy** je garde toujours un calepin sous la main.

**hang** *verb* 1 être [6] accroché; **there was a mirror hanging on the wall** il y avait un miroir accroché au mur; 2 **to hang something** accrocher [1] quelque chose; **we**

446

**hung the mirror on the wall** nous avons accroché le miroir au mur.

- **to hang around** traîner [1]; **we were hanging around outside the cinema** on traînait devant le cinéma.
- **to hang down** pendre [3].
- **to hang on** attendre [3]; **hang on a second!** attends une seconde!.
- **to hang up** (*on the phone*) raccrocher [1]; **she hung up on me** elle m'a raccroché au nez (*literally: she hung up on my nose*).
- **to hang something up** accrocher [1] quelque chose; **you can hang your coat up in the hall** tu peux accrocher ton manteau dans l'entrée.

**hang-gliding** *noun* deltaplane *Masc.*; **to go hang-gliding** faire du deltaplane.

**hangover** *noun* gueule *Fem.* de bois; **to have a hangover** avoir la gueule de bois.

**happen** *verb* **1** se passer [1]; **what's happening?** qu'est-ce qui se passe?; **it happened in June** ça s'est passé en juin; **2 what's happened to the can-opener?** où est l'ouvre-boîte?; **3 if you happen to see Jill** si par hasard tu vois Jill.

**happily** *adverb* **1** joyeusement; **she smiled happily** elle a souri joyeusement; **2** (*willingly*) volontiers; **I'll happily do it for you** je le ferai pour toi volontiers.

**happiness** *noun* bonheur *Masc.*

**happy** *adjective* heureux (*Fem.* heureuse); **a happy child** un enfant heureux; **Happy Birthday!** Bon anniversaire!

**harbour** *noun* port *Masc.*

**hard** *adjective* **1** dur; **to go hard** durcir; **2** (*difficult*) difficile; **a hard question** une question difficile; **it's hard to know ...** il est difficile de savoir ....
**hard** *adverb* **1 to work hard** travailler dur; **2 to try hard** faire beaucoup d'efforts.

**hard-boiled egg** *noun* œuf *Masc.* dur.

**hard disk** *noun* (*in a computer*) disque *Masc.* dur.

**hardly** *adverb* **1** à peine; **I can hardly hear him** je l'entends à peine; **2 hardly any** presque pas de; **there's hardly any milk** il n'y a presque pas de lait; **3 hardly ever** presque jamais; **I hardly ever see them** je ne les vois presque jamais; **4 there was hardly anybody** il n'y avait presque personne.

**hard up** *adjective* fauché (*informal*).

**hare** *noun* lièvre *Masc.*

**harm** *noun* **it won't do you any harm** ça ne te fera pas de mal.
**harm** *verb* **to harm somebody** faire [10] du mal à quelqu'un; **they did not harm him** ils ne lui ont pas fait de mal; **a cup of coffee won't harm you** une tasse de café ne te fera pas de mal.

**harmful** *adjective* nuisible.

**harmless** *adjective* inoffensif (*Fem.* inoffensive).

**harvest** *noun* récolte *Fem.*; **to get the harvest in** faire [10] la récolte.

**hat** *noun* chapeau *Masc.* (*plural* chapeaux).

447

a
b
c
d
e
f
g
**h**
i
j
k
l
m
n
o
p
q
r
s
t
u
v
w
x
y
z

**hate** *verb* détester [1]; **I hate geography** je déteste la géographie.

**hatred** *noun* haine *Fem.*

**haunted** *adjective* hanté.

**have** *verb* **1** avoir [5]; **Anna has three brothers** Anna a trois frères; **how many sisters do you have?** tu as combien de sœurs?; **2 to have got** avoir [5]; **we've got a dog** nous avons un chien; **what have you got in your hand?** qu'est-ce que tu as à la main?; **3** (*to form past tenses, some verbs in French take 'avoir' and some 'être'*) **I've finished** j'ai fini; **have you seen the film?** est-ce que tu as vu le film?; **Rosie hasn't arrived yet** Rosie n'est pas encore arrivée; **he had left** il était parti; **4 to have to do** devoir [8] faire; **I have to phone my mum** je dois appeler ma mère; **5** prendre [64] (*food, drink, a shower*); **we had a coffee** nous avons pris un café; **what will you have?** qu'est-ce que tu prends?; **I'll have an omelette** je prends une omelette; **I'm going to have a shower** je vais prendre une douche; **6 to have lunch** déjeuner [1]; **to have dinner** (*in the evening*) dîner [1]; **7 to have something done** faire [10] faire quelque chose; **I'm going to have my hair cut** je vais me faire couper les cheveux.

**hawk** *noun* faucon *Masc.*

**hay** *noun* foin *Masc.*

**hay fever** *noun* rhume *Masc.* des foins.

**hazelnut** *noun* noisette *Fem.*

**he** *pronoun* il; **he lives in Manchester** il habite à Manchester; **he's my brother** c'est mon frère.

**head** *noun* **1** tête *Fem.*; **he had a cap on his head** il avait une casquette sur la tête; **at the head of the queue** à la tête de la queue; **2** (*of school*) directeur *Masc.*, directrice *Fem.*; **3** (*when tossing a coin*) **"heads or tails?' – 'heads'** 'pile ou face?' – 'face' (*note that it is in fact 'tails or heads' in French*).

● **to head for something** se diriger [52] vers quelque chose; **Liz headed for the door** Liz s'est dirigée vers la porte.

**headache** *noun* **I've got a headache** j'ai mal à la tête.

**headlight** *noun* phare *Masc.*

**headline** *noun* gros titre *Masc.*; **to hit the headlines** faire la une.

**headmaster** *noun* directeur *Masc.*

**headmistress** *noun* directrice *Fem.*

**headphones** *plural noun* casque *Masc. singular.*

**headquarters** *noun* **1** (*of organization*) siège *Masc.* social; **2** (*military*) quartier *Masc.* général.

**headteacher** *noun* directeur *Masc.*, directrice *Fem.*

**health** *noun* santé *Fem.*

**health centre** *noun* centre *Masc.* médico-social.

**healthy** *adjective* **1** (*person*) **to be healthy** être en bonne santé; **2 a healthy diet** une alimentation saine.

**heap** *noun* tas *Masc.*; **I've got heaps of things to do** j'ai un tas de choses à faire.

**hear** *verb* **1** entendre [3]; **I can't hear you** je ne t'entends pas; **I can't hear anything** je n'entends rien; **2** apprendre [64] (*news*); **I hear you've bought a dog** j'apprends que tu as acheté un chien.

● **to hear about something** entendre [3] parler de quelque chose; **have you heard about the concert?** as-tu entendu parler du concert?

● **to hear from somebody** avoir [5] des nouvelles de quelqu'un; **have you heard from Amanda?** as-tu des nouvelles d'Amanda?

**hearing aid** *noun* Sonotone™ *Masc.*

**heart** *noun* **1** cœur *Masc.*; **to learn something by heart** apprendre quelque chose par cœur; **2** (*in cards*) cœur; **the jack of hearts** le valet de cœur.

**heart attack** *noun* crise *Fem.* cardiaque.

**heat** *noun* chaleur *Fem.*
**heat** *verb* **1** chauffer [1]; **the soup's heating** la soupe est en train de chauffer; **2 to heat something** faire [10] chauffer quelque chose; **I'll go and heat the soup** je vais faire chauffer la soupe.

● **to heat something up** faire [10] réchauffer quelque chose; **I'm heating up the sauce** je fais réchauffer la sauce.

**heater** *noun* radiateur *Masc.*

**heather** *noun* bruyère *Fem.*

**heating** *noun* chauffage *Masc.*

**heatwave** *noun* vague *Fem.* de chaleur.

**heaven** *noun* paradis *Masc.*

**heavy** *adjective* **1** lourd; **my rucksack's really heavy** mon sac à dos est très lourd; **2** (*busy*) chargé; **I've got a heavy day tomorrow** j'ai une journée chargée demain; **3 heavy rain** des pluies fortes.

**heavy metal** *noun* (*music*) hard rock *Masc.*

**hectic** *adjective* **a hectic day** une journée mouvementée.

**hedge** *noun* haie *Fem.*

**hedgehog** *noun* hérisson *Masc.*

**heel** *noun* talon *Masc.*

**height** *noun* **1** (*of a person*) taille *Fem.*; **2** (*of a building*) hauteur *Fem.*; **3** (*of a mountain*) altitude *Fem.*

**helicopter** *noun* hélicoptère *Masc.*

**hell** *noun* enfer *Masc.*; **it's hell here!** c'est infernal ici!

**hello** *exclamation* **1** (*polite*) bonjour!; **2** (*informal*) salut!; **3** (*on the telephone*) allô!

**helmet** *noun* casque *Masc.*

**help** *noun* aide *Fem.*; **do you need any help?** est-ce que tu as besoin d'aide?

**help** *verb* **1** aider [1]; **to help somebody to do** aider quelqu'un à faire; **can you help me move the table?** peux-tu m'aider à déplacer la table?; **2 to help yourself to something** se servir [71] de quelque chose; **help yourselves to vegetables** servez-vous de légumes; **help yourself!** sers-toi!; **3 help!** au secours!

a
b
c
d
e
f
g
**h**
i
j
k
l
m
n
o
p
q
r
s
t
u
v
w
x
y
z

**helper** noun aide Masc. & Fem.; **helpers are needed to run charity stalls** on a besoin de bénévoles pour tenir les stands de la fête de charité.

**helpful** adjective (person) serviable.

**helping** noun portion Fem.; **would you like a second helping of chips?** est-ce que tu veux reprendre des frites?

**hem** noun ourlet Masc.

**hen** noun poule Fem.

**her** pronoun **1** la, l' (before a vowel or silent 'h'); **I know her** je la connais; **I can hear her** je l'entends; **listen to her!** écoute-la!; **I saw her last week** je l'ai vue la semaine dernière; **2** (to her) lui; **I gave her my address** je lui ai donné mon adresse; **3** (after a preposition) elle; **with her** avec elle; **without her** sans elle; (in comparisons) **he's older than her** il est plus âgé qu'elle.

**her** adjective **1** (before a masculine noun) son; **her brother** son frère; **her book** son livre; **2** (before a feminine noun) sa; **her sister** sa sœur; **her house** sa maison (but 'sa' becomes 'son' before a feminine noun beginning with a vowel or silent 'h') **her address** son adresse; **3** (before a plural noun) ses; **her children** ses enfants; **4** (with parts of the body) le, la, les; **she had a glass in her hand** elle avait un verre à la main; **she's washing her hands** elle se lave les mains.

**herb** noun herbe Fem.

**herd** noun troupeau Masc (plural troupeaux).

**here** adverb **1** ici; **not far from here** pas loin d'ici; **2** là; **Tom isn't here at the moment** Tom n'est pas là en ce moment; **3 here is** voilà; **here's my address** voilà mon adresse; **4 here are** voilà; **here are the photos** voilà les photos; **and here they are!** et les voilà!

**hero** noun héros Masc.

**heroin** noun héroïne Fem.

**heroine** noun héroïne Fem.

**herring** noun hareng Masc.

**hers** pronoun **1** (for a masculine noun) le sien; **I took my hat and she took hers** j'ai pris mon chapeau et elle a pris le sien; **2** (for a feminine noun) la sienne; **I gave her my address and she gave me hers** je lui ai donné mon adresse et elle m'a donné la sienne; **3** (for a masculine plural noun) les siens; **I've invited my parents and Karen's invited hers** j'ai invité mes parents et Karen a invité les siens; **4** (for a feminine plural noun) les siennes; **I showed her my photos and she showed me hers** je lui ai montré mes photos et elle m'a montré les siennes; **5** à elle; **the green one's hers** le vert est à elle; **it's hers** c'est à elle.

**herself** pronoun **1 she's hurt herself** elle s'est blessée; **2 she said it herself** elle l'a dit elle-même; **3 she did it by herself** elle l'a fait toute seule.

**hesitate** verb hésiter [1]; **to hesitate to do** hésiter à faire.

**heterosexual** adjective, noun hétérosexuel Masc., hétérosexuelle Fem.

**hi** *exclamation* salut!

**hiccups** *plural noun* **to have the hiccups** avoir le hoquet.

**hidden** *adjective* caché.

**hide** *verb* **1** (*person*) se cacher [1]; **she hid behind the door** elle s'est cachée derrière la porte; **2 to hide something** cacher [1] quelque chose; **who's hidden the chocolate?** qui a caché le chocolat?

**hide-and-seek** *noun* **to play hide-and-seek** jouer à cache-cache.

**hi-fi** *noun* chaîne *Fem.* hi-fi.

**high** *adjective* **1** haut; **on a high shelf** sur une étagère haute; **the wall is very high** le mur est très haut; **how high is the wall?** quelle est la hauteur du mur?; **the wall is two metres high** le mur fait deux mètres de hauteur; **2** (*number, price, temperature*) élevé; **food prices are very high** les prix de la nourriture sont très élevés; **3 at high speed** à grande vitesse; **4 high winds** des vents violents; **5 a high voice** une voix aiguë.

**Highers**, **Advanced Highers** *noun plural* baccalauréat *Masc.*, bac *Masc.* (*informal*) (*Students take 'le bac' at the end of their secondary education. You can explain Highers briefly as follows: Les Highers sont un examen qui sanctionne l'avant-dernière année d'école secondaire en Écosse. On passe les Highers dans cinq matières au maximum. En dernière année, certains lycéens passent également les Advance Highers dans un maximum de trois matières, qui ont déjà fait l'objet de l'un de leurs*

*Highers. Ces deux examens sont notés de A à C et permettent de s'inscrire à l'université).*

**high-heeled** *adjective* à hauts talons; **high-heeled shoes** des chaussures à hauts talons.

**high jump** *noun* saut *Masc.* en hauteur.

**highly** *adverb* extrêmement.

**hijack** *verb* **to hijack a plane** détourner [1] un avion.

**hijacker** *noun* pirate *Masc.* de l'air.

**hijacking** *noun* détournement *Masc.*

**hike** *noun* randonnée *Fem.*; **to go on a hike** faire une randonnée.

**hiker** *noun* randonneur *Masc.*, randonneuse *Fem.*

**hiking** *noun* randonnée *Fem.*

**hilarious** *adjective* hilarant.

**hill** *noun* **1** (*in landscape*) colline *Fem.*; **you can see the hills** on voit les collines; **2** (*hillside*) coteau *Masc.* (*plural* coteaux); **the houses on the hill** les maisons sur le coteau; **3** (*sloping street or road*) **to go up the hill** monter; **you go up the hill to the church and then turn right** vous montez jusqu'à l'église et vous tournez à droite.

**him** *pronoun* **1** le, l' (*before a vowel or silent 'h'*); **I know him** je le connais; **I can hear him** je l'entends; **listen to him!** écoute-le!; **I saw him last week** je l'ai vu la semaine dernière; **2** (*to him*) lui; **I gave him my address** je lui ai donné mon adresse; **3** (*after a preposition*) lui; **with him** avec lui; **without him** sans

a
b
c
d
e
f
g
**h**
i
j
k
l
m
n
o
p
q
r
s
t
u
v
w
x
y
z

## himself

lui; (*in comparisons*) **she's older than him** elle est plus âgée que lui.

**himself** *pronoun* **1** he's hurt **himself** il s'est blessé; **2** he said it **himself** il l'a dit lui-même; **3** he did **it by himself** il l'a fait tout seul.

**Hindu** *adjective* hindou.

**hip** *noun* hanche *Fem.*

**hippie** *noun* hippie *Masc. & Fem.*

**hippopotamus** *noun* hippopotame *Masc.*

**hire** *noun* location *Fem.*; **car hire** location de voitures; **for hire** à louer. **hire** *verb* louer [1]; **we're going to hire a car** nous allons louer une voiture.

**his** *adjective* **1** (*before a masculine noun*) son; **his brother** son frère; **his book** son livre; **2** (*before a feminine noun*) sa; **his sister** sa sœur; **his house** sa maison (*but 'sa' becomes 'son' before a feminine noun beginning with a vowel or silent 'h'*) **his address** son adresse; **3** (*before a plural noun*) ses; **his children** ses enfants; **4** (*with parts of the body*) le, la, les; **he had a glass in his hand** il avait un verre à la main; **he's washing his hands** il se lave les mains.

**his** *pronoun* **1** (*for a masculine noun*) le sien; **I took my hat and he took his** j'ai pris mon chapeau et il a pris le sien; **2** (*for a feminine noun*) la sienne; **I gave him my address and he gave me his** je lui ai donné mon adresse et il m'a donné la sienne; **3** (*for a masculine plural noun*) les siens; **I've invited my parents and Steve's invited his** j'ai invité mes parents et Steve a invité

les siens; **4** (*for a feminine plural noun*) les siennes; **I showed him my photos and he showed me his** je lui ai montré mes photos et il m'a montré les siennes; **5** à lui; **the green car's his** la voiture verte est à lui; **it's his** c'est à lui.

**historic** *adjective* historique.

**history** *noun* histoire *Fem.*

**hit** *noun* **1** (*song*) tube *Masc.* (*informal*); **their latest hit** leur dernier tube; **2** (*success*) succès *Masc.*; **the film is a huge hit** le film a un succès fou. **hit** *verb* **1** frapper [1]; **to hit the ball** frapper la balle; **2** to hit your head **on something** se cogner [1] la tête contre quelque chose; **3** heurter [1]; **the car hit a tree** la voiture a heurté un arbre; **4** to be hit by a car (*person*) être [6] renversé par une voiture.

**hitch** *noun* problème *Masc.*; **there's been a slight hitch** il y a eu un petit problème. **hitch** *verb* **to hitch a lift** faire [10] du stop (*informal*).

**hitchhike** *verb* faire [10] du stop (*informal*); **we hitchhiked to Dijon** nous sommes allés à Dijon en stop.

**hitchhiker** *noun* autostoppeur *Masc.*, autostoppeuse *Fem.*

**hitchhiking** *noun* autostop *Masc.*

**HIV-negative** *adjective* séronégatif (*Fem.* séronégative).

**HIV-positive** *adjective* séropositif (*Fem.* séropositive).

**hobby** *noun* passe-temps *Masc.*

**hockey** *noun* hockey *Masc.*; **to play hockey** jouer au hockey.

**hockey stick** *noun* crosse *Fem.* de hockey.

**hold** *verb* **1** tenir [77]; **to hold something in your hand** tenir quelque chose à la main; **can you hold the torch?** est-ce que tu peux tenir la lampe?; **2** (*contain*) contenir [77]; **a jug which holds a litre** un pichet qui contient un litre; **3 to hold a meeting** organiser [1] une réunion; **4 can you hold the line, please** ne quittez pas, s'il vous plaît; **5 hold on!** (*wait*) attends!; (*on telephone*) ne quittez pas!

● **to hold somebody up** (*delay*) retenir [77] quelqu'un; **I was held up at the dentist's** j'ai été retenu chez le dentiste.

● **to hold something up** (*raise*) lever [50] quelque chose; **he held up his glass** il a levé son verre.

**hold-up** *noun* **1** retard *Masc.*; **2** (*traffic jam*) bouchon *Masc.*; **3** (*robbery*) hold-up *Masc.*

**hole** *noun* trou *Masc.*

**holiday** *noun* **1** vacances *Fem. plural*; **where are you going for your holiday?** où est-ce que vous partez en vacances?; **have a good holiday!** bonnes vacances!; **to be away on holiday** être en vacances; **to go on holiday** partir en vacances; **the school holidays** les vacances scolaires; **2** (*from work*) congé *Masc.*; **I'm taking two days' holiday next week** je prends deux jours de congé la semaine prochaine; **3 a public holiday** un jour férié; **Monday's a holiday** lundi est férié.

**holiday home** *noun* résidence *Fem.* secondaire.

**Holland** *noun* Hollande *Fem.*; **to Holland** en Hollande; **in Holland** en Hollande.

**hollow** *adjective* creux (*Fem.* creuse).

**holly** *noun* houx *Masc.*

**holy** *adjective* saint.

**home** *noun* maison *Fem.*; **I was at home** j'étais à la maison; **to stay at home** rester à la maison; **make yourself at home** fais comme chez toi.

**home** *adverb* **1** chez soi; **Susie's gone home** Susie est rentrée chez elle; **I'll call in and see you on my way home** je passerai te voir en rentrant chez moi; **2 to get home** rentrer; **we got home at midnight** nous sommes rentrés à minuit.

**homeless** *adjective* sans abri; **the homeless** les sans-abri *Masc. plural.*

**homemade** *adjective* fait maison; **homemade cakes** des gâteaux faits maison.

**home match** *noun* match *Masc.* à domicile.

**homeopathic** *adjective* homéopathique.

**homesick** *adjective* **to be homesick** avoir le mal du pays.

**homework** *noun* devoirs *Masc. plural*; **I did my homework** j'ai fait mes devoirs; **my French homework** mes devoirs de français; (*written*) mon devoir de français.

**homosexual** *adjective*, *noun* homosexuel (*Fem.* homosexuelle).

**honest** *adjective* honnête.

**honestly** *adverb* franchement.

a
b
c
d
e
f
g
h
i
j
k
l
m
n
o
p
q
r
s
t
u
v
w
x
y
z

**honesty** *noun* honnêteté *Fem.*

**honey** *noun* miel *Masc.*

**honeymoon** *noun* voyage *Masc.* de noces; **they're going to Paris on their honeymoon** ils partent à Paris en voyage de noces.

**honeysuckle** *noun* chèvrefeuille *Masc.*

**honour** *noun* honneur *Masc.*

**hood** *noun* capuchon *Masc.*

**hook** *noun* **1** crochet *Masc.*; **2 to take the phone of the hook** décrocher le téléphone.

**hooligan** *noun* voyou *Masc.*

**hooray** *exclamation* hourra!

**Hoover™** *noun* aspirateur *Masc.*

**hoover** *verb* passer [1] l'aspirateur; **I hoovered my bedroom** j'ai passé l'aspirateur dans ma chambre.

**hope** *noun* espoir *Masc.*; **to give up hope** perdre espoir.

**hope** *verb* espérer [24]; **we hope you'll be able to come** nous espérons que vous allez pouvoir venir; **hoping to see you on Friday** en espérant te voir vendredi; **here's hoping!** espérons que ça marchera!; **I hope so** je l'espère; **I hope not** j'espère que non.

**hopefully** *adverb* avec un peu de chance; **hopefully, the film won't have started** avec un peu de chance, le film n'aura pas commencé.

**hopeless** *adjective* nul (*Fem.* nulle) (*informal*); **I'm completely hopeless at geography** je suis complètement nul en géographie.

**horizon** *noun* horizon *Masc.*

**horizontal** *adjective* horizontal (*Masc. plural* horizontaux).

**horn** *noun* **1** (*of an animal*) corne *Fem.*; **2** (*of a car*) klaxon *Masc.*; **to sound your horn** klaxonner; **3** (*musical instrument*) cor; **to play the horn** jouer du cor.

**horoscope** *noun* horoscope *Masc.*

**horrible** *adjective* **1** affreux (*Fem.* affreuse); **the weather was horrible** il a fait un temps affreux; **2** (*person*) désagréable; **she's really horrible!** elle est vraiment désagréable; **he was really horrible to me** il a été vraiment désagréable avec moi.

**horrific** *adjective* terrible; **a horrific accident** un terrible accident.

**horror** *noun* horreur *Fem.*

**horror film** *noun* film *Masc.* d'épouvante.

**horse** *noun* cheval *Masc.* (*plural* chevaux).

**horse chestnut** *noun* **1** (*tree*) marronnier *Masc.*; **2** (*nut*) marron *Masc.*

**horse racing** *noun* courses *Fem. plural* hippiques.

**horseshoe** *noun* fer *Masc.* à cheval.

**hose** *noun* tuyau *Masc.* (*plural* tuyaux).

**hosepipe** *noun* tuyau *Masc.* d'arrosage.

**hospital** *noun* hôpital *Masc.* (*plural* hôpitaux); **to be in hospital** être à l'hôpital; **to be taken into hospital** être hospitalisé.

**hospitality** *noun* hospitalité *Fem.*

**host** *noun* hôte *Masc.*, hôtesse *Fem.*; **my host family is very nice** ma famille d'accueil est très sympathique.

**hostage** *noun* otage *Masc.*

**hostel** *noun* **youth hostel** auberge *Fem.* de jeunesse.

**hostess** *noun* hôtesse *Fem.*; **an air hostess** une hôtesse de l'air.

**hot** *adjective* **1** chaud; **a hot drink** une boisson chaude; **be careful, the plates are hot!** fais attention, les assiettes sont très chaudes!; **2** (*a person*) **to be hot** avoir chaud; **I'm hot** j'ai chaud; **I'm very hot** j'ai très chaud; **I'm too hot** j'ai trop chaud; **3** (*the weather or temperature in a room*) **it's hot today** il fait chaud aujourd'hui; **it's very hot in the kitchen** il fait très chaud dans la cuisine; **4** (*food: spicy*) épicé; **the curry's too hot for me** le curry est trop épicé pour moi.

**hot dog** *noun* hot-dog *Masc.*

**hotel** *noun* hôtel *Masc.*

**hour** *noun* heure *Fem.*; **two hours later** deux heures plus tard; **we waited for two hours** nous avons attendu pendant deux heures; **two hours ago** il y a deux heures; **to be paid by the hour** être payé à l'heure; **every hour** toutes les heures; **half an hour** une demi-heure; **a quarter of an hour** un quart d'heure; **an hour and a half** une heure et demie.

**hourly** *adjective* toutes les heures; **there is an hourly bus** il y a un bus par heure; **the trains leave hourly** il y a des trains toutes les heures.

**house** *noun* **1** maison *Fem.*; **to buy a house** acheter une maison; **2 at somebody's house** chez quelqu'un; **I'm at Judy's house** je suis chez Judy; **I'm going to Judy's house tonight** je vais chez Judy ce soir; **I phoned from Judy's house** j'ai téléphoné de chez Judy.

**housewife** *noun* femme *Fem.* au foyer.

**housework** *noun* ménage *Masc.*; **to do the housework** faire le ménage.

**how** *adverb* **1** comment; **how did you do it?** comment l'as-tu fait?; **how are you?** comment allez-vous?; **2 how much?** combien?; **how much money do you have?** tu as combien d'argent?; **how much is it?** (*price*) ça coûte combien?; **3 how many?** combien?; **how many brothers do you have?** tu as combien de frères?; **4 how old are you?** quel âge as-tu?; **5 how far is it?** c'est à quelle distance d'ici?; **how far is it to Paris?** Paris est à quelle distance d'ici?; **6 how long will it take?** ça va prendre combien de temps?; **how long have you known her?** tu la connais depuis combien de temps?

**however** *adverb* cependant.

**hug** *noun* **to give somebody a hug** serrer quelqu'un dans ses bras; **she gave me a hug** elle m'a serré dans ses bras.

**huge** *adjective* immense.

**hum** *verb* fredonner [1].

**human** *adjective* humain.

a b c d e f g h i j k l m n o p q r s t u v w x y z

**human being** *noun* être *Masc.* humain.

**humour** *noun* humour *Masc.*; **to have a sense of humour** avoir le sens de l'humour.

**hundred** *number* **1** cent; **two hundred** deux cents; **two hundred and ten** deux cent dix (*note that there is no 's' on 'cent' when it is followed by another number*); **a hundred people** cent personnes; **2 about a hundred** une centaine; **about a hundred people** une centaine de personnes; **hundreds of people** des centaines de personnes.

**Hungary** *noun* Hongrie *Fem.*

**hunger** *noun* faim *Fem.*

**hungry** *adjective* **to be hungry** avoir faim; **I'm hungry** j'ai faim.

**hunt** *verb* **1** chasser [1] (*an animal*); **2** rechercher [1] (*person*).

**hunting** *noun* chasse *Fem.*; **fox-hunting** la chasse au renard.

**hurricane** *noun* ouragan *Masc.*

**hurry** *noun* **to be in a hurry** être pressé; **I'm in a hurry** je suis pressé. **hurry** *verb* se dépêcher [50]; **I must hurry** je dois me dépêcher; **he hurried home** il s'est dépêché de rentrer chez lui; **hurry up!** dépêche-toi!

**hurt** *verb* **1 to hurt somebody** faire [10] mal à quelqu'un; **you're hurting me!** tu me fais mal!; **that hurts!** ça fait mal!; **2 my back hurts** j'ai mal au dos; **3 to hurt yourself** se faire [10] mal; **did you hurt yourself?** est-ce que tu t'es fait mal?
**hurt** *adjective* **1** (*in an accident*) blessé; **three people were hurt**

trois personnes ont été blessées; **2** (*in feelings*) blessé; **she felt hurt** elle était blessée.

**husband** *noun* mari *Masc.*

**hutch** *noun* clapier *Masc.*

**hygienic** *adjective* hygiénique.

**hymn** *noun* cantique *Masc.*

**hypermarket** *noun* hypermarché *Masc.*

**hyphen** *noun* trait *Masc.* d'union.

**hypnotize** *verb* hypnotiser [1].

# Ii

**I** *pronoun* **1** je, j' (*before a vowel or a silent 'h'*); **I am Scottish** je suis écossais; **I have two sisters** j'ai deux sœurs; **2** moi; **Robert and I** Robert et moi; **Tony and I left before you** Tony et moi sommes partis avant vous.

**ice** *noun* **1** glace *Fem.*; **2** (*on the roads*) verglas *Masc.*; **3** (*in a drink*) glaçons *Masc. plural.*

**iceberg** *noun* iceberg *Masc.*

**ice cream** *noun* glace *Fem.*; **a chocolate ice cream** une glace au chocolat.

**ice-cube** *noun* glaçon *Masc.*

**ice hockey** *noun* hockey *Masc.* sur glace.

**ice rink** *noun* patinoire *Fem.*

**ice-skating** *noun* **to go ice-skating** faire [10] du patin à glace.

**icing** *noun* glaçage *Masc.*

**icon** *noun* icône *Fem.*

**icy** *adjective* **1** verglacé (*a road*); **2** (*very cold*) glacial; **an icy wind** un vent glacial.

**idea** *noun* idée *Fem.*; **what a good idea!** quelle bonne idée!; **I've no idea** je n'ai aucune idée.

**ideal** *adjective* idéal (*Masc. plural* idéaux).

**identical** *adjective* identique; **identical twins** des vrais jumeaux.

**identification** *noun* identification *Fem.*

**identify** *verb* identifier [1].

**identity card** *noun* carte *Fem.* d'identité.

**idiom** *noun* idiome *Masc.*

**idiot** *noun* idiot *Masc.*, idiote *Fem.*

**idiotic** *adjective* bête.

**idyllic** *adjective* idyllique.

**i.e.** c-à-d (*short for: c'est-à-dire*).

**if** *conjunction* **1** si, s' (*before 'il' and 'ils'*); **if Sue's there** si Sue est là; **if it rains** s'il pleut; **if I won the lottery** si je gagnais la loterie; **if not** sinon; **2 if only** ... si seulement ...; **if only you'd told me** si seulement tu me l'avais dit; **3** even if même si; **even if it snows** même s'il neige; **4 if I were you** ... à ta place ...; **if I were you, I'd forget it** à ta place je n'y penserais plus.

**ignore** *verb* **1** ignorer [1] (*a person*); **2** ne pas écouter [1] (*what somebody says*); **3 just ignore it** ne fais pas attention.

**ill** *adjective* malade; **to fall ill, to be taken ill** tomber [1] malade; **I feel ill** je ne me sens pas bien.

**illegal** *adjective* illégal (*Masc. plural* illégaux).

**illegible** *adjective* illisible.

**illness** *noun* maladie *Fem.*

**illusion** *noun* illusion *Fem.*

**illustrated** *adjective* illustré.

**illustration** *noun* illustration *Fem.*

**image** *noun* image *Fem.*; ★ **he's the spitting image of his father** c'est son père tout craché.

**imagination** *noun* imagination *Fem.*; **to show imagination** faire preuve d'imagination.

**imaginative** *adjective* plein d'imagination.

**imagine** *verb* imaginer [1]; **imagine that you're very rich** imagine que tu es très riche; **you can't imagine how hard it was!** tu ne peux pas t'imaginer combien c'était difficile!

**imitate** *verb* imiter [1].

**imitation** *noun* imitation *Fem.*

**immediate** *adjective* immédiat.

**immediately** *adverb* immédiatement; **I rang them immediately** je les ai appelés immédiatement; **immediately before** juste avant; **immediately after** juste après.

**immigrant** *noun* immigré *Masc.*, immigrée *Fem.*.

**immigration** *noun* immigration *Fem.*

**impact** *noun* impact *Masc.*

**impatience** *noun* impatience *Fem.*

a
b
c
d
e
f
g
h
i
j
k
l
m
n
o
p
q
r
s
t
u
v
w
x
y
z

**impatient** *adjective* **1** impatient;
**2 to get impatient with somebody**
s'impatienter [1] contre quelqu'un.

**impatiently** *adverb* avec
impatience.

**imperfect** *noun* (*of a verb*)
imparfait *Masc.*; **in the imperfect** à
l'imparfait.

**import** *noun* produit *Masc.* importé.
**import** *verb* importer [1].

**importance** *noun* importance
*Fem.*

**important** *adjective* important.

**impossible** *adjective* impossible;
**it's impossible to find a telephone**
il est impossible de trouver un
téléphone.

**impressed** *adjective*
impressionné.

**impression** *noun* impression
*Fem.*; **to make a good impression
on somebody** faire bonne
impression sur quelqu'un; **I got the
impression he was hiding
something** j'avais l'impression
qu'il cachait quelque chose.

**impressive** *adjective*
impressionnant.

**improve** *verb* **1 to improve
something** améliorer [1] quelque
chose; **2** (*get better*) s'améliorer [1];
**the weather is improving** le temps
s'améliore.

**improvement** *noun* **1** (*a clear
change for the better*) amélioration
*Fem.*; **2** (*gradual progress*) progrès
*Masc.* plural (*in schoolwork, for
example*).

**in** *preposition, adverb* **1** dans; **in my
pocket** dans ma poche; **in the**
newspaper dans le journal; **in the
kitchen** dans la cuisine; **in my class**
dans ma classe; **I was in the bath**
j'étais dans mon bain; **2** à; **in Oxford**
à Oxford; **a house in the country**
une maison à la campagne; **in
school** à l'école; **in the sun** au soleil;
**the girl in the pink shirt** la fille à la
chemise rose; **3** en; **in France** en
France (*BUT*) **in Portugal** au
Portugal (*'en' for feminine countries,
'au' for most masculine countries*); **in
town** en ville; **in French** en français;
**4** (*time expressions*) **in May** en mai;
**in '94** en quatre-vingt-quatorze; **in
winter** en hiver; **in summer** en été;
(*BUT*) **in spring** au printemps; **in
the morning** le matin; **at eight in
the morning** à huit heures du
matin; **in the night** pendant la nuit;
**I'll phone you in ten minutes** je
t'appellerai dans dix minutes; **she
did it in five minutes** elle l'a fait en
cinq minutes; **5** (*talking about a
group*) de; **the tallest boy in the
class** le garçon le plus grand de la
classe; **the biggest city in the
world** la ville la plus grande du
monde; **6 in time** à temps; **7 in the
photo** sur la photo; **8 in the rain**
sous la pluie; **9 dressed in white**
habillé en blanc; **10 to come in**
entrer; **to go in** entrer; **we went
into the cinema** nous sommes
entrés dans le cinéma; **to run in**
entrer en courant; **11 to be in** être
là; **Mick's not in at the moment**
Mick n'est pas là en ce moment.

**incident** *noun* incident *Masc.*

**include** *verb* comprendre [64];
**dinner is included in the price** le

dîner est compris dans le prix; **service included** service compris.

**including** *preposition* (y) compris; **£50 including VAT** cinquante livres TVA comprise; **everyone, including children** tout le monde, y compris les enfants; **including Sundays** y compris les dimanches; **not including Sundays** sans compter les dimanches.

**income** *noun* revenu *Masc.*

**income tax** *noun* impôt *Masc.* sur le revenu.

**inconvenient** *adjective* **1** incommode (*a place or an arrangement*); **2** inopportun (*a time*).

**increase** *noun* augmentation *Fem.* (*in price, for example*). **increase** *verb* augmenter [1]; **the price has increased by £10** le prix a augmenté de dix livres.

**incredible** *adjective* incroyable.

**incredibly** *adverb* (*very*) extrêmement; **the film's incredibly boring** le film est extrêmement ennuyeux.

**indeed** *adverb* **1** (*to emphasize*) vraiment; **she's very pleased indeed** elle est vraiment très contente; **I'm very hungry indeed** j'ai vraiment très faim; **thank you very much indeed** merci beaucoup; **2** (*certainly*) bien sûr; **'can you hear his radio?' – 'indeed I can!'** 'entends-tu sa radio?' – 'bien sûr que oui!'

**indefinite article** *noun* (*in grammar*) article *Masc.* indéfini.

**independence** *noun* indépendance *Fem.*

**independent** *adjective* indépendant; **an independent school** une école privée.

**index** *noun* index *Masc.*

**index finger** *noun* index *Masc.*

**India** *noun* Inde *Fem.*; **in India** en Inde; **to India** en Inde.

**Indian** *noun* Indien *Masc.*, Indienne *Fem.* **Indian** *adjective* indien (*Fem.* indienne).

**indicate** *verb* indiquer [1].

**indication** *noun* indication *Fem.*

**indigestion** *noun* indigestion *Fem.*; **to have indigestion** avoir une indigestion.

**indirect** *adjective* indirect.

**individual** *noun* individu *Masc.* **individual** *adjective* **1** individuel (*Fem.* individuelle) (*a serving or a contribution, for example*); **2 individual tuition** des cours particuliers.

**indoor** *adjective* couvert; **an indoor swimming pool** une piscine couverte.

**indoors** *adverb* à l'intérieur; **it's cooler indoors** il fait plus frais à l'intérieur; **to go indoors** rentrer.

**industrial** *adjective* industriel (*Fem.* industrielle).

**industrial estate** *noun* zone *Fem.* industrielle.

**industry** *noun* industrie *Fem.*; **the advertising industry** l'industrie de la publicité.

**inefficient** *adjective* inefficace.

a
b
c
d
e
f
g
h
i
j
k
l
m
n
o
p
q
r
s
t
u
v
w
x
y
z

**inevitable** *adjective* inévitable.

**inevitably** *adverb* inévitablement.

**inexperienced** *adjective* inexpérimenté.

**infant school** *noun* école *Fem.* maternelle.

**infected** *adjective* qui s'est infecté.

**infection** *noun* infection *Fem.*; **an eye infection** une infection de l'œil; **a throat infection** une angine.

**infectious** *adjective* contagieux (*Fem.* contagieuse).

**infinitive** *noun* infinitif *Masc.*; **in the infinitive** à l'infiinitif.

**inflammable** *adjective* inflammable.

**inflatable** *adjective* pneumatique (*a mattress or a boat*).

**inflate** *verb* gonfler [1] (*a mattress or boat*).

**inflation** *noun* inflation *Fem.*

**influence** *noun* influence *Fem.*; **to be a good influence on somebody** avoir une bonne influence sur quelqu'un.

**influence** *verb* influencer [61].

**inform** *verb* informer [1]; **to inform somebody that** informer quelqu'un du fait que; **they informed us that there was a problem** ils nous ont informés du fait qu'il y avait un problème; **to inform somebody of something** informer quelqu'un de quelque chose.

**informal** *adjective* **1** simple (*a meal or event, for example*); **2** (*language*) familier (*Fem.* familière); **an informal expression** une expression familière.

**information** *noun* renseignements *Masc. plural*; **I need some information about flights to Paris** j'ai besoin de quelques renseignements sur les vols vers Paris; **a piece of information** un renseignement.

**information desk**, **information office** *noun* bureau *Masc.* des renseignements.

**information technology** *noun* informatique *Fem.*

**infuriating** *adjective* exaspérant.

**ingredient** *noun* ingrédient *Masc.*

**inhabitant** *noun* habitant *Masc.*, habitante *Fem.*

**initials** *plural noun* initiales *Fem. plural*; **put your initials here** marquez vos initiales ici.

**initiative** *noun* initiative *Fem.*

**injection** *noun* piqûre *Fem.*; **to give somebody an injection** faire [10] une piqûre à quelqu'un.

**injure** *verb* blesser [1].

**injured** *adjective* blessé.

**injury** *noun* blessure *Fem.*

**ink** *noun* encre *Fem.*

**in-laws** *noun* beaux-parents *Masc. plural.*

**inner** *adjective* intérieur.

**innocent** *adjective* innocent.

**insane** *adjective* fou (*Fem.* folle).

**inscription** *noun* inscription *Fem.*

**insect** *noun* insecte *Masc.*; **an insect bite** une piqûre d'insecte.

**insect repellent** *noun* insectifuge *Masc.*

**insert** *verb* insérer [24].

**inside** *noun* intérieur *Masc.*; **the inside of the oven** l'intérieur du four.

**inside** *preposition* à l'intérieur de; **inside the cinema** à l'intérieur du cinéma.

**inside** *adverb* à l'intérieur; **she's inside, I think** elle est à l'intérieur, je crois; **to go inside** rentrer.

**inside out** *adjective, adverb* à l'envers.

**insincere** *adjective* peu sincère.

**insist** *verb* **1** insister [1]; **if you insist** puisque tu insistes; **to insist on doing** insister pour faire; **he insisted on paying** il a insisté pour payer; **2 to insist that** affirmer [1] que; **Ruth insisted I was wrong** Ruth a affirmé que j'avais tort.

**insomnia** *noun* insomnie *Fem.*

**inspector** *noun* inspecteur *Masc.*, inspectrice *Fem.*

**install** *verb* installer [1].

**instalment** *noun* (*of a story or serial*) épisode *Masc.*

**instance** *noun* **for instance** par exemple.

**instant** *noun* instant *Masc.*; **come here this instant!** viens ici tout de suite!

**instant** *adjective* **1** instantané (*coffee or soup*); **2** (*immediate*) immédiat (*an effect or a success, for example*).

**instantly** *adverb* immédiatement.

**instead** *adverb* **1 Ted couldn't go, so I went instead** Ted ne pouvait pas y aller, donc je suis allé à sa place; **we didn't go to the concert, we went to Lucy's instead** au lieu

d'aller au concert, nous sommes allés chez Lucy; **2 instead of** au lieu de; **instead of pudding I had cheese** j'ai pris le fromage au lieu d'un dessert; **instead of playing tennis we went swimming** au lieu de jouer au tennis nous sommes allés à la piscine.

**instinct** *noun* instinct *Masc.*

**institute** *noun* institut *Masc.*

**institution** *noun* institution *Fem.*

**instruct** *verb* **to instruct somebody to do** donner [1] l'ordre à quelqu'un de faire; **the teacher instructed us to stay together** le professeur nous a donné l'ordre de rester en groupe.

**instructions** *plural noun* instructions *Fem. plural*; **follow the instructions on the packet** suivez les instructions sur l'emballage; **'instructions for use'** 'mode d'emploi'.

**instructor** *noun* moniteur *Masc.*, monitrice *Fem.*; **my skiing instructor** mon moniteur de ski.

**instrument** *noun* instrument *Masc.*; **to play an instrument** jouer d'un instrument.

**insulin** *noun* insuline *Fem.*

**insult** *noun* insulte *Fem.*
**insult** *verb* insulter [1].

**insurance** *noun* assurance *Fem.*; **travel insurance** l'assurance voyage; **do you have medical insurance?** est-ce que vous avez une assurance maladie?

**intelligence** *noun* intelligence *Fem.*

**intelligent** *adjective* intelligent.

a
b
c
d
e
f
g
h
**i**
j
k
l
m
n
o
p
q
r
s
t
u
v
w
x
y
z

a
b
c
d
e
f
g
h
**i**
j
k
l
m
n
o
p
q
r
s
t
u
v
w
x
y
z

**intend** *verb* **1** vouloir [14]; **as I intended** comme je le voulais; **2 to intend to do** avoir [5] l'intention de faire; **we intend to spend the night in Rome** nous avons l'intention de passer la nuit à Rome.

**intensive** *adjective* intensif (*Fem.* intensive).

**intensive care** *noun* **in intensive care** en réanimation.

**intention** *noun* intention *Fem.*; **I have no intention of paying** je n'ai aucune intention de payer.

**interest** *noun* **1** (*hobby*) centre *Masc.* d'intérêt; **what are your interests?** quels sont vos centres d'intérêt?; **2** (*keenness*) intérêt *Masc.*; **he has an interest in jazz** il a un intérêt pour le jazz.

**interest** *verb* intéresser [1]; **that doesn't interest me** ça ne m'intéresse pas.

**interested** *adjective* **to be interested in** s'intéresser à; **Sean's very interested in cooking** Sean s'intéresse beaucoup à la cuisine.

**interesting** *adjective* intéressant.

**interfere** *verb* **1 to interfere with something** (*to fiddle with it*) toucher [1] quelque chose; **don't interfere with my computer!** ne touche pas mon ordinateur; **2 to interfere in** se mêler [1] à (*someone else's affairs*).

**interior** *adjective* intérieur.

**interior designer** *noun* designer *Masc. & Fem.*

**international** *adjective* international (*Masc. plural* internationaux).

**Internet** *noun* Internet *Masc.*; **on the Internet** sur Internet.

**Internet cafe** *noun* cybercafé *Masc.*; **where is there an Internet cafe?** où est-ce qu'il y a un cybercafé?

**interpret** *verb* (*act as an interpreter*) faire [10] l'interprète.

**interpreter** *noun* interprète *Masc. & Fem.*

**interrupt** *verb* interrompre [69].

**interruption** *noun* interruption *Fem.*

**interval** *noun* entracte *Masc.* (*in a play or concert*).

**interview** *noun* **1** (*for a job*) entretien *Masc.*; **a job interview** un entretien; **2** (*in a newspaper, on TV or radio*) interview *Fem.*

**interview** *verb* interviewer [1] (*on TV, radio*).

**interviewer** *noun* interviewer *Masc.*

**into** *preposition* **1** dans; **he's gone into the bank** il est entré dans la banque; **I put the cat into his basket** j'ai mis le chat dans son panier; **we all got into the car** nous sommes tous montés dans la voiture; **2 to go into town** aller en ville; **Mum's gone into town** Maman est allée en ville; **to get into bed** se mettre au lit; **to translate into French** traduire en français; **to change pounds into euros** changer des livres sterling en euros; **3 to be into jazz** être fana du jazz (*informal*).

**introduce** *verb* présenter [1]; **she introduced me to her brother** elle m'a présenté à son frère; **can I introduce you to my mother?** je te présente ma mère.

**introduction** *noun* (*in a book*) introduction *Fem.*

**intuition** *noun* intuition *Fem.*

**invade** *verb* envahir [2].

**invalid** *noun* malade *Masc. & Fem.*

**invasion** *noun* invasion *Fem.*

**invent** *verb* inventer [1].

**invention** *noun* invention *Fem.*

**inventor** *noun* inventeur *Masc.*, inventrice *Fem.*

**inverted commas** *plural noun* guillemets *Masc. plural*; **in inverted commas** entre guillemets.

**investigation** *noun* (*by police*) enquête *Fem.*; **an investigation into the fire** une enquête sur l'incendie.

**invisible** *adjective* invisible.

**invitation** *noun* invitation *Fem.*; **an invitation to dinner** une invitation à dîner.

**invite** *verb* inviter [1]; **Kirsty invited me to lunch** Kirsty m'a invité à déjeuner; **he's invited me out on Tuesday** il m'a invitée à sortir avec lui mardi.

**inviting** *adjective* **1** appétissant (*a meal*); **2** accueillant (*a room*).

**invoice** *noun* facture *Fem.*

**involve** *verb* **1** nécessiter [1]; **it involves a lot of work** cela nécessite beaucoup de travail; **2** (*to affect*) concerner [1]; **the play will involve everybody** le spectacle va concerner tout le monde; **two cars were involved** deux voitures ont été concernées; **3 to be involved in**

participer [1] à; **I am involved in the new project** je participe au nouveau projet.

**Iran** *noun* Iran *Masc.*

**Iraq** *noun* Iraq *Masc.*

**Ireland** *noun* Irlande *Fem.*; **in Ireland** en Irlande; **to Ireland** en Irlande; **the Republic of Ireland** la République d'Irlande.

**Irish** *noun* **1** (*the language*) irlandais *Masc.*; **2** (*the people*) **the Irish** les Irlandais *Masc. plural*. **Irish** *adjective* irlandais.

**Irishman** *noun* Irlandais *Masc.*

**Irish Sea** *noun* mer *Fem.* d'Irlande.

**Irishwoman** *noun* Irlandaise *Fem.*

**iron** *noun* **1** (*for clothes*) fer *Masc.* à repasser; **2** (*the metal*) fer *Masc.* **iron** *verb* repasser [1].

**ironing** *noun* repassage *Masc.*; **to do the ironing** faire le repassage.

**ironing board** *noun* planche *Fem.* à repasser.

**ironmonger's** *noun* quincaillerie *Fem.*

**irregular** *adjective* irrégulier (*Fem.* irrégulière).

**irresponsible** *adjective* irresponsable.

**irritable** *adjective* irritable.

**irritate** *verb* irriter [1].

**irritating** *adjective* irritant.

**Islam** *noun* Islam *Masc.*

**Islamic** *adjective* islamique.

**island** *noun* île *Fem.*

**isolated** *adjective* isolé.

**Israel** *noun* Israël *Masc.*

a
b
c
d
e
f
g
h
i
j
k
l
m
n
o
p
q
r
s
t
u
v
w
x
y
z

**Israeli** *noun* Israélien *Masc.*, Israélienne *Fem.*
**Israeli** *adjective* israélien (*Fem.* israélienne).

**issue** *noun* **1** (*something you discuss*) question *Fem.*; **a political issue** une question politique; **2** (*of a magazine*) numéro *Masc.*
**issue** *verb* (*hand out*) distribuer [1].

**IT** *noun* (*short for information technology*) informatique *Fem.*

**it** *pronoun* **1** (*as the subject*) il (*when it stands for a masculine noun*); elle (*when it stands for a feminine noun*); **'where is my bag?' – 'it's in the kitchen'** 'où est mon sac?'– 'il est dans la cuisine'; **'how old is your car?' – 'it's five years old'** 'quel âge a ta voiture?' – 'elle a cinq ans'; **2** (*as the object*) le (*when it stands for a masculine noun*); la (*when it stands for a feminine noun*); l' (*before a vowel or silent 'h'*); **his new book? I know it** son nouveau livre? je le connais; **his address? I know it** son addresse? je la connais; **where's my book? I've lost it** où est mon livre? je l'ai perdu; **3 yes, it's true** oui, c'est vrai; **it doesn't matter** ça ne fait rien; **4 who is it?** qui c'est?; **it's me** c'est moi; **what is it?** qu'est-ce que c'est?; **5 it's raining** il pleut; **it's a nice day** il fait beau; **it's two o'clock** il est deux heures.

**Italian** *noun* **1** (*the language*) italien *Masc.*; **2** (*person*) Italien *Masc.*, Italienne *Fem.*
**Italian** *adjective* **1** italien (*Fem.* italienne); **Italian food** la cuisine italienne; **2** d'italien (*a teacher or a*

*lesson*); **my Italian class** mon cours d'italien.

**italics** *noun* italique *Masc.*; **in italics** en italique.

**Italy** *noun* Italie *Fem.*; **in Italy** en Italie; **to Italy** en Italie.

**itch** *verb* **my back is itching** j'ai le dos qui me démange; **this sweater itches** ce pull me gratte.

**item** *noun* article *Masc.*

**its** *determiner* son (*before a masculine noun or a feminine noun beginning with a vowel or silent 'h'*); sa (*before a feminine noun*); ses (*before a plural noun*); **the dog has lost its collar** le chien a perdu son collier; **the dog's in its kennel** le chien est dans sa niche; **its ear** son oreille; **its toys** ses jouets.

**itself** *pronoun* **1** se, s' (*before a vowel or silent 'h'*); **the cat is washing itself** le chat se lave; **2 he left the dog by itself** il a laissé le chien tout seul.

**ivory** *noun* ivoire *Masc.*

**ivy** *noun* lierre *Masc.*

# Jj

**jack** *noun* **1** (*in cards*) valet *Masc.*; **the jack of clubs** le valet de trèfle; **2** (*for a car*) cric *Masc.*

**jacket** *noun* veste *Fem.*

**jacket potato** *noun* pomme *Fem.* de terre en robe des champs.

**jackpot** *noun* gros lot *Masc.*; **to win the jackpot** gagner le gros lot.

a b c d e f g h i j k l m n o p q r s t u v w x y z

**jagged** *adjective* dentelé.

**jail** *noun* prison *Fem.*
**jail** *verb* emprisonner [1].

**jam** *noun* **1** (*that you eat*) confiture *Fem.*; **raspberry jam** la confiture de framboises; **2 a traffic jam** un embouteillage.

**Jamaica** *noun* Jamaïque *Fem.*

**Jamaican** *noun* Jamaïquain *Masc.*, Jamaïquaine *Fem.*
**Jamaican** *adjective* jamaïquain.

**jammed** *adjective* coincé.

**January** *noun* janvier *Masc.*; **in January** en janvier.

**Japan** *noun* Japon *Masc.*; **in Japan** au Japon.

**Japanese** *noun* **1** (*the language*) japonais *Masc.*; **2** (*person*) Japonais *Masc.*, Japonaise *Fem.*; **the Japanese** les Japonais *Masc. plural.*
**Japanese** *adjective* japonais.

**jar** *noun* (*small*) pot *Masc.*; (*large*) bocal *Masc.* (*plural* bocaux); **a jar of jam** un pot de confiture.

**javelin** *noun* javelot *Masc.*

**jaw** *noun* mâchoire *Fem.*

**jazz** *noun* jazz *Masc.*

**jealous** *adjective* jaloux (*Fem.* jalouse).

**jealousy** *noun* jalousie *Fem.*

**jeans** *noun* jean *Masc.*; **my jeans** mon jean; **a pair of jeans** un jean.

**jelly** *noun* gelée *Fem.*

**jellyfish** *noun* méduse *Fem.*

**jersey** *noun* **1** (*a pullover*) pull-over *Masc.*; **2** (*for football*) maillot *Masc.*

**Jersey** *noun* Jersey *Fem.*

**Jesus** *noun* Jésus *Masc.*; **Jesus Christ** Jésus-Christ.

**jet** *noun* jet *Masc.*

**jet lag** *noun* décalage *Masc.* horaire.

**jetty** *noun* jetée *Fem.*

**Jew** *noun* Juif *Masc.*, Juive *Fem.*

**jewel** *noun* bijou *Masc.* (*plural* bijoux).

**jeweller's** *noun* bijouterie *Fem.*

**jeweller** *noun* bijoutier *Masc.*, bijoutière *Fem.*

**jewellery** *noun* bijoux *Masc. plural.*

**Jewish** *adjective* juif (*Fem.* juive).

**jigsaw** *noun* puzzle *Masc.*

**job** *noun* **1** (*paid work*) emploi *Masc.*; **a job as a secretary** un emploi comme secrétaire; **he's got a job** il a trouvé un emploi; **out of a job** sans emploi; **what's your job?** qu'est-ce que vous faites comme travail?; **a job offer** une offre d'emploi; **2** (*a task*) travail *Masc.*; **it's not an easy job** ce n'est pas un travail facile; **she made a good job of it** elle a fait un bon travail.

**jobless** *adjective* sans emploi.

**jockey** *noun* jockey *Masc.*

**jog** *verb* **to go jogging** faire [10] du jogging.

**join** *verb* **1** (*become a member of*) s'inscrire [38] à; **I've joined the judo club** je me suis inscrit au club de judo; **2** (*to meet up with*) rejoindre [49]; **I'll join you later** je vous rejoindrai plus tard.

● **to join in 1** participer [1]; **Ruth never joins in** Ruth ne participe jamais; **2 to join in something** participer [1] à quelque chose; **won't**

a b c d e f g h i j k l m n o p q r s t u v w x y z

**a**

you join in the game? veux-tu participer au jeu?

**b**

**joiner** *noun* menuisier *Masc.*

**c**

**joint** *noun* **1** (*of meat*) rôti *Masc.*; **a joint of beef** un rôti de bœuf; **2** (*in your body*) articulation *Fem.*

**d**

**joint** *adjective* **1 the joint winners** les lauréats ex aequo.

**e**

**f**

**joke** *noun* (*a funny story*) plaisanterie *Fem.*; **to tell a joke** raconter une plaisanterie.

**g**

**joke** *verb* plaisanter [1]; **you must be joking!** tu plaisantes!

**h**

**i**

**joker** *noun* (*in cards*) joker *Masc.*

**j**

**Jordan** *noun* Jordanie *Fem.*

**k**

**journalism** *noun* journalisme *Masc.*

**l**

**journalist** *noun* journaliste *Masc. & Fem.*; **Sean's a journalist** Sean est journaliste.

**m**

**n**

**journey** *noun* **1** (*a long one*) voyage *Masc.*; **our journey to Turkey** notre voyage en Turquie; **2** (*shorter: to work or school*) trajet *Masc.*; **a bus journey** un trajet en bus.

**o**

**p**

**q**

**joy** *noun* joie *Fem.*

**r**

**joy-riding** *noun* rodéo *Masc.* à la voiture volée.

**s**

**t**

**joystick** *noun* (*for computer games*) manette *Fem.* de jeu.

**u**

**Judaism** *noun* judaïsme *Masc.*

**v**

**judge** *noun* juge *Masc.*

**judge** *verb* estimer [1] (*a time or distance*).

**w**

**x**

**judgement** *noun* jugement *Masc.*

**judo** *noun* judo *Masc.*; **he does judo** il fait du judo.

**y**

**z**

**jug** *noun* pot *Masc.*

**juggle** *verb* jongler [1].

**juice** *noun* jus *Masc.*; **two orange juices please** deux jus d'orange s'il vous plaît.

**juicy** *adjective* juteux (*Fem.* juteuse).

**jukebox** *noun* jukebox *Masc.*

**July** *noun* juillet *Masc.*; **in July** en juillet.

**jumble sale** *noun* vente *Fem.* de charité.

**jumbo jet** *noun* gros-porteur *Masc.*

**jump** *noun* saut *Masc.*; **a parachute jump** un saut en parachute.

**jump** *verb* sauter [1].

**jumper** *noun* pull *Masc.*

**junction** *noun* **1** (*of roads*) carrefour *Masc.*; **2** (*of motorways*) échangeur *Masc.*; **3** (*on railway*) nœud *Masc.* ferroviaire.

**June** *noun* juin *Masc.*; **in June** en juin.

**jungle** *noun* jungle *Fem.*

**junior** *adjective* primaire; **a junior school** une école primaire; **the juniors** les élèves du primaire.

**junk** *noun* (*real rubbish*) bric-à-brac *Masc.*

**junk food** *noun* **you shouldn't eat junk food** tu devrais manger correctement (*there is no word for junk food in French, so you will need to express it differently, according to the context*).

**junk shop** *noun* magasin *Masc.* de brocante.

**jury** *noun* jury *Masc.*

**just** *adverb* **1** juste; **just before midday** juste avant midi; **just after**

the church juste après l'église; **just for fun** juste pour rire; **2 to have just done** venir de faire; **Tom has just arrived** Tom vient d'arriver; **Helen had just called** Helen venait d'appeler; **3 to be just doing** être en train de faire; **I'm just finishing the ironing** je suis en train de finir le repassage; **4** (*only*) ne ...que; **he's just a child** il n'est qu'un enfant; **there's just me and Justine** il n'y a que moi et Justine; **5 just coming!** j'arrive!

**justice** *noun* justice *Fem.*

**justify** *verb* justifier [1].

# Kk

**kangaroo** *noun* kangourou *Masc.*

**karaoke** *noun* karaoké *Masc.*

**karate** *noun* karaté *Masc.*

**kebab** *noun* brochette *Fem.*

**keen** *adjective* **1** (*enthusiastic*) enthousiaste; **you don't look too keen** tu n'as pas l'air très enthousiaste; **2** (*committed*) passionné; **he's a keen photographer** c'est un photographe passionné; **3 I'm not keen on fish** je n'aime pas trop le poisson; **4 to be keen on doing** (or **to do**) avoir très envie de faire; **I'm not keen on camping** je n'ai pas très envie de faire du camping.

**keep** *verb* **1** garder [1]; **I kept the letter** j'ai gardé la lettre; **will you keep my seat?** veux-tu garder ma place?; **they kept her in hospital** ils l'ont gardée à l'hôpital; **to keep a secret** garder un secret; **2 to keep somebody waiting** faire [10] attendre quelqu'un; **3** (*to store*) ranger [52]; **I keep my bike in the garage** je range mon vélo dans le garage; **where do you keep saucepans?** où rangez-vous les casseroles?; **4 to keep on doing** continuer [1] à faire; **she kept on talking** elle a continué à parler; **keep straight on** continuez tout droit; **5 to keep on doing** (*time after time*) **he keeps on ringing me up** il n'arrête pas de m'appeler; **6** (*stay*) rester [1]; **keep calm!** restez calme!; **keep out of the sun** reste à l'abri du soleil; **7 to keep a promise** tenir [77] sa promesse.

**keep fit** *noun* gymnastique *Fem.* d'entretien.

**kennel** *noun* **1** (*for one dog*) niche *Fem.*; **2** (*for boarding*) **kennels** chenil *Masc.*.

**kerb** *noun* bord *Masc.* du trottoir.

**ketchup** *noun* ketchup *Masc.*

**kettle** *noun* bouilloire *Fem.*; **to put the kettle on** mettre l'eau à chauffer.

**key** *noun* **1** (*for a lock*) clé *Fem.*; **a bunch of keys** un trousseau de clés; **2** (*on a piano or typewriter*) touche *Fem.*

**keyboard** *noun* (*for a piano or a computer*) clavier *Masc.*

**keyhole** *noun* trou *Masc.* de serrure.

**keyring** *noun* porte-clés *Masc.*

**kick** *noun* **1** (*from a person or a horse*) coup *Masc.* de pied; **to give somebody a kick** donner un coup

467

# kick

de pied à quelqu'un; **2** (*in football*) tir *Masc.*; ★ **to get a kick out of doing** prendre plaisir à faire.

**kick** *verb* **to kick somebody** donner [1] un coup de pied à quelqu'un; **to kick the ball** donner un coup de pied dans le ballon.

● **to kick off** donner [1] le coup d'envoi.

**kick-off** *noun* coup *Masc.* d'envoi.

**kid** *noun* gosse *Masc. & Fem.* (*child*); **Dad's looking after the kids** Dad s'occupe des gosses.

**kidnap** *verb* enlever [50].

**kidnapper** *noun* ravisseur *Masc.*, ravisseuse *Fem.*

**kidney** *noun* **1** (*part of your body*) rein *Masc.*; **2** (*for eating*) rognon *Masc.*

**kill** *verb* tuer [1]; **she was killed in an accident** elle a été tuée dans un accident.

**killer** *noun* (*murderer*) meurtrier *Masc.*, meurtrière *Fem.*

**kilo** *noun* kilo *Masc.*; **a kilo of sugar** un kilo de sucre; **five euros a kilo** cinq euros le kilo.

**kilogramme** *noun* kilogramme *Masc.*

**kilometre** *noun* kilomètre *Masc.*

**kilt** *noun* kilt *Masc.*

**kind** *noun* sorte *Fem.*; **all kinds of people** toutes sortes de gens.

**kind** *adjective* gentil (*Fem.* gentille); **Marion was very kind to me** Marion a été très gentille avec moi.

**kindness** *noun* gentillesse *Fem.*

**king** *noun* roi *Masc.*; **King George** le roi Georges; **the king of hearts** le roi de cœur.

**kingdom** *noun* royaume *Masc.*; **the United Kingdom** le Royaume-Uni.

**kiosk** *noun* **1** (*for newspapers or snacks*) kiosque *Masc.*; **2** (*for a phone*) cabine *Fem.*

**kipper** *noun* hareng *Masc.* fumé.

**kiss** *noun* baiser *Masc.*; **to give somebody a kiss** embrasser quelqu'un.
**kiss** *verb* embrasser [1]; **kiss me!** embrasse-moi!; **we kissed each other** nous nous sommes embrassés.

**kit** *noun* **1** (*of tools*) trousse *Fem.*; **a tool kit** une trousse à outils; **2** (*clothes*) affaires *Fem. plural*; **where's my football kit?** où sont mes affaires de foot?; **3** (*for making a model, a piece of furniture, etc*) kit *Masc.*

**kitchen** *noun* cuisine *Fem.*; **the kitchen table** la table de la cuisine.

**kitchen foil** *noun* papier *Masc.* d'aluminium.

**kitchen garden** *noun* jardin *Masc.* potager.

**kitchen roll** *noun* essuie-tout *Masc.*

**kite** *noun* (*toy*) cerf-volant *Masc.*; **to fly a kite** faire voler un cerf-volant.

**kitten** *noun* chaton *Masc.*

**kiwi fruit** *noun* kiwi *Masc.*

**knack** *noun* don *Masc.*

**knee** *noun* genou *Masc.* (*plural genoux*); **on (your) hands and knees** à quatre pattes.

**kneel** *verb* se mettre [11] à genoux.

**knickers** *plural noun* petite culotte *Fem.*

**knife** *noun* couteau *Masc.* (*plural* couteaux).

**knight** *noun* (*in chess*) cavalier *Masc.*

**knit** *verb* tricoter [1].

**knitting** *noun* tricot *Masc.*

**knob** *noun* bouton *Masc.*

**knock** *noun* coup *Masc.*; **a knock on the head** un coup à la tête; **a knock at the door** un coup à la porte.
**knock** *verb* **1** (*to bang*) cogner [1]; **I knocked my arm on the table** je me suis cogné le bras contre la table; **2 to knock on something** (*a person*) frapper [1] à (*the door*).

● **to knock down 1** (*in a traffic accident*) renverser [1] (*a person*); **2** (*to demolish*) démolir [2] (*an old building*).

● **to knock out 1** (*to make unconscious*) assommer [1]; **2** (*in sport, to eliminate*) éliminer [1].

**knocker** *noun* heurtoir *Masc.*

**knot** *noun* nœud *Masc.*; **to tie a knot in something** nouer [1] quelque chose.

**know** *verb* **1** (*know a fact*) savoir [70]; **do you know where Tim is?** sais-tu où est Tim?; **I know they've moved house** je sais qu'ils ont déménagé; **he knows it by heart** il le sait par cœur; **yes, I know** oui, je sais; **you never know!** on ne sait jamais!; **2** (*be personally acquainted with*) connaître [27] (*a person, place, book, or music, for example*); **do you know the Jacksons?** est-ce que tu connais les Jackson?; **all the people**

**I know** tous les gens que je connais; **I don't know his mother** je ne connais pas sa mère; **3 to know how to do** savoir [70] faire; **Steve knows how to make couscous** Steve sait faire du couscous; **Liz knows how to mend it** Liz sait le réparer; **4 to know about** être [6] au courant de (*the latest news*); **5 to know about** s'y connaître [27] en (*machines, cooking, etc*); **Lindy knows about computers** Lindy s'y connaît en informatique.

**knowledge** *noun* connaissance *Fem.*

**knuckle** *noun* articulation *Fem.* des doigts.

**koala** *noun* koala *Masc.*

**Koran** *noun* Coran *Masc.*

**kosher** *adjective* kascher.

# Ll

**lab** *noun* labo *Masc.*

**label** *noun* étiquette *Fem.*

**laboratory** *noun* laboratoire *Masc.*

**Labour** *noun* les travaillistes *Masc. plural*; **to vote for the Labour party** voter pour les travaillistes; **the Labour Party** le parti travailliste.

**lace** *noun* **1** (*for a shoe*) lacet *Masc.*; **2** (*for curtains, for example*) dentelle *Fem.*

**lad** *noun* gars *Masc.*

**ladder** *noun* (*for climbing, or in your tights*) échelle *Fem.*

a
b
c
d
e
f
g
h
i
j
k
l
m
n
o
p
q
r
s
t
u
v
w
x
y
z

# ladies

**ladies** *noun* (*lavatory*) toilettes *Fem.* *plural*; (*on a sign*) **'Ladies'** 'Dames'.

**lady** *noun* dame *Fem.*; **ladies and gentlemen** mesdames et messieurs.

**ladybird** *noun* coccinelle *Fem.*

**lager** *noun* bière *Fem.* blonde.

**laid-back** *adjective* relaxe.

**lake** *noun* lac *Masc.*; **Lake Geneva** le lac Léman.

**lamb** *noun* agneau *Masc.* (*plural* agneaux); **a leg of lamb** un gigot.

**lame** *adjective* boiteux (*Fem.* boiteuse); **he is lame** il boite.

**lamp** *noun* lampe *Fem.*

**lamp-post** *noun* réverbère *Masc.*

**lampshade** *noun* abat-jour *Masc.* (*plural* abat-jour).

**land** *noun* **1** terre *Fem.*; **I can see land** je vois la terre; **2** (*property*) terrain *Masc.*; **a piece of land** un terrain.
**land** *verb* **1** (*plane, passenger*) atterrir [2]; **2** (*leave a ship*) débarquer [1].

**landing** *noun* **1** (*on the stairs*) palier *Masc.*; **2** (*of a plane*) atterrissage *Masc.*; **3** (*from a boat*) débarquement *Masc.*

**landlady** *noun* propriétaire *Fem.*

**landlord** *noun* propriétaire *Masc.*

**landscape** *noun* paysage *Masc.*

**lane** *noun* **1** (*a country path*) chemin *Masc.*; **2** (*of a motorway*) voie *Fem.*

**language** *noun* **1** (*French, Italian, etc*) langue *Fem.*; **a foreign language** une langue étrangère; **2** (*way of speaking*) langage *Masc.*; **bad language** un langage grossier.

**language lab** *noun* laboratoire *Masc.* de langues.

**language school** *noun* école *Fem.* de langue.

**lap** *noun* **1** (*your knees*) genoux *Masc.* *plural*; **on my lap** sur mes genoux; **2** (*in races*) tour *Masc.* de piste.

**laptop** *noun* portable *Masc.*

**larder** *noun* garde-manger *Masc.*

**large** *adjective* **1** grand (*goes before the noun*); **a large number** un grand nombre; **a large house** une grande maison; **2** gros (*Fem.* grosse) (*a piece, part, animal*) (*goes before the noun*); **a large piece of cake** un gros morceau de gâteau; **3** nombreux (*Fem.* nombreuse) (*crowd or family*); **I come from a large family** je viens d'une famille nombreuse.

**laser** *noun* laser *Masc.*

**laser beam** *noun* rayon *Masc.* laser.

**laser printer** *noun* imprimante *Fem.* laser.

**last** *adjective* dernier (*Fem.* dernière); **the last time** la dernière fois; **last week** la semaine dernière; **last night** (*in the evening*) hier soir; (*in the night*) cette nuit.
**last** *adverb* **1** (*in final position*) (*to arrive or leave*) en dernier; **Rob arrived last** Rob est arrivé en dernier; **at last!** enfin!; **2** (*most recently*) **I last saw him in May** la dernière fois que je l'ai vu était en mai.
**last** *verb* durer [1]; **the play lasted two hours** le spectacle a duré deux heures.

**late** *adjective, adverb* **1** en retard; **we're late** nous sommes en retard; **they arrived late** ils sont arrivés en retard; **to be late for something** être en retard pour quelque chose; **we were late for the film** nous étions en retard pour le film; **2 to be late** (*a bus or train*) avoir du retard; **the train was an hour late** le train a eu une heure de retard; **3** (*late in the day*) tard; **we got up late** nous nous sommes levés tard; **the chemist is open late** la pharmacie est ouverte tard; **late last night** tard hier soir; **too late!** trop tard!

**lately** *adverb* ces derniers temps.

**later** *adverb* plus tard; **I'll explain later** j'expliquerai plus tard; **see you later!** à tout à l'heure!

**latest** *adjective* **1** dernier (*Fem.* dernière); **the latest news** les dernières nouvelles; **2 at the latest** au plus tard.
**latest** *noun* **the latest in audio equipment** le dernier cri en matière d'équipement hifi.

**Latin** *noun* latin *Masc.*

**laugh** *noun* rire *Masc.*; **to do something for a laugh** faire quelque chose pour rigoler (*informal*).
**laugh** *verb* **1** rire [68]; **everybody laughed** tout le monde a ri; **2 to laugh at** se moquer [1] de; **I tried to explain but they laughed at me** j'ai essayé d'expliquer mais ils se sont moqués de moi.

**laughter** *noun* rire *Masc.*

**launch** *noun* (*of a ship, product, spacecraft*) lancement *Masc.*.
**launch** *verb* **1** (*product, spacecraft*) lancer [61]; **2** (*ship*) mettre [11] à l'eau.

**launderette** *noun* laverie *Fem.* automatique.

**laundry** *noun* **1** (*in hotel etc*) laverie *Fem.*; **2** (*shop*) blanchisserie *Fem.*

**lavatory** *noun* toilettes *Fem. plural*; **to go to the lavatory** aller aux toilettes.

**lavender** *noun* lavande *Fem.*

**law** *noun* **1** loi *Fem.*; **it's against the law** c'est interdit; **2** (*subject of study*) droit *Masc.*

**lawn** *noun* pelouse *Fem.*

**lawnmower** *noun* tondeuse *Fem.* à gazon.

**lawyer** *noun* avocat *Masc.*, avocate *Fem.*

**lay** *verb* **1** (*put*) poser [1]; **she laid the card on the table** elle a posé la carte sur la table; **2** (*spread out*) étaler [1]; **we laid newspaper on the floor** nous avons étalé du papier journal sur le parquet; **3 to lay the table** mettre [11] la table.

**lay-by** *noun* aire *Fem.* de stationnement.

**layer** *noun* couche *Fem.*

**laziness** *noun* paresse *Fem.*

**lazy** *adjective* paresseux (*Fem.* paresseuse).

**lead**¹ *noun* **1** (*when you are ahead*) **to be in the lead** être en tête; **Baxter's in the lead** Baxter est en tête; **we have a lead of three points** nous avons trois points d'avance; **2** (*electric*) fil *Masc.*; **3** (*for a dog*) laisse *Fem.*; **on a lead** en laisse.

a
b
c
d
e
f
g
h
i
j
k
l
m
n
o
p
q
r
s
t
u
v
w
x
y
z

# lead

**lead** *adjective* (*a role or a singer*) principal (*Masc. plural* principaux).
**lead** *verb* **1** mener [50]; **the path leads to the sea** le chemin mène à la mer; **2 to lead the way** montrer [1] le chemin; **3 to lead to something** entraîner [1] quelque chose (*an accident or problems, for example*).

**lead**[2] *noun* (*the metal*) plomb *Masc.*

**leader** *noun* **1** (*of a gang*) chef *Masc.*; **2** (*of a political party*) dirigeant *Masc.*, dirigeante *Fem.*; **3** (*in a competition*) premier *Masc.*, première *Fem.*.

**lead-free petrol** *noun* essence *Fem.* sans plomb.

**lead singer** *noun* chanteur principal *Masc.*, chanteuse principale *Fem.*

**leaf** *noun* feuille *Fem.*

**leaflet** *noun* dépliant *Masc.*

**league** *noun* (*in sport*) championnat *Masc.*

**leak** *noun* fuite *Fem.*; **a gas leak** une fuite de gaz.
**leak** *verb* (*a bottle or a roof*) fuir [44].

**lean** *adjective* (*meat*) maigre.
**lean** *verb* **1 to lean on something** s'appuyer [41] contre quelque chose; **2** (*prop*) appuyer [41]; **lean the ladder against the tree!** appuie l'échelle contre l'arbre!; **3** (*a person*) se pencher [1]; **to lean out of the window** se pencher par la fenêtre; **lean forward a bit** penche-toi un peu en avant.

**leap** *verb* sauter [1].
**leap year** *noun* année *Fem.* bissextile.

**learn** *verb* apprendre [64]; **to learn Russian** apprendre le russe; **to learn (how) to drive** apprendre à conduire.

**learner** *noun* apprenant *Masc.*, apprenante *Fem.*; **to be a fast learner** apprendre vite.

**learner driver** *noun* élève *Masc. & Fem.* d'auto-école.

**least** *adverb, adjective, pronoun* **1** le moins; **I like the blue shirt least** c'est la chemise bleue que j'aime le moins; **2** (*followed by a noun*) le moins de; **Tony has the least money** c'est Tony qui a le moins d'argent; **3** (*followed by an adjective*) le moins, la moins, les moins (*according to the gender and number of the noun going with the adjective*); **the least expensive hotel** l'hôtel le moins cher; **the least expensive car** la voiture la moins chère; **the least expensive shoes** les chaussures les moins chères; **4 the least** (*the slightest*) le moindre, la moindre (*according to the gender of the noun that follows*); **I haven't the least idea** je n'ai pas la moindre idée; **5 at least** (*at a minimum*) au moins; **at least twenty people** au moins vingt personnes; **6 at least** (*at any rate*) du moins; **at least, I think she's a teacher** du moins, je crois qu'elle est professeur.

**leather** *noun* cuir *Masc.*; **a leather jacket** un blouson en cuir.

**leave** *noun* congé *Masc.*; **three days' leave** trois jours de congé.

**leave** *verb* **1** (*go away*) partir [58]; **they're leaving tomorrow** ils vont partir demain; **we left at six** nous sommes partis à six heures; **2** (*go away from*) quitter [1]; **I left the office at five** j'ai quitté le bureau à cinq heures; **Guy left school at sixteen** Guy a quitté l'école à seize ans; **3** (*go out of*) sortir [72] de; **she left the cinema at ten** elle est sortie du cinéma à dix heures; **4** (*deposit*) laisser [1]; **you can leave your coats in the hall** vous pouvez laisser vos manteaux dans l'entrée; **5** (*not do*) laisser [1]; **let's leave the washing up!** laissons la vaisselle!; **6** (*forget*) oublier [1]; **he left his umbrella on the train** il a oublié son parapluie dans le train; **7 be left** rester [1]; **there are two pancakes left** il reste deux crêpes; **we have ten minutes left** il nous reste dix minutes; **I don't have any money left** il ne me reste plus d'argent.

**lecture** *noun* **1** (*at university*) cours *Masc.* magistral (*plural* cours magistraux); **2** (*public*) conférence *Fem.*

**lecturer** *noun* professeur *Masc.* à l'université.

**ledge** *noun* **1** (*of a window*) rebord *Masc.*; **2** (*on a cliff*) corniche *Fem.*

**leek** *noun* poireau *Masc.* (*plural* poireaux).

**left** *noun* gauche *Fem.*; **to drive on the left** conduire à gauche; **turn left at the church** tournez à gauche à l'église; **on my left** à ma gauche. **left** *adjective* gauche; **his left foot** son pied gauche.

**left-click** *noun* clic *Masc.* sur le bouton gauche de la souris. **left-click** *verb* **to left-click the icon** cliquer [1] en appuyant sur le bouton gauche de la souris.

**left-hand** *adjective* **the left-hand side** la gauche.

**left-handed** *adjective* gaucher *Masc.*, gauchère *Fem.*

**left luggage office** *noun* consigne *Fem.*

**leftovers** *plural noun* restes *Masc. plural.*

**leg** *noun* **1** (*of a person or a horse*) jambe *Fem.*; **my left leg** ma jambe gauche; **to break your leg** se casser la jambe; **2** (*of other animals*) patte *Fem.*; **3** (*of a table or chair*) pied *Masc.*; **4** (*in cooking*) **a leg of chicken** une cuisse de poulet; **a leg of lamb** un gigot; ★ **to pull somebody's leg** faire [10] marcher quelqu'un.

**legal** *adjective* légal (*Masc. plural* légaux).

**legend** *noun* **1** (*story*) légende *Fem.*; **2** (*person*) légende *Fem.*

**leggings** *plural noun* caleçon *Masc.*

**leisure** *noun* loisirs *Masc. plural*; **in my leisure time** pendant mes loisirs.

**leisure centre** *noun* centre *Masc.* de loisirs.

**lemon** *noun* citron *Masc.*; **a lemon yoghurt** un yaourt au citron.

**lemonade** *noun* limonade *Fem.*

**lemon juice** *noun* jus *Masc.* de citron.

**lend** *verb* prêter [1]; **to lend something to somebody** prêter

a
b
c
d
e
f
g
h
i
j
k
l
m
n
o
p
q
r
s
t
u
v
w
x
y
z

quelque chose à quelqu'un; **I lent Judy my bike** j'ai prêté mon vélo à Judy; **will you lend it to me?** veux-tu me le prêter?

**length** *noun* longueur *Fem.*

**lens** *noun* **1** (*in a camera*) objectif *Masc.*; **2** (*in spectacles*) verre *Masc.*; **3 contact lenses** les lentilles *Fem. plural* de contact.

**Lent** *noun* Carême *Masc.*

**lentil** *noun* lentille *Fem.*

**Leo** *noun* Lion *Masc.*; **I'm Leo** je suis Lion.

**leotard** *noun* justaucorps *Masc.*

**lesbian** *noun* lesbienne *Fem.*

**less** *pronoun, adjective, adverb*
**1** moins; **Richard eats less** Richard mange moins; **2** (*before a noun*) moins de; **less traffic** moins de circulation; **less time** moins de temps; **3** (*before an adjective or adverb*) moins; **less interesting** moins intéressant; **less quickly than us** moins vite que nous; **4 less than** moins de; **less than three hours** moins de trois heures; **less than a kilo** moins d'un kilo; **5 less than** (*in comparisons*) moins que; **you spent less than me** tu as dépensé moins que moi.

**lesson** *noun* **1** (*class*) cours *Masc.*; **the history lesson** le cours d'histoire; **to take tennis lessons** prendre des cours de tennis; **2** (*one in a planned series*) leçon *Fem.*; **a driving lesson** une leçon de conduite.

**let**¹ *verb* **1** (*allow*) **to let somebody do** laisser [1] quelqu'un faire; **she lets me borrow her bike** elle me

laisse emprunter son vélo; **will you let me go alone?** veux-tu me laisser y aller toute seule?; **the police let us through** la police nous a laissés passer; **let me see** (*show me*) laisse-moi voir; **2** (*as a suggestion or a command*) **let's go!** allons-y!; **let's not talk about it** n'en parlons pas; **let's see, if Tuesday is the third** ... voyons, si mardi est le trois ...; **let's eat out** si on mangeait au restaurant?

● **to let off 1** tirer [1] (*fireworks*); **2** faire [10] exploser (*a bomb*); **3** (*to excuse from*) dispenser [1] de (*homework*).

**let**² *verb* (*to rent out*) louer [1]; **'flat to let'** 'appartement à louer'.

**lethal** *adjective* mortel (*Fem.* mortelle)

**letter** *noun* lettre *Fem.*; **a letter for you from Delia** une lettre pour toi de Delia; **G is the letter after F** G est la lettre après F.

**letter box** *noun* boîte *Fem.* à lettres.

**lettuce** *noun* salade *Fem.*; **two lettuces** deux salades.

**leukaemia** *noun* leucémie *Fem.*

**level** *noun* niveau *Masc.* (*plural* niveaux); **at street level** au niveau de la rue.
**level** *adjective* **1** droit (*a shelf or floor*); **2** plat (*ground*).

**level crossing** *noun* passage *Masc.* à niveau.

**lever** *noun* levier *Masc.*

**liar** *noun* menteur *Masc.*, menteuse *Fem.*

**liberal** *adjective* libéral (*Masc. plural* libéraux); **the Liberal Democrats** le parti libéral-démocrate.

**liberty** *noun* liberté *Fem.*

**Libra** *noun* Balance *Fem.*; **Sean's Libra** Sean est Balance.

**librarian** *noun* bibliothécaire *Masc. & Fem.*; **Mark's a librarian** Mark est bibliothécaire.

**library** *noun* bibliothèque *Fem.*; **the public library** la bibliothèque municipale.

**licence** *noun* **1** (*for driving or fishing*) permis *Masc.*; **a driving licence** un permis de conduire; **2** (*for a TV*) redevance *Fem.*

**lick** *verb* lécher [24].

**lid** *noun* couvercle *Masc.*; **she took the lid off** elle a enlevé le couvercle.

**lie** *noun* mensonge *Masc.*; **to tell a lie** (or **lies**) mentir [53].
**lie** *verb* **1** (*to be stretched out*) être [6] allongé; **Jimmy was lying on the bed** Jimmy était allongé sur le lit; **my coat lay on the bed** mon manteau était sur le lit; **2 to lie down** se coucher [1]; (*for a little while*) s'allonger [52]; **come and lie down in the sun** viens t'allonger au soleil; **3** (*not to tell the truth*) mentir [53].

**lie-in** *noun* **to have a lie-in** faire la grasse matinée.

**lieutenant** *noun* lieutenant *Masc.*

**life** *noun* vie *Fem.*; **all her life** toute sa vie; **full of life** plein de vie; **that's life!** c'est la vie!

**lifebelt** *noun* bouée *Fem.* de sauvetage.

**lifeboat** *noun* canot *Masc.* de sauvetage.

**lifeguard** *noun* maître nageur *Masc.*; **is there a lifeguard at the pool?** est-ce que la piscine est surveillée?

**life jacket** *noun* gilet *Masc.* de sauvetage.

**life-style** *noun* style *Masc.* de vie.

**lift** *noun* **1** ascenseur *Masc.*; **let's take the lift** prenons l'ascenseur; **2** (*a ride*) **to give somebody a lift to the station** déposer quelqu'un à la gare; **Tom gave me a lift home** Tom m'a déposé chez moi; **can I give you a lift?** puis-je vous déposer quelque part?
**lift** *verb* soulever [50]; **he lifted the box** il a soulevé le carton.

**light** *noun* **1** (*electric*) lumière *Fem.*; **will you turn the light on?** veux-tu allumer la lumière?; **to turn off the light** éteindre la lumière; **2** (*streetlight*) réverbère *Masc.*; **3** (*a headlight for a car*) phare *Masc.*; **are your lights on?** as-tu allumé tes phares?; **4** (*an indicator on a machine*) voyant *Masc.*; **5 traffic lights** les feux *Masc. plural*; **the lights were green** le feu était au vert; **6 have you got a light?** tu as du feu?

**light** *adjective* **1** (*in colour*) clair; **light blue eyes** des yeux bleu clair; **2** (*not night*) **it gets light at six** il fait jour à six heures; **3** (*not heavy*) léger (*Fem.* légère); **a light sweater** un pull léger; **a light breeze** une brise légère.

**light** *verb* **1** allumer [1] (*the oven, the fire, or a cigarette*); **we lit a fire**

a
b
c
d
e
f
g
h
i
j
k
l
m
n
o
p
q
r
s
t
u
v
w
x
y
z

nous avons fait un feu; **2** craquer [1] (*a match*).

**light bulb** *noun* ampoule *Fem*.

**lighter** *noun* briquet *Masc*.

**lighthouse** *noun* phare *Masc*.

**lightning** *noun* éclairs *Masc. plural*; **a flash of lightning** un éclair; **to be struck by lightning** être frappé par la foudre.

**light switch** *noun* interrupteur *Masc*.

**like**[1] *preposition, conjunction*
**1** comme; **like me** comme moi; **like this** comme ça; **like a duck** comme un canard; **like I said** comme j'ai dit; **what's it like?** c'est comment?; **what was the weather like?** quel temps faisait-il?; **2 to look like** ressembler [1] à; **Cindy looks like her father** Cindy ressemble à son père.

**like**[2] *verb* **1** aimer [1] (bien); **I like fish** j'aime bien le poisson; **I don't like snakes** je n'aime pas les serpents; **Mum likes travelling** Maman aime bien voyager; **I like Renoir best** je préfère Renoir; **2 I would like** je voudrais; **would you like a coffee?** est-ce que tu voudrais un café?; **what would you like to eat?** qu'est-ce que tu veux manger?; **yes, if you like** oui, si tu veux.

**likely** *adjective* probable; **it's not very likely** ce n'est pas très probable; **she's likely to phone** elle va probablement appeler.

**lilac** *noun* lilas *Masc*.

**lily** *noun* lys *Masc*.

**lily of the valley** *noun* muguet *Masc*.

**lime** *noun* citron *Masc*. vert.

**limit** *noun* limitation *Fem*.; **the speed limit** la limitation de vitesse.

**limp** *noun* **to have a limp** boiter [1].

**line** *noun* **1** ligne *Fem*.; **a straight line** une ligne droite; **six lines of text** six lignes de texte; **to draw a line** tirer un trait; **2 a railway line** (*from one place to another*) une ligne de chemin de fer; **on the railway line** (*the track*) sur la voie ferrée; **3** (*a queue of people or cars*) file *Fem*.; **to stand in line** faire la queue; **4** (*telephone*) ligne *Fem*.; **the line's bad** la ligne est mauvaise; **hold the line, please** ne quittez pas.
**line** *verb* doubler [1] (*a coat*).

**linen** *noun* lin *Masc*.; **a linen jacket** une veste en lin.

**lining** *noun* doublure *Fem*.

**link** *noun* rapport *Masc*.; **what's the link between the two?** quel est le rapport entre les deux?.
**link** *verb* relier [1] (*two places*); **the terminals are linked by a shuttle service** les terminaux sont reliés par une navette.

**lino** *noun* linoléum *Masc*.

**lion** *noun* lion *Masc*.

**lip** *noun* lèvre *Fem*.

**lip-read** *verb* lire [51] sur les lèvres.

**lipstick** *noun* rouge *Masc*. à lèvres.

**liquid** *noun, adjective* liquide *Masc*.

**liquidizer** *noun* mixer *Masc*.

**list** *noun* liste *Fem*.

**listen** *verb* **1** écouter [1]; **I wasn't listening** je n'écoutais pas; **2 to**

**listen to** écouter [1]; **listen to the music** écoutez la musique; **you're not listening to me** tu ne m'écoutes pas.

**listener** *noun* (*to the radio*) auditeur *Masc.*, auditrice *Fem.*

**literally** *adverb* littéralement.

**literature** *noun* littérature *Fem.*

**litre** *noun* litre *Masc.*; **a litre of milk** un litre de lait.

**litter** *noun* (*rubbbish*) détritus *Masc.* plural.

**litter bin** *noun* poubelle *Fem.*

**little** *adjective, pronoun* **1** (*small*) petit (*goes before the noun*); **a little boy** un petit garçon; **a little break** une petite pause; **2** (*not much*) peu (de); **they have little money** ils ont peu d'argent; **we have very little time** nous avons très peu de temps; **3 a little** un peu (de); **4 we have a little money** nous avons un peu d'argent; **just a little, please** juste un peu, s'il vous plaît; **it's a little late** c'est un peu tard; **a little more** un peu plus; **a little less** un peu moins; ★ **little by little** petit à petit.

**little finger** *noun* petit doigt *Masc.*

**live**[1] *verb* **1** (*in a house or town*) habiter [1]; **Susan lives in York** Susan habite à York; **we live in a flat** nous habitons dans un appartement; **they live at number 57** ils habitent au numéro cinquante-sept; **we're living in the country now** nous habitons à la campagne maintenant; **2** (*be or stay alive, spend one's life*) vivre [82]; **lions live in Africa** les lions vivent en Afrique; **they live on fruit** ils vivent de fruits; **they live together** ils vivent ensemble.

**live**[2] *adjective* **1** en direct (*a broadcast*); **a live concert** un concert en direct; **a broadcast live from Wembley** une émission en direct de Wembley; **2** (*alive*) vivant.

**lively** *adjective* animé (*a party or restaurant, for example*).

**liver** *noun* foie *Masc.*

**living** *noun* vie *Fem.*; **to earn a living** gagner sa vie.

**living room** *noun* salle *Fem.* de séjour.

**lizard** *noun* lézard *Masc.*

**load** *noun* **1** (*on a lorry*) chargement *Masc.*; **a (lorry-)load of bricks** un camion de briques; **2 a bus-load of tourists** un autobus plein de touristes; **3 loads of** des tas de (*informal*); **loads of people** des tas de gens; **they've got loads of money** ils sont bourrés de fric (*informal*).
**load** *verb* charger [52]; **a lorry loaded with wood** un camion chargé de bois.

**loaf** *noun* pain *Masc.*; **a loaf of wholemeal bread** un pain complet.

**loan** *noun* prêt *Masc.*
**loan** *verb* prêter [1].

**loathe** *verb* détester [1]; **I loathe getting up early** je déteste me lever tôt.

**lobster** *noun* homard *Masc.*

**local** *noun* **1** (*a pub*) pub *Masc.* du coin; **2 the locals** (*people*) les gens du coin.
**local** *adjective* **the local library** la

a b c d e f g h i j k **l** m n o p q r s t u v w x y z

bibliothèque du coin; **the local newspaper** le journal local.

**locally** *adverb* de façon locale; **they only advertise locally** ils ne font de publicité que dans la région.

**lock** *noun* **1** (*with a key*) serrure *Fem.*; **2** (*on a canal*) écluse *Fem.*
**lock** *verb* **to lock the door** fermer [1] la porte à clé; **the door was locked** la porte était fermée à clé.

**locker** *noun* casier *Masc.*

**locker room** *noun* vestiaire *Masc.*

**lodger** *noun* locataire *Masc. & Fem.*

**loft** *noun* grenier *Masc.*

**log** *noun* bûche *Fem.*; **a log fire** un feu de bois.

**logical** *adjective* logique.

**lollipop** *noun* sucette *Fem.*

**London** *noun* Londres; **to London** à Londres; **a day in London** une journée à Londres; **the London streets** les rues de Londres.

**Londoner** *noun* Londonien *Masc.*, Londonienne *Fem.*

**loneliness** *noun* solitude *Fem.*

**lonely** *adjective* **1** seul; **to feel lonely** se sentir [53] seul; **2** (*a place*) isolé.

**long** *adjective, adverb* **1** long (*Fem.* longue); **a long film** un film long; **a long day** une longue journée; **it's an hour long** ça dure une heure; **2 a long time** longtemps; **he stayed for a long time** il est resté longtemps; **I've been here for a long time** je suis là depuis longtemps; **a long time ago** il y a longtemps; **this won't take long** ça ne prendra pas longtemps; **3 how long?** combien de

temps?; **how long have you been here?** tu es là depuis combien de temps?; **long ago** il y a longtemps; **4 a long way** loin; **it's a long way to the cinema** le cinéma est loin d'ici; **5 all night long** toute la nuit.
**long** *verb* **to long to do** avoir [5] très envie de faire; **I'm longing to see you** j'ai très envie de te voir.

**long-distance call** *noun* (*within the country*) appel *Masc.* interurbain.

**longer** *adverb* **no longer** ne ...plus; **I no longer know** je ne sais plus; **they no longer live here** ils n'habitent plus ici.

**long jump** *noun* saut *Masc.* en longueur.

**longlife milk** *noun* lait *Masc.* longue conservation.

**loo** *noun* toilettes *Fem. plural.*

**look** *noun* **1** (*a glance*) coup *Masc.* d'œil; **to have a look at something** jeter un coup d'œil à quelque chose; **2** (*a tour*) **to have a look round the town** faire un tour dans la ville; **to have a look round the shops** faire les magasins; **3 to have a look for** chercher (*something you've lost*).
**look** *verb* **1** regarder [1]; **I wasn't looking** je ne regardais pas; **to look out of the window** regarder par la fenêtre; **2 to look at** regarder [1]; **Andy was looking at the photos** Andy regardait les photos; **3** (*to seem*) avoir [5] l'air; **Melanie looks pleased** Melanie a l'air contente; **the salad looks delicious** la salade a l'air délicieuse; **4 to look like** ressembler [1] à; **Sally looks like her aunt** Sally ressemble à sa tante;

they look like each other ils se ressemblent; **what does the house look like?** comment est la maison?; **it looks like rain** on dirait qu'il va pleuvoir.

● **to look after 1** s'occuper [1] de; **Dad's looking after the baby** Papa s'occupe du bébé; **2** surveiller [1] (*luggage*)**to look for** chercher [1]; **I'm looking for the keys** je cherche les clés.

● **to look forward to something** attendre [3] quelque chose avec impatience (*a party or a trip, for example*)

● **to look out** (*to be careful*) faire [10] attention; **look out, it's hot!** (fais) attention, c'est chaud!

● **to look something up** chercher [1] quelque chose (*in a dictionary or directory*); **you can look it up in the dictionary** tu peux le chercher dans le dictionnaire.

**loose** *adjective* **1** (*a screw or knot*) desserré; **2** (*a garment*) ample; **3 loose change** la petite monnaie; ★ **I'm at a loose end** je ne sais pas trop quoi faire.

**lorry** *noun* camion *Masc.*

**lorry driver** *noun* routier *Masc.*

**lose** *verb* **1** perdre [3]; **we lost** nous avons perdu; **we lost the match** nous avons perdu le match; **Sam's lost his watch** Sam a perdu sa montre; **2 to get lost** se perdre [3]; **we got lost in the woods** nous nous sommes perdus dans les bois.

**loss** *noun* perte *Fem.*

**lost** *adjective* perdu; **I'm lost** je suis perdu; **are you lost?** vous êtes perdu?

**lost property** *noun* objets *Masc. plural* trouvés.

**lot** *noun* **1 a lot** beaucoup; **Jason eats a lot** Jason mange beaucoup; **I spent a lot** j'ai beaucoup dépensé; **he's a lot better** il va beaucoup mieux; **2 a lot of** beaucoup de; **a lot of coffee** beaucoup de café; **lots of people** beaucoup de gens; **'what are you doing tonight?'** – **'not a lot'** 'qu'est-ce que tu fais ce soir?' – 'pas grand-chose'.

**lottery** *noun* loterie *Fem.*; **to win the lottery** gagner à la loterie.

**loud** *adjective* **1** fort; **in a loud voice** d'une voix forte; **2 to say something out loud** dire quelque chose à haute voix.

**loudly** *adverb* fort.

**loudspeaker** *noun* haut-parleur *Masc.* (*plural* haut-parleurs).

**lounge** *noun* **1** (*in a house or hotel*) salon *Masc.*; **2** (*in an airport*) **the departure lounge** la salle d'embarquement.

**love** *noun* **1** amour *Masc.*; **to be in love with somebody** être amoureux (*Fem.* amoureuse) de quelqu'un; **she's in love with Jake** elle est amoureuse de Jake; **Gina sends her love** Gina t'embrasse; **with love from Charlie** amitiés, Charlie; **2** (*in tennis*) zéro *Masc.*

**love** *verb* **1** aimer [1] (*a person*) **I love you** je t'aime; **2** aimer beaucoup (*place, suggestion*); **she loves London** elle aime beaucoup Londres; **I'd love to come** j'aimerais beaucoup venir; **3** adorer [1] (*activity, thing*); **I love dancing** j'adore danser; **Wayne loves**

a b c d e f g h i j k **l** m n o p q r s t u v w x y z

seafood Wayne adore les fruits de mer.

**lovely** *adjective* 1 (*to look at*) joli; **a lovely dress** une jolie robe; **their garden is lovely** leur jardin est très joli; **a lovely house** une belle maison; 2 **it's a lovely day** il fait très beau; **we had lovely weather** il a fait très beau; 3 (*food, meal*) délicieux (*Fem.* délicieuse).

**lover** *noun* 1 (*general*) partenaire *Masc. & Fem.*; 2 (*of married man*) maîtresse *Fem.*; (*of married woman*) amant *Masc.*

**low** *adjective* bas (*Fem.* basse); **a low table** une table basse; **at a low price** à prix bas; **in a low voice** à voix basse.

**lower** *adjective* (*not as high*) inférieur.
**lower** *verb* baisser [1].

**low-fat milk** *noun* lait *Masc.* écrémé.

**loyalty** *noun* loyauté *Fem.*; **loyalty card** carte *Fem.* de fidélité.

**luck** *noun* chance *Fem.*; **good luck!** bonne chance!; **bad luck!** pas de chance!; **with a bit of luck** avec un peu de chance.

**luckily** *adverb* heureusement; **luckily for them** heureusement pour eux.

**lucky** *adjective* 1 **to be lucky** (*a person*) avoir de la chance; **we were lucky** nous avons eu de la chance; 2 **to be lucky** (*bringing luck*) porter bonheur; **it's supposed to be lucky** c'est censé porter bonheur; **my lucky number** mon numéro porte-bonheur.

**luggage** *noun* bagages *Masc. plural*; **my luggage is in the boot** mes bagages sont dans le coffre.

**lump** *noun* 1 (*of earth*) motte *Fem.*; 2 (*piece*) morceau *Masc.* (*plural* morceaux); 3 (*swelling*) grosseur *Fem.*

**lunch** *noun* déjeuner *Masc.*; **to have lunch** déjeuner [1]; **we had lunch in Oxford** nous avons déjeuné à Oxford.

**lunch break** *noun* pause-déjeuner *Fem.*

**lunch hour**, **lunch time** *noun* heure *Fem.* du déjeuner.

**lung** *noun* poumon *Masc.*

**Luxembourg** *noun* 1 (*country*) Luxembourg *Masc.*; **to Luxembourg** au Luxembourg; **in Luxembourg** au Luxembourg; 2 (*city*) Luxembourg; **in Luxembourg** à Luxembourg.

**luxurious** *adjective* luxueux (*Fem.* luxueuse).

**luxury** *noun* luxe *Masc.*; **a luxury hotel** un hôtel de luxe.

**lyrics** *plural noun* paroles *Fem. plural.*

# Mm

**mac** *noun* imper *Masc.* (*informal*).

**macaroni** *noun* macaronis *Masc. plural*; **we had macaroni** nous avons mangé des macaronis.

**machine** *noun* machine *Fem.*

**machinery** *noun* machines *Fem. plural.*

**mackerel** *noun* maquereau *Masc.* (*plural* maquereaux).

**mad** *adjective* **1** fou (*Fem.* folle); **she's completely mad!** elle est complètement folle!; **2** (*angry*) furieux (*Fem.* furieuse); **my mum will be mad!** ma mère sera furieuse!; **3 to be mad about something** adorer quelque chose; **she's mad about horses** elle adore les chevaux.

**madam** *noun* madame *Fem.*

**madman** *noun* fou *Masc.*

**madness** *noun* folie *Fem.*

**magazine** *noun* magazine *Masc.*

**maggot** *noun* asticot *Masc.*

**magic** *noun* magie *Fem.*
**magic** *adjective* **1** magique; **a magic wand** une baguette magique; **2** (*great*) super.

**magician** *noun* **1** (*wizard*) magicien *Masc.*; **2** (*conjurer*) prestidigitateur *Masc.*

**magnet** *noun* aimant *Masc.*

**magnificent** *adjective* magnifique.

**magnifying glass** *noun* loupe *Fem.*

**magnolia** *noun* magnolia *Masc.*

**mahogany** *noun* acajou *Masc.*

**maiden name** *noun* nom *Masc.* de jeune fille.

**mail** *noun* courrier *Masc.*; **email** (*electronic mail*) courrier *Masc.* électronique.

**mail order** *noun* **to buy something by mail order** acheter quelque chose par correspondance; **a mail order catalogue** un catalogue de vente par correspondance.

**main** *adjective* principal (*Masc. plural* principaux); **the main entrance** l'entrée principale.

**main course** *noun* plat *Masc.* principal.

**mainly** *adverb* principalement.

**main road** *noun* route *Fem.* principale.

**maize** *noun* maïs *Masc.*

**major** *adjective* majeur.
**major** *noun* commandant *Masc.*

**Majorca** *noun* Majorque *Fem.*

**majority** *noun* majorité *Fem.*

**make** *noun* marque *Fem.*; **what make is your bike?** de quelle marque est ton vélo?
**make** *verb* **1** faire [10]; **I made an omelette** j'ai fait une omelette; **she made her bed** elle a fait son lit; **he made me wait** il m'a fait attendre; **she makes me laugh** elle me fait rire; **two and three make five** deux et trois font cinq; **2** fabriquer [1]; **they make computers** ils fabriquent des ordinateurs; **'made in France'** 'fabriqué en France'; **3** rendre [3]; **to make somebody happy** rendre quelqu'un heureux; **that makes me hungry** ça me donne faim; **4** gagner [1] (*money*); **he makes forty pounds a day** il gagne quarante livres par jour; **to make a living** gagner sa vie; **5** (*force*) **to make somebody do something** obliger [52] quelqu'un à faire quelque chose; **she made him give the money back** elle l'a obligé à rendre l'argent; **6 to make a meal**

a
b
c
d
e
f
g
h
i
j
k
l
**m**
n
o
p
q
r
s
t
u
v
w
x
y
z

préparer [1] un repas; **7 to make a phone call** passer [1] un coup de fil; **I have to make a few phone calls** je dois passer quelques coups de fil; **8 I can't make it tonight** je ne peux pas venir ce soir.

● **to make something up 1** inventer [1] quelque chose; **she made up an excuse** elle a inventé une excuse; **2 to make it up** (*after a quarrel*) se réconcilier [1]; **they've mad it up now** il se sont maintenant réconciliés

**make-up** *noun* maquillage *Masc.*; **to put on your make-up** se maquiller; **Jo's putting on her make-up** Jo est en train de se maquiller; **I don't wear make-up** je ne me maquille pas.

**male** *adjective* **1** mâle (*animal*); **a male rat** un rat mâle; **2** (*sex : on a form*) masculin; **3 a male rôle** un rôle pour homme; **a male voice** une voix d'homme; **a male student** un étudiant.

**male chauvinist** *noun* macho *Masc.*

**mall** *noun* centre *Masc.* commercial.

**Malta** *noun* Malte *Fem.*

**mammal** *noun* mammifère *Masc.*

**man** *noun* homme *Masc.*; **modern man is taller than his ancestors** l'homme moderne est plus grand que ses ancêtres.

**manage** *verb* **1** diriger [52] (*business, team*); **she manages a travel agency** elle dirige une agence de voyages; **2** (*cope*) se débrouiller [1]; **I can manage** je me débrouille; **3 to manage to do**

réussir [2] à faire; **he managed to open the door** il a réussi à ouvrir la porte; **I didn't manage to get in touch with her** je n'ai pas réussi à la contacter.

**management** *noun* **1** gestion *Fem.*; **a management course** un cours de gestion; **2** direction; **a meeting with management** une réunion avec la direction.

**manager** *noun* **1** (*of a company or a bank*) directeur *Masc.*, directrice *Fem.*; **2** (*of a shop or restaurant*) gérant *Masc.*, gérante *Fem.*; **3** (*in sport and entertainment*) manager *Masc.*

**manageress** *noun* gérante *Fem.*

**managing director** *noun* directeur *Masc.* général, directrice *Fem.* générale.

**mandarin (orange)** *noun* mandarine *Fem.*

**mango** *noun* mangue *Fem.*

**mania** *noun* manie *Fem.*

**maniac** *noun* fou *Masc.*, folle *Fem.*; **she drives like a maniac!** elle conduit comme une folle!

**mankind** *noun* humanité *Fem.*

**man-made** *adjective* (*fibre*) synthétique.

**manner** *noun* **1 in a manner of speaking** pour ainsi dire; **2 to have good manners** être poli; **it's bad manners to talk like that** ce n'est pas poli de parler comme ça.

**manpower** *noun* main-d'œuvre *Fem.*

**mansion** *noun* demeure *Fem.*

**mantelpiece** *noun* cheminée *Fem.*

**manual** *noun* manuel *Masc.*

**manufacture** *verb* fabriquer [1].

**manufacturer** *noun* fabricant *Masc.*

**manure** *noun* fumier *Masc.*

**many** *adjective, pronoun*
1 beaucoup (de); **does she have many friends?** est-ce qu'elle a beaucoup d'amis?; **we didn't see many people** nous n'avons pas vu beaucoup (de) gens; **not many** pas beaucoup; **there aren't many onions left** il ne reste pas beaucoup d'oignons; **many of them forgot** beaucoup d'entre eux ont oublié;
2 **very many** beaucoup (de); **there aren't very many glasses** il n'y a pas beaucoup de verres; 3 **so many** tant; **I have so many things to do!** j'ai tant de choses à faire!; 4 **so many** autant de; **I've never eaten so many strawberries** je n'ai jamais mangé autant de fraises;
5 **as many as** autant que; **you can take as many as you like** tu peux en prendre autant que tu veux; 6 **too many** trop (de); **I've got too many things to do** j'ai trop de choses à faire; **there were too many people** il y avait trop de monde; **that's far too many!** c'est beaucoup trop!;
7 **how many?** combien?; **how many are there?** il y en a combien?; **how many sisters have you got?** tu as combien de sœurs?; **how many are there left?** il en reste combien?

**map** *noun* 1 carte *Fem.*; **a road map** une carte routière; 2 (*of a town*) plan *Masc.*

**marathon** *noun* marathon *Masc.*

**marble** *noun* 1 marbre *Masc.*; **a marble fireplace** une cheminée en marbre; 2 bille; **to play marbles** jouer aux billes.

**march** *noun* (*demonstration*) manifestation *Fem.*
**march** *verb* (*demonstrators*) défiler [1].

**March** *noun* mars *Masc.*; **in March** en mars.

**mare** *noun* jument *Fem.*

**margarine** *noun* margarine *Fem.*

**margin** *noun* marge *Fem.*

**marijuana** *noun* marijuana *Fem.*

**mark** *noun* 1 (*at school*) note *Fem.*; **I got a good mark for my French homework** j'ai eu une bonne note pour mon devoir de français; **what mark did you get for French?** tu as eu combien en français?; 2 (*stain*) tache *Fem.*
**mark** *verb* corriger [52]; **the teacher marks our homework** le professeur corrige nos devoirs.

**market** *noun* marché *Masc.*

**marketing** *noun* marketing *Masc.*

**marmalade** *noun* confiture *Fem.* d'oranges amères.

**maroon** *adjective* bordeaux; **a maroon jumper** un pull bordeaux.

**marriage** *noun* mariage *Masc.*

**married** *adjective* marié; **a married couple** un couple marié; **they've been married for twenty years** ils sont mariés depuis vingt ans.

**marry** *verb* 1 **to marry somebody** épouser [1] quelqu'un; **she married a Frenchman** elle a épousé un Français; 2 **to get married** se marier [1]; **they got married in July** ils se sont mariés en juillet.

a
b
c
d
e
f
g
h
i
j
k
l
**m**
n
o
p
q
r
s
t
u
v
w
x
y
z

## marvellous

**marvellous** *adjective* merveilleux (*Fem.* merveilleuse); **the weather's marvellous** il fait un temps merveilleux.

**marzipan** *noun* pâte *Fem.* d'amandes.

**mascara** *noun* mascara *Masc.*

**masculine** *noun* (*in French and other grammars*) masculin *Masc.*; **in the masculine** au masculin.

**mash** *verb* écraser [1] (*vegetables*).

**mashed potatoes** *noun* purée *Fem.* de pommes de terre.

**mask** *noun* masque *Masc.*

**mass** *noun* 1 **a mass of** une masse de; 2 **masses of** beaucoup de; **they've got masses of money** ils ont beaucoup d'argent; **there's masses left over** il en reste beaucoup; 3 (*religious*) messe *Fem.*; **to go to mass** aller à la messe.

**massacre** *noun* massacre *Masc.*

**massage** *noun* massage *Masc.*

**massive** *adjective* énorme.

**master** *verb* maîtriser [1].

**masterpiece** *noun* chef-d'œuvre *Masc.* (*plural* chefs-d'œuvre).

**mat** *noun* 1 (*doormat*) paillasson *Masc.*; 2 (*to put under a hot dish*) dessous-de-plat *Masc.*; 3 **a table mat** un set de table.

**match** *noun* 1 allumette *Fem.*; **a box of matches** une boîte d'allumettes; 2 (*sports*) match *Masc.* (*plural* matchs); **a football match** un match de foot; **to watch the match** regarder [1] le match; **to win the match** gagner [1] le match; **to lose the match** perdre [3] le match.

**match** *verb* être [6] assorti à; **the jacket matches the skirt** la veste est assortie à la jupe.

**matching** *adjective* **matching curtains and cushions** des rideaux et des coussins assortis.

**mate** *noun* copain *Masc.*, copine *Fem.* (*informal*); **I'm going out with my mates tonight** je sors avec mes copains ce soir.

**material** *noun* 1 (*fabric*) tissu *Masc.*; 2 (*information*) documentation *Fem.*; 3 (*substance*) matière *Fem.*; **raw materials** les matières *Fem. plural* premières.

**mathematics** *noun* mathématiques *Fem. plural*.

**maths** *noun* maths *Fem. plural*; **I like maths** j'aime bien les maths; **Anna's good at maths** Anna est forte en maths.

**matter** *noun* **what's the matter?** qu'est-ce qu'il y a? **matter** *verb* 1 **the things that matter** les choses importantes; **it matters a lot to me** c'est très important pour moi; 2 **it doesn't matter** ça ne fait rien; **it doesn't matter if it rains** ça ne fait rien s'il pleut; 3 **it doesn't matter** (*whether one thing or another*) ça n'a pas d'importance; **you can write it in French or English, it doesn't matter** tu peux l'écrire en français ou en anglais, ça n'a pas d'importance.

**mattress** *noun* matelas *Masc.*

**mature** *adjective* mûr.

**maximum** *noun* maximum *Masc.*; **the maximum possible** le maximum possible.

**maximum** *adjective* maximum (*does not change in the feminine or plural*); **the maximum temperature** la température maximum; **maximum profits** les bénéfices maximum.

**May** *noun* mai *Masc.*; **in May** en mai.

**may** *verb* **1** she may be ill elle est peut-être malade; **we may go to Spain** nous irons peut-être en Espagne; **2** (*asking permission*) **may I close the door?** est-ce que je peux fermer la porte?

**maybe** *adverb* peut-être; **maybe not** peut-être pas; **maybe he's forgotten** il a peut-être oublié; **maybe they've got lost** ils se sont peut-être perdus.

**May Day** *noun* le Premier Mai.

**mayonnaise** *noun* mayonnaise *Fem.*

**mayor** *noun* maire *Masc.*

**mayoress** *noun* mairesse *Fem.*

**me** *pronoun* **1** me, m' (*before a vowel or silent 'h'*); **she knows me** elle me connaît; **can you help me, please?** est-ce que tu peux m'aider, s'il te plaît?; **can you lend me a pen?** peux-tu me prêter un stylo?; **can you give me your address?** peux-tu me donner ton adresse?; **2** (*after a preposition*) moi; **I took her with me** je l'ai emmenée avec moi; **they left without me** ils sont partis sans moi; **3** (*in commands*) moi; **listen to me!** écoute-moi!; **wait for me!** attends-moi!; **excuse me!** excusez-moi!; **4** (*in comparisons*) **than me** que moi; **she's older than me** elle est

plus âgée que moi; **5 me too!** moi aussi!

**meadow** *noun* pré *Masc.*

**meal** *noun* repas *Masc.*; **they have three meals a day** ils mangent trois fois par jour.

**mean** *verb* **1** vouloir [14] dire; **what do you mean?** qu'est-ce que tu veux dire?; **what does that mean?** qu'est-ce que ça veut dire?; **that's not what I meant** ce n'est pas ce que je voulais dire; **2 to mean to do** avoir [5] l'intention de faire; **I meant to phone my mother** j'avais l'intention d'appeler ma mère; **3 to be meant to do** devoir faire; **she was meant to be here at six** elle devait être là à six heures.

**mean** *adjective* **1** (*with money*) radin (*informal*); **2** (*unkind*) méchant; **she's really mean to her brother** elle est vraiment méchante avec son frère; **what a mean thing to do!** c'est vraiment méchant!

**meaning** *noun* sens *Masc.*

**means** *noun* moyen *Masc.*; **a means of transport** un moyen de transport; **a means of doing** un moyen de faire; **we have no means of contacting him** nous n'avons aucun moyen de le contacter; **by means of** au moyen de; **by all means** certainement.

**meantime** *noun* **for the meantime** pour le moment; **in the meantime** pendant ce temps.

**meanwhile** *adverb* pendant ce temps; **meanwhile she was waiting at the station** pendant ce temps, elle attendait à la gare.

a
b
c
d
e
f
g
h
i
j
k
l
**m**
n
o
p
q
r
s
t
u
v
w
x
y
z

**measles** *noun* rougeole *Fem.*

**measure** *verb* mesurer [1].

**measurements** *plural noun*
1 (*of a room or an object*) dimensions *Fem. plural*; **the measurements of the room** les dimensions de la pièce; 2 (*of a person*) mensurations *Fem. plural*; **my chest measurement** mon tour de poitrine; **my waist measurement** mon tour de taille.

**meat** *noun* viande *Fem.*

**Mecca** *noun* Mecque *Fem.*

**mechanic** *noun* mécanicien *Masc.*; **he's a mechanic** il est mécanicien.

**mechanical** *adjective* mécanique.

**medal** *noun* médaille *Fem.*; **the gold medal** la médaille d'or.

**media** *noun* **the media** les médias *Masc. plural.*

**medical** *noun* visite *Fem.* médicale; **to have a medical** passer une visite médicale.

**medical** *adjective* médical (*Masc. plural* médicaux); **do you have medical insurance?** est-ce que vous avez une assurance-maladie?

**medicine** *noun* 1 médicament *Masc.*; **I'd like some cough medecine** je voudrais un médicament pour la toux; 2 (*subject of study*) médecine *Fem.*; **she's studying medicine** elle fait des études de médecine; 3 **alternative medecine** la médecine douce.

**medieval** *adjective* médiéval, du moyen-âge.

**Mediterranean** *noun* **the Mediterranean** la Méditerranée.

**medium** *adjective* moyen (*Fem.* moyenne).

**medium-sized** *noun* de taille moyenne.

**meet** *verb* 1 (*by chance*) rencontrer [1]; **I met Rosie outside the baker's** j'ai rencontré Rosie devant la boulangerie; 2 (*by appointment*) retrouver [1]; **I'll meet you outside the cinema at six** je te retrouverai devant le cinéma à six heures; 3 se retrouver [1]; **we're meeting at six** nous allons nous retrouver à six heures; 4 (*get to know*) faire [10] la connaissance de; **I met a French girl last week** j'ai fait la connaissance d'une Française la semaine dernière; 5 **Tom, have you met Oskar?** Tom, est-ce que tu connais Oskar?; 6 (*off a train, bus, etc*) venir [81] chercher; **my dad's meeting me at the station** mon père vient me chercher à la gare.

**meeting** *noun* réunion *Fem.*; **there's a meeting at ten o'clock** il y a une réunion à dix heures; **she's in a meeting** elle est en réunion.

**megabyte** *noun* mégaoctet *Masc.*

**melody** *noun* mélodie *Fem.*

**melon** *noun* melon *Masc.*

**melt** *verb* 1 fondre [3]; **it melts in your mouth** ça fond dans la bouche; 2 **to melt something** faire [10] fondre quelque chose; **melt the butter in a saucepan** faites fondre le beurre dans une casserole.

**member** *noun* membre *Masc.*; **she's a member of the Labour Party** elle est membre du parti travailliste.

486

**metal**

**Member of Parliament** *noun* député *Masc.*

**membership** *noun* adhésion *Fem.*

**membership card** *noun* carte *Fem.* de membre.

**membership fee** *noun* cotisation *Fem.*

**memorial** *noun* **a war memorial** un monument aux morts.

**memorial service** *noun* messe *Fem.* commémorative.

**memorize** *verb* **to memorize something** apprendre [64] quelque chose par cœur.

**memory** *noun* **1** (*of a person or computer*) mémoire *Fem.*; **you have a good memory!** tu as bonne mémoire!; **I have a bad memory** je n'ai pas de mémoire; **2** (*of the past*) souvenir *Masc.*; **I have good memories of my stay in France** j'ai de bons souvenirs de mon séjour en France.

**mend** *verb* réparer [1].

**meningitis** *noun* méningite *Fem.*

**mental** *adjective* mental (*Masc. plural* mentaux); **a mental illness** une maladie mentale; **a mental hospital** un hôpital psychiatrique.

**mention** *verb* mentionner [1].

**menu** *noun* menu *Masc.*; **on the menu** au menu; **is there a set menu?** est-ce qu'il y a un menu à prix fixe?

**mercy** *noun* pitié *Fem.*

**merge** *verb* **1** (*roads*) se rejoindre [49]; **2** (*documents*) fusionner [1].

**meringue** *noun* meringue *Fem.*

**merit** *noun* mérite *Masc.*

**mermaid** *noun* sirène *Fem.*

**merry** *adjective* **1** joyeux (*Fem.* joyeuse); **Merry Christmas** Joyeux Noël; **2** (*from drinking*) éméché (*informal*).

**merry-go-round** *noun* manège *Masc.*

**mess** *noun* désordre *Masc.*; **my papers are in a mess** mes papiers sont dans le désordre; **to make a mess** mettre du désordre; **to clear up the mess** mettre de l'ordre; **what a mess!** quelle pagaille! (*informal*).

- **to mess about** faire [10] l'imbécile; **stop messing about!** arrête de faire l'imbécile!

- **to mess about with something** jouer [1] avec quelque chose; **it's dangerous to mess about with matches** il est dangereux de jouer avec les allumettes.

- **to mess something up** mettre [11] la pagaille dans quelque chose (*informal*); **you've messed up all my papers** tu as mis la pagaille dans tous mes papiers.

**message** *noun* message *Masc.*; **a telephone message** un message téléphonique.

**messenger** *noun* messager *Masc.*

**messy** *adjective* **1** **it's a messy job** c'est un travail salissant; **2** **he's a messy eater** il mange n'importe comment; **her writing's really messy** elle écrit n'importe comment.

**metal** *noun* métal *Masc.* (*plural* métaux).

487

a
b
c
d
e
f
g
h
i
j
k
l
m
n
o
p
q
r
s
t
u
v
w
x
y
z

**meter** *noun* **1** (*electricity, gas, taxi*) compteur *Masc.*; **to read the meter** relever le compteur; **2 a parking meter** un parcmètre.

**method** *noun* méthode *Fem.*

**Methodist** *noun* méthodiste *Masc. & Fem.*; **I'm a Methodist** je suis méthodiste.

**metre** *noun* mètre *Masc.*

**metric** *adjective* métrique.

**Mexican** *noun* Mexicain *Masc.*, Mexicaine *Fem.*
**Mexican** *adjective* mexicain.

**Mexico** *noun* Mexique *Masc.*; **in Mexico** au Mexique; **to Mexico** au Mexique.

**microchip** *noun* puce *Fem.*

**microphone** *noun* microphone *Masc.*

**microscope** *noun* microscope *Masc.*

**microwave oven** *noun* four *Masc.* à micro-ondes.

**midday** *noun* midi *Masc.*; **at midday** à midi.

**middle** *noun* **1** milieu *Masc.*; **in the middle of the room** au milieu de la pièce; **in the middle of the night** au milieu de la nuit; **2 to be in the middle of doing** être en train de faire; **when she phoned I was in the middle of washing my hair** quand elle a appelé j'étais en train de me laver les cheveux.

**middle-aged** *adjective* d'un certain âge; **a middle-aged lady** une dame d'un certain âge.

**middle-class** *adjective* de la classe moyenne; **a middle-class** family une famille de la classe moyenne.

**Middle-East** *noun* Moyen-Orient *Masc.*; **in the Middle East** au Moyen-Orient.

**middle finger** *noun* majeur *Masc.*

**midge** *noun* moucheron *Masc.*

**midnight** *noun* minuit *Masc.*; **at midnight** à minuit.

**Midsummer's Day** *noun* la Saint Jean.

**midwife** *noun* sage-femme *Fem.*

**might** *verb* 'are you going to phone him?' – 'I might' 'est-ce que tu vas l'appeler? – 'peut-être'; **I might invite Jo** j'inviterai peut-être Jo; **Amanda might know** Amanda le saurait peut-être; **he might have forgotten** il a peut-être oublié.

**migraine** *noun* migraine *Fem.*

**mike** *noun* micro *Masc.* (*informal*).

**mild** *adjective* doux (*Fem.* douce); **it's quite mild today** il fait plutôt doux aujourd'hui.

**mile** *noun* **1** mille *Masc.* (*the French use kilometres for distances; to convert miles roughly to kilometres, multiply by 8 and divide by 5*) **the village is ten miles from Oxford** le village est à seize kilomètres d'Oxford; **2 it's miles better!** c'est dix fois meilleur!

**mileage** *noun* kilométrage *Masc.*; **what's the mileage on your car?** elle a combien de kilomètres, votre voiture?

**military** *adjective* militaire.

**milk** *noun* lait *Masc.*; **full-cream milk** le lait entier; **skimmed milk** le lait écrémé; **semi-skimmed milk** le lait demi-écrémé.

**milk** *verb* traire [78].

**milk chocolate** *noun* chocolat *Masc.* au lait.

**milk jug** *noun* pot *Masc.* à lait.

**milkman** *noun* laitier *Masc.*

**milk shake** *noun* milk-shake *Masc.*

**millennium** *noun* millénaire *Masc.*

**millimetre** *noun* millimètre *Masc.*

**million** *noun* million *Masc.*; **a million people** un million de personnes; **two million people** deux millions de personnes.

**millionaire** *noun* millionnaire *Masc.*

**mimic** *verb* imiter [1].

**mince** *noun* viande *Fem.* hachée.

**mind** *noun* 1 esprit *Masc.*; **it crossed my mind that ...** il m'est venu à l'esprit que ...; **2 to change your mind** changer d'avis; **I've changed my mind** j'ai changé d'avis; **3 to make up your mind** se décider; **I can't make up my mind** je n'arrive pas à me décider.

**mind** *verb* **1** surveiller [1]; **can you mind my bag for me?** est-ce que tu peux surveiller mon sac?; **2** s'occuper [1] de (*baby*); **could you mind the baby for ten minutes?** est-ce que tu peux t'occuper du bébé pendant dix minutes?; **3 do you mind if ...?** est-ce que cela vous dérange si ...?; **do you mind if I close the door?** est-ce que cela vous dérange si je ferme la porte?; **I don't mind** cela ne me dérange pas; **I don't mind the heat** la chaleur ne me dérange pas; **4 mind the step!**

attention à la marche!; **5 never mind!** peu importe!

**mine**[1] *noun* mine *Fem.*; **a coal mine** une mine de charbon.

**mine**[2] *pronoun* **1** (*for a masculine noun*) le mien; **she took her hat and I took mine** elle a pris son chapeau et j'ai pris le mien; **2** (*for a feminine noun*) la mienne; **she gave me her address and I gave her mine** elle m'a donné son adresse et je lui ai donné la mienne; **3** (*for a masculine plural noun*) les miens; **Karen's invited her parents and I've invited mine** Karen a invité ses parents et j'ai invité les miens; **4** (*for a feminine plural noun*) les miennes; **she showed me her photos and I showed her mine** elle m'a montré ses photos et je lui ai montré les miennes; **5** à moi; **the green one's mine** le vert est à moi; **it's mine** c'est à moi.

**miner** *noun* mineur *Masc.*

**mineral water** *noun* eau *Fem.* minérale.

**miniature** *noun, adjective* miniature *Fem.*

**minibus** *noun* minibus *Masc.*

**minimum** *noun* minimum *Masc.*; **a minimum of** un minimum de. **minimum** *adjective* minimum (*does not change in the feminine or plural*); **the minimum age** l'âge minimum; **minimum safety measures** des mesures de sécurité minimum; **the minimum amount** le minimum.

**miniskirt** *noun* mini-jupe *Fem.*

a
b
c
d
e
f
g
h
i
j
k
l
m
n
o
p
q
r
s
t
u
v
w
x
y
z

a
b
c
d
e
f
g
h
i
j
k
l
**m**
n
o
p
q
r
s
t
u
v
w
x
y
z

**minister** *noun* **1** (*in government*) ministre *Masc.*; **2** (*of a church*) pasteur *Masc.*

**ministry** *noun* ministère *Masc.*

**minor** *adjective* mineur.

**minority** *noun* minorité *Fem.*

**mint** *noun* **1** (*herb*) menthe *Fem.*; **2** (*sweet*) bonbon *Masc.* à la menthe.

**minus** *preposition* moins; **seven minus three is four** sept moins trois égale quatre; **it was minus ten this morning** il a fait moins dix ce matin.

**minute**[1] *noun* minute *Fem.*; **just a minute!** une minute!; **I'll be ready in two minutes** je serai prêt dans deux minutes; **it's five minutes' walk from here** c'est à cinq minutes à pied d'ici.

**minute**[2] *adjective* minuscule; **the bedrooms are minute** les chambres sont minuscules.

**miracle** *noun* miracle *Masc.*

**mirror** *noun* **1** glace *Fem.*; **I looked at myself in the mirror** je me suis regardé dans la glace; **2** (*rearview mirror in a car*) rétroviseur *Masc.*

**misbehave** *verb* se conduire [26] mal.

**mischief** *noun* **to get up to mischief** faire des bêtises.

**mischievous** *adjective* coquin.

**miser** *noun* avare *Masc. & Fem.*

**miserable** *adjective* **1** malheureux (*Fem.* malheureuse); **he was miserable without her** il était malheureux sans elle; **I feel really miserable today** je n'ai vraiment pas le moral aujourd'hui;

**2 it's miserable weather** il fait un sale temps; **3 she gets paid a miserable wage** elle gagne un salaire de misère.

**misery** *noun* souffrance *Fem.*; **he was in misery** il était extrêmement malheureux.

**misfire** *verb* tomber [1] à plat; **our plans misfired** nos projets sont tombés à plat.

**misfortune** *noun* malheur *Masc.*

**misjudge** *verb* **1** mal évaluer [1]; **she misjudged the distance** elle a mal évalué la distance; **2** mal juger [52] (*a person*); **everybody had misjudged her** tout le monde l'avait mal jugée.

**mislay** *verb* égarer [1]; **I've mislaid my keys** j'ai égaré mes clés.

**misleading** *adjective* trompeur (*Fem.* trompeuse); **it's a misleading advertisement** c'est une publicité trompeuse.

**Miss** *noun* Mademoiselle; **Miss Jones** Mademoiselle Jones; (*written as*) Mlle Jones.

**miss** *verb* **1** rater [1]; **she missed her train** elle a raté son train; **I missed the film** j'ai raté le film; **the ball missed the goal** le ballon a raté le but; **missed!** raté!; **2** manquer [1]; **he's missed several classes** il a manqué plusieurs cours; **to miss an opportunity** manquer une occasion; **3 I miss you** tu me manques; **she's missing her sister** sa sœur lui manque; **I miss France** la France me manque.

**missile** *noun* missile *Masc.*

**missing** *adjective* **1** manquant; **she's found the missing pieces** elle a trouvé les pièces manquantes; **the missing link** le chaînon manquant; **2 there's a plate missing** il manque une assiette; **there are three forks missing** il manque trois fourchettes; **3 to go missing** disparaître; **several things have gone missing lately** plusieurs choses ont disparu récemment; **three people are missing** trois personnes ont disparu.

**missionary** *noun* missionnaire *Masc. & Fem.*

**mist** *noun* brume *Fem.*

**mistake** *noun* **1** erreur *Fem.*; **by mistake** par erreur; **it was my mistake** c'était une erreur de ma part; **2** faute *Fem.*; **a spelling mistake** une faute d'orthographe; **you've made lots of mistakes** tu as fait beaucoup de fautes; **3 to make a mistake** (*be mistaken*) se tromper; **sorry, I made a mistake** je suis désolé, je me suis trompé.

**mistake** *verb* **I mistook you for your brother** je vous ai pris pour votre frère.

**mistaken** *adjective* **to be mistaken** se tromper; **you're mistaken** tu te trompes.

**mistletoe** *noun* gui *Masc.*

**misty** *adjective* brumeux (*Fem.* brumeuse); **a misty morning** un matin brumeux; **it's misty this morning** il y a de la brume ce matin.

**misunderstand** *verb* mal comprendre [64]; **I misunderstood** j'ai mal compris.

**misunderstanding** *noun* malentendu *Masc.*; **there's been a misunderstanding** il y a eu un malentendu.

**mix** *noun* **1** mélange *Masc.*; **a good mix of people** un bon mélange de gens; **2 a cake mix** une préparation pour gâteau.

**mix** *verb* **1** mélanger [52]; **mix all the ingredients together** mélangez tous les ingrédients; **2 to mix with** fréquenter [1]; **she mixes with lots of interesting people** elle fréquente beaucoup de gens intéressants.

● **1** mélanger [52]; **you've mixed up all my papers** tu as mélangé tous mes papiers; **you've got it all mixed up!** tu mélanges tout! (*story*); **2** (*confuse*) confondre [69]; **I get him mixed up with his brother** je le confonds avec son frère

**mixed** *adjective* varié; **a mixed programme** un programme varié.

**mixed salad** *noun* salade *Fem.* composée.

**mixed school** *noun* école *Fem.* mixte.

**mixer** *noun* batteur *Masc.* électrique.

**mixture** *noun* mélange *Masc.*; **it's a mixture of jazz and rock** c'est un mélange de jazz et de rock.

**moan** *verb* râler [1] (*informal*); **stop moaning!** arrête de râler!

**mobile home** *noun* mobile home *Masc.*

**mobile phone** *noun* téléphone *Masc.* portable.

**mock** *noun* (*mock exam*) examen *Masc.* blanc.

a
b
c
d
e
f
g
h
i
j
k
l
m
n
o
p
q
r
s
t
u
v
w
x
y
z

a

**mock** *verb* se moquer [1] de; **stop mocking me!** arrête de te moquer de moi!

b

c

**model** *noun* 1 (*type*) modèle *Masc.*; **the latest model** le dernier modèle; 2 (*fashion model*) mannequin *Masc.*; **she's a model** elle est mannequin de luxe; 3 (*of a plane, car, etc*) modèle *Masc.* réduit; **he makes models** il fait des modèles réduits; 4 (*of a building*) maquette *Fem.*; **a model of Westminster Abbey** une maquette de l'Abbaye de Westminster.

d

e

f

g

h

**model aeroplane** *noun* modèle *Masc.* réduit d'avion.

i

j

**model railway** *noun* chemin *Masc.* de fer miniature.

k

**model village** *noun* village *Masc.* miniature.

l

m

**modem** *noun* modem *Masc.*

n

**moderate** *adjective* modéré.

o

**modern** *adjective* moderne.

**modernize** *verb* moderniser [1].

p

**modern languages** *noun* langues *Fem. plural* vivantes.

q

r

**modest** *adjective* modeste.

**modify** *verb* modifier [1].

s

**moisture** *noun* humidité *Fem.*

t

**moisturizer** *noun* 1 (*lotion*) lait hydratant *Masc.*; 2 (*cream*) crème *Fem.* hydratante.

u

v

**mole** *noun* 1 (*animal*) taupe *Fem.*; 2 (*on skin*) graine *Fem.* de beauté.

w

**molecule** *noun* molécule *Fem.*

x

**molehill** *noun* taupinière *Fem.*

y

**moment** *noun* 1 instant *Masc.*; **he'll be here in a moment** il sera là dans un instant; **at any moment** à tout

z

instant; 2 **at the moment** en ce moment; **at the right moment** au bon moment.

**Monaco** *noun* Monaco.

**monarchy** *noun* monarchie *Fem.*

**monastery** *noun* monastère *Masc.*

**Monday** *noun* lundi *Masc.*; **on Monday** lundi; **I'm going out on Monday** je sors lundi; **see you on Monday!** à lundi!; **on Mondays** le lundi; **the museum is closed on Mondays** le musée est fermé le lundi; **every Monday** tous les lundis; **last Monday** lundi dernier; **next Monday** lundi prochain.

**money** *noun* argent *Masc.*; **I don't have enough money** je n'ai pas assez d'argent; **to make money** gagner de l'argent; **they gave me my money back** (*in a shop*) ils m'ont remboursé.

**money box** *noun* tirelire *Fem.*

**mongrel** *noun* chien *Masc.* bâtard.

**monitor** *noun* (*on computer*) moniteur *Masc.*

**monk** *noun* moine *Masc.*

**monkey** *noun* 1 singe *Masc.*; 2 **you little monkey!** petit galopin! (*informal*).

**monotonous** *adjective* monotone.

**monster** *noun* monstre *Masc.*

**month** *noun* mois *Masc.*; **in the month of May** au mois de mai; **this month** ce mois-ci; **next month** le mois prochain; **we're leaving next month** nous allons partir le mois prochain; **last month** le mois dernier; **every month** tous les mois; **in two months' time** dans deux mois; **at the end of the month** à la fin du mois.

**monthly** *adjective* mensuel (*Fem.* mensuelle); **a monthly payment** une mensualité.

**monument** *noun* monument *Masc.*

**mood** *noun* humeur *Fem.*; **to be in a good mood** être de bonne humeur; **to be in a bad mood** être de mauvaise humeur; **I'm not in the mood** ça ne me dit rien.

**moody** *adjective* lunatique.

**moon** *noun* lune *Fem.*; **by the light of the moon** au clair de lune; ★ **to be over the moon** être aux anges (*literally: to be at the level of the angels*).

**moonlight** *noun* clair *Masc.* de lune; **by moonlight** au clair de lune.

**moor** *noun* lande *Fem.*; **the Yorkshire moors** les landes du Yorkshire.
**moor** *verb* amarrer [1] (*a boat*).

**moped** *noun* mobylette™ *Fem.*

**moral** *noun* morale *Fem.*; **the moral of the story** la morale de l'histoire.
**moral** *adjective* moral (*Masc. plural* moraux).

**morale** *noun* moral *Masc.*; **to boost somebody's morale** remonter le moral à quelqu'un; **he's been trying to boost morale** il essaie de leur remonter le moral.

**morals** *noun* moralité *Fem.*

**more** *adverb* **1** plus; **more interesting** plus intéressant; **more difficult** plus difficile; **more slowly** plus lentement; **more easily** plus facilement; **2 more ...than** plus ...que; **the book's more interesting** than the film le livre est plus intéressant que le film.

**more** *adjective* **1** plus de; **they have more money than we do** ils ont plus d'argent que nous; **I'll have a little more milk** je prendrai un peu plus de lait; **2** (*of something you have already*) encore de; **would you like some more cake?** voulez-vous encore du gâteau?; **a few more glasses** encore quelques verres.

**more** *pronoun* **1** plus; **he eats more than me** il mange plus que moi; **2** (*of something you have already*) encore; **we need three more** il nous en faut encore trois; **I'll have a little more** je prendrai un peu plus; **I don't want any more** je n'en veux plus; **3 more and more** de plus en plus; **books are getting more and more expensive** les livres coûtent de plus en plus cher; **it takes more and more time** ça prend de plus en plus de temps; **4 more or less** plus ou moins; **it's more or less finished** c'est plus ou moins fini.

**morning** *noun* **1** matin *Masc.*; **this morning** ce matin; **tomorrow morning** demain matin; **yesterday morning** hier matin; **in the morning** le matin; **she doesn't work in the morning** elle ne travaille pas le matin; **on Friday mornings** le vendredi matin; **at six o'clock in the morning** à six heures du matin; **2** (*as a period of time spent doing something*) matinée; **I spent the whole morning doing the washing-up** j'ai passé toute la matinée à faire la vaisselle.

# Morocco

**Morocco** noun Maroc Masc.; to Morocco au Maroc; in Morocco au Maroc.

**mortgage** noun crédit Masc. (immobilier).

**Moscow** noun Moscou; in Moscow à Moscou.

**Moslem** noun musulman Masc., musulmane Fem.

**mosque** noun mosquée Fem.

**mosquito** noun moustique Masc.; a mosquito bite une piqûre de moustique.

**most** adjective, adverb, pronoun **1** (followed by a plural noun) la plupart de; **most children like chocolate** la plupart des enfants aiment le chocolat; **most of my friends** la plupart de mes amis; **2** (followed by a singular noun) presque tout; **they've eaten most of the chocolate** ils ont mangé presque tout le chocolat; **3 most of the time** la plupart du temps; **4 the most** (followed by adjective) le plus, la plus, les plus; **the most interesting film** le film le plus intéressant; **the most exciting story** l'histoire la plus passionnante; **the most boring books** les livres les plus ennuyeux; **5 the most** (followed by noun) le plus de; **I've got the most time** c'est moi qui ai le plus de temps; **6 the most** (after verb) le plus; **what I hate most is the noise** ce que je déteste le plus, c'est le bruit.

**moth** noun **1** (butterfly) papillon Masc. de nuit; **2** (clothes moth) mite Fem.

**Mother's Day** noun la fête des Mères (in France the last Sunday in May).

**mother** noun mère Fem.; my mother ma mère; Kate's mother la mère de Kate.

**mother-in-law** noun belle-mère Fem. (plural belles-mères).

**motion** noun mouvement Masc.

**motivated** adjective motivé.

**motivation** noun motivation Fem.

**motor** noun moteur Masc.

**motorbike** noun moto Fem.

**motorboat** noun bateau Masc. à moteur.

**motorcyclist** noun motocycliste Masc. & Fem.

**motorist** noun automobiliste Masc. & Fem.

**motor racing** noun course Fem. automobile.

**motorway** noun autoroute Fem.

**mouldy** adjective moisi.

**mountain** noun montagne Fem.; in the mountains à la montagne.

**mountain bike** noun VTT Masc. (short for 'vélo tout-terrain').

**mountaineer** noun alpiniste Masc. & Fem.

**mountaineering** noun alpinisme Masc.; to go mountaineering faire de l'alpinisme.

**mountainous** adjective montagneux (Fem. montagneuse).

**mouse** noun souris Fem. (both the animal and for a computer).

ENGLISH-FRENCH

**mousse** *noun* mousse *Fem.*;
**chocolate mousse** la mousse au
chocolat.

**moustache** *noun* moustache *Fem.*;
**a man with a moustache** un
moustachu.

**mouth** *noun* bouche *Fem.*

**mouthful** *noun* bouchée *Fem.*

**mouth organ** *noun* harmonica
*Masc.*; **to play the mouth organ**
jouer de l'harmonica.

**move** *noun* **1** (*to a different house*)
déménagement *Masc.*; **2** (*in a game*)
**your move!** à toi de jouer!
**move** *verb* **1** bouger [52]; **she
didn't move** elle n'a pas bougé;
**2 move up a bit** pousse-toi un peu;
**3** enlever [50] (*an object*); **can you
move your bag, please?** peux-tu
enlever ton sac, s'il te plaît?; **4** (*car,
traffic*) avancer [61]; **the traffic was
moving slowly** la circulation
avançait lentement; **5 to move
forward** avancer [61]; **he moved
forward a step** il s'est avancé d'un
pas; **6** (*move house*) déménager [52];
**we're moving on Tuesday** nous
déménageons mardi; **they've
moved to France** ils se sont
installés en France.

● **to move in** emménager [52]; **when
are you moving in?** quand est-ce
que tu emménages?

● **to move out** déménager [52]; **we're
moving out next week** nous
déménageons la semaine prochaine.

**movement** *noun* mouvement *Masc.*

**movie** *noun* film *Masc.*; **to go to the
movies** aller au cinéma.

**moving** *adjective* **1** en marche; **a
moving vehicle** un véhicule en
marche; **2** (*emotionally*) émouvant;
**it's a very moving film** c'est un film
très émouvant.

**mow** *verb* tondre [3]; **to mow the
grass** tondre la pelouse.

**mower** *noun* tondeuse *Fem.* à gazon.

**MP** *noun* député *Masc.*; **she is an MP**
elle est député.

**Mr** *noun* Monsieur (*usually
abbreviated to 'M.'*); **Mr Angus
Brown** M. Angus Brown.

**Mrs** *noun* Madame (*usually
abbreviated to 'Mme'*); **Mrs Mary
Hendry** Mme Mary Hendry.

**Ms** *noun* Madame (*usually
abbreviated to 'Mme'; note that there
is no direct equivalent to 'Ms' in
French, but 'Madame' may be used
whether the woman is married or
not*).

**much** *adjective, adverb, pronoun*
**1** beaucoup; **she doesn't eat much**
elle ne mange pas beaucoup; **we
don't go out much** nous ne sortons
pas beaucoup; **much more**
beaucoup plus; **much shorter**
beaucoup plus court; **2** (*followed by
a noun*) beaucoup de; **we don't have
much time** nous n'avons pas
beaucoup de temps; **there isn't
much butter left** il ne reste pas
beaucoup de beurre; **3 very much**
beaucoup; **thank you very much**
merci beaucoup; **I don't watch
television very much** je ne regarde
pas beaucoup la télé; **4 very much**
(*followed by a noun*) beaucoup de;
**there isn't very much milk** il n'y a
pas beaucoup de lait; **5 not much**

a
b
c
d
e
f
g
h
i
j
k
l
m
n
o
p
q
r
s
t
u
v
w
x
y
z

pas beaucoup; **'do you have a lot of homework?' – 'no, not much'** 'est-ce que tu as beaucoup de devoirs?' – 'non, pas beaucoup'; **6 so much** tellement; **we liked it so much!** nous l'avons tellement aimé!; **I have so much to do!** j'ai tellement de choses à faire!; **7 so much** autant; **you shouldn't have given me so much** tu n'aurais pas dû m'en donner autant; **8 as much as** autant que; **you can take as much as you like** tu peux en prendre autant que tu veux; **9 too much** trop (de); **her parents give her too much money** ses parents lui donnent trop d'argent; **that's far too much!** c'est beaucoup trop!; **10 how much?** combien (de)?; **how much is it?** ça coûte combien?; **how much do you want?** tu en veux combien?; **how much sugar do you want?** tu veux combien de sucre?

**mud** *noun* boue *Fem.*

**muddle** *noun* désordre *Masc.*; **to be in a muddle** être en désordre.

**muddy** *adjective* **1** (*path, road*) boueux (*Fem.* boueuse); **2** (*shoes, clothes*) couverts de boue; **your boots are all muddy** tes bottes sont couvertes de boue.

**mug** *noun* grande tasse *Fem.*; **a mug of coffee** une grande tasse de café. **mug** *verb* **to mug somebody** agresser [1] quelqu'un; **to be mugged** se faire [10] agresser; **my brother was mugged in the park** mon frère s'est fait agresser au parc.

**mugging** *noun* agression *Fem.*

**multiplication** *noun* multiplication *Fem.*

**multiply** *verb* multiplier [1]; **to multiply six by four** multiplier six par quatre.

**mum, mummy** *noun* **1** mère *Fem.*; **Tom's mum** la mère de Tom; **I'll ask my mum** je vais demander à ma mère; **2** (*within the family or as a name*) maman *Fem.*; **mum's not back yet** maman n'est pas encore rentrée.

**mumps** *noun* oreillons *Masc. plural.*

**murder** *noun* meurtre *Masc.* **murder** *verb* assassiner [1].

**murderer** *noun* assassin *Masc.*

**muscle** *noun* muscle *Masc.*

**muscular** *adjective* musclé.

**museum** *noun* musée *Masc.*; **to go to the museum** aller au musée.

**mushroom** *noun* champignon *Masc.*; **a mushroom salad** une salade aux champignons.

**music** *noun* musique *Fem.*; **pop music** la musique pop; **classical music** la musique classique.

**musical** *noun* comédie *Fem.* musicale. **musical** *adjective* **1 a musical instrument** un instrument de musique; **2 they're a very musical family** ils sont très musiciens dans la famille.

**musician** *noun* musicien *Masc.*, musicienne *Fem.*

**Muslim** *noun* musulman *Masc.*, musulmane *Fem.*

**mussel** *noun* moule *Fem.*

**must** *verb* **1** falloir [43] (*to express obligation 'falloir' is used as an impersonal verb*) **we must leave**

# Nn

**now** il faut partir maintenant (*the construction 'il faut que' is followed by a verb in the subjunctive*) **I must tell you something** il faut que je te dise quelque chose; **you must be there at eight** il faut que tu sois là à huit heures; **you must learn the vocabulary** il faut que tu apprennes le vocabulaire; **2** (*expressing probability*) devoir [8]; **you must be tired** tu dois être fatigué; **it must be five o'clock** il doit être cinq heures; **he must have forgotten** il a dû oublier.

**mustard** *noun* moutarde *Fem.*

**mutter** *verb* marmonner [1].

**my** *adjective* **1** (*before a masculine noun*) mon; **my brother** mon frère; **my book** mon livre; **2** (*before a feminine noun*) ma; **my sister** ma sœur; **my house** ma maison (*but 'ma' becomes 'mon' before a feminine noun beginning with a vowel or silent 'h'*) **my address** mon adresse; **3** (*before a plural noun*) mes; **my children** mes enfants; **4** (*with parts of the body*) le, la, les; **I had a glass in my hand** j'avais un verre à la main; **I'm washing my hands** je me lave les mains.

**myself** *pronoun* **1** **I've hurt myself** je me suis blessé; **2** **I said it myself** je l'ai dit moi-même; **3** **by myself** tout seul; **I did it by myself** je l'ai fait tout seul.

**mysterious** *adjective* mystérieux (*Fem.* mystérieuse).

**mystery** *noun* **1** mystère *Masc.*; **2** (*book*) roman *Masc.* policier.

**myth** *noun* mythe *Masc.*

**mythology** *noun* mythologie *Fem.*

**nail** *noun* **1** (*on finger or toe*) ongle *Masc.*; **to bite your nails** se ronger [52] les ongles; **2** (*metal*) clou *Masc.* **nail** *verb* clouer [1].

**nailbrush** *noun* brosse *Fem.* à ongles.

**nailfile** *noun* lime *Fem.* à ongles.

**nail scissors** *noun* ciseaux *Masc. plural* à ongles.

**nail varnish** *noun* vernis *Masc.* à ongles.

**nail varnish remover** *noun* dissolvant *Masc.*

**naked** *adjective* nu.

**name** *noun* **1** nom *Masc.*; **I've forgotten her name** j'ai oublié son nom; **what's your name?** comment vous appelez-vous?; **my name is Joy** je m'appelle Joy; **2** (*of a book or film*) titre *Masc.*

**nanny** *noun* nurse *Fem.*

**nap** *noun* petit somme *Masc.*; **to have a nap** faire un petit somme.

**napkin** *noun* serviette *Fem.*

**nappy** *noun* couche *Fem.*

**narrow** *adjective* étroit; **a narrow street** une rue étroite.

**nasty** *adjective* **1** (*mean*) méchant; **that was a nasty thing to do** c'était méchant; **2** (*unpleasant*) désagréable; **that's a nasty job** c'est une tâche désagréable; **3** (*bad*) mauvais; **a nasty smell** une mauvaise odeur.

**nation** *noun* nation *Fem.*

a
b
c
d
e
f
g
h
i
j
k
l
**m**
**n**
o
p
q
r
s
t
u
v
w
x
y
z

**national** *adjective* national (*Masc. plural* nationaux).

**national anthem** *noun* hymne *Masc.* national.

**nationality** *noun* nationalité *Fem.*

**national park** *noun* parc *Masc.* national (*plural* parcs nationaux).

**Nativity** *noun* nativité *Fem.*

**natural** *adjective* naturel (*Fem.* naturelle).

**naturally** *adverb* naturellement.

**nature** *noun* nature *Fem.*

**nature reserve** *noun* réserve *Fem.* naturelle.

**naughty** *adjective* vilain.

**nausea** *noun* nausée *Fem.*

**navel** *noun* nombril *Masc.*

**navigate** *verb* naviguer [1].

**navy** *noun* marine *Fem.*; **my uncle's in the navy** mon oncle est dans la marine.

**navy-blue** *adjective* bleu marine; **navy-blue gloves** des gants bleu marine.

**near** *adjective* proche; **the nearest shop** le magasin le plus proche.
**near** *adverb, preposition* 1 près; **they live quite near** ils habitent tout près; **to come nearer** s'approcher; 2 **near (to)** près de; **near the station** près de la gare.

**nearby** *adverb* tout près; **there's a park nearby** il y a un parc tout près.

**nearly** *adverb* presque; **nearly empty** presque vide; **we're nearly there** nous sommes presque arrivés.

**neat** *adjective* 1 (*well-organized*) bien rangé; **a neat desk** un bureau bien rangé; 2 soigné (*a garden, your clothes, or the way you look*).

**neatly** *adverb* avec soin.

**necessarily** *adverb* **not necessarily** pas forcément.

**necessary** *adjective* nécessaire; **if necessary** si besoin est.

**neck** *noun* 1 (*of a person*) cou *Masc.*; 2 (*of a garment*) encolure *Fem.*

**necklace** *noun* collier *Masc.*

**nectarine** *noun* nectarine *Fem.*

**need** *noun* **there's no need, I've done it already** inutile, c'est fait; **there's no need to wait** inutile d'attendre.
**need** *verb* 1 avoir [5] besoin de; **we need bread** nous avons besoin de pain; **they need help** ils ont besoin d'aide; **everything you need** tout ce qu'il vous faut; 2 (*to have to*) devoir [8]; **I need to drop in at the bank** je dois passer par la banque; 3 **you needn't decide today** tu n'es pas obligé de décider aujourd'hui; **you needn't wait** tu n'es pas obligé d'attendre.

**needle** *noun* aiguille *Fem.*

**negative** *noun* (*of a photo*) négatif *Masc.*

**neglected** *adjective* mal entretenu.

**neighbour** *noun* voisin *Masc.*, voisine *Fem.*; **we're going round to the neighbours'** on va chez les voisins.

**neighbourhood** *noun* quartier *Masc.*; **a nice neighbourhood** un quartier agréable.

**neither** *conjunction* 1 **neither ... nor** ni ...ni; **I have neither the time**

**nor the money** je n'ai ni le temps ni l'argent; **2 neither do I** moi non plus; **'I don't like fish' – 'neither do I'** 'je n'aime pas le poisson' – 'moi non plus' (*translations using 'non plus' can be used for many similar replies*) **'I wasn't invited' – 'neither was I'** 'je n'ai pas été invité' – 'moi non plus'; **"I didn't like the film' – 'neither did Kirsty'** je n'ai pas aimé le film' – 'Kirsty non plus'; **3 'which do you like?' – 'neither'** 'lequel aimes-tu?' – 'ni l'un ni l'autre'.

**nephew** *noun* neveu *Masc.* (*plural* neveux).

**nerve** *noun* **1** (*in the body*) nerf *Masc.*; **2 to lose one's nerve** perdre son courage; **3 you've got a nerve!** tu as un sacré culot! (*informal*); ★ **he gets on my nerves** il me tape sur les nerfs (*informal*).

**nervous** *adjective* nerveux (*Fem.* nerveuse); **to feel nervous** (*before a performance or an exam*) avoir le trac (*informal*).

**nervous breakdown** *noun* dépression *Fem.* nerveuse.

**nest** *noun* nid *Masc.*

**net** *noun* **1** (*for fishing or in tennis*) filet *Masc.*; **2** (*in football*) filets *Masc. plural*.

**Netherlands** *noun* Pays-Bas *Masc. plural*; **in the Netherlands** aux Pays-Bas.

**nettle** *noun* ortie *Fem.*

**network** *noun* réseau *Masc.* (*plural* réseaux).

**neutral** *noun* (*in a gearbox*) point *Masc.* mort; **to be in neutral** être au point mort.

**neutral** *adjective* neutre.

**never** *adjective* **1** ne ... jamais; **Ben never smokes** Ben ne fume jamais; **I've never seen the film** je n'ai jamais vu le film; **2** jamais; **'have you ever been to Spain?' – 'no, never'** 'est-ce que tu es déjà allé en Espagne?' – 'non, jamais'; **3 never again** plus jamais; **4 never mind!** peu importe!

**new** *adjective* **1** (*different or unknown to you*) nouveau (*Fem.* nouvelle); **have you seen their new house?** as-tu vu leur nouvelle maison?; **Debbie's new boyfriend** le nouveau copain de Debbie; **2** (*brand new*) neuf (*Fem.* neuve); **it's a new car** c'est une voiture neuve.

**newcomer** *noun* nouveau venu *Masc.* (*plural* nouveaux venus), nouvelle venue *Fem* (*plural* nouvelles venues).

**news** *plural noun* **1** (*everyday gossip*) nouvelle *Fem.*, nouvelles *Fem.* plural; **a piece of good news** une bonne nouvelle; **I've got good news** j'ai de bonnes nouvelles; **any news?** y a-t-il des nouvelles?; **2** (*on TV*) journal *Masc.*; **the midday news** le journal de midi; **3** (*on the radio*) **the news** les informations.

**newsagent** *noun* marchand *Masc.* de journaux; **at the newsagent's** chez le marchand de journaux.

**newspaper** *noun* journal *Masc.* (*plural* journaux).

**newsreader** *noun* présentateur *Masc.*, présentatrice *Fem.*

**New Year** *noun* le Nouvel An; **Happy New Year!** Bonne Année!

**New Year's Day** *noun* le jour de l'An.

a
b
c
d
e
f
g
h
i
j
k
l
m
n
o
p
q
r
s
t
u
v
w
x
y
z

**a**
**b**
**c**
**d**
**e**
**f**
**g**
**h**
**i**
**j**
**k**
**l**
**m**
**n**
**o**
**p**
**q**
**r**
**s**
**t**
**u**
**v**
**w**
**x**
**y**
**z**

**New Year's Eve** *noun* la Saint-Sylvestre.

**New Zealand** *noun* Nouvelle-Zélande *Fem.*

**New Zealander** *noun* Néo-Zélandais *Masc.*, Néo-Zélandaise *Fem.*

**next** *adjective* 1 prochain; **the next train is at ten** le prochain train est à dix heures; **next week** la semaine prochaine; **next Thursday** jeudi prochain; **next year** l'année prochaine; **the next time I see you** la prochaine fois que je te verrai; 2 (*following*) suivant; **I saw her the next week** je l'ai vue la semaine suivante; **the next day** le lendemain; **the letter arrived the next day** la lettre est arrivée le lendemain; 3 (*next-door*) voisin; **in the next room** dans la pièce voisine.

**next** *adverb* 1 (*afterwards*) ensuite; **what did he say next?** qu'est-ce qu'il a dit ensuite?; 2 (*now*) maintenant; **what shall we do next?** qu'est-ce qu'on fait maintenant?; 3 **next to** à côté de; **the girl next to Pat** la fille à côté de Pat; **it's next to the baker's** c'est à côté de la boulangerie.

**next door** *adverb* à côté; **they live next door** ils habitent à côté; **the girl next door** la fille d'à côté.

**nice** *adjective* 1 (*pleasant*) agréable; **we had a nice evening** nous avons passé une soirée agréable; **Brighton's a nice town** Brighton est une ville agréable; **have a nice time!** amusez-vous bien!; 2 (*attractive to look at*) joli; **that's a nice dress** elle est jolie, cette robe; 3 (*kind, friendly*) sympathique (*a*

*person*); **she's really nice** elle est vraiment sympathique; 4 **to be nice to somebody** être gentil avec quelqu'un; **she's been very nice to me** elle a été très gentille avec moi; 5 (*tasting good*) bon (*Fem.* bonne); **let's have a nice cup of tea** si on prenait une bonne tasse de thé; 6 (*weather*) **it's a nice day** il fait beau; **we had nice weather** il a fait beau.

**nick** *verb* (*steal*) piquer [1] (*informal*).

**nickname** *noun* surnom *Masc.*

**niece** *noun* nièce *Fem.*

**night** *noun* 1 (*before you go to bed*) soir *Masc.*; **what are you doing tonight?** qu'est-ce que tu fais ce soir?; **see you tonight!** à ce soir!; **I saw Greg last night** j'ai vu Greg hier soir; 2 (*after bedtime*) nuit *Fem.*; **it's cold at night** il fait froid la nuit; **to stay the night with somebody** coucher chez quelqu'un.

**night club** *noun* boîte *Fem.* de nuit.

**nightie** *noun* chemise *Fem.* de nuit.

**nightingale** *noun* rossignol *Masc.*

**nightmare** *noun* cauchemar *Masc.*; **to have a nightmare** faire un cauchemar.

**night-time** *noun* nuit *Fem.*

**nil** *noun* zéro *Masc.*; **they won four-nil** ils ont gagné quatre à zéro.

**nine** *number* neuf *Masc.*; **Jake's nine** Jake a neuf ans.

**nineteen** *number* dix-neuf *Masc.*; **Kate's nineteen** Kate a dix-neuf ans.

**ninety** *number* quatre-vingt-dix *Masc.*

**ninth** *number* neuvième; **on the ninth floor** au neuvième étage; **the ninth of June** le neuf juin.

**nitrogen** *noun* azote *Masc.*

**no** *adverb* non; **I said no** j'ai dit non; **no thank you** non merci.
**no** *adjective* **1** pas de; **we've got no bread** nous n'avons pas de pain; **no problem!** pas de problème!; **2** (*on a notice*) **'no smoking'** 'défense de fumer'; **'no parking'** 'stationnement interdit'.

**nobody** *pronoun* personne; **'who's there?' – 'nobody'** 'qui est là?' – 'personne'; **there's nobody in the kitchen** il n'y a personne dans la cuisine; **nobody knows me** personne ne me connaît; **nobody answered** personne n'a répondu.

**nod** *verb* (*to say yes*) faire [10] oui de la tête; **he nodded** il a fait oui de la tête.

**noise** *noun* bruit *Masc.*; **to make a noise** faire du bruit.

**noisy** *adjective* bruyant.

**none** *pronoun* **1** (*not one*) aucun (*Fem.* aucune); **'how many students failed the exam?' – 'none'** 'combien d'étudiants ont raté l'examen?' – 'aucun'; **none of the girls knows him** aucune des filles ne le connaît; **2 there's none left** il n'y en a plus; **there are none left** il n'y en a plus.

**nonsense** *noun* bêtises *Fem. plural*; **to talk nonsense** dire des bêtises; **nonsense! she's at least thirty!** tu dis des bêtises! elle a au moins trente ans!

**non-smoker** *noun* non-fumeur *Masc.*

**non-stop** *adjective* direct (*a train or flight*).
**non-stop** *adverb* sans arrêt; **she talks non-stop** elle parle sans arrêt.

**noodles** *plural noun* nouilles *Fem. plural*.

**noon** *noun* midi *Masc.*; **at (twelve) noon** à midi.

**no-one** *pronoun* personne; **'who's there?' – 'no-one'** 'qui est là?' – 'personne'; **there's no-one in the kitchen** il n'y a personne dans la cuisine; **no-one knows me** personne ne me connaît; **no-one answered** personne n'a répondu.

**nor** *conjunction* **1 neither ...nor** ni ...ni; **I have neither the time nor the money** je n'ai ni le temps ni l'argent; **2 nor do I** moi non plus; **'I don't like fish' – 'nor do I'** je n'aime pas le poisson' – 'moi non plus'; (*translations using 'non plus' can be used for many similar replies*) **'I wasn't invited' – 'nor was I'** je n'ai pas été invité' – 'moi non plus'.

**normal** *adjective* **1** normal (*Masc. plural* normaux); **2** (*usual*) habituel (*Fem.* habituelle).

**normally** *adverb* normalement.

**Normandy** *noun* Normandie *Fem.*; **in Normandy** en Normandie.

**north** *noun* nord *Masc.*; **in the north** au nord.
**north** *adjective, adverb* nord (*never agrees*); **the north side** le côté nord;

501

a

**a north wind** un vent du nord; **north of Paris** au nord de Paris.

b

**North America** *noun* Amérique *Fem.* du Nord.

c

**North American** *noun* Nord-Américain *Masc.*, Nord-Américaine *Fem.*

d

e

**North American** *adjective* nord-américain.

f

**northeast** *noun* nord-est *Masc.* **northeast** *adjective* **in northeast England** au nord-est de l'Angleterre.

g

h

**Northern Ireland** *noun* Irlande *Fem.* du Nord.

i

j

**North Pole** *noun* pôle *Masc.* Nord.

k

**North Sea** *noun* **the North Sea** la mer du Nord.

l

m

**northwest** *noun* nord-ouest *Masc.* **northwest** *adjective* **in northwest England** au nord-ouest de l'Angleterre.

**n**

o

**Norway** *noun* Norvège *Fem.*; **in Norway** en Norvège.

p

**Norwegian** *noun* **1** (*person*) Norvégien *Masc.*, Norvégienne *Fem.*; **2** (*language*) norvégien *Masc.* **Norwegian** *adjective* norvégien (*Fem.* norvégienne).

q

r

s

t

**nose** *noun* nez *Masc.*; **to blow your nose** se moucher [1].

u

**nosebleed** *noun* **to have a nosebleed** saigner [1] du nez.

v

w

**nostril** *noun* narine *Fem.*

x

**not** *adverb* **1** pas; **not on Saturdays** pas le samedi; **not all alone!** pas tout seul!; **not bad** pas mal; **not at all** pas du tout; **not yet** pas encore; **2** (*when used with a verb*) ne ...pas;

y

z

**it's not my car** ce n'est pas ma voiture; **I don't know** je ne sais pas; **Sam didn't phone** Sam n'a pas appelé; **we decided not to wait** nous avons décidé de ne pas attendre; **3 I hope not** j'espère que non.

**note** *noun* **1** (*a short letter*) mot *Masc.*; **she left me a note** elle m'a laissé un mot; **2 to take notes** prendre [64] des notes; **3** (*a banknote*) billet *Masc.*; **a ten-pound note** un billet de dix livres; **4** (*in music*) note *Fem.*; (*on the keyboard*) touche *Fem.*

**notebook** *noun* carnet *Masc.*

**notepad** *noun* bloc-notes *Masc.* (*plural* blocs-notes).

**nothing** *pronoun* **1** rien; **'what did you say?' – 'nothing'** 'qu'est-ce que tu as dit?' – 'rien'; **2** (*with an adjective*) **nothing new** rien de nouveau; **there's nothing new** il n'y a rien de nouveau; **3** (*when used with a verb*) ne ...rien; **she knows nothing** elle ne sait rien; **but there was nothing there** mais il n'y avait rien; **I saw nothing** je n'ai rien vu; **nothing's happening** il ne se passe rien; **4 nothing has changed** rien n'a changé.

**notice** *noun* **1** (*a sign*) panneau *Masc.* (*plural* panneaux); **2** (*an advertisement*) annonce *Fem.*; **3 don't take any notice of her!** ne fais pas attention à elle!; **4 to do something at short notice** faire quelque chose à la dernière minute. **notice** *verb* remarquer [1]; **I didn't notice anything** je n'ai rien remarqué.

**noticeable** *adjective* visible.

**notice board** *noun* panneau *Masc.* d'affichage.

**nought** *noun* zéro *Masc.*

**noun** *noun* nom *Masc.*

**novel** *noun* roman *Masc.*

**novelist** *noun* romancier *Masc.*, romancière *Fem.*

**November** *noun* novembre *Masc.*; **in November** en novembre.

**now** *adverb* **1** maintenant; **where is he now?** où est-il maintenant?; **they've got six children now** ils ont six enfants maintenant; **2 he's busy just now** il est occupé en ce moment; **I saw her just now in the corridor** je viens de la voir dans le couloir; **3 do it right now!** fais-le tout de suite!; **4 now and then** de temps en temps.

**nowadays** *adverb* de nos jours; **nowadays they are quite common** de nos jours, ils sont assez fréquents.

**nowhere** *adjective* **1** nulle part; **nowhere in France** nulle part en France; **2 there's nowhere to park** il n'y a pas d'endroit pour se garer.

**nuclear** *adjective* nucléaire; **a nuclear power station** une centrale nucléaire.

**nude** *noun* **in the nude** nu.
**nude** *adjective* nu.

**nuisance** *noun* **it's a nuisance** c'est embêtant.

**numb** *adjective* **1** (*with cold*) engourdi; **my fingers are numb with cold** j'ai les doigts engourdis

par le froid; **2** (*with an anaesthetic*) insensible.

**number** *noun* **1** (*of a house, telephone, or account*) numéro *Masc.*; **I live at number thirty-one** j'habite au numéro trente-et-un; **my new phone number** mon nouveau numéro de téléphone; **2** (*a written figure*) chiffre *Masc.*; **the third number is a 7** le troisième chiffre est un 7; **3** (*an amount*) nombre *Masc.*; **a large number of visitors** un grand nombre de visiteurs.

**number plate** *noun* plaque *Fem.* d'immatriculation.

**nun** *noun* religieuse *Fem.*

**nurse** *noun* infirmier *Masc.*, infirmière *Fem.*; **Janet's a nurse** Janet est infirmière.

**nursery** *noun* **1** (*for children*) crèche *Fem.*; **2** (*for plants*) pépinière *Fem.*

**nursery school** *noun* école *Fem.* maternelle.

**nursing** *noun* profession *Fem.* d'infirmier/d'infirmière; **she went into nursing** elle est devenue infirmière.

**nut** *noun* **1** (*walnut*) noix *Fem.*; **2** (*almond*) amande *Fem.*; **3** (*peanut*) cacahuète *Fem.*; **4** (*for a bolt*) écrou *Masc.*

**nutmeg** *noun* noix *Fem.* de muscade.

**nylon** *noun* nylon *Masc.*

# Oo

**oak** *noun* chêne *Masc.*

a
b
c
d
e
f
g
h
i
j
k
l
m
**n**
**o**
p
q
r
s
t
u
v
w
x
y
z

**oar** *noun* rame *Fem*.

**oasis** *noun* oasis *Fem*.

**oats** *noun* avoine *Fem*.; **porridge oats** les flocons d'avoine.

**obedient** *adjective* obéissant.

**obey** *verb* obéir [2] à (*a person*); **to obey the rules** respecter [1] les règlements.

**object** *noun* objet *Masc*.
**object** *verb* soulever [50] des objections; **if you don't object** si vous n'avez pas d'objection.

**objection** *noun* objection *Fem*.

**oblong** *adjective* rectangulaire.

**oboe** *noun* hautbois *Masc*.; **to play the oboe** jouer du hautbois.

**obscene** *adjective* obscène.

**observe** *verb* observer [1].

**obsessed** *adjective* obsédé; **she's obsessed with her diet** elle est obsédée par son régime.

**obsession** *noun* obsession *Fem*.; **she has an obsession with cleanliness** elle est obsédée par la propreté.

**obstacle** *noun* obstacle *Masc*.

**obstinate** *adjective* têtu.

**obstruct** *verb* gêner [1] (*people or the traffic*).

**obtain** *verb* obtenir [77].

**obvious** *adjective* évident.

**obviously** *adverb* **1** (*of course*) évidemment; **'do you want to come too?' – 'obviously, but it's a bit difficult'** 'veux-tu nous accompagner?' – 'évidemment, mais c'est un peu difficile'; **2** (*looking at something*) manifestement; **the**

**house is obviously empty** la maison est manifestement vide.

**occasion** *noun* occasion *Fem*.; **a special occasion** une grande occasion.

**occasional** *adjective* **he sends us the occasiona lcard** il nous envoie une carte de temps en temps.

**occasionally** *adverb* de temps en temps.

**occupation** *noun* **1** (*job*) profession *Fem*.; **2** (*of territory*) occupation *Fem*.

**occupied** *adjective* occupé.

**occur** *verb* **1** **it occurs to me that my cousins live nearby** il me vient à l'esprit que mes cousins habitent tout près; **it never occurred to me** cela ne m'est pas venu à l'idée; **2** (*happen*) avoir [5] lieu; **the accident occurred on Monday** l'accident a eu lieu lundi.

**ocean** *noun* océan *Masc*.

**o'clock** *adverb* **at ten o'clock** à dix heures; **it's three o'clock** il est trois heures.

**October** *noun* octobre *Masc*.; **in October** en octobre.

**octopus** *noun* pieuvre *Fem*.

**odd** *adjective* **1** (*strange*) bizarre; **that's odd, I'm sure I heard the phone** c'est bizarre, je suis sûr d'avoir entendu le téléphone; **2** (*number*) impair; **three is an odd number** trois est un chiffre impair; **3** **to be the odd one out** être l'exception.

**odds and ends** *plural noun* bricoles *Fem. plural*.

**of** *preposition* **1** de; **a kilo of tomatoes** un kilo de tomates; **the end of my work** la fin de mon travail; **2** (*note that 'de le' becomes 'du' and 'de les' becomes 'des'*) **the beginning of the concert** le début du concert; **the name of the flower** le nom de la fleur; **the parents of the children** les parents des enfants; **3 Ray has four horses but he's selling three of them** Ray a trois chevaux mais il en vend trois; **we ate a lot of it** nous en avons mangé beaucoup; **4 two of us** deux d'entre nous; **5 the sixth of June** le six juin; **6 made of** en; **a bracelet made of silver** un bracelet en argent.

**off** *adverb, adjective, preposition* **1** (*switched off*) éteint; **is the telly off?** est-ce que la télé est éteinte?; **to turn off the lights** éteindre la lumière; **2** (*tap, water, gas*) fermé; **to turn off the tap** fermer le robinet; **3** (*turned off at the meter*) coupé; **the gas and electricity were off** le gaz et l'électricité étaient coupés; **4 to be off** (*to leave*) s'en aller [7]; **I'm off** je m'en vais; **5 a day off** un jour de congé; **Caroline took three days off work** Caroline a pris trois jours de congé; **to be off sick** être malade; **Maya's off school today** Maya n'est pas à l'école aujourd'hui; **6** (*cancelled*) annulé; **the match is off** le match est annulé; **7 '20% off shoes'** '20% de remise sur les chaussures'.

**offence** *noun* **1** (*crime*) délit *Masc.*; **2 to take offence** s'offenser [1]; **he takes offence easily** il s'offense facilement.

**offer** *noun* **1** offre *Fem.*; **a job offer** une offre d'emploi; **2 'on (special) offer'** 'en promotion'.

**offer** *verb* **1** offrir [56] (*a present, a reward, or a job*) **he offered her a chair** il lui a offert une chaise; **2 to offer to do** proposer [1] de faire; **Blake offered to drive me to the station** Blake m'a proposé de me conduire à la gare.

**office** *noun* bureau *Masc.* (*plural* bureaux); **he's still at the office** il est toujours au bureau; **Sue works in the same office** Sue travaille dans le même bureau.

**office block, office building** *noun* immeuble *Masc.* de bureaux.

**officer** *noun* officier *Masc.*

**official** *adjective* officiel (*Fem.* officielle); **the official version** la version officielle.

**off-licence** *noun* magasin *Masc.* de vins et de spiritueux.

**offside** *adjective* hors jeu.

**often** *adverb* souvent; **he's often late** il est souvent en retard; **how often do you see Rosie?** est-ce que tu vois Rosie souvent?; **I'd like to see Eric more often** j'aimerais voir Eric plus souvent.

**oil** *noun* **1** huile *Fem.*; **olive oil** l'huile d'olive; **suntan oil** l'huile solaire; **2** (*crude oil*) pétrole *Masc.*

**oil painting** *noun* peinture *Fem.* à l'huile (*both the activity and the object*).

**oil rig** *noun* plateforme *Fem.* pétrolière.

**oil slick** *noun* marée *Fem.* noire.

**oil tanker** *noun* pétrolier *Masc.*

a
b
c
d
e
f
g
h
i
j
k
l
m
n
o
p
q
r
s
t
u
v
w
x
y
z

**ointment** *noun* pommade *Fem.*

**okay** *adjective* **1** d'accord; **okay, tomorrow at ten** d'accord, demain à dix heures; **is it okay with you if I don't come till Friday?** ça te va si je ne viens que vendredi?; **2** (*person*) sympa (*informal*); **Daisy's okay** Daisy est sympa; **3** (*nothing special*) pas mal; **the film was okay** le film n'était pas mal; **4** (*not ill*) **are you okay?** ça va?; **I've been ill but I'm okay now** j'ai été malade, mais ça va mieux maintenant.

**old** *adjective* **1** (*not young, not new*) vieux, vieil (*before a vowel or silent 'h'*) (*Fem.* vieille); **an old man** un vieux monsieur; **an old lady** une vieille dame; **an old tree** un vieil arbre; **old people** les personnes âgées; **bring some old clothes** apporte de vieux vêtements; **2** (*previous*) ancien (*Fem.* ancienne); **our old car was a Rover** notre ancienne voiture était une Rover; **I've only got their old address** je n'ai que leur ancienne adresse; **3** (*talking about age*) **how old are you?** tu as quel âge?; **James is ten years old** James a dix ans; **a two-year-old child** un enfant de deux ans; **4 my older sister** ma sœur aînée; **she's older than me** elle est plus âgée que moi; **he's a year older than me** il a un an de plus que moi.

**old age** *noun* vieillesse *Fem.*

**old age pensioner** *noun* retraité *Masc.*, retraitée *Fem.*

**old-fashioned** *noun* **1** (*clothes, music, style*) démodé; **2** (*a person*) vieux jeu (*never agrees*); **my parents are so old-fashioned** mes parents sont si vieux jeu.

**olive** *noun* olive *Fem.*

**olive oil** *noun* huile *Fem.* d'olive.

**Olympic Games, Olympics** *plural noun* Jeux Olympiques *Masc.* plural.

**omelette** *noun* omelette *Fem.*; **a cheese omelette** une omelette au fromage.

**omit** *verb* omettre [11].

**on** *preposition* **1** sur; **on the desk** sur le bureau; **on the road** sur la route; **on the beach** sur la plage; **2** (*in expressions of time*) **on March 21st** le 21 mars; **he's arriving on Tuesday** il arrive mardi; **it's shut on Saturdays** c'est fermé le samedi; **on rainy days** quand il pleut; **3** (*for buses, trains, etc*) **she arrived on the bus** elle est arrivée en bus; **I met Jackie on the bus** j'ai vu Jackie dans le bus; **I slept on the plane** j'ai dormi dans l'avion; **let's go on our bikes!** allons-y à vélo!; **4 on TV** à la télé; **on the radio** à la radio; **on video** en vidéo; **5 on holiday** en vacances; **on strike** en grève. **on** *adjective* **1** (*switched on*) **to be on** (*TV, light, oven*) être [6] allumé; (*radio, machine*) être en marche; **all the lights were on** toutes les lumières étaient allumées; **is the radio on?** est-ce que la radio est en marche?; **I've put the oven on** j'ai allumé le four; **2** (*happening*) **what's on on TV?** qu'est-ce qu'il y a à la télé?; **what's on this week at the cinema?** qu'est-ce qui passe cette semaine au cinéma?

**once** *adverb* **1** une fois; **I've tried once already** j'ai déjà essayé une fois; **try once more** essaie encore une fois; **once a day** une fois par jour; **more than once** plus d'une fois; **2 at once** (*immediately*) tout de suite; **the doctor came at once** le médecin est venu tout de suite; **3 at once** (*at the same time*) à la fois; **I can't do two things at once** je ne peux pas faire deux choses à la fois.

**one's** *determiner* son, sa, ses; **one does one's best** on fait de son mieux; **to pay for one's car** payer sa voiture; **to love one's children** aimer ses enfants; **to wash one's hands** se laver les mains.

**one** *number* un (*Fem.* une); **one son** un fils; **one apple** une pomme; **if you want a pen I've got one** si tu veux un stylo j'en ai un; **at one o'clock** à une heure.
**one** *pronoun* **1** on; **one never knows** on ne sait jamais; **2 this one** celui-ci (*Fem.* celle-ci); **I like that bike, but this one's cheaper** j'aime bien ce vélo-là, mais celui-ci est moins cher; **do you want the red tie or this one?** veux-tu la cravate rouge ou celle-ci?; **3 that one** celui-là (*Fem.* celle-là); **'which video?' – 'that one'** 'quelle vidéo?' – 'celle-là'; **4 which one?** lequel? (*Fem.* laquelle?); **'my foot's hurting' – 'which one?'** 'j'ai mal au pied' – 'auquel?'; **'she borrowed a skirt from me' – 'which one?'** 'elle m'a emprunté une jupe' – 'laquelle?'

**oneself** *noun* **1 to wash oneself** se laver; **to hurt oneself** se blesser; **2** (*for emphasis*) soi-même; **one has to do everything oneself** il faut

tout faire soi-même; **3 (all) by oneself** tout seul (*Fem.* toute seule).

**one-way street** *noun* sens *Masc.* unique.

**onion** *noun* oignon *Masc.*; **onion soup** la soupe à l'oignon.

**only** *adjective* **1** seul; **the only free seat** la seule place libre; **the only thing to do** la seule chose à faire; **2 an only child** un enfant unique.
**only** *adverb, conjunction* **1** (*with a verb*) ne ...que; **they've only got two bedrooms** ils n'ont que deux chambres; **Anne's only free on Fridays** Anne n'est libre que le vendredi; **there are only three left** il n'en reste que trois; **2** seulement; **'how long did they stay?' – 'only two days'** 'ils sont restés combien de temps?' – 'deux jours seulement'; **3** (*but*) mais; **I'd walk, only it's raining** j'irais à pied, mais il pleut.

**onto** *preposition* sur.

**open** *noun* **in the open** en plein air.
**open** *adjective* **1** (*not shut*) ouvert; **the door's open** la porte est ouverte; **the baker's is not open** la boulangerie n'est pas ouverte; **2 in the open air** en plein air.
**open** *verb* **1** ouvrir [30]; **can you open the door for me?** est-ce que tu peux ouvrir la porte?; **Sam opened his eyes** Sam a ouvert les yeux; **the bank opens at nine** la banque ouvre à neuf heures; **2 the door opened slowly** la porte s'est ouverte lentement.

**open-air** *adjective* en plein air; **an open-air swimming pool** une piscine en plein air.

**opener** *noun* **1** (*for bottles*) décapsuleur *Masc.*; **2** (*for cans*) ouvre-boîte *Masc.*

**opening** *noun* **1** (*space*) ouverture *Fem.*; **2** (*opportunity*) occasion *Fem.*; **there are few openings for recent graduates** il y a peu de débouchés pour les jeunes diplômés.

**opera** *noun* opéra *Masc.*

**operate** *verb* (*medically*) opérer [24]; **will they have to operate?** est-ce qu'il va falloir qu'ils opèrent?

**operation** *noun* opération *Fem.*; **to have an operation** se faire opérer; **she's had an operation** elle s'est fait opérer.

**opinion** *noun* avis *Masc.*; **in my opinion** à mon avis.

**opinion poll** *noun* sondage *Masc.*

**opponent** *noun* adversaire *Masc. & Fem.*

**opportunity** *noun* occasion *Fem.*; **to have the opportunity of doing** avoir l'occasion de faire; **I took the opportunity to visit the museum** j'ai profité de l'occasion pour visiter le musée.

**opposed** *adjective* **to be opposed to something** être [6] opposé à quelque chose; **they are opposed to any change of the rules** ils s'opposent à un changement des règles.

**opposite** *noun* contraire *Masc.*; **no, quite the opposite** non, tout le contraire.

**opposite** *adjective* **1** opposé (*a direction, side, or view, for example*); **she went off in the opposite direction** elle est partie dans la direction opposée; **2** (*facing*) d'en face; **in the house opposite** dans la maison d'en face.

**opposite** *adverb* en face; **they live opposite** ils habitent en face.

**opposite** *preposition* en face de; **opposite the station** en face de la gare.

**opposition** *noun* opposition *Fem.*

**optician** *noun* opticien *Masc.*, opticienne *Fem.*

**optimistic** *adjective* optimiste.

**option** *noun* choix *Masc.*; **we have no option** nous n'avons pas le choix.

**optional** *adjective* facultatif (*Fem.* facultative).

**or** *conjunction* **1** ou; **English or French?** anglais ou français?; **today or Tuesday?** aujourd'hui ou mardi?; **2** (*in negatives*) **I don't have a cat or a dog** je n'ai ni un chat ni un chien; **not in June or July** ni en juin ni en juillet; **3** (*or else*) sinon; **phone Mum, or she'll worry** appelle maman, sinon elle va s'inquiéter.

**oral** *noun* (*an exam*) oral *Masc.* (*plural* oraux); **the French oral** l'oral de français.

**orange** *noun* (*the fruit*) orange *Fem.*; **an orange juice** un jus d'orange. **orange** *adjective* orange (*never changes*); **my orange socks** mes chaussettes orange.

**orchard** *noun* verger *Masc.*

**orchestra** *noun* orchestre *Masc.*

**order** *noun* **1** (*arrangement*) ordre *Masc.*; **in the right order** dans le bon ordre; **in the wrong order** dans le mauvais ordre; **in alphabetical**

**order** dans l'ordre alphabétique; **2** (*in a restaurant or café*) commande *Fem.*; **can I take your orders?** puis-je prendre vos commandes?; **3 'out of order'** 'en panne'; **4 in order to do** pour faire; **we hurried in order to be on time** nous nous sommes dépêchés pour arriver à l'heure.

**order** *verb* **1** (*in a restaurant or a shop*) commander [1]; **we ordered steaks** nous avons commandé des steacks; **2** réserver [1] (*a taxi*).

**ordinary** *adjective* ordinaire.

**organ** *noun* **1** (*in music*) orgue *Masc.*; **to play the organ** jouer de l'orgue; **2** (*of body*) organe *Masc.*

**organic** *adjective* biologique (*food*).

**organization** *noun* organisation *Fem.*

**organize** *verb* organiser [1].

**orienteering** *noun* course *Fem.* d'orientation.

**original** *adjective* original (*Masc. plural* originaux); **the original version was better** la version originale était meilleure; **it's a really original novel** c'est un roman très original.

**originally** *adverb* à l'origine; **originally we wanted to take the car** à l'origine nous voulions prendre la voiture.

**Orkneys** *plural noun* **the Orkneys** les Orcades *Fem. plural.*

**ornament** *noun* bibelot *Masc.*

**orphan** *noun* orphelin *Masc.*, orpheline *Fem.*

**ostrich** *noun* autruche *Fem.*

**other** *adjective* **1** autre; **the other day** l'autre jour; **we took the other road** nous avons pris l'autre route; **give me the other one** donne-moi l'autre; **where are the others?** où sont les autres?; **the other two cars** les deux autres voitures; **2 every other week** une semaine sur deux; **3 somebody or other** quelqu'un; **something or other** quelque chose; **somewhere or other** quelque part.

**otherwise** *adverb* (*in other ways*) à part ça; **the flat's a bit small but otherwise it's lovely** l'appartement n'est pas très grand mais à part ça il est très bien.

**otherwise** *conjunction* (*or else*) sinon; **I'll phone home, otherwise they'll worry** je vais appeler chez moi, sinon ils vont s'inquiéter.

**ought** *verb* ('*ought*' *is translated by the conditional tense of* '*devoir*' [8]) **I ought to go now** je devrais partir maintenant; **they ought to know the address** ils devraient savoir l'adresse; **you oughtn't to have any problems** vous ne devriez pas avoir des problèmes.

**our** *adjective* **1** notre; **our house** notre maison; **2** (*before a plural noun*) nos; **our parents** nos parents; **3** (*with parts of the body*) le, la, les; **we'll go and wash our hands** on va se laver les mains.

**ours** *pronoun* **1** (*for a masculine noun*) le nôtre; **their garden's bigger than ours** leur jardin est plus grand que le nôtre; **2** (*for a feminine noun*) la nôtre; **their house is smaller than ours** leur maison est plus petite que la nôtre; **3** (*for a

a
b
c
d
e
f
g
h
i
j
k
l
m
n
o
p
q
r
s
t
u
v
w
x
y
z

plural noun) les nôtres; **they've invited their friends and we've invited ours** ils ont invité leurs amis et nous avons invité les nôtres; **4** à nous; **the green one's ours** le vert est à nous; **it's ours** c'est à nous; **a friend of ours** un ami à nous.

**ourselves** pronoun **1** nous; **we introduced ourselves** nous nous sommes présentés; **2** (for emphasis) nous-mêmes; **in the end we did it ourselves** finalement nous l'avons fait nous-mêmes.

**out** adverb **1** (outside) dehors; **it's cold out there** il fait froid dehors; **out in the rain** sous la pluie; **they're out in the garden** ils sont dans le jardin; **2 to go out** sortir [72]; **she went out an hour ago** elle est sortie il y a une heure; **Mr. Barnes is out** Monsieur Barnes est sorti; **are you going out this evening?** est-ce que tu sors ce soir?; **Alison's going out with Danny at the moment** Alison sort avec Danny en ce moment; **he's asked me out** il m'a invitée à sortir avec lui; **3 to go out of the room** sortir de la pièce; **he threw it out of the window** il l'a jeté par la fenêtre; **to drink out of a glass** boire dans un verre; **she took the photo out of her bag** elle a pris la photo dans son sac.

**out** adjective (light, fire) éteint; **are all the lights out?** est-ce que toutes les lumières sont éteintes?; **the fire was out** le feu était éteint.

**outdoor** adjective (an activity or sport) de plein air; **an outdoor restaurant** un restaurant en plein air.

**outdoors** adverb en plein air.

**outing** noun sortie Fem.; **to go on an outing** faire une sortie.

**outline** noun (of an object) contour Masc.

**out-of-date** adjective **1** (no longer valid) périmé; **my passport's out of date** mon passeport est périmé; **2** (old-fashioned) démodé; **they played out-of-date music** ils ont joué la musique démodée.

**outside** noun extérieur Masc.; **it's blue on the outside** c'est bleu à l'extérieur.
**outside** adjective extérieur.
**outside** adverb dehors; **it's cold outside** il fait froid dehors.
**outside** preposition devant (a building); **I'll meet you outside the cinema** on se retrouve devant le cinéma.

**outskirts** noun périphérie Fem.; **on the outskirts of York** à la périphérie de York.

**outstanding** adjective exceptionnel (Fem. exceptionnelle).

**oval** adjective ovale.

**oven** noun four Masc.; **I've put it in the oven** je l'ai mis au four.

**over** preposition **1** (above) au-dessus de; **there's a mirror over the sideboard** il y a un miroir au-dessus du buffet; **2** (involving movement) par-dessus; **she jumped over the fence** elle a sauté par-dessus la clôture; **he threw the ball over the wall** il a jeté la balle par-dessus le mur; **3 over here** par ici; **the drinks are over here** les boissons sont par ici; **4 over there** là-bas; **she's over**

**there talking to Julian** elle est là-bas en train de discuter avec Julian; **5** (*more than*) plus de; **it will cost over a hundred pounds** ça coûtera plus de cent livres; **he's over sixty** il a plus de soixante ans; **6** (*during*) pendant; **over the weekend** pendant le weekend; **over Christmas** à Noël; **7** (*finished*) terminé; **when the meeting's over** quand la réunion sera terminée; **it's all over now** c'est terminé maintenant; **8 over the phone** par téléphone; **to ask someone over** inviter quelqu'un; **can you come over on Saturday?** peux-tu venir chez moi samedi?; **9 all over the place** partout; **all over the house** partout dans la maison.

**overcast** *adjective* couvert.

**overcrowded** *adjective* bondé.

**overdose** *noun* **1** (*of drugs*) overdose *Fem.*; **2** (*of medicine*) surdose *Fem.*

**overflow** *verb* déborder [1].

**overseas** *adverb* à l'étranger; **Dave works overseas** Dave travaille à l'étranger.

**oversleep** *verb* se réveiller [1] trop tard.

**overtake** *verb* doubler [1] (*another car*).

**overtime** *noun* **to work overtime** faire [10] des heures supplémentaires.

**overweight** *adjective* (*a person*) trop gros (*Fem.* trop grosse).

**owe** *verb* devoir [8]; **I owe Rick ten pounds** je dois dix livres à Rick.

**owing** *adjective* **1** (*to pay*) à payer; **there's five pounds owing** il y a cinq livres à payer; **2 owing to** en raison de; **owing to the snow** en raison de la neige.

**owl** *noun* hibou *Masc.* (*plural* hiboux).

**own** *adjective* **1** propre (*goes before the noun*); **my own computer** mon propre ordinateur; **I've got my own room** j'ai une chambre à moi; **2 on your own** tout seul (*Fem.* toute seule); **Annie did it on her own** Annie l'a fait toute seule.

**own** *verb* posséder [24].

**owner** *noun* propriétaire *Masc. & Fem.*

**oxygen** *noun* oxygène *Masc.*

**oyster** *noun* huître *Fem.*

**ozone layer** *noun* couche *Fem.* d'ozone.

# Pp

**pace** *noun* **1** (*a step*) pas *Masc.*; **2** (*the speed you walk at*) allure *Fem.*; **at a brisk pace** à vive allure.

**Pacific** *noun* **the Pacific Ocean** l'océan *Masc.* Pacifique.

**pack** *noun* **1** paquet *Masc.*; **2 a pack of cards** un jeu de cartes.

**pack** *verb* **1** faire [10] ses bagages; **I haven't packed yet** je n'ai pas encore fait mes bagages; **2 I'll pack my case tonight** je ferai ma valise ce soir; **have you packed my red shirt?** as-tu mis ma chemise rouge dans la valise?

a
b
c
d
e
f
g
h
i
j
k
l
m
n
o
p
q
r
s
t
u
v
w
x
y
z

**package** *noun* paquet *Masc.*

**package holiday**, **package tour** *noun* voyage *Masc.* organisé.

**packed lunch** *noun* panier-repas *Masc.*

**packet** *noun* 1 paquet *Masc.*; **a packet of biscuits** un paquet de biscuits; 2 (*bag*) sachet *Masc.*; **a packet of crisps** un sachet de chips.

**packing** *noun* **to do your packing** faire ses bagages.

**pad** *noun* (*of paper*) bloc-notes *Masc.*

**paddle** *noun* (*for a canoe*) pagaie *Fem.*
**paddle** *verb* (*at the seaside*) **to go paddling** faire [10] trempette.

**padlock** *noun* cadenas *Masc.*

**page** *noun* page *Fem.*; **on page seven** à la page sept.

**pain** *noun* douleur *Fem.*; **I've got a pain in my leg** j'ai mal à la jambe; **to be in pain** souffrir [73]; ★ **Eric's a real pain (in the neck)** Eric est vraiment pénible.

**painful** *adjective* douloureux (*Fem.* douloureuse).

**painkiller** *noun* analgésique *Masc.*

**paint** *noun* peinture *Fem.*; **'wet paint'** 'peinture fraîche'.
**paint** *verb* peindre [60]; **to paint something pink** peindre quelque chose en rose.

**paintbrush** *noun* pinceau *Masc.* (*plural* pinceaux).

**painter** *noun* peintre *Masc.*

**painting** *noun* (*picture*) tableau *Masc.* (*plural* tableaux); **a painting by Monet** un tableau de Monet.

**pair** *noun* 1 paire *Fem.*; **a pair of socks** une paire de chaussettes; **a pair of scissors** une paire de ciseaux; 2 **a pair of jeans** un jean; **a pair of trousers** un pantalon; **a pair of knickers** un slip; 3 **to work in pairs** travailler en groupes de deux.

**Pakistan** *noun* Pakistan *Masc.*; **in Pakistan** au Pakistan; **to Pakistan** au Pakistan.

**Pakistani** *noun* Pakistanais *Masc.*, Pakkistanaise *Fem.*.
**Pakistani** *adjective* pakistanais.

**palace** *noun* palais *Masc.*

**pale** *adjective* pâle; **pale green** vert pâle (*never changes*); **pale green curtains** des rideaux vert pâle; **to turn pale** pâlir [2].

**palm** *noun* 1 (*of your hand*) paume *Fem.*; 2 (*a palm tree*) palmier *Masc.*

**pan** *noun* (*saucepan*) casserole *Fem.* 1 **a pan of water** une casserole d'eau; 2 (*frying-pan*) poêle *Fem.*

**pancake** *noun* crêpe *Fem.*

**panel** *noun* 1 (*on radio or TV*) (*for a discussion*) invités *Masc.* plural (*i.e. guests*); (*for a quiz show*) jury *Masc.*; 2 (*for a wall or a bath, for example*) panneau *Masc.* (*plural* panneaux).

**panel game** *noun* jeu *Masc.* (*plural* jeux).

**panic** *noun* panique *Fem.*
**panic** *verb* s'affoler [1]; **don't panic!** pas de panique!

**pannier** *noun* (*on a bike*) sacoche *Fem.*

**panther** *noun* panthère *Fem.*

**panties** *noun* petite culotte *Fem.*

512

**pantomime** *noun* spectacle *Masc.* pour enfants.

**pants** *plural noun* slip *Masc.*

**paper** *noun* **1** papier *Masc.*; **a sheet of paper** une feuille de papier; **2 a paper cup** un gobelet en carton; **a paper hanky** un mouchoir en papier; **3** (*newspaper*) journal *Masc.* (*plural* journaux); **it was in the paper** c'était dans le journal.

**paperback** *noun* livre *Masc.* de poche.

**paperclip** *noun* trombone *Masc.* (*because of its shape*).

**paper shop** *noun* magasin *Masc.* de journaux.

**paper towel** *noun* essuie-tout *Masc.*

**parachute** *noun* parachute *Masc.*

**parachuting** *noun* parachutisme *Masc.*; **to go parachuting** faire du parachutisme.

**parade** *noun* défilé *Masc.*

**paradise** *noun* paradis *Masc.*

**paraffin** *noun* pétrole *Masc.*

**paragraph** *noun* paragraphe *Masc.*; **'new paragraph'** 'à la ligne'.

**parallel** *adjective* parallèle.

**paralysed** *adjective* paralysé.

**parcel** *noun* paquet *Masc.*

**pardon** *noun* **I beg your pardon** pardon; **pardon?** pardon?

**parent** *noun* parent *Masc.*; **my parents are Scottish** mes parents sont écossais; **a parents' evening** une réunion pour les parents d'élèves.

**Paris** *noun* Paris; **Marie lives in Paris** Marie habite à Paris.

**Parisian** *noun* Parisien *Masc.*, Parisienne *Fem.*
**Parisian** *adjective* parisien (*Fem.* parisienne).

**park** *noun* **1** parc *Masc.*; **a theme park** un parc à thème; **2 a car park** un parking.
**park** *verb* **1** se garer [1]; **you can park outside the house** vous pouvez vous garer devant la maison; **2 to park a car** garer [1] une voiture; **where did you park the car?** où as-tu garé la voiture?

**parking** *noun* stationnement *Masc.*; **'no parking'** 'stationnement interdit'.

**parking meter** *noun* parcmètre *Masc.*

**parking space** *noun* place *Fem.*

**parking ticket** *noun* PV *Masc.* (*informal*).

**parliament** *noun* parlement *Masc.*

**parrot** *noun* perroquet *Masc.*

**parsley** *noun* persil *Masc.*

**part** *noun* **1** partie *Fem.*; **part of the garden** une partie du jardin; **the last part of the concert** la dernière partie du concert; **that's part of your job** ça fait partie de votre travail; **2 to take part in something** participer à quelque chose; **3** (*a role in a play*) rôle *Masc.*; **4 spare parts** pièces *Fem. plural* détachées.

**particular** *adjective* particulier (*Fem.* particulière); **nothing in particular** rien de particulier.

**particularly** *adverb* **1** (*unusually*) spécialement; **not particularly interesting** pas spécialement intéressant; **2** (*in particular*) surtout; **particularly as it's our last day** surtout que c'est notre dernier jour.

**parting** *noun* (*in your hair*) raie *Fem.*

**partly** *adverb* en partie.

**partner** *noun* **1** (*in a game*) partenaire *Masc.*; **2** (*the person you live with*) partenaire *Masc. & Fem.*; **3** (*in business*) associé *Masc.*, associée *Fem.*

**partridge** *noun* perdrix *Fem.*

**part-time** *adjective, adverb* à temps partiel; **part-time work** du travail à temps partiel; **to work part-time** travailler à temps partiel.

**party** *noun* **1** fête *Fem.*; **a Christmas party** une fête de Noël; **to have a birthday party** faire une fête d'anniversaire; **2** (*more formal, in the evening*) soirée *Fem.*; **we've been invited to a party at the Smiths' house** nous sommes invités à une soirée chez les Smith; **3** (*group*) groupe *Masc.*; **a party of schoolchildren** un groupe d'élèves; **a rescue party** une équipe de secouristes; **4** (*in politics*) parti *Masc.*; **the Labour party** le parti travailliste.

**party game** *noun* jeu *Masc.* de société (*plural* jeux de société).

**pass** *noun* **1** (*to let you in*) laisser-passer *Masc.* (*plural* laisser-passer); **2 a bus pass** une carte de bus; **3** (*a mountain pass*) col *Masc.*; **4** (*in an exam*) **to get a pass in history** être reçu en histoire.

**pass** *verb* **1** (*go past*) passer [1] devant (*a place or building*); **we passed your house** nous sommes passés devant chez toi; **2** (*to overtake*) doubler [1] (*a car*); **3** (*give*) passer [1]; **could you pass me the paper please?** peux-tu me passer le journal s'il te plaît?; **4** (*time*) passer [1]; **the time passed slowly** le temps passait lentement; **5** (*in an exam*) être [6] reçu; **did you pass?** as-tu été reçu?; **to pass an exam** être reçu à un examen.

**passage** *noun* **1** (*a corridor*) couloir *Masc.*; **2** (*a piece of text*) passage *Masc.*

**passenger** *noun* **1** (*in a car, plane, or ship*) passager *Masc.*, passagère *Fem.*; **2** (*in a train, bus, or underground*) voyageur *Masc.*, voyageuse *Fem.*

**passerby** *noun* passant *Masc.*, passante *Fem.*

**passion** *noun* passion *Fem.*

**passionate** *adjective* passionné.

**passive** *noun* passif *Masc.* **passive** *adjective* passif (*Fem.* passive).

**Passover** *noun* Pâque *Fem.* juive.

**passport** *noun* passeport *Masc.*; **an EU passport** un passeport de l'UE.

**password** *noun* mot *Masc.* de passe.

**past** *noun* passé *Masc.*; **in the past** au passé.

**past** *adjective* **1** (*recent*) dernier (*Fem.* dernière) (*goes before the noun*); **in the past few weeks**

pendant les dernières semaines; **2** (*over*) fini; **winter is past** l'hiver est fini.

**past** *preposition, adverb* **1 to walk or drive past something** passer devant quelque chose; **we went past the school** nous sommes passés devant l'école; **Ray went past in his new car** Ray est passé dans sa nouvelle voiture; **2** (*the other side of*) après; **it's just past the post office** c'est juste après la poste; **3** (*talking about time*) **ten past six** six heures dix; **half past four** quatre heures et demie; **a quarter past two** deux heures et quart.

**pasta** *noun* pâtes *Fem. plural*; **I don't like pasta** je n'aime pas les pâtes.

**paste** *verb* coller [1]; **to cut and paste the table** copier-coller le tableau.

**pasteurized** *adjective* pasteurisé.

**pastry** *noun* pâte *Fem.*

**patch** *noun* **1** (*fabric, for mending*) pièce *Fem.*; **2** (*of snow or ice*) plaque *Fem.*; **3** (*of blue sky*) coin *Masc.*

**path** *noun* chemin *Masc.*; (*very narrow*) sentier *Masc.*

**pathetic** *adjective* (*useless, hopeless*) lamentable.

**patience** *noun* **1** patience *Fem.*; **2** (*card game*) réussite *Fem.*

**patient** *noun* patient *Masc.*, patiente *Fem.*

**patient** *adjective* patient.

**patiently** *adverb* avec patience.

**patio** *noun* terrasse *Fem.*

**patrol** *noun* patrouille *Fem.*

**patrol car** *noun* voiture *Fem.* de police.

**pattern** *noun* **1** (*on wallpaper or fabric*) motif *Masc.*; **2** (*dressmaking*) patron *Masc.*; **3** (*knitting*) modèle *Masc.*

**pause** *noun* pause *Fem.*

**pavement** *noun* trottoir *Masc.*; **on the pavement** sur le trottoir.

**paw** *noun* patte *Fem.*

**pawn** *noun* pion *Masc.*

**pay** *noun* salaire *Masc.*

**pay** *verb* **1** payer [59]; **I'm paying** c'est moi qui paie; **to pay cash** payer comptant; **2 to pay for something** payer [59] quelque chose; **Tony paid for the drinks** Tony a payé les boissons; **it's all paid for** c'est tout payé; **3 to pay by credit card** régler [24] par carte de crédit; **to pay by cheque** régler par chèque; **4 to pay somebody back** (*money*) rembourser [1] quelqu'un; **5 to pay attention** faire [10] attention; **6 to pay a visit to somebody** rendre [3] visite à quelqu'un.

**paydesk** *noun* caisse *Fem.*

**payment** *noun* paiement *Masc.* (*of a bill*) règlement *Masc.*

**pay phone** *noun* téléphone *Masc.* public.

**PC** *noun* (*computer*) PC *Masc.*

**pea** *noun* petit pois *Masc.*

**peace** *noun* paix *Fem.*

**peaceful** *adjective* paisible (*day, scene*).

**peach** *noun* pêche *Fem.*

**peacock** *noun* paon *Masc.*

**peak** noun (of a mountain) pic Masc.

**peak period** (for holidays) période Fem. de pointe.

**peak rate** noun (for phoning) tarif Masc. rouge.

**peak time** noun (for traffic) heures Fem. plural de pointe.

**peanut** noun cacahuète Fem.

**peanut butter** noun beurre Masc. de cacahuètes.

**pear** noun poire Fem.

**pearl** noun perle Fem.

**peasant** noun paysan Masc., paysanne Fem.

**pebble** noun 1 (on the road) caillou Masc. (plural cailloux); 2 (on a beach) galet Masc.

**peculiar** adjective bizarre.

**pedal** noun pédale Fem.
**pedal** verb pédaler [1].

**pedal boat** noun pédalo™ Masc.

**pedestrian** noun piéton Masc.

**pedestrian crossing** noun passage Masc. pour piétons.

**pedestrian precinct** noun zone Fem. piétonne.

**pee** noun to have a pee faire [10] pipi (informal) .

**peel** noun 1 (of an apple) peau Fem.; 2 (of an orange) écorce Fem.
**peel** verb éplucher [1] (fruit, vegetables).

**peer** verb to peer at something regarder [1] quelque chose attentivement.

**peg** noun 1 (hook) patère Fem.; 2 a clothes peg une pince à linge; 3 a tent peg un piquet.

**pen** noun stylo Masc.; a felt pen un stylo-feutre.

**penalty** noun 1 (a fine) amende Fem.; 2 (in football) penalty Masc.; 3 (in rugby) pénalité Fem.

**penalty area** noun surface Fem. de réparation.

**pence** plural noun pence Masc. plural.

**pencil** noun crayon Masc.; to write in pencil écrire au crayon.

**pencil case** noun trousse Fem.

**pencil sharpener** noun taille-crayon Masc.

**pendant** noun pendentif Masc.

**penfriend** noun correspondant Masc., correspondante Fem.; my French pen-friend is called Christelle ma correspondante française s'appelle Christelle.

**penguin** noun pingouin Masc.

**penis** noun pénis Masc.

**penknife** noun canif Masc.

**penny** noun penny Masc.

**pension** noun retraite Fem.

**pensioner** noun retraité Masc., retraitée Fem.

**people** plural noun 1 gens Masc. plural; **people round here** les gens d'ici; **nice people** des gens sympathiques; 2 (when you're counting them) personnes Fem. plural; **ten people** dix personnes; **several people** plusieurs personnes; **how many people have you asked?** tu as invité combien de personnes?; 3 **people say he's very rich** on dit qu'il est très riche.

**ENGLISH-FRENCH**

**pepper** noun 1 (*spice*) poivre Masc.; 2 (*vegetable*) poivron; **a green pepper** un poivron vert.

**peppermill** noun moulin Masc. à poivre.

**peppermint** noun menthe Fem.; **peppermint tea** le thé à la menthe.

**per** preposition par; **ten pounds per person** dix livres par personne.

**per cent** adverb pour cent; **sixty per cent of students** soixante pour cent des étudiants.

**percentage** noun pourcentage Masc.

**percussion** noun percussion Fem.; **to play percussion** jouer des percussions.

**perfect** adjective 1 parfait; **she speaks perfect English** elle parle un anglais parfait; 2 (*ideal*) idéal (Masc. plural idéaux); **the perfect place for a picnic** l'endroit idéal pour un pique-nique.

**perfectly** adverb parfaitement.

**perform** verb 1 jouer [1] (*a piece of music or a play*); 2 chanter [1] (*a song*).

**performance** noun 1 (*playing or acting*) interprétation Fem.; **a wonderful performance of Macbeth** une superbe interprétation de Macbeth; 2 (*show*) spectacle Masc.; **the performance starts at eight** le spectacle commence à huit heures; 3 (*the results of a team or company*) performance Fem.

**performer** noun artiste Masc. & Fem.

**perfume** noun parfum Masc.

**perhaps** adverb peut-être; **perhaps it's in the drawer?** c'est peut-être dans le tiroir?; **perhaps he's missed the train** il a peut-être raté le train.

**period** noun 1 période Fem.; **a two-year period** une période de deux ans; 2 (*in school*) cours Masc.; **a forty-five-minute period** un cours de quarante-cinq minutes; 3 (*menstruation*) règles Fem. plural; **during your period** pendant vos règles.

**perm** noun permanente Fem.

**permanent** adjective permanent.

**permanently** adverb en permanence.

**permission** noun permission Fem.; **to get permission to do** obtenir la permission de faire.

**permit** noun permis Masc. **permit** verb permettre [11]; **to permit somebody to do** permettre à quelqu'un de faire; **smoking is not permitted** il est interdit de fumer; **weather permitting** si le temps le permet.

**person** noun personne Fem.; **there's room for one more person** il y a de la place pour une autre personne; **in person** en personne.

**personal** adjective personnel (Fem. personnelle).

**personality** noun personnalité Fem.

**personally** adverb personnellement; **personally, I'm against it** personnellement, je suis contre.

517

**a**
**b**
**c**
**d**
**e**
**f**
**g**
**h**
**i**
**j**
**k**
**l**
**m**
**n**
**o**
**p**
**q**
**r**
**s**
**t**
**u**
**v**
**w**
**x**
**y**
**z**

**personal stereo** *noun* baladeur *Masc.*

**perspiration** *noun* transpiration *Fem.*

**persuade** *verb* persuader [1]; **to persuade somebody to do** persuader quelqu'un de faire; **we persuaded Tim to wait a bit** nous avons persuadé Tim d'attendre un peu.

**pessimistic** *adjective* pessimiste.

**pest** *noun* **1** (*greenfly for example*) insecte *Masc.* nuisible; **2** (*annoying person*) casse-pieds *Masc. & Fem.*

**pester** *verb* harceler [45].

**pet** *noun* **1** animal *Masc.* de compagnie (*plural* animaux de compagnie); **do you have a pet?** avez-vous un animal de compagnie?; **a pet dog** un chien; **2** (*favourite person*) chouchou *Masc.*, chouchoute *Fem.*; **Julie is teacher's pet** Julie est la chouchoute du prof.

**petal** *noun* pétale *Masc.*

**pet name** *noun* petit nom *Masc.*

**petrol** *noun* essence *Fem.*; **to fill up with petrol** faire le plein d'essence; **to run out of petrol** tomber en panne d'essence.

**petrol station** *noun* station *Fem.* d'essence.

**petticoat** *noun* jupon *Masc.*

**pharmacist** *noun* pharmaciste *Masc. & Fem.*

**pharmacy** *noun* pharmacie *Fem.*

**pheasant** *noun* faisan *Masc.*

**philosophy** *noun* philosophie *Fem.*

**phone** *noun* téléphone *Masc.*; **she's on the phone** elle est au téléphone;

**I was on the phone to Sophie** j'étais au téléphone avec Sophie; **you can book by phone** on peut réserver par téléphone.

**phone** *verb* **1** téléphoner [1]; **while I was phoning** pendant que je téléphonais; **2 to phone somebody** appeler [18] quelqu'un; **I'll phone you tonight** je t'appellerai ce soir.

**phone book** *noun* annuaire *Masc.*

**phone box** *noun* cabine *Fem.* téléphonique.

**phone call** *noun* appel *Masc.*; **phone calls are free** les appels sont gratuits; **to make a phone call** téléphoner.

**phone card** *noun* télécarte *Fem.*

**phone number** *noun* numéro *Masc.* de téléphone.

**photo** *noun* photo *Fem.*; **to take a photo** prendre une photo; **to take a photo of somebody** prendre quelqu'un en photo; **I took a photo of their house** j'ai pris leur maison en photo.

**photocopier** *noun* photocopieuse *Fem.*

**photocopy** *noun* photocopie *Fem.*
**photocopy** *verb* photocopier [1].

**photograph** *noun* photo *Fem.*; **to take a photograph** prendre une photo; **to take a photograph of somebody** prendre quelqu'un en photo.
**photograph** *verb* photographier [1].

**photographer** *noun* photographe *Masc. & Fem.*

**photography** *noun* photographie *Fem.*

**phrase** *noun* expression *Fem.*

**phrase-book** *noun* manuel *Masc.* de conversation.

**physical** *adjective* physique.

**physicist** *noun* physicien *Masc.*, physicienne *Fem.*

**physics** *noun* physique *Fem.*

**physiotherapist** *noun* kinésithérapeute *Masc. & Fem.*

**physiotherapy** *noun* kinésithérapie *Fem.*

**pianist** *noun* pianiste *Masc. & Fem.*

**piano** *noun* piano *Masc.*; **to play the piano** jouer du piano; **Steve played it on the piano** Steve l'a joué au piano; **a piano lesson** une leçon de piano.

**pick** *noun* **take your pick!** choisis!
**pick** *verb* **1** (*to choose*) choisir [2]; **pick a card** choisis une carte; **2** (*for a team*) sélectionner [1]; **I've been picked for Saturday** j'ai été sélectionné pour samedi; **3** cueillir [35] (*fruit or flowers*).

• **to pick up 1** (*lift*) prendre [64]; **he picked up the papers and went out** il a pris les papiers et il est sorti; **2** (*collect together*) ramasser [1]; **I'll pick up the toys** je ramasserai les jouets; **3** (*to collect*) venir [81] chercher; **I'll pick you up at six** je viendrai te chercher à six heures; **I'll pick up the keys tomorrow** je viendrai chercher les clés demain; **4** (*learn*) apprendre [64]; **you'll soon pick it up** tu vas vite l'apprendre.

**pickpocket** *noun* pickpocket *Masc.*

**picnic** *noun* pique-nique *Masc.*; **to have a picnic** pique-niquer.

**picture** *noun* **1** (*a painting*) tableau *Masc.* (*plural* tableaux); **a picture by Renoir** une tableau de Renoir; **he painted a picture of a horse** il a peint un cheval; **2** (*a drawing*) dessin *Masc.*; **draw me a picture of your little sister** dessine-moi ta petite sœur; **3** (*in a book*) illustration *Fem.*; **a book with lots of pictures** un livre avec beaucoup d'illustrations; **4** (*the cinema*) **the pictures** le cinéma; **to go to the pictures** aller au cinéma.

**pie** *noun* **1** (*sweet*) tarte *Fem.*; **an apple pie** une tarte aux pommes; **2** (*savoury*) tourte *Fem.*; **a meat pie** une tourte à la viande.

**piece** *noun* **1** (*a bit*) morceau *Masc.* (*plural* morceaux); **a big piece of cheese** un gros morceau de fromage; **2** (*that you fit together*) pièce *Fem.*; **the pieces of a jigsaw** les pièces d'un puzzle; **to take something to pieces** démonter [1] quelque chose; **3 a piece of furniture** un meuble; **four pieces of luggage** quatre valises; **a piece of information** un renseignement; **that's a piece of luck!** c'est un coup de chance!; **4** (*coin*) pièce *Fem.*; **a two-euro piece** une pièce de deux euros.

**pier** *noun* jetée *Fem.*

**pierced** *adjective* percé; **to have pierced ears** avoir les oreilles percées.

**pig** *noun* cochon *Masc.*

**pigeon** *noun* pigeon *Masc.*

**piggy bank** *noun* tirelire *Fem.*

a
b
c
d
e
f
g
h
i
j
k
l
m
n
o
p
q
r
s
t
u
v
w
x
y
z

**pigsty** noun porcherie Fem.; **your room is a pigsty** ta chambre est une vraie porcherie.

**pigtail** noun natte Fem.

**pile** noun 1 (a neat stack) pile Fem.; **a pile of plates** une pile d'assiettes; 2 (a heap) tas Masc.; **a pile of dirty shirts** un tas de chemises sales.

• **to pile something up** (neatly) empiler [1] quelque chose; (in a heap) entasser [1] quelque chose.

**pilgrimage** noun pèlerinage Masc.; **to go on a pilgrimage** faire [10] un pèlerinage.

**pill** noun comprimé Masc.; **the pill** (contraceptive) la pilule.

**pillar** noun pilier Masc.

**pillar box** noun boîte Fem. aux lettres.

**pillow** noun oreiller Masc.

**pillowcase** noun taie Fem. d'oreiller.

**pilot** noun pilote Masc.

**pimple** noun bouton Masc.

**pin** noun 1 (for sewing) épingle Fem.; 2 **a three-pin plug** une prise à trois fiches.

• **to pin up** 1 épingler [1] (a hem); 2 accrocher [1] (a notice).

**PIN** noun (personal identification number) code Masc. confidentiel.

**pinball** noun flipper Masc.; **to play pinball** jouer au flipper; **a pinball machine** un flipper.

**pinch** noun (of salt, for example) pincée Fem.

**pinch** verb 1 (steal) piquer [1]; **somebody's pinched my bike** on m'a piqué mon vélo; 2 **to pinch somebody** pincer [61] quelqu'un.

**pine** noun pin Masc.; **a pine table** une table en pin.

**pineapple** noun ananas Masc.

**pine cone** noun pomme Fem. de pin.

**ping-pong** noun ping-pong Masc.; **to play ping-pong** jouer au ping-pong.

**pink** adjective rose.

**pip** noun (in a fruit) pépin Masc.

**pipe** noun 1 (for gas or water) tuyau Masc. (plural tuyaux); 2 (to smoke) pipe Fem.; **he smokes a pipe** il fume la pipe.

**pirate** noun pirate Masc.

**pirated** adjective piraté; **a pirated video** une vidéo piratée.

**Pisces** noun Poissons Masc. plural; **Amanda is Pisces** Amanda est Poissons.

**pistachio** noun pistache Fem.

**pit** noun fosse Fem.

**pitch** noun terrain Masc.; **a football pitch** un terrain de foot.
**pitch** verb **to pitch a tent** dresser [1] une tente.

**pity** noun 1 **what a pity!** quel dommage!; **it would be a pity to miss the beginning** ce serait dommage de rater le début; 2 (feeling sorry for somebody) pitié Fem.
**pity** verb **to pity somebody** plaindre [31] quelqu'un.

**pizza** noun pizza Fem.

**place** noun 1 endroit Masc.; **in a warm place** dans un endroit chaud;

**Rome is a wonderful place** Rome est un endroit merveilleux; **all over the place** partout; **2** (*a space*) place *Fem.*; **a place for the car** une place pour la voiture; **is there a place for me?** y a-t-il une place pour moi?; **will you keep my place?** veux-tu me garder ma place?; **to change places** changer de place; **3** (*in a race*) place *Fem.*; **in first place** à la première place; **4 at your place** chez toi; **we'll go round to Zafir's place** on ira chez Zafir; **5 to take place** avoir [5] lieu; **the competition will take place at four** le concours aura lieu à quatre heures.

**place** *verb* mettre [11]; **he placed his cup on the table** il a mis sa tasse sur la table.

**plain** *noun* plaine *Fem.*

**plain** *adjective* **1** simple; **plain cooking** une cuisine simple; **2** (*unflavoured*) nature; **a plain yoghurt** un yaourt nature; **3** (*not patterned*) uni; **plain curtains** des rideaux unis.

**plait** *noun* natte *Fem.*

**plan** *noun* **1** projet *Masc.*; **what are your plans for this summer?** quels sont vos projets pour cet été?; **to go according to plan** se passer comme prévu; **everything went according to plan** tout s'est passé comme prévu; **2** (*a map*) plan *Masc.*

**plan** *verb* **1 to plan to do** avoir [5] l'intention de faire; **we're planning to leave at eight** nous avons l'intention de partir à huit heures; **2** (*make plans for*) préparer [1]; **Ricky's planning a trip to Italy** Ricky prépare un voyage en Italie;

**3** (*organize*) organiser [1]; **I'm planning my day** j'organise ma journée; **4** (*to design*) concevoir [66] (*a house or garden*); **a well-planned kitchen** une cuisine bien conçue.

**plane** *noun* avion *Masc.*; **we went by plane** nous avons pris l'avion.

**planet** *noun* planète *Fem.*

**plank** *noun* planche *Fem.*

**plant** *noun* plante *Fem.*; **a house plant** une plante d'intérieur. **plant** *verb* planter [1].

**plaster** *noun* **1** (*sticking plaster*) pansement *Masc.* adhésif; **2** (*for walls*) plâtre *Masc.*; **3 to have your leg in plaster** avoir la jambe dans le plâtre.

**plastic** *noun* plastique *Masc.*; **a plastic bag** un sac en plastique.

**plate** *noun* assiette *Fem.*

**platform** *noun* **1** (*in a station*) quai *Masc.*; **the train arriving at platform six** le train qui entre en gare quai numéro six; **2** (*for lecturing or performing*) estrade *Fem.*

**play** *noun* pièce *Fem.*; **a play by Molière** une pièce de Molière; **our school is putting on a play** notre école monte une pièce.

**play** *verb* **1** jouer [1]; **the children were playing with a ball** les enfants jouaient avec un ballon; **they play all kinds of music** ils jouent toutes sortes de musique; **who's playing Hamlet?** qui est-ce qui joue Hamlet?; **2** jouer [1] à (*a game*); **to play tennis** jouer au tennis; **they were playing cards** ils jouaient aux cartes; **3** jouer [1] de (*a musical instrument*); **Helen plays the violin**

Helen joue du violon; **4** mettre [11] (*a tape, CD, or record*); **play me your new CD** mets-moi ton nouveau CD.

**player** *noun* **1** (*in sport*) joueur *Masc.*, joueuse *Fem.*; **a football player** un joueur de foot; **2** (*musician*) musicien *Masc.*, musicienne *Fem.*

**playground** *noun* cour *Fem.* de récréation.

**playgroup** *noun* halte-garderie *Fem.*

**playing card** *noun* carte *Fem.* à jouer.

**playing field** *noun* terrain *Masc.* de sport.

**playroom** *noun* salle *Fem.* de jeux.

**plaza** *noun* **a shopping plaza** un centre commercial.

**pleasant** *adjective* agréable.

**please** *adverb* s'il vous plaît; (*less formal*) s'il te plaît; **two coffees, please** deux cafés, s'il vous plaît; **could you turn the TV off, please?** est-ce que tu peux éteindre la télé s'il te plaît?

**pleased** *adjective* content; **I was really pleased!** j'étais très content!; **she was pleased with her present** elle était contente de son cadeau; **pleased to meet you!** enchanté!

**pleasure** *noun* plaisir *Masc.*

**plenty** *pronoun* **1** (*lots*) beaucoup; **there's plenty of bread** il y a beaucoup de pain; **he's got plenty of money** il a beaucoup d'argent; **2** (*quite enough*) **we've got plenty of time for a coffee** nous avons largement le temps de prendre un

café; **thank you, that's plenty!** merci, ça suffit largement!

**pliers** *noun* pince *Fem.*

**plot** *noun* (*of a film or novel*) intrigue *Fem.*

**plough** *verb* labourer [1].

**plug** *noun* **1** (*electrical*) prise *Fem.*; **2** (*in a bath or sink*) bonde *Fem.*; **to pull out the plug** retirer la bonde.

**plum** *noun* prune *Fem.*; **a plum tart** une tarte aux prunes.

**plumber** *noun* plombier *Masc.*; **he's a plumber** il est plombier.

**plump** *adjective* potelé.

**plunge** *verb* plonger [52].

**plural** *noun* pluriel *Masc.*; **in the plural** au pluriel.

**plus** *preposition* plus; **three children plus the baby** trois enfants plus le bébé.

**p.m.** *adverb* (*French people usually express times after midday in terms of the 24-hour clock*) **1** at two p.m. à quatorze heures; **at nine p.m.** à vingt-et-une heures; **2** (*however, you can also use 'de l'après-midi', for times up to 6 p.m. and 'du soir' for times after that*) **at two p.m.** à deux heures de l'après-midi; **at nine p.m.** à neuf heures du soir.

**poached egg** *noun* œuf *Masc.* poché.

**pocket** *noun* poche *Fem.*

**pocket money** *noun* **1** (*for child*) argent *Masc.* de poche; **2** (*for small purchases*) petites dépenses *Fem. plural.*

**poem** *noun* poème *Masc.*

**poet** *noun* poète *Masc.*

**poetry** *noun* poésie *Fem.*

**point** *noun* **1** (*tip*) pointe *Fem.*; **the point of a nail** la pointe d'un clou; **2** (*in time*) moment *Masc.*; **at that point the police arrived** à ce moment-là, la police est arrivée; **3 to get the point** comprendre; **I don't get the point** je ne comprends pas; **what's the point of waiting?** à quoi bon attendre?; **there's no point phoning, he's out** ça ne sert à rien d'appeler, il est sorti; **that's not the point** il ne s'agit pas de ça; **4 that's a good point!** c'est vrai!; **5 from my point of view** de mon point de vue; **6 her strong point** son point fort; **7** (*in scoring*) point *Masc.*; **fifteen points to eleven** quinze points à onze; **8** (*in decimals*) (*in French, a comma is used for the decimal point, so 6,75*) **6 point 4** 6 virgule 4 (*this is how you say it aloud*).

**point** *verb* **1** indiquer [1]; **a notice pointing to the station** un panneau qui indiquait la gare; **James pointed out the cathedral** James nous a montré la cathédrale; **2** (*with finger*) montrer [1] du doigt; **he pointed at one of the children** il a montré l'un des enfants du doigt; **3 I'd like to point out that I'm paying** je vous signale que c'est moi qui paie.

**pointless** *adjective* inutile; **it's pointless to keep on ringing** c'est inutile de continuer de sonner.

**poison** *noun* poison *Masc.*
**poison** *verb* empoisonner [1].

**poisonous** *adjective* **1** toxique (*chemical or gas*); **2** vénéneux (*Fem.* vénéneuse) (*toadstools or berries*);

**3** venimeux (*Fem.* venimeuse) (*snake or insect*).

**poker** *noun* **1** (*for fire*) tisonnier *Masc.*; **2** (*card game*) poker *Masc.*

**Poland** *noun* Pologne *Fem.*; **in Poland** en Pologne.

**polar bear** *noun* ours *Masc.* polaire.

**pole** *noun* **1** (*for a tent*) mât *Masc.*; **2** (*for skiing*) bâton *Masc.*; **3 the North Pole** le pôle Nord.

**Pole** *noun* (*a Polish person*) Polonais *Masc.*, Polonaise *Fem.*

**police** *noun* **the police** la police; **the police are coming** la police arrive (*note that a singular verb is used after 'la police'*).
**police** *verb* surveiller [1].

**police car** *noun* voiture *Fem.* de police.

**policeman** *noun* agent *Masc.* de police.

**police station** *noun* commissariat *Masc.* de police.

**policewoman** *noun* femme *Fem.* policier.

**policy** *noun* **1** (*plan of action*) politique *Fem.*; **2** (*document*) police *Fem.*

**polish** *noun* **1** (*for furniture*) cire *Fem.*; **2** (*for shoes*) cirage *Masc.*
**polish** *verb* cirer [1] (*shoes or furniture*).

**Polish** *noun, adjective* polonais *Masc.*

**polite** *adjective* poli; **to be polite to somebody** être poli avec quelqu'un.

**political** *adjective* politique.

523

a
b
c
d
e
f
g
h
i
j
k
l
m
n
o
p
q
r
s
t
u
v
w
x
y
z

**politician** *noun* homme *Masc.* politique, femme *Fem.* politique.

**politics** *noun* politique *Fem.*

**polluted** *adjective* pollué.

**pollution** *noun* pollution *Fem.*

**polo-necked** *adjective* à col roulé; **a polo-necked jumper** un pull à col roulé.

**polythene bag** *noun* sac *Masc.* en plastique.

**pond** *noun* **1** (*large*) étang *Masc.*; **2** (*smaller*) mare *Fem.*; **3** (*in a garden*) bassin *Masc.*

**pony** *noun* poney *Masc.*

**ponytail** *noun* queue *Fem.* de cheval.

**poodle** *noun* caniche *Masc.*

**pool** *noun* **1** (*swimming pool*) piscine *Fem.*; **2** (*in the country*) étang *Masc.*; **3** (*puddle*) flaque *Fem.*; **4** (*game*) billard *Masc.* américain; **to have a game of pool** jouer au billard américain; **5 the football pools** le loto sportif; **to do the pools** jouer au loto sportif.

**poor** *adjective* **1** pauvre; **a poor area** un quartier pauvre; **a poor family** une famille pauvre; **poor Tanya's failed her exam** la pauvre Tanya a raté son examen; **2** (*bad*) mauvais; **this is poor work** c'est du mauvais travail; **the weather was pretty poor** le temps était assez mauvais.

**pop** *noun* pop *Masc.*; **a pop concert** un concert de pop; **a pop star** un pop star; **a pop song** une chanson pop.

● **to pop into** faire [10] un saut à; **I'll just pop into the bank** je vais juste faire un saut à la banque.

**popcorn** *noun* pop-corn *Masc.*

**pope** *noun* pape *Masc.*

**poppy** *noun* coquelicot *Masc.*

**popular** *adjective* populaire.

**population** *noun* population *Fem.*

**porch** *noun* porche *Masc.*

**pork** *noun* porc *Masc.*; **a pork chop** une côtelette de porc.

**porridge** *noun* porridge *Masc.*

**port** *noun* **1** port *Masc.*; **the ferry was in port** le ferry était au port; **2** (*wine*) porto *Masc.*

**portable computer** *noun* ordinateur *Masc.* portable.

**porter** *noun* **1** (*at a station or airport*) porteur *Masc.*; **2** (*in a hotel*) portier *Masc.*

**portion** *noun* (*of food*) portion *Fem.*

**portrait** *noun* portrait *Masc.*

**Portugal** *noun* Portugal *Masc.*; **to Portugal** au Portugal; **in Portugal** au Portugal.

**Portuguese** *noun* **1** (*language*) portugais *Masc.*; **2** (*a person*) Portugais *Masc.*, Portugaise *Fem.* **Portuguese** *adjective* portugais.

**posh** *adjective* chic (*never changes*); **a posh house** une maison chic.

**position** *noun* position *Fem.*

**positive** *adjective* **1** (*sure*) sûr; **I'm positive he's left** je suis sûr qu'il est parti; **2** (*enthusiastic*) positif (*Fem.* positive); **her reaction was very positive** sa réaction était très

**positive**; **try to be more positive** essaie d'être plus positif.

**possess** *verb* posséder [24].

**possessions** *plural noun* affaires *Fem. plural*; **all my possessions are in the flat** toutes mes affaires sont dans l'appartement.

**possibility** *noun* possibilité *Fem.*

**possible** *adjective* possible; **it's possible** c'est possible; **if possible** si possible; **as quickly as possible** le plus vite possible.

**possibly** *adverb* 1 (*maybe*) peut-être; **'will you be at home at midday?' – 'possibly'** 'est-ce que tu seras chez toi à midi?' – 'peut- être'; 2 (*for emphasis*) **how can you possibly believe that?** mais comment donc peux-tu croire ça?; **I can't possibly arrive before Thursday** je ne peux vraiment pas arriver avant jeudi.

**post** *noun* 1 poste *Fem.*; **to send something by post** envoyer quelque chose par la poste; 2 (*letters*) courrier *Masc.*; **is there any post for me?** y a-t-il du courrier pour moi?; 3 (*a pole*) poteau *Masc.*; 4 (*a job*) poste *Masc.* **post** *verb* **to post a letter** mettre [11] une lettre à la poste.

**postbox** *noun* boîte *Fem.* à lettres.

**postcard** *noun* carte *Fem.* postale.

**postcode** *noun* code *Masc.* postal.

**poster** *noun* 1 (*for decoration*) poster *Masc.*; **I've bought an Oasis poster** j'ai acheté un poster d'Oasis; 2 (*advertising*) affiche *Fem.*; **I saw a poster for the concert** j'ai vu une affiche pour le concert.

**postman** *noun* facteur *Masc.*; **has the postman been?** est-ce que le facteur est passé?

**post office** *noun* poste *Fem.*; **the post office is on the right** la poste est à droite.

**postpone** *verb* **to postpone something** remettre [11] quelque chose à plus tard.

**postwoman** *noun* factrice *Fem.*

**pot** *noun* 1 (*jar*) pot *Masc.*; **a pot of honey** un pot de miel; 2 (*teapot*) théière *Fem.*; **I'll make a pot of tea** je vais faire du thé; 3 **the pots and pans** les casseroles *Fem. plural*; ★ **to take pot luck** manger à la fortune du pot.

**potato** *noun* pomme *Fem.* de terre; **fried potatoes** des pommes de terre sautées; **mashed potatoes** de la purée.

**potato crisps** *plural noun* chips *Masc. plural*.

**pottery** *noun* poterie *Fem.*

**pound** *noun* 1 (*money*) livre *Fem.*; **fourteen pounds** quatorze livres; **how much is that in pounds?** c'est combien en livres sterling?; 2 (*in weight*) livre *Fem.*; **a pound of apples** une livre de pommes.

**pour** *verb* 1 verser [1] (*liquid*); **he poured the milk into the pan** il a versé le lait dans la casserole; 2 servir [71] (*a drink*); **to pour the tea** servir le thé; **I poured him a drink** je lui ai servi à boire; 3 (*with rain*) **it's pouring** il pleut à verse.

**poverty** *noun* pauvreté *Fem.*

**powder** *noun* poudre *Fem.*

a
b
c
d
e
f
g
h
i
j
k
l
m
n
o
p
q
r
s
t
u
v
w
x
y
z

**power** *noun* 1 (*electricity*) courant
*Masc.*; 2 (*energy*) énergie *Fem.*;
**nuclear power** l'énergie nucléaire;
3 (*over other people*) pouvoir *Masc.*;
**to be in power** être au pouvoir.

**power cut** *noun* coupure *Fem.* de
courant.

**powerful** *adjective* puissant.

**power point** *noun* prise *Fem.* de
courant.

**power station** *noun* centrale
*Fem.* électrique.

**practical** *adjective* pratique.

**practical joke** *noun* farce *Fem.*

**practically** *adverb* pratiquement.

**practice** *noun* 1 (*for sport*)
entraînement *Masc.*; **hockey
practice** l'entraînement de hockey;
2 (*for an instrument*) **to do your
piano practice** travailler [1] son
piano; 3 **to be out of practice** être
rouillé; 4 **in practice** en pratique.

**practise** *verb* 1 travailler [1]
(*music, language, etc*); **a week in
Berlin to practise my German** une
semaine à Berlin pour travailler
mon allemand; 2 (*in a sport*)
s'entraîner [1]; **the team practises
on Wednesdays** l'équipe s'entraîne
le mercredi.

**praise** *verb* **to praise somebody
for something** féliciter [1]
quelqu'un de quelque chose.

**pram** *noun* landau *Masc.*

**prawn** *noun* crevette *Fem.*

**pray** *verb* prier [1].

**prayer** *noun* prière *Fem.*

**precaution** *noun* précaution *Fem.*;
**to take precautions** prendre ses
précautions.

**precinct** *noun* **a shopping
precinct** un quartier commerçant;
**a pedestrian precinct** une zone
piétonne.

**precious** *adjective* précieux (*Fem.*
précieuse).

**precise** *adjective* précis.

**precisely** *adverb* précisément; **at
eleven o'clock precisely** à onze
heures précises.

**preface** *noun* préface *Fem.*

**prefer** *verb* préférer [24]; **I prefer
coffee to tea** je préfère le café au
thé.

**pregnancy** *noun* grossesse *Fem.*

**pregnant** *adjective* enceinte.

**prejudice** *noun* préjugé *Masc.*; **a
prejudice** un préjugé; **to fight
against racial prejudice** lutter
contre les préjugés raciaux.

**prejudiced** *adjective* **to be
prejudiced** avoir des préjugés.

**preliminary** *adjective*
préliminaire.

**première** *noun* première *Fem.* (*of a
play or film*).

**prep** *noun* devoirs *Masc. plural*; **my
English prep** mes devoirs d'anglais.

**preparation** *noun* 1 préparation
*Fem.*; 2 **the preparations for** les
préparatifs *Masc. plural* pour; **our
preparations for Christmas** nos
préparatifs pour Noël.

**prepare** *verb* préparer [1]; **to
prepare somebody for** préparer
quelqu'un à (*a surprise or shock*).

**prepared** *adjective* prêt; **I'm prepared to pay half** je suis prêt à en payer la moitié; **to be prepared for the worst** s'attendre [3] au pire.

**preposition** *noun* préposition *Fem.*

**prep school** *noun* école *Fem.* primaire privée.

**prescribe** *verb* prescrire [38].

**prescription** *noun* ordonnance *Fem.*; **on prescription** sur ordonnance.

**presence** *noun* présence *Fem.*; **in my presence** en ma présence.

**presence of mind** *noun* présence *Fem.* d'esprit.

**present** *noun* 1 (*a gift*) cadeau *Masc.* (*plural* cadeaux); **to give somebody a present** offrir un cadeau à quelqu'un; 2 (*the time now*) présent *Masc.*; **in the present (tense)** au présent; **that's all for the present** c'est tout pour le moment.
**present** *adjective* 1 (*attending*) présent; **is Tracy present?** est-ce que Tracy est présente?; **to be present at** assister [1] à; **fifty people were present at the funeral** cinquante personnes ont assisté à l'enterrement; 2 (*existing now*) actuel (*Fem.* actuelle); **the present situation** la situation actuelle; 3 **at the present time** actuellement.
**present** *verb* 1 remettre [11] (*a prize*); 2 (*introduce*) présenter [1].

**presenter** *noun* (*on TV*) présentateur *Masc.*, présentatrice *Fem.*

**presently** *adverb* (*soon*) bientôt.

**president** *noun* président *Masc.*, présidente *Fem.*

**press** *noun* **the press** la presse.
**press** *verb* 1 (*to push*) appuyer [41]; **press here to open** appuyez ici pour ouvrir; 2 appuyer [41] sur (*a button, switch, or pedal*); **he pressed the button** il a appuyé sur le bouton.

**press conference** *noun* conférence *Fem.* de presse.

**pressure** *noun* pression *Fem.*

**pressure gauge** *noun* indicateur *Masc.* de pression.

**pressure group** *noun* groupe *Masc.* de pression.

**pretend** *verb* **to pretend to do** faire [10] semblant de faire; **he's pretending not to hear** il fait semblant de ne pas entendre.

**pretty** *adjective* joli (*goes before the noun*); **a pretty dress** une jolie robe.
**pretty** *adverb* plutôt; **it was pretty silly** c'était plutôt bête.

**prevent** *verb* **to prevent somebody from doing** empêcher [1] quelqu'un de faire; **there's nothing to prevent you from leaving** rien ne vous empêche de partir.

**previous** *adjective* précédent.

**previously** *adverb* auparavant.

**price** *noun* prix *Masc.*; **the price per kilo** le prix du kilo; **CDs have gone up in price** les CD ont augmenté.

**price list** *noun* liste *Fem.* des prix.

**price ticket** *noun* étiquette *Fem.*

**prick** *verb* piquer [1]; **to prick your finger** se piquer le doigt.

**pride** *noun* fierté *Fem.*

a
b
c
d
e
f
g
h
i
j
k
l
m
n
o
p
q
r
s
t
u
v
w
x
y
z

**priest** noun prêtre Masc.

**primary school** noun école Fem. primaire.

**primary (school) teacher** noun instituteur Masc., institutrice Fem.

**prime minister** noun Premier ministre Masc.

**primrose** noun primevère Fem.

**prince** noun prince Masc.; **Prince Charles** le prince Charles.

**princess** noun princesse Fem.; **Princess Anne** la princesse Anne.

**principal** noun (of a college) directeur Masc., directrice Fem. **principal** adjective (main) principal (Masc. plural principaux).

**principle** noun principe Masc.; **on principle** par principe; **that's true in principle** cela est vrai en principe.

**print** noun 1 (letters) caractères Masc. plural; **in small print** en petits caractères; 2 (a photo) tirage Masc.; **a colour print** un tirage en couleur.

**printer** noun imprimante Fem.

**print-out** noun copie Fem. papier.

**prison** noun prison Fem.; **in prison** en prison.

**prisoner** noun prisonnier Masc., prisonnière Fem.

**private** adjective 1 privé; **a private school** une école privée; **'private property'** 'propriété privée'; 2 particulier (Fem. particulière) (lesson); **to have private lessons** prendre des cours particuliers.

**privately** adverb en privé.

**prize** noun prix Masc.; **to win a prize** gagner un prix.

**prize-giving** noun distribution Fem. des prix.

**prizewinner** noun gagnant Masc., gagnante Fem.

**probable** adjective probable.

**probably** adverb probablement.

**problem** noun problème Masc.; **it's a serious problem** c'est un grave problème; **no problem!** pas de problème!

**process** noun 1 processus Masc.; 2 **to be in the process of doing** être en train de faire.

**procession** noun 1 (in parade) défilé Masc.; 2 (at religious festival) procession Fem.

**produce** noun (food) produits Masc. plural. **produce** verb produire [26]; **I produced my passport** j'ai produit mon passeport; **it produces a lot of heat** ça produit beaucoup de chaleur.

**producer** noun (of a film or programme) metteur Masc. en scène.

**product** noun produit Masc.

**production** noun 1 (of a film or opera) production Fem.; 2 (of a play) mise Fem. en scène; **a new production of Hamlet** une nouvelle mise en scène de Hamlet; 3 (by a factory) production Fem.

**profession** noun profession Fem.

**professional** noun professionnel Masc., professionnelle Fem.; **he's a professional** c'est un professionnel. **professional** adjective professionnel (*Fem.* professionnelle); **she's a professional singer** c'est une chanteuse professionnelle.

**professor** *noun* professeur *Masc.*

**profile** *noun* profil *Masc.*

**profit** *noun* bénéfice *Masc.*

**profitable** *adjective* rentable.

**program** *noun* **a computer program** un programme informatique.

**programme** *noun* **1** (*for a play or an event*) programme *Masc.*; **2** (*on TV or radio*) émission *Fem.*

**programmer** *noun* programmateur *Masc.*, programmatrice *Fem.*

**progress** *noun* **1** progrès *Masc.*; **to make progress** faire des progrès; **2 to be in progress** être en cours.

**project** *noun* **1** (*at school*) dossier *Masc.*; **2** (*a plan*) projet *Masc.*; **a project to build a bridge** un projet pour construire un pont.

**projector** *noun* projecteur *Masc.*

**promise** *noun* promesse *Fem.*; **to make a promise** faire une promesse; **to break a promise** manquer à sa promesse; **it's a promise!** c'est promis! **promise** *verb* **to promise to do** promettre [11] de faire; **I've promised to be home by ten** j'ai promis de rentrer avant dix heures.

**promote** *verb* **to be promoted** être [6] promu.

**promotion** *noun* promotion *Fem.*

**prompt** *adjective* rapide; **a prompt reply** une réponse rapide.

**promptly** *adjective* **1** (*at once*) immédiatement; **he promptly fell off again** il est retombé immédiatement; **2** (*quickly*) rapidement; **please reply promptly** répondez rapidement s'il vous plaît; **3 promptly at nine o'oclock** à neuf heures précises.

**pronoun** *noun* pronom *Masc.*

**pronounce** *verb* prononcer [61]; **it's hard to pronounce** c'est difficile à prononcer.

**pronunciation** *noun* prononciation *Fem.*

**proof** *noun* preuve *Fem.*; **there's no proof that** ... rien ne prouve que ....

**propaganda** *noun* propagande *Fem.*

**propeller** *noun* hélice *Fem.*

**proper** *adjective* **1** (*real, genuine*) vrai; **a proper doctor** un vrai médecin; **I need a proper meal** j'ai besoin d'un vrai repas; **2** (*correct*) bon (*Fem.* bonne); **the proper answer** la bonne réponse; **the proper tool** le bon outil; **in its proper place** à sa place.

**properly** *adverb* comme il faut; **hold it properly** tiens-le comme il faut; **is it properly wrapped?** est-ce que c'est emballé comme il faut?

**property** *noun* (*your belongings*) affaires *Fem. plural*, propriété *Fem.*; **'private property'** 'propriété privée'.

**proposal** *noun* proposition *Fem.*

**propose** *verb* **1** (*suggest*) proposer [1]; **2** (*marriage*) **he proposed to her** il l'a demandée en mariage.

**prostitute** *noun* prostituée *Fem.*

a
b
c
d
e
f
g
h
i
j
k
l
m
n
o
p
q
r
s
t
u
v
w
x
y
z

**protect** *verb* protéger [15].

**protection** *noun* protection *Fem.*

**protein** *noun* protéine *Fem.*

**protest** *noun* protestation *Fem.*; **in spite of their protests** malgré leurs protestations.
**protest** *verb* **1** (*to grumble*) protester [1]; **he protested, but** ... il a protesté, mais ...; **2** (*demonstrate*) manifester [1].

**Protestant** *noun, adjective* protestant *Masc.*, protestante *Fem.*

**protester** *noun* manifestant *Masc.*, manifestante *Fem.*

**protest march** *noun* manifestation *Fem.*

**proud** *adjective* fier (*Fem.* fière).

**prove** *verb* prouver [1].

**proverb** *noun* proverbe *Masc.*

**provide** *verb* fournir [2].

**provided** *conjunction* à condition que; **provided you do it now** à condition que tu le fasses maintenant (*note that a verb in the subjunctive is needed*).

**province** *noun* province *Fem.*

**prune** *noun* pruneau *Masc.* (*plural* pruneaux).

**PS** (*at end of letter*) P.S.

**psychiatrist** *noun* psychiatre *Masc. & Fem.*; **he's a psychiatrist** il est psychiatre.

**psychological** *adjective* psychologique.

**psychologist** *noun* psychologue *Masc. & Fem.*; **she's a psychologist** ele est psychologue.

**psychology** *noun* psychologie *Fem.*

**PTO** TSVP (= *tournez s'il vous plaît*).

**pub** *noun* pub *Masc.*

**public** *noun* **the public** le public; **in public** en public.
**public** *adjective* **1** public (*Fem.* publique); **2 the public library** la bibliothèque municipale.

**public address system** *noun* sonorisation *Fem.*

**public holiday** *noun* jour *Masc.* férié; **January 1 is a public holiday** le premier janvier est férié.

**publicity** *noun* publicité *Fem.*

**public school** *noun* école *Fem.* privée.

**public transport** *noun* transports *Masc. plural* en commun.

**publish** *verb* publier [1].

**publisher** *noun* éditeur *Masc.*

**pudding** *noun* (*dessert*) dessert *Masc.*; **for pudding we've got strawberries** comme dessert nous avons des fraises.

**puddle** *noun* flaque *Fem.*

**puff** *noun* (*of smoke*) bouffée *Fem.*

**puff pastry** *noun* pâte *Fem.* feuilletée.

**pull** *verb* tirer [1]; **pull hard!** tire fort!; **to pull a rope** tirer sur une corde; **he pulled a letter out of his pocket** il a tiré une lettre de sa poche; ★ **you're pulling my leg!** tu me fais marcher!
● **to pull down** baisser [1] (*a blind*).
● **to pull in** (*at the roadside*) s'arrêter [1].

**pullover** *noun* pull-over *Masc.*

**pulse** *noun* pouls *Masc.*; **the doctor took my pulse** le médecin a pris mon pouls.

**pump** *noun* pompe *Fem.*; **a bicycle pump** une pompe à vélo.
**pump** *verb* pomper [1]; **they were pumping the water out of the cellar** ils pompaient l'eau de la cave.
• **to pump up** gonfler [1] (*a tyre*).

**pumpkin** *noun* citrouille *Fem.*

**punch** *noun* **1** (*in boxing*) coup *Masc.* de poing; **2** (*drink*) punch *Masc.*
**punch** *verb* **1 to punch somebody** donner [1] un coup de poing à quelqu'un; **he punched me** il m'a donné un coup de poing;
**2** composter [1] (*a ticket*).

**punctual** *adjective* ponctuel (*Fem.* ponctuelle).

**punctuation** *noun* ponctuation *Fem.*

**punctuation mark** *noun* signe *Masc.* de ponctuation.

**puncture** *noun* crevaison *Fem.*; **we had a puncture on the way** nous avons crevé en route.

**punish** *verb* punir [2].

**punishment** *noun* punition *Fem.*

**pupil** *noun* élève *Masc. & Fem.*

**puppet** *noun* marionnette *Fem.*

**puppy** *noun* chiot *Masc.*; **a labrador puppy** un chiot labrador.

**pure** *adjective* pur.

**purple** *adjective* violet (*Fem.* violette).

**purpose** *noun* **1** but *Masc.*; **what was the purpose of her call?** quel était le but de son appel?; **2 on purpose** exprès; **she did it on**

**purpose** elle l'a fait exprès; **he closed the door on purpose** il a fait exprès de fermer la porte.

**purr** *verb* ronronner [1].

**purse** *noun* porte-monnaie *Masc.* (*plural* porte-monnaie).

**push** *noun* **to give something a push** pousser [1] quelque chose.
**push** *verb* **1** pousser [1]; **he pushed me** il m'a poussé; **2** (*to press*) appuyer [41] sur (*a bell or button*); **3 to push somebody to do** pousser [1] quelqu'un à faire; **his teacher is pushing him to sit the exam** son prof le pousse à passer l'examen.
• **to push something away** repousser [1] quelque chose; **she pushed her plate away** elle a repoussé son assiette.

**pushchair** *noun* poussette *Fem.*

**put** *verb* **1** mettre [11]; **you can put the cream in the fridge** tu peux mettre la crème au frigo; **where did you put my bag?** où est-ce que tu as mis mon sac?; **put your suitcase here** mets ta valise ici; **2** (*write*) écrire [38]; **put your address here** écris ton adresse ici.
• **to put away** ranger [52]; **I'll put the shopping away** je vais ranger les courses.
• **to put back 1** remettre [11]; **I put it back in the drawer** je l'ai remis dans le tiroir; **2** (*postpone*) remettre [11]; **the meeting has been put back until Thursday** la réunion a été remise à jeudi.
• **to put down** poser [1]; **she put the vase down on the table** elle a posé le vase sur la table.
• **to put off 1** (*postpone*) remettre

a
b
c
d
e
f
g
h
i
j
k
l
m
n
o
**p**
q
r
s
t
u
v
w
x
y
z

[11]; **he's put off my lesson till Thursday** il a remis ma leçon à jeudi; **2** (*turn off*) éteindre [60] (*a light or TV*); **don't forget to put off the lights** n'oublie pas d'éteindre la lumière; **3 to put somebody off something** dégoûter [1] quelqu'un de quelque chose; **it really put me off Chinese food!** ça m'a vraiment dégoûté de la nourriture chinoise!; **4 to be put off** (*doing something*) se décourager [52]; **don't be put off!** ne te décourage pas!

● **to put on 1** mettre [11] (*clothing, make-up, CD*); **I'll just put my shoes on** je vais juste mettre mes chaussures; **il a mis Oasis** he's put on Oasis; **2** (*switch on*) allumer [1] (*a light or heating*); **could you put the lamp on?** est-ce que tu peux allumer la lampe?; **3** monter [1] (*a play*); **we're putting on a French play** nous sommes en train de monter une pièce française.

● **to put out 1** (*put outside*) sortir [72]; **have you put the rubbish out?** as-tu sorti les ordures?; **2** éteindre [60] (*a fire, light, or cigarette*); **I've put the lights out** j'ai éteint la lumière; **3 to put out your hand** tendre [3] la main.

● **to put through** passer [52]; **I'll put you through to the manager** je vous passe le responsable.

● **to put up 1** lever [50] (*your hand*); **I put up my hand** j'ai levé la main; **2** mettre [11] (*picture*); **I've put up some photos in my room** j'ai mis des photos dans ma chambre; **3** afficher [1] (*a notice*); **4** augmenter [1] (*the price*); **they've put up the price of the tickets** ils ont augmenté le prix des billets; **5** (*for the night*) héberger [52]; **can you put me up on Friday?** est-ce que tu peux m'héberger vendredi?

● **to put up with something** supporter [1]; **I don't know how she puts up with it** je ne sais pas comment elle le supporte.

**puzzle** *noun* (*jigsaw*) puzzle *Masc.*

**puzzled** *adjective* perplexe.

**pyjamas** *plural noun* pyjama *Masc. singular*; **a pair of pyjamas** un pyjama; **where are my pyjamas?** où est mon pyjama?

**pylon** *noun* pilône *Masc.*

**Pyrenees** *noun* les Pyrénées *Fem. plural*; **in the Pyrenees** dans les Pyrénées.

# Qq

**quail** *noun* caille *Fem.*

**qualification** *noun* **1** diplôme *Masc.* (*certificate, exam, degree*); **2 qualifications** qualifications *Fem. plural*; **vocational qualifications** les qualifications professionnelles.

**qualified** *adjective* **1** qualifié; **she's a qualified ski instructor** c'est une monitrice de ski qualifiée; **2** (*having a degree or a diploma*) diplômé; **a qualified architect** un architecte diplômé.

**qualify** *verb* **1** (*to be eligible*) avoir [5] droit à; **we don't qualify for a reduction** nous n'avons pas droit à une réduction; **2** (*in sport*) se qualifier [1].

**quality** *noun* qualité *Fem.*; **good quality vegetables** des légumes de bonne qualité.

**quantity** *noun* quantité *Fem.*

**quarantine** *noun* quarantaine *Fem.*

**quarrel** *noun* dispute *Fem.*; **to have a quarrel** se disputer [1]. **quarrel** *verb* se disputer [1]; **they're always quarrelling** ils sont tout le temps en train de se disputer.

**quarry** *noun* carrière *Fem.*

**quarter** *noun* **1** quart *Masc.*; **a quarter of the class** le quart de la classe; **three quarters of the class** les trois quarts de la classe; **2 a quarter past ten** dix heures et quart; **a quarter to ten** dix heures moins le quart; **a quarter of an hour** un quart d'heure; **three quarters of an hour** trois quarts d'heure; **an hour and a quarter** une heure et quart.

**quarter-final** *noun* quart *Masc.* de finale.

**quartet** *noun* quatuor *Masc.*; **a jazz quartet** un quatuor de jazz.

**quay** *noun* quai *Masc.*

**queen** *noun* reine *Fem.*; **Queen Elizabeth** la reine Elizabeth; **the Queen Mother** la reine mère.

**query** *noun* question *Fem.*; **are there any queries?** y a-t-il des questions?

**question** *noun* question *Fem.*; **to ask a question** poser une question; **I asked her a question** je lui ai posé une question; **it's a question of time** c'est une question de temps; **it's out of the question!** c'est hors de question!

**question** *verb* interroger [52].

**question mark** *noun* point *Masc.* d'interrogation.

**questionnaire** *noun* questionnaire *Masc.*; **to fill in a questionnaire** remplir un questionnaire.

**queue** *noun* **1** (*of people*) queue *Fem.*; **to stand in a queue** faire la queue; **2** (*of cars*) file *Fem.* **queue** *verb* faire [10] la queue; **we were queueing for check-in** nous faisions la queue pour l'enregistrement.

**quick** *adjective* **1** rapide; **a quick lunch** un déjeuner rapide; **it's quicker on the motorway** c'est plus rapide par l'autoroute; **to have a quick look at something** jeter un coup d'il rapide à quelque chose; **2 quick! there's the bus!** vite! voilà le bus!; **be quick!** dépêche-toi!

**quickly** *adverb* vite; **I'll just quickly phone my mother** je vais vite appeler ma mère.

**quiet** *adjective* **1** (*silent*) silencieux (*Fem.* silencieuse); **the children are very quiet** les enfants sont très silencieux; **2 to keep quiet** se taire [76]; **please keep quiet** taisez-vous, s'il vous plaît; **3** (*gentle*) doux (*Fem.* douce); **some quiet music** de la musique douce; **in a quiet voice** à voix basse; **4** (*peaceful*) tranquille; **a quiet street** une rue tranquille; **a quiet day at home** une journée tranquille à la maison.

**quietly** *adverb* **1** (*to move*) sans bruit; **he got up quietly** il s'est levé

a b c d e f g h i j k l m n o p **q** r s t u v w x y z

# quilt

sans bruit; **2** (*speak*) doucement;
**3** (*read or play*) en silence.

**quilt** *noun* couette *Fem.*

**quite** *adverb* **1** assez; **it's quite cold
outside** il fait assez froid dehors;
**that's quite a good idea** c'est une
assez bonne idée; **he sings quite
well** il chante assez bien; **quite
often** assez souvent; **2 not quite** pas
tout à fait; **the meat's not quite
cooked** la viande n'est pas tout à
fait cuite; **3 quite a lot of** pas mal
de; **we've got quite a lot of friends
here** nous avons pas mal d'amis ici;
**quite a few people** pas mal de gens.

**quiz** *noun* quiz *Masc.*

**quotation** *noun* (*from a book*)
citation *Fem.*

**quotation marks** *plural noun*
guillemets *Masc. plural*; **in quotation
marks** entre guillemets.

**quote** *noun* **1** (*from a book*) citation
*Fem.*; **2** (*estimate*) devis *Masc.*; **3 in
quotes** entre guillemets.
**quote** *verb* citer [1].

# Rr

**rabbi** *noun* rabbin *Masc.*

**rabbit** *noun* lapin *Masc.*

**rabbit hutch** *noun* clapier *Masc.*

**rabies** *noun* rage *Fem.*

**race** *noun* **1** (*a sports event*) course
*Fem.*; **a cycle race** une course
cycliste; **to have a race** faire la
course; **2** (*an ethnic group*) race *Fem.*

**racer** *noun* (*bike*) vélo *Masc.* de
course.

**racetrack** *noun* **1** (*for horses*)
champ *Masc.* de course; **2** (*for cars*)
circuit *Masc.*; **3** (*for cycles*) piste *Fem.*

**racial** *adjective* racial (*Masc. plural*
raciaux); **racial discrimination** la
discrimination raciale.

**racing** *noun* courses *Fem. plural.*

**racing car** *noun* voiture *Fem.* de
course.

**racing driver** *noun* pilote *Masc.* de
course.

**racism** *noun* racisme *Masc.*

**racist** *noun*, *adjective* raciste *Masc. &
Fem.*

**rack** *noun* (*for luggage*) porte-
bagages *Masc.*

**racket** *noun* **1** (*for tennis*) raquette
*Fem.*; **here's your tennis racket**
voici ta raquette de tennis; **2** (*noise*)
vacarme *Masc.*

**radar** *noun* radar *Masc.*

**radiation** *noun* radiation *Fem.*

**radiator** *noun* radiateur *Masc.*

**radio** *noun* radio *Fem.*; **to listen to
the radio** écouter la radio; **to hear
something on the radio** entendre
quelque chose à la radio.

**radioactive** *adjective* radioactif
(*Fem.* radioactive).

**radio-controlled** *adjective*
téléguidé.

**radio station** *noun* station *Fem.*
de radio.

**radish** *noun* radis *Masc.*

**radius** *noun* rayon *Masc.*

**raffle** *noun* tombola *Fem.*

**raft** *noun* radeau *Masc.*

**rag** *noun* chiffon *Masc.*

**rage** *noun* colère *Fem.*; **she's in a rage** elle est furieuse; ★ **it's all the rage** ça fait fureur.

**raid** *noun* **1** hold-up *Masc.*; **2** (*by the police*) rafle *Fem.*

**rail** *noun* **1** (*the railway*) **to go by rail** prendre le train; **2** (*on a balcony or bridge*) balustrade *Fem.*; **3** (*on stairs*) rampe *Fem.*; **4** (*for a train*) rail *Masc.*

**railing(s)** *noun* grille *Fem.*

**rail strike** *noun* grève *Fem.* des cheminots.

**railway** *noun* **1** (*the system*) chemin *Masc.* de fer; **the railways** les chemins de fer; **2 a railway line** une ligne de chemin de fer (*from one place to another*); **3 on the railway line** sur la voie ferrée (*the rails*).

**railway carriage** *noun* wagon *Masc.*

**railway station** *noun* gare *Fem.*; **opposite the railway station** en face de la gare.

**rain** *noun* pluie *Fem.*; **in the rain** sous la pluie.
**rain** *verb* pleuvoir [63]; **it's raining** il pleut; **it's going to rain** il va pleuvoir.

**rainbow** *noun* arc-en-ciel *Masc.* (*plural* arcs-en-ciel).

**raincoat** *noun* imperméable *Masc.*

**raindrop** *noun* goutte *Fem.* de pluie.

**rainfall** *noun* niveau *Masc.* de précipitations.

**rainy** *adjective* pluvieux (*Fem.* pluvieuse).

**raise** *verb* **1** (*lift up*) lever [50]; **she raised her head** elle a levé la tête; **2** (*increase*) augmenter [1] (*a price or a salary*); **3 to raise money for something** collecter [1] des fonds pour quelque chose; **4** (*to raise the alarm*) donner [1] l'alarme; **5** (*to raise somebody's spirits*) remonter [1] le moral à quelqu'un.

**raisin** *noun* raisin *Masc.* sec.

**rake** *noun* rateau *Masc.* (*plural* rateaux).

**rally** *noun* **1** (*a meeting*) rassemblement *Masc.*; **2** (*for sport*) rallye *Masc.*; **3** (*in tennis*) échange *Masc.*

**rambler** *noun* randonneur *Masc.*, randonneuse *Fem.*

**rambling** *noun* randonnée *Fem.*

**ramp** *noun* (*for a wheelchair, for example*) rampe *Fem.*

**ranch** *noun* ranch *Masc.*

**range** *noun* **1** (*a choice*) gamme *Fem.*; **we offer a range of sports** nous vous proposons une gamme de sports; **in a wide range of colours** dans un grand choix de coloris; **a top-of-the-range computer** un ordinateur haut de gamme; **2** (*of mountains*) chaîne *Fem.*

**rap** *noun* rap *Masc.* (*music*).

**rape** *noun* viol *Masc.*
**rape** *verb* violer [1].

**rare** *adjective* **1** rare; **a rare bird** un oiseau rare; **2** saignant (*a steak*); **medium-rare** à point.

**rarely** *adverb* rarement.

**rash** *noun* rougeurs *Fem. plural*; **I've got a rash on my arms** j'ai des

rougeurs sur les bras.
**rash** *adjective* irréfléchi; **a rash decision** une décision irréfléchie.

**raspberry** *noun* framboise *Fem.*;
**raspberry jam** la confiture de framboises; **a raspberry tart** une tarte aux framboises.

**rat** *noun* rat *Masc.*

**rate** *noun* **1** (*a charge*) tarif *Masc.*;
**what are the rates for children?** quels sont les tarifs pour les enfants?; **reduced rates** les tarifs réduits; **2** (*a level*) taux *Masc.*; **a high cancellation rate** un taux élevé d'annulation; **3 at any rate** en tout cas.

**rather** *adverb* **1** plutôt; **I'm rather busy** je suis plutôt occupé; **2 rather than** plutôt que; **in summer rather than winter** en été plutôt qu'en hiver; **3 I'd rather wait** je préfère attendre; **they'd rather come on Thursday** ils préfèrent venir jeudi;
**4 rather a lot of** pas mal de; **I've got rather a lot of shopping to do** j'ai pas mal de courses à faire.

**rave** *noun* rave *Masc.* (*a party*).

**raw** *adjective* cru.

**ray** *noun* rayon *Masc.*

**razor** *noun* rasoir *Masc.*

**razor blade** *noun* lame *Fem.* de rasoir.

**RE** *noun* éducation *Fem.* religieuse.

**reach** *noun* portée *Fem.*; **out of reach** hors de portée; **within reach** (*of your hand*) à portée de main; **within easy reach of the sea** à proximité de la mer.
**reach** *verb* **1** arriver [1] à; **when you reach the church** quand vous

arrivez à l'église; **to reach a decision** arriver à une décision;
**2 to reach the final** arriver [1] à la finale.

**react** *verb* réagir [2].

**reaction** *noun* réaction *Fem.*

**read** *verb* lire [51]; **what are you reading at the moment?** qu'est-ce que tu lis en ce moment?; **I'm reading a detective novel** je lis un roman policier; **he read out the list** il a lu la liste à haute voix.

**reading** *noun* lecture *Fem.*; **I don't much like reading** je n'aime pas beaucoup la lecture; **some easy reading for the beach** de la lecture facile pour la plage.

**ready** *adjective* prêt; **supper's not ready yet** le dîner n'est pas encore prêt; **are you ready to leave?** est-ce que tu es prêt à partir?; **to get ready** se préparer [1]; **I'm getting ready to go out** je me prépare pour sortir; **I was getting ready for bed** je me préparais pour me coucher; **I'll get your room ready** je vais préparer ta chambre.

**real** *adjective* vrai; **it's a real diamond** c'est un vrai diamant; **he's a real bore** c'est un vrai casse-pieds; **is that his real name?** est-ce que c'est son vrai nom?; **her real father is dead** son vrai père est mort.

**realistic** *adjective* réaliste.

**reality** *noun* réalité *Fem.*

**realize** *verb* se rendre [3] compte; **I hadn't realized** je ne m'en étais pas rendu compte; **I didn't realize he was French** je ne me suis pas rendu compte qu'il était français; **do you**

**realize what time it is?** tu te rends compte de l'heure qu'il est?

**really** *adverb* vraiment; **not really** pas vraiment; **is it really midnight?** est-il vraiment minuit?; **the film was really good** le film était vraiment très bon; **really?** c'est vrai?

**rear** *noun* arrière *Masc.* **rear** *adjective* arrière; **the rear door** la porte arrière.

**reason** *noun* raison *Fem.*; **the reason for the delay** la raison du retard; **the reason why I phoned** la raison pour laquelle j'ai appelé.

**reasonable** *adjective* raisonnable.

**reassure** *verb* rassurer [1].

**reassuring** *adjective* rassurant.

**rebel** *noun* rebelle *Masc. & Fem.*

**rebellion** *noun* rébellion *Fem.*, révolte *Fem.*

**rebuild** *verb* reconstruire [26].

**receipt** *noun* reçu *Masc.*

**receive** *verb* recevoir [66].

**receiver** *noun* combiné *Masc.*; **to pick up the receiver** décrocher [1].

**recent** *adjective* récent.

**recently** *adverb* récemment.

**reception** *noun* 1 réception *Fem.*; **he's waiting at reception** il attend à la réception; **a big wedding reception** une grande réception de mariage; **2 to get a good reception** avoir un bon accueil.

**receptionist** *noun* réceptionniste *Masc. & Fem.*

**recipe** *noun* recette *Fem.*; **can I have the recipe for your salad?** est-ce que je peux prendre la recette de ta salade?

**reckon** *verb* penser [1]; **I reckon it's a good idea** je pense que c'est une bonne idée.

**recognize** *verb* reconnaître [27].

**recommend** *verb* conseiller [1]; **can you recommend a dentist?** est-ce que vous pouvez me conseiller un dentiste?; **I recommend the fish soup** je vous conseille la soupe de poisson.

**recommendation** *noun* recommandation *Fem.*

**record** *noun* 1 record *Masc.*; **it's a world record** c'est le record mondial; **record sales for the CD** des ventes record pour le CD; **the hottest summer on record** l'été le plus chaud qu'on ait jamais enregistré; **2 to keep a record of something** noter quelque chose; **3** (*music*) disque *Masc.*; **a Miles Davis record** un disque de Miles Davis; **4** (*office files*) dossier *Masc.*; **I'll just check your records** je vais juste vérifier votre dossier. **record** *verb* (*on tape or CD*) enregistrer [1]; **they're recording a new album** ils sont en train d'enregistrer un nouvel album.

**recorder** *noun* 1 flûte *Fem.* à bec; **to play the recorder** jouer de la flûte à bec; **2 a cassette recorder** un magnétophone à cassettes; **a video recorder** un magnétoscope.

**recording** *noun* enregistrement *Masc.*

a
b
c
d
e
f
g
h
i
j
k
l
m
n
o
p
q
r
s
t
u
v
w
x
y
z

**record player** *noun* tourne-disque *Masc.*

**recover** *verb* se remettre [11]; **she's recovered now** elle s'est maintenant remise.

**recovery** *noun* (*from an illness*) rétablissement *Masc.*

**recovery vehicle** *noun* camion *Masc.* de dépannage.

**rectangle** *noun* rectangle *Masc.*

**rectangular** *adjective* rectangulaire.

**recycle** *verb* recycler [1].

**red** *adjective* 1 rouge; **a red shirt** une chemise rouge; **a bright red car** une voiture rouge vif; **to go red** rougir [2]; 2 roux (*Fem.* rousse) (*hair*); **to have red hair** avoir les cheveux roux.

**Red Cross** *noun* **the Red Cross** la Croix-Rouge.

**redcurrant** *noun* groseille *Fem.*; **redcurrant jelly** la gelée de groseilles.

**redecorate** *verb* refaire [10]; **they've redecorated the kitchen** ils ont refait la cuisine.

**redo** *verb* refaire [10].

**reduce** *verb* réduire [68]; **they've reduced the price** ils ont réduit le prix; **to reduce speed** ralentir [2].

**reduction** *noun* réduction *Fem.*

**redundant** *adjective* **to be made redundant** être licencié.

**reel** *noun* (*of cotton*) bobine *Fem.*

**refer** *verb* **refer to** parler [1] de; **she's referring to you** elle parle de vous.

**referee** *noun* (*in sport*) arbitre *Masc.*

**reference** *noun* références *Fem. plural* (*for a job*); **she gave me a good reference** elle m'a fourni de bonnes références.

**reference book** *noun* ouvrage *Masc.* de référence.

**refill** *noun* recharge *Fem.*

**reflect** *verb* refléter [24].

**reflection** *noun* 1 (*in a mirror*) image *Fem.*; 2 (*thought*) réflexion *Fem.*; **on reflection** à la réflexion.

**reflexive** *adjective* **a reflexive verb** un verbe réfléchi.

**refreshing** *adjective* rafraîchissant.

**refreshment** *noun* rafraîchissement *Masc.*

**refrigerator** *noun* réfrigérateur *Masc.*

**refuge** *noun* refuge *Masc.*; **a mountain refuge** un refuge (de montagne); **to take refuge in** se réfugier [1] dans.

**refugee** *noun* refugié *Masc.*, refugiée *Fem.*

**refund** *noun* remboursement *Masc.* **refund** *verb* rembourser [1].

**refusal** *noun* refus *Masc.*

**refuse** *noun* (*rubbish*) ordures *Fem. plural.*
**refuse** *verb* refuser [1]; **I refused** j'ai refusé; **he refuses to help** il refuse de nous aider.

**regards** *plural noun* amitiés *Fem. plural*; **'regards to your parents'** 'mes amitiés à vos parents'; **Nat**

religious

**sends his regards** tu as le bonjour de Nat.

**reggae** *noun* reggae *Masc.*

**region** *noun* région *Fem.*

**regional** *adjective* régional (*Masc. plural* régionaux).

**register** *noun* (*in school*) cahier *Masc.* des absences.
**register** *verb* s'inscrire [38].

**registered letter** *noun* lettre *Fem.* recommandée.

**registration number** *noun* numéro *Masc.* d'immatriculation (*of a vehicle*).

**regret** *verb* regretter [1].

**regular** *adjective* régulier (*Fem.* régulière); **regular visits** des visites régulières.

**regularly** *adverb* régulièrement.

**regulation** *noun* règlement *Masc.*

**rehearsal** *noun* répétition *Fem.*

**rehearse** *verb* répéter [24].

**reheat** *verb* réchauffer [1].

**reign** *noun* règne *Masc.*

**rein** *noun* rêne *Fem.*

**reject** *verb* rejeter [48].

**related** *adjective* apparenté; **we're not related** nous ne sommes pas apparentés.

**relation** *noun* **my relations** ma famille; **there were just relations and close friends** il n'y avait que la famille et des amis proches; **she's got relations in France** elle a de la famille en France.

**relationship** *noun* relations *Fem. plural*; **we have a good relationship** nous avons de bonnes relations.

**relative** *noun* membre *Masc.* de la famille; **there were a few relatives at the funeral** il y avait quelques membres de la famille à l'enterrement; **all my relatives** toute ma famille.

**relatively** *adverb* relativement.

**relax** *verb* se détendre [3]; **I'm going to relax and watch telly tonight** je vais me détendre en regardant la télé ce soir.

**relaxation** *noun* détente *Fem.*

**relaxed** *adjective* détendu.

**relaxing** *adjective* reposant.

**relay race** *noun* course *Fem.* de relais.

**release** *noun* **1** nouveauté *Fem.*; **this week's new releases** les nouveautés de la semaine; **2** (*of a prisoner or hostage*) libération *Fem.*
**release** *verb* **1** sortir [72] (*a record or a video*); **2** libérer [24] (*a person*).

**relevant** *adjective* pertinent.

**reliable** *adjective* fiable.

**relief** *noun* soulagement *Masc.*; **what a relief!** quel soulagement!

**relieve** *verb* soulager [52] (*pain*).

**relieved** *adjective* soulagé; **I was relieved to hear you'd arrived** j'ai été soulagé d'apprendre que tu étais arrivé.

**religion** *noun* religion *Fem.*

**religious** *adjective* **1** croyant (*a person*); **Jane's not religious** Jane n'est pas croyante; **2** religieux (*Fem.* religieuse) (*art or music, for example*).

a
b
c
d
e
f
g
h
i
j
k
l
m
n
o
p
q
r
s
t
u
v
w
x
y
z

**reluctant** *adj* réticent; **he's reluctant to go** il est peu disposé à y aller.

**rely** *verb* **to rely on somebody** compter [1] sur quelqu'un; **I'm relying on you for Saturday** je compte sur toi pour samedi.

**remain** *verb* rester [1].

**remains** *plural noun* restes *Masc. plural*; **the remains of the chicken** les restes du poulet; **the remains of a castle** les restes d'un château.

**remark** *noun* remarque *Fem.*; **to make remarks about** faire des remarques sur.

**remarkable** *adjective* remarquable.

**remarkably** *adverb* remarquablement.

**remember** *verb* **1** se souvenir [81]; **I don't remember** je ne me souviens plus; **2 to remember something** se souvenir [81] de quelque chose; **I can't remember the number** je ne me souviens pas du numéro; **3 to remember to do** ne pas oublier [1] de faire; **remember to shut the door** n'oublie pas de fermer la porte; **I remembered to bring the CDs** je n'ai pas oublié d'apporter les CD.

**remind** *verb* rappeler [18] **1 to remind somebody to do** rappeler à quelqu'un de faire; **remind your mother to pick me up** rappelle à ta mère de venir me chercher; **2** faire [10] penser; **it reminds me of Paris** ça me fait penser à Paris; **he reminds me of Frank** il me fait penser à Frank; **oh, that reminds me** ... tiens, j'y pense ....

**remote** *adjective* isolé.

**remote control** *noun* télécommande *Fem.*

**remove** *verb* enlever [50]; **he removed his jacket** il a enlevé sa veste; **the chairs had all been removed** quelqu'un avait enlevé toutes les chaises.

**renew** *verb* renouveler [18] (*a passport or licence*).

**rent** *noun* loyer *Masc.*
**rent** *verb* louer [1]; **Simon's rented a flat** Simon a loué un appartement.

**rental** *noun* location *Fem.*

**reorganize** *verb* réorganiser [1].

**repair** *noun* réparation *Fem.*
**repair** *verb* réparer [1]; **to get something repaired** faire [10] réparer quelque chose; **we've had the television repaired** nous avons fait réparer la télévision.

**repay** *verb* rembourser [1]; **he repaid me the money he owed me** il m'a remboursé l'argent qu'il me devait.

**repeat** *noun* reprise *Fem.* (*of a programme*).
**repeat** *verb* répéter [24].

**repeatedly** *adverb* à plusieurs reprises.

**repertoire** *noun* répertoire *Masc.*

**repetitive** *adjective* répétitif (*Fem.* répétitive).

**replace** *verb* remplacer [61].

**replacement** *noun* **1** (*person*) remplaçant *Masc.*, remplaçante *Fem.*; **2** (*thing*) **can you find me a replacement?** est-ce que vous pouvez le/la remplacer?

**replay** *verb* **1** (*game*) rejouer [1];
**2** (*video*) repasser [1].

**reply** *noun* réponse *Fem.*; **I didn't get
a reply to my letter** je n'ai pas reçu
de réponse à ma lettre; **there's no
reply** ça ne répond pas (*on the
telephone*).
**reply** *verb* répondre [3]; **I still
haven't replied to the letter** je n'ai
toujours pas répondu à la lettre.

**report** *noun* **1** (*of an event*) compte
rendu *Masc.*; **2** (*school report*)
bulletin *Masc.* scolaire.
**report** *verb* **1** signaler [1] (*a
problem or accident*); **we've
reported the theft** nous avons
signalé le vol; **2** se présenter [1]; **I
had to report to reception** je
devais me présenter à la réception.

**reporter** *noun* journaliste *Masc. &
Fem.*

**represent** *verb* représenter [1].

**representative** *noun*
représentant *Masc.*, représentante
*Fem.*.

**reproach** *noun* reproche *Masc.*
**reproach** *verb* reprocher [1].

**reproduction** *noun* reproduction
*Fem.*

**reptile** *noun* reptile *Masc.*

**republic** *noun* république *Fem.*

**reputation** *noun* réputation *Fem.*;
**a good reputation** une bonne
réputation; **she has a reputation
for honesty** elle a la réputation
d'être honnête.

**request** *noun* demande *Fem.*; **on
request** sur demande.
**request** *verb* demander [1].

**rescue** *noun* secours *Masc.*; **to
come to somebody's rescue** venir
au secours de quelqu'un.
**rescue** *verb* sauver [1]; **they
rescued the dog** ils ont sauvé le
chien.

**rescue party** *noun* équipe *Fem.* de
secours.

**rescue worker** *noun* secouriste
*Masc. & Fem.*

**research** *noun* recherche *Fem.*; **for
research into Aids** pour la
recherche sur le Sida; **to do
research** faire des recherches.
**research** *verb* **to research into**
faire [10] des recherches sur; **a well-
researched programme** un
programme bien documenté.

**resemblance** *noun*
ressemblance *Fem.*

**resemble** *verb* ressembler [1] à;
**she resembles her aunt** elle
ressemble à sa tante.

**reservation** *noun* (*a booking*)
réservation *Fem.*; **to make a
reservation** faire une réservation.

**reserve** *noun* **1** réserve *Fem.*; **we
have some in reserve** nous en
avons en réserve; **2 a nature
reserve** une réserve naturelle;
**3** (*for a match*) remplaçant *Masc.*,
remplaçante *Fem.*.
**reserve** *verb* réserver [1]; **this
table is reserved** cette table est
réservée.

**reservoir** *noun* réservoir *Masc.*

**resident** *noun* résident *Masc.*,
résidente *Fem.*

a
b
c
d
e
f
g
h
i
j
k
l
m
n
o
p
q
**r**
s
t
u
v
w
x
y
z

a

b **residential** *adjective* résidentiel (*Fem.* résidentielle); **a residential area** un quartier résidentiel.

c **resign** *verb* démissionner [1].

d **resignation** *noun* (*from a post*) démission *Fem.*

e **resist** *verb* résister [1] à (*an offer or temptation*); **I can't resist!** je ne peux pas résister!

f

g **resit** *verb* repasser [1] (*an exam*).

h **resort** *noun* 1 (*for holidays*) **a holiday resort** un lieu de villégiature; **a ski resort** une station de ski; **a seaside resort** une station balnéaire; 2 **as a last resort** en dernier recours.

i

j

k

l **respect** *noun* respect *Masc.* **respect** *verb* respecter [1].

**respectable** *adjective* respectable.

m

n **respectful** *adjective* respectueux (*Fem.* respectueuse).

o **responsibility** *noun* responsabilité *Fem.*

p

q **responsible** *adjective* 1 (*to blame*) responsable; **he's responsible for the delay** il est responsable du retard; 2 (*in charge*) responsable; **I'm responsible for booking the rooms** je suis responsable de la réservation des chambres; 3 (*reliable*) sérieux (*Fem.* sérieuse); **he's not very responsible** il n'est pas très sérieux.

r

s

t

u

v

w **rest** *noun* 1 **the rest** le reste; **the rest of the day** le reste du jour; **the rest of the bread** le reste du pain; 2 (*the others*) les autres; **the rest have gone home** les autres sont rentrés; 3 repos *Masc.*, ; **ten days'**

x

y

z

**complete rest** dix jours de repos total; **to have a rest** se reposer [1]; 4 (*a short break*) pause *Fem.*; **to stop for a rest** faire une pause.

**rest** *verb* (*have a rest*) se reposer [1].

**restaurant** *noun* restaurant *Masc.*

**restful** *adjective* reposant.

**restless** *adjective* nerveux (*Fem.* nerveuse).

**restore** *verb* restaurer [1]

**restrain** *verb* retenir [77].

**restrict** *verb* limiter [1].

**restriction** *noun* limitation *Fem.*

**result** *noun* 1 résultat *Masc.*; **the exam results** les résultats des examens; 2 **as a result** par conséquent; **as a result we missed the ferry** par conséquent nous avons raté le ferry.

**retire** *verb* (*from work*) prendre [64] sa retraite; **she retires in June** elle prend sa retraite en juin; **for retired people** pour les retraités.

**retirement** *noun* retraite *Fem.*

**return** *noun* 1 retour *Masc.*; **the return journey** le voyage de retour; **by return of post** par retour de courrier; 2 **in return** en échange; **in return for his help** en échange de son aide; ★ **many happy returns!** bon anniversaire!

**return** *verb* 1 (*come back*) revenir [81]; **he returned ten minutes later** il est revenu dix minutes plus tard; 2 (*get home*) rentrer [1]; **to return from holiday** rentrer de vacances; **I'll ask her to phone as soon as she returns** je lui demanderai de vous appeler dès qu'elle rentrera; 3 (*to give back*) rendre [3]; **Gemma's**

**never returned the video** Gemma n'a jamais rendu la vidéo.

**return fare** *noun* prix *Masc.* d'un billet aller-retour.

**return ticket** *noun* billet *Masc.* aller-retour.

**reunion** *noun* réunion *Fem.*; **a class reunion** une réunion d'anciens élèves.

**reveal** *verb* révéler [24].

**revenge** *noun* vengeance *Fem.*; **to get one's revenge on someone** se venger [52] de quelqu'un.

**reverse** *noun* **1** (*of a coin*) revers *Masc.*; **2** (*of a page*) dos *Masc.*; **3** (*opposite*) **the reverse is true** le contraire est vrai; **4** (*gear*) marche *Fem.* arrière.
**reverse** *verb* **1** (*in a car*) faire [10] marche arrière; **he reversed the car out of the garage** il a sorti la voiture du garage en marche arrière; **2 to reverse the charges** faire [10] un appel en PCV.

**review** *noun* (*of a book, play, or film*) critique *Fem.*
**review** *verb* faire [10] la critique de (*a play or concert*); **the film was well reviewed** le film a eu une bonne critique.

**revise** *verb* réviser [1]; **Tessa's busy revising for her exams** Tessa est en train de réviser pour ses examens.

**revision** *noun* révision *Fem.*

**revive** *verb* ranimer [1].

**revolting** *adjective* infect; **the sausages are revolting** les saucisses sont infectes.

**revolution** *noun* révolution *Fem.*; **the Fench Revolution** la Révolution française.

**revolving door** *noun* porte *Fem.* à tambour.

**reward** *noun* récompense *Fem.*; **a £100 reward** cent livres de récompense.
**reward** *verb* récompenser [1].

**rewarding** *adjective* enrichissant.

**rewind** *verb* rembobiner [1] (*a cassette or video*).

**rhinoceros** *noun* rhinocéros *Masc.*

**rhubarb** *noun* rhubarbe *Fem.*

**rhyme** *noun* rime *Fem.*

**rhythm** *noun* rythme *Masc.*

**rib** *noun* côte *Fem.*

**ribbon** *noun* ruban *Masc.*

**rice** *noun* riz *Masc.*; **chicken and rice** du poulet au riz; **rice pudding** le riz au lait.

**rich** *adjective* riche; **we're not very rich** nous ne sommes pas très riches; **the rich and the poor** les riches et les pauvres.

**rid** *adjective* **to get rid of something** se débarrasser de quelque chose; **we got rid of the car** nous nous sommes débarrassés de la voiture.

**riddle** *noun* devinette *Fem.*

**ride** *noun* tour *Masc.*; **to go for a ride (on a bike)** faire [10] un tour à vélo; **to go for a ride (on a horse)** faire une promenade à cheval.
**ride** *verb* **1 to learn to ride a bike** apprendre [64] à faire du vélo; **can you ride a bike?** sais-tu faire du vélo?; **2 to learn to ride (a horse)** apprendre [64] à monter à cheval;

a
b
c
d
e
f
g
h
i
j
k
l
m
n
o
p
q
r
s
t
u
v
w
x
y
z

I've never ridden a horse je ne suis jamais monté à cheval.

**rider** *noun* **1** (*on a horse*) cavalier *Masc.*, cavalière *Fem.*; **2** (*on a bike*) cycliste *Masc. & Fem.*; **3** (*on a motorbike*) motocycliste *Masc. & Fem.*

**ridiculous** *adjective* ridicule.

**riding** *noun* équitation *Fem.*; **to go riding** faire [10] de l'équitation.

**riding school** *noun* école *Fem.* d'équitation.

**rifle** *noun* fusil *Masc.*

**right** *noun* **1** (*not left*) droite *Fem.*; **on the right** à droite; **on my right** à ma droite; **2** (*to do something*) droit *Masc.*; **the right to strike** le droit de grève; **you have no right to say that** tu n'as pas le droit de dire ça.

**right** *adjective* **1** (*not left*) droit; **my right hand** ma main droite; **2** (*correct*) bon (*Fem.* bonne); **the right answer** la bonne réponse; **the right telephone number** le bon numéro de téléphone; **the right amount of** la bonne quantité de; **is this the right address?** est-ce que c'est la bonne adresse?; **3 to be right** (*a person*) avoir [5] raison; **you see, I was right** tu vois, j'avais raison; **4 you were right to stay at home** tu as bien fait de rester chez toi; **he was right not to say anything** il a bien fait de ne rien dire; **5** (*moral*) bien; **it's not right to talk like that** ce n'est pas bien de parler comme ça.

**right** *adverb* **1** (*direction*) à droite; **turn right at the lights** tournez à droite aux feux; **2** (*correctly*) comme il faut; **you're not doing it right** tu ne le fais pas comme il faut; **3** (*completely*) tout; **right at the**

bottom tout au fond; **right at the beginning** tout au début; **right now** tout de suite; **right in the middle** en plein milieu; **4** (*okay*) bon; **right, let's go** bon, allons-y.

**right-click** *noun* clic *Masc.* sur le bouton droit de la souris.

**right-hand** *adjective* **on the right-hand side** à droite.

**right-handed** *adjective* droitier (*Fem.* droitière).

**rind** *noun* **1** (*on fruit*) peau *Fem.*; **2** (*on cheese*) croûte *Fem.*

**ring** *noun* **1** (*on the phone*) **to give somebody a ring** appeler [18] quelqu'un; **2** (*for your finger*) bague *Fem.*; **3** (*circle*) cercle *Masc.*; **4 there was a ring at the door** on a sonné à la porte.

**ring** *verb* **1** (*a bell or phone*) sonner [1]; **the phone rang** le téléphone a sonné; **2** (*phone*) appeler [18]; **I'll ring you tomorrow** je t'appellerai demain; **could you ring for a taxi?** est-ce que tu peux appeler un taxi?

• **to ring back** rappeler [18]; **I'll ring you back later** je te rappellerai tout à l'heure.

• **to ring off** raccrocher [1].

**ring road** *noun* rocade *Fem.*

**rinse** *verb* rincer [61].

**riot** *noun* émeute *Fem.*

**rioting** *noun* émeutes *Fem. plural.*

**rip** *verb* déchirer [1].

**ripe** *adjective* mûr; **are the tomatoes ripe?** est-ce que les tomates sont mûres?

**rip-off** *noun* **it's a rip-off!** c'est de l'arnaque!

**rise** *noun* **1** hausse *Fem.*; **a rise in price** une hausse de prix; **2 a pay rise** une augmentation.
**rise** *verb* **1** (*the sun*) se lever [50]; **when the sun rose** quand le soleil s'est levé; **2** (*prices*) augmenter [1].

**risk** *noun* risque *Masc.*; **to take risks** prendre des risques.
**risk** *verb* risquer [1]; **he risks losing his job** il risque de perdre son emploi.

**rival** *noun* rival *Masc.* (*plural* rivaux), rivale *Fem.*

**river** *noun* **1** rivière *Fem.*; **we picnicked on the edge of a river** nous avons pique-niqué au bord d'une rivière; **2** fleuve *Masc.*; **the rivers of Europe** les fleuves de l'Europe (*'fleuve' is only used for a river which flows directly into the sea like the Thames in Britain or the Seine in France*).

**Riviera** *noun* **the French Riviera** la Côte d'Azur.

**road** *noun* **1** route *Fem.*; **the road to London** la route de Londres; **2** (*in a town*) rue *Fem.*; **the butcher's is on the other side of the road** la boucherie est de l'autre côté de la rue; **3 across the road** en face; **they live across the road from us** ils habitent en face de chez nous.

**road accident** *noun* accident *Masc.* de la route.

**road map** *noun* carte *Fem.* routière.

**roadside** *noun* **by the roadside** au bord de la route.

**road sign** *noun* panneau *Masc.* de signalisation (*plural* panneaux de signalisation).

**roadworks** *plural noun* travaux *Masc. plural*.

**roast** *noun* rôti *Masc.*
**roast** *adjective* rôti; **roast potatoes** les pommes de terre rôties; **roast beef** le rôti de bœuf.

**rob** *verb* **1** voler [1] (*a person*); **2** dévaliser [1] (*a bank*).

**robber** *noun* voleur *Masc.*, voleuse *Fem.*

**robbery** *noun* vol *Masc.*; **a bank robbery** un hold-up.

**robot** *noun* robot *Masc.*

**rock** *noun* **1** (*a big stone*) rocher *Masc.*; **she was sitting on a rock** elle était assise sur un rocher; **2** (*the material*) roche *Fem.*; **3** (*music*) rock *Masc.*; **a rock band** un groupe de rock; **to dance rock and roll** danser le rock.

**rock climbing** *noun* escalade *Fem.*; **to go rock climbing** faire de l'escalade.

**rocket** *noun* fusée *Fem.*

**rocking horse** *noun* cheval *Masc.* à bascule.

**rock star** *noun* rock-star *Fem.*

**rocky** *adjective* rocailleux (*Fem.* rocailleuse).

**rod** *noun* **a fishing rod** une canne à pêche.

**role** *noun* rôle *Masc.*; **to play the role of** jouer le rôle de.

**roll** *noun* **1** rouleau *Masc.* (*plural* rouleaux); **a roll of fabric** un rouleau de tissu; **a roll of**

a
b
c
d
e
f
g
h
i
j
k
l
m
n
o
p
q
r
s
t
u
v
w
x
y
z

**a**

sellotape™ un rouleau de scotch™;
**a toilet roll** un rouleau de papier
hygiénique; **2 a bread roll** un petit
pain.

**roll** *verb* rouler [1].

- **to roll something up 1** rouler [1]
(*a carpet*); **2** retrousser [1] (*sleeves*);
**he rolled up his sleeves** il a
retroussé ses manches

**roller** *noun* rouleau *Masc.* (*plural*
rouleaux).

**rollerblades** *plural noun* rollers
*Masc. plural.*

**rollercoaster** *noun* montagnes
*Fem. plural* russes (*literally: Russian
mountains*).

**roller skates** *plural noun* patins
*Masc. plural* à roulettes.

**Roman Catholic** *noun, adjective*
catholique *Masc. & Fem.*

**romantic** *adjective* romantique.

**roof** *noun* toit *Masc.*

**roof rack** *noun* galerie *Fem.*

**rook** *noun* **1** (*in chess*) tour *Fem.*;
**2** (*bird*) freux *Masc.*

**room** *noun* **1** pièce *Fem.*; **she's in the
other room** elle est dans l'autre
pièce; **it's the biggest room in the
house** c'est la pièce la plus grande
de la maison; **a three-room flat** un
appartement à trois pièces; **2** (*a
bedroom*) chambre *Fem.*; **Freda's in
her room** Freda est dans sa
chambre; **I tidied my room last
night** j'ai rangé ma chambre hier
soir; **3** (*space*) place *Fem.*; **enough
room for two** assez de place pour
deux; **very little room** très peu de
place.

**roommate** *noun* camarade *Masc. &
Fem.* de chambre.

**root** *noun* racine *Fem.*

**rope** *noun* corde *Fem.*

**rose** *noun* rose *Fem.*

**rosebush** *noun* rosier *Masc.*

**rot** *verb* pourrir [2].

**rota** *noun* tableau *Masc.* de service.

**rotten** *adjective* pourri.

**rough** *adjective* **1** (*scratchy*)
rugueux (*Fem.* rugueuse); **2** (*vague*)
approximatif (*Fem.* approximative);
**a rough idea** une idée
approximative; **3** (*stormy*) agité; **a
rough sea** une mer agitée; **in rough
weather** par gros temps; **4** (*difficult*)
**to have a rough time** passer par
une période dificile; **5 to sleep
rough** dormir à la dure.

**roughly** *adjective* (*approximately*)
**roughly ten per cent** à peu près dix
pour cent; **it takes roughly three
hours** ça prend à peu près trois
heures.

**round** *noun* **1** (*in a tournament*)
manche *Fem.*; **2** (*of cards*) partie *Fem.*;
**3 a round of drinks** une tournée;
**it's my round** c'est ma tournée.
**round** *adjective* rond; **a round table**
une table ronde.
**round** *preposition* **1** autour de;
**round the city** autour de la ville;
**round my arm** autour de mon bras;
**they were sitting round the table**
ils étaient assis autour de la table;
**2 to go round the shops** faire les
magasins; **to go round a museum**
visiter un musée; **it's just round the
corner** c'est tout près.
**round** *adverb* **1 to go round to**

**somebody's house** aller chez quelqu'un; **we invited Sally round for lunch** nous avons invité Sally à déjeuner; **2 all the year round** toute l'année.

**roundabout** *noun* **1** (*for traffic*) rond-point *Masc.*; **2** (*in a fairground*) manège *Masc.*

**route** *noun* **1** (*that you plan*) itinéraire *Masc.*; **the best route is via Calais** le meilleur itinéraire est par Calais; **2 a bus route** un parcours de bus.

**routine** *noun* routine *Fem.*

**row**[1] *noun* **1** rang *Masc.*; **in the front row** au premier rang; **in the back row** au dernier rang; **2** rangée *Fem.*; **a row of books** une rangée de livres; **3 four times in a row** quatre fois de suite.

**row**[2] *verb* (*in a boat*) ramer [1]; **it's your turn to row** c'est à toi de ramer; **we rowed across the lake** nous avons traversé le lac à la rame.

**row**[3] *noun* **1** (*a quarrel*) dispute *Fem.*; **to have a row** se disputer; **they've had a row** ils se sont disputés; **I had a row with my parents** je me suis disputé avec mes parents; **2** (*noise*) vacarme *Masc.*; **they were making a terrible row!** ils faisaient un vacarme pas possible!

**rowing** *noun* aviron *Masc.*; **to go rowing** faire [10] de l'aviron.

**rowing boat** *noun* barque *Fem.*

**royal** *adjective* royal (*Masc. plural* royaux); **the royal family** la famille royale.

**rub** *verb* frotter [1]; **to rub your eyes** se frotter les yeux.

● **to rub something out** effacer [61] quelque chose.

**rubber** *noun* **1** (*an eraser*) gomme *Fem.*; **2** (*material*) caoutchouc *Masc.*; **rubber soles** des semelles en caoutchouc.

**rubbish** *noun* **1** (*for the bin*) ordures *Fem. plural*; **2** (*nonsense*) bêtises *Fem. plural*; **you're talking rubbish!** tu dis des bêtises!

**rubbish** *adjective* nul (*Fem.* nulle); **the film was rubbish** le film était nul; **they're a rubbish band** c'est un groupe nul.

**rubbish bin** *noun* poubelle *Fem.*

**rucksack** *noun* sac *Masc.* à dos.

**rude** *adjective* **1** impoli; **that's rude** c'est impoli; **2 a rude joke** une plaisanterie grossière; **a rude word** un gros mot.

**rug** *noun* **1** tapis *Masc.*; **2** (*a blanket*) couverture *Fem.*

**rugby** *noun* rugby *Masc.*; **to play rugby** jouer au rugby; **a rugby match** un match de rugby.

**ruin** *noun* ruine *Fem.*; **in ruins** en ruines.

**ruin** *verb* **1** abîmer [1]; **you'll ruin your jacket** tu vas abîmer ta veste; **2** gâcher [1] (*day, holiday*); **it ruined my evening** ça m'a gâché la soirée.

**rule** *noun* **1** règle *Fem.*; **the rules of the game** les règles du jeu; **2 the school rules** le règlement de l'école; **3 as a rule** en général.

**ruler** *noun* règle *Fem.*; **I've lost my ruler** j'ai perdu ma règle.

**rum** *noun* rhum *Masc.*

**rumour** *noun* rumeur *Fem.*

a
b
c
d
e
f
g
h
i
j
k
l
m
n
o
p
q
r
s
t
u
v
w
x
y
z

**run** *noun* **1** to go for a run courir [29]; **2** (*in cricket*) point *Masc.*; **to score fifteen runs** marquer quinze points; **3 in the long run** à long terme.

**run** *verb* **1** courir [29]; **I ran ten kilometres** j'ai couru dix kilomètres; **he ran across the pitch** il a traversé le terrain en courant; **Kitty ran for the bus** Kitty a couru pour attraper le bus; **2** (*organize*) organiser [1]; **who's running this concert?** qui est-ce qui organise ce concert?; **3** diriger [52] (*a business*); **he ran the firm for forty years** il a dirigé l'entreprise pendant quarante ans; **4** (*a train or bus*) circuler [1]; **the buses don't run on Sundays** les bus ne circulent pas le dimanche; **5 to run a bath** faire [10] couler un bain.

- **to run away** s'enfuir [44].
- **to run into** rentrer [1] dans; **the car ran into a lamppost** la voiture est rentrée dans un réverbère.
- **to run out of something: we've run out of bread** il ne reste plus de pain; **I'm running out of money** je n'ai presque plus d'argent.
- **to run somebody over** écraser [1] quelqu'un; **you'll get run over!** tu vas te faire écraser!

**runner** *noun* coureur *Masc.*, coureuse *Fem.*

**runner-up** *noun* second *Masc.*, seconde *Fem.*

**running** *noun* (*for exercise*) course *Fem.*

**running** *adjective* **1 running water** l'eau courante; **2 three days running** trois jours de suite; **six times running** six fois de suite.

**runway** *noun* piste *Fem.*

**rush** *noun* (*a hurry*) **to be in a rush** être pressé; **sorry, I'm in a rush** désolé, je suis pressé.

**rush** *verb* **1** (*hurry*) se dépêcher [1]; **I must rush!** il faut que je me dépêche!; **2** (*run*) se précipiter [1]; **she rushed into the street** elle s'est précipitée dans la rue; **3 Louise was rushed to hospital** on a emmené Louise d'urgence à l'hôpital.

**rush hour** *noun* heures *Fem. plural* de pointe; **in the rush hour** aux heures de pointe.

**Russia** *noun* Russie *Fem.*; **in Russia** en Russie.

**Russian** *noun* **1** (*a person*) Russe *Masc. & Fem.*; **2** (*the language*) russe *Masc.*

**Russian** *adjective* russe.

**rust** *noun* rouille *Fem.*

**rusty** *adjective* rouillé.

**rye** *noun* seigle *Masc.*

# Ss

**Sabbath** *noun* **1** (*Jewish*) sabbat *Masc.*; **2** (*Christian*) dimanche *Masc.*

**sack** *noun* **1** sac *Masc.*; **2 to get the sack** être mis à la porte.

**sack** *verb* **to sack somebody** mettre [11] quelqu'un à la porte.

**sacred** *adjective* sacré.

**sacrifice** *noun* sacrifice *Masc.*

**sad** *adjective* triste.

**saddle** *noun* selle *Fem.*

**saddlebag** *noun* sacoche *Fem.*

**sadly** *adverb* **1** tristement; **she looked at me sadly** elle m'a regardé tristement; **2** (*unfortunately*) malheureusement.

**safe** *adjective* **1** (*out of danger*) hors de danger; **to feel safe** se sentir en sécurité; **2** (*not dangerous*) pas dangereux (*Fem.* pas dangereuse); **the path is safe** le sentier n'est pas dangereux; **it's not safe** c'est dangereux.

**safety** *noun* sécurité *Fem.*

**safety belt** *noun* ceinture *Fem.* de sécurité.

**safety pin** *noun* épingle *Fem.* de nourrice.

**Sagittarius** *noun* Sagittaire *Masc.*; **Kylie's Sagittarius** Kylie est Sagittaire.

**sail** *noun* voile *Fem.*

**sailing** *noun* voile *Fem.*; **to go sailing** faire [10] de la voile; **she does a lot of sailing** elle fait beaucoup de voile.

**sailing boat** *noun* voilier *Masc.*

**sailor** *noun* marin *Masc.*

**saint** *noun* saint *Masc.*, sainte *Fem.*

**sake** *noun* **1** **for your mother's sake** par égard pour ta mère; **2** **for heaven's sake** nom de Dieu!

**salad** *noun* salade *Fem.*; **a tomato salad** une salade de tomates.

**salad dressing** *noun* vinaigrette *Fem.*

**salami** *noun* saucisson *Masc.*

**salary** *noun* salaire *Masc.*

**sale** *noun* **1** (*selling*) vente *Fem.*; **the sale of the house** la vente de la maison; **'for sale'** 'à vendre'; **2** **the sales** les soldes *Fem. plural*; **I bought it in the sales** je l'ai acheté en solde.

**sales assistant** *noun* vendeur *Masc.*, vendeuse *Fem.*

**salesman** *noun* représentant *Masc.*; **he's a salesman** il est représentant.

**saleswoman** *noun* représentante *Fem.*

**saliva** *noun* salive *Fem.*

**salmon** *noun* saumon *Masc.*

**salt** *noun* sel *Masc.*

**salty** *adjective* salé.

**Salvation Army** *noun* armée *Fem.* du Salut.

**same** *adjective* **1** même; **she said the same thing** elle a dit la même chose; **her birthday's the same day as mine** son anniversaire est le même jour que le mien; **at the same time** en même temps; **their car's the same as ours** ils ont la même voiture que nous; **2** **the same** (*after verb*) pareil; **the two bikes are not the same** les deux vélos ne sont pas pareils; **it's not the same** ce n'est pas pareil.

**sample** *noun* échantillon *Masc.*; **a free sample** un échantillon gratuit.

**sand** *noun* sable *Masc.*

**sandal** *noun* sandale *Fem.*; **a pair of sandals** une paire de sandales.

**sand castle** *noun* château *Masc.* de sable (*plural* châteaux de sable).

**sandpaper** *noun* papier *Masc.* de verre.

a
b
c
d
e
f
g
h
i
j
k
l
m
n
o
p
q
r
s
t
u
v
w
x
y
z

a   **sandwich** *noun* sandwich *Masc.*; **a ham sandwich** un sandwich au jambon.

b

c   **sanitary towel** *noun* serviette *Fem.* hygiénique.

d   **Santa Claus** *noun* le père Noël.

e   **sarcasm** *noun* sarcasme *Masc.*

f   **sarcastic** *adjective* sarcastique.

   **sardine** *noun* sardine *Fem.*

g   **satchel** *noun* cartable *Masc.*

h   **SARS** *noun* pneumopathie *Fem.* atypique.

i   **satellite** *noun* satellite *Masc.*

j   **satellite dish** *noun* antenne *Fem.* parabolique.

k

l   **satellite television** *noun* télévision *Fem.* par satellite.

m   **satisfactory** *adjective* satisfaisant.

n   **satisfied** *adjective* satisfait.

o   **satisfy** *verb* satisfaire [10].

p   **satisfying** *adjective* **1** (*pleasing*) satisfaisant; **2 a satisfying meal** un repas consistant.

q

r   **Saturday** *noun* samedi *Masc.*; **on Saturday** samedi; **I'm going out on Saturday** je sors samedi; **see you on Saturday!** à samedi!; **on Saturdays** le samedi; **the museum is closed on Saturdays** le musée est fermé le samedi; **every Saturday** tous les samedis; **last Saturday** samedi dernier; **next Saturday** samedi prochain; **to have a Saturday job** travailler le samedi.

s

t

u   **sauce** *noun* sauce *Fem.*

v   **saucepan** *noun* casserole *Fem.*

w

x   **saucer** *noun* soucoupe *Fem.*

y

z

**sausage** *noun* **1** saucisse *Fem.*; **2** (*salami*) saucisson *Masc.*

**savage** *noun* sauvage *Masc. & Fem.*

**save** *verb* **1** (*rescue*) sauver [1]; **to save somebody's life** sauver la vie à quelqu'un; **the doctors saved his life** les médecins lui ont sauvé la vie; **2** mettre [11] de côté (*money, food*); **I've saved £60** j'ai mis soixante livres de côté; **3** (*avoid spending*) économiser [1]; **I walk to school to save money** je vais à l'école à pied pour économiser de l'argent; **4 to save time** gagner [1] du temps; **we'll take a taxi to save time** on va prendre un taxi pour gagner du temps; **5** (*on a computer*) sauvegarder [1].

• **to save up** mettre [11] de l'argent de côté; **I'm saving up to go to Spain** je mets de l'argent de côté pour aller en Espagne.

**savings** *plural noun* économies *Fem. plural*; **I've spent all my savings** j'ai dépensé toutes mes économies.

**savoury** *adjective* salé; **I prefer savoury things to sweet things** j'aime mieux les choses salées que les choses sucrées.

**saw** *noun* scie *Fem.*

**sawdust** *noun* sciure *Fem.*

**sax** *noun* saxo *Masc.* (*informal*); **to play the sax** jouer du saxo.

**saxophone** *noun* saxophone *Masc.*; **to play the saxophone** jouer du saxophone.

**say** *verb* **1** dire [9]; **what did you say?** qu'est-ce que tu as dit?; **she says she's tired** elle dit qu'elle est fatiguée; **he said to wait here** il a dit d'attendre ici; **as they say** comme on dit; **that goes without saying** cela va sans dire; **2 to say something again** répéter [24] quelque chose.

**saying** *noun* dicton *Masc.*; **as the saying goes** comme on dit.

**scab** *noun* croûte *Fem.*

**scale** *noun* **1** (*of a map or model*) échelle *Fem.*; **large-scale** à grande échelle; **2** (*extent*) ampleur *Fem.*; **the scale of the disaster** l'ampleur du désastre; **3** (*in music*) gamme *Fem.*; **4** (*of a fish*) écaille *Fem.*

**scales** *noun* **1** balance *Fem. singular*; **kitchen scales** une balance de cuisine; **2 bathroom scales** un pèse-personne *Masc. singular*.

**scallop** *noun* coquille *Fem.* Saint-Jacques.

**scalp** *noun* cuir *Masc.* chevelu.

**scandal** *noun* **1** scandale *Masc.*; **2** (*gossip*) ragots *Masc. plural*.

**Scandinavia** *noun* Scandinavie *Fem.*

**Scandinavian** *adjective* scandinave.

**scanner** *noun* scanner *Masc.*

**scar** *noun* cicatrice *Fem.*

**scarce** *adjective* rare.

**scarcely** *adverb* à peine.

**scare** *noun* **1** panique *Fem.*; **it caused a scare** cela a provoqué une panique; **2 a bomb scare** une alerte à la bombe.
**scare** *verb* **to scare somebody** faire [10] peur à quelqu'un; **you scared me!** tu m'as fait peur!

**scarecrow** *noun* épouvantail *Masc.*

**scared** *adjective* **to be scared** avoir [5] peur; **I'm scared!** j'ai peur; **to be scared of** avoir [5] peur de; **he's scared of dogs** il a peur des chiens; **I'm scared of falling** j'ai peur de tomber.

**scarf** *noun* **1** (*silky*) foulard *Masc.*; **2** (*long, warm*) écharpe *Fem.*

**scary** *adjective* effrayant.

**scene** *noun* **1** (*of an incident or a crime*) lieux *Masc. plural*; **to be on the scene** être sur les lieux; **the scene of the crime** le lieu du crime; **2** (*world*) monde *Masc.*; **on the music scene** dans le monde de la musique; **3 scenes of violence** des incidents violents; **4 to make a scene** faire une scène.

**scenery** *noun* **1** (*landscape*) paysage *Masc.*; **2** (*theatrical*) décors *Masc. plural*.

**scent** *noun* parfum *Masc.*

**scented** *adjective* parfumé.

**schedule** *noun* programme *Masc.*

**scheduled flight** *noun* vol *Masc.* régulier.

**scheme** *noun* projet *Masc.*

**scholarship** *noun* bourse *Fem.*

**school** *noun* école *Fem.*; **at school** à l'école; **to go to school** aller à l'école.

**schoolbook** *noun* livre *Masc.* scolaire.

**schoolboy** *noun* écolier *Masc.*

**schoolchildren** *plural noun* écoliers *Masc. plural*.

a
b
c
d
e
f
g
h
i
j
k
l
m
n
o
p
q
r
s
t
u
v
w
x
y
z

**schoolfriend** *noun* camarade *Masc. & Fem.* de classe.

**schoolgirl** *noun* écolière *Fem.*

**science** *noun* science *Fem.*; **I like science** j'aime la science; **the science teacher** le prof des sciences.

**science fiction** *noun* science-fiction *Fem.*

**scientific** *adjective* scientifique.

**scientist** *noun* scientifique *Masc. & Fem.*

**scissors** *plural noun* ciseaux *Masc. plural*; **a pair of scissors** une paire de ciseaux.

**scoff** *verb* (*eat*) bouffer [1] (*informal*).

**scoop** *noun* **1** (*utensil*) cuillère *Fem.* à glace; **2** (*content*) boule *Fem.*; **how many scoops would you like?** vous voulez combien de boules?

**scooter** *noun* **1** (*motor scooter*) scooter *Masc.*; **2** (*for a child*) trottinette *Fem.*

**score** *noun* score *Masc.*; **the score was three two** le score était trois à deux.
**score** *verb* **1** marquer [1]; **Lenny scored a goal** Lenny a marqué un but; **I scored three points** j'ai marqué trois points; **2** (*keep score*) compter [1] les points.

**Scorpio** *noun* Scorpion *Masc.*; **Jess is Scorpio** Jess est Scorpion.

**Scot** *noun* Écossais *Masc.*, Écossaise *Fem.*; **the Scots** les Écossais *Masc. plural*.

**Scotland** *noun* Écosse *Fem.*; **in Scotland** en Écosse; **to Scotland** en Écosse; **Pauline's from Scotland** Pauline est écossaise.

**Scots** *adjective* écossais; **a Scots accent** un accent écossais.

**Scotsman** *noun* Écossais *Masc.*

**Scotswoman** *noun* Écossaise *Fem.*

**Scottish** *adjective* écossais; **a Scottish accent** un accent écossais.

**scout** *noun* scout *Masc.*

**scrambled eggs** *noun* œufs *Masc. plural* brouillés.

**scrap** *noun* **a scrap of paper** un bout de papier.

**scrapbook** *noun* album *Masc.*

**scrape** *verb* gratter [1].

**scratch** *noun* **1** (*on your skin*) égratignure *Fem.*; **2** (*on a surface*) rayure *Fem.*; ★ **to start from scratch** partir de zéro.
**scratch** *verb* (*scratch yourself*) se gratter [1]; **to scratch your head** se gratter la tête.

**scream** *noun* cri *Masc.*
**scream** *verb* crier [1].

**screen** *noun* écran *Masc.*; **on the screen** à l'écran.

**screw** *noun* vis *Fem.*
**screw** *verb* visser [1].

**screwdriver** *noun* tournevis *Masc.*

**scribble** *verb* griffonner [1].

**scrub** *verb* récurer [1] (*a saucepan*); **to scrub your nails** se brosser [1] les ongles.

**scuba diving** *noun* plongée *Fem.* sous-marine.

**sculptor** *noun* sculpteur *Masc.*, sculpteuse *Fem.*; **Rebecca's a sculptor** Rebecca est sculpteur.

**sculpture** *noun* sculpture *Fem.*

**sea** *noun* mer *Fem.*

**seafood** *noun* fruits *Masc. plural* de mer; **I love seafood** j'adore les fruits de mer.

**seagull** *noun* mouette *Fem.*

**seal** *noun* (*animal*) phoque *Masc.* **seal** *verb* coller [1] (*envelope*).

**seaman** *noun* marin *Masc.*

**search** *verb* 1 fouiller [1]; **I've searched my desk but I can't find the letter** j'ai fouillé dans mon bureau mais je ne trouve pas la lettre; **the police searched the house/the room** la police a fouillé la maison/la chambre; 2 **to search for** chercher [1]; **I've been searching everywhere for the scissors** j'ai cherché les ciseaux partout. **search** *noun* fouille *Fem.*

**seashell** *noun* coquillage *Masc.*

**seasick** *adjective* **to be seasick** avoir le mal de mer.

**seaside** *noun* **at the seaside** au bord de la mer.

**season** *noun* saison *Fem.*; **the rugby season** la saison de rugby; **strawberries are not in season at the moment** ce n'est pas la saison des fraises en ce moment; **off-season prices** des prix hors saison.

**season ticket** *noun* carte *Fem.* d'abonnement.

**seat** *noun* 1 siège *Masc.*; (*in a car*) **the front seat** le siège avant; **the back seat** le siège arrière; **take a seat** assieds-toi; 2 (*in a cinema, theatre, etc*) place *Fem.*; **to book a seat** réserver une place; **can you keep my seat?** est-ce que tu peux garder ma place?

**seatbelt** *noun* ceinture *Fem.* de sécurité.

**seaweed** *noun* algues *Fem. plural.*

**second** *noun* seconde *Fem.*; **can you wait a second?** est-ce que tu peux attendre une seconde? **second** *adjective* 1 deuxième; **for the second time** pour la deuxième fois; 2 **the second of July** le deux juillet.

**secondary school** *noun* 1 collège *Masc.* (*up to the end of the equivalent of Year 10*); 2 lycée *Masc.* (*for the equivalent of Years 11 to 13*).

**second class** *noun* (*category*) deuxième classe *Fem.*; **a second class team** une équipe de niveau très moyen.

**secondhand** *adjective, adverb* d'occasion; **a secondhand bike** un vélo d'occasion; **I bought it secondhand** je l'ai acheté d'occasion.

**secondly** *adverb* deuxièmement.

**secret** *noun* secret *Masc.*; **to keep a secret** garder un secret; **in secret** en secret. **secret** *adjective* secret (*Fem.* secrète); **a secret plan** un projet secret.

**secretarial college** *noun* école *Fem.* de secrétariat.

**secretary** *noun* secrétaire *Masc. & Fem.*; **she's a secretary** elle est

# secretly

a b c d e f g h i j k l m n o p q r s t u v w x y z

**secretly** *adverb* secrètement.

**sect** *noun* secte *Fem.*

**section** *noun* section *Fem.*

**security** *noun* sécurité *Fem.*

**security guard** *noun* vigile *Masc.*; **he's a security guard** il est vigile.

**see** *verb* **1** voir [13]; **I saw Lindy yesterday** j'ai vu Lindy hier; **have you seen the film?** est-ce que tu as vu le film?; **I haven't see her for ages** ça fait une éternité que je ne l'ai pas vue; **I'll see what I can do** je vais voir ce que je peux faire; **2 to be able to see** voir [13]; **I can't see anything** je ne vois rien; **3 see you!** salut!; **see you on Saturday!** à samedi!; **see you soon!** à bientôt!
- **to see to something** s'occuper [1] de quelque chose; **Jo's seeing to the drinks** Jo s'occupe des boissons.

**seed** *noun* graine *Fem.*; **to plant seeds** semer des graines.

**seem** *verb* **1** paraître [57]; **it seems odd to me** ça me paraît bizarre; **it seems he's left** il paraît qu'il est parti; **2** (*look, appear to be*) avoir [5] l'air; **he seems a bit shy** il a l'air un peu timide; **the museum seems to be closed** le musée a l'air d'être fermé.

**seesaw** *noun* tapecul *Masc.*

**select** *verb* sélectionner [1].

**selection** *noun* sélection *Fem.*

**self-confidence** *noun* confiance *Fem.* en soi; **she doesn't have much self-confidence** elle n'a pas beaucoup de confiance en elle.

**self-confident** *adjective* plein d'assurance; **he's very self-confident** il est très sûr de lui.

**self-conscious** *adjective* timide.

**self-contained** *noun* **a self-contained flat** un appartement indépendant.

**self-employed** *noun* **the self-employed** les travailleurs indépendants *Masc. plural.*
**self-employed** *adjective* **to be self-employed** travailler à son compte; **my parents are self-employed** mes parents travaillent à leur compte.

**selfish** *adjective* égoïste.

**self-service** *adjective* **a self-service restaurant** un self (*informal*).

**sell** *verb* vendre [3]; **to sell something to somebody** vendre quelque chose à quelqu'un; **I sold him my bike** je lui ai vendu mon vélo; **the house has been sold** la maison a été vendue; **the concert's sold out** il ne reste plus de billets pour le concert.

**sell-by date** *noun* date *Fem.* limite de vente.

**seller** *noun* vendeur *Masc.*, vendeuse *Fem.*

**Sellotape™** *noun* Scotch™ *Masc.*
**Sellotape™** *verb* **to sellotape something** scotcher [1] quelque chose (*informal*).

**semi** *noun* maison *Fem.* jumelée (*literally: a twinned house*); **we live in a semi** nous habitons dans une maison jumelée.

**semicircle** *noun* demi-cercle *Masc.*

**semicolon** *noun* point-virgule *Masc.*

**semi-detached house** *noun* maison *Fem.* jumelée (*literally: a twinned house*); **we live in a semi-detached house** nous habitons dans une maison jumelée.

**semi-final** *noun* demi-finale *Fem.*

**semi-skimmed milk** *noun* lait *Masc.* demi-écrémé.

**send** *verb* envoyer [40]; **to send something to somebody** envoyer quelque chose à quelqu'un; **I sent her a present for her birthday** je lui ai envoyé un cadeau pour son anniversaire.

● **to send back: to send somebody back** renvoyer [40] quelqu'un; **to send something back** renvoyer [40] quelque chose.

**sender** *noun* expéditeur *Masc.*, expéditrice *Fem.*

**senior citizen** *noun* personne *Fem.* du troisième âge.

**sensation** *noun* **1** (*feeling*) sensation *Fem.*; **2** (*impact*) sensation *Fem.*; **she caused a sensation** elle a fait sensation.

**sensational** *adjective* sensationnel (*Fem.* sensationnelle).

**sense** *noun* **1** sens *Masc.*; **common sense** le bon sens; **it doesn't make sense** ça n'a pas de sens; **it makes sense** ça paraît logique; **to have a sense of humour** avoir le sens de l'humour; **she has no sense of humour** elle n'a aucun sens de l'humour; **2 the sense of smell** l'odorat *Masc.*; **the sense of touch** le toucher.

**sensible** *adjective* raisonnable; **she's very sensible** elle est très raisonnable; **it's a sensible decision** c'est une décision raisonnable.

**sensitive** *adjective* sensible; **for sensitive skin** pour peaux sensibles.

**sentence** *noun* **1** phrase *Fem.*; **écris une phrase en français** write a sentence in French; **2 the death sentence** la peine de mort.
**sentence** *verb* condamner [1]; **to be sentenced to death** être condamné à mort.

**sentimental** *adjective* sentimental (*Masc. plural* sentimentaux).

**separate** *adjective* **1** à part; **in a separate pile** dans une pile à part; **on a separate sheet of paper** sur une feuille à part; **2** (*different*) autre; **that's a separate problem** c'est un autre problème; **3 they have separate rooms** ils ont chacun leur chambre.
**separate** *verb* **1** séparer [1]; **2** (*a couple*) se séparer [1].

**separately** *adverb* séparément.

**separation** *noun* séparation *Fem.*

**September** *noun* septembre *Masc.*; **in September** en septembre.

**sequel** *noun* suite *Fem.*

**sequence** *noun* **1** série *Fem.*; **a sequence of events** une série d'événements; **2 in sequence** dans l'ordre; **3** (*in a film*) séquence *Fem.*

**sergeant** *noun* **1** (*in the police*) brigadier *Masc.*; **2** (*in the army*) sergent *Masc.*

a
b
c
d
e
f
g
h
i
j
k
l
m
n
o
p
q
r
s
t
u
v
w
x
y
z

**a**

**b**

**serial** *noun* feuilleton *Masc.*

**series** *noun* série *Fem.*; **a television series** une série télévisée.

**c**

**d**

**e**

**f**

**g**

**serious** *adjective* **1** sérieux (*Fem.* sérieuse); **a serious discussion** une discussion sérieuse; **are you serious?** sérieusement?; **2** grave (*illness, injury, mistake, problem*); **we have a serious problem** nous avons un grave problème.

**h**

**i**

**j**

**k**

**l**

**seriously** *adverb* **1** sérieusement; **seriously, I have to go now** sérieusement je dois partir maintenant; **seriously?** vraiment?; **2 to take somebody seriously** prendre quelqu'un au sérieux; **3** gravement (*ill, injured*); **she is seriously ill** elle est gravement malade.

**m**

**n**

**servant** *noun* domestique *Masc. & Fem.*

**o**

**p**

**q**

**r**

**serve** *noun* (*in tennis*) service *Masc.*; **it's my serve** c'est à moi de servir. **serve** *verb* **1** (*in tennis*) servir [71]; **2** servir; **can you serve the vegetables, please?** est-ce que tu peux servir les légumes, s'il te plaît?; **they served the fish with a lemon sauce** ils ont servi le poisson accompagné d'une sauce au citron; ★ **it serves him right** c'est bien fait pour lui.

**s**

**t**

**u**

**v**

**w**

**x**

**y**

**z**

**service** *noun* **1** (*in a restaurant, from a company, etc*) service *Masc.*; **the service is very slow** le service est très lent; **service is included** le service est compris; **is there a maid service?** est-ce qu'il y a une femme de ménage?; **2 the emergency services** les services des urgences; **3** (*church service*) office *Masc.*; **4** (*of a*

car or machine*) révision *Fem.*
**service** *verb* réviser [1] (*a car or a machine*).

**service area** *noun* aire *Fem.* de services.

**service charge** *noun* service *Masc.*; **what is the service charge?** le service est de combien?; **there is no service charge** le service est compris.

**service station** *noun* station-service *Fem.* (*plural* stations-service).

**serviette** *noun* serviette *Fem.*

**session** *noun* séance *Fem.*

**set** *noun* **1** (*for playing a game*) jeu *Masc.* (*plural* jeux); **a chess set** un jeu d'échecs; **2 a train set** un petit train; **3** (*in tennis*) set *Masc.*
**set** *adjective* fixe; **at a set time** à une heure fixe; **a set menu** un menu fixe.
**set** *verb* **1** fixer [1] (*date, time*); **2** établir [2] (*record*); **3 to set the table** mettre [11] la table; **to set an alarm clock** mettre [11] un réveil; **I've set my alarm for seven** j'ai mis mon réveil à sept heures; **4 to set a watch** régler [24] une montre; **5** (*sun*) se coucher [1].

● **to set off** partir [58]; **we're setting off at ten** nous allons partir à dix heures; **they set off for Paris yesterday** ils sont partis pour Paris hier.

● **to set off something 1** faire [10] partir (*firework*); **2** faire [10] exploser (*bomb*); **3** déclencher [1] (*alarm*).

• **to set out** partir [58]; **they set out for Paris yesterday** ils sont partis pour Paris hier.

**settee** *noun* canapé *Masc.*

**settle** *verb* régler [24] (*a bill or a problem*).

**seven** *number* sept; **Rosie's seven** Rosie a sept ans.

**seventeen** *number* dix-sept; **Jonny's seventeen** Jonny a dix-sept ans.

**seventh** *adjective* septième; **on the seventh floor** au septième étage; **the seventh of July** le sept juillet.

**seventies** *plural noun* **the seventies** les années soixante-dix; **in the seventies** aux années soixante-dix.

**seventieth** *adjective* soixante-dixième; **it's her seventieth birthday** elle fête ses soixante-dix ans.

**seventy** *number* soixante-dix; **my grandma's seventy** ma grand-mère a soixante-dix ans.

**several** *adjective, pronoun* plusieurs; **I've seen her several times** je l'ai vue plusieurs fois; **I've read several of her novels** j'ai lu plusieurs de ses romans; **he took several** il en a pris plusieurs.

**severe** *adjective* **1** (*person*) sévère; **2** (*weather*) rigoureux (*Fem.* rigoureuse); **3** (*injuries*) grave.

**sew** *verb* coudre [28].

**sewer** *noun* égout *Masc.*

**sewing** *noun* couture *Fem.*; **I like sewing** j'aime la couture.

**sewing machine** *noun* machine *Fem.* à coudre.

**sex** *noun* **1** (*gender*) sexe *Masc.*; **2** (*intercourse*) rapports *Masc. plural* sexuels; **to have sex with someone** coucher avec quelqu'un.

**sex education** *noun* éducation *Fem.* sexuelle.

**sexism** *noun* sexisme *Masc.*

**sexist** *adjective* sexiste; **sexist remarks** des propos sexistes.

**sexual** *adjective* sexuel (*Fem.* sexuelle).

**sexual harassment** *noun* harcèlement *Masc.* sexuel.

**sexuality** *noun* sexualité *Fem.*

**sexy** *adjective* sexy.

**shabby** *adjective* miteux (*Fem.* miteuse).

**shade** *noun* **1** (*of a colour*) ton *Masc.*; **a pretty shade of green** un joli vert; **2 in the shade** à l'ombre.

**shadow** *noun* ombre *Fem.*

**shake** *verb* **1** (*tremble*) trembler [1]; **my hands are shaking** j'ai les mains qui tremblent; **2 to shake something** secouer [1] quelque chose; **3 to shake hands with somebody** serrer [1] la main à quelqu'un; **she shook hands with me** elle m'a serré la main; **we shook hands** nous nous sommes serré la main; **4 to shake your head** (*meaning no*) faire [10] non de la tête.

**shaken** *adjective* bouleversé; **I was shaken by the news** j'ai été bouleversé par la nouvelle.

**shall** *verb* **shall I come with you?** tu veux que je t'accompagne?; **shall**

a
b
c
d
e
f
g
h
i
j
k
l
m
n
o
p
q
r
s
t
u
v
w
x
y
z

557

we stop now? si on s'arrêtait maintenant?

**shallow** *adjective* peu profond; **the water's very shallow here** l'eau est très peu profonde ici.

**shallow end** *noun* partie *Fem.* la moins profonde de la piscine.

**shambles** *noun* pagaille *Fem.* (*informal*); **it was a total shambles!** ça a été la pagaille complète!

**shame** *noun* 1 honte *Fem.*; **shame on you!** tu devrais avoir honte!; 2 **what a shame!** quel dommage!; **it's a shame she can't come** c'est dommage qu'elle ne puisse pas venir (*note that 'c'est dommage que' is followed by a verb in the subjunctive*).

**shameful** *adjective* honteux (*Fem.* honteuse).

**shampoo** *noun* shampooing *Masc.*; **I bought some shampoo** j'ai acheté du shampooing.

**shamrock** *noun* trèfle *Masc.*

**shandy** *noun* panaché *Masc.*; **a half of shandy** un demi panaché.

**shape** *noun* forme *Fem.*

**share** *noun* 1 part *Fem.*; **your share of the money** ta part de l'argent; **he paid his fair share** il a payé sa part; 2 (*in a company*) action *Fem.*
**share** *verb* partager [52]; **I'm sharing a room with Emma** je partage une chambre avec Emma.
• **to share out** partager [52], répartir [58].

**shark** *noun* requin *Masc.*

**sharp** *adjective* 1 (*knife*) bien aiguisé; **this knife isn't very sharp**

ce couteau ne coupe pas très bien; 2 **a sharp pencil** un crayon bien taillé; 3 **a sharp bend** un virage brusque; 4 (*clever*) intelligent.

**sharpen** *verb* 1 (*a pencil*) tailler [1]; 2 (*a knife*) aiguiser [1].

**sharpener** *noun* taille-crayon *Masc.*

**shave** *verb* 1 (*have a shave*) se raser [1]; **he's just shaving** il est en train de se raser; 2 **to shave your legs** se raser [1] les jambes; **to shave off your beard** se raser la barbe.

**shaver** *noun* **an electric shaver** un rasoir électrique.

**shaving cream** *noun* crème *Fem.* à raser.

**shaving foam** *noun* mousse *Fem.* à raser.

**she** *pronoun* elle; **she's in her room** elle est dans sa chambre; **she's a student** elle est étudiante; **she's a very good teacher** c'est un très bon prof; **here she is!** la voici!; **there she is!** la voilà!

**shed** *noun* remise *Fem.*

**sheep** *noun* mouton *Masc.*

**sheepdog** *noun* chien *Masc.* de berger (*plural* chiens de berger).

**sheer** *adjective* 1 pur; **it's sheer stupidity!** c'est de la pure bêtise!; 2 (*tights*) extra-fin.

**sheet** *noun* 1 (*for a bed*) drap *Masc.*; 2 **a sheet of paper** une feuille de papier; **a blank sheet** une feuille blanche; 3 (*of glass or metal*) plaque; ★ **to be as white as a sheet** être blanc comme un linge; **she was as white as a sheet** elle était blanche comme un linge.

**shelf** *noun* **1** (*in the home*) étagère *Fem.*; **a set of shelves** une étagère; **2** (*in a shop, in a fridge*) rayon *Masc.*

**shell** *noun* **1** (*of an egg or a nut*) coquille *Fem.*; **2** (*seashell*) coquillage *Masc.*; **3** (*explosive*) obus *Masc.*

**shellfish** *noun* fruits *Masc. plural* de mer.

**shelter** *noun* **1** abri *Masc.*; **in the shelter of** à l'abri de; **to take shelter from the rain** se mettre à l'abri de la pluie; **2 a bus shelter** un abribus™.

**shepherd** *noun* berger *Masc.*

**sheriff** *noun* shérif *Masc.*

**sherry** *noun* sherry *Masc.*

**Shetland Islands** *noun* îles *Fem. plural* Shetland.

**shield** *noun* bouclier *Masc.*

**shift** *noun* service *Masc.*; **the night shift** le service de nuit; **to be on night shift** être de nuit.
**shift** *verb* **to shift something** déplacer [61] quelque chose; **can you help me shift this table?** est-ce que tu peux m'aider à déplacer cette table?

**shifty** *adjective* louche; **he looks a bit shifty** il a l'air un peu louche; **a shifty-looking guy** un type un peu louche.

**shin** *noun* tibia *Masc.*

**shine** *verb* briller [1].

**shiny** *adjective* brillant.

**ship** *noun* **1** bateau *Masc.*; **2 a passenger ship** un paquebot; **3** (*large naval vessel*) navire *Masc.*

**shipbuilding** *noun* construction *Fem.* navale.

**shipyard** *noun* chantier *Masc.* naval.

**shirt** *noun* **1** (*man's*) chemise *Fem.*; **2** (*woman's*) chemisier *Masc.*

**shiver** *verb* frissonner [1].

**shock** *noun* **1** choc *Masc.*; **it was a shock** ça a été un choc; **it gave me a shock** j'ai eu un choc; **2 an electric shock** une décharge; **to get an electric shock** prendre une décharge.
**shock** *verb* choquer [1].

**shocked** *adjective* choqué.

**shocking** *adjective* choquant.

**shoe** *noun* chaussure *Fem.*; **a pair of shoes** une paire de chaussures.

**shoelace** *noun* lacet *Masc.*

**shoe polish** *noun* cirage *Masc.*

**shoe shop** *noun* magasin *Masc.* de chaussures.

**shoot** *verb* **1** (*fire*) tirer [1]; **to shoot at somebody** tirer sur quelqu'un; **she shot him in the leg** elle lui a tiré une balle dans la jambe; **he was shot in the arm** il a reçu une balle dans le bras; **2** (*kill*) abattre [21]; **he was shot by terrorists** il a été abattu par des terroristes; **3** (*execute*) fusiller [1]; **4** (*in football, hockey*) shooter [1]; **5 to shoot a film** tourner [1] un film.

**shooting** *noun* tir *Masc.*

**shop** *noun* magasin *Masc.*; **a shoe shop** un magasin de chaussures; **to go round the shops** faire les magasins.

**shop assistant** *noun* vendeur *Masc.*, vendeuse *Fem.*; **Brad's a shop assistant** Brad est vendeur.

a
b
c
d
e
f
g
h
i
j
k
l
m
n
o
p
q
r
s
t
u
v
w
x
y
z

a
b
c
d
e
f
g
h
i
j
k
l
m
n
o
p
q
r
s
t
u
v
w
x
y
z

**shopkeeper** *noun* commerçant
*Masc.*, commerçante *Fem.*

**shoplifter** *noun* voleur *Masc.* à
l'étalage, voleuse *Fem.* à l'étalage.

**shoplifting** *noun* vol *Masc.* à
l'étalage.

**shopping** *noun* courses *Fem. plural*;
**can you put the shopping away?**
est-ce que tu peux ranger les
courses?; **I've got a lot of shopping
to do** j'ai beaucoup de courses à
faire; **to go shopping** (*for food*) faire
des courses; (*for fun, to buy clothes or
presents*) faire du shopping.

**shopping bag** *noun* sac *Masc.* à
provisions.

**shopping centre** *noun* centre
*Masc.* commercial.

**shopping trolley** *noun* 1 (*in a
supermarket*) chariot *Masc.*;
2 (*personal*) caddie™ *Masc.*

**shop window** *noun* vitrine *Fem.*

**shore** *noun* côte *Fem.*

**short** *adjective* 1 court; **a short
dress** une robe courte; **she has
short hair** elle a les cheveux courts;
2 **a short break** une petite pause; **to
go for a short walk** faire une petite
promenade; **it's a short walk from
the station** c'est à quelques minutes
à pied de la gare; 3 **to be short of
something** ne pas avoir beaucoup
de quelque chose; **we're a bit short
of money at the moment** nous
n'avons pas beaucoup d'argent en ce
moment; **we're getting short of
time** il ne nous reste pas beaucoup
de temps.

**shortage** *noun* pénurie *Fem.*

**shortbread** *noun* sablé *Masc.*

**shortcrust pastry** *noun* pâte
*Fem.* brisée.

**short cut** *noun* raccourci *Masc.*; **we
took a short cut** nous avons pris un
raccourci.

**shorten** *verb* 1 (*clothes*) raccourcir
[2]; 2 (*a stay, journey*) écourter [1].

**shortly** *adverb* bientôt.

**shorts** *plural noun* short *Masc.*
*singular*; **a pair of shorts** un short;
**my red shorts** mon short rouge.

**short-sighted** *adjective* myope;
**I'm short-sighted** je suis myope.

**short story** *noun* nouvelle *Fem.*

**shot** *noun* 1 (*from a gun*) coup *Masc.*
de feu (*plural* coups de feu); 2 (*a
photo*) photo *Fem.*; **I took several
shots of the garden** j'ai pris
plusieurs photos du jardin.

**shotgun** *noun* fusil *Masc.* de chasse
(*plural* fusils de chasse).

**should** *verb* 1 (*'should' meaning
'ought to' is translated by the
conditional tense of 'devoir'*) devoir
[8]; **you should ask Simon** tu
devrais demander à Simon; **the
potatoes should be cooked now**
les pommes de terre devraient être
cuites maintenant; 2 (*'should have'
is translated by the past conditional
tense of 'devoir'*) **you should have
told me** tu aurais dû me le dire; **I
shouldn't have stayed** je n'aurais
pas dû rester; 3 (*'should' meaning
'would' is translated by the
conditional tense of the verb*) **I
should forget it if I were you** à ta
place je l'oublierais; 4 **I should
think** à mon avis; **I should think**

**he's forgotten** à mon avis, il a oublié.

**shoulder** *noun* épaule *Fem.*

**shoulder bag** *noun* sac *Masc.* à bandoulière.

**shout** *noun* cri *Masc.*
**shout** *verb* crier [1]; **stop shouting!** arrêtez de crier!; **they shouted at us to come back** ils nous ont crié de revenir.

**shovel** *noun* pelle *Fem.*

**show** *noun* **1** (*on stage*) spectacle *Masc.*; **we went to see a show** nous sommes allés voir un spectacle; **2** (*on TV*) émission; **he has a TV show** il a une émission à la télé; **3** (*exhibition*) salon; **the motor show** le salon des automobiles.
**show** *verb* **1** montrer [1]; **to show something to somebody** montrer quelque chose à quelqu'un; **I'll show you my photos** je te montrerai mes photos; **to show somebody how to do** montrer à quelqu'un comment on fait; **he showed me how to make pancakes** il m'a montré comment on fait les crêpes; **2 it shows!** ça se voit!
● **to show off** frimer [1] (*informal*).

**shower** *noun* **1** (*in a bathroom*) douche *Fem.*; **to have a shower** prendre une douche; **2** (*of rain*) averse *Fem.*

**show-jumping** *noun* saut *Masc.* d'obstacles.

**show-off** *noun* frimeur *Masc.*, frimeuse *Fem.* (*informal*).

**shriek** *verb* hurler [1].

**shrimp** *noun* crevette *Fem.*

**shrine** *noun* autel *Masc.*

**shrink** *verb* rétrécir [2].

**Shrove Tuesday** *noun* mardi *Masc.* gras.

**shrug** *verb* **to shrug your shoulders** hausser [1] les épaules.

**shuffle** *verb* **to shuffle the cards** battre [21] les cartes.

**shut** *adjective* fermé; **the shops are shut** les magasins sont fermés.
**shut** *verb* fermer [1]; **can you shut the door please?** est-ce que tu peux fermer la porte, s'il te plaît?; **the shops shut at six** les magasins ferment à six heures.
● **to shut up** (*be quiet*) se taire [76]; **shut up!** tais-toi!

**shutter** *noun* volet *Masc.*

**shuttle** *noun* navette *Fem.*; **there's a shuttle service from the airport** il y a une navette de l'aéroport.

**shuttlecock** *noun* volant *Masc.*

**shy** *adjective* timide.

**shyness** *noun* timidité *Fem.*

**Sicily** *noun* Sicile *Fem.*; **to Sicily** en Sicile; **in Sicily** en Sicile.

**sick** *adjective* **1** (*ill*) malade; **2 to be sick** (*vomit*) vomir [2]; **I was sick several times** j'ai vomi plusieurs fois; **to feel sick** avoir [5] mal au cœur; **3 a sick joke** une plaisanterie malsaine; **4 to be sick of something** en avoir assez de quelque chose; **I'm sick of staying at home every night** j'en ai assez de rester à la maison tous les soirs.

**sickness** *noun* maladie *Fem.*

**side** *noun* **1** côté *Masc.*; **on the other side of the street** de l'autre côté de la rue; **on the wrong side** du mauvais côté; **I'm on your side** (*I agree with you*) je suis de ton côté; **2** (*edge*) bord *Masc.*; **at the side of the road** au bord de la route; **by the side of the pool** au bord de la piscine; **3** (*team*) équipe; **she plays on our side** elle joue dans notre équipe; **4 to take sides** prendre parti; **5 side by side** côte à côte.

**sideboard** *noun* buffet *Masc.*

**sideburns** *noun* pattes *Fem. plural.*

**side-effect** *noun* effet *Masc.* secondaire.

**side street** *noun* petite rue *Fem.*

**siege** *noun* siège *Masc.*

**sieve** *noun* passoire *Fem.*

**sigh** *noun* soupir *Masc.*
**sigh** *verb* pousser [1] un soupir.

**sight** *noun* **1** spectacle *Masc.*; **it was a marvellous sight** c'était un spectacle merveilleux; **2 at the sight of** à la vue de; **3** (*eyesight*) vue *Fem.*; **to have poor sight** avoir une mauvaise vue; **to know somebody by sight** connaître quelqu'un de vue; **out of sight** caché; **4 to see the sights** visiter les attractions touristiques.

**sightseeing** *noun* tourisme *Masc.*; **to do some sightseeing** faire du tourisme.

**sign** *noun* **1** (*notice*) panneau *Masc.* (*plural* panneaux); **there's a sign on the door** il y a un panneau sur la porte; **2** (*trace, indication*) signe *Masc.*; **3** (*of the Zodiac*) signe *Masc.*; **what sign are you?** tu es de quel signe?

**sign** *verb* **1** signer [1]; **to sign a**

cheque signer un chèque; **2** (*using sign language*) communiquer [1] en langage par signes.

● **to sign on** (*as unemployed*) s'inscrire [38] au chômage.

**signal** *noun* signal *Masc.* (*plural* signaux).

**signature** *noun* signature *Fem.*

**significance** *noun* importance *Fem.*

**significant** *adjective* important.

**sign language** *noun* langage *Masc.* par signes.

**signpost** *noun* poteau *Masc.* indicateur (*plural* poteaux indicateurs).

**silence** *noun* silence *Masc.*

**silent** *adjective* silencieux (*Fem.* silencieuse).

**silicon chip** *noun* puce *Fem.* électronique.

**silk** *noun* soie *Fem.*
**silk** *adjective* en soie; **a silk shirt** une chemise en soie.

**silky** *adjective* soyeux (*Fem.* soyeuse).

**silly** *adjective* idiot; **it was a really silly thing to do** c'était vraiment idiot.

**silver** *noun* argent *Masc.*
**silver** *adjective* **a silver spoon** une cuillère en argent; **a silver medal** une médaille d'argent.

**SIM card** *noun* carte *Fem.* SIM.

**similar** *adjective* semblable.

**similarity** *noun* ressemblance *Fem.*

**simmer** *verb* to simmer something faire [10] mijoter quelque chose.

**simple** *adjective* facile.

**simplify** *verb* simplifier [1].

**simply** *adverb* simplement.

**sin** *noun* péché *Masc.*

**since** *preposition, adverb, conjunction* **1** depuis (*notice that French uses the present tense where English uses 'have done' or 'have been doing'*) **I have been in Paris since Saturday** je suis à Paris depuis samedi; **I've been learning French since last year** j'apprends le français depuis l'année dernière; **2** depuis que (*the same thing happens with tenses here as above*) **since I have known him** depuis que je le connais; **since I've been learning French** depuis que j'apprends le français; **3 I haven't seen her since** je ne l'ai pas revue depuis; **I haven't seen her since Monday** je ne l'ai pas revue depuis lundi; **since when?** depuis quand?; **4** (*because*) puisque; **since it was raining, the match was cancelled** puisqu'il pleuvait le match a été annulé.

**sincere** *adjective* sincère.

**sincerely** *adverb* **Yours sincerely** (*in a business letter*) Veuillez agréer Madame (*or* Monsieur) l'expression de mes sentiments distingués; (*to somebody you know*) Cordialement (*in French there are very formal and rigid formulae for signing letters*).

**sing** *verb* chanter [1].

**singer** *noun* chanteur *Masc.*, chanteuse *Fem.*

**singing** *noun* **1** chant *Masc.*; **a singing lesson** une leçon de chant; **2 I like singing** j'aime chanter.

**single** *noun* aller *Masc.* simple; **a single to Lyons, please** un aller simple pour Lyon, s'il vous plaît. **single** *adjective* **1** (*not married*) célibataire; **2 a single room** une chambre pour une personne; **a single bed** un lit pour une personne; **3 not a single** pas un seul, pas une seule; **I haven't had a single reply** je n'ai pas reçu une seule réponse.

**single parent** *noun* **she's a single parent** elle élève ses enfants toute seule; **a single-parent family** une famille monoparentale.

**singles** *plural noun* (*in tennis*) simple *Masc. singular*; **the women's singles** le simple dames; **the men's singles** le simple messieurs.

**singular** *noun* singulier *Masc.*; **in the singular** au singulier.

**sink** *noun* évier *Masc.* **sink** *verb* couler [1].

**sir** *noun* monsieur *Masc.*; **yes, sir** oui, Monsieur.

**siren** *noun* sirène *Fem.*

**sister** *noun* sœur *Fem.*; **my sister's ten** ma sœur a dix ans.

**sister-in-law** *noun* belle-sœur *Fem.* (*plural* belles-sœurs).

**sit** *verb* **1** s'asseoir [20]; **you can sit on the sofa** tu peux t'asseoir sur le canapé; **I can sit on the floor** je peux m'asseoir par terre; **2 to be sitting** être [6] assis; **Leila was**

a
b
c
d
e
f
g
h
i
j
k
l
m
n
o
p
q
r
s
t
u
v
w
x
y
z

sitting on the sofa Leila était
assise sur le canapé; **3 to sit an
exam** passer [1] un examen; **she's
sitting her driving test on
Thursday** elle passe son permis
jeudi.

● **to sit down** s'asseoir [20]; **he sat
down on a chair** il s'est assis sur
une chaise; **do sit down** asseyez-
vous.

**sitcom** noun comédie Fem. de
situation (plural comédies de
situation).

**site** noun **1 a building site** un
chantier; **2 a camping site** un
camping; **3 an archaeological site**
un site archéologique.

**sitting room** noun salon Masc.

**situated** adjective **to be situated**
être situé; **the house is situated in
a small village** la maison est située
dans un petit village.

**situation** noun situation Fem.

**six** number six; **Harry's six** Harry a
six ans.

**sixteen** number seize; **Alice is
sixteen** Alice a seize ans.

**sixth** adjective sixième; **on the
sixth floor** au sixième étage; **the
sixth of July** le six juillet.

**sixty** number soixante; **she's sixty**
elle a soixante ans.

**size** noun **1** grandeur Fem.; **it
depends on the size of the house**
ça dépend de la grandeur de la
maison; **2** (precise measurements)
dimensions Fem. plural; **what size is
the window?** quelles sont les
dimensions de la fenêtre?; **3** (in
clothes) taille Fem.; **what size do you**

**take?** quelle taille faites-vous?; **4** (of
shoes) pointure; **I take a size thirty-
eight** je fais du trente-huit.

**skate** noun **1 an ice skate** un patin
à glace; **2 a roller skate** un patin à
roulettes.
**skate** verb **1** (ice-skate) faire [10] du
patin à glace; **2** (roller-skate) faire
[10] du patin à roulettes.

**skateboard** noun skateboard
Masc.

**skateboarding** noun skateboard
Masc.; **to do** (or **go**) **skateboarding**
faire du skateboard.

**skater** noun patineur Masc.,
patineuse Fem.

**skating** noun **1** (ice) patin Masc. à
glace; **to go skating** faire du patin à
glace; **2 roller-skating** le patin à
roulettes; **to go roller-skating** faire
du patin à roulettes.

**skating rink** noun patinoire Fem.

**skeleton** noun squelette Masc.

**sketch** noun **1** (drawing) croquis
Masc.; **2** (comedy routine) sketch
Masc.

**ski** noun ski Masc.
**ski** verb faire [10] du ski; **he can ski**
il sait faire du ski.

**ski boot** noun chaussure Fem. de
ski.

**skid** verb déraper [1]; **the car
skidded** la voiture a dérapé.

**skier** noun skieur Masc., skieuse Fem.

**skiing** noun ski Masc.; **to go skiing**
faire du ski.

**ski lift** noun remonte-pente Masc.

**skill** noun compétence Fem.

**skimmed milk** *noun* lait *Masc.* écrémé.

**skin** *noun* peau *Fem.* (*plural* peaux).

**skinhead** *noun* skinhead *Masc.* & *Fem.*

**skinny** *adjective* maigre.

**skip** *noun* (*for rubbish*) benne *Fem.*
**skip** *verb* 1 sauter [1] (*a meal, part of a book*); **I skipped a few chapters** j'ai sauté quelques chapitres; **2 to skip a lesson** sécher un cours (*informal*).

**ski pants** *noun* fuseau *Masc.* singular; **I bought some ski pants** j'ai acheté un fuseau.

**skipping rope** *noun* corde *Fem.* à sauter.

**skirt** *noun* jupe *Fem.*; **a long skirt** une jupe longue; **a straight skirt** une jupe droite; **a mini-skirt** une mini-jupe.

**ski suit** *noun* combinaison *Fem.* de ski.

**skittles** *plural noun* quilles *Fem. plural*; **to play skittles** jouer aux quilles.

**skull** *noun* crâne *Masc.*

**sky** *noun* ciel *Masc.*

**skyscraper** *noun* gratte-ciel *Masc.* (*plural* gratte-ciel).

**slam** *verb* claquer [1]; **she slammed the door** elle a claqué la porte.

**slang** *noun* argot *Masc.*

**slap** *noun* claque *Fem.*
**slap** *verb* **to slap somebody** donner [1] une claque à quelqu'un.

**slate** *noun* ardoise *Fem.*

**slave** *noun* esclave *Masc.* & *Fem.*

**sledge** *noun* luge *Fem.*

**sledging** *noun* **to go sledging** faire [10] de la luge.

**sleep** *noun* sommeil *Masc.*; **I had a good sleep** j'ai bien dormi; **to go to sleep** s'endormir [37].
**sleep** *verb* dormir [37]; **she's sleeping** elle dort.

**sleeping bag** *noun* sac *Masc.* de couchage.

**sleeping pill** *noun* somnifère *Masc.*

**sleepy** *adjective* **to be sleepy** avoir [5] sommeil; **I feel sleepy** j'ai sommeil; **he was getting sleepy** il commençait à avoir sommeil.

**sleet** *noun* neige *Fem.* fondue.

**sleeve** *noun* manche *Fem.*; **a long-sleeved jumper** un pull à manches longues; **a short-sleeved shirt** une chemise à manches courtes; **to roll up your sleeves** retrousser ses manches.

**slice** *noun* tranche *Fem.*; **a slice of ham** une tranche de jambon.
**slice** *verb* **to slice something** couper [1] quelque chose en tranches.

**slide** *noun* 1 (*photo*) diapositive *Fem.*; 2 (*hairslide*) barrette *Fem.*; 3 (*for sliding down*) toboggan *Masc.*

**slight** *adjective* léger (*Fem.* légère); **there is a slight problem** il y a un léger problème.

**slightly** *adverb* légèrement.

**slim** *adjective* mince.
**slim** *verb* **I'm slimming** je fais un régime.

a
b
c
d
e
f
g
h
i
j
k
l
m
n
o
p
q
r
s
t
u
v
w
x
y
z

**sling** *noun* écharpe *Fem.*; **to have your arm in a sling** avoir le bras en écharpe.

**slip** *noun* **1** (*mistake*) erreur *Fem.*; **2** (*petticoat*) (*from waist*) jupon *Masc.* (*full-length*) combinaison *Fem.*
**slip** *verb* **1** (*slide*) glisser [1]; **2 it had slipped my mind** j'avais oublié.

**slipper** *noun* pantoufle *Fem.*

**slippery** *adjective* glissant.

**slope** *noun* pente *Fem.*

**slot** *noun* fente *Fem.*

**slot machine** *noun* **1** (*games machine*) machine *Fem.* à sous; **2** (*vending machine*) distributeur *Masc.* automatique.

**slow** *adjective* **1** lent; **the service is a bit slow** le service est une peu lent; **2 my watch is slow** ma montre retarde.
● **to slow down** ralentir [2].

**slowly** *adverb* **1** lentement; **he got up slowly** il s'est levé lentement; **2** (*speak, drive*) doucement; **can you speak more slowly, please?** est-ce que vous pouvez parler plus doucement, s'il vous plaît?

**slug** *noun* limace *Fem.*

**slum** *noun* quartier *Masc.* démuni.

**slush** *noun* neige *Fem.* fondue.

**sly** *adjective* (*person*) rusé; ★ **on the sly** en douce.

**smack** *noun* claque *Fem.*
**smack** *verb* **to smack somebody** donner [1] une claque à quelqu'un.

**small** *adjective* petit (*goes before the noun*); **a small dog** un petit chien.

**smart** *adjective* **1** (*well-dressed, posh*) chic; **a smart restaurant** un restaurant chic; **2** (*clever*) intelligent.

**smash** *noun* **a car smash** un accident de voiture.
**smash** *verb* casser [1]; **they smashed a window** ils ont cassé une vitre.

**smashing** *adjective* formidable.

**smell** *noun* odeur *Fem.*; **a nasty smell** une mauvaise odeur; **there's a smell of burning** ça sent le brûlé.
**smell** *verb* **1** sentir [58]; **I can't smell anything** je ne sens rien; **I can smell lavender** ça sent la lavande; **2** (*smell bad*) sentir [58] mauvais; **the drains smell** les égouts sentent mauvais.

**smelly** *adjective* qui sent mauvais; **her smelly dog** son chien qui sent mauvais.

**smile** *noun* sourire *Masc.*
**smile** *verb* sourire [68].

**smoke** *noun* fumée *Fem.*
**smoke** *verb* fumer [1]; **she doesn't smoke** elle ne fume pas; **he smokes a pipe** il fume la pipe.

**smoked** *adjective* fumé; **smoked salmon** du saumon fumé.

**smoker** *noun* fumeur *Masc.*, fumeuse *Fem.*

**smoking** *noun* 'no smoking' 'défense de fumer'; **to give up smoking** arrêter de fumer.

**smooth** *adjective* **1** lisse; **a smooth surface** une surface lisse; **2** (*person*) mielleux (*Fem.* mielleuse).

**smug** *adjective* suffisant.

**smuggle** *verb* **to smuggle something** faire [10] passer quelque chose en contrebande.

**smuggler** *noun* **1** contrebandier *Masc.*, contrebandière *Fem.*; **2 a drugs smuggler** un passeur de drogue.

**smuggling** *noun* **1** contrebande *Fem.*; **2** (*of drugs or arms*) trafic *Masc.*

**snack** *noun* casse-croûte *Masc.*

**snack bar** *noun* sandwicherie *Fem.*, snack-bar *Masc.*

**snail** *noun* escargot *Masc.*

**snake** *noun* serpent *Masc.*

**snap** *noun* (*card game*) bataille *Fem.*
**snap** *verb* **1** (*break*) casser [1]; **2 to snap your fingers** faire [10] claquer ses doigts.

**snapshot** *noun* photo *Fem.*

**snarl** *verb* gronder [1].

**snatch** *verb* arracher [1]; **to snatch something from somebody** arracher quelque chose à quelqu'un; **he snatched my book** il m'a arraché mon livre; **she had her bag snatched** on lui a arraché son sac.

**sneak** *verb* **to sneak in** entrer [1] furtivement; **to sneak out** sortir [72] furtivement; **he sneaked up on me** il s'est approché de moi sans faire de bruit.

**sneeze** *verb* éternuer [1].

**sniff** *verb* renifler [1].

**snob** *noun* snob *Masc. & Fem.*

**snobbery** *noun* snobisme *Masc.*

**snooker** *noun* snooker *Masc.*; **to play snooker** jouer au snooker.

**snooze** *noun* somme *Masc.*; **to have a snooze** faire un petit somme.

**snore** *verb* ronfler [1].

**snow** *noun* neige *Fem.*
**snow** *verb* neiger [52]; **it's snowing** il neige; **it's going to snow** il va neiger.

**snowball** *noun* boule *Fem.* de neige (*plural* boules de neige).

**snowdrift** *noun* congère *Fem.*

**snowman** *noun* bonhomme *Masc.* de neige (*plural* bonshommes de neige).

**snowy** *adjective* enneigé; **it was very snowy** il y avait beaucoup de neige.

**so** *conjunction, adverb* **1** tellement; **he's so lazy** il est tellement paresseux; **the coffee's so hot I can't drink it** le café est tellement chaud que je n'arrive pas à le boire; **2 not so** moins; **our house is a bit like yours, but not so big** notre maison est un peu comme la vôtre, mais moins grande; **3 so much** tellement; **I hate it so much!** je le déteste tellement!; **4 so much, so many** tellement de; **I have so much work to do** j'ai tellement de travail à faire; **we've got so many problems** nous avons tellement de problèmes; **5** (*therefore*) donc; **he got up late, so he missed his train** il s'est levé tard, donc il a raté son train; **6** (*starting a sentence*) alors; **so what's your name?** alors, tu t'appelles comment?; **so what shall we do?** alors, qu'est-ce qu'on fait?; **so what?** et alors?; **7 so do I, so did I** moi aussi; **'I live in Leeds' – 'so do I'** 'j'habite à Leeds' – 'moi aussi'; **'I hated the film' – 'so did I'** 'j'ai détesté le film' – 'moi aussi'; **so am I**

moi aussi; **so do we** nous aussi; **8 I think so** je crois; **I hope so** j'espère.

**soak** *verb* tremper [1].

**soaked** *adjective* trempé; ★ **to be soaked to the skin** être trempé jusqu'aux os (*literally: to be soaked to the bones*).

**soaking** *adjective* trempé; **soaking wet** trempé.

**soap** *noun* **1** savon *Masc.*; **a cake of soap** un savon; **2** (*soap opera: on TV*) feuilleton *Masc.*

**soap powder** *noun* lessive *Fem.*

**sober** *adjective* **to be sober** ne pas avoir bu; **he's sober** il n'a pas bu; **are you sure she's sober?** tu es sûr qu'elle n'a pas bu?

**soccer** *noun* football *Masc.*; **to play soccer** jouer au football.

**social** *adjective* social (*Masc. plural* sociaux).

**socialism** *noun* socialisme *Masc.*

**socialist** *noun, adjective* socialiste *Masc. & Fem.*

**social security** *noun* **1** aide *Fem.* sociale; **to be on social security** recevoir de l'aide sociale; **2 the social security** (*the system*) sécurité sociale *Fem.*

**social worker** *noun* travailleur *Masc.* social (*plural* travailleurs sociaux), travailleuse *Fem.* sociale; **she's a social worker** elle est travailleuse sociale.

**society** *noun* société *Fem.*

**sociology** *noun* sociologie *Fem.*

**sock** *noun* chaussette *Fem.*; **a pair of socks** une paire de chaussettes.

**socket** *noun* (*power point*) prise *Fem.* de courant (*plural* prises de courant).

**sofa** *noun* canapé *Masc.*

**sofa bed** *noun* canapé-lit *Masc.*

**soft** *adjective* doux (*Fem.* douce); ★ **to have a soft spot for somebody** avoir un faible pour quelqu'un.

**soft drink** *noun* boisson *Fem.* non alcoolisée.

**soft toy** *noun* peluche *Fem.*

**software** *noun* logiciel *Masc.*

**soil** *noun* terre *Fem.*

**solar energy** *noun* énergie *Fem.* solaire.

**soldier** *noun* soldat *Masc.*

**solicitor** *noun* **1** (*dealing with property or documents*) notaire *Masc.*; **she's a solicitor** elle est notaire; **2** (*dealing with lawsuits*) avocat *Masc.*, avocate *Fem.*; **she's a solicitor** elle est avocate.

**solid** *adjective* **1** massif (*Fem.* massive); **a table made of solid pine** une table en pin massif; **a solid gold ring** une bague en or massif; **solid silver** argent massif; **2** (*not flimsy*) solide; **a solid structure** une structure solide.

**solo** *noun* solo *Masc.*; **a guitar solo** un solo de guitare.
**solo** *adjective, adverb* en solo; **a solo album** un album en solo; **to play solo** jouer en solo.

**soloist** *noun* soliste *Masc. & Fem.*

**solution** *noun* solution *Fem.*

**solve** *verb* résoudre [67].

**some** *adjective, adverb* **1** (*followed by a singular noun*), du (*with a masculine noun*), de la (*with a feminine noun*), de l' (*with a noun beginning with a vowel or silent 'h'*); **would you like some butter?** voulez-vous du beurre?; **may I have some salad?** puis-je avoir de la salade?; **can you lend me some money?** est-ce que tu peux me prêter de l'argent?; **2** (*followed by a plural noun*) des; **I've bought some apples** j'ai acheté des pommes; **3** (*referring to something that has been mentioned*) en; **'would you like butter?' – 'thanks, I've got some'** 'veux-tu du beurre?' – 'merci, j'en ai'; **he's eaten some of it** il en a mangé un peu; **4 some people think he's wrong** il y a des gens qui pensent qu'il a tort; **5 some day** un de ces jours.

**somebody**, **someone** *pronoun* quelqu'un; **there's somebody in the garden** il y a quelqu'un dans le jardin.

**somehow** *adverb* **1** d'une manière ou d'une autre; **I've got to finish this essay somehow** je dois finir cette rédaction d'une manière ou d'une autre; **2 I somehow think they won't come** quelque chose me dit qu'ils ne viendront pas.

**somersault** *noun* **1** (*child's*) galipette *Fem.*; **2** (*gymnast's*) roulade *Fem.*; **3** (*diver's*) saut *Masc.* périlleux.

**something** *pronoun* quelque chose; **I've got something to tell you** j'ai quelque chose à te dire; **something pretty** quelque chose de joli; **something interesting** quelque chose d'intéressant; **there's something wrong** il y a quelque chose qui ne va pas; **their house is really something!** leur maison c'est vraiment quelque chose!; **a guy called Colin something or other** un type qui s'appelle Colin quelque chose.

**sometime** *adverb* un de ces jours; **give me a ring sometime** appelle-moi un de ces jours; **I'll ring you sometime next week** je t'appellerai dans le courant de la semaine prochaine.

**sometimes** *adverb* quelquefois; **I sometimes take the train** quelquefois je prends le train.

**somewhere** *adverb* quelque part; **I've put my bag down somewhere** j'ai posé mon sac quelque part; **I've met you somewhere before** je vous ai déjà vu quelque part.

**son** *noun* fils *Masc.*

**song** *noun* chanson *Fem.*

**son-in-law** *noun* gendre *Masc.*

**soon** *adverb* **1** bientôt; **it will soon be the holidays** c'est bientôt les vacances; **see you soon!** à bientôt; **2 as soon as** dès que; **as soon as she arrives** dès qu'elle arrivera; **as soon as possible** dès que possible; **3 it's too soon** c'est trop tôt.

**sooner** *adverb* **1** plus tôt; **we should have started sooner** nous aurions dû commencer plus tôt; **2 I'd sooner wait** je préfère attendre; ★ **sooner or later** tôt ou tard.

**soprano** *noun* soprano *Masc. & Fem.*

a
b
c
d
e
f
g
h
i
j
k
l
m
n
o
p
q
r
s
t
u
v
w
x
y
z

**sore** noun plaie Fem.

**sore** adjective **to have a sore leg** avoir mal à la jambe; **to have a sore throat** avoir mal à la gorge; **my arm's sore** j'ai mal au bras; ★ **it's a sore point** c'est un sujet délicat.

**sorry** adjective **1** désolé; **I'm really sorry** je suis vraiment désolé; **sorry to disturb you** je suis désolé de vous déranger; **I'm sorry I forgot your birthday** je suis désolé d'avoir oublié ton anniversaire; **2 sorry!** excusez-moi!; **3 sorry?** comment?; **4 to feel sorry for somebody** plaindre [31] quelqu'un.

**sort** noun sorte Fem.; **what sort of music do you like?** tu aimes quelle sorte de musique?; **all sorts of** toutes sortes de; **for all sorts of reasons** pour toutes sortes de raisons.

• **to sort something out 1** mettre [11] de l'ordre dans (room, desk, papers, possessions); **I must sort out my room tonight** je dois mettre de l'ordre dans ma chambre ce soir; **2** s'occuper [1] de (problem, arrangement); **Liz is sorting it out** Liz s'en occupe.

**so-so** adjective moyen (Fem. moyenne); **'how was the film?' – 'so-so'** 'c'était comment le film?' – 'moyen'.

**soul** noun **1** âme Fem.; **2** (music) soul Masc.

**sound** noun **1** (noise) bruit ; **the sound of voices** le bruit des voix; **2** (volume) volume; **to turn down the sound** baisser le volume.

**sound** verb **it sounds easy** ça a l'air facile; **it sounds as if she's happy** elle a l'air d'être heureuse.

**sound asleep** adjective profondément endormi.

**sound effect** noun effet Masc. sonore.

**soundtrack** noun bande Fem. sonore.

**soup** noun soupe Fem.; **mushroom soup** la soupe aux champignons.

**soup plate** noun assiette Fem. creuse la soupe.

**soup spoon** noun cuillère Fem. à soupe.

**sour** adjective **1** (taste) aigre; **2 the milk has gone sour** le lait a tourné.

**south** noun sud Masc.; **in the south** au sud.

**south** adjective, adverb sud (never agrees); **the south side** le côté sud; **a south wind** un vent du sud; **south of Paris** au sud de Paris.

**South Africa** noun Afrique Fem. du Sud.

**South America** noun Amérique Fem. du Sud.

**South American** noun Sud-Américain Masc., Sud-Américaine Fem.

**South American** adjective sud-américain.

**southeast** noun sud-est Masc.

**southeast** adjective **in southeast England** au sud-est de l'Angleterre.

**South Pole** noun pôle Masc. Sud.

**southwest** noun sud-ouest Masc.

**southwest** adjective **in southwest England** au sud-ouest de l'Angleterre.

**souvenir** *noun* souvenir *Masc.*

**soya** *noun* soja *Masc.*

**soy sauce** *noun* sauce *Fem.* de soja.

**space** *noun* **1** (*room*) place *Fem.*; **is there enough space?** est-ce qu'il y a de la place?; **there's enough space for two** il y a de la place pour deux; **2** (*gap*) espace *Masc.*; **leave a space** laissez un espace; **3** (*outer space*) espace *Masc.*; **in space** dans l'espace.

**spacecraft** *noun* engin *Masc.* spatial.

**spade** *noun* **1** pelle *Fem.*; **2** (*in cards*) pique *Masc.*; **the queen of spades** la reine de pique.

**spaghetti** *noun* spaghetti *Masc. plural.*

**Spain** *noun* Espagne *Fem.*; **in Spain** en Espagne; **to Spain** en Espagne.

**Spaniard** *noun* Espagnol *Masc.*, Espagnole *Fem.*

**spaniel** *noun* épagneul *Masc.*

**Spanish** *noun* **1** (*language*) espagnol *Masc.*; **I'm learning Spanish** j'apprends l'espagnol; **2 the Spanish** (*people*) les Espagnols *Masc. plural.*
**Spanish** *adjective* espagnol; **Pedro is Spanish** Pedro est espagnol.

**spank** *verb* **to spank somebody** donner [1] une fessée à quelqu'un.

**spanner** *noun* clé *Fem.* anglaise.

**spare** *adjective* (*part, battery*) de rechange; **we have a spare ticket** nous avons un billet de trop.
**spare** *verb* **I can't spare the time** je n'ai pas le temps; **can you spare a moment?** est-ce que tu as un instant?

**spare part** *noun* pièce *Fem.* de rechange.

**spare room** *noun* chambre *Fem.* d'amis.

**spare time** *noun* temps *Masc.* libre; **in my spare time** dans mon temps libre.

**spare wheel** *noun* roue *Fem.* de secours.

**sparkling** *adjective* **sparkling (mineral) water** l'eau (minérale) pétillante; **sparkling wine** le vin mousseux.

**sparrow** *noun* moineau *Masc.* (*plural* moineaux).

**speak** *verb* **1** parler [1]; **do you speak French?** est-ce que vous parlez français?; **spoken French** le français parlé; **2 to speak to somebody** parler [1] à quelqu'un; **she's speaking to Mike** elle parle à Mike; **I've never spoken to her** je ne lui ai jamais parlé; **I'll speak to him about it** je vais lui en parler; **3 who's speaking?** (*on the phone*) c'est qui à l'appareil?

**speaker** *noun* **1** (*on a music system*) enceinte *Fem.*; **2** (*at a public lecture*) conférencier *Masc.*, conférencière *Fem.*; **3** (*of a language*) **a French speaker** un/une francophone; **an English speaker** un/une anglophone.

**spear** *noun* lance *Fem.*

**special** *adjective* spécial (*Masc. plural* spéciaux).

**specialist** *noun* spécialiste *Masc. & Fem.*

**specialize** *verb* to specialize in être [6] spécialisé dans; **we specialize in French cars** nous sommes spécialisés dans les voitures françaises.

**specially** *adverb* **1** spécialement; **not specially** pas spécialement; **the poems have been specially chosen for small children** les poèmes ont été spécialement choisis pour les petits enfants; **2** (*specifically*) exprès; **I came specially in order to see you** je suis venu exprès pour te voir; **I made this cake specially for you** j'ai fait ce gâteau exprès pour toi.

**species** *noun* espèce *Fem.*

**specific** *adjective* précis.

**spectacles** *noun* lunettes *Fem. plural.*

**spectacular** *adjective* spectaculaire.

**spectator** *noun* spectateur *Masc.*, spectatrice *Fem.*

**speech** *noun* discours *Masc.*; **to make a speech** faire un discours.

**speechless** *adjective* muet (*Fem.* muette); **to be speechless with rage** rester muet de colère; **I was speechless** j'étais stupéfait.

**speed** *noun* vitesse *Fem.*; **at top speed** à toute vitesse; **what speed was he doing?** il roulait à quelle vitesse?; **a twelve-speed bike** un vélo à douze vitesses.

● **to speed up** accélérer [24].

**speeding** *noun* excès *Masc.* de vitesse; **he was fined for speeding** il a reçu une contravention pour excès de vitesse.

**speed limit** *noun* limitation *Fem.* de vitesse.

**spell** *noun* (*of time*) période *Fem.*; **a cold spell** une période de temps froid; **sunny spells** des éclaircies *Fem. plural.*

**spell** *verb* **1** (*in writing*) écrire [38]; **how do you spell it?** ça s'écrit comment?; **how do you spell your surname?** ça s'écrit comment, ton nom de famille?; **2** (*out loud*) épeler [18].

**spell checker** *noun* correcteur *Masc.* orthographique.

**spelling** *noun* orthographe *Fem.*; **a spelling mistake** une faute d'orthographe.

**spend** *verb* **1** dépenser [1] (*money*); **I've spent all my money** j'ai dépensé tout mon argent; **2** passer [1] (*time*); **we spent three days in Paris** nous avons passé trois jours à Paris; **she spends her time writing letters** elle passe son temps à écrire des lettres.

**spice** *noun* épice *Fem.*

**spicy** *adjective* épicé; **he doesn't like spicy food** il n'aime pas les choses épicées.

**spider** *noun* araignée *Fem.*

**spill** *verb* renverser [1]; **I've spilled my wine on the carpet** j'ai renversé mon vin sur la moquette.

**spinach** *noun* épinards *Masc. plural*; **do you like spinach?** est-ce que tu aimes les épinards?

**spine** *noun* colonne *Fem.* vertébrale.

**spiral** *noun* spirale *Fem.*

**spiral staircase** *noun* escalier *Masc.* en colimaçon.

**spire** *noun* flèche *Fem.*

**spirit** *noun* 1 (*energy*) énergie *Fem.*; 2 **to get into the spirit of the occasion** se mettre dans l'ambiance.

**spirits** *noun* 1 (*alcohol*) alcools *Masc.* plural forts; 2 **to be in good spirits** être de bonne humeur.

**spit** *verb* cracher [1]; **to spit something out** cracher quelque chose.

**spite** *noun* 1 **in spite of** malgré; **we decided to go in spite of the rain** nous avons décidé d'y aller malgré la pluie; 2 (*nastiness*) méchanceté *Fem.*; **to do something out of spite** faire quelque chose par méchanceté.

**spiteful** *adjective* méchant.

**splash** *noun* 1 (*noise*) plouf *Masc.*; 2 **a splash of colour** une touche de couleur.
**splash** *verb* éclabousser [1].

**splendid** *adjective* splendide.

**splinter** *noun* écharde *Fem.*

**split** *verb* 1 (*with an axe or a knife*) fendre [3]; **to split a piece of wood** fendre un morceau de bois; 2 (*come apart*) se fendre [3]; **the lining has split** la doublure s'est fendue; 3 (*divide up*) partager [52]; **they split the money between them** ils ont partagé l'argent entre eux.

● **to split up** 1 (*a couple or group*) se séparer [1]; 2 **she's split up with her boyfriend** elle a rompu avec son copain.

**spoil** *verb* 1 gâcher [1]; **it completely spoiled the evening** ça a complètement gâché la soirée; **to**

**spoil the surprise** gâcher la surprise; 2 gâter [1] (*a child*).

**spoiled** *adjective* gâté; **a spoiled child** un enfant gâté.

**spoilsport** *noun* trouble-fête *Masc. & Fem.*

**spoke** *noun* (*of a wheel*) rayon *Masc.*

**spokesman** *noun* porte-parole *Masc.* (*plural* porte-parole).

**spokeswoman** *noun* porte-parole *Masc.* (*plural* porte-parole).

**sponge** *noun* éponge *Fem.*

**sponge bag** *noun* trousse *Fem.* de toilette.

**sponge cake** *noun* génoise *Fem.*

**sponsor** *noun* sponsor *Masc.*
**sponsor** *verb* sponsoriser [1].

**spontaneous** *adjective* spontané.

**spooky** *adjective* 1 (*atmosphere*) sinistre; 2 **a spooky story** une histoire qui fait froid dans le dos.

**spoon** *noun* cuillère *Fem.*; **a soup spoon** une cuillère à soupe; **a teaspoon** une petite cuillère.

**spoonful** *noun* cuillère *Fem.*

**sport** *noun* sport *Masc.*; **to be good at sport** être bon en sport; **my favourite sport** mon sport préféré.

**sports bag** *noun* sac *Masc.* de sport.

**sports car** *noun* voiture *Fem.* de sport.

**sports centre** *noun* centre *Masc.* sportif.

**sports club** *noun* club *Masc.* sportif.

**sportsman** *noun* sportif *Masc.*

a
b
c
d
e
f
g
h
i
j
k
l
m
n
o
p
q
r
**s**
t
u
v
w
x
y
z

**sportswear** *noun* vêtements *Masc.* *plural* de sport.

**sportswoman** *noun* sportive *Fem.*

**sporty** *adjective* sportif (*Fem.* sportive); **she's very sporty** elle est très sportive.

**spot** *noun* 1 (*in fabric*) pois *Masc.*; **a red tie with black spots** une cravate rouge aux pois noirs; 2 (*on your skin*) bouton; **I've got spots** j'ai des boutons; **to be covered in spots** être couvert de boutons; 3 (*stain*) tache *Fem.*; **you've got a spot on your tie** tu as une tache sur ta cravate; 4 (*spotlight*) projecteur *Masc.*; (*in the home*) spot *Masc.*; 5 **on the spot** (*immediately*) sur-le-champ; **we'll do it for you on the spot** nous le ferons sur-le-champ; 6 (*at hand*) sur place; **they have experts on the spot** ils ont des experts sur place.
**spot** *verb* repérer [24]; **I spotted her in the crowd** je l'ai repérée dans la foule.

**spotless** *adjective* impeccable.

**spotlight** *noun* 1 projecteur *Masc.*; 2 (*in the home*) spot *Masc.*

**spotty** *adjective* (*pimply*) boutonneux (*Fem.* boutonneuse).

**spouse** *noun* époux *Masc.*, épouse *Fem.*

**sprain** *noun* entorse *Fem.*
**sprain** *verb* **to sprain your ankle** se faire [10] une entorse à la cheville.

**spray** *noun* (*spray can*) bombe *Fem.*
**spray** *verb* vaporiser [1] (*liquid*).

**spread** *noun* pâte *Fem.* à tartiner; **cheese spread** le fromage à tartiner.
**spread** *verb* 1 (*news or a disease*) se propager [52]; 2 étaler [1] (*butter, jam, cement, glue, etc.*).

**spreadsheet** *noun* (*on a computer*) tableur *Masc.*

**spring** *noun* 1 (*the season*) printemps *Masc.*; **in the spring** au printemps; **spring flowers** les fleurs du printemps; 2 (*made of metal*) ressort *Masc.*; 3 (*providing water*) source *Fem.*

**spring-cleaning** *noun* grand nettoyage *Masc.* de printemps.

**springtime** *noun* printemps *Masc.*; **in springtime** au printemps.

**spring water** *noun* eau *Fem.* de source.

**sprint** *noun* sprint *Masc.*
**sprint** *verb* courir [2] à toute vitesse.

**sprinter** *noun* sprinteur *Masc.*, sprinteuse *Fem.*

**sprout** *noun* (*Brussels sprout*) chou *Masc.* de Bruxelles (*plural* choux de Bruxelles).

**spy** *noun* espion *Masc.*, espionne *Fem.*
**spy** *verb* **to spy on somebody** espionner [1] quelqu'un.

**spying** *noun* espionnage *Masc.*

**squabble** *verb* se disputer [1].

**square** *noun* 1 (*shape*) carré; 2 (*in a town or village*) place *Fem.*; **the village square** la place du village; ★ **to go back to square one** retourner à la case départ.
**square** *adjective* carré; **a square box** une boîte carrée; **three square metres** trois mètres carrés; **the**

574

room is four metres square la pièce fait quatre mètres carrés.

**squash** *noun* 1 (*drink*) sirop *Masc.*; **orange squash** le sirop d'orange; 2 (*sport*) squash *Masc.*; **to play squash** jouer au squash.

**squeak** *verb* 1 (*door, hinge*) grincer [61]; 2 (*person, animal*) pousser [1] un petit cri.

**squeeze** *verb* 1 serrer [1] (*somebody's arm, hand, etc*); 2 presser [1] (*toothpaste*).

**squid** *noun* calmar *Masc.*

**squirrel** *noun* écureuil *Masc.*

**stab** *verb* poignarder [1].

**stable** *noun* écurie *Fem.* **stable** *adjective* stable.

**stack** *noun* 1 (*pile*) pile *Fem.*; 2 **stacks of** plein de; **she's got stacks of CDs** elle a plein de CD.

**stadium** *noun* stade *Masc.*

**staff** *noun* 1 (*of a company*) personnel *Masc.*; 2 (*in a school*) professeurs *Masc. plural.*

**stage** *noun* 1 (*for a performance*) scène *Fem.*; **on stage** sur scène; 2 (*phase*) stade *Masc.*; **at this stage of the project** à ce stade du projet; **at this stage it's hard to know** pour l'instant il est difficile de savoir.

**staggered** *adjective* (*amazed*) stupéfié.

**stain** *noun* tache *Fem.* **stain** *verb* tacher [1].

**stainless steel** *noun* inox *Masc.*; **a stainless steel sink** un évier en inox.

**stair** *noun* 1 (*step*) marche *Fem.*; 2 **stairs** escalier *Masc.*; **I met her on the stairs** je l'ai croisée dans l'escalier.

**staircase** *noun* escalier *Masc.*

**stale** *adjective* (*bread*) rassis.

**stalemate** *noun* (*in chess*) pat *Masc.*

**stall** *noun* 1 (*at a market or fair*) stand *Masc.*; 2 **the stalls** (*in a theatre*) l'orchestre *Masc. singular.*

**stammer** *noun* **to have a stammer** bégayer [59]. **stammer** *verb* bégayer [59].

**stamp** *noun* timbre *Masc.* **stamp** *verb* 1 affranchir [2] (*a letter*); 2 **to stamp your foot** taper [1] du pied.

**stamp album** *noun* album *Masc.* de timbres.

**stamp collection** *noun* collection *Fem.* de timbres.

**stand** *verb* 1 être [6] debout; **several people were standing** plusieurs personnes étaient debout; 2 (*when you say somebody is standing somewhere 'standing' is not usually translated*) **we were standing outside the cinema** nous étions devant le cinéma; **I'm standing here waiting for you** je suis là en train de t'attendre; 3 (*bear*) supporter [1]; **I can't stand her** je ne la supporte pas; **I can't stand waiting** je ne supporte pas d'attendre.

● **to stand for something** (*be short for*) être [6] l'abréviation de; **'UN' stands for 'United Nations'** 'UN' est l'abréviation de 'United

a b c d e f g h i j k l m n o p q r **s** t u v w x y z

a
b
c
d
e
f
g
h
i
j
k
l
m
n
o
p
q
r
**s**
t
u
v
w
x
y
z

Nations'.

• **stand up** se lever [50]; **everybody stood up** tout le monde s'est levé.

**standard** *noun* niveau *Masc.*; **her work is of a high standard** son travail est d'un bon niveau; **the standard of living** le niveau de vie.
**standard** *adjective* standard; **the standard price** le prix standard.

**Standard grades** *noun plural*
You can explain Standard grades as follows: Ce sont des examens que les lycéens écossais passent à l'âge d'environ 16 ans dans six ou sept matières. La meilleure note que l'on peut obtenir est 1 et la note la plus basse est 7. Une fois qu'ils ont obtenu leurs Standard grades, de nombreux étudiants se préparent pour les Highers; SEE **Highers**.

**stands** *noun* (*in a stadium*) tribune *Fem. singular.*

**staple** *noun* agrafe *Fem.*
**staple** *verb* agrafer [1]; **to staple the pages together** agrafer les feuilles.

**stapler** *noun* agrafeuse *Fem.*

**star** *noun* **1** (*in the sky*) étoile *Fem.*; **2** (*person*) vedette; **he's a film star** c'est une vedette de cinéma.
**star** *verb* **to star in a film** être [6] la vedette d'un film.

**stare** *verb* regarder [1] fixement; **he was staring at me** il me regardait fixement; **what are you staring at?** qu'est-ce que tu regardes?

**star sign** *noun* signe *Masc.* astrologique; **what star sign are you?** de quelle signe êtes-vous?

**start** *noun* **1** début *Masc.*; **at the start** au début; **at the start of the book** au début du livre; **from the start** dès le début; **we knew from the start that it was dangerous** nous savions dès le début que c'était dangereux; **2 to make a start on something** commencer à faire quelque chose; **I've made a start on my homework** j'ai commencé à faire mes devoirs; **3** (*of a race*) départ *Masc.*
**start** *verb* **1** commencer [61]; **the film starts at eight** le film commence à huit heures; **I've started the book** j'ai commencé le livre; **2 to start doing** commencer [61] à faire; **I've started learning Spanish** j'ai commencé à apprendre l'espagnol; **3 to start a business** créer [32] une entreprise; **4 to start a car** faire [10] démarrer une voiture; **she started the car** elle a fait démarrer la voiture; **the car wouldn't start** la voiture n'a pas voulu démarrer.

**starter** *noun* (*in a meal*) entrée *Fem.*; **what would you like as a starter?** qu'est-ce que vous voulez comme entrée?

**starve** *verb* mourir [54] de faim; **I'm starving!** je meurs de faim!

**state** *noun* **1** état *Masc.*; **the house is in a very bad state** la maison est en très mauvais état; **2** (*administrative*) état *Masc.*; **the state** l'État; **3 the States** les États-Unis *Masc. plural*; **they live in the States** ils habitent aux États-Unis.
**state** *verb* **1** déclarer [1] (*intention, opinion*); **2** indiquer [1] (*address, income, occupation, reason, etc.*).

**stately home** *noun* château *Masc.* (*plural* châteaux).

**statement** *noun* déclaration *Fem.*

**station** *noun* gare *Fem.*; **the railway station** la gare; **the bus station** la gare routière; **the police station** le commissariat; **a radio station** une station de radio.

**stationary** *adjective* à l'arrêt.

**stationer's** *noun* papeterie *Fem.*

**stationery** *noun* papeterie *Fem.*

**statistics** *noun* **1** (*subject*) statistique *Fem.*; **2 the statistics** (*figures*) les statistiques.

**statue** *noun* statue *Fem.*

**status** *noun* position *Fem.*

**stay** *noun* séjour *Masc.*; **our stay in Paris** notre séjour à Paris; **enjoy your stay!** bon séjour!
**stay** *verb* **1** rester [1]; **I'll stay here** je reste ici; **how long are you staying?** vous restez combien de temps?; **2** (*with time*) **we're going to stay in Berlin for three days** nous allons passer trois jours à Berlin; **3** (*at somebody's house*) **to stay with somebody** aller [7] chez quelqu'un; **I'm going to stay with my sister this weekend** je vais chez ma sœur ce weekend; **4** (*be temporarily lodged*) loger [52]; **where are you staying?** où est-ce que vous logez?

● **to stay in** rester [1] à la maison; **I'm staying in tonight** je reste à la maison ce soir.

**steady** *adjective* **1** stable; **a steady job** un emploi stable; **2** régulier (*Fem.* régulière); **a steady increase** une augmentation régulière;

**3** (*hand, voice*) ferme; **4 to hold something steady** bien tenir quelque chose.

**steak** *noun* steack *Masc.*; **steak and chips** un steack frites.

**steal** *verb* voler [1].

**steam** *noun* vapeur *Fem.*

**steam engine** *noun* locomotive *Fem.* à vapeur.

**steam iron** *noun* fer *Masc.* à vapeur.

**steel** *noun* acier *Masc.*

**steep** *adjective* raide; **a steep slope** une pente raide.

**steeple** *noun* **1** (*spire*) flèche *Fem.*; **2** (*bell tower*) clocher *Masc.*

**steering wheel** *noun* volant *Masc.*

**step** *noun* **1** pas *Masc.*; **to take a step forwards** faire un pas en avant; **to take a step backwards** faire un pas en arrière; **2** (*stair*) marche *Fem.*; **'mind the step'** 'attention à la marche'.

● **to step back** faire [10] un pas en arrière.

● **to step forward** faire [10] un pas en avant.

● **to step into** entrer [1] dans (*a lift*).

**stepbrother** *noun* demi-frère *Masc.* (*plural* demi-frères).

**stepdaughter** *noun* belle-fille *Fem.* (*plural* belles-filles).

**stepfather** *noun* beau-père *Masc.*

**stepladder** *noun* escabeau *Masc.* (*plural* escabeaux).

**stepmother** *noun* belle-mère *Fem.*

**stepsister** *noun* demi-sœur *Fem.* (*plural* demi-sœurs).

a b c d e f g h i j k l m n o p q r s t u v w x y z

a
b
c
d
e
f
g
h
i
j
k
l
m
n
o
p
q
r
**s**
t
u
v
w
x
y
z

**stepson** *noun* beau-fils *Masc.* (*plural* beaux-fils).

**stereo** *noun* chaîne *Fem.* stéréo (*plural* chaînes stéréo).

**sterling** *noun* sterling *Masc.*; **in sterling** en livres sterling.

**stew** *noun* ragoût *Masc.*

**steward** *noun* steward *Masc.*

**stewardess** *noun* hôtesse *Fem.*

**stick** *noun* **1** bâton *Masc.*; **2 a walking stick** une canne; **3 a hockey stick** une crosse de hockey. **stick** *verb* **1** (*with glue*) coller [1]; **2** (*put*) mettre [11]; **stick them on my desk** mets-les sur mon bureau.

**sticker** *noun* autocollant *Masc.*

**sticky** *adjective* **1** poisseux (*Fem.* poisseuse); **my hands are sticky** j'ai les mains poisseuses; **2** adhésif (*Fem.* adhésive); **sticky paper** le papier adhésif.

**sticky tape** *noun* Scotch™ *Masc.*

**stiff** *adjective* **1 to feel stiff** avoir [5] des courbatures; **to have stiff legs** avoir des courbatures dans les jambes; **2 to be bored stiff** s'ennuyer [41] à mourir; **to be scared stiff** être [6] mort de peur.

**still** *adjective* **1 sit still!** tiens-toi tranquille!; **keep still!** ne bouge pas!; **2 still mineral water** l'eau minérale non-gazeuse. **still** *adverb* **1** toujours; **do you still live in London?** est-ce que tu habites toujours à Londres?; **I've still not finished** je n'ai toujours pas fini; **he's still working** il est toujours en train de travailler; **2** encore; **there's still a lot of beer left** il reste encore beaucoup de bière; **3 better still** encore mieux.

**sting** *noun* piqûre *Fem.*; **a wasp sting** une piqûre de guêpe. **sting** *verb* piquer [1]; **I was stung by a bee** je me suis fait piquer par une abeille.

**stink** *noun* odeur *Fem.*; **what a stink!** ça pue! **stink** *verb* puer [1]; **it stinks of cigarette smoke in here** ça pue la cigarette ici.

**stir** *verb* remuer [1].

**stitch** *noun* **1** (*in sewing*) point *Masc.*; **2** (*in knitting*) maille *Fem.*; **3** (*surgical*) point *Masc.* de souture (*plural* points de souture).

**stock** *noun* **1** (*in a shop*) stock *Masc.*; **to have something in stock** avoir quelque chose en stock; **2** (*supply*) réserve; **I always have a stock of pencils** j'ai toujours une réserve de crayons; **3** (*for cooking*) bouillon; **chicken stock** le bouillon de poulet. **stock** *verb* (*in a shop*) vendre [3]; **they don't stock dictionaries** ils ne vendent pas les dictionnaires.

● **to stock up on something** s'approvisionner [1] en quelque chose.

**stock cube** *noun* bouillon-cube *Masc.*

**stock exchange** *noun* Bourse *Fem.* (des valeurs).

**stocking** *noun* bas *Masc.*

**stomach** *noun* estomac *Masc.*

**stomachache** *noun* **to have stomachache** avoir mal au ventre.

**stone** *noun* **1** pierre *Fem.*; **a stone wall** un mur en pierre; **2** (*pebble*) caillou *Masc.*; **3** (*in fruit*) noyau *Masc.* (*plural* noyaux).

**stool** *noun* tabouret *Masc.*

**stop** *noun* arrêt *Masc.*; **the bus stop** l'arrêt de bus.
**stop** *verb* **1** s'arrêter [1]; **he stopped in front of the shop** il s'est arrêté devant le magasin; **the music stopped** la musique s'est arrêtée; **does the train stop in Dijon?** est-ce que le train s'arrête à Dijon?; **2 to stop somebody/something** arrêter [1] quelque chose/quelqu'un; **she stopped me in the street** elle m'a arrêté dans la rue; **3 to stop doing** arrêter [1] de faire; **he's stopped smoking** il a arrêté de fumer; **she never stops asking questions** elle n'arrête pas de poser des questions; **4 to stop somebody doing** empêcher [1] quelqu'un de faire; **there's nothing to stop you going on your own** rien ne t'empêche d'y aller tout seul.

**stopwatch** *noun* chronomètre *Masc.*

**store** *noun* (*shop*) magasin *Masc.*
**store** *verb* **1** garder [1]; **2** (*on a computer*) mémoriser [1].

**storey** *noun* étage *Masc.*; **a three-storey house** une maison à trois étages.

**stork** *noun* cigogne *Fem.*

**storm** *noun* **1** (*wind*) tempête *Fem.*; **a snowstorm** une tempête de neige; **a rainstorm** une tempête de pluie; **2** (*thunderstorm*) orage *Masc.*

**stormy** *adjective* orageux (*Fem.* orageuse).

**story** *noun* histoire *Fem.*; **to tell a story** raconter une histoire.

**stove** *noun* (*cooker*) cuisinière *Fem.*

**straight** *adjective* **1** droit; **a straight line** une ligne droite; **2 to have straight hair** avoir les cheveux raides.
**straight** *adverb* **1** (*in direction*) droit; **go straight ahead** continuez tout droit; **2** (*in time*) directement; **he went straight to the doctor's** il est allé directement chez le médecin; **3 straight away** tout de suite.

**straightforward** *adjective* simple.

**strain** *noun* stress *Masc.*; **the strain of the last few weeks** le stress de ces dernières semaines; **to be a strain** être stressant.
**strain** *verb* **1** se faire [10] mal à (*part of the body*); **he's strained his back** il s'est fait mal au dos; **2** (*a muscle*) se froisser [1]; **3** (*vegetables, rice*) égoutter [1].

**strange** *adjective* bizarre; **a strange situation** une situation bizarre.

**stranger** *noun* inconnu *Masc.*, inconnue *Fem.*

**strangle** *verb* étrangler [1].

**strap** *noun* **1** (*on case, bag, camera*) courroie *Fem.*; **2** (*on a garment*) bretelle *Fem.*; **3** (*of a watch*) bracelet *Masc.*; **a watchstrap** un bracelet de montre; **4** (*on a shoe*) lanière *Fem.*

**strapless** *adjective* sans bretelles.

a
b
c
d
e
f
g
h
i
j
k
l
m
n
o
p
q
r
s
t
u
v
w
x
y
z

**straw** noun paille Fem. (both the material and for drinking with); **a straw hat** un chapeau de paille.

**strawberry** noun fraise Fem.; **strawberry jam** la confiture de fraises; **a strawberry yoghurt** un yaourt à la fraise.

**stray** adjective **a stray dog** un chien perdu.

**stream** noun (small river) ruisseau Masc. (plural ruisseaux).

**street** noun rue Fem.; **I met Simon in the street** j'ai croisé Simon dans la rue.

**streetlamp** noun réverbère Masc.

**street map** noun plan Masc. de la ville.

**streetwise** adjective dégourdi.

**strength** noun force Fem.

**stress** noun stress Masc.
**stress** verb (emphasize) souligner [1]; **to stress the importance of something** souligner l'importance de quelque chose.

**stretch** verb **1** (garment) se déformer [1]; **this jumper has stretched** ce pull s'est déformé; **2** (shoes) s'élargir [2].

**stretcher** noun brancard Masc.

**stretchy** adjective élastique.

**strict** adjective strict.

**strike** noun grève Fem.; **to go on strike** faire grève; **to be on strike** être en grève.
**strike** verb **1** (hit) frapper [1]; **2** (clock) sonner [1]; **the clock struck six** l'horloge a sonné six heures; **3** (go on strike) faire [10] grève.

**striker** noun **1** (in football) buteur Masc.; **2** (person on strike) gréviste Masc. & Fem.

**striking** adjective frappant; **a striking resemblance** une ressemblance frappante.

**string** noun **1** (for tying) ficelle Fem.; **2** (for a musical instrument) corde Fem.

**strip** noun bande Fem.
**strip** verb (undress) se déshabiller [1].

**strip cartoon** noun bande Fem. dessinée.

**stripe** noun rayure Fem.

**striped** adjective rayé.

**stroke** noun **1** (style of swimming) nage Fem.; **2** (medical) attaque Fem.; **to have a stroke** avoir une attaque; ★ **a stroke of luck** un coup de chance.
**stroke** verb caresser [1].

**stroll** noun **to go for a stroll** faire une petite promenade.
**stroll** verb se promener [50].

**strong** adjective **1** (person, drink) fort; **2** (feeling) puissant; **3** (material) solide.

**strongly** adverb **1** (believe) fermement; **2** (support) fortement; **3** (advise, oppose) vivement.

**struggle** noun **1** lutte Fem.; **the struggle for independence** la lutte pour l'indépendance; **a power struggle** une lutte pour le pouvoir; **2 it's been a struggle** ça a été très dur.
**struggle** verb **1** (to obtain something) se battre [21]; **they have struggled to survive** ils se sont

battus pour survivre; **2** (*physically, in order to escape or reach something*) se débattre [21]; **3** (*have difficulty in doing*) avoir [5] du mal à faire; **I'm struggling to finish my homework** j'ai du mal à finir mes devoirs.

**stub** *noun* **a cigarette stub** un mégot.

• **to stub out** écraser [1] (*a cigarette*).

**stubborn** *adjective* têtu.

**stuck** *adjective* **1** (*jammed*) coincé; **the drawer's stuck** le tiroir est coincé; **2** (*person*) **to get stuck** rester coincé (*in a lift, traffic jam, or place*).

**stud** *noun* **1** (*on a belt or jacket*) clou *Masc.*; **2** (*on a boot*) clou *Masc.*; **3** (*earring*) boucle *Fem.* d'oreille.

**student** *noun* étudiant *Masc.*, étudiante *Fem.*

**studio** *noun* **1** (*film, TV*) studio *Masc.*; **2** (*artist's*) atelier *Masc.*

**studio flat** *noun* studio *Masc.*

**study** *verb* **1** réviser [1]; **he's busy studying for his exams** il est en train de réviser pour ses examens; **2** faire [10] des études de (*a subject*); **she's studying medicine** elle fait des études de médecine.

**stuff** *noun* **1** (*things*) trucs *Masc. plural* (*informal*); **we can put all that stuff in the attic** on peut mettre tous ces trucs au grenier; **2** (*personal belongings*) affaires *Fem. plural*; **you can leave your stuff at my house** tu peux laisser tes affaires chez moi; **3** (*substance*) truc *Masc.* (*informal*); **some antiseptic stuff** un truc antiséptique.

**stuff** *verb* **1** (*shove*) fourrer [1] (*informal*); **she stuffed some things into a suitcase** elle a fourré quelques affaires dans une valise; **2** farcir [2] (*chicken, turkey, vegetables*); **stuffed aubergines** des aubergines farcies.

**stuffing** *noun* (*for cooking*) farce *Fem.*

**stuffy** *adjective* (*airless*) étouffant.

**stumble** *verb* (*trip*) trébucher [1].

**stunned** *adjective* (*amazed*) stupéfait.

**stunning** *adjective* sensationnel (*Fem.* sensationnelle).

**stunt** *noun* (*in a film*) cascade *Fem.*

**stuntman** *noun* cascadeur *Masc.*

**stuntwoman** *noun* cascadeuse *Fem.*

**stupid** *adjective* bête; **that was really stupid** c'était vraiment bête; **to do something stupid** faire une bêtise.

**stutter** *noun* **to have a stutter** bégayer [59].
**stutter** *verb* bégayer [59].

**style** *noun* **1** style *Masc.*; **a style of living** un style de vie; **he has his own style** il a son propre style; **2** (*fashion*) mode *Fem.*; **it's the latest style** c'est la dernière mode.

**subject** *noun* **1** sujet *Masc.*; **the subject of my talk** le sujet de mon exposé; **2** (*at school*) matière *Fem.*; **my favourite subject is biology** ma matière préférée c'est la biologie.

**submarine** *noun* sous-marin *Masc.* (*plural* sous-marins).

a
b
c
d
e
f
g
h
i
j
k
l
m
n
o
p
q
r
s
t
u
v
w
x
y
z

**subscription** *noun* abonnement *Masc.*; **to take out a subscription to** s'abonner à.

**subsidy** *noun* subvention *Fem.*

**substance** *noun* substance *Fem.*

**substitute** *noun* (*person*) remplaçant *Masc.*, remplaçante *Fem.* **substitute** *verb* substituer [1].

**subtitled** *adjective* (*film*) sous-titré.

**subtitles** *plural noun* sous-titres *Masc. plural.*

**subtle** *adjective* subtil.

**subtract** *verb* soustraire [78].

**suburb** *noun* banlieue *Fem.*; **a suburb of Edinburgh** une banlieue d'Édimbourg; **in the suburbs of London** dans la banlieue de Londres.

**suburban** *adjective* de banlieue.

**subway** *noun* (*underpass*) passage *Masc.* souterrain.

**succeed** *verb* réussir [2]; **to succeed in doing** réussir à faire; **we've succeeded in contacting her** nous avons réussi à la contacter.

**success** *noun* succès *Masc.*; **a great success** un grand succès.

**successful** *adjective* **1** réussi; **he's a successful writer** c'est un écrivain à succès; **2 to be successful in doing** réussir à faire.

**successfully** *adverb* avec succès.

**such** *adverb* **1** tellement; **they're such nice people!** ils sont tellement gentils!; **I've had such a busy day!** j'ai eu une journée tellement chargée!; **it's such a long way** c'est tellement loin; **it's such a**

pity c'est tellement dommage; **2 such a lot of** tellement de; **I've got such a lot of things to tell you!** j'ai tellement de choses à te dire!; **3 such as** comme; **in big cities such as Glasgow** dans les grandes villes comme Glasgow; **4 there's no such thing** ça n'existe pas.

**suck** *verb* sucer [61].

**sudden** *adjective* soudain; ★ **all of a sudden** tout d'un coup.

**suddenly** *adverb* **1** tout d'un coup; **he suddenly started to laugh** tout d'un coup il s'est mis à rire; **suddenly the light went out** tout d'un coup la lumière s'est éteinte; **2 to die suddenly** mourir subitement.

**suede** *noun* daim *Masc.*; **a suede jacket** une veste en daim.

**suffer** *verb* souffrir [73].

**sufficiently** *adverb* suffisamment.

**sugar** *noun* sucre *Masc.*; **would you like sugar?** est-ce que tu veux du sucre?; **brown sugar** le sucre roux.

**suggest** *verb* suggérer [24]; **he suggested I should speak to you abou it** il m'a suggéré de vous en parler.

**suggestion** *noun* suggestion *Fem.*; **to make a suggestion** faire une suggestion.

**suicide** *noun* suicide *Masc.*; **to commit suicide** se suicider.

**suit** *noun* **1** (*man's*) costume *Masc.*; **2** (*woman's*) tailleur *Masc.*

**suitable** *adjective* **1** (*clothing*) approprié; **I don't have any suitable shoes** je n'ai pas de

**suitcase** *noun* valise *Fem.*

**sulk** *verb* bouder [1].

**sum** *noun* **1** somme *Fem.*; **a sum of money** une somme d'argent; **a large sum** une grosse somme; **2** (*calculation*) calcul *Masc.*

● **to sum up** résumer [1].

**summarize** *verb* résumer [1].

**summary** *noun* résumé *Masc.*

**summer** *noun* été *Masc.*; **in summer** en été; **summer clothes** les vêtements d'été; **the summer holidays** les grandes vacances.

**summertime** *noun* été *Masc.*; **in summertime** en été.

**summit** *noun* sommet *Masc.*

**sun** *noun* soleil *Masc.*; **in the sun** au soleil.

**sunbathe** *verb* se bronzer [1].

**sunblock** *noun* crème *Fem.* écran total.

**sunburn** *noun* coup *Masc.* de soleil.

**sunburned** *adjective* **1** (*tanned*) bronzé; **2 to get sunburned** (*burned*) attraper un coup de soleil.

**Sunday** *noun* dimanche *Masc.*; **on Sunday** dimanche; **I'm going out on Sunday** je sors dimanche; **see you on Sunday!** à dimanche!; **on Sundays** le dimanche; **the museum is closed on Sundays** le musée est fermé le dimanche; **every Sunday** tous les dimanches; **last Sunday** dimanche dernier; **next Sunday** dimanche prochain.

**sunflower** *noun* tournesol *Masc.*; **sunflower oil** l'huile *Fem.* de tournesol.

**sunglasses** *plural noun* lunettes *Fem. plural* de soleil.

**sunlight** *noun* soleil *Masc.*

**sunny** *adjective* **1 it's a sunny day** il fait du soleil; **it's going to be sunny** il va faire du soleil; **2** (*place*) ensoleillé; **in a sunny corner of the garden** dans un coin ensoleillé du jardin.

**sunrise** *noun* lever *Masc.* du soleil.

**sunroof** *noun* toit *Masc.* ouvrant.

**sunset** *noun* coucher *Masc.* du soleil.

**sunshine** *noun* soleil *Masc.*

**sunstroke** *noun* insolation *Fem.*; **to get sunstroke** attraper une insolation.

**suntan** *noun* bronzage *Masc.*; **to get a suntan** bronzer.

**suntan lotion** *noun* lotion *Fem.* solaire.

**suntan oil** *noun* huile *Fem.* solaire.

**super** *adjective* formidable; **we had a super time!** c'était formidable!

**supermarket** *noun* supermarché *Masc.*

**supernatural** *adjective* surnaturel (*Fem.* surnaturelle).

**superstitious** *adjective* superstitieux (*Fem.* superstitieuse).

**supervise** *verb* surveiller [1].

**supervisor** *noun* **1** (*in a shop*) responsable *Masc. & Fem.*; **2** (*in a factory*) contremaître *Masc.*

a
b
c
d
e
f
g
h
i
j
k
l
m
n
o
p
q
r
s
t
u
v
w
x
y
z

a
b
c
d
e
f
g
h
i
j
k
l
m
n
o
p
q
r
**s**
t
u
v
w
x
y
z

**supper** *noun* dîner *Masc.*; **I had supper at Sandy's** j'ai dîné chez Sandy.

**supplement** *noun* supplément *Masc.*

**supplies** *plural noun* (*of food*) provisions *Fem. plural*.

**supply** *noun* 1 (*stock*) réserves *Fem. plural*; 2 **to be in short supply** être difficile à trouver.
**supply** *verb* fournir [2]; **the school supplies the paper** c'est l'école qui fournit le papier; **to supply somebody with something** fournir quelque chose à quelqu'un.

**supply teacher** *noun* suppléant *Masc.*, suppléante *Fem.*

**support** *noun* soutien *Masc.*; **he has a lot of support** il a beaucoup de soutien.
**support** *verb* 1 (*back up*) soutenir [77]; **her teachers have really supported her** ses professeurs l'ont vraiment soutenue; 2 être [6] supporter de (*a team*); **Graeme supports Liverpool** Graeme est supporter de Liverpool; 3 (*financially*) **to support a family** subvenir [81] aux besoins d'une famille.

**supporter** *noun* supporter *Masc.*; **a Manchester United supporter** un supporter de Manchester United.

**suppose** *verb* **I suppose she's forgotten** elle a sans doute oublié.

**supposed** *adjective* **to be supposed to do** être censé faire; **you're supposed to wear a helmet** on est censé porter un casque; **he**

was supposed to be here at six il devait être là à six heures.

**sure** *adjective* sûr; **are you sure?** tu es sûr?; **are you sure you've had enough to eat?** tu es sûr que tu as assez mangé?; **are you sure you saw her?** tu es sûr de l'avoir vue?; **'can you shut the door?' – 'sure!'** 'peux-tu fermer la porte?' – 'bien sûr!'

**surely** *adverb* quand même; **surely she couldn't have forgotten!** elle ne peut pas avoir oublié quand même!

**surf** *noun* écume *Fem.*
**surf** *verb* **to surf the Net/Web** surfer [1] Internet/le web.

**surface** *noun* surface *Fem.*

**surfboard** *noun* planche *Fem.* de surf (*plural* planches de surf).

**surfer** *noun* 1 (*on the sea*) surfeur *Masc.*, surfeuse *Fem.*; 2 (*on the Net*) cybernaute *Masc. & Fem.*, internaute *Masc. & Fem.*

**surfing** *noun* surf *Masc.*; **to go surfing** faire du surf.

**surgeon** *noun* chirurgien *Masc.*; **she's a surgeon** elle est chirurgien.

**surgery** *noun* 1 (*procedure*) chirurgie *Fem.*; **to have surgery** se faire opérer; **laser surgery** la chirurgie au laser; 2 (*doctor's*) cabinet *Masc.* médical; **the dentist's surgery** le cabinet dentaire.

**surname** *noun* nom *Masc.* de famille (*plural* noms de famille).

**surprise** *noun* surprise *Fem.*; **what a surprise!** quelle surprise!

**surprised** *adjective* étonné; **I was surprised to see her** j'ai été étonné de la voir.

**surprising** *adjective* étonnant.

**surrender** *verb* **1** (*soldiers*) se rendre [3]; **2** (*country*) capituler [1]; **3** livrer [1] (*a town, castle*).
**surrender** *noun* (*by sportsman*) abandon *Masc.*; (*by army*) capitulation *Fem.*

**surround** *verb* **1** encercler [1]; **2 to be surrounded by** être [6] entouré de; **she's surrounded by friends** elle est entourée d'amis.

**survey** *noun* enquête *Fem.*

**survive** *verb* survivre [82].

**survivor** *noun* survivant *Masc.*, survivante *Fem.*

**suspect** *noun* suspect *Masc.*, suspecte *Fem.*
**suspect** *adjective* douteux (*Fem.* douteuse).
**suspect** *verb* soupçonner [1].

**suspend** *verb* **1** (*hang*) suspendre [3]; **2 to be suspended** (*from school*) être [6] exclu.

**suspense** *noun* suspense *Masc.*

**suspicious** *adjective* **1** méfiant; **to be suspicious of** se méfier de; **2 a suspicious parcel** un paquet suspect; **3 a suspicious-looking individual** un individu louche.

**swallow** *noun* (*bird*) hirondelle *Fem.*
**swallow** *verb* avaler.

**swan** *noun* cygne *Masc.*

**swap** *verb* **1** échanger [52]; **do you want to swap?** tu veux qu'on échange?; **he's swapped his bike**

for a computer il a échangé son vélo contre un ordinateur; **2 to swap seats with somebody** changer [52] de place avec quelqu'un.

**swear** *verb* (*use bad language*) utiliser [1] des gros mots; **he swears a lot** il utilise beaucoup de gros mots.

**swearword** *noun* gros mot *Masc.*

**sweat** *noun* transpiration *Fem.*
**sweat** *verb* transpirer [1].

**sweater** *noun* pull *Masc.*

**sweatshirt** *noun* sweatshirt *Masc.*

**swede** *noun* (*vegetable*) rutabaga *Masc.*

**Swede** *noun* Suédois *Masc.*, Suédoise *Fem.*

**Sweden** *noun* Suède *Fem.*; **in Sweden** en Suède; **to Sweden** en Suède.

**Swedish** *noun* (*language*) suédois *Masc.*
**Swedish** *adjective* suédois.

**sweep** *verb* balayer [59].

**sweet** *noun* **1** bonbon *Masc.*; **I bought her some sweets** je lui ai acheté des bonbons; **2** (*dessert*) dessert *Masc.*
**sweet** *adjective* **1** (*food*) sucré; **I try not to eat sweet things** j'essaie d'éviter les choses sucrées; **2** (*kind*) gentil (*Fem.* gentille); **she's a really sweet person** elle est vraiment gentille; **it was really sweet of him** c'était vraiment gentil de sa part; **3** (*cute*) mignon (*Fem.* mignonne); **he looks really sweet in that hat!** il est mignon avec ce chapeau!

**sweetcorn** *noun* maïs *Masc.*

a
b
c
d
e
f
g
h
i
j
k
l
m
n
o
p
q
r
s
t
u
v
w
x
y
z

**swell** *verb* (*part of the body*) enfler [1].

**swelling** *noun* enflure *Fem.*; **he has a swelling on his knee** il a le genou enflé.

**swerve** *verb* faire [10] un écart; **the car swerved to avoid the dog** la voiture a fait un écart pour éviter le chien.

**swim** *noun* **to go for a swim** aller [7] se baigner.

**swim** *verb* nager [52]; **can he swim?** est-ce qu'il sait nager?; **to swim across a lake** traverser [1] un lac à la nage.

**swimmer** *noun* nageur *Masc.*, nageuse *Fem.*; **she's a strong swimmer** c'est une bonne nageuse.

**swimming** *noun* natation *Fem.*; **to go swimzming** faire de la natation.

**swimming cap** *noun* bonnet *Masc.* de bain.

**swimming costume** *noun* maillot *Masc.* de bain.

**swimming pool** *noun* piscine *Fem.*

**swimming trunks** *noun* maillot *Masc.* de bain.

**swimsuit** *noun* maillot *Masc.* de bain.

**swindle** *noun* escroquerie *Fem.*; **what a swindle!** quelle escroquerie!

**swing** *noun* balançoire *Fem.*

**Swiss** *noun* (*person*) Suisse *Masc. & Fem.*; **the Swiss** les Suisses *Masc.* plural.

**Swiss** *adjective* suisse.

**switch** *noun* **1** (*button type: electrical*) bouton *Masc.*; **2** (*up-down type*) interrupteur *Masc.*

**switch** *verb* (*change*) changer [52] de; **to switch places** changer de place.

- **to switch something off** éteindre [60] quelque chose.

- **to switch something on** allumer [1] quelque chose.

**Switzerland** *noun* Suisse *Fem.*; **in Switzerland** en Suisse; **to Switzerland** en Suisse.

**swollen** *adjective* enflé.

**swop** *verb* SEE **swap**.

**sword** *noun* épée *Fem.*

**swordfish** *noun* espadon *Masc.*

**sycamore** *noun* sycomore *Masc.*

**syllabus** *noun* programme *Masc.*; **to be on the syllabus** être au programme.

**symbol** *noun* symbole *Masc.*

**symbolic** *adjective* symbolique.

**sympathetic** *adjective* compréhensif (*Fem.* compréhensive).

**sympathize** *verb* **to sympathize with somebody** comprendre [64] quelqu'un; **I sympathize with her** je la comprends.

**sympathy** *noun* compassion *Fem.*

**symphony** *noun* symphonie *Fem.*

**symphony orchestra** *noun* orchestre *Masc.* symphonique.

**symptom** *noun* symptôme *Masc.*

**synagogue** *noun* synagogue *Fem.*

**synthesizer** *noun* synthétiseur *Masc.*

**synthetic** *adjective* synthétique.

**syringe** *noun* seringue *Fem.*

**system** *noun* système *Masc.*

# Tt

**table** *noun* table *Fem.*; **on the table** sur la table; **to lay the table** mettre la table; **to clear the table** débarrasser la table.

**tablecloth** *noun* nappe *Fem.*

**table football** *noun* baby-foot *Masc.*

**tablemat** *noun* **1** (*for individual plates*) set *Masc.* de table; **2** (*for dish*) dessous-de-plat *Masc.*

**tablespoon** *noun* grande cuillère *Fem.*; (*in recipes*) **a tablespoon of flour** une cuillère à soupe de farine.

**tablet** *noun* comprimé *Masc.*

**table tennis** *noun* ping-pong™ *Masc.*; **to play table tennis** jouer au ping-pong.

**tabloid** *noun* quotidien *Masc.* populaire.

**tackle** *noun* **1** (*in football*) tacle *Masc.*; **2** (*in rugby*) plaquage *Masc.*
**tackle** *verb* **1** (*in football or hockey*) tacler [1]; **2** s'attaquer [1] à (*a job or problem*).

**tact** *noun* tact *Masc.*

**tactful** *adjective* plein de tact; **that wasn't very tactful** ça a manqué un peu de tact.

**tactic** *noun* tactique *Fem.*

**tadpole** *noun* têtard *Masc.*

**tail** *noun* **1** queue *Fem.*; **2** 'heads or tails?' – 'tails'** 'pile ou face?' – 'pile'.

**tailor** *noun* tailleur *Masc.*

**take** *verb* **1** prendre [64]; **he took a chocolate** il a pris un chocolat; **take my hand** prends ma main; **I**
took the bus j'ai pris le bus; **to take a holiday** prendre des vacances; **do you take sugar?** est-ce que vous prenez du sucre?; **who's taken my keys?** qui a pris mes clefs?; **it takes two hours** ça prend deux heures; **he took the news badly** il a mal pris la nouvelle; **2** (*to accompany*) emmener [50] (*a person*); **I'm taking Jake to the doctor's** j'emmène Jake chez le médecin; **I must take the car to the garage** je dois emmener la voiture au garage; **3** (*carry away*) emporter [1]; **she's taken some work to do at home** elle a emporté du travail pour faire chez elle; **4 to take something up(stairs)** monter [1] quelque chose; **could you take these towels up?** est-ce que tu peux monter ces serviettes?; **5 to take something down(stairs)** descendre [3] quelque chose; **Cheryl's taken the cups down** Cheryl a descendu les tasses; **6** accepter [1] (*a credit card or a cheque*); **do you take cheques?** est-ce que vous acceptez les chèques?; **7** passer [1] (*an exam*); **she's taking her driving test tomorrow** elle passe son permis demain; **8 it takes a lot of courage** il faut beaucoup de courage; **9 what size do you take?** quelle taille faites-vous?

- **to take something apart** démonter [1] quelque chose.

- **to take something back** rapporter [1] quelque chose.

- **to take off 1** (*a plane*) décoller [1]; **2** enlever [50] (*clothes or shoes*); **he took off his shirt** il a enlevé sa chemise; **3** déduire [26] (*money*); **he**

a
b
c
d
e
f
g
h
i
j
k
l
m
n
o
p
q
r
s
t
u
v
w
x
y
z

**took five pounds off the price** il a déduit cinq livres du prix

• **to take out 1** (*from a bag or pocket*) sortir [72]; **Eric took out his wallet** Eric a sorti son porte-feuille; **2 he's taking me out to lunch** il m'emmène déjeuner; **she took me out to the theatre** elle m'a emmenée au théâtre

**takeaway** *noun* **1** (*a meal*) repas *Masc.* à emporter; **an Indian takeaway** un repas indien à emporter; **2** (*where you buy it*) restaurant *Masc.* qui fait des plats à emporter.

**take-off** *noun* décollage *Masc.* (*of a plane*).

**tale** *noun* histoire *Fem.*

**talent** *noun* talent *Masc.*; **to have a talent for something** être doué pour quelque chose.

**talented** *adjective* doué; **he's really talented** il est vraiment doué.

**talk** *noun* **1** (*a chat*) conversation *Fem.*; **I had a talk with Roy about it** j'ai eu une conversation avec Roy à ce sujet; **2** exposé *Masc.*; **she's giving a talk on Hungary** elle fait un exposé sur la Hongrie.

**talk** *verb* **1** parler [1]; **I was talking to Jeevan about football** je parlais du foot avec Jeevan; **what's he talking about?** de quoi parle-t-il?; **we'll talk about it later** on en parlera plus tard; **2** (*to gossip*) bavarder [1]; **they're always talking** ils n'arrêtent pas de bavarder.

**talkative** *adjective* bavard; **he's not exactly talkative!** on ne pourrait pas dire qu'il est bavard!

**tall** *adjective* **1** grand; **she's very tall** elle est très grande; **I'm 1.7 metres tall** je mesure un mètre soixante-dix; **2** haut (*a building or tree*).

**tambourine** *noun* tambourin *Masc.*

**tame** *adjective* apprivoisé (*an animal*).

**tampon** *noun* tampon *Masc.*

**tan** *noun* bronzage *Masc.*; **to get a tan** bronzer.
**tan** *verb* bronzer [1]; **I tan easily** je bronze facilement.

**tangerine** *noun* mandarine *Fem.*

**tank** *noun* **1** (*for petrol or water*) réservoir *Masc.*; **2 a fish tank** un aquarium; **3** (*military*) char *Masc.*

**tanker** *noun* **1** (*ship*) navire-citerne *Masc.*; **2** (*on road*) camion-citerne *Masc.*

**tanned** *adjective* bronzé.

**tap** *noun* **1** robinet *Masc.*; **to turn on the tap** ouvrir le robinet; **to turn off the tap** fermer le robinet; **the hot tap** le robinet d'eau chaude; **2** (*a pat*) petite tape *Fem.*
**tap** *verb* taper [1].

**tap-dancing** *noun* claquettes *Fem. plural*; **to do tap-dancing** faire des claquettes.

**tape** *noun* **1** cassette *Fem.*; **my tape of the Stones** ma cassette des Stones; **I've got it on tape** je l'ai en cassette; **2 sticky tape** scotch™.
**tape** *verb* enregistrer [1]; **I want to tape the film** je veux enregistrer le film.

**tape measure** *noun* mètre *Masc.* à ruban.

**tape recorder** *noun* magnétophone *Masc.*

**tapestry** *noun* tapisserie *Fem.*

**tar** *noun* goudron *Masc.*

**target** *noun* cible *Fem.*

**tart** *noun* tarte *Fem.*; **a raspberry tart** une tarte aux framboises.

**tartan** *adjective* écossais; **a tartan skirt** une jupe écossaise.

**task** *noun* tâche *Fem.*

**taste** *noun* goût *Masc.*; **the taste of onions** le goût des oignons; **in bad taste** de mauvais goût.
**taste** *verb* 1 goûter [1]; **do you want to taste?** tu veux goûter?; **the soup tastes horrible** la soupe a un goût infect; 2 **to taste of** avoir [5] un goût de; **it tastes of strawberries** ça a un goût de fraises.

**tasty** *adjective* savoureux (*Fem.* savoureuse).

**tattoo** *noun* tatouage *Masc.*; **he's got a tattoo on his arm** il a un tatouage sur le bras.

**Taurus** *noun* Taureau *Masc.*; **Josephine's Taurus** Josephine est Taureau.

**tax** *noun* 1 impôts *Masc.* plural; 2 (*on goods*) taxe *Fem.*

**taxi** *noun* taxi *Masc.*; **by taxi** en taxi; **to take a taxi** prendre un taxi.

**taxi driver** *noun* chauffeur *Masc.* de taxi.

**taxi rank** *noun* station *Fem.* de taxis.

**TB** *noun* tuberculose *Fem.*

**tea** *noun* 1 thé *Masc.*; **a cup of tea** une tasse de thé; **to have tea** prendre le thé; 2 (*evening meal*) dîner *Masc.*

**teabag** *noun* sachet *Masc.* de thé.

**teach** *verb* 1 apprendre [64]; **she's teaching me Italian** elle m'apprend l'italien; **that'll teach you!** ça t'apprendra!; 2 enseigner [1]; **her mum teaches maths** sa mère enseigne les maths; 3 **to teach yourself something** apprendre [64] quelque chose tout seul; **Anne taught herself Italian** Anne a appris l'italien toute seule.

**teacher** *noun* 1 (*in a secondary school*) professeur *Masc.*; **my mother's a teacher** ma mère est professeur; **our biology teacher** notre professeur de biologie; 2 (*in primary school*) instituteur *Masc.*, institutrice *Fem.*; **she's a primary school teacher** elle est institutrice.

**teaching** *noun* enseignement *Masc.*

**team** *noun* équipe *Fem.*; **a football team** une équipe de foot; **our team won** notre équipe a gagné.

**teapot** *noun* théière *Fem.*

**tear**[1] *noun* (*a rip*) accroc *Masc.*; **I've got a tear in my jeans** j'ai un accroc dans mon jean.
**tear** *verb* 1 déchirer [1]; **you've torn your shirt** tu as déchiré ta chemise; **she tore up my letter** elle a déchiré ma lettre; 2 se déchirer [1]; **be careful, it tears easily** attention, ça se déchire facilement.
● **to tear off, to tear open** 1 (*carefully*) détacher [1]; 2 (*violently*) arracher [1].

**tear**[2] *noun* (*when you cry*) larme *Fem.*; **to be in tears** être en larmes;

to burst into tears fondre en larmes.

**tease** *verb* **1** taquiner [1] (*a person*); **2** tourmenter [1] (*an animal*).

**teaspoon** *noun* petite cuillère *Fem.*; (*in recipes*) a teaspoonful of ... une cuillère à café de ....

**teatime** *noun* l'heure *Fem.* du dîner (*evening meal*).

**tea towel** *noun* torchon *Masc.*

**technical** *adjective* technique.

**technical college** *noun* lycée *Masc.* technique.

**technician** *noun* technicien *Masc.*, technicienne *Fem.*

**technique** *noun* technique *Fem.*

**techno** *noun* techno *Fem.* (*music*).

**technological** *adjective* technologique.

**technology** *noun* technologie *Fem.*; information technology l'informatique *Fem.*

**teddy bear** *noun* nounours *Masc.*

**teenage** *adjective* **1** adolescent (*Fem.* adolescente); they have a teenage son ils ont un fils adolescent; **2** (*films, magazines, etc.*) pour les jeunes; a teenage magazine un magazine pour les jeunes.

**teenager** *noun* **1** jeune *Masc. & Fem.*; a group of teenagers une bande de jeunes; **2** (*more precisely*) adolescent *Masc.*, adolescente *Fem.*; when I was a teenager quand j'étais adolescent.

**teens** *plural noun* adolescence *Fem.*; he's in his teens c'est un adolescent.

**tee-shirt** *noun* tee-shirt *Masc.*

**telegraph pole** *noun* poteau *Masc.* télégraphique.

**telephone** *noun* téléphone *Masc.*; on the telephone au téléphone. **telephone** *verb* appeler [18]; I'll telephone the bank je vais appeler la banque.

**telephone box** *noun* cabine *Fem.* téléphonique.

**telephone call** *noun* coup *Masc.* de téléphone.

**telephone card** *noun* carte *Fem.* de téléphone.

**telephone directory** *noun* annuaire *Masc.*

**telephone number** *noun* numéro *Masc.* de téléphone.

**telescope** *noun* télescope *Masc.*

**televise** *verb* téléviser [1]; they're televising the match on va téléviser le match.

**television** *noun* télévision *Fem.*; she was watching television elle regardait la télévision; I saw it on television je l'ai vu à la télévision.

**television programme** *noun* émission *Fem.* de télévision.

**tell** *verb* **1** to tell somebody something dire [9] quelque chose à quelqu'un; that's what she told me c'est ce qu'elle m'a dit; I told him it was silly je lui ai dit que c'était idiot; have you told Sara? est-ce que tu l'as dit à Sara?; **2** to tell somebody to do dire [9] à quelqu'un de faire; he told me to do it myself il m'a dit de le faire moi-même; she told me not to wait elle m'a dit de ne pas attendre;

**3** (*explain*) **can you tell me how to do it?** est-ce que vous pouvez m'expliquer comment on le fait?; **4** raconter [1] (*a story*); **tell me about your holiday** raconte-moi tes vacances; **5** (*to see*) voir [13]; **you can tell it's old** on voit bien que c'est ancien; **you can tell she's cross** on voit bien qu'elle est fâchée; **I can't tell them apart** je n'arrive pas à les distinguer.

**telly** *noun* télé *Fem.*; **to watch telly** regarder la télé; **I saw her on telly** je l'ai vue à la télé.

**temp** *noun* intérimaire *Masc. & Fem.*

**temper** *noun* **to be in a temper** être en colère; **to lose your temper** se mettre en colère.

**temperature** *noun* **1** température *Fem.*; **the oven temperature** la température du four; **2 to have a temperature** avoir de la fièvre.

**temple** *noun* temple *Masc.*

**temporary** *adjective* temporaire.

**temptation** *noun* tentation *Fem.*

**tempted** *adjective* tenté; **I'm really tempted to go** je suis vraiment tenté d'y aller.

**tempting** *adjective* tentant.

**ten** *number* dix *Masc.*; **Harry's ten** Harry a dix ans.

**tend** *verb* **to tend to do** avoir [5] tendance à faire; **he tends to talk a lot** il a tendance à beaucoup parler.

**tendency** *noun* tendance *Fem.*; **to have a tendency to** avoir [5] tendance à.

**tender** *adjective* tendre.

**tennis** *noun* tennis *Masc.*; **to play tennis** jouer au tennis.

**tennis ball** *noun* balle *Fem.* de tennis.

**tennis court** *noun* tennis *Masc.*

**tennis player** *noun* joueur de tennis *Masc.*, joueuse de tennis *Fem.*

**tennis racket** *noun* raquette *Fem.* de tennis.

**tenor** *noun* ténor *Masc.*

**tenpin bowling** *noun* bowling *Masc.*; **to go tenpin bowling** jouer au bowling.

**tense** *noun* **the present tense** le présent; **in the future tense** au futur.
**tense** *adjective* tendu.

**tent** *noun* tente *Fem.*

**tenth** *number* dixième *Masc.*; **on the tenth floor** au dixième étage; **the tenth of April** le dix avril.

**term** *noun* **1** (*in school*) trimestre *Masc.*; **2 to be on good terms with somebody** être en bons termes avec quelqu'un.

**terminal** *noun* **1** (*at an airport*) aérogare *Fem.*; **terminal two** l'aérogare numéro deux; **2 a ferry terminal** une gare maritime; **3** (*a computer terminal*) terminal *Masc.* (*plural* terminaux).

**terrace** *noun* **1** (*of a house or hotel*) terrasse *Fem.*; **2 the terraces** (*at a stadium*) les gradins *Masc. plural*.

**terrible** *adjective* épouvantable; **the weather was terrible** il a fait un temps épouvantable.

**terribly** *adverb* **1** (*very*) très; **not terribly clean** pas très propre;

a
b
c
d
e
f
g
h
i
j
k
l
m
n
o
p
q
r
s
t
u
v
w
x
y
z

591

a

**2** (*badly*) affreusement mal; **I played terribly** j'ai joué affreusement mal.

b

c

**terrific** *adjective* **1 at a terrific speed** à une vitesse folle; **a terrific amount** une quantité énorme; **2 terrific!** formidable!

d

e

**terrified** *adjective* terrifié.

f

**terrify** *verb* terrifier [1].

g

**territory** *noun* territoire *Masc.*

h

**terrorism** *noun* terrorisme *Masc.*

i

**terrorist** *noun* terroriste *Masc. & Fem.*

j

k

**test** *noun* **1** (*in school*) contrôle *Masc.*; **we've got a maths test tomorrow** nous avons un contrôle de maths demain; **2** (*of your skills or patience*) test *Masc.*; **3** (*medical*) analyse *Fem.*; **a blood test** une analyse de sang; **4 a driving test** un examen de permis de conduire; **she's doing her driving test on Friday** elle passe son permis vendredi; **he passed his driving test** il a eu son permis.

l

m

n

o

p

**test** *verb* **1** (*in school*) contrôler [1]; **2 to test something out** essayer [59] quelque chose.

q

**test tube** *noun* éprouvette *Fem.*

r

**text** *noun* texte *Masc.*

s

**text** *verb* **to text someone** envoyer [40] un texto à quelqu'un; **I'll text you tomorrow** je t'enverrai un texto demain.

t

u

v

w

**textbook** *noun* manuel *Masc.*

x

**text message** *noun* texto™ *Masc.*

y

**Thames** *noun* **the Thames** la Tamise.

z

**than** *preposition, conjunction* **1** que; **their new album's better than the last one** leur nouveau CD est meilleur que le dernier; **they have more money than we do** ils ont plus d'argent que nous; **2** (*for quantities*) de; **more than forty** plus de quarante; **more than thirty years** plus de trente ans.

**thank** *verb* remercier [1].

**thanks** *plural noun* **1** merci; **no thanks** non merci; **thanks a lot** merci beaucoup; **thanks for your letter** merci pour ta lettre; **2 with thanks for** avec mes remerciements pour; **3 thanks to** grâce à; **it was thanks to Micky** c'était grâce à Micky.

**thank you** *adverb* merci; **thank you very much for the cheque** merci beaucoup pour le chèque; **no thank you** non merci; **a thank-you letter** une lettre de remerciements.

**that** *adjective* **1** ce (*Fem.* cette) (*but 'ce' becomes 'cet' before a masculine noun beginning with a vowel or a silent 'h'*) **that dog** ce chien; **that man** cet homme; **that blue car** cette voiture bleue; **2 that one** celui-là *Masc.*, celle-là *Fem.*; **'which cake would you like?' – 'that one, please'** 'tu veux quel gâteau?' – 'celui-là, s'il te plaît'; **I like all the dresses but I'm going to buy that one** j'aime toutes les robes mais je vais acheter celle-là.

**that** *adverb* **1 it's not that silly** ce n'est pas si idiot que ça; **their house isn't that big** leur maison n'est pas si grande que ça; **2 it was that high** c'était haut comme ça.

**that** *pronoun* **1** (*before verb 'être'*) ce, c' (*before a vowel*); **that's not true** ce n'est pas vrai; **that's not what you told me** ce n'est pas ce que tu m'as dit; **what's that?** qu'est-ce que c'est?; **that smells good** ça sent bon; **who's that?** c'est qui?; **where's that?** c'est où?; **is that Mandy?** c'est Mandy?; **2** ça; **did you see that?** tu as vu ça?; **that's my bedroom** ça c'est ma chambre; **3** qui; **the book that's on the table** le livre qui est sur la table; **4** que, qu' (*before a vowel or a silent 'h'*); **the book that I lent you** le livre que je t'ai prêté.

**that** *conjunction* que, qu' (*before a vowel or a silent 'h'*); **I knew that he was wrong** je savais qu'il avait tort.

**thaw** *noun* fonte *Fem.* des neiges.

**the** *definite article* **1** (*before a noun which is masculine in French*) le, l' (*before a vowel or silent 'h'*) **the cat** le chat; **the tree** l'arbre; **2** (*before a noun which is feminine in French*) la, l' (*before a vowel or silent 'h'*) **the table** la table; **the orange** l'orange; **3** les (*before all plural nouns*); **the windows** les fenêtres.

**theatre** *noun* théâtre *Masc.*; **to go to the theatre** aller au théâtre.

**theft** *noun* vol *Masc.*

**their** *adjective* leur (*plural* leurs); **their flat** leur appartement; **their mother** leur mère; **their presents** leurs cadeaux.

**theirs** *pronoun* **1** le leur (*when standing for a masculine noun*); **our garden's smaller than theirs** notre jardin est plus petit que le leur; **2** la leur (*when standing for a feminine noun*); **your house is bigger than theirs** votre maison est plus grande que la leur; **3** les leurs (*when standing for a plural noun*); **our children are older than theirs** nos enfants sont plus âgés que les leurs; **4** à eux, à elles; **the yellow car's theirs** la voiture jaune est à eux; **it's theirs** c'est à eux.

**them** *pronoun* **1** les; **I know them** je les connais; **I don't know them** je ne les connais pas; **listen to them!** écoute-les!; **I saw them last week** je les ai vus la semaine dernière; **2** (*to them*) leur; **I gave them my address** je leur ai donné mon adresse; **3** (*after a preposition*) eux (*Fem.* elles); **I'll go with them** j'irai avec eux; (*if they are all female*) j'irai avec elles; **without them** sans eux, sans elles; (*in comparisons*) **she's older than them** elle est plus âgée qu'eux; (*if all female*) elle est plus âgée qu'elles.

**theme** *noun* thème *Fem.*

**theme park** *noun* parc *Masc.* de loisirs.

**themselves** *pronoun* **1** se; **they've helped themselves** ils se sont servis; **2** (*for emphasis*) eux-mêmes *Masc.*, elles-mêmes *Fem.*; **the boys can do it themselves** les garçons peuvent le faire eux-mêmes; **the girls will tell you themselves** les filles vous le diront elles-mêmes.

**then** *adverb* **1** (*next*) ensuite; **I wash up and then I make the bed** je fais la vaisselle et ensuite je fais le lit; **I went to the post office and then the bank** je suis allé à la poste et ensuite à la banque; **2** (*at that time*) à l'époque; **we were living in York**

a
b
c
d
e
f
g
h
i
j
k
l
m
n
o
p
q
r
s
**t**
u
v
w
x
y
z

**then** nous habitions à York à l'époque; **3** (*in that case*) alors; **then why worry?** alors pourquoi s'inquiéter?; **that's all right then** ça va alors; **4 by then** déjà; **by then it was too late** il était déjà trop tard.

**theory** *noun* théorie *Fem.*; **in theory** en théorie.

**there** *adverb* **1** là; **put it there** mets-le là; **stand there** mettez-vous là; **they're in there** ils sont là; **2 over there** là-bas; **she's over there talking to Mark** elle est là-bas en train de discuter avec Mark; **down there** là-bas; **3 up there** là-haut; **look up there!** regarde là-haut!; **4** y (*when the place 'there' stands for has already been mentioned*); **I've seen photos of Oxford but I've never been there** j'ai vu des photos d'Oxford mais je n'y suis jamais allé; **yes, I'm going there on Tuesday** oui, j'y vais mardi; **5 there is** il y a; **there's a cat in the garden** il y a un chat dans le jardin; **there was no bread** il n'y avait pas de pain; **yes, there's enough** oui, il y en a assez; **6 there are** il y a; **there are plenty of seats** il y a beaucoup de places; **7 there they are!** les voilà!; **there she is!** la voilà!; **there's the bus coming!** voilà le bus qui arrive!

**therefore** *adverb* donc.

**thermometer** *noun* thermomètre *Masc.*

**these** *adjective* ces; **these books** ces livres.

**they** *pronoun* **1** ils (*when standing for a masculine noun*); **'where are the knives?' – 'they're in the drawer'** 'où sont les couteaux?'– 'ils

sont dans le tiroir'; **2** elles (*when standing for a feminine noun*); **I bought some apples but they're not very nice** j'ai acheté des pommes mais elles ne sont pas très bonnes.

**thick** *adjective* épais (*Fem.* épaisse); **a thick layer of butter** une couche épaisse de beurre.

**thickness** *noun* épaisseur *Fem.*

**thief** *noun* voleur *Masc.*, voleuse *Fem.*

**thigh** *noun* cuisse *Fem.*

**thin** *adjective* **1** mince (*a slice or a person*); **2** (*too thin, skinny*) maigre; **she's got terribly thin** elle a beaucoup maigri.

**thing** *noun* **1** (*an object*) chose *Fem.*; **shops full of pretty things** des magasins remplis de jolies choses; **she told me some surprising things** elle m'a raconté des choses étonnantes; **2** (*a whatsit*) truc *Masc.* (*informal*); **tu peux utiliser ce truc-là pour l'ouvrir** you can use that thing to open it; **that thing next to the hammer** ce truc à côté du marteau; **3 things** (*belongings*) affaires *Fem. plural*; **you can put your things in my room** tu peux mettre tes affaires dans ma chambre; **4 the best thing to do is** ... ce qu'il faut faire, c'est ...; **the thing is, I've lost her address** ce qu'il y a, c'est que j'ai perdu son adresse; **how are things with you?** comment ça va?

**think** *verb* **1** (*believe*) croire [33]; **do you think they'll come?** tu crois qu'ils vont venir?; **no, I don't think so** non, je ne crois pas; **I think he's already left** je crois qu'il est déjà parti; **2** penser [1]; **I'm thinking**

about you je pense à toi; **Tony thinks it's silly** Tony pense que c'est bête; **what do you think of my new jacket?** qu'est-ce que tu penses de ma nouvelle veste?; **what do you think of that?** qu'en penses-tu?; **3** (*to think carefully*) réfléchir [2]; **he thought for a moment** il a réfléchi un instant; **I've thought it over carefully** j'y ai bien réfléchi; **4** (*imagine*) imaginer [1]; **just think! we'll soon be in Spain!** imagine! on va bientôt être en Espagne!; **I never thought it would be like this!** je n'avais jamais imaginé que ce serait comme ça.

**third** *noun* tiers *Masc.*; **a third of the population** un tiers de la population.
**third** *adjective* troisième; **on the third floor** au troisième étage; **the third of March** le trois mars.

**thirdly** *adverb* troisièmement.

**Third World** *noun* tiers-monde *Masc.*

**thirst** *noun* soif *Fem.*

**thirsty** *adjective* **to be thirsty** avoir [5] soif; **I'm thirsty** j'ai soif; **we were all thirsty** nous avions tous soif.

**thirteen** *number* treize *Masc.*; **Ahmed's thirteen** Ahmed a treize ans.

**thirty** *number* trente *Masc.*

**this** *adjective* **1** ce (*before a masculine noun*), cet (*before a masculine noun beginning with a vowel or a silent 'h'*), cette (*before a feminine noun*); **this paintbrush** ce pinceau; **this tree** cet arbre; **this cup** cette tasse; **this morning** ce matin; **this evening** ce soir; **this afternoon** cet après-midi; **2 this one** celui-ci *Masc.*, celle-ci *Fem.*; **if you need a pen you can use this one** si tu as besoin d'un stylo tu peux utiliser celui-ci; **if you want a lamp you can borrow this one** si tu veux une lampe tu peux emprunter celle-ci.
**this** *pronoun* **1** ça; **can you hold this for a moment?** est-ce que tu peux prendre ça un instant?; **2 what's this?** qu'est-ce que c'est?; **this is Tracy speaking** (*on the phone*) c'est Tracy à l'appareil; **3** (*in introductions*) **this is my sister Carla** je te présente ma sœur Carla.

**thistle** *noun* chardon *Masc.*

**thorn** *noun* épine *Fem.*

**thorough** *adjective* **1** (*search*) minutieux (*Fem.* minutieuse); **2** (*person*) consciencieux (*Fem.* consciencieuse).

**those** *adjective* ces; **those books** ces livres.
**those** *pronoun* ceux-là *Masc.*, celles-là *Fem.*; **if you want some knives you can take those** si tu veux des couteaux tu peux prendre ceux-là; **if you want some plates you can take those** si tu veux des assiettes tu peux prendre celles-là.

**though** *conjunction, adverb* **1** bien que (*followed by a verb in the subjunctive*); **though it's cold** bien qu'il fasse froid; **though he's older than she is** bien qu'il soit plus âgé qu'elle; **2 it was a good idea, though** et pourtant, c'était une bonne idée.

**thought** *noun* pensée *Fem.*

a
b
c
d
e
f
g
h
i
j
k
l
m
n
o
p
q
r
s
t
u
v
w
x
y
z

595

**thoughtful** *adjective*
1 (*considerate*) gentil (*Fem.* gentille);
**it was really thoughtful of you**
c'était vraiment gentil de ta part;
2 (*deep in thought*) pensif (*Fem.*
pensive).

**thoughtless** *adjective* irréfléchi.

**thousand** *number* 1 mille *Masc.*; **a
thousand** mille; **three thousand**
trois mille; 2 **thousands of** des
milliers de; **there were thousands
of tourists in Venice** il y avait des
milliers de touristes à Venise.

**thread** *noun* fil *Masc.*
**thread** *verb* enfiler [1] (*a needle*).

**threat** *noun* menace *Fem.*

**threaten** *verb* menacer [61]; **to
threaten to do** menacer de faire.

**three** *number* trois *Masc.*; **Oskar's
three** Oskar a trois ans.

**three-quarters** *noun* trois-
quarts *Masc. plural*; **three-quarters
full** plein aux trois-quarts.

**thrilled** *adjective* ravi; **I was
thrilled to hear from you** j'ai été
ravi d'avoir de tes nouvelles.

**thriller** *noun* thriller *Masc.*

**thrilling** *adjective* palpitant.

**throat** *noun* gorge *Fem.*; **to have a
sore throat** avoir mal à la gorge.

**through** *preposition* 1 (*across*) à
travers; **through the forest** à
travers la forêt; **the water went
right through** l'eau est passée à
travers; **the police let us through**
la police nous a laissés passer;
2 (*via*) par; **the train went through
Leeds** le train est passé par Leeds;
**through the window** par la fenêtre;
**I know them through my cousins**

je les connais par mes cousins; 3 **to
go through something** traverser
quelque chose; **we went through
the park** nous avons traversé le
parc; 4 **right through the day** toute
la journée.
**through** *adjective* direct (*a train or
flight*).

**throughout** *preposition*
**throughout the match** pendant
tout le match; **throughout the
world** partout dans le monde.

**throw** *verb* 1 jeter [48]; **I threw the
letter into the bin** j'ai jeté la lettre
dans la poubelle; **he threw the
book on the floor** il a jeté le livre
par terre; 2 (*taking aim*) lancer [61];
**throw me the ball!** lance-moi le
ballon!; **we were throwing
snowballs** on lançait des boules de
neige.

● **to throw something away** jeter
[48] quelque chose; **I've thrown
away the old newspapers** j'ai jeté
les vieux journaux.

● **to throw somebody out** expulser
[1] quelqu'un.

● **to throw something out** jeter [48]
quelque chose (*rubbish*).

● **to throw up** vomir [2].

**thumb** *noun* pouce *Masc.*

**thump** *verb* taper [1].

**thunder** *noun* tonnerre *Masc.*; **a
peal of thunder** un roulement de
tonnerre.

**thunderstorm** *noun* orage *Masc.*

**thundery** *adjective* orageux (*Fem.*
orageuse).

**Thursday** *noun* jeudi *Masc.*; **on
Thursday** jeudi; **I'm going out on**

**Thursday** je sors jeudi; **see you on Thursday!** à jeudi!; **on Thursdays** le jeudi; **the museum is closed on Thursdays** le musée est fermé le jeudi; **every Thursday** tous les jeudis; **last Thursday** jeudi dernier; **next Thursday** jeudi prochain.

**thyme** *noun* thym *Masc.*

**tick** *verb* **1** (*tick-tock*) faire [10] tic-tac; **2** (*on paper*) cocher [1]; **tick the box** cochez la case.

**ticket** *noun* **1** billet *Masc.* (*for a plane, a train, an exhibition, a theatre or cinema*) **two tickets for the concert** deux billets pour le concert; **2** (*for the underground, the bus, or left luggage*) ticket *Masc.*; **a bus ticket** un ticket de bus; **3 a parking ticket** un PV (*informal*).

**ticket inspector** *noun* contrôleur *Masc.*

**ticket office** *noun* (*at a station*) guichet *Masc.*

**tickle** *verb* chatouiller [1].

**tide** *noun* marée *Fem.*; **at high tide** à marée haute; **the tide is out** c'est la marée basse.

**tidy** *adjective* **1** bien rangé (*a room*); **2** soigné (*homework*); **3** ordonné (*a person*).
**tidy** *verb* ranger [52]; **I'll tidy (up) the kitchen** je rangerai la cuisine.

**tie** *noun* **1** cravate *Fem.*; **a red tie** une cravate rouge; **2** (*in a match*) match *Masc.* nul.
**tie** *verb* **1** nouer [1]; **to tie your shoelaces** nouer ses lacets; **2 to tie a knot in something** faire [10] un nœud à quelque chose; **3** (*in a*

*match*) **we tied two all** nous avons fait match nul, deux partout.

**tiger** *noun* tigre *Masc.*

**tight** *adjective* **1** juste; **the skirt's a bit tight** la jupe est un peu juste; **these shoes are too tight** ces chaussures me serrent; **2** (*close-fitting*) moulant; **she was wearing a tight dress** elle portait une robe moulante.

**tighten** *verb* serrer [1].

**tightly** *adverb* fermement.

**tights** *plural noun* collant *Masc. singular*; **a pair of purple tights** un collant violet.

**tile** *noun* **1** (*on a floor or wall*) carreau *Masc.* (*plural* carreaux); **2** (*on a roof*) tuile *Fem.*

**till**[1] *preposition, conjunction* **1** jusqu'à; **they're here till Sunday** ils sont là jusqu'à dimanche; **till then** jusque là; **till now** jusqu'à présent; **2 not till** pas avant; **she won't be back till ten** elle ne sera pas rentrée avant dix heures; **we won't know till Monday** nous ne le saurons pas avant lundi.

**till**[2] *noun* caisse *Fem.*; **pay at the till** payez à la caisse.

**time** *noun* **1** (*on the clock*) heure *Fem.*; **what time is it?** quelle heure est-il?; **it's time for lunch** c'est l'heure du déjeuner; **on time** à l'heure; **ten o'clock French time** dix heures heure française; **2** (*an amount of time*) temps *Masc.*; **we've got lots of time** nous avons beaucoup de temps; **there's not much time left** il ne reste plus beaucoup de temps; **for a long time**

a b c d e f g h i j k l m n o p q r s **t** u v w x y z

597

longtemps; **from time to time** de temps en temps; **3** (*moment*) moment *Masc.*; **is this a good time to phone?** est-ce que c'est le bon moment pour vous appeler?; **at times** par moments; **for the time being** pour le moment; **any time now** d'un moment à l'autre; **4** (*in a series*) fois *Fem.*; **six times** six fois; **the first time** la première fois; **the first time I saw you** la première fois que je t'ai vu; **three times a year** trois fois par an; **three times two is six** trois fois deux égalent six; **5 to have a good time** bien s'amuser [1]; **we had a really good time** nous nous sommes très bien amusés; **have a good time!** amusez-vous bien!

**time off** *noun* **1** (*free time*) temps *Masc.* libre; **2** (*leave*) congé *Masc.*

**timetable** *noun* **1** (*in school*) emploi *Masc.* du temps; **2** (*for trains or buses*) horaire *Masc.*; **the bus timetable** l'horaire des bus.

**tin** *noun* boîte *Fem.*; **a tin of tomatoes** une boîte de tomates.

**tin-foil** *noun* papier *Masc.* aluminium.

**tinned** *adjective* en conserve; **tinned peas** des petits pois en conserve.

**tin opener** *noun* ouvre-boîte *Masc.*

**tinted** *adjective* teinté.

**tiny** *adjective* minuscule.

**tip** *noun* **1** (*the end*) bout *Masc.*; **the tip of my finger** le bout de mon doigt; **2** (*money*) pourboire *Masc.*; **3** (*a useful hint*) tuyau *Masc.* (*plural* tuyaux) (*informal*).

**tip** *verb* **1** (*to give money to*) donner [1] un pourboire à; **we tipped the waiter** nous avons donné un pourboire au garçon; **2** verser [1] (*liquid*).

**tiptoe** *noun* **on tiptoe** sur la pointe des pieds.

**tired** *adjective* **1** fatigué; **I'm tired** je suis fatigué; **you look tired** tu as l'air fatigué; **2 to be tired of** en avoir assez de; **I'm tired of London** j'en ai assez de Londres; **I'm tired of watching TV** j'en ai assez de regarder la télé.

**tiring** *adjective* fatigant.

**tissue** *noun* (*a paper hanky*) kleenex™ *Masc.*; **do you have a tissue?** est-ce que tu as un kleenex?

**tissue paper** *noun* papier *Masc.* de soie.

**title** *noun* titre *Masc.*

**to** *preposition* **1** (*to a place or person*) à (*note that 'à + le' becomes 'au' and 'à + les' becomes 'aux'*) **to go to London** aller à Londres; **give the book to Leila** donne le livre à Leila; **I'm going to school** je vais à l'école; **she's gone to the office** elle est partie au bureau; **a letter to parents** une lettre aux parents; **from Monday to Friday** du lundi au vendredi; **2** (*with names of countries*) **they're going to Spain** ils vont en Espagne; (*BUT*) **they're going to Japan** ils vont au Japon (*'en' with feminine countries, 'au' with most masculine countries*); **3** à; **I have nothing to do** je n'ai rien à faire; **I had a lot of homework to do** j'avais beacoup de devoirs à faire; **we're ready to go** nous sommes prêts à partir; **it's easy to do** c'est facile à faire; **4** (*to somebody's house, shop, surgery*) chez; **I went round to Paul's house** je suis allé chez Paul; **we're going to the Browns' for supper** on va dîner chez les Brown; **I'm going to the dentist's tomorrow** je vais chez le dentiste demain; **she's gone to the hairdresser's** elle est allée chez le coiffeur; **5** (*talking about the time*) **it's ten to nine** il est neuf heures moins dix; **it's twenty to** il est moins vingt; **6** (*in order to*) pour; **he gave me some money to buy a sandwich** il m'a donné de l'argent pour acheter un sandwich.

**toad** *noun* crapaud *Masc.*

**toadstool** *noun* champignon *Masc.*; **a poisonous toadstool** un champignon vénéneux.

**toast** *noun* **1** pain *Masc.* grillé; **two slices of toast** deux tranches de pain grillé; **2** (*to your health*) toast *Masc.*; **to drink a toast to the future** lever un verre à l'avenir.

**toaster** *noun* grille-pain *Masc.*

**tobacco** *noun* tabac *Masc.*

**tobacconist's** *noun* bureau *Masc.* de tabac.

**today** *noun* aujourd'hui *Masc.*; **today's her birthday** c'est son anniversaire aujourd'hui.

**toe** *noun* doigt *Masc.* de pied; **my big toe** mon gros orteil.

**toenail** *noun* ongle *Masc.* de pied.

**toffee** *noun* caramel *Masc.*

**together** *adverb* **1** ensemble; **Kate and Lenny arrived together** Kate et Lenny sont arrivés ensemble; **2** (*at the same time*) en même temps; **they all left together** ils sont tous partis en même temps.

**toilet** *noun* toilettes *Fem. plural*; **where's the toilet?** où sont les toilettes?; **she's gone to the toilet** elle est allé aux toilettes.

**toilet paper** *noun* papier *Masc.* hygiénique.

**toilet roll** *noun* rouleau *Masc.* de papier hygiénique.

**token** *noun* **1** (*for a machine or game*) jeton *Masc.*; **2 a record token** un chèque-cadeaux *Masc.* pour disque.

**tolerant** *adjective* tolérant.

**toll** *noun* **1** péage *Masc*; **2** (*number of dead*) nombre *Masc.*; **the death toll is now 25** le nombre de victimes s'élève maintenant à 25.

**tomato** *noun* tomate *Fem.*; **a tomato salad** une salade de tomates; **tomato sauce** la sauce tomate.

**tomorrow** *adverb* demain; **I'll do it tomorrow** je le ferai demain; **tomorrow afternoon** demain après-midi; **tomorrow morning** demain matin; **tomorrow night** demain soir; **the day after tomorrow** après-demain.

**ton** *noun* tonne *Fem.*; **she gets tons of letters** elle reçoit des tonnes de lettres.

**tone** *noun* **1** (*on an answerphone*) tonalité *Fem.*; **speak after the tone** parlez après la tonalité; **2** (*of a voice or a letter*) ton *Masc.*

**tongue** *noun* langue *Fem.*; **to stick your tongue out** tirer la langue;

a
b
c
d
e
f
g
h
i
j
k
l
m
n
o
p
q
r
s
**t**
u
v
w
x
y
z

a
b
c
d
e
f
g
h
i
j
k
l
m
n
o
p
q
r
s
**t**
u
v
w
x
y
z

★ **it's on the tip of my tongue** je l'ai sur le bout de la langue.

**tonic** *noun* Schweppes™ *Masc.*; **a gin and tonic** un gin tonic.

**tonight** *adverb* **1** (*this evening*) ce soir; **I'm going out with my mates tonight** je sors avec les copains ce soir; **2** (*after bedtime*) cette nuit.

**tonsillitis** *noun* angine *Fem.*

**too** *adverb* **1** trop; **it's too expensive** c'est trop cher; **too often** trop souvent; **2 too much, too many** trop; **it takes too much time** ça prend trop de temps; **there are too many accidents** il y a trop d'accidents; **he eats too much** il mange trop; **3** (*as well*) aussi; **Karen's coming too** Karen vient aussi; **me too!** moi aussi!

**tool** *noun* outil *Masc.*

**tool box** *noun* boîte *Fem.* à outils.

**tool kit** *noun* trousse *Fem.* à outils.

**tooth** *noun* dent *Fem.*; **to brush your teeth** se brosser les dents.

**toothache** *noun* mal *Masc.* de dents; **to have toothache** avoir mal aux dents.

**toothbrush** *noun* brosse *Fem.* à dents.

**toothpaste** *noun* dentifrice *Masc.*

**top** *noun* **1** haut *Masc.* (*of a page, a ladder, or stairs*); **at the top of the stairs** en haut de l'escalier; **2** (*of a container or box*) dessus *Masc.*; **it's on top of the chest-of-drawers** c'est sur la commode; **3** (*of a mountain*) sommet *Masc.*; **4** (*a lid*) (*of a pen*) capuchon *Masc.*; (*of a bottle*) capsule *Fem.*; **5** (*to wear*) haut *Masc.*; **6 to be at the top of the list** être en

tête de la liste.

**top** *adjective* **1** (*a step or floor*) dernier (*Fem.* dernière); **it's on the top floor** c'est au dernier étage; **2** de haut (*a bunk*); **3** du haut (*a shelf*); **4 in the top left-hand corner** en haut à gauche; ★ **and on top of all that** et par-dessus le marché; ★ **it was a bit over the top** c'était un peu exagéré.

**topic** *noun* sujet *Masc.*

**topping** *noun* garniture *Fem.*; **which topping would you like on your pizza?** vous voulez une pizza à quoi?

**torch** *noun* lampe *Fem.* de poche.

**torn** *adjective* déchiré.

**tornado** *noun* tornade *Fem.*

**tortoise** *noun* tortue *Fem.*

**torture** *noun* torture *Fem.*
**torture** *verb* torturer [1].

**Tory** *noun* conservateur *Masc.*, conservatrice *Fem.*

**total** *noun* total *Masc.*
**total** *adjective* total (*Masc. plural* totaux).

**totally** *adverb* complètement.

**touch** *noun* **1** (*contact*) **to get in touch with somebody** prendre contact avec quelqu'un; **to stay in touch with somebody** rester en contact avec quelqu'un; **2 we've lost touch** on s'est perdu de vue; **I've lost touch with her recently** je l'ai perdue de vue récemment; **3** (*a little bit*) petit peu *Masc.*; **a touch of vanilla** un petit peu de vanille; **it was a touch embarrassing** c'était un petit peu gênant.
**touch** *verb* toucher [1].

**touched** *adjective* touché.

**touching** *adjective* touchant.

**tough** *adjective* 1 dur; **the meat's a bit tough** la viande est un peu dure; **it's a tough area** c'est un quartier dur; **things are a bit tough at the moment** la vie est un peu dure en ce moment; **a tough guy** un dur; 2 robuste; **you need to be tough to survive** il faut être robuste pour survivre!; **a tough fabric** un tissu robuste; 3 (*tough luck*) tant pis; **tough, you're too late** tant pis pour toi, tu arrives trop tard.

**tour** *noun* 1 visite *Fem.*; **we did the tour of the castle** nous avons fait la visite du château; **a tour of the city** une visite de la ville; 2 **a package tour** un voyage organisé; 3 (*by a band or theatre group*) tournée *Fem.*; **to go on tour** partir en tournée. **tour** *verb* (*performer*) être [6] en tournée; **they're touring the States** ils sont en tournée aux États-Unis.

**tourism** *noun* tourisme *Masc.*

**tourist** *noun* touriste *Masc. & Fem.*

**tourist information office** *noun* syndicat *Masc.* d'initiative.

**tournament** *noun* tournoi *Masc.*; **a tennis tournament** un tournoi de tennis.

**tow** *verb* **to be towed away** (*by the police*) être [6] emmené à la fourrière; (*by a breakdown truck*) être [6] remorqué.

**towards** *preposition* en direction de; **she went off towards the lake** elle est partie en direction du lac.

**towel** *noun* serviette *Fem.*

**tower** *noun* tour *Fem.*; **the Eiffel Tower** la tour Eiffel.

**tower block** *noun* tour *Fem.*

**town** *noun* ville *Fem.*; **to go into town** aller en ville.

**town centre** *noun* centre-ville *Masc.*

**town hall** *noun* mairie *Fem.*

**toxic** *adjective* toxique.

**toy** *noun* jouet *Masc.*; **a toy car** une petite voiture.

**toyshop** *noun* magasin *Masc.* de jouets.

**trace** *noun* trace *Fem.*; **there was no trace of it** il n'en restait aucune trace.
**trace** *verb* retrouver [1].

**tracing paper** *noun* papier *Masc.* calque.

**track** *noun* 1 (*for sport*) piste *Fem.*; **a track event** une épreuve de vitesse; **a racing track** (*for cars*) un circuit; 2 (*a path*) chemin *Masc.*; 3 (*song*) chanson; **this is my favourite track** c'est ma chanson préférée.

**track suit** *noun* survêtement *Masc.*

**tractor** *noun* tracteur *Masc.*

**trade** *noun* (*a profession*) métier *Masc.*

**trademark** *noun* marque *Fem.*; **registered trademark** marque déposée.

**trade union** *noun* syndicat *Masc.*

**tradition** *noun* tradition *Fem.*

**traditional** *adjective* traditionnel (*Fem.* traditionnelle).

**traffic** *noun* circulation *Fem.*

**traffic island** *noun* refuge *Masc.*

a
b
c
d
e
f
g
h
i
j
k
l
m
n
o
p
q
r
s
**t**
u
v
w
x
y
z

a

b

c

d

e

f

g

h

i

j

k

l

m

n

o

p

q

r

s

**t**

u

v

w

x

y

z

**traffic jam** *noun* embouteillage *Masc.*

**traffic lights** *plural noun* feux *Masc. plural.*

**traffic warden** *noun* contractuel *Masc.*, contractuelle *Fem.*

**tragedy** *noun* tragédie *Fem.*

**tragic** *adjective* tragique.

**trail** *noun* (*a path*) sentier *Masc.*; **a nature trail** un sentier écologique.

**trailer** *noun* remorque *Fem.*

**train** *noun* train *Masc.*; **he's coming by train** il prend le train; **I met her on the train** je l'ai rencontrée dans le train; **the train to York** le train pour York.

**train** *verb* **1** former [1] (*a student*); **2 to train to be something** suivre [75] une formation de quelque chose; **he's training to be a nurse** il suit une formation d'infirmier; **3** (*in sport*) s'entraîner [1]; **the team trains on Saturdays** l'équipe s'entraîne le samedi.

**trainee** *noun* stagiaire *Masc. & Fem.*

**trainer** *noun* **1** (*of an athlete or a horse*) entraîneur *Masc.*, entraîneuse *Fem.*; **2** (*shoe*) basket *Masc.*; **my new trainers** mes nouveaux baskets.

**training** *noun* **1** (*for a career*) formation *Fem.*; **2** (*for sport*) entraînement *Masc.*

**train ticket** *noun* billet *Masc.* de train.

**train timetable** *noun* horaire *Masc.* des trains.

**tram** *noun* tramway *Masc.*

**tramp** *noun* clochard *Masc.*, clocharde *Fem.*

**trampoline** *noun* trampoline *Masc.*

**transfer** *noun* **1** (*of money*) virement *Masc.*; **2** (*of employee, footballer*) transfert *Masc.*; **3** (*sticker*) décalcomanie *Fem.*

**transform** *verb* transformer [1].

**transistor** *noun* transistor *Masc.*

**translate** *verb* traduire [26]; **to translate something into French** traduire quelque chose en français.

**translation** *noun* traduction *Fem.*

**translator** *noun* traducteur *Masc.*, traductrice *Fem.*; **I'd like to be a translator** j'aimerais être traducteur.

**transparent** *adjective* transparent.

**transplant** *noun* **1** (*operation*) transplantation *Fem.*; **2** (*organ*) transplant *Masc.*

**transport** *noun* transport *Masc.*; **air transport** le transport aérien; **public transport** les transports en commun.

**trap** *noun* piège *Masc.*

**travel** *noun* voyages *Masc. plural*; **foreign travel** les voyages à l'étranger; **a travel brochure** une brochure de voyages.

**travel** *verb* voyager [52].

**travel agency** *noun* agence *Fem.* de voyages.

**travel agent** *noun* agent *Masc.* de voyages.

**traveller's cheque** *noun* chèque-voyage *Masc.* (*plural* chèques-voyage).

**traveller** *noun* **1** voyageur *Masc.*, voyageuse *Fem.*; **2** (*gypsy*) nomade *Masc. & Fem.*

**travelling** *noun* voyages *Masc. plural*; **I like travelling** j'aime partir en voyage.

**travel-sick** *noun* **to be** or **get travel-sick** souffrir [73] du mal de voyage.

**tray** *noun* plateau *Masc.* (*plural* plateaux).

**tread** *verb* **to tread on something** marcher [1] sur quelque chose.

**treasure** *noun* trésor *Masc.*

**treat** *noun* **1 I took them to the circus as a treat** je les ai emmenés au cirque pour leur faire plaisir; **2** (*food*) gâterie *Fem.*; **it's a little treat** c'est une petite gâterie.
**treat** *verb* **1** traiter [1]; **he treats his dog well** il traite bien son chien; **the doctor who treated you** le médecin qui vous a traité; **2 to treat somebody to something** offrir [56] quelque chose à quelqu'un; **I'll treat you to a drink** je vous offre à boire; **I treated myself to a new dress** je me suis offert une nouvelle robe.

**treatment** *noun* traitement *Masc.*

**treaty** *noun* traité *Masc.*

**tree** *noun* arbre *Masc.*

**tree trunk** *noun* tronc *Masc.* d'arbre.

**tremble** *verb* trembler [1].

**tremendous** *adjective* fantastique; **a tremendous victory/ defeat** une victoire/défaite écrasante.

**trend** *noun* **1** (*a fashion*) mode *Fem.*; **2** (*a tendency*) tendance *Fem.*

**trendy** *adjective* branché.

**trial** *noun* (*legal*) procès *Masc.*.

**triangle** *noun* triangle *Masc.*

**tribe** *noun* tribu *Fem.*

**tribute** *noun* hommage *Masc.*; **many tributes were paid to the Pope** de nombreuses personnes ont rendu hommage au Pape.

**trick** *noun* **1** (*by a conjuror, or as a joke*) tour *Masc.*; **to play a trick on somebody** jouer un tour à quelqu'un; **2** (*a knack*) astuce *Fem.*; **it doesn't work, there must be a trick to it** ça ne marche pas, il doit y avoir une astuce.
**trick** *verb* rouler [1]; **he tricked me!** il m'a roulé!

**tricky** *adjective* délicat; **it's a tricky situation** c'est une situation délicate.

**tricycle** *noun* tricycle *Masc.*

**trim** *verb* couper [1] (*hair or fabric*).

**Trinidad** *noun* (île de) la Trinité.

**Trinidadian** *noun* Trinidadien *Masc.*, Trinidadienne *Fem.*
**Trinidadian** *adjective* trinidadien (*Fem.* trinidadienne).

**trip** *noun* voyage *Masc.*; **a trip to Florida** un voyage en Floride; **he's on a business trip** il est en voyage d'affaires; **a day trip to France** une excursion d'une journée en France.
**trip** *verb* (*to stumble*) trébucher [1]; **Nicky tripped over a stone** Nicky a trébuché sur un gros caillou.

**triple** *verb* tripler [1]; **the price has tripled** le prix a triplé.

a
b
c
d
e
f
g
h
i
j
k
l
m
n
o
p
q
r
s
t
u
v
w
x
y
z

**triumph** *noun* triomphe *Masc.*

**trolley** *noun* chariot *Masc.*

**trombone** *noun* trombone *Masc.*; **to play the trombone** jouer du trombone.

**troops** *plural noun* troupes *Fem. plural.*

**trophy** *noun* trophée *Masc.*

**tropical** *adjective* tropical (*Masc. plural* tropicaux).

**trot** *verb* trotter [1].

**trouble** *noun* **1** problèmes *Masc. plural*; **we've had trouble with the car** nous avons eu des problèmes avec la voiture; **the trouble is, I've forgotten the number** le problème, c'est que j'ai oublié le numéro; **2** (*personal problems*) ennuis *Masc. plural*; **Steph's in trouble** Steph a des ennuis; **what's the trouble?** qu'est-ce qui ne va pas?; **3** (*difficulty*) **to have trouble doing** avoir du mal à faire; **I had trouble finding a seat** j'ai eu du mal à trouver une place; **it's not worth the trouble** cela ne vaut pas la peine; **it's no trouble!** ça ne me dérange pas!

**trousers** *plural noun* pantalon *Masc. singular*; **my old trousers** mon vieux pantalon; **a new pair of trousers** un pantalon neuf.

**trout** *noun* truite *Fem.*

**truant** *noun* **to play truant** faire [10] l'école buissonnière; **she's playing truant** elle fait l'école buissonnière.

**truck** *noun* camion *Masc.*

**true** *adjective* vrai; **a true story** une histoire vraie; **is that true?** c'est vrai?; **it's true she's**

**absent-minded** c'est vrai qu'elle est distraite.

**truly** *adverb* vraiment.

**trump** *noun* atout *Masc.*; **spades are trumps** atout pique.

**trumpet** *noun* trompette *Fem.*; **to play the trumpet** jouer de la trompette.

**trunk** *noun* **1** (*of a tree*) tronc *Masc.*; **2** (*of an elephant*) trompe *Fem.*; **3** (*a suitcase*) malle *Fem.*

**trunks** *plural noun* **swimming trunks** maillot *Masc.* de bain.

**trust** *noun* confiance *Fem.*

**trust** *verb* **I trust her** je lui fais confiance.

**truth** *noun* vérité *Fem.*; **to tell the truth, I'd completely forgottten** à vrai dire, j'avais complètement oublié.

**try** *noun* essai *Masc.*; **it's my first try** c'est mon premier essai; **to have a try** essayer [59]; **you should give it a try** tu devrais l'essayer.

**try** *verb* essayer [59]; **to try to do** essayer de faire; **I'm trying to open the door** j'essaie d'ouvrir la porte; **to try hard to do** faire [10] de gros efforts pour faire.

● **to try something on** essayer [59] quelque chose (*a garment*).

**T-shirt** *noun* tee-shirt *Masc.*

**tub** *noun* **1** (*food container*) pot *Masc.*; **2** (*bath*) baignoire *Fem.*

**tube** *noun* tube *Masc.*

**tuberculosis** *noun* tuberculose *Fem.*

**Tuesday** *noun* mardi *Masc.*; **on Tuesday** mardi; **I'm going out on**

**Tuesday** je sors mardi; **see you on Tuesday!** à mardi!; **on Tuesdays** le mardi; **the museum is closed on Tuesdays** le musée est fermé le mardi; **every Tuesday** tous les mardis; **last Tuesday** mardi dernier; **next Tuesday** mardi prochain.

**tug** *verb* tirer [1].

**tuition** *noun* cours *Masc. plural*; **piano tuition** des cours de piano; **private tuition** des cours particuliers.

**tulip** *noun* tulipe *Fem.*

**tumble-drier** *noun* sèche-linge *Masc.*

**tumbler** *noun* verre *Masc.* droit.

**tummy** *noun* estomac *Masc.*

**tuna** *noun* thon *Masc.*

**tune** *noun* air *Masc.*

**Tunisia** *noun* Tunisie *Fem.*; **in Tunisia** en Tunisie.

**tunnel** *noun* tunnel *Masc.*; **the Channel Tunnel** le tunnel sous la Manche.

**turban** *noun* turban *Masc.*

**turf** *noun* gazon *Masc.*

**turkey** *noun* dinde *Fem.*

**Turkey** *noun* Turquie *Fem.*; **in Turkey** en Turquie; **to Turkey** en Turquie.

**Turkish** *noun* turc *Masc.* (*language*). **Turkish** *adjective* turc (*Fem.* turque).

**turn** *noun* **1** (*in a game*) tour *Masc.*; **it's your turn** c'est ton tour; **whose turn is it?** c'est à qui le tour?; **it's Jane's turn to play** c'est à Jane de jouer; **to take turns driving**

conduire à tour de rôle; **2** (*in a road*) virage *Masc.*

**turn** *verb* **1** tourner [1]; **turn your chair round** tourne ta chaise; **turn left at the next set of lights** tournez à gauche aux prochains feux; **2** (*become*) devenir [81]; **she turned red** elle est devenue rouge.

● **to turn back** faire [10] demi-tour; **we turned back** nous avons fait demi-tour.

● **to turn off 1** (*from a road*) tourner [1]; **2** (*switch off*) éteindre [60] (*a light, an oven, a TV or radio*) fermer [1] (*a tap*) couper [1] (*gas or electricity*).

● **to turn on** allumer [1] (*the oven, TV, radio, or a light*) ouvrir [30] (*a tap*).

● **to turn out 1 to turn out well** bien se terminer [1]; **the holiday turned out badly** les vacances se sont mal terminées; **it all turned out alright in the end** finalement tout s'est arrangé; **2 it turned out that I was wrong** il s'est avéré que j'avais tort

● **to turn over 1** (*roll over*) se retourner [1]; **2** tourner [1] (*a page*).

● **to turn up 1** (*to arrive*) arriver [1]; **they turned up an hour later** ils sont arrivés une heure plus tard; **2** augmenter [1] (*the gas or the heating*); **3** (*make louder*) **can you turn up the volume?** est-ce que tu peux monter le son?

**turning** *noun* virage *Masc.*; **take the third turning on the right** prenez la troisième rue à gauche.

**turnip** *noun* navet *Masc.*

**turquoise** *adjective* turquoise.

**turtle** *noun* tortue *Fem* marine.

**turtle dove** *noun* tourterelle *Fem.*

a
b
c
d
e
f
g
h
i
j
k
l
m
n
o
p
q
r
s
t
u
v
w
x
y
z

a

**TV** *noun* télé *Fem.*; **I saw her on TV** je l'ai vue à la télé.

b

**tweezers** *noun* pince *Fem. singular* à épiler.

c

d

**twelfth** *number* douzième; **on the twelfth floor** au douzième étage; **the twelfth of May** le douze mai.

e

f

**twelve** *number* **1** douze *Masc.*; **Tara's twelve** Tara a douze ans; **2 at twelve o'clock** (*midday*) à midi; (*midnight*) à minuit.

g

h

**twenty** *number* vingt *Masc.*; **Marie's twenty** Marie a vingt ans; **twenty-one** vingt-et-un; **twenty-five** vingt-cinq.

i

j

k

**twice** *adverb* deux fois; **I've asked him twice** je lui ai demandé deux fois; **twice as much** deux fois plus.

l

**twig** *noun* brindille *Fem.*

m

**twilight** *noun* crépuscule *Masc.*

n

o

p

**twin** *noun* jumeau *Masc.* (*plural* jumeaux), jumelle *Fem.*; **Helen and Tim are twins** Helen et Tim sont jumeaux; **her twin sister** sa sœur jumelle.

q

r

**twin** *verb* **Oxford is twinned with Grenoble** Oxford est jumelée avec Grenoble.

s

**twist** *verb* tordre [3].

t

**two** *number* deux *Masc.*; **Ben's two** Ben a deux ans; **two by two** deux par deux.

u

v

**type** *noun* type *Masc.*; **what type of computer is it?** c'est quel type d'ordinateur?

w

x

**type** *verb* (*on a typewriter*) taper [1]; **I'm learning to type** j'apprends à taper à la machine; **I was busy typing some letters** j'étais en train de taper des lettres.

y

z

**typewriter** *noun* machine *Fem.* à écrire.

**typical** *adjective* typique.

**typing** *noun* dactylographie *Fem.*; **her typing is awful** elle tape très mal.

**tyre** *noun* pneu *Masc.*

# Uu

**UFO** *noun* ovni *Masc.*

**ugly** *adjective* laid.

**UK** *noun* (*short for United Kingdom*) Royaume-Uni *Masc.*

**ulcer** *noun* ulcère *Masc.*

**Ulster** *noun* Irlande *Fem.* du Nord.

**umbrella** *noun* parapluie *Masc.*

**umpire** *noun* arbitre *Masc.*

**UN** *noun* O.N.U. *Fem.* (*short for Organisation des Nations Unies*).

**unable** *adjective* **to be unable to do** ne pas pouvoir faire; **he's unable to come** il ne peut pas venir.

**unanimous** *adjective* unanime.

**unattractive** *adjective* peu attrayant (*person, place*).

**unavoidable** *adjective* inévitable.

**unbearable** *adjective* insupportable.

**unbelievable** *adjective* incroyable.

**uncertain** *adjective* incertain; **I'm uncertain whether they're coming** je ne suis pas sûr qu'ils viennent.

**unchanged** *adjective* inchangé.

**uncivilized** *adjective* barbare.

**uncle** noun oncle Masc.; **my Uncle Julian** mon oncle Julian.

**uncomfortable** adjective **1** inconfortable (shoes or a chair); **2** pénible (a journey or a situation).

**uncommon** adjective rare.

**unconscious** adjective (out cold) sans connaissance; **Tessa's still unconscious** Tessa est toujours sans connaissance.

**under** preposition **1** (underneath) sous; **under the bed** sous le lit; **perhaps it's under there** c'est peut-être là-dessous; **2** (less than) moins de; **under £20** moins de vingt livres; **children under five** les enfants de moins de cinq ans.

**under-age** noun **to be under-age** être mineur (Fem. mineure).

**underclothes** plural noun sous-vêtements Masc. plural.

**undercooked** adjective pas assez cuit.

**underestimate** verb sous-estimer [1].

**underground** noun (a railway) métro Masc.; **I saw her on the underground** je l'ai vue dans le métro; **shall we go by underground?** on prend le métro? **underground** adjective souterrain; **an underground carpark** un parking souterrain.

**underline** verb souligner [1].

**underneath** preposition sous; **it's underneath these papers** c'est sous ces papiers. **underneath** adverb dessous; **look underneath** cherche dessous.

**underpants** plural noun slip Masc. singular; **my underpants** mon slip.

**underpass** noun **1** (pedestrian) passage Masc. souterrain; **2** (for traffic) passage Masc. inférieur.

**understand** verb comprendre [64]; **I don't understand** je ne comprends pas; **I couldn't understand what he was saying** je n'ai pas compris ce qu'il disait.

**understandable** adjective **that's understandable** ça se comprend.

**understanding** noun compréhension Fem. **understanding** adjective compréhensif (Fem. compréhensive); **he was very understanding** il a été très compréhensif.

**underwear** noun sous-vêtements Masc. plural.

**undo** verb **1** défaire [10] (a button or a lock); **2** ouvrir [30] (a parcel).

**undone** adjective **to come undone** se défaire [10].

**undress** verb **to get undressed** se déshabiller [1]; **I got undressed** je me suis déshabillé.

**unemployed** noun **the unemployed** les chômeurs; **work for the unemployed** du travail pour les chômeurs. **unemployed** adjective au chômage; **she's unemployed** elle est au chômage.

**unemployment** noun chômage Masc.

**uneven** adjective irrégulier (Fem. irrégulière).

**unexpected** adjective imprévu.

**unexpectedly** *adverb* (*to happen, arrive*) à l'improviste.

**unfair** *adjective* injuste; **it's unfair to young people** c'est injuste pour les jeunes.

**unfashionable** *adjective* démodé.

**unfasten** *verb* défaire [10].

**unfit** *adjective* **I'm terribly unfit** je ne suis pas du tout en forme.

**unfold** *verb* déplier [1].

**unforgettable** *adjective* inoubliable.

**unfortunate** *adjective* regrettable.

**unfortunately** *adverb* malheureusement.

**unfriendly** *adjective* pas très sympathique.

**unfurnished** *adjective* non meublé.

**ungrateful** *adjective* ingrat.

**unhappy** *adjective* malheureux (*Fem.* malheureuse).

**unhealthy** *adjective* **1** maladif (*Fem.* maladive) (*a person*); **2** malsain (*food*).

**unhurt** *adjective* indemne.

**uniform** *noun* uniforme *Masc.*; **in school uniform** en uniforme scolaire.

**uninhabited** *adjective* inhabité.

**union** *noun* (*a trade union*) syndicat *Masc.*

**Union Jack** *noun* **the Union Jack** le drapeau du Royaume-Uni.

**unique** *adjective* unique.

**unit** *noun* **1** (*for measuring, for example*) unité *Fem.*; **2** (*in a kitchen*) élément *Masc.*; **3** (*a hospital department*) service *Masc.*

**United Kingdom** *noun* Royaume-Uni *Masc.*

**United Nations** *noun* O.N.U (*Organisation des Nations Unies*).

**United States (of America)** *plural noun* États-Unis *Masc. plural*; **in the United States** aux États-Unis; **to the United States** aux États-Unis.

**universe** *noun* univers *Masc.*

**university** *noun* université *Fem.*; **to go to university** aller à l'université.

**unjust** *adjective* injuste.

**unkind** *adjective* pas gentil (*Fem.* pas gentille).

**unknown** *adjective* inconnu.

**unleaded petrol** *noun* essence *Fem.* sans plomb.

**unless** *conjunction* **unless he does it** à moins qu'il ne le fasse; **unless you tell her** à moins que tu ne le lui dises (*note that 'à moins que' is followed by a subjunctive*).

**unlike** *adjective* **1 unlike me, she hates dogs** contrairement à moi, elle déteste les chiens; **2 it's unlike her to be late** ce n'est pas son genre d'être en retard.

**unlikely** *adjective* peu probable; **it's unlikely** c'est peu probable.

**unlimited** *adjective* illimité.

**unload** *verb* décharger [52].

**unlock** *verb* ouvrir [30]; **the car's unlocked** la voiture est ouverte.

**unlucky** *adjective* **1** to be unlucky (*a person*) ne pas avoir de chance; **I was unlucky, it was shut** je n'ai pas eu de chance, c'était fermé; **2 thirteen is an unlucky number** le treize porte malheur.

**unmarried** *adjective* célibataire.

**unnatural** *adjective* anormal (*Masc. plural* anormaux).

**unnecessary** *adjective* inutile; **it's unnecessary to book** il est inutile de réserver.

**unpack** *verb* défaire [10]; **I unpacked my rucksack** j'ai défait mon sac à dos; **I'll just unpack and then come down** je vais juste défaire ma valise et puis je descendrai.

**unpaid** *adjective* **1** impayé (*a bill*); **2** non rémunéré (*work*).

**unpleasant** *adjective* désagréable.

**unplug** *verb* débrancher [1].

**unpopular** *adjective* impopulaire.

**unrealistic** *adjective* peu réaliste.

**unreasonable** *adjective* pas raisonnable; **he's being really unreasonable** il n'est vraiment pas raisonnable.

**unrecognizable** *adjective* méconnaissable.

**unreliable** *adjective* peu fiable (*information or equipment*); **he's unreliable** on ne peut pas compter sur lui.

**unroll** *verb* dérouler [1].

**unsafe** *adjective* dangereux (*Fem.* dangereuse) (*wiring, for instance*).

**unsatisfactory** *adjective* insatisfaisant.

**unscrew** *verb* dévisser [1].

**unshaven** *adjective* pas rasé.

**unsuccessful** *adjective* to be unsuccessful ne pas réussir; **I tried, but I was unsuccessful** j'ai essayé mais je n'ai pas réussi; **an unsuccessful attempt** un essai vain.

**unsuitable** *adjective* inapproprié.

**untidy** *adjective* en désordre; **the house is always untidy** la maison est toujours en désordre.

**untie** *verb* défaire [10].

**until** *preposition* **1** jusqu'à; **until Monday** jusqu'à lundi; **until the tenth** jusqu'au dix; **until now** jusqu'à présent; **until then** jusque-là; **2 not until** pas avant; **not until September** pas avant septembre; **it won't be finished until Friday** ce ne sera pas fini avant vendredi.

**unusual** *adjective* peu commun; **an unusual beetle** un scarabée peu commun; **storms are unusual in June** c'est rare d'avoir des orages au mois de juin.

**unwilling** *adjective* to be unwilling to do ne pas vouloir faire; **he's unwilling to wait** il ne veut pas attendre.

**unwrap** *verb* déballer [1].

**up** *preposition, adverb* **1** (*out of bed*) to be up être levé; **Liz isn't up yet** Liz n'est pas encore levée; **to get up** se lever [50]; **we got up at six** nous nous sommes levés à six heures; **I was up late last night** je me suis couché tard hier soir; **2** (*higher up*)

a
b
c
d
e
f
g
h
i
j
k
l
m
n
o
p
q
r
s
t
**u**
v
w
x
y
z

en haut; **hands up!** haut les mains!; **up on the roof** en haut sur le toit; **up here** ici; **up there** là-haut; **we went up the road** nous avons remonté la rue; **it's just up the road** c'est tout près; **up in Glasgow** à Glasgow; **3** (*wrong*) **what's up?** qu'est-ce qui se passe?; **what's up with him?** qu'est-ce qu'il a?; **4 up to** jusqu'à; **up to here** jusqu'ici; **up to fifty people** jusqu'à cinquante personnes; **she came up to me** elle s'est approchée de moi; **5 what's she up to?** qu'est-ce qu'elle fait?; **it's up to you (to decide)** c'est à toi de décider; ★ **time's up!** c'est l'heure!

**update** *noun* mise *Fem.* à jour; **here's an update on the delays** voici une mise à jour des retards.

**update** *verb* **1** (*revise*) mettre [11] à jour (*timetables or information*); **2** moderniser [1] (*styles or furnishings*).

**upheaval** *noun* bouleversement *Masc.*

**uphill** *adverb* en montée.

**upright** *adjective* droit; **put it upright** mets-le droit; **to stand upright** se tenir droit.

**upset** *noun* **a stomach upset** une indigestion.
**upset** *adjective* contrarié; **he's upset** il est contrarié.
**upset** *verb* **to upset somebody** contrarier [1] quelqu'un.

**upside down** *adjective* à l'envers.

**upstairs** *adverb* en haut; **Mum's upstairs** maman est en haut; **to go upstairs** monter [1].

**up-to-date** *adjective* **1** (*in fashion*) moderne; **2** (*information*) à jour.

**upwards** *adjective* vers le haut.

**urgent** *adjective* urgent.

**urgently** *adverb* d'urgence; **she wants to see you urgently** elle veut vous voir d'urgence.

**US** *noun* U.S.A. *Masc. plural.*

**us** *pronoun* nous; **she knows us** elle nous connaît; **they saw us** ils nous ont vus; **he gave us a cheque** il nous a donné un chèque; **with us** avec nous.

**USA** *noun* U.S.A. *Masc. plural.*

**use** *noun* **1** emploi *Masc.*; **the instructions for use** le mode d'emploi; **2 it's no use** ça ne sert à rien; **it's no use phoning** ça ne sert à rien de téléphoner.
**use** *verb* utiliser [1]; **we used the dictionary** nous avons utilisé le dictionnaire; **to use something to do** se servir [71] de quelque chose pour faire; **I used a knife to open the parcel** je me suis servi d'un couteau pour ouvrir le paquet.

● **to use up 1** consommer [1] (*food or petrol*); **2** dépenser [1] (*money*).

**used** *adjective* **1 to be used to something** être [6] habitué à quelque chose; **I'm not used to cats** je ne suis pas habitué aux chats; **I'm not used to it!** je n'ai pas l'habitude; **2 to be used to doing something** avoir [5] l'habitude de faire quelque chose; **I'm not used to eating in restaurants** je n'ai pas l'habitude de manger au restaurant; **3 to get used to** s'habituer à; **I've got used to living here** je me suis habitué à

a b c d e f g h i j k l m n o p q r s t u v w x y z

habiter ici; **you'll get used to it!** tu t'y habitueras!

**used** *verb* **they used to live in the country** ils habitaient à la campagne avant; **she used to smoke** elle fumait avant.

**useful** *adjective* utile.

**useless** *adjective* nul (*Fem.* nulle); **this knife's useless** ce couteau est nul; **you're completely useless!** tu es complètement nul!

**user** *noun* utilisateur *Masc.*, utilisatrice *Fem.*

**user-friendly** *adjective* convivial (*Masc. plural* conviviaux).

**usual** *adjective* habituel (*Fem.* habituelle); **it's the usual problem** c'est le problème habituel; **as usual** comme d'habitude; **it's colder than usual** il fait plus froid que d'habitude.

**usually** *adjective* d'habitude; **I usually leave at eight** d'habitude je pars à huit heures.

**utensil** *noun* ustensile *Masc.*

**vacancy** *noun* **1** (*in a hotel*) 'vacancies' 'chambres libres'; **'no vacancies'** 'complet'; **2 a job vacancy** un poste vacant.

**vacant** *adjective* libre.

**vaccinate** *verb* vacciner [1].

**vaccination** *noun* vaccination *Fem.*

**vacuum** *noun* vide *Masc.*
**vacuum** *verb* passer [1] l'aspirateur; **I'm going to vacuum my room** je vais passer l'aspirateur dans ma chambre.

**vacuum cleaner** *noun* aspirateur *Masc.*

**vagina** *noun* vagin *Masc.*

**vague** *adjective* vague.

**vaguely** *adverb* vaguement.

**vain** *adjective* vaniteux (*Fem.* vaniteuse); **in vain** en vain.

**Valentine's Day** *noun* la Saint-Valentin.

**valentine card** *noun* carte *Fem.* pour la Saint-Valentin.

**valid** *adjective* valable.

**valley** *noun* vallée *Fem.*

**valuable** *adjective* **1** de valeur; **to be valuable** avoir de la valeur; **that watch is very valuable** cette montre a une grande valeur; **2** (*appreciated*) précieux (*Fem.* précieuse); **he gave us some valuable information** il nous a donné des renseignements précieux.

**value** *noun* valeur *Fem.*
**value** *verb* apprécier [1] (*somebody's help, opinion, or friendship*).

**van** *noun* (*small*) fourgon *Masc.*, (*large*) camionnette *Fem.*

**vandal** *noun* vandale *Masc. & Fem.*

**vandalism** *noun* vandalisme *Masc.*

**vandalize** *verb* vandaliser [1].

**vanilla** *noun* vanille *Fem.*; **a vanilla ice cream** une glace à la vanille.

**vanish** *verb* disparaître [27].

a
b
c
d
e
f
g
h
i
j
k
l
m
n
o
p
q
r
s
t
**u**
**v**
w
x
y
z

611

# variety

a b c d e f g h i j k l m n o p q r s t u **v** w x y z

**variety** *noun* variété *Fem.*

**various** *adjective* plusieurs; **there are various ways of doing it** il y a plusieurs façons de le faire.

**vary** *verb* varier [1]; **it varies a lot** ça varie beaucoup.

**vase** *noun* vase *Masc.*

**VAT** *noun* TVA *Fem.*

**VCR** *noun* magnétoscope *Masc.*

**VDU** *noun* console *Fem.*

**veal** *noun* veau *Masc.*

**vegan** *noun* végétalien *Masc.*, végétalienne *Fem.*

**vegetable** *noun* légume *Masc.*

**vegetarian** *noun, adjective* végétarien *Masc.*, végétarienne *Fem.*; **he's vegetarian** il est végétarien.

**vehicle** *noun* véhicule *Masc.*

**vein** *noun* veine *Fem.*

**velvet** *noun* velours *Masc.*

**vending machine** *noun* distributeur *Masc.* automatique.

**ventilation** *noun* aération *Fem.*

**verb** *noun* verbe *Masc.*

**verdict** *noun* verdict *Masc.*

**verge** *noun* 1 (*the roadside*) accotement *Masc.*; 2 **to be on the verge of doing** être [6] sur le point de faire; **I was on the verge of leaving** j'étais sur le point de partir.

**version** *noun* version *Fem.*

**versus** *preposition* contre; **Bath versus Chelsea** Bath contre Chelsea.

**vertical** *adjective* vertical (*Masc. plural* verticaux).

**vertigo** *noun* vertige *Masc.*

**very** *adverb* **it's very difficult** c'est très difficile; **very well** très bien; **very much** beaucoup.
**very** *adjective* 1 **the very person I need!** exactement la personne qu'il me faut!; **the very thing he was looking for** exactement ce qu'il cherchait; 2 **in the very middle** en plein milieu; **at the very end** tout à la fin; **at the very front** tout devant.

**vest** *noun* maillot *Masc.* de corps.

**vet** *noun* vétérinaire *Masc. & Fem.*; **she's a vet** elle est vétérinaire.

**via** *preposition* **to go via** passer par; **we're going via Dover** nous allons passer par Douvres; **we'll go via the bank** on va passer par la banque.

**vicar** *noun* pasteur *Masc.*

**vicious** *adjective* 1 méchant (*a dog*); 2 brutal (*Masc. plural* brutaux) (*an attack*).

**victim** *noun* victime *Fem.*

**victory** *noun* victoire *Fem.*

**video** *noun* 1 (*film*) vidéo *Fem.*; **to watch a video** regarder une vidéo; **I've got it on video** je l'ai en vidéo; 2 (*cassette*) cassette *Fem.* vidéo; **I bought a video** j'ai acheté une cassette vidéo; 3 (*video recorder*) magnétoscope *Masc.*
**video** *verb* enregistrer [1]; **I'll video it for you** je te l'enregistrerai.

**video cassette** *noun* cassette *Fem.* vidéo.

**video game** *noun* jeu *Masc.* vidéo (*plural* jeux vidéo).

**video recorder** *noun* magnétoscope *Masc.*

**video shop** *noun* vidéoclub *Masc.*

**view** *noun* **1** vue *Fem.*; **a room with a view of the lake** une chambre avec vue sur le lac; **2** (*opinion*) avis *Masc.*; **in my view** à mon avis; **a point of view** un point de vue.

**viewer** *noun* (*on TV*) téléspectateur *Masc.*, téléspectatrice *Fem.*

**viewpoint** *noun* point *Masc.* de vue.

**vigorous** *adjective* vigoureux (*Fem.* vigoureuse).

**vile** *adjective* abominable.

**villa** *noun* villa *Fem.*

**village** *noun* village *Masc.*

**villager** *noun* villageois *Masc.*, villageoise *Fem.*

**vine** *noun* vigne *Fem.*

**vinegar** *noun* vinaigre *Masc.*

**vineyard** *noun* vignoble *Masc.*

**violence** *noun* violence *Fem.*

**violent** *adjective* violent.

**violin** *noun* violon *Masc.*; **to play the violin** jouer du violon.

**violinist** *noun* violoniste *Masc.* & *Fem.*

**virgin** *noun* vierge *Fem.*

**Virgo** *noun* Vierge *Fem.*; **Robert's Virgo** Robert est Vierge.

**virtual reality** *noun* réalité *Fem.* virtuelle.

**virus** *noun* **1** (*in medicine*) virus *Masc.*; **2** (*in computing*) virus *Masc.*; **anti-virus software** un logiciel antivirus.

**visa** *noun* visa *Masc.*

**visible** *adjective* visible.

**visit** *noun* **1** (*stay*) séjour *Masc.*; **my last visit to France** mon dernier séjour en France; **2** visite *Fem.* (*to a house, museum*).

**visit** *verb* **1** visiter [1] (*museum, castle, town*); **2** aller [7] voir (*a person*); **we visited Auntie Pat at Christmas** nous sommes allés voir tante Pat à Noël.

**visitor** *noun* **1** invité *Masc.*, invitée *Fem.*; **we've got visitors tonight** on a des invités ce soir; **2** (*a tourist*) visiteur *Masc.*, visiteuse *Fem.*

**visual** *adjective* visuel (*Fem.* visuelle).

**vital** *adjective* indispensable; **it's vital to book** il est indispensable de réserver.

**vitamin** *noun* vitamine *Fem.*

**vivid** *adjective* **1** (*colour*) vif (*Fem.* vive); **2** **to have a vivid imagination** exagérer.

**vocabulary** *noun* vocabulaire *Masc.*

**vocational** *adjective* professionnel (*Fem.* professionnelle).

**vodka** *noun* vodka *Masc.*

**voice** *noun* voix *Fem.*

**volcano** *noun* volcan *Masc.*

**volleyball** *noun* volley-ball *Masc.*; **to play volleyball** jouer au volley-ball.

**volume** *noun* volume *Masc.*; **could you turn down the volume?** est-ce que tu peux baisser le volume?

**voluntary** *adjective* **1** (*not compulsory*) volontaire; **2** **to do voluntary work** travailler bénévolement.

a
b
c
d
e
f
g
h
i
j
k
l
m
n
o
p
q
r
s
t
u
v
w
x
y
z

a

**volunteer** *noun* **1** (*for a job*) volontaire *Masc. & Fem.*; **2** (*in charity work*) bénévole *Masc. & Fem.*

b

**vomit** *verb* vomir [2].

c

**vote** *noun* vote *Masc.*; **she got 20 votes** elle a obtenu 20 votes.

d

**vote** *verb* voter [1]; **she always votes Green** elle vote toujours pour les Verts.

e

f

**voucher** *noun* bon *Masc.*

g

**vowel** *noun* voyelle *Fem.*

h

**voyage** *noun* voyage *Masc.*

i

**vulgar** *adjective* vulgaire.

j

k

# Ww

l

m

**waffle** *noun* (*to eat*) gaufre *Fem.*

n

**wage(s)** *noun* salaire *Masc.*

o

**wagon** *noun* **1** (*for transport*) chariot *Masc.*; **2** (*on railway*) wagon *Masc.* de marchandises.

p

**waist** *noun* taille *Fem.*

q

**waistcoat** *noun* gilet *Masc.*

r

**waist measurement** *noun* tour *Masc.* de taille.

s

**wait** *noun* attente *Fem.*; **an hour's wait** une heure d'attente.

t

**wait** *verb* **1** attendre [3]; **they're waiting in the car** ils attendent dans la voiture; **she kept me waiting** elle m'a fait attendre; **2 to wait for** attendre [3]; **wait for me!** attends-moi!; **wait for the signal** attendez le signal; **3 I can't wait to open it!** j'ai hâte de l'ouvrir!

u

v

w

x

**waiter** *noun* serveur *Masc.*

y

z

**waiting list** *noun* liste *Fem.* d'attente.

**waiting room** *noun* salle *Fem.* d'attente.

**waitress** *noun* serveuse *Fem.*

**wake** *verb* **1** réveiller [1] (*somebody else*); **Jess woke me at six** Jess m'a réveillé à six heures; **2** se réveiller [1]; **I woke (up) at six** je me suis réveillé à six heures; **wake up!** réveille-toi!

**Wales** *noun* pays *Masc.* de Galles; **in Wales** au pays de Galles; **to Wales** au pays de Galles.

**walk** *noun* promenade *Fem.* (*a little stroll*) tour *Masc.*; **to go for a walk** faire une promenade; **we went for a walk in the woods** nous avons fait une promenade dans la forêt; **we'll go for a little walk round the village** on va faire un petit tour au village; **to take the dog for a walk** promener [50] le chien; **it's about five minutes' walk from here** c'est à environ cinq minutes à pied d'ici. **walk** *verb* **1** marcher [1]; **I like walking on sand** j'aime marcher sur le sable; **2** (*walk around*) se promener [50]; **we walked around the old town** nous nous sommes promenés dans la vieille ville; **3** (*go*) aller [7]; **I'll walk to the bus stop with you** j'irai avec toi jusqu'à l'arrêt de bus; **4** (*on foot rather than by car or bus*) aller [7] à pied; **it's not far, we can walk** ce n'est pas loin, on peut y aller à pied.

**walkie-talkie** *noun* talkie-walkie *Masc.* (*plural* talkies-walkies).

**walking** *noun* (*hiking*) randonnée *Fem.*; **we're going walking in**

**Scotland** nous allons faire de la randonnée en Écosse.

**walking distance** *noun* **it's within walking distance of the sea** c'est à quelques minutes à pied de la mer.

**walking stick** *noun* canne *Fem.*

**walkman™** *noun* walkman™ *Masc.*

**wall** *noun* **1** (*of a house*) mur *Masc.*; **2** (*of a city*) muraille *Fem.*; **the southern wall was destroyed** la muraille sud a été détruite; **the city walls** les fortifications de la ville.

**wallet** *noun* portefeuille *Masc.*

**wallpaper** *noun* papier *Masc.* peint.

**walnut** *noun* noix *Fem.* (*plural* noix).

**wander** *verb* **to wander around town** se balader [1] en ville; **to wander off** s'éloigner [1].

**want** *noun* **all our wants** tous nos besoins.

**want** *verb* vouloir [14]; **do you want some coffee?** tu veux du café?; **what do you want to do?** qu'est-ce que tu veux faire?; **I don't want to bother him** je ne veux pas le déranger.

**war** *noun* guerre *Fem.*

**ward** *noun* salle *Fem.* (*in a hospital*).

**wardrobe** *noun* **1** (*cupboard*) armoire *Fem.*; **2** (*clothes*) garde-robe *Fem.*

**warehouse** *noun* entrepôt *Masc.*

**warm** *adjective* **1** chaud; **a warm drink** une boisson chaude; **it's warm today** il fait chaud

aujourd'hui; **I am warm** j'ai chaud; **are you warm enough?** as-tu assez chaud?; **I'll keep your dinner warm** je tiendrai ton dîner au chaud; **2** (*friendly*) chaleureux (*Fem.* chaleureuse); **a warm welcome** un accueil chaleureux.

**warm** *verb* chauffer [1]; **warm the plates** chauffez les assiettes.

● **to warm up 1** (*the weather*) s'adoucir [2]; **2** (*an athlete*) s'échauffer [1]; **3** (*to heat up*) réchauffer [1] (*food*); **I'll warm up some soup for you** je vous réchaufferai de la soupe

**warmth** *noun* chaleur *Fem.*

**warn** *verb* prévenir [81]; **I warn you, it's expensive** je vous préviens que c'est cher; **to warn somebody to do** conseiller [1] à quelqu'un de faire; **he warned me to lock the car** il m'a conseillé de fermer la voiture.

**warning** *noun* avertissement *Masc.*

**wart** *noun* verrue *Fem.*

**wash** *noun* **to give something a wash** laver [1] quelque chose; **to have a wash** se laver.

**wash** *verb* laver [1]; **I've washed your jeans** j'ai lavé ton jean; **to wash your hands** se laver les mains; **I washed my hands** je me suis lavé les mains; **to wash your hair** se laver les cheveux; **to get washed** se laver; **to wash the dishes** faire [10] la vaisselle.

● **to wash up** faire [10] la vaisselle.

**washbasin** *noun* lavabo *Masc.*

**washing** *noun* **1** (*dirty*) linge *Masc.* sale; **2** (*clean*) linge *Masc.*

a
b
c
d
e
f
g
h
i
j
k
l
m
n
o
p
q
r
s
t
u
v
**w**
x
y
z

**washing machine** *noun* machine *Fem.* à laver.

**washing powder** *noun* lessive *Fem.*

**washing-up** *noun* vaisselle *Fem.*; **to do the washing-up** faire la vaisselle.

**washing-up liquid** *noun* liquide *Masc.* à vaisselle.

**wasp** *noun* guêpe *Fem.*

**waste** *noun* **1** (*of food, money, paper*) gaspillage *Masc.*; **2** (*of time*) perte *Fem.*; **it's a waste of time** c'est une perte de temps.
**waste** *verb* **1** gaspiller [1] (*food, money, paper*); **2** perdre [3] (*time*); **you're wasting your time** tu perds ton temps.

**waste-bin** *noun* poubelle *Fem.*

**wastepaper-basket** *noun* corbeille *Fem.* à papier.

**watch** *noun* montre *Fem.*; **my watch is fast** ma montre avance; **my watch is slow** ma montre retarde.
**watch** *verb* **1** (*to look at*) regarder [1]; **I was watching TV** je regardais la télé; **2** (*keep a check on*) surveiller [1]; **watch the time** surveille l'heure; **3** (*to be careful*) faire [10] attention; **watch you don't spill it** fais attention de ne pas le renverser; **watch out for black ice** faites attention au verglas; **watch out!** attention!

**water** *noun* eau *Fem.*
**water** *verb* arroser [1]; **to water the plants** arroser les plantes.

**watercolours** *noun* peinture *Fem.* pour aquarelle.

**waterfall** *noun* cascade *Fem.*

**watering can** *noun* arrosoir *Masc.*

**water melon** *noun* pastèque *Fem.*

**waterproof** *adjective* imperméable.

**water-skiing** *noun* ski *Masc.* nautique; **to go water-skiing** faire du ski nautique.

**water sports** *plural noun* sports *Masc. plural* nautiques.

**wave** *noun* **1** (*in the sea*) vague *Fem.*; **2** (*with your hand*) signe *Masc.*; **she gave him a wave from the bus** elle lui a fait signe du bus.
**wave** *verb* **1** (*with your hand*) saluer [1] de la main; **2** (*flap*) agiter [1] (*your ticket or the newspaper, for example*).

**wax** *noun* cire *Fem.*

**way** *noun* **1** (*a route or road*) chemin *Masc.*; **the way to town** le chemin pour aller en ville; **we asked the way to the station** nous avons demandé le chemin pour aller à la gare; **on the way back** sur le chemin de retour; **on the way** en route; **'way in'** 'entrée'; **'way out'** 'sortie'; **2** (*direction*) direction *Fem.*; **which way did he go?** en quelle direction est-il parti?; **come this way** venez par ici; **to be in the way** gêner le passage; **3** (*side*) sens *Masc.*; **the right way up** à l'endroit; **the wrong way round** à l'envers; **4** (*distance*) **it's a long way** c'est loin; **Terry went all the way to York** Terry est allé jusqu'à York; **5** (*manner*) façon *Fem.*; **a way of talking** une façon de parler; **he does it his way** il le fait à sa façon; **either way, she's wrong** de toute façon elle

**weigh**

a tort; **do it this way** fais-le comme ceci; **6 no way!** pas question!; **7 by the way** à propos.

**way in** *noun* entrée *Fem.*

**way out** *noun* sortie *Fem.*

**we** *pronoun* nous; (*informally*) on; **we live in Carlisle** nous habitons Carlisle; **we're going to the cinema tonight** on va au cinéma ce soir.

**weak** *adjective* **1** (*feeble*) faible; **her voice was weak** sa voix était faible; **2** léger (*Fem.* légère) (*coffee or tea*).

**wealth** *noun* fortune *Fem.*; **the wealth of the nation** la richesse de la nation.

**wealthy** *adjective* riche.

**weapon** *noun* arme *Fem.*

**wear** *noun* **children's wear** vêtements *Masc. plural* pour enfants; **sports wear** vêtements de sport.

**wear** *verb* porter [1]; **Tamsin's wearing her trainers** Tamsin porte ses baskets; **she often wears red** elle est souvent en rouge; **to wear make-up** se maquiller [1].

**weather** *noun* temps *Masc.*; **what's the weather like?** quel temps fait-il?; **in fine weather** quand il fait beau; **the weather was cold** il faisait froid; **the weather here is terrible** il fait un temps affreux ici.

**weather forecast** *noun* météo *Fem.*; **the weather forecast says it will rain** selon la météo il va pleuvoir.

**web** *noun* **1** (*spider's*) toile *Fem.*; **2** (*Internet*) **the Web** le web *Masc.*, la Toile *Fem.*

**web site** *noun* site *Masc.* internet.

**wedding** *noun* mariage *Masc.*

**Wednesday** *noun* mercredi *Masc.*; **on Wednesday** mercredi; **I'm going out on Wednesday** je sors mercredi; **see you on Wednesday!** à mercredi!; **on Wednesdays** le mercredi; **the museum is closed on Wednesdays** le musée est fermé le mercredi; **every Wednesday** tous les mercredis; **last Wednesday** mercredi dernier; **next Wednesday** mercredi prochain.

**weed** *noun* mauvaise herbe *Fem.*

**week** *noun* semaine *Fem.*; **last week** la semaine dernière; **next week** la semaine prochaine; **this week** cette semaine; **for weeks** pendant des semaines; **a week today** aujourd'hui en huit.

**weekday** *noun* **on weekdays** en semaine.

**weekend** *noun* week-end *Masc.*; **last weekend** le weekend dernier; **next weekend** le weekend prochain; **they're coming for the weekend** ils vont passer le weekend chez nous; **I'll do it at the weekend** je le ferai pendant le week-end; **have a nice weekend!** bon weekend!

**weekly** *adverb* une fois par semaine; **I see her weekly** je la vois toutes les semaines.

**weekly** *adjective* hebdomadaire; **a weekly magazine** un magazine hebdomadaire.

**weigh** *verb* peser [50]; **to weigh something** peser quelque chose; **how much do you weigh?** combien pèses-tu?; **I weigh 50 kilos** je pèse cinquante kilos; **to weigh yourself** se peser.

a
b
c
d
e
f
g
h
i
j
k
l
m
n
o
p
q
r
s
t
u
v
w
x
y
z

**weight** *noun* poids *Masc.*; **to put on weight** prendre du poids; **to lose weight** perdre du poids.

**weightlifting** *noun* haltérophilie *Fem.*

**weird** *adjective* bizarre.

**welcome** *noun* accueil *Masc.*; **they gave us a warm welcome** ils nous ont fait un accueil chaleureux; **welcome to Oxford!** bienvenue à Oxford!.

**welcome** *adjective* bienvenu; **you're welcome any time** vous êtes toujours les bienvenus; **'thank you!' – 'you're welcome!'** 'merci!' – 'de rien!'

**welcome** *verb* accueillir [35].

**well**[1] *noun* puits *Masc.*

**well**[2] *adverb* **1 to feel well** se sentir bien; **I'm very well, thank you** ça va très bien, merci; **2** bien; **Terry played well** Terry a bien joué; **the operation went well** l'opération s'est bien passée; **well done!** bravo!; **3 as well** aussi; **Kevin's coming as well** Kevin vient aussi; **4** alors; **well then, what's the problem?** alors, quel est le problème?; **5 very well then, you can go** très bien, tu peux y aller.

**well-behaved** *adjective* sage.

**well-done** *adjective* bien cuit (*a steak*).

**wellington (boot)** *noun* botte *Fem.* en caoutchouc.

**well-known** *adjective* célèbre.

**well-off** *adjective* aisé.

**Welsh** *noun* **1 the Welsh** (*people*) les Gallois *Masc. plural*; **2** (*language*) gallois *Masc.*
**Welsh** *adjective* gallois.

**Welshman** *noun* Gallois *Masc.*

**Welshwoman** *noun* Galloise *Fem.*

**west** *noun* ouest *Masc.*; **in the west** à l'ouest.
**west** *adjective, adverb* ouest (*never agrees*); **the west side** le côté ouest; **a west wind** un vent d'ouest; **west of Paris** à l'ouest de Paris.

**western** *noun* (*a film*) western *Masc.*

**West Indian** *noun* Antillais *Masc.*, Antillaise *Fem.*
**West Indian** *adjective* antillais.

**West Indies** *plural noun* Antilles *Fem. plural*; **in the West Indies** aux Antilles.

**wet** *adjective* **1** (*damp*) mouillé; **the grass is wet** l'herbe est mouillée; **we got wet** nous nous sommes fait mouiller; **2 a wet day** un jour de pluie.

**whale** *noun* baleine *Fem.*

**what** *pronoun, adjective* **1** qu'est-ce que (*in questions as the object of a verb*); **what did you say?** qu'est-ce que tu as dit?; **what's she doing?** qu'est-ce qu'elle fait?; **what did you buy?** qu'est-ce que tu as acheté?; **what is it?** qu'est-ce que c'est?; **what's the matter?** qu'est-ce qu'il y a?; **2** qu'est-ce qui (*in questions as the subject of the verb*); **what's happening?** qu'est-ce qui se passe?; **3** ce que (*relative pronoun as the object of the verb*); **tell me what you bought** dis-moi ce que tu as acheté; **4** ce qui (*relative pronoun as the* *subject of a verb*); **she told me what had happened** elle m'a dit ce qui s'était passé; **5** quel *Masc.*, quelle *Fem.*; **what's your address?** quelle est ton adresse?; **what country is it in?** c'est dans quel pays?; **what colour is it?** c'est de quelle couleur?; **what make is it?** c'est quelle marque?; **6 what's her name?** elle s'appelle comment?; **what?** comment?

**wheat** *noun* blé *Masc.*

**wheel** *noun* roue *Fem.*; **the spare wheel** la roue de rechange; **the steering wheel** le volant.

**wheelbarrow** *noun* brouette *Fem.*

**wheelchair** *noun* fauteuil *Masc.* roulant.

**when** *adverb, conjunction* quand; **when is she arriving?** quand est-ce qu'elle arrive?; **when's your birthday?** c'est quand, ton anniversaire?; **it was raining when I went out** il pleuvait quand je suis sorti.

**where** *adverb, conjunction* où; **where are the plates?** où sont les assiettes?; **where do you live?** tu habites où?; **where are you going?** où vas-tu?; **I don't know where they live** je ne sais pas où ils habitent.

**whether** si; **I don't know whether he's back or not** je ne sais pas s'il est rentré ou non.

**which** *adjective* quel (*Fem.* quelle); **which CD did you buy?** quel CD as-tu acheté?

**which** *pronoun* **1** (*which one*) lequel *Masc.*, laquelle *Fem.*; **'I saw your brother' – 'which one?'** 'j'ai

vu ton frère – lequel?'; **'I saw your sister' – 'which one?'** 'j'ai vu ta sœur' – 'laquelle?'; **which of these jackets is yours?** laquelle de ces vestes est à toi?; **2** (*relative pronoun*) qui (*as the subject of the verb*); **the lamp which is on the table** la lampe qui est sur la table; **3** (*relative pronoun*) que (*as object of the verb*); **the book which you borrowed from me** le livre que tu m'as emprunté.

**while** *noun* **for a while** pendant quelque temps; **she worked here for a while** elle a travaillé ici pendant quelque temps; **after a while** au bout d'un moment.
**while** *conjunction* pendant que; **you can make some tea while I'm finishing my homework** tu peux faire du thé pendant que je finirai mes devoirs.

**whip** *noun* (*for a horse*) cravache *Fem.*
**whip** *verb* fouetter [1]; **whipped cream** la crème fouettée.

**whirlpool** *noun* tourbillon *Masc.*

**whiskers** *plural noun* moustaches *Fem. plural.*

**whisky** *noun* whisky *Masc.*

**whisper** *noun* chuchotement *Masc.*; **to speak in a whisper** chuchoter [1].
**whisper** *verb* chuchoter [1].

**whistle** *noun* sifflet *Masc.*
**whistle** *verb* siffler [1].

**white** *noun* blanc *Masc.*; **an egg white** un blanc d'œuf.
**white** *adjective* blanc (*Fem.*

a b c d e f g h i j k l m n o p q r s t u v w x y z

blanche); **a white shirt** une chemise blanche.

**white coffee** *noun* café *Masc.* au lait.

**Whitsun** *noun* Pentecôte *Fem.*

**who** *pronoun* **1** (*in questions*) qui; **who wants some chocolate?** qui veut du chocolat?; **2** (*relative pronoun*) qui (*as subject of the verb*); **my friend who lives in Paris** mon ami qui habite à Paris; **3** (*relative pronoun*) que (*as object of the verb*); **the friends who we invited** les amis que nous avons invités.

**whole** *noun* **the whole of the class** la classe tout entière; **on the whole** dans l'ensemble.
**whole** *adjective* tout; **the whole family** toute la famille; **the whole morning** toute la matinée; **the whole time** tout le temps; **the whole world** le monde entier.

**wholemeal** *adjective* complet (*Fem.* complète); **wholemeal bread** le pain complet.

**whom** *pronoun* **1** que; **the person whom I saw** la personne que j'ai vue; **2** (*after a preposition*) qui; **the person to whom I wrote** la personne à qui j'ai écrit.

**whose** *pronoun, adjective* **1** à qui; **whose is this jacket?** à qui est cette veste?; **whose shoes are these?** à qui sont ces chaussures?; **whose is it?** à qui c'est?; **I know whose it is** je sais à qui c'est; **2** dont; **the man whose car has been stolen** le monsieur dont la voiture a été volée.

**why** *adverb* pourquoi; **why did she phone?** pourquoi a-t-elle

appelé?; **nobody knows why he did it** personne ne sait pourquoi il l'a fait.

**wicked** *adjective* **1** (*bad*) méchant; **2** (*brilliant*) génial (*Masc. plural* géniaux).

**wide** *adjective* **1** large; **the Thames is very wide here** la Tamise est très large ici; **a piece of paper 20 cm wide** une feuille de papier de vingt centimètres de large; **2 a wide range** une vaste gamme.
**wide** *adverb* **the door was wide open** la porte était grande ouverte.

**wide awake** *adjective* complètement éveillé.

**widen** *verb* élargir [2].

**widow** *noun* veuve *Fem.*

**widower** *noun* veuf *Masc.*

**width** *noun* largeur *Fem.*

**wife** *noun* femme *Fem.*

**wig** *noun* perruque *Fem.*

**wild** *adjective* **1** sauvage (*an animal or plant*); **wild birds** les oiseaux sauvages; **2** (*crazy*) fou (*Fem.* folle) (*idea, party, person*); **3 to be wild about something** être un fana de quelque chose.

**wild life** *noun* **a programme on wild life in Africa** un programme sur la nature en Afrique.

**wild life park** *noun* réserve *Fem.* naturelle.

**will** *verb* **1** (*if you are unsure of the future tense of a French verb, you can check in the verb tables in the centre of the dictionary*) **I'll see you soon** je te reverrai bientôt; **he'll be pleased**

to see you il sera content de te voir; **it won't rain** il ne pleuvra pas; **there won't be a problem** il n'y aura pas de problème; **2** aller [7] (*can be used for the immmediate future*); **I'll phone them at once** je vais les appeler tout de suite; **3** (*in offers and requests*) **will you have a drink?** est-ce que vous prenez quelque chose à boire?; **will you help me?** est-ce que tu peux m'aider?; **'will you write to me?' – 'of course I will!'** 'est-ce que tu m'écriras?' – 'bien sûr que oui!'; **4 he won't open the door** il ne veut pas ouvrir la porte; **the car won't start** la voiture ne veut pas démarrer; **the drawer won't open** je n'arrive pas à ouvrir le tiroir.

**willing** *adjective* **to be willing to do** être prêt à faire; **I'm willing to pay half** je suis prêt à payer la moitié.

**willingly** *adverb* volontiers.

**willow** *noun* saule *Masc.*; **a weeping willow** un saule pleureur.

**win** *noun* victoire *Fem.*; **our win over Everton** notre victoire sur Everton. **win** *verb* gagner [1]; **we won!** nous avons gagné!; **Rovers won by two goals** Rovers ont gagné de deux buts.

**wind**[1] *noun* vent *Masc.*; **the North wind** le vent du nord.

**wind**[2] *verb* **1** enrouler [1] (*a wire or a rope, for example*); **2** remonter [1] (*a clock*).

**wind farm** *noun* ferme *Fem.* d'éoliennes.

**wind instrument** *noun* instrument *Masc.* à vent.

**window** *noun* **1** (*in a building*) fenêtre *Fem.*; **to look out of the window** regarder par la fenêtre; **2** (*in a car, bus, train*) vitre *Fem.*

**windscreen** *noun* pare-brise *Masc.* (*plural* pare-brise).

**windscreen wipers** *plural noun* essuie-glace *Masc.*

**windsurfing** *noun* planche *Fem.* à voile; **to go windsurfing** faire [10] de la planche à voile.

**windy** *adjective* **1** venteux (*Fem.* venteuse) (*a place*); **2 it's windy today** il fait du vent aujourd'hui.

**wine** *noun* vin *Masc.*; **a glass of white wine** un verre de vin blanc.

**wing** *noun* **1** aile *Fem.*; **2** (*in sport*) ailier *Masc.*

**wink** *verb* **to wink at somebody** faire [10] un clin d'œil à quelqu'un.

**winner** *noun* gagnant *Masc.*, gagnante *Fem.*

**winning** *adjective* gagnant.

**winnings** *plural noun* gains *Masc. plural.*

**winter** *noun* hiver *Masc.*; **in winter** en hiver.

**wipe** *verb* essuyer [41]; **I'll just wipe the table** je vais juste essuyer la table; **to wipe your nose** se moucher [1].

● **to wipe up** (*dishes*) essuyer [41] la vaisselle.

**wire** *noun* fil *Masc.*; **an electric wire** un fil électrique.

**wire netting** *noun* grillage *Masc.*

**wise** *adjective* sage.

**wish** *noun* **1** vœu *Masc.* (*plural* vœux); **make a wish!** fais un vœu!;

a b c d e f g h i j k l m n o p q r s t u v **w** x y z

a
b
c
d
e
f
g
h
i
j
k
l
m
n
o
p
q
r
s
t
u
v
**w**
x
y
z

**2** (*a desire*) désir *Masc.*; **3 best wishes on your birthday** meilleurs vœux pour ton anniversaire.

**wish** *verb* **1 I wish he were here** si seulement il était ici; **2 I wished him happy birthday** je lui ai souhaité un bon anniversaire.

**wit** *noun* esprit *Masc.*

**witch** *noun* sorcière *Fem.*

**with** *preposition* **1** avec; **with James** avec James; **with me** avec moi; **with pleasure** avec plaisir; **beat the eggs with a fork** battez les œufs avec une fourchette; **he took his umbrella with him** il a pris son parapluie; **2** (*at the house of*) chez; **we're staying the night with Frank** on va passer la nuit chez Frank; **3** (*in descriptions*) **a girl with red hair** une fille aux cheveux roux; **the boy with the broken arm** le garçon au bras cassé; **4** de; **filled with water** rempli d'eau; **covered with mud** couvert de boue; **red with rage** rouge de colère.

**without** *preposition* sans; **without you** sans toi; **without sugar** sans sucre; **without a sweater** sans pull; **without looking** sans regarder.

**witness** *noun* témoin *Masc.*

**witty** *adjective* spirituel (*Fem.* spirituelle).

**wizard** *noun* magicien *Masc.*

**wolf** *noun* loup *Masc.*

**woman** *noun* femme *Fem.*; **a woman friend** une amie; **a woman doctor** une femme médecin.

**wonder** *noun* **1** merveille *Fem.*; **2 it's no wonder you're tired** ce n'est pas étonnant si tu es fatigué.

**wonder** *verb* se demander [1]; **I wonder why** je me demande pourquoi; **I wonder where Jake is** je me demande où est Jake.

**wonderful** *adjective* merveilleux (*Fem.* merveilleuse).

**wood** *noun* bois *Masc.*; **the lamp is made of wood** la lampe est en bois.

**wooden** *adjective* en bois.

**woodwork** *noun* menuiserie *Fem.*

**wool** *noun* laine *Fem.*

**woollen** *adjective* en laine.

**word** *noun* **1** mot *Masc.*; **a long word** un mot long; **what's the French word for 'window'?** comment dit-on 'window' en français?; **in other words** autrement dit; **to have a word with somebody** parler avec quelqu'un; **2** (*promise*) **to give somebody your word** donner sa parole à quelqu'un; **he broke his word** il n'a pas tenu parole; **3 the words of a song** les paroles d'une chanson.

**word processing** *noun* traitement *Masc.* de texte.

**word processor** *noun* machine *Fem.* à traitement de texte.

**work** *noun* travail *Masc.* (*plural* travaux); **Mum's at work** maman est au travail; **I've got some work to do** j'ai du travail à faire; **he's out of work** il est sans emploi; **Ben's off work** (*sick*) Ben est en arrêt de travail; (*on holiday*) Ben est en congé.

**work** *verb* **1** travailler [1]; **she works in an office** elle travaille dans un bureau; **Dad works at home** papa travaille à domicile;

**Ruth works in advertising** Ruth travaille dans la publicité; **he works nights** il travaille de nuit; **2** (*to operate*) se servir [71] de; **can you work the video?** sais-tu te servir du magnétoscope?; **3** (*function*) marcher [1]; **the dishwasher's not working** le lave-vaisselle est en panne; **that worked really well!** ça a bien marché!

● **to work out 1** (*understand*) comprendre [64]; **I can't work out why** je ne comprends pas pourquoi; **2** (*exercise*) s'entraîner [1]; **3** (*to go well*) (*a plan*) marcher [1]; **4** (*calculate*) calculer [1]; **I'll work out how much it would cost** je vais calculer combien ç coûterait

**worked up** *adjective* **to get worked up** s'énerver [1].

**worker** *noun* (*in a factory*) ouvrier *Masc.*, ouvrière *Fem.*

**worker** *noun* ouvrier *Masc.*, ouvrière *Fem.*

**work experience** *noun* stage *Masc.*; **to do work experience** faire un stage; **to be on work experience** être en stage.

**working-class** *adjective* ouvrier (*Fem.* ouvrière); **a working-class background** un milieu ouvrier.

**work of art** *noun* œuvre *Fem.* d'art.

**workshop** *noun* atelier *Masc.*

**workstation** *noun* (*computer*) poste *Masc.* de travail (*plural* postes de travail).

**world** *noun* monde *Masc.*; **the best in the world** le meilleur du monde;

the Western world les pays occidentaux.

**World Cup** *noun* **the World Cup** la Coupe du Monde.

**world war** *noun* guerre *Fem.* mondiale; **the Second World War** la Seconde Guerre mondiale.

**worm** *noun* ver *Masc.*

**worn out** *adjective* **1** (*a person*) épuisé; **2** (*clothes or shoes*) complètement usé.

**worried** *adjective* inquiet (*Fem.* inquiète); **they're worried** ils s'inquiètent; **to be worried about** s'inquiéter pour; **we're worried about Susan** nous nous inquiétons pour Susan.

**worry** *noun* soucis *Masc. plural.*

**worry** *verb* s'inquiéter [24]; **don't worry!** ne t'inquiète pas!; **there's nothing to worry about** il n'y a pas de quoi s'inquiéter.

**worrying** *adjective* inquiétant.

**worse** *adjective* pire; **it was even worse than the last time** c'était encore pire que la dernière fois; **to get worse** empirer [1]; **the weather's getting worse** le temps empire; **things are getting worse and worse** ça va de pire en pire.

**worst** *adjective* **the worst** le plus mauvais; **it was the worst day of my life** ça a été la journée la plus mauvaise de ma vie; **if the worst comes to the worst** au pire.

**worth** *adjective* **to be worth** valoir [80]; **how much is it worth?** ça vaut combien?; **to be worth doing** valoir la peine de faire; **it's worth trying** ça vaut la peine d'essayer;

a b c d e f g h i j k l m n o p q r s t u v w x y z

it's not worth it ça ne vaut pas la peine.

**would** *verb* **1 would you like something to eat?** voulez-vous quelque chose à manger?; **2 he wouldn't answer** il n'a pas voulu répondre; **the car wouldn't start** la voiture n'a pas voulu démarrer; **3 I would like an omelette** je voudrais une omelette; **I'd like to go to the cinema** j'aimerais aller au cinéma; **that would be a good idea** ce serait une bonne idée; **if we asked her she would help us** elle nous aiderait, si nous le lui demandions.

**wound** *noun* blessure *Fem.*
**wound** *verb* blesser [1].

**wrap** *verb* emballer [1]; **I'm going to wrap (up) my presents** je vais emballer mes cadeaux; **could you wrap it for me please?** voulez-vous me faire un paquet cadeau, s'il vous plaît?

**wrapping paper** *noun* papier *Masc.* cadeau.

**wreck** *noun* **1** (*of a crashed car or plane*) épave *Fem.*; **2 I feel a wreck!** je suis une loque!
**wreck** *verb* **1** détruire [26]; **2** gâcher [1] (*plans, occasion*); **it completely wrecked my evening!** ça m'a complètement gâché la soirée!

**wrestler** *noun* catcheur *Masc.*, catcheuse *Fem.*

**wrestling** *noun* catch *Masc.*

**wrinkle** *noun* ride *Fem.*

**wrinkled** *adjective* ridé.

**wrist** *noun* poignet *Masc.*

**write** *verb* écrire [38] (*a letter or a story*); **I'll write her a letter** je lui écrirai une lettre; **to write to somebody** écrire à quelqu'un; **I wrote to Jean yesterday** j'ai écrit à Jean hier.

● **to write down** noter [1]; **I wrote down her name** j'ai noté son nom.

**writer** *noun* écrivain *Masc.*

**writing** *noun* écriture *Fem.*

**wrong** *adjective* **1** (*not correct*) mauvais; **the wrong answer** la mauvaise réponse; **it's the wrong address** ce n'est pas la bonne adresse; **I've brought the wrong file** je n'ai pas apporté le bon classeur; **you've got the wrong number** vous vous êtes trompé de numéro; **2 to be wrong** (*mistaken*) se tromper; **I was wrong** je me suis trompé; **I was wrong when I said it was finished** je me suis trompé en disant que c'était fini; **3 what's wrong?** qu'est-ce qu'il y a?; **4** (*false*) faux (*Fem.* fausse); **the information was wrong** les renseignements étaient faux.

# Xx

**xerox™** *noun* photocopie *Fem.*
**xerox™** *verb* photocopier [1].

**Xmas** *noun* Christmas.

**X-ray** *noun* radio *Fem.*; **I saw the X-rays** j'ai vu les radios.
**X-ray** *verb* faire [10] une radio de; **they X-rayed her ankle** ils ont fait une radio de sa cheville.

# Yy

**yacht** *noun* **1** (*sailing boat*) voilier *Masc.*; **2** (*large luxury boat*) yacht *Masc.*

**yawn** *verb* bâiller [1].

**year** *noun* **1** an *Masc.*; (*the whole period*) année *Fem.*; **six years ago** il y a six ans; **the whole year** toute l'année; **they lived in Moscow for years** ils ont habité Moscou pendant des années; **2** (*for someone's age*) an *Masc.*; **he's seventeen years old** il a dix-sept ans; **a two-year-old child** un enfant de deux ans; **3** (*in secondary schools in France the years go from 'sixième', the equivalent of Year 7, to 'terminale', the equivalent of Year 13*); **I'm in Year 10** je suis en troisième; **I'm in Year 11** je suis en seconde.

**yearly** *adjective* annuel (*Fem.* annuelle); **a yearly event** un événement annuel.
**yearly** *adverb* tous les ans; **he goes to Normandy yearly** il va en Normandie tous les ans.

**yell** *verb* hurler [1].

**yellow** *adjective* jaune.

**yes** *adverb* **1** oui; **yes, I know** oui, je sais; **'is Tom in his room?' – 'yes, he is'** 'est-ce que Tom est dans sa chambre?' – 'oui'; **2** (*answering a negative*) si; **'you don't want to go, do you?' – 'yes, I do!'** 'tu ne veux pas y aller, n'est-ce pas?' – 'mais si!'; **'you haven't finished, have you?' – 'yes, I have'** 'tu n'as pas fini?' – 'si si'.

**yesterday** *adverb* hier; **I saw her yesterday** je l'ai vue hier; **yesterday afternoon** hier après-midi; **yesterday morning** hier matin; **the day before yesterday** avant-hier.

**yet** *adverb* **not yet** pas encore; **it's not ready yet** ce n'est pas encore prêt.

**yoga** *noun* yoga *Masc.*

**yoghurt** *noun* yaourt *Masc.*; **a banana yoghurt** un yaourt à la banane.

**yolk** *noun* jaune *Masc.* d'œuf (*plural* jaunes d'œuf).

**you** *pronoun* **1** tu (*'tu' is the familiar way of talking to family members, close friends, and people of your own age; 'vous' is more polite*); **do you want to go to the cinema tonight?** tu veux aller au cinéma ce soir?; **2** te (*the object form of 'tu'*); **I'll lend you my bike** je te prêterai mon vélo; **I'll invite you** je t'inviterai; **I'll write to you** je t'écrirai; **3** toi (*after prepositions and in comparisons*); **I'll go with you** j'irai avec toi; **he's older than you** il est plus âgé que toi; **4** (*more polite or to several people*) vous; **can you tell me where the station is, please?** est-ce que vous pouvez m'indiquer la gare, s'il vous plaît?; **I'll invite you all!** je vous inviterai tous!

**young** *adjective* jeune; **he's younger than me** il est plus jeune que moi; **Tessa's two years younger than me** Tessa a deux ans de moins que moi; **young people** les jeunes.

a
b
c
d
e
f
g
h
i
j
k
l
m
n
o
p
q
r
s
t
u
v
w
x
**y**
z

**your** *adjective* **1** ton *Masc.*, ta *Fem.* (*plural* tes) (*this is the familiar way of talking to family members, close friends, and people of your own age; 'vous' is more polite*) **I met your Dad** j'ai rencontré ton père; **I like your skirt!** j'aime bien ta jupe!; **you've forgotten your CDs!** tu as oublié tes CD; **2** (*more polite or to several people*) votre (*plural* vos); **thank you for your hospitality** merci pour votre hospitalité; **you can all bring your friends** vous pouvez tous amener vos amis.

**yours** *pronoun* **1** le tien *Masc.*, la tienne *Fem.* (*plural* les tiens *Masc.*, les tiennes *Fem.*) (*this is the familiar way of talking to somebody of your own age or belonging to your family; otherwise you should use 'vôtre'*) **my brother's younger than yours** mon frère est plus jeune que le tien; **2** (*formally or to several people*) le vôtre *Masc.*, la vôtre *Fem.* (*plural* les vôtres ); **my children are younger than yours** mes enfants sont plus jeunes que les vôtres; **3** à toi, à vous (*polite form*); **is this pen yours?** est-ce que ce stylo est à toi?

**yourself** *pronoun* **1** (*informal*) te; (*formal*) vous; **you'll hurt yourself** tu vas te faire mal; **2** (*for emphasis*) toi-même; (*formal*) vous-même; **did you do it yourself?** est-ce que tu l'as fait toi-même?; **3 all by yourself** tout seul (*Fem.* toute seule).

**yourselves** *pronoun* **1** vous; **help yourselves** servez-vous; **2** (*for emphasis*) vous-mêmes; **did you do it yourselves?** est-ce que vous l'avez fait vous-mêmes?

**youth** *noun* **1** (*stage in life*) jeunesse *Fem.*; **2** (*young people*) les jeunes *Masc. plural*; **today's youth** les jeunes d'aujourd'hui; **3** (*young male*) jeune *Masc.*

**youth hostel** *noun* auberge *Fem.* de jeunesse (*plural* auberges de jeunesse).

**Yugoslavia** *noun* Yougoslavie *Fem.*; **the former Yugoslavia** l'ex-Yougoslavie.

# Zz

**zany** *adjective* loufoque.

**zebra** *noun* zèbre *Masc.*

**zebra crossing** *noun* passage *Masc.* pour piétons.

**zero** *noun* zéro *Masc.*

**zigzag** *verb* zigzaguer [1].

**zip** *noun* fermeture *Fem.* éclair™.

**zodiac** *noun* zodiaque *Masc.*; **the signs of the zodiac** les signes du zodiaque.

**zone** *noun* zone *Fem.*

**zoo** *noun* zoo *Masc.*

**zoom lens** *noun* zoom *Masc.*

# FRENCH LIFE AND CULTURE

# The year in France

## le jour de l'an
New Year's Day. It's a public holiday in France.

## Id-al-Fitr
The date of this Muslim festival varies from year to year. It is celebrated mainly by people from North Africa (Algeria, Tunisia, etc), the largest Muslim group in France.

## la Fête des Rois
Feast of the Three Kings: 6th January. Cake shops sell a special cake containing a whole bean or almond, or a plastic figure. Whoever gets it in their piece of cake wears the golden cardboard crown that decorates the cake.

## la Saint Valentin
St Valentine's Day: 14th February. The custom of people sending a special message to someone they love is growing in France.

## le 1er avril
April Fool's Day. People play tricks on each other: the tricks are called *poissons d'avril* (April fish).

## Pâques
Easter. Children often look for chocolate eggs or rabbits hidden in the garden. Easter Monday is a public holiday, but Good Friday (le *vendredi saint*) is not.

## le 1er mai
1st May: a public holiday.

## le huit mai
8th May: a public holiday celebrating the end of World War II.

## le quatorze juillet
14th July: the French National Day, and a public holiday. It celebrates the storming of the Bastille prison in 1789, an event which launched the French Revolution. There are street fairs, firework displays, music and dancing in all French towns. Many people set off on holiday at about this time.

## le 15 août
15th August: Feast of the Assumption. Many people return home from their summer holidays around the time of this public holiday.

## le 1er novembre
1st November: All Saints Day. A public holiday, on which many people put flowers on the graves of relatives and friends who have died.

## le 11 novembre
11th November. A public holiday that commemorates the end of World War I, which was largely fought in France.

## Noël
Christmas. People often excshange presents on Christmas Eve, before going to Midnight Mass. On Christmas Day they have a big meal, and the traditional cake is a richly decorated Christmas log (*la bûche de Noël*).

## le Réveillon
New Year's Eve party. People like to dance and see the New Year in with champagne.

# Food and drink

**baguette**
The name of the most popular French bread.

**boucherie**
A butcher's shop. A *boucherie chevaline* sells horse meat.

**boulangerie**
A baker's shop, which sells pain (bread), *croissants, pains au chocolat* (rolls with a chocolate filling), etc

**charcuterie**
A delicatessen shop that sells ham, sausages, cold meats, salads, etc

**café**
A French cafe serves coffee, alcoholic drinks, sandwiches and often simple meals. In tourist spots, you often pay more if you sit than if you stand at the counter.

**Champagne**
The area of Champagne, east of Paris has given its name to the sparkling wine that is produced there. Wines are often called by the areas where they are produced, e.g. Bordeaux, Bourgogne (from Burgundy).

**Chantilly**
Fresh, sweetened whipped cream.

**chips**
Crisps. Chips, French fries, are called *frites*.

**crêpes**
Pancakes. A *crêperie* serves both sweet and savoury pancakes, e.g. pancakes filled with ham or cheese.

**fruits de mer**
Sea food, such as mussels, shrimps, lobster.

**glaces**
Ice creams. Flavours include e.g. *cassis* (blackcurrant), *pistache* (pistachio nut), *noisette* (hazelnut), *citron vert* (lime), and many others.

**menthe à l'eau**
Mint cordial in chilled water: one of the cheapest and most thirst-quenching drinks available in a café.

**plat du jour**
Meal of the day, e.g. in a cafe or restaurant.

**pâtisserie**
A shop which sells cakes, tarts and biscuits, usually made on the premises.

**ratatouille**
A spicy vegetable dish made with tomatoes, onions, garlic, courgettes and often aubergine.

**salade composée**
A mixed salad.

**veau**
Veal, the meat from a calf, is widely available in France.

# Life at School

## arts plastiques
The school subject we call 'art'. It is a compulsory subject in French *collèges*.

## bac
The end-of-school exam taken by pupils who have stayed at school to the age of 18. *Bac* is short for *baccalauréat*.

## brevet
The exam taken at the age of 15 or 16 by pupils leaving school.

## Carnet de notes et de correspondance
A book in which pupils write information which the school wants to send home, e.g. information about school trips.

## classe de neige
A week which younger pupils (under 12s) spend in the mountains, with skiing lessons as part of their curriculum.

## collège
State school for pupils aged 11-15.

## éducation civique
A compulsory school subject in which pupils are taught how the country is governed, and what people's rights and duties are.

## journée scolaire
The school day. The length of the school day varies, but can be from 8.30 a.m. to 5 p.m.

## lycée
State school for 15-18 year olds.

## redoubler
Pupils who fail in too many subjects have to repeat the year *(redoubler)* instead of going on to a higher class.

## rentrée
The return to school in September. Shops are full of products for pupils going back to school, and the issue of school are widely discussed in the media.

## sixième
Pupils begin *collège* when they are about 11 years old. The years are called:

*sixième* (6th) = Year 7
*cinquième* (5th) = Year 8
*quatrième* (4th) = Year 9
*troisième* (3rd) = Year 10

## vacances scolaires
School holidays are usually:

- one week in October / November
- two weeks at Christmas
- two weeks in February
- two weeks at Easter
- about eight weeks in summer, from early July to early September

630

# On holiday in France

**aire**
Motorway services.

**Arc de Triomphe, Paris**
A grand arch, built in 1836 at the meeting-point of 13 roads. From the top there is a grand view down the wide avenue called the Champs-Élysées to a similar arch in front of the Louvre palace.

**Bretagne**
Brittany. A popular tourist area, with a rocky coast and sandy beaches.

Many people speak Breton, a Celtic language, and road signs are often in both French and Breton.

**chambre d'hôte**
You see this sign outside houses which offer bed-and-breakfast accommodation.

**Champs-Élysées**
The grandest street in Paris, lined with luxury shops, cafes and hotels. It stretches from the *Arc de Triomphe* to the *Louvre* palace.

**Corse**
The island of Corsica, in the Mediterranean, has been French since 1768.

**Côte d'Azur**
The French Riviera, the most fashionable stretch of the French Mediterranean coast, including St Tropez, Cannes, Nice, Monte Carlo, etc

**Dordogne**
The area along the Dordogne river, famous for its fortified towns and villages.

**gîte rural**
A self-catering holiday house or flat.

**grottes**
Underground caves and caverns. Some still have paintings from prehistoric times.

**Loire**
The longest river in France, famous for its many beautiful castles and palaces (*châteaux*) within a small area near Tours, e.g.

- Chambord, reputed to a have a tower for every day of the year,

- Chenonceaux, built across the river Cher.

**Louvre**
The Louvre used to be a royal palace. It is now one of the world's largest and richest museums of paintings (e.g. the Mona Lisa), sculptures, and other works of art.

**météo**
The weather forecast, on the internet, on TV, in newspapers, etc

**métro**
The Paris underground. The fast trains serving the suburbs are called RER. A carnet of 10 tickets is cheaper than 10 individual tickets.

**tour Eiffel**
Built by Gustave Eiffel in 1889, 100 years after the French Revolution, the Eiffel Tower was the highest structure in the world. It is 320 metres high. You can climb the stairs to the second storey, or take a lift to the top.

## Midi

Midi means 'south', and le Midi refers to the south of France.

## Mont Saint-Michel

This tiny island, reached by a causeway from the border between Brittany and Normandy, is one of the most popular tourist attractions in France. It is named after its Benedictine abbey begun in 966 AD.

## Monaco

A tiny country on the Mediterranean coast, near Nice, famous for its fashionable luxury marina. The Monaco Grand Prix is raced on the streets of the town.

## Monte Carlo

The part of Monaco which houses the famous casino.

## Provence

Part of the south of France, near the Rhone delta. Its Roman remains, the associations with the painter Van Gogh, and its hot, sunny climate, make it a popular tourist area.

## Routes nationales

The main roads in France. They are numbered in red (N1, N2, etc). Smaller roads, *routes départementales*, are numbered in yellow (D1, D2, etc).

## SNCF

The name of French railways. Some main lines operate high-speed trains called *le TGV*.

## toutes directions

Follow the *toutes directions* (all directions) signs when you want to leave the town centre.

## Versailles

The enormous and magnificent royal palace built in the town of Versailles, outside Paris, as from the 17th century. Louis XIV, sometimes called the Sun King, had his court here.

# Life in France

## bal public
Many events end with a *bal public:* dancing for all in the town or village square.

## boules
A game in which players from two teams throw or roll metal balls on an earth pitch, aiming to get as close as possible to the jack (a small wooden ball). The game, very popular in France, is also called *pétanque.*

## carte d'identité
French people have an identity card. It can be used instead of a passport to travel within the EU.

## code postal
Postcode. French postcodes have five figures and no letters.

## département
France is divided into 95 *départements.* Each has a number, e.g. central Paris is 75. This number is used in postcodes and as the last two numbers on car number plates.

## fête
A party. In summer, many towns and villages have *fêtes*, with music, stalls, dancing, etc.

## fête nationale
The French national day: 14th July.

## Hôtel de Ville
Town hall.

## Maghreb
The name given to the North of Africa (Morocco, Algeria, Tunisia). There are many people from these countries living and working in France.

## pédalos
Pedal-boats that can be hired on many larger lakes.

## République
France is a republic, with a president *(président)* at its head. The president is elected every seven years.

## Roland-Garros
A big stadium in Paris. International tennis competitions are held here.

## Stade de France
With a capacity of 80 000 for football and rugby matches, 75 000 for athletics or 100 000 for concerts, this stadium in the north of Paris is France's biggest. It was opened in 1998.

## Tour de France
The world's most famous cycle race takes place in July.

## VTT
Mountain bikes.

# Did you know ... ?

★ that most French motorways (autoroutes) charge tolls (péage), but that many are free?

★ that comics (bandes dessinées or BD) are very popular in France?

★ that French letter boxes (boîtes aux lettres) are yellow?

★ that shops are often closed (fermés) at lunchtime, but are open (ouvert) late into the evening?

★ that France is the biggest country in western Europe?

★ that there are about 169 million speakers of French (Francophones) in the world?

★ that the French call the English Channel La Manche (the Sleeve)?

★ that Marseille was founded by the Greeks in about 600BC?

★ that the French national anthem is called the Marseillaise because it was soldiers from Marseille who first sang it in Paris?

★ that Médecins Sans Frontières is an organisation that sends doctors to countries hit by crises such as war or famine?

★ that le Mont Blanc (4807m), on the border between France and Italy, is western Europe's highest mountain?

★ that some museums (musées) are free for young people, and that some are free for all visitors on the first Sunday in the month?

★ that a big piece of meat in a restaurant is called a pavé (paving stone)?

★ that the French national police are organised in two forces (la police, les gendarmes) and that officers in both forces are armed?

★ that the usual place to buy stamps is in a tobacconist's shop (tabac)?

★ that the EU is known as l'UE (Union Européenne) and the UN is known as l'ONU (Organisation des Nations Unies)?